STEVENS' HANDBOOK OF EXPERIMENTAL PSYCHOLOGY

STEVENS' HANDBOOK OF EXPERIMENTAL PSYCHOLOGY

Second Edition

VOLUME 1: Perception and Motivation

Edited by

RICHARD C. ATKINSON
RICHARD J. HERRNSTEIN
GARDNER LINDZEY
R. DUNCAN LUCE

68-302

WILEY

A Wiley-Interscience Publication
JOHN WILEY & SONS
New York / Chichester / Brisbane / Toronto / Singapore

Library of Congress Cataloguing in Publication Data:

Handbook of Experimental psychology.
    Stevens' handbook of experimental psychology.

    Rev. ed. of: Handbook of experimental psychology
edited by S.S. Stevens. 1951.
    "A Wiley-Interscience publication."
    Includes bibliographies and index.
    Contents: v. 1. Perception and motivation —
v. 2. Learning and cognition.
    1. Psychology, Experimental. I. Stevens, S. S.
(Stanley Smith), 1906–1973. II. Atkinson, Richard C.

III. Title. [DNLM: 1. Cognition. 2. Learning
3. Motivation. 4. Perception. 5. Psychophysiology.

WL 102 H2355]
BF181.H336 1988   150   87-31637
ISBN 0-471-04203-X (v. 1)
IBSN 0-471-04207-2 (v. 2)

CONTRIBUTORS

GERARD P. BAERENDS, Ph.D.
Emeritus Professor of Ethology and Ecology
Department of Behavioural Biology
University of Groningen
Groningen, The Netherlands

LINDA M. BARTOSHUK, Ph.D.
Fellow, John B. Pierce Foundation
Professor, Departments of Epidemiology and
    Public Health
Yale University
School of Medicine
New Haven, Connecticut

WILLIAM S. CAIN, Ph.D.
Fellow, John B. Pierce Foundation
Professor, Departments of Epidemiology and
    Psychology
Yale University
New Haven, Connecticut

TERRYL T. FOCH, Ph.D.
Danville, California

DAVID M. GREEN, Ph.D.
Graduate Research Professor
Department of Psychology
University of Florida
Gainesville, Florida

IRA J. HIRSH, Ph.D.
Mallinckrodt Distinguished University
    Professor of Psychology and Audiology
Washington University
Senior Scientist, Central Institute for the Deaf
Saint Louis, Missouri

JULIAN HOCHBERG, Ph.D.
Centennial Professor of Psychology
Department of Psychology
Columbia University
New York, New York

BARTLEY G. HOEBEL, Ph.D.
Professor, Department of Psychology
Princeton University
Princeton, New Jersey

CARROLL E. IZARD, Ph.D.
Unidel Professor
Department of Psychology
University of Delaware
Newark, Delaware

NELSON YUAN-SHENG KIANG, Ph.D.
Eaton-Peabody Professor
Whitaker College of Health Sciences,
    Technology and Management
Massachusetts Institute of Technology
Cambridge, Massachusetts
Director, Eaton-Peabody Laboratory
Massachusetts Eye and Ear Infirmary
Professor of Physiology
Department of Otology and Laryngology
Harvard Medical School
Boston, Massachusetts

CAROL L. KRUMHANSL, Ph.D.
Associate Professor, Department of Psychology
Cornell University
Ithaca, New York

R. DUNCAN LUCE, Ph.D.
Victor S. Thomas Professor of Psychology
Department of Psychology
Harvard University
Cambridge, Massachusetts

GERALD E. McCLEARN, Ph.D.
Director, Institute for the Study of
    Human Development
The Pennsylvania State University
University Park, Pennsylvania

CONTRIBUTORS

WILLIAM T. PEAKE, Sc.D.
Professor of Electrical and Bioengineering
Department of Electrical Engineering and
    Computer Science
Massachusetts Institute of Technology
Cambridge, Massachusetts
Massachusetts Eye and Ear Infirmary
Boston, Massachusetts

E. N. PUGH, Jr., Ph.D.
Professor, Department of Psychology
University of Pennsylvania
Philadelphia, Pennsylvania

PAUL ROZIN, Ph.D.
Professor, Department of Psychology
University of Pennsylvania
Philadelphia, Pennsylvania

PATRICIA M. SAXTON, Ph.D.
Scientist
Institute for Neuroscience
University of Delaware
Newark, Delaware

JONATHAN SCHULL, Ph.D.
Assistant Professor, Department of Psychology
Haverford College
Haverford, Pennsylvania

GERALD WESTHEIMER, Ph.D., F.R.S.
Professor of Physiology
Department of Physiology-Anatomy
University of California, Berkeley
Berkeley, California

PREFACE

Stanley Smith Stevens' original *Handbook of Experimental Psychology*, published in 1951, comprised 36 chapters in six sections, all in one large volume. Here, the number of chapters has shrunk to 27, the sections to four, and the whole made more manageable as two volumes. The shrinkage is not in experimental psychology, for what has vanished are mainly importations into psychology from other disciplines. The original *Handbook* had chapters on the neuron, on synapses, on neural maturation, on the mathematics of growth curves, and on the anatomy of motor systems. Also missing are topics that now seem less pertinent to experimental psychology than they did right after World War II, such as engineering psychology, equipment design, and manpower training. As experimental psychology developed, it grew less dependent on other sciences and focused more sharply on its own territory.

Experimental psychology has grown differentially. What was a single chapter on Cognitive Processes has become a section of nine chapters in the present edition, a full third of the entire undertaking. The section on Sensory Processes has been transformed into Perception, a shift away from the physical and physiological to the more purely psychological. Physics and physiology remain, as they must, but the hope is that they make more meaningful contact with psychology's variables. The section on Motivation has grown from three chapters to five, almost all of the growth owing to the enriching convergence of behavioral biology and experimental psychology. The section on Learning and Adjustment changed its name to Learning and ceded Cognitive Processes and Speech and Language to other sections. It abandoned a mixture of substantive and methodological chapter topics that has become unwieldy, and it now presents four fundamental issues of simple learning: conditioning processes, stimulus discrimination, response strength, and the physiology of learning and memory.

This work is not so much a revision of Stevens' *Handbook* as it is a tribute to its editor. Although the present editors had quite different relations with our predecessor, all of us were significantly influenced by him in our work, and we are unified in our admiration for him as a scientist, scholar, and person. It is difficult to say anything about Smitty without saying a great deal. Here space permits us only to point to his distinguished contributions to sensory psychology and measurement, and to his Harvard presence for four decades, where in his highly individual manner he molded generations of experimental psychologists. So, too, did his *Handbook* shape experimental psychology in its time. Readers who are not familiar with him and his work may wish to consult his fascinating autobiography, which says much of interest about him and about our science (S. S. Stevens, *Autobiography*. In G. Lindzey (ed.), *A History of Psychology in Autobiography, Vol VI*. New York: Appleton-Century-Crofts, 1974, pp 395–420).

Conversations among the editors about a possible new edition of Stevens' *Handbook* began in the fall of 1977. The old edition was out of date and out of print, but the question was whether a new one of so comprehensive a scope would be useful at a time when fine handbooks in perception, learning, and other specialized areas of experimental psychology have become available. Or were the fissures within experimental psychology so deep, we wondered, that it was pointless to try to span them in a single work. We came to believe that the very fractionation of our subject that almost deterred us could be blamed in part on the lack of a contemporary *Handbook*. Experimental psychology has more coherence than is reflected in the specialized textbooks, handbooks, journals, and monographs of our time, or so we thought. Wiley, publisher of the original *Handbook*, agreed. The next step was to try to discover whether colleagues elsewhere agreed as well.

In the summer of 1978, a tentative outline, drafted by the editors, was sent to several dozen psychologists and other scholars. They were asked for advice on the idea of a new edition, on our outline, and on possible authors. Their answers helped mold our tentative plan into the present *Handbook*. Because of their generous response to our inquiry, the outline was extensively revised, a list of prospective authors drawn up, and, most significantly, the editors felt encouraged to proceed with the project. We acknowledge, but cannot fully repay, our debt to these consultants by listing their names.

Authors were recruited to write chapters of a level of scholarship sufficient to serve the needs of scholars and a level of clarity to serve those of beginning graduate students in experimental psychology. That was Stevens' conception of his *Handbook*, as it is the present editors'. All who were asked accepted or provided advice, about the outline of the *Handbook* or about alternative authors. Soon we had the assemblage here represented. Only the enduring and versatile George A. Miller turns up as author in both editions, although several others of the original authors helped as consultants.

Also enduring is Geraldine Stone Stevens, whom Stevens gratefully acknowledged in his Preface. We are grateful to her, too, for allowing us to grace this edition with "Stevens" in its title, for advice about how to put a handbook together, for editing about one-third of the chapters, and for her enthusiasm and encouragement.

The editors needed further help as the chapters came in. The reviewers listed below provided expertise where the editors' expertise fell short. Their criticisms and suggestions were often detailed, and occasionally fundamental. We know we speak not just for ourselves but also for the authors when we express most earnest thanks to these reviewers for accepting the largely thankless task of careful editorial reading and commenting. Much, though not all, of this edition's long delay from conception to publication is accounted for by the slow pace of the successive exchanges from reviewer to author and back again, always via an editor.

But the delay would have been worse, perhaps infinite, had it not been for the efforts of Susan Herrnstein, of whom we write, as Stevens wrote of Geraldine Stone Stevens in his Preface, that "she did more work on this handbook than anyone else." Detecting a vacuum, Susan Herrnstein took administrative command—organizing, advising, and keeping the communication and paper flowing among editors, authors, publisher, and, at last, printer. Despite a schedule already too busy, she found the time and energy to do the work that needed to be done when the rest of us did not. We cannot begin to repay our debt to her, but our profound gratitude we can at least acknowledge here.

R.C.A.
R.J.H.
G.L.
R.D.L.

29 January 1988
Cambridge, MA
La Jolla, CA
Stanford, CA

Consultants

Jack A. Adams
Abram Amsel
S. Howard Bartley
William H. Batchelder
Frank A. Beach
Robert C. Bolles
Robert M. Boynton
J. Douglas Carroll
Russell M. Church
Charles N. Cofer
F.I.M. Craik
Robert G. Crowder
M.R. D'Amato
Hallowell Davis
James Deese
Victoria A. Fromkin
Wendell R. Garner
Norman Geschwind
James J. Gibson
Bert F. Green, Jr.
Sebastian P. Grossman
Norman Guttman
Eliot Hearst
Ernest R. Hilgard
Robert A. Hinde
Earl Hunt
Tarow Indow
Paul A. Kolers
John I. Lacey
Alvin A. Liberman

Frank A. Logan
George Mandler
Lawrence E. Marks
A.A.J. Marley
Edwin Martin
George A. Miller
Thomas O. Nelson
Allen Newell
Irwin Pollack
Michael I. Posner
J.O. Ramsay
Floyd Ratliff
Robert A. Rescorla
Lorrin A. Riggs
Rudolph W. Schulz
Charles P. Shimp
B.F. Skinner
Richard L. Solomon
Norman E. Spear
J.E.R. Staddon
Saul Sternberg
N.S. Sutherland
Philip Teitelbaum
Garth J. Thomas
Richard F. Thompson
Endel Tulving
William Uttal
Bernice M. Wenzel
Wayne Wickelgren

Reviewers

Norman Anderson
Phipps Arabie
Elizabeth Bates
Ursula Bellugi-Klima
Gordon Bower
Robert Boynton
Herbert Clark
Michael Domjan
Richard L. Doty
Trygg Engen
E. Bruce Goldstein
Isidore Gormezano
James L. Gould
Bruce P. Halpern
Katherine S. Harris
Julian Hochberg
J.A. Scott Kelso
Walter Kintsch
Michael Kubovy
Herschel Leibowitz
Steve Link
John C. Loehlin
George Mandler
James L. McGaugh

William J. McGill
Donald R. Meyer
Jeffrey Miller
Richard Millward
John A. Nevin
Donald Norman
Carl Pfaffman
Leo Postman
Howard Resnikoff
David Rumelhart
Richard Shiffrin
Edward Smith
Larry R. Squire
Saul Sternberg
Patrick Suppes
Delbert O. Thiessen
Garth J. Thomas
Richard F. Thompson
William Vaughan, Jr.
Allan R. Wagner
Wayne Wickelgren
Thomas Wickens
Frederic L. Wightman

CONTENTS

CONTENTS FOR VOLUME 2

PERCEPTION

Chapter 1

MEASUREMENT, SCALING, AND PSYCHOPHYSICS

R. Duncan Luce, *Harvard University*

Carol L. Krumhansl, *Cornell University*

INTRODUCTION

To most physical scientists, the term *measurement* brings to mind issues of precision, reliability, bias, and technique. One takes for granted that the attribute in question—be it the velocity of light, the mass of an electron, or the diameter of the sun—is measurable, that it can be quantified in a consistent and meaningful way. In the physical sciences very precise systems of measurement have been developed that permit largely observer-free descriptions of physical objects and events. But think back to the early history of physics, when the very nature of many measures was a matter of doubt and debate, and most measurement systems in use resulted from the needs of trade and commerce, not physical theory. True, there were strong intuitive notions of what we now call force, weight, mass, time, velocity, momentum, work, heat, and temperature, but it took a great deal of effort to develop methods for measuring these attributes of physical systems and to understand the relations among them. In the process, it became necessary to introduce some far less intuitive but equally important measures, such as entropy, kinetic and potential energy, acceleration, impedance, and charge.

Psychological measurement is in a comparable, floundering state with informal concepts that seem to admit of degree or amount, but whose means of measurement remain crude, controversial, and uncertain. Subjectively, our sensations of hunger, loudness, and sweetness are no less real than our sensations of force, energy, and acceleration. Moreover, for both psychological and physical attributes, our sensations suggest a measurement system that codes the degree or amount of the attribute or property in question. However, it is important to recognize an essential difference between the objectives of physical and psychological measurement. Physics studies certain properties of space, matter, and radiation, not the sensations they engender, although there is no doubt that in its early development physics was strongly guided, and sometimes misguided, by these sensations. In psychology, we are concerned with the sensations themselves, and this difference poses a challenge to develop measures that are appropriate for our special purposes. The system of measurement that develops in psychology will undoubtedly turn out to resemble that of physics in certain fundamental ways, but new problems requiring novel solutions are also likely to emerge.

Physics and its applications exhibit three distinct levels of theory. First, there are the primitive relations among attributes that determine both the measurement representations and the interconnections among measures, as reflected in the structure of physical units. Second, there are the various laws of physics that are expressed entirely in terms of these measures, such as the basic equations of electromagnetic theory (Maxwell's equations), of hydrodynamics, of kinetics, and of statistical mechanics. And third, certain particular systems are modeled and the equations are solved for those cases. An example is the force exerted on a particular airfoil in a particular fluid flow, or the movement of the needle of a voltmeter when placed across a particular circuit under particular conditions. Keep in mind that, at each of the three levels, important regularities are found, all of which are called laws; those of measurement, those of general physical processes, and those of particular physical systems. Although they all express regularities, they are obviously not all of the same type, since they differ in generality.

If three distinct levels really can be distinguished, at which level does the psychophysicist operate when studying loudness? If a scale of loudness is developed, is it (1) an example of measurement, (2) a part of some psychophysical theory, or (3) the manifestation of the operation of a mechanism? In the first case, it must eventually be shown to arise as the representation of a lawful qualitative structure. In the second, it is best thought of as a construct whose ultimate status is not necessarily clear; often constructs of theories eventually become basic measures, once the situation is better understood. And in the third, it may best be thought of as a random variable, reflecting the probabilistic character of a mechanism, but not necessarily having anything to do with fundamental measurement.

We discuss the first separately and then lump the other two.

The Strategy of Measurement and Scaling in Psychophysics

In following this strategy we suppose that the sensations themselves are attributes of the organism, comparable in many ways to the properties of physical objects. As such, these attributes are assumed to be highly stable and regular, and thus they can be subjected to careful analytical study and represented numerically in a manner analogous to physical measurement. This approach is concerned not only with the assignment of numerical values to the psychological states, but also with the way in which the observed psychological measures possess various formal properties of the number system into which they are being mapped. For the purpose of this chapter, we will refer to this as the measurement approach.

If this approach is followed and succeeds, one anticipates the discovery of general laws relating the sensations to physical attributes. That is, the measured sensations are expected to correspond systematically to the physical quantities that give rise to them. This is the point of view, more or less explicit, that has informed the tradition of psychophysical measurement that began with Fechner (1860) and received major impetus in this century by Thurstone (1927), Stevens (1951, 1975; see the latter for numerous references), and many others. For example, sound intensity, that is, the amplitude of the pressure wave impinging on the eardrum, is a well-understood physical attribute that is highly correlated with the sensation called loudness. It is, however, by no means identical to it. For one thing, the relationship is not linear; twice the amplitude does not give rise to twice the perceived loudness. Moreover loudness is affected by the frequency of the sound as well as by its intensity. A more striking example, perhaps, is color vision. Light stimuli are described at the physical level by the energy at each of an infinity of wavelengths, but perceptually this infinite-dimensional space is mapped onto the much simpler, three-dimensional structure of the psychological color space. Thus, the relation between the physical stimulus and the corresponding psychological response may be quite complex, although this approach assumes that the relation is lawful.

For the measurement view to prevail in psychophysics or, more generally, in psychology, or even more generally, in biology, it appears necessary for some structure of interconnected scales to arise, much as exists in physics. This would mean a complex pattern of reductions of some psychological scales to others, with a resulting simple pattern of units, and quite possibly some simple connection with the scales of physics. This appears to be the program that Stevens was pursuing; we discuss it below. To anticipate, Stevens attempted to argue that the psychological scales of intensity are all power functions of the primary physical scales that manipulate each attribute. Moreover he attempted to show that a consistent pattern of power functions holds among the scales of intensity, suggesting a single underlying attribute of psychological intensity. Were that true, then psychophysical measurement would simply enlarge the system of physical measures, just as electromagnetic theory did in the second half of the last century, and one could anticipate the development of psychological theories involving these sensory (and perhaps other) variables on the model established in physics.

Within this tradition of measurement there are a number of subschools and points of view. Perhaps most notable is the division between axiomatizers and scalers. The axiomatizers (whose approach is exemplified in Krantz, Luce, Suppes & Tversky, 1971, Narens, 1985, and Roberts, 1979) tend to treat the following type of problem: If a body of (potential) qualitative observations satisfies certain primitive laws—axioms that capture properties of these observations—then is it possible to find a numerical structure that accurately summarizes these observations? In technical terms, the question is: To which numerical structures is the set of qualitative observations isomorphic? An isomorphism is a one-to-one mapping between structures under which the structure of the one maps into that of the other. It is also desirable to have an explicit process whereby the numerical structure can be constructed from the qualitative one. This literature, which is a part of 'applicable mathematics,' is purely mathematical in character, but the choice of structures to be studied is greatly influenced by the type of application intended. The objective of this approach is to illuminate the range of possible situations that permit the development of a measurement system, to determine the type of system that is appropriate, and to provide at least one method for its construction.

The scalers pose a different, often more immediately useful, problem. They are concerned with transforming psychological data, which are for the most part fallible in the sense of exhibiting a certain amount of inconsistency and irregularity, into some familiar numerical representation. For example, the question may be how best to locate points in some geometrical, often metric, space so as to represent the psychological relationships among stimuli? This approach accepts the fallible nature of the data, and is, therefore, not so much concerned with verifying that the data satisfy specific properties entailed by the chosen representation as with searching for the best possible fit of the data within the chosen class of representations. The fit between the original data and the solution is evaluated in some global, statistical sense.

In the short run, this scaling approach has proved to be very directly usable. In the long run, solving some of the deeper questions posed by the axiomatic approach to measurement, such as defining the possibilities for measurement, discovering how complexes of structures interrelate (as, for example, those underlying the system of physical units), and determining what kinds of statements are meaningful in a measurement structure, may have more profound implications for progress in psychology.

The Strategy of Mechanisms in Psychophysics

The second major strategy for describing psychophysical attributes is to focus on sensory and other mechanisms in the organism. This strategy is directed at analyzing the internal systems responsible for the transduction, transformation, storage, and interpretation of sensory information. In this view, the organism is likened to an information processing machine, with the sensations corresponding to certain aspects of its internal workings, perhaps the firing patterns of various key neurons that are monitored by an executive control system. This was probably the implicit view of most psychophysicists working on sensations in the 19th century, including the remarkable Helmholtz (1867). It is certainly the dominant point of view of psychophysicists working in this century. Consequently, we will call this the psychophysical approach, and the last part of the chapter will be devoted to a summary of some classical and contemporary work in this field. In that section, a distinction is made between local psychophysics, which is concerned primarily with sensory mechanisms that serve to discriminate stimuli that are physically little different, and global psychophysics, which is directed toward understanding the apprehension of sensations over the full dynamic range of the physical signal. The dividing line between local and global psychophysics is fuzzy in much the same way as is the transition from day to night. Global psychophysics, with its concern for the relation between sensations and the numerically measured physical stimulus has close ties with measurement theory, which will be discussed first.

What is to be Measured?

Before turning to the theory of measurement, it may be well to consider for a moment the question of what it is that is to be measured. Psychologists are interested in a wide variety of behaviors in humans and animals, and obviously the interests of the investigator determine to a large extent which of the observable behaviors receive attention. Once this choice has been made, the investigator faces the problem of devising an appropriate set of experimental measures that are sensitive to the attributes of interest. In this step, investigators are necessarily guided to a significant degree by their own intuitions, but if a number of different measures converge on a single conclusion, there is more reason to be confident of the findings.

Because of the diversity of interests in psychology, there are many different answers to the question, what is to be measured? The attributes of interest can be physical, physiological, or purely psychological. In general, external, physical measures, such as age, sex, and weight, tend to be easy to measure but difficult or impossible to manipulate by experimental procedures. Consequently, studies employing these variables tend to make comparisons across different subject groups. Internal physiological measures, such as hormone levels, neuronal firing rate, and blood pressure, are usually more difficult to obtain, but they are still reducible to some physically defined values. Of these, some can be varied over a wide range depending on the experimental conditions; others are less susceptible to experimental manipulation. Purely psychological variables pose very difficult and important problems of measurement. Some are

usually viewed as relatively enduring characteristics of the individual, such as intelligence, authoritarianism, and the number of items that can be held in short-term memory. Others are characteristic of the momentary state of the individual, and they may vary over a wide range, depending on the external conditions immediately preceding the time at which the measurement is made. The external conditions are often referred to as stimuli when they are varied intentionally in a controlled manner.

Psychophysical measures of sensory states are of the latter type. The stimuli typically used in these studies have the desirable feature of inducing an internal state rapidly and of permitting a shift from one state to another in a matter of seconds or at worst minutes (the ear adjusts exceedingly rapidly, the eye is more leisurely, and taste receptors require even more time). By common convention, psychophysical stimuli that readily alter the internal states are called 'signals.'

At this time, physiological techniques have not been sufficiently developed to permit direct access to many of the sensory states of interest. So for the most part the emphasis in psychophysical experiments is on carefully controlled changes in the external signals. Does this mean that we can assume that there is a one-to-one correspondence between signals and sensory states? Unfortunately, the data strongly suggest that the variability in the induced sensory states is far greater than can be accounted for by uncontrolled variation in the physical signal that gives rise to the sensation. Much of the theoretical and experimental work in psychophysics is an attempt to contend with the imperfect relation between signals and sensory states as reflected in the observer's responses. Perhaps physiological techniques will some day allow us to sidestep this difficult problem, but in the meantime we proceed by labeling the internal states, albeit imperfectly, by the signals used to generate them, and confine ourselves to stimuli that bring about rapid sensory changes.

AXIOMATIC MEASUREMENT

Our aim in this section is to convey a sense of the nature of the work in axiomatic measurement, not to provide a comprehensive summary of the literature pertaining to measurement.

Not only would that be impossible in the space available, but much of the work in this area is technical in character, and thus inappropriate for a general presentation. We will, for the most part, ignore the technical details that lie beneath the results we describe. Nevertheless, it should be kept in mind that measurement theory is quite distinct from the majority of work in psychology, which is of an empirical, inductive character. In contrast, measurement theory proceeds in the deductive fashion of mathematics: certain formal properties are defined and theorems are proved. These theorems take the form of assertions that, if certain properties are true of the structure in question, then certain conclusions follow as a matter of pure logic. Measurement theory is a subpart of that branch of mathematics that studies ordered algebraic systems; however, the impetus for its development is not purely mathematical but comes from the need to place measurement in the social sciences on a firm foundation. The special character of the measurement approach reflects concerns that arise from empirical studies in the social sciences, particularly psychology. Despite the theoretical nature of this work, it has the potential to be applied to experimental situations, and to the extent that the application is successful it may help the investigator to summarize and organize complex sets of observations, to develop models and theories, and to reach a deeper level of understanding of the phenomena under study.

Representation and Uniqueness Theorems

Most results in measurement theory come in pairs (for more complete discussions, see Krantz et al., 1971; Roberts, 1979; Suppes & Zinnes, 1963). The first specifies conditions (axioms) under which it is possible to find numerical representation of the qualitative information. In other words, it formulates properties of a qualitative set of observations that are adequate for a certain kind of measurement system or scale to be appropriate. Such a result is called a representation theorem. The second type of result, called a uniqueness theorem, determines how unique the resulting measure or scale is. In other words, once we know that measurement is possible, the uniqueness theorem describes all other representations that are possible using the same numerical relations and operations. We illustrate these two types of theorems in several important cases.

Orderings and Ordinal Measurement

All measurement, whether within the axiomatic or scaling tradition, begins with a method that orders the objects or events under study according to the attribute of interest. At least half— some would say more—of the practical measurement problem is solved by finding a satisfactory method for ordering the stimuli according to the attribute in question. Over time, the methods may change and improve, but concern for refining the method should not mask the fact that it is merely a way to elicit the qualitative ordering of the attribute. Once a method has been adopted, we can turn our attention to the rest of the measurement problem, namely, finding a numerical representation.

To study internal states, which is our focus here, there is little to do but to ask the subject which of two signals produces more or less of the psychological attribute in question. For example, the subject may be questioned which of two signals is louder, brighter, or whatever. There are any number of variants on this basic strategy; for example, subjects may compare two pairs of stimuli and judge which of the two is the more similar in terms of certain specified, or possibly even unspecified, attributes.

There are some peculiar features to such reports about internal states. In principle, one should be able to ask questions about any internal state to which the observer has some access, but in practice those that change slowly, such as hunger, are difficult to compare, possibly because of the severe burden placed on memory. Thus we are limited to states that change rapidly, and even so we must take care to minimize the memory load.

In addition, we have no way of being certain, except perhaps by examining the data for internal consistency, that the subjects are accurately reporting their internal states. Even if the same response is given every time the same pair of signals is presented—which is rarely the case —we find ourselves in a somewhat uncertain position until physiological measures of internal states become available that closely correlate with verbal reports. Lacking these techniques, we are left with one of two strategies in the face of fluctuations in the observer's responses. One is to attribute these fluctuations to errors of measurement and to deal with them statistically. For example, one can present two signals, a and b, many times, and say that a has more of the attribute in question than does b if this is the observer's judgment on the majority of trials. Alternatively, one can try to build theories to account for the nature of the variability that arises in the mapping between signals and internal states. Some suggested theories for doing this are described later.

For the moment, assume that we have a set of order judgments from an observer, and consider the question of exactly what properties we might expect these judgments to exhibit. Suppose that we denote the set of signals in the experiment by $A = \{a, b, c, \ldots\}$, where a typical element, say b, is simply a way to identify or label a well-defined procedure for presenting a particular signal to the subject. Let $a \gtrsim b$ stand for the observer's report that the sensation generated by a has at least as much of the attribute as that generated by b. Put another way, $\gtrsim$ consists of all ordered pairs of signals for which the observer asserts that the first member of the pair has at least as much of the attribute as the second member of the pair. In technical terms, $\gtrsim$ is called a *relation* on the set of signals A. The first property that we expect the judgments to exhibit is *transitivity*: if whenever $a \gtrsim b$ and $b \gtrsim c$ are both true, then $a \gtrsim c$ will also hold in the data. In practice, this rarely holds without exception, but it appears to be approximately true for many of the senses that have been investigated. It seems plausible also that this would be true of the internal states if we had direct access to them, and whatever failures are observed in the data may simply result from the imperfect match between signals and internal states. There also seems to be no problem in assuming that the relation $\gtrsim$ is *connected*: for any two signals, a and b, either $a \gtrsim b$ or $b \gtrsim a$ or both. (When $a \gtrsim b$ and $b \gtrsim a$ are both true, we say that a is *indifferent* to b and write $a \sim b$.) Any relation that is both connected and transitive is said to be a *weak order*. These minimal assumptions seem to be likely to hold quite generally for many sets of elicited judgments.

Having made these definitions, we can turn to the measurement problem in which we are really interested. The question is whether there is a way of assigning numbers to signals, say the number $\phi(a)$ to signal a, such that the observed

order relation on the set of signals is mirrored by the order of the numbers into which they are mapped. In other words, can we find a function, ϕ, from A into the real numbers that is *order preserving* in the following sense: for all a, b in A, $a \gtrsim b$ if and only if $\phi(a) \geq \phi(b)$? That is to say, the numerical representation is such that the number assigned to a is greater than or equal to the number assigned to b in just those cases in which a is judged to have at least as much of the property as b. This is the representation question, and the answer to it is a qualified Yes. An order preserving function can always be found if A is either finite or denumerable (which means that the signals can be enumerated by using the integers). When A is infinite and not denumerable, a stricter requirement, of a somewhat technical nature, is needed for the function to exist. This requirement is that the set A must include a denumerable subset that acts in A in the same way as the rational numbers (the fractions) act in the set of real numbers, namely, that it is dense in the sense that between any two distinct numbers there is a rational number. This result, precisely formulated, is known as the Cantor-Birkhoff Theorem (see Section 2.1 of Krantz et al., 1971, or Sec. 3.1 of Roberts, 1979). This is the first major result of measurement theory.

It might seem that the major objective of measurement has been accomplished, namely, that of finding a numerical scale to represent the set of signals. However, the answer to the second measurement question, uniqueness, is disappointing. It turns out that any strictly increasing function of the obtained scale ϕ is just as good as the original scale. This means that if $\phi^*(x)$ is given by $f[\phi(x)]$, where f is any strictly increasing function whatsoever, then it is also an order preserving numerical representation. Scales that are unique only up to such transformations are known as *ordinal scales*. (This term and those of ratio, interval, and log interval scales to be defined below were introduced by Stevens, 1946.)

To make this point more concrete and to illustrate why this kind of scale is problematic, consider the example where $\phi^*(x) = f[\phi(x)] = \phi^3(x) + 2$. This is a monotonic increasing function of ϕ—because $f[\phi(a)] > f[\phi(b)]$ if and only if $\phi(a) > \phi(b)$—and so according to the uniqueness result this new ϕ^* is also an order preserving scale. We call this result disappointing because nothing about numbers except their order is invariant. Suppose a, b, and c are such that $\phi(a) + \phi(b) = \phi(c)$. Then for our transformation,

$$
\begin{aligned}
\phi^*(c) &= \phi^3(c) + 2 = [\phi(a) + \phi(b)]^3 + 2 \\
&\neq \phi(a)^3 + 2 + \phi(b)^3 + 2 \\
&= \phi^*(a) + \phi^*(b).
\end{aligned}
$$

In words, this means that addition is not invariant under scale changes, that is, $\phi^*(c) \neq \phi^*(a) + \phi^*(b)$. Multiplication also is not invariant under scale changes. And so we do not have available to us any of the power of the numbers, and much of the point of measurement is lost. For example, statistics such as the mean and variance are not invariant. Only summary statistics based on frequency, such as the median, are not changed in going from one ordinal scale to another.

In order to gain greater uniqueness, more structure than just order is required of the empirical relational structure. We now turn to two major, related approaches to the problem of obtaining greater uniqueness of the measurement scale.

Extensive Structures: Combining Objects

Many physical attributes have, in addition to order, the property that if two objects, both possessing the attribute, are combined, then the combination also exhibits the same attribute. For example, not only can weights be ordered by placing them in the two pans of an equal-arm balance and seeing which pan drops, but if the two objects are combined by placing both in one pan, the combination so formed also has weight. We use the symbol $\circ$ to denote the operation of combining objects, so that $a \circ b$ means the combination of a with b. And we use the general term *concatenation* to refer to the process of combining two objects.

There are three kinds of properties to be expected in a system having both an order relation $\succsim$ and a concatenation operation $\circ$: those that involve only $\succsim$, those that involve only the concatenation operation $\circ$, and those that involve both $\succsim$ and $\circ$. The first we have described already: $\succsim$ is a weak order. The second arises by considering what happens when the concatenation operation is applied more than once, as for example, when a and b are first combined, and c is then added to them, written as $(a \circ b) \circ c$. An alternative would be

first to combine b and c, giving $b \circ c$, and then to combine this with a, giving $a \circ (b \circ c)$. At least for the pan balance situation, we would expect the following to hold: if there is some weight d that balances $(a \circ b) \circ c$, then it should also balance $a \circ (b \circ c)$, and if d does not balance $(a \circ b) \circ c$, then it also should not balance $a \circ (b \circ c)$. In symbols, $(a \circ b) \circ c \sim d$ if and only if $a \circ (b \circ c) \sim d$. Because the indifference relation $\sim$ of a weak order is transitive, this property, called *weak associativity*, is normally abbreviated as

$$(a \circ b) \circ c \sim a \circ (b \circ c).$$

Many operations, such as addition and multiplication of numbers, and sums and products of matrices, exhibit associativity. However, not all operations are associative; for example, the averaging operation defined by $x \circ y = (x + y)/2$ fails associativity, because $(x \circ y) \circ z = [(x + y)/2 + z]/2$ is not in general equal to $x \circ (y \circ z) = [x + (y + z)/2]/2$.

Another property one would expect is: $a \circ b \sim b \circ a$. This is called *commutativity*. It is clearly true of the weight example, and indeed it follows as a consequence of the additive representation. Nevertheless we need not assume it explicitly because it follows logically from the other axioms.

We next evolve two properties involving both $\circ$ and $\succsim$. The first comes from considering two equivalent objects c and c', written as $c \sim c'$—in the case of weight, two objects that balance exactly. If an additional object a is added to the pan containing c, then that side of the balance will drop (so long as the balance is in a vacuum, or the objects have density greater than air). This property, known as *positivity*, says that for any a in A if $c \sim c'$, then $a \circ c \succ c'$. The second property is again concerned with a situation in which $c \sim c'$, and c is combined with an object a. However, in this case c' is combined with yet another object b. Intuitively, it seems plausible that if $a \succsim b$, then combining c with a and combining c' with b should not change the ordering; that is, $a \circ c \succsim b \circ c'$ should hold. Going the other way, if $a \circ c \succsim b \circ c'$, then taking away c and c' should preserve the ordering of a and b, so that $a \succsim b$. Together these are summarized as:

if $c \sim c'$, then $a \succsim b$ if and only if

$$a \circ c \succsim b \circ c'.$$

This property is called *monotonicity* (or *independence*).

These definitions allow us to state the next important result in measurement theory. This result says that if $\succsim$ is a weak order, if $\circ$ is weakly associative, and if both positivity and monotonicity hold (together with some more technical assumptions, such as solvability and the Archimedean axioms, which we need not go into here), then there is a mapping ϕ of A into the positive real numbers that preserves the order relation $\succsim$ and is such that the concatenation operation $\circ$ in A corresponds to addition in the real numbers. In symbols, the function ϕ that maps A into the real numbers has the properties that, for all a and b in A,

(i) $a \succsim b$ if and only if $\phi(a) \geq \phi(b)$,

and

(ii) $\phi(a \circ b) = \phi(a) + \phi(b)$.

Any qualitative structure that has a representation with these two properties is called an *extensive structure*.

The answer to the question of the uniqueness is now most satisfactory. The representation is unique to the extent that any other representation that preserves the order relation and maps the concatenation operation into addition is related to the first by a positive multiplicative constant. That is, if ϕ and ϕ^* are two representations, then it must be the case that $\phi^*(a) = k\phi(a)$ for all a in A, where k is some positive number. Families of representations that have the property of being unique up to a multiplicative constant are called *ratio scales*. Moreover if we choose to map a particular object of A into the number 1, that is, to make it the unit, then the representation is uniquely specified. (For a more detailed discussion of extensive measurement, see Sec. 3.1, 3.4, 3.6 of Krantz et al., 1971, or Sec. 3.6 of Roberts, 1979).

In physics there are a number of cases, including the measurement of mass, length, and time, in which a positive, monotonic, associative operation of the required sort exists. However, there are others for which either there is no suitable concatenation operation, as with density or momentum, or an operation exists but it fails to meet one or another of the needed properties, as with temperature. In psychology few operations that one can think of preserve any attribute of interest, and by and large those

that do fail to satisfy one or another of the properties needed for extensive measurement. Given this, why have we bothered to describe extensive measurement here? There are two reasons. First, it is the basis for certain fundamentally important scales in physics, and it has been taken by many philosophers of science as the prototype of successful measurement. Second, extensive measurement is central to the development of the rest of axiomatic measurement theory in that nearly every other result in the theory either reduces to extensive measurement (although not necessarily in a trivial or obvious way) or is in some way a generalization of it.

From here, there are two general avenues of development. One is to consider cases that have an operation with properties different from or weaker than those required for extensive measurement, or both. For example, only a minor modification allows probability to be treated as extensive measurement. For this case, let A be the set of possible chance events, and let $a \succsim b$ mean that event a is at least as probable as event b. Let the operation $\circ$ be the union of disjoint (i.e., mutually exclusive) events. Note that this operation differs from that of extensive measurement because it is defined for only some of the pairs of elements of A, namely, those events that are disjoint. Nevertheless, a modification of the theory of extensive measurement yields the usual probability representation that is finitely additive. This has played some role in research on decision theory, and such qualitative theories of probability may turn out to have important philosophic implications, as described later. The second avenue of development that may be followed is to abandon entirely the notion of an operation. We turn next to an approach that does this, at least on the surface.

Conjoint Structures: Trading off Factors

Thus far we have confined ourselves to the situation in which the set of objects being studied varies in just one physical variable. Many cases of interest, however, involve multiple, independently varying factors. Much of science, including psychology, studies tradeoffs between such factors, Examples in psychology are stimulus pairs consisting of an amount of food and a delay of its receipt that are equally rewarding; pairs of intensities and frequencies of pure tones that are equally loud; and pairs of luminances and durations that are equally detectable. More generally, one can ask which of two different sets of factors exhibits more of the psychological attribute; is 5 sec of access to a food tray after a 3-sec delay more or less preferred than 2 sec of access following a 1-sec delay; is a 60-dB SPL, 500-Hz tone more or less loud than a 50-dB, 1000-Hz tone; is 50 msec of a 100 troland light flash more or less detectable than a 20-msec, 500-troland flash?

The stimuli in these two-factor situations can be described as pairs (a, p), where a labels the amount or level of factor A, and p labels the amount of factor P. The set of all such pairs (a, p) is called the *Cartesian product* of A and P, denoted $A \times P$. Given a factorial structure of this sort, we can ask subjects to order the pairs (a, p) for some psychological attribute, such as preference, loudness, or detectability. This, then, gives an order on the set $A \times P$, and the measurement question is: How can this psychological structure be represented numerically? At first glance, it appears that this is just the ordinal measurement case described earlier, which was unsatisfactory because the numerical representation was so lacking in uniqueness. It turns out, however, that if the numerical representation is required to reflect both the factorial structure of the pairs and the obtained pattern of tradeoffs, then the representation is much more unique than an ordinal scale.

Perhaps it will help to understand the solution to this representation problem if we first give one of many examples from physics. Suppose A is the set of all possible homogeneous substances, such as lead, water, oxygen, and so on, and P represents a set of containers. Thus (a, p) refers to the amount of substance labeled a just sufficient to fill the container labeled p. Let the ordering $\gtrsim$ be that induced on $A \times P$ by mass, as measured by a pan balance in a vacuum. From physics, we know that there is a positively valued numerical scale of mass m on $A \times P$, of density ϱ on A, and of volume V on P, such that for all a in A and p in P,

$$m(a, p) = \varrho(a) V(p),$$

or, for short, $m = \varrho V$. That is, a number can be assigned to each pair (a, p) that is equal to the product of the number assigned to a and the number assigned to p. The factorial structure and the trading off of the factors in this situation are represented by the separate numerical

mappings for A and P, the product of which gives the representation for $A \times P$. A representation of this sort is called a *product representation*.

In fact, it turns out that more can be said than this. There is a mass concatenation operation, which is denoted here as $\circ_m$ on $A \times P$, such that

$$m[(a, p) \circ_m (b, q)] = m(a, p) + m(b, q).$$

In addition, there is a volume concatenation operation $\circ_v$ on P such that

$$V(p \circ_v q) = V(p) + V(q).$$

In words, there is some concatenation operation (placing the two filled containers on one side of the pan balance) on the pairs of substances and containers that corresponds to addition of the numerical values on the volume scale V.

Keeping this example in mind, we turn now to the general measurement problem: under what conditions does a weak order, $\gtrsim$, on $A \times P$ have a product representation, and how unique is it? The answer must somehow involve the interplay between the order relation and the factorial structure. We now define two properties that must govern this interplay in order for a representation of the desired sort to exist. The first property says that, if two pairs have the same level on one factor, then the same order on the pairs should obtain, independently of what this common factor is. In symbols, for all a, b in A, and p, q in P

$$(a, p) \gtrsim (b, p) \text{ if and only if } (a, q) \gtrsim (b, q)$$

and $(a, p) \gtrsim (a, q)$ if and only if $(b, p) \gtrsim (b, q)$.

It should be clear why this property, called *independence*, is essential if an ordering on the separate factors A and P is to exist. For example, if $(a, p) \gtrsim (b, p)$ but $(a, q) \prec (b, q)$, then it would be impossible to assign any numbers to a and b that are consistent with the ordering on the factorial structure, $A \times P$. Such a failure of independence is reminiscent of interactions between factors in the context of analysis of variance. Consider a two-factor experiment in which two variables are being simultaneously varied. If it turns out that there is a significant interaction between the factors, then no general statements can be made about the main effects of each of the factors taken singly.

Note that if independence holds, we may define an order $\gtrsim_A$ on A by: $a \gtrsim_A b$ if and only

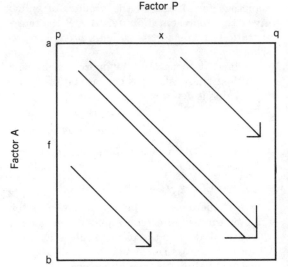

Figure 1.1. Graphical representation of the double cancellation property. An arrow means that the stimulus pair at the foot of the arrow dominates the pair at the head of the arrow. Each single arrow is an antecedent assumption; the double arrow is the conclusion.

if for some p and so for all p in P, $(a, p) \gtrsim (b, p)$. In like manner, $\gtrsim_P$ is defined on P. These are referred to as *induced orders*.

The second property needed for a multiplicative representation, called *double cancellation*, is less familiar, but equally important, and is described with reference to Figure 1.1.

Each of the two factors has three levels: a, f, and b are the levels of A, and p, x, and q are those of P. The requirement is that whenever the obtained judgments exhibit the ordering indicated by the single arrows, $(f, p) \gtrsim (b, x)$ and $(a, x) \gtrsim (f, q)$, then they must also exhibit the ordering indicated by the double arrows, $(a, p) \gtrsim (b, q)$.

With these definitions in hand, we now state the measurement result for this case. It can be shown (Debreu, 1960a; Luce & Tukey, 1964; Krantz et al., 1971, chap. 6) that if these two properties, independence and double cancellation, hold together with some more, rather technical assumptions (again some form of solvability and an Archimedean axiom), then a multiplicative representation of positive scale values exists on the factors. That is to say, there exists a positive, real-valued mapping ψ_A on A, and ψ_P on P, such that

$(a, p) \gtrsim (b, q)$ if and only if

$$\psi_A(a)\psi_P(p) \geq \psi_A(b)\psi_P(q).$$

Moreover, if $\psi_A\psi_P$ is one such representation, any other must be of the form $\gamma\psi_A^\alpha\psi_P^\alpha$, where α and γ are both positive numbers. Families of representations that are invariant up to this kind of power transformation are called *log-interval scales*.

A completely equivalent representation, in the sense of containing the same information, is produced by taking the logarithm of the multiplicative representation. If $\phi_A = \log \psi_A$ and $\phi_P = \log \psi_P$, then $\phi_A + \phi_P = \log \psi_A\psi_P$ is an additive representation, and it is unique up to the affine transformation of the form $\alpha\phi_A + \alpha\phi_P + \beta$, where α is greater than zero and $\beta = \log \gamma$. Such families are called *interval scales*. As with the ratio scales found for extensive measurement, the unit or scale factor is not fixed. For the interval scales there is an additional degree of freedom, the exponent α in the case of log interval scales and the additive constant β in the case of pure interval scales. Thus, these two scale types are slightly less unique than are ratio scales, but this additional degree of freedom does not pose serious difficulties. In fact, the three scale types, ratio, interval, and log interval, are exactly the ones that have proved most useful in well-developed physical theories involving measurement.

Earlier we said that many of the measurement situations that have been studied have a close tie in one way or another to extensive measurement, in which there is a concatenation operation ∘. In the example given earlier in this section with physical substances and containers, we discussed the existence of such operations. The general relationship between conjoint and extensive measurement is not too complicated to be outlined here. Suppose A and P each have a smallest element, denoted a_0 and p_0, respectively, under the induced orderings $\gtrsim_A$ on A and $\gtrsim_P$ on P defined by: $a \gtrsim_A b$ if $(a, p) \gtrsim (b, p)$ for all p, and $p \gtrsim_P q$ if $(a, p) \gtrsim (a, q)$ for all a. For each a in A, let $\pi(a)$ be that element of P such that $(a, p_0) \sim (a_0, \pi(a))$. This means that the 'interval' on A with end points a and a_0 is just matched by the interval on P with end points p_0 and $\pi(a)$. Now, we would like to combine the interval from a_0 to a with that from a_0 to any b in A; this gives the concatenation $a \circ b$. In order to see the trick for doing this, it

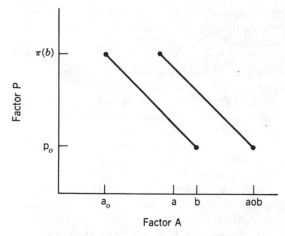

Figure 1.2. Graphical representation of the function $\pi(b)$ and of the operation $a \circ b$. Stimulus pairs on the same curve are equivalent.

may be well to follow the steps in Figure 1.2. The first step is to map the interval from a_0 to b onto P, by finding $\pi(b)$ such that $(a_0, \pi(b))$ is indifferent to (b, p_0). For example, if the structure consists of pairs of substances and amounts ordered by mass, then $\pi(b)$ denotes the container such that the amount of substance a_0 has the same mass as the amount of substance b that fills container p_0. The interval from p_0 to $\pi(b)$ is then mapped back onto A, using a as the bottom of the interval. That is, we look for the element $a \circ b$ such that $(a \circ b, p_0) \sim [a, \pi(b)]$. So in the example $a \circ b$ is that substance in the amount filling container p_0 that has the same mass as substance a in the amount filling container $\pi(b)$. If this can be found (i.e., if such an $a \circ b$ exists for all a and b in A), then the double cancellation property ensures that the operation $\circ$ thus defined is associative. Indeed, it can be shown that A with the induced ordering $\succsim_A$ and the concatenation operation is an extensive structure, and so there is an additive scale of ϕ_A on A. By a similar argument one can construct a scale ϕ_P on P. Then one shows that the numerical ordering of $\phi_A + \phi_P$ corresponds to the qualitative ordering of $\succsim$. By this trick, the proof of the conjoint case is reduced to the extensive measurement situation. (If no minimal elements exist in either A or P, then additional problems are encountered, but they can be overcome.) The theory of conjoint measurement just described for two factors generalizes naturally to any finite, but fixed, number of factors, but the two-

factor case illustrates the essential points. Later, in the section on functional measurement, we consider the case in which the number of factors is not fixed.

Proximity Structures: The Judgment of Similarity

To this point we have assumed that the subject orders (some of) the stimuli; such data are often called *dominance data*. It is also possible and common to get subjects to judge how close or similar two stimuli are. For example, if a, b, c, d are stimuli, then we may ask the subject to judge whether a is closer to b than c is to d; if so, we write $(a, b) \precsim (c, d)$. Such data, often called *proximity data*, form an ordering $\precsim$ of $A \times A$.

A number of axiomatic theories exist for proximity data, leading to various sorts of representations for these data. The simplest, which is very closely related to additive conjoint measurement, results in a mapping ϕ of A into the real numbers such that

$$(a, b) \precsim (c, d) \text{ if and only if}$$
$$\phi(a) - \phi(b) \le \phi(c) - \phi(d).$$

Rather more important, and somewhat trickier to axiomatize, is the representation

$$(a, b) \precsim (c, d) \text{ if and only if}$$
$$|\phi(a) - \phi(b)| \le |\phi(c) - \phi(d)|,$$

where $|x|$ denotes the absolute magnitude of x, independent of its sign. These axiom systems can be found in chapter 4 of Krantz et al. (1971).

More important for scaling purposes are representations not into the real numbers, but into some sort of geometric space, especially some type of metric space. These representations are described in detail under *Scaling of Proximity Data*, and a discussion of the axiomatic basis for this can be found in Beals, Krantz, and Tversky (1968).

A rather different approach has been taken by Tversky (1977), who followed in spirit earlier ideas for probability models, which are described below. The essential idea is that stimuli can be thought of as collections of features or attributes. His feature-matching model postulates that similarity data can be accounted for by three sets of features: those the objects share and those that are unique to each of the two objects. More specifically, let A be the features or properties of object a and B those of object b.

The model assumes that the more features that are held in common by the two objects—that is, the more features in the intersection A and B, $A \cap B$—the greater will be the similarity measure. Unique features—those of a not shared by b and those of b not shared by a, denoted $A - B$ and $B - A$, respectively—are assumed to subtract from judged similarity. Tversky has provided conditions (axioms) under which there exists a function f that assigns numerical values to sets of features such that the observed similarity data are monotonically related to the following equation:

$$S(a, b) = \theta f(A \cap B) - \alpha f(A - B)$$
$$- \beta f(B - A),$$

where θ, α, and β are positive constants. This expression incorporates the assumption that shared features add to and unique features subtract from the overall similarity between a and b.

This feature-matching model is extremely general. The constants, θ, α, and β, allow for the possibility that different tasks may induce the subject to place different emphasis on the shared and distinctive features. For example, if the subject is to rate how much alike the stimuli are, greater emphasis may be placed on the shared features than if the subject's task focuses on differences between objects. Moreover, tasks that are directional in character—for example, when the question is how much the first object is like the second object—may place greater emphasis on, say, the unique features of the first object than on those of the second. This allows the model to account for frequently obtained asymmetric similarity measures, that is, cases in which the measured similarity of a to b is different from that of b to a. In addition, the features of the objects need not be either equal in number or equally salient. This difference may be reflected in certain kinds of similarity measures, such as when some members of the set of objects turn out to be correctly identified more often than other members. Finally, the model may account for particular kinds of context effects, in which specific features or properties become important or salient because they are useful for dividing the set of objects into convenient subsets. We note that, although the feature-matching model is extremely general and powerful, no method yet exists for determining

the appropriate features or for finding the required numerical function for the set of features.

Scaling Arising from Representation Theorems

Each axiom system for measurement leads to a family of numerical representations or a scale, and to the extent that the proof is constructive it leads in principle to a scaling method. However, since not all scaling methods have received a measurement treatment, we have elected to discuss them later in a separate section. But before leaving the topic of measurement, we illustrate the major device for constructing a scale in the case of extensive measurement.

Suppose a is any element of the stimulus set. Let $a_1, a_2, \ldots, a_n, \ldots$ be distinct objects in the set that are each equivalent to a. Then in an extensive structure, which is associative, we define the concept of n copies of a, denoted na, to be

$$na = a_1 \circ a_2 \circ \cdots \circ a_n.$$

Note that if ϕ is an additive representation in the sense of $\phi(a \circ b) = \phi(a) + \phi(b)$, then $\phi(na) = n\phi(a)$. Now, to carry out an approximate construction, some element e is chosen to be the unit and is assigned $\phi(e) = 1$. Suppose we wish to estimate ϕ to an accuracy of ε. Choose n to be an integer such that $n > 1/\varepsilon$. For any element a, first find na and then search for that integer m such that

$$me \precsim na \precsim (m + 1)e.$$

The existence of such an m must be assured by an axiom of the system, called, the Archimedean axiom. Note that if ϕ exists,

$$m = m\phi(e) = \phi(me) \leq n\phi(a) \leq \phi[(m + 1)e]$$
$$= (m + 1)\phi(e) = m + 1,$$

and so

$$m/n \leq \phi(a) \leq m/n + 1/n.$$

Thus, to an accuracy better than ε, $\phi(a) = m/n$.

This is basically the method by which physical scales were originally developed, and this method can readily be extended to the conjoint measurement case. A psychological application of this method in the conjoint case was carried out by Levelt, Riemersma, and Bunt (1972). In that study subjects judged binaural loudness, with different intensities presented to the two ears. They found that, to a good approximation, loudness is additive across the two ears and that for each ear it is a power function of physical intensity (see the section on magnitude estimation). Because there is considerable variability in such judgments, there is room for error. For this reason, Falmagne (1976) developed a modified method based on median responses, and data reported in his studies suggest that the picture may not be as simple as indicated by Levelt et al.

The method just described is usable only when one is working with very fine-grained dimensions so that elements with specific properties can be found. In psychology this is not often the case, because only a small number of levels of each of the factors can be generated, and one must then solve a finite system of linear inequalities. The theory for this is well developed and there are frequently used computer packages for solving the equations. (See the later section on functional measurement for an approach to the finite, factorial case.)

Meaningfulness and Invariance

As we have seen, fundamental measurement involves the search for numerical structures that mimic in all essentials the structure of the set of empirical observations. One's interest in finding such representations is primarily that they place at one's disposal all the powerful tools of mathematical analysis, including the calculus, probability theory and stochastic processes, statistics, Fourier analysis, etc. Valuable as this is—it has been a major feature of the flowering of physics during the past 300 years—dangers may arise from the fact that, once an empirical structure is mapped into numbers, the numbers tend to assume a life of their own, inviting assertions that go beyond what was actually captured in the measurement.

As an example, suppose $\gtrsim$ is a weak order on the set $\{a, b, c, d, e\}$ that ranks the elements in alphabetical order. Each of the two numerical

representations shown in Table 1.1 is an equally suitable representation of this ranking. Observe that 2, 6, and 8 are values of both representations, and, of course, $2 + 6 = 8$ is a truth of arithmetic. But does this arithmetical statement correspond to something that is true of the empirical structure, the alphabetical ordering of a, b, c, d, and e? One suspects that the answer is No, but is the reason clear? One might say that the addition operation does not correspond to an empirical truth because the empirical structure has no operation that is mapped into the numerical operation $+$. Although true, this is irrelevant. Often numerical operations are meaningful, even though they do not correspond explicitly to anything in the qualitative structure. Recall, for example, that multiplication (or addition) meaningfully enters into the representation of conjoint structures, even though nothing corresponds to it directly in the empirical situation.

Why, then, is the statement $2 + 6 = 8$ not meaningful in our example? A more subtle observation, and one that is closer to the point, is that addition does not remain invariant when we substitute one perfectly acceptable representation for another. That is, addition of the values for representation 1 does not correspond to addition of the values for representation 2. To see this, let f be the function that takes representation 1 into representation 2, so that $f(8) = 6$, $f(6) = 4$, and $f(2) = 1$. Now, if the operation of addition were invariant under this mapping, it would mean that $f(2 + 6)$ should be equal to $f(2) + f(6)$. But this is not true, since $f(2 + 6) = f(8) = 6$ and $f(2) + f(6) = 1 + 4 = 5$, which are not equal. So the addition operation is not invariant, and this is the real reason that it makes no sense to add scale values in this case. Before formalizing this more precisely, we turn briefly again to the concept of scale types.

Scale Types

We have already indicated how mappings between different, equally good numerical representations can be used to classify the measurement scales. Stevens (1946, 1951) first brought this to the attention of psychologists, and he isolated three distinct cases that appear to be important in psychology, and indeed also in physics. These cases differ in the kinds of operations that are invariant under mappings between equivalent representations. The most restrictive condition

Table 1.1.

Object	Representation 1	Representation 2
a	10	8
b	8	6
c	6	4
d	4	2
e	2	1

that can be applied to these mappings is that the representation be unique except for multiplication by a positive constant (often called a similarity transformation), as was true for extensive measurement. As was noted earlier, measurement with this degree of uniqueness is called *ratio measurement* and the family of representations is called a *ratio scale*.

Stevens also singled out those empirical structures that have both a ratio scale representation and also a largest element. Examples of a largest element are the velocity of light and the certain event in probability measurement. If the value of one, or any other fixed value, is assigned to the largest element, then no transformations are permitted; Stevens called these *absolute scales*. It is true that such boundedness causes special theoretical problems, but it is not really useful to treat those structures as more constrained than other ratio scales.

We return to the question raised above: when is a numerical statement involving the operation of addition invariant under all possible representations within the scale? The answer is that this is true only for ratio measurement. This can be seen by noting that the transformation f from one scale to another must be increasing and it must satisfy the following constraint: for all positive real x and y

$$f(x + y) = f(x) + f(y).$$

This is known to be true only if $f(x) = \alpha x$, where α is some fixed positive constant (Aczél, 1966). It is easy to verify that such functions have the required property; it is more difficult to prove that they are the only ones that do. So, in order for $+$ to be invariant in the class of representations, the scale must be of the ratio type.

A less restrictive condition that can be applied to the mappings between equivalent representations is that the mappings take the form of a positive linear (or affine) transformation, $\alpha x + \beta$, $\alpha > 0$. The scales that have this property are called *interval scales*. Note that since β can be any real number, the numerical values can be either positive or negative. If, however, we apply an exponential transformation, $\gamma e^{\alpha x}$ with $\gamma = e^{\beta} > 0$, all values in the new representation are positive numbers, addition is transformed to multiplication, and the new representations are related to one another by the power transformation, ηx^{ν}, $\eta > 0$, $\nu > 0$. Such a family of representations is called a *log-interval*

scale because a logarithmic transformation converts them into an interval scale.

The weakest case is ordinal measurement, where the measurement representations differ from one another by strictly increasing function, and any such function generates another representation. Because only order information is invariant under mappings between the representations, these are called *ordinal scales*. Some researchers, including Stevens, choose to class many : one mappings as measurement, calling these *nominal scales*. We omit them here because we believe measurement should be defined as involving additional structure such as ordering relations.

Symmetric Structures

For some years measurement theorists have wondered whether there might exist interesting empirical structures with scales of strength intermediate between ordinal and interval and between interval and ratio. In fact, there are at least two classes of structures that are not ratio, interval, or ordinal and whose scale types have never been characterized. These are semiorders (Suppes & Zinnes, 1963), which model algebraic thresholds, and Coombs's preference model in which a common ordering is folded about individual points to yield the preference orders of individuals (see below). Recently, Narens (1981a, b, 1985) has significantly clarified these issues.

Consider mappings of a structure that transform it *onto* itself while preserving its structure —in other words, mappings that represent it on itself. This is exactly what a scale transformation does in the numerical representation, but we can also study such mappings in the empirical structure itself. They are called *automorphisms*, and their existence corresponds to symmetries in the structure. Only symmetric structures have automorphisms, and the greater the degree of symmetry, the richer the set—technically, group—of automorphisms. One way to describe this richness is as follows. Let M be an integer, and suppose that each set of M distinct points can be mapped by an automorphism into any other set of M distinct points that are ordered in the same way as the first set; we then say the structure is *M-point homogeneous*. Thus, for example, a structure with an interval scale representation is 2-point homogeneous since with positive linear transformation one can always find one that maps the point (x, y), $x > y$, into (u, v), $u > v$.

A second notion characterizes the redundancy of the automorphisms. If N points can be mapped into another N points, can the mapping be done in more than one way? If not—that is, whenever two automorphisms agree at N distinct points, they are the same automorphisms—then the structure is said to be *N-point unique*. We can easily verify that an interval scale structure is 2-point unique. A structure is said to be of *scale type* (M, N), if M is the largest value for which it is M-point homogeneous and N is the smallest value for which it is N-point unique. It is easy to show that $M \leq N$.

Narens has established the following. For structures that are of type (M, M), and that have a representation onto either the real numbers or the positive real numbers—this means a highly dense set of objects—then

(i) $M = 1$ if and only if there is a ratio scale representation.

(ii) $M = 2$ if and only if there is an interval scale representation.

(iii) There are no (M, M) structures for which $M > 2$.

Later it was shown that if a structure on the real numbers is both M-point homogeneous, $M > 1$, and N-point unique for some N, then it is 2-point unique and has a representation whose automorphisms form a subgroup of the linear transformations of an interval scale (Alper 1984, 1987). This means they are of the form $x \rightarrow \alpha x + \beta$, but not necessarily every transformation of this type is an automorphism. Thus, for structures with $M \geq 1$, the only case beyond ratio and interval is that with $M = 1$ and $N = 2$. Very little is known about the cases with either $M = 0$ or $N = \infty$ (defined to be those that are not N-point unique for any finite N). Examples of $M = 0$ structures are probability measures over events defined on a continuum; and examples of $N = \infty$ are threshold structures called semiorders.

Luce and Narens (1985) have studied all possible structures with a concatenation operation. They established that the most general ratio scale structure on the positive real numbers must have a numerical operation of the form: for all real x and y, $x \circ y = yf(x/y)$, where f is a strictly increasing function and $f(x)/x$ is strictly decreasing. And the most general interval scale on the real numbers has an operation of the form: there are constants a and b that are both between 0 and 1, such that for all real x and y,

$$x \circ y = \begin{cases} ax + (1 - a)y, & x \geq y, \\ bx + (1 - b)y, & x \leq y. \end{cases}$$

Luce and Narens show that this leads to a possible theory for choices among monetary gambles. It is similar to and only slightly more complicated than the well-known subjective expected utility theory (see Ch. 10 of Vol. 2), except that it does not presuppose a high degree of rationality on the part of the decision maker. Further generalizations are in Luce (1986b).

Structure and Reference Invariance

That addition is a meaningful concept if and only if measurement is at the level of a ratio scale is a special case of the following more general concept. Consider any numerical relation, by which we mean some collection R of k-tuples $(x_1, x_2, \ldots, x_k)$, where k is a fixed integer and the order of the elements matter. Such a k-tuple is called an (ordered) pair when $k = 2$, a triple when $k = 3$, and a quadruple when $k = 4$. Addition is an example of such a relation since it consists of all triples (x_1, x_2, x_3) for which, in the usual notation, $x_1 + x_2 = x_3$. Another example is quadruples (x_1, x_2, x_3, x_4) that satisfy the cross-ratio property $x_1 x_4 = x_2 x_3$. Now the property we want to isolate—call it structure invariance (in the numerical structure)—requires a relation R to be invariant under the admissible transformations that take one measurement representation into another, that is, the automorphisms of the representation. More formally, a relation R on the real numbers is *structure invariant* relative to a measurement theory if whenever $(x_1, x_2, \ldots, x_k)$ is in R and whenever f is a transformation that takes one representation into another, then $[f(x_1), f(x_2), \ldots, f(x_k)]$ is also in R. This is a first condition that must be met if R is to be called a meaningful numerical relation vis-à-vis a particular measurement structure. Is there more to meaningfulness?

Consider a numerical relation R and a particular representation ϕ of the empirical structure. We can then ask about all the k-tuples $(a_1, a_2, \ldots, a_k)$ in the empirical structure that map under ϕ into R, that is, such that $[\phi(a_1), \phi(a_2),$

..., $\phi(a_k)$] is an element of R. Let this set of empirical k-tuples be denoted by $S(R, \phi)$, which makes explicit that it depends on the choice of both R and ϕ. Now, if the numerical relation R corresponds to something empirical—that is, has an invariant meaning back in the empirical structure—then $S(R, \phi)$ should not in fact depend on ϕ. This is to say, if ϕ and ψ are both representations, $S(R, \phi) = S(R, \psi)$. If this holds for all representations, we say R is *reference invariant*.

It is interesting that when measurement is onto all real numbers or onto all the positive reals, then it can be shown that a numerical relation is reference invariant if and only if it is structure invariant. So nothing new has been added in these cases, although when measurement is not onto an open real interval, such as the positive reals, the two concepts may not agree.

A natural question to raise is: what conditions must an empirical relation S satisfy in order that it map onto a reference-invariant numerical relation? One might first think that any relation defined in the empirical structure could arise, but that is not true. Only some relations S can be said to be empirically meaningful. The answer is found by looking at the automorphisms of the structure, and the requirement is that S map into itself under each automorphism. Such structure invariant relations (in the empirical structure) can be shown to correspond exactly to the numerical relations that are reference invariant.

For measurement situations in which the empirical structures are so rich that the numerical measurements are onto either the real numbers or the positive real numbers, we accept these three equivalent concepts—structure invariance in the empirical structure, structure invariance in the numerical structure, and reference invariance—as a characterization of meaningfulness. (It is unclear which of the three, if any, is the correct definition when they do not agree.) These concepts of meaningfulness have evolved through the work of Adams, Fagot, and Robinson, 1965; Luce, 1978; Narens, 1981a, b, 1985; Pfanzagl, 1968; Suppes and Zinnes, 1963; as well as unpublished work. Much still remains to be done to explicate this concept fully.

The remainder of the section outlines two applications of these ideas. One is very important in physics and potentially important in psychology; the other has been a source of controversy in psychology for several decades.

Dimensional Invariance

The scales of physics are all very neatly tied together, as is reflected in the pattern of their units. One can select a set of independent scales as basic—one common, but by no means unique, choice is mass, length, time, charge, and temperature—and the units of all other measures can be expressed as products of powers of these. If the corresponding units are gram, meter, second, coulomb, and kelvin, then that of energy is gm^2/s^2, of impedance is $gm^2/c^2 s$, etc. This arises in part because many multiplicative conjoint structures exist that establish intimate connections between scales and in part because there is a simple compatibility between a number of concatenation operations and the conjoint structures in situations in which those scales enter. For example, kinetic energy E, mass m and velocity v are related by $E = (1/2) mv^2$. This complex of interrelated empirical structures can all be represented by a numerical structure called a multiplicative vector space. Physicists have long asserted that the relations in the vector space that correspond to physical laws must satisfy invariance under certain transformations of the vector space called similarities because they generalize the one-dimensional transformations of a ratio scale. This invariance property, known as *dimensional invariance*, is a special case of the measurement-theoretic concept of meaningfulness, just defined (Luce, 1978).

Dimensional invariance of physical laws was shown many years ago (Buckingham, 1914; Krantz et al., 1971, Theorem 10.4) to impose severe constraints on the numerical form of physical laws, and it leads to an analytical technique called dimensional analysis. Often one can arrive at the form of a physical law, sometimes determined completely except for a numerical constant, merely by knowing the relevant variables and without solving any of the basic equations for the dynamics involved. A good reference to the method and its applications is Sedov (1959). So far no effective use has been made in psychology of dimensional methods, the reason being, in part at least, that no one has seen how to add any purely psychological variables to the dimensional structure of physics. For more detailed discussions (see Krantz et al.,

1971, vol. 1, chap. 10; vol. 3 (in preparation); Luce, 1978).

Meaningfulness and Statistics

The major impact of the measurement concept of meaningfulness in psychology has concerned statistics, and, unfortunately, a considerable amount of controversy and confusion about the matter has ensued. Ever since Stevens emphasized the importance of scale type, it has been realized that the meaningfulness of any assertion involving a statistic, such as the mean, median, standard deviation, and so on, depends upon the scale type of the measurement. Consider, for example, the mean of k measurements $x_1, x_2, \ldots, x_k$, namely,

$$\bar{x} = \frac{1}{k} \sum_{i=1}^{k} x_i,$$

and let u be another measurement. Then the equation $\bar{x} = u$ is a relation that is reference invariant for both a ratio and an interval scale, but clearly not for an ordinal scale. Table 1.2 summarizes a number of reference-invariant (i.e., meaningful) statements or propositions for different scale types when the measurement is onto either the reals or the positive reals, as is appropriate. In each case, one can verify the assertion simply by testing to see whether the statement satisfies numerical structure invariance. For example, the statement $\bar{x} = y + u$ is meaningful for a ratio scale, since multiplying each of the values by a positive constant α results in the mathematically equivalent statement $\alpha\bar{x} = \alpha y + \alpha u$. However, the same statement is not meaningful for an interval scale, since $\bar{x} = y + u$ is not equivalent to $(\alpha\bar{x} + \beta) = (\alpha\bar{y} + \beta) + (\alpha u + \beta)$. *It should be noted that it is not the statistic per se that is or is not meaningful, but rather the proposition in which it appears.*

The problem is to pass from this table, which is not especially controversial, to statistical practice, which is. One extreme position is that, for example, one must never perform a t test, which involves the statistic $\sqrt{k - 1}(\bar{x} - u)/s_x$ (see Table 1.2 for symbols), unless the observations come from a ratio scale. The reason given is that this statistic is only invariant under ratio scale transformations. The opposite extreme view is that measurement considerations are totally irrelevant to any statistical inference which, after all, has to do with some property of a set of numbers and not where they came from. As is often the case when two contradictory statements are each based on somewhat plausible arguments, neither is wholly right nor wholly wrong. Krantz et al. (in preparation) argue in detail the following view of the matter.

For any of this to make sense we must be working with an empirical situation that has both a measurement structure (including, at a minimum, an ordering) and a probability aspect. Viewed one way, the empirical structure is a qualitative measurement structure that admits some sort of numerical measurement representation. Viewed another way, the empirical structure is a population on which various numerical functions (called random variables) may be

Table 1.2. Examples of meaningful propositions

Sample statistic	Formula	Scale type	Meaningful propositions
Mean	$\bar{x} = \frac{1}{x} \sum_{i=1}^{k} x_i$	ratio interval	$\bar{x} = u,\ \bar{x} = \bar{y} + u$ $\bar{x} = u,\ \bar{x} - u = \bar{y} - v$
Median	that x_j of $x_1, \ldots, x_{2k+1}$ such that $x_i < x_j$ for exactly k i's	ordinal	x_j is the median of $x_1, \ldots, x_{2k+1}$
Geometric mean	$\bar{x}_g = \exp\left[\frac{1}{k} \sum_{i=1}^{k} \log x_i\right]$	log interval	$\bar{x}_g = w,\ \bar{x}_g = \bar{y}_g,\ \bar{x}_g u = \bar{y}_g v$
Standard deviation	$s_x = \left[\frac{1}{k} \sum_{i=1}^{k} (x_i - \bar{x})^2\right]^{1/2}$	ratio interval	$s_x = u$ $s_x = \tau s_y$
Coefficient of variation	$s_x/\bar{x}$	ratio	$\frac{s_x}{\bar{x}} = \tau$

defined, and the underlying probability structure induces a probability distribution for each random variable. Both structures can exist, and they are in no way contradictory. Some of the random variables are also order preserving, but we may not assume that each order-preserving random variable forms a measurement representation.

Often we are interested in random variables that are distributed in a particular way, the most common one being the Gaussian (often called the normal) distribution. There is absolutely no reason to expect that an order-preserving random variable with a particular distribution function, say, the Gaussian, is also a mapping that preserves the measurement aspects of the situation. Moreover, one must not be misled about this in the following deceptive situation. Suppose the measurement structure forms an interval scale, so that positive affine transformations take one measurement mapping into another. Note that the same affine transformations also take one Gaussian random variable into another Gaussian random variable. Nevertheless, we have no reason to expect any but a monotonic relation between a measurement mapping and a Gaussian random variable.

An example may help. Physical time differences, such as reaction times, form an extensive structure and so have a ratio scale representation. Reaction times in a particular experiment have some (necessarily non-Gaussian) distribution. It is quite conceivable, however, that some nonlinear, but monotonic, transformation of the reaction times may have a Gaussian distribution, which of course is invariant under multiplication by a positive constant. Those two ratio invariances in no way force the two scales—physical time and that transformation of it that is Gaussian distributed in a particular reaction time experiment—to be linearly related. In general, one is at great risk in making, and under considerable obligation to defend, the assumption that the measurement mapping, which of course is a random variable, has a particular distribution function, say the Gaussian.

That being the case, it is essential to distinguish clearly the two kinds of hypotheses that one can formulate. First there are propositions about the structure of the population itself, and for these to be meaningful they must exhibit measurement-theoretic reference invariance. And then there are those that make assertions about samples of observations that are reported in terms of a random variable whose distribution is known or is assumed to be known. We call hypotheses of the first type *population meaningful* and those of the second type, *distribution meaningful*.

Observe that since an order-preserving random variable whose distribution is specified does not, in general, coincide with any measurement representation (although they are monotonically related), a hypothesis that is population meaningful need not be distribution meaningful, and conversely. This means that if we are going to perform any statistical test concerning a population-meaningful hypothesis, it must be of a distribution-free (i.e., a nonparametric) character. In contrast, a distribution-meaningful hypothesis can (and should) be tested using the full strength of the distribution information. In practice, this applies to Gaussian methods and to those derived from the Gaussian, such as *t* tests, *F* tests, and the like. It becomes the responsibility of the scientist to formulate carefully and explicitly the type of hypothesis under consideration, and then it will be transparently clear whether or not to use distribution or distribution-free methods. Roughly speaking, if the hypothesis concerns the structure of the underlying population, use a distribution-free test; if it concerns a random variable of known distribution, use tests appropriate to that distribution. In the example of reaction time, if the hypothesis is about some aspect of the measurement of time itself, use a distribution-free test; if it is about reaction times that are known to follow some law (e.g., a Wald distribution), then use that information to design a suitable test, often by transforming the random variable into one with a Gaussian distribution.

SCALING

Measurement theory, as just discussed, is concerned with properties (formulated as axioms in the mathematical model) of an empirical structure that allow measurement scales to be constructed. Scaling, on the other hand, is concerned with the process of assigning numbers to objects subject to certain structural constraints so as to reflect, as well as possible, the regularities exhibited by a set of empirical observations. The structural constraints are imposed by the particular class of models being applied to the data. In other words, the scaling problem is one of finding how best to recast a set of (usually fallible) data into a particular numerical representation within a chosen class of representations. Although some scaling techniques have arisen from axiomatic treatments of a measurement problem (see the earlier sections on proximity structures and scaling in extensive and conjoint measurement), for many scaling techniques the measurement problem either has not been solved or has been treated only incompletely. For this reason, we elect to discuss scaling as a separate topic, as is done generally in psychology. For example, the *Annual Review of Psychology* regularly surveys the field (Carroll & Arabie, 1980; Cliff, 1973; Ekman & Sjöberg, 1965; Young, 1984; Zinnes, 1969). A second reason for doing this is that, even for those cases in which the representation problem has been solved, actual data rarely satisfy the axioms exactly, presumably because of error or noise in the data.

Types of Data and the Choice of Model

Scaling techniques have been developed for several different types of data. As we noted earlier, two basic types are distinguished: dominance (or order) and proximity (or similarity). Dominance data establish an ordering on the set of objects, for example, when a subject orders pairs of objects or stimuli in terms of brightness, loudness, or preference. Proximity data arise when, instead, the relative closeness or similarity of pairs of objects is judged. Sometimes these judgments are obtained directly by asking the observer to give ratings of similarity, relatedness, dissimilarity, or distance; at other times, judgment is obtained indirectly by using either confusion errors in identification, the time it takes to discriminate between two alternatives, or measures of co-occurrence or substitutability. In addition to comparisons between elements of the same type, as in the above examples, there are also cases in which the data represent comparisons between elements from different sets. Examples are: the likelihood that certain behaviors will be exhibited in different situations, the degree to which an individual endorses various attitude statements, and a person's scores on subtests within a test battery. A much more complete taxonomy

of these data types is provided by Coombs (1964), Coombs, Dawes, and Tversky (1970), Shepard (1972), and Carroll and Arabie (1980).

In recent years, the number of scaling models proposed, as well as the concurrent development of sophisticated computational methods for fitting the models to sets of observations (Carroll & Arabie, 1980), has increased rapidly. Two basic types of models can be distinguished: spatial and nonspatial. Spatial models assign to each object in the stimulus domain a point or vector in some dimensionally organized coordinate space, and interobject proximity is represented either as interpoint distances or as angles between vectors. Nonspatial models, in contrast, represent proximity either by determining clusters of stimuli, that is, partitions of the stimulus set, or by finding a best-fitting tree structure in which proximity is related to the maximum height in the tree of the path joining two objects or the length of the path joining two objects. In addition, hybrid models with both spatial and nonspatial components have been developed by Carroll (1976).

Because, for many types of data, algorithms exist for fitting several different classes of models, an important task is how to delimit the situations in which one class of models, rather than another, is more appropriate. Although this problem of selecting the appropriate model is far from being resolved, various approaches have been suggested. One is to determine whether certain assumptions underlying the model in question are reasonably well supported by the set of data. Another is to compare some overall measure for closeness of fit when different models are subjected to the same data, or to determine whether certain distributional properties, such as skewness, entailed by the various classes of representations are matched by the distributional properties of the data (e.g., Pruzansky, Tversky & Carroll, 1982). A third approach considers the question of the interpretability of the obtained solutions when different models are imposed, a judgment that is often difficult and rather subjective. Each of these approaches has some inherent difficulties, and the theoretical basis for selecting the class of model for a particular scaling application is currently less well developed than the computational methods for obtaining a scaling solution, once the class of models has been chosen. In this review, we limit our attention to models and methods that are currently considered the best established; more complete coverage is provided in the reviews by Carroll and Arabie (1980) and Young (1984).

Dominance Data

Methods Based on Numerical Data: Functional Measurement

Functional measurement (Anderson, 1974a, b, 1981, 1982, and numerous references in these articles and books) is in some ways similar to the feature-matching model of Tversky (1977) described earlier. Both approaches assume that the objects under study can be considered as collections of properties or features, and the number of properties need not be the same for all objects. In this respect, both approaches differ from conjoint measurement, which requires that the objects being compared exhibit a fixed factorial structure. Moreover, both the feature-matching model and functional measurement assume that values can be assigned to the features, which are then combined in some algebraic way, often a weighted average.

However, there are important differences between these two approaches. First, whereas the feature-matching model applies to similarity data, functional measurement applies to ratings of collections of attributes. In a typical experiment, the subject is presented with collections of attributes—for example, honesty, dependability, and introversion—and is asked to rate the collection of attributes according to some criterion, such as how likable a person is who exhibits them. A second difference is that the feature-matching model has been studied axiomatically, whereas work in functional measurement has not been directed at the question of observable properties needed for a representation of the desired type to exist (see, however, Luce, 1981; McClelland, 1980). Instead, to the extent that the rating data can be fitted numerically by the chosen type of representation, this is taken as simultaneous confirmation of both the form of the representation and the measurement assumptions that have been made about the response scale. This position has been strongly attacked by various authors, especially in a careful critique by Birnbaum (1982). Third and lastly, whereas methods have not been developed to estimate the feature values required by the feature-matching model,

methods are available to accomplish this for a number of models that come under the classification of functional measurement.

Of the different models considered in functional measurement, the three most prevalent are weighted averaging, adding, and multiplying. Adding, as in conjoint measurement, and averaging, as in computing a mean, are distinct models, although there are situations in which they cannot be distinguished. For example, if equal weights are used with averaging and the number of factors is fixed, there is no difference. If, however, either the weights are unequal or the number of factors vary, then the two models are distinct. For example, consider scale values that when added, yield

$$1 + 2 + 3 > 4 + 1;$$

but when they are averaged with equal weights the order is reversed since $6/3 = 2 < 5/2$. (There has been a controversy over the exact conditions under which it is possible to distinguish the adding model from the unequal weight-averaging model in the two-factor case.)

In either the averaging or adding case, the approach taken employs a factorial design: the subjects rate a number of situations that are described as combinations of levels of the various factors. Each situation can be rated a number of times, and since both adding and averaging models are additive in character, the statistical method of analysis of variance can be used to evaluate the fit of the model. In addition, graphical displays of the ratings as a function of the different, multiple factors, can be examined for characteristics that either support or reject the chosen type of representation. For example, if an averaging model holds and one manipulates two factors, then a plot of the mean ratings against one of the factors, with the other one treated as a parameter, yields a series of parallel curves, one for each value of the parameter, that can be superimposed by vertical shifts. This characteristic of averaging and adding models plays an important role in applications of functional measurement. If the model is rejected as a result of the analysis of variance or of using properties of the graphical displays, then two paths are available: either search for some nonlinear transformation of the rating data that improves the fit of the representation, or attempt to fit a different kind of representation.

The work in this area is extensive; not only

have many different models been considered within this framework, but various kinds of context and serial position effects have been analyzed. For an overview of this work, see Anderson (1970a, b, 1972, 1974a, b, 1976, 1981, 1982). (An example of this method applied to psychophysical data is given later in this chapter.)

Methods Based on Individual Differences: Unfolding

Psychology is beset with individual differences, that is, different response patterns from different individuals, and for the most part these pose difficulties for measurement. Under some conditions, however, they can help to solve the problem of finding a numerical representation, a point emphasized by Coombs (1950, 1964). He developed a method, designed initially as a theory of preferential choice behavior, that makes use of individual differences to obtain a numerical scale for the set of objects under consideration. Although his method, called unfolding, has played little role in psychophysics, we describe it briefly since it bears on measurement more generally. This approach makes two assumptions. First, the stimuli are assumed to vary along a single dimension (although the multidimensional case has been developed and is discussed below). Second, all subjects are assumed to have the same psychological order on the set of stimuli. As an example, let the stimuli be cups of coffee ordered by the amount of sugar added, from none to fully saturated, in 25-mg steps, so that the set of physical stimuli can be represented as in Figure 1.3. Almost everyone will agree that they are ordered by increasing sweetness; for this judgment there are no individual differences.

Suppose, further, that the subjective sensation of sweetness grows more rapidly than the amount of sugar, so that the subjective representation appears as in Figure 1.4. Of course, we do not start out knowing the subjective representation; its discovery is one objective of the unfolding technique. This is done by using the

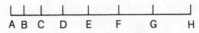

Figure 1.4. Hypothetical subjective spacing of the cups of coffee according to sweetness.

subjects' preference ratings for the set of stimuli. These are assumed to be generated as follows: each subject has an ideal point along the subjective representation—that subject's ideal concentration of sugar—such that the closer a stimulus is to the ideal point, the more it is preferred. Clearly, subjects' preference orders are not all the same. At one extreme is the person who likes unsweetened coffee and whose preference order, therefore, is the inverse of the sweetness order. For others the ideal level lies somewhere in between. Consider a person with the ideal point at F, so whose preferences are therefore ordered as the distance along the representation folded around the ideal point F as in Figure 1.5. Collapsing these points onto one line, we see that, for this individual, the resulting preference order is F > E > G > D > H > C > B > A. If all subjects have a common subjective representation, and if it is related to the preference orderings by folding around different ideal points, then only certain patterns of preferences can arise. To the extent that this is true, it is possible in principle to find the common subjective representation. The problem, which is mathematically quite complicated, can be solved in specific cases using computer programs developed for this purpose.

The method has also been extended to the multidimensional case (Bennett & Hays, 1960). As in the one-dimensional model, the basic data are the preference orderings of individuals for a set of entities. The solution consists of two sets of points in a multidimensional metric space (see section on Multidimensional Scaling); one set of points corresponding to the objects, and

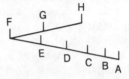

Figure 1.5. The subjective scale is folded about the "ideal" sweetness located at stimulus F. The preference order for a person for whom F is the ideal sweetness is read off by the order of stimuli from F to the right.

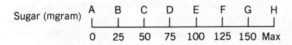

Figure 1.3. Stimuli defined in terms of the number of milligrams of sugar in a cup of coffee.

the other to the subjects' ideal points. Preferences for each person are ordered by the distance between objects and that person's ideal point, with shorter distances corresponding to more preferred objects. A somewhat more general model is one in which individuals are permitted to have different weights for the several dimensions of the space, as in individual-differences multidimensional scaling, to be described later. In an alternative formulation, individuals are represented as vectors, rather than as points, in the multidimensional space, such that preferences are related to the order in which the stimulus points project onto the subject's vector. (See Carroll, 1972, 1980, and below, vol. 2, chap. 12, for a more complete discussion of these different model for individual differences in preference data.)

Probabilistic Data

Most of the measurement ideas discussed earlier either arose from or are closely parallel to problems in physics. For example, the concept of dimension, the development of measuring techniques and instruments, and the discovery of laws describing how observable quantities are related to each other are all problems of physics that reappear in many other sciences. But the sciences differ on questions about variability or inconsistency of measurement. Variability that is large in proportion to magnitude is exceedingly common in the social and behavioral sciences and, though rare in fundamental physics, it occurs in others of the complex "hard" sciences such as biology and geology.

For the most part, the variability that appears in physical measurement is attributed either to inaccuracy in the measuring instrument or to uncontrolled variability in the experimental treatment of the system under study. In these instances one attempts to eliminate the variability in order to arrive at laws that are free from error, and with advancing knowledge these attempts have often been successful in physics and chemistry. In parts of geology and biology variability appears to be inherent to the objects of study, not just to their preparation and observation, in which case the problem is identical to that encountered in the social and behavioral sciences: how to develop useful generalizations in the face of gross, irreducible variability?

Two major approaches to the problem are available. The one treats it as a nuisance to be dealt with by statistical methods. The focus is on ways to extract from a set of observations a few statistics that are representative of the entire population. For example, measures of central tendency—mean, mode, or median—are often accepted as representative values, and they are incorporated into algebraic measurement and substantive models. Variability in this approach is reduced simply by increasing sample size. This is the path taken by the vast majority of statistical methods used in the social sciences, and it is also widely used in the physical sciences.

The other approach treats variability not as a nuisance, but as an important and interesting element of the empirical problem. The issue then becomes one of trying to explain it, to predict it, and to develop measurement models consistent with it. These models are the topic of this section. Two quite different types of models have been proposed, whose origins are often attributed to Thurstone (1927) and Luce (1959), although both authors make clear that their formulations arose from earlier work. Even though these two systems begin with rather different intuitions about the psychological mechanisms involved and use somewhat different mathematical concepts, they often arrive at similar predictions, making it difficult to decide clearly in favor of one. Each system provides a method for scaling stimuli on a single dimension, and each provides an account of the observed variability in responses. Moreover, the important point is that each is applicable to a wide variety of psychological problems, ranging from psychophysical studies of stimuli with precisely measurable physical characteristics to choice data about objects so complex or abstract that no precise physical description of them is really possible.

Random Variable Models
Thurstone took the observed variability at face value: he assumed that the impact of a stimulus —virtually any stimulus—on a person differs on different occasions. By that he meant that the internal representation of the stimulus in the mind (or nervous system) is not always the same. For the perception of a brief light flash, there are enough sources of variability in the transduction, transmission, and processing of the stimulus that it is impossible to deny variability

in the representation. With more complex stimuli, the reasons appear to be different. Consider choosing between two novels to buy for a friend. At one instant you think one is better, but later you alter your view, possibly reflecting a change in emphasis on the several characteristics of the novels. In both cases, however, the model assumes that the momentary reaction to a stimulus can be represented as a single point along a numerical representation of the relevant choice attribute. That point is determined by some unknown "discriminal process" whereby ". . . the organism identifies, distinguishes, discriminates, or reacts to stimuli" (Thurstone, 1927). Repeated presentations of the stimulus yield a distribution of values, which he called the *discriminal dispersion*. For the most part, this terminology has been replaced by the language of probability theory, which we now present.

The set of possible distinct outcomes under consideration—for example, the various internal states that can arise from a stimulus—is called the *sample space*. The elements of this set, which are mutually exclusive and exhaustive, are called *sample points*. Any numerical function X that assigns to each sample point s a number $X(s)$ is called a *random variable*. Such an assignment of numbers may be quite arbitrary—for example, the number 0 when a coin comes up heads and 1 when it comes up tails —or it may have a quite natural meaning—for example, the time in milliseconds it takes a person to make a detection response. In the present context we are thinking of a hypothetic numerical representation of the internal state. We often distinguish between those random variables that are *discrete*, in the sense that their values can be mapped onto a subset of the integers, as in the coin example, and those that are *continuous*, in the sense that they assume values on a real interval (continuum) as in the reaction time example.

Associated to each random variable is a measure of how it varies from occurrence to occurrence. For a random variable X and for each real number x, let $F_X(x)$ denote the probability that the observed value of X is x or less; the function F_X is called the *(cumulative) distribution function* of X. When there is no ambiguity, we suppress the name X and simply write F for the distribution function. For a discrete random variable with possible values $x_1 < x_2 <$

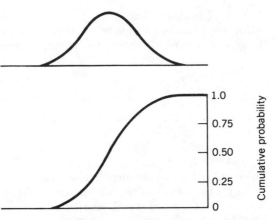

Figure 1.6. The relation between a (cumulative) distribution function and the corresponding probability density function.

. . . $x_i < $ . . . , we can assign a probability value f_i to each x_i, in which case $F(x)$ is just the sum of all the f_i for which $x_i \leqslant x$. For a continuous random variable we can sometimes work in an analogous way, that is, we can assign a value $f(x)$ to each possible value x so that $F(x)$ is the sum (technically, the integral) of all the $f(y)$ for which $y \leq x$. The function f (which, if it exists, and we will assume that it does, is the derivative of F) is called the *probability density function*. Figure 1.6 shows graphically one example of the relation between F and f.

Often a density function tells us more than we care to deal with, in which case we attempt to collapse it so as to retain only the information that concerns us. Such summary quantities are called *statistics*. Perhaps the most important statistics are the mean—sometimes called the first moment—which is a measure of central tendency, and the standard deviation or its square, the variance or second moment about the mean, which is a measure of dispersion or variability. For discrete distributions, they are defined by:

$$\mu = \sum_{i=1}^{n} x_i f_i \quad \text{and} \quad \sigma = \left[\sum_{i=1}^{n} (x - \mu)^2 f_i \right]^{1/2}$$

and for continuous distributions by:

$$\mu = \int_{-\infty}^{\infty} x f(x)\, dx$$

and

$$\sigma = \left[\int_{-\infty}^{\infty} (x - \mu)^2 f(x)\, dx \right]^{1/2}.$$

One of the most important distributions to arise in probability theory is the so-called *Gaussian* or *normal*, whose density function is:

$$f(x) = \frac{1}{\sqrt{2\pi}\sigma} e^{-(x-\mu)^2/2\sigma^2}$$

It can be shown that its mean is μ and variance is σ^2. The density function has the familiar bell shape shown at the top of Figure 1.6. With the mean set at 0 and variance at 1, it is then called the standard Gaussian distribution, and tables of its probability density and cumulative distribution functions are readily available.

Given these concepts, we can now describe Thurstone's model. The internal representation of a stimulus is assumed to be a random variable which in Thurstone's original paper was assumed to be Gaussian distributed, although later authors have considered other possible distributions. If they are Gaussian, then the problem of describing the internal representations of different stimuli is reduced to knowing for each stimulus its mean and variance, and the correlations between the random variables.

To see how this model might be applied, suppose that on each trial an observer sees two brief flashes of light and the task is to say which seemed brighter. Let the two internal representations be the random variables X_1 and X_2, where the one with larger mean (μ_1 or μ_2) corresponds to the more intense flash; however, it is the one with the larger observed value that appears brighter at any given presentation. The model says that the subject will report the first stimulus as brighter when $X_1 > X_2$ and the second when $X_2 > X_1$. If the difference in the means is small relative to the variability, for example, $\mu_1 - \mu_2 < (1/4)(\sigma_1^2 + \sigma_2^2)^{1/2}$, then on some proportion of the trials the sign of $X_1 - X_2$ will not agree with the sign of $\mu_1 - \mu_2$, in which case the response will be incorrect. In fact, if X_1 and X_2 are both Gaussian distributed and have a correlation of ρ_{12} then it can be shown that $X_1 - X_2$ will also be Gaussian distributed, that its mean is $\mu_1 - \mu_2$ and that its variance is $\sigma_1^2 + \sigma_2^2 - 2\rho_{12}\sigma_1\sigma_2$, which we call σ^2. Assuming that $\mu_2 > \mu_1$, the probability of a correct response is the probability that $X_2 - X_1 > 0$; this is equivalent to the probability that a standard Gaussian random variable has a value in excess of $(\mu_2 - \mu_1)/\sigma$. This line of reasoning will be pursued further in the section on *Psycho-physics*, where we will see that, though in principle it is possible to perform experiments to check the assumption of Gaussian distributions, in practice it is quite difficult to make the experiments adequately sensitive to small deviations from the Gaussian distribution.

In actual applications of the model, we almost never have direct access to the parameters—mean, variance, and correlation—of the probability distributions. Rather, the process is one of working backwards from the observed choice probabilities to the parameters of the model. For simplicity, it has often been assumed that the random variables are uncorrelated and that they have equal variances (Thurstone's Case 5), and so the means are the only parameters of interest. Note that the means form a measure of the stimuli, and the common variance constitutes a unit of measurement. With the computer algorithms now available it is unnecessary to make special assumptions, and nonconstant variance models are frequently fitted to data.

The model generalizes in a natural way to choices from more than two possibilities. Suppose n stimuli are presented and that they have internal representations $X_1, X_2, \ldots, X_n$, then the identification of the "largest" stimulus entails selecting the one with the largest observed value. The mathematics of this n-alternative choice model can be worked out in detail when it is assumed that the representations are independent of each other.

Strength-of-Alternative Models

We turn now to the second approach to the problem of modeling variability in responses. Since these models were developed to explain general choice behavior, including preferences, psychophysical judgments, and learning, we adopt that general terminology. The approach assumes that the choice alternatives are represented internally not as random variables, but as unique numbers that characterize the relative strengths of the alternatives. Economists and statisticians refer to these as constant utility models in contrast to the random utility models discussed previously. In the strength models, variability arises in the overt responses not because the psychological representation of the stimulus is variable but because the choice process among the representations is itself inherently variable. Thus the two models are conceptually quite distinct, but in important special cases they are closely related, as we shall see.

A particular strength-of-alternative model involving only pairs of alternatives was postulated by Bradley and Terry (1952); Luce (1959) generalized it to choices among finite sets of alternatives, and, more important, he provided an axiomatic treatment of it. At the cornerstone of this development is a postulate, sometimes called the "choice axiom" (not to be confused with the important "axiom of choice" in mathematics), which can be formulated in two parts. The first, more substantive condition, states that choices from subsets behave like conditional probabilities in the larger set. Specifically, suppose a is an alternative in a set A of alternatives which in turn is a subset of S. Denote by $P_S(a)$ the probability of selecting a when S is the choice set, by $P_A(a)$ the same probability when A is the choice set, and by $P_S(A)$ the sum of all $P_S(b)$ where b ranges over A. The assumption is that if all of these probabilities differ from 0 and 1, they are related by

$$P_S(a) = P_S(A) P_A(a).$$

The second part deals with probabilities of 0 and 1. Suppose a and b are two elements of S and that, when a choice is offered between just a and b, a is never selected. Then it is assumed that a may be deleted from S without altering in any way the probabilities of choosing from S. Both of these conditions are, in principle, empirically testable.

A number of consequences follow from these simple assumptions. The first and most useful is that there is a ratio scale v over all the alternatives such that if $P_A(a) \neq 0$ or 1,

$$P_A(a) = \frac{v(a)}{\displaystyle\sum_{b \text{ in } A} v(b)}.$$

Put another way, there are strengths associated with the alternatives, and probabilities of choice are given by these strengths normalized by the total amount of strength of the alternatives under consideration. A second consequence, which follows readily from the first, is known as the constant ratio rule: the ratio $P_A(a)/P_A(b)$ has the same value for every choice set A that includes both a and b. A third consequence holds only among the binary probabilities. Writing $P(a, b)$ for $P_{\{a,b\}}(a)$, the product

rule asserts

$$P(a, b) P(b, c) P(c, a) = P(a, c) P(c, b) P(b, a).$$

A fourth consequence, also limited to binary probabilities, is strong stochastic transitivity: If $P(a, b) \geq 1/2$ and $P(b, c) \geq 1/2$, then $P(a, c) \geq P(a, b)$ and $P(a, c) \geq P(b, c)$.

It should be realized that this model is a special example of a constant utility model. The general form continues to assume a scale v defined over the alternatives and that $P_A(a)$ is some function of all $v(b)$ where b ranges over the set a. The choice model just given entails a special function of the vs. For example, in the binary case the general model is of the form

$$P(a, b) = G[v(a), v(b)],$$

where G is a function that is increasing in the first variable and decreasing in the second one and $G(x, x) = 1/2$. Krantz (1964) has shown that this binary form is equivalent to the observable property of satisfying strong stochastic transitivity. Falmagne (1985), in an important theoretical book, has studied how various properties of P limit the form of G.

There is a close relation between Luce's model and Case 5 of Thurstone. If we define $u(a) = \ln v(a)$, then the binary probabilities can be written

$$P(a, b) = 1/[1 + e^{-[u(a) - u(b)]}].$$

This is called the logistic distribution, and is known to be similar to the Gaussian distribution. The question has been raised: is the choice model in general an example of a Thurstone model? Block and Marschak (1960) have shown that it is. More recently, McFadden (1974) and Yellott (1977) have shown that if one restricts oneself to distributions that, apart from their means, are identical (a shift family), and if there are at least three alternatives, then a necessary and sufficient condition for an independent random variable model to have the same probabilities as a choice model is that the random variables have the double exponential distribution

$$F(x) = e^{-e^{-ax+b}},$$

which in fact is quite close to the Gaussian distribution function except in the tails. This distribution is important in statistics in connection with the problem of the distribution of the largest of a very large number of independent, identically distributed random variables. Yellott

(1977) stated some plausible conditions on choices that give rise to this distribution.

Several empirical studies have attempted to evaluate one or another property of the choice model. The earlier studies were summarized by Luce (1977). As a generalization, the choice model holds up fairly well when the choice set is a highly heterogeneous collection of alternatives, but it fails when the set has some natural structure. Indeed, the failure appears to be a characteristic of all strength-of-alternative models. The type of structure that presents problems is one in which the set of alternatives breaks into subgroups that share certain features or properties. An example, given by Debreu (1960b), illustrates the problem. Suppose you are indifferent between two quite distinct alternatives, a and b, so that $P(a, b) = 1/2$. Let a third alternative c be added that is almost identical to a, for example, a second copy of a phonograph record. One would expect that c could be substituted for a, yielding $P(c, b) = 1/2$. Thus $v(a) = v(b) = v(c)$. And so if all three are presented, any strength model predicts that the probability of choosing b is 1/3, which is contrary to intuition which says that b will continue to be selected with probability 1/2 and a and c jointly will be chosen with probability 1/2. Perhaps the best known experimental demonstration of this problem was presented by Rumelhart and Greeno (1971). They asked subjects which one person they would most like to spend an hour with out of nine celebrities, including three athletes, three movie stars, and three politicians. They found that the observed choice probabilites strongly violated the model given above.

Strength-of-Aspects Models

It seems clear from both the examples and data that an adequate choice model must take into account the similarities among the alternatives. The first to recognize this and to suggest a solution to the problem was Restle (1961). His model, which is for the binary case, assumes that each alternative is described by a collection of features or aspects, each of which has associated with it a numerical value. When a choice is being made, it is assumed that those aspects that are common to the alternatives are ignored as irrelevant and the choice is based on applying the Luce choice model to the values of the aspects possessed by one but not both of the alternatives. Rumelhart and Greeno (1971) found that this model gave a much improved account of their data.

Tversky (1972) extended Restle's model to the general case, which he called the elimination-by-aspects approach. As in Restle's formulation, each alternative consists of a collection of aspects, and a numerical measure is assumed to exist over the aspects. At each step of the decision process an aspect is selected from all those alternatives still available, where the probability of selection is computed from the numerical values by Luce's model. All alternatives not possessing this aspect are then eliminated from further consideration. This process of eliminating alternatives continues until only one alternative remains, and that is the choice. This model includes as special cases both Restle's (by restricting it to the binary case) and Luce's (by assuming that any aspect shared by any two alternatives is shared by all). The difficulty with this model is that, if there are n alternatives, then a very large number, $2^n - 2$, of parameters must be estimated.

To alleviate that problem Tversky and Sattath (1979) proposed a restricted, but plausible version of the model which reduces the number of parameters to $2n - 2$. This model represents the alternatives and their aspects as related by a treelike structure, and was dubbed the elimination-by-tree model. In the tree, each terminal node is associated with a single alternative, and each link of the tree is associated with the set of aspects that is shared by all the alternatives that include that link, but is not possessed by any of the other alternatives. The process of elimination involves selecting at each stage a link from the tree with a probability that is proportional to its length, which is a parameter of the model. All alternatives that do not include that link are thereby eliminated. The process continues until all alternatives are eliminated but one. They have shown that this model is equivalent to one in which it is assumed that the examination of aspects follows a strict hierarchical order. This model is still quite general, but it has a reasonable number of parameters.

It should be noted that this last class of models deviates rather markedly from the measurement models with which we began, which associated a single number with each alternative. At present it is not clear how, within the measurement framework, to deal with the phenomenon of choice among a set of alternatives that has a similarity structure.

Proximity Data

The scaling methods just discussed all rest on the idea that a single numerical value is associated with each stimulus, even though in some cases (conjoint and functional measurement) the stimuli themselves have several components. We turn next to several methods that ask whether data about stimuli, whose psychological organization may or may not be understood, can be represented by various classes of more complex spatial and nonspatial models. The representation, which as before is inferred from relational data about the stimuli, is no longer in terms of points on a line, but is something far more deeply geometric in character. Perhaps the best understood psychological example of such an inference arises in color vision. Here the physical stimuli have infinitely many dimensions because they are energy distributions over an infinity of wave lengths—and the data are judgments about whether two different energy distributions are seen as being the same color, that is, whether they are metameric matches. The result, which is by no means obvious, is that, in terms of color distinctions, the stimuli lie in only a three-dimensional space. For people who are color blind, the number of dimensions is reduced to two or, rarely, to one. To see that this reduction to three dimensions is not obvious, consider auditory energy distributions over frequency, again an infinite-dimensional stimulus space. No one has ever discovered the auditory analogue of a metameric match: namely, two quite different acoustic energy distributions that sound exactly the same.

The color example is misleading in the sense that this is an area with a well-developed theory. It is far more common, in practice, for the following methods to be used in an exploratory fashion, by seeking to uncover the structure of the psychological representation in uncharted areas. As such, the models make weak assumptions about the way in which the stimuli are organized. Some models assume a spatial structure; others postulate a set of clusters or a tree structure. Some years ago the methods entailed heroic computational efforts, but now almost any scientist has easy access to standard pro-

grams for all the methods we shall describe. This has meant that attention can be refocused on the conceptual and theoretical issues involved, not on tricks to simplify the computations.

Vectors and Euclidean Representations

The first multidimensional spaces to be considered by psychologists were the vector spaces that had originated in physics. Physicists, in their search for laws to describe the motion of material bodies, had become concerned with such concepts as velocity, acceleration, and force. For these quantities, it is not sufficient to specify their magnitudes; one must specify their directions as well. A force that acts in one direction definitely does not have the same effect as a force of equal magnitude in a different direction. Thus the real number system, while sufficient to specify magnitudes, had to be generalized in some way to specify direction also.

Such a generalized quantity is called a *vector*. A three-dimensional one, such as an ordinary force, can be specified as a triple of numbers (x_1, x_2, x_3), where each component x_i specifies the magnitude of the force acting in each of three orthogonal directions which we identify by the indices 1, 2, and 3. The ratios of the component forces, such as x_2/x_3, specify the direction of the force, and its overall magnitude is given by $(x_1^2 + x_2^2 + x_3^2)^{1/2}$. To illustrate the usefulness of this notational system, consider the problem of describing the net effect of two different forces acting on a single point: $\vec{x} = (x_1, x_2, x_3)$ and $\vec{y} = (y_1, y_2, y_3)$. Their sum is defined to be

$$\vec{x} + \vec{y} = (x_1 + y_1, x_2 + y_2, x_3 + y_3).$$

Clearly this concept of a sum can be extended to any finite number of three-dimensional vectors. Also the concept of a vector can be extended to any finite dimensionality, not just to three.

Several points are worth commenting on. First, in defining the sum of two vectors, they must have the same dimensionality. Second, many different vector pairs can give rise to the same vector sum, just as a real number can be viewed as the sum of infinitely many pairs of real numbers. Third, the underlying coordinate system has no unique status: the axes may be rotated in any way so long as they remain orthogonal to each other, and vector addition is equally valid in the new system of axes.

A second operation, called *scalar multiplica-*

tion, is defined as follows: let $\vec{x}$ be a vector and c a number, then

$$c\vec{x} \;=\; (cx_1, \, cx_2, \, cx_3).$$

For example, doubling the magnitude of a force while maintaining its direction is done by scalar multiplication with $c = 2$. (There are other multiplicative operations defined for vectors, in particular, dot and cross products, but they do not concern us here.)

The example of force is used not only because it is familiar, but also because it is closely analogous to color perception (Krantz, 1974). There is, of course, the superficial similarity that both domains are three dimensional. For color, this appears as the familiar trichromacy principle: any color can be matched either by some mix of three primary colors, or by adding in an appropriate amount one of the primaries to the given color and matching that by a mix of the other two primaries. In other words, every color has a natural representation as a three-dimensional vector composed of the amounts of the primaries needed to match it. Also, as in the force example, the choice of the axes (in this case, primaries) is highly arbitrary. The restriction on the choice of primaries is that no mixture of two match the third.

More important than the three dimensionality of the color example is the fact that vector addition has a natural interpretation in color mixing. If two light sources are mixed together, the resulting color matches the color that is produced by adding together the components of the three-dimensional vectors that represent the two lights. This rule of color mixing, called Grassman's law of addition, holds extremely well over a large range, and it maps directly onto the physiological mechanisms for color coding. Of course, many different sets of colors can add to produce the same color, just as many distinct sets of forces can sum to the same resultant. Finally, scalar multiplication in color vectors simply means an overall change in the energy of each of the components.

In what follows we shall need vectors in n dimensions, $\vec{x} = (x_1, x_2, \ldots, x_n)$ and we shall also need the concept of vector difference:

$$\vec{x} - \vec{y} \;=\; \vec{x} + (-1)\vec{y}$$

$$=\; (x_1 - y_1, x_2 - y_2, \ldots, x_n - y_n).$$

Note that the magnitude of $\vec{x} - \vec{y}$ is:

$$[(x_1 - y_1)^2 + (x_2 - y_2)^2 + \cdots + (x_n - y_n)^2]^{1/2}.$$

Factor Analysis

The technique of factor analysis, the first example of multidimensional scaling to arise in psychology, originated in an attempt to uncover the component factors in tests of intelligence. It was stated in special cases by Spearman (1904) and was put in modern form by Thurstone (1947); recent texts are by Harman (1976) and Cattell (1978). Although the method has been and still is widely used in psychology and other fields, such as sociology, it has not been extensively applied by psychophysicists. For this reason and because of certain limitations to be noted later, we discuss it only briefly.

Exploratory factor analysis attempts to reduce a set of variables to a smaller number of hypothetical variables, called factors. The basic data are the values for each of the variables under consideration—for example, performance on a set of test items or ratings of a group of objects—that are provided by a number of individual respondents. The profiles of values are then intercorrelated over the individuals to give a derived measure of similarity between each pair of variables. It is implicit in calculating a correlation that the values are each measured on an interval scale, because on any weaker scale the correlation coefficient is not invariant (meaningful). It is these derived similarity measures, the correlations, that are the input to factor analysis. This fact is an important limitation of the method when it is compared with other methods described later.

The method of factor analysis then poses the question: when we treat the cosine of the angle between two vectors as the correlation between them, what is the smallest vector space in which we can embed a set of hypothetical vectors, one for each variable, so as to recover all the observed correlations up to some degree of approximation. Slightly more generally, let the variable $\vec{X}$ represent, for example, performance on a test. This variable is assumed to be composed of a unique component $\vec{U}$ and weightings $c_1, c_2, \ldots, c_k$ on the several distinct factors. These factors can be represented as unit vectors —1 in the ith coordinate and 0 on all other coordinates—that are mutually orthogonal; call them $\vec{F}_1, \vec{F}_2, \ldots, \vec{F}_k$. Thus,

$$\vec{X} \;=\; c_1\vec{F}_1 + c_2\vec{F}_2 + \cdots + c_k\vec{F}_k + \vec{U}.$$

If the unique term is ignored, then, because the $\vec{F}_i$ are unit vectors, we see that $\vec{X} =$

$(c_1, c_2, \ldots, c_k)$. The method attempts to recover these vectors.

It should be noted that the coordinates represent just one orthogonal basis for the vector space. Other, equally good ones can be obtained by rotations which will, of course, systematically change the numerical representations of the vectors. And if one chooses there is the possibility of using nonorthogonal factors. There are subtle questions about how to select from the infinity of possibilities one system of factors that has special meaning. Usually this is done by developing an interpretation for one set of factors, paying special attention to those variables that have particularly heavy factor loadings on just one of the factors. In this connection, it should be noted that implicit in the method is the assumption of a causal relationship between the common factors and the observed correlations; this is plausible in some settings and not in others. In any event, the method itself is unable to assess whether factorial causation is reasonable in any particular context; it must be argued from substantive knowledge of the area under investigation.

The few attempts to employ factor analysis in psychophysics have for the most part been deemed failures. For example, applied to color perception (Ekman, 1954), factor analysis resulted in five factors, which exceeds the three known to be correct. The problem is that, even if the assumption is wrong that variables can be represented as the sum of weighted factors, the model can always accommodate the data by introducing a sufficiently large number of factors. If one already knows the answer, it is easy to tell when the analysis leads to too many factors; if one does not, a considerable element of judgment enters into accepting or rejecting the fit of the model to the data. A related problem with the method is that the solution obtained is in the form of a matrix of factor weights which, especially when the number of factors is large, is often not readily interpretable.

Properties of Distance

Correlation is only one measure of similarity, and in some contexts not a very natural one. Similarity can be measured directly, as when a subject rates how similar two stimuli are, or indirectly, as when we observe probabilities of confusion between pairs of stimuli. For those measures of similarity it was unclear how to use

factor analysis since the measures did not have any natural interpretation as the angle between vectors. This led to the proposal that similarity could be thought of as inversely related to the distance between points in a metric space where the points corresponded to the stimuli. In the first stages of the development of this method (Torgerson, 1958), it was postulated that distance in a metric space is strictly proportional to the inverse of the similarity measure being used. More recently, so-called nonmetric methods (Kruskal, 1964a, b; Shepard, 1962) assume only that distance decreases with increases in similarity, and the exact form of the function is left to be determined by the data.

If $\hat{x}$ and $\hat{y}$ are two vectors—each of dimension n—the distance between them is defined as the magnitude of $\hat{x} - \hat{y}$, that is,

$$d(\hat{x}, \hat{y}) = \left[\sum_{i=1}^{n} (x_i - y_i)^2 \right]^{1/2}.$$

Mathematicians have noted that this measure exhibits three crucial properties that they have come to accept as characterizing anything one would ever want to call a distance; they are known as the metric axioms:

(i) $d(\hat{x}, \hat{y}) \geq 0$ and $d(\hat{x}, \hat{y}) = 0$ if and only if $\hat{x} = \hat{y}$,

(ii) $d(\hat{x}, \hat{y}) = d(\hat{y}, \hat{x})$,

(iii) $d(\hat{x}, \hat{z}) \leq d(\hat{x}, \hat{y}) + d(\hat{y}, \hat{z})$.

The first says that distance is a nonnegative quantity that assumes the value 0 only when the vectors are identical. The second says distance is a symmetric concept. And the third is the famous triangle inequality, so called because the tips of the three vectors potentially define a triangle whose sides are the three distances in question.

Obviously, similarity data can be represented by distances only to the extent that analogous constraints hold in the data. There is usually no difficulty with property (i). There is more often difficulty with (ii). For example, in a confusion matrix, the probability of confusing stimulus a with stimulus b is frequently different from that of confusing b with a. In such cases, symmetry is generally artificially imposed, for example, by using the average of the two estimated probabilities. Property (iii), the triangle inequality, is somewhat more difficult to state for similarities, especially when it is related nonlinearly to distances. However, qualitatively, it entails the following: if each of two objects is quite similar to a third, then the two must be at least moderately similar to each other. Tversky (1977; Tversky & Gati, 1982) has noted a number of cases in which the metric axioms are systematically violated and has argued against the application of multidimensional models (see Krumhansl, 1978, for further discussion). In many cases, however, the assumptions of spatial models are reasonably well supported.

Nonmetric Multidimensional Procedures

The term nonmetric is somewhat misleading in this context. It refers to the fact that only ordinal properties of the data are employed; it does not mean that the representation achieved is nonmetric since, in fact, all the representations we shall discuss are in metric spaces. What is important, however, is that, in finding the metric representation, only the relative ordering of the similarity values is used, not their differences or ratios or any numerical property other than order. In other words, multidimensional scaling solutions are invariant under monotonic increasing transformations of the data. So one attractive aspect of the method is the exceedingly weak assumption made about the nature of the measurement scale.

On first hearing about this, it seems quite surprising that the solution can possibly have metric properties. However, when the number of objects being scaled is large relative to the number of dimensions of the metric space, all the interobject similarity orderings actually place much more rigid constraints on the possible configurations than most people would anticipate. This statement follows more from computational experience than from detailed mathematical understanding.

Although there are a number of methods (see Carroll & Arabie, 1980 and Young, 1984, for reviews), we will concentrate on the one that is both the most general and the most commonly used. These nonmetric methods arrive at a final spatial configuration and a nonlinear mapping of similarity into distance through a series of successive approximations. At each step of the iteration, the interpoint distances in the current configuration are compared to the interobject similarity data. A measure called "stress" is computed of the extent to which the distances

fail to be ordered inversely to the similarities, and at the next stage the points are moved so as to reduce the stress value and, hence, the number and magnitude of the discrepancies. The iterations are continued until changes in stress become negligible.

As an example, consider the application of multidimensional scaling (Shepard, 1962) to Ekman's (1954) color data. In the original study, Ekman asked observers to rate the "qualitative similarity" of pairs of colors drawn from a set of fourteen colors ranging from 434 nm to 674 nm. The two-dimensional scaling solution obtained by Shepard is shown in Figure 1.7. This entails a reduction of the data matrix of average ratings for the $14 \times 13/2 = 91$ distinct pairs of colors to $14 \times 2 = 28$ coordinate parameters, less a few because the origin, the orientation of the axes, and the unit of the scales are arbitrary. Although this is a substantial reduction, scaling techniques of this sort typically estimate a large number of parameters as compared to most other types of mathematical models.

The main purpose of the method is not simply to reduce the number of parameters needed to describe the data, but to do so in a way that makes possible some understanding of the structure of the data matrix. This is carried out by examining the relative positions of objects in the multidimensional solution and attempting to identify what is common to objects that are close together or, if the objects are widely dispersed, to try to find a system of axes that can give meaning to the locations of the object points. Almost always, the solution has to be rotated in order to uncover a dimensional interpretation. In the present example, the method produces the conventional color circle, which is brought out by the smooth contour drawn through the fourteen points.

Interpretability and Goodness-of-Fit

A major virtue of this scaling approach is the ease of visualizing the results, at least when two or at most three dimensions are involved. Low dimensionality facilitates our ability to discover a meaningful set of axes or interpretable clusters of objects. So it is important not to go to more dimensions than are absolutely necessary. However, the choice of the number of dimensions is not always simple and must be based on several considerations. For a fixed number of objects, the stress value decreases as the number

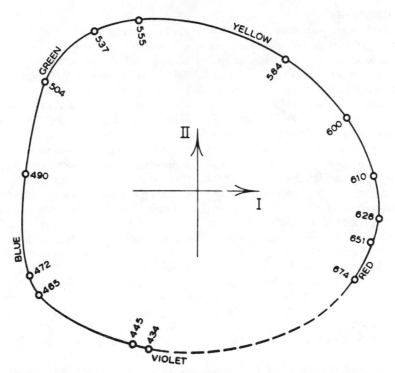

Figure 1.7. Shepard's multidimensional scaling analysis of Ekman's (1954) similarity data for 14 colors, which are identified by their wavelength in nanometers (nm). From "The Analysis of Proximities: Multidimensional Scaling with an Unknown Distance Function" by R.N. Shepard, 1962, *Psychometrika*, *27*, p. 236. Copyright 1962 by Psychometrika. Reprinted by permission.

of dimensions increases. Put another way, the desired inverse monotonic relation between the similarity data and interpoint distances is met more and more closely as the number of dimensions increases. The expense is in terms of our ability to understand what the dimensions mean. Indeed, in higher dimensional solutions some dimensions may serve only to account for error or noise in the data, for which no substantive interpretation is really possible. There is, therefore, a trade-off between ease in visualizing, reliability, and interpretability on the one side and goodness-of-fit on the other side. There is no rigorous solution to this tradeoff; judgment is required. Shepard (1974) discussed this and other issues that arise in the application of multidimensional scaling.

Non-Euclidean Metrics

So far we have assumed that the solution will be found in the ordinary (Euclidean) metric in a vector space, but in fact other choices are possible. Perhaps the most familiar is the so-called city-block metric in which distances add up along a rectilinear grid. For example, in two dimensions

$$d(\check{x}, \check{y}) = |x_1 - y_1| + |x_2 - y_2|,$$

where $|z|$ means the absolute value of the quantity z. Attneave (1950), Shepard (1964, 1974), Carroll and Wish (1974b), Garner (1976) and others have argued that for certain types of stimuli, for example, those that vary along "separable" dimensions, this metric represents psychological distance better than does the more common Euclidean metric. Another metric space, which arises in studies in the geometry of visual space perception (Luneburg, 1947; Indow, 1979), is the Riemannian space of constant curvature. Computer algorithms exist for several other types of metrics. The scientist must therefore make a choice among them, either on *a priori* grounds or by analyzing the data in several ways and then judging which gives the most parsimonious or plausible explanation.

Individual Differences

As described, these scaling methods apply to the data from a single source, usually an individual. If different people yield different data, as they usually do, then as many distinct solutions will result as there are people. Yet, if the method is getting at something fundamental about human perception, cognition, or choice behavior, we anticipate that the solutions should be in some sense closely related. The literature includes two attempts to implement this intuition and to devise methods to use the data from a number of respondents simultaneously. One, the unfolding method, has already been discussed.

The other, proposed by Carroll and Chang (1970), posits that all individuals use the same fundamental dimensions, though they accord the dimensions different weights in establishing similarities. This view suggests the following modification of the usual Euclidean distance measures:

$$d_i(x, y) = \left[\sum_{j=1}^{n} w_{ij}(x_j - y_j)^2 \right]^{1/2},$$

where w_{ij} is the weight assigned by subject i to dimension j.

The solution, which is arrived at by techniques that are called three-way multidimensional scaling methods, yields an object space and a subject weight space. The object space describes the psychological structure of the stimuli for the group of subjects. The subject weight space tells how much weight each subject gives to each of the dimensions of the object space. Techniques of this type often assume something more than ordinal measurement scales, usually interval scales. Despite this requirement and their greater costliness in computation time, they have a number of advantages. First, individual differences are accounted for very simply, and the subject weights may be meaningfully interpreted. As an example, Figure 1.8 shows the object space and the subject weight space for Helm's (1964) data on color perception arrived at by Carroll and Wish (1974a) using three-way multidmensional scaling. The group stimulus space exhibits the familiar color circle; the subject weight space shows the weights given the two dimensions by ten normal and four color-deficient subjects. The color-deficient subjects gave lower weights to the second (red-green) dimension than did the subjects with normal color vision. A second advantage of the individual-differences scaling method is that the solution is no longer invariant (except in special circumstances) under rotations of the axes, as can easily be checked using the distance expression given above. Indeed, if there are sufficient individual differences, the axes are nearly uniquely determined. Finally, because the solution is based on more input data than a single similarity matrix, a higher dimensional solution can typically be supported without the risk that it is simply fitting random noise in the proximity matrix.

One must not conclude, however, that such individual multidimensional scaling necessarily captures all the individual differences that arise. There may be idiosyncratic classifications that appear to have little to do with differential weighting of dimensions. For example, some people think of the food swordfish as a meat rather than a fish. Some people may vacillate in their representation of a stimulus in a dimensional structure. And people may very well disagree on the dimensional decomposition of stimuli: rectangles by length and height versus by area and length of a diagonal.

Clustering

Although geometric nearness is a notion of similarity, and an important one, the concept of similarity seems somewhat more general than that. It has something to do with how much two things have in common and how much they do not. We have previously seen this idea exploited in the probabilistic strength-of-aspects models. Here we discuss methods that presuppose not a probability data structure, but simply measures of similarity. The techniques are aimed, once again, at uncovering the structure in the data, but the representations arrived at are much weaker than the spatial ones just discussed. Basically, the idea is to sort the objects into relatively homogeneous subgroups. Within each subgroup, the objects have some degree of similarity, and the interpretation of the result depends on identifying what it is they have in common. Through this type of procedure, psychologically salient features or properties of the stimulus domain can be determined. The basic appeal of methods of this kind for psychology is that categorization of objects on the basis of their similarities and differences seems to be a fundamental aspect of human and animal behavior (Herrnstein & de Villiers, 1980).

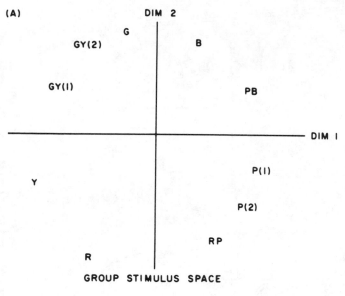

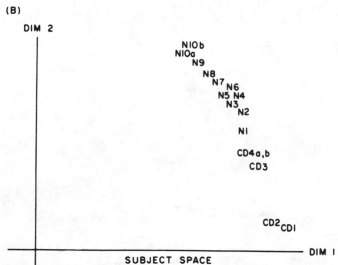

Figure 1.8. Carroll and Wish's individual-differences, multidimensional-scaling solution for Helm's (1964) color data: R = red; Y = yellow; GY(1) = green yellow; GY(2) = green yellow but with more green than GY(1); G = green; B = blue; PB = purple blue; N refers to subjects with normal color vision; CD refers to color-deficient subjects. From "Models and Methods for Three-Way Multidimensional Scaling" by J.D. Carroll and M. Wish in *Contemporary Developments in Mathematical Psychology, Volume II.* W.H. Freeman and Company. Copyright 1974. Reprinted by permission.

Quite a number of different techniques exist, some of which were developed in biology for constructing taxonomies (Sneath & Sokal, 1973). The type of solution obtained depends on the particular algorithm. Some methods produce a tree structure, in which points or nodes on the branches correspond to objects, and these are successively joined together by other branches, until all objects are connected in some way in the tree. The tree is required to be such that any two objects are connected by one and only one path along the branches of the tree. Other algorithms produce clusters that subdivide the set of objects into homogeneous

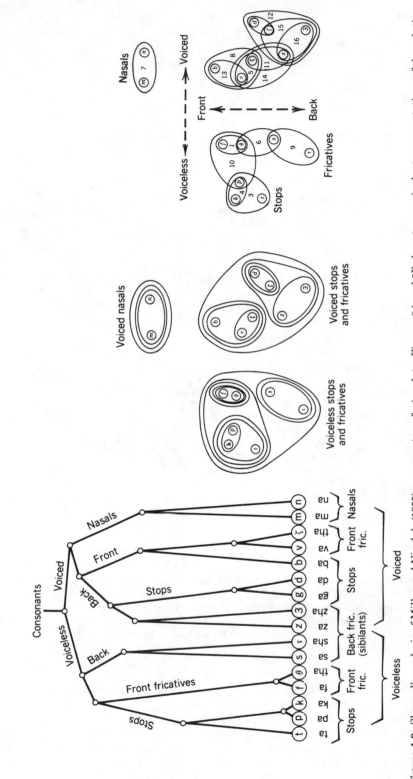

Figure 1.9. Shepard's analysis of Miller and Nicely's (1955) consonant confusion data. Figures 9A and 9B show two equivalent representations of the solution obtained using the hierarchical clustering method. Figure 9C shows the solution obtained using the nonhierarchical, additive clustering method. From "Multidimensional Scaling, Tree-Fitting and Clustering" by R.N. Shepard, 1980, *Science, 210*, pp. 390–398. Copyright 1980 by the AAAS. Reprinted by permission.

subsets. In some cases these clusters are required to be nonoverlapping; in others, the clusters must be hierarchically organized so that small subsets are successively joined to other objects and subsets until all objects are finally joined into one large set. Still other methods allow for the possibility of partially overlapping subsets. Several considerations, including the scale type of the original data, implicit assumptions of the method about properties of the data, and computational efficiency, play a role in the choice of the most appropriate method.

Methods for Obtaining Tree Structures

One tree model frequently fitted to psychological data represents the similarity between any two objects as the height of the path joining the two objects in a tree in which all points are equally distant from some highest point (root) of the tree (Hartigan, 1975; Jardine, Jardine & Sibson, 1967; Johnson, 1967). Objects that are most similar are joined at lower levels in the tree, whereas dissimilar objects are joined together only at higher levels in the tree. Figure 1.9A shows Shepard's (1980) application of Johnson's (1967) method to the consonant confusion data collected by Miller and Nicely (1955). To facilitate interpretation, the branches of the tree structure are labeled by the features that apply to the various objects at the ends of the branches. Trees of this sort are called ultrametric because, once two objects have been joined together, they must be equally distant from any third object to which they are joined at a higher level. This is called the ultrametric property. For example, g and d cluster first, and so their distances to any other consonant, say, b, are assumed to be equal. This is a strong assumption about the data, one that is satisfied only rarely. Before turning to methods that relax this assumption, however, it should be noted that ultrametric trees can be equivalently represented as hierarchically organized clusters. Figure 1.9B shows the solution displayed as clusters imposed on the two-dimensional scaling solution of the same data.

Methods for fitting more general tree models to proximity data have subsequently been developed by Carroll (1976), Cunningham (1978), and Sattath and Tversky (1977). These methods allow some or all of the interior, or nonterminal, nodes of the tree to correspond to objects or stimuli. In addition, these methods define an alternative metric on the tree, in which the distance between any two objects is represented by the length of the path joining the two nodes of the tree. This metric definition makes weaker assumptions about the data than the ultrametric property, but still requires that the data conform to a condition, called the four-point condition or additive inequality, which is stronger than the triangle inequality discussed earlier. Other generalizations include the option of simultaneously fitting more than one tree to a set of data, and even of combining multiple tree representations with a multidimensional spatial component (Carroll, 1976). Figure 1.10 shows Carroll and Pruzansky's (1980) application of the multiple tree model to Miller and Nicely's (1955) data. Two trees were obtained with the first tree interpretable as grouping consonants by voicing

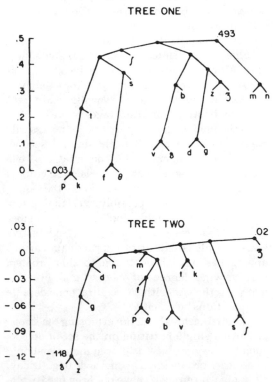

Figure 1.10. Carroll and Pruzansky's application of the multiple tree model to Miller and Nicely's (1955) data. From "Discrete and Hybrid Scaling Models" by J.D. Carroll and S. Pruzansky in *Similarity and Choice* (p. 122) by E.D. Lantermann and H. Geger (eds.), 1980, Bern: Hans Huber. Copyright 1980 by Bell Telephone Laboratories, Incorporated. Reprinted by permission.

and nasality and the second tree as related to place of articulation.

Methods for Obtaining Clusters

Certain methods produce a collection of subsets or clusters rather than a tree structure. The objective of these clustering methods is to group together objects that are similar and to separate dissimilar objects into different clusters. In other words, the representation obtained should group together objects into relatively homogeneous subsets. This objective is formalized in a variety of different clustering criteria which specify how the clusters are to be formed. Certain methods are nonmetric in the sense that the solution obtained is invariant under any (increasing) monotonic transformation of the data, but most methods assume stronger numerical properties. Although a thorough discussion of clustering algorithms is beyond our scope, two issues should be noted briefly. First, there are difficulties in ensuring that the solution obtained is optimal in the sense of maximizing an objectively defined measure of the goodness of fit. More specifically, the iterative algorithms are such that the decision to join (or subdivide) clusters at one stage is not reevaluated in light of its implications for later stages of the process. Thus the final configuration does not necessarily maximize the overall fit to the data. A second, related point concerns the computational efficiency of the algorithms. The basic difficulty is that the number of possible solutions—the assignment of the objects to possibly overlapping subsets—grows extremely rapidly as the number of objects increases, making an exhaustive search of all possibilities impractical. Various approaches have been taken to this problem with varying degrees of success, and, even so, many of the algorithms require considerable computational capacity.

Nonhierarchical, nonoverlapping methods produce a single partition on the set of objects such that every object is placed in one and only one subset or cluster. The methods (e.g., Diday, 1974; MacQueen, 1967) have not been used extensively in psychology. In contrast, the hierarchical clustering method, which produces a set of hierarchically nested subsets, has been used in a number of psychological applications, possibly because there exist simple algorithms for obtaining a solution to this model. It is equivalent to an ultrametric tree and was discussed in the last section. One development (Shepard & Arabie, 1979, Arabie & Carroll, 1980) allows for partly overlapping subsets. The basic assumption of this later model, which is called additive clustering, is that the objects have properties with associated weights, and the observed similarity between two objects is the sum of the weights associated with those properties. Each feature corresponds to a subset of objects that possess that feature. Figure 1.9C shows Shepard's (1980) application of this model to the Miller and Nicely (1955) data. As can be seen, the solution consists of a number of partly overlapping subsets, suggesting that this model provides a better account of the consonant confusion data than the more restrictive hierarchical clustering model.

Comparison of Spatial and Nonspatial Methods

Because spatial and nonspatial models yield solutions that are quite different—the one fundamentally geometric and the other lattice-like—they clearly must capture different aspects of the structure existing in the data. Spatial models are suited to structures that can be reasonably thought of as homogeneously organized along one or several dimensions and in which there is a reasonably continuous tradeoff among dimensions, as is reflected in the distance measure used. When such homogeneity is lacking, when objects seem to group themselves into distinct classes that are not geometric in character, then nonspatial models become more appropriate. Which type of nonspatial model is best suited to the data depends on the exact structural features that are found, such as whether there exist nesting or hierarchical relations.

If the data are of one type and the other type of model is used to analyze them, the results can be misleading. For example, experience suggests that the application of multidimensional scaling to data with a lattice structure has the consequence of causing some structured subsets to collapse into a point, thereby obliterating their fine structure. Kruskal (1977) has suggested that the spatial models are generally best at bringing out the global features of the data, whereas the nonspatial methods tend to highlight local, nongeometric structure. Since the data do not often announce clearly their character, it is usually wise to treat such methods as distinctly exploratory, and to apply as many as possible to see what each reveals—maintaining, of course, a degree of skepticism about what is real and what is due to chance features of the data. In this regard, there are few substitutes for the analysis of additional bodies of independent data.

PSYCHOPHYSICS

Most psychophysicists, though interested in various scaling problems, approach these measurement questions differently from the ways just discussed. One group, much the larger, is concerned with data and descriptive models of various kinds of sensory interactions that result in confusions of one sort or another. The topics include detection, discrimination, intensity-time tradeoffs, masking, and the like. We group these studies together under the heading *Local Psychophysics* because the focus is on stimulus changes that are small enough to cause confusions among stimuli. In the process of trying to account for these data, sensory measures arise as parameters in the models.

The second group attempts to deal with the full dynamic range of sensory dimension—differences so large that there is no chance whatever of confusions between the extreme signals in the range. These topics we call *Global Psychophysics*. The methods used include absolute identification and confusion matrices, category scaling, and various methods of magnitude estimation and production and of cross-modal matching. In some methods, measures of stimuli are inferred indirectly through a model such as Thurstone's; in others the responses are treated rather directly as measurement representations.

The final section—*The Elusive Bridge*—discusses attempts that have been made to bridge the results and models of these two domains. Although this is, in a sense, the oldest theoretical problem in psychophysics, it remains unresolved.

Local Psychophysics

Random Variable Representations of Signals

The central problem of classical psychophysics, as defined by its founder Fechner (1860), was how to characterize the relation between events in the external physical environment and internal sensations in the observer. In Fechner's work the problem was interpreted as solvable using internal thresholds, that is, finding those points along the physical dimension that correspond to discontinuous transition points in perception. This orientation reflects the belief that differences between sensations can be detected, but that their absolute magnitudes are less well apprehended.

Two kinds of thresholds were distinguished: absolute or detection thresholds, defined as those values of physical dimensions below which the stimulus is not detected at all but above which it is; and relative or difference thresholds, defined as the least differences along a dimension needed to perceive a distinction. The value on the physical dimension corresponding to this subjective just noticeable difference (jnd) was called a difference threshold or limen. The experimental methods developed to estimate such thresholds are many, and summaries may be found in Gescheider (1976), Guilford (1954), Kling and Riggs (1972), and elsewhere.

For both absolute and difference thresholds, one finds empirically a smooth rather than discontinuous transition between response states —present versus absent or same versus different —as the physical magnitude or difference is varied. At the level of responses, observers are neither absolutely consistent nor infinitely sensitive. These facts have led to several types of theories to account for them as well as to statistical definitions of thresholds.

Almost without exception, modern accounts offered for confusions among signals involve the assumption that the signals are represented numerically in the brain and that these representations exhibit some degree of variability. Put another way, the signals are represented as random variables, as was assumed by Thurstone.

Although two major questions about such a postulate immediately come to mind, they have not yet been fully resolved to everyone's satisfaction. The first has to do with the dimensionality of the representation. How can we assume it to be one-dimensional when we know well that each signal activates a number of peripheral neurons and so involves, at least, a vector representation? Basically, two approaches have been taken. The one is to suppose that for the type of one-dimensional question that psychophysicists typically ask, for example, which of two signals is the larger, the central nervous system amalgamates the vector, perhaps by some form of addition, into a single random variable. If the components of the vector are random, statistically independent, and of comparable size, the central limit theorem shows that the distribution of the sum will be approximately Gaussian, which is what is usually assumed in Thurstonian models. Various specific models have postulated other forms of amalgamation, without, however, a great deal of detailed evidence to guide the modeling.

The other approach, which was taken in laying the foundations of the theory of signal detectability (see, e.g., Green & Swets, 1966/1974), is to use a simple statistical device. Suppose there are only two possible signals s_1 and s_2 and the internal observation is some vector $\hat{x}$, then there is some probability density f_i of observing $\hat{x}$ when signal s_i is presented, and the likelihood ratio l of the observation is defined to be

$$l(\hat{x}) = f_1(\hat{x})/f_2(\hat{x}).$$

Obviously, this is a number. For each number l, consider the set X_1 of values $\hat{x}$ such that $l(\hat{x}) = l$. Thus the probability that the likelihood value l would arise is the same as the probability that an observation lies in X_1. Of course, this probability depends upon which signal is presented, and the likelihood ratio thus has one distribution of values when s_1 is presented and another when s_2 is presented. Under plausible assumptions, these distributions can be shown to be Gaussian. And so the problem is reduced to the two-signal version of the Thurstone model in which the decision variable is likelihood ratio. This is acceptable so long as attention is confined to two signals, but it does not generalize in a satisfactory way to the N-signal, one-dimensional Thurstone model, which is what one typically uses when there are more than two signals that vary on only one physical dimension.

The second major issue has been whether the random variable is discrete or continuous; that is, should it be thought of as quantal in character, and so take on integral values, or might it take on any number as a value? True thresholds are one consequence of discreteness. Such discreteness could arise in at least two quite distinct ways. One is that the stimuli themselves are physically discrete; the other is that the nervous system is in some way discrete. We take up each of these points of view briefly.

At least for absolute thresholds, it is possible for a physical threshold to be imposed by the quantal structure of matter and energy. Can the eye detect one or a very few quanta of light? This question was posed by Hecht, Schlaer, and Pirenne (1942). Since there was evidence that a single quantum of light was enough to activate a single photoreceptor, the question arose as to how many receptors would need to be excited to detect a flash of light. The problem would be easy if one could cause a known number of quanta to impinge on the retina, but that is not possible. The number of quanta emitted by a light source is a random variable that follows what is known as the Poisson distribution: the probability that n quanta will be emitted given that the mean number is μ, is $\mu^n e^{-\mu}/n!$. Thus we know the distribution of the number that will arrive at the cornea, but that is much greater than the number that will actually be absorbed by the photopigments. A few quanta are lost by reflection, and many are absorbed as they travel through the optical medium. These losses, which can be estimated, apply with equal likelihood to each quantum independently and so do not alter the Poisson character of the distribution, but they do reduce its mean value. A family of curves, each showing the probability of obtaining n or more quanta as a function of the average number of quanta arriving at the receptor level, can be calculated and they are shown in Figure 1.11. In order to answer the question of how many quanta are required for detection, one compares with these curves the observed probability of a detection response as a function of the mean number of quanta estimated to arrive at the receptor level. The best-fitting curve led to the conclusion that between five and seven excited photoreceptors are sufficient to detect a flash of light. Sakitt (1972) has refined the procedure and has estimated an even smaller number, two.

The point of this example is that at absolute threshold, at least, a careful consideration of the variability inherent in the stimulus at the sensory transducer appears to be adequate to account for most, if not all, of the variability in the responses. Nothing comparable has been done for audition or for difference thresholds.

The other major quantal approach began with Fechner, who believed there were true sensory thresholds. It was refined by Békésy (1930) who suggested that true thresholds arise because the number of neural cells that are activated (at

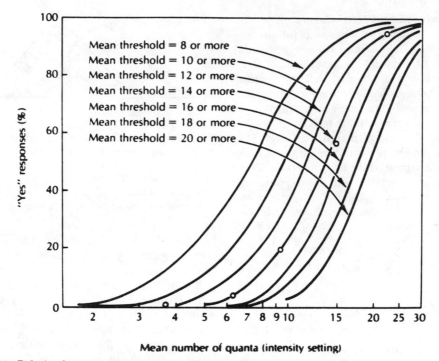

Figure 1.11. Relative frequency of detecting a visual stimulus as a function of the mean number of light quanta estimated to reach the retina. The plotted curves are those predicted by different quantal thresholds (numbers shown on curves) assuming a Poisson distribution of quanta. From *Visual Perception* (p. 77) by T.N. Cornsweet, 1970, New York: Academic Press. Copyright 1970 by Academic Press. Reprinted by permission.

some level of the nervous system) is the critical variable in intensity discrimination, and that it is a discrete, not continuous, variable. This led to the prediction that the probability of detection or discrimination changes linearly with a suitable measure of signal intensity. Stevens and Volkmann (1940) restated the theory, and Stevens, Morgan, and Volkmann (1941) provided some relevant data. There have subsequently been a number of summaries and critiques of the idea and experiments (Corso, 1956, 1973; Gescheider, 1976; Krantz, 1969; Luce, 1963c; Treisman, 1977; Wright, 1974). Almost everyone agrees that any version of the theory that attempts to explain discrimination data by the involvement of only two discrete states is wrong. Most psychophysicists have generalized that conclusion to the entire concept of a discrete representation. So far as we can tell, this sweeping conclusion goes far beyond the data; however, it has proved very difficult to devise a clean experiment that can reveal discreteness in the representation if it is there. So we turn to the popular continuous representation.

Historically, the theory of signal detectability first entered psychophysics for vision (Tanner & Swets, 1954), following from earlier engineering work conducted during World War II for the detection of electromagnetic signals. In that form it had certain special features—(1) that the decision axis is a likelihood ratio, and (2) that the decision maker is ideal in the sense of behaving optimally in extracting information from the physical stimulus—but for most psychological applications those features have not mattered. When stripped of these interpretations, signal detection is just the random variable model of Thurstone with Gaussian distributed random variables. Still, it has had an impact in psychophysics that far exceeded Thurstone's. What was new and very important was the recognition that performance in such a situation is controlled by two independent factors: the signals used and the subject's motivation. When looked at this way, it also turns out to be the general approach taken in statistical decision theory. For a detailed exposition of the theory, see Green and Swets (1966/1974).

Error Tradeoffs and ROC Curves

The general decision problem is as follows: one of two events called stimuli can occur; there is some form of internal evidence, called data, about which one did occur; and the decision maker, called a subject or observer in a psychological experiment, is to infer from the evidence which event occurred and is to respond accordingly. When dealing with signal detection, the two events are the presentation either of a signal s or of no signal n; the evidence is the Thurstonian random variable; and the responses are Yes (Y) there was a signal, or No (N) there was none. We can visualize the situation in two ways. First, we can form a table of possibilities

$$
\text{Presentation} \quad
\begin{array}{c}
s \\
n
\end{array}
\begin{array}{c}
\overbrace{\hphantom{xxxxx}}^{Y} \quad \overbrace{\hphantom{xxxxx}}^{N} \\
\left[
\begin{array}{cc}
\text{hit} & \text{miss} \\
\text{false} & \text{correct} \\
\text{alarm} & \text{rejection}
\end{array}
\right].
\end{array}
$$

When data are collected and classed in this way, they give rise to the following table of estimated conditional probabilities:

$$
\begin{array}{c}
s \\
n
\end{array}
\begin{array}{c}
\overbrace{\hphantom{xxxxxxxxxx}}^{Y} \qquad \overbrace{\hphantom{xxxxxxxxxx}}^{N} \\
\left[
\begin{array}{cc}
P(Y|s) & P(N|s) = 1 - P(Y|s) \\
P(Y|n) & P(N|n) = 1 - P(Y|n)
\end{array}
\right].
\end{array}
$$

Here $P(Y|s)$ denotes the probability of saying Yes when the signal s is presented, and so on. Second, we can visualize it in terms of two distributions which correspond to whether the signal has or has not been presented (Figure 1.12). Obviously the subject should respond Y when the value of the random variable is large enough, and N when it is small enough. Indeed, if we assume that the subject selects a criterion β to divide the range into Y and N intervals, we have the picture shown in Figure 1.13. This dif-

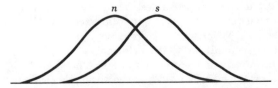

Figure 1.12. Hypothetical distributions of internal observations for those trials on which a signal (s) in noise is presented and on those trials on which only noise (n) appears.

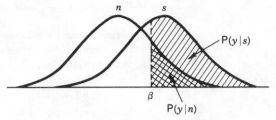

Figure 1.13. One possible response criterion β for the distributions shown in Figure 1.12. Whenever the internal observation is to the right of β, the "Yes" response is made. The probability of a "Yes" response on signal and noise trials is given by the shaded areas of the corresponding density functions.

fers from Thurstone's model, in that the parameter β is explicitly assumed to be under the subject's control.

There is no obviously unique choice for β. As β is made larger, both Y probabilities get smaller, which means that the error $P(Y|n)$ is reduced at the expense of making the error $P(N|s) = 1 - P(Y|s)$ larger. As β is made smaller, $P(N|s)$ is reduced, but $P(Y|n)$ is increased. Thus, according to the model there is an error tradeoff, called the power of a test by statisticians, and it can be plotted. Actually, it is conventional in psychophysics to plot $P(Y|s)$ versus $P(Y|n)$, and to call the resulting curve either a receiver operating characteristic (ROC) curve or an isosensitivity curve. An example for equal-variance Gaussian distributions with unit separation between the distributions is shown in Figure 1.14.

All of this is tidy theoretically, but does it have anything to do with human performance? For nearly a century no one realized that it did; however, once the theory was available psychophysicists undertook to study it. They argued that subjects would try to select β so as to perform well in the eyes of the experimenter, which in practice means in terms of the feedback provided the subject about the quality of performance. Instructions, relative frequency in presenting the signal versus the noise, and payoffs have all been successfully used to manipulate β. Differences in values of β are thought to underlie subjects' confidence judgments, and these are often used as a quick way to develop an ROC curve. Figure 1.15 presents an example using vibration to the finger as the stimulus. There is no doubt today that performance depends on both the signal and the reinforcement conditions.

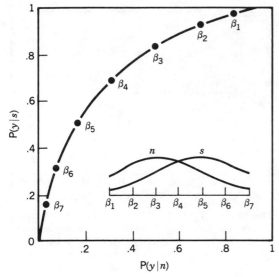

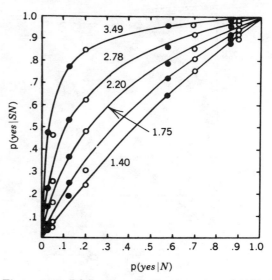

Figure 1.14. For the distributions of signal and noise shown, an illustration of how the ROC curves are generated by varying β. The area to the right of β on the n curve shows the probability of saying "Yes" when there is no signal; the corresponding area on the signal distribution shows the probability of saying "Yes" when the signal is presented. The value for signal is plotted on the ordinate; that for noise alone is plotted on the abscissa. From *Psychophysics: Method and Theory* (p. 79) by G.A. Gescheider, 1976, Hillsdale, NJ: Lawrence Erlbaum Associates, Inc. Copyright 1976 by Lawrence Erlbaum Associates, Inc. Reprinted by permission.

Figure 1.15. ROC curves for the detection of 60-Hz vibrations to the fingertip. The curves are labeled with the peak-to-peak amplitude of the stimulus in microns. The subjects' expectancy of the signal's being applied was varied by instruction. From *Psychophysics: Method and Theory* (p. 21) by G.A. Gescheider, 1976, Hillsdale, NJ: Lawrence Erlbaum Associates, Inc. Copyright 1976 by Lawrence Erlbaum Associates, Inc. Reprinted by permission.

If the internal representation is discrete rather than continuous, as in the neural quantum theory, then the predicted ROC curve is a series of discrete points (Blackwell, 1953; Luce, 1963c; Norman, 1964). However, by certain strategies involving some false reporting, these points can be transformed into a continuous ROC curve in which linear segments connect the points. There are as many segments as there are relevant states. Krantz (1969) showed that ROC data are inconsistent with the two-state model, but the three-state model has never been rejected by ROC data. The reason is, of course, that three straight lines can approximate the Gaussian ROC curves so well that a huge amount of data would be needed to reduce the binomial variability enough to distinguish the two curves.

In the forced-choice design—in which the signal appears in exactly one of two time or space intervals and the subject is asked to say which—slightly better separation appears between the theories. Atkinson (1963) and Luce (1963c) showed for the two-state case, and Norman (1964) for the general case, that the forced-choice ROC curve has a major linear segment of slope 1. Figure 1.16 shows the data for one subject plotted in both probability coordinates and Gaussian coordinates (where the Gaussian ROC curve is a straight line). It is by no means obvious which curve fits the data better. Study of forced-choice ROC curves has never been pursued intensively.

Psychometric Functions and d'

From Fechner to the appearance of signal detectability theory, the major summary of the data was the probability $P(Y|s)$ as a function of a physical measure of s. This plot is often called the *psychometric function* although in special literatures other terms are used, such as frequency-of-seeing curve. Using the usual logarithmic measure of the physical scale—often called a decibel scale both in audition, where it originated, and in vision—the psychometric function often resembles the cumulative Gaussian distribution, as shown in Figure 1.17.

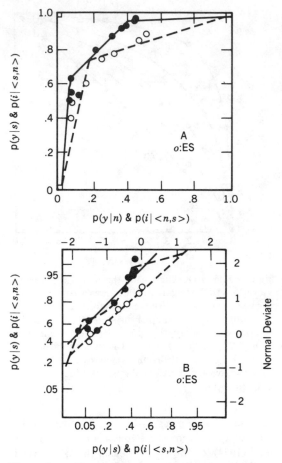

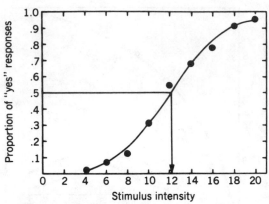

Figure 1.17. Typical psychometric function obtained by varying the signal strength in a Yes-No detection procedure. The threshold is defined to be the signal intensity that is detected exactly 50 percent of the time. From *Psychophysics: Methods and Theory* (p. 61) by G.A. Gescheider, 1976, Hillsdale, NJ: Lawrence Erlbaum Associates, Inc. Copyright 1976 by Lawrence Erlbaum Associates, Inc. Reprinted by permission.

Figure 1.16. Yes-No (open circles) and two-alternative forced-choice (closed circles) pure-tone detection data for a single subject. The ROC curves were manipulated by varying the payoffs. (a) The two sets of data fitted by the two-state, low threshold model. (b) The same data fitted by Gaussian ROC curves (the fitted curves are straight lines because the axes are the z-scores corresponding to the probabilities). Also shown is the transformed two-state ROC curve for the two-alternative, forced-choice procedure. From "Sensory Thresholds, Response, Biases, and the Neural Quantum Theory" by D.A. Norman, 1964, *Journal of Mathematical Psychology*, p. 116. Copyright 1964 by Academic Press. Reprinted by permission.

Laming (1986) has presented a careful study of the form of psychometric functions, establishing appreciable differences for increment versus forced-choice procedures and developing a theory of their origins.

Such data, and their explanation as a muddied true threshold, lead naturally to a statisti-

cal estimation of the threshold; and if the explanation is rejected, it simply becomes a statistical definition of the threshold. In increment detection against a background level, the psychometric function runs from 0, when the signal is never detected, to 1, when it always is. The threshold is defined to be that intensity leading to 1/2 on the psychometric function, that is, a 50–50 chance of detecting the signal. For forced-choice discrimination studies, the function runs from 1/2 to 1, and the threshold or limen is defined as the change leading to a probability of 3/4.

Once one is aware of the ROC curve, it becomes clear, however, that the classic psychometric function is not very satisfactory. The problem is that, if the subject can vary β, then it is very important that the experimenter does not allow the subject to vary β with the magnitude of the signal. One way to achieve this is to randomize the intensities of s so that the subject cannot know on any trial what value is pitted against noise and so cannot correlate his choice of β with the signal level. Even so, there are statistical problems, because the experimenter usually attempts to hold $P(Y|n)$ to a very small value, which implies that one is attempting to estimate $P(Y|s)$ on the steepest part of the ROC curve. Thus any error that is made in estimating $P(Y|n)$—which can be quite sizable unless the sample size is enormous—is amplified as an

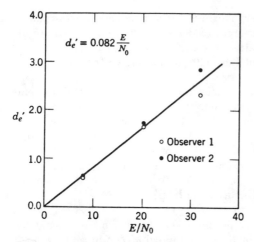

Figure 1.18. Estimated values of d' for detection of a pure tone as a function of signal strength (E/N_0) measured in decibels. From *Signal Detection Theory and Psychophysics* (p. 190) by D.M. Green and J.A. Swets, 1974, New York: John Wiley & Sons, Inc. Copyright 1974 John Wiley & Sons, Inc. Reprinted by permission of John Wiley & Sons, Inc.

error in estimating $P(Y|s)$ that is five to ten times larger. The net result is that the psychometric function is usually not estimated precisely, and even statistical estimates of thresholds are subject to large errors.

Observe that, in the Thurstone model, the impact of increasing signal strength is to increase the separation of the two distributions. However, just how significant the difference of the means is depends on the spread of the density functions. This suggests using the following normalized measure of their separation:

$$d' = (\mu_s - \mu_n)/\sqrt{\sigma_s^2 + \sigma_n^2}.$$

A plot of this function, assuming that we can estimate it, as a function of signal strength is totally unaffected by the choice of the response criterion β. An example is shown in Figure 1.18. A number of authors use this rather than the traditional psychometric functions, but others object that it is too dependent on the theory's being correct. A less theory-bound measure is the area under the entire ROC curve. Although that is expensive to measure directly, there is a simple equivalent way to find it, to which we now turn.

It is fairly common practice not to use a Yes–No procedure of the sort discussed, but a two-alternative forced-choice procedure. It is not difficult to show that the same model applies but that the value of d' is increased by a factor of $\sqrt{2}$, which corresponds to the fact that the subject really has twice as much information. It can be shown that, when the criterion is set halfway between the two distributions, the proportion of correct responses in the force-choice procedure exactly equals the area under the ROC curve in the corresponding Yes–No experiment (Green & Swets, 1966/1974, pp. 45–47). This type of psychometric function seems acceptable to both camps and is widely used.

Speed-accuracy Tradeoffs

Although the time a subject takes to respond is ignored in most psychophysical studies, it has the potential to give us additional information about the processing of the signals. Moreover it places an interesting further demand on the theorist who must simultaneously account for the subject's choices and the time it has taken to make them.

There is a question of experimental procedure: When we record response times, should we emphasize to the subject the fact they are being recorded? The brief signals usually employed certainly encourage the subject to attend just to that time, but if the subject is not motivated to respond as fast as possible we cannot be sure what irrelevant delays may enter into the response times. And since response times usually become briefer when pressure is applied, some experimenters, though not all, feel it best to impose such pressure. However, doing so can result in another problem, namely, anticipatory responses. These are responses that originate before the signal is actually presented. Responses made before the signal is presented are clearly anticipatory, but presumably some of the responses that follow signal onset were also initiated by something other than the signal. Attempts to reduce the tendency for anticipatory responses include the introduction of (1) variable times between a warning signal and the reaction signal, (2) catch trials on which no signal is presented at all, and (3) choice-reaction paradigms in which the subject is obliged to make a discriminative response.

It is well established that it takes longer—on the order of 75–100-msec longer—to identify one of two distinct signals than it does to detect the onset of either. Choice reactions are always slower than simple ones, though it is not certain whether this is due to a difference in the decision process or in the preparation to make the response.

A second fact is that, when pressed for time, subjects can usually adjust their behavior with respect to speed but at some cost in accuracy of performance. This was first studied explicitly by Fitts (1966), and later studies by Pew (1969), Lappin and Disch (1972), Laming (1968), Link (1975, 1978), and Link and Heath (1975) have established nearly linear relations between mean reaction time and one or another of several measures of accuracy—information transmitted, log odds of being correct, d', $(d')^2$, and a measure suggested by the random walk model of Link. In order to study this relation, some experimental technique is required to manipulate simultaneous changes in speed and accuracy. For example, Green and Luce (1973) ran a Yes–No detection study in which the signals were response terminated. They employed a time deadline, which was varied over conditions from 250 to 2000 msec, such that responses after the deadline drew fines, whereas those before it, but not before signal onset, were paid off with accuracy. The resulting tradeoff, plotted as d' versus the overall mean reaction time (there was little difference in the means for the four stimulus-response cells), is shown in Figure 1.19A. These data are much like the results of other speed-accuracy studies. The data in the other three panels were obtained using a slightly modified procedure in which the deadline applied only to signal trials, not to noise trials. Under these conditions the mean times to signals are faster than to noise, and so there are two distinct speed-accuracy tradeoffs for each subject. It is worth noting that the rate of change is roughly doubled by imposing the deadline on signal trials only.

Green and Luce offered a possible explanation in terms of two different types of information processing, called counting and timing models. Assume that the sensory intensity information is encoded as the variable firing rates of neural pulses; the task then for the subject is basically to infer from a neural sample whether it arose from the faster or slower rate. In the counting mode, the rate is estimated as the ratio of the number of counts obtained in a fixed observation time (determined by the deadline) to that time, whereas, in the timing mode it is estimated as the inverse ratio of the time taken to obtain a fixed number of counts to that num-

ber. This difference is adequate to explain the different tradeoffs. Link (1978) offered an alternative account in terms of a random walk model, but Luce (1986a) has shown that it is not satisfactory.

A somewhat uneven, but useful, general reference to the entire subject of reaction times, and to the theoretical models that have been studied, is Welford's (1980) edited volume. A general survey of models and closely related experiments is given by Luce (1986a).

Global Psychophysics

Any psychophysical experiment is said to be global if the following condition is met: The range of possible signals used in an experimental run is such that if the two extreme values were run in a 2-stimulus absolute identification design, they would be identified almost perfectly. (In such an experiment one of the two signals is presented on each trial according to a random schedule unknown to the subject, and the subject is required to say whether it is the louder or softer signal, the brighter or dimmer signal, or whatever. After each trial the subject is informed whether or not the response on that trial was correct.)

There are two comments to be made about this definition. First, it is ambiguous because "almost perfectly," like "beyond a reasonable doubt," is subject to interpretation. Do we mean 99.9 percent, 99 percent, 90 percent, 75 per cent, or what? The intuition is that, in fact, the extreme stimuli are sufficiently separated so that discrimination between them can be perfect, although in practice lapses of attention may occur that drop the observed performance below 100 percent. So probably 99 percent is a suitable criterion. Certainly 75 percent is far too low, as is 90 percent.

Second, it is implicit in the distinction between global and local psychophysics that there is some difference either of procedure or results or both. The difference in procedure is obvious. In local psychophysics attention was mainly on experimental designs in which performance in identifying or discriminating two signals is imperfect, and one studies those imperfections. By definition, in global psychophysics one has reached the point where, for at least the two most extreme signals, one can no longer study them in the same way, and a different approach is required. The differences in results we will come to presently.

There are two strong motives for carrying out global studies as well as local ones. First, our ordinary environment is psychophysically a global one, at least some of the time. To be sure, much of the time the range of variation in signal intensity is quite small, but at other times it is decidedly not small. So if we are to understand human performance in the natural environment, we must either extrapolate from local experiments or use global experiments, or both. Second, when we try to extrapolate from local data, we find that gross errors in prediction

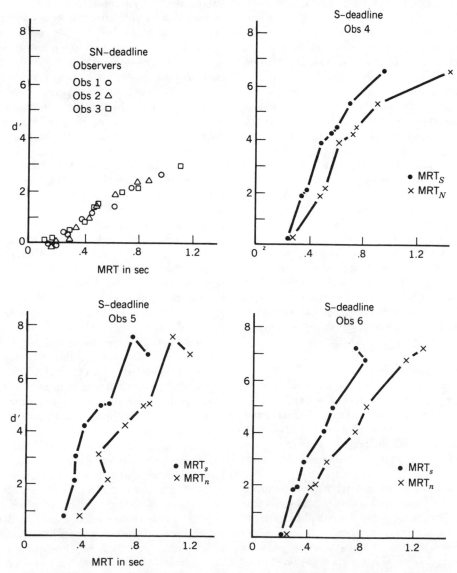

Figure 1.19. The speed-accuracy tradeoff obtained by varying a response-time deadline in an auditory detection experiment. Accuracy is measured by d' and speed by mean reaction time (MRT). (a) Data for three subjects when the deadline was applied to all trials. (b, c, d) Data for individual subjects when the deadline was applied only to signal trials. For these cases, the time data are separated for signal and noise trials, because they were appreciably different. From "Speed and Accuracy Tradeoff in Auditory Detection" by D.M. Green and R.D. Luce in *Attention and Performance, IV* (p. 564) by S. Kornblum (ed.), 1973, New York: Academic Press. Copyright 1973 by Academic Press. Reprinted by permission.

arise. This apparently was not really recognized until the early 1950s when facts of the following type were noticed. For auditory intensity, two signals 5 dB apart can be absolutely identified with almost perfect accuracy, so any experiment with a range greater than 5 dB is global. In particular, consider the absolute identification of one of 20 signals, successively spaced 5 dB apart over a 95 dB range from 15 dB to 110 dB. Since successive pairs can be identified perfectly, the natural extrapolation is that each of the 20 can be also. The facts are otherwise. A great many identification errors occur, and to get perfect identification of equally spaced signals over a 95-dB range, the number of signals must be reduced to about 7, spaced about 15 dB apart. This phenomenon was first reported by Pollack (1952) for pitch and by Garner (1953) for loudness, and it has since been shown to hold for every unidimensional psychophysical domain. It was brought forcefully to psychologists' attention in the classic paper of Miller (1956), whose "magical number" 7 in the title refers, in part, to the 7 we have just mentioned.

Such facts mean we must collect and study global as well as local data, and some of these data are described in the present section. They also mean that a theoretical account is needed for the discrepancy between global and local results, and various approaches are discussed in the next section.

Types of Global Experiments

Most of the local designs use pairs of stimuli, and the experimenter observes the nature of the errors subjects make when trying to distinguish between them. By definition of a global situation, this approach no longer makes any sense. Something else must be done. Several ideas have been pursued.

One major distinction is whether the subject is required to classify signals in some manner (the different methods are described later) or to identify absolutely the signals. In the latter case, the subject knows there is an ensemble of n signals and is provided with some one-to-one code to identify them. As individual signals are presented the subject attempts to identify them, using this code. Often the signals are ordered along one physical dimension, in which case the code is their ranking on that dimension or some variant of it, such as the left-right ordering of a bank of keys. No real judgment is required of the

subject, who simply attempts to make correct identifications. In this experiment each response is correct or not, and so information feedback and payoffs may be (and usually are) used. In this respect, absolute identification (AI) experiments are a natural extension of those employed in local situations. Of course, rank ordering of stimuli is closely related to AI, but it is usually carried out by allowing the observer to make paired comparisons.

Since AI experiments have a nice objectivity about them, why do anything else? The reason is that they do not permit us to study directly one important aspect of the global situation, namely, the way in which the subjective attribute grows with the physical signal. If loudness is the attribute, how does it depend on the auditory signal, its intensity and frequency, or in the case of noise, its band of frequencies? We do not seem to gain much information about that from AI experiments, and we are forced to use other designs in which the subjects' responses provide evidence about their subjective judgments. There is no way around it; we are asking for, and we hope to receive, assertions about the subjects' perceptions of the signals. There are no right or wrong answers; our only criterion can be internal consistency of bodies of data and repeatability, which presumably would not be achieved, were the responses based on something other than the signal presented. Nevertheless, it is well to keep in mind that this part of the so-called hard science of psychophysics is just as soft as any other part of psychology that asks about the nature of internal states.

We distinguish three broad types of classification procedures.

First, there are tradeoff methods. To use these methods the experimenter must be prepared to manipulate at least two physical variables that affect the attribute in question, and the subject is required to judge when the two signals exhibit the same amount of the attribute. In some cases, judgment can be replaced by a detectability criterion as, for example, when duration-intensity tradeoffs are studied at threshold. But in general, judgment is required. Working with superthreshold signals, one may still ask if one intensity-duration flash of light is just as bright as another intensity-duration flash; or whether one intensity-frequency tone is as loud as another; or which distributions of wavelength of light are seen as the identical color (metameric matches). This is a valuable technique, closely related to both conjoint and functional measurement, but it does not provide as much immediate information about the structure of sensations as do the next two types of judgmental methods. Moreover, in modern practice, tradeoff studies are often subsumed under the method of magnitude estimation, as we do below.

Both of the next two methods ask the subjects to judge how signals differing along a single dimension relate to each other. In the first method, the subject is asked to partition the subjective domain into equal intervals. In the second, the subject is asked to report something about the ratio relation between two signals. We will mention three equal-interval procedures. The first is bisection, in which the subject is to find or report which signal x 'bisects' the interval bounded by two given signals, a and b. (One can also ask for proportions other than equality, although that is rarely done.) The second is categorizing or rating, in which the subject is told to place the signals, usually presented one at a time, into k categories that are 'equally spaced' along a subjective continuum. Of course, AI is the very special case of a category experiment in which the subject knows $k = n$. Although in principle there is no restriction on k, usually $k < n$ and the most commonly used values vary from as few as 7 to as many as 20 or 30. Anderson (1974a, p. 232) recommends 20. An obvious drawback with the category method is that, if the subject keeps the category boundaries fixed, the distribution of the signals has a powerful impact on the frequency with which the categories are used (Parducci, 1965; Parducci & Perrett, 1971; Mellers & Birnbaum, 1982). This can be an issue, since subjects appear to grow uncomfortable over highly uneven response distributions. A third technique, called 'graphical rating', has the subject mark a point on a line interval as the response to the signal. In recent years, Anderson has used this method instead of category scaling (see Anderson, 1981, for discussion and references). We group all three of these methods under the heading of *partition methods*.

At least five ratio methods must be mentioned. In the method of fractionation, the subject is presented with a signal a and is to select x such that x is some fixed fraction (often 1/2) of a. In the method of ratio response, signals a and b are presented and the subject is to report the subjective ratio of b to a. In the method of magnitude estimation, single signals are presented and the subject is asked to assign a number to each presentation so that ratios among responses reflect the subjective ratios of the signals. Thus, for example, if s_{n-1} and s_n are the signals on trials $n - 1$ and n, if the response R_{n-1} was made to s_{n-1}, and if s_n stands in the subjective ratio r to s_{n-1} then the instruction is to make the response $R_n = rR_{n-1}$. In this sense, magnitude estimation is a natural generalization of the method of ratio responses. In like manner, magnitude production generalizes fractionation by requiring the subject to assign signals to input numbers so that the signal assignments will maintain subjective ratios that agree with the ratios of the numbers. In what follows, we will report results based on the magnitude methods, but not on fractionation and ratio response. Finally, the method of cross-modal matching is a natural generalization of magnitude estimation and production. Consider two distinct modalities such as sound intensity and light intensity. If one can magnitude estimate sounds —assign numbers systematically to the sounds —and magnitude produce light intensity— assign lights systematically to numbers—then presumably one can systematically assign lights to sounds.

Most people, when first encountering these methods, are at ease with absolute identification and partitioning, but feel that the magnitude methods and especially cross-modal matching are really rather ridiculous. After all, what does it mean to match a light to a sound? Any match will do. If so, then presumably you are willing to match a barely detectable light to the sound of a nearby thunderclap. No . . . the light must be considerably brighter than that, indeed it should be one of the brightest you can imagine, say an equally rapid glance at the sun. (Neither lights so bright nor sounds so loud are actually used in these experiments.) So something more than order is involved, and the data are, in fact, highly systematic.

Because global psychophysics rests on the judgments of subjects, it is an area of controversy and uncertainty. Usually the greater the uncertainty, the stronger the expressed convictions of the advocates. Some authors are convinced that one method gets the right answers, whereas other methods exhibit bias, error, or

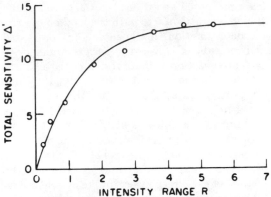

Figure 1.20. Performance as a function of signal range in the absolute identification of individual presentations of signals selected at random from a set of ten auditory signals equally spaced in decibels. Performance is measured by total sensitivity, which is the sum of d' for each of the successive 2×2 submatrices. Range is measured in bels = dB/10. From "Intensity Perception. II. Resolution in One-Interval Paradigms" by L.D. Braida and N.I. Durlach, 1972, *Journal of the Acoustical Society of America*, p. 491. Copyright 1972 by the American Institute of Physics. Reprinted by permission.

worse. Our stance is more eclectic. The task, in part, is to understand how the different methods are related. After all, exactly the same signal presentation can occur under several different methods; the only real difference is in what the subject has been asked to do with the information acquired about the signal.

Absolute Identification

We have already cited one of the major findings of the AI literature: local results do not predict global ones. To see what is involved, we wish to present a measure of performance either against the range for a fixed number of signals or against the number of signals for a fixed range. Three different, but closely related, measures of performance are found in the literature. The easiest to understand is percentage of correct responses. The next easiest is a d' measure that is computed as follows: the confusions between each successive pair of signals are treated as two-stimulus data, d' is calculated, and those values are summed over all successive pairs to yield what is called Δ' (an exact description is

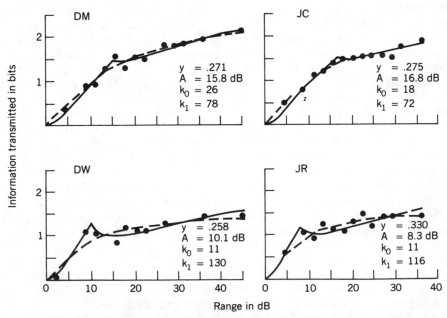

Figure 1.21. Performance as a function of signal range in the absolute identification of ten auditory signals. Performance in this case is measured by the amount of information transmitted, which is nearly linear with total sensitivity (see Figure 1.20). The solid line and the parameter values represent the attention band model, and the dashed line is for the Braida–Durlach model, which assumes that the variance of the internal representation grows linearly with the square of the range in decibels. From "Attention Bands in Absolute Identification" by R.D. Luce, D.M. Green, and D.L. Weber, 1976, *Perception & Psychophysics, 20,* p. 51. Copyright 1976 by The Psychonomic Society, Inc. Reprinted by permission.

given in the appendix of Luce, Green & Weber, 1976). With a fixed number of equally spaced signals, increasing the range would, one might imagine, cause Δ' to increase at least linearly. Figure 1.20 shows a plot for sound intensity, and we see that up to about 20-dB the growth is linear, after which it is much slower. A third measure often used (especially in the literature of the 1950s) is the amount of information transmitted. If P_{ij} is the probability of response j to signal i, P_j is the probability of response j, and if we assume that the signals are equally likely to occur, then $-\Sigma_i \Sigma_j P_{ij} \log_2(P_{ij}/P_j)$ is the information transmitted. For further explanation, see Coombs et al. (1970), Garner (1962), or Miller (1953). Figure 1.21 shows this measure as a function of the number of signals in a fixed range. Again, packing in more than about seven signals in a very wide range does not lead to improved performance. (The theoretical curves will be discussed later.)

There are at least two things to be understood here. The first is why the global data are inconsistent with the local. We go into that in the next major section. The second is why the limit of 7 ± 2 absolutely identifiable signals is so at variance with our everyday experience—everyone absolutely identifies many more than seven faces, or sounds, or even phonemes. The difference is one versus several dimensions. For example, Pollack (1953) used pure tones that varied in both intensity and frequency. The maximum information transmitted on each alone was 1.8 bits for intensity and 1.7 for frequency, corresponding to perfect identification of 3.5 and 3.3 signals, respectively. But when frequency and intensity were combined, information transmitted increased to 3.1 bits or the equivalent of perfect identification of 8.6 signals. Pollack and Ficks (1954) found that for complex stimuli with eight factors, each having two categories, transmission of 7.4 bits of information was achieved, which corresponds to 169 perfectly identifiable signals.

The use of any of these gross measures—percent correct, information transmitted, or Δ'—masks another characteristic of absolute identification data, namely, that the signals at the end of the range are far more accurately identified than those in the middle. This is illustrated in the curves of Figure 1.22. (The differences among the curves will be described later.) A number of papers have attempted to explore

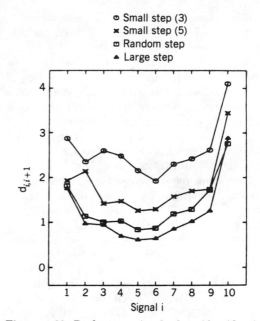

Figure 1.22. Performance in absolute identification as a function of the ordinal position (equal decibel steps) of the signal presented for the four different presentation schedules discussed in the text. The performance measure is the value of d' obtained by collapsing the entire data matrix around two successive signals and treating it as a 2×2 absolute identification. From "The Bow and Sequential Effects in Absolute Identification" by R.D. Luce, D.M. Green, R. Nosofsky, and A.F. Smith, 1982, *Perception & Psychophysics*, *32*, p. 399. Copyright 1982 by The Psychonomics Society, Inc. Reprinted by permission.

this phenomenon, which is sometimes called an edge effect (Berliner & Durlach, 1973; Berliner, Durlach & Braida, 1977; Braida & Durlach, 1972; Durlach & Braida, 1969; Gravetter & Lockhead, 1973; Luce, Nosofsky, Green & Smith, 1982; Lippman, Braida & Durlach, 1976; Weber, Green & Luce, 1977). Without going into detail, it is a robust phenomenon that has little to do with the stimuli themselves. As the range varies, the improved performance at the edge moves with it —except when one begins a session with a large range and then unbeknownst to the subject contracts the range, in which case the subject continues to perform poorly at the new edge as if it were an interior point in the longer range. Neither practice nor differential payoff seems able to overcome the edge effect. Some portion of the edge effect can be attributed to the fact that the end signals have only one neighbor to be confused with. But even if that is taken into account (Berliner et al., 1977; Weber et al., 1977), a substantial effect remains, at least for the more intense signals.

A second phenomenon, one that is often viewed as a mere nuisance, is the presence of pronounced sequential effects in the data. These may be closely related to why the local and global data are so different. The existence and magnitude of these effects were first emphasized by Lockhead and his students (Holland & Lockhead, 1968; Ward, 1972; Ward & Lockhead, 1970, 1971) and they have continued to be investigated (Purks, Callahan, Braida & Durlach, 1980; Green & Luce, 1974; Jesteadt, Luce & Green, 1977; Luce, Nosofsky, Green & Smith, 1982; Luce & Nosofsky, 1984). Three major conclusions appear warranted. First, changes in both sensitivity and response criteria appear to underlie these effects (Nosofsky, 1983). Second, substantial changes in response criteria are made on a trial-by-trial basis (Luce, Nosofsky et al., 1982; Purks et al., 1980). Third, changes in sensitivity are made more slowly and seem to be evident only when some form of signal clustering occurs over a number of trials (Luce & Nosofsky, 1984). As an example of clustering, Luce, Nosofsky et al. (1982) ran subjects in three conditions, in all of which the signals were used equally often in the long run. In one condition, the signals were chosen at random, in a second they were selected from three adjacent signals centered on the one that had occurred on the preceding trial (small step-3), and in a third they were selected from three adjacent signals far from the one on the preceding trial (large step-3). The d' data were shown previously in Figure 1.22, where we see that the random and large-step data are really the same, but the small steps are displaced upward by about 1, with the result that performance approaches that of a local AI experiment, despite the wide range of signals actually used. Note that the large-step data make it clear that the effect is not due to increased predictability of the responses. We return to these results in discussing the bridges between local and global psychophysics.

Partition Methods

Over the years, there has been a desultory use of partition methods in psychophysics, although those methods and rankings are widely used in the rest of psychology. Various authors (see chapter 5 of Stevens, 1975, for a discussion) have reported results on bisection experiments, and category scales have been discussed, especially in connection with the magnitude methods (Stevens & Galanter, 1957; Stevens, 1975). But not until the extensive work of N.H. Anderson and his collaborators has there been such a strong push to use partition methods in psychophysics. He has on different occasions used categorizing or rating scales, ranking, and graphical rating scales (see Anderson, 1981, p. 344, and 1982).

The category rating method has two salient features. First, the number of categories is almost always fewer—usually, substantially fewer—than the number of stimuli, which means that signals that are perfectly distinguishable locally must be grouped together. Second, this fact immediately raises the question of what principles the subject should use to class stimuli together. The emphasis usually given is that categories should correspond to subjectively equal intervals, and the models proposed generally assume that this is what is done. To the degree that the models fit the data, Anderson argues, the assumption is tested and found acceptable. The compromise implicit in the method is to accept a loss in evidence about the subject's discriminating power—by using only a few categories—in order to gain evidence about the subject's relative spacing of stimuli. The method presumably becomes more informative as more different stimuli are used, since that allows a more precise definition of the subjectively equal intervals.

Consider the simplest example, bisection. Here the method involves presenting two signals, a and b, that differ on some dimension, and then exploring the infinite set of intermediate signals to find the one, x, that bisects the interval a to b, that is, in a two-category design, x is half the time classed with a and half the time with b. The assumed model is that

$$\psi(b) - \psi(x) = \psi(x) - \psi(a)$$

so that

$$\psi(x) = (1/2)[\psi(a) + \psi(b)], \qquad (1)$$

where ψ denotes the psychological measure on the stimulus dimension.

Weiss (1975) ran a factorial design using patches of gray and searched for and found a function ψ that fitted Equation 1 well. As a function of reflectance R, ψ is of the form of a power function $\psi(R) = \alpha R^\beta$ with $\beta = 0.2$. Anderson

(1976, p. 107) reports comparable results. In addition, Weiss had his subjects rate the overall grayness of pairs of stimuli s_i and s_j, which he assumed satisfied

$$r = w\psi(s_i) + (1 - w)\psi(s_j), \quad 0 < w < 1,$$

and he had them rate the difference in grayness, which presumably satisfied

$$r = C[\psi(s_i) - \psi(s_j)].$$

Although there were some systematic discrepancies, especially for individual subjects in the differencing task, he found a good fit with essentially the same power function. Weiss (1975) also had his subjects divide the interval into either three or four equal sections, but in both cases the natural generalization of Equation 1 failed to hold. Anderson (1977) applied the same methods to the bisection of length and found it impossible to fit the data by Equation 1.

We now turn to Anderson's more general approach, called functional measurement, which we discussed briefly in the earlier section on scaling. The principles of this method have been restated by him a number of times (e.g., Anderson, 1970, 1974a, b, 1976, 1981, 1982), with his two recent books providing by far the most comprehensive coverage. The main steps of functional measurement are:

1. Factorial designs, in which multiple variables are manipulated independently, are used to pit two or more variables against one another as they affect the dependent variable under study. The motive for this is clear: one wants to study how subjects integrate stimulus information. This is not very controversial, although in some contexts other ways of studying stimulus integration are more usual, such as finding stimulus combinations that leave the dependent variable unchanged (equal-attribute contours).

2. The dependent measure is subject-generated numbers on some sort of partition scale. (The use of such response scales is controversial; see below.)

3. These numbers are then analyzed according to one of several simple algebraic representations—adding factors, weighted averaging of factors, or multiplying factors are the most common—which formalize various notions of possible stimulus integration. If that is unsuccessful, the data are in essence treated as ordinal, nonlinear transformations are employed,

and the best fitting model is selected. In a surprising number of cases, no transformation is used. Whichever model is apparently correct is then called the *psychological law* for that situation.

For factorial designs, there are very simple ways of estimating the parameters of the averaging model, and the goodness of fit of the model to the data is evaluated statistically. In some studies analysis of variance techniques have been used, but when nonlinear monotonic transformations are employed, distribution-free methods are recommended.

4. If the fit is good, the psychological law embodied in the algebraic representation, together with the rating scale method, are said to be jointly validated. This highly controversial contention has been carefully discussed and criticized by Birnbaum (1982). The basic issue, as in all measurement representations, is that, when one set of representations combined by one psychological law fits the data, then an infinity of other combinations will fit equally well. It is unclear which should be selected (this is discussed further below). Moreover,

(a) The partition scale design, or its transformed values if that was necessary, as well as the stimulus parameters estimated from it are said to form interval scales because the algebraic models are invariant under affine transformations and, under assumptions of stimulus continuity, they are invariant only under affine transformations.

(b) The estimated parameters may be plotted against a physical measure of the factor in question, and that relation is referred to as a *psychophysical law*, about which more will be said.

(c) Considerable attention is paid to the question of whether the same psychophysical law arises from different types of stimulus integration involving the same factors. One possibility is that only one psychophysical law is involved, although different integrations of it may take place. It is an empirical matter to decide whether this is true.

As an example, Anderson (1972) reports two studies on lifted weights. Both were 5×5 fac-

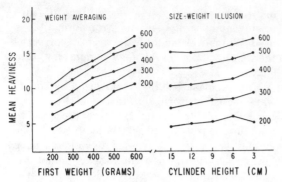

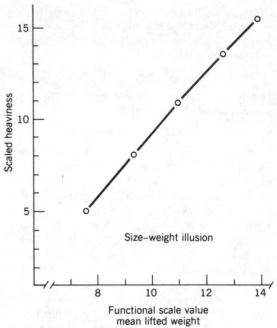

Figure 1.23 Mean category ratings of heaviness in two procedures: in (a) two weights are "averaged"; in (b) the weight and volume of the container are varied. From "Cross-Task Validation of Functional Measurement" by N.H. Anderson, 1972, *Perception & Psychophysics*, *12*, No. 5, p. 390. Copyright 1972 by The Psychonomics Society, Inc. Reprinted by permission.

Figure 1.24. Scale values of weight estimated from the two sets of data shown in Figure 1.23 are plotted against each other to show a linear relation. From "Cross-Task Validation of Functional Measurement" by N.H. Anderson, 1972, *Perception & Psychophysics*, *12*, No. 5, p. 390. Copyright by The Psychonomics Society, Inc. Reprinted by permission.

torial designs; the response in one was to the average weight of two successive liftings, and in the other the response was to a single lifting of a cylinder that varied in both weight and height. The data are shown in Figure 1.23. The parallelism in both cases supports the averaging model, and the resulting psychological scales are linearly related, as shown in Figure 1.24.

A major factor about all global scaling methods, including partition scaling, is the impact of context on the subject's response. Knowing the signal presented determines only partly the response made; the total context of the other signals in the experiment also matters a great deal. As we said in the special case of absolute identification, the response is seriously affected both by the location of the signal in the total range of other signals and by events on the immediately preceding trial, especially when the two signals are moderately close together. All this and more applies to general partition methods. A first attempt to discuss the phenomenon was the adaptation level theory of Helson (1964), which in essence says that responses are affected by some average of all the signals used in the experiment. A rather more unified theory has been put forward and tested in detail by Parducci and his collaborators (Parducci, 1965; Parducci, Calfee, Marshall & Davidson, 1960; Parducci & Perrett, 1971). The essential idea is to modify a theory of Thurstone's (see *Scaling: Random Variable Models*) to take into account two conflicting tendencies, the one to

subdivide the subjective scale into equal intervals and the other to use each response category equally often. Each subject is assumed to weight these two tendencies differently. By varying the spacing of the signals, one can systematically affect the frequency with which categories are used if equal spacing is maintained, and the model leads to a very systematic account of the data.

Magnitude Estimation

As noted earlier, magnitude estimation is in many ways similar to category scaling. The most notable differences are, first, that the number of categories is very large (e.g., any positive number in a voice response or any integer from 1 to 1000 or 10,000 in an online computer setup) and, second, subjects are asked to respond so as to preserve subjective ratios, not subjective differences, of the signals.

The most pervasive finding is that for signal intensity, or what Stevens called prothetic attri-

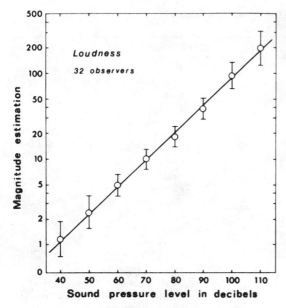

Figure 1.25. Magnitude estimates (geometric means of 32 observers) of the loudness of a 1000-Hz tone as a function of signal intensity. Both coordinates are logarithmic. From *Psychophysics: Introduction to Its Perceptual, Neural, and Social Prospects* (p. 28) by S.S. Stevens, 1975, New York: John Wiley & Sons, Inc. Copyright 1975 by John Wiley & Sons, Inc. Reprinted by permission of John Wiley & Sons, Inc.

butes, the central tendency of the response is approximately a power function of stimulus intensity as measured physically on an additive scale, that is,

$$\psi = \alpha \phi^\beta,$$

where ψ is the measure of central tendency in the magnitude response and ϕ is the physical measure. Most commonly, the geometric mean of the numerical response is used to estimate ψ. Observe that by taking logarithms, Stevens' law becomes

$$\log \psi = \beta \log \phi + \log \alpha$$

and it is usual to plot the data in logarithmic coordinates. In this form it is easy to tell if the points fall on a straight line and to get an approximate estimate of the exponent β from the slope using linear regression. Some typical data are shown in Figure 1.25.

Often the data deviate from Stevens' law in either of two ways. First, at low intensities, the slope increases. Such curvature can be exaggerated in various ways, for example, (1) by

hearing loss due to nerve degeneration (Hallpike & Hood, 1959), (2) by masking by noise (Stevens & Guirao, 1967) or (3) by masking light by light (Stevens, 1975). Various authors have suggested that this can be accommodated by generalizing Stevens' law to

$$\psi = \alpha(\phi - \phi_0)^\beta + \psi_0.$$

In fact, one can take either $\phi_0 = 0$ or $\psi_0 = 0$ and do rather well with just one extra parameter, and it has not been easy to decide which choice is the better.

The other departure arises when the procedures for data collection and analysis are changed. Stevens advocated collecting only a few observations (usually 2 each) from a few stimuli (usually 5 to 10) from a moderate number of subjects (usually 10), and then he averaged over subjects and responses for each signal. He placed some value on using untrained, inexperienced subjects. This style is quite contrary to the hoary traditions of local psychophysics, where well-trained observers and hundreds and thousands of observations are standard. When hundreds of magnitude estimates are collected from each of 20–30 signals and the data are plotted for individual subjects, we find not only appreciable individual differences in the rate of growth with intensity but also rather systematic and sizable departures from a power function (see, e.g., Green & Luce, 1974). These deviations, which can run up to 5 or 10 percent of the range (in logarithmic measure), do not disappear if the data are separated into time quarters and plotted separately. Just how stable they are over prolonged periods of time is not certain. Teghtsoonian and Teghtsoonian (1971) studied estimated exponents for individual subjects and found high correlations (0.8) on data collected with small time separations, but they dropped to much lower values (0.4) with a day's delay and were virtually zero after several months. However, Engeland and Dawson (1974) repeated the Teghtsoonians' study, again using length and area, and Logue (1976) did it using loudness, and both found moderately high correlations after 11 weeks. Whether or not individual differences are important, the rest of the data presented here are averaged results because they are mainly what is available in the literature.

Stevens explored a wide range of stimulus attributes and tabulated the average exponent for each attribute; these are shown in Table 1.3.

Table 1.3. Representative exponents of the power functions relating subjective magnitude to stimulus magnitude[a]

Continuum	Measured exponent	Stimulus condition
Loudness	0.67	Sound pressure of 3000-hertz tone
Vibration	0.95	Amplitude of 60 hertz on finger
Vibration	0.6	Amplitude of 250 hertz on finger
Brightness	0.33	5° Target in dark
Brightness	0.5	Point source
Brightness	0.5	Brief flash
Brightness	1.0	Point source briefly flashed
Lightness	1.2	Reflectance of gray papers
Visual length	1.0	Projected line
Visual area	0.7	Projected square
Redness (saturation)	1.7	Red-gray mixture
Taste	1.3	Sucrose
Taste	1.4	Salt
Taste	0.8	Saccharine
Smell	0.6	Heptane
Cold	1.0	Metal contact on arm
Warmth	1.6	Metal contact on arm
Warmth	1.3	Irradiation of skin, small area
Warmth	0.7	Irradiation of skin, large area
Discomfort, cold	1.7	Whole body irradiation
Discomfort, warm	0.7	Whole body irradiation
Thermal pain	1.0	Radiant heat on skin
Tactual roughness	1.5	Rubbing emery cloths
Tactual hardness	0.8	Squeezing rubber
Finger span	1.3	Thickness of blocks
Pressure on palm	1.1	Static force on skin
Muscle force	1.7	Static contractions
Heaviness	1.45	Lifted weights
Viscosity	0.42	Stirring silicone fluids
Electric shock	3.5	Current through fingers
Vocal effort	1.1	Vocal sound pressure
Angular acceleration	1.4	5-Second rotation
Duration	1.1	White noise stimuli

[a] *Note.* From *Psychophysics: Introduction to Its Perceptual, Neural and Social Properties* (p. 15) by S.S. Stevens, 1975, New York: John Wiley & Sons, Inc. Copyright © 1975 by John Wiley & Sons, Inc. Reprinted by permission of John Wiley & Sons, Inc.

Teghtsoonian (1971) noted a systematic correlation between the value of the exponent and the size of the physical range as measured by the ratio of the most intense signal acceptable to the least intense detectable. To at least a first approximation, the exponents are such that exactly the same range of responses is used for each attribute; this relation is shown in the theoretical curve plotted in Figure 1.26. One conjecture that is consistent with these data is that all intensive modalities are ultimately encoded in neural cells of the same type, and the response range simply reflects the range of firing rates for these cells.

Others are considerably less confident that the exponents have any very firm meaning. Warren and Warren (1963) and Warren (1981) have argued that they arise from learning experiences and reflect more about our physical environment than they do about the sensory systems. For a recent critique of this, see the comments following Warren (1981). Poulton (1968) reviewed a number of factors, including stimulus spacing, that affect the estimate. Robinson (1976) showed how instructions can bias the exponent. King and Lockhead (1981) ran subjects with information feedback based on three quite different exponents, and their subjects were easily able to produce responses consistent with each of the three different exponents. And general laboratory experience indicates that the exponents are quite responsive to

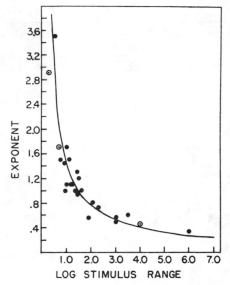

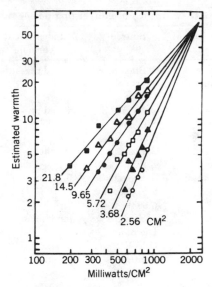

Figure 1.26. Estimated exponents of Stevens's power law as a function of the number of logarithmic steps (factors of ten) in the estimated dynamic range of the stimulus measured using the standard ratio scales of physics. Each point corresponds to a different physical attribute. The smooth curve is βR = constant, where β is the exponent and R is the range. From "On the Exponents in Stevens' Law and the Contents in Ekman's Law" by R. Teghtsoonian, 1971, *Psychological Review*, p. 73. Copyright 1971 by the American Psychological Association. Reprinted by permission of the author.

Figure 1.27. Magnitude estimates of warmth as a function of power per unit area, with area of application as a parameter. From "Families of Converging Power Functions" by J.C. Stevens in *Sensation and Measurement* (p. 163) by H.R. Moskowitz, B. Scharf, and J.C. Stevens (eds.), 1974, Dordrecht: D. Reidel Publishing Company. Copyright 1974 by D. Reidel Publishing Company, Dordrecht, Holland. Reprinted by permission.

instructions. For example, if one urges the subjects to reduce the variability of their responses, some react by reducing the exponent, that is, by narrowing the total range of responses, which indeed does reduce variability. All of these findings suggest that it may prove difficult to affix any precise meaning to the values of the exponents.

Once one has a technique such as magnitude estimation or category scaling, it is natural to use it to explore the tradeoffs—what Anderson calls the psychological law—among the physical variables that affect this attribute. We present several examples using magnitude estimation. It is often the case that if a secondary parameter is varied and log ψ is plotted against log ϕ, then the functions extrapolated to extreme values converge to a single point. An example is subjective warmth plotted as a function of irradiance with the area radiated as a parameter of the curves (see Figure 1.27). The point of convergence is approximately the

threshold of burning pain. J.C. Stevens (1974) has summarized a number of these families of functions and the interpretation of the point of convergence (see Table 1.4).

Another example is the joint effect of signal duration and intensity. This has frequently been studied by detection methods, but it is also possible to explore the tradeoff for suprathreshold studies by using either magnitude estimation or determining curves of equal attribute. Figure 1.28 shows the data for brightness. Similar data for loudness are shown in Figure 1.29. Note that the point at which the subjective attribute becomes independent of signal duration is at about 150 msec for loudness, and this point does not depend on intensity; whereas, for brightness it varies from 15 msec for the most intense signals to 500 msec for the least intense.

Although we have not mentioned it to this point, the response structure in both category and magnitude estimation is rather more complicated than just the mean response to a signal. Just as for absolute identification, there are major sequential effects (Holland & Lockhead, 1968; Mashhour, 1964; Mashhour & Hosman,

Table 1.4. Families of converging power functions[a]

Continuum	Source	Independent variable	Parameter	Approximate convergence	Possible significance
Auditory volume	S.S. Stevens & Terrace (1962)	sound pressure	frequency	140 dB SPL	tickling & pain
Auditory density	Guirao & S.S. Stevens (1964)	sound pressure	frequency	130–150 dB SPL	tickling & pain
Heaviness	J.C. Stevens & Rubin (1970)	weight	volume	8 kg	maximum heft
Brightness	J.C. Stevens & S.S. Stevens (1963)	luminance	level of light adaptation	10^9 cd m^{-2}	solar luminance
Brightness	S.S. Stevens & Diamond (1965)	luminance	glare angle	2×10^5 cd m^{-2}	glare luminance
Brightness	J.C. Stevens (1967)	luminance	size of inhibitory surround	32 cd m^{-2}	surround luminance
Cold	Marks & J.C. Stevens (1972)	lowering of irradiation from neutral	duration	1 W cm^{-2} below neutral	pain threshold?
Warmth	J.C. Stevens & Marks (1971)	3-s irradiation of forehead	areal extent	0.8 W cm^{-2}	pain threshold
Warmth	J.C. Stevens & Marks (1971)	3-s irradiation of back	areal extent	0.8 W cm^{-2}	pain threshold
Warmth	Marks & J.C. Stevens (1973)	0.5-s irradiation of forehead	areal extent	2.3 W cm^{-2}	pain threshold
Warmth	J.C. Stevens & Marks (unpublished)	3-s irradiation of forearm	areal extent	1.0 W cm^{-2}	pain threshold
Warmth	J.C. Stevens & Marks (unpublished)	3-s irradiation of cheek	areal extent	0.9 W cm^{-2}	pain threshold
Warmth	J.C. Stevens, Marks, & Simonson (unpublished)	3-s irradiation of calf	areal extent	0.9 W cm^{-2}	pain threshold

[a] *Note.* From "Families of Converging Power Functions" by J.C. Stevens in *Sensation and Measurement* (p. 161) by H.R. Moskowitz, B. Scharf, and J.C. Stevens (eds.), 1974, Dordrecht: D. Reidel Publishing Company. Copyright 1974 by D. Reidel Publishing Company, Dordrecht, Holland. Reprinted by permission.

1968; Jesteadt, Luce & Green, 1977; Ward & Lockhead, 1970; Ward, 1973, 1979). For example, the correlation between responses to successive signals is near zero when the signals are widely separated but rises to more than 0.8 when they are very close or identical (Baird, Green & Luce, 1980; Jesteadt 1977; Green, Luce & Duncan, 1977). Although there have been attempts to model sequential effects (Luce, Baird, Green & Smith, 1980; Staddon, King & Lockhead, 1980), at present they are not well understood. One suspects they are closely related to the sequential effects in absolute identification, but exact comparisons do not exist.

A final phenomenon, described primarily by Baird (for a summary and references, see Baird & Noma, 1978, pp. 108–110) but known to all who run magnitude estimation experiments, is that all subjects exhibit strong number preferences. Usually something of the order of 80 percent of the responses are accounted for by 10 to 20 numbers, such as 1, 2, 3, 4, 5, 10, 15, 20, 25, 30, 40, 50,

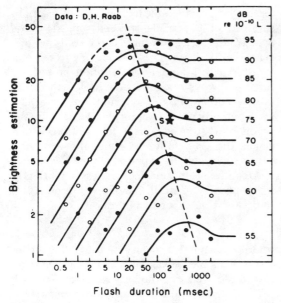

Figure 1.28. Log magnitude estimates of brightness as a function of log duration with luminance as a parameter. The dotted line indicates the approximate point at which additional observing time does not affect the estimate. From "Duration, Luminance, and the Brightness Exponent" by S.S. Stevens, 1966, *Perception & Psychophysics, 1*, p. 98. Copyright 1966 by The Psychonomic Society, Inc. Reprinted by permission.

75, 100, 125, 150, 250, 300, 400, 500, 600, 750, 800, 900, 1000. Little is known about this, but it is pervasive, and no one's model of magnitude estimation or category scaling takes it into account.

Cross-Modal Matching

If ϕ_1 and ϕ_2 are two intensive physical measures and the corresponding subjective scales are

$$\psi_1 = \alpha_1 \phi_1^{\beta_1} \quad \text{and} \quad \psi_2 = \alpha_2 \phi_2^{\beta_2},$$

then matching seems to mean choosing $\psi_1 = \psi_2$, and so

$$\phi_1 = \alpha_{12} \phi_2^{\beta_{12}}$$

where $\beta_{12} = \beta_2/\beta_1$. Not only is a power function predicted, but its exponent is uniquely determined. We see from this that if a third modality is introduced, it follows that

$$\beta_{13} = \frac{\beta_3}{\beta_1} = \frac{\beta_2}{\beta_1} \cdot \frac{\beta_3}{\beta_2} = \beta_{12}\beta_{23} \tag{2}$$

It is not quite so straightforward to test these predictions as it might seem; the reason is an empirical asymmetry. In practice a signal is presented in one modality and is matched by one in another modality. Of course, the procedures can be reversed, and if this is done it turns out that $\beta_{ji} \neq 1/\beta_{ij}$. Stevens & Guirao (1963) called

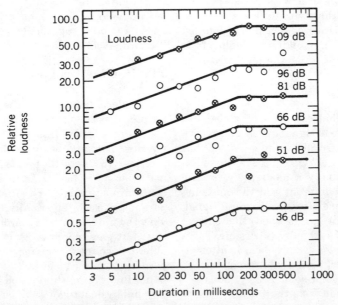

Figure 1.29. Log magnitude estimation of loudness as a function of log duration with intensity in decibels as a parameter. From "Brightness and Loudness as Functions of Stimulus" by J.C. Stevens and J.W. Hall, 1966, *Perception & Psychophysics, 1*, p. 324. Copyright 1966 by The Psychonomic Society, Inc. Reprinted by permission.

this a regression effect, although there is no proved connection to the well-known statistical phenomenon of regression. The effect probably is closely related to the fact that we do not get the same estimates of the relation between ψ and ϕ from magnitude estimation and magnitude production.

Stevens opted to use the geometric mean $(\beta_{ij}/\beta_{ji})^{1/2}$ as his estimate of the symmetrical exponent relating dimension i to j. Using this exponent and Equation 2 to make predictions, he obtained an average absolute error of 4 percent for one set of nine modalities each matched to handgrip, and 11 percent for another of 10 modalities matched to loudness. Baird, Green & Luce (1980), working with extensive data for three subjects, were considerably less successful. A study by Daning (1983) of cross-modal matches involving four modalities was, however, very encouraging. A careful study of estimation, production, and matching for three or more modalities and individual subjects is badly needed.

If there are individual differences in the exponents and if they are interrelated in systematic ways, then exponents must be highly correlated over subjects. This has been found to hold in a variety of cases (see references in Rule & Markley, 1971). They argue that the individual differences have more to do with the use of numbers in responding than with differences in the sensory systems. Until much more detailed studies are carried out on individual subjects, it will not be known whether the predicted relations really hold or not.

Reaction Time

Another measure that can be used globally is simple reaction time to signal onset. The experiment is simple to describe, although somewhat difficult to perform well. On each trial there is a warning signal, usually a moderately intense signal in a modality different from the one being studied. At some time after the warning signal, the reaction signal occurs and the subject attempts to respond as rapidly as possible. There are serious methodological problems in attempting to get the subject actually to respond to the reaction signal and to prevent anticipations of it using time estimation from the warning signal. Two procedures are commonly followed to discourage this practice. In one, the time between the warning signal and the reaction signal, the

foreperiod, is constant, but on a small fraction, say, 0.1, of the trials the reaction signal is omitted. Responses on these catch trials are evidence that the subject is not waiting to respond to the reaction signal. In the other procedure, there is always a signal, but the length of the wait is random. Various distributions have been used, but only one makes any sense, namely, the exponential (or geometric) distribution, which makes the probability of a signal's occurring during any small, fixed period of time a constant.

Mean reaction time decreases systematically with intensity (Cattell, 1886), and Piéron (1914) suggested that it took the form

$$\overline{RT} = r + kI^{-\beta},$$

where I is signal intensity and r, k, β are constants. This has been shown to summarize some data quite well, but not visual data (Kohfeld, 1971; Mansfield, 1976). Because the magnitude data satisfy Stevens' law, some effort has been made to show that a basic linear relation holds between reaction time and subjective loudness or brightness. However, at least one study is not consistent with that hypothesis (Kohfeld, Santee & Wallace, 1981).

An adequate psychophysical theory should account for both the scaling of data, by whatever means, and the response times that are involved. As yet, no fully adequate theory has been developed, although a number of partial ones have been suggested (see Luce, 1986a, and Welford, 1980).

The Elusive Bridge

A considerable portion of the history of psychophysics can be viewed as a search for a way to construct a bridge from local to global psychophysics. The field began with such an attempt (Fechner, 1860), and the problem remains unsolved and ever more taxing as new data add to the constraints that must be satisfied. Another, and perhaps more intellectually satisfying, way to view the problem is as a search for a comprehensive, but parsimonious, psychophysical theory, able to account for the results from the various paradigms, both local and global. The implicit belief underlying this search is that a unifying psychophysical theory will be found rather than simply a collection of special theories, one for loudness, another for brightness, still another for warmth, and so on. The reason for this hope

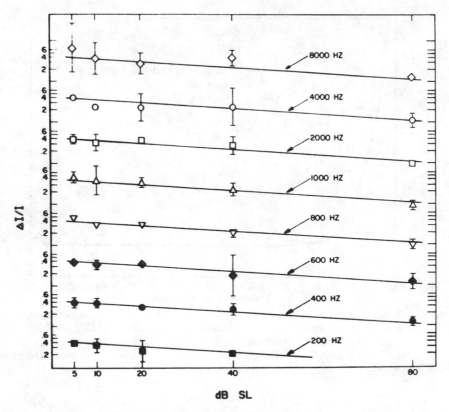

Figure 1.30. The near miss to Weber's law for pure-tone intensity with frequency as a parameter. $\Delta I/I$ in decibels is plotted against I in decibels. The common theoretical curve is $\Delta I/I = I^{-0.072}$. From "Intensity Discrimination as a Function of Frequency and Sensation Level" by W. Jesteadt, C.C. Wier, and D.M. Green, 1977, *Journal of the Acoustical Society of America*, p. 171. Copyright 1977 by the American Institute of Physics. Reprinted by permission.

is the intuition that once the transduction of a signal is completed, which admittedly varies substantially among modalities, then possibly the central nervous system deals with all intensive modalities in the same way when responding to the kinds of questions posed in psychophysical experiments. It seems reasonably clear that such a comprehensive theory does not exist for qualitative (what Stevens called metathetic) attributes, such as hue, pitch, taste, and the like. So, in what follows our attention will be confined, as it has been throughout much of the chapter, to attributes having to do with intensity.

Weber Functions

The most obvious bridge from local to global psychophysics is simply to state how local performance varies over the whole range of the attribute. We denote by $\Delta\phi$ the size of the increment required at physical intensity ϕ in order to

achieve a certain level of performance in discrimination—say 75 percent correct in a two-interval, forced-choice design or 50 percent correct identification in a single-interval design. Then, one can ask how $\Delta\phi$ or, more conveniently when ϕ is a ratio scale, how the so-called Weber fraction $\Delta\phi/\phi$ varies with ϕ. That relation is known as a Weber function. Plots of it for a pure tone, for noise, and for white light are shown in Figures 1.30, 1.31 and 1.32. Observe that for noise the Weber fraction is constant over a substantial part of the range; when that obtains, Weber's law, $\Delta\phi = k\phi$, is said to hold. It used to be thought that Weber's law was a rather good approximation to the Weber function for many intensive attributes, which is why it was called a law. However, with better measurements it has become clear that it is at best an approximation. The curve shown in Figure 1.31, which fits the noise data rather well, is the slight

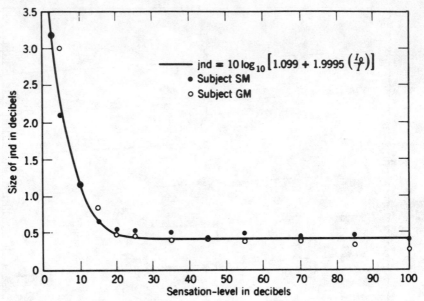

Figure 1.31. The Weber fraction in decibels versus noise power density in decibels for white noise. The generalized Weber's law is shown fitted to the data. (Adapted from Miller, 1947.) From "Discrimination" by R.D. Luce in *Handbook of Mathematical Psychology* (p. 203) by R.D. Luce, R.R. Bush, and E. Galanter (eds.), 1963, New York: John Wiley & Sons, Inc. Copyright 1963 by John Wiley & Sons, Inc. Reprinted by permission of John Wiley & Sons, Inc.

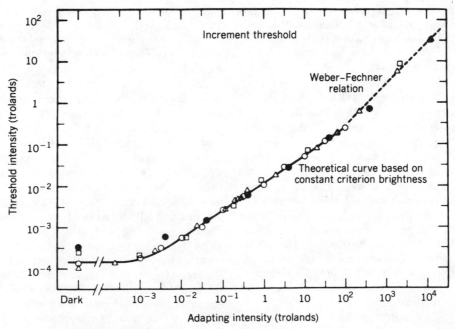

Figure 1.32. Increment thresholds versus intensity of a light flash, showing the transition to Weber's law well above threshold. Open symbols represent human observers; solid symbols represent retinal ganglion cells of cat. Reprinted with permission from *Vision Research*, *16*, R.J.W. Mansfield, "Visual Adaptation: Retinal Transduction, Brightness and Sensitivity," Copyright 1976, Pergamon Press, Ltd.

generalization of Weber's law to $\Delta\phi = k\phi + c$; another relation, with a third parameter, fits even better (Falmagne, 1974). For the pure tones, the data are all well fitted by a still different generalization $\Delta\phi = k\phi^{1-\rho}$, where $\rho = 0.072$. This latter relation has been called the 'near miss to Weber's law' (McGill & Goldberg, 1968). Rabinowitz, Lim, Braida and Durlach (1976) argued that the Weber function for pure tones is actually piecewise linear. For additional material on visual discrimination, see Rushton (1965), and for a general discussion of Weber functions, Falmage (1985) and Laming (1986).

The Psychophysical Law

The Weber function only tells us something about how the variability of performance changes with intensity; it does not really say anything about the subjective growth of sensation with intensity. This hypothesized relation, which is commonly called the psychophysical law, has been the focus of two major and numerous minor efforts; we turn to the major ones.

Fechner (1860) first posed the problem of relating global attributes of sensation to local ones, and he believed he had solved it. Nevertheless, well over a century later the problem is still open. Consider the just noticeable difference (jnd) in intensity—which is often taken to be the change in intensity that results in some fixed value for the probability of detecting the change, as in the Weber function, or some closely related estimate using sequential methods. Fechner asserted that the jnd could be used as a unit of measurement. He assumed that at the subjective level all such changes are equivalent to one another. This was plausible on the assumption of a discrete representation and so the existence of true thresholds. Specifically, if ϕ is the physical measure and ψ the corresponding subjective one, and if $\Delta\phi$ is the just discriminable physical change, then for the corresponding subjective change, $\Delta\phi$ to be constant, we have

$$\Delta\psi = \psi(\phi + \Delta\phi) - \psi(\phi) = \text{constant.} \quad (3)$$

On the assumption that $\Delta\phi$ satisfies Weber's law, it is not difficult to see that

$$\psi = \alpha \log \phi/\phi_0 \quad (4)$$

is a solution to Equation 3, where α and ϕ_0 are free parameters. (Fechner presented a general scheme for solving Equation 3 for any Weber function which, though it leads to the correct answer when Weber's law holds, is incorrect in general; for a detailed discussion see Falmagne, 1971, 1974, 1985, Krantz, 1971, and Luce & Edwards, 1958.) The logarithmic solution came to be called Fechner's law.

Fechner's approach is valid only if the untested assumption that $\Delta\psi$ is constant is correct. Almost from the beginning objections were raised to it, based on the recurrent observation that invariant stimulus ratios seem to correspond, at least roughly, to invariant sensations (Plateau, 1872). For example, changing the overall illumination from bright sunlight to the dimness of dusk does not seem greatly to alter the relative intensities within a scene. This is not implied by Fechner's law. Nevertheless, these objections did not prevail in the debates at the end of the 19th century nor for the first 30 years of this century until practical experience and experiments cast it in serious doubt. Were it correct, loudness would grow with decibels; yet engineers who quieted noisy environments to some fraction of their original levels using decibel measures always disappointed their clients. The engineers' 50 percent seemed subjectively very different from what had been expected. These, and other observations, were the background that led to the introduction of ratio estimates (Richardson & Ross, 1930) and ended in Stevens's (see 1975 for a full list of references) systematic and prolonged attack on Fechner's law and to its proposed replacement, Stevens' law. For a detailed history of these early studies, see Marks (1975, Chapter 1).

Stevens took seriously the notion that intensity ratios are of fundamental importance in sensory processing, and he developed his methods of magnitude estimation and production and of cross-modal matching to take advantage of this apparently major property. In addition, he argued forcefully that Fechner's approach of tying local variability to the growth of the scale was inherently misguided, because there is no necessary relation between the scale value and the amount of variability at that point along the scale. (This observation is easier to accept for continuous representations than for discrete ones.) He cited physical examples, such as a voltmeter, to bolster his point. Rather, he argued, the growth of sensation can be observed directly, and as we noted in the section on magnitude estimation he found (approximately)

$$\psi = \alpha\phi^\beta, \tag{5}$$

that is, Stevens' law. He was not concerned with the variability in the responses in these global experiments; his focus was explicitly on the central tendency, and the variability he considered as no more than noise of measurement. [This is slightly misleading since Stevens was earlier involved in studying Békésy's (1930) neural quantum theory of discrimination (Stevens et al., 1941), but although he discussed it in his book that was published posthumously (Stevens, 1975), it was largely isolated from his work on the psychophysical law.] Thus there really was no closing of the chasm between local and global matters, since the local concerns itself almost exclusively with questions of variability.

Category versus Magnitude Scales

The debate between differences and ratios, logarithms and power functions is far from resolved, as we shall see in this and the next subsection. In recent years, Anderson and his students have strongly urged, in essence, that the differencing of Fechner is more adequate than the ratioing of Stevens. Put their way, scaling should be done by partition methods, not magnitude ones. The raw empirical facts relating category and magnitude scales are moderately simple and uniform, as was first shown by Stevens and Galanter (1957). Category scales are concave relative to the corresponding magnitude scale and, in fact, tend to approximate a logarithmic function. The degree of concavity is affected by a number of things, especially by the number of categories used.

Torgerson (1961) first raised the question, whether there are two distinct subjective operations when subjects are asked to respond in these two ways, or only a single one. The latter seems a real possibility since the two scales are roughly logarithmically related and the logarithm is the function that converts a ratio into a difference. Indeed, if there were two distinct operations, we should then be able to find different orderings of pairs of stimuli depending on which operation is used. This is because we have many examples in which ratios and differences give different orders, such as

$$6/4 < 2/1 \quad \text{and} \quad 6 - 4 > 2 - 1.$$

The data (see Birnbaum, 1978 and 1982, for a

summary and other references) have not exhibited any such nonmonotonicity, and so the current conclusion is that there is a single operation available to the subjects. Accepting that raises two questions: does that operation involve differences or ratios, and is the same psychophysical mapping used under both sets of instructions? As yet there is no agreed-upon answer to either question and, in fact, the two questions are not independent. It is agreed, however, that an experiment designed to answer these questions would necessarily be quite complex, and would involve judgments about differences of two pairs of ratios and ratios of two pairs of ratios. Such judgments appear to be at, or perhaps beyond, the limits of subjects' capabilities (Birnbaum, 1979; Hagarty & Birnbaum, 1978; Eisler, 1978). In any event, there is no consensus yet on which operation should be viewed as basic.

Random Variable Representations

Following Fechner but preceding Stevens there was Thurstone, whose model and the closely related signal detectability theory we have already treated in some detail. According to his argument each signal results in an internal numerical representation which varies from presentation to presentation. In probability terms, the internal representation is a random variable. This view was implicit in Fechner and in such work as Urban (1910) and others during the first quarter of the century, especially among those concerned with mental test theory, but it was first made explicit by Thurstone (1927, 1959). Given such representations of signals, one develops a theory for category experiments by assuming that the range of possible values of the representations is partitioned into a number of intervals equal to the number of response categories (Torgerson, 1954). Responses are made according to the interval within which the representation falls. Usually, the intervals are defined by giving the location of the mean boundary points between successive intervals.

Accepting this point of view, one can, in principle, estimate the means and variances of the random variables and the mean boundary values from data on the identifiability of signals. A plot of the mean signal representation against intensity is the psychophysical law and if the variance were constant, it would support Fechner's assumption of constant subjective variability (in Thurstone's paper this was called Case 5 of the model). Much of the work of Braida and Durlach and their colleagues has been an attempt to do just that.

One major problem with all this is that the representation lacks uniqueness. Given that a particular Thurstonian model fits a body of data, any strictly increasing transformation of the psychophysical scale leads to another Thurstonian representation that fits it equally well, albeit with different distributions of the random variables. In practice, it is customary—it began with Thurstone, although he was quite tentative about it—to limit attention to Gaussian distributions, in which case the means are uniquely determined up to positive affine (interval scale) transformations. And when this is done, a logarithmic psychophysical law and constant variances give a good account of the data (Braida & Durlach, 1972; Durlach & Braida, 1969; Kornbrot, 1978, 1980). But the issue is, why assume the Gaussian? This has no stronger intuitive appeal than does Fechner's constancy of subjective just noticeable differences. It is sometimes argued that the Gaussian postulate can be tested by studying the form of ROC curves, which in principle is true. But in practice the data are so variable and other distributions differ so slightly from the Gaussian that it is rather futile to try to decide on the basis of ROC curves (as evidence of the problem, see Wandell & Luce, 1978).

If one takes seriously the existence of an internal representation, one might assume that it is used in a more or less direct fashion in magnitude estimates, in which case the variability of those estimates should reflect that of the internal representation. This line was followed by Green & Luce (1974), and although it is reasonably clear that the distributions of magnitude estimates are not Gaussian, their exact form is much more difficult to determine than had been anticipated because of the very strong sequential effects that exist. We turn to that problem together with the problem of the major impact of signal range on absolute identification.

If one fits an equal-variance, Gaussian Thurstone model to the data obtained using different ranges, the variance grows systematically with range. Independently, Durlach and Braida (1969) and Gravetter and Lockhead (1973) concluded that the variance is of the form $AR^2 + B$ where A and B are estimated constants, and R is the stimulus range as measured by the logarithm of the ratio of the maximum to the minimum stimulus used, measured in physical units. (Actually, Gravetter and Lockhead, 1973, and Weber et al., 1977, have shown that a more subtle definition of range is needed, but that given above is satisfactory when the signals are more or less evenly spaced over the range.) The fit of this model is shown in Figure 1.20, p. 50. It is generally agreed that this is an empirical result in need of further explanation. Almost certainly, it does not mean what it seems to, namely, that the variance of the signal representation as such grows with range. There is little reason to believe that brief signals occurring on other trials many seconds away directly affect the representation of the signal in the peripheral nervous system. Certainly this does not happen in the auditory system and it is unlikely to be a major factor in the visual system either. The apparent change in the variance more likely has something to do with central access to the peripheral information.

Several ideas have been proposed. Berliner and Durlach (1973) suggested that the end points of the signal range serve as well-defined anchors for the location of the category boundaries, and that the farther a boundary is from the nearest anchor the more variable its location. Qualitatively, at least, this accounts nicely for both the range effect and for the bow (or edge) effect. There is, however, no account provided of the mechanisms involved in both establishing anchors and generating more variability as the distance from an anchor increases.

A second proposal, by Green and Luce (1974), assumes that the central nervous system can access all the information available for only a narrow band of intensities—something of the order of 15 ± 5 dB for sound intensity—and for a signal falling outside this attention band only a fraction, roughly 10 percent, of the information is accessed. Since the band may be located anywhere on the stimulus continuum, this is a postulate of focused neural sampling. If one simply assumes that on each trial the band is located at random in the range being used, it accounts nicely for the range effects, an example of which is shown in Figure 1.21, p. 50 (Luce et al., 1976). If in addition, one assumes that there is a greater tendency to locate the band at the ends of the range than at the midrange, then perhaps the bow is explained. Shifts in the location of the band that depend on the pattern of signal presentation can potentially account for some of the sequential effects (Luce & Green, 1978). Of course, as was noted earlier, there is clear evidence that criterion shifts are also involved in the trial-by-trial sequential effects.

Other models have been suggested by Marley and Cook (1984, 1986), Treisman (1985), and Treisman and Williams (1984).

Although there has been some progress in understanding why the global data are so different from the local, the topic is still exceedingly controversial and fluid. No one has come up with a comprehensive model, one that explains local discrimination, accounts for global methods such as magnitude estimation, production, and cross-modal matching, gives a detailed explanation of both the sensitivity and criterion sequential effects, and has a natural explanation for response times and their distributions. Anything less is not really satisfactory, although the steps in reaching that goal will surely be more modest.

Possible Relations to Measurement Theory

Clearly, psychophysicists doing global experiments, whether they use partition or magnitude methods, are in a sense measuring something. We may therefore ask: do their data satisfy any of the axiomatic theories of measurement and, if so, does the structure of the scales that result mesh with the highly structured family of scales from physics?

Anderson, using partition methods, has quite explicitly attempted to fit the numerical responses obtained from stimuli with a factor structure to several simple representations, and when the fit is good he interprets that as evidence favoring both the model and the procedures. The resulting scales are unique up to the scale character of the model, usually an interval scale. Stevens and his followers have not been quite so explicit and systematic in fitting the data from magnitude methods to factorial models, but in some cases they have and in others it is obviously possible to do so. Moreover, Levelt et al. (1972) and Falmagne (1976) have explicitly used methods from conjoint measurement to develop additive scales of loudness where the two factors were the two ears; interestingly, the loudness functions for the separate ears were power functions

of intensity. And, although we have not talked much of theories for metathetic attributes, mention should be made of Krantz's (1974/1975) very careful measurement analysis of metameric color matches which leads to a representation of color as multiplicative vector space.

So, to a considerable degree, the measurement carried out in global psychophysics is consistent with the representations developed in the theory of measurement. To a much lesser degree, some study has taken place of the adequacy of the axioms underlying these representations. It is probably safe to assume that, as measurement theory becomes more familiar to psychologists, the relations between these models and global scales will become far more explicit and deeper.

Now, what can be said about the structure of the resulting scales? Recall that in physics one can select a basic set of five (or possibly six, depending on how one chooses to treat angle) extensive quantities so that all other scales are products of powers of the basic ones. Does anything of the sort exist in psychophysics and, if so, how does it relate to the physical structure?

If we accept the view of the Anderson school, with its resulting interval scales and additivity or averaging across factors, the answer is either No, there is no comparable structure, or Maybe, if one works with the exponential of the observed scales, but that introduces free exponents in the scale. No work along these lines has yet been done. If we accept the Stevens school and its belief that the exponents are fixed by the modality, then a possibility exists, although it cannot yet be said to have been fully explored. Let us try to be a bit more explicit as to what is needed.

Stevens attempted to establish by means of cross-modal matches that every magnitude scale of physical intensity is a power function of every other one, and that of any three modalities, the exponents relating any two pairs predict the exponent relating the third pair. Although he provided some support for this based on average data, it remains somewhat uncertain whether it holds for individual subjects and whether estimation followed by production can predict the cross-modal function.

Stevens's data hint at the possibility of a single sensory dimension of intensity. At the moment, however, we cannot really say more than that there is a hint, for no one has actually pushed these studies through in the detail necessary to know whether the various intensity scales exhibit a structure similar to the scales of physics. One cannot but be concerned by the demonstration (King & Lockhead, 1981) that the exponents can easily be shifted by as much as a factor of 3 and by the earlier data that the exponents are affected by a variety of experimental manipulations (Poulton, 1968). Clearly, much more work, using the data from individual subjects, is needed before we will be able to develop any clear picture of the structure of psychophysical scales.

ACKNOWLEDGMENTS

We have had useful comments on drafts from N.H. Anderson, P. Arabie, J.C. Baird, and two anonymous readers. Although we have modified the text as a result of these comments, we are of course solely responsible for what is said.

REFERENCES

Aczél, J. (1966). *Lectures on functional equations and their applications.* New York: Academic Press.

Adams, E.W., Fagot, R.F., & Robinson, R.E. (1965). A theory of appropriate statistics. *Psychometrika, 30,* 99–127.

Alper, T.M. Groups of homeomorphisms of the real line. (AB Thesis, Harvard University, 1984).

Alper, T.M. (1987). A classification of all order-preserving homeomorphism groups of the reals that satisfy finite uniqueness. *Journal of mathematical psychology, 31,* 135–154.

Anderson, N.H. (1970a). Functional measurement and psychophysical judgment. *Psychological Review, 77,* 154–170.

Anderson, N.H. (1970b). Averaging model applied to the size-weight illusion. *Perception & Psychophysics, 8,* 1–4.

Anderson, N.H. (1972). Cross-taste validation of functional measurement. *Perception & Psychophysics, 12,* 389–395.

Anderson, N.H. (1974a). Algebraic models in perception. In E.C. Carterette & M.P. Freidman (Eds.), *Handbook of perception,* Vol. 2 (pp. 215–298). New York: Academic Press.

Anderson, N.H. (1974b). Information integration theory: A brief survey. In D.H. Krantz, R.C. Atkinson, R.D. Luce, & P. Suppes (Eds.), *Contemporary developments in mathematical psychology.* Vol. 2 (pp. 236–305). San Francisco: Freeman.

Anderson, N.H. (1976). Integration theory, functional measurement, and the psychophysical law. In H.-G. Geissler & Yu.M. Zubrodin (Eds.), *Advances in psychophysics* (pp. 93–130). Berlin: VEB Deutscher Verlag.

Anderson, N.H. (1977). Failure of additivity in bisection of length. *Perception & Psychophysics, 22,* 213–222.

Anderson, N.H. (1981). *Foundations of information integration theory.* New York: Academic Press.

Anderson, N.H. (1982). *Methods of information integration theory.* New York: Academic Press.

Arabie, P., & Carroll, J.D. (1980). MAPCLUS: A mathematical programming approach to fitting the ADCLUS model. *Psychometrika, 45,* 211–235.

Atkinson, R.C. (1963). A variable sensitivity theory of signal detection. *Psychological Review, 70,* 91–106.

Attneave, F. (1950). Dimensions of similarity. *American Journal of Psychology, 63,* 516–556.

Baird, J.C., Green, D.M., & Luce, R.D. (1980). Variability and sequential effects in cross-modality matching of area and loudness. *Journal of Experimental Psychology: Human Perception and Performance, 6,* 277–289.

Baird, J.C., & Noma, E. (1978) *Fundamentals of scaling and psychophysics.* New York: Wiley.

Beals, R., Krantz, D.H., & Tversky, A. (1978). Foundations of multidimensional scaling. *Psychological Review, 75,* 127–143.

Békésy, G. von (1930). Über das Fechnersche Gesetz und seine Bedeutung für die Theorie der akustischen Beobachtungsfehler und die Theorie des Hörens. *Annalen der Physik,* Ser. 5, 7, 329–359.

Bennett, J., & Hays, W.L. (1960). Multidimensional unfolding: Determining the dimensionality of ranked preference data. *Psychometrika, 25,* 27–43.

Berliner, J.E., & Durlach, N.I. (1973). Intensity perception. IV. Resolution in roving-level discrimination. *Journal of the Acoustical Society of America, 53,* 1270–1287.

Berliner, J.E., Durlach, N.I., & Braida, L.D. (1977). Intensity perception. VII. Further data on roving-level discrimination and the resolution and bias edge effects. *Journal of the Acoustical Society of America, 61,* 1577–1585.

Birnbaum, M.H. (1978). Differences and ratios in psychological measurement. In F. Restle & N.J. Castellan, Jr. (Eds.), *Cognitive theory,* Vol. 3 (pp. 33–74). Hillsdale, NJ: Erlbaum.

Birnbaum, M.H. (1979). Reply to Eisler: On the subtraction theory of stimulus comparison. *Perception & Psychophysics, 25,* 150–156.

Birnbaum, M.H. (1982). Controversies in psychological measurement. In B. Wegener (Ed.), *Social attributes and psychological measurement* (pp. 401–485).

Hillsdale, NJ: Erlbaum.

Blackwell, H.R. (1953). Psychophysical thresholds: Experimental studies of methods of measurement. *Engineering Research Bulletin* 36. Ann Arbor: University of Michigan.

Block, H.D., & Marschak, J. (1960). Random orderings and stochastic theories of responses. In I. Olkin, S. Ghurye, W. Hoeffding, W. Madow, & H. Mann (Eds.), *Contributions to probability and statistics* (pp. 97–132). Stanford, CA: Stanford University Press.

Braida, L.D., & Durlach, N.I. (1972). Intensity perception. II. Resolution in one-interval paradigms. *Journal of the Acoustical Society of America, 51,* 483–502.

Bradley, R.A., & Terry, M.E. (1952). Rank analysis of incomplete block designs. I. The method of paired comparisons. *Biometrika, 39,* 324–345.

Buckingham, E. (1914). On physically similar systems: Illustrations of the use of dimensional equations. *Physical Review, 4,* 345–376.

Carroll, J.D. (1972). Individual differences and multidimensional scaling. In R.N. Shepard, A.K. Romney, & S.B. Nerlove (Eds.), *Multidimensional scaling,* Vol. I (pp. 105–155). New York: Seminar Press.

Carroll, J.D. (1976). Spatial, non-spatial, and hybrid models for scaling. *Psychometrika, 41,* 439–463.

Carroll, J.D. (1980). Models and methods for multidimensional analysis of preferential choice (or other dominance) data. In E.D. Lantermann & H. Feger (Eds.), *Similarity and choice* (pp. 234–289). Bern: Hans Huber.

Carroll, J.D., & Arabie, P. (1980). Multidimensional scaling. In M.R. Rosenzweig & L.W. Porter (Eds.), *Annual review of psychology,* Vol. 31 (pp. 607–649). Palo Alto, CA: Annual Reviews.

Carroll, J.D., & Chang, J.J. (1970). Analysis of individual differences in multidimensional scaling via an N-way generalization of 'Eckart–Young' decomposition. *Psychometrika, 35,* 238–319.

Carroll, J.D., & Pruzansky, S. (1980). Discrete and hybrid scaling models. In E.D. Lantermann & H. Feger (Eds.), *Similarity and choice* (pp. 108–139). Bern: Hans Huber.

Carroll, J.D., & Wish, M. (1974a). Models and methods for three-way multidimensional scaling. In D.H. Krantz, R.C. Atkinson, R.D. Luce, & P. Suppes (Eds.), *Contemporary developments in mathematical psychology,* Vol. 2 (pp. 57–105). San Francisco: Freeman.

Carroll, J.D., & Wish, M. (1974b) Multidimensional perceptual models and measurement methods. In E.C. Carterette & M.P. Friedman (Eds.), *Handbook of perception,* Vol. 2 (pp. 391–447). New York: Academic Press.

Cattell, J.McK. (1886). The influence of intensity of the stimulus on the length of reaction times. *Brain, 8,* 512–515.

Cattell, R.B. (1978). *The scientific use of factor analysis in behavioral and life sciences.* New York: Plenum Press.

Cliff, N. (1973). Scaling. In P.H. Mussen & M.R. Rosenzweig (Eds.), *Annual review of psychology,* Vol. 24 (pp. 473–506). Palo Alto: Annual Reviews.

Coombs, C.H. (1950). Psychological scaling without a unit of measurement. *Psychological Review, 57,* 145–158.

Coombs, C.H. (1964). *A theory of data.* New York: Wiley.

Coombs, C.H., Dawes, R.M., & Tversky, A. (1970). *Mathematical psychology: An elementary introduction.* Englewood Cliffs, NJ: Prentice-Hall.

Corso, J.F. (1956). The neural quantum theory of sensory discrimination. *Psychological Bulletin, 53,* 371–393.

Corso, J.F. (1973). Neural quantum controversy in sensory psychology. *Science, 181,* 467–468.

Cornsweet, T.N. (1970). *Visual perception.* New York: Academic Press.

Cunningham, J.P. (1978). Free trees and bidirectional trees as representation of psychological distance. *Journal of Mathematical Psychology, 17,* 165–188.

Daning, R. (1983). Intraindividual consistencies in cross-modal matching across several continua. *Perception & Psychophysics, 33,* 516–522.

Debreu, G. (1960a). Topological methods in cardinal utility theory, In K.J. Arrow, S. Karlin, & P. Suppes (Eds.), *Mathematical methods in the social sciences, 1959* (pp. 16–26). Stanford: Stanford University Press.

Debreu, G. (1960b). [Review of R.D. Luce, Individual choice behavior: A theoretical analysis]. *American Economic Review, 50,* 186–188.

Diday, E. (1974). Optimization in non-hierarchical clustering. *Pattern Recognition, 6,* 17–33.

Durlach, N.I., & Braida, L.D. (1969). Intensity perception. I. Preliminary theory of intensity resolution. *Journal of the Acoustical Society of America, 46,* 372–383.

Eisler, H. (1978). On the ability to estimate differences: A note on Birnbaum's subtraction model. *Perception & Psychophysics, 24,* 185–189.

Ekman, G. (1954). Dimensions of color vision. *Journal of Psychology, 38,* 467–474.

Ekman, G., & Sjöberg, L. (1965). Scaling. In P.R. Farnsworth, O. McNemar, & Q. McNemar (Eds.), *Annual review of psychology,* Vol. 16 (pp. 451–474). Palo Alto: Annual Reviews.

Engeland, W., & Dawson, W.E. (1974). Individual differences in power functions for a 1-week inter-session interval. *Perception & Psychophysics, 15,* 349–352.

Falmagne, J.-C. (1971). The generalized Fechner problem and discrimination. *Journal of Mathematical Psychology, 8,* 22–43.

Falmagne, J.-C. (1974). Foundations of Fechnerian psychophysics. In D.H. Krantz, R.C. Atkinson, R.D. Luce & P. Suppes (Eds.), *Contemporary developments in mathematical psychology,* Vol. 2 (pp. 127–159). San Francisco: Freeman.

Falmagne, J.-C. (1976). Random conjoint measurement and loudness summations. *Psychological Review, 83,* 65–79.

Falmagne, J.-C. (1985). *Elements of psychophysical theory.* New York: Oxford University Press.

Fechner, G.T. (1860). *Elemente der Psychophysik.* Leipzig: Breitkopf and Hartel. (Translation of Vol. 1 by H.E. Adler [D.H. Howes & E.G. Boring, Eds.], *Elements of psychophysics.* New York: Holt, Rinehart and Winston, 1966.)

Fitts, P.M. (1966). Cognitive aspects of information processing, III. Set for speed versus accuracy. *Journal of Experimental Psychology, 71,* 849–857.

Garner, W.R. (1953). An informational analysis of absolute judgments of loudness. *Journal of Experimental Psychology, 46,* 373–380.

Garner, W.R. (1962). *Uncertainty and structure as psychological concepts.* New York: Wiley.

Garner, W.R. (1976). Interaction of stimulus dimensions in concept and choice processes. *Cognitive Psychology, 8,* 98–123.

Gescheider, G.A. (1976). *Psychophysics: Method and theory.* Hillsdale, NJ: Erlbaum.

Gravetter, F., & Lockhead, G.R. (1973). Criterial range as a frame of reference for stimulus judgments. *Psychological Review, 80,* 203–216.

Green, D.M., & Luce, R.D. (1973). Speed–accuracy tradeoff in auditory detection. In S. Kornblum (Ed.), *Attention and performance,* Vol. 4 (pp. 547–569). New York: Academic Press.

Green, D.M., & Luce, R.D. (1974). Variability of magnitude estimates: A timing theory analysis. *Perception & Psychophysics, 15,* 291–300.

Green, D.M., Luce, R.D., & Duncan, J.E. (1977). Variability and sequential effects in magnitude production and estimation of auditory intensity. *Perception & Psychophysics, 22,* 450–456.

Green, D.M., & Swets, J.A. (1966). *Signal detection theory and psychophysics.* New York: Wiley. (Reprinted, Huntington, NY: Kruger, 1974.)

Guilford, J.P. (1954). *Psychometric methods* (2nd ed.). New York: McGraw-Hill.

Hagarty, M., & Birnbaum, M.H. (1978). Nonmetric tests of ratio vs. subtraction theories of stimulus comparison. *Perception & Psychophysics, 24,* 121–129.

Hallpike, C.S., & Hood, J.D. (1959). Observations upon the neurological mechanism of loudness recruitment phenomenon. *Acta Otolaryngologica, 50,* 472–486.

Harman, H.H. (1976). *Modern factor analysis* (3rd ed.). Chicago: University of Chicago Press.

Hartigan, J.A. (1975). *Clustering algorithms.* New York: Wiley.

Hecht, S., Schlaer, S., & Pirenne, M.H. (1942). Energy, quanta, and vision. *Journal of General Psychology, 25,* 819–840.

Helm, C.E. (1964). Multidimensional ratio scaling analysis of perceived color relations. *Journal of the Optical Society of America, 54,* 256–262.

Helmholtz, H. von. (1962). *Treatise on physiological optics,* Vol. 3. J.P.C. Southall (Ed.). New York: Dover. (Translated from the 3rd German edition, 1867).

Helson, H. (1964). *Adaptation-level theory.* New York: Harper & Row.

Herrnstein, R.J., & de Villiers, P.A. (1980). Fish as a natural category for people and pigeons. In G. Bower (Ed.), *The psychology of learning and motivation,* Vol. 14 (pp. 60–96). New York: Academic Press.

Holland, M.K., & Lockhead, G.R. (1968). Sequential effects in absolute judgments of loudness. *Perception & Psychophysics, 3,* 409–414.

Indow, T. (1979). Alleys in visual space. *Journal of Mathematical Psychology, 19,* 221–258.

Jardine, C.J., Jardine, N., & Sibson, R. (1967). The structure and construction of taxonomic hierarchies. *Mathematical Biosciences, 1,* 173–179.

Jesteadt, W., Luce, R.D., & Green, D.M. (1977). Sequential effects in judgments of loudness. *Journal of Experimental Psychology: Human Perception and Performance, 3,* 92–104.

Jesteadt, W., Wier, C.C., & Green, D.M. (1977). Intensity discrimination as a function of frequency and sensation level. *Journal of the Acoustical Society of America, 61,* 169–177.

Johnson, S.C. (1967). Hierarchical clustering schemes. *Psychometrika, 32,* 241–254.

King, M., & Lockhead, G.R. (1981). Response scales and sequential effects in judgment. *Perception & Psychophysics, 30,* 599–603.

Kling, J.W., & Riggs, L.A. (Eds.). (1972). *Woodworth & Schlosberg's Experimental psychology* (3rd ed.). Vol. 1, *Sensation and perception.* New York: Holt, Rinehart and Winston.

Kohfeld, D.L. (1971). Simple reaction time as a function of stimulus intensity in decibels of light and sound. *Journal of Experimental Psychology, 88,*

251–257.

Kohfeld, D.L., Santee, J.L., & Wallace, N.D. (1981). Loudness and reaction times: I. *Perception & Psychophysics, 29,* 535–549.

Kornbrot, D.E. (1978). Theoretical and empirical comparison of Luce's choice reaction model and logistic Thurstone model of categorical judgment. *Perception & Psychophysics, 24,* 193–208.

Kornbrot, D.E. (1980). Attention bands: Some implications for categorical judgment. *British Journal of Mathematical and Statistical Psychology, 32,* 1–16.

Krantz, D.H. (1964). The scaling of small and large color differences (Doctoral dissertation, University of Pennsylvania, 1964). Ann Arbor, MI: *University Microfilms,* 1964, No. 65-5777.

Krantz, D.H. (1969). Threshold theories of signal detection. *Psychological Review, 76,* 308–324.

Krantz, D.H. (1971). Integration of just-noticeable differences. *Journal of Mathematical Psychology, 8,* 591–599.

Krantz, D.H. (1974). Measurement theory and qualitative laws in psychophysics. In D.H. Krantz, R.C. Atkinson, R.D. Luce & P. Suppes (Eds.), *Contemporary developments in mathematical psychology,* Vol. 2 (pp. 160–199). San Francisco: Freeman.

Krantz, D.H. (1975). Color measurement and color theory. I. Representation theorem for Grassman structures. II. Opponent-colors theory. *Journal of mathematical psychology, 12,* 283–303; 304–327.

Krantz, D.H., Luce, R.D., Suppes, P., & Tversky, A. (1971) *Foundations of measurement,* Vol. 1. New York: Academic Press. (Vols. 2 and 3 in preparation).

Krumhansl, C. (1978). Concerning the applicability of geometric models to similarity data: The interrelationship between similarity and spatial density. *Psychological Review, 85,* 415–463.

Kruskal, J.B. (1964a). Multidimensional scaling by optimizing goodness of fit to a nonmetric hypothesis. *Psychometrika, 29,* 1–28.

Kruskal, J.B. (1964b). Nonmetric multidimensional scaling: A numerical method. *Psychometrika, 29,* 115–129.

Kruskal, J.B. (1977). The relationship between multidimensional scaling and clustering. In J. Van Ryzin (Ed.), *Classification and clustering* (pp. 17–44). New York: Academic Press.

Laming, D.R.J. (1968). *Information theory of choice-reaction times.* New York: Academic Press.

Laming, D.R.J. (1986). *Sensory analysis.* New York: Academic Press.

Lappin, J.S., & Disch, K. (1972). The latency operating characteristic. I. Effects of stimulus probability on choice reaction time. *Journal of Experimental Psychology, 92,* 419–427.

Levelt, W.J.M., Riemersma, J.B., & Bunt, A.A. (1972). Binaural additivity in loudness. *British Journal of Mathematical and Statistical Psychology, 25,* 51–68.

Link, S.W. (1975). The relative judgment theory of two choice response times. *Journal of Mathematical Psychology, 12,* 114–135.

Link, S.W. (1978). The relative judgment theory analysis of response time deadline experiments. In N.J. Castellan, Jr., & F. Restle (Eds.), *Cognitive theory,* Vol. 2 (pp. 117–138). Hillsdale, NJ: Erlbaum.

Link, S.W., & Heath, R.A. (1975). A sequential theory of psychological discrimination. *Psychometrika, 40,* 77–105.

Lippman, R.P., Braida, L.D., & Durlach, N.I. (1976). Intensity perception. V. Effect of payoff matrix on absolute identification. *Journal of the Acoustical Society of America, 59,* 121–134.

Logue, A.W. (1976). Individual differences in magnitude estimation of loudness. *Perception & Psychophysics, 19,* 279–280.

Luce, R.D. (1959). *Individual choice behavior: A theoretical analysis.* New York: Wiley.

Luce, R.D. (1963a). Detection and recognition. In R.D. Luce, R.R. Bush, & E. Galanter (Eds.), *Handbook of mathematical psychology.* Vol. 1 (pp. 103–189). New York: Wiley.

Luce, R.D. (1963b) Discrimination. In R.D. Luce, R.R. Bush & E. Galanter (Eds.), *Handbook of mathematical psychology,* Vol. 1 (pp. 191–243). New York: Wiley.

Luce, R.D. (1963c). A threshold theory for simple detection experiments. *Psychological Review, 70,* 61–79.

Luce, R.D. (1977). The choice axiom after twenty years. *Journal of Mathematical Psychology, 15,* 215–233.

Luce, R.D. (1978). Dimensionally invariant numerical laws correspond to meaningful qualitative relations. *Philosophy of Science, 45,* 1–16.

Luce, R.D. (1981). Axioms for the averaging and adding representations of functional measurement. *Mathematical Social Sciences, 1,* 139–144.

Luce, R.D. (1986a). *Response times.* New York: Oxford University Press.

Luce, R.D. (1986b). Uniqueness and homogeneity in real relational structures. *Journal of Mathematical Psychology, 30,* 391–415.

Luce, R.D., Baird, J.C., Green, D.M., & Smith, A.F. (1980). Two classes of models for magnitude estimation. *Journal of Mathematical Psychology, 22,* 121–148.

Luce, R.D., & Edwards, W. (1958). The derivation of subjective scales from just noticeable differences. *Psychological Review, 65,* 227–237.

Luce, R.D., & Green, D.M. (1978). Two tests of a neural attention hypothesis in auditory psychophysics. *Perception & Psychophysics, 23,* 363–371.

Luce, R.D., Green, D.M., & Weber, D.L. (1976). Attention bands in absolute identification. *Perception & Psychophysics, 20,* 49–54.

Luce, R.D. & Narens, L. (1985). Classification of concatenation measurement structures according to scale type. *Journal of mathematical psychology, 29,* 1–72.

Luce, R.D., & Nosofsky, R. (1984). Sensitivity and criterion effects in absolute identification. In S. Kornblum & J. Requin (Eds.), *Preparatory states and processes* (pp. 3–25). Hillsdale, NJ: Erlbaum.

Luce, R.D., Nosofsky, R.M., Green, D.M., & Smith, A.F. (1982). The bow and sequential effects in absolute identification. *Perception & Psychophysics, 32,* 397–408.

Luce, R.D., & Tukey, J.W. (1964). Simultaneous conjoint measurement: A new type of fundamental measurement. *Journal of Mathematical Psychology, 1,* 1–27.

Luneburg, R.K. (1947). *Mathematical analysis of binocular vision.* Princeton, NJ: Princeton University Press.

MacQueen, J. (1967). Some methods for classification and analysis of multivariate observations. In L.M. LeCam & J. Neyman (Eds.), *Proceedings of the Fifth Berkeley Symposium on Mathematical Statistics and Probability,* Vol. 1 (pp. 281–297). Berkeley: University of California Press.

Mansfield, R.J.W. (1976). Visual adaption: Retinal transduction, brightness and sensitivity. *Vision Research, 16,* 679–690.

Marks, L.E. (1974). *Sensory processes: The new psychophysics.* New York: Academic Press.

Mashhour, M. (1964). *Psychophysical relations in the perception of velocity.* Stockholm: Almquist and Wiksell.

Mashhour, M., & Hosman, J. (1968). On the new "psychophysical law": A validation study. *Perception & Psychophysics, 3,* 367–375.

Marley, A.A.J., & Cook, V. T. (1984). A fixed rehearsal capacity interpretation of limits on absolute identification performance. *British journal of mathematical and statistical psychology, 37,* 136–151.

Marley, A.A.J., & Cook, V. T. (1986). A limited capacity rehearsal model for psychophysical judgments applied to magnitude estimation. *Journal of mathematical psychology, 30,* 339–390.

McClelland, G.H. (1980). *Axioms for the weighted linear model.* Unpublished manuscript.

McFadden, D. (1974). Conditional logit analysis of qualitative choice behavior. In P. Zarembka (Ed.), *Frontiers in econometrics* (pp. 105–142). New York: Academic Press.

McGill, W.J., & Goldberg, J.P. (1968). A study of the near-miss involving Weber's law and pure-tone intensity discrimination. *Perception & Psychophysics, 4,* 105–109.

Mellers, B.A., & Birnbaum, M.H. (1982). Loci of contextual effects in judgment. *Journal of Experimental Psychology: Human Perception and Performance, 8,* 582–601.

Miller, G.A. (1947). Sensitivity to changes in the intensity of white noise and its relation to masking and loudness. *Journal of the Acoustical Society of America, 19,* 609–619.

Miller, G.A. (1953). What is information measurement? *American Psychologist, 8,* 3–11.

Miller, G.A. (1956). The magical number seven, plus or minus two: Some limits on our capacity for processing information. *Psychological Review, 63,* 81–97.

Miller, G.A., & Nicely, P.E. (1955). An analysis of perceptual confusions among some English consonants. *Journal of the Acoustical Society of America, 27,* 338–352.

Narens, L. (1981a). A general theory of ratio scalability with remarks about the measurement-theoretic concept of meaningfulness. *Theory and Decision, 13,* 1–70.

Narens, L. (1981b). On the scales of measurement. *Journal of Mathematical Psychology, 24,* 249–275.

Narens, L. (1985). *Abstract measurement theory.* Cambridge, MA: MIT.

Norman, D.A. (1964). Sensory thresholds, response biases, and the neural quantum theory. *Journal of Mathematical Psychology, 1,* 88–120.

Nosofsky, R.M. (1983). Information integration and the identification of stimulus noise and criterial noise in absolute judgment. *Journal of Experimental Psychology: Human Perception and Performance, 9,* 299–309.

Parducci, A. (1965). Category judgment: A range-frequency model. *Psychological Review, 72,* 407–418.

Parducci, A., Calfee, R.C., Marshall, L.M., & Davidson, L.P. (1960). Context effects in judgment: Adaptation level as a function of the mean, midpoint, and median of the stimuli. *Journal of Experimental Psychology, 60,* 65–77.

Parducci, A., & Perrett, L.F. (1971). Category rating scales: Effects of relative spacing and frequency of stimulus values. *Journal of Experimental Psychology, 89,* 427–452.

Pew, R.W. (1969). The speed-accuracy operating characteristic. *Acta Psychologica, 30,* 16–26.

Pfanzagl, J. (1971). *Theory of measurement* (2nd ed.). New York: Wiley.

Piéron, H. (1914). Recherches sur les lois de variation des temps de latence sensorielle en fonction des intensités excitatrices. *L'Année Psychologique, 20,* 17–96.

Plateau, J.A.F. (1872). Sur la mesure des sensations physiques, et sur la loi qui lie l'intensité de ces sensation à l'intensité de la cause excitante. *Bulletin de l'Academie Royale de Belgique, 33,* 376–388.

Pollack, I. (1952). Information in elementary auditory displays. *Journal of the Acoustical Society of America, 24,* 745–750.

Pollack, I. (1953). The information of elementary auditory displays, II. *Journal of the Acoustical Society of America, 25,* 765–769.

Pollack, I., & Ficks, L. (1954). Information of elementary multidimensional auditory displays. *Journal of the Acoustical Society of America, 26,* 155–158.

Poulton, E.C. (1968). The new psychophysics: Six models for magnitude estimation. *Psychological Bulletin, 69,* 1–19.

Pruzansky, S., Tversky, A., & Carroll, J.D. (1982). Spatial versus tree representations of proximity data. *Psychometrika, 47,* 3–24.

Purks, S.R., Callahan, D.J., Braida, L.D., & Durlach, N.I. (1980). Intensity perception. X. Effect of preceding stimulus on identification performance. *Journal of the Acoustical Society of America, 67,* 634–637.

Rabinowitz, W.M., Lim, J.S., Braida, L.D., & Durlach, N.I. (1976). Intensity perception. VI. Summary of recent data on deviations from Weber's law for 1000-Hz tone pulses. *Journal of the Acoustical Society of America, 59,* 1506–1509.

Restle, F. (1961). *Psychology of judgment and choice.* New York: Wiley.

Richardson, L.F., & Ross, J.S. (1930). Loudness and telephone current. *Journal of General Psychology, 3,* 280–306.

Roberts, F.S. (1979). *Measurement theory.* Vol. 7 of *Encyclopedia of Mathematics and Its Applications.* Reading, MA: Addison-Wesley.

Robinson, G.H. (1976). Biasing power law exponents by magnitude estimation instructions. *Perception & Psychophysics, 19,* 80–84.

Rule, S.J., & Markley, R.P. (1971). Subject differences in cross-modal matching. *Perception & Psychophysics, 9,* 115–117.

Rumelhart, D.L., & Greeno, J.G. (1971). Similarity between stimuli: An experimental test of the Luce and Restle choice models. *Journal of Mathematical Psychology, 8,* 370–381.

Rushton, W.A.H. (1965). The Ferrier Lecture: Visual adaptation. *Proceedings of the Royal Society* (Lond.), B162, 20–46.

Sakitt, B. (1972). Counting every quantum. *Journal of Physiology, 223,* 131–150.

Sattath, S., & Tversky, A. (1977). Additive similarity trees. *Psychometrika, 42,* 319–345.

Sedov, L.I. (1959). *Similarity and dimensional methods in mechanics.* (M. Holt & M. Friedman, Trans.). New York: Academic Press. (Original Russian work published 1943; translation from 1956 edition.)

Shepard, R.N. (1962). The analysis of proximities: Multidimensional scaling with an unknown distance function. I, II. *Psychometrika, 27,* 125–140; 219–246.

Shepard, R.N. (1964). Attention and the metric structure of the stimulus space. *Journal of Mathematical Psychology, 1,* 54–87.

Shepard, R.N. (1972). A taxonomy of some principal types of data and of multidimensional methods for their analysis. In R.N. Shepard, A.K. Romney, & S.B. Nerlove (Eds.) (pp. 23–47). *Multidimensional scaling.* Vol. 1, *Theory.* New York: Seminar Press.

Shepard, R.N. (1974). Representation of structure in similarity data: Problems and prospects. *Psychometrika, 39,* 373–421.

Shepard, R.N. (1980). Multidimensional scaling, tree-fitting, and clustering. *Science, 210,* 390–398.

Shepard, R.N., & Arabie, P. (1979). Additive clustering: Representation of similarities as combinations of discrete overlapping properties. *Psychological Review, 86,* 87–123.

Sneath, P.H.A., & Sokal, R.R. (1973). *Numerical taxonomy.* San Francisco: Freeman.

Spearman, C. (1904). "General intelligence": Objectively determined and measured. *American Journal of Psychology, 15,* 201–293.

Staddon, J.E.R., King, M., & Lockhead, G.R. (1980). On sequential effects in absolute judgment experiments. *Journal of Experimental Psychology: Human Perception and Performance, 6,* 290–301.

Stevens, J.C. (1974). Families of converging power functions. In H.R. Moskowitz, B. Scharf, & J.C. Stevens (Eds.), *Sensation and measurement* (pp. 157–165). Dordrecht, Holland: Reidel.

Stevens, J.C., & Hall, J.W. (1966). Brightness and loudness as functions of stimulus duration. *Perception & Psychophysics, 1,* 319–327.

Stevens, S.S. (1946). On the theory of scales of measurement. *Science, 103,* 677–680.

Stevens, S.S. (1951). Mathematics, measurement and psychophysics. In S.S. Stevens (Ed.), *Handbook of experimental psychology* (pp. 1–49). New York: Wiley.

Stevens, S.S. (1966). Duration, luminance, and the brightness exponent. *Perception & Psychophysics, 1,* 96–103.

Stevens, S.S. (1975). *Psychophysics: Introduction to its perceptual, neural, and social prospects.* New York: Wiley.

Stevens, S.S., & Galanter, E.H. (1957). Ratio scales and category scales for a dozen perceptual continua. *Journal of Experimental Psychology, 54*, 377–411.

Stevens, S.S., & Guirao, M. (1963). Subjective scaling of length and area and the matching of length to loudness and brightness. *Journal of Experimental Psychology, 66*, 177–186.

Stevens, S.S., & Guirao, M. (1967). Loudness functions under inhibition. *Perception & Psychophysics, 2*, 459–465.

Stevens, S.S., Morgan, C.T., & Volkman, J. (1941). Theory of neural quantum in the discrimination of loudness and pitch. *American Journal of Psychology, 54*, 315–335.

Stevens, S.S., & Volkman, J. (1940). The quantum theory of discrimination. *Science, 92*, 583–585.

Suppes, P., & Zinnes, J.L. (1963). Basic measurement theory. In R.D. Luce, R.R. Bush, & E. Galanter (Eds.), *Handbook of mathematical psychology*, Vol. 1 (pp. 1–76). New York: Wiley.

Tanner, W.P., Jr., & Swets, J.A. (1954). A decision-making theory of visual detection. *Psychological Review, 61*, 401–409.

Teghtsoonian, R. (1971). On the exponents in Stevens' law and the constant in Ekman's law. *Psychological Review, 78*, 71–80.

Teghtsoonian, M., & Teghtsoonian, R. (1971). How repeatable are Stevens' power law exponents for individual subjects? *Perception & Psychophysics, 10*, 147–149.

Thurstone, L.L. (1927). A law of comparative judgment. *Psychological Review, 34*, 273–286.

Thurstone, L.L. (1947). *Multiple factor analysis*. Chicago: University of Chicago Press.

Thurstone, L.L. (1959). *The measurement of values*. Chicago: University of Chicago Press.

Torgerson, W.S. (1954). A law of categorical judgment. In L.H. Clark, *Consumer behavior* (pp. 92–93). New York: New York University Press.

Torgerson, W.S. (1958). *Theory and methods of scaling*. New York: Wiley.

Torgerson, W.S. (1961). Distance and ratios in psychophysical scaling. *Acta Psychologica, 19*, 201–205.

Treisman, M. (1977). Neural quantum theory: How strongly does the occurrence of rational intercept ratios support it? *Acta Psychologica, 41*, 327–334.

Treisman, M. (1985). The magical number seven and some other features of category scaling: Properties of a model for absolute judgment. *Journal of mathematical psychology, 29*, 175–230.

Treisman, M., & Williams, T.C. (1984). A theory of criterion setting with an application to sequential dependencies. *Psychological review, 91*, 68–111.

Tversky, A. (1972). Elimination by aspects: A theory of choice. *Psychological Review, 79*, 281–299.

Tversky, A. (1977). Features of similarity. *Psychological Review, 84*, 327–352.

Tversky, A., & Gati, I. (1982). Similarity, separability, and the triangle inequality. *Psychological Review, 89*, 123–154.

Tversky, A., & Sattath, S. (1979). Preference trees. *Psychological Review, 86*, 542–573.

Urban, F.M. (1910). The method of constant stimuli and its generalizations. *Psychological Review, 17*, 229–259.

Wandell, B., & Luce, R.D. (1978). Pooling peripheral information: Averages versus extreme values. *Journal of Mathematical Psychology, 17*, 220–235.

Ward, L.M. (1972). Category judgments of loudness in the absence of an experimenter-induced identification function: Sequential effects of power-function fit. *Journal of Experimental Psychology, 94*, 179–184.

Ward, L.M. (1973). Repeated magnitude estimations with a variable standard: Sequential effects and other properties. *Perception & Psychophysics, 13*, 193–200.

Ward, L.M. (1979). Stimulus information and sequential dependencies in magnitude estimation and cross-modality matching. *Journal of Experimental Psychology: Human Perception and Performance, 5*, 444–459.

Ward, L.M., & Lockhead, G.R. (1970). Sequential effects and memory in category judgments. *Journal of Experimental Psychology, 84*, 27–34.

Ward, L.M., & Lockhead, G.R. (1971). Response system processes in absolute judgment. *Perception & Psychophysics, 9*, 73–78.

Warren, R.M. (1981). Measurement of sensory intensity. *Behavioral and Brain Sciences, 4*, 175–223.

Warren, R.M., & Warren, R.P. (1963). A critique of S.S. Stevens' "New psychophysics." *Perceptual and Motor Skills, 16*, 797–810.

Weber, D.L., Green, D.M., & Luce, R.D. (1977). Effects of practice and distribution of auditory signals on absolute identification. *Perception & Psychophysics, 22*, 223–231.

Weiss, D.J. (1975). Quantifying private events: A functional measurement analysis of equisection. *Perception & Psychophysics, 17*, 351–357.

Welford, A.T. (Ed.) (1980). *Reaction times*. New York: Academic Press.

Wright, A.A. (1974). Psychometric and psychophysical theory within a framework of response bias. *Psychological Review, 81*, 322–347.

Yellott, J.I., Jr. (1977). The relationship between Luce's choice axiom, Thurstone's theory of comparative judgment and the double exponential distribution. *Journal of Mathematical Psychology, 15,* 109–144.

Young, F.W. (1984). Scaling. In M.R. Rosenzweig & L.W. Porter (Eds.), *Annual review of psychology,*

vol. 35 (pp. 55–81). Palo Alto: Annual Reviews.

Zinnes, J.L. (1969). Scaling. In P.H. Mussen & M.R. Rosenzweig (Eds.), *Annual review of psychology,* Vol. 20 (pp. 447–478). Palo Alto: Annual Reviews.

Chapter 2

VISION: PHYSICS AND RETINAL PHYSIOLOGY

E.N. Pugh, Jr., *University of Pennsylvania*

And thus is the universe knit together. The atomic motions of a distant star still have sufficient influence at this great distance to set the electrons in our eye in motion, and so we know about the stars.

Richard P. Feynman
Lectures on Physics

This chapter outlines the physical and physiological processes by which light energy is transformed by the visual system into the neural signals that form the basis of the visual world. The nature of light itself is considered, as are those fundamental aspects of chemistry and physics that govern the interaction of light with matter. This leads to a consideration of physical optics and then physiological optics—that is, the characterization of the image-forming elements of the eye that produce the retinal image, the proximal stimulus of vision. Next the chapter discusses the initial stage of visual processing, photoreception and phototransduction, at which light energy is transduced into neural signals in the photoreceptors. Finally, the chapter considers some of the retinal processes governing light and dark adaptation, the processes by which the visual system adjusts itself to the ambient illumination conditions.

The complexity of the scientific material considered and the limitations of space have necessitated compromises in this chapter. The physics of vision is a highly technical subject. The interaction of light with matter is a quantum mechanical event, and the full explanation of how a photon of light triggers a significant neural signal requires some discussion of quantum theory. Modern visual optics also encompasses issues of formidable technical complexity and employs many tools of mathematical physics. Biophysical analyses have placed understanding of neural events throughout the visual system on an increasingly technical level. I recognize the impossibility of presenting a satisfactory, self-contained, introductory exposition of such technical matters, and I realize that not all readers will be interested in such material. Nonetheless, I have included some basic mathematical formulae that provide insights into visual physics and physiology. In dealing with the neurophysiology and neuroanatomy of the visual system, some familiarity with the basic principles and methods of neurobiology will be helpful (e.g., Kuffler & Nicholls, 1976).

LIGHT

Electromagnetic fields originate in the acceleration of charged particles such as the electron. Such fields propagate in a vacuum with a velocity $c = 3.0 \times 10^8$ m/sec, one of the fundamental physical constants. The characteristic oscillation periods of the charged particle determine the frequency, v, which is related to the propagation velocity in a vacuum, c, and the wavelength, λ, by the formula,

$$c = \lambda v \qquad (2.1)$$

Maxwell condensed the laws governing electricity and magnetism into a single set of differential equations that characterize the electromagetic field, the propagation of which we call *electromagnetic radiation*. Planck, Einstein, Bohr, de Broglie, Born, Schrödinger, Heisenberg and others contributed to the development of the quantum theory, which initially served to explain such phenomena as the energy distribution of the black body radiator and the photoelectric effect, but eventually provided the basis for an all-encompassing theory of matter and radiation. Of special significance to vision is the basic proposition of quantum mechanics that the electromagnetic field can only receive and give up energy in packets or "quanta." The quantal energy, E, of a single photon of frequency v is given by the relationship,

$$E = hv \qquad (2.2)$$

where Planck's constant h $= 6.63 \times 10^{-27}$ erg.sec.

Light comprises a region of the electromagnetic spectrum, in which the wavelengths in a vacuum range from about 350 nanometers to about 750 nanometers; or, applying equation 2.1, ranging in frequencies from 9×10^{14} to 4×10^{14} Hertz. Combining equations 2.1 and 2.2 we compute the energy of a single photon of light of 350 nm light to be 5.7×10^{-12} ergs or 3.5 eV, and the energy of a single photon of light of 750 nm to be 1.8 eV ($1 eV = 1.6 \times 10^{-12}$ ergs). The significance for vision of this window in the spectrum arose in part because many organic molecules—including the pigments that initiate vision—absorb radiant energy in the waveband 350 nm to 750 nm. Absorption can only occur when the energy of a photon, given in equation 2.2, matches the difference in energy levels between the ground state of an electron and a low-lying, unoccupied excited state.

Interaction of Light and Matter: Physical Nature of Absorption

Figure 2.1*a* is a diagram of 11-*cis* retinal, an isomeric configuration of vitamin A aldehyde. This molecule, or its close relative, 11-*cis*, 3-dehydroretinal, form the essential light-absorbing structure or *chromophore* in all known visual pigments. By virtue of the system of alternating double and single bonds joining nuclei 5 through 16, the molecule possesses a cloud of 12 π-electrons, which occupy *orbitals* that extend above and below the plane of the nuclei. Absorption of a photon from the electromagnetic field promotes one of the π-electrons from its ground state to an unoccupied orbital of higher energy: The excited molecule is less stable and can relax to the lower energy state determined by thermal equilibrium by any of several pathways—fluorescence, internal conversion of the photon energy into vibrational energy, or by undergoing a chemical change such as isomerization. This latter event is the initial even in vision. The following provides a brief tutorial of the quantum theory of absorption.

Matter and energy are unitary, a fact expressed in the celebrated Einstein relation,

$$E = mc^2. \qquad (2.3)$$

de Broglie proposed that every material particle has a characteristic wavelength. Combining equations 2.1 through 2.3, one arrives at the simple formula $\lambda = h/mc$. Now mc is the *momentum* of the photon. Thus, by analogy, one has the expression $\lambda = h/p$, where $p = mv$ is the momentum of a particle with velocity v. Since the total energy, E, of a particle in a potential field is the sum of its kinetic and potential energy, $E = T + V$, where $T = mv^2/2$, one has

$$\lambda = h/\sqrt{2m(E - V)} \qquad (2.4)$$

for the de Broglie wavelength of a particle in a vacuum. Electrons were shown to produce diffraction patterns consistent with equation 2.4 soon after de Broglie proposed the relation. Schrödinger extended de Broglie's analysis by

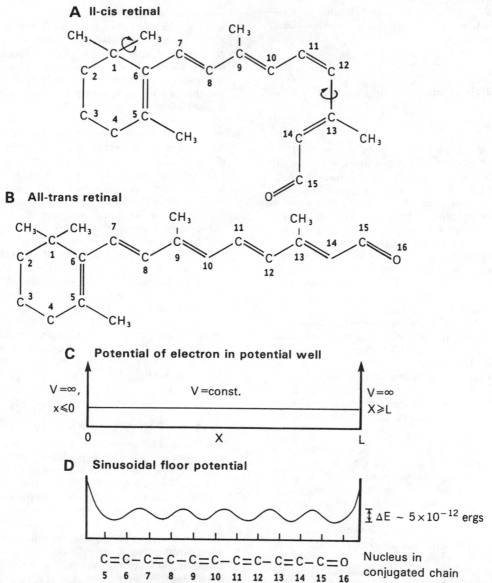

Figure 2.1. (a) Diagram of 11-*cis* (more properly, 6s-*cis*, 11-*cis*, 12s-*cis*) retinal, the aldehyde of vitamin A. (Hydrogen atoms bound to various carbon atoms, which complete the four pairs of shared electrons of each carbon, have been left off for clarity.) This molecule (or its close relative, 11-*cis*, 3-dehydro-retinal) forms the chromophore, or essential light absorbing element in all known visual pigments. By virtue of the system of alternating double and single bonds between nuclei at positions 5 through 16, the molecule possesses 12π electrons that occupy orbitals that extend above and below the plane of the nuclei. These orbitals tend to fuse and overlap, giving the single bonds some double-bond character and vice-versa. Absorption of a photon near the wavelength of peak absorption promotes one of the π-electrons from its ground state to an unoccupied orbital of higher energy, $\pi \to \pi^*$ transition. The molecule can relax from this excited state in several different ways, one of which is to isomerize to all-*trans* retinal.

(b) All-*trans* retinal, which is discussed in the text as an example of a conjugated system.

(c) A very simple treatment of the electrostatic potential of the π-electrons of all-*trans* retinal imagines it as an infinite potential well of potential V extending from one end of the conjugated chain to the other. A solution to Schroedinger's one-dimensional wave equation is given in the text for this case.

(d) A slightly more sophisticated model of the potential, which recognizes that the potential energy is lower in the neighborhood of the nominal double bonds. Models of the potential must take into consideration details of geometry and influence of other energy nearby charges (e.g., the methyl groups attached to carbons 9, 13) to give a full account of the extinction spectrum.

taking the classical time-independent wave equation (here given for the one-dimensional case),

$$\frac{d^2\psi}{dx^2} + \left(\frac{2\pi}{\lambda}\right)^2 \psi = 0 \qquad (2.5)$$

and, substituting in de Broglie's relation for λ:

$$\left(\frac{-h^2}{8\pi^2 m}\right)\frac{d^2\psi}{dx^2} + (V - E)\,\psi = 0 \qquad (2.6)$$

For the single electron (with mass $m = 9.11 \times 10^{-28}$ gm) of the hydrogen atom, the potential field V is the coulombic or electrostatic potential between the hydrogen nucleus (the proton) and the electron. The solutions of (2.6) for a given m only exist for certain discrete values of the energy E; these are known as the *eigenvalues*. Thus, the permissible energy states of a particle obeying these relations are *quantized*. This is the essence of quantum mechanics. A solution ψ to Schrödinger's wave equation is called a *wavefunction* or *orbital* for the particle. (The full three-dimensional version of the wave equation, (2.6), usually must be employed, however, and the potential V may be very complicated.) In accord with Einstein's suggestion that the square of the electromagnetic wave be considered as proportional to the probability of finding a photon at a given point in space, ψ^2 was taken as proportional to the probability of finding the particle of matter (the electron) at a given point.

Chemistry is concerned with the electrons in atoms and molecules that take part in chemical bonding. Quantum chemistry describes the wavefunctions or orbitals (and therefore probability densities) of the electrons; bonding results in new stable orbital configurations of the electrons of the contributing atoms. In *sigma bonds* the pair of bonding electrons have a wavefunction cylindrically symmetric about an axis joining the two nuclei. Double bonds, in which the bonding nuclei share two pairs of electrons, have a π-bond in addition to a sigma bond; the π-orbitals are characterized by a wavefunction with a zero or node at the axis joining the nuclei and symmetry about a line perpendicular to the internuclear axis. In a *conjugated* system with alternating double and single bonds, such as that shown in Figures 2.1a and 2.1b, the π-orbitals overlap and fuse, delocalizing the electrons, and giving the structure planar rigidity.

Figure 2.1b is a diagram of all-*trans* retinal, the aldehyde of vitamin A. The nuclei 5 through 16 form a conjugated system with a total of 12 π-electrons. A simple particle-in-a-box approxi-

mation to the potential V (see Figure 2.1c) and the Hückel theory assumption that the π-electrons may be treated separately (i.e., with mathematical separability) from the remaining (sigma) bonding electrons, converts equation 2.6 into a simple one-dimensional wave equation, like that of a vibrating string. The square normalized solutions to equation 2.6 are $\psi_n(x) = \sqrt{2/L}\sin(n\pi x/L)$, which can be seen by substitution in equation 2.6 to have eigenvalues $E_n = n^2 h^2/8mL^2$. Note that n gives the number of nodes or zero-crossings in the wavefunction, and that the higher n is the greater E_n is. Let $2N$ be the number of π-electrons. By virtue of the Pauli exclusion principle, each orbital can be occupied by two electrons (with opposite spin.) In the *electronic ground state* the first N π-orbitals will be occupied with two electrons each—in this case $N = 6$. The absorption of a photon with energy $E = h\nu = hc/\lambda$ will raise one electron from an occupied to an empty orbital, if the electronic transition is permissible and if the energy difference between the two states matches that of the photon. The longest wavelength (minimally energetic) electronic transition will result from an electron going from the highest occupied to the lowest unoccupied orbital; thus $\Delta E_{\min} = E_{N+1} - E_N = h^2(2N + 1)/8mL^2$ and so,

$$\lambda_{\max} = hc/\Delta E_{\min}$$
$$= (8mc/h)\,(L^2/(2N + 1)) \qquad (2.7)$$

The result of equation 2.7 is of course a rough approximation. For all-trans retinal (Figure 2.1b) dissolved in a non-polar solvent in which light propagates with a speed $c = c_0/1.4$, where $c_0 = 3 \times 10^8$ cm/sec is the speed *in vacuo*, the observed $\lambda_{\max}$ is 375 nm (Sperling, 1973). Equation 2.7 yields the value $\lambda_{\max} = 375$ nm for $L = 14.3$ Å. The sum of the bond lengths between nuclei 5 to 16, determined by X-ray diffraction, is 15.3 Å (Sperling, 1973). An improvement can be made in describing the long-wave maxima of a sequence of conjugated compounds of increasing chain length if the potential V is assumed to vary sinusoidally, as in Figure 2.1d (Kuhn, 1959). In fact, much more detailed models can be built using methods such as the "linear combination of molecular orbitals" (e.g., Abrahamson & Japar, 1972). The simple formula 2.7 does reveal that the longest wavelength absorption maximum depends directly on the square of the length of the conjugated chain, and inversely on the number of π-electrons. The expression 2.7, however, does not show two very important aspects of light absorption. It does not explain the absolute probability that an incident photon of the appropriate energy will induce the electronic transition (this probability is called the **extinction coefficient**). Although the extinction coefficient has the dimensions of a cross-section, it is essentially a quantum mechanical property, for it depends on the degree to which the electronic transition is permissible or probable. Second, the formula does not reveal that the absorption spectrum will be "smeared" into a broad band, and not be a line. This is due to vibrational modes of the molecule (the internuclear distances vary at characteristic frequencies) and rotational modes (the electron-charge clouds have a certain amount of rotational freedom). In summary, the initial event in vision is the absorption of a photon by a visual pigment chromophore: a π-electron in the conjugated chain is boosted from its ground state to a higher energy orbital (excited state).[1]

Light and Matter: Scattering

Light propagation through a transparent medium of index of refraction, n, can be described as a retardation of the wave propagation velocity to $v = c/n$. The physical origin of this effect lies in the fact that the electric field induced by an accelerating charge in a region past a transparent boundary is the sum of the electric field that would be present if there were no transparent material, and the electric field generated by the oscillation of the electrons in the transparent medium—the latter being induced by the original electric field. That is, the index of refraction results from the fact that the *forward scattered* component of the electric field is phase-retarded. Although we will not consider the physical theory of the refractive index, note that such properties as the dependence of the refractive index on the material, the wavelength dependence of the refractive index, the absorption of light by refractile materials at certain wavelengths, etc., cannot be understood without reference to the physical theory of scattering.[2]

Light Measurement and Units

Radiometric Units

Since vision depends on the rate at which quanta of light are absorbed in the photoreceptors, the most appropriate units to describe light are quantal units. Historically, however, the use of energy rather than quantal units has taken precedence, and the understanding of many basic facts and papers in vision still requires familiarity with energy units. (Recall that equation 2.2, the Planck–Einstein formula, gives the relation between quantal and energy units). In this section we shall discuss both types of radiometric units.

Figure 2.2a shows a diagram of a radiant source of area dA_1 and a receiving surface of area dA_2. One considers the emission in a direction that makes an angle ε_1 with the normal $\boldsymbol{n}_1$ to the emitting surface; $d\omega_1$ is a limiting solid angle in this direction. The normal $\boldsymbol{n}_2$ to the receiving surface makes an angle ε_2 with the incident radiation, assumed to be a plane wave locally. Table 2.1, from Wyszecki and Stiles (1967), gives the definition of the various radiometric quantities in terms of the components of Figure 2.2. For monochromatic radiation of wavelength, λ, these may be converted readily to quantum units by equation 2.2, $E = h\nu = hc/\lambda$, which gives the energy in ergs of a single photon. In specifying the light irradiating the retina, the most appropriate unit would be irradiance in quantum units, e.g., quanta $\times$ sec^{-1} $\times$ cm^{-2} or quanta $\times$ sec^{-1} $\times$ deg^{-2}. A difficulty with both energy and quantal units arises because the retina is not equally sensitive to all wavelengths, and so summing the quanta (or energy) in a broad-band source would clearly misrepresent a light's visual effectiveness. Some method of weighting the irradiance or radiant intensity in each waveband by the relative spectral sensitivity of the eye is needed. Thus we have photometric units.

---

[1] For an introduction to the ideas in this section, the reader is referred to *Quantum Chemistry* (student edition) by J.P. Lowe. W. Kauzmann's *Quantum Chemistry*, a classic text in the field, is reasonably accessible. The chapter by Abrahamson & Japar in the *Handbook of Sensory Physiology* (1972) provides a fairly detailed treatment of these ideas, specifically oriented toward vision. A briefer treatment, also oriented toward vision, can be found in Appendix II of R.W. Rodieck's valuable book, *The Vertebrate Retina*.

[2] (An excellent introductory treatment of the physical theory can be found in Chapters 28 through 33 of Vol. I of Feynman's *Lectures on Physics*.)

Table 2.1.

Term	Symbol	Defining Equation	Explanatory Notes and Formulas	Units
Radiant energy	P_e			erg
Radiant flux			$d^2 P_e = L_e \dfrac{dA_1 \cos \varepsilon_1 \, dA_2 \cos \varepsilon_2}{r^2}$ = flux from source element dA_1 incident on receiver element dA_2	$erg\ s^{-1}$
Radiant emittance	M_e	$M_e = \dfrac{dP_e}{dA_1}$	dA_1: surface element of source	$erg\ s^{-1}\ cm^{-2}$
Irradiance	E_e	$E_e = \dfrac{dP_e}{dA_2}$	dA_2: surface element of receiver	$erg\ s^{-1}\ cm^{-2}$
Radiant intensity	I_e	$I_e = \dfrac{dP_e}{d\omega_1}$	$d\omega_1$: element of solid angle with apex (1) at surface of source	$erg\ s^{-1}\ sr^{-1}$
Radiance	L_e	$L_e = \dfrac{d^2 P_e}{dA_1 \cos \varepsilon_1 \, d\omega_1}$ $= \dfrac{d^2 E_e}{dA_2 \cos \varepsilon_2 \, d\omega_2}$ $= \dfrac{d(E_e)_n}{d\omega_2}$	ε_1: angle between given direction (1)–(2) and normal n_1 of dA_1 ε_2: angle between given direction (1)–(2) and normal n_2 of dA_2 $d\omega_2$: element of solid angle with apex (2) at surface of receiver S: portion of sphere surface r: radius of sphere, also distance between (1) of dA_1 and (2) of dA_2 c: velocity of radiant energy in vacuo $dA_1 \cos \varepsilon_1$: dA_1 orthogonally projected on plane perpendicular to given direction (1)–(2) $dA_2 \cos \varepsilon_2$: dA_2 orthogonally projected on plane perpendicular to given direction (1)–(2) $d(E_e)_n = \dfrac{dE_e}{dA_2 \cos \varepsilon_2}$ $d\omega_1 = \dfrac{dA_2 \cos \varepsilon_2}{r^2}$ $d\omega_2 = \dfrac{dA_1 \cos \varepsilon_1}{r^2}$	$erg\ s^{-1}\ cm^{-2}\ sr^{-1}$
Solid angle	ω	$\omega = \dfrac{S}{r^2}$		sr (steradian)
Frequency	ν			s^{-1}
Wavelength	λ	$\lambda = c/\nu$		cm
Wavenumber	ν'	$\nu' = \nu/c$		cm^{-1}

Note. If radiometric quantities are considered over small intervals of the spectrum, their respective symbols are correspondingly designated by the index ν, λ, or ν'. For example: $L_{e\lambda} = dL_e/d\lambda$ which is the spectral radiance taken over the wavelength interval $d\lambda$ at λ.

A

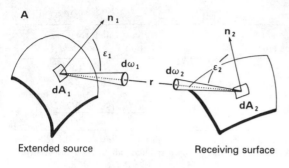

Extended source Receiving surface

B

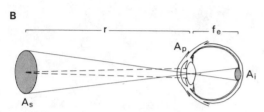

Figure 2.2. (a) Geometric quantities involved in radiometry. A surface differential dA_1 of the emitting source A_1 is considered radiating in the direction of the differential area dA_2 of receiving surface A_2. The surface normal n_1 at dA_1 makes an angle ε_1 with the direction of emission under consideration; the surface normal n_2 of the receiving surface makes an angle ε_2 with the direction considered. The distance between the emitter and receiver is r, and $d\omega_1$ and $d\omega_2$ represent differential solid angles. Table 2.1 (from Wyszecki & Stiles, 1982) gives the formal defintions of the various radiometric quantities.

(b) Geometric analysis showing that retinal illuminance produced by a homogeneous extended source of luminance L_v is independent of viewing distance. Hatched areas represent two-dimensional surfaces of areas A_s, A_p, and A_i. r is distance of luminous source of area A_s from eye; A_p, the area of entrance pupil of eye; f_e, the posterior nodal distance of eye; A_i, the surface area of retinal image of source. Dotted lines show how pupil restricts bundle of rays collected from single point on surface. The solid angle subtended by the pupil at the source (dashed lines) is A_p/r^2, and thus varies inversely with r^2; the solid visual angle subtended by the source at the eye (solid line) is A_s/r^2. Thus, the total luminous flux through the pupil is $F = A_s L_v A_p/r^2$, and the flux per unit solid visual angle $F/(A_s/r^2) = L_v A_p$, which is independent of r.

Photometric Units

There are two types of photometric units, scotopic and photopic. They are defined with respect to two internationally standardized spectral weighting functions, the *scotopic* and the *photopic luminosity functions*, V'_λ and V_λ, respectively (Table 2.4, second and third columns). By definition, the scotopic (photopic) luminosity of an arbitrary light is the weighted sum of energy or of power in each component waveband multiplied by the respective luminosity coefficient. Thus, two sources with spectral radiance distributions $E_{1\lambda}$ and $E_{2\lambda}$ have equal scotopic effectiveness if and only if,

$$\int E_{1\lambda} V'_\lambda \, d\lambda \;=\; \int E_{2\lambda} V'_\lambda \, d\lambda.$$

Likewise, two radiance distributions have equal photopic effectiveness if the equation just given holds with V'_λ replaced by V_λ. As we shall see below (p. 114) the scotopic luminosity curve has a virtually certain physiological interpretation: it represents the average in vivo absorption spectrum of the rod pigment, rhodopsin. The photopic luminosity curve cannot be assigned so simple a physiological interpretation as the scotopic curve, but it is nonetheless the internationally standardized spectral weighting function for daylight and normal roomlight conditions.

The terms **luminous flux** (unit—the *lumen*), **luminous intensity** (unit—the *candela* = 1 lumen/steradian), **luminance** (unit—*candela/meter²*), and **illuminance** (unit—*lumen/meter²*) correspond exactly to their radiometric counterparts. To obtain lumens, F, from watts, P_e, one multiplies the latter by the luminous efficiency factor, $K_m = 680$ lumens/watt (photopic) or $K'_m = 1745$ lumens/watt (scotopic). For example, $1\,\text{mW}$ of monochromatic light of wavelength $\lambda = 600\,\text{nm}$ corresponds to a luminous flux of $K_m V_\lambda \times 10^{-3} = 680 \times 0.631 \times 0.001 = 0.429$ photopic lumens.

There are some limits to using photometric units. The first is that V_λ, unlike V'_λ, is not proportional to a single visual pigment's absorption spectrum, and therefore, only gives a rough indication of the overall excitation of the photopic visual system. V_λ is a linear combination of the standard (CIE) observer's color matching functions, and is thus a linear combination of the average foveal cone pigment spectra (see p. 118). However, the short-wavelength sensitive cones make insignificant contribution to luminosity (defined in terms of flicker sensitivity). Thus, the photometric units will not clearly indicate how strongly these cones are excited by any given light. Also, the mid-wave sensitive cone pigment absorption is overestimated by V_λ in the long-wave region of the spectrum. Second,

Table 2.2. Unit conversion for photopic vision

	Quanta $\times$ sec^{-1} $\times$ deg^{-2} (at cornea)	Quanta absorbed cone^{-1} $\times$ sec^{-1}
Photopic trolands	$\dfrac{\lambda \times 10^{3.35}}{V_\lambda}$	$\dfrac{\lambda_{max}\tau_{\lambda max}S_\lambda \times 10^{-1.11}}{V_\lambda}$
Quanta $\times$ sec^{-1} $\times$ deg^{-2}	1	$\dfrac{\lambda_{max}\tau_{\lambda max}S_\lambda \times 10^{-4.46}}{\lambda}$

Table 2.2 and 2.3 give in each entry, a factor which converts by multiplication a number with the unit given by the row label to a number with the unit given by the column; e.g., 1 photopic td of λ_{max} = 555 nm light corresponds to about 44 quanta absorbed cone^{-1} $\times$ sec^{-1}, for $\tau_{\lambda max}S_\lambda$ = 1. In this table:

λ = wavelength in nanometers
V_λ = photopic luminosity function (Table 2.4)
S_λ = normalized cone absorption spectrum (energy basis at cornea; see Table 2.4))
$\tau_{\lambda max}$ = ocular media transmissivity at cone λ_{max}

Assumptions made in Table 2.2 are:
foveal cone entrance aperture diameter = 2.4 μm*
foveal cone optical density = 0.45 (45 μm outer segment)
foveal cone collecting area = $\pi(1.2)^2(1 - 10^{-0.45})$ = 2.92 μm^2
eye accommodated for ∞, posterior nodal distance 16.7 mm†

*Miller and Bernard (1983).
†This means that 1 μm^2 = $10^{-4.93}$ deg^2 of retina.

variation from individual to individual in luminosity functions can be large, particularly in the region of the spectrum below 520 nm where the macular pigment and lens density can be significant. This limitation applies to both scotopic and photopic luminosity functions.

One photometric unit that has had broad utility in vision is the *troland*, named after the visual psychophysicist/physiologist Leonard Thompson Troland. One troland is the retinal illuminance (luminous flux per unit retinal area) that results when an observer with a pupil area of 1 mm^2 views a distributed source that has a luminance of 1 cd $\times$ m^{-2}. One td (troland) correspond to a radiant intensity of 10^{-6} lumens/steradian of the retina. Tables 2.2 and 2.3 give conversions

from trolands to quantal units. The troland unit not only incorporates the standard photopic spectral weighting function, but also embodies a fundamental insight in both radiometry and photometry: for a fixed pupil aperture, the retinal illuminance (irradiance) caused by a homogeneous extended source of constant luminance (radiance) is independent of its distance from the viewer. Figure 2.2b shows why this independence of illuminance from viewing distance holds. The extended source, with area, A_s, and luminance, L_v, at a distance, r, from an observer with pupil area, A_p, causes a luminous flux $F_v = (L_v A_s A_p)/r^2$ through the observer's pupil. Since this flux is distributed evenly over the retinal image with area A_i, the retinal illumi-

Table 2.3. Unit conversion for scotopic vision

	Quanta $\times$ sec^{-1} $\times$ deg^{-2} (at cornea)	Quanta absorbed rod^{-1} $\times$ sec^{-1}
Scotopic trolands	$\dfrac{\lambda \times 10^{2.94}}{V'_\lambda}$	$\lambda \times 10^{-2.01}$
Quanta $\times$ sec^{-1} $\times$ deg^{-2}	1	$V'_\lambda \times 10^{-4.95}$

λ = wavelength in nanometers
V'_λ = scotopic luminosity function
    = media transmissivity $\times$ rhodopsin absorption spectrum in the rods, normalized at cornea (see p. xx)

Assumptions made:
rod diameter = 2 μm
rod λ_{max} optical density = 0.35
rod collecting area = $\pi(1 - 10^{-0.35})$ = 1.74 μm^2
eye media transmissivity at rod λ_{max} = 0.55

Table 2.4. Normalized spectral sensitivities for photopic and scotopic vision (energy basis, at cornea)

λ	V'_λ	V_λ	$S_{1\lambda}$	$S_{2\lambda}$	$S_{3\lambda}$
400	0.0093	0.0004	0.1742	0.0046	0.0042
410	0.0348	0.0012	0.3632	0.0097	0.0087
420	0.0966	0.0040	0.6612	0.0189	0.0159
430	0.1988	0.0116	0.9043	0.0307	0.0234
440	0.3281	0.0230	1.0000	0.0478	0.0302
450	0.4550	0.0380	0.9161	0.0637	0.0345
460	0.5670	0.0600	0.8018	0.0862	0.0414
470	0.6760	0.0910	0.6930	0.1307	0.0628
480	0.7930	0.1390	0.4071	0.1892	0.1023
490	0.9040	0.2080	0.2777	0.2677	0.1624
500	0.9820	0.3230	0.1646	0.3976	0.2636
510	0.9970	0.5030	0.0959	0.5968	0.4242
520	0.9350	0.7100	0.0475	0.8105	0.6184
530	0.8110	0.8620	0.0256	0.9445	0.7751
540	0.6500	0.9540	0.0125	1.0000	0.8858
550	0.4180	0.9950	0.0055	0.9898	0.9564
560	0.3288	0.9950	0.0024	0.9259	0.9959
570	0.2076	0.9520	0.0012	0.8090	1.0000
580	0.1212	0.8700	0.0010	0.6530	0.9671
590	0.0655	0.7570	0.0007	0.4786	0.8965
600	0.0332	0.6310	0.0004	0.3188	0.7967
610	0.0159	0.5030		0.1941	0.6721
620	0.0074	0.3810		0.1105	0.5314
630	0.0033	0.2650		0.0586	0.3810
640	0.0015	0.1750		0.0297	0.2571
650	0.0007	0.1070		0.0143	0.1596
660	0.0003	0.0610		0.0072	0.0916
670	0.0001	0.0320		0.0033	0.0483
680	0.00005	0.0170		0.0015	0.0258
690	0.0000	0.0082		0.0008	0.0124
700	0.0000	0.0041			0.0063

λ = wavelength in nm
V'_λ = scotopic luminosity function
V_λ = photopic luminosity function
$S_{1\lambda}$ = short-wave sensitive cone absorption spectrum
$S_{2\lambda}$ = mid-wave sensitive cone absorption spectrum
$S_{3\lambda}$ = long-wave sensitive cone absorption spectrum

The three cone spectra are tabulated as if measured at the cornea (i.e., they implicitly incorporate, as do the scotopic and photopic luminosity functions, the ocular media transmissivity). The cone spectra are from Smith and Pokorny (1975), as tabulated by Boynton and Wisowaty (1980) and are calculated from specific linear combinations of small-field color matching functions, based upon the Konig loss theory of dichromacy (see p. 120).

Two lights with spectral energy distributions $E_{1\lambda}$ and $E_{2\lambda}$ at the cornea have equal effectiveness for the ith cone class if

$$\int E_{1\lambda} S_{i\lambda} d\lambda = \int E_{2\lambda} S_{i\lambda} d\lambda$$

To convert the spectrum $S_{i\lambda}$ to a quantal basis, divide by λ: $S'_{i\lambda} = S_{i\lambda}/\lambda$. Then, lights with quantal energy distributions $Q_{1\lambda}$, $Q_{2\lambda}$ at the cornea are equivalent for the ith cone class

whenever

$$\int Q_{1\lambda} S'_{i\lambda} d\lambda = \int Q_{2\lambda} S'_{i\lambda} d\lambda$$

Because the cone spectra given in the table are (roughly) normalized, rather than absolute, their use in computing the number of quanta absorbed per cone with the formulae in Table 2.2 requires an additional multiplicative constant for each cone class. The required constant is the product of the ocular media transmissivity and the absolute absorption coefficient of the cone pigment at the cone λ_{max}: This constant is estimated to be 0.1087, 0.5559, and 0.6024, respectively for the short-wave, mid-wave and long-wave sensitive cones. The lower value of this constant for the short-wave cones is due to the lower transmissivity of the ocular media in the short wavelengths.

---

nance is $E_v = (L_v A_s A_p)/ (A_i r^2)$. The area of the retinal image, A_i, however, is inversely proportional to the square of the distance of the source: $A_i = (f_e^2 A_s)/r^2$, where f_e is the posterior nodal distance of the eye (see p. 87). Thus, we find

$$E_v = L_v A_p/f_e^2$$

This means the retinal illuminance is directly proportional to the luminance of the source and the pupil area, and inversely proportional to the square of the posterior nodal distance of the eye (essentially, the eye's radius)—but not dependent on the distance of the extended source.

IMAGE FORMATION AND OPTICAL PERFORMANCE

When the wavelength of a radiation is vanishingly small compared with the size of the device or target interacting with it, and the energy of the photon is small compared with the sensitivity of the device, rectilinear propagation obtains in homogeneous media and the approximations of Geometrical Optics (laws that can be deduced from Snell's Law and the geometry of refractive surfaces) are appropriate. However, since the dimensions of the photoreceptors of vision are comparable to the wavelengths of light, and because photoreceptors are sensitive enough to signal the absorption of single photons, both

A very valuable reference text for the material presented in this section is G. Wyszecki and W.S. Stiles's (1982) *Color Science.* There is also a great wealth of information about all aspects of quantifying and measuring visual stimuli, visual optics, and basic visual psychophysical data.

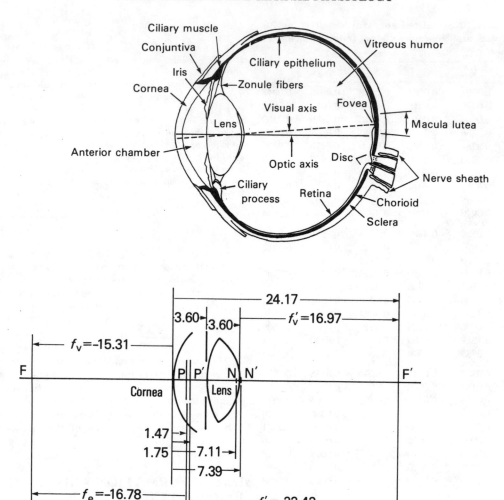

Figure 2.3. (a) Schematic diagram of coronal section of right eye emphasizing features relevant to optical performance of the eye (after Walls, 1942).

(b) The unaccomodated Gullstrand schematic eye, drawn approximately to the scale of Figure 2.3A. P and P' are the principal planes, N and N' the nodal points (p. 87). F is the anterior principal focus, F' the posterior principal focus; f_e and f_e' the anterior and posterior vertex focal lengths. All numbers indicate distances in millimeters. From "Visual Optics" by A.G. Bennett and J.L. Francis in *The Eye*, Volume 4 (p. 104) by H. Davson (ed.), 1962, New York: Academic Press. Copyright 1962 by Academic Press. Reprinted by permission.

wave and particle aspects of light play roles in the physics of vision. To the psychophysicist it is noteworthy that both the most dramatic manifestation in vision of the quantum nature of light, the response to of single photons by retinal rods (see p. 126); and the most celebrated manifestation in vision of the wave nature of light, the Stiles–Crawford effect (see p. 102), were discovered in psychophysical experiments. None-

theless, Geometrical Optics remains central and appropriate to the description of image formation by the eye.

Schematic Eye

Figure 2.3A presents a horizontal cross-section of the adult human eye, showing its principal features. From the perspective that considers

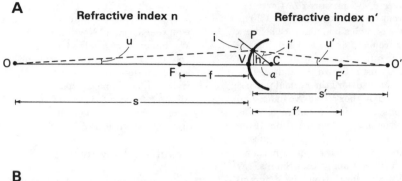

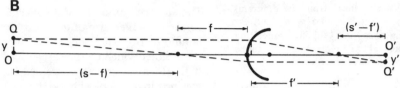

Figure 2.4. (a) Refraction at a spherical refractive surface separating media of indices n and n', drawn roughly to scale for $n = 1$, $n' = 1.33$. OO' describes an axis perpendicular to the surface, intersecting the surface at the vertex V. The center of the surface is C. P is a particular point on the surface, hit by a ray from O, at an angle of incidence i; the ray emerges at angle i'. a is the angle made by a line from C to P with the axis. F is the anterior focal point: rays emitted from the axis at this point emerge parallel from the refractive surface. F' is the posterior focal point: paraxial rays parallel to the axis striking the surface are brought to focus at F'.

(b) Imaging of an off-axis point Q by a spherical refractive surface. Q' is the image point. The various distance relations are described in the text.

the eye as an optical system, its key components are the cornea and lens, along with the fluid-filled chambers that support the former and house the latter. The optical significance of the cornea and lens is that they constitute the *refracting* or light-bending boundaries which enable the eye to focus an image on the light-sensitive cells of the retina.

For the understanding of the optical performance of the eye and for the routine treatment of optical defects, it is of great utility to have a model or "schematic eye" that represents the essential optical features from the perspective of Geometrical Optics. The researchers of Helmholtz and others in the 19th century culminated in Gullstrand's schematic eye, shown in Figure 2.3B, for which the latter received the Nobel prize in 1911. In the next two sections we will present an elementary introduction to the Geometrical Optics analysis of the eye. Detailed treatment can be found in a number of sources, for example in the thorough chapters by Bennett and Francis in Vol. IV of **The Eye**, edited by Davson, or the excellent reference work, **Color Science**, by Wyszecki and Stiles (1982).

Refraction at a Spherical Surface

When a plane wave[3] of light reaches a planar boundary between two transparent media of refractive indices n and n', the speed of propagation of the wave is altered according to the reaction $v = c/n$, $v' = c/n'$, where c is the velocity of propagation in a vacuum, and v, v' are the velocities in the regions with refractive indices n and n', respectively. Assuming that the plane wave remains a plane wave upon passing to the second medium, one may readily deduce Snell's Law,

$$n \times \sin(i) = n' \times \sin(i'), \qquad (2.8)$$

where the angles i and i' are measured from the normal to the surface. Note that a ray, which is an idealized line perpendicular to the wavefront, is refracted toward the normal to the surface in passing from a region of a lower to one of higher refractive index.

Consider media of refractive indices n and n', where $n' > n$, separated by a spherical boundary as shown in Figure 2.4A; in this figure

---

[3]For a *plane wave*, all the surfaces for which a propagating disturbance have constant phase are planes, each perpendicular to the propagation direction.

the distances are to be measured in Cartesian coordinates from the boundary vertex V. The idealized cornea is such a boundary. Consider a ray emanating from a point O and striking the surface at P. The tangent plane at the point P is normal to the radius, r, drawn through P. This ray will be refracted toward the normal in passing to the region of higher refractive index, and cross the axis at some point, O', and required by the spherical symmetry of the situation. If the three angles, u, u', and a are small enough that the 1st term in Taylor series approximations, $\sin(x) = x$, $\tan(x) = x$ apply, then Snell's Law becomes $ni = n'i'$, where (from the diagram) we see that $i = a + u$, and $i' = a - u'$. By writing the angles as their tangents, cancelling the common factor h, and rearranging the terms in Snell's Law, we have the formula

$$\frac{n'}{s'} + \frac{n}{s} = \frac{(n' - n)}{r} \qquad (2.9)$$

In this formula s is positive when it lies to the left of the vertex V of the curved surface, and s' is positive when it lies to the right of V. The value of h plays no role in the region for which the approximations are valid, so the same relation holds for any ray from O striking any point on the surface within some critical range of h. The region for which the rays are close to the optic axis and for which the 1st term Taylor series approximations are valid is known as the *paraxial* or *Gaussian* region (Gauss was the first to apply these approximations systematically). Thus, the formula shows that for any point on the left-hand axis there corresponds a unique point on the right-hand axis. By letting $s \to \infty$, one obtains a special value, $s' = f'$, the back focal length. Similarly, by letting $s' \to \infty$, one obtains a special value $s = f$, the first focal length of the refractive surface.

Consider now a point Q which lies a vertical distance y off the optic axis but in the paraxial region (Figure 2.4B). If we were to draw a line through C from Q we would simply have a second axis, and thus any family of rays emanating from Q and striking the surface will converge at a point Q', and in general any point in the left-hand space will have one *conjugate point* in the right-hand space. In the paraxial region if OQ is perpendicular to the axis, the image $O'Q'$ will also be perpendicular to the axis. To obtain the Q' coordinate we find the magnification ratio, y'/y. By similar triangles $y/f' = y'/(s' - f')$, and $y'/f = y/(s - f)$. Thus, the magnification ratio is

$$y'/y = f/(s - f)$$
$$= (s' - f')/f' \qquad (2.10)$$

Defining the "reduced" distances $x = s - f$, $x' = s' - f'$ (see Figure 2.3B), we also have equation from 2.10 Newton's formula, $xx' = ff'$. We have thus specified for each point with coordinates (s, y) in the left-hand or "object" space a unique set of coordinates (s', y') in the right-hand or "image" space. (Radial symmetry allows neglect of the third coordinate, but in practice one must be quite careful about the signs of the various quantities.)

Refracting Power

The *surface power*, F, of a spherical refracting surface is a measure of its ability to converge a bundle of rays: it is defined to be the index of refraction divided by the respective focal length. If the focal length is expressed in meters, the power is in *diopters*, abbreviated D. For a spherical surface separating transparent media of refractive indices n, n' as in Figure 2.4, the refracting power is given by (see equation 2.9)

$$F = (n'/f') = (n' - n)/r \qquad (2.11)$$

With this formula one can readily compute the power of the various refracting surfaces of the eye. These are given in Table 2.5. Perhaps the most notable fact is that most of the refractive power of the eye is contributed by the anterior surface of the cornea, a feature that results from the relatively large difference between the indices of refraction of air and the cornea. It should be kept in mind, however, that it is by approximation that one treats the refractive surfaces as spherical, coaxial, and isotropic.

The total power of a "thin" lens may be computed by summing the powers of its first and second surfaces. For example, application of equation 2.11 gives a power of $7.7\,D$ for the anterior surface of the crystalline lens and $12.8\,D$ for the posterior surface (unaccommodated eye), as shown in Table 2.5. (Note that the curvature of the posterior surface is negative.) The total power of the lens, $20.3\,D$, is approximately the sum of the two surface powers. The eye as a whole cannot be treated accurately as a combination of thin lenses in close contact, but its total power is approximately the sum of the powers of its component refracting surfaces. Exact formulae for computing the total power of the eye are derived in most optical texts. The concept of optical power plays a key role in the routine characterization and correction of optical defects.

Table 2.5. Gullstrand schematic eye no. 2 parameters

	Unaccommodated	Accommodated 8.62 D
Radii of curvature		
Cornea	$r_1 = 7.80\,\text{mm}$	$7.80\,\text{mm}$
Lens		
anterior	$r_2 = 10.00\,\text{mm}$	$5.00\,\text{mm}$
posterior	$r_3 = -6.00\,\text{mm}$	$-5.00\,\text{mm}$
Refractive indices		
Air	$n_1 = 1.000$	
Aqueous	$n_2 = 1.336$	
Lens	$n_3 = 1.413$	
Vitreous	$n_4 = 1.336$	
Surface powers		
Cornea	$F_1 = 43.08\ \text{Diopters}$	$43.08\,D$
Lens		
anterior	$F_2 = 7.70\,D$	$15.40\,D$
posterior	$F_3 = 12.83\,D$	$15.40\,D$
Equivalent powers		
Lens	$20.28\,D$	$30.13\,D$
Eye as whole	$59.60\,D$	$68.22\,D$

Reduced Schematic Eye

In the paraxial region (see p. 86, Figure 2.3) of a spherical refractive surface, a planar region perpendicular to the optical axis in the object space is imaged as a planar region in the image space. This general property of ideal paraxial optics forms the basis of reducing any combination of coaxial, spherical refractive surfaces to a single "equivalent lens," providing one measures the distances in the object and image spaces from the *principal planes* (see Figure 2.3B). These planes have the defining property that objects in the first are imaged with unit magnification in the second. The first and second focal points of the reduced system are defined in the same way as for the single refracting surface: they are the positions to which rays entering on one side parallel to the axis converge on the other. Using only these abstract properties of the principal planes, one may derive (e.g., Longhurst, 1967) Newton's formula, $xx' = ff'$, which applies exactly in the reduced system when the distances x and x' are measured from the principal planes. The two conjugate axial points N and N' that have the property that a ray through N is conjugate to a parallel ray through N' are called the *nodal points*; these play a central role in the paraxial theory of complex optical systems.

A number of attempts have been made to construct an equivalent optical system for the eye. In the case of Gullstrand's schematic eye, Figure 2.3B, as in all other schematic eyes, the principal planes come out within a fraction of a millimeter of one another (Westheimer, 1972). Coalescing them into a single plane allows formal representation of the eye's optics as a single equivalent spherical refractive surface of radius 5.55 mm separating air from a medium of refractive index 4/3. This representation of the eye's dioptrics is known as a *reduced eye*. Applying equation 2.11, one obtains a refractive power of 60 D; applying equation 2.9 for an object at $s = \infty$, one finds that the image plane, the retina, lies 22.2 mm behind the surface vertex, or 16.7 mm behind the center of the surface. A ray striking the eye normal to this fictitious surface passes undeviated to the retina. The value 16.7 mm is thus worth remembering, for with it one can readily compute the retinal size of any target at optical infinity, simply by knowing the angle that the target subtends at the eye. For example, a basketball (dia. c. 9 inches) at 100 yds. has a retinal image of $(0.25/100) \times 16.7 = 0.042\,\text{mm}$. For analysis of the imaging of objects not at optical infinity a schematic eye can still be derived, but one must include the effects of accommodation, considered in the next section, on the components.

Accommodation

The human eye has the ability to change its focal length by virtue of the elasticity of the biconvex crystalline lens; this change is called accommodation. If, for an unaccommodated eye, the image of an infinitely distant object falls on the retina, the eye is called *emmetropic*; for such an eye the retina is in the back focal plane. When the eye accommodates to bring into focus a near object, the lens power increases, mainly by a decrease in the radius of curvature of the anterior surface from about 10 mm to a minimum of 5 mm. Table 2.5 includes the optical properties of an eye accommodated 8.62 D. For such an eye the plane conjugate with the retina is 12 cm from the first principal plane. This may be deduced by assuming that the distance from the nodal point to the retina is the same for the reduced eye, in both accommodated and unaccommodated states, and applying of equations 2.9 and 2.11 with $F = 59.6$ and $F = 68.2 D$.

Optical Defects

For the emmetropic eye, objects at optical infinity are in focus on the retina, and accommodation allows near objects to be brought into focus. For the *myopic* eye, however, the image of a distant object is formed in front of the retina, and there is a finite *far point*, beyond which objects cannot be imaged clearly. Myopia typically arises from elongation of the eye, but may also derive from increased curvature of the cornea, or even from change in refractive indicates that result in increased power in the unaccommodated eye. The myopic eye is called nearsighted since only near objects can be brought into focus, and the *near point*, the closest distance at which objects can be imaged clearly, lies closer than the normal near point distance, which may be taken to be 12 cm for the standard eye accommodated 8.6 D. A lens with negative curvature placed in front of the eye diverges incoming parallel rays from a distant object, giving a virtual image that lies at or nearer than the eye's far point. The dioptric powers of the spectacle lens and the eye approximately sum, so the appropriate negative lens is one which cancels the excess power of the unaccommodated myopic eye—i.e., one whose power in diopters is the negative of the power of a lens whose focal length is the distance from the myopic eye to its far point.

The *hyperopic* (or hypermetropic) eye is characterized by a defect in dioptric power. Distant objects cannot be brought into focus by the unaccommodated eye, for their focal plane lies behind the retina. The near point of the fully accommodated hyperopic eye lies farther away than that of the emmetropic eye. The appropriate correction for the hyperopic eye is a positive lens, which increases its power in the unaccommodated state, such that infinitely distant objects are in focus, without accommodation.

A third common optical defect of the eye is *astigmatism*. This condition typically results from a cornea that is not spherically symmetric. In the simplest case the eye will have two distinct axes perpendicular to the line of sight, such that objects at a given distance along one or the other axis can be brought simultaneously into focus, but not objects along both axes. The correction for this condition is an oriented cylindrical lens, which makes the optical power along the two axes equal. Such cylindrical correction can be combined with a spherical lens to correct concomitant myopia or hyperopia. For more complexity irregular corneal distortions, no general spectacle correction is possible, but with a contact lens contoured on the inner surface to match the distortion, almost any condition could, in principle, be corrected.

The condition known as *presbyopia* results from the gradual loss of elasticity in the crystalline lens of the aging eye; the ability to accommodate is gradually impaired and ultimately lost, at a rate of about 0.3 diopters per year, beginning at age 15 or earlier (Westheimer, 1972).

Another optical defect of the eye which is of interest is *chromatic aberration*, which results from the fact that no single refractive material can simultaneously refract all wavelengths of light to the same degree. Over the range of 400 to 700 nm there is a discrepancy of about 2 D on the optical axis with the short wavelengths being refracted more strongly than the long (Bedford & Wyszecki, 1957).

Pupil System

Consider a point source imaged on the retina—e.g., an emmetropic eye viewing a star. The pupil will obviously limit the bundle of rays from the star that will enter the eye. The total flux entering the eye from the point source will be proportional to the size of the pupil, and thus, to a first aproximation the irradiance at the retinal image will be proportional to the pupil area. When fully dark adapted, the adult pupil has a diameter of about 6 to 7 mm, and under bright illumination can constrict to about 2.5 mm, giving about a seven-fold range of intensity control. Light and dark adapation, however, occur over a far greater range (6 or more decades), and pupillary size control can account for only a minor part.

Actually, the physical pupil size does not determine the bundle of rays that enters the eye, but rather, the *entrance pupil* which is the virtual image of the real pupil formed by the cornea in object space and is about 13% larger than the real pupil. The image of the pupil formed by the lens is known as the *exit pupil*. All rays forming part of the retinal image pass through the exit pupil. The ray which passes through the center of the exit pupil is called the *chief ray*; it is the central ray of the Gaussian or geometrical image, regardless of whether or not the image is in focus. The angle at the exit pupil made by the chief rays of two points in object space is essentially invariant over accommodation states, and thus uniquely specifies the angular separation between the central point of the images of two point sources. Because the angle that the chief ray makes with the entrance pupil is uniquely related to the angle it makes with the exit pupil, the preferred method of specifying an object's position in object space is its angular position relative to the center of the entrance pupil (Westheimer, 1972).

Optical Performance: Resolution and Modulation Transfer

The task of an image-forming optical system is to represent in the image plane the distribution of luminance in the front focal or object plane of the system. The actual performance of an optical system in this task cannot be readily characterized within the framework of Geometrical Optics. We now consider two characterizations of the optical performance of an imaging system, resolution and modulation transfer, and discuss how these characterizations can be made within the framework called Fourier Optics.

Diffraction Limitation on Resolution Imposed by Finite Pupil Size

What is the minimal angular separation between two stars that the unaccommodated emmetropic eye can resolve? In Geometric Optics a ray is an infinitesimal, so from this standpoint, one might expect two distinct points in object space, no matter how close together, to be imaged at separate points in the image space. In reality, both the wave and the quantum nature of light limit the resolving power of any optical instrument, including the eye. For now we shall concentrate on the former limitation, and put off the discussion of quantum fluctuations for a subsequent section.

A basic formula for characterizing the angular resolving power, $(\Delta\theta)_{min}$, of an optical device forming images of "infinitely" distant objects—a telescope, as well as an eye—is

$$(\Delta\theta)_{min} = 1.22 \, \lambda/D \qquad (2.12)$$

where $(\Delta\theta)$ is in radian angular measure, D, is the diameter of the entrance pupil of the device and λ the wavelength of the light. Thus, for the human eye with a pupil diameter of 2 mm and a wavelength of 550 nm, the predicted resolution is $(1.22 \times 550 \times 10^{-9} \text{m})/(2 \times 10^{-3} \text{m}) = 3.4 \times 10^{-4}$ radians, or equivalently, 1.2 minutes of arc. This is about one inch at a distance of 100 yds, or put in terms of the distance on the retina (see p. 87), it is $3.4 \times 10^{-4} \times 16.7 \text{mm} = 5.7 \, \mu\text{m}$. For magnitude comparison, we note that the center-to-center spacing between the finest foveal receptors is about $3 \, \mu\text{m}$; the significance of this spacing is discussed further on p. 97.

The resolution limitation expressed in equation 2.12 is derived from two physical principles. The first, the principle of superposition of electric fields, states that the field induced by a collection of oscillators at a given point is the vectorial sum of the fields induced by the individual oscillators. The second is that the power transmitted by an electromagnetic wave per unit area is proportional to the square of the amplitude of the electric field. The electromagnetic field induced at the retina by a distant point source (assuming an emmetropic eye) is equivalent to the superposition of the electric fields induced by a uniform distribution of linear electron

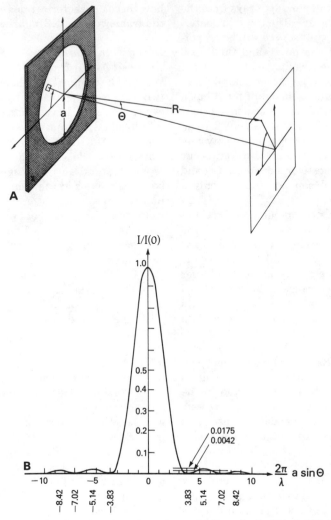

Figure 2.5. (a) Geometry in the situation that gives rise to the Fraunhofer "far-field" diffraction pattern for a circular aperture. Light from a distant point source (not shown) passes through a circular aperture and is imaged at a great distance from the aperture on a plane parallel to the planar aperture. (By using a focusing lens, the image plane can be brought closer without altering the pattern.) a is the radius of the aperture. θ is the angle made between the ray emerging from the center of the aperture and striking the image plane perpendicularly, and a ray from the center of the aperture to an arbitrary point on the image plane.

(b) Intensity distribution of the radially symmetric Fraunhofer far-field diffraction pattern for circular aperture with radius a (diameter $D = 2a$). The central maximum is shown as the Airy disk. For small angles $\sin \theta = \theta$, and so at the first minimum $\theta = (3.83\,\lambda)/(2\pi a) = 1.22\,(\lambda/D)$, giving equation (2.12) of the text. From Eugene Hecht and Alfred Zajac, OPTICS, © 1974, Addison-Wesley, Reading, Massachusetts, pg. 352, Fig. 10.28. Reprinted with permission.

oscillators across the pupil aperture. The mathematical combination of these electric fields requires detailed consideration of the phases of the fields induced by each oscillator at each retinal point, and the resultant field, by definition, produces a *diffraction pattern* of intensity. For a circular aperture (Figure 2.5A) such as the pupil of the eye and coherent illumination of the aperture, the diffraction pattern has the form whose radial cross-section is given in Figure 2.5B. The region of the central peak of this distribution is known as the Airy disk, in

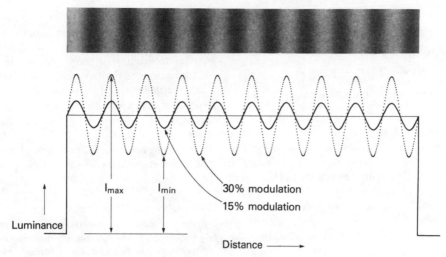

Figure 2.6. (a) One-dimensional sinusoidal luminance profile; contrast c. 30%.

(b) Definition of contrast or fraction modulation: $m = (I_{max} - I_{min})/(I_{max} + I_{min})$. Two levels of modulation are shown, 0.30 and 0.15. The arrows indicate the maximum and minimum luminance of the wave with 30% contrast; the straight line represents the mean luminance. The abscissa represents a space or time coordinate.

honor of George Biddel Airy, the British astronomer who first derived the distribution. (A derivation of this, the Fraunhofer far-field diffraction pattern for a circular aperture, can be found in most optics texts, such as in Hecht & Zajac, 1974.) By **Rayleigh's criterion** two Airy disks are said to be *resolved* when the center of one disk falls on the first minimum of the second; for monochromatic light, the first minimum of an Airy disk is at $\Delta\theta = 1.22 \, \lambda/D$. Thus we arrive at equation 2.12. Although Rayleigh's criterion of resolution is useful by virtue of being specific and memorable, it is also arbitrary, and cannot be thought of as constituting an absolute limit or "threshold" for angular resolution.

Whereas there is an arbitrariness in characterizing the resolving power of an optical device, characterization of the ability of an optical system to transmit *contrast* or *depth of modulation* is not at all arbitrary. Figure 2.6 shows what is meant by contrast. If an optical system had perfect contrast transfer, all modulation in the object plane would be faithfully represented in the image plane. In fact, images are always degraded to some degree; this degradation results both from diffraction effects due to a finite pupil (the image of any point in object space is necessarily smeared—Figure 2.5) and from imperfections in the optics (such as chromatic and

spherical abberations). When the modulation in the object plane is sinusoidal, the ratio of the contrast of the image to the contrast of the object is known as the **modulation transfer function** (e.g., Westheimer, 1960). This function provides a truly rigorous characterization of the performance of an optical system under any specified conditions. It is interesting to note in this context, that D/λ (in cycles/radian where D is pupil diameter and λ is wavelength) constitutes an absolute upper limit on the highest spatial frequency that can be transmitted by a diffraction-limited system with a circular aperture (Linfoot, 1964): Above this cutoff frequency, even 100 percent modulation in the object produces no modulation in the image. Thus, for a 2 mm pupil, the highest spatial frequency transmitted by the eye is 63 cycles/degree. We now give a somewhat expanded treatment of the ideas just presented.

Fourier Optics

Fourier Optics is a term used to describe the application of Fourier analysis, or more generally, linear systems analysis to optical problems (e.g., Linfoot, 1964). In vision, Fourier Optics offers an elegant way of giving a unified operational treatment to all the factors that contribute to the spreading of light in the image plane.

A *linear system* is a function, L, on a space that satisfies two properties:

(i) $L(aI) = aL(I)$ (scaling)   (2.13a)

(ii) $L(I_1 + I_2) = L(I_1) + L(I_2)$

                  (superposition)   (2.13b)

For present purposes (incoherent source) I refers to the intensity distribution in the object plane and $L(I)$ is the intensity distribution in the image plane. The optical system is *space invariant* or *isoplanatic* if moving the object in the object plane alters only the position of the image in the image plane, but does not change its intensity distribution.

Although all optical systems, including the eye, obey the superposition principle, equation 2.13a and b over the range of intensities achievable with most incoherent sources, in general such systems are not space invariant except for a modest angular extent about the center of the entrance pupil. In the isoplanatic region, however, the system is completely characterized by its **point-spread function**, the image it forms in the image plane of a point source of light in the object plane. The centrality of the point-spread function arises because an arbitrary distribution can be considered (and mathematically represented) as the superposition of point sources. Close in significance to the point-spread function is the **line-spread function**, the image formed by the system of an infinitesimally thin luminous line in the object plane. One-dimensional object distributions can be represented as the superposition of line sources, so knowledge of the line-spread function allows computation of the image of an arbitrary source intensity distribution that varies only in one-dimension.

If an optical system has the same line-spread function for lines of any orientation, it is said to be *isotropic*. An astigmatic system is anisotropic. An isotropic system has a circularly symmetric point spread function, and the point-spread and line-spread functions are equivalent, in that either can be derived from the other.

In addition to the point-spread and line-spread functions, the concept of the **optical modulation transfer function** plays a fundamental role in Fourier optics. A fundamental property of any linear system is that the output to a pure sine wave input is a pure sine wave, with possible differential attenuation of amplitude and differential shift in phase across frequencies. The optical modulation transfer function describes the amplitude attenuation as a function of the spatial frequency of the input. If the system is isoplanatic and isotropic, the optical modulation transfer function is the Fourier (cosine) transformation of the line-spread function. In the optical sections below we sketch the relationship among they key concepts of Fourier Optics, and review results from applying them to the characterization of the optical performance of the human eye.

POINT-SPREAD FUNCTION

As discussed previously (p. 89), the preferred coordinates to employ in describing visual imagery are the angular subtenses, measured from the centers of the entrance and exit pupil, respectively. Following Westheimer (1972), we label the object coordinates (a, b), $-\pi < a, b < +\pi$. Although there is a small angular magnification difference between entrance and exit pupil coordinates, we make the two sets of coordinates comparable by the following device. "Reinvert" the image by the rigid transformation that maps every point in image space back onto its Gaussian or geometric conjugate point in object space: in effect, mathematically "project" the retinal image back onto the object plane.

Of fundamental significance to the characterization of any invariant linear system is the **impulse response function**, the output or response of the system to the Dirac δ-function:

$$j(a, b) = L[\delta(a, b)] \quad \delta(a, b) = 1, \quad a = b = 0$$

$$\delta(a, b) = 0, \quad \text{otherwise}$$

$$(2.14)$$

In an optical system the impulse response is called the point-spread function. Figure 2.7 shows an idealization of the point-spread function for an optical system with a circular aperture. In an ideal or diffraction-limited optical system (no significant aberrations) with a circular pupil, the point-spread functions is that given in Figure 2.5B. Note that the point-spread function, when expressed in these coordinates, is independent of all parameters of the optical system (e.g., focal length), except the pupil aperture and the wavelength of light. Its great utility is that it characterizes the isoplanatic optical system even when the optics are not aberration-free. Intuitively, every intensity distribution $I_o(a, b)$ in object space can be thought of as composed of the linear superposition of δ-functions,

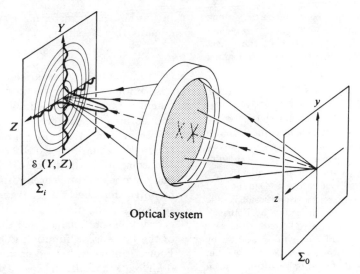

Figure 2.7. Diagram of the point-spread function of an optical system. Σ_o is the source plane, with point source centered at the origin. Σ_i is the image plane, showing the electric field amplitude distribution (for coherent source) or intensity distribution (for coherent source). In the text the point-spread function is represented in terms of angular coordinates measured from the centers of the entrance and exit pupils of the optical systems. From Eugene Hecht and Alfred Zajac, OPTICS, © 1974, Addison-Wesley, Reading, Massachusetts, p. 350, Fig. 10.26, Reprinted by permission.

represented as an integral of these functions over object space:

$$I_o(a, b) = \iint I_o(a', b')$$
$$\times \ \delta(a' - a, b' - b) \ da'db' \quad (2.15)$$

If one knows how the optical system responds to the δ-function, then by virtue of linearity, one can compute its response, I_i, to an arbitrary light distribution, I_o, by integrating its responses to the elementary components:

$$I_i(a, b) = L[I_o(a, b)]$$
$$= \iint I_o(a', b')j(a' - a, b' - b) \ da'db'$$
$$(2.16a)$$

The operation implicit in equation 2.16 in which the image intensity at (a, b) is computed as the sum of the intensities $I_o(a', b')$ at every point (a', b') in object space, weighted by the point spread value $j(a' - a, b' - b)$, is known as a *convolution* and is often written in the short-hand notation:

$$I_i = I_o * j \quad (2.16b)$$

A fundamental property of a linear system which plays an important role in visual optics can be obtained by taking the Fourier transform of both sides of equation 2.16. By letting

(ω_a, ω_b) be the transform coordinates (these coordinates have units of cycles/deg), one finds

$$F_i(\omega_a, \omega_b) = F_o(\omega_a, \omega_b) \times F_j(\omega_a, \omega_b) \quad (2.17)$$

In words, *the Fourier transform of the image is the transform of the object multiplied by the transform of the point-spread function.* It should be kept in mind that F_i, F_o, F_j are, in the general case of an arbitrary linear system, complex numbers. However, if the function j is an even function of each coordinate, then F_j is a purely real-valued function. This condition will certainly hold if the point-spread junction j is radially symmetric. In the following sections we will see the utility of these relations.

LINE-SPREAD FUNCTION. If the object intensity distribution is a luminous line, e.g.,

$$I_l(a, b) = 1, a = 0$$

$$0, \text{otherwise}$$

then the image distribution is the convolution of I_l with the point-spread function, and is called the line-spread function L:

$$L = I_l * j \quad (2.18)$$

If the point-spread function is radially symmetric, then there is a unique line-spread function, and either of the two functions may be derived from the other (Clark-Jones, 1958; Gubisch, 1967; Linfoot, 1964; Marchand, 1965). If the intensity distribution I_o in object space varies only along the one coordinate, then the image intensity distribution is the convolution of the object distribution with the line-spread function along that coordinate, i.e.,

$$I_i = L * I_o \qquad (2.19)$$

The significance of this fact is both theoretical and empirical. Theoretically, any linear system must transform sine waves into sine waves: The amplitude and phase, however, of the output sine wave may vary with the frequency. For an isotropic optical system, the line-spread is an even function, and therefore, transmission results in no phase shifts. Furthermore, by Fourier's Theorem, any function may be expressed as a linear combination of sine waves, and so by knowing the response to sine waves we can predict the image distribution resulting from an arbitrary object intensity distribution. Empirically, one-dimensional sine wave distributions are relatively easy to generate with CRT displays.[4]

Physical Measurement of the Line-Spread Function

Flamant (1955) developed a method for objectively measuring the line-spread function. She imaged a thin, luminous line on the retina. A small amount of light is reflected back by the fundus of the eye, and since the retina was conjugate with the line source in the optical system, the eye's optics reimaged the retinal image back at the source. By arranging a beam-splitter in front of the eye, the reflected image could be cast upon a photographic plate. Assuming that the fundus acts as a perfect diffuser, and that the forward and reverse traverses through the eye's optics are equivalent, the observed image is the convolution (see equation 2.19) of the source image twice, with the line-spread function, L:

$$I_i = L * L * I_l \qquad (2.20)$$

In the Fourier transform, or spatial frequency domain, this is simply,

$$F_i = F_L^2 \qquad (2.20')$$

(A scalar factor that arises from the media absorption losses and the fundal reflection coefficient has been omitted.) Thus, the Fourier transform of the observed image is the square of the transform of the line-spread function. By taking the square root of the image transform, and computing the inverse Fourier transform one obtains the line-spread function. It should be noted that the Fourier transform of the line source is unity (it is a δ-function in the one coordinate that varies), and that the symmetry of the line-spread function guarantees that its Fourier transform has no imaginary components —all frequencies are in "cosine phase." Flamant's technique was used by Campbell and Gubisch (1966), Krauskopf (1962), and by Westheimer and Campbell (1962), employing a photomultiplier behind a slit rather than a photographic plate for analysis of the reflected image. Campbell and Gubisch (1966) have performed the most exhaustive measurements with the technique, and also demonstrated that the fundus acts as a diffuse reflector. Figure 2.8 shows the average line-spread functions they obtained for various pupil sizes. Also, shown as dotted lines, the line-spread functions were calculated for an ideal achromatic diffraction-limited optical system with the same pupil sizes. The deviations from ideality, most notable at the larger pupil diameters, presumably result from optical aberrations, and from light-scatter within the eye.

Optical Modulation Transfer Function and Contrast Sensitivity Function

As noted above, a light distribution can be characterized in terms of its local *contrast*. In essence, this is the deviation of the intensity of each point of the image from the spatial mean intensity. Figure 2.6 shows how contrast is defined, in the simple case of a spatial intensity distribution that varies sinusoidally in one coordinate. The equation for such an intensity distribution can be written

$$I_o(a) = \bar{I}_o[1 + m \cos(\omega a)] \qquad (2.21)$$

Here the units of ω are cycles/deg, and a is in degrees and m is the contrast or *depth of modulation* from the mean level $\bar{I}_0$. A fundamental

---

[4]There are numerous introductory treatments of Fourier analysis and Linear Systems Theory, for example, *Introduction to Linear Systems Analysis* by R.G. Brown and J.W. Nilsson, or *Linear Systems* by R.J. Schwarz and B. Friedland. F. Hecht and A. Zajac's text *Optics* provides an excellent introductory treatment of Fourier optics (as well as geometrical optics). Westheimer's (1972) chapters in *The Handbook of Sensory Physiology* give a very good Fourier optics treatment of the human eye.

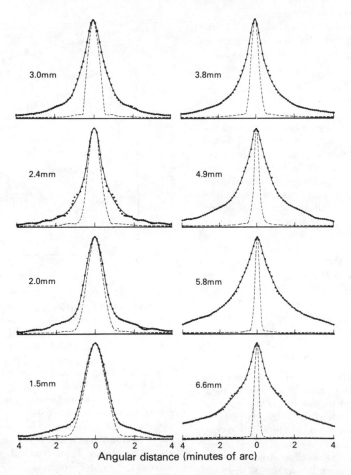

Figure 2.8. Average line-spread functions (points) of the human eye for various pupil diameters obtained by Campbell and Gubisch (1966) with Flamant's fundus reflection technique (equations 2.20, 2.21) using a broadband white light. The dotted lines represent the theoretical line-spread functions for a diffraction limited optical system with the same pupil size under the same viewing conditions (incoherent white light). The narrowest line-spread functions occur with pupils of about 2 to 2.5 mm. Below 2 mm diffraction causes spread; above 2.5 mm various optical aberrations cause the line-spread to deviate greatly from diffraction-limited ideality. From "Optical Quality of the Human Eye" by F.W. Campbell and R.W. Gubisch, 1966, *Journal of Physiology, 186*, p. 571. Copyright 1966 by The Physiological Society. Reprinted by permission.

property of a linear system is that the output to a sinusoidal input is a sinusoidal output. The system may, however, alter the relative amplitudes and phases of sine waves of different frequencies. For a linear optical system with a symmetric line-spread function, however, the phase term is always zero. Thus, the image on the retina of the sinusoidal distribution given in equation 2.21 is

$$I_i(a) = \bar{I}_i[1 + m'(\omega) \cos(\omega a)] \quad (2.22)$$

(For convenience we may consider the steady or dc component $\bar{I}_i$ of equation 2.22 to be the same

at that of 2.21, although a transmission scale factor is omitted.) By definition, the ratio of the image contrast to the physical contrast is the modulation transfer function: $t(\omega) = m'(\omega)/m$. Now, I_i must also be the convolution of I_o with the line-spread function:

$$I_i = L * I_o \quad (2.23)$$

By taking the Fourier transform of both sides of equation 2.23 after substituting in the formulae in equations 2.21 and 2.22, one can verify the important fact that *the modulation transfer function is the Fourier transform of the line-spread function.* (The more general theorem in linear systems analysis is that the modulation transfer function is the modulus of the Fourier transform of the impulse response function.)

LeGrand (1937) pointed out that two coherent sources, imaged near the nodal point of the eye (see Figure 2.4), would form interference fringes on the retina, in the manner of the classic double-slit experiment of Thomas Young. (See, e.g., Hecht & Zajac, 1974, p. 275). Such interference fringes have a sinusoidal distribution across the retina, and a contrast independent of the dioptric apparatus of the eye. Suppose two such monochromatic, coherent sources are separated by a lateral distance d, and let α be the angle that a ray arriving at a given point on the retina (originating midway between the sources) makes with the optic axis. The resultant electric field at a given point on the retina arrives from the more distant source with an approximate phase lag (in radians) $\Delta\varphi$, where

$$\Delta\varphi = [2\pi d \sin \alpha]/\lambda$$

$$= [2\pi d\alpha]/\lambda$$

and the latter approximation holds for small α (α is in units of radians). If the electric field intensity at the retina due to the two sources (considered in isolation) is I_1 and I_2, respectively, then the field intensity across the retina in the neighborhood of the optical axis is given, according to the principle of superposition and the square law relation between field strength and intensity, by

$$I(\alpha) = I_1 + I_2 + 2\sqrt{I_1 I_2} \cos [2\pi d\alpha/\lambda]$$

$$= 2I [1 + \cos (2\pi d\alpha/\lambda)], \quad I_1 = I_2$$

$$(2.24)$$

To vary the spatial frequency of the fringes, the inter-source distance d is varied. Byram (1944a, 1944b) describes some fascinating experiments with the technique in a prescient analysis of visual acuity.

Westheimer (1959) realized that the optical modulation transfer function could be measured with the interference fringe technique with the observer serving as a null detector. First, by diluting the fringes with noncoherent light (taking care to keep the mean illuminance constant), one measures the threshold contrast at each spatial frequency. The resultant **contrast sensitivity function** does not depend on the eye's dioptrics. Second, one measures the contrast sensitivity function with normal viewing

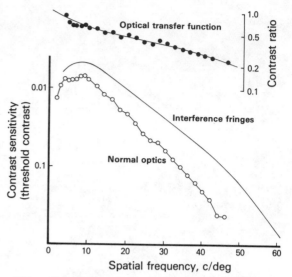

Figure 2.9. Psychophysical estimation of the optical modulation transfer function. The middle curve (no points) represents the foveal spatial modulation threshold function (contrast sensitivity function) for interference fringes generated on the retina with a helium neon laser, and demodulated with incoherent light. The lower curve (open symbols) is the spatial modulation threshold function for normal viewing of sinusoidally modulated gratings with 2 mm pupil. The upper curve (solid symbols) is the logarithmic difference of the two lower curves, and is an estimate of the demodulation caused by the eye's optics at each spatial frequency. From "Optical and Retinal Factors Affecting Visual Resolution" by F.W. Campbell and D.G. Green, 1965, *Journal of Physiology*, *181*, p. 586. Copyright 1965 by The Physiological Society. Reprinted by permission.

(the sinusoidal spatial distributions can be produced, for example, with a suitable oscilloscope). Third, at each frequency one finds the ratio of the two contrast sensitivity functions; this ratio must be the factor by which the eye's dioptrics demodulates the sine wave. The availability of lasers, which produce very pure coherent light, has made this technique quite feasible, and many clinical applications, such as characterizing the retinal performance of eyes with optical defects, have appeared.

Campbell and Green (1965) performed an extensive series of measurements with this combination technique. Figure 2.9 gives some of their results for one observer. The deduced optical transfer function, which is the ratio of the two contrast sensitivity functions, attenuates higher spatial frequencies considerably less than the optical transfer function deduced with the best data collected with Flamant's technique. The discrepancies between the two techniques are thought to be due to the chromatic aberration and to the intraocular scatter that occur in the purely physical measurements, but play no differential role in the psychophysical experiments (Campbell & Gubisch, 1966). In this context, we note that the Stiles–Crawford effect (see p. 102) will reduce the effectiveness of scattered light that hits the cones off-axis. It is important to emphasize that the measurements of the modulation transfer and line-spread functions that we have been discussing are only valid in the immediate vicinity of the visual axis. Analysis of the eye's off-axis performance has been carried out by Jennings and Charman, (1981).

PHOTORECEPTION

The Photoreceptor Cells: Rods and Cones

Figure 2.10 (left panel) is a schematic diagram of the retina derived by Dowling and Boycott (1966) from their electron micrographic studies of the rhesus monkey and the human, showing the cell types and synaptic connectivity they found. Figure 2.10 (right panel) shows a radial section of human peripheral (i.e., non-foveal) retina, with identification of the major regions of the retina and its landmarks. Note, for example, in the inner segment layer the five, large, darkly stained cell bodies. These are the inner segments of five cones.

The output segment layer is composed of the rod and cone photoreceptor outer segments containing the visual pigment and biochemical machinery that *transduces* light energy into electrical signals. Signals from the receptors are relayed synaptically to bipolar cells, and from the bipolars (again synaptically) to the ganglion cells, whose axons exit the eye in the optic nerve. Horizontal and amacrine cells, in the outer and inner plexiform layers, respectively, modify the transmission of information between photoreceptors and bipolars, and between bipolars and ganglion cells.

Spatial Sampling by the Retinal Mosaic

The adult human retina comprises about 125 million rod and 6.4 million cone photoreceptors (Osterberg, 1935), whose distribution is far from uniform. When the normal observer *fixates* a target, the image is centered on a small, highly specialized region of the retina known as the *fovea*. Figure 2.11 shows a diagram of this area of the retina. The neurons of the inner retina connecting with the foveal receptors are displaced laterally, forming a depression whose widest extent is about 5 deg visual angle (1500 μm) in diameter. (Recall that for a posterior nodal distance of 16.7 mm, 1 deg of visual angle corresponds to 290 μm on the retina.) The central 1 deg and possibly even 2 deg of the fovea is rod free, as judged by anatomical (Polyak, 1941) and psychophysical evidence (Cabello & Stiles, 1950). The central 2 deg is shown in more detail in Figure 2.11B; here the cones are longer and slender than elsewhere in the retina. The spacing of foveal cones is determined by the tight hexagonal packing of the inner segments (Figure 2.11B, inset) at the level of the outer-limiting membrane: The best modern histology places the center-to-center spacing of the finest foveal cones at $d_{cc} = 3.0\,\mu m$ (Snyder & Miller, 1977; see Miller, 1979a for a detailed review of cone spacing). Although the outer segment diameter of cones in the central fovea is only about 1 to 1.5 μm, it is the spacing d_{cc} that determines the **Nyquist frequency** v_N, which is the highest spatial frequency that can be unambiguously reconstructed according to the Whittaker–Shannon sampling theorem (Snyder & Miller, 1977):

$$v_N = f/[d_{cc}\sqrt{3}\,(57.3)] \qquad (2.25)$$

Here v_N is given in cycles/degree, $f = 16.7$ mm is the posterior nodal distance, $d_{cc} = 3 \times 10^{-3}$ mm is the cone spacing, 57.3 is the factor for converting from radian measure to degrees and $\sqrt{3}$ is a factor from the two-dimensional sampling theorem for a hexagonal array (Petersen & Middleton, 1962; Synder & Miller, 1977). The value obtained is $v_N = 56$ cycles/degree. It is noteworthy that the highest spatial frequency sinusoid that can be resolved in normal viewing is 50 to 60 cycles/degree. this acuity is achieved with a pupil diameter of about $D = 2.5$ mm. The highest angular frequency passed by a diffraction limited system at $\lambda = 555$ nm with this size pupil is

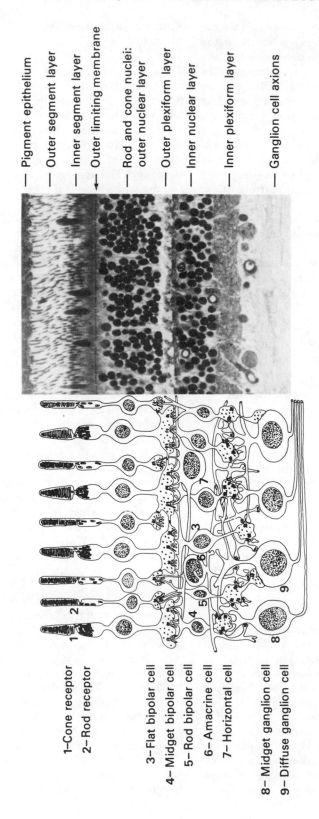

Figure 2.10. Left panel: schematic diagram of synaptic organization of monkey retina, modified from Dowling and Boycott (1966) to match the micrograph of right panel. Note that the size of the schematic cells has been increased for clarity, while preserving the proper vertical positions.
Right panel: Phase-contrast micrograph of the human retina, showing layers of retina. (Courtesy of Adolph Cohen.) Modified from "Organization of the Primate Retina: Electron Microscopy" by J. Dowling and B. Boycott, 1966, *Proc. Roy. Soc.*, *B166*, p. 104.

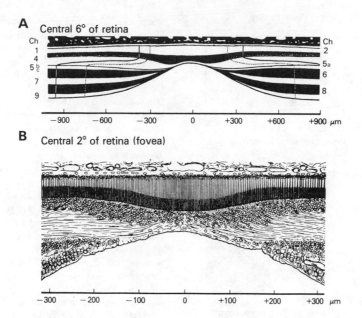

Figure 2.11. (a) Schematic diagram of the layers seen in horizontal cross section of the central 9 degrees of the human retina (1 deg corresponds to 291 μm for an eye with posterior nodal distance of 16.7 mm). Ch, choroidal layer; 1, pigment epithelial cell layer separated by a line from the distal tips of layer 2, layer of outer and inner segments of receptors. The outer limiting membrane separates layer 2 from layer 4, the outer nuclear layer formed by photoreceptor cell bodies. Layer 5 is the outer plexiform, where horizontal and cell processes and bipolar dendrites converge on cone pedicles. Layer 6 is the inner nuclear layer and contains the cells bodies of the bipolar cells, and also of horizontal and amacrine cells, which make lateral connections in the outer and inner plexiform respectively. (Figure 2.10). Layer 8 is the ganglion cell body layer, and layer 9 the ganglion cells axons that exit eye and form the optic nerve. From *The Retina* (Fig. 38, Illustrations) by S.L. Polyak, 1941, Chicago; University of Chicago Press. Reprinted by permission.

(b) Schematic diagram of the fovea, the central 2 degrees of the human retina. Note that the inner segments of the foveal cones are here shaded dark. Also note the variation in the size and shape of the cones, even in this restricted area of the retina. From *The Retina* (Fig. 38, Illustrations) by S.L. Polyak, 1941, Chicago; University of Chicago Press. Reprinted by permission.

$D/57.3\lambda = 78$ cycles/degree (see p. 97). However, the actual cutoff of the optical modulation transfer is lower due to aberrations and scatter, and lies very close to 60 cycles/degree. Thus, the optical transfer of the eye appears well matched to the spatial sampling of the finest cones.

Figure 2.12A shows the density distribution of cones and rods along a horizontal meridian through the fovea. The normal human retina contains three spectrally distinct cones classes (p. 118). The detailed trichromatic cone mosaic is not known, but histological evidence (Marc & Sperling, 1977; Ahnelt, Kolb, & Pflug, 1987) and human psychophysical data (Wilmer, 1950; Williams, MacLeod, & Hayhoe, 1981a, 1981b; Demonasterio, Schein, & McCrane 1981; Castano & Sperling, 1982) support the view that the

distribution of cones containing the short-wavelength sensitive pigment is quite different from those of the cones containing the long-wave and mid-wave sensitive pigments. Absent for all practical purposes in the foveola (central 25 min of arc), the short-wave cone density peaks at about 1 deg eccentricity, as shown in Figure 2.12B. The work of Williams et al. (1981a) argues that the short-wave cone spacing about 15 to 20 min from the center of the fovea is roughly 10 min of arc, 5 to 10 times the spacing between the other cones in the same retinal region. Marc and Sperling (1977) and the previous psychophysical work of Brindley (1954) lend some support to the idea that the long-wave sensitive cones may also be less dense in the fovea (and elsewhere) than the mid-wave sensitive cones.

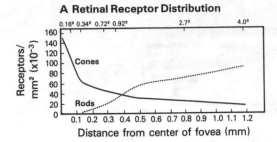

A Retinal Receptor Distribution

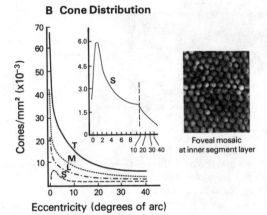

B Cone Distribution

Foveal mosaic
at inner segment layer

Eccentricity (degrees of arc)

Figure 2.12. (a) Density distribution of rods and cones of human retina along a horizontal meridian through the fovea (Osterberg, 1935). For more recent evidence, see Curcio et al., 1987. From "Topography of the Layer of Rods and Cones in the Human Retina" by G. Osterberg, 1935, *Acta Ophthal.*, Suppl. 6, pp. 1 – 103.

(b) Density distribution of various cone types in baboon retina (Marc & Sperling, 1977). *S* labels the curve for the short-wave sensitive cones; *L* for the long-wave sensitive; *M* for the mid-wave sensitive; and *T* the total cone distribution. The upper inset shows on a magnified scale the perpendicular distribution of the short-wave sensitive cones. From "Chromatic Organization of Primate Cones" by R.C. Marc and H.G. Sperling, 1977, *Science, 196*, pp. 454 – 456. Copyright 1977 by the AAAS. Reprinted by permission.

(c) Micrograph of a tangential slice through the foveal region of the monkey retina taken at the ellipsoid level of the inner segments. Note that tight "hexagonal" packaging. Center-to-center spacing is 3.0 μm. Courtesy of W.H. Miller. See Williams (1985) for a more extensive picture and analysis of foveal mosaic.

It bears emphasis that the Nyquist frequency of the sampling theorem is not to be understood as a frequency limit beyond which there can be no output modulation (as is the case for the analogue filtering done by the eye's optics).

With digital sampling a wave of frequency above the Nyquist limit can produce output modulation, but this will appear aliased at a lower frequency. Indeed, it now seems apparent (as reported by Byram, 1944a; Williams & Collier, 1983; Williams 1985) that interference fringes formed on the retina by bypassing the optics (see p. 96) can be detected at frequencies up 130 to 150 cycles/degree. Miller and Bernard (1983) have shown that the cutoff at 150 cycles/degree is unlikely to be due to receptor disarray (Yellott, 1983), but rather to demodulation caused by the finite entrance aperture of the foveal cones, which is about 2.3 μm at the inner segment where wave-guiding (see p. 104) begins. It seems likely, however, that randomness in the positioning of cones in the near periphery (say, at 5 deg eccentricity, where the optical m.t.f. is almost the same as for the fovea) plays an important role in demodulating spatial frequencies that would be aliased (Yellot, 1983). A striking example of aliasing has been described by Williams, Collier, & Thompson (1983), who demonstrated that under conditions in which grating detection is determined by signals from the short-wavelength sensitive cones, an observer can discriminate a high-frequency grating (say, 30 cycles/deg) from a homogeneous field, although only gratings of spatial frequency less than 13 cycles/deg can be seen as gratings. The results can be interpreted in terms of aliasing due to sparse sampling, and randomness in the short-wave cone mosaic. The sampling of the retinal image by non-receptor elements also constitutes digital filtering. In the retinal periphery the rod spacing is very close to the foveal cone spacing, and poor peripheral acuity and much greater spatial summation (Barlow, 1958) is due to the lower sampling frequency of more central non-receptor units. Aliasing of high spatial frequencies should occur if the image itself contains modulation at such frequencies, and the mosaic of neurons is sufficiently regular.

Physical Structure of the Rods and Cones

Photoreceptors are differentiated into two principal regions, the *outer segment* and the *inner segment*. Figure 2.13A shows a human rod and human cones from various retinal regions, from von Greef (1900), as discussed and confirmed with modern histological techniques by Miller and Snyder (1973). There is a dramatic and systematic variation in the length of the outer and inner segments, both in the ratio of the diameter

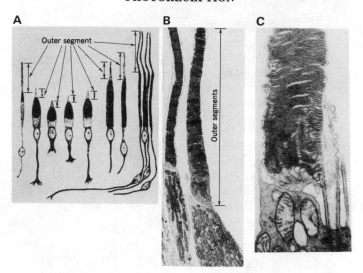

Figure 2.13. (a) Drawings of human rod (left-most structure) and human cones taken from various parts of the retina. The cones are arranged from the left in order of degree of eccentricity of position in the retina from which they were taken. The four cones at the right are from the fovea. Note the large variation in inner segment diameter and outer segment length as a function of eccentricity. From von Greef (1902) as republished by Miller and Snyder (1973). Reprinted with permission from *Vision Research*, p. 2187, W. Miller and A.W. Snyder, Copyright 1973, Pergamon Press, Ltd.

(b) Electron micrographs of a human rod and cone from the near periphery. The dense mitochondria of the inner segment are visible. The full width of the cone inner segment cannot be seen in this micrograph. Courtesy of Adolph Cohen.

(c) Electron micrograph of human rod showing the lamellar or "disk" membranes of the outer segment, the ciliary "backbone" which connects outer and inner segments, and several inner segment mitochondria. The lamellar membranes are continually manufactured at the base of the outer segment and removed at the distal tips of the rods, with a cycle time of about two weeks. Some of the disorder of disk membrane organization is due to tissue preparation. Courtesy of Adolph Cohen.

of the outer to inner segment, and in the degree of taper of the inner segment. The inner segment immediately below the outer segment (the *ellipsoid* region) contains a very dense mass of mitochondria which supply the enormous metabolic demands of the cell (see p. 123). The dense mitochondrial and outer segment regions, with refractive indices high relative to the extracellular space, cause the receptors to act as *waveguides* (like fiber-optic bundles) trapping light that enters the guide's acceptance angle (Miller, 1979b; Snyder, Pask, & Mitchell, 1973; see also (p. 104). The wider inner segment cross-section of cones at the ellipsoid (the waveguide entrance) increases the cell's light collecting area. Below the ellipsoid region is the paraboloid region containing the Golgi apparatus where proteins are synthesized, the myoid (a region that can alter its length in many vertebrates), the nuclear region, and the pedicle

(cone) or spherule (rod) where synapses are made with the secondary neurons of the retina.

The outer segment of the photoreceptor is the site of photon absorption and transduction. Figure 2.13B, from Cohen (1969), shows electron micrographs of a human rod and cone. In each case the outer segment comprises a large number of *lamellar* or *disk bilayer membranes* (Figure 2.13C), with repeat period c. 300 Å, as determined from X-ray diffraction studies (Blaurock and Wilkins, 1969; Gras & Worthington, 1969). The light absorbing visual pigment of the photoreceptors is an *integral membrane protein*; that is, the pigment protein molecules reside in (and span) the c. 50 Å thick disk membranes. The surface density of the pigment molecules is about 25,000 to 30,000 molecules/μm^2. This estimate of the surface density comes primarily from microspectrophotometric analysis of the pigments of individual photoreceptors (Liebman,

1972; see p. 111). Since a typical human rod outer segment is about 1.7 μm in diameter and about 25 μm long, it contains about 850 disks having 4.5 μm^2 surface area (each with two sides containing pigment). Thus a human rod has a total of 10^8 molecules of visual pigment, at an apparent concentration (relative to total outer segment volume) of c. 3 mM.

There are two universal structural differences between rods and cones. First, in cones the lamellar membranes themselves constitute the envelope or *plasma membrane* of the outer segment. In rods all but a very few basal disk membranes are completely separated from one another and from the plasma membrane (Cohen, 1968; Yoshikami, Robinson, & Hagins, 1974). Second, in rods the inner segment is approximately the same diameter as the outer segment, whereas in cones the inner segment is 2 to 5 times wider than the outer segment, with the greatest ratio occurring in the peripheral retina.

Directional Sensitivity of the Retina

Figure 2.14A diagrams a simplified version of a very important optical device employed in visual science—the **Maxwellian view**—named after its inventor, the physicist James Clerk Maxwell.[5] A point source of light, S_1, illuminates a lens, L, which in turn forms an image, S_1', of the source near the plane of the observer's pupil, and, in this case, centered on the optic axis. The distance of the lens from the eye is l'. Under these conditions the lens appears uniformly illuminated to the observer, and produces a retinal illuminance $I(l'/l)^2$, where I is the luminous intensity (in lumens/sterad) of the source in the direction of the lens, and the assumption is made that the image S_1' is smaller than the entrance pupil. (To convert to the troland unit, note that $1\,\mathrm{td} = 10^{-6}$ lumens/sterad.)

If an identical source, S_2, of the same intensity as S_1 is situated off-axis, so that its small pupillary image S_2' now falls near the edge of the dilated pupil, the apparent brightness of the lens produced by S_2 alone will be less than that produced by S_1. This effect is called the **Stiles–Crawford effect of the first kind** (*SC–I effect*), and can be quantified by a variety of techniques.

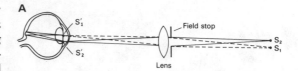

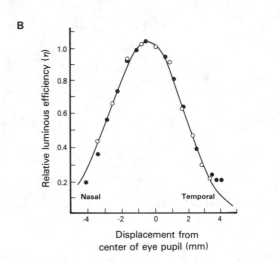

Figure 2.14. (a) Diagram of simple Maxwellian view optical system. Two point sources illuminate a converging lens with identical intensity I lumens/sterad; the observer is accommodated for the lens distance and the beam is stopped down very near the lens. The lens produce an image of the source in the plane of the observer's pupil. The luminous flux captured by the lens from either source is $I\,(\pi r^2)/l^2$, where l is the distance from the source to the lens. Since the lens subtends a solid angle $(\pi r^2)/(l')^2$ at the eye, where l' is the distance from the pupil to the lens, the retinal illumination in lumens/sterad is given by $I(l'/l)^2$. Since the two light sources identically illuminate the same stop, each causes the identical retinal illumination of the same image area.

(b) Measurements of the Stiles–Crawford effect of the first kind with an apparatus such as that shown in Figure 2.14A. The abscissa gives the displacement of the Maxwellian image from the center of the pupil. The ordinate gives the relative visual effectiveness of lights entering through various pupil positions. The visual effectiveness of light entering at the edge of the dilated pupil is seen to have only 20 percent the effectiveness of that entering the pupil center. Open and filled circles represent replications of experiment in same observer. From "The Stiles-Crawford Effects and their Significance in Vision" by B.H. Crawford in *Handbook of Sensory Physiology, Vol. VII/4* (p. 471) by L.M. Hurvich and D. Jameson (eds.), 1972, New York: Springer-Verlag. Copyright 1972 by Springer-Verlag, Reprinted by permission.

[5]An excellent treatment of the Maxwellian view can be found in Westheimer (1966).

Figure 2.14B shows the effect as measured with detection thresholds by Stiles and Crawford (1933). Note that the angle of incidence of the light reaching a given point on the retina (say the central fovea) changes by at most 15 deg as S_2' moves to the pupillary edge—this can be readily deduced from Figure 2.4, since the distance of the retina from the pupil is c. 20 mm, and the maximum radius of the pupil is c. 4 mm. One practical consequence of cone directional selectivity is the minimization of the effect of optical aberrations caused by rays passing through the pupil's edge. Another is the reduction of the effect of interocularly scattered light.

There is no doubt that, as hypothesized by Stiles and Crawford, the SC-I directional sensitivity results from the shape and orientation of the photoreceptors (see Crawford, 1972, for a review). One compelling line of evidence is that retinal conditions that cause the receptors to lose their normal orientation (e.g., a buckling of the retina) alter directional sensitivity (Dunnewold, 1964; Frankhauser, Enoch, & Cibis, 1961). Another line of evidence is the correlation between the magnitude of the SC-I effect and retinal eccentricity (Westheimer, 1967), which is expected because of the systematic shape variation in the cones (see Figure 2.13A and below). Another source of evidence is photoreceptor electrophysiology: intracellular voltage recordings from single turtle cones (Baylor & Fettiplace, 1975) show them to have directional sensitivity closely comparable to the psychophysical phenomenon. It is notable that the photoreceptors from different parts of the retina are not all perpendicular to the retinal surface, but rather have their axes oriented toward a point near the center of the exit pupil (Enoch & Laties, 1971; Laties, 1969; Laties & Enoch, 1971; Laties, Liebman, & Campbell, 1968). Psychophysical evidence has shown that this orientation is actively maintained through some trophic influence of light (Applegate & Bonds, 1981; Enoch, Birch, & Birch, 1979), and it seems quite likely that this influence is exerted through the directional sensitivity of the individual photoreceptors. Although it is sometimes stated that rods exhibit no directional sensitivity, this is only relatively true. Under appropriate conditions rods do exhibit directional sensitivity (Alpern, Ching, & Kitahara, 1983; Enoch, 1975), although the effect is relatively minor compared to that of cones.

Stiles (1937) found that most monochromatic lights seen in Maxwellian view alter their hue depending upon the position of pupil entry. This effect is called the **Stiles–Crawford effect of the second kind** (*SC-II effect*). This effect was reasoned by Stiles to be due to different cone classes exhibiting distinctive wavelength dependencies in their individual directional selectivity, a conclusion borne out by the work of Enoch and Stiles (1961), and by the more recent work of Alpern and Kitahara (1983).

Theories of Directional Sensitivity

Rod and cone photoreceptors, because of their shape and refractile properties alone are *light-guides*—i.e., independent of their absorption properties, they tend to trap radiant energy that flows through their acceptance angle, in the same way that a fiber-optics strand traps light. Figure 2.15A shows how this light-trapping property can be modelled with geometric optics. The index of refraction inside the cell, n_i, is higher than that of the extracellular space, n_o, due to the greater material density. (Without interstices between outer segments, no waveguiding could occur.) Consequently, from Snell's Law (equation 2.8), light rays that enter the guide undergo *total internal reflection* if

$$\sin(i) > \sin(i_c) = n_o/n_i \qquad (2.26)$$

(This condition is found by putting $i' = 90°$ in Snell's Law.) The condition for total internal reflection may also be written as

$$\alpha < \alpha_c \simeq \sin(\alpha_c) = \sqrt{1 - (n_o/n_i)^2} \qquad (2.26')$$

where α is the angle a meridional ray makes with the central axis of the guide, and $\sin(\alpha_c) = \cos(i_c)$ from the geometry. Assuming $n_o = 1.34$ and $n_i = 1.38$ (Miller & Snyder, 1973), the condition applies for $\alpha < 14°$. The cone photoreceptors constitute *tapered light guides*; perhaps the most important consequence of the tapering is the enhancement of the light-collecting area compared with total pigment cross-section, a fact emphasized by O'Brien (1951) in his review of his work on visual resolution. Winston and Enoch (1971) elaborated a model cone based on geometrical optics. Baylor and Fettiplace (1975) demonstrated that this model gives a reasonable account of the directional sensitivity of turtle cones, and that the light-collecting efficiency of the turtle cone outer segment (1.5 to 2.5 μm diameter) is enhanced more than 10 times by the wider, tapering inner segment (7 to 12 μm diameter). Another "geometrical optics" model of the Stiles–Crawford effect is due to P.L. Walraven and M.A. Bouman (1960). This model

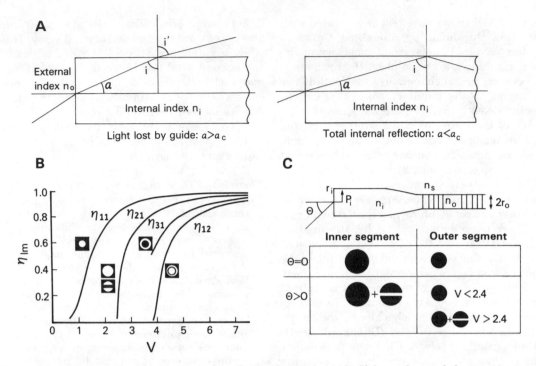

Figure 2.15. (a) Conditions for total internal reflection by a light-guide. If the angle α made by a ray intersecting the meridianal ray at the entrance to the guide is larger than a critical angle α_c (equation 2.26′), light will exit the guide; for angles $\alpha < \alpha_c$ the wave will undergo total internal reflection and be trapped by the guide. From "Chapter A.2" by A.W. Snyder in *Photoreceptor Optics—Theoretical Principles* (p. 40) by A.W. Snyder and R. Menzel (eds.), 1975, New York: Springer-Verlag. Copyright 1975 by Springer-Verlag. Reprinted by permission.

(b) Modal patterns propagating in cylindrical waveguides. The abscissa gives the waveguide parameter, $V = \pi n_i (D/\lambda) \sin(\alpha_c)$ (equation 2.27) which is determined by the indices of refraction inside and outside the guide, the diameter D of the guide and the wavelength of light λ; V is thus a structural property of a cylindrical guide. The ordinate gives the fraction of light transmitted within the guide in each modal pattern as a function of V, and sketches the various modal patterns. From "Chapter A.2" by A.W. Snyder in *Photoreceptor Optics —Theoretical Principles* (p. 45) by A.W. Snyder and B. Menzel (eds.), 1975, New York: Springer-Verlag. Copyright 1975 by Springer-Verlag. Reprinted by permission.

(c) Waveguide model of tapered guide such as human cone by Snyder and Pask (1973). For axial propagation (light entering through the center of the pupil) only mode 11 is excited. For off-axis propagation modal pattern 21 may be excited, depending critically on the value of the waveguide parameter V, which is near the critical value 2.4. From "Chapter A.7 by C. Pask & A.W. Snyder in *Photoreceptor Optics*—Theory of the Stiles–Crawford Effect of the Second Kind (p. 153) by A.W. Snyder & B. Menzel (eds.), 1975, New York: Springer-Verlag. Copyright by Springer-Verlag.

postulates that there is a wavelength-independent leakage of light out of the tapering outer segment of the cone, due to the failure of total internal reflection. This theory gives a reasonable fit to SC-I data, as well as to data of psychophysically isolated cones (Alpern & Kitahara, 1983; Zwas, 1979), but is difficult to reconcile with the exact physical structure of human cones.

Explanations of the Stiles–Crawford effects based upon purely geometrical optics suffer from a logical flaw. Because the dimensions of the human cone outer segments are near the wavelengths of visible lights, a full electromagnetic analysis (i.e., solution of Maxwell's equations subject to the specific boundary conditions of the guide) is required (Snyder & Pask, 1973). Snyder, Pask, and Mitchell (1973) have demonstrated that detailed geometrical optics ray-tracing yields an incorrect calculation of directional sensitivity for a cylindrical guide, as compared with the exact calculation based on electromagnetic wave theory. In all waveguides light propagates in *modes*, coherent distributions of energy "localized in the vicinity of the guide by total internal reflection, and with well defined phase velocity" (Snitzer, 1961). The modal patterns for various guides have been well characterized mathematically (Snitzer, 1961; Snyder, 1969a, 1969b), and modal patterns have been observed in human retinal specimens (Enoch, 1961). Snyder (see Snyder, 1975, for a tutorial review) has emphasized in many articles that the waveguide parameter

$$V = (\pi D/\lambda) \sqrt{n_i^2 - n_o^2}$$
$$= \pi n_i (D/\lambda) \sin (\alpha_c) \qquad (2.27)$$

determines which modes are excited in a cylindrical guide with entrance diameter D, internal index n_i, external or cladding index n_o, and light wavelength λ. Note that V includes a product of the light-trapping parameter, $\sin (\alpha_c)$, (critical angle for total internal reflection in the guide—see equation 2.26') and the reciprocal of the diffraction parameter, λ/D. Figure 2.15B shows the fraction of light transmitted (represented by the symbol $\eta_{1,m}$) within the receptor as a function of the waveguide parameter V, and schematic diagrams of the modes most likely to be excited in photoreceptors. Only modes 11 and 21 are likely to be of much significance for receptors the size of human rods of foveal cones. Snyder and Pask (1973) have presented a formal model of the SC-I effect (specifically its wavelength dependence) based on waveguide theory, and have elaborated this to a theory of the SC-II effect (Snyder & Pask, 1975). Figure 2.15C shows a schematic of the foveal cone used in the Snyder–Pask theory, and diagrams the modal patterns that propagate in the inner and outer segment; the propagation of modal pattern 21 depends critically on V, which probably lies very close to the human cone cut-off $V = 2.4$. As the angle of incidence changes, the light captured in each mode drops, and in addition the total distribution of power among the modes that lie above cut-off changes, requiring detailed reanalysis of the absorption by the pigment from the power in each model. The theory has greatly advanced thinking about the Stiles–Crawford effects, but due in part to the sensitivity of the theory to very small changes in the parameters (whose values are not known with sufficiency accuracy), to the difficulty of assessing some of the approximations involved, and very likely to the heterogeneity of shape of the cone populations upon which the SC measurements have been made (Figures 2.11B, 2.12A), it cannot be said to be a definitive explanation at this time.

Visual Pigments

General Characterization

Vision is initiated by the absorption of a light quantum or photon by a visual pigment molecule. Although visual pigments differ greatly in λ_{max} (wavelength of maximal sensitivity) and to a lesser extent in their spectral bandwidth, the visual pigment of the rods, *rhodopsin*, which is by far the most thoroughly studied pigment, serves to illustrate the most important features of visual pigments.

Rhodopsin is a protein of molecular weight 39,000 daltons (Daemen, DeGrip, & Jansen, 1972; Hubbard, 1954) comprising 348 amino acid residues, as shown in Figure 2.16B (Ovchinnikov, 1982; Hargrave et al., 1983). About 50 percent of the protein is within the 25 to 30 Å hydrocarbon core of of the membrane, 25 percent in the hydrophilic surface of the membrane and extradiskal space, and 25 percent in the intradiskal space, as shown in Figure 2.16A (Dratz & Hargrave, 1983). The amino acid chain curls through the membrane in seven helices, and the diameter of the molecule in the hydrocarbon core is about 20 Å. Figure 2.17 shows a schematic of the disk membrane. The average spacing between rhodopsin molecules in the disk membrane is about 60 Å, but the individual rhodopsin molecules are free to diffuse rotationally (Cone, 1972; Poo & Cone, 1973) and laterally (Liebman & Entine, 1974; Poo & Cone, 1973) within the lipid membrane; the lateral diffusion coefficient is $5 \times 10^{-9} \, cm^2/sec$. The mobility of rhodopsin in the membrane may play an important role in early steps in transduction. The chromophore of the pigment, shown in Figure 2.1A, is the 11-*cis* aldehyde of vitamin A (the corresponding alcohol). It is covalently attached to the protein at the ε-amino group of lysine residue no. 296 by a Schiff base (C=N bond at the 15th carbon—Bownds, 1967; Morton & Pitt, 1955), which is probably protonated in native rhodopsin. The site of attachment lies within the hydrophobic core of the membrane, as shown in Figure 2.16A, and the chromophore is oriented with its long-axis parallel to the disk surface (Schmidt, 1938; Liebman, 1962).

Absorption of a photon by a rhodopsin molecule is a quantum mechanical event: An elec-

---

For a tutorial review, see Abrahamson and Japar (1972). For more recent, detailed reviews of the very large literature of this field see Birge (1981) and Honig & Ebrey (1974).

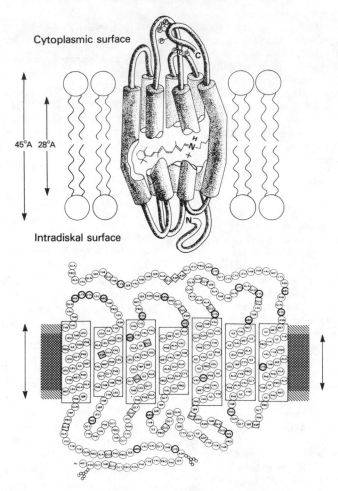

Figure 2.16. (a) Crude three-dimensional structural configuration of rhodopsin, showing the seven helical regions and connecting loops. From "The Structure of Rhodopsin in the Rod Outer Segment Disk Membrane" by E.A. Dratz and P.A. Hargrave, 1983, *Trends in Biochem. Science*, p. 128. Copyright 1983 Elsevier Science Publishers. Reprinted by permission.

(b) Overall amino acid sequence of bovine rhodopsin, with most likely configuration of components. The portions above the boxed regions are the carboxy-terminus and the loops in the cytoplasmic space. The boxed regions represent seven helical regions that lie within the lipid behavior. The amino-terminus and loops lying below the boxes lie inside the intra-diskal space. From "The Structure of Bovine Rhodopsin" by P.A. Hargrave, *et al.*, 1983, *Biophys. Struct. Mech.*, *9*, p. 242. Copyright 1983 by Springer-Verlag. Reprinted by permission.

tron in the π-cloud of the conjugated chain is promoted to a higher energy non-bonding orbital. The photon-activated molecule, which has a lifetime of the order of a picosecond, can dissipate its additional energy in several ways. First, it can fluoresce, emitting a photon that contains most of the energy absorbed, and thus relax to a lower energy state. This occurs with probability c. 0.005 (Guzzo & Pool, 1968). Second, the energy can be conserved in "internal conversion"; for example, it can be dissipated in the excited vibrational modes of the molecule and be lost as heat. Third, the energy can cause a change in the state of the molecule itself. The only chemical change that occurs with significant probability is the *isomerization* of the chromo-

Rod disk membrane

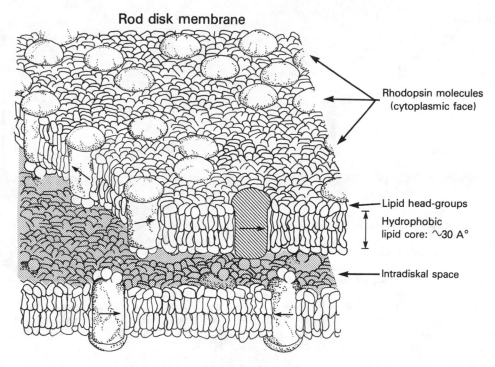

Rhodopsin molecules
(cytoplasmic face)

Lipid head-groups

Hydrophobic
lipid core: ∿30 A°

Intradiskal space

Figure 2.17. Schematic diagram of a portion of a rod disk. The dominant species of each face of the membrane are phospholipids, having hydrophilic head groups and hydrophobic fatty acid tails; each face of the membrane is composed of two layers of oppositely oriented phospholipids. Rhodopsin molecules of about 30 Å diameter are the dominant integral membrane component, spanning the lipid bilayer. The rhodopsin molecules (and lipids as well) diffuse both rotationally and laterally within the membrane; the arrows indicate dipole axes of the chromophores, which lie in the plane of the membrane but have random orientation with respect to one another. Inside the living rod a number of other proteins are known to be attached as "ectoproteins" to the disk surface (p. xx). From "The Structure of Rhodopsin in the Rod Outer Segment Disk Membrane" by E.A. Dratz and P.A. Hargrave, 1983, *Trends in Biochem. Science*, p. 130. Copyright 1983 Elsevier Science Publishers, Reprinted by permission.

phore to the all-*trans* configuration, as shown in Figure 2.18 (Kropf & Hubbard, 1958; Hubbard & Kropf, 1958, 1959), which occurs with a probability (*quantum efficiency*) of c. 0.65 (Dartnall, 1972b—see p. 110). Isomerization leads to a series of thermally driven changes in the pigment which can be observed spectroscopically. The names and approximate life-times of these intermediates are given in Figure 2.19. Collectively, the series of changes undergone by the molecule upon photon absorption is known as *bleaching*, since the apparent color of the pigment in broad band light (at room temperature) changes from a rich purple to orange to pale yellow and finally becomes colorless. At body temperature and normal pH the first immediate with any significant lifetime is metarhodopsin II. It should be noted, however, that the later thermal steps are

not irreversible until the chromophore actually separates from the opsin moiety.

A general physical theory of photopigments must account quantitatively for the general red-shift in λ_{max} that occurs when the chromophore (λ_{max} in free solution, c. 380 nm) is attached to the opsin, for the high quantum efficiency of the primary photochemical event, for the specific differences in λ_{max} and bandwidth among various visual pigments, as well as for a wealth of additional quantitative details of visual pigment chemistry (such as the spectra and thermal stability of the bleaching intermediates). Honig, Greenberg, Dinur, and Ebney (1976) have presented a theoretical model of the pigment molecule based on (1) the protonation of the Schiff base and the close association of the proton with a neighboring counterion (as originally

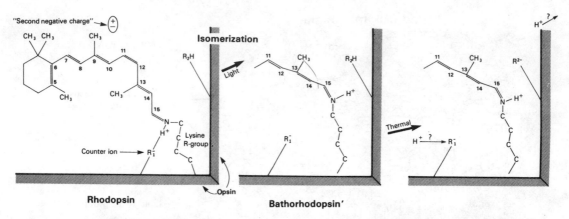

Figure 2.18. Schematic diagram of the initial event in visual transduction. The absorption of a photon excites one of the π-electrons of the chromophore to a non-bonding π* orbital. With probability c. 0.65 the chromophore relaxes by isomerization about the 11–12 double bond. In doing so a proton attached to the nitrogen of the lysine residue of rhodopsin (the site of chromophore attachment) is thought to be separated from its neutralizing counter-ion, R_1^-. Work is thus performed in the charge separation, and conserved as potential energy. Further thermally and ionically driven processes cause the protein itself to gradually undergo conformation changes that permit it to interact differentially with other disk membrane proteins. From "Photosomerization, Energy Storage and Charge Separation: A Model for Light Energy Transduction in Visual Pigment and Bacteriorhodopsin" by B. Honig and T. Ebrey, 1979, *Proc. Natl. Acad. Sci.*, *76*, p. 2506. Reprinted by permission.

suggested by Kropf & Hubbard, 1958) and (2) the positioning of additional negatively charged or polar groups by the protein in the neighborhood of the chromophore ring. Honig et al. (1976) have performed quantum-mechanical calculations reproducing many quantitative properties of visual pigment spectroscopy. Birge (1981) and Honig and Ebrey (1974) review recent work on such theoretical models. Honig, Ebrey, Callender, Dinur, and Ottolenghi (1979) have also proposed a model, reproduced in part schematically in Figure 2.18, to explain how the energy that induces the chromophore isomerization can be conserved. The idea is

> "that the essential goal of photoisomerization is charge separation, and that this alone can account for the characteristic properties of the primary event" (Honig et al., 1979, p. 2504).

Rod photoreceptors reliably generate signals in response to single photon absorptions (see p. 126), and yet the visual system is not overwhelmed by noise from the photoreceptors in the dark. It follows that primary photochemical events must have both a high probability of occurring once a photon is absorbed, and a low possibility of being triggered by thermal energy alone. The

high thermal stability of the rhodopsin (100 to 1000 times greater than the thermal stability of the isolated chromosphere), can be deduced from psychophysical observations (Barlow, 1956; Denton & Pirenne, 1954). For example, consider a psychophysical experiment measuring absolute threshold for a stimulus falling upon a 1 deg retinal patch in the near periphery (Stiles, 1939). One can think of the 10^4 rods and thus, 10^{12} pigments molecules in this retinal patch, as being all wired to one detector. Given that a single isomerization produces an event that can be registered at the detector with fair reliability, if thermal isomerization were frequent, the retinal patch would be swamped with thermal shot noise—for example, if the rate of thermal isomerization were as high as 10^{-9}/sec, the patch with its 10^{12} rhodopsin molecules would generate 1000 dark events per sec, and the ability of an observer to reliably detect 10 or so isomerizations due to a brief flash falling on this retinal area would be severely compromised. Recently it has been established by direct recording from single rods that the rate of thermal excitation events in primate rods at 37°C is about 0.006 events/rod/sec, or about 6×10^{-11}/sec/molecule (Baylor, Nunn, & Schnapf, 1984).

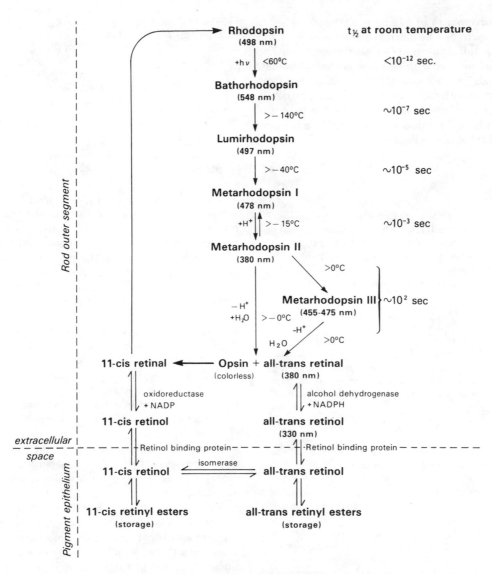

Figure 2.19. Diagram of the rhodopsin bleaching/regeneration cycle. Rhodopsin absorbs a photon and upon isomerization becomes a spectrally distinct species, bathorhodopsin with $\lambda_{max} = 548$ nm, which is stable at temperatures below $-140°$ C. The λ_{max}, temperatures of stability, and life-times at room temperature are similarly shown for the other intermediates. The first spectral intermediate with appreciable lifetime relative to the photoreceptor's light response is metarhodopsin II; this latter is always in equilibrium with metarhodopsin I, but the equilibrium is strongly tilted in the direction of meta II at cellular pH and temperature. The all-*trans* chromophore can reach the point of separation from the opsin via either of two paths, although it seems that the meta III path is somewhat less probable. Opsin will recombine spontaneously again with 11-*cis* retinal to regenerate the pigment. Transport proteins and several enzymes are required for maintaining a supply of 11-*cis* retinal and getting it to the outer segment from storage sites in the pigment epithelium.

Once the charge separation of the protonated Schiff base from its counterion has been induced by isomerization (Figure 2.18), further thermally and ionically driven processes trigger changes in the rhodopsin molecule's conformation: These changes allow it to interact differentially with other proteins and membrane structures (see p. 131).

Measurements of Pigment Extracts

Rhodopsin can be extracted from rods by detergent solubilization of the membrane lipids and studied in vitro with classic spectrophotometric methods. A vast store of information has been gathered with these methods (see, e.g., Dartnall, 1972a), and we can only convey a few essential points here. The absorption of light by a pigment in solution obeys Beer's Law,

$$\frac{dI_\lambda}{dl} = -\alpha_\lambda C I_\lambda \qquad (2.28)$$

where $I_\lambda(l)$ is the irradiance (quanta $\times$ cm^{-2} $\times$ sec^{-1}) at depth l, C is the concentration (molecules $\times$ cm^{-3}) and α_λ is a proportionality constant known as the *extinction coefficient*, with the units of a cross-section (cm^2/molecule). Integration equation 2.27 across a pathlength, L, gives

$$I_\lambda(L) = I_\lambda(0) \exp(-\alpha_\lambda CL) \qquad (2.29)$$

where $I_\lambda(0) = I_{\text{inc},\lambda}$ is the quantal flux incident on the sample, and $I_\lambda(L) = I_{\text{trans},\lambda}$ is the quantal flux transmitted through the sample at wavelength λ. The *density* of any absorbing substance at a particular wavelength, λ, is defined by

$$D_\lambda = \log_{10}(I_{\text{inc},\lambda}/I_{\text{trans},\lambda}) \qquad (2.30)$$

The usual convention in spectroscopy is to have a pathlength of 1 cm and to express the concentration in molar units; in this convention the extinction coefficient, ε_{max}, has units of liters/(mole $\times$ cm) or equivalently, cm^2/mmole. At the λ_{max} of rhodopsin, $\varepsilon_{\text{max}} = 40{,}000$ (Wald & Brown, 1953; reviewed in Dartnall, 1972); this translates to an apparent λ_{max} cross-section of $\alpha_{\lambda\text{max}} = 1.5 \times 10^{-16}$ cm^2/molecule. [$\varepsilon_{\text{max}} = (N_A \times 10^{-3}/\ln(10)) \times \alpha_{\lambda\text{max}}$, where N_A is Avagadro's number]. The extinction coefficient, as well as the shape of the extinction spectrum, are determined by the quantum mechanical properties of the molecule and should not be taken as indicating the exact physical size of the chromophore.

The probability that an absorbed photon leads to chromophore isomerization and thus to bleaching is known as the *quantum efficiency* of bleaching, and is given the symbol γ. Dartnall (1957) described the bleaching of visual pigment in the absence of regeneration by the equation

$$\frac{dC}{dt} = \frac{\gamma I_{\text{abs}}}{L} \qquad (2.31)$$

where C is a concentration, $I_{\text{abs}} = I_{\text{inc}}[1 - \exp(-\alpha_\lambda CL)]$ is in units of quanta $\times$ cm^{-2} $\times$ sec^{-1}, and L is the pathlength. If the pigment is in dilute solution, i.e., if $1 - \exp(-\alpha_\lambda C_D L) = \alpha_\lambda C_D L$, where C_D is the concentration of the pigment in the dark before any bleaching commences, then the solution to equation 2.31 is

$$p(t) = \exp(-a\gamma It) \qquad (2.32)$$

where $p(t) = C(t)/C_D$. The product $\alpha_{\text{max}\gamma}$ (or $\varepsilon_{\text{max}\gamma}$) is known as the *photosensitivity* (Dartnall, 1972b).

The photosensitivity of the pigment in photoreceptors is increased over that measured in solution by two effects: first, the chromophores in the disk membranes are oriented with their dipole axis (long axis of the conjugated chain) parallel to the disk and perpendicular to the axis of light propagation; second, the ratio of inner segment to outer segment diameter can, subject to the losses in the waveguide, increase the effective light-collecting area of the outer segment. The latter effect has been discussed in the context of the directional sensitivity (see p. 103). The former effect increases the absorption efficiency 50 percent over what it would be were molecules randomly oriented in solution, and gives rise to the *dichroism* of the rods—the specific absorbance of the outer segment is 4 to 5 times greater when the E-vector of plane-polarized light is parallel to the disks than when it is perpendicular, for light propagating perpendicular to the long axis (Leibman, 1962; Schmidt, 1938).

Hubbard and Wald (1951) demonstrated that rhodopsin would spontaneously regenerate when cattle opsin (fully bleached rhodopsin) was incubated with 11-*cis* retinal. The only other retinal isomer they found to generate a pigment was 9-*cis* retinal; the resultant pigment is called isorhodopsin. Subsequent work has led to a more detailed picture of regeneration (Henselman & Cusanovich, 1976). Without an exogenous source of 11-*cis* (or 9-*cis*) retinal, completely bleached retinas regenerate at most a few percent of their pigment; this percentage regeneration is probably due to a small endogenous store of chromophore solubilized in the lipids of the rods themselves. In the frog, this endogenous store is capable of supporting a complete and relatively rapid regeneration from small (< 0.15) fractional bleaches (Azuma, Azuma, & Sickel, 1977), but the situation is likely different in different species (Baumann, 1972).

Pigment regeneration following larger fractional bleaches requires a greater supply of 11-*cis* chromophore, supplied by the pigment epithelium. Bridges and Alvarez (1987) and Bernstein, Law, and Rando (1987) have established the existence of an enzymatic mechanism in pigment epithelium membranes that catalyzes the reconversion of all-trans retinol to 11-*cis* retinol. Furthermore, because retinal, retinol and retinyl esthers are all quite insoluble in water, specific transport mechanisms are required for moving them through various compartments (e.g., Liou, Bridges, Fong, Alverez, & Gonzalez-Fernandez, 1982); additional enzymes regulate the interconversion of the various storage and transport forms of the chromophore (Bridges, 1976; Futterman, 1965). Figure 2.19 gives a summary picture of the overall rhodopsin cycle, bleaching and regeneration; many details remain to be worked out. Species differences, especially in the regeneration portion of the cycle, are certainly significant. The picture also leaves out the recycling of the entire rod outer segment, consisting of continuous disk membrane synthesis at the basal disks, and circadian phagocytosis at the distal tips by the pigment epithelium (Young, 1967, 1976); in primates, full resynthesis of each rod occurs about every 12 days.

Microspectrophotometry

In the 1960's spectrophotometric techniques were developed for measuring the pigment in single photoreceptors. Measurements by Brown (1961), Liebman (1962), Liebman and Entine (1964), Marks (1963), and others enormously broadened our knowledge of photopigments, especially cone pigments, which had proven very difficult to study with isolation techniques. The difficulties arose in part due to the relative paucity of cones in most species, but in addition to lability of cone pigments in detergent solutions. (See Liebman, 1972 for an excellent review of the principles of microspectrophotometry, and the literature up to that point.) Significant among the findings have been the nearly universal absolute densities of the pigments in the cells of 0.014 to 0.017 optical density units/μm, the confirmation of the linear dichroism (establishing that the long axis of the chromophore is oriented in a plane parallel to the disk membrane surface), and the mobility or diffusion of pigment molecules in the bilayer membrane (Liebman & Entine, 1974; Poo & Cone, 1973).

Early microspectrophotometric work on primate receptors confirmed the existence of several distinct photoreceptor pigments (Marks, Dobelle, & MacNichol, 1964). Measurements with improved instruments demonstrated rhesus monkey cones to fall into four non-overlapping classes: rods with rhodopsin; cones with mean peak absorption at c. 415 nm, 535 nm, and 565 nm, respectively (Bowmaker, Dartnall, Lythgoe, & Mollon, 1978; Bowmaker et al., 1980). Dartnall, Bowmaker, & Mollon (1983) measured the absorbance of 147 cones from seven human eyes removed for malignant growths, and found cells of four spectrally distinct classes. These, and their estimated λ_{max}s are as follows: rods, λ_{max} = 496.3 $\pm$ 2.3 nm (n = 39); short-wave sensitive cones, λ_{max} = 419 $\pm$ 3.6 nm (n = 5); mid-wave cones, λ_{max} = 530.8 $\pm$ 3.5 nm (n = 45); long-wave cones, λ_{max} = 558.4 $\pm$ 5.2 nm (n = 58). The latter authors also found evidence for two subpopulations of mid-wave and long-wave cones, that is—the distributions of spectra for these two cone types had clear and statistically significant bimodality.

Reflection Densitometry

The fundus of the human eye reflects light: This is why an opthalmologist can view the fundus with an ophthalmoscope. Rushton, Weale (for reviews of their work, see Rushton, 1972 and Weale, 1965), and more recently a number of other laboratories, have developed optical/electronic instruments for measuring the visual pigments in the living eye with the light reflected from the fundus. The essence of these instruments is that one or more measuring light beams is focused in Maxwellian view on a region of the retina, whose pigment content can be altered by a bleaching beam (usually alternated with the measuring beam(s)). A beam-splitter/collecting lens arrangement is used to gather the light reflected back through the pupil and focus it onto a highly sensitive photomultiplier for electronic recording. Some differential measure between the fully bleached and a completely dark adapted or partially bleached condition is taken as the data.

Perhaps the greatest difficulty faced by fundal reflectometry is that the normal human pigment epithelium is filled with densely absorbing melanin granules, with the result that only 1×10^{-4} or less of the light incident on a given area of retina is actually reflected back through the pupil. A second formidable difficulty (which manifests itself at the point when one begins to interpret measurements made with reflection densitometers) is *stray light*—that is, light which is collected by the photomultiplier, but which has not taken a path through the outer segments. Additional practical and theoretical difficulties result from the instability of observer fixation, from the presence of blood vessels anterior to the retina, and from the heterogeneity of receptors in some parts of the retina. The effect of these difficulties inherent in reflection densitometry is that any quantitative use of fundal reflectometry necessarily involves a physical *model* (explicit or implicit) of all the light paths that the measuring light can take to reach the photomultiplier, as was clearly realized by Rushton (1956a, 1972). Space does not permit a fuller discussion of these modeling problems, but the interested reader is urged to consider the analyses of Rushton (1956a, 1972), Weale (1965), Alpern and Pugh (1974) and others who have explicitly confronted them.

Despite the difficulties in quantitative interpretation of fundal reflectometry measurements, the technique has greatly increased our knowledge of human pigments and of their bleaching and regeneration kinetics in normal and abnormal eyes, and has developed into an important research instrument in ophthalmology. Because of the much greater numerosity of rods in the retina, the reflection densitometer has provided more information about human rhodopsin than about other pigments. Investigations with the instrument, however, have established the existence of two of the three cone pigments in the normal trichromat's fovea (Baker & Rushton, 1965; Rushton & Henry, 1968)—the short-wavelength sensitive pigment has so far eluded densitometry—and shown that protanopic and deuteranopic dichromats each lack one of the two measurable pigments (Rushton, 1963, 1965). More recently, it has been demonstrated that anomalous trichromats possess two measurable pigments, but that the separation between the pigments varies within each class (Alpern & Wake, 1977). Many advances in the field of retinal densitometry can be expected—such as the development of efficient clinical instruments based upon television technology (Kilbride, Read, Fishman, & Fishman, 1983). The photosensitivity of human visual pigments *in vivo*, measured with the reflection

densitometer, is higher than would be expected from *in vitro* measurements, even after the factor of 3/2 required by the orientation of the chromophores in the plane of the disks is accounted for. Densitometry literature is remarkably consistent on this high photosensitivity (Alpern, 1971; Alpern & Pugh, 1974; Ripps & Weale, 1969; Rushton, 1956a, 1972; Weale, 1965). For example, human rhodopsin in the rods has an apparent $\varepsilon_{max}\gamma = 90,000\,cm^2/mmole$ (Alpern & Pugh, 1974), about twice what would be expected from *in vitro* measurements. The most probable explanation is optical funneling by the waveguiding properties of the photoreceptors (see p. 103). This explanation gives a good account of the factor by which human cone pigments are more photosensitive than rods (Brindley, 1966).

The density (equations 2.29 and 2.30) estimates of human visual pigments have risen since the earliest densitometric analysis (Rushton, 1956b). The value in recent literature for human rhodopsin, 0.35 (Alpern & Pugh, 1974; Zwas & Alpern, 1976) is about what one would expect from the known length of the rod outer segment (c. $25\,\mu m$), and from the microspectrophotometrically measured intrinsic density of c. $0.015/\mu m$. Foveal cone pigment densities have been estimated to be slightly larger (e.g., King-Smith, 1973), consistent with the greater length of foveal cone outer segments.

Another fundamental aspect of visual pigment chemistry is the *rate of regeneration* after bleaching. The regeneration reaction (Henselman & Cusanovich, 1976; Hubbard & Wald, 1951) *per se* is

free opsin + 11-*cis* retinal → rhodopsin.

The differential equation form of this bimolecular reaction is

$$\frac{dC}{dt} = kM(C_D - C) \qquad (2.33)$$

where C is the concentration of rhodopsin in the rods at time t, M is the concentration of free 11-*cis* retinal in the outer segment, C_D is the fully dark adapted rhodopsin concentration, and k is a second-order rate constant. If the amount of free 11-*cis* far exceeds the amount of free opsin, or the amount is held constant by another mechanism, then equation 2.33 becomes pseudo-first order and the solution becomes $C(t) = C_D[1 -$

exp $(-kMt)$], where $1/kM$ is the time constant of the observed regeneration. If one divides both sides of equation 2.33 by C_D, then one can write the equation in terms of $p(t) = C(t)/C_D$, the fraction of regenerated pigment. Rushton (see Rushton, 1972) and others (e.g., Alpern, 1971) have in many places presented densitometric data that support the view that in man rhodopsin regenerates roughly exponentially, with a time constant of 5 to 7 min after a large bleach. Assuming that bleaching and regeneration proceed independently of one another, Rushton combined equation 2.33 with the bleaching equation 2.31, to generate predictions of the rhodopsin concentration under arbitrary regimes of light and dark. Actually, the two processes cannot be strictly independent, since before a photoisomerized molecule can regenerate, it must pass through a series of dark reactions (Figure 2.19), which has more than one step with a long time constant. We reiterate that the pigment epithelium is absolutely necessary for regeneration from large bleaches, and that this almost surely entails the recruitment of enzymatic mechanisms for interconversion of the precursors of 11-*cis* retinal, and transport mechanisms for bringing the 11-*cis* or an appropriate precursor (probably 11-*cis* retinol) into the rod outer segment. Human patients who have abnormalities of the uvea-pigment epithelial interface have abnormally slow rhodpsin regeneration kinetics (Alpern & Krantz, 1981), a fact that underscores the role of pigment epithelial mechanisms in normal regeneration. One must keep in mind that in different species (e.g., frog, rat, cat, man) the regeneration process follows quite different kinetics (Baumann, 1972), and in no other case but man are apparent first-order kinetics obeyed.

Human cone pigments regenerate 3 to 4 times faster than human rhodopsin, typically with a time constant of c. 2 min (Alpern, Masseidvaag, & Ohba, 1971; Hollins & Alpern, 1973; Rushton, 1958, 1963, 1965; Rushton & Henry, 1968). It should be kept in mind that the cone disks are patent to the extracellular space, whereas the rod disks are fully enclosed within the plasma membrane, and thus regeneration from a substantial bleaching exposure in rods entails an extra delay and energetically demanding step: transport of replacement 11-*cis* chromophore from the pigment epithelium across the rod plasma membrane.

Scotopic Vision

Purkinje Shift

When one undergoes full dark adaptation in an appropriately dim environment, a number of striking phenomenological changes occur. Most lights or reflecting surfaces appear colorless. A light eccentric to fixation appears brighter than when fixated. The relative brightness of different light changes in comparison with their relative brightness under light-adapted conditions. For example, a 480 nm light and a 580 nm light matched for brightness under daylight conditions appear grossly mismatched in brightness when viewed at the same relative intensity under dark-adapted conditions. This latter phenomenon is known as the **Purkinje shift**. The relative visual effectiveness of spectral lights under daylight (photopic) and nighttime (scotopic) conditions are quantified in the internationally standardized (CIE, Commission Internationale d'Eclairage) photopic and scotopic luminosity functions, V_λ and V_λ', respectively (see p. 82). In the latter part of the 19th and early part of the 20th century many observations related to, and quantifying the Purkinje shift, were assembled into the Duplex Theory of the Retina, ably summarized in Hecht's (1937) thorough treatment, "Rods, Cones and the Chemical Basis of Vision."

The Invariance Laws of Scotopic Vision

Central among the observations forming the foundation of the Duplicity Theory are the Scotopic Invariance Laws. An important notion requisite for understanding these laws is that of an *action spectrum*, which is a graph or table giving the energy (quanta, quantal flux, etc.) needed in each spectral band to achieve some criterion effect. The effect might be a fixed amount of pigment bleached, a certain amplitude electrophysiological response, a psychophysical threshold, flicker fusion frequency or a brightness match.

Consider some visual function, say flicker fusion frequency, which can be measured as a function of light intensity, and thus for which we can measure an action spectrum. Following Krantz (1975) we say that a function f which maps light distributions to real numbers is invariant, if

$$f(A) = f(B) \Rightarrow f(q^\star A) = f(q^\star B) \qquad (2.34)$$

where A and B represent lights of arbitrary

spectral distribution and the operation "*" means neutral scaling (attenuation at all wavelengths by the same factor), in this case by the scalar quantity q. If we focus attention on spectral lights of unit intensity, 1_λ, then an action spectrum is a special set of scalars $q_c(\lambda)$, satisfying the property $f(q_c(\lambda)*1_\lambda) = $ constant. Invariance is a necessary and sufficient condition for a given visual function f to have a unique spectral sensitivity, for without it action spectra determined for different criteria are not proportional to one another. Scotopic flicker fusion (CFF) is invariant, which has the consequence that all scotopic flicker action spectra are proportional to one another regardless of the criterion (2 Hz fusion, 6 Hz fusion, etc.) chosen. Another way to state this is that when $f = $ CFF is plotted as a function of $q(\lambda)$, the scalar intensity of the light, the functions for different λ are parallel on a logarithmic axis (Hecht, 1937). Invariance is in fact a property of all scotopic visual functions, including acuity versus intensity, flicker fusion (Hecht, 1937), threshold versus intensity (Stiles, 1939), etc. Thus, all scotopic visual functions are governed (for a given eye) by a single spectral sensitivity.

The Photopigment Explanation of the Scotopic Invariance Laws

All scotopic action spectra from a given eye are identical when normalized. This fundamental property can be explained by the following propositions:

1. Only photoreceptors containing one and the same visual pigment (viz., rhodopsin) are active under scotopic conditions;
2. For a photoreceptor, the isomerization of any one molecule of pigment is identical in effect to the isomerization of any other;
3. Any criterion visual effect employed in determining a scotopic action spectrum is produced by a constant number of (or spatio-temporal distribution of) isomerizations.

The second of these three propositions was called the **Principle of Univariance** by William Rushton (Naka & Rushton, 1966). The principle really operates at two distinct levels, the molecular level of the photopigment, and the physiological level of the photoreceptor response. At the molecular level it is the assertion that there is a single event, chromophore isomerization, that triggers all visual effects of light. At the physiological level, it is the assertion that all of the pigment molecules in a photoreceptor are equivalent physiologically (a proposition that may not be absolutely correct (Schnapf, 1983), but is very reasonable when given the statistical context of a psychophysical experiment). It is relatively easy to see how propositions (1) through (3) above, imply the Invariance Laws discussed in the prior section. On the other hand, it is important to note that the converse does not follow: Invariance does not logically require Univariance for its explanation, and there are situations in which invariance is apparently obeyed, and yet other implications of Univariance are violated (e.g., Pugh, 1976; Sirovich & Abramov, 1977).

The third proposition stated above—that is, that any criterion effect employed in generating a scotopic action spectrum is produced by a wavelength-invariant spatio-temporal distribution of isomerizations—is one of the great *linking hypotheses* in vision, for it provides a rigorous bridge between certain behavioral and psychophysical data and a chemical/physiological substrate.

Figure 2.20 shows data that embody the ideas in the previous paragraphs, and illustrates a fundamental quantitative relationship implicit in propositions (1) through (3). Figure 2.20A gives the log *spectral sensitivities* (log reciprocal action spectra, normalized) of 10 single rods from three macaque monkeys, obtained by Baylor, Nunn, and Schnapf (1984) with the suction electrode technique (see pp. 124–127). In this case propositions (1) and (2) are assumed in force, so that a criterion response of a rod occurs when a constant number n of isomerizations are caused by light flashes of each wavelength: from equations (2.28) through (2.30) a constant number n of isomerizations is given by $n = Aq_c(\lambda)\gamma[1 - \exp(-\alpha_\lambda CL)]$. Here A is the geometrical cross section of the rod in μm^2, $q_c(\lambda)$ is the flux density of the beam in quanta/μm^2 required to give the criterion response, γ the quantum efficiency of isomerization, α_λ is the extinction coefficient, C is the pigment concentration in the rod, and L is the path length through the rod. Since the rod is illuminated from the side and has diameter of only 2 μm (i.e., $L \simeq 2 \mu m$), the argument of the exponential term is no larger than 0.04, so that

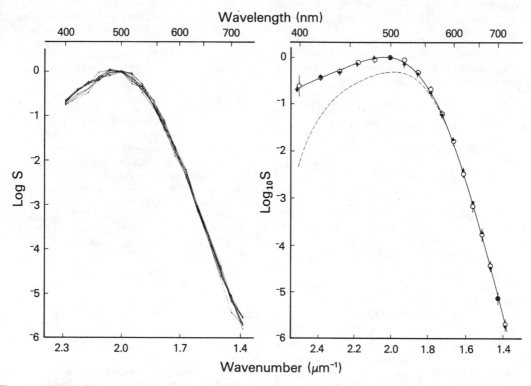

Figure 2.20. (a) Spectral sensitivities (normalized reciprocal action spectra) of 10 macaque rods whose light-induced membrane currents were measured with the suction electrode technique. Because the rods are only about $2\,\mu$m in diameter, the action spectrum can be shown to be proportional to the extinction spectrum of rhodopsin. Because the rods are being used as null detectors (i.e., the flash intensity at each wavelength is varied to bring the response to a constant magnitude), the spectrum can be measured over a far greater range than is possible with microspectrophotometric techniques. From "The Photocurrent Noise and Spectral Sensitivity of Rods of the Monkey" by D.A. Baylor, B.J. Nunn, and J.L. Schnapf, *Journal of Physiology, 357,* pp. 583, 585. Copyright 1984 by The Physiological Society. Reprinted by permission.

(b) Filled symbols show the average spectral sensitivity data of Figure 2.20A. Open symbols show the scotopic spectral sensitivities of a population of young male observers (Crawford, 1949). Crawford's data have been "uncorrected" for a lens absorption spectrum (Wyszecki & Stiles, 1967, p. 216) with density 1.62 at 400 nm, and an axial absorption maximum of 0.36. From "The Photocurrent Noise and Spectral Sensitivity of Rods of the Monkey" by D.A. Baylor, B.J. Nunn, and J.L. Schnapf, 1984, *Journal of Physiology, 357,* pp. 583, 585. Copyright 1984 by The Physiological Society. Reprinted by permission.

$n = Aq_c(\lambda)\gamma\alpha_\lambda CL$. Dividing the right hand side of this last expression by its value at $\lambda = \lambda_{\max}$, we have $S_\lambda = q_c(\lambda_{\max})/q_c(\lambda) = \alpha_\lambda/\alpha_{\lambda\max}$. In words, the spectral sensitivity curve is proportional to the extinction spectrum of the rod pigment rhodopsin.

Figure 2.20B compares the average spectral sensitivity data of Figure 2.20A with the average scotopic spectral sensitivity of Crawford (1949). The appropriate analysis here requires all three of propositions (1) through (3). For the case of human psychophysical data we assume

that $q_c(\lambda)$ represents the number of quanta required at the cornea to produce the criterion effect (a visual threshold for a homogeneously illuminated patch of retina). The number N of isomerizations at threshold is thus given by $N = \tau_\lambda q_c(\lambda)\,AF\,[1 - \exp(-\alpha_\lambda CL)]$, where here τ_λ is the transmissivity of the ocular media between the cornea and the receptor layer, A is the area of the retina illuminated, F is the packing fraction of the rods in the region, and L is the pathlength of the rods when seen end on (about $25\,\mu$m). Again, dividing both sides of the expression in the previous sentence by the value at λ_{max}, we have the following fundamental deduction:

the spectral sensitivity of scotopic vision is proportional to the media-corrected absorption spectrum of rhodopsin.

This deduction can be expressed symbolically:

$$S_\lambda = \tau_\lambda [1 - \exp(-\alpha_\lambda CL)]/$$
$$\tau_{\lambda max}[1 - \exp(-\alpha_{\lambda max}CL)]$$
$$= (\tau_\lambda/\tau_{\lambda max})[1 - 10^{-D(\lambda)}]/$$
$$[1 - 10^{-D(\lambda max)}] \qquad (2.35)$$

where $S_\lambda = q_c(\lambda_{max})/q_c(\lambda)$ is the normalized spectral sensitivity (measured at the cornea), α_λ is the extinction spectrum of human rhodopsin, C is the concentration of rhodpsin in the rods, L is the pathlength of light traversing the rods axially, and $D(\lambda)$ is a density spectrum incorporating the other parameters in the way indicated. To show that Crawford's spectral sensitivity data are consistent with the extinction spectrum inferred from the monkey rod data of Figure 2.20A, Baylor, Nunn, and Schnapf (1984) corrected the psychophysical measurements for a lens transmissivity spectrum (Wyszecki & Stiles, 1982, p. 216) with density 1.62 at 400 nm, and assumed in axial pigment density $D(\lambda_{max}) = 0.36$: Given these two assumptions equation 2.35 may be solved for $D(\lambda)$, which is proportional to α_λ. The agreement between the rhodopsin extinction spectrum inferred from the monkey rods and that inferred from Crawford's psychophysical results is manifestly excellent. Other comparisons of rhodopsin spectra with human scotopic spectral sensitivity data have shown general agreement (e.g., Alpern & Pugh, 1974; Bowmaker et al., 1980; Wald & Brown, 1958), but none so good nor over so extensive a spectral range as that in Figure 2.20B.

A few additional comments about the generality of equation 2.35 are called for. First, it represents an idealization of the actual physical condition of the rhodopsin in the retina: The pigment is not in a solution, but embedded in membranes which in turn are encased in structures that approach the wavelength of light in diameter, and can produce perturbations in the spectral properties of the cells. Although to be more true to the actual physical situation, a waveguide approach is required, the exact properties of the cell that must be modeled are too poorly known at present to make the attempt worthwhile. Second, the media correction term, τ_λ, differs in systematic ways from one eye to another. Third, the effective axial density of the pigment may not be the same in different eyes, and may even vary from one region to another of the retina (certainly this would be true for the cone pigments). Finally, the extinction spectrum itself may not be absolutely identical from one eye to another (Bowmaker, Loew, & Liebman, 1975). The result of these points is that the theory or model embodied in equation 2.35 is more likely to be used in conjunction with scotopic spectral sensitivity data to estimate the parameters pigment density, extinction λ_{max}, and media transmissivity rather than to test the particular physical model it embodies. In other words, because the Univariance principle is believable, the model embodied in equation 2.35 takes on a normative aspect—something like it must be true!

Photopic Vision

Grassmann's Laws of Metameric Color Matching

Scotopic vision is *monochromatic*—any light can be matched in effectiveness to any other by adjustment of their relative intensities. In striking contrast, photopic vision is *trichromatic*, requiring three independent variables to make lights match. The story of man's gradual realization that trichromacy results from the physiology of the eye and brain and not from the physics of light is a fascinating chapter in the history and philosophy of science. Chapter 8 of Brindley (1970) presents a readable introduction to this history. Certainly Thomas Young in 1802 grasped the basic nature of trichromacy (although Young failed to make a clear distinction between perceived color and the physics of light):

Now, as it is almost impossible to conceive each sensitive point of the retina to contain an infinite number of particles, each capable of vibrating in perfect unison with every possible undulation, it becomes necessary to suppose the number limited; for instance, to the three principal colours, red, yellow and blue . . . and that each is capable of being put into motion less or more forcibly by undulations differing less or more from a perfect unison . . . each sensitive filament of the nerve may consist of three portions, one for each principal colour. (Quoted in Brindley, 1970, p. 203.)

One can find variation of opinion on just what the term trichromacy means, and in particular one finds the term is used to refer both to psychophysical phenomena and to the physiological explanation of these phenomena. The clearest operational definition of the concept comes from the framework of human metameric color matching, and specifically from the formal statement of the laws obeyed by symmetric color matches, known as **Grassmann's Laws** in honor of Grassmann (1853), who formulated them. The context of systematic metameric color matches is a small region of the central retina (no more than 10 deg). The observer views a split field, and an apparatus (typically a Maxwellian view) allows independent adjustment of the intensities of several light beams that can illuminate either side of the field. The notation adopted here is that of Krantz (1975), and the student is urged to consult Krantz's important paper for a rigorous and thorough treatment of these ideas. A, B, C, etc. refer to arbitrary spectral distributions; "*" signifies neutral attenuation ($t*A$ means attenuation of the spectrum $A(\lambda)$ at all wavelengths by the factor t where $0 < t < 1$); the symbol "$\oplus$" signifies physical superposition of spectra ($A \oplus B$ is the spectral distribution formed by adding the energy $A(\lambda) + B(\lambda)$, at every wavelength, λ); the special symbol "$\sim$" refers to the psychophysical matching operation itself, and signifies that the two halves of the split field are matched by an observer. A true metameric match renders the two sides of the match field completely indiscriminable, although discrimination experiments are rarely done with humans in practice. Grassmann's Laws (Krantz's reformulation) follow:

1. **Law of Neutral Attenuation**. If a light A matches a light B, then the match is preserved if both sides of the match are attenuated by a common neutral density filter. In notation,

$$A \sim B \Rightarrow t*A \sim t*B \qquad (2.36)$$

2. **Law of Superposition (Additivity)**. Two lights A and B are metameric to one another if and only if for any third light C the mixtures $A \oplus C$ and $B \oplus C$ are metameric; the admixture (or subtraction) of a common light to the two sides of a matching field leaves the two sides matched.

In notation,

$$A \sim B \Leftrightarrow \text{for all } C, A \oplus C \sim B \oplus C$$

$$(2.37)$$

3. **Law of Trichromacy**. (i) For the normal observer, given any four lights A, B, C, and D a match can always be made by adjusting the intensity and the position (which side of the matching field) of only three of them. (ii) There exists a set of three lights such that no non-trivial match can be made among them by any adjustment of position and intensity. In notation,

(i) Given any four lights A, B, C, and D there exist scalars t_A, t_B, t_C such that

$$D \sim t_A^* A \oplus t_B^* B \oplus t_C^* C$$

(ii) There exist lights U, V, W such that no match can be made among them alone.

The first two laws state that color matches are preserved under *neutral attenuation*, and *superposition* of a common light. The Law of Trichromacy has two parts. The first states that any four lights A, B, C, and D are *linearly dependent*—that is, a match can always be made by scalar adjustment of the intensity and/or position of three of them, say A, B, and C. Care must be taken in the interpretation of the scalar coefficients—negative scalars are usually required for one or more of the components, meaning that those components must be admixed to the side of the field containing D. The second part states that there exists a set of three lights that are *linearly independent* (in fact there are a large number of such sets). Any such set is called a set of *primaries* for color matching; for an arbitrary light D and a particular set of primaries U, V, and W, the scalars $t_U(D)$, $t_V(D)$, $t_W(D)$ in the matching equation 2.38 are called *tristimulus values* for D. When $D = 1_\lambda$ (i.e., D ranges over the set of spectral lights) then the scalars $t_U(1_\lambda)$, $t_V(1_\lambda)$, $t_W(1_\lambda)$ are called the *color matching functions* for that set of primaries.

Physically distinct lights that match under symmetric viewing conditions are called *metamers*; the matching operation divides the infinite dimensional space of spectral distributions into metameric equivalence classes. It has been recognized since Grassmann that the laws of metameric matching permit the mapping of the metameric equivalence classes onto a three-dimensional real vector space (a rigorous proof is given in Krantz, 1975); given a set of primaries U, V, W, one particular representation of the vector space is in terms of the tristimulus coordinates (t_U, t_V, t_W). Once the color matching functions have been measured for a particular set of primaries, then the vector representation of any other light can be computed by virtue of Grassmann's Law of Additivity, since any other light can be represented as the superposition of spectral lights. The two sets of tristimulus values of a light for any two distinct sets of primaries are related by a nonsingular linear transformation, which can be represented as a 3×3 matrix of coordinates (see Wyszecki & Stiles, 1982). Because of Grassmann's Laws, international standards of color matching functions have been codified from the data of a series of experiments by Guild, Wright, Stiles, and others (see Wyszecki & Stiles, 1982), and serve as the basis for standardizing dyes, paints, color television, etc. Figure 2.21 shows color matching functions for monochromatic primaries of wavelengths 436 nm, 546 nm, and 700 nm.

Note that the characterization of normal photopic vision in terms of the properties of metameric matching says nothing at all about the perceptual qualities of photopic lights, and that Grassmann's Laws and the vector space representation of metamers made possible by these laws are logically (although obviously not ontologically) independent of the physiological theory of color matches, discussed in the next section.

The Pigment Theory of Color Matching

The essential tenets of the generally accepted theory of metameric color matching are two:

1. the Univariance Principle which states that within each photoreceptor, isomerizations produced by quanta of different wavelengths are indistinguishable; and

2. the hypothesis that a metameric match is established when the quantum catch rate for each of the three classes of cones is equated on each side of the matching field.

The Univariance Principle was discussed in the context of scotopic vision (see p. 114). The second tenet is a novel linking proposition, and ranks with the similar (but simpler) proposition stated for scotopic vision (see p. 114) as one of the great *linking hypotheses* of vision.

To express the pigment theory of matches formally, we assume that one side of the matching field is illuminated with a monochromatic light of $\mathbf{1}_\lambda$ unit quantum intensity $q(\lambda)$, and that three monochromatic primaries U, V, and W are admixed as necessary to make the maximum saturation match,

$$q(\lambda) * \mathbf{1}_\lambda \sim t_U(\mathbf{1}_\lambda) * U + t_V(\mathbf{1}_\lambda) * V + t_W(\mathbf{1}_\lambda) * W$$

$$(2.39)$$

Letting $S_{1\lambda}$, $S_{2\lambda}$, and $S_{3\lambda}$ represent the absorption spectra of the three classes of foveal cones at the cornea (i.e., as they would be measured with light entering the eye through the ocular media), each cone's quantum catch from the primaries can be written as the sum of three terms, which sum to the catch from the monochromatic light:

$$S_{1\lambda} q(\lambda) = S_{1U} t_U(\mathbf{1}_\lambda) + S_{1V} t_V(\mathbf{1}_\lambda) + S_{1W} t_W(\mathbf{1}_\lambda)$$
$$S_{2\lambda} q(\lambda) = S_{2U} t_U(\mathbf{1}_\lambda) + S_{2V} t_V(\mathbf{1}_\lambda) + S_{2W} t_W(\mathbf{1}_\lambda)$$
$$S_{3\lambda} q(\lambda) = S_{3U} t_U(\mathbf{1}_\lambda) + S_{3V} t_V(\mathbf{1}_\lambda) + S_{3W} t_W(\mathbf{1}_\lambda),$$

$$(2.40)$$

where $t_U(\mathbf{1}_\lambda)$, $t_V(\mathbf{1}_\lambda)$, and $t_W(\mathbf{1}_\lambda)$ are the color matching functions (see Figure 2.21) for the three primaries U, V, and W for a unit quantum spectrum $\mathbf{1}_\lambda$. In effect, each time a trichromatic observer makes a symmetric color match he is solving three simultaneous linear equations in three unknowns—the three tristimulus values for the match. (If the value of a color matching function is negative at a wavelength, then the primary must be admixed to the side of the field containing λ.) In words, the theorem embodied in equation 2.40 is:

Each of the three foveal cone classes has a spectral sensitivity (at the cornea) that is a linear combination of any set of color matching functions.

One proof can be found in Brindley (1957). Krantz (1975) presents a more formal derivation based upon linear algebraic principles, and in particular upon the properties of the "dual space" of linear functionals, whose vector basis the three normal pigments form. A major difference between the result embodied in equation

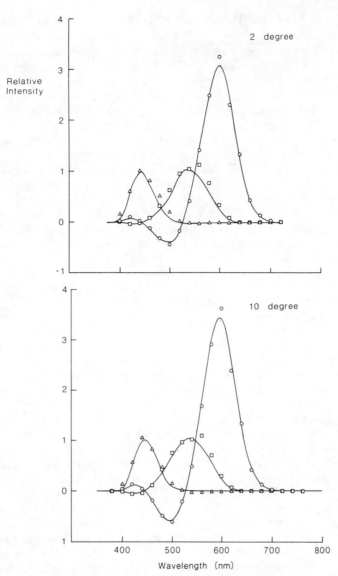

Figure 2.21. Upper panel. The smooth curves are tristimulus values for metameric matches to an equal-quantum monochromatic spectrum derived from the small-field (foveal, 2 deg) color-matching data of Stiles and Burch (1955): the curves give the retinal quantal flux of each of three monochromatic primaries (645.2 nm, 526.3 nm, and 444.4 nm) required to make a metameric match to a monochromatic light of unit flux whose wavelength is given by the abscissa. The symbols give the tristimulus values predicted by Baylor, Nunn, and Schnapf (1987) from their monkey cone extinction spectra, shown in Figure 2.22. The pigments were assumed to have peak axial optical densities of 0.27; the macular pigment density at 460 nm was assumed to be 0.29, and the lens density at 400 nm to be 1.22 (the spectra for the latter were obtained from tabulated spectra in Wyszecki & Stiles, 1982).

Lower panel. The smooth curves are tristimulus values for metameric matches to an equal-quantum monochromatic spectrum derived from the large-field (foveally centered, 10 deg) color-matching data of Stiles and Burch (1959), as described for the upper panel. The symbols give the tristimulus values predicted by Baylor et al. (1987) from the monkey cone extinction spectra assuming peak axial cone densities of 0.17, macular pigment density at 460 nm of 0.13, and lens density at 400 nm of 1.13.

The differences in the estimates of the parameters (peak axial cone density, macular pigment) are roughly consistent with regional variation in these quantities in the retina (see Figure 2.11), assuming the matches are computed on the basis of averaging across the relevant photoreceptor population. From "Spectral Sensitivity of Cones of the Monkey. *Macaca fascicularis*" by D.A. Baylor, B.J. Nunn, and J.L. Schnapf, 1987, *Journal of Physiology, 390*, 145–160. Copyright 1987 by The Physiological Society. Reprinted by permission.

2.40 and that obtained for the one-dimensional case of scotopic vision, is that equation 2.40 of itself gives no way to derive from the psycho-physically measured color matching functions the three cone absorption spectra. Furthermore, the three pigments cannot be argued to be known in advance with any precision. Thus, the problem remains to determine exactly what the three underlying cone spectral sensitivities are. The history of attempts to determine them by various logical and empirical artifices goes back into the last century, and is punctuated with great names like Helmholtz, Schrödinger, Stiles, and others. An excellent treatment can be found in Wyszecki and Stiles (1982).

Candidate Pigment Spectra; Reduction Dichromacy; Pigment Variation

The most well known method of deriving the three cone spectral sensitivities is based on a hypothesis proposed by Koenig and Dieterici (1892). The hypothesis is that each major form of *dichromacy* results from loss of one of the three spectra: *protanopia*, the loss of the most long-wave sensitive; *deuteranopia*, the mid-wave sensitive; and *tritanopia*, the short-wave sensitive. Given the Koenig loss hypothesis, and the color matching functions of normals and of the three classes of dichromats, it is possible to derive (see Wyszecki & Stiles, 1982) the three cone spectral sensitivities. The effort by Thomson and Wright (1952) and the more recent essays by Vos and Walraven (1971), Smith and Pokorny (1975), Estevez (1979) and Vos (1978) are notable in this regard; most color scientists agree that the derived sensitivities are reasonable estimates. Table 2.4 gives cone spectral sensitivities deduced from color matching data on the basis of the Koenig hypothesis by Smith and Pokorny (1975). These spectral sensitivities have been widely used in theoretical modeling in color theory (see, for example, a detailed discussion of them by Boynton & Wisowaty, 1980).

Difficulties arise in treating spectra derived with the Koenig loss hypothesis as the cone spectral sensitivities of an arbitrary color normal observer. First, it is quite clear that there is systematic variation among color normals in color matches; the Koenig spectra are in effect measured at the cornea, so any variation in the transmissivity of the eye media across observers invalidates their general use (Smith, Pokorny, &

Starr, 1976); such variation is especially large in the region of the spectrum below 500 nm where both macular pigment and lens absorption are significant. A second difficulty has arisen in experiments when the Koenig hypothesis is directly put to the test: that is, when dichromats are confronted with color matches made by normal trichromats, they do not generally accept them (Alpern, Bastian, & Moeller, 1982; Alpern & Moeller, 1977), although for any given dichromat usually there can be found a normal trichromat whose matches the dichromat will accept. Finally, there is systematic variation in both normal and dichromatic matches (Alpern & Pugh, 1977; Smith, Pokorny, & Starr, 1976) that can be ruled out by the rescaling procedure of W.D. Wright as due to any photostable pre-retinal filter.

Resolution of some of the problems that have plagued efforts to determine human cone action spectra will come in the near future with suction electrode recordings of individual cones from ennucleated eyes. The first report of human cone action spectra so determined has appeared (Schnapf, Kraft, & Baylor, 1987). An extensive series of such measurements on cones of macaque monkeys has already been reported (Baylor, Nunn, & Schnapf, 1987). Macaques are known from behavioral work to have cone spectra very similar to humans' (DeValois, Morgan, Polson, Mead, & Hull, 1974). Figure 2.22 presents spectra of 41 macaque monkey cones—16 long-wave sensitive, 20 mid-wave sensitive, and 5 short-wave sensitive—from 5 monkeys measured with the suction electrode action spectrum technique by Baylor et al. (1987). As discussed above (see Figure 2.20), the action spectrum determined by transversely illuminating a photoreceptor in a suction electrode is reciprocally proportional to the pigment extinction spectrum. Figure 2.21 presents a comparison of the best human 2 deg (Stiles & Burch, 1955) and 10 deg (Stiles & Burch, 1959) color matching functions (curves; with predictions (symbols) derived from average monkey cone extinction spectra, employing equations 2.35 and 2.40, as described in Baylor et al. (1987). The conclusions to be drawn are that cones with the extinction spectra in Figure 2.22 could be the basis of the color matching functions, and that the spectra of these cones are likely very close, and possibly identical, to the average normal human cone extinction spectra.

Because the data of Figure 2.22 are action

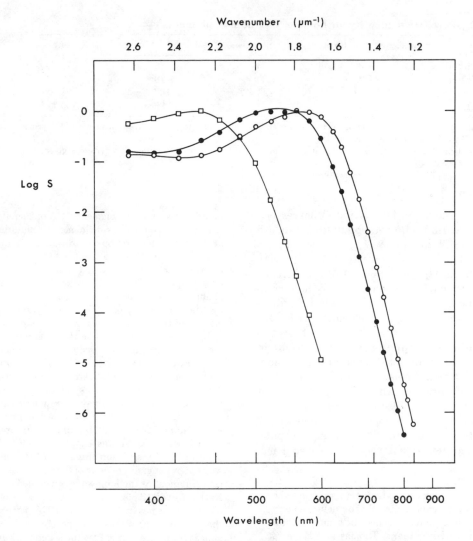

Figure 2.22. Average spectral sensitivities (reciprocal action spectra) of 5 short-wave sensitive, 19 mid-wave sensitive and 16 long-wave sensitive cones from macaque monkey cones, measured with suction electrode technique. The standard deviations of λ_{max} for the mid-wave and long-wave cone populations were 1.4 and 0.9 nm, indicating very little variation in extinction spectra across the population of 5 animals. From "Spectral Sensitivity of Single Cones of the Monkey, *Macaca Fascicularis*" by D.A. Baylor, B.J. Nunn, and J.L. Schnapf, 1987, Journal of Physiology, *390*, pp. 145–160. Copyright 1987 by the Physiological Society. Reprinted by permission.

spectra, the variation of the data points is essentially wavelength-independent. This feature allows far more accurate determination of the extinction coefficient away from the absorption peak than any densitometric technique, since the latter techniques rely on measurement of the fraction of light absorbed, which diminishes very rapidly away from λ_{max}. The mean values of the λ_{max}s reported by Baylor et al. (1987) for the three

classes of monkey cones are 565 nm, 538 nm, and 435 nm. The discrepancy of these values from microspectrophotometrically determined λ_{max}s of monkey (565 nm, 535 nm and 415 nm) and human (558 nm, 531 nm, and 419 nm) is noteworthy, but could be due to slight differences in the procedure of determining λ_{max} for the rather broad, flat-topped spectral distributions. The standard deviations of the λ_{max}s determined by the action

Table 2.6. Percentage identity[1] or homology[2] of human pigments[3]

	Rhodopsin	Short-wave	Mid-wave	Long-wave
Rhodopsin	100	75	73	73
Short-wave	42	100	79	79
Mid-wave	41	44	100	99
Long-wave	40	43	96	100

[1]Identity, meaning that the same amino acid residue occupies a given position in the linear sequence of the protein, is given in the table by entries above the diagonal.
[2]Homology, defined in terms of sets of subsitutable residues that have related functional properties is given in the table by entries below the diagonal.
[3]Source: Nathans, Thomas, and Hogness (1986).

spectra technique are 1.0, 1.3, and 1.4 nm respectively, about 1/3 to 1/5 the population standard deviations of human cone λ_{max}s estimated from microspectrophotometry (see p. 111) or psychophysics (e.g., Alpern & Pugh, 1977). Difference in measurement precision amongst the techniques is the first hypothesis that will have to be examined in the effort to account for the discrepancy in λ_{max} dispersion. This hypothesis certainly will be tested in the near future by direct measurement of the action spectra of a substantial population of human cones with the suction electrode technique. Another hypothesis that may account for the discrepancy in variation of λ_{max} is that the human population is genetically more heterogeneous than the macaque population in the genes that specify the visual pigments.

It has now become possible to examine the population genome directly for heterogeneity in the cone pigment genes. In a monumental investigation, Nathans, Thomas and Hogness (1986) used recombinant genetic technology to isolate and clone the DNA of the human cone pigments. Their investigation proved the position of the genes for the long-wave and mid-wave sensitive pigments to be on the q-arm of the X-chromosome, as predicted by conventional genetics (Kalmus, 1965); the short-wave pigment gene residues on the seventh; the rhodopsin gene resides on the third chromosome. Table 2.6 shows the percentage homology and identity for the amino acid residue sequences of the four human visual pigments. Perhaps even more remarkable than the near identity of the long- and mid-wave opsins is that the color normal population varies in the number of copies of the mid-wave pigment gene with different individuals having 1, 2, or 3 copies per long-wave pigment gene. In a subsequent study, Nathans, Piantanida, Eddy, Shows, and Hogness (1986)

investigated the cone pigment DNA of 25 males with phenotypic colour deficiencies, including protanopia, deuteranopia, protanomaly and deuteranomaly. This study confirmed the modern interpretation of Koenig and Dieterici's (1892) loss hypothesis, by showing that some phenotypic deuteranopes are completely missing the gene that specifies the mid-wave pigment, and that some phenotypic protanopes are completely missing the gene that specifies the long-wave pigment. Other red/green dichromats have various fragments of DNA from the functionally absent pigment. In striking contrast to dichromats, color anomalous individuals, have an almost bewildering array of fragments and combinations of the two X-chromosome genes. For example, two out of ten anomalous individuals whose DNA was examined had eight copies of one restriction fragment of the mid-wave pigment gene per copy of the same restriction fragment of the long-wave pigment. While Nathans et al. (1986) propose reasonable recombination schemes that explain the DNA patterns they have seen, at present there is nothing approaching a theory of how these genetic variations produce the phenotypic variation in anomalous color vision. The central problem for such theory will be to explain how changes in amino acid sequence give rise to pigments with different λ_{max}s, a deep structure–function problem involving quantum mechanical calculations.

PHOTOTRANSDUCTION

Photoreceptor Electrophysiology

The function of the photoreceptor is to generate electrical signals that convey the rate of light absorption in the outer segment to the neurons of the inner retina. *Transduction*, the actual conversion of light into an electrical event at the cell membrane, occurs in the outer segment. In transmitting the signal to synapses with secondary neurons, the photoreceptor behaves as an electrical cable: the membrane hyperpolarization induced by light propagates down the cell to the region of synaptic contact with bipolar and horizontal cells (the rod spherule or cone pedicle), and causes a decrease in the rate of synaptic transmitter release. We now give a brief summary of the photoreceptor as transducer and cable.

Photoreceptors, like all cells, maintain ionic gradients (or "batteries") across their plasma membrane at the expense of metabolic energy. Since the cell membrane is permeable to water, the maintenance of relatively high concentration of external Na^+ (100 to 150 mM) and of relatively low internal Na^+ serves to balance the outward osmotic pressure that would be generated by the soluble organic molecules (polypeptides, nucleotides, etc., which are usually negatively charged). Internal electrical neutrality is achieved in part by having a relatively high internal potassium concentration; external potassium is relatively low (1 to 3 mM). The internal concentrations of sodium and potassium are maintained against their gradients by an ATP-consuming pump (an integral, trans-membrane protein) that transports 3 Na ions and countertransports 2 to 3 K ions per ATP molecule hydrolyzed.

A fundamental feature of the vertebrate photoreceptor is that it maintains in the dark a steady *dark current*, which flows in a loop between outer and inner segments as demonstrated by Hagins, Penn, and Yoshikami (1970) in the retina of the rat, whose rods are quite similar to those of primates. The spatially integrated magnitude of the dark current in a rat rod is c. 70 pA—that is, 70×10^{-12} amperes (Hagins et al., 1970). In isolated macaque monkey rods, the dark current magnitude is near the same value (Baylor, Nunn, & Schnapf, 1984). The metabolic load of this current is large: To maintain steady state in the dark in the face of a 50 pA current leak, a rod must pump out about $3 \times 10^8 Na^+$ ions/sec/rod (1 monovalent ion carries a charge of 1.6×10^{-16} coulombs). The Na-pumping in turn requires consumption of about 10^8 ATP molecules/sec/rod, or for the whole human retina, about 2×10^{16} ATP/sec, requiring about 5 nanomoles oxygen/sec for oxidative metabolism. The oxygen demand of

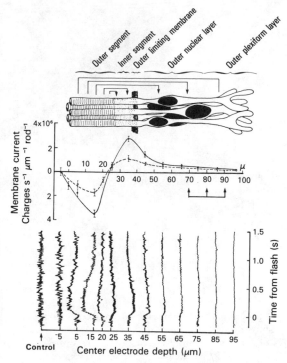

Figure 2.23. Spatial distribution of rat rod photocurrents. On the left is shown the current that flows across the rod membrane in response to a flash yielding about 100 isomerizations. A yoked triplex of extracellular microelectrodes centered on the value given in the left-hand ordinate was advanced into the retina from the receptor tips; by computing an appropriately weighted difference of the first spatial derivatives of extracellular voltage in the longitudinal direction with the electrodes, the current flowing across the membrane in response to the flash could be computed.

In the middle are shown the amplitudes of the average response to 16 flashes for flashes of 100 and 400 isomerizations. In the outer segment region the photocurrent is outward; in the inner segment, inward, summing to zero over the whole rod.

On the right is shown a sketch of the rod layer drawn to scale. From "Signal Transmission Along Retinal Rods and the Origin of the Electroretinographic A-Wave" by R.D. Penn and W.S. Hagins, 1969, *Nature, 223,* p. 204.

the retina is as high as that of any other tissue.

Light transiently suppresses the dark current; this effect is somewhat easier to measure than the dark current (requiring less d.c. electrical stability), and is known as the *photocurrent.* Figure 2.23 shows the spatial (source/sink)

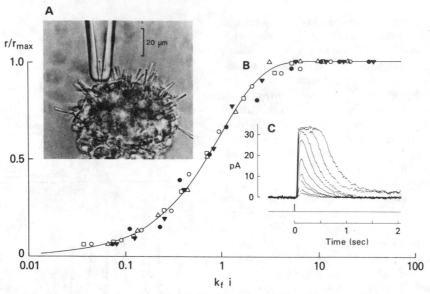

Figure 2.24. (a) Photograph of a monkey rod, attached to a small chip of retina, held in a suction pipette, as it would be for making the recordings in C.

(b) Normalized photocurrent amplitude vs. intensity curves for 7 monkey rods, obtained from data such as shown in C.

(c) Photocurrents of monkey rod recorded with suction pipette technique. Rod outer segment, with rod attached to a small portion of retina, was sucked into the suction pipette as shown in A; membrane current recorded with the technique of Baylor, Lamb, and Yau (1979a). Responses to 11 msec flashes of graded intensity are shown; the responses to the less intense flashes are averages of several sweeps. The most intense flash caused c. 500 isomerizations; the least intense, c. 2. All results in this figure from Baylor, Nunn, and Schnapf (1984.) From "The Photocurrent Noise and Spectral Sensitivity of Rods of the Monkey, *Macaca fasicularis*" by D.A. Baylor, B.J. Nunn, and J.L. Schnapf, 1984, *Journal of Physiology, 357*, p. 579. Copyright 1984 by The Physiological Society. Reprinted by permission.

distribution of rat rod photocurrents, as measured by Hagins et al. (1970). The maximal photocurrent exactly cancels the full dark current (Penn & Hagins, 1972). Light flashes of graduated intensity give rise to graded decrements in the dark current (Figure 2.24A) whose peak magnitudes obey a saturation relation (Bader, MacLeish, & Schwartz, 1979; Baylor, Lamb, & Yau, 1979a; Baylor, Nunn, & Schnapf, 1984; Hagins et al., 1970; Penn & Hagins, 1972). As shown in Figure 2.24B for macaque monkey rods, this saturation relation can be represented as

$$J/J_{max} = 1 - \exp(-K_f i) \qquad (2.41)$$

where J is the peak amplitude of the photocurrent produced by a flash of i isomerizations, J_{max} is the absolute maximal photocurrent, and K_f the fraction of dark current suppressed per isomerization by dim flashes. (By Taylor series expansion of the exponential in equation 2.41, for flash intensities such that $i \ll 1/K_f$, $J/J_{max} = K_f i$). In rat rods (Hagins et al., 1970), in toad

rods (Baylor et al., 1979a), and in macaque monkey rods (Baylor et al., 1984), K_f is about 0.03 to 0.05 —that is, 1 isomerization shuts down about 3 to 5 percent of the standing dark current.

In most neurons permeabilities for the cations Na^+ and K^+ dominate the cell's membrane potential. Given that $[Na^+]$ is higher outside than inside, the sign of the outer segment dark current (outer segment inward) argues that in the dark there must be a net influx of Na^+, down its diffusion gradient into the outer segment. By similar logic the outward dark current of the inner segment is carried primarily by K^+ flowing outward, down its diffusion gradient. Thus, *the primary effect of light on the rod membrane is to suppress the Na^+ conductance of the outer segment*. Consistent with this view of the primary effect of light is the universal finding of intracellular membrane potential recordings from photoreceptors: Light *hyperpolarizes* the rod membrane, that is, drives it toward the c. $-80\,mV$ Nernst potential of K^+ (Fain & Lisman, 1981;

Owen & Torre, 1981), the cation whose permeability would be expected to dominate the membrane potential when Na^+ permeability is blocked.

Characterization of the Light Response

Rod photocurrents give a number of clues about the nature of the transduction process (Figure 2.24A). Below about 20 isomerizations per flash the dark-adapted rod light responses are *linear with light*—that is, are identical in shape when normalized. The shape of the normalized linear response to a brief flash, the *temporal impulse response*, is important for the characterization of the temporal events in transduction. In the range of response linearity each photon absorbed contributes an essentially identical incremental response. Figure 2.25 shows the mean response of a monkey rod to 264 nominally identical dim flashes; this is the cell's photocurrent impulse response. The impulse response is characterizable as *multi-stage* or *multi-order* (see caption, Figure 2.25), a feature noted by Fuortes & Hodgkin (1964) in their treatment of *Limulus* photopotentials. The term multi-order means that to fit the linear response with an analytical expression, one has to employ the equivalent of the mathematical convolution of a series of four or more

single exponential decays stages: In electrical terminology, one concatenates several RC filters (Fuortes & Hodgkin, 1964; Penn & Hagins, 1972); in chemical terminology, one cascades several chemical reactions (Baylor, Hodgkin, & Lamb, 1974). The characterization of the transduction process as multi-stage is parametric and far from unique; fitting schemes based upon other principles (e.g., Payne & Howard, 1981) have been proposed. Nonetheless, most researchers agree that several distinct, cascaded delay stages (chemical reactions, transmembrane transport, and retarded diffusion) underlie the rod impulse response.

A second fundamental feature of the rod impulse response is gain. One characterization of this gain is in terms of energy units. The energy of a single photon of light of wavelength 500 nm is $2.5\,eV$ (see p. 76). In macaque monkey rods a single isomerization causes a displacement across the membrane of a charge of about $0.2\,pC$, or 1.4×10^6 monovalent ions (Figure 2.25; Baylor, Nunn, & Schnapf, 1984; see below). Since the membrane potential E_m is about $-30\,mV$, the work done in response to a single isomerization is $W = q|E_m| = 4.2 \times 10^4\,eV$, for a gain of about 10^4. Thus, the cell behaves as a photomultiplier, enormously amplifying the energy of a single photon. The amplification, of course, is

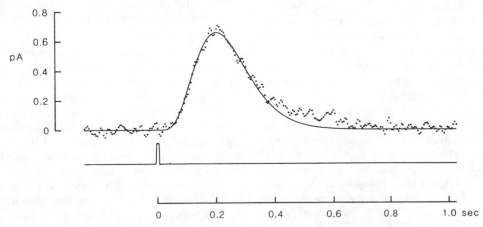

Figure 2.25. Monkey rod impulse response. Average of 264 photocurrent responses of a monkey rod to very dim 11 msec flashes, which was estimated to produce (on average) 0.8 isomerizations/flash. The response can be taken as the form of the single photon response. Smooth curve is the impulse response of a cascade of six identical low-pass ("RC") filters in series. Recording temperature, 36°C; saturating response, 22 pA. From "The Photocurrent Noise and Spectral Sensitivity of Rods of the Monkey, *Macaca fascicularis*" by D.A. Baylor, B.J. Nunn, and J.L. Schnapf, 1984, *Journal of Physiology, 357*, p. 381. Copyright 1984 by The Physiological Society. Reprinted by permission.

achieved at the expense of metabolic energy, most notably in the maintenance of the dark current. Since each open Na$^+$ channel in the outer segment is likely admitting hundreds to thousands of cations/sec in the dark, each channel blocked during the light response contributes an energy gain equal to its closure lifetime times its individual dark current in ions/sec when open, times the membrane potential.

A third fundamental feature of the rod photocurrent is its ability to reliably signal the absorption of single photons. (Cones cannot do this, having considerably lower gain, and more membrane noise.) A compelling argument based upon psychophysical evidence that rods can reliably signal single photon absorptions comes from a simple computation showing that an observer can detect a flash with a probability substantially higher than the probability that any single rod is absorbing two or more quanta. If in a retinal region containing N rods Q quanta are absorbed, then

$$\begin{aligned}
&\text{Prob(any of } N \text{ rods absorbs 2} \\
&\quad \text{or more of } Q \text{ quanta)} \\
&= 1 - \text{Prob}(Q \text{ rods absorb exactly} \\
&\quad \text{one quantum each)} \\
&= 1 - [N/N]\,[(N-1)/N]\,[(N-2)/N] \\
&\quad \ldots [(N-Q+1)/N] \\
&= Q(Q-1)/2N, \quad \text{if } Q \ll N \quad (2.42)
\end{aligned}$$

In their classical psychophysical experiments Hecht, Schlaer, and Pirenne (1942) measured human absolute threshold (60% detection in a Yes/No paradigm, with low false alarm rate) to be 50 to 150 quanta at the cornea. Modern estimates of the preretinal media transmissivity (c. 0.5 at 510 nm) and rhodopsin optical density (c. 0.35) predict that as many as 30 percent of these were absorbed by the c. 500 rods subtended by their target's geometrical image. Thus, the computation of equation 2.42 with their results leaves the question moot as to whether rods can signal single photon absorptions. Absolute threshold measurements by Hallett (1969), Sakitt (1972), Stiles (1939), and others, however, more than suffice to make the argument stick (Brindley, 1970). While psychophysical evidence that rods can signal single photon absorptions is compelling, uncertainties of ocular media transmissivity, internal noise, and observer criteria make it difficult to estimate the actual quantum efficiency of the event—that

is, the conditional probability that an absorbed photon gave rise to an elementary rod signal. Barlow's (1956) analysis concluded that a photon at the cornea must generate a retinal event with a probability between 0.1 and 0.3, which requires the quantum efficiency of the single-isomerization photoresponse to be greater than 40 percent.

Membrane potential recordings from *Limulus* and other invertebrate cells confirmed the existence of photon shot noise in the 1950s and 1960s (e.g., Borsellino & Fuortes, 1968; Fuortes & Yeandle, 1964; Yeandle, 1958; Yeandle & Srebro, 1970; see Fuortes & O'Bryan, 1973, for a review). In 1975, Fain recorded with microelectrodes the membrane potential of single toad rods (which are about 3 times the diameter and 2.5 times the length of human rods) at light intensities (0.6 to 0.2 quanta abs/flash) that would be expected to yield quantum fluctuations in response. However, in the toad retina the receptors are electrically coupled by gap junctions, enabling the potentials to spread through a syncetium of rods, diminishing their magnitude by 90 percent in the impaled cell, and rendering it extremely difficult to measure the response to single photons above the high impedance microelectrode noise. In the late 1970s the suction pipette technique developed by Yau, Lamb, and Baylor (1977) proved capable of measuring the membrane current generated by single photon absorptions in toad rods (Baylor, Lamb, & Yau, 1979b). This technique has now been applied successfully to monkey rods (Baylor, Nunn, & Schnapf, 1984).

Figure 2.26A shows a trace of macaque rod outer segment membrane current measured by Baylor, Nunn, and Schnapf (1984) with the suction electrode technique. At the instants marked by the tick marks, the cell was stimulated by a series of nominally identical dim flashes of 0.6 photons/μm^2. Note that for most of the flashes there appears to be no response that rises above the noise of the trace; in a few instances, however, responses clearly resulted. This response variability, which is not seen for more intense flashes, results from the facts that photon absorptions from a fixed intensity flash necessarily follow a Poisson distribution, whose variance is equal to its mean. The intuitive analysis of results such as those shown in Figure 2.26A is strengthened by analysis of the histograms of peak response amplitudes to a large series of identical dim flashes, chosen so that most of

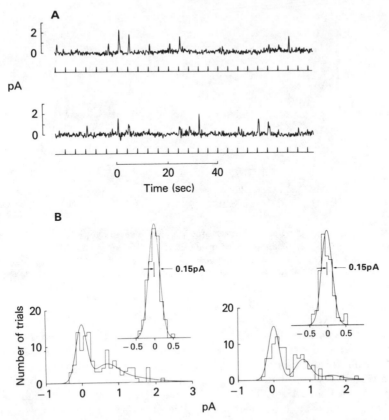

Figure 2.26. (a) Amplitude variation in monkey rod photocurrent response to very dim flashes. At each point marked by tic on abscissa, an 11 msec flash of 0.6 photons/μm^2, λ = 500 nm was delivered. From "The Photocurrent Noise and Spectral Sensitivity of Rods of the Monkey, *Macaca fascicularis*" by D.A. Baylor, B.J. Nunn, and J.L. Schnapf, 1984, *Journal of Physiology, 357,* pp. 587, 588. Copyright 1984 by The Physiological Society. Reprinted by permission.

(b) Histograms of peak amplitudes of responses of two rods to a large series of flashes, such as shown in Figure 2.26A. Smooth curves fit to data calculated from a four-parameter theory: Poisson distribution of events with mean peak amplitude a, occurring at mean rate m/trial; convoluted with the Poisson variation is a gaussian variation in event amplitude, with standard deviation σ_1, and an independent dark gaussian noise of standard deviation σ_0. For the left histogram, a = 0.68 pA, m = 0.70, σ = 0.30 pA, σ_0 = 0.15 pA. For the right histogram, a = 0.81 pA, m = 0.54, σ_1 = 0.20 pA, σ_0 = 0.15 pA. Insets are amplitude histograms of trials with no flashes. From "The Photocurrent Noise and Spectral Sensitivity of Rods of the Monkey, *Macaca fascicularis*" by D.A. Baylor, B.J. Nunn, and J.L. Schnapf, 1984, *Journal of Physiology, 357,* pp. 587, 588. Copyright 1984 by The Physiological Society. Reprinted by permission.

the flashes apparently give no response at all. Figure 2.26B shows such histograms for two monkey rods (Baylor, Nunn, & Schnapf, 1984). The amplitude histograms were derived from the individual trials by fitting the normalized ensemble average (mean of all responses) to each individual flash response. The insets are histograms for interleaved trials of complete darkness. The smooth curves drawn through the histograms are consistent with the idea that the response amplitude variations are generated by a Poisson process, assuming additional Gaussian amplitude variation in the dark, and in the response to each photon (see Baylor et al., 1979b, for details). From these and related data Baylor, Nunn, and Schnapf (1984) estimate the mean single photon response of a monkey rod to have an amplitude of c. 0.7 pA, with a time to peak of c. 190 msec (see Figure 2.25).

Baylor et al. (1979b) in their elegant paper

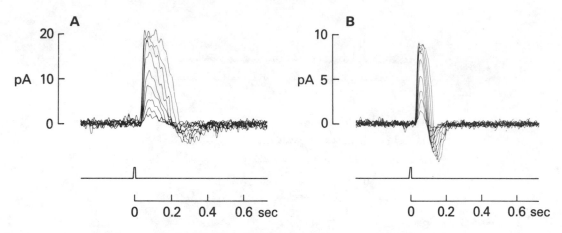

Figure 2.27. Superimposed photocurrent responses of a long-wave sensitive (a) and a mid-wave sensitive (b) monkey cone to a series of 10 msec flashes graded in about two-fold increments of intensity. From "Spectral Sensitivity of Single Cones in the Retina of *Macaca fascicularis*" by B.J. Nunn, D.A. Baylor, and J.L. Schnapf, 1985, reprinted by permission from *Nature, 309* (5965), pp. 264–266. Copyright © 1985 Macmillan Journals Limited. Reprinted by permission.

analyzing the single photon responses of toad rods, show with several analyses that the mean peak photocurrent/photoisomerization in toad is c. 1 pA, with a time to peak of about 1 to 2 sec under their experimental conditions. They also demonstrated that the single photon response is spectrally univariant (i.e., does not depend on the wavelength of the light—see p. 114), and by comparing microspectrophotometric measurements of bleaching and rod responses to single photons for the first time obtained a quantitative estimate of the quantum efficiency of the single photon response, 0.5 ± 0.1, a value slightly lower but very close to the quantum efficiency of bleaching, 0.67.

Baylor, Nunn, and Schnapf (1987) have used the suction electrode technique to characterize the photocurrents of macaque monkey cones as well as those of rods. Figure 2.27 shows response series for a long-wave sensitive cone and for a mid-wave sensitive cone (cf. Figure 2.22). Monkey cone photocurrents differ from those of rods in four fundamental ways. First, cone photocurrents are much less sensitive to light: Cones, despite having maximal photocurrents comparable to those of rods, produce around 0.01 pA/isomerization at response peak as opposed to 0.7 pA/ isomerization in rods. Second, dark-adapted cones are 2 to 4 times faster than rods: time to peak of linear response (impulse response) was 60 to 100 msec in cones, but 150 to 250 msec in

rods. Third, cone photocurrents are strikingly biphasic, whereas those of rods are monophasic (compare Figures 2.24, 2.25 and 2.27); this difference extends to the linear or dim-flash impulse response. Fourth, monkey rod photocurrents show little desensitization in response to steady illumination other than that due to the response compression resulting from their limited response range: To a good approximation, the step response (to arbitrarily long steps) is the integral of the impulse response, the linear flash response in the presence of a steady light. Monkey cone photocurrents, on the other hand show genuine desensitization in response to steady illumination (see p. 146). These differences in rod and cone photocurrents must reflect interesting differences in their transduction mechanisms. On the other hand, recent evidence suggests that rods and cones in vertebrates have a similar light-activated biochemical mechanism (see p. 133).

The differences between primary rod and cone photocurrents provide insight into several psychophysical phenomena. Absolute threshold in the fovea requires multiple isomerizations per cone, probably as many as seven (Brindley, 1970, p. 189); absolute scotopic threshold usually is achieved when no individual rod absorbs more than 1 photon per flash. This difference in absolute photopic and scotopic thresholds is due at least in part to the difference in intrinsic sensitivities of the two cells types. The psychophysically measured photopic temporal modulation threshold function (m.t.f.) shows a low frequency decline (bandpass characteristic), whereas, the scotopic temporal m.t.f. shows no such decline. This difference in m.t.f.'s is expected because of the difference between rod and cone impulse responses. If the visual system as a whole acts as a linear system at the modulation threshold (De Lange, 1958), the modulation threshold curve will be proportional to the modulus of the Fourier transform of the underlying impulse response. The modulus of the Fourier transform of a biphasic impulse response has a low-frequency roll-off, whereas that of a monophasic impulse response has no low-frequency roll-off. It should be kept in mind that it is the change in photoreceptor voltage at the synapse that drives the change in synaptic transmitter release, not the photocurrent per se. Nonetheless, in the linear response range of each class of photoreceptor one can reasonably expect the photocurrent and photovoltage to be proportional to each other.

Specific Hypotheses about the Phototransduction Process

In the report of their classic investigation of horseshoe crab photovoltages, Fuortes and Hodgkin (1964) discuss the possibility that light produces an activator whose concentration regulates the light-sensitive conductance. Baylor and Fuortes (1970) argued their recordings from turtle cones to be consistent with the hypothesis that light produces a "substance which decreases the permeability of membrane channels acting as a shunt of the membrane in darkness." Many subsequent investigations of vertebrate phototransduction have been focused by the insight that the transduction process in rods requires an *internal transmitter* between disk membranes and the plasma membrane. This requirement follows from two premises: First, the rhodopsin molecules that initiate the normal light response are integrally embedded in disk membranes; second (with the exception of a few basal disks), the disk membranes are not continuous with the envelope or plasma membrane of the rod (see p. 102, and Olive, 1980, for discussion of these premises). Only two substances have been hypothesized to be the internal transmitter of rod

excitation: the divalent cation Ca^{2+} (calcium) and the cyclic nucleotide cGMP (cyclic guanosine monophosphate). The evidence now overwhelmingly supports the cGMP hypothesis. A brief review of the theories based upon these two substances follows. For more extensive reviews, see Applebury and Chabre (1986), Miller (1981), Pugh and Cobbs (1986), and Stryer (1986).

The Calcium Hypothesis

The hypothesis that Ca^{2+} is the internal transmitter was proposed by Yoshikami and Hagins (1970). According to the hypothesis, Ca^{2+} is released from the rod disks by light (perhaps through a pore formed by photoactivated rhodopsin), diffuses through the cytoplasm to the plasma membrane, and there transiently reduces the Na^+ conductance, perhaps by binding directly to it. A number of experimental results have been taken to support the calcium hypothesis, including the following. (1) Elevated external Ca^{2+} reduces the outer segment Na^+ conductance, as does light (Yoshikami & Hagins, 1973). (2) Elevated Ca^{2+} is much more effective on the inside than outside of the plasma membrane in reducing the Na^+ conductance (Hagins & Yoshikami, 1974, 1977). (3) Rods contain the requisite amount of Ca^{2+} in the bound state, mostly inside the disks (Schnettkamp, 1979; Szuts & Cone, 1977). (4) Light causes a transient increase in Ca^{2+} in the extracellular space around the outer segment; (5) the time course of the appearance of this increase closely parallels the photocurrent; (6) the number of extra Ca^{2+}s that appear in the extra-cellular space per photon is quite high—hundreds to thousands (Gold & Korenbrot, 1980; Yoshikami, George, & Hagins, 1980). Yoshikami et al. (1980) argue that the most likely explanation of the light-triggered increase in extra-cellular Ca^{2+} is a transient increase in intracellular Ca^{2+}. The fact that Ca^{2+} appears outside the cell against its relatively large electrochemical gradient, $\simeq -110\,mV$, means that work must be done to extrude it from the rod. Evidence (Yau & Nakatani, 1984) supports the hypothesis that the mechanism that performs this work is a Na/Ca exchange carrier, which uses the energy stored in the transmembrane Na gradient that is maintained by the Na/K pump.

Although the Calcium Hypothesis proved extremely productive in generating information about rods, it is now certain that it is false. The following findings cannot be reconciled with it.

(1) The light-sensitive conductance has been found to be quite permeable to Ca^{2+} (Yau &

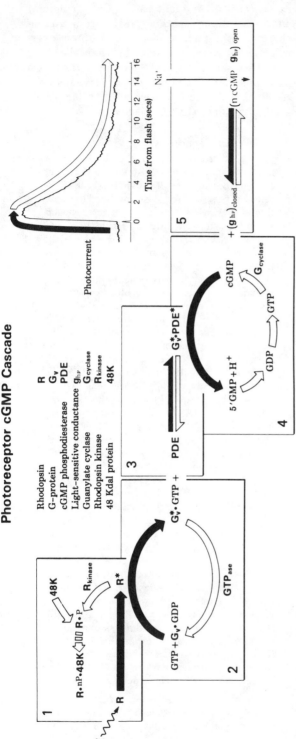

Figure 2.28. A schematic diagram of the cGMP Cascade Theory of Phototransduction. In this diagram the filled arrows represent events that lead to the closure of the light-sensitive conductance, g_{hv}; events that lead to the reopening of the conductance are represented as open arrows. Arched arrows indicate enzymatic catalysis; straight arrows indicate binding interactions. Each of the five boxes represent a physically distinct stage, involving both a forward and reverse reaction(s). This scheme was derived from work of many investigations.

Forward reactions (filled arrows)

(1) Photon absorption by rhodopsin, R, transforms it to an enzymatically active state, R^*. (2) In its active state, R^* catalyzes the exchange of GTP and GDP on GTP-binding protein, G_v, converting it to its active form, G_v^*·GTP. (3) G_v^* (or the separated α-subunit) activates phosphodiesterase, PDE, by binding. (4) PDE* catalyzes the hydrolysis of cGMP. (5) The catalyzed breakdown of cGMP causes the cytoplasm concentration of cGMP to fall, causing the binding reaction between cGMP and the cGMP-gated conductance, g_{hv}, to be driven toward the unbound state, in which the conductance is impermeable to Na$^+$, thereby decreasing the dark current of the outer segment. As the K$^+$ current of the inner segment (that balanced the outer segment Na$^+$ current at rest in the dark) continues to flow out, the cell hyperpolarizes.

Restoration reactions (open arrows)

(1) Photoactivated rhodopsin, R^*, is inactivated by phosphorylation and subsequent binding of 48K protein. (2) G_v^*·GTP is inactivated by the hydrolysis of the terminal phosphate of GTP, rendering the protein back into its inactive form G_v·GDP. (3) G_v·GDP lowered affinity for PDE causes it to be released, inactivating PDE*. (4) [cGMP] in the cytoplasm is restored by the enzyme guanylate cyclase, G-cyclase, which acts upon the relatively large pool of GTP maintained by enzymes that rephosphorylate GMP and GDP to GTP. (5) As [cGMP] rises in the outer segment, the binding reaction to the cGMP-gated channel is driven toward the bound state, reestablishing permeability of some of the channels to Na$^+$.

The glaring omission in this diagram is the role of Ca^{2+}. The latter ion leaks in with Na$^+$ through the open cGMP-gated channel and is pumped out by an Na/Ca exchange, to maintain steady state. When the inward leak is stopped by light, the pumping continues, causing the [Ca^{2+}]$_i$ to drop. It is thought that this change in internal calcium acts as a signal to stimulate G-cyclase or perhaps speed up one or more of the other inactivating steps in the cascade. Summary of the work of many laboratories.

Nakatani, 1984), and very large inward currents carried purely by Ca^{2+} (300 pA or greater, corresponding to more than $10^9 Ca^{2+}$ ions/sec) take more than 5 sec to shut down the dark current. In contrast, a step of light delivering 4500 isomerizations/sec during this large Ca^{2+} influx shuts off the dark current in c. 0.2 sec. Reconciling these observations would require that the light step release Ca^{2+} internally at a rate greatly exceeding $[(5/0.2) \times 10^9]/4500 = 6 \times 10^6 Ca^{2+}$/sec/isomerization, a release stoichiometry much higher than estimated from experiments in which there is a measured increase in extracellular Ca^{2+}. Furthermore, analysis shows that the increase in extracellular Ca^{2+} triggered by light can be accounted for quantitatively by assuming merely that light stops the inward flux of Ca^{2+} through the light-sensitive conductance (Yau & Nakatani, 1985a).

(2) Infusion of calcium buffers into rods has shown that these substances actually increase, rather than decrease the rod's sensitivity to light, as predicted by the Calcium Hypothesis (Lamb, Matthews, & Torre, 1986; Matthews, Torre, & Lamb, 1985).

(3) Definitive evidence against the Calcium Hypothesis has been obtained by measuring the luminescence of the calcium-binding photoprotein aequorin, infused into salamander rods (McNaughton, Cervetto, & Nunn, 1986). This investigation directly demonstrated that outer segment free Ca^{2+} decreases in the rod during the light response, in direct conflict with the key tenet of the hypothesis. This decrease was previously inferred by Yau and Nakatani (1985a) from their measurements of the Na/Ca exchange current.

The Cyclic GMP Hypothesis

W.H. Miller proposed that a cyclic nucleotide might act as an internal transmitter in visual transduction, in analogy with the theory of Sutherland that cyclic AMP acts as an internal messenger in many cell types. Miller's proposal launched (Bitensky, Gorman, & Miller, 1971) a field of investigation that gradually uncovered a richly interconnected set of enzymes in the outer segment, whose final common path seems to be the regulation of the cyclic nucleotide, cyclic GMP (reviewed in Miller, 1981). Figure 2.28 presents a scheme of the phototransduction theory based upon the **cGMP hypothesis**. In this diagram the filled arrows represent the excitatory events initiated by light (hv) which lead to closure of the light-regulated conductance (g_{hv}); the open arrows represent events

that lead to restoration of the baseline condition. Arched arrows represent catalysis, or enzymatic amplification steps; straight arrows representing binding reactions.

Consider the excitatory chain, segregated into five stages by boxes 1 through 5 in Figure 2.28.

(1) Light isomerizes the chromophore of rhodopsin (Figure 2.18), inducing a sequence of changes (see Figure 2.19) that cause the protein to adopt a distinct conformation, R*, which is thought to be identical with the spectroscopically defined intermediate, Metarhodopsin II (see Figure 2.19). R* is inactivated primarily by phosphorylation (Bownds et al., 1972; Liebman & Pugh, 1980).

(2) Photoactivated rhodopsin, R* is an enzyme, catalyzing the binding of GTP to G_v, a GTP-binding protein (Baehr, Morita, Swanson, & Applebury, 1982; Fung & Stryer, 1980; Godchaux & Zimmerman, 1979), an 80 Kdal protein (alias G-protein, transducin) present in amounts about 1/10 that of rhodpsin, and attached by ionic bonds to the disk surface. Each R* is capable of catalyzing the attachment of GTP to about 500 G-proteins/sec.

(3) In the GTP-complexed form, G-protein activates (Fung, Hurley, & Stryer, 1981) another outer segment enzyme, cGMP phosphodiesterase (PDE) (Bitensky, Wheeler, Aloni, Vetury, & Matuo, 1978).

(4) PDE, a c. 180 kDal protein, catalyzes the hydrolysis of the $3'$ phospho–ester bond of cyclic GMP (Baehr, Devlin, & Applebury, 1979; Miki, Baraban, Boyce, & Bitensky, 1975; Yee & Liebman, 1978). PDE, which is normally attached to the disk membrane surface by ionic bonds, is present in amounts of about 1/50 to 1/100 that of rhodopsin, and each enzyme molecule can catalyze the hydrolysis of up to 2000 molecules/sec of cGMP.

(5) Cyclic GMP, in the dark or resting state opens, by direct binding, the channel protein, g_{hv}, that carries the light-sensitive current. The steady-state gating of the conductance obeys the Hill relation

$$[g_{hv}]_{open}/[g_{hv}]_{total} = [cGMP]^N/$$
$$\{[cGMP]^N + (K_D)^N\} \quad (2.43)$$

where [cGMP] is the concentration of cGMP in the outer segment cytoplasm, $N \simeq 3$ is the Hill coefficient or cooperativity index, and $K_D \simeq 20 \mu M$ is the concentration of cGMP that causes 50 percent of the channels to be opened. Since only about 5 percent of g_{hv} is open in the dark, [cGMP] at rest is a few μm. The discovery of this truly novel form of gating—by direct cyclic nucleotide binding—was made by a team of Russian investigators, Fesenko, Kolesnikov, & Lyubarsky (1985), who studied the ionic currents of isolated patches of rod outer segment membrane which were perfused with nucleotides. Characterization of the cGMP-activated conductance by them and by others established the identity of the cGMP-gated conductance with the previously operationally characterized light-regulated conductance (Matthews, 1986, 1987; Yau & Nakatani, 1985b), and that it is a channel protein (Cook, Hanke, & Kaupp, 1987; Haynes, Kay, & Yau, 1986; Zimmerman & Baylor, 1986). The cGMP binding equilibrium is established in a few milliseconds (Cobbs & Pugh, 1985, 1987), so when outer segment [cGMP] is lowered by light activated PDE, the channels that carry the dark current are rapidly closed.

There is virtually no doubt at this time about the identity of the excitatory events leading from photon absorption to closure of g_{hv}—that is, the events represented in Figure 2.28 by the filled arrows. Some quantitative issues about the excitatory chain do remain unresolved, but these do not constitute serious hindrances to acceptance of the cGMP cascade theory. In contrast with the confident state of knowledge about the excitatory chain of events, knowledge about the events that restore the photoreceptor to the pre-response baseline is somewhat insecure, and a number of issues remain unresolved. The open arrows in Figure 2.28 represent a working hypothesis under investigation by many laboratories. The principle behind the hypothesis is that each of the excitatory events must be reversed.

In the first restoration step, R* loses its catalytic activity by virtue of two reactions, multiple phosphorylation and by binding of a protein known as 48 K protein. In the second state, activated G-protein, G_v^*, becomes inactivated by the hydrolysis of GTP to GDP. Third, PDE* is inactivated by the unbinding of inactivated G-protein. Fourth, outer segment [cGMP] rises as guanylate cyclase (the enzyme that catalyzes the synthesis of cGMP from GTP) is able to overtake PDE-catalyzed hydrolysis. Fifth, as cGMP rises, it pushes the binding equilibrium of the cGMP-gated conductance toward the open state, allowing Na^+ to enter the outer segment, restoring the dark current. The difficulty with most of these steps is that the in vitro data which show them to exist also show them too slow to participate in the relatively rapid baseline restoration in vivo. (For discussion of the unresolved problems concerning

these steps, the reader is referred to the review articles cited at the beginning of this section.) Nonetheless, it seems likely that many of the outstanding problems will be resolved with improved techniques, and that a biochemically realistic model of the single-photon response explaining these features will not be long in coming. In addition to the problems associated with the recovery steps of the cGMP cascade, another major unresolved problem concerns the role of Ca^{2+} in the cell.

A Negative Feedback Hypothesis for the Role of Calcium in Transduction

The profound effects of altered $[Ca^{2+}]$ on the dark current and on the photocurrent kinetics cited above in the discussion of the Calcium Hypothesis suggest that even if Ca^{2+} is not the internal transmitter of excitation it plays an important regulatory role in photoreceptors. The recognition that Ca^{2+} permeates g_{hv}, the cGMP-regulated conductance, and is pumped out by an Na/Ca exchanger, has led to the realization that in the normal course of the photoresponse the outer segment dynamically regulates its internal Ca^{2+}: the exchange pump continues to remove internal Ca^{2+} while the inward leak is stopped by the hydrolysis of cGMP, causing $[Ca^{2+}]_i$ to drop (Yau & Nakatani, 1985a). By infusing rods with substantial amounts of calcium buffers, thereby slowing the rate of change of $[Ca^{2+}]_i$ attendant on a change in the inward flux through g_{hv}, Lamb, Matthews, and Torre (1986) and Torre, Matthews, and Lamb (1986) demonstrated that the normal, rapid lowering of $[Ca^{2+}]$ during a light response is critical for the restoration of the pre-flash baseline condition. Based upon their observations, Torre et al. (1986) propose the hypothesis that the normal role of Ca^{2+} is as a *low-pass filtered, negative feedback signal derived from the dark current.* Lowered $[Ca^{2+}]_i$ speeds up recovery to baseline by its effect on one or more of the restoration steps (open arrows, Figure 2.28) in the cascade. Elevated or static $[Ca^{2+}]_i$ retards baseline restoration after a light flash, prolonging the photocurrent, because the Ca^{2+}-sensitive step is retarded. The signal is a *negative* feedback because increasing the influx of Ca^{2+} through g_{hv} leads, after a flash, to a relative decrease in [cGMP] and therefore a decrease in dark current; conversely, decreasing the influx of Ca^{2+} through g_{hv} leads to a more rapid increase in [cGMP] and restoration of the dark current. Low-pass filtering is effected through the cell's calcium buffering—a change in influx of Ca^{2+} is only seen after the natural buffering is overcome. The Calcium Negative Feedback Hypothesis of Torre et al. (1986) may prove to be the critical insight in a comprehensive theory of transduction and photoreceptor light adaptation. Accordingly, a steady background of light causes lowered $[Ca^{2+}]_i$, which in turn speeds up the kinetics of one or more restoration steps in the cascade, as predicted by Baylor et al. (1974) in their classic study of light-adaptation in turtle cones.

The biochemical step or steps affected by Ca^{2+} have not been unequivocally established. Modulation of guanylate cyclase by Ca^{2+} (Fleishman & Denisevich, 1979) has the correct sign to account for the major effects of experimentally manipulated calcium cited above. For example, since elevated Ca^{2+} inhibits cyclase, this manipulation can be expected to lower [cGMP], causing the dark current to diminish, according to equation 2.43. Other evidence points to an inhibitory effect of elevated Ca^{2+} on one of the early steps in the inactivation of the cascade, perhaps on the phosphorylation of rhodopsin.

Phototransduction in Cone Photoreceptors

Cones and rods share many properties: both are divided into inner segments containing synaptic termination, nucleus and mitochrondria, and outer segment composed of stacks of lamellar membranes densely packed with photopigment molecules (see p. 101); both hyperpolarize in response to light; both have dark currents modulated locally by light. Cones differ from rods, however, in several dramatic ways. First, the lamellar membranes of cones are themselves the plasma membrane. Second, the intrinsic gain of the photoresponse (e.g., in pA/photon absorbed or μV/photon absorbed at response peak) of a cone of any given retina is typically 1/100 or 1/1000 that of a rod. Third, the speed of the photocurrent response in a dark-adapted cone of a given retina is typically 5 to 10 times faster than in a rod of the same retina. Fourth, in retinas where light-adaptation occurs in the photoreceptors, cones light-adapt—that is, change their gain and speed in response to a step of light—much more quickly than rods (see Pugh & Cobbs, 1986 for a review).

Evidence has accumulated that cones and rods share much the same phototransduction machinery. Cones have a cGMP-regulated conductance in their outer segment membranes (Haynes & Yau, 1985; Cobbs, Barkdoll, & Pugh, 1985). Cones have a cGMP cascade, with a distinct G-protein and phosphodiesterase (Hurwitz et

al., 1985; Lerea et al., 1986; Nakatani & Yau, 1986). Given such similarity with rods in their biochemical machinery, how might their striking differences arise? It is tantalizing to hypothesize that an extension of the Calcium Negative Feedback Hypothesis might provide an explanation.

Because the lamellar membranes are also the plasma membrane in cones, cones of any given retina typically have a much higher surface/volume ratio. Consider a cone and a rod with the same length, l, and radius, r, with the lamellar membranes spaced at an interval $\Delta l \simeq$ 300 Å. The internal cytoplasmic volume of the two outer segments will be the same, but the surface areas will be $S_{rod} = 2\pi rl$ and $S_{cone} = 2\pi r^2 l/\Delta l$, respectively. Thus, the relative surface/volume ratios of the two cells will be $r/\Delta l$. For a human foveal cone and peripheral rod (each having a diameter of about 2 μm) the cone will have a 30 times greater surface/volume ratio. (Note that the cone will also have greater capacitance.) In some retinas small cones have up to a 200-fold greater surface/volume ratio of the large rods. It is evident that given a comparable dark current (and inward flux of Ca^{2+} through g_{hv}) that the Na/Ca exchanger in a cone should be able to modulate $[Ca^{2+}]_i$ much more rapidly than in a rod. Thus, in the framework of the Calcium Negative Feedback Hypothesis of Lamb and colleagues, the *morphology of cone outer segments might in part be the basis of their faster photocurrent kinetics and ability to light adapt more rapidly than rods.*

Synaptic Transmission of Photoreceptor Signals

The role of the photoreceptor in transduction is completed when the hyperpolarization initiated by the closing of the outer segment, light-sensitive conductance is transmitted passively down the relatively short inner segment cable, reaching the rod spherule or cone pedicle, and there altering the rate of synaptic transmitter release onto the secondary neurons, bipolar, and horizontal cells. In accordance with the general physiological rule that depolarization is the electrical event that stimulates synaptic transmitter release, it has widely been held that the hyperpolarization of rods and cones decreases the rate of synaptic transmitter release (Dacheux & Miller, 1975; Trifonov, 1968). A substantial body of evidence supports the hypothesis that the transmitters released by vertebrate photoreceptors include one or both of the similar negative amino acids, *L*-aspartate or *L*-glutamate (Cervetto & MacNichol, 1972; Miller & Schwartz, 1983; Murakami, Ohtsuka, & Shimazaki, 1975; Schwartz, 1981; Slaughter & Miller, 1983). Early work demonstrated that these compounds depolarized bipolar and/or horizontal cells, and could block the transmission of light signals to second order neurons, although the relatively high concentrations of the amino acids required to produce these effects cast some doubt on the conclusion that they were the actual transmitters. More recently, in toad retinas, mechanisms of both uptake and release for aspartate and glutamate from photoreceptors have been demonstrated (Miller & Schwartz, 1983). Specific high-affinity receptors for glutamate that activate the light-regulated conductances of depolarizing bipolar cells have been described (Nawy & Copenhagen, 1987). Since there is very strong evidence for ion channels directly gated by glutamate in some neurons (e.g., Cull-Candy & Usowicz, 1987; Jahr & Stevens, 1987), it seems highly likely that the transmitter at the photoreceptor-depolarizing bipolar cell is glutamate. It must be kept in mind, however, that vertebrate photoreceptors make two morphologically distinct types of chemical synapses—a *ribbon* synapse, and a *basal contact*. Although the ribbon synapse is perhaps the better known, the basal contact is the only type found between photoreceptors and one type of bipolar cell in primate (Kolb, 1970; Missotten, 1965). Furthermore, both calcium dependent (presumable vesicle release) and calcium independent mechanisms of release of candidate transmitters from photoreceptors have been described (Miller & Schwartz, 1983). It thus seems likely that there are several photoreceptor transmitters and mechanisms of transmitter release.

SIGNAL TRANSMISSION IN THE RETINA

Anatomy and Physiology of Inner Retina: Overview

The primate retina contains five basic neuronal types, which are found in all vertebrate retinas: *photoreceptors, bipolar cells, ganglion cells, horizontal cells, and amacrine cells*. (A sixth type, the *interplexiform cell*, which carries centrifugal

information, also has been described.) As shown in Figure 2.10, cell somas occur in three layers: the *outer nuclear layer*, containing the nuclei of the rods and cones; the *inner nuclear layer*, containing the cell bodies of bipolar cells, most horizontal and amacrine cells, and a few ganglion cells; and the *ganglion cell layer*, containing the cell bodies of some amacrine cells and most ganglion cells. Synapses between photoreceptors and bipolar cells occur in the *outer plexiform layer*. Horizontal cells have processes and synaptic terminations all confined to the outer plexiform layer. Bipolar cells transfer information from photoreceptors to the *inner plexiform layer*, where the processes of bipolar cells contact the dendrites of amacrine and ganglion cells. Amacrine cells have all their synaptic contacts confined to the inner plexiform layer. Ganglion cells are solely reponsible for carrying information from the retina to higher visual centers. The axons of the ganglion cells, which total about 1,000,000, or 1 percent of the number of photoreceptors, gather and merge into small bundles, eventually exiting the eye in the optic disk. In the foveal region of the primate retina (see Figure 2.11), the cell bodies of the cones and of all the inner retinal neurons (as well as all blood vessels) are displaced to the side, serving to minimize light scattering in this critical region of the retinal image (see p. 99).

Anatomically, each retinal cell type may be characterized by its location, morphology, arborization pattern, pattern of synaptic contacts, and so forth. Many of these properties may depend on retinal eccentricity, so ideally, cell types should be characterized in restricted regions. One useful anatomical descriptor is the *coverage factor*, defined as the average retinal area occupied by a cell type's dendritic arbor, multiplied by the spatial density of the cells of that type. A coverage factor of 2, for example, indicates modest overlap of dendritic arbors. Coverage factors as high as 60 have been observed. Physiologically, each retinal cell type can be crudely characterized by (1) its receptive field

---

The anatomical descriptions of the primate retina given here are taken largely from the work of Boycott and Dowling (1969), and Kolb (1970), who in turn make contact with earlier authors' work such as that by Cajal (1893) and Polyak (1941). Rodieck's (1973) thorough book on the topic and his recent review (Rodieck, 1987) of anatomy of the primate retina were heavily consulted.

and (2) by the sign of its response to light. The *receptive field* is defined as that region of the retina which when illuminated causes the cell to respond. A cell may respond to light either by *depolarizing* or *hyperpolarizing*: For retinal cells other than photoreceptors, a depolarizing response is generally called an "on" response, and a hyperpolarizing response is called "off." Most retinal cells respond to light with only graded changes in polarization. Only ganglion cells and some amacrines generate action potentials: as in other spiking neurons, the electrical event that initiates the action potential is depolarization.

Since the seminal work of Kuffler (1953) it has been clear that the receptive fields of retinal cells have spatial organization: in the ganglion cells he studied, light falling in the central region of the receptive field could either increase their firing rate or decrease it. Typically, surrounding the receptive field center there is a region which, when illuminated, has the opposite sign effect as light falling in the center. A ganglion cell is called *on-center* if it depolarizes (firing rate increases) when light falls in the receptive field center. An *off-center* cell is one which hyperpolarizes (decreases its firing rate) in response to light falling in its receptive field center. Many retinal cells do not have the classic center/surround organization (e.g., directionally selective cells in rabbit). Such cells require distinct classification schemes.

Outer Plexiform Layer

The terminations of cones and rods where synapses with bipolars are made, are known as *cone pedicles* and *rod spherules*, respectively; the terms reflect distinct morphologies (see Figure 2.10). The flattened pedicles of the cones form a basement below which there are no rod spherules; the rod spherules, however, are staggered to accommodate the relatively high rod spatial density at eccentricities where both rods and cones are found. The retinal layer just central to the cone pedicle basement is the outer plexiform layer, which is composed primarily of processes of bipolar and horizontal cells. (In some treatises, the outer plexiform includes the photoreceptor terminals.) Cone pedicles in primates are flattened and wide (typically 6 to $10\,\mu m$ in diameter), and contain many (20 or more) invaginations into which processes of horizontal and bipolar cells insert and make

synaptic contact in an orderly arrangment known as a *triad*. The two processes that form the lateral aspect of the triad are from horizontal cells; usually set deeper than the two later processes, the central process in the triad is from a bipolar cell. A deep staining *synaptic ribbon* with associated synaptic vesicles invariably lies presynaptic to the triad. Synapses without invagination are also formed on cone pedicles. Synapses of bipolars and horizontal cells with rods are made either in 1 to 2 invaginations (each with 3 to 7 processes) in the rod spherule or superficially upon the spherule. Rods and cones in some mammalian species also form *gap junctions* (electrically conducting synapses), which play functional roles in signal transmission. Under conditions of moderate scotopic illumination, cat rod-generated signals are transmitted through cone pedicles to cone bipolars (Nelson, 1977; see below).

In primate retinas, cones make synapses with two major anatomical classes of bipolar cells (see Figure 2.10): *invaginating bipolars*, and *flat bipolars* (Boycott & Dowling, 1969). Invaginating bipolars donate the central element in cone triads, and except in the fovea, typically make multiple synapses with each of several cones. Flat bipolars make superficial synapses upon cone pedicles (i.e., invaginations). The distinction between invaginating and flat cone bipolars corresponds to distinct physiology: Invaginating cone bipolars *depolarize* to illumination in their receptive field centers (i.e., are "on-center"), whereas flat cone bipolars *hyperpolarize* (i.e. are "off-center") (reviewed in Kaneko, 1979). Exceptions of this rule of physiological-anatomical correspondence have been found.

Invaginating and flat cone bipolar cells in primates seem to be divided into two subclasses each: diffuse and midget. *Midget invaginating cone bipolar cells*, which are found in the central retina, appear to synapse on single cone pedicles; they may make 25 or more invaginating synapses in the single pedicle, no doubt insuring a high degree of signal transmission reliability. *Midget flat bipolars* likewise appear to make their superficial synapses with single cone pedicles. Like the invaginating midget bipolars, midget flat bipolars may make more than 20 synapses on a single pedicle (Kolb, 1970). *Diffuse* bipolar cells (Mariani, 1981), which are of either the invaginating or flat type, in contrast with the midget bipolars, make synapses with seven or more cone pedicles. Diffuse bipolars do not appear to populate the central fovea, but can be found within $750\,\mu m$ of its center (see Figure 2.11). Rods bipolar cells form a distinct class from cone bipolars, and apparently make synapses only with rods (Boycott & Dowling, 1969). Rod bipolar dendrites penetrate above the basement formed by the cones pedicles and have a staggered appearance, synapsing with as many as 45 rod spherules, which because of their density are not aligned in a retinal single plane. The rod bipolar in cat hyperpolarizes in response to light in its receptive field center, and is thus, off-center (Nelson, Kolb, Famiglietti, & Gouras, 1976). The typology of primate bipolars is probably not complete. Detailed reconstruction of bipolars from serial electron micrographs in a restricted central region of cat retina have revealed seven distinct subclasses of cone bipolar (Maguire, Stevens, & Sterling, 1984; Sterling, 1983).

Two distinct classes of primate *horizontal cells* have been described (Kolb, Mariani, & Gallego, 1980; Rodieck, 1985). The first class makes synaptic contact as the lateral element in cone triads with all the cones in its synaptic field, and thus makes contact at the ribbon synapses with both long- and mid-wave cones. Strangely enough, several millimeters away from the point at which it makes synapses with cones, the class I horizontal typically sends a thin process which arborizes and makes contact with a number of rods. Calculations suggest that the two ends of the cell are very poorly electrically coupled. Class II horizontal cells do not contact every cone pedicle within range of their dendritic field. They could conceivably make ribbon synapse contact with only one spectral class of cones. In many fish retinas there are horizontal cells that are "color coded": in some regions of the spectrum they respond by hyperpolarizing, and in others by depolarizing (these are the so called C-type S-potentials, named after Svaetichin, who discovered them). These cells clearly receive opposite-signed inputs from two types of cones. At present there is no direct evidence that any of the horizontal cells of primates are color coded in this sense.

An hypothesis about the role of horizontal cells in the retina is that they are responsible for the inhibitory surround of bipolar receptive fields. The lateral inhibitory signals from horizontals apparently shift the bipolar response versus intensity curve, so that the center of the response range is shifted toward the mean illumination level of the horizontal receptive field (Werblin, 1974). Although this shifting of the bipolar response curve represents an overall desensitization (more light is required to achieve a given amplitude response), the cells become capable of responding to lights that would, prior to the shift, drive them into saturation, and in this sense the shift can be described as a sensitization. In some retinas horizontal cells feed back signals that depolarize cones (Baylor, Fuortes, & O'Bryan, 1971), presumably through the lateral elements of the triadic processes invaginating cone pedicles. Although this feedback could be the basis for the effect of surrounding illumination on bipolar sensitivity, experiments by Werblin (1974) support the notion of a direct effect of horizontal cell activity on the bipolar membrane.

Inner Plexiform Layer

The inner plexiform layer is the retinal region where bipolars relay information to ganglion cells. An important distinguishing feature of this layer is *sublamination*: This feature is due to the stratification of the branching of the process of several types of bipolar and ganglion cells. In cat retina, Famiglietti and Kolb (1975) established that there are two distinct populations of ganglion cells, one whose dendrites stratify in the outer third of the outer plexiform (sublamina a), and the other branching in the inner part (sublamina b) of the inner plexiform. They put forward and confirmed with electrophysiological recording and dye injection (Nelson, Famiglietti, & Kolb, 1978) the hypothesis that the ganglion cells branching in the outer portion of the inner plexiform were off-center ganglion cells, and that those branching in the inner portion (sublamina b) of the inner plexiform were on-center cells. Bipolar cells have their synaptic terminals either in sublamina a or in sublamina b: it had been thought that those bipolars that terminate in sublamina a were off-center cells, and those terminating in sublamina b were on-center, but this generality is not without exceptions (Sterling, 1983). Nonetheless, it remains clear that distinctive stratification patterns can correspond to distinct physiological functions and that the on- and off-response systems in the retina maintain some functional independence. Combined physiological and anatomical results of the sort obtained for cat retina are not available for primate retina. Although outer plexiform stratification patterns in primate suggests that the on- and off-center systems in primates will follow the pattern established in cat, the primate retina's requirement of encoding signals from the three cone types has no doubt given rise to some interesting differences in anatomical connections.

Amacrine cells in all vertebrates show a wide variety of morphology. In cat retina perhaps as many as 22 types can be distinguished on the basis of their patterns of branching in the inner plexiform layer (Kolb, Nelson, & Mariani, 1981), and the different cell types may use eight or more distinct synaptic transmitters. Their complexity is illustrated by the extensively studied type AII amacrine first described by Famiglietti and Kolb (1975), a type which is found in abundance (coverage factor, c. 5) in the retinas of cat, dog and rhesus monkey. This cell has a relatively small field, and is "bistratified" (i.e., branches in two sublamina of the inner plexiform layer). The branches in sublamina b receive direct inputs from rod bipolar terminals and also make large gap junctions with cone bipolars; in sublamina a, where the AII amacrines output lies, the cell makes synapses with other amacrines, with cone bipolars, and with ganglion cells. Functionally, the AII amacrine is driven mainly by signals from rods (Nelson et al., 1976). It may be the sole route for signals from rod bipolars to drive ganglion cells and thus exit the retina. The delineation of the functional roles of the many other types of amacrine cells that have been distinguished on the basis of Golgi stains and electron micrography must await combined physiological and anatomical studies. It can be expected that they will be shown to perform a variety of interesting spatial and temporal filtering of signals in the inner retina.

Ganglion Cells

Enroth-Cugell and Robson (1966), in recording from cat retinal ganglion cells stimulated with sinusoidal gratings, noted two highly distinctive response patterns. One class of cells, which they called *X-cells*, obeyed *"linear spatial summation"*: (1) a grating stimulus that covered the receptive field could be positioned so that modulation of the contrast in time (by square wave modulation) gave rise to no response (Figure 2.29); (2) a drifting grating gave rise to a response with constant mean, and with modulation frequency in synchrony with the passage of the grating. A second class of cells, which they called Y-cells, had the property that no null position for the grating could be found (Figure 2.29); these latter cells responded to drifting gratings with a poorly modulated firing rate. Other investigators have noted correlative properties of the two cell types (reviewed for example, in Lennie, 1980), such as more sustained (X) versus more transient (Y) responses, to steps of contrast, and relatively slower conduction velocities for X-cells than Y-cells.

Hochstein and Shapley (1976a) developed the most rigorous scheme for distinguishing X- and Y-cells. Their scheme compares the first and second harmonic component (obtained by Fourier analysis) of the responses to stationary gratings sinusoidally modulated in time. *The first harmonic of X-cells' responses shows a strong sinusoidal spatial phase dependence* (Figure 2.30A), with clear null position, and *X-cells show almost no second harmonic* response component. These characteristics are not strongly dependent on grating spatial frequency. The first harmonic of Y-cell responses (Figure 2.30B) shows a spatial phase dependence like that of X-cells. In striking contrast to the behavior of X-cells, however, *Y-cells showed a strong second-harmonic response component* at all spatial frequencies.

The response characteristics of X-cells can be accounted for by assuming that (1) photoreceptor responses to local contrast modulation (at the modulation depths employed) are linear; (2) summation of inputs from different regions of the receptive field is linear; and (3) spatiotemporal separability obtains, so that the temporal "impulse response" of different local regions of the receptive field are the same (Shapley & Lennie, 1985). These properties are, in effect, those postulated by the "difference of two-Gaussians" (DOG) model of the receptive field proposed by Rodieck (1965). In this model of the receptive field, the center mechanism is considered to summate its input signals with a Gaussian weighting function of one sign, the surround, with a wider and less sensitive Gaussian profile of the opposite sign; temporal properties of the center and surround are considered homogeneous across the receptive field. One significant and generally accepted feature of the DOG model is that the inhibitory surround mechanism actually has its greatest effectiveness in the

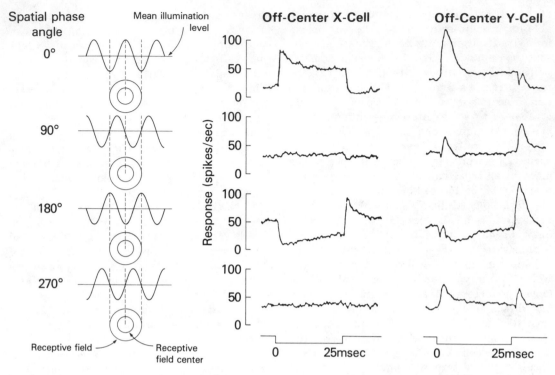

Figure 2.29. Responses (spike rates) of a cat retinal off-center *X*-cell and an off-center *Y*-cell to sine-wave gratings (see Figure 2.6), set at various positions (phases) with respect to the receptive field center, and square-wave modulated temporally, as shown in the stimulus marker traces below the responses. Note the two null positions in the *X*-cell series. From "The Contrast Sensitivity of Retinal Ganglion Cells of the Cat" by C. Enroth-Cugall and J.E. Robson, 1966, *Journal of Physiology, 187,* p. 526. Copyright 1966 by The Physiological Society. Reprinted by permission.

very center of the receptive field. Enroth-Cugell and Robson (1966), and others since, have shown the DOG model to provide a good description of the spatial behavior of X-cells. Y-cells are not describable in terms of the simple DOG model. Hochstein and Shapley (1976b) explained the response properties of Y-cells by postulating a population of rectifying (nonlinear) subunits distributed throughout (and probably well beyond) the classic receptive field (center and surround) of these cells.

As discussed above, a correspondence has been established in cat retina between the response sign of ganglion cells and their dendritic branching in the inner plexiform layer. A distinct anatomical typology of cat retinal ganglion cells based upon size of the dendritic field was established by Boycott and Wässle (1974). They showed that at each retinal eccentricity two very distinct ganglion cell populations were

readily distinguished: alpha cells, with large soma and axons, and wide fields (180 to 1000 μm diameter), sparse branching, and coverage factor c. 1.5; and beta cells, with medium soma and axons, dense dendritic branching, and high coverage factor, c. 11 (Sterling, 1983). Each type of cell is represented at all retinal eccentricities, although the size of the dendritic fields of both types increases monotonically from central retina to periphery. Alpha-cells constitute a constant fraction of about 4 percent of the ganglion cells of cat at each retinal eccentricity, while the beta-cells are about 60 to 70 percent of the ganglion cells in the central retina (Peichl & Wässle, 1979). A signal advance in the correlation of retinal anatomy and physiology has been the identification of the X/Y functional classification in the cat retina with the alpha/beta anatomical distinction. This identification in cat of two distinct sets of single unit behavior

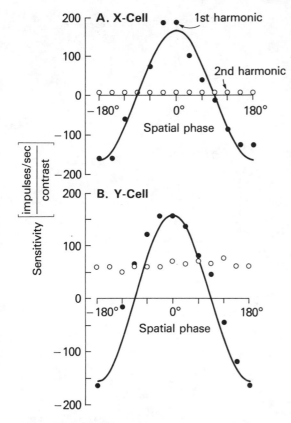

Figure 2.30. Sensitivity (impulses/sec/contrast) of the first-harmonic (filled circles) and second-harmonic (open circles) components of the responses of a cat X-cell (a) and a Y-cell (b) to spatial sine-wave gratings placed at various positions (spatial phases) in the receptive field and modulated sinusoidally in time. Both cell types show strong spatial phase dependence in the first harmonic. The X-cell shows almost no second harmonic component, whereas the Y-cell shows a second-harmonic component that does not depend on the grating position. From "Quantitative Analysis of Retinal Ganglion Cell Classifications" by S. Hochstein and R. Shapley, 1976, *Journal of Physiology, 262,* p. 252. Copyright 1966 by The Physiological Society. Reprinted by permission.

with two specific anatomical substrates assumes even greater significance in view of the finding that the X/Y functional distinction applies to vertebrate retinas as different as those of goldfish, cat and primate.

From single cell recordings in macaque retina, DeMonasterio (1978a, 1978b) classified ganglion cells as either X or Y using a test similar to the stationary grating test employed by Enroth-Cugell and Robson (1966). Figure 2.31 shows

results from two cells from the central 20° of macaque retina; the cell of 2.31A is X-like; the cell of 2.31B is Y-like. DeMonasterio found that 95 percent (147/155) of the cells classified as having "Type I opponent-coded receptive fields" (Wiesel & Hubel, 1966; see below) were X-like. Most of the 77 additional ganglion cells studied by DeMonasterio (1978a) with the procedure of Figure 2.31 and independently classified on the basis of spectral properties of their receptive fields as "Types III and IV" (Wiesel & Hubel, 1966) showed some degree of nonlinear spatial summation.

Two recent studies (Derrington & Lennie, 1984; Kaplan & Shapley, 1982) of large populations of single units of macaque lateral geniculate nucleus (LGN), the primary relay station in the pathway from retina to striate cortex, demonstrated with the rigorous test of Hochstein and Shapley (1976a), that the four upper layers of the LGN (the so called parvocellular layers) are populated exclusively by X-like cells. The two lower layers of the LGN (the magnocellular layers, containing Wiesel and Hubel's (1966) Type III and Type IV units) contain a small but definite fraction of Y-cells, although too, most units were X-like. Based upon the principle (Lennie, 1980) that LGN neurons preserve the properties of their retinal afferents with essentially no modification, these studies reinforce the notion that a large majority of primate retinal ganglion cells are X-cells.

Primate X- and Y-cells differ strikingly from their cat counterparts in their response to lights of different wavelengths. In primate the center and antagonistic surround of most ganglion cells are apparently dominated by signals from spectrally distinct cone classes. Figure 2.32 shows a receptive field analysis of a ganglion cell from the study of DeMonasterio (1978a): excitation of the long-wave sensitive (L) cones in the receptive field center depolarized the cell, whereas, excitation of the mid-wave sensitive (M) cones in the surround hyperpolarized the unit. Cells such as that of Figure 2.32, which are polarized in opposite directions by inputs from distinct cone classes, are called generically, *chromatically opponent* or *opponent coded cells.* Evidence (reviewed in Gouras & Zrenner, 1981; Zrenner, 1983) from retinal recordings supports the view that opponent coded ganglion cells fall into three distinct groups: L/M, M/L, and S/(M + L). Here L/M means long-wave cone

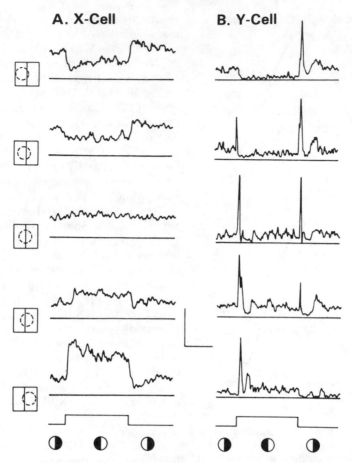

Figure 2.31. Responses of monkey X and Y ganglion cells to square-wave reversal of contrast between two halves of a circular bipartite field. The position of the circular stimulus, with respect to the receptive field center, is indicated by the position of the circles at left with respect to the bisected rectangle (the bisecting line goes through the receptive field center). The timing of the temporal modulation with respect to the responses is shown below. The X-cell, but not the Y-cell, shows a null position. From "Properties of Concentrically Organized X and Y Ganglion Cells of Macaque Retina" by F.M. de Monasterio, 1978, *Journal of Neurophysiology, 41*, 1402. Copyright 1978 by The American Physiological Society. Reprinted by permission.

dominated center and mid-wave cone dominated antagonistic surround, and so forth. In the dark-adapted state the nature and degree of opponency and apparent spatial organization may vary much more than under light-adapted conditions.

A recent analysis of a large population of macaque LGN units having receptive fields within 10 deg of the fovea with an elegant chromatic modulation technique (Derrington, Krauskopf, & Lennie, 1984) has demonstrated that when adapted to a white field of c. 4500 td. most parvocellular units fall rather clearly into one

of three chromatically opponent classes. The L/M and M/L classes, for which the input signals weights from the cone classes were approximately balanced, were the largest classes; S/(M + L) units comprised a third, less populous class. These results corroborate previous findings (DeValois, Abramov, & Jacobs, 1966; Wiesel & Hubel, 1966) demonstrating the chromatic coding of LGN units, and strengthen the conclusion that under light-adapted conditions the spatially linear primate X-cells have quite homogeneous chromatic coding properties.

Primate midget ganglion cells, which are the

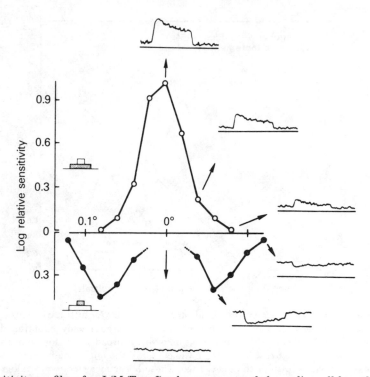

Figure 2.32. Sensitivity profiles of an L/M (Type I) color-opponent coded ganglion cell from the monkey retina. The center profile (open circles) was obtained with a 620 nm spot of 0.01 deg, pulsed upon a 520 nm background of 3.4×10^{10} quanta $\times$ deg^{-2} $\times$ sec^{-1}. Surround profile obtained with a 520 nm spot of 0.02 deg, pulsed on a 620 nm background of 6.2×10^{11} quanta $\times$ deg^{-2} $\times$ sec^{-1}. Traces shown were the average of 30 responses at each indicated position. Note the relatively narrow width of the spatial tuning curve. From "Center and Surround Mechanisms of Opponent-Color X and Y Ganglion Cells of Retina of Macaques" by F.M. de Monasterio, 1978, *Journal of Neurophysiology, 41*, p. 1427. Copyright 1978 by The American Physiological Society. Reprinted by permission.

dominant ganglion cell type of the primate retina, and the almost exclusive ganglion cell receiving input from the fovea (Polyak, 1941; Rodieck, 1987), coexist with a smaller population of parasol and giant ganglion cells (Polyak, 1941), such that in every retinal eccentricity where both the cell types are found, the giant and parasol cells have a dendritic spread about $4\times$ that of the midget cells (Rodieck, 1987). Both cell groups have members which ramify in either the outer third or middle third of the inner plexiform, probably indicating both on-center and off-center subtypes of both midget and parasol cells. Midget cells project to the parvocellular levels of the LGN, whereas the parasol ganglion cells project to the magnocellular layers (Leventhal, Rodieck & Dreher, 1981; Perry, Oehler, & Cowey, 1984). Although primate LGN magnocellular units do not exhibit such strong Y-like behavior as magnocellular

units in cat, cross-species antibody studies (Hendry, Hockfield, Jones, & McKay, 1984) and more general analysis leads to the conclusion that primate midget and parasol cells correspond to the beta- and alpha-cells respectively of the cat (Rodieck, 1987).

LIGHT ADAPTATION

The human visual system, like the visual system of many other vertebrates, functions effectively from starlight to bright sunlight, over a 7 to 8 log unit variation of mean retinal illumination. The capacity to function over such a large input range is a considerable evolutionary achievement, because the visual system is constructed of neural elements of limited dynamic range. (Dynamic range is used here to mean the range above prevailing noise levels in a cell over which

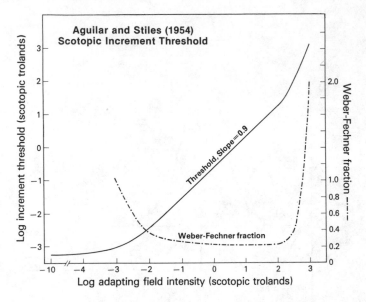

Figure 2.33. Human parafoveal increment threshold curve. Thresholds for fully dark-adapted human observers for a 9 deg diameter, 1 sec flash, measured in the presence of a large, steady adapting field of the retinal illumination indicated by the abscissa. The adapting field was a broad band, long-wave stimulus, and was presented in Maxwellian view (Figure 2.14) through the center of the pupil; the test flash was mid-wave, and presented in Maxwellian view through the pupil edge. These latter measures were taken to insure greater isolation of the scotopic (rod-dominated) system from the photopic. Cone-intrusion in detection occurs just above the highest point in the curve. Average data of 5 observers. From "Saturation of the Rod Mechanism of the Retina at High Levels of Stimulation" by M. Aguilar and W.S. Stiles, 1954, *Optica Acta, 1*, p. 91.

responses are linear.) As a first example, consider the case of the primate rod, which can respond reliably to single rhodopsin isomerizations. To be a reliable signal, the single photon response must have sufficient amplitude to exceed a variety of intrinsic noise (Baylor, Matthews, & Yau, 1980; Baylor, Nunn, & Schnapf, 1984; Yoshikami & Hagins, 1973). As a consequence of the amplitude of the single photon response, and the rod's compressive nonlinearity (equation 2.41) the linear range of the flash-response of a rod is about 1 to 30 isomerizations, or 1.5 log units, and the entire useful operating range for steady lights is certainly less than 3 log units. As a second example, consider the cat ganglion cells that Barlow, Levick, and Yoon (1971) showed could generate c. 3 spikes/isomerization in their receptive field at absolute threshold. Since the upper limit on spike frequency is a few hundred/sec, the dynamic range of such dark adapted ganglion cells is not much more than 2 log units. Clearly, the visual system must have mechanisms that allow it both to be exquisitely

sensitive at the dimmest levels of illumination and to operate effectively at high illuminations.

Light adaptation is the general term applied to all processes by which the visual system adjusts itself to the level of illumination. The term light adaptation encompasses all changes in light sensitivity resultant upon altered illumination. Sensitivity is usually measured psychophysically as reciprocal threshold (e.g., Figure 2.33), or physiologically as (response amplitude)/ (illumination intensity).

One strategy evolved by the visual system for dealing with the competing demands of sensitivity and limited dynamic range is the *use of parallel pathways*, with differential intrinsic sensitivities of the pathways. This strategy is employed in all duplex retinas (retinas with rods and cones) and is fundamental to the distinction between photopic and scotopic systems (Hecht, 1937). The strategy may be employed more generally than in the case of photopic vs. scotopic pathways. Rod signals in cat retina have at least two distinct pathways by which to reach ganglion cells, and these appear to differ considerably in sensitivity (Smith, Freed, & Sterling, 1986).

A second general strategy evolved by the visual system for coping with the sensitivity/dynamic range dilemma is *gain change*. The gain of a neuron is the output per unit input for a small (perturbation) input: For example, spikes/quantum or spikes/(stimulus contrast) for ganglion cells. *Adaptational gain change* is an adjustment to increased mean retinal illumination that decreases the linear or perturbation response of a given cell type. For discussion, it is worth identifying three types of gain control, all of which play some role in light adaptation: (1) *pigment depletion*, (2) *pure compressive non-linearity*, (3) *automatic gain control*. Pigment depletion accounts for none of the light adaptation in the human retina below 3000 photopic trolands, but does play a role in photopic adaptation above this level of retinal illumination. Compressive non-linearity in cell responses also accounts for some adaptation, but in general the intensity range of response compression below response saturation (e.g., equation 2.41) is much too narrow for compression to be effective as a mechanism of gain regulation over many log units. Automatic gain control includes all processes by which the visual system alters its gain, while preserving a significant range of linear response. It encompasses both changes within individual cells (e.g., photoreceptors) and changes in functional relationships (e.g., pooling, feedback) among cells. Automatic gain control is central to the visual system's ability to operate sensitively over a wide range of illumination.

An Important Achievement of Light Adaptation: Constant Contrast Sensitivity

The function of the visual system is to provide information about the physical character of objects in the environment. A physical property of an object of great interest to an animal whose visual system could extract information about it is the *surface reflectance distribution*. This distribution is the fraction of illumination scattered back from local patches of the surface, including the angular and wavelength dependence of the scattering. Although the reflectance distribution is an intrinsic, invariant property of a surface, because ambient illumination varies diurnally over 7 to 8 log units, the retinal image distribution of any surface undergoes drastic diurnal intensity variation. *A primary function of retinal light adaptation is to adjust sensitivity within the retina in order to maintain approximately constant retinal response to surfaces over the widest range of retinal illumination.* The case for this thesis has been argued most eloquently by Shapley and Enroth-Cugell (1984).

If the retinal activity representing surfaces is to remain relatively constant over a wide intensity range, there must exist an intensity-invariant property of the image of a surface to which cells can respond. A physical parameter of the retinal image of a surface that remains invariant over changes in illumination is contrast. Contrast (see Figure 2.6) is defined as the incremental or decremental change from the mean intensity at a point (x, y) in the image, divided by the mean intensity:

$$c(x, y) = [I(x, y) - \bar{I}]/\bar{I}$$
$$= \Delta I(x, y)/\bar{I} \qquad (2.43)$$

The thesis of Shapley and Enroth-Cugell (1984) may be rephrased thusly: *Automatic gain controls exist in the retina that allow it to respond with constant contrast sensitivity over a wide range of mean illumination.* The evidence they reviewed supports the view that a hierarchy of sensitivity-regulating mechanisms exist within retinas that allow them to approximate the ideal of constant contrast sensitivity.

Psychophysical Evidence

Figure 2.33 presents the average results from the classical psychophysical investigation of scotopic incremental sensitivity by Aguilar and Stiles (1954). Over the 4 log unit range of mean retinal illuminances 0.01 to 100 scotopic td, the increment threshold for detecting a 200 msec, 9 deg diameter parafoveal target obeys, to a good approximation **Weber's Law**:

$$\Delta I/\bar{I} = 0.2 \qquad (2.44)$$

The value of 0.2 is known as the Weber, Fechner, or Weber–Fechner fraction. Its reciprocal is the *contrast sensitivity* under the stated conditions. Comparison of equations 2.43 and 2.44 shows that *over the range of obedience to Weber's Law, constancy of contrast sensitivity obtains.* Incremental saturation (the step upward deviation from Weber's law in Figure 2.33) of the scotopic system effectively bars the scotopic system from contributing to contrast detection above 1000 scotopic td (3000 to 5000 isomerizations/sec/rod). The likely cause of this incremental saturation lies in the compressive (saturating) response function of the primate rod itself (Baylor, Nunn, & Schnapf, 1984; see below).

Under normal broadband illumination conditions (as opposed to the special chromatic adaptation conditions employed by Aguilar and Stiles to isolate the scotopic system over the widest possible range) the photopic system dominates the threshold above approximately 10 scotopic td. Many investigations (e.g., Stiles, 1939; Whittle & Challands, 1969) have shown that above about 10 td the photopic visual system obeys Weber's Law for the detection of moderately large test targets (e.g., 1 deg diameter) of moderate to long duration, with an approximate (foveal) Weber fraction of 0.02 to 0.05. Unlike that of the scotopic system, the incremental sensitivity of the photopic system for detection of a white or neutral flash upon a steady-state background never rises significantly above the slope-1, or Weber line. Thus, *for the detection of moderately large and long-duration targets imposed upon steady backgrounds, the human visual system exhibits constant contrast sensitivity,* and so possesses a basis for a luminance-invariant response to reflecting surfaces.

Whittle and Challands (1969), in a dichoptic matching paradigm, demonstrated that the brightness of a target was determined by its contrast: Above about 10 to 100 td suprathreshold, lights of equal contrast were judged to be equally bright, although the retinal illuminances varied widely. These data support the view that brightness constancy is based upon signals from mechanisms that respond with constant contrast sensitivity.

Weber Law behavior, however, is not exhibited for all incremental targets under all adaptation conditions. In particular, for small and/or brief targets incremental sensitivity declines with increasing mean illumination in a fashion that more closely approximates the Rose–de Vries or square-root law,

$$\Delta I / \sqrt{I} = \text{const}$$

as shown, for example, by Barlow (1957) for the scotopic system. The square root law can be deduced as the optimum performance of a quantum-fluctuation-limited system.

Contrast sensitivity of the human system is thus seen to be dependent on both spatial and temporal frequency content of targets: direct measurements of contrast sensitivity functions for lights sinusoidally modulated in space and/or time have explicitly demonstrated this dependence. Daitch and Green (1969) for example, using scotopic targets sinusoidally modulated in space (see Figure 2.6), presented in 200 msec trials, found roughly constant contrast sensitivity (equivalent Weber fraction, 0.1) for 0.5 cycles/deg over the range 0.01 to 1 scotopic td. For a 2 cycles/deg target, however, the contrast sensitivity increased with increasing intensity, in a fashion predicted from the square-root law. Van Nes and Bouman (1967) have provided the most extensive results on the dependence of foveal contrast sensitivity on the mean retinal illuminance. At the low spatial frequency of 0.5 cycles/deg Weber Law behavior obtains above 0.01 td; for high spatial frequencies, however, contrast sensitivity continues to improve with mean illumination well into the photopic range, reaching Weber behavior at all spatial frequencies only above 100 td or so.

Physiological Evidence: Photoreceptor Gain Control

The photoreceptors of many poikilothermic vertebrates have been shown to decrease their gain (incremental linear response amplitude to a dim flash) in the presence of steady illumination. Among the photoreceptors proven by direct electrophysiological recording to light-adapt thus, are skate rods (Dowling & Ripps, 1972), mudpuppy (salamander) rods (Norman & Werblin, 1974), turtle cones (Baylor & Hodgkin, 1974), gekko (lizard) rods (Kleinschmidt & Dowling, 1975), and toad rods (Bastian & Fain, 1979; Baylor et al., 1979b; Baylor, Matthews, & Yau, 1980; Fain, 1975). Light adaptation in these cells can be characterized as a lateral shift of a relatively invariant response-vs.-log-intensity function as a function of mean quantal absorption rate. At each level of mean illumination the cell has a linear operating range, and to first approximation, incremental responses obeys Weber's law at sufficiently high intensities.

In species where comparisons are appropriate and have been made, cones and rods show quantitative differences in sensitivity to adaptation fields. In toad and turtle rods a steady light of 5

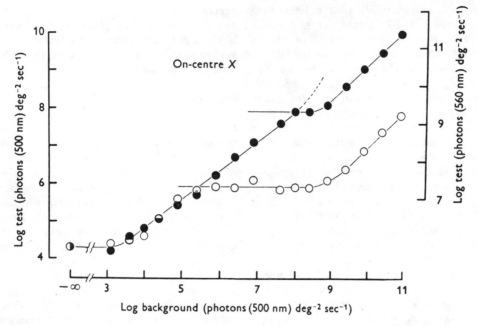

On-centre X

Figure 2.34. Increment threshold curves for a single cat on-center X-cell. Open circles are thresholds measured for a long-wave flash; filled circles, for a mid-wave ("blue-green") flash. Each curve shows two distinct branches or components, which obey the Invariance principle (p. xx), as seen in the classic psychophysical study of Stiles (1939). The threshold upon the lower, more sensitive branch is determined by signals from rods; that upon the upper branch is determined by signals from cones. The left-hand ordinate gives a scale equated for rods, the right-hand, for cones. Below background intensities of $10^{7.5}$ photons $\times$ sec^{-1} $\times$ deg^{-2}, the rod-dominated, but not the cone-dominated segment, of the curve rises, showing that the gain control is not at the ganglion cell level, and that it operates relatively independently for the rod and cone inputs under these conditions, in the sense that the desensitization affecting the response to the rods' signal is not reflected in the sensitivity to cone signals. From "Convergence of Rod and Cone Signals in the Cats' Retina" by C. Enroth-Cugell, B.G. Hertz, and P. Lennie, 1977, *Journal of Physiology, 269,* p. 279. Copyright 1977 by The Physiological Society. Reprinted by permission.

to 10 isomerizations/sec will reduce the flash sensitivity by a factor of 2 (Bastian & Fain, 1979; Baylor & Hodgkin, 1974; Baylor, Matthews, & Yau, 1980; Fain, 1975); for turtle cones flash sensitivity is halved by an adapting light of 2000 isomerizations/sec (Baylor & Hodgkin, 1974).

Light-induced sensitivity changes in vertebrate photoreceptor sensitivity have been shown to be coupled usually to changes in the time scale or speed of the linear (impulse) response at each mean illumination, in a manner similar to that originally found by Fuortes and Hodgkin (1964) in *Limulus*. The faster impulse response allows the visual system to react more rapidly when plenty of light is available. In a dim environment, however, speed is sacrificed to gain sensitivity. The most thorough characterization of the effects of light adaptation on the impulse response of photoreceptors is the

classic study of Baylor and Hodgkin (1974) of turtle cones.

Mammalian rods show little if any gain change in response to steady illumination. This failure of mammalian rods to light-adapt in the fashion of amphibian and reptilian rods has been found by Penn and Hagins (1972) and Green (1973) in rat rods and by Sakmann and Filion (1972) in cat with measurements of massed rod responses, and by Baylor, Nunn, & Schnapf (1984) in suction electrode measurements of single macaque rods. Apparently mammalian rods do not have some regulatory mechanism(s) possessed by fish, amphibian, and reptilian rods. Mammalian rods simply summate the effects of quanta absorbed from background and test: Since the mean duration (integrating time) of the response to a single photon is c. 0.1 sec (see Figure 2.24), mammalian rods operate linearly in response to steady lights up to c. 100 td (500 quanta/rod/sec, or 50 quanta/rod/integrating time). Thus, because the mammalian rod is responding linearly to the adapting lights that produce Weber Law adaptational behavior (0.01 to 100 scotopic td, Figure 2.34) and because the form of the compressive nonlinearity (equation 2.41) of the mammalian rod response cannot give rise to Weber's Law, most mammalian scotopic light adaptation must be attributed to the action of neurons central to the rods.

Little information is available at present on light adaptation of mammalian cones. The investigations of Boynton and Whitten (1970) and of Valeton and van Norren (1983) of massed cone responses from the monkey retina led to opposite conclusions: The former concluded that only a saturating nonlinearity was present, the latter that a true automatic gain control was operative. The more extensive data of Valeton and Van Norren show sub-Weber light adaptation to backgrounds from 10^2 to 10^4 td—about 0.4 log units of adaptation/log unit background increase. This sub-Weber adaptation appears to be due to an automatic gain control intrinsic to the cones. From 10^4 to 10^6 td, the incremental responses of the monkey cone massed responses follow Weber's Law. This Weber behavior can be demonstrated to be a consequence of bleaching adaptation, the diminishment of the ability to absorb light that occurs as pigment is depleted. No data regarding change in speed of mammalian cones during light adaptation have been published, although psychophysical data (critical duration data and temporal modulation transfer data) show that light adaptation in the range 50 to 1000 td does speed up the temporal resolution of the system as a whole (DeLange, 1958; Kelly, 1972), rendering it likely that some response speed-up occurs in light-adapted mammalian cones.

Bleaching Adaptation in Cones

By analysis of the equations of bleaching and regeneration (assuming independence of the processes) one can demonstrate that in the intensity range of significant bleaching, the quantal absorption from steady lights asymptotes to a constant (Alpern, Rushton, & Torii, 1970; Shevell, 1979). If a constant incremental absorption is required to achieve the threshold, Weber's Law follows as a consequence (e.g., Alpern et al., 1970). Geisler (1978) and Shevell (1979) present psychophysical evidence demonstrating that bleaching adaptation plays a significant role in the light adaptation of the human photopic system at illumination intensities above 3000 to 5000 photopic trolands.

Horizontal Cells

In most species horizontal cells seem to follow the adaptation of the photoreceptors. In turtle horizontal cells driven exclusively by long-wave sensitive cones (Norman & Perlman, 1979) and in skate horizontal cells driven by rods (Dowling & Ripps, 1971) exhibit Weber behavior, mimicking the respective receptor gain control mechanisms. Mammalian horizontal cells may be an important exception to the rule: Cat horizontal cells obey Weber's Law from roughly 1 to 100 scotopic td (at which intensity incremental saturation sets in), and yet cat rods seem to behave as other mammalian rods (Sakman & Filion, 1972), having no significant gain control.

Bipolar Cells

In some retinas—for example, mudpuppy (Thibos & Werblin, 1978; Werblin, 1974) and catfish (Naka, Chan, & Yasui, 1979)—bipolar cells exhibit automatic gain control. Rod signals that desensitize the bipolars seem to arrive from horizontal cells over a large spatial extent (Thibos & Werblin, 1978) and perhaps act by shunting the signals from the receptors that drive the bipolar directly. Again, no general rule seems applicable to all species; dogfish (Ashmore & Falk, 1980) shows no bipolar gain control, and yet indirect evidence supports the view that some gain control operates directly in the bipolar cells that feed cat X and Y receptive field centers (Shapley & Enroth-Cugell, 1984). One fact supporting a bipolar gain control in cat is that Y-cells show some local adaptation in the receptive field center (see below). Horizontal cells generally have larger, not smaller, receptive fields than ganglion cells at a given retinal location, and thus would not be a good candidate for a site of adaptation having a finer spatial grain that the ganglion cells.

Ganglion Cells

Ganglion cells in all species that have been studied light-adapt. Adaptation invariably occurs

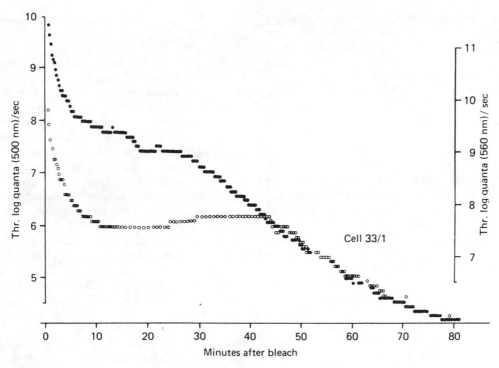

Figure 2.35. Dark adaptation of a cat retinal X-cell after two successive 90% rhodopsin bleaches. Filled symbols represent thresholds measured for a mid-wave (blue-green) test flash; open symbols, thresholds for a long-wave (red) flash. As in the increment threshold curves of Figure 2.34, each curve in this figure has two distinct component branches: the threshold on the upper branch is determined by signals from cones, the threshold on the lower branch by signals from rods. Clearly, the sensitivity is regulated at a site distal to the cell in the retina. From "Recovery of Cat Retinal Ganglion Cell Sensitivity Following Pigment Bleaching" by A.B. Bonds and C. Enroth-Cugell, 1979, *Journal of Physiology*, *295*, p. 55. Copyright 1979 by The Physiological Society. Reprinted by permission.

at or before the signals leave the retina. In cat retinal ganglion cells under scotopic conditions, the adaptation state is determined by the flux falling on the ganglion cell's center, and only that which falls on the center (Cleland & Enroth-Cugell, 1968; Enroth-Cugell & Shapley, 1973—reviewed in Shapley & Enroth-Cugell, 1984). Ganglion cells with larger receptive field centers begin light adapting at lower intensities than cells with smaller centers, and steady light falling upon the antagonistic surround affects the steady-state discharge, but not the gain, of the center. Typically, cat ganglion cells' light adaptation is well described by the formula (Shapley & Enroth-Cugell, 1984)

$$\Delta I/\Delta I_O = [1 + (I_B/I_{RO})]^p \qquad (2.45)$$

where ΔI represents the light required for a criterion response upon the background, I_B; ΔI_O is the amount required in the dark; I_{RO} is a constant that depends on the size of the receptive field center; and p is about 0.9 ($p = 1$ corresponds to Weber behavior). Note that Aguilar and Stiles's (1954) human psychophysical data (Figure 2.33) are also well described by this equation.

In a two-color adaptation paradigm like that used by Aguilar and Stiles, Enroth-Cugell, Hertz and Lennie (1977), demonstrated (Figure 2.35) that the response of a cat ganglion cell to its cone inputs can remain unadapted over an intensity range which causes the rod inputs to desensitize more than two log units in gain. This result provides compelling evidence that gain control occurs distal to the ganglion cell, and that the cone and rod pathways to the ganglion cell have independent gain regulation.

Although in all species the adaptation receptive field—a profile of intensities of small spots required to reduce sensitivity a criterion amount

—of the ganglion cell center response corresponds reasonably well with the excitatory receptive field center, in rat (Green et al., 1977; Tong & Green, 1977), goldfish (Easter, 1968) and frog (Burkhardt & Berntson, 1972) local adaptation within the receptive field center is observed, indicating that subunits with their own adaptation processes pool to form the center mechanism. Cat Y-cells are like the ganglion cells of rat and frog is showing local adaptation in the center, but the smaller X-cells show little local adaptation. It seems likely that automatic gain control mechanisms (and not mere compressive nonlinearities) are the basis of adaptation seen at the ganglion cell level, for ganglion cells exhibit a fair extent of response linearity at each adaptation level. Strong compressive nonlinearities without a shift in operating characteric (in, say, bipolar cells) would not allow such linear response range about each adaptation level.

DARK ADAPTATION

Light adaptation comprises, in its operational definition, all decrease in visual sensitivity that occurs as a result of increased retinal illumination. As has been seen, this broad definition encompasses a variety of mechanisms. Similarly, *dark adaptation* in its operational sense comprises all increase in visual sensitivity that follows a decrease in mean retinal illumination.

A standard paradigm for studying dark adaptation is the exposure of a dark-adapted retina to a relatively brief (say, less than 2 minutes) adapting light, followed by measurement of the return of sensitivity in the dark to its fully dark-adapted maximum. Figure 2.35 (Bonds & Enroth-Cugell, 1979) shows two adaptation curves of a single X-cell of cat retina measured after consecutive adaptation exposures that bleached 90 percent of the rhodopsin. The curves were measured with two different test wavelengths: (a) a blue/green test (c. 500 nm, effective) and (b) a red test. These data show a classic cone/rod break, as well as the spectral (shape) invariance of the two component branches (above, p. 113). Clearly, as in light adaptation (Figure 2.34), sensitivity during dark adaptation is regulated at a site distal to the ganglion cell in cat, since the rod recovery in the curve proceeds during the cone plateau—that is, at a time

when the cone response sensitivity does not change.

In many dark adaptation experiments a modest to substantial amount of visual pigment is bleached by the adapting exposure, and the adapting exposure may be quantified in these terms. Given the variety of mechanisms involved in light adaptation in the broad sense, one is led to expect dark adaptation from a more highly to a less highly light-adapted state to reflect the recovery or relaxation of the variety of mechanisms that govern light adaptation. It does.

Few physiological studies have attempted to characterize explicitly mechanisms that govern distinct components of dark adaptation (other than the classic cone/rod component distinction), although there are ample physiological data (Bonds & Enroth-Cugell, 1979; Dodt & Echte, 1961; Donner & Reuter, 1965, 1968; Dowling, 1963; Grabowski & Pak, 1975; Green, Dowling, Siegel, & Ripps, 1975; Kleinschmidt & Dowling, 1975) and psychophysical data (Crawford, 1946; Hecht, Haig, & Chase, 1937; Pugh, 1975; Rushton & Powell, 1972) demonstrating the existence of at least two components of the scotopic dark adaptation curve. The components typically have apparent time constants separated by an order of magnitude—for example, c. 20 and 200 sec in man for a bleach of 0.5 percent of the rhodopsin (Pugh, 1975; Lamb, 1981). Distinct components of dark adaptation have been observed in the receptors themselves. In their seminal study of turtle cone adaptation Baylor & Hodgkin (1974) found evidence for distinct recovery components with time constants of the order of 0.1, 1.0, 10, and 100 sec. These distinct components manifested themselves to varying degrees, depending on the prior adaptation intensity, with the longer time constant recovery components becoming more salient at the extinction of the more intense adapting or bleaching fields.

The work of many investigations, both physiological and psychophysical, has shown that pigment depletion and subsequent regeneration alone fails grossly to provide a quantitative explanation of dark adaptation. For example, a rhodopsin bleach of 0.5 percent causes a threshold elevation of more than two log units at the extinction of the bleaching exposure (Blakemore & Rushton, 1965; Pugh, 1975); a 99 percent bleach would be required to explain this amount of theshold elevation on the basis of pigment depletion alone. On the other hand, psychophysical studies (Crawford, 1946; Mote & Riopelle, 1953; Pugh, 1975) have shown that the time course of human scotopic dark adaptation is identical for adapting exposures that bleach the same amount of visual pigment, if the duration of the exposure is under 30 sec, for bleaches ranging from 0.01 to 99 percent. It seems extremely unlikely that any mechanism at or past the rod synapse could integrate the effects of bleaching exposures of such varied intensity and duration to give perfect I × T tradeoff, especially since all the exposures render the rods into the region of incremental response saturation. Thus, *it is reasonable to believe that the amount of pigment bleached* (or something functionally dependent upon it) *plays a dominant role in determining the state of dark adaptation* in the standard dark adaptation paradigm *for exposures that bleach more than 0.01 percent.*

Direct evidence for a role of bleached pigment in determining the state of dark adaptation has come from studies of receptor responses in isolated retinas. As noted above, when isolated from the pigment epithelium, the retina cannot regenerate bleached pigment, if the bleaching exposure exceeds a few percent—although regeneration following small bleaches is observed (Azuma et al., 1977; Cone & Brown, 1969; Goldstein, 1970). When more than about 2 percent of the pigment is bleached in the normal eye, then, full regeneration requires that 11-*cis* chromophores be transported from pigment epithelial cells via a specific transport pathway which includes interstitial retinol binding proteins (Bridges et al., 1984; Chader & Wiggert, 1984; Saari et al., 1982) and likely, specific outer segment membrane surface receptor molecules. Following a bleaching exposure greater than 2 percent, the receptors of an isolated retina exhibit a large, persistent threshold elevation that far exceeds that expected on the basis of pigment depletion. If, however, chromophore is supplied exogenously (in the form of 11-*cis* retinal or 11-*cis* retinol), pigment regenerates and sensitivity recovers. This important and robust effect of exogenously induced pigment regeneration on the return of receptor sensitivity has been shown in a number of species with several different techniques—skate (Pepperberg et al., 1976, 1978); rabbit (Pepperberg & Masland, 1978); rat (Albani, Noll, & Yoshikami, 1980); and bullfrog (Perlman, Nodes, & Pepperberg, 1982). Both

pigment regeneration and sensitivity increase appear to begin the moment exogenous chromophore is supplied, and can be effected by delivering the highly water-insoluble chromophore in ethanol-containing Ringers (Clack & Pepperberg, 1982; Pepperberg et al., 1976, 1978) or via liposomes (Albani, Noll, & Yoshikami, 1980; Yoshikami & Noll, 1978). Human disease conditions that affect the relationship between the retina and the pigment epithelium retard both pigment regeneration and the recovery of sensitivity following a bleach (Alpern & Krantz, 1981).

No single relationship between bleached pigment and retinal sensitivity exists that is quantitatively correct for all species and all bleach levels. However, the Dowling–Rushton relation,

$$\log [S_F(t)/S_{FD}] = \alpha[1 - p(t)] \quad (2.46)$$

where $S_F(t)$ is sensitivity at time t, S_{FD} is sensitivity in the fully dark-adapted state, and $p(t)$ is the fraction of pigment present, provides a reasonable account of a considerable body of data, both scotopic (Alpern, 1971; Blakemore & Rushton, 1965; Dowling, 1963; Dowling & Ripps, 1971, 1972; Ripps, Mehaffey, & Siegel, 1981) and photopic (Hollins & Alpern, 1973). Although this formula has no obvious theoretical interpretation, it serves to illustrate the powerful desensitizing effect of a relatively small amount of bleached pigment—in human rods, for example, $\alpha \simeq 20$, meaning a 10 percent bleach causes a two log units threshold elevation. It also embodies the large difference between scotopic and photopic dark adaptation: in man, $1 - p(t) = \exp(-t/\tau)$, with $\tau \simeq 400$ sec in the scotopic case, and $\tau \simeq 100$ sec in photopic dark adaptation. A number of exceptions to equation 2.46 have been noted, however, in subhuman retinas (e.g., Bonds & Enroth-Cugell, 1979).

A theoretical interpretation of the effects of bleached pigment has been given by the dark light hypothesis of Barlow. Barlow (1956) proposed that thermally-induced isomerizations of rhodopsin produce a steady rain of "dark noise" above which dark-adapted thresholds have to be detected, and developed a consistent signal detection theory of absolute threshold based upon this assumed noise. Barlow (1964) hypothesized that in addition, after a bleaching exposure, a "dark light" is generated in the receptors as long as bleached pigment is present. This hypothesis neatly explains the famous Crawford "equivalent background transformation" (Crawford, 1937), which associates with each state of dark adaptation a unique real light background that has identical threshold elevating effects on any test target. Furthermore, Barlow's hypothesis predicts that a bleached-induced afterimage should match in brightness the (retinally stabilized) equivalent background at each point during dark adaptation —a result found by Barlow and Sparrock (1964).

Lamb (1981) expanded Barlow's dark light hypothesis, proposing that by virtue of the reversibility of the bleaching steps prior to the separation of the all-*trans* chromophore from the opsin (Figure 2.19), after a substantial bleach some of the photoproduct could back up to an earlier step in the sequence, and trigger events that are identical to that triggered by an absorbed photon. Lamb developed a quantitative model based upon this kinetic scheme which allowed him to compute the rate of dark equivalent isomerizations. By analyzing an extensive set of human scotopic dark adaptation curves (ranging from 0.5 percent to 98 percent initial rhodopsin bleach) Lamb demonstrated that distinct components corresponding to several decay steps could be extracted, and that the implicit rate constants were reasonable in the light of values known for the decay of the human rhodopsin spectral intermediates.

In a suction electrode experiment in which he measured the outer segment membrane current of single toad receptors after a 1 percent bleach, Lamb (1980) demonstrated the existence of quantum-bump-like events that had the same power spectrum as the single photon response. Similar dark shot-noise events have been observed by Ashmore and Falk (1981) in the bipolar cells of dogfish after a weak bleach. Baylor, Nunn, and Schnapf (1984) measured dark adaptation of macaque monkey rods with the suction electrode technique. During dark adaptation the membrane current exhibited a step-like recovery. The step-like events are of a magnitude that would result from the sudden blockage or opening of a region of about $1 \mu m$, or $1/20$ of the monkey rod outer segment. Unlike the post-bleaching events seen by Lamb in toads or Ashmore and Falk in dogfish, the monkey rod dark noise events have a character very distinct from the single-photon response. Nonetheless, it remains plausible that they would be interpreted by the visual system as photon-like

events. Thus, it seems likely that Barlow's dark light hypothesis is approximately correct, although the biochemical nature of the bleaching-induced dark events in primates remains unknown, and other events in the outer segment and inner retina no doubt also contribute to some rapid components of dark adaptation under various conditions.

CONCLUSION

The student who has worked his/her way through the material of this chapter will no doubt correctly conclude that the edifice of ocular physics and retinal physiology has a solid foundation. He/she may also conclude that the same material provides little reason for psychologists to believe that they have something to contribute to the understanding of how the nervous system actually constructs the perceptual world. This psychologist/physiologist believes the latter conclusion to be quite incorrect. Many of the fundamental developments in visual science originated in insights and derived motivation from psychophysical experimentation. Consider the five following examples.

(1) The realization that Grassmann's Laws, and in particular, the Trichromacy of photopic vision (pp. 116–122) are consequences of the encoding of the retinal image by three classes of cone photoreceptors stands as one of the great milestones in man's efforts to understand which aspects of his perceptual world result from properties of the nervous system, and which from the physics of light. Only very recently has the physiology of primate cones (Baylor, Nunn, & Schnapf, in press) begun to catch up to psychophysics, and the data of psychophysics continues to supply phsyiologists with insights and hypotheses to test.

(2) The great insights that the retina of most vertebrates is duplex (Hecht, 1937), and that scotopic vision is based upon signals generated in a class of photoreceptors so sensitive that they can reliably signal single photon absorptions (p. 126; Hecht, Schlaer, & Perinne, 1942) originated in psychophysics. Again, only recently has retinal physiology (Barlow, Levick, & Yoon, 1971; Baylor, Nunn, & Schnapf, 1984; Hagins, Penn, & Yoshikami, 1970)—guided and motivated by the earlier psychophysics—been able

to demonstrate directly and go beyond what was known from psychophysics.

(3) The extraordinary acuity of human foveal vision has motivated increasingly more sophisticated techniques for characterizing the eye's optics (p. 96) and the foveal cone mosaic (p. 99). Here again, psychophysics provides the yardsticks by which the anatomy and physiology of central vision must be gauged.

(4) The marvelous ability of the human visual system to function efficiently over a 10 million-fold range of retinal illuminations (p. 142), as measured in psychophysical experiments, motivated the search for retinal automatic gain control mechanisms and led to the insight (Shapley & Enroth-Cugell, 1984) that the goal of such gain control mechanisms might be preserving constant contrast sensitivity, so that surface reflectances could be perceived.

(5) The encoding of the signals from foveal cones into chromatically opponent signals was predicted from psychophysical results (Boynton, Ikeda, & Stiles, 1964; Guth, 1965; Jameson & Hurvich, 1955; Sperling & Harwerth, 1971) many years before being directly observed in primate recordings (p. 139). Again, psychophysical experimentation and analysis motivated the search for mechanisms and led to the development of sophisticated techniques (Derrington, Krauskopf, & Lennie, 1984) for quantifying the chromatic coding of single cells. The insight (Ingling & Martinez-Uriegas, 1985) that the same chromatically coded primate X-cells can carry signals that are used by different central neurons to construct luminosity or achromatic percepts (just as the cones generate signals that drive several different types of ganglion cells) should provide impetus for the search for the central mechanism of luminosity.

A lesson that the psychologist may draw from these examples is that psychophysics has a great deal indeed to offer in understanding how the nervous system functions, and ultimately, how it builds the perceptual world. As the frontiers in research in the visual system move centrad, psychophysicists can and must continue to provide insights, intuitions, and principles that guide physiological research.

My thanks to T.D. Lamb, R.W. Rodieck, & R.L. Shapley for helpful comments on this manuscript. I am indebted to D.A. Baylor, A.I. Cohen, W.H. Miller, and R.L. Shapley for providing materials used in preparation of the figures.

REFERENCES

Abramhamson, E.W. & Japar, S.M. (1972). Principles of the interaction of light and matter. In H.J.A. Dartnall (Ed.), *Handbook of sensory physiology* (Vol. VII Sec. 1, pp. 1–32). New York: Springer.

Aguilar, M. & Stiles, W.S. (1954). Saturation of the rod mechanism of the retina at high levels of stimulation. *Optica Acta, 1*, 59–65.

Ahnelt, P.K., Kolb, H., & Pflug, R. (1987). Identification of a subtype of cone photoreceptor, likely to be blue-sensitive, in the human retina. *Journal of Comparative Neurology, 255*, 18–34.

Albani, C., Nöll, G.N., & Yoshikami, S. (1980). Rhodopsin regeneration, calcium and the control of dark current in vertebrate rods. *Photochemistry and Photobiology, 32*, 515–520.

Alpern, M. (1971). Rhodopsin kinetics in the human eye. *Journal of Physiology, 217*, 447–471.

Alpern, M., Bastian, B., & Moeller, J. (1982). In search of the elusive long-wave fundamental. *Vision Research, 22*, 627–634.

Alpern, M., Ching, C.C., & Kitahara, K. (1983). The directional sensitivity of retinal rods. *Journal of Physiology, 43*, 577–592.

Alpern, M. & Kitahara, K. (1983). The directional sensitivities of the Stiles colour mechanisms. *Journal of Physiology, 338*, 627–649.

Alpern, M. & Krantz, D.H. (1981). Visual pigment kinetics in abnormalities of the uvea-retina interface in man. *Investigative Ophthalmology and Visual Science, 20*, 183–203.

Alpern, M., Masseidvaag, F., & Ohba, N. (1971). The kinetics of cone visual pigment in man. *Vision Research, 11*, 539–549.

Alpern, M. & Moeller, J. (1977). The red and green cone visual pigments of deuteranomalous trichromacy. *Journal of Physiology, 266*, 647–675.

Alpern, M. & Pugh, E.N. Jr. (1974). The density and photosensitivity of human rhodopsin in the living retina. *Journal of Physiology, 237*, 341–370.

Alpern, M. & Pugh, E.N. Jr. (1977). Variation in the action spectrum of erythrolabe among deuteranopes. *Journal of Physiology, 266*, 613–646.

Alpern, M., Rushton, W.A.H., & Torii, S. (1970). Signals from cones. *Journal of Physiology, 207*, 463–475.

Alpern, M. & Wake, T. (1977). Cone pigments in human deutan colour vision defects. *Journal of Physiology, 266*, 595–610.

Applebury, M.L. & Chabre, M. (1986). Interaction of photoactivated rhodopsin with photoreceptor proteins: The cGMP cascade. In H. Stieve (Ed.), *The molecular mechanism of photoreception* (pp. 51–66). Berlin: Springer.

Applegate, A. & Bonds, A.B. (1981). Induced movement of receptor alignment toward a new pupillary aperture. *Investigative Ophthalmology and Visual Science, 21,* 869–873.

Ashmore, J.F. & Falk, G. (1980). Responses of rod bipolar cells in the dark adapted retina of the dogfish. *Scyliorhinus canicula. Journal of Physiology, 300,* 115–150.

Ashmore, J.F. & Falk, G. (1981). Photon-like signals following weak rhodopsin bleaches. *Nature, 289,* 489–491.

Azuma, K., Azuma, M., & Sikel, W. (1977). Regeneration of rhodopsin in frog rod outer segments. *Journal of Physiology, 271,* 747–759.

Bader, C.R., MacLeish, P.R., & Schwartz, E.A. (1979). A voltage-clamp study of the light response in solitary rods of the tiger salamander. *Journal of Physiology, 296,* 1–26.

Baehr, W., Devlin, M.J., & Applebury, M.L. (1979). Isolation and characterization of cGMP phosphodiesterase from bovine rod outer segments. *Journal of Biological Chemistry, 254,* 11669–11677.

Baehr, W., Morita, E.A., Swanson, R.J., & Applebury, M.L. (1982). Characterization of bovine rod outer segment G-protein. *Journal of Biological Chemistry, 257,* 6452–6460.

Baker, H.D. & Rushton, W.A.H. (1965). The red-sensitive pigment in normal cones. *Journal of Physiology, 176,* 56–72.

Barlow, H.B. (1956). Retinal noise and absolute threshold. *Journal of the Optical Society of America, 46,* 634–639.

Barlow, H.B. (1957). Increment thresholds at low intensities considered as signal/noise discriminations. *Journal of Physiology, 141,* 337–350.

Barlow, H.B. (1958). Temporal and spatial summation in human vision at different background intensities. *Journal of Physiology, 141,* 337–350.

Barlow, H.B. (1964). Dark adaptation: A new hypothesis. *Vision Research, 4,* 47–58.

Barlow, H.B., Levick, W.R., & Yoon, M. (1971). Responses to single quanta of light in retinal ganglion cells of cat. *Vision Research, 11* (Suppl. 3), 87–101.

Barlow, H.B. & Sparrock, J.M.B. (1964). The role of afterimages in dark adaptation. *Science, 144,* 1309–1344.

Bastian, B.L. & Fain, G.L. (1979). Light adaptation in toad rods: Requirement for an internal messenger which is not calcium. *Journal of Physiology, 297,* 493–520.

Baumann, C.L. (1972). The regeneration and renewal of visual pigments in vertebrates. In H.J.A. Dartnall (Ed.), *Handbook of sensory physiology* (Vol. VII Sec. 2, pp. 395–416). New York: Springer.

Baylor, D.A. & Fettiplace, R. (1975). Light path and photon capture in turtle photoreceptors. *Journal of Physiology, 248,* 433–464.

Baylor, D.A. & Fuortes, M.G.F. (1970). Electrical responses of single cones in the retina of the turtle. *Journal of Physiology, 207,* 77–92.

Baylor, D.A., Fuortes, M.G.F., & O'Bryan, P.M. (1971). Receptive fields of single cones in the retina of turtle. *Journal of Physiology, 214,* 256–294.

Baylor, D.A. & Hodgkin, A.L. (1974). Changes in time scale and sensitivity in turtle photoreceptors. *Journal of Physiology, 242,* 729–758.

Baylor, D.A., Hodgkin, A.L., & Lamb, T.D. (1974). The electrical response of turtle cones to flashes and steps of light. *Journal of Physiology, 242,* 685–727.

Baylor, D.A., Lamb, T.D., & Yau, K.-W. (1979a). The membrane current of single rod outer segments. *Journal of Physiology, 288,* 589–611.

Baylor, D.A., Lamb, T.D., & Yau, K.-W. (1979b). Responses of retinal rods to single photons. *Journal of Physiology, 288,* 613–634.

Baylor, D.A., Matthews, G., & Yau, K.-W. (1980). Two components of electrical dark noise in toad retinal rod outer segments. *Journal of Physiology, 309,* 591–621.

Baylor, D.A., Nunn, B.J., & Schnapf, J.L. (1984). The photocurrent, noise and spectral sensitivity of rods of the monkey, *Macaca fascicularis. Journal of Physiology, 357,* 575–607.

Baylor, D.A., Nunn, B.J., & Schnapf, J.L. (1987). Spectral sensitivity of cones of the monkey, *Macaca fascicularis. Journal of Physiology, 390,* 145–160.

Bedford, R.E. & Wyszecki, E. (1957). Axial chromatic aberration of the human eye. *Journal of the Optical Society of America, 47,* 564–570.

Bennett, A.G. & Francis, J.L. (1962). Visual optics. In H. Davson (Ed.), *The eye.* (Vol. 4, pp. 3–207). New York: Academic.

Bernstein, P.S., Law, W.C., & Rando, R.R. (1987). Isomerization of all-*trans* retinoids to 11-*cis* in vitro. *Proceedings of the National Academy of Sciences, 84,* 1849–1853.

Birge, R.R. (1981). Photophysics of light transduction in rhodopsin and bacteriorhodopsin. *Annual Review of Biophysics and Bioengineering, 10,* 315–354.

Bitensky, M.W., Gorman, R.E., & Miller, W.H. (1971). Adenyl cyclase as a link between photon capture and changes in membrane permeability of frog photoreceptors. *Proceedings of the National Academy of Sciences, 68,* 561–562.

Bitensky, M.W., Wheeler, G.L., Aloni, B., Vetury, S., & Matuo, Y. (1978). Light and GTP-activated photoreceptor phosphodiesterase regulation by a light-activated GTP-ase. *Advances in Cyclic Nucleotide Research, 9,* 553–572.

Blakemore, C.B. & Rushton, W.A.H. (1965). The rod increment threshold during dark adaptation in normal and rod monochromat. *Journal of Physiology, 181*, 629–640.

Blaurock, A.E. & Wilkins, M.H.F. (1969). Structure of frog photoreceptor membranes. *Nature, 223*, 906–909.

Bonds, A.B. & Enroth-Cugell, C. (1979). Recovery of cat retinal ganglion cell sensitivity following pigment bleaching. *Journal of Physiology, 295*, 47–68.

Borsellino, A. & Fuortes, M.G.F. (1968). Responses to single photons in visual cells of *Limulus*. *Journal of Physiology, 196*, 507–539.

Bowmaker, J.K., Dartnall, H.J.A., Lythgoe, J.N., & Mollon, J.D. (1978). The visual pigments of rods and cones in the rhesus monkey, *Macaca mulatta*. *Journal of Physiology, 274*, 329–348.

Bowmaker, J.K., Dartnall, H.J.A., & Mollon, J.D. (1980). Microspectrophotometric demonstration of four classes of photoreceptor in an old world primate, *Macaca fascicularis*. *Journal of Physiology, 298*, 131–143.

Bowmaker, J.K., Loew, E.R., & Liebman, P.A. (1975). Variation in λ_{max} of rhodopsin from individual frogs. *Vision Research, 15*, 997–1003.

Bownds, D. (1967). Site of attachment of retinal in rhodopsin. *Nature, 216*, 1178–1181.

Bownds, D., Dawes, J., Miller, J., & Stahlman, M. (1972). Phosphorylation of frog photoreceptor membranes induced by light. *Nature New Biology, 237*, 125–127.

Boycott, B.B. & Dowling, J.E. (1969). Organization of the primate retina: Light microscopy. *Philosophical Transactions of The Royal Society of London B, 255*, 109–184.

Boycott, B.B. & Wässle, H. (1974). The morphological types of ganglion cells of the domestic cat retina. *Journal of Physiology, 240*, 397–419.

Boynton, R.M., Ikeda, M., & Stiles, W.S. (1964). Interactions among chromatic mechanisms as inferred from positive and negative increment thresholds. *Vision Research, 4*, 87–117.

Boynton, R.M. & Whitten, D.N. (1970). Visual adaptation in monkey cones: Recording of late receptor potentials. *Science, 170*, 1423–1426.

Boynton, R.M. & Wisowaty, J. (1980). Equations for chromatic discrimination models. *Journal of the Optical Society of America, 79*, 1471–1476.

Bridges, C.D.B. (1976). Vitamin A and the role of the pigment epithelium during bleaching and regeneration of rhodopsin in the frog eye. *Experimental Eye Research, 22*, 435–455.

Bridges, C.D.B. & Alvarez, R.A. (1987). The visual cycle operates via an isomerase acting on all-*trans* retinol in the pigment epithelium. *Science, 236*, 1678–1680.

Bridges, C.D.B., Alvarez, R.A., Fong, S.-L., Gonzalez-Fernandez, F., Lam, D.M.K., & Lion, E.I. (1984). Visual cycle in the mammalian eye: Retinoid-binding proteins and the distribution of 11-*cis* retinols. *Vision Research, 24*, 1581–1594.

Brindley, G.S. (1957). Two theorems in colour vision. *Quarterly Journal of Experimental Psychology, 9*, 101–105.

Brindley, G.S. (1966). The deformation phosphene and the tunnelling of light into rods and cones. *Journal of Physiology, 188*, 24–25P.

Brindley, G.S. (1970). *Physiology of the retina and visual pathway* (2nd ed.). London: A. Edward Arnold.

Brown, P.K. (1961). A system for microspectrophotometering employing a commercial recording spectrophotometer. *Journal of the Optical Society of America, 51*, 1000–1008.

Brown, R.G. & Nilsson, J.W. (1962). *Introduction to linear systems analysis*. New York: Wiley.

Burkhardt, D.A. & Berntson, G.G. (1972). Light adaptation and excitation: Lateral spread of signals within the frog retna. *Vision Research, 12*, 1095–1111.

Byram, G.M. (1944a). The physical and photochemical basis of resolving power. 1. The distribution of illumination in retinal images. *Journal of the Optical Society of America, 34*, 571–591.

Byram, G.M. (1944b). The physical and photochemical basis of resolving power. 2. Visual acuity and the photochemistry of the retina. *Journal of the Optical Society of America, 34*, 712–738.

Byzov, A.L. & Trifonov, Y.A. (1968). The response to electric stimulation of horizontal cells in the carp retina. *Vision Research, 8*, 817–822.

Cabello, J. & Stiles, W.S. (1950). Sensibilidad de bastones y conos en la parafovea. *Anales de la Real Sociedad Espanola de Fisica y Quimica A, XLVI*, 251–282.

Cajal, S.R. (1983). La retine de vertebres. *La cellule, 9*, 17–257.

Campbell, F.W. & Green, D.G. (1965). Optical and retinal factors affecting visual resolution. *Journal of Physiology, 181*, 576–593.

Campbell, F.W. & Gubisch, R.W. (1966). Optical quality of the human eye. *Journal of Physiology, 186*, 558–578.

Castano, J.A. & Sperling, H.G. (1982). Sensitivity of the blue-sensitive cones across the central retina. *Vision Research, 22*, 661–673.

Cervetto, L. & MacNichol, E.F. Jr. (1972). Inactivation of horizontal cells in the turtle retina by glutamate and asparate. *Science, 178*, 767–768.

Chader, G.J. & Wiggert, B. (1984). Interphotoreceptor retinoid-binding protein: Characteristics in bovine and monkey retina. *Vision Research, 24*, 1605–1614.

Clack, J.W. & Pepperberg, D.R. (1982). Desensitization of skate photoreceptors by bleaching and background light. *Journal of General Physiology*, *80*, 863–883.

Clark-Jones, R. (1958). On the point- and line-spread functions of photographic images. *Journal of the Optical Society of America*, *48*, 934–937.

Cleland, B.G. & Enroth-Cugell, C. (1968). Quantitative aspects of sensitivity and summation in the cat retina. *Journal of Physiology*, *206*, 73–91.

Cobbs, W.H., Barkdoll, A.E., III, & Pugh, E.N. Jr. (1985). Cyclic GMP increases photocurrent and light sensitivity of retinal cones. *Nature*, *317*, 64–66.

Cobbs, W.H. & Pugh, E.N. Jr. (1985). Cyclic GMP can increase rod outer-segment light-sensitive current 10-fold without delay of excitation. *Nature*, *313*, 585–587.

Cobbs, W.H. & Pugh, E.N. Jr. (1987) Kinetics and components of the flash photocurrent of isolated retinal rods of the larval salamander, *Ambystoma tigrinum*. *Journal of Physiology*, in the press.

Cohen, A.I. (1968). New evidence supporting the linkage to extracellular space of outer segment saccules of frog cones but not rods. *Journal of Cell Biology*, *37*, 424–444.

Cohen, A.I. (1969). Rods, cones and visual excitation. In B.R. Straatsma, M. Hall, R.A. Allen, & F. Crescitelli (Eds.), *The retina* (pp. 31–62). Los Angeles: Univ. of Calif. Press.

Cone, R.A. (1972). Rotational diffusion of rhodopsin in the visual receptor membrane. *Nature New Biology*, *236*, 39–43.

Cone, R.A. & Brown, P.K. (1969). Spontaneous regeneration of rhodopsin in the isolated rat retina. *Nature*, *221*, 818–820.

Cook, N.J., Hanke, W., & Kaupp, U.B. (1987). Identification, purification and functional reconstitution of the cyclic-GMP-dependent channel from rod photoreceptors. *Proceedings of the National Academy of Sciences*, *84*, 585–589.

Crawford, B.H. (1937). The change of visual sensitivity with time. *Proceedings of the Royal Society of London B*, *134*, 283–302.

Crawford, B.H. (1946). Photochemical laws and visual phenomena. *Proceedings of the Royal Society of London B*, *134*, 283–302.

Crawford, B.H. (1949). The scotopic visibility function. *Proceedings of the Physical Society B*, *62*, 321–334.

Crawford, B.H. (1972). The Stiles-Crawford effects and their significance in vision. In L.M. Hurvich & D. Jameson (Eds.), *Handbook of sensory physiology*, (Vol. VII Sec. 4, pp. 470–483). New York: Springer.

Cull-Candy, S.G. & Usowicz, M.M. (1987). Multiple-conductance channels activated by excitatory amino acids in cerebellar neurons. *Nature*, *325*, 525–527.

Curcio, C.A., Sloan, K.R., Packer, O., Hendrickson, A.E. & Kalina, R.E. (1987). Distribution of cones in human and monkey retina: individual variability and radial asymmetry. *Science*, *236*, 579–582.

Dacheux, R.F. & Miller, R.F. (1975). Photoreceptor-bipolar cell transmission in the perfused retina eyecup of the mudpuppy. *Science*, *191*, 963–965.

Daemen, F.J.M., DeGrip, W.J., & Jansen, P.A.A. (1972). Biochemical aspects of the visual process. XX. The molecular weight of rhodopsin. *Biochem. Biophys. Acta*, *271*, 419–428.

Daitch, J.M. & Green, D.G. (1969). Contrast sensitivity of the human peripheral retina. *Vision Research*, *9*, 947–952.

Dartnall, H.J.A. (1957). *The visual pigments*. New York: Wiley.

Dartnall, H.J.A. (1972a). Photochemistry of vision. In H.J.A. Dartnall (Ed.), *Handbook of sensory physiology* Vol. VII. Sec. 4. New York: Springer.

Dartnall, H.J.A. (1972b). Photosensitivity. In H.J.A. Dartnall (Ed.), *Handbook of sensory physiology*, Vol. VII. Sec. 4. New York: Springer.

Dartnall, H.J.A., Bowmaker, J.K., & Mollon, J.D. (1983). Human visual pigments: Microspectrophotometric results from the eyes of seven persons. *Proceedings of the Royal Society of London B*, *220*, 115–130.

Davson, H. (1962). *The eye*. New York: Academic.

DeLange, H. (1958). Research into the dynamic nature of the human-fovea-cortex systems with intermittent and modulated light. I. Attenuation characteristics with white and colored light. *Journal of the Optical Society of America*, *48*, 777–784.

DeMonasterio, F.M. (1978a). Center and surround membranes of opponent-color X & Y ganglion cells of retina of macaques. *Journal of Neurophysiology*, *41*, 1418–1434.

DeMonasterio, F.M. (1978b). Properties of concentrically organized X and Y ganglion cells of macaque retina. *Journal of Neurophysiology*, *41*, 1394–1417.

DeMonasterio, F.M., Schein, S.J., & McCrane, E.P. (1981). Staining of blue-sensitive cones of the macaque retina by a fluorescent dye. *Science*, *213*, 1278–1281.

Denton, E.J. & Pirenne, M.H. (1954). The absolute sensitivity and functional stability of the human eye, *Journal of Physiology*, *123*, 417–442.

Derrington, A.M., Krauskopf, J. & Lennie, P. (1984). Chromatic mechanisms in lateral geniculate nucleus of macaque. *Journal of Physiology*, *357*, 241–265.

Derrington, A.M. & Lennie, P. (1984). Spatial and temporal contrast sensitivities of neurones in lateral geniculate nucleus of macaque. *Journal of Physiology, 357,* 219–240.

DeValois, R.L., Abramov, I., & Jacobs, G.H. (1966). Analysis of response patterns of LGN cells. *Journal of the Optical Society of America, 56,* 966–977.

DeValois, R., Morgan, H.C., Polson, M., Mead, W.R., & Hull, E.M. (1974). Psychophysical studies on monkey vision. I. Macaque luminosity and color vision tests. *Vision Research, 14,* 53–67.

Dodt, E. & Echte, K. (1961). Dark and light adaptation in pigmented and white rat measured by electroretinogram threshold. *Journal of Neurophysiology, 24,* 427–445.

Donner, K.O. & Reuter, T. (1965). The dark adaptation of single units in the frog's retina and its relation to the regeneration of rhodopsin. *Vision Research, 5,* 615–632.

Donner, D.O. & Reuter, T. (1968). Visual adaptation of the rhodopsin rods in the frog's retina. *Journal of Physiology, 199,* 59–87.

Dowling, J.E. (1963). Neural and photochemical mechanisms of visual adaptation in the rat. *Journal of General Physiology, 46,* 1287–1301.

Dowling, J.E. & Boycott, B.B. (1966). Organization of the primate retina: Electron microscopy. *Proceedings of the Royal Society of London B, 166,* 80–111.

Dowling, J.E. & Ripps, H. (1971). S-potentials in the skate retina: Intracellular recordings during light and dark adaptation. *Journal of General Physiology, 58,* 163–189.

Dowling, J.E. & Ripps, H. (1972). Adaptation in skate photoreceptors. *Journal of General Physiology, 60,* 698–719.

Dratz, E.A. & Hargrave, P.A. (1983). The structure of rhodopsin and the rod outer segment disk membrane. *Trends in Biological Science, 8,* 128–131.

Dunnewold, C.J.W. (1964). *On the Campbell and Stiles-Crawford effects and their clinical importance.* Soesterberg: Institute for Perception. The Netherlands.

Easter, S.S. (1968). Adaptation in goldfish retina. *Journal of Physiology, 195,* 273–281.

Enoch, J.M. (1961). Nature of the transmission of energy in the retinal receptors. *Journal of the Optical Society of America, 51,* 1122–1126.

Enoch, J.M. (1975). Vertebrate rod photoreceptors are directionally selective. In A.W. Snyder & D. Menzel (Eds.), *Photoreceptor optics* (pp. 17–37). New York: Springer.

Enoch, J.M., Birch, D.G., & Birch, E.E. (1979). Monocular light exclusion for a period of days reduces directional sensitivity of the human retina. *Science, 206,* 705–707.

Enoch, J.M. & Laties, A.M. (1971). An analysis of retinal receptor orientation. II. Predictions for psychophysical tests. *Investigative Ophthalmology and Visual Science, 10,* 959–970.

Enoch, J.M. & Stiles, W.S. (1961). The color change of monochromatic light with retinal angle of incidence. *Optica Acta, 8,* 329–358.

Enroth-Cugell, C., Hertz, B.G., & Lennie, P. (1977). Convergence of rod and cone signals in the cat's retina. *Journal of Physiology, 269,* 297–318.

Enroth-Cugell, C. & Robson, J.E. (1966). The contrast sensitivity of retinal ganglion cells of the cat. *Journal of Physiology, 187,* 517–552.

Enroth-Cugell, C. & Shapley, R.M. (1973). Flux, not retinal illumination, is what cat retinal ganglion cells really care about. *Journal of Physiology, 233,* 311–326.

Estevez, O. (1979). On the fundamental data-base of normal and dichromatic vision. Ph.D. Thesis, University of Amsterdam, Krips Repro Mepel, Amsterdam.

Fain, G.L. (1975). Quantum sensitivity of rods in the toad retina. *Science, 187,* 838–841.

Fain, G.L. & Lisman, J.E. (1981). Membrane conductances of photoreceptors. *Progress in Biophysics and Molecular Biology, 37,* 91–147.

Famiglietti, E.V. & Kolb, H. (1975). A bistratified amacrine cell and synaptic circuitry in the inner plexiform layer of the retina. *Brain Research, 84,* 293–300.

Fesenko, E.E., Kolesnikov, S.S., & Lyubarsky, A.L. (1985). Induction by cyclic GMP of cationic conductance in plasma membrane of retinal rod outer segment. *Nature, 313,* 310–313.

Feynman, R.P., Leighton, R.B., & Sands, M. (1965). *The Feynman lectures on physics.* Menlo Park, CA: Addison-Wesley.

Flamant, F. (1955). Etude de la repartition de lumiere dans l'image retinienne d'une fente. *Revue d'Optique, 34,* 433–459.

Fleishman, D. & Denisevich, M. (1979). Guanylate cyclase of isolated bovine retinal rod axoneme. *Biochemistry, 18,* 5060–5066.

Frankhauser, F., Enoch, J.M., & Cibis, P. (1961). Receptor orientation in retinal pathology. *American Journal of Ophthalmology, 52,* 767–783.

Fung, B.K.-K., Hurley, J.B., & Stryer, L. (1981). Flow of information in the light-triggered cyclic nucleotide cascade of vision. *Proceedings of the National Academy of Sciences, 78,* 152–156.

Fung, B.K. & Stryer, L. (1980). Photolyzed rhodopsin catalyzes the exchange of GTP for bound GDP in retinal rod outer segments. *Proceedings of the National Academy of Sciences, 77,* 2500–2504.

Fuortes, M.G.F. & Hodgkin, A.L. (1964). Changes in time scale and sensitivity in the ommatidia of *Limulus*. *Journal of Physiology, 172*, 239–263.

Fuortes, M.G.F. & O'Bryan, P.M. (1973). Responses to single photons. In M.G.F. Fuortes (Ed.), *Handbook of sensory physiology* (Vol. VII. Sec. 2 pp. 321–338). New York: Springer.

Fuortes, M.G.F. & Yeandle, S. (1964). Probability of occurrence of discrete potential waves in the eye of *Limulus*. *Journal of General Psychology, 47*, 443–463.

Futterman, S. (1965). Stoichiometry of vitamin A metabolism during light adaptation. In C.N. Graymore (Ed.), *Biochemistry of the retina* pp. 16–21. London: Academic.

Geisler, W.S. (1978). The effects of photopigment depletion on brightness and threshold. *Vision Research, 18*, 269–278.

Godchaux, W. & Zimmermann, W.F. (1979). Membrane-dependent guanine nucleotide binding and GTPase activities of soluble protein from bovine r.o.s. *Journal of Biological Chemistry, 254*, 7874–7884.

Gold, G.H. & Korenbrot, J.I. (1980). Light-induced calcium release by intact retinal rods. *Proceedings of the National Academy of Sciences, 77*, 5557–5561.

Goldstein, E.B. (1970). Cone pigment regeneration in the isolated frog retina. *Vision Research, 10*, 1065–1068.

Gouras, P. & Zrenner, E. (1981). Color vision: A review from a neurophysiological perspective. *Progress in Sensory Physiology, 1*, 139–179.

Grabowski, S.R. & Pak, W.L. (1975). Intracellular recordings of rod responses during dark adaptation. *Journal of Physiology, 247*, 363–391.

Gras, W.J. & Worthington, C.R. (1969). X-ray analysis of retinal photoreceptors. *Proceedings of the National Academy of Sciences, 63*, 233–238.

Grassmann, H. (1853). Zur Theorie der Farbenmischung. *Poggendorfs Annalen der Physik., 84*, 69–84.

Greef, R. von (1902). *A guide to microscopic examination of the eye*. Philadelphia: Blackiston.

Green, D.G. (1973). Scotopic and photopic components of the rat electroretinogram. *Journal of Physiology, 228*, 781–797.

Green, D.G., Dowling, J.E., Siegel, I.M., & Ripps, H. (1975). Retinal mechanisms of visual adaptation in the skate. *Journal of General Physiology, 65*, 483–502.

Green, D.G., Tong, L., & Cicerone, C.M. (1977). Lateral spread of light adaptation in the rat retina. *Vision Research, 17*, 479–486.

Gubisch, R.W. (1967). Optical performance of the human eye. *Journal of the Optical Society of America, 57*, 407–415.

Guth, S.L. (1965). Luminance addition: General considerations and some results at foveal threshold. *Journal of the Optical Society of America, 55*, 718–722.

Guzzo, A.V. & Pool, E.L. (1968). Visual pigment fluorescence. *Science, 159*, 312–314.

Hagins, W.A., Penn, R.D., & Yoshikami, S. (1970). Dark current and photocurrent in retinal rods. *Biophys. J., 10*, 380–412.

Hagins, W.A. & Yoshikami, S. (1974). A role for Ca^{2+} in excitation of retinal rods and cones. *Experimental Eye Research, 18*, 299–305.

Hagins, W.A. & Yoshikami, S. (1977). Intracellular transmission of visual excitation in photoreceptors: Electrical effects of chelating agents introduced into rods by vesicle fusion. In H.B. Barlow & P. Fatt (Eds.), *Vertebrate photoreception* (pp. 97–138). New York: Academic.

Hallett, P.E. (1969). The variations in visual threshold measurement. *Journal of Physiology, 202*, 403–419.

Hargrave, P.A., McDowell, J.H., Curtis, D.R., Wang, J.K., Juszczak, E., Fong, S.-L., Rao, J.K.M., & Argos, P. (1983). The structure of bovine rhodopsin. *Biophysics of Structure and Mechanism, 9*, 235–244.

Haynes, L.W., Kay, A.R., & Yau, K.-W. (1986). Single cyclic GMP-activated channel activity in excised patches of rod outer segment membranes. *Nature, 321*, 66–69.

Haynes, L.W. & Yau, K.-W. (1985). Cyclic GMP-sensitive conductance in outer segment membranes of catfish cones. *Nature, 317*, 61–64.

Hecht, E. & Zajac, A. (1974). *Optics*. New York: Addison-Wesley.

Hecht, S. (1937). Rods, cones and the chemical basis of vision. *Physiological Reviews, 17*, 239–290.

Hecht, S., Haig, C., & Chase, A.M. (1937). The influence of light adaptation on subsequent dark adaptation of the eye. *Journal of General Physiology, 20*, 831–850.

Hecht, S., Schlaer, S., & Piarenne, M.H. (1942). Energy, quanta and vision. *Journal of General Physiology, 25*, 819–840.

Hendry, S.H.C., Hockfield, E.G., Jones, E.G., & McKay, R. (1984). Monoclonal antibody that identifies subsets of neurones in the central visual system of monkey and cat. *Nature, 307*, 267–269.

Henselman, R.A. & Cusanovich, M.A. (1976). Characterization of the recombination of rhodopsin. *Biochemistry, 15*, 5321–5325.

Hochstein, S. & Shapley, R. (1976a). Linear and nonlinear subunits in cat Y retinal ganglion cells. *Journal of Physiology, 262*, 265–284.

Hochstein, S. & Shapley, R. (1976b). Quantitative analysis of retinal ganglion cell classifications. *Journal of Physiology, 262*, 265–284.

Hollins, M. & Alpern, M. (1973). Dark adaptation and visual pigment regeneration in human cones. *Journal of General Physiology, 62*, 430–447.

Honig, B. & Ebrey, T. (1974). The structure and the spectra of the chromophore of the visual pigments. *Annual Review Biophysics & Bioengineering, 3*, 151–177.

Honig, B., Ebrey, T., Callender, R.H., Dinur, U., & Ottolenghi, M. (1979). Photoisomerization, energy storage and charge separation: A model for light energy transduction in visual pigment and bacteriorhodopsin. *Proceedings of the National Academy of Sciences, 76*, 2503–2507.

Honig, B., Greenberg, A.D., Dinur, U., & Ebrey, T. (1976). Visual-pigment spectra: Implications of the protonation of the retinal Schiff-base. *Biochemistry, 15*, 4593–4599.

Hubbard, R. (1954). The molecular weight of rhodopsin and the nature of the rhodopsin-digitonin complex. *Journal of General Physiology, 37*, 381–399.

Hubbard, R. & Kropf, A. (1958). The action of light on rhodopsin. *Proceedings of the National Academy of Sciences, 44*, 130–145.

Hubbard, R. & Kropf, A. (1959). Molecular aspects of visual excitation. *Annals of the New York Academy of Sciences, 81*, 388–398.

Hubbard, R. & Wald, G. (1951). The mechanism of rhodopsin synthesis. *Proceedings of the National Academy of Sciences, 37*, 69–79.

Hurwitz, R.L., Bunt-Milam, A.H., Chang, M.L., & Beavo, J.A. (1985). cGMP phosphodiesterase in rod and cone outer segments of the retina. *Journal of Biological Chemistry, 260*, 568–573.

Ingling, C.R. & Martinez-Uriegas, E. (1985). The spatiotemporal properties of the r-g X-cell channel. *Vision Research, 25*, 33–38.

Jahr, C.E. & Stevens, C.F. (1987). Glutamate activates multiple single channel conductances in hippocampal neurons. *Nature, 325*, 522–525.

Jameson, D. & Hurvich, L.M. (1955). Some quantitative aspects of an opponent colors theory. I. Chromatic responses and spectral saturating. *Journal of the Optical Society of America, 45*, 546–552.

Jennings, J.A.M. & Charman, W.N. (1981). Off-axis image quality in the human eye. *Vision Research, 21*, 445–456.

Kalmus, H. (1965). *Diagnosis and genetics of defective color vision*. New York: Pergamon.

Kaneko, A. (1979). Physiology of the retina. *Annual Review of Neuroscience, 2*, 169–192.

Kaplan, E. & Shapley, R.M. (1982). X and Y cells in the lateral geniculate nucleus of macaque monkeys. *Journal of Physiology, 330*, 125–143.

Kauzmann, W. (1957). *Quantum chemistry*. New York: Academic.

Kelly, D.H. (1972). Flicker. In D. Jameson & L. Hurvich (Eds.), *Handbook of sensory physiology* (Vol. VII. Sec. 4, pp. 273–330). New York: Springer.

Kilbride, P.E., Read, J.S., Fishman, G.A., & Fishman, M. (1983). Determination of human cone pigment density difference spectra in spatially resolved regions of the fovia. *Vision Research, 23*, 1341–1350.

King-Smith, P.E. (1973). The optical density of erythrolabe determined by retinal densitometry using the self-screening method. *Journal of Physiology, 230*, 535–549.

Kleinschmidt, J. & Dowling, J.E. (1975). Intracellular recordings from Gecko photoreceptors during light and dark adaptation. *Journal of General Physiology, 66*, 617–648.

Koenig, A. & Dieterici, C. (1892). Die Grundempfindungen in normalen und anormalen Farbensystemen und ihre Intensititatsverteilung im Spectrum. *Zeitschrift fur Psychologie und Physiologie der Sinnesorg, 4*, 241–347.

Kolb, H. (1970). Organization of the outer plexiform layer of the primate retina: Electron microscopy of Golgi-impregnated cells. *Philosophical Transactions of the Royal Society of London B, 258*, 261–283.

Kolb, H., Mariani, A.P., & Gallego, A. (1980). A second type of horizontal cell in the monkey retina. *Journal of Comparative Neurology, 189*, 31–44.

Kolb, H., Nelson, R., & Mariani, A. (1981). Amacrine cells, bipolar cells and ganglion cells of the cat retina: A Golgi study. *Vision Research, 21*, 1081–1114.

Krantz, D.H. (1975). Color measurement and color theory. I. Representation theorem for Grassmann structures. *Journal of Mathematical Psychology, 12*, 283–303.

Krauskopf, J. (1962). Light distribution in human retinal images. *Journal of the Optical Society of America, 52*, 1046–1050.

Kropf, A. & Hubbard, R. (1958). The mechanism of bleaching rhodopsin. *Annals of the New York Academy of Sciences, 74*, 266–280.

Kuffler, S.W. (1953). Discharge patterns and functional organization of mammalian retina. *Journal of Neurophysiology, 16*, 37–68.

Kuffler, S.W. & Nicholls, J.G. (1976). *From neuron to brain*. Sunderland, Mass.: Sinauer.

Kuhn, H. & Dryer, W.J. (1972). Light dependent phosphorylation of rhodopsin by ATP. *Federation of Biochemical Societies Letters, 20*, 1–6.

Kuhn, M. (1959). The electron gas theory of the color natural and artificial dyes. *Fortschritte der Chemie organischer Naturstoffe, 16*, 169–205.

Lamb, T.D. (1980). Spontaneous quantal events induced in toad rods by pigment bleaching. *Nature, 287*, 349–351.

Lamb, T.D. (1981). The involvement of rod photoreceptors in dark adaptation. *Vision Research, 21,* 1773–1782.

Lamb, T.D., Matthews, H.R., & Torre, V. (1986). Incorporation of calcium buffer into salamander retinal rods: A rejection of the calcium hypothesis of phototransduction. *Journal of Physiology, 372,* 315–349.

Lamb, T.D., McNaughton, P.A., & Yan, K.-W. (1981). Spatial spread of activation and background densitization in toad rod outer segments. *Journal of Physiology, 319,* 463–496.

Laties, A. (1969). Histochemical techniques for the study of photoreceptor orientation. *Tissue and Cell, 1,* 63–81.

Laties, A. & Enoch, J.M. (1971). An analysis of retinal receptor orientation. I. Angular relationships of neighboring photoreceptors. *Investigative Ophthalmology, 10,* 69–77.

Laties, A.M., Liebman, P.A., & Campbell, C.E.M. (1968). Photoreceptor orientation in the primate eye, *Nature, 218,* 172–173.

LeGrand, Y. (1937). Diffusion de la lumiere dans l'oeil. *Revue d'Optique, 16,* 201–241.

Lennie, P. (1980). Parallel visual pathways: A review. *Vision Research, 20,* 561–594.

Lerea, C.L., Somers, D.E., Hurley, J.B., Klock, I.B., & Bunt-Milam, A.H. (1986). Identification of specific transducin α subunits in retinal rod and cone photoreceptors. *Science, 234,* 77–79.

Leventhal, A.G., Rodieck, R.W., & Dreher, B. (1981). Retinal ganglion cells in the old world monkey: morphology and central projections. *Science, 213,* 1139–1142.

Liebman, P. (1972). Microspectrophotometry of photoreceptors. In H.J.A. Dartnall (Ed.), *Handbook of sensory physiology,* Vol. VII. Sec. 1 (pp. 481–528). New York: Springer.

Liebman, P.A. (1962). *In situ* microspectrophotometric studies on the pigments of single retinal rods. *Biophysical Journal, 2,* 161–178.

Liebman, P.A. & Entine, G. (1964). Sensitive low-light-level microspectrophotometer detection of photosensitive pigments of retinal cones. *Journal of the Optical Society of America, 54,* 1451–1459.

Liebman, P.A. & Entine, G. (1974). Lateral diffusion of visual pigment in photoreceptor disk membranes. *Science, 185,* 457–459.

Liebman, P.A. & Pugh, E.N. Jr. (1980). ATP mediates rapid reversal of cGMP phosphodiesterase activation in visual receptor membranes. *Nature, 287,* 734–736.

Linfoot, H.H. (1964). *Fourier methods in optical image evaluation.* New York: Focal.

Liou, G.I., Bridges, C.D.B., Fong, S.-L., Alverez, R.A.,

& Gonzalez-Fernadez, F. (1982). Vitamin A transport between retina and pigment epithelium: An interstitial protein carrying endogenous retinal (interstitial retinal binding protein). *Vision Research, 22,* 1457–1468.

Longhurst, R.S. (1967). *Geometrical and physical optics* (2nd ed.). London: Jarrold & Sons.

Lowe, J.P. (1978). *Quantum chemistry.* New York: Academic Press.

MacNaughton, P.A., Cervetto, L., & Nunn, B.J. (1986). Measurement of the intracellular free calcium concentration in salamander rods. *Nature, 322,* 261–263.

Maguire, B.A., Stevens, J.K., & Sterling, P. (1984). Microcircuitry of bipolar cells in cat retina. *Journal of Neuroscience, 4,* 2920–2938.

Marc, R.E. & Sperling, H.G. (1977). Chromatic organization of primate cones. *Science, 196,* 454–456.

Marchand, E.W. (1965). From point to line-spread function: The general case. *Journal of the Optical Society of America, 55,* 352–354.

Mariani, A.P. (1981). A diffuse, invaginating cone bipolar cell in primate retina. *Journal of Comparative Neurology, 197,* 661–671.

Marks, L., Dobelle, W.H., & MacNichol, E.F., Jr. (1964). Visual pigments of single primate cones. *Science, 143,* 1181–1183.

Marks, W.B. (1963). *Difference spectra of the visual pigment spectra in single goldfish cones.* Unpublished doctoral dissertation, Johns Hopkins University.

Matthews, G. (1986). Comparison of the light-sensitive and cyclic GMP-sensitive conductances of the rod photoreceptor: Noise characteristics. *Journal of Neuroscience, 6,* 2521–2526.

Matthews, G. (1987). Single-channel recordings demonstrate that cGMP opens the light-sensitive ion channel of the rod photoreceptor. *Proceedings of the National Academy of Sciences, 84,* 299–302.

Matthews, H.R., Torre, V., & Lamb, T. (1985). Effects on the photoresponse of calcium buffers and cyclic GMP incorporated into the cytoplasm of retinal rods. *Nature, 313,* 582–585.

Miki, N., Baraban, J.M., Boyce, J.J., & Bitenski, M.W. (1975). Purification and properties of the light activated cyclic nucleotide phosphodiesterase of r.o.s. *Journal of Biological Chemistry, 250,* 6320–6327.

Miller, A.M. & Schwartz, E.A. (1983). Evidence for the identification of synaptic transmitters released by photoreceptors of the toad retina. *Journal of Physiology, 334,* 325–349.

Miller, W.H. (1979a). Intraocular filters. In H. Atrum (Ed.), *Handbook of sensory physiology,* Vol. VII. Sec. 6A (pp. 69–143). Berlin: Springer-Verlag.

Miller, W.H. (1979b). Receptor-optic waveguide effects. *Investigative Ophthalmology, 13,* 556–559.

Miller, W.H. (1981). Calcium and cGMP. In W.H. Miller (Ed.), *Current topics in membranes and transport*. Vol. 15. *Molecular mechanisms of photoreceptor transduction* (pp. 441–445). New York: Academic.

Miller, W.H. & Bernard, G.D. (1983). Averaging over the foveal receptor aperture curtails aliasing. *Vision Research, 23*, 1365–1369.

Miller, W.H. & Snyder, A.W. (1973). Optical functions of human peripheral cones. *Vision Research, 13*, 2185–2194.

Morton, R.A. & Pitt, G.A.J. (1955). pH and the hydrolysis of indicator yellow. *Biochemical Journal, 59*, 128–134.

Missotten, L. (1965). *The ultrastructure of the retina*. Brussels: Arscia.

Mote, F.A. & Riopelle, A.J. (1953). Effect of varying the intensity and duration of pre-exposure on subsequent dark adaptation in the human eye. *Journal of Comparative Physiological Psychology, 62*, 430–447.

McGuire, B.A., Stevens, J.K., & Sterling, P. (1984). Microcircuitry of bipolar cells in cat retina. *Journal of Neuroscience, 4*, 2920–2938.

Murakami, M., Ohtsuka, T., & Shimazaki, H. (1975). Effects of aspartate and glutamate on the bipolar cells in the carp retina. *Vision Research, 15*, 456–458.

Naka, K.-I., Chan, R.Y., & Yasui, S. (1979). Adaptation in catfish retina. *Journal of Neurophysiology, 42*, 441–454.

Naka, K.-I. & Rushton, W.A.H. (1966). An attempt to analyze color reception by electrophysiology. *Journal of Physiology, 185*, 556–586.

Nakatani, K. & Yau, K.-W. (1986). Light-suppressible, cyclic GMP-activated current recorded from a dialyzed cone preparation. *Investigative Ophthalmology and Visual Science, 27*, 300a.

Nathans, J., Piantanida, T.P., Eddy, R.L., Shows, T.B., & Hogness, D.S. (1986). Molecular genetics of inherited variation in human color vision. *Science, 232*, 203–210.

Nathans, J., Thomas, D., & Hogness, D.S. (1986). Molecular genetics of human color vision: The genes encoding blue, green and red pigments. *Science, 232*, 193–202.

Nawy, S. & Copenhagen, D.R. (1987). Multiple classes of glutamate receptor on depolarizing bipolar cells in retina. *Nature, 325*, 56–58.

Nelson, R. (1977). Cat cones have rod input: A comparison of response properties of cones and horizontal cell bodies in the retina of the cat. *Journal of Comparative Neurology, 172*, 109–136.

Nelson, R., Kolb, H., Famiglietti, E.V., & Gouras, P. (1976). Neural responses in rod and cone systems of the cat retina. *Investigative Ophthalmology and Visual Science, 15*, 946–953.

Nelson, R.E., Famiglietti, E.V., & Kolb, H. (1978). Intracellular staining reveals different levels of stratification for ON- and OFF-center ganglion cells in cat retina. *Journal of Neurophysiology, 41*, 472–483.

Norman, R.A. & Perlman, I. (1979). Signal transmission from rod cones to horizontal cells in the turtle retina. *Journal of Physiology, 286*, 509–524.

Norman, R.A. & Werblin, F.S. (1974). Control of retinal sensitivity. I. Light and dark adaptation of vertebrate rods and cones. *Journal of General Physiology, 63*, 37–61.

Nunn, B.J. & Baylor, D.A. (1982). Visual transduction in the retinal rods of the monkey *Macaca fascicularis. Nature, 299*, 726–728.

O'Brien, B. (1951). Vision and resolution in the central retina. *Journal of the Optical Society of America, 41*, 882–894.

Olive, J. (1980). The structural organization of mammalian retinal disk membrane. *International Review of Cytology, 64*, 107–169.

Osterberg, G. (1935). Topography of the layer of rods and cones in the human retina. *Acta Ophthalmologica* (Supplement), *6*, 1–103.

Ovchinnikov, Y.A. (1982). Rhodopsin and bacteriorhodopsin: Structure-function relationships. *Federation of Biochemical Societies Letters, 148*, 179–191.

Owen, W.G. & Torre, V. (1981). Ionic studies of vertebrate rods. In W.H. Miller (Ed.), *Molecular mechanisms of photoreceptor transduction* (pp. 33–57). New York: Academic.

Payne, R. & Howard, J. (1981). Response of an insect photoreceptor: A simple log-normal model. *Nature, 290*, 415–416.

Peichl, L. & Wässle, H. (1979). Size, scatter and coverage of ganglion cell receptive field centers in the cat retina. *Journal of Physiology, 291*, 117–141.

Penn, R.D. & Hagins, W.A. (1969). Signal transmission along retinal rods and the origin of the electroretinographic a-wave. *Nature, 223*, 201–205.

Penn, R.D. & Hagins, W.A. (1972). Kinetics of the photocurrent of retinal rods. *Biophysical Journal, 12*, 1073–1094.

Pepperberg, D.R., Brown, P.K., Lurie, M., & Dowling, J. E. (1978). Visual pigment and photoreceptor sensitivity in the isolated skate retina. *Journal of General Physiology, 71*, 369–396.

Pepperberg, D.R., Lurie, M., Brown, P.K., & Dowling, J.E. (1976). Visual adaptation: Effects of externally applied retinal on the light-adapted isolated skate retina. *Science, 191*, 394–396.

Pepperberg, D.R. & Masland, R.H. (1978). Retinal-induced sensitization of light-adapted rabbit photo-receptors. *Brain Research, 151*, 194–200.

Perlman, J.I., Nodes, B.R., & Pepperberg, D.R. (1982). Utilization of retinoids in the bullfrog retina. *Journal of General Physiology, 80*, 885–913.

Perry, V.H. & Cowey, A. (1981). The morphological correlates of X- and Y- like retinal ganglion cells in the retina of monkeys. *Experimental Eye Research, 43*, 226–228.

Perry, V.H., Oehler, R., & Cowey, A. (1984). Retinal ganglion cells that project to the dorsal lateral geniculate nucleus in the monkey. *Neuroscience, 12*, 1125–1137.

Petersen, D.P. & Middleton, D. (1962). Sampling and reconstruction of wave-number limited functions in N-dimensional Euclidean spaces. *Information & Control, 5*, 279–323.

Polyak, S.L. (1941). *The retina*. Chicago: University of Chicago Press.

Poo, M.M. & Cone, R.A. (1973). Lateral diffusion of rhodopsin in photoreceptor membranes. *Nature, 247*, 438–441.

Pugh, E.N. Jr. (1975). Rushton's paradox: Dark rod adaptation after flash photolysis. *Journal of Physiology, 248*, 413–431.

Pugh, E.N. Jr. (1976). The nature of the π_1 color mechanism of W.S. Stiles. *Journal of Physiology, 257*, 713–747.

Pugh, E.N. Jr. & Cobbs, W.H. (1986). Visual transduction in vertebrate rods and cones: A tale of two transmitters, calcium and cyclic GMP. *Vision Research, 26*, 1613–1643.

Ripps, H., Mehaffey, L., & Siegel, I.M. (1981). Rhodopsin kinetics in the cat retina. *Journal of General Physiology, 77*, 317–334.

Ripps, H. & Weale, R.A. (1969). Flash bleaching of rhodopsin in the human retina. *Journal of Physiology, 200*, 151–161.

Rodieck, R.W. (1965). Quantitative analysis of cat retinal ganglion cell response to visual stimuli. *Vision Research, 18*, 159–173.

Rodieck, R.W. (1973). *The vertebrate retina*. San Francisco: Freeman.

Rodieck, R.W. (1987). *The primate retina*. In H.D. Stecklis (Ed.), *Comparative Primate Biology*, Vol. 4, Neuroscience. New York: Alan R. Liss, Inc.

Rushton, W.A.H. (1956a). The difference spectrum and photosensitivity of rhodopsin in the living human eye. *Journal of Physiology, 134*, 11–29.

Rushton, W.A.H. (1956b). The rhodopsin density in human rods. *Journal of Physiology, 134*, 30–46.

Rushton, W.A.H. (1958). Kinetics of cone pigments measured objectively on the living human fovea. *Annals of the New York Academy of Science, 74*, 291–304.

Rushton, W.A.H. (1963). Cone pigment kinetics in the protanope. *Journal of Physiology, 168*, 374–388.

Rushton, W.A.H. (1965). Cone pigment kinetics in the deuteranope. *Journal of Physiology, 176*, 38–45.

Rushton, W.A.H. (1972). Visual pigments in man. In H.J.A. Dartnall (Ed.), *Handbook of sensory physiology*, Vol. VII, Sec. 4 (pp. 364–394). New York: Springer.

Rushton, W.A.H. & Henry, G.H. (1968). Bleaching and regeneration of cone pigments in man. *Vision Research, 8*, 617–631.

Rushton, W.A.H. & Powell, D.S. (1972). The early phase of dark adaptation. *Vision Research, 12*, 1083–1093.

Saari, J., Bredberg, C., & Garwin, G. (1982). Identification of the endogenous retinoids associated with three cellular retinoid-binding proteins from bovine retina and retinal pigment epithelium. *Journal of Biological Chemistry, 257*, 13329–13333.

Sakitt, B. (1972). Counting every quantum. *Journal of Physiology, 223*, 131–150.

Sakman, B. & Filion, M. (1972). Light adaptation of the late receptor potential in the cat retina. In G.B. Arden (Ed.), *Advances in experimental medicine and biology* (Vol. 24, pp. 87–93). New York: Plenum.

Schmidt, W.J. (1938). Polarisationsoptische Analyses eines Eiweiss-Lipoid-Systems, erlautert am Aussenglied der Sehzellen. *Kolloidzeitschrift, 85*, 137–148.

Schnapf, J. (1983). Dependence of the single photon response on longitudinal position of absorption in toad rod outer segments. *Journal of Physiology, 343*, 147–159.

Schnapf, J., Kraft, T.W., & Baylor, D.A. (1987). Spectral sensitivity of human cone photoreceptors. *Nature, 324*, 439–442.

Schnettkamp, P.P.M. (1979). Calcium translocation and storage of isolated intact cattle rod outer segments in darkness. *Biochemica Biophysica Acta, 554*, 441–459.

Schwartz, E.A. (1981). First events in vision: The generation of responses in vertebrate rods. *Journal of Cell Biology, 90*, 271–278.

Schwarz, R.J. & Friedland, B. (1965). *Linear systems*. New York: McGraw-Hill.

Shapley, R. & Enroth-Cugell, C. (1984). Visual adaptation and retinal gain controls. *Progress in Retinal Research, 3*, 263–346.

Shapley, R. & Lennie, P. (1985). Spatial frequency analysis in the visual system. *Annual Review of Neuroscience, 8*, 547–583.

Shevell, S.K. (1979). Similar threshold functions from contrasting neural signal models. *Journal of Mathematical Psychology, 19*, 1–17.

Sirovich, L. & Abramov, I. (1977). Photopigments and pseudo-pigments. *Vision Research, 17,* 5–16.

Slaughter, M.M. & Miller, R.F. (1983). An excitatory amino acid antagonist blocks cone input to sign-conserving second order retinal neurons. *Science, 219,* 1230–1232.

Smith, R.G., Freed, M.A., & Sterling, P. (1986). Microcircuitry of the dark adapted cat retina: Functional architecture of the rod-cone network. *Journal of Neuroscience, 6,* 3505–3517.

Smith, V.C. & Pokorny, J. (1975). Spectral sensitivity of the foveal cone photopigments between 400 nm and 500 nm. *Vision Research, 15,* 161–171.

Smith, V.C., Pokorny, J., & Starr, S.J. (1976). Variability of color-mixture data. I. Inter-observer variability in the unit coordinates. *Vision Research, 16,* 1087–1094.

Snitzer, E. (1961). Cylindrical dialectic waveguide modes. *Journal of the Optical Society of America, 51,* 491–498.

Snyder, A.W. (1969a). Excitation and scattering on a dielectric of optical fiber. *IEEE Transactions on Microwave Theory and Techniques, 17,* 1138–1144.

Snyder, A.W. (1969b). Asymptotic expression for eigenvalues and eigenfunctions of a dialectic of optical waveguide. *IEEE Transactions on Microwave Theory and Techniques, 17,* 1130–1138.

Snyder, A.W. (1975). Photoreceptor optics—Theoretical principles. In A.W. Snyder & R. Menzel (Eds.), *Photoreceptor optics* (pp. 38–55). New York: Springer.

Snyder, A.W. & Miller, W.H. (1977). Photoreceptor diameter and spacing for highest resolving power. *Journal of the Optical Society of America, 67,* 696–698.

Snyder, A.W. & Pask, C. (1973). The Stiles–Crawford effect: Explanation and consequences. *Vision Research, 13,* 1115–1137.

Snyder, A.W. & Pask, C. (1975). A theory of the Stiles–Crawford effect of the second kind. In A.W. Synder & R. Menzel (Eds.), *Photoreceptor optics* (pp. 145–174). New York: Springer.

Snyder, A.W., Pask, C., & Mitchell, D.J. (1973). Light acceptance property of an optical fiber. *Journal of the Optical Society of America, 63,* 59–64.

Sperling, H.E. & Harwerth, F.S. (1971). Red-green cone interactions in the increment-threshold spectral sensitivity of primates. *Science, 172,* 180–184.

Sterling, P. (1983). Microcircuitry of the cat retina. *Annual Review of Neurosciences, 6,* 149–185.

Sperling, W. (1973). Conformations of 11-*cis* retinal. pp. 19–28 in H. Langer (Ed.), *Biochemistry and physiology of visual pigments.* Berlin: Springer.

Stiles, W.A. (1937). The luminous efficiency of monochromatic rays entering the pupil at different points and a new color effect. *Proceedings of the Royal Society of London B, 123,* 90–118.

Stiles, W.S. (1939). The directional sensitivity of the retina and the spectral sensitivities of the rods and cones. *Proceedings of the Royal Society of London B, 127,* 64–105.

Stiles, W.S. & Burch, J.M. (1955). Interim report to the Commission Internationale de l'Eclairage, Zurich, 1955, on the National Physical Laboratory's investigation of color matching. *Optica Acta, 2,* 168–181.

Stiles, W.S. & Crawford, B.H. (1933). The luminous efficiency of rays entering the pupil at different points. *Proceedings of the Royal Society of London B, 112,* 428–450.

Stryer, L. (1986). Cyclic GMP cascade of vision. *Annual Review of Neurosciences, 9,* 87–119.

Szuts, E.F. & Cone, R.A. (1977). Calcium content of frog rod outer segments and disks. *Biochemica Biophysica Acta, 468,* 194–208.

Thibos, L.N. & Werblin, F.S. (1978). The response properties of the steady antagonistic surrounds in the mudpuppy retina. *Journal of Physiology, 278,* 101–116.

Thomson, L.C. & Wright, W.D. (1953). The convergence of the tritanopic confusion loci and the derivation of the fundamental response-functions. *Journal of the Optical Society of America, 43,* 890–894.

Tong, L. & Green, D.G. (1977). Adaptation pools and excitation receptive fields of rat retinal ganglion cells. *Vision Research, 17,* 1233–1236.

Torre, V., Matthews, H.R., & Lamb, T.D. (1986). Role of calcium in regulating the cyclic GMP cascade of phototransduction in retinal rods. *Proceedings of the National Academy of Sciences, 83,* 7109–7113.

Trifonov, Y.A. (1968). Study of synaptic transmission between the photoreceptor and the horizontal cell using electrical stimulation of the retina. *Biofizika, 13,* 809–817.

Valeton, M.J. & Van Norren, D. (1983). Light adaptation of primate cones: An analysis based on extracellular data. *Vision Research, 23,* 1539–1547.

Van Nes, F.L. & Bouman, M.A. (1967). Spatial modulation transfer in the human eye. *Journal of the Optical Society of America, 57,* 401–406.

Vos, J.J. (1978). Colorimetric and photometric properties of a 2-fundamental observer. *Color Research & Applications, 3,* 125–128.

Vos, J.J. & Walraven, P.L. (1971). On the derivation of the foveal receptor primaries. *Vision Research, 11,* 799–818.

Wald, G. & Brown, P.K. (1958). Human rhodopsin. *Science, 127,* 222–226.

Wald, G. & Brown, P.K. (1953). The molar extinction of rhodopsin. *Journal of General Physiology*, *37*, 189–200.

Walls, G.L. (1942). *The Vertebrate Eye and its Adaptive Radiation.* Cranbrook Institute of Science, Bulletin No. 19. Bloomfield Hills, Michigan.

Walraven, P.L. & Bouman, M.A. (1960). Relation between directional sensitivity and spectral response curves in human cone vision. *Journal of the Optical Society of America*, *50*, 780–784.

Weale, R.A. (1965). Vision and fundus reflectometry: A review. *Photochemistry & Photobiology*, *4*, 67–87.

Werblin, F.S. (1974). Control of retinal sensitivity. II. Lateral interaction at the outer plexiform layer. *Journal of General Physiology*, *63*, 62–87.

Westheimer, G. (1959). A new method of measuring visual resolution at the retina. *Journal of the Optical Society of America*, *49*, 504.

Westheimer, G. (1960). Modulation thresholds for sinusoidal light distributions on the retina. *Journal of Physiology*, *152*, 67–74.

Westheimer, G. (1966). The Maxwellian view. *Vision Research*, *6*, 669–682.

Westheimer, G. (1967). Dependence of the magnitude of the Stiles–Crawford effect on retinal location. *Journal of Physiology*, *192*, 209–215.

Westheimer, G. (1972). Optical properties of vertebrate eyes. In M.G.F. Fuortes (Ed.), *Handbook of sensory physiology* (Vol. VII, Sec. 2, pp. 449–482). New York: Springer.

Westheimer, G. & Campbell, F.W. (1962). Light distribution in the image formed by the living human eye. *Journal of the Optical Society of America*, *52*, 1040–1045.

Whittle, P. & Challands, P.D.C. (1969). The effect of background luminance of the brightness of flashes. *Vision Research*, *9*, 1095–1110.

Wiesel, T.N. & Hubel, D.H. (1966). Spatial and chromatic interactions in the lateral geniculate body of the rhesus monkey. *Journal of Neurophysiology*, *29*, 1115–1156.

Williams, D.R. (1985). Aliasing in human foveal vision. *Vision Research*, *25*, 195–206.

Williams, D.R. & Collier, R. (1983). Consequences of spatial sampling by a human photoreceptor mosaic. *Science*, *221*, 385–387.

Williams, D.R., Collier, R.J., & Thompson, B.J. (1983). Spatial resolution of the short wavelength mechanism. In J. Mollon & T. Sharpe (Eds.), *Color vision* (pp. 487–503). New York: Academic.

Williams, D.R., MacLeod, D.I.A., & Hayhoe, M.M. (1981a). Foveal tritanopia. *Vision Research*, *21*, 1341–1356.

Williams, D.R., MacLeod, D.I.A., & Hayhoe, M.M.

(1981b). Punctuate sensitivity of the blue-sensitive mechanism. *Vision Research*, *21*, 1357–1376.

Wilmer, E.N. (1950). The monochromatism of the central fovea in red-green blind subjects. *Journal of Physiology* (London) *110*, 377–385.

Winston, R. & Enoch, J.M. (1971). Retinal cone as an ideal light collector. *Journal of the Optical Society of America*, *61*, 1120–1121.

Wyszecki, G. & Stiles, W.S. (1967). *Color science.* New York: Wiley.

Wyszecki, G. & Stiles, W.S. (1982). *Color science* (2nd ed.). New York: Wiley.

Yau, K.W., Lamb, T.D., & Baylor, D.A. (1977). Light-induced fluctuations in membrane current of single toad rod outer segments. *Nature*, *269*, 79–80.

Yau, K.W. & Nakatani, K. (1984). Electrogenic Na–Ca exchange in retinal rod outer segment. *Nature*, *311*, 661–663.

Yau, K.-W. & Nakatani, K. (1985a). Light-induced reduction of cytoplasmic free calcium in retinal rod outer segment. *Nature*, *313*, 579–581.

Yau, K.-W. & Nakatani, K. (1985b). Light-suppressible, cyclic-GMP-sensitive conductance in the plasma membrane of a truncated rod outer segment. *Nature*, *317*, 252–255.

Yeandle, S. (1958). *Limulus* quantum bumps. *American Journal of Ophthalmology*, *46*, 82–87.

Yeandle, S. & Srebro, R. (1970). Latency fluctuations of discrete waves in the *Limulus* photoreceptor. *Journal of the Optical Society of America*, *60*, 398–401.

Yee, R. & Liebman, P.A. (1978). Light-activated phosphodiesterase of the rod outer segment. *Journal of Biological Chemistry*, *253*, 8902–8909.

Yellott, J. (1983). Spatial consequences of photoreceptor sampling in the Rhesus retina. *Science*, *221*, 382–385.

Yoshikami, S., George, S., & Hagins, W.A. (1980). Light-induced calcium fluxes from the outer segment layer of vertebrate retina. *Nature*, *286*, 395–398.

Yoshikami, S. & Hagins, W.A. (1970). Ionic basis of dark current and photocurrent of retinal rods. *Biophysical Journal*, *10*, 60a.

Yoshikami, S. & Hagins, W.A. (1973). Control of dark current in vertebrate rods and cones. In H. Langer (Ed.), *Biochemistry and physiology of visual pigments* (pp. 245–255). New York: Springer.

Yoshikami, S. & Noll, G.N. (1978). Isolated retinas synthesize visual pigments from retinal congeners delivered by liposomes. *Science*, *200*, 1393–1395.

Yoshikami, S., Robinson, W.E., & Hagins, W.A. (1974). Topology of the outer segment membranes of retinal rods and cones revealed by a fluorescent probe. *Science*, *185*, 1176–1179.

Young, R.W. (1967). The renewal of photoreceptor cell outer segments. *Journal of Cell Biology, 33,* 61–80.

Young, R.W. (1976). Visual cells and the concept of renewal. *Investigative Ophthalmology and Visual Science, 15,* 700–725.

Zimmerman, A.L. & Baylor, D.A. (1986). Single-channel currents from the cyclic GMP sensitive conductance retinal rod outer segments. *Nature, 321,* 70–72.

Zrenner, E. (1983). Neurophysiological aspects of color vision in the primate retina. In J. Mollon & T. Sharpe (Eds.), *Color vision* (pp. 195–210). London: Academic.

Zwas, F. (1979). Wavelength variation in directional sensitivity of the long- and medium-wave sensitive foveal cones of red-green dichromats. *Vision Research, 19,* 1067–1076.

Zwas, F. & Alpern, M. (1976). The density of human rhodopsin in the rods. *Vision Research, 16,* 121–128.

Chapter 3

VISION: SPACE AND MOVEMENT

Gerald Westheimer, *University of California, Berkeley*

Visual experiences, besides having brightness and chromatic qualities, have the fundamental attributes of space and time. The most elementary stimulation of the visual pathways leads to a sensory experience with spatial and temporal signatures, whose intrinsic nature is not further analyzable by scientific means.

To the extent that they do not share properties with perceptual processes in general, the temporal aspects of visual perception have their origin in the limitations of the retinal apparatus to handle high-frequency light signals.

In the usual categorical classification, where time and space are regarded as fundamental dimensions, the time rate of spatial changes, that is, movement, would be regarded as a hybrid. But detailed psychophysical analysis now permits us to to view movement as a singular attribute of a visual percept.

SPACE PERCEPTION

Basic Concepts

Mechanical, electrical or x-ray excitation of the retina in an alert observer leads to a visual experience, called phosphene, to which a spatial location can be assigned. By means of phosphenes it is possible, for example, to test the functional integrity of the retina and central visual pathways, even when the cornea or lens

of the eye is opaque to light. Phosphenes have been used in the convincing demonstration of the inverted relation between the outside world and the retinal image; mechanical stimulation of the temporal edge of the retina causes a light sensation that is localized in the opposite direction, that is, a direction equivalent in location to a real object on the nasal side.

Basic to the study of spatial vision is the optical mapping of the object space onto the retina. The retina may be regarded as a two-dimensional surface, each point of which corresponds to an incoming light ray. The sheaf of incoming rays can be thought of as converging on the eye's entrance pupil. Any particular object point is, for the purposes of retinal imagery, associated with one of these rays—called line of sight—and is, therefore, characterized by two angular parameters, corresponding to the two positional parameters that describe a point on the retina. The world of objects is, of course, three dimensional, and hence there is a residual ambiguity; a retinal point can be stimulated by all objects lying on the same line of sight. However, information about the third dimension can still be extracted by means of an elaborate apparatus for teasing out differences arising from variations in target distances from the eye.

Because the visual process is necessarily based on this optical arrangement, the usual coordinates for specifying the position of a visual target are two angles expressing the direction of its line of sight in the two dimensions needed to place it in the sheaf of incoming rays. Distance from the observer along the line of sight is the third dimension. If the eye is held stationary, the visual field, that is, the totality of the lines of sight on which objects can yield a visual sensation, extends to about 90 degrees temporally and at least 60 degrees upwards, downwards, and nasally (Figure 3.1). Functional capabilities are not uniform within this visual field. Visual acuity, to be discussed below, is best in the center where the retina has a specially adapted structure, the fovea. A normal subject, when asked to look at a target, moves the eye so as to bring the foveal line of sight onto the target. This is called fixation. The oculomotor apparatus can generate eye movements that extend to a total of about 90 degrees horizontally and somewhat more vertically. The field of fixation, which describes the full extent of possible eye positions, should not be confused with the visual field, which refers to the full range of target directions within which visual sensations can be elicited for a stationary eye.

Since in the human both eyes are directed forward, their visual fields overlap to a considerable extent; the binocular field measures about 90 degrees in diameter in all directions. The overlapping of the visual fields of the two eyes makes interesting demands on the anatomical arrangement of the visual pathways to accommodate the desired interaction between the projections of equivalent directions in the visual field as processed by the two eyes individually.

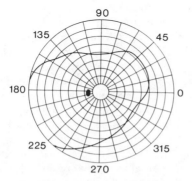

Figure 3.1. Visual field of the left eye as seen by the subject. Polar coordinates define the meridians and eccentricity, expressed in visual angle. Filled-in area shows the blind spot, which is situated in the nasal retina and hence falls into the temporal hemifield.

The most commonly used coordinate system for the visual field is the polar system, because it follows naturally from the existence of the fovea and also because, as we shall see later, most visual performances change as a function of distance from the fovea to the retinal periphery. The basic concept here is the meridian, defined as a plane containing the anteroposterior axis of the eye. The horizontal meridian bisects the visual field into its upper and lower halves, and the vertical meridian into right and left, or nasal and temporal hemifields. Meridians are specified according to their orientation: the vertical meridian is usually the 90–270 degree meridian, and the horizontal the 0–180 degree meridian. Along any meridian, the distance from the fovea is called eccentricity, also expressed in degrees. Using the words upper, lower, nasal, and temporal for the outside projection of the visual field will avoid ambiguity. For example, the blind spot of an eye can then be specified as situated 12 degrees along the temporal horizontal meridian, as 5 degrees wide, and as 7.5 degrees in vertical extent. Finally, by identifying also the radial distance from the eye along any line of sight, we have a complete specification of the eye's object space given in terms most natural to the structural organization of the visual system: two angular measures of the direction of the line of sight, for example, orientation of the meridian and eccentricity along that meridian, and a linear measure of the distance from the eye along that line of sight. By coordinate transformation one can easily map this into a three-dimensional x-y-z Euclidean space centered on the eye, but it must be understood that these coordinates move with the eye. As occasion demands, coordinates centered on the eye, the head, or the body may have to be distinguished.

Object Space and Visual Space

The preceding description of a coordinate system refers to the placement of targets for stimulation of the visual system. It is the object space, and the laws of Euclidean geometry apply to it for all practical purposes. In studying visual psychophysical and perceptual phenomena, we base our findings on subjects' responses. As was mentioned earlier, a spatial quality is associated with even the simplest visual sensation, and while the nature of this set of spatial attributes of a subjective visual impression defies further analysis, the relation between its members certainly does not. Visual spatial psychophysics thus uses as its raw material the response of conscious subjects to specific questions concerning the relation between the spatial attributes of visual sensations. In the simplest experiments visual sensations are associated unambiguously with physical light stimuli—objects whose characteristics we can specify with arbitrary precision. The distinction between physical object space and the subjective ordering of the spatial attributes of arrays of visual percepts (i.e., visual space), is fundamental, and one needs to be comfortable with it before proceeding. If the two manifolds, physical object space and subjective visual space, were always coincident and had identical characteristics, there would be no lengthy discussion of visual perception. As it is, there are innumerable differences between the two spaces, some trivial in nature and some of fundamental character; they become tractable in principle once it is understood that the problem consists in mapping the two spaces on each other.

At the beginning psychophysical level, much the same set of concepts can serve for the two spaces. For example, we can investigate whether equal distances in one space correspond to equal distances in the other. The experiment would be carried out as follows. The observer looks at a line on a board that stands at some distance from him in a frontoparallel plane. A marker is placed in the middle of the line, and the observer reports whether the two halves of the line are of equal length. The experiment can be carried out with all the refinements of the best psychophysical procedures. In the end we can determine where the marker has to be placed for the two line segments to be subjectively equal in length. So far as subjective visual space is concerned, the segments are now equal. If they are also equal in object space, the observer's perception is veridical.

In actual fact, veridicality of spatial perception is the exception rather than the rule. In elementary and popular accounts of visual perception much is made of the many situations in which relations in one space are grossly discrepant from relations in the other—the so-called visual illusions. The seasoned psychophysicist needs no reminder of this lack of concordance; the catalogue of visual illusions is

long and needlessly discouraging if the purpose of the exercise is a scientific review of the topic.

Exact concordance is not, of course, necessary. There may be a universal law that contains the mathematical rules or perhaps only the computational algorithms by which one space may be mapped on the other. Well-behaved spaces in geometry are characterized completely by their metric, which is the rule for determining distances within the space. Some spaces such as the ordinary Euclidean space have simple metrics. If visual space had a metric, it would simplify our discussion immensely. Once determined experimentally and given adequate expression, it would allow the prediction of a spatial relation between percepts. Unfortunately, no such metric is available. In color vision the situation is different. Although the metric of color space is not a simple mathematical expression, it is nevertheless available in numerical form; it permits, for example, the design of a uniform chromaticity domain in which all just noticeable differences (jnd) of chromaticities are equidistant. But even there, difficulties soon arise—such phenomena as the Bezold-Brücke effect and the various simultaneous and successive color contrast effects make the approach to color perception via metrics of color spaces an incomplete enterprise. The approach now favors instead an analysis of the underlying physiological mechanisms, which, though they lack the conceptual simplicity of a metrical mathematical space, have a reasonably satisfying explanatory power.

Psychophysics: Spatial versus Brightness Criteria

Another tradition in psychophysics that is helpful is the distinction between intensive and extensive aspects of vision. The studies presented in this chapter are distinct from those intended to elucidate the mechanism for the sensation of brightness. The spatial attribute of visual sensation is best illustrated by the questions asked of the observer and by the manipulations carried out by the experimenter with stimuli. When studying the light sense, the experimenter usually varies the luminance of targets and asks the subject whether, for example, two patches are equally bright, or whether a field is uniform or has just perceptible brightness differences. On the other hand, when studying the space sense, the experimenter asks the subject questions about the spatial attribute of the percept, such as: Did you see one or two lines? Was the line vertical? Was this pattern in front of that pattern?

This difference in approach is best illustrated by the rather simple first question one might ask for the visual space sense: How small must a target be to be seen? Experiments here can be carried out without any apparatus. One measures the width of a telephone wire and backs off until it just can or cannot be seen against a uniform sky. A wire 1 cm wide needs an observation distance of several kilometers to be at the threshold of visibility. In conformity with the convention of expressing visual spatial magnitudes in terms of angles subtended at the eye's entrance pupil, the threshold width of a line is found to be less than 1 sec of arc visual angle under ideal observation conditions (Hecht & Mintz, 1939). This is indeed a small quantity, but on further analysis the situation becomes less surprising.

It is helpful at this stage to have recourse to the distinction between the distal and the proximal stimulus, which can be succinctly stated for visual space perception. Basic to the approach is the convention that there is a real world in which the laws of physics apply, and that there are objects with definable properties of length, mass, position, temperature, and so on, that are subject to lawful transformations. The laws of geometrical and physical optics are examples.

One begins with the spatial configurations of objects confronting the observer. The scene can, in principle, be characterized with arbitrary detail by photography, photometry, or any of a variety of optical or electrical tools. This gives the distal stimulus. Visual processing in the central nervous system does not, however, operate on this pattern of external light sources, but rather on the spatial distribution of light excitation impinging on the retina of the subject's eye. Transduction of the external light distribution by the optics of the eye yields the retinal light distribution. As it happens, we are well informed about the optical imaging within the eye, and we can, for all practical purposes, factor out its contributions when we are searching for lawful relations between objects and the associated visual perceptions. Fechner, who first thoughtfully analyzed the situation in 1860,

coined the term *outer psychophysics* for the study between the distal stimulus and the associated perception, and the term *inner psychophysics* for the relation starting with the proximal stimulus.

For human vision in the center of the retina, the difference between the distal and the proximal stimulus can be most concisely stated by referring to the eye's line-spread function, that is, the distribution of light in the retinal image of a theoretical infinitesimally narrow line stimulus. Diffraction, optical aberrations of the eye, scatter of light in the ocular media, and so on, spread the light into a bell-shaped distribution with a half-width at half-height of, at best, 1 minute of arc. This means that on the retina even the narrowest line target ends up with a width covering several retinal receptors. The visibility of any small target—small with reference to the 1 or 2 min of arc width of the line-spread function—will then depend not on its dimension in detail, but on the total energy it delivers to the retina. Whether a star is detected depends only on its intensity and the background luminance, not on its diameter (Figure 3.2).

The visibility of a dark line against a bright background creates a slightly more complicated situation. The line creates a dimple in the uniform level of background retinal illuminance; the shape then is that of the eye's line-spread function (no target can have a smaller image), but the depth of the dimple depends on the width of the line (Figure 3.2b). As the target line is widened, the image contrast increases. Although the test for finding the narrowest dark line that can be seen may be carried out in the space domain (by increasing line width until threshold visibility is reached), the threshold determiner is contrast. The minimum target size that can be detected is, therefore, not a test that addresses the spatial sense of the eye in the stricter meaning. We have here a good example of the insight that can be gained by distinguishing between distal and proximal stimuli.

The eye's line-spread function can vary considerably with physiological changes in refractive state, accommodation, pupil size, corneal transparency, and more. On occasion some care may be needed before concluding that changes in spatial thresholds are not caused by changes in the optical transduction properties of the eye.

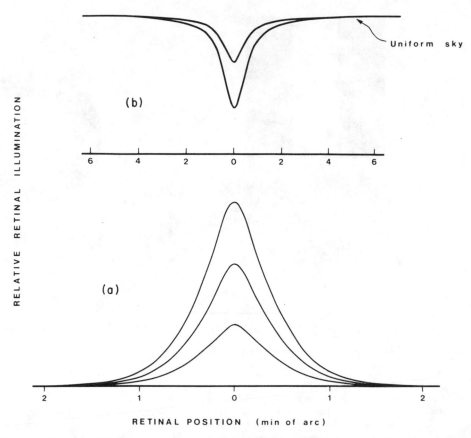

Figure 3.2. (a) Retinal light distribution in images of stars of three different magnitudes. Because the objects are smaller than the eye's point-spread function, the images all have the same light distribution (the point-spread function), differing only in relative height. Whether the star is visible depends on whether the total light received produces a brightness jnd. (b) Cross-sectional light distribution for the retinal image of thin wires seen against a uniform sky. If the wires are much thinner than the width of the eye's line-spread function, the dimple in the uniform light level due to the sky will have the inverted shape of the line-spread function; depth of dimple depends on wire thickness. Threshold width of wire is determined by the luminance jnd for this light distribution under the viewing conditions.

Fine Grain of Visual Space: Visual Acuity

We will return later to more global aspects of visual space perception. Of long-standing interest and utility has been the study of the fine grain of visual space; the connection between psychophysical responses and their physical and physiological substrates is most immediate here and the psychophysical experiments least complicated.

In the attempt to understand the structure of the visual spatial sense, we have learned very little of how finely divisible it is by investigating the smallest target that can just be seen. As has just been pointed out, that determination rests on the contrast detection limit of the light sense. We make better progress by formulating questions that address the space sense in its own terms. For example: Are there two point objects present or is there only one? When we reduce the distance separating a double star until a subject no longer sees it as double, we reach the spatial resolution limit, which has for a long time been thought to be the measure of the fineness of the grain of visual space. A variety of targets can be used for testing this so-called visual acuity. Conceptually the simplest is in fact a variant of this double-star test, namely, a pair of bars separated by a space equal in

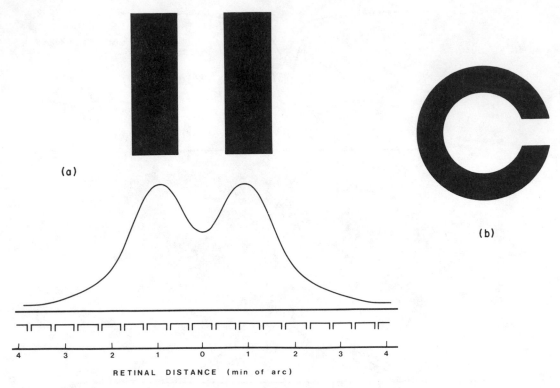

(a)

(b)

RETINAL DISTANCE (min of arc)

Figure 3.3. (a) Double bar acuity test, made of two bars and intervening space, all of equal width, in a 3 × 3 matrix of space modules. The whole pattern is magnified or reduced to reach resolution threshold; the measure is that of the size module. At resolution threshold, the retinal light distribution is shown to scale below the pattern. The mosaic of individual receptors in the human fovea is also shown. (b) Visual acuity is usually tested with letters whose features (e.g. gap in C) is 1/5 of total letter size. For a 20/20 letter, the feature subtends 1 min of arc; for a 20/40 letter, 2 min of arc, etc.

thickness to the bars (Figure 3.3). By increasing or decreasing the size of this pattern, we can determine when the subject is just able to determine that the lines are double. The bar width is taken as the minimum angle of resolution (or mar). Under ideal conditions it is somewhat less than one minute of arc in the human fovea. Normal or 20/20 visual acuity is taken to be a mar of 1 min of arc, and the scale of visual acuity is reciprocal to the just resolvable pattern dimension in minutes of arc of visual angle.

The mar is not closely dependent on the pattern used for its measurement. Clinical tests use letters with feature dimension, for example, gap size in the letter C, corresponding to the mar. Thus a 20/20 letter C has a gap of 1 min of arc, a 20/40 C has a 2-min-of-arc gap, and so on (Figure 3.3b). Another common pattern for testing visual acuity is a grating, or a repetitive double bar configuration. Its spatial frequency,

that is, the number of lines per unit of visual angle, can be varied to determine threshold resolution. A coarse grating that is easily resolvable can also be changed in contrast to test the eye's contrast detection, thus giving interesting information about the light sense.

Coordinated Physiological Processes

As much as any other psychophysical exploration of the visual space sense, visual acuity currently illustrates the form of the psychophysicist's ultimate aim. It was most clearly articulated over two generations by Mach (1885/1922):

Now, sensations can be analyzed psychologically—per se, immediately—(as was done, for example by Johannes Müller), or the associated physiological processes can be studied by physical methods (as is preferred by the current school of physiologists) or, finally, one can pursue the connection between what is psychologically observable and the coordinated physiological processes. We aspire to the latter aim wherever it seems within reach, because it goes farthest and because observations then attack at all points and one kind of investigation supports the other. (p. 49)

Analysis of visual acuity by physical methods starts with the description of the proximal stimulus, that is, with the light distribution in the retinal image of the test object. For a double bar stimulus, this has the appearance, illustrated above in Figure 3.3a, of two peaks flanking a trough. As the pattern is reduced, the peak-trough ratio approaches unity, that is, the trough fills in and the peaks disappear. When below the resolution limit, the pattern is in principle indistinguishable from the image of a single, somewhat wider bar. There is thus a physical limit to visual acuity that no optical system can escape.

But the mere existence of a trough between two peaks in the image does not ensure that the whole organism can perform the task of resolution. The light distribution containing the necessary information has to be passed into the relevant anatomical structures—the retinal receptors—which means that the associated compartmentalization inevitably introduces a grain to the neural image whose smallest elements are determined by receptor size and spacing. These two factors, optical spreading and anatomical grain, have been adequately characterized by measurements with photocells and the microscope. In the human fovea, receptors are densely packed and have a diameter whose equivalent in object space is about 1/2 min of arc. This means that true resolution could not be achieved with pattern elements smaller than 1/2 min of arc. The match between the width of the line-spread function and the receptor spacing, which is desirable if the information transfer is to be maximized, is reasonable here (Figure 3.3a), but this situation does not obtain in the periphery for photopic vision, where the cones are wider apart.

Modern physiological methods have added a further element of information. It is possible to record neural firing of single nerve cells in the retina and farther along the visual pathways and to measure their receptive fields, that is, the area in the eye's object space within which

stimuli can elicit responses. Two pieces of data emerge from this kind of investigation, the size of the receptive field and the overlap of receptive fields of adjoining neurons (Hubel & Wiesel, 1974; Dow, Snyder, Vautin & Bauer, 1981). Insofar as the mapping of the retina onto these cell layers is at all orderly—and that seems to be the case at least so far as the lateral geniculate nucleus and the first cortical stages are concerned—the grain appears to be somewhat coarser than at the retina. The best behavioral measurements of visual acuity cannot, at the present time, be accommodated by the performance of central neurons. The reason may simply be that the neurons with the smallest receptive fields and the least overlap of adjoining receptive fields in the cortex of the alert primate have not yet been recorded.

But whatever the size of the individual receptive fields, processing visual acuity requires a comparison of light stimulus strength in three adjoining regions of the visual field, which must be set off from each other and individually distinguishable. A decision stage must follow that would say Yes to two peaks separated by a trough and No to a blob without a dividing trough. This raises the question of a remapping of the retinal image in terms of templates more complex than direct position-by-position representation. The celebrated findings of Hubel and Wiesel (1977) concerning orientation have demonstrated that such remapping does, in fact, occur. So far as visual acuity is concerned, we do not yet know the template or how far along in the stream of information flow it is encountered.

In the meantime, less restricted search than single unit studies is underway in an attempt to characterize the processing mechanism of visual acuity. Mach's agenda for "the connection between what is psychologically observable and the coordinated physiological processes" is being pursued in investigations that range from the recording of brain responses evoked electrically (e.g., by Regan, 1972) or magnetically (e.g., by Williamson & Kaufman, 1981) to behavioral studies of animals with lesions of the striate cortex (by Berkley & Sprague, 1979).

The Fine Grain of Visual Space: Hyperacuity

An array of spatial thresholds point to the existence of a grain of visual space that is much finer than what is demanded by visual acuity—the hyperacuities. Even in the last century various spatial capabilities with exceedingly low thresholds have been discovered, but not until definitive anatomical measurements of the retinal receptors were made was their lack of compatibility with receptor size recognized. For, although receptors are not much less than one minute of arc in diameter, these kinds of spatial thresholds can be as low as just a few seconds of arc. The best known of these is vernier or alignment acuity, but many other patterns can be discriminated with hyperacuity thresholds (Figure 3.4).

For example, an observer manifests keen sensitivity in detecting the direction of a sudden target displacement (Basler, 1909). This step displacement threshold of a simple line or spot of light is much less than the mar—10–12 seconds of arc as against 30–40 sec of arc. The lowest hyperacuity thresholds, however, are obtained when two features are present simultaneously and the detection involves an estimate of their relative locations, either in the direction of the line joining the two features (Figure 3.4a)

or perpendicular to the line joining them (Figure 3.4b). Such thresholds may be as low as 5 sec of arc or less.

It is necessary to dispel an implication that hyperacuity violates any laws of physics. It is true that diffraction, rooted in the electromagnetic theory and consonant with the uncertainty relation as applied to photons, does set a limit to resolution, that is, the decision whether a certain light distribution originated from a single or a double source. But the localization of the centroid of a statistical distribution of quantal absorptions—which is an ultimate physicalist description of the substrate of a hyperacuity response—can be achieved with arbitrary precision without running counter to any laws of physics (Westheimer, 1981).

The actual mechanism subserving the elaboration of a manifold with the fine texture demanded by the hyperacuities has yet to be discovered. The school of thought that seeks a detailed mapping of all values of target attributes in single cortical cells would want an ensemble of cortical cells, each with a spatial local sign differing from its neighbor's by as little as 3 sec

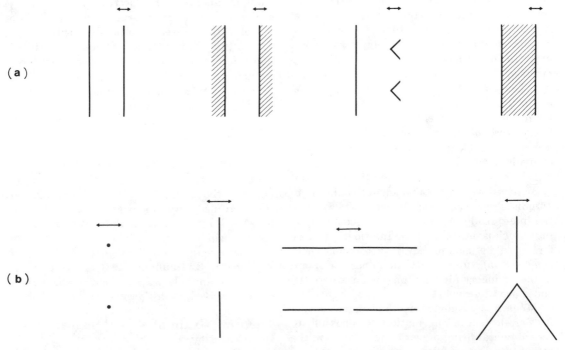

Figure 3.4. Patterns in which components can be localized relative to each other with the precision considerably finer than receptor dimensions—hyperacuity. (a) Relative localization is in direction of line joining components. (b) Relative localization is in direction perpendicular to line joining components.

of arc (Barlow, 1981); this means that the cortical mosaic would need many more cells than the
retinal mosaic for spatial local signs alone, not
to mention such other attributes as orientation,
for which an individual system of mapping has
been demonstrated. The alternative would be a
mapping of local sign differences of adjoining
features in a more fluid fashion, for example, in
a way that would enable this measure to be read
out with great relative though not absolute precision. That view is favored by the fact that
hyperacuity is robust to a common movement of
the involved targets, and by the discovery of
interference effects between adjoining features
within a small flanking zone.

Stereoscopic Depth Discrimination

The discussion so far has concerned the sensation of location in a two-dimensional continuum, and one eye would have sufficed to carry
out all measurements studied so far. There is,
however, one more basic spatial attribute available to those who have normal binocular vision
—that of stereoscopic depth. This attribute is
not a consequence of learning, nor is it derived
from a detailed analysis of other sense data;
rather it is an independent response category.
That is an important distinction, because, as
will be seen later, a great deal of information is
inherent in the ordinary, two-dimensional visual
image available to a single eye that permits
decisions to be made concerning the relative
depth of targets in object space. The binocular
stereoscopic sense of depth, based on processing
the minute pattern differences in the two eyes,
appears quite early in infancy and seems to
develop faster than ordinary visual acuity
(Held, Birch & Gwiazda, 1980). In certain abnormalities of binocular vision—for example, in
strabismus—this stereoscopic sense of depth
may be absent, and it may be deficient in characteristic ways even in otherwise normal visual
systems (Richards, 1971).

The geometrical basis of binocular stereoscopic vision is illustrated in Figure 3.5. When
any configuration is shown tilted out of the
frontoparallel plane, the two eyes see somewhat
different aspects. The horizontal visual angle
between equivalent feature components is different in the retinal image of the two eyes. This
is called binocular disparity. Disparity discrimination is the fundamental element of stereo-

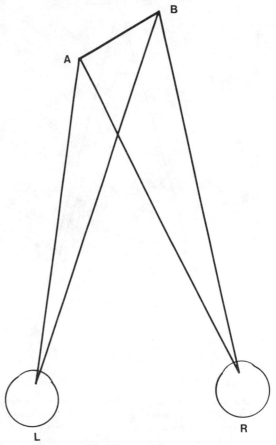

Figure 3.5. Construction showing geometrical basis
for stereoscopic depth perception. Horizontal section
containing both eyes and a line segment AB tilted out
of the frontoparallel plane, away from the eye at the
right. The line segment subtends a larger visual angle
at the right eye than at the left eye of the subject.

scopic vision. In a typical subject under the
right conditions, the disparity threshold is
lower than that for monocular hyperacuity
(Berry, 1948). Minute pattern differences that
cannot be detected monocularly can be seen
when given in the form of a binocular horizontal
disparity (Westheimer and McKee, 1979).

The stereoscopic depth threshold is usually
expressed in the disparity angle, and after some
training it can have a value as low as 3–10 sec of
arc. To relate it to the real object space, a simple
construction is necessary (Figure 3.6) which
leads to the following equation: $dx = a \cdot ds/x \cdot x \cdot k$, where a, x, and dx are distances in meters,
ds is the threshold disparity in seconds of arc,
and k is a constant equal to 206,000. In the

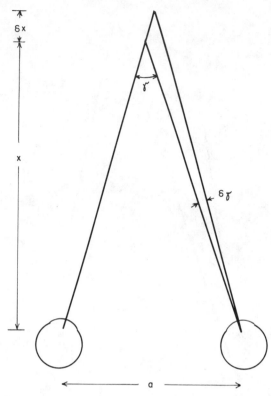

Figure 3.6. Stereoacuity: relation between just-discriminable binocular disparity $\delta\gamma$ and angle γ, and the involved distance parameters: a, subject's inter-ocular distance; x, observation distance; and δx, just discriminable depth. $\delta\gamma = (a/x^2)\delta x$.

typical subject, the interocular distance a is about 0.065 meter. It is instructive to calculate the minimum detectable depth under certain conditions. Based on a threshold of 10 sec of arc, the jnd for stereoscopic depth at 25 cm is 1/20 mm (which may be verified by looking at the profile on a coin) and just over 1 mm at 1 meter. When these values are applied to the just detectable tilt of a pattern out of the frontoparallel plane (Figure 3.5), a 4 in (10 cm) board at a distance of 1 meter would be seen as tilted away from the observer on one side if it is less than one degree out of the frontoparallel plane.

Ever since the discovery of its geometrical basis by Wheatstone in 1838, stereopsis has vied with color as the favorite facet of vision for theorists and experimentalists alike. A large number of factors affecting stereo thresholds has been studied, which cannot be given justice in a beginning overview. Not only do they relate

to the associated visual variables such as luminance, adaptation, duration, retinal position, chromaticity, and so on (where by and large the effects are what may be expected for a visual function demanding precise retinal localization) but also to the particular variables that have to do with the need for detailed spatial information coming to the cortex through the two eyes. Of special interest in this connection are the requirements for simultaneity, both of the occurrence of the two uniocular stimuli (Mitchell and O'Hagan, 1972), and of the two members of the target pair that constitute the minimum configuration for good stereoacuity (Westheimer, 1979). On the other hand, the requirements for pattern similarity in the two eyes are not quite as demanding as one might think, and for the members of the target pair in a stereoacuity test they are quite lax. Of considerable significance for theories of the physiological basis of stereopsis is the observation that the target configuration can be in parallel motion across the two retinas without detriment to stereopsis and even, to a limited extent, in motion in the opposite direction in the two eyes, that is, toward or away from the observer (Westheimer and McKee, 1978).

A fundamental processing apparatus has been described above for the three dimensions of the outside world. Expressed in angular measure at the eye's entrance pupils, there is a two-dimensional picture for each eye and a method of extracting information about the distance of targets from the observer by processing the difference between the target's aspect on the two retinas. All this can be imagined as a mapping of the three-dimensional manifold of the outside world onto a related internal representation. Studying such responses as visual acuity, hyperacuity, and stereoscopic acuity may give one an indication of the minimum grain of this internal representation in terms of the object-sided magnitude of the jnd's, each in its own dimension.

Significance of Neurophysiological Findings

In the brightness domain, fruitful interaction has taken place between psychophysical investigations, in particular, of the jnd and the physiological study of the visual apparatus. In principle, the search seeks correlation between the perception of brightness differences or patterns or the perceived brightness invariances (constancies) on the one hand, and the neuronal discharges on the other. In the wake of these researches, spatial aspects of perception have taken on new meaning. For example, the interaction effects of adjoining fields of different luminances—which have attracted the interest of psychophysicists since Mach—have been found to be related to spatial characteristics of neuronal excitability in the retina and higher visual pathways (center and surround organization of receptive fields, Kuffler, 1953). More recently, central neurons have been described whose receptor fields have much more elaborate configurations. These range from the well-substantiated elongated shapes of Hubel and Wiesel's simple cortical neurons to those whose fields have been described as complex or hypercomplex, to fields tuned to repetitive patterns (Pollen & Ronner, 1975), and even to cells in the association areas of monkey brains said to have shapes resembling monkey hands (Gross, Rocha-Miranda & Bender, 1972).

Characterizing the shapes of the receptive fields of cells in the primate cortex is a taxing and difficult task, particularly in the alert animal where such factors as eye movement and attention need to be controlled. And it becomes more so when the associated visual variables, such as binocularity, three-dimensional depth, chromaticity, adaptation, spatial context and so on are taken into account. The procedure involves finding the adequate stimulus, that is, the kind of stimulus that needs the least change in energy to elicit a response. In neurophysiological exploration, cell discharge is usually regarded as response. Defining what a cell does, as practiced by neurophysiologists, then, is to outline the cell's adequate stimulus. Once this is understood, analysis of psychophysiological linking hypotheses (Brindley, 1960) leads to a clearer view of what can be learned about the functioning of the visual apparatus by neurophysiological experiments on single cells.

Orientation sensitivity for line targets provides an excellent example of the current situation of psychophysics vis-à-vis single-cell neurophysiology. As early as 1893, the American psychologist Jastrow investigated the threshold for detecting line-orientation differences and found it to be less than one degree. After Hubel and Wiesel found that the receptive fields of many cortical neurons were elongated (line units), and after it was demonstrated that this property of cortical cells was present even in the alert primate, the range of orientations to which these cells would respond became the subject of intensive investigation. Estimates of this orientation tuning vary, but are never below several degrees. The experimental procedure is to present lines of many orientations and to measure the nerve impulse strength as a function of target-line orientation. The tuning curve can be characterized by its half-width at half-height. If this number is, say, 5 degrees, the presentation of a line 5 degrees away from the optimum orientation should elicit a response half as strong as a response at the optimum orientation. Firing strength of these cells also depends on such factors as line length and light intensity. A given impulse output of this cell, say, of half maximum strength, can therefore arise from a variety of stimulus situations, for example, optimum orientation at low contrast, or good contrast but less than optimal orientation, either clockwise or counterclockwise.

From this example it can be seen that a chasm still separates even the best single-cell neurophysiology from the behavior of the total organism. A comparison of results from the two disciplines requires, of course, that the same species of animal be used. Behavioral data are not always available on cats, the species used most widely for single cell recording. Fortunately, monkeys seem not to differ significantly from humans in spatial visual thresholds so that, if concordance between psychophysical thresholds and single-cell firing rates is sought, recordings from the alert monkey may readily be compared with human psychophysical data.

Even though single-unit analysis may not reach the ultimate expectation of a reductionist approach to behavior, it has nevertheless had an important impact on the mode of studying visual processing. When Helmholtz made his contribution to physiological optics in the 1850s and 1860s, his strength lay in the application of physical methods to the study of the substrates of vision. If visual acuity, which has already been treated in this chapter, is used as an example, we find that Helmholtz dealt with the diffraction limit, the effect of light scatter and aberrations in the eye, the size of the retinal receptors, and the resultant compartmentalization of light. He then compared the expected resolution, given all these factors, with the measured acuity in normal subjects. The values matched. This leaves open the implication that there is a point-by-point representation of object space in the neural system. This representation could, of course, be topologic rather than metrically identical. But the general idea was that if, for example, a triangle were shown to the eyes, there would be three small regions on the cortical representation corresponding to the apexes and some sort of connecting lines of excitation between them. This one-to-one correspondence between the object world and the cortical projection was a centerpiece of Helmoltz's thinking, and it continued to guide anatomists and histologists in their successful quest for a detailed map of the visual projections. No matter how disparate their standpoint seemed to be, it was also part of many Gestalt approaches —witness Köhler's postulating of physical fields on the brain surface that were isomorphic with target configurations (1924). This postulate at one time was taken so seriously that Sperry and Miner (1955) carried out an experiment showing that the recognition of shapes by trained cats did not cease when dielectric material was implanted in their cortexes, presumably confusing the electric fields in the cortex.

Diverse Representations and a Single Visual Space

It thus becomes apparent why the discovery of complex-shaped receptive fields in the visual system—center and surround in the retina, elongated, sometimes with inhibiting end zones in the cortex—aroused such interest among scientists concerned with the nature of processing visual signals. The center and surround organization of retinal ganglion cells provided a physiological substrate for a variety of psychophysical and perceptual phenomena—Mach bands, Herrmann grids, simultaneous contrast. These effects are no longer regarded as superimposed on an orderly (if not linear, at least monotonic) transmission and re-creation of the visual scene in the cortex but are now accepted as an integral part of this transmission process.

While the influence of this change in point of view was fairly immediate and not too wrenching for our attitudes toward the perception of brightness (and to some extent color), it has barely begun to be felt concerning space per-

ception. Brightness is presumably a singular visual quality, that is, it can have only one value at a time in any location. The value may be a complex, time-dependent function of retinal illuminance, and, in particular, it will not be independent of the values at other places in visual space. But how are we to look at space in a similar way? There are no decisive impediments to thinking of a warped, time-varying, content-dependent representation of space, but the difficulty arises when we try to envisage a variety of parallel spatial representations that should still add up to no more than a single-valued three-dimensional manifold.

Suppose, for the sake of illustration, that line orientations are processed by a separate mechanism, independent of the mechanism that processes corners. How then would a quadrangle be elaborated? How can all the possible conflicts between the manifolds (of lines, orientations, corners, distances between opposing sides, angles between adjoining sides, parallelism of opposing sides, and any other attributes of the figure that may be processed independently) be resolved to yield not only a single pattern that can participate in, say, figure-ground relations, but also a united impression of but a single visual space? It is not surprising, therefore, that some properties of well-behaved spaces are not obeyed in visual space (Foley, 1964). But the central nervous system's capacity to unify signals from a number of separate topographic representations should not be underestimated; after all, it is known to occur in various sense modalities, so why not within what was previously taken as a single quality of one modality? Yet it will be difficult to free oneself from the concept that visual space is an indivisible construct serving as a vehicle for objects. As Kant put it: "One cannot imagine that there is no space, though one can conceive of there being no objects in it."

Veridicality: Illusions and Figural Aftereffects

One can best achieve a unitary description of perceived spatial relations when the objects are shown in isolation in time and space. This is evident when the observer's task is to make judgments involving very simple criteria, for example, which is the closer of two lines? It still applies for a variety of criteria that are not quite so simple. Examples include the deviation of a

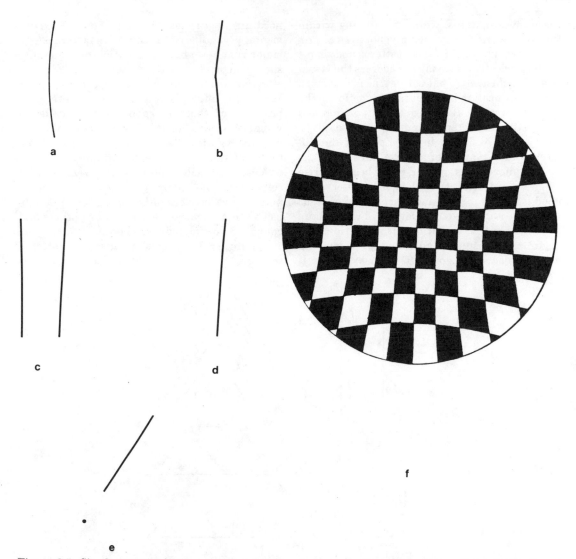

Figure 3.7. Simple patterns for investigating relations between purely spatial aspects of visual stimuli and responses: (a) Is the line straight or curved? (Guillery, 1899; Watt & Andrews, 1982); (b) Is this a straight line or a chevron? (Guillery, 1899; Andrews, Butcher & Buckley, 1973); (c) Are the two lines parallel? (Mach, 1861); (d) Is the line vertical or tilted? (Jastrow, 1893); (e) Would the line, if extended, pass through the dot? (Salomon, 1947; Wenderoth, Beh & White 1978); (f) Is the pattern, when viewed from a distance of 3 in., a rectangular checker-board? (Helmholtz, 1866).

contour from a straight line, in the sense either of a curvature or of an angle between two line segments. More sophisticated yet are such criteria as to whether a point is aligned with a line segment, whether two angles are equal, or whether a grid is a rectangular checkerboard. In all these cases (Figure 3.7) there is the benchmark of veridicality, because the target patterns in object space can be accurately set for the

criterion, and the observer's verbal response is about as uncontaminated as a measure of the character of his visual space as is ever likely to be available. And, of course, the refinement of modern psychophysical methods can be given full scope here, as can also the nonverbal behavioral procedures applied to infants (Dobson & Teller, 1978) and experimental animals.

When other physiological variables enter,

these investigations, while still staying within the framework of rigorous psychophysical procedures in their use of object patterns and simple subjective responses, may not address the visual system exclusively. That will be true for example, when the question involves the perception of the vertical in a visual pattern. Head position and the vestibular system cannot be factored out as easily then as in an investigation of the difference in curvature of a pair of arcs.

Complications, however, really begin to arise when the patterns can no longer be observed in good isolation in time and space. A voluminous literature is devoted to situations in which more or less serious deviations from veridicality occur as a result of adjoining or competing visual objects (Gregory, 1978; Frisby, 1980). It

need not be stressed in a handbook of experimental psychology that cognitive factors play a major role here, but the addition of even quite simple geometrical components can produce startling alterations in visual space responses. When the effect is due to the simultaneous presence of these components it is called a visual illusion; when it is due to a pattern shown previously, it is called a figural aftereffect. True to the mission of this chapter, the phenomena to be described will relate to observers' spatial responses. The many phenomena of similar nature that concern other qualities of a subject's visual experience, such as brightness and color, are considered elsewhere.

Figure 3.8 illustrates a variety of patterns that give rise to visual responses at obvious

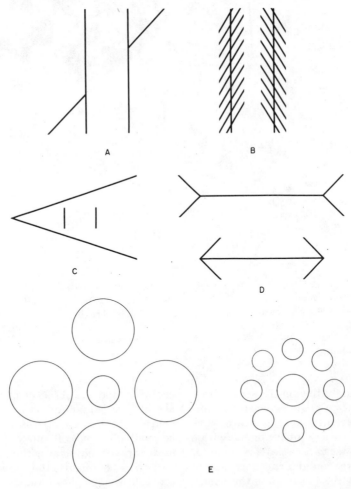

Figure 3.8. Geometrical optical illusions of (a) Poggendorff, (b) Zöllner, (c) Ponzo, (d) Müller-Lyer, and (e) Ebbinghaus.

variance with the geometrical measures that can quickly be applied to the objects. They are just a few samples from the enormous arsenal of so-called geometrical optical illusions (Luckiesh, 1965; Coren & Girgus, 1978). Efforts have been made to invent simple rules to account for them, for example, the statement that obtuse angles are seen as smaller than acute ones, which would help explain the Poggendorff illusion. Usually such rules fail to cover a large enough segment of the illusions to make them appealing.

More global theories of visual illusions have been proposed in abundance. When they can be tested, they usually do not prevail. An example is the eye movement theory, according to which the illusion is the result of real or attempted eye movements to trace out the patterns. But the illusions still obtain with flash presentations or with stabilized retinal imagery. Visual illusions played a role in the more general Gestalt theories of perception (Koffka, 1935) in which forces, fields, or organizing principles were hypothesized to provide a unified account of perceptual phenomena. These theories no longer attract the following they did a couple of generations ago. The reason lies in the vague nature of the notions they employ, which most readers now feel can be given too many properties at will as the observed facts demand them.

This is not to say that the subject of visual illusion is or should be devoid of theory. Aside from the curiosity engendered by visual illusions and their capacity to elicit admonishing stances ("What you say you saw is not what is out there!"), the interest in them rests precisely in the hope that their study will provide the key to the understanding of the underlying processes. If a sorting system made consistent mistakes, these mistakes might help us figure out how the system operates. In view of present-day strong physiological biases, understanding the underlying processes usually means knowing what neural transmission system is at work. Visual illusions should thus be regarded as a tool to help characterize the neural sorting that the messages undergo in their passage from the eye to higher association centers. Consistent missorting can suggest specific operating properties of neural circuits and, in a more general way, can be used to analyze the system.

Closely related to visual illusions are the figural aftereffects associated with the pioneering researches of Gibson (1933) and Köhler and Wallach (1944). Inspection of certain figures causes spatial distortion in subsequently observed figures. An example of a figural aftereffect pattern is shown in Figure 3.9. Some temporal aspects of this phenomenon can be well analyzed. Figure 3.10a depicts the decay of a figural aftereffect and Figure 3.10b the relation between the duration of inspection of the original figure and the strength of the aftereffect. Some figural aftereffects, however, occur with even momentary (30-msec) exposure of the inducing figure (Sekular & Littlejohn, 1974).

An illustration of the way illusions and figural aftereffects can be used as analytical tools is given by the study of Mitchell and Ware (1974), in which the tilt aftereffect was employed, that is, the appearance of tilt in a line following the observation of a grating pattern of a different orientation. The magnitude of this effect is small but easily measured. Mitchell and Ware had the observer view the inducing grating pattern with one eye while they measured the resulting aftereffect on a test line shown either to the same eye or to the other eye. They found the interocular transfer of the tilt aftereffect absent in patients with certain defects in binocular vision (strabismus) and derived some conclusions about the channeling of impulses from the two eyes through cortical structures in these patients in contrast to normal subjects.

Configurations That are not Explicitly Delineated

From a consideration of visual illusions and figural aftereffects it becomes apparent that the gamut of spatial visual perception cannot be covered by simple geometrical formulations. This view is reinforced by several demonstrations of even more complex kinds of processing. A naive view, based on geometrical thinking, might demand that a configuration, to be processed as such, needs explicit delineation. But, as can be seen in Figure 3.11, the triangle defined by the missing sectors of the three circles is not really outlined, but still has a compelling presence.

The well-known reversible figures (Figure 3.12) constitute another case in point. A stationary pattern assumes one of two distinct appearances in temporal alternation. Certain processes must be at work that try to resolve the ambiguity

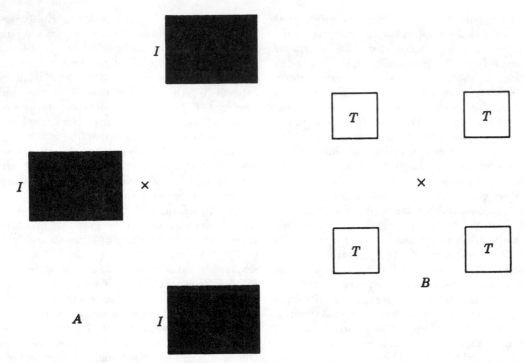

Figure 3.9. Demonstration of figural affereffect after Köhler and Wallach (1944). Inspection of configuration in a (steady fixation on × for at least 30 sec) changes the perceived separation of the test squares on the two sides of the fixation square in b: right test squares appear displaced toward each other, left squares away from eath other. From Graham, C.H. Visual perception in S.S. Stevens (Ed.), *Handbook of Experimental Psychology.* New York: John Wiley & Sons, Inc. 1951, p. 907.

inherent in the geometry of the retinal image of the pattern, and these processes have a dynamic character that manifests itself in the reversing of the percepts.

Theories of Transformation Processes in Visual Perception

It is clear now that there is more to the process of visual space perception than the creation of an optical image on the retina and its transduction by the receptor cells. Over the decades, changes have occurred in what has been regarded as an understanding of the processes intervening between the retinal image and the description of the percept by the observer (see Hochberg, 1981, for an outline of this development). Helmholtz, who was very much aware of the gap separating the two, did not attempt much of a physiological interpretation and, instead, evoked the observer's judgment.

During the first half of the twentieth century, a more formal structure of intervening processing was advanced by the Gestalt school of psychologists. This school tried to formulate rules by which the spatially distributed excitation on the retina could be organized into coherent percepts. These rules were tacitly assumed to reside in the observer, although at the outset not in any anatomical structure. In other words, the sensory input from the outside world was subjected, during its transmission, to transformations that could be expressed in some kinds of laws. Because these laws were not always framed in ways that permitted unambiguous predictions, they did not find universal favor among physiological psychologists. As we saw earlier, Köhler's attempt (1924) at a translation into simplistic physiological notions was not a success.

The picture has changed fundamentally in the last three decades. The discovery that the retinal image is funneled through neural cells with a "Mexican-hat" receptive field has solidified a variety of notions that started with Mach and Hering. The fundamental significance of these points of view is that they look to neural processing by elements in the visual pathway for

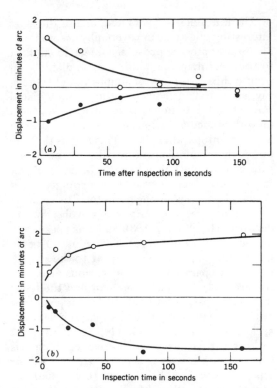

Figure 3.11. A configuration need not be delineated by explicit contours. A triangle is implied by the open sectors of the three disks though it is not explicitly outlined (after Kanisza, 1976).

Figure 3.10. (a) Time course of decay of the figural aftereffect in Figure 3.9. Ordinates indicate the position shifts necessary for the right test squares (open circles) and left test squares (closed circles) to appear equally far apart. (b) Maximum displacement induced by inspection pattern in Fig. 1.9 on the test pattern, as a function of inspection time (after Hammer, 1949). From Graham, C.H. Visual perception in S.S. Stevens (Ed.), *Handbook of Experimental Psychology*. New York: John Wiley & Sons, Inc. 1951, p. 910.

obtains for any of a large class of patterns. If the interest is in retinal processing, the most appropriate function is a circularly symmetrical Mexican-hat function or a Bessel function bullseye (Kelly, 1962). A good deal of processing in the visual cortex involves cells with elongated receptive fields that also display a center and surround organization. They are well addressed

the reconciliation of any dissonances between the retinal image and the observer's spatial percept.

Since the characterization of single-cell properties is a continuing process, the theoretical formulations develop apace. The most successful of these has its physiological support in the band-pass transmitting nature of cells whose receptive fields have a center and surround organization. These cells do not respond well to slowly changing input patterns, either in time or space, nor can they follow very high-frequency inputs. This means that when one tests them with a given kind of pattern in a range of sizes, the briskest response is obtained for an intermediate span, and their response falls off for both larger and smaller sizes. This behavior

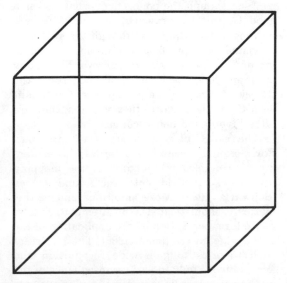

Figure 3.12. Necker cube, a reversible figure. The line drawing can represent either of two aspects of a three-dimensional structure, a cube; they are perceived in alternation, only one at a time.

by a Gaussian wave-packet pattern, that is, a grating with a Gaussian function as the envelope (Watson, Barlow & Robson, 1981), and they respond to sine-wave gratings over a limited range of spatial frequencies (Albrecht, deValois, & Thorell, 1980). This is the origin of the so-called Fourier theory of vision (Campbell, 1974), which sees the sine-wave grating as the basis function for the visual process.

The ideal outcome of the application of any of these formulations—and hence their original premise—is that one can predict the response to any object configuration by decomposing it into its component basis functions and determining the response to each component. For example, in the Fourier formulation one would first perform a Fourier analysis of the object pattern and then multiply each Fourier component by the response of the system to that component. The success of such an enterprise depends on the level at which it is applied. It works perfectly for the retinal image, which obeys all the rules of linearity demanded by such theories. It has also been applied with good results to the analysis of the responses of single cortical cels and to psychophysical threshold studies. But for an analysis of more global perceptual responses, this kind of theory falls short of the mark. This is quite evident in the phenomena illustrated above in Figures 3.7 and 3.8.

Even though the concepts of what makes a good Gestalt, as drawn up in the 1920s, are no longer appealing, and though the synthesis of visual percepts from center and surrounding or "line" units appears unrewarding, many attempts have been made to modernize the theory of visual space perceptions. Consonant with the style of most other sciences, they are often given a mathematical cast.

The range of new concepts is enormous. For instance, a search is underway for explanatory principles in the topographic mapping of the visual field onto the visual cortex (Schwartz, 1980). More ambitious and mathematically sophisticated is the attempt to characterize form perception by the application of Lie group algebra (Hoffman, 1966). The failure of such theories to gain wide recognition and acceptance is only in part a consequence of the mathematical skills they demand. The example of the Luneburg (1947) theory of non-Euclidean visual space illustrates the sort of problems encountered by this kind of formulation.

About a hundred years ago, one of the most interesting questions in psychophysics was that of the horopter. Suppose a subject looks at a fixation point in the midline some distance in front of him. An array of simple visual targets, say, short rods, is shown without much visual context, and the subject is required to set them up with binocular vision so that they appear to be in a frontoparallel plane. This means that the targets mark out a frontoparallel plane in the subject's (virtual) visual space. In (real) object space, however, the rods are arranged in a curve, which is called the horopter. The shape of the horopter seems to vary with the observation distance (Hillebrand, 1893), and it is possible to lay out a series of curves that would, if populated with simple targets, appear to the subject to be frontoparallel planes at various distances (Figure 3.13). Similarly, one can find the locus in object space of targets that satisfy other criteria, so far as the subject's spatial judgments are concerned. For example, pairs of light sources can be placed at increasing distances from a subject, who is then asked to set their separation so that they appear to be equal distances apart—Blumenfeld's (1913) so-called equidistant alleys (Figure 3.14). In a complementary experiment, the subject's settings follow the criterion of parallelism, that is, the lights are to be arranged to mark out a pair of lines that appear to be parallel. The equidistant and parallel alleys are not coincident, a characteristic of non-Euclidean spaces—witness the fact that two meridians of longitude on the surface of a sphere both intersect the equator at right angles, that is, they are parallel, and yet their distance apart does not remain constant. Luneburg, who was a mathematician, took these observations and a few related ones (such as the universal appearance of the sky as a dome), formulated the hypothesis of a hyperbolic, or non-Euclidean, visual space of constant curvature, and proceeded to make an estimate of its metric. This constitutes a powerful step because it permits the mathematical expression of the apparent distance of observed objects in terms of the physical location of the targets, and of a very few constant parameters which mark the particular relation between the Euclidean object space and the subject's visual space.

Luneburg's was a very cohesive approach, expressed in better conceptual and numerical detail than most, but its promise was never

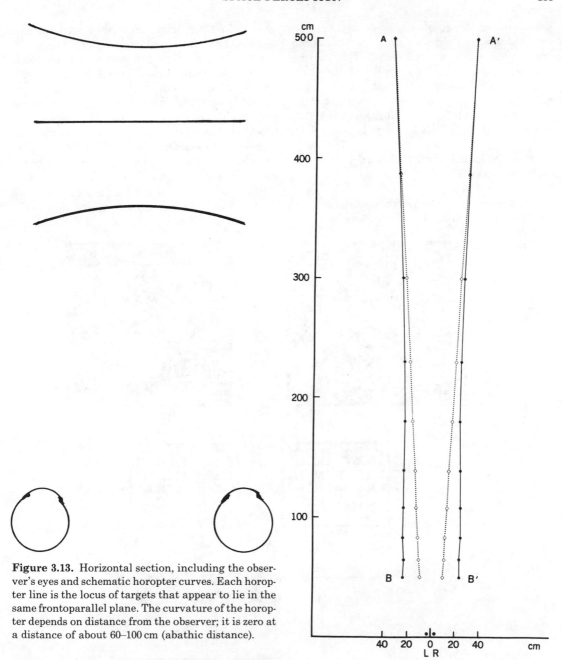

Figure 3.13. Horizontal section, including the observer's eyes and schematic horopter curves. Each horopter line is the locus of targets that appear to lie in the same frontoparallel plane. The curvature of the horopter depends on distance from the observer; it is zero at a distance of about 60–100 cm (abathic distance).

Figure 3.14. Horizontal section including the observer's two eyes (L and R) and schematic Blumenfeld alleys. The solid lines represent the locations of the target pairs that appear to be the same distance apart; i.e., separation AA′ appears equal to separation BB′ (equidistant alleys). The dotted lines represent the location of target pairs that have been arranged to give the appearance of an alley with parallel sides.

fulfilled. When the real world is confronted, too many simple and complex variations occur for a skeleton formulation of a hyperbolic visual space with constant curvature to yield predictions in any useful sense. For example, a visual space of constant curvature would not demonstrate why the moon apparently changes in diameter as its distance from the horizon increases (Leibowitz, 1965). There seem to be never-ending dissonances between psychophysical findings and rigorous models built along traditional mathematical lines. That mathematical models may be inapplicable for quite fundamental reasons is a point raised by one of this century's greatest mathematicians, von Neumann, in his last published work (von Neumann, 1958).

Computational Theories and Algorithms

The failure of traditional mathematical theories —which are patterned more or less after the

successful approach to modern physics—to gain some permanent standing in visual space perception makes it appropriate to look more closely at theories that use mathematics in less conventional ways. One such approach is that of David Marr (1982) and his associates. Recognizing that the problem of visual space perception is so vast that it must be broken down into manageable components and for the moment ignoring color, they have addressed themselves to the early stages of visual information processing —those stages that occur between the presence of a spatial light distribution on the retina, the so-called gray-level array, and the separation

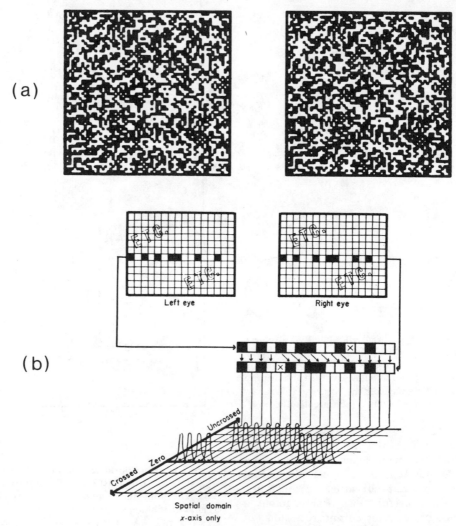

Figure 3.15. (a) Random dot stereogram. From *Seeing* (p. 79) by J. Frisby, 1980, Oxford: Oxford University Press. Reprinted by permission. (b) Scheme of feature matching, disparity detection, and global processing necessary to perceive different depth planes in a random dot stereogram (courtesy J.I. Nelson).

of figure from ground. Using what is now generally called a computational approach, they postulate that this light distribution is convolved with an array of spatial filters that vaguely resemble the neural cells with receptive field characteristics described by Kuffler (1953) and Hubel and Wiesel (1977), as well as with other receptive fields likely to exist, such as corners, roof-shaped intensity profiles, and so on. The result of this operation is what they call the primal sketch, namely, the description of the gray-level pattern in a vocabulary of kinds of intensity change (e.g., edge, line, blob) and their associated parameters (position, orientation, termination point). Of particular importance in the Marr approach is the second step, which proposes that grouping takes place within the parameter space to create the next higher aggregates. The rules according to which grouping occurs are reminiscent of those used earlier by Gestalt psychologists and suggest that processing of this kind is indeed taking place as a percept is elaborated. Because they try to transcend the findings of neurophysiology while at the same time deploying them, Marr's propositions are having an important heuristic influence on current research.

Efforts to take the step from the purely local to more global accounts of perception assume other forms. Texture (Julesz, 1981) and symmetry (Barlow & Reeves, 1979) are examples of attributes that are currently being defined and characterized. One of the most striking demonstrations of the operation of global processes in perception is the random dot stereograms associated with Bela Julesz (1971) (Figure 3.15a). They arouse curiosity because the patterns emerge only after the stereoscopic depth detection; no patterns are seen in the two monocular views.

The actual mechanism by which depth is observed in random dot stereograms bears closer analysis. Basic to the process is the presence throughout the field of small discretely circumscribed picture elements. Depth differences could never appear in a stereogram that was uniform and without fine structure. The usual random dot stereogram is made of a square checkerboard whose elementary constituent squares are randomly dark or light, but any other array of small features would do. Figure 3.15b shows two views of a single line of a random dot stereogram and how some homologous components are displaced in one eye relative to the other, that is, how disparity is introduced. To recognize depth it is necessary to be able to associate equivalent elements of structure seen on the two retinas, even though different (not overlapping) sets of elements appear with different disparities. It is this ability to force a global correlation of picture elements into sets according to their disparity that distinguishes performance in a random dot stereogram from an ordinary binocular stereoscopic task. Simple disparity detection (local stereopsis) is a prerequisite, but the difficult part of the task is to create the association of a coherent aggregate, which is the essence of perceiving depth in a random dot stereogram. That is obviously a much higher-order task, as is manifest in the poor performance of some people with good local stereopsis, and the fact that the thresholds and time needed for a response are much higher than with simple line stereograms. The real interest of random dot sterograms is not that they test stereopsis—that can be done more effectively with other patterns—but that they make us aware of the underlying sophisticated process of matching pattern elements into a cohesive aggregate according to disparity, and of the decisions about removing local ambiguities that it implies (Marr & Poggio, 1976).

The foregoing discussion has centered on the recognition of depth through the use of the binocular disparity apparatus. But that is not the only resource available to a subject for discerning fore and aft differences. In the real world a variety of clues enable distinctions to be made about the apparent location in the third dimension of targets the observer sees. In their totality, these clues are more powerful than the binocular disparity cue and can easily override it (Metzger, 1953, p. 302). They account for the flawless performance of the occasional one-eyed pilot who relies on the so-called monocular clues to make distance judgments. Figure 3.16 illustrates some of these clues, which are discussed in more detail in specialized texts (e.g., Gibson, 1950). Inspection of the figures makes it clear just how many intermediate steps, of the kind hinted at by Marr and his colleagues, must intervene between the receipt in the visual cortex of the information transmitted from the retinal image and the elaboration of the percept, including decisions on the relative three-dimensional placement of the seen targets.

More detailed analyis of the mechanisms

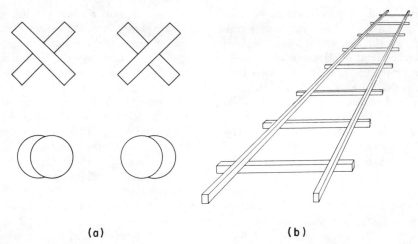

(a)   (b)

Figure 3.16. Natural visual scenes contain many cues, other than binocular disparity, from which the relative depth location of objects can be surmised. They include dynamic cues, involving relative motion of targets or the observer's motor responses, such as eye or head motions. Stationary displays may also contain cues, of which three are illustrated schematically here. (a) *Interposition*: contours of nearer figures interrupt those of more distant ones. (b) *Relative size and linear perspective*: patterns known to have relative constant size in the real world (human figures, automobiles, railroad ties) subtend smaller visual angles when they are more distant. Convergence of contours implies, according to the laws of perspective, that they are receding.

underlying these clues is beyond the scope of this chapter. But there are some indications of how this may be accomplished. Leaning on the findings of neurophysiology—so effective a strategy for some of the simpler visual functions—will not provide a viable option unless the basis of that kind of research can be broadened significantly. But observations from neuropathology, largely anecdotal in nature, are contributing to a body of information that is beginning to outline the perimeter of the subject. After World War I, Gelb and Goldstein (1929) analyzed by behavioral means the spatial processing abilities of patients with cerebral lesions. The aim of their research was to postulate spatial representation of the outside world in regions of the brain other than the visual cortex, because some of their patients with lesions in such areas could recognize individual features present in their visual field without being able to develop the correct spatial relations between them.

This dissociation of feature processing from detailed relative localization of features, shown above to be a part of hyperacuity responses also, is strikingly illustrated in the drawings of patients recovering from strokes (Jung, 1974). Analysis by modern psychophysical procedures has yet to be attempted in this area. A beginning

is being made, however, by A. Treissman, who has used the method of reaction times to demonstrate that subjects can more quickly distinguish an item with a particular spatial attribute from the remaining members of an array than they can assign specific position to it within the array. This opens up the reanalysis of the concept of Marr's primal sketch in a way that would decouple the presence of features in a general area of the visual field from their precise positions within the field.

Reaction time has also been used as an analytical tool in an interesting way by Shepard and Metzler (1971) to characterize the amount of processing involved in the identification of objects that were presented to observers with various degrees of spatial rotation. They found that the reaction time required to identify whether a pair of two-dimensional drawings representing the same simple three-dimensional object was a linear function of the angle required to superimpose the pair—the task required about one additional second for each 60 degrees of rotation. This research approaches experimentally Shepard's (1981) much deeper propositions concerning geometrical fundaments of spatial constancies. In brief, spatial constancies are seen as an expression of neural coding of the kinematic laws of object displacement in our three-dimensional object space: successively seen configurations whose transformations obey these laws are recognized as having an underlying identity.

MOVEMENT

An object is said to have moved when it occupies different positions at different times. Thus both time and space enter into a discussion of movement perception. The perception of time through visual signals has not been studied in much detail, apart from the phenomena associated with flicker (i.e., the upper limits of interruption at which lights appear to remain on continuously), and the phenomena of critical duration and the Bunsen-Ross law (i.e., the intensity-duration trade-off for very short exposures). Both these topics are of significance for the processing of brightness signals, but they do not address in a substantial fashion the rules according to which our perception of time is elaborated.

While both a displacement in position dx and an interval in time dt are involved in a movement, the essence of the quality of motion rests on their interrelation. The power of what is known as differential calculus lies in the conjoining of differentials into derivatives, that is dx/dt, and their manipulation as entities. The fundamental question concerning motion perception is whether more is involved than just the detection that at a later time an object is in a different place; in other words, is motion a perceptual quality *sui generis*? An important impetus to this question came from the realization that a target need not actually move physically for an observer to perceive it to move. Apparent motion was a major constituent in the development of Gestalt psychology, in which one of the most important documents, Wertheimer's 1912 monograph, dealt with the seeing of motion. Wertheimer subjected the topic of apparent motion to detailed investigation. Two lines, separated by a small distance, were exposed separately with a time delay. When the spatial and temporal intervals were chosen appropriately, the observer reported seeing a movement, the so-called phi phenomenon. The effect is compelling and the locale to which the movement is assigned is the space between the two asynchronously exposed objects.

In studying the detailed conditions under which the phenomenon was observed, Wertheimer found, for example, that the target need not consist of an identical pair: phi movement is still seen when one object is a vertical line and the other a horizontal one. Wertheimer distinguished between the phi phenomenon of apparent movement, and the appearances of quiet simultaneity and quiet succession, which were reported when the asynchronies were shorter and longer, respectively, than those optimal for phi. The earlier values of typical asynchronies for these three conditions—30, 60, and 200 msec—have recently been revised by Westheimer and McKee (1977) who reported a significant influence of target separation. In the fovea, phi is seen for asynchronies as short as 3 msec, provided the targets are only a few minutes of arc apart. They also discovered that two monocularly induced phi movements in opposite directions can give a phi movement in depth.

As distinct from apparent movement, where only the dx and dt values need be assigned distinct values, the study of real movement always confounds parameters of distance and time. Thus, when a range of velocities is chosen for an experiment and the distance that the target travels is fixed, the duration of exposure will of necessity have to vary. in the present context, interest centers on visual motion primarily as a sensory process and eye movements should therefore not be involved. In fact, the perception of motion is an important aspect in the initiation of pursuit eye movements (Rashbass, 1961). Once the eyes start moving in response to a moving target—and this may occur after a delay of 200 msec, or even less if the target movement and position are predictable—the retinal motion is no longer equal to the target motion but is the difference between the target motion and the eye motion. This may not matter in a practical situation in which the effect of the total system is being considered as, for example, in the visual acuity for moving targets exposed for periods lasting more than a few hundredths of a second. When the focus of research is solely on the sensory aspects of target motion, there are two possible ways to avoid the contaminating effect of eye motions. The simpler of the two is to restrict exposure duration to less than 200 msec and randomize target motion to prevent predictive eye movement. The other is to stabilize retinal images, but that is a rather cumbersome and instrument-intensive procedure.

Using a random-dot technique, Nakayama and Tyler (1981) decoupled motion-sensitive from position-sensitive mechanisms and concluded that motion is a distinct attribute of a visual percept.

Both absolute and relative thresholds for motion sensitivity have been studied. The minimum target velocity at which movement can be detected under optimal conditions of luminance and fixation is about 3 min of arc per second for 1/8-second exposure, and this can be improved by a factor of about 10 for much longer durations (Leibowitz, 1955a). The displacement of the target for these minimal conditions is smaller than a cone diameter. This accords with the earlier observations of von Fleischl (1883) and Basler (1909) who recognized in these findings the likelihood that the visual acuity threshold of 1 min of arc could be bettered as the minimum spatial module of the visual system. The presence of a reference framework improves performance only when the exposure is extended (Leibowitz, 1955b), providing a hint that under these conditions, where the threshold may be as low as 0.3 min of arc per second, the detection is not so much of movement as of the change in target position over time.

Differential movement sensitivity gives a Weber fraction of about 0.05 (McKee, 1981), and this can be demonstrated to be a consequence of the accurate detection of onset differences in adjoining retinal regions, since the results obtained for velocity differences for real targets can be mimicked by discontinuous (hopping) displacements.

The implication of much of the work on detection of real and apparent motion is that there is indeed a mechanism for processing motion and that this mechanism can be addressed in a variety of ways. Basic to the processing is the asynchronous stimulation of adjoining retinal regions with the appropriate parameters of distance and time. Confirmation of this view is seen in the presence of neurons in the rabbit retina (Barlow & Levick, 1965), for which an adequate stimulus consists of motion in a limited range of directions and velocities. While comparable neurons do not seem to exist in the primate retina (DeMonasterio & Gouras, 1975), analysis of response properties of primate cortical neurons in terms of their "velocity tuning" has been a rewarding topic (Movshon, 1975).

The perception of motion aftereffects consti-

tutes a further clue to the processing of movement via a separate mechanism. Well described by the term *waterfall effect* is the illusion of motion in a stationary visual world that follows the inspection of a moving pattern. The induced apparent motion has a direction opposite to that of the inducing motion. There is room for different interpretations of the mechanism by which this aftereffect arises. For example, there may be fatigue or adaptation of one of the pair of opposing processes dealing with motion along the opposing directions associated with one meridian (up and down, or right and left). But the essence of the waterfall illusion, in its relation to motion perception, is that it points to a channeling of motion information apart from that of the underlying displacement and time changes in the retinal image; the features and their positions relative to each other are preserved during the course of the aftereffect, but there is a compelling sense of motion. Studies of the time course and spatial confinement of motion aftereffects can help outline the characteristics of the motion-specific processing.

It would be rash, however, to assign a set of too singular properties to the movement-processing channels of the visual system, as is illustrated by the following observation. If the set of three disks at the top of Figure 3.17 is replaced after an interval of 50 msec or more by the set of three disks in the bottom line of the figure, the subject reports movement of the whole pattern, that is, the appearance of a sideward displacement of all three disks. If, however, the interval between the presentation of the top and bottom sets of three disks is shorter than 30 msec, a single disk appears to be jumping back and forth across the middle two to flank them alternately at right and left (Pantle & Picciano, 1976). This kind of observation has led Braddick (1974) to postulate motion detection via either (1) a short-range mechanism operating over small retinal distances, affecting neurons like those found in the rabbit retina, and subject to motion aftereffects, or (2) a long-range mechanism operating over much larger retinal distances and not subject to motion aftereffects. To disentangle these two mechanisms requires elaborate experiments (Anstis, 1978), because they are likely to reside fairly far apart in the central nervous system. In particular, the long-range mechanism probably requires more elaborate preprocessing than the short in order

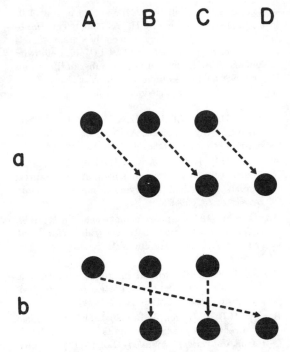

Figure 3.17. Pantle and Picciano's (1976) experiment is interpreted as demonstrating that there are two separate motion systems in human vision. Three disks were presented first in stations A, B, and C, for 200 msec and, after an interstimulus interval (ISI), in stations B, C, and D for another 200 msec. For ISIs of 50 msec or longer, observers reported the group of three disks to move *in toto* (scheme a). For ISIs of 30 msec or less, they reported the outer disk as moving from A to D while the other two disks remained stationary (scheme b).

to detect certain components of similarity between the two patterns whose appearance in different places at different times is interpreted as motion.

Another interesting example of channeling of movement information was described by Regan and Beverley (1980). By suitable selection of stimuli, they discovered independence of adaptation to purely sideways motion and to the "zooming" motion that occurs when a target approaches the observer.

The definition of motion as a displacement in time invites some interesting questions in the realm of binocular vision, because it is clearly possible to distribute the successive presentations between the two eyes. This was first done by Mach's student Dvorak (1872), who showed a moving spot stroboscopically to the two eyes

alternately and found that observers reported differences in depth. These differences in depth are similar to those discovered later by Pulfrich (1922). To see the Pulfrich effect, a subject fixates a stationary target while a pendulum oscillates in the subject's frontoparallel plane. When both eyes receive the same retinal illuminance from the moving pendulum, its trajectory remains in the frontoparallel plane, but if one eye receives less light (as, for example, when a neutral filter is placed over that eye only) the pendulum now appears to trace out an ellipse in depth. In other words, when it moves towards the eye with the dimmer retinal image, it seems to be in front of the fixation plane, and when it moves in the opposite direction, it appears behind the fixation plane. The origin of this effect lies in the longer action time taken for retinal and retinocortical conduction events for lower retinal illuminances. Thus the cortical signals arriving at any instant through the two eyes originated at different positions of the pendulum: the signal that comes through the eye with the filter originated at an earlier position of the pendulum. This time difference has been converted into a position difference and, in that particular aspect of binocular viewing, into a disparity and hence a difference in depth.

In the Pulfrich experiments the time differences were only indirectly under the experimenter's control. Békésy (1969) improved on this situation by devising a method of showing a pendulum-like target to stationary eyes in which one eye's target trajectory could be delayed by amounts determined by the experimenter or the subject. When the minimal depth deviation of the target was determined, it was found to correspond to an interocular time difference of 0.05 msec for the optimal conditions of oscillation frequency and amplitude of a target under photopic viewing conditions.

More recently interest has shifted to related experiments with discontinuously presented targets, in which temporal and spatial intervals of target presentation and interocular delays can be manipulated separately. The general question centers around the ability of the binocular apparatus to associate features appearing on the two retinas with both binocular disparity and asynchrony. The conclusion drawn from a series of experiments (Morgan, 1979; Burr & Ross, 1979) is that the filling in of stroboscopically flashed targets to yield a single trajectory of apparent motion is done separately in the two monocular projections, that is, it occurs before stereopsis (Morgan, 1976). The depth at which such targets appear at any one moment is determined by the disparity of the individual filled-in apparent motion trajectories of the two eyes at that moment, and not by the disparity of the targets when they were actually exposed. This has given rise to discussions of hypothetical processes of interpolation (Barlow, 1981; Crick, Marr & Poggio, 1981; Fahle & Poggio, 1981) by which fairly accurate temporal and spatial localization in flight, so to speak, can be achieved, based on information garnered at stations moderately far apart. The time span involved is of the order of 25 msec and the spatial extent is of the order of 10 min of arc.

The processes that are involved in associating simple features presented with spatial and temporal disparities in the two eyes can also operate to impose structure to a field of dots appearing randomly in time and position, as on a television screen without a station signal (Tyler, 1974; Smith, 1975). When an intensity-reducing filter is placed over one eye during the viewing of such a field, the observer soon reports seeing the dots organize themselves into a horizontally disposed vortex, that is, sheets of dots moving in one direction in planes in front of the screen and others moving in the opposite direction behind the screen. The apparent depth effects conform with those of the Pulfrich phenomenon. But since there is no coherence in the random target, the coherence observed must have its origin in the merging of target pairs of appropriate asynchrony and spatial placement into effectively single stimuli with the appropriate motion and binocular disparity.

REFERENCES

This chapter does not supersede Graham's chapter "Visual Perception" in the first edition but reviews the topic from a perspective of 30 years later. The reader is referred to Graham (1951) for many facets of visual space perception that still remain well grounded. Earlier encyclopedic reviews that continue to be useful are those of Hofmann (1920, 1925/1970) and Tschermak (1931); a contemporary one has been presented by Uttal (1981). Specialized texts containing important material include Berliner (1948), Gibson (1950), and Ogle (1950). The Zeitgeist of the 1950s is well captured in Graham (1965) and that of the 1970s in a symposium volume by Harris (1980). The *Handbook of Sensory Physiology*, especially Volumes VII/4 (Jameson & Hurvich, 1972) and VIII (Held, Leibowitz & Teuber, 1978), features a large number of illuminating reviews, as does Volume V of the *Handbook of Perception* (Carterette & Friedman, 1975).

Albrecht, D.G., DeValois, R.L., & Thorell, L.G. (1980). Visual cortical neurons: Are bars or gratings the optimal stimuli? *Science, 207*, 88–90.

Andrews, D.P., Butcher, A.K., & Buckely, B.R. (1973). Acuities for spatial arrangement in line figures: Human and ideal observers compared. *Vision Research, 13*, 599–620.

Anstis, S.M. (1978). Apparent movement. In R. Held, H.W. Leibowitz, & H.-L. Teuber (Eds.), *Handbook of sensory physiology*, Vol. VIII. Berlin: Springer-Verlag.

Barlow, H.B. (1981). Critical limiting factors in the design of the eye and visual cortex. *Proceedings of the Royal Society* (Lond.), *B212*, 1–34.

Barlow, H.B., & Levick, W.R. (1965). The mechanism of directionally selective units in the rabbit's retina. *Journal of Physiology* (Lond.), *178*, 477–504.

Barlow, H.B., & Reeves, B.C. (1979). The versatility and absolute efficiency of detecting mirror symmetry in random dot displays. *Vision Research, 19*, 783–793.

Basler, A. (1909). Ueber das Sehen von Bewegungen. *Pflugers Archiv für die gesamte Physiologie, 128*, 427–430.

Békésy, G. von. (1969). The smallest time difference the eyes can detect with sweeping stimulation. *Proceedings of the National Academy of Sciences 64*, 142–147.

Berkley, M.A., & Sprague, J.M. (1979). Striate cortex and visual acuity functions in the cat. *Journal of Comparative Neurology, 187*, 679–702.

Berliner, A. (1948). *Lectures on visual physiology*. Chicago: Professional Press.

Berry, R.N. (1948). Quantitative relations among vernier, real depth, and stereoscopic depth acuities. *Journal of Experimental Psychology, 38*, 708–721.

Blumenfeld, W. (1913). Untersuchungen über die scheinbare Grösse im Sehraum. *Zeitschrift für Psychologie, 65*, 241.

Braddick, O. (1974) A short-range process in apparent motion. *Vision Research, 14*, 519–528.

Brindley, G.S. (1960). *Physiology of the retina and visual pathway*. London: Arnold.

Burr, D.C., & Ross, J. (1979). How does binocular delay give information about depth? *Vision Research, 19*, 523–532.

Campbell, F.W. (1974). The transmission of spatial information through the visual system. In F.O. Schmitt & F.G. Worden (Eds.), *The neurosciences, Third Study Program*, Cambridge, MA: M.I.T. Press. pp. 95–103.

Carterette, E.C. & Friedman, M.P. (Eds.) (1975). *Handbook of perception. Seeing.* Vol. V. New York: Academic Press.

Coren, S., & Girgus, J.S. (1978). *Seeing is deceiving: The psychology of visual illusions.* Hillsdale, NJ: Erlbaum.

Crick, F.H.C., Marr, D., & Poggio, T. (1981). An information-processing approach to understanding the visual cortex. In F.O. Schmitt (Ed.), *The organization of the cerebral cortex.* Cambridge, MA: M.I.T. Press. pp. 505–533.

DeMonasterio, F.M., & Gouras, P. (1975). Functional properties of ganglion cells of the rhesus monkey retina. *Journal of Physiology* (Lond.), *251*, 167–195.

Dobson, V., & Teller, D.Y. (1978). Visual acuity in human infants: A review and comparison of behavioral and electrophysiological studies. *Vision Research, 18*, 1469–1484.

Dow, B.M., Snyder, A.Z., Vautin, R.G., & Bauer, R. (1981). Magnification factor and receptive field size in foveal striate cortex of the monkey. *Experimental Brain Research, 44*, 213–239.

Dvorak, V. (1872) Ueber Analoga der persönlichen Differenz zwischen beiden Augen und den Netzhautstellen desselben Auges. *Sitzungberichte der königlichen böhmischen Gesesellschaft*, Prag, pp. 65–72.

Fahle, M., & Poggio, T. (1981). Visual hyperacuity: Spatio-temporal interpolation in vision. *Proceedings of the Royal Society* (Lond.), *B213*, 451–477.

Fechner, G.T. (1860). *Elemente der Psychophysik.* Leipzig: Breitkopf und Härtel.

Fleischl, E. von (1883). Die Verteilung der Sehnervenfasern über die Zapfen der menschlichen Netzhaut. *Sitzungberichte des Akademie Wissenschaften, Wien (Math.-nat. Kl.*, Abeilung 3), *87*, 246–252.

Foley, J.M. (1964). Desarguesian property of visual space. *Journal of the Optical Society of America, 54*, 684–692.

Frisby, J.P. (1980). *Seeing.* Oxford: Oxford University Press.

Gelb, A., & Goldstein, K. (1920). *Psychologische Analysen hirnpathologischer Fälle.* Barth, Leipzig, 1929.

Gibson, J. J. (1933). Adaptation, after-effect, and contrast in the perception of curved lines. *Journal of Experimental Psychology, 16*, 1–31.

Gibson, J.J. (1950). *The perception of the visual world.* Boston: Houghton Mifflin.

Graham, C.H. (1951). Visual perception. In S.S. Stevens (Ed.), *Handbook of experimental psychology.* New York: Wiley. pp. 868–920.

Graham, C.H. (Ed.) (1965). *Vision and visual perception.* New York: Wiley.

Gregory, R.L. (1978). *Eye and brain: The psychology of seeing*, 3rd ed. New York: McGraw-Hill.

Gross, C.H., Rocha-Miranda, C.E., & Bender, D.B. (1972). Visual properties of neurons in inferotemporal cortex of the macaque. *Journal of Neurophysiology, 35*, 96–111.

Guillery, H. (1899). Messende Untersuchungen über den Formensinn. *Pflügers Archiv der gesamte Physiologie, 75*, 466.

Hammer, E.R. (1949). Temporal factors in figural after-effects. *American Journal of Psychology, 62*, 337–354.

Harris, C.S. (Ed.). (1980). *Visual coding and adaptibility.* Hillsdale, NJ: Erlbaum.

Hecht, S., & Mintz, E.U. (1939). The visibility of single lines at various illuminations and the retinal basis of visual resolution. *Journal of General Physiology, 22*, 593–612.

Held, R., Birch, R., & Gwiazda, J. (1980). Stereoacuity of the human infant. *Proceedings of the National Academy of Sciences, 77*, 5572–5574.

Held, R., Leibowitz, H.W., & Tueber, H.-L. (Eds.), (1978). *Perception.* Vol. VIII of *Handbook of Sensory Physiology.* Berlin: Springer-Verlag.

Helmholtz, H. (1924). *Helmholtz's Treatise on physiological optics*, Trans. J.P.C. Southall, 3 vols. Mensha, WI: Optical Society of America. (Original work, *Handbuch der physiologischen Optik*, 1856/66).

Hillebrand, F. (1893). Die Stabilität der Raumwerte auf der Netzhaut. *Zeitschrift für Psychologie, 5*, 1–60.

Hochberg, J. (1981). Levels of perceptual organization. In M. Kubovy, & Pomerantz, J.R. (Eds.), *Perceptual organization.* Hillsdale, NJ: Erlbaum.

Hoffman, W.C. (1966). The Lie algebra of visual perception. *Journal of Mathematical Psychology, 3*, 65–98.

Hofmann, F.B. (1970). *Die Lehre vom Raumsinn des Auges.* Berlin: Springer-Verlag. (Reprint of Vol. III of *Handbuch der gesamten Augenheilkunde.* Place of publ.: Graefe-Saemisch, 1920, 1925).

Hubel, D.H., & Wiesel, T.N. (1974). Uniformity of monkey striate cortex: A parallel relationship between field size, scatter and magnification factor. *Journal of Comparative Neurology, 158*, 295–306.

Hubel, D.H., & Wiesel, T.N. (1977). Functional architecture of macaque monkey cortex. *Proceedings of the Royal Society* (Lond.), *B198*, 1–59.

Jameson, D., & Hurvich, L.M. (Eds.) (1972). *Visual psychophysics*, Vol. VII/4 of *Handbook of sensory physiology.* Berlin: Springer-Verlag.

Jastrow, J. (1893). On the judgement of horizontal, vertical and oblique positions of lines. *American Journal of Psychology, 5*, 220–223.

Julesz, B. (1971) *Foundations of cyclopean perception.* Chicago: Chicago University Press.

Julesz, B. (1981) Textons, the elements of texture perception, and their interactions. *Nature, 290*, 91–97.

Jung, R. (1974). Neuropsychologie und Neurophysiologie des Kontur- und Formsehens in Zeichnung und Malerei. In H.H. Wieck (Ed.), *Psychopathologie musischer Gestaltungen.* Stuttgart: Schattauer, pp. 29–88.

Kanizsa, G. (1976). Subjective contours. *Scientific American, 234*(4), 48–52.

Kelly, D.H. (1962). *New Stimuli in vision.* Lexington, MA: Itek.

Koffka, K. (1935). *Principles of Gestalt psychology.* New York: Harcourt, Brace.

Köhler, W. (1924). *Die physischen Gestalten in Ruhe und im stationären Zustand.* Erlangen: Philosophische Akademie.

Köhler, W. & Wallach, H. (1944). Figural after-effects. *Proceedings American Philosophical Society, 88*, 269–357.

Kuffler, S. W. (1953). Discharge patterns and functional organization of mammalian retina. *Journal of Neurophysiology, 16*, 37–68.

Leibowitz, H.W. (1955a). The relation between the rate threshold for the perception of movement and luminance for various durations of exposure. *Journal of Experimental Psychology, 49*, 209–214.

Leibowitz, H.W. (1955b). Effect of reference lines on the discrimination of movement. *Journal of the Optical Society of America, 45*, 829–830.

Leibowitz, H.W. (1965). *Visual perception.* New York: Macmillan.

Luckiesh, M. (1965). *Visual illusions.* New York: Dover.

Luneburg, R.K. (1947) *Mathematical analysis of binocular vision.* Princeton, NJ: Princeton University Press.

Lupp, U., Hauske, G., & Wolf, W. (1978). Different systems for the visual detection of high and low spatial frequencies. *Photographic Science and Engineering, 22*, 80–84.

Mach, E. (1861). Ueber das Sehen von Lagen und Winkeln durch die Bewegung des Auges. *Sitzungberichte der Akademie der Wissenschaften, Wien., 43*(2), 215–221.

Mach, E. (1922). *Die Analyse der Empfindungen,* Jena: Fischer.

Marr, D. (1982). *Vision.* San Francisco: Freeman.

Marr, D., & Poggio, T. (1976). Cooperative computation of stereo disparity. *Science, 194*, 283–287.

McKee, S.P. (1981). A local mechanism for differential velocity detection. *Vision Research, 21*, 491–500.

Metzger, W. (1953). *Gesetze des Sehens.* Frankfurt a.M.: Kramer.

Mitchell, D.M., & O'Hagan, S. (1972). Accuracy of stereoscopic localization of small line segments that differ in size and orientation for the two eyes. *Vision Research, 12*, 437–454.

Mitchell, D.M., & Ware, C. (1974). Interocular transfer of a visual after-effect in normal and stereoblind humans. *Journal of Physiology* (Lond.), *243*, 739–756.

Morgan, M.J. (1976). The Pulfrich effect and the filling in of apparent motion. *Perception, 5*, 187–195.

Morgan, M.J. (1979). Perception of continuity in stroboscopic motion: A temporal frequency analysis. *Vision Research, 19*, 491–500.

Movshon, J.A. (1975). The velocity tuning of single units in cat striate cortex. *Journal of Physiology* (Lond.), *249*, 445–468.

Nakayama, K., & Tyler, C.W. (1981). Psychophysical isolation of movement sensitivity by removal of familiar position cues. *Vision Research, 21*, 427–433.

Nelson, J.I. (1975). Globality and stereoscopic fusion in binocular vision. *Journal of Theoretical Biology, 49*, 1–88.

Neumann, J. von. (1958). *The computer and the brain.* New Haven: Yale University Press.

Ogle, K.N. (1950). *Researches in binocular vision.* Philadelphia: Saunders.

Pantle, A.J., & Picciano, L. (1976). A multi-stable movement display: Evidence for two separate motion systems in humans. *Science, 193*, 500–502.

Pollen, D.A., & Ronner, S.F. (1975). Periodic excitability changes across the receptive fields of complex cells in the striate and parastriate cortex of the cat. *Journal of Physiology* (Lond.), *245*, 667–697.

Pulfrich, C. (1922). Die Stereoskopie im Dienste der isochromen und heterochromen Photometrie. *Naturwissenschaften, 10*, 533.

Rashbass, C. (1961). The relationship between saccadic and smooth tracking eye movements. *Journal of Physiology* (Lond.), *159*, 326–338.

Regan, D. (1972). *Evoked potentials in psychology, sensory physiology and clinical medicine.* London: Chapman & Hall.

Regan, D., & Beverley, K.I. (1980). Visual responses to changing size and sideways motion for different directions of motion in depth. *Journal of the Optical Society of America, 60*, 1289–1296.

Richards, W. (1971). Anomalous stereoscopic depth perception. *Journal of the Optical Society of America, 61*, 410–414.

Salomon, A. (1947). Visual field factors in the perception of direction. *American Journal of Psychology, 60,* 68–88.

Schwartz, E. (1980). Computational anatomy and functional architecture of striate cortex: A spatial mapping approach to perceptual coding. *Vision Research, 20,* 645–670.

Sekular, R., & Littlejohn, J. (1974). Tilt after-effects following very brief exposures. *Vision Research, 14,* 151–152.

Shepard, R.N. (1981). Psychophysical complementarity. In M. Kubovy & J.R. Pomerantz (Eds.), *Perceptual organization.* Hillsdale, NJ: Erlbaum. pp. 271–341.

Shepard, R.N., & Metzler, J. (1971). Mental rotation of three-dimensional objects. *Science, 171,* 701–703.

Smith, R.A. (1975). Motion effect and after effect that are contingent upon depth. *Journal of the Optical Society of America, 65,* 1180.

Sperry, R.W., & Miner, N. (1955). Pattern perception following insertion of mica plates into the visual cortex. *Journal of Comparative and Physiological Psychology, 48,* 463–469.

Treismann, A.M., & Gelader, G. (1980). A feature-integration theory of attention. *Cognitive Psychol. 12,* 97–136.

Tschermak, A. (1931). Optischer Raumsinn. In A. Bethe, G.V. Bergmann, G. Emden, & A. Ellinger (Eds.), *Handbuch der normalen und pathologischen Physiologie,* Vol. XII/2. Berlin: Springer. pp. 834–1000.

Tyler, C.W. (1974). Stereopsis in dynamic visual noise. *Nature, 250,* 781–782.

Uttal, W.R. (1981) *A taxonomy of visual processes.* Hillsdale, NJ: Erlbaum.

Watson, A., Barlow, H., & Robson, J. (1981). What does the eye see best? *Investigative Ophthalmology and Visual Science* (Suppl.), 20(3), 178. Abstract.

Watt, R.J., & Andrews, D.P. (1982). Contour curvature analysis: Hyperacuities in the discrimination of detailed shape. *Vision Research, 22,* 449–460.

Wenderoth, P., Beh, H., & White, D. (1978). Perceptual distortion of an oblique line in the presence of an abutting vertical line. *Vision Research, 18,* 923–930.

Wertheimer, M. (1912). Experimentelle Studien über das Sehen von Bewegungen. *Zeitschrift für Psychologie, 61,* 161–265.

Westheimer, G. (1979). Cooperative neural processes involved in stereoscopic acuity. *Experimental Brain Research, 36,* 585–597.

Westheimer, G. (1981). Visual hyperacuity. *Progress in Sensory Physiology, 1,* 1–30.

Westheimer, G., & McKee, S.P. (1977). Perception of temporal order in adjacent visual stimuli. *Vision Research, 17,* 887–892.

Westheimer, G., & McKee, S.P. (1978). Stereoscopic acuity for moving retinal images. *Journal of the Optical Society of America, 68,* 450–455.

Westheimer, G., & McKee, S.P. (1979). What prior uniocular processing is necessary for stereopsis? *Investigative Ophthalmology and Visual Science, 18,* 614–621.

Williamson, S.J., & Kaufman, L. (1981). Biomagnetism. *Journal of Magnetism and Magnetic Materials, 22,* 129–202.

Chapter 4

VISUAL PERCEPTION

Julian Hochberg, *Columbia University*

INTRODUCTION

The term, perception refers most generally to our sensory experiences of the world, and of the people, objects, and events that comprise it. The term refers as well to the process by which an internal representation of the world is obtained from sensory information about objects and events in the world. The study of perception consists then of attempts to explain why things appear as they do. That study has been pursued from several different major theoretical orientations which differ substantially in their goals, and in what they take to be adequate data and explanations.

In the past century and a half, a great deal of perceptual research has been done, and much more knowledge has been gained—and very often, rediscovered—than can possibly be summarized in a single place. I have tried to concentrate on those areas of research that seem most relevant to current theoretical or practical interests, but the reader should know that many other areas lie buried in the archives, any of which areas may regain importance at any time.

A Historical Division

This chapter has three main historical divisions. The first division is the early background of inquiry pursued primarily by artists and philosophers, who were interested in how we perceive pictures and why one object is an effective surrogate for another (that is, why the pictorial objects provide a perception that is similar to that provided by some scene). The conceptual tools used to deal with this problem were essentially those of physics and geometry.

The second division is what we consider the classical period of psychology, which ran from approximately 1850 to 1950. The primary theoretical concerns during this period were those of neurophysiologists and psychologists—what are the irreducible sensory elements and mechanisms by which our nervous systems analyze the information in proximal stimulation, and what are the processes by which, from those

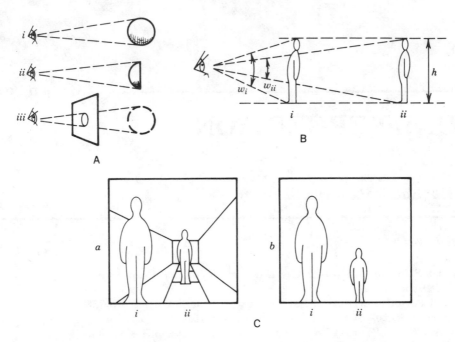

Figure 4.1. *Distal world and proximal stimulation.*

(A) Different objects (distal stimuli) can provide the same light to the eye (proximal stimulation): a sphere (i) and a half sphere (ii) can provide the same proximal stimulation—pattern of light—to the eye, and so can (iii) a picture of the object (under the proper conditions).

(B) The same object can provide different light to the eye. Man (i) and (ii) are the same height (h) but they provide different light to the eye. The usual measure of the latter is in terms of visual angle, and (ωii) is smaller than (ωi). It is this decrease of ω with distance that underlies linear perspective and the related depth cues in Figure 4.2 and 4.4.

(C) Both distal and proximal stimulus measures will (under different conditions) serve to predict what we perceive. For example, viewed in context (a), the two men are likely to look of equal height, with the apparent height determined by their distal height; viewed out of context (b), their apparent sizes will be close to their visual angles, ω.

sensory analyses, we arrive at our perception of the distal properties of objects and events in the world? The major areas of application lay in *visual science*, providing foundations for the fields of visual prosthesis (e.g., optometry and ophthalmology), for the visual media (e.g., photography, print, and eventually television), and for the study of the visual interface between man and machine (a field currently called *human factors*). These applications provided motivation for much of the research that gave the field its rich base of technical data.

The third division, the present period, which started around 1950, is a time of tremendous ferment that continues unabated. The problems of perception continue to engage the other disciplines I have mentioned, but now Computer Science is a further major presence in the field,

providing tools, concepts, and motivation in several several distinct but closely related ways (pp. 248f).

The body of this chapter is divided unevenly into these three historical sections. However, within each, substantial reference will be made to relevant work from other periods, and within each we will pay particular attention to the division between the three types of explanations that have characterized the various approaches: (1) explanations that are primarily an account of the *stimulus pattern*; (2) explanations that take *neurophysiology* into account (or that have as their aim the explication of neurophysiology); and (3) *psychological explanations*, which draw upon principles that cannot be found in the physical stimulation and are not expressed in terms of neurophysiology.

I wish to stress that many of the theories that have been offered, such as "direct theory" (pp. 201f, 240ff) and "unconscious inference" (pp. 211f, 226f), are not explanations in themselves, but are arguments about the terms in which explanations should be couched. These theories are vacuous until they are fleshed out with specific details, and then if they are to be viable and useful they must draw from all three domains.

ATTEMPTS AT A STIMULUS ACCOUNT: THE EARLY MODERNS AND CONTEMPORARY CONCERNS WITH THE ISSUES THEY RAISED

First, we consider a general issue that runs through all attempts to account for our perceptions of the world and that raises a fundamental distinction.

An Essential Distinction: Distal Environment and Proximal Stimulation

Distal properties are those measured at the physical object or event—a man's height, an object's reflectance, and so on. When perceptions are truthful or *veridical*, appearance of objects vary according to their distal properties in the world. A grapefruit (Figure 4.1A) looks and feels spherical—just as a box would look and feels cubic—in accordance with its physical form, and two men (Figure 4.1B) correctly appear of equal height because they are so. In much of our daily lives, and indeed in many fields of psychological study, this account suffices.

But perceptions are not always veridical, nor do we necessarily know by any internal evidence when they are not. A stick, even though it is straight, when it is half immersed in water looks bent because the light received from it by the eye has been refracted. We must therefore distinguish two ways in which the world can be described: by its *distal* properties and by its *proximal* properties. Many distal properties are relatively constant or *invariant*, that is, they change little or not at all from one occasion to the next—the straightness of the stick, the sphericity of the grapefruit, the heights of the two men. Other distal properties are inconstant and variable—the object's distance from the

viewer, the illumination that falls upon it, the velocity with which it moves, its changes in shape if it is a nonrigid object.

Proximal properties are measured at or near the relevant sense organ; *proximal stimulation* refers to the physical energies that affect the sense organ and that provide the channels through which we learn about the distal properties. The distinction between distal and proximal properties is particularly clear in the case of the *distance senses*. In vision, the proximal stimulation is the pattern of light that falls on the retina of the eye; in audition or hearing it is the pattern of atmospheric pressure waves that enter the ear. Because both viewers and observed objects move about, and because viewing conditions change, most proximal stimulation is inconstant and variable. In Figure 4. 1B, the two men at different distances provide different proximal stimuli—that is, different arrays of light to the eye, and different retinal images that are formed within the eye—even though they are equal in distal size.

Because it is difficult to measure the image on the eye, and because for some purposes it is not necessary to know where within the scene the gaze is directed, we often take as the proximal stimulus pattern a projection that is intermediate between the distal stimulus and the retinal image, namely, the *optic array*. The optic array is the sheaf of light rays that originates in the environment and that confronts the viewer's eye. It is to be distinguished from the retinal image actually formed within the eye, which depends on the momentary direction of the viewer's gaze. Both the optic array and the retinal image must be distinguished from the effective retinal response to the retinal image, because as we will see (in Figure 4.8) the sensitivity of the retinal surface varies greatly from one region to another. The optic array is thus a statement only about the physical field of potential stimulation that can be sampled by the viewer's gaze from that station point.

In most practical situations, it is much easier to know what distal object confronts a viewer, and to measure it, than to know precisely what the proximal stimulus pattern is. And to the degree that we perceive the world correctly, of course, our perceptions will be in correspondence with the distal properties of the things around us. In many cases, therefore, an account of the distal stimuli in the world will suffice as an explanation of what people see and of how they and animals act (given their motives, opportunites, etc.).

But the description of one's distal environment does not always account for what we perceive, nor can it by itself explain our perceptions. And this is where the problems of perception start (and, historically, the problems of experimental psychology in general: Boring, 1942; Hochberg, 1962, 1984b).

Perception often differs from reality (i.e., from the distal measure), and in many of these situations, like that discussed in Figure 4.1C, the contents of the proximal stimulus pattern itself account for the discrepancy. Thus, the apparent difference in the sizes of the two men in Figure 4.1Cb is caused by the visual angles that they subtend, and not by their physical sizes.

However, the proximal pattern cannot in general provide unambiguous information about the distal environment, so that very different objects or events may provide the same light to the eye and therefore be indistinguishable. In Figure 4.1A, the viewer cannot tell the difference between the grapefruit (*i*) and the half grapefruit (*ii*), because both present the same proximal stimulus to the eye. So does (*iii*), which is a color photograph of the grapefruit —as a flat, pigmented plane it is a distal object totally different from the spherical fruit, but it is under certain circumstances (see p. 200; and Ames, 1925) indistinguishable from the sphere and hemisphere of which it is equally well a *surrogate* stimulus. Conversely, things that are the same can provide different proximal stimulation, and therefore appear to be different. In Figure 4.1C, if the two men at different distances are viewed out of their context they will likely appear to be of different sizes (1Cb).

Accordingly, there are many situations in which we can better account for what we see in terms of the proximal rather than the distal stimulus, as when we perceive a half grapefruit as a whole, a picture as an object, two equally tall men being of different heights. Much of what we now know about perception consists of having learned about the principles that relate proximal to distal stimulation. We will continue to encounter examples of such analyses throughout this chapter. Elucidating this relationship is the first step toward an explanation of perception. But it can only be a first step, because proximal stimulation simply *cannot* specify distal characteristics unambiguously unless auxiliary assumptions or constraints are made.

Because most of the issues and applications of perceptual psychology arise in connection with this point, it will recur in various guises throughout this chapter. The proximal stimulus for vision is essentially a two-dimensional array of light that will fit equally well to any one of an indefinitely large set of distal stimuli. Simply changing the value of the third dimension for any of the points in the two-dimensional array yields a new distal layout in three dimensions, but leaves the array itself unchanged. One cannot specify three dimensions in two. Sometimes, however, it is argued (p. 241) that because the moving viewer receives changing images, which provide a dimension of change, the proximal stimulus is really three dimensional; but by that argument the distal stimulus may also change, so that the problem remains intact unless one assumes an unchanging and rigid distal stimulus (pp. 244ff.).

This abstract issue became concrete when first artists and then philosophers noted the implications of the fact that three-dimensional space can be conveyed by two-dimensional pictures.

Artists, Philosophers and Physicists Before the 1850s

One way to produce a picture would be to make a surrogate object that offers the eye exactly the same pattern of light as that offered by the scene itself. The techniques of artificial perspective introduced or reintroduced by Brunelleschi in 1420, and codified by Alberti in 1435, provided a picture plane that could approximately meet this requirement (see White, 1957). At the beginning of the sixteenth century, Leonardo urged the artist to discover the characteristics of the two-dimensional image provided by a three-dimensional world by tracing the outlines of the objects on a plane of glass interposed between his eye and the scene (Figure 4.2A) The same method was in fact used to provide pictures of existing scenes—by carefully tracing the scene or, with the growth of appropriate technology, by photographic or video camera—with no need for the artist to learn anything.

The features that result from projecting

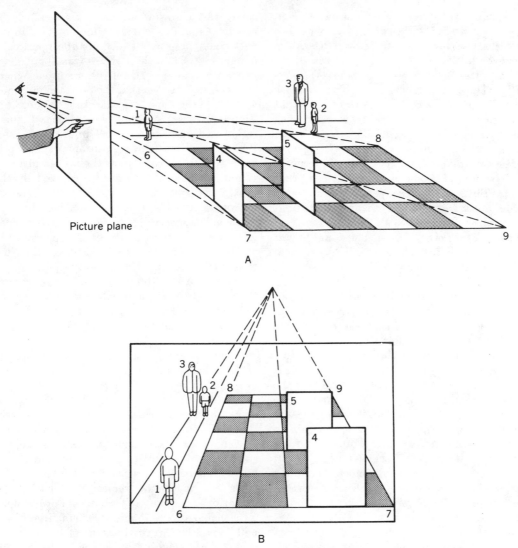

Picture plane

A

B

Figure 4.2. *Pictures and the pictorial depth cues.*

(A) Leonardo's instructions: trace scenes carefully on glass panes to learn how to make pictures—flat objects that produce the same effects as some scene in space.

(B) The tracing made at (A). The tracing itself can serve as a picture (this procedure eventually became photography). More important, the artist can note the characteristics—what we now call the *pictorial depth cues* —that are provided to the eye by a flat plane that intersects the light to the eye from a scene and that, when painted on canvas, will in turn provide the eye with light that is at least in some respects the same as that provided by a layout of objects and surfaces in three-dimensional space.

A partial listing of the major pictorial depth cues are: (a) *linear perspective* (e.g., lines that are parallel in space project tracings that converge with represented distance); (b) *familiar size*: the man (3) and the boy (1) project images of equal size; given that the man is known to be larger, he must be farther; (c) *relative size:* the boys at (1) and (2), even if they were unfamiliar objects, would, because of their similarity of shape, be likely to be of equal size; their difference in size in the picture becomes a cue as to their different distances; (d) *interposition*: the object whose contours are not interrupted (4) is thereby indicated as being in front of the object whose contours are interrupted (5); (e) *texture-density gradient*: the homogeneously distributed markings on the "playing field" (6, 7, 8, 9) increase in density with represented distance; (g) *aerial perspective* (not shown here): in exterior scenes, increasing distance through the air results in lessened contrast, lessened detail, and loss of the warm colors (reds and yellows).

normal three-dimensional scenes on two dimensions, as shown in Figure 4.2B, include what are now called the monocular or pictorial *depth cues* (Woodworth, 1938): (1) *linear perspective*, (1) *familiar size*, (3) *relative size*, and (4) *interposition*. The picture traced on the plane of glass is merely a measure of the pattern of light that the scene reflects to the eye. (For recent geometrical analysis, see Sedgwick, 1980.) These cues, and the growing science of optics seemed to offer an explanation of perception in terms of the physical and geometrical properties of that pattern. But even the most perfect picture must be inherently ambiguous, in that the same light at the eye is offered by both the flat surrogate and the very different three-dimensional layout it represents. And the pattern of light provided to the eye by the scene itself is also inherently ambiguous.

This is what made pictures, and visual perception, of interest to the philosophers: how can we know anything to be true, given that all our sense data must, like vision, be ambiguous?

With certain viewing conditions—a stationary monocular viewer, and a larger viewing distance—Figure 4.1A(i) to (iii) all provide the same proximal stimulus pattern (and indeed are then perceived alike). The fact is, however, that the world about us, and the objects within it, normally look definite enough, and we do not normally mistake a real scene for a flat but perfect picture. Something more than the proximal stimulus pattern, and therefore something beyond the physics of light or sound, would seem to be at work.

Here the study of perception departs from physical analysis and must draw on one or both of two other disciplines—one physiological, the other psychological. To most psychologists, a complete account includes both.

It was in making this point that Berkeley in 1709 offered his New Theory of Vision, arguing that the information in the sensory stimulation is inherently unable to specify any definite sets of objects or events in the world, and that our perceptions of those objects and events must therefore be learned through our experiences with the world. This doctrine, known as *empiricism*, was developed in the course of pursuing the philosophical implications of the proposition that our knowledge of the world can only be gained through our senses. By Berkeley's argument, because our sense data must necessarily rest on what we have here called the proximal stimulus pattern, which is itself inherently ambiguous about such distal properties as distance, size, and shape, our ideas about those properties must have some other source. Where could we get the idea that the two men in Figure 4.1B are of the same height, or that the object in Figure 4.1A is a sphere, if the proximal stimulation does not provides the information? For Berkeley, as for many philosophers and psychologists before and since, the idea of distance is not a single sense datum provided by the proximal visual stimulus alone. It is a complex or compound idea, originally learned by connecting or *associating* the visual sensory idea given by the retinal image of the sphere, as in the case of Figure 4.1A, with the nonvisual (tactual and kinesthetic) sensory experiences of reaching out and touching the sphere or with the experiences of the numbers of steps, and so on, that would be needed to touch the man, given the size of his retinal image in Figure 4.1B.

The properties of the world are thus explained as complex ideas, not as *direct perceptions* produced in the viewer by the proximal stimulation. The direct and simple effects of proximal stimulation were called *sensations*, and were thought to consist of the simpler properties such as visual color and extent, tactual pressure, and so on—those properties that correspond plausibly to properties of the proximal stimulation. To these are added the remembered packets of sensations from past experiences. For example, if the visual angle subtended by a familiar beach ball should be a retinal extent of 11.3 degrees, that would signify the bodily sensations provided by five strides to a viewer whose habitual stride is two feet long. Just as our ideas about the meanings of names and other words are learned from, and composed of, the associations provided by their usage in the world, our perceptions of distal properties (e.g., size, distance, etc.) were thought to be learned from the world and consist of having learned the packets of proximal stimuli that are provided in association by the regularities of the world.

This argument was intended to show that physics cannot explain our perceptions, and that the structure that we have learned from our experiences with the world provide an essential (indeed, *the* essential) element of any explanation of perception. This empiricist point of view has been immensely influential, but it has not gone unopposed.

In 1838, more than a century after Berkeley's analysis, Wheatstone studied the consequence of the fact that the two eyes, with their difference in viewpoints, called *binocular parallax*, receive slightly different optic arrays for scenes in depth (Figure 4.3A). Objects that lie nearer to or farther from the plane that contains the point at which the eyes are *converged* fall on different places in the two eyes, a factor called *binocular disparity* (Figure 4.3B). The amount and direction of the disparity is therefore a potential depth cue, and an effective one, as Wheatstone showed in inventing a *stereoscope* with which to provide a separate array to each eye. With disparities of less than about 15 min of arc, the doubling of the images is not seen; instead, the single object is perceived in its appropriate depth relationship.

An analysis of how the geometry of binocular vision specifies a simple depth relationship is shown in Figure 4.3C. This suggests a possible innate basis for depth perception, although we should note that the stereoscope itself shows that, to the philosopher, binocular vision must also be ambiguous, inasmuch as each eye receives only a flat image, yet the viewer perceives a convincingly three-dimensional layout.

The latest version of the opposition to Berkeley's argument rests on the "direct theory" of J.J. Gibson (1950, 1979), who maintained that in a normal environment the optic array of a moving viewer provides information sufficient to specify for the nervous system all of the important properties of the scenes and events in the physical world, and that our perceptions of these distal properties are in some important sense *direct* responses to that information. That information arises primarily in consequence of *motion parallax*: objects at different distances in the world are displaced to different extents in the optic array by any movement of the viewer (Figure 4.4A). As sketched in Figure 4.4B, one can readily find aspects of the optic array that reflect an object's relative distal size, and so on, that remain *invariant* even though the object's distance (and therefore the optic array and retinal image it provides to the eye) may vary.

Attempts at a purely physical account of perception continue. The optic array is almost equivalent in meaning to the picture plane of a motion picture or video display, and what makes it important today is our need to learn more about how to generate pictorial surrogates from principles, as opposed to tracing them or otherwise copying the world: This need arises because computers now provide an increasing proportion of the pictures that we confront. To do so, the computers must draw upon the rules by which three-dimensional layouts are projected in two-dimensional arrays, so that nonexistent layouts can be pictured just as existing scenes can be photographed. This study is, of course, really a branch of physics, but it must be pursued with the limitations and contributions of the human viewer firmly in mind, a requirement that is seldom met by those most interested in examining the information that might in principle be retrieved from stimulation.

But surrogates (p. 198) are therefore more than merely a means of pictorial communication. To the degree that the viewer responds identically to different objects or scenes, comparison of those objects tell us about the limits of the information that the sense organ can pick up, and about how the brain uses that information.

The earliest scientific example of that point was Newton's famous experiment in visual sensation, showing in 1672 that with mixtures of three narrow wavelengths of light—for example, narrow bands of light that look red, green, and blue—one could match the appearance of all of the other colors of the spectrum and of any scene. An appropriate mix of three colors can serve as surrogate for any and all colors (Figure 4.5). *This is not a fact about photic energy* (the light itself remains unchanged by the mixture); it is a fact about our sensory nervous systems. Newton himself realized this, and we will see that physiological explanations of color mixture figure heavily in the classical account of perception.

Physiological explanations of perception have been offered for centuries. In 1650 Descartes introduced the idea of the *reflex arc*—we obtain sensory information through the actions of sensory nerves, and execute behaviors through the action of motor nerves. Hobbes (1651) explained false perceptions of light (e.g., in afterimages) as caused by activity of the optic nerve, *which is interpreted by the brain as external light because the latter would normally be the cause of such activity.* And Hartley, in 1791, proposed that (1)

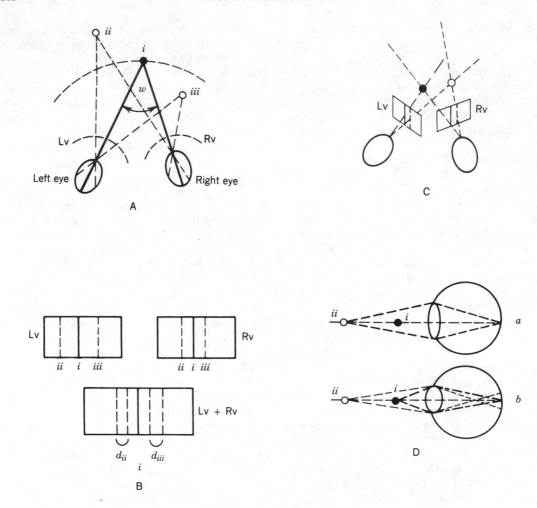

Figure 4.3. *Nonpictorial depth cues.*

(A) *Convergence and binocular parallax.* Because the two eyes have different viewpoints, their optic arrays (Lv and Rv) differ, that is, display *binocular parallax*, for objects at different distances. If the eyes are converged (angle ω) so as to bring point (i) to the fovea of each, the retinal images projected by points that are nearer or farther than (i) will fall on noncorresponding points in the two eyes (i.e., points which would not coincide if one retina could be superimposed on the other), as shown at (Lv + Rv) in (B).

(B) The two eyes' views (Lv and Rv) and their superimposed combination (Lv + Rv). The image of (i), and of any other point that is at the same distance from the viewer, falls on corresponding points in the two fields of view, and is single. All other points are doubled, with separations or *disparities* (d_{ii}, d_{iii}) whose sizes and directions reflect the place where each point lies relative to the plane of (i). You can notice the double images by holding your finger before some distant object and alternately fixating your finger (in which case the object will double) and fixating the object (your finger will double). If a disparity is relatively small (less than 15 min of visual angle) the disparity is not detected as such, but provides instead an impression of real depth, or *patent stereopsis*. Wheatstone in 1838 devised *stereoscopes* for providing the eyes with appropriately disparate views.

(C) The objects are seen to be located in space where the rays through the two views intersect. (This diagram was, in its essentials, first drawn by Kepler in 1622; see Kaufman, 1974.)

We will be concerned with stereoscopic vision at several points in this chapter (pp. 217, 226ff, 254). See also Ch. 3.

(D) Given two objects at different distances, the lens of the eye must change its curvature or *accommodation* in order to bring the light from each into focus on the retina. At (a) the lens is focused for (ii), and its image is sharp; at (b) the lens is focused for (i), and the image of (ii) is blurred.

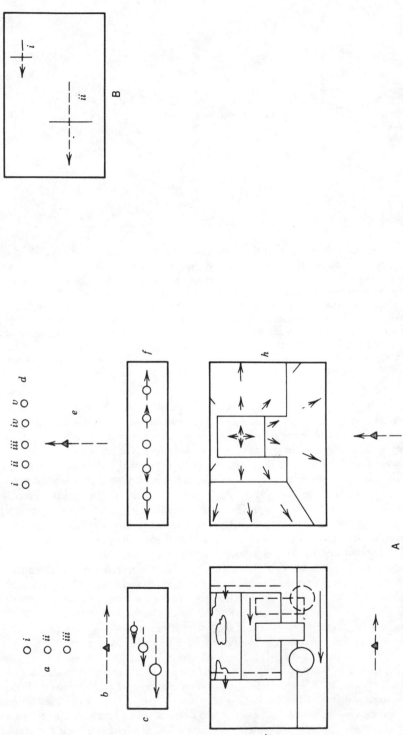

Figure 4.4. *Motion-provided information about surfaces in space.* The shaded triangle represents a moving viewer, its apex indicating the direction of gaze. (A) Two components of motion parallax: if a viewer moves to the right (b) while looking at a row of posts, shown from above at (a), because of motion parallax the nearer rods are displaced more in the optic array (c), providing a *gradient* of velocities that comprises an example of *motion perspective*. If the viewer (e) moves toward, and keeps his or her gaze fixed on, one of a row of object (d), other objects in the field of view (f) will move outward with velocities that depend on their distance from the direction of motion (iii), on the velocity of the viewer, and on the relative nearness of each object (for a plane surface, that would amount to specifying its slant, which is here perpendicular to the line of sight). This *optical expansion pattern* (or its reverse, if the viewer is moving away from the surface) therefore potentially provides information about all these distal variables (Gibson, Olum, & Rosenblatt, 1955; Gordon, 1965; Hay, 1966; Koenderink and van Doorn, 1981; Prazdny, 1980, 1983; Purdy, 1958). More complex examples of (c) and (f) are shown at (g) and (h), respectively.

(B) Although movement provides changing or transforming images of the world, many of the unchanging distal properties of objects in space find their counterpart in invariant properties of the transformations caused by the viewer's motion relative to the objects. Thus, if the viewer moves rightward past two rods of equal height, their sizes divided by their velocities in the optic array will be equal.

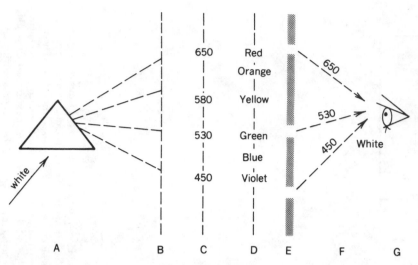

A   B   C   D   E   F   G

Figure 4.5. *Newton's experiment.* White light (A) is bent by a prism as a function of wavelength (as we now know), spreading the wavelengths out in an orderly spectrum (B). The visible spectrum (C), comprising *photic energy,* runs approximately from 450 to 700 nanometers (nm). To the eye, the spectrum ranges in color from violet to red (D). Many textbooks are written as though wavelength were the physical correlate of color, but—as Newton knew—that is not so. If three narrow slits are made in a cardboard mask (E) so as to pass three bands of light that are then recombined as at (F) and presented to the eye of a viewer (G), the appearance of any single wavelength or combination of wavelengths in the entire spectrum, including *white,* can (in essence) be matched exactly by an appropriate mixture of the three wavelengths. This phenomenon is psychological and physiological, not physical, as is shown by the fact that when the three are combined to white, passing the combination through the prism once again yields only those three wavelengths, not the entire spectrum.

each simple sensory idea corresponds to the actions of a specialized sensory nerve, and (2) a simple mental *image,* or idea that occurs in the absence of sensory stimulation, does so because (as Hobbes had suggested) the appropriate nerve has been caused to act by something other than the sensory stimulation to which it normally responds. *Association* of ideas, and perceptual learning, presumably occur because when two nerves are frequently caused to respond to simultaneous or closely successive stimulation, they will become connected in such a way that even if only one is stimulated it will cause the other to respond as well.

This picture that we have just sketched of perception and of the function of the nervous system has been close to consensus for a long time, and in its general outlines it is substantially the model of brain process that was proposed by Hebb in 1949 and was tested by computer simulations in the 1960s (Rosenblatt, 1962; cf. Minsky and Pappert, 1969).

The scientific study of perception, growing naturally from this speculative philosophical

background, began with physiological psychology. In 1838, Johannes Mueller argued that the apparently seamless and infinitely varied world that we perceive is found upon analysis to consist of separable neural channels of sensory experience. Such sensory *modalities* as vision, hearing, and taste depend on the action of some specific and identifiable part of the sensory nervous system (see Chapters 2, 5 and 9, in this Volume, and therefore reflect only indirectly the actual state of the physical world.

Phenomena that are not simply or elegantly accounted for by physical stimulation alone make far greater sense once we accept some version of Mueller's formulation (known as the *law of specific nerve energies*); for example, if you press your finger to one side of your closed eyelid, you will see a faint light, called a *pressure phosphene*. It occurs because pressure stimulates the optic nerve fibers, and the action of those fibers, regardless of source, is sensed as light. Again, if you first stare at a bright light and then close your eyes (or otherwise provide a dark background) you will see its positive *afterimage,* whereas with a gray or light background you will see its negative afterimage. The afterimages are caused the fatigue or lessened sensitivity of those nerve fibers that were stimulated by the light.

THE CLASSICAL PERIOD: PERCEPTUAL PSYCHOLOGY AND PHYSIOLOGY FROM 1850 TO 1950, AND THE CURRENT STATUS OF THE RESEARCH THEN INITIATED

From Optic Array to Neural Activity

The basic facts of color as described by Newton in 1672 are sketched in Figure 4.5. Given those facts, the most parsimonious model of visual perception was offered by Young in 1802 and adapted by Helmholtz some 50 years later—that color perception is mediated by three kinds of specialized receptor neurons in the retina called *cones*. Each kind of receptor—each *channel*—is responsive to most of the spectrum of photic energy, but each has a different sensitivity function (Figure 4.6), being most sensitive to light that looks red, green, and blue, respectively. The retina of the eye was envisioned as a mosaic composed of independent triads of the three cones; the light projected to the eye by any scene would then be analyzed at each point into the three component colors. The information in the retinal image presented by any scene would be *transduced* by these receptor triads into a set of neural activities from which the brain could recover the information (in effect, reconstitute the retinal image) with limits set both by the spectral sensitivities of the receptors (Figure 4.6) and by their spatial resolution (i.e., their size and spacing: Figure 4.7Bii).

Two kinds of research bore most directly on this theory: research that attempted to map the sensitivity of each type of cone to the wavelengths that comprise the visible spectrum; and research that mapped the spatial resolution of the retinal mosaic, that is, what detail the eye could be expected to resolve. The former research was pursued by an illustrious line of physicists and physiologists, beginning with J. Clerk Maxwell and Hermann von Helmholtz, and continues today in laboratories of Visual Science (see Chapter 2). The method used was some version of the matching task implied by Figure 4.6—what proportions of three component

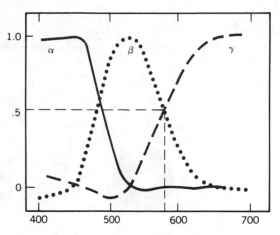

Figure 4.6. *The Young-Helmholtz theory: units of analysis of color.* To explain the facts of Figure 4.5. Thomas Young proposed in 1802 that three types of receptors, here labeled alpha, beta and gamma, are each responsive to a broad range of wavelengths, but have different sensitivities across the spectrum. Hermann von Helmholtz adopted and developed this theory 50 years later, presenting the three hypothetical sensitivity curves shown: the x-axis shows each wavelength in the visible spectrum; the y-axis indicates how much of each of three single wavelengths is needed to match the appearance of each wavelength on the x-axis. Thus a single wavelength of 580 nm (which looks yellow) stimulates equally the beta and gamma cones; so does an equal mixture of two wavelengths of light—light of 530 nm (which looks green) and of 650 nm (which looks red) —so that a patch of 580 nm and one of 530 nm + 650 nm, will look the same (yellow).

All possible hues that can be seen at any point could be accounted for with these three types of receptors, each responding independently to a range of wavelengths. (We will consider an alternative theory in Figure 4.18.) The three types of receptors—cone cells, called for by this hypothesis, are now known to exist. In addition to these cones, we have the rod cells, which all respond similarly to different wavelengths and are therefore "color blind." A more detailed introductory treatment of this topic is in Goldstein, 1984, and surveys of recent research are found in Chapter 2 and in Boynton, 1979 and Hurvich, 1981.

wavelengths is needed to make a patch of light appear identical to each of the wavelengths in the spectrum?

Resolution is measured by procedures designed to determine the smallest gap that the viewer can detect (the *minimum separable*) at each point in the visual field, using patterns like those in Figure 4.7B. Dimensions in the retinal

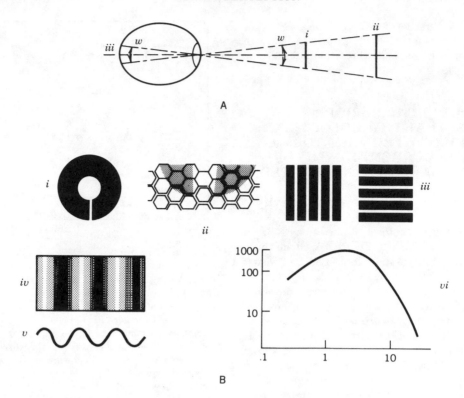

Figure 4.7. *Visual angle, acuity and resolution: a mosaic for the analysis of the retinal image.* The independent receptor cells in Helmholtz's theory (Figure 4.6) serve not only to analyze the myriad hues that we can perceive into three basic sensory responses. They also provide units for the analysis of any spatial patterns of light on the retinal image into a specific array of sensory responses. Imagine the retina as a sheet of receptors (rods and cones), each of which responds independently to the light that falls upon it. The size and spacing of the receptor cells then determine what detail can be discerned, and what patterns will be distinguishable or indistinguishable from each other.

(A) Note first that we measure the proximal visual stimulus in visual angle, ω, which provides the same information about the extent of the retinal image (iii) regardless of the distance of the object in space (i, ii).

(B) The main measure of *acuity*, or ability to resolve detail, is the smallest gap that can be detected, or *minimum separable*: for example, the viewer is given a ring like (i), with gaps of varying width, and required to detect the orientation (up, down, right, left). This measure is particularly appropriate for the mosaic model. Helmholtz thought that the minimum separable provided an estimate of cone size, by the logic of the sketch at (ii). An alternative measure that is frequently used is a grid (iii): the fineness of the lines and spacing is varied, and the subject's task is to detect the orientation of the lines.

In recent years, the gratings used have not been sharp, as at (iii), but are graded (iv) so as to provide a sine wave of brightness and darkness, as shown by the brightness curve at (v). The subject's task is to detect the presence or orientation of a grating of a particular fineness, or *spatial frequency* (number of cycles per degree of visual angle), and of a particular contrast (ratio of brightest portion to darkest portion); if the grating is undetectable, the contrast is increased. Obtaining this measure over a range of spatial frequencies generates contrast sensitivity functions, as at (vi), in which the x-axis is the range of spatial frequencies tested, and the y-axis is the contrast needed to detect the grating.

This measure has many practical advantages over the minimum separable for use in visual science and engineering; for example, it provides a more meaningful comparison of the limitations of some imaging and display system, such as a particular television device, and the capacities of the viewer's visual system. This measure is also theoretically interesting because it is compatible with the theory that the retinal image is analyzed by a set of spatial frequency channels— neural units of response that are most sensitive to a particular spatial frequency—just as the minimum separable is compatible with a mosaic picture of retinal function. The spatial-frequency channel theory is discussed on pp. 228ff in this chapter, and at greater length in Chapter 3.

image are measured in degrees of the *visual angle* subtended at the eye (Figure 4.7A). The familiar eye chart measures the minimum separable; in recent decades, the viewer's ability to detect the orientation of a grating of bars of dark and light that follow a sine function (Figure 7Biv) has been increasingly studied. The sine waves can be made to vary in amplitude or contrast (bright to dark ratio) and in *spatial frequency* (cycles per degree of visual angle; see Figure 4.7Bv). Such gratings are used to provide *contrast sensitivity functions* that indicate the amplitude of the bright to dark difference needed at each spatial frequency over the range of such frequencies as are being considered (Figure 4.7Bvi). One advantage of this measure is its applicability to the visual Fourier notions described on p. 228.

Factors Intervening Between Optic Array and Neural Counterpart

The optic array is only *potential* stimulus information. How much of that information will in fact be available in retinal response depends on the eye movements that the viewer elects to make and on the differences in detail that can be resolved at different places in the retina.

In fact, resolution or acuity falls off rapidly with eccentricity from the center of the retina, that is, the *fovea* in Figure 4.8. The fovea is only about 2 deg in extent. In order to obtain detailed information about any part of the optic array that is not within the fovea, therefore, the eye must be moved so as to bring the retinal image of that part of the array within the fovea. This is accomplished by a set of balanced muscles, external to each eye, that provide several distinct classes of eye movements, including the *ballistic saccades*: these are abrupt jumps in which the eye is so "tossed" as to bring to the fovea some point that fell initially in peripheral vision. Thus, the information in the optic array is not available to the nervous system until the eye has moved to bring different parts of it to the appropriately sensitive region within the retinal image. Indeed, how much of the array is ever projected as retinal image depends upon eye movements that the viewer *chooses* to make. These movements are chiefly saccades, and the saccades therefore comprise the basic oculomotor tool for the exploration of the optic array. Their essential characteristics are as

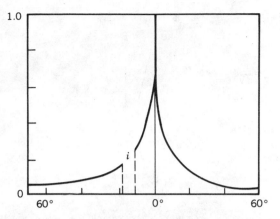

Figure 4.8. *The acuity distribution within the momentary glance: fovea versus periphery.* Regardless of the amount of information in the optic array, if the information is not picked up by the retina, it cannot affect our perceptions. The actual field of view within which we can pick up small detail, the *fovea*, is itself very small—approximately 1.5 degrees (about six or seven letters on this page at normal reading distance). Outside the fovea, in *peripheral vision*, only larger features can be discerned. The acuity distribution, as shown here, shows the percentage of maximum acuity (as measured by the minimum separable in Figure 4.7) that is available at the different degrees of eccentricity (in visual angle) from the center of the fovea (at 0 degrees on the figure). The gap at (i) is the blind spot, where the optic nerve exits the retina, and where no visual information is acquired.

follows:

1. In order to preserve the spatial information in the retinal image (e.g., that a red point lies between a blue point and another red point, or that the three lie on the corners of a triangle), our visual systems must be able to identify *where* each part of the retina lies with respect to the other parts. Each receptor—or group of receptors —must have its own *local sign* (Riggs, 1964). With each saccade, the correspondence between each local sign and the optic array changes (Figure 4.9), so that the images on the retina are constantly moving. Despite this movement of the retinal image, however, the world does not in general seem to move. Why is that? Several possible answers have received attention. *Suppression* is one possibility, in other words, displacements of the

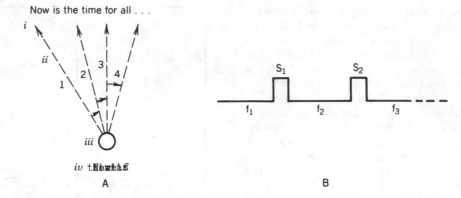

Figure 4.9. *The glances that sample the optic array.* In order to bring detail from different parts of the optic array to foveal vision, the eye moves by means of *ballistic saccades*—jumps that are not guided en route, but that move the fovea abruptly to a specific place previously seen only in peripheral vision.

(A) Reading displays some of the essential features of saccadic eye movements. Note first that such movements are *elective*: the viewer is not compelled by the stimulus pattern to make these movements but undertakes them in order to answer a visual question. Confronted by the strings of letters (i), the reader might take the four glances (ii), directing the eye (iii) successively as shown.

(B) The eye pauses during fixation periods (f1, f2, f3) that are at least 150 to 200 msec long. The saccades themselves (s1, s2) occupy a shorter interval (say, 50 msec), so that the actual rate of movement is a sporadic function as shown.

The fact that the eye can bring some feature that falls in peripheral vision to the fovea implies that the retina has a set of *local signs* that identify the retinal location of any particular stimulus. But the spatial (distal) significance of the local sign must change with each eye movement. The viewer must be able to separate the views from each other and to some degree to keep track of how the successive glimpses fit together. Lacking these abilities, the first four foveal views of the sentence at (Ai) would merely be the superimposed jumble at (Aiv).

retinal image that occur subsequent to saccades might be ignored or suppressed (Wallach and Lewis, 1966; Sperling and Speelman, 1965). Another possibility is *compensation*. The amount that the eye had been signaled to move might be subtracted from the displacement of the image (Helmholtz, 1863; von Holst, 1954). Still another is that we respond to what is *invariant* despite the translation or displacement of the retinal image. When we move our eye, all parts of the visual field are displaced together and essentially to an equal extent in the retinal image, so that relationships within the image remain unchanged. This might be the stimulus that leads us to perceive a change in viewing direction rather than movement of environment (Gibson, 1950; Johansson, 1977). For recent analyses and review, see Matin (1982, 1986).

2. Whether a saccade will be made, and where it will be directed, depends both on

the viewer's task and on the pattern of stimulation available to peripheral vision, that is the retinal image well outside the fovea (Buswell, 1935; Hochberg & Brooks, 1978). This is now an important field of research in connection with the reading process (McConkie & Rayner, 1975; McConkie & Zola, 1984), but its general importance is this: the optic array is only *potential* stimulus information, and how much of it is even sampled by the retinal image depends upon the saccades that the viewer elects to make.

3. Saccades are rapidly executed, but have relatively long latencies (Figure 4.9B), so that three or four per second is about the highest rate that can be sustained. The information that is obtained from two separate places in the optic array may be separated by substantial periods of time, therefore these processes are even slower than saccadic movements, especially if the places are at different distances so that the

eyes, focus and angle of convergence must change (see Figure 4.3; Hallett, 1986).

All this makes the relationship between the optic array and our perceptions of the world more remote and precarious. Two other factors that affect the relationship between the optic array and the retinal image depend on internal muscles of the eye: the curvature of the eye's lens (its *accommodation*) and the size of the pupil (or aperture in the iris). The lens changes in its curvature in order to help bring the light from objects that lie at different distances from the eye to form a focused image on the retina. The curvature, or degree of accommodation, is (within certain limits) different, depending on the distance of the objects that are in focus. The degree of accommodation therefore provides a potential depth cue (Gogel, 1969b; Hochberg, 1971; Owens & Leibowitz, 1976; Wallach & Floor, 1971). This is also a source of potential information about space, but it is not information that is included in present accounts of the optic array, and indeed we must note that only those parts of the array that are in sharp focus at any time will provide detail within the retinal image.

Theoretical and Practical Uses of Such Analyses and Findings

Such research provides the basis for visual science and its many applications—from the prescription of spectacles to the design of television characteristics. It was also the foundation of the classical view of the perceptual process in general. That view is diagrammed in Figure 4.10. First comes the physical object, with its distal physical properties of distance, size, shape, reflectance (surface color). These properties affect the visual sense only through the light they reflect to the sensitive rods and cones. All things that cause these cells to respond in the same way elicit the same sensory experience, such as the light coming from the object itself, the light produced by some surrogate of that object, the effects of mechanical or electrical stimulation of the eye, and so on. The response to a set of different events in terms of a smaller number of events comprises an *encoding process*. Since different objects and events can produce the same responses, information about the world clearly is lost in this

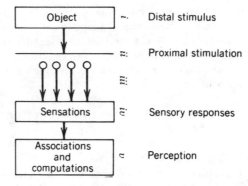

Figure 4.10. *The classical model of perception.* A simple schematic diagram of the classical theory starts with (i) the Distal Stimulus—attributes of some object, such as its size, reflectance, position in space, and so on. These are reflected in (ii) the pattern of Proximal Stimulation, which consists of the parcels of differing visual angle, ω, that differ in their luminance and wavelength. Because of the regularities in the world, the proximal stimulus pattern will contain informative patterns or cues about the physical properties of objects and layouts in the world. The proximal stimulus pattern is analyzed by (iii), the sensory receptors, which provide sensory responses that vary at each point in color and brightness and that are patterned according to the cues in the proximal stimulus pattern. Drawing on associations that have been built up in dealing with the world, we perceive (v), those distal object properties of size, reflectance, position in space, and so on, that are most likely to have provided the set of sensory responses (iv).

encoding process. This is what makes surrogates possible, and provides a tool with which to study the structure and function of the nervous system.

This conception of the visual system is now exemplified by the television camera. Television, like the Helmholtzian visual system, analyzes the countless objects and events of the world into the different combinations of a set of three colors arrayed in a spatial mosaic. It is important that such a simple set will suffice both for the Helmholtzian theory and for television as a medium. In both cases, the remaining properties of the objects that we perceive in the world—their bodily sizes and forms, their reflectances, their distances and movements in three-dimensional space—all go beyond the stimulus per se, and must therefore be supplied by the viewer.

The simplest theory about how the viewer

supplies those properties was inherited from the centuries of philosophical empiricism that we outlined above, that is, that we have learned the perceptual properties of objects from our experiences with the world. We now turn to a further description of empiricism.

Psychological Theories of Perception: Mental Structure

The Constancies

The problem that empiricism was intended to solve is illustrated in Figures 4.11 and 4.12: In most situations in the real world, the region of stimulation that is projected to the eye does not by itself provide information about object properties. Even if the two gray disks on the cube (Figure 4.11) are of identical lightness of *reflectance* (R), the luminous energy each provides to the eye is different (L_1, L_2) if the illumination falling on each is different (E_1, E_2). Another example of how the stimulation projected to the eye by an object does not provide information about the object's properties is shown in Figure 4.12, in which two rods of the same physical size are at different distances. Even when the two rods are of the same physical size (H), the size of the retinal image each provides differs if the rods lie at different distances (Di, Dii).

Nevertheless we tend to perceive such object properties correctly, despite changing retinal stimulation. There is a considerable literature based on the following paradigm. The subject is asked to choose that value of some distal property of one object (e.g., its reflectance or its size) that will cause it to appear equal to another object in what may be a different situation (e.g., under different illumination or distance). For virtually every case in which we can vary distal and proximal properties independently—size and retinal extent, reflectances and luminance at the eye, perceived place in space and direction of gaze—the matches that subjects make are, at least under certain task instructions (Brunswik, 1956; Leibowitz & Harvey, 1967), closer to distal than to proximal equality. That is, subjects tend to judge two physically identical rods as equal even when their retinal images are different. For a general systematic review, see Hochberg (1971) and a collection of readings by Epstein (1977).

The classical theory held that this *object con-*

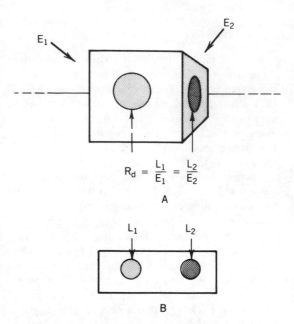

$$R_d = \frac{L_1}{E_1} = \frac{L_2}{E_2}$$

A

B

Figure 4.11. *Constancy of object properties: reflectance.* Objects may be the same or may differ in their reflectance, that is, in the percentage of the light falling on them that they reflect to the eye—and they may also receive equal or different illumination. (A) The two disks here are unequally illuminated (E1, E2). The luminances that each provides the eye are therefore different: L1 = R1 × E1, L2 = R2 × E2. If the two disks have equal reflectances, the two luminances will differ. Viewed without context—through what is called a *reduction screen* (B), which is some device that obscures the surroundings—they indeed look different. Nevertheless, despite such changes in luminance, when viewed in context (A) the reflectances tend to appear equal. In the classical theory, the perceived illuminations (E) are taken into account in arriving at perceptions of reflectance. Solving for reflectance, we get R = L ÷ E, and since the disk's reflectances (Rd) are in fact equal, the ratios of L ÷ E are equal.

Similar constancy is found for hue, so the general term color constancy is often used. For more detailed introductory treatment, see Goldstein, 1984; for a comprehensive survey of the earlier literature on this issue, see Hochberg, 1971.

stancy, as it is now known, is achieved when the viewer takes the conditions of seeing into account, in effect by using the depth cues in Figure 4.12B to perceive depths i and ii, and then using the latter to infer the object sizes from the retinal sizes; or similarly, by using cues to perceive the illuminations E_1 and E_2 in Figure 4.11 and then by using the latter to infer the

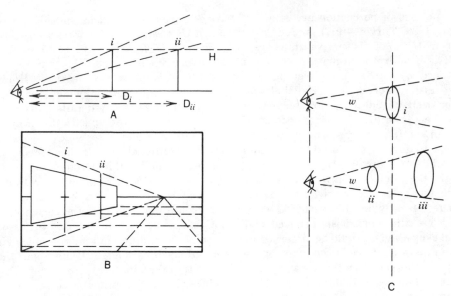

Figure 4.12. *Constancy of object properties: size.* As we have seen in Figures 4.1B and 4.7A, as an object's distance changes, its visual angle changes. At (A), each pole of height (H) and at distance (D) provides a visual angle ω = arc tan H ÷ D.

(B) Nevertheless, the perceived size of invariant objects tends to be constant when viewed in context (see Figure 4.1C), at least for near distances (although we should note that the degree of size constancy depends on the viewer's attitude, i.e., whether instructed to attend to distal or proximal size; Brunswik, 1956; Leibowitz and Harvey, 1967). Within the classical model, the explanation is that we perceive size by taking perceived distance into account, and that in turn must depend on appropriate use of the depth cues (Figures 4.2 and 4.3).

(C) A strong example of the relationship between perceived size and perceived distance should make this point clear. After looking at a strong light at some distance (i), the retina is left with an afterimage of fixed size (ω). If the viewer now looks at a nearer or a more distant surface, the after image will look smaller (ii) or larger (iii), as it must in order to fit the formula, H = D × tan ω. The fact that the size of the afterimage appears proportional to the distance of the surface on which it is seen to lie is called *Emmert's Law.*

For a more detailed introductory treatment, see Goldstein, 1984. For discussions of the extensive research literature, see Hochberg, 1971, Epstein, 1977, and Sedgwick, 1986.

reflectances of the parts of the scene from their luminances.

This explanation is now commonly called *unconscious inference.* It assumes that the viewer has learned the constraints in the physical world (e.g., that $L = R \times I$, etc.). These constraints, once learned, provide a mental structure that mirrors the physical relationship between the attributes of the object and those of sensory stimulation, permitting the viewer to infer or compute the former from the latter.

The empiricist theory is attractive for three reasons. First, it is economical. Only as much innate structure is attributed to the organism as is needed to respond differently to the different discernible fundamental properties, and these are chosen as the smallest set into which the sensory world can be analyzed. The rest of the nervous system need have no structure except to learn (or to form associations). In the second place, at a time when only mechanical views of casual explanation were available for thinking about such things, it did not seem plausible that sensory mechanisms could exist that would respond directly to distance or to other distal properties in general. Third, because learning from the world so readily accounts for the perception of distal properties, it is not logically necessary to think up and speculate about possible innate mechanisms.

This account of perceptual inferences is a *psychological* theory of perception, one that is still of considerable influence. It has many adherents today (e.g., Gillam, Gregory, Rock), but even if it did not it would still be important, if only because it is named as the target whenever empiricist theories of perception are attacked (see Gibson, 1966; Turvey, 1977), and because significant features of it survive in current theories. It is usually the arguments that had been advanced by earlier empiricist philosophers that are attacked. The Helmholtzian account, as well as contemporary empiricist theories, differ from the earlier versions of empiricism in significant ways, as they must in order to come to terms with more than 250 years of thought and 100 years of data.

Although their critics have not always noticed the fact, classical empiricist theories have changed greatly in the last 250 years. Several of the earlier empiricists believed that the simplest sensory ideas could be discerned by careful examination of one's thoughts or by introspection, whereas later theorists since at least the time of James Mill, John Stuart Mill, and Hermann von Helmholtz have assumed that the fundamental units or elements of perception are *not* open to introspection, and therefore cannot be directly observed, but instead must be arrived at by indirect means. Furthermore, just as the experience of "white" is not deducible from its components—that is, white is not a reddish-greenish-bluish color—so in general the way things look cannot be predicted from the appearances of the simple sensations to which the proximal stimulus gives rise. The elements of perceptual experience and the processes by which they combine have thus both been relegated to the status of hidden machinery, leaving them without immediate consequence in the explanation or prediction of perception.

The theory has changed in other critical ways as well. To Berkeley, what is learned and brought to each perceptual situation is a specific set of associations (e.g., the number of paces discussed in connection with Figure 4.1B). To Helmholtz, approximately 150 years later, the viewer has learned a set of *expectations* (e.g., expectations about how the proximal stimulation would change if the viewer moves slightly to the left, etc.). In these accounts of perception, it is the set of such expectations that comprise our perception of the object, and those expectations follow *rules* that are learned from the regularities of the environment.

To paraphrase somewhat, the major predictive constraint that is offered by Helmholtz to link perception and proximal stimulation is this:

We perceive just that distal state of affairs in the world that would, under normal circumstances, provide the effective proximal stimulus distribution we receive.

This formula is the heart of Helmholtz's position and is accepted by many psychologists today (pp. 213f). Many details must be spelled out, however, before this explanation can be made either usable or testable. We should note now that although the classical theory is often treated as monolithic (Köhler, 1929; Koffka, 1935; Gibson, 1966), Helmholtz's rule does not necessarily entail either the notion that sensations are the elements of experience, nor the notion that perception is based on associative learning. Very different kinds of underlying perceptual machinery might bring about the same perceptual principle.

Indeed, the learning processes that could underlie the computations that are implied by Helmholtz's rule have never been formally and explicitly worked out. What we would now call *look-up tables* (e.g., with grouped entries for L, E and R) would be compatible with theories about associative learning. However, Helmholtz and others often wrote as though we learn to apply the *rules* that mirror those of the physical world. But they do not say explicitly by what processes such abstract principles—as distinguished from look-up tables listing the elements of sense data—are learned.

It is therefore misleading to propose some version of Helmholtz's rule, as many theorists have done over the years, while still claiming that in so doing one is opposing Helmholtz. Some better justification for one's pronouncements should be found.

In summary, according to the classical theory the sense organs analyze the world into *fundamental sensations*, and those sensations normally occur in characteristic patterns because of the regularities of the physical world (the depth cues in Figure 4.2 are examples of such characteristic patterns).

By learning these regularities and their meanings, it was held, we learn to perceive the physical world and its properties. Thus, the constancies are thought of as interactions that occur between responses to the parts of a pattern or scene, so that the response to one region depends on the response to another. Since the elements of the sensory nervous system that analyze the scene were thought to be independent of each other, the interaction was attributed to some central process by which the inference is executed, so that the interaction is an adaptation to the physical regularities of the world.

But there are other interactions—also known for centuries—that require explanation, for example, the *illusions*, which must be seriously considered by any theory in which perception is thought to reflect the structure of the world.

The Illusions

As artists and architects have known since antiquity, the physical properties that we perceive rarely coincide with those we measure. It is currently fashionable to emphasize that we normally perceive the world *veridically*, that is, in accordance with physical measure, but the facts do not support this assertion. Robust and systematic perceptual errors, or illusions, are manifest in every dimension that can be measured. Erroneous perceptions of length, size, shape (or curvature), and angle appear, with the names normally attributed to them, in the geometric illusions of Figure 4.13. And lightness contrast makes the identical gray half-rings in Figure 4.14 appear of different lightness at the top.

Such errors appear at first to provide a serious challenge to the explanation of the constancies that we have just considered. The classical explanation of the constancies was, as we have just seen, that they result from perceptual learning of the regularities in the world —that we take the depth cues into account in judging objects' sizes, take the cues to illumination into account in judging their lightnesses, and so on. As an explanation of the constancies, it sounds plausible that our perceptual experience with the world should teach us to perceive it correctly. It is not self-evident, however, why such experience should cause us to experience illusions, although we will see that just that explanation has in fact been offered for most of the illusions.

Many psychologists today, following Helmholtz, explain the illusions as examples of the principle that I have called Helmholtz's rule. Helmholt explained contrast (Figure 4.14A), as a mistaken inference that occurs because we habitually base our estimates of the illumination, E, on the luminance that would be provided by surrounds of average reflectance. A

surround of abnormally high reflectance leads to an overestimate of E, and therefore to an underestimate of $R(t)$. And many psychologists have, over the years, argued that at least some of the geometrical illusions, such as the Müller-Lyer (Figure 4.13A) and the Ponzo illusion (Figure 4.13C) result from "misapplied size constancy" (Thiery, 1896; Tolman and Brunswik, 1935; Tausch, 1954; Gregory, 1963). Distance must be discounted in judging size (Figure 4.1C; see Emmert's law, in Figure 4.12C). In the real world, systematically converging contours are normally the sign of distance (Figure 4.2); so in the patterns of Figures 4.13A and 4.13C the diagonal lines affect the apparent length of the lines they enclose in a way that would normally provide size constancy but here provides an illusion. Many psychologists today support some version of this perspective explanation (Day, 1972; Gillam, 1971; Gregory, 1963; Kaufman and Rock, 1962; Leibowitz and Pick, 1972), and anthropological data have been brought to its support (Segal, Campbell, & Herskowitz, 1966). It should be stressed however that these illusions can be explained on other grounds (see Coren and Girgus 1978; Hochberg, 1971), that the anthropological evidence has been questioned (Jahoda, 1966), and that it is not clear how other illusions such as Figure 4.13D can be explained in these terms. It seems probable that the stronger illusions, which include 4.13A and 4.13D, are multiply caused. If even some of the phenomena are due not to experience but to interactions between the receptors—a lack of independence in their spatial contributions— that is an important limitation on the strong empiricist position and what it can accomplish. But if even only some of the illusory phenomena are due to unconscious inference, that fact would be important in assessing those theories that aspire to greater parsimony by dispensing with unconscious inference (the so-called direct theories, p. 240ff). For reviews of the literature see Hochberg, 1971; Kaufman, 1974; and Coren and Girgus, 1978.

As summarized in this simple way, the classical theory seemed to be economical and elegant, and the principles of learning seemed to be at hand. From Hobbes in 1651 to James Mill in 1829, the British empiricist philosophers had discussed in great detail how the laws of association, offered in essence by Aristotle, would serve to build from those simple sensations our

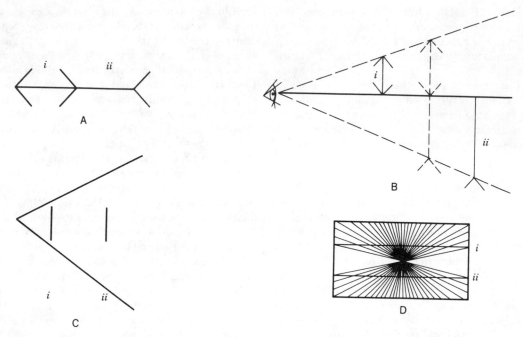

Figure 4.13. *Misperceptions of object properties: the "geometrical illusions."* Figure 4.12 was concerned with perceptual departures from the proximal stimulus (ω) in the direction of correct perception of distal (object) size. A large class of deviations from both distal and proximal values, known for well over a century, are called *illusions*. The geometrical illusions are misperceptions of size or shape. Three particularly robust illusions are shown here. In (A) and (C), i and ii are in fact of equal size; in (D), they are straight and parallel.

(A) Müller-Lyer illusion.

(B) It is to be expected from the classical model in Figure 4.10 that we tend to see the world correctly (i.e., as in Figures 4.11 and 4.12), but at first thought the illusions would appear to be inexplicable by that account. Further thought suggests explanations consistent with the classical model in many cases. If the diagonal lines on the pattern at (A) act as the depth cue of linear perspective (Figure 4.2), side i will be taken as nearer and hence smaller (see Figure 4.12B) and side ii will be taken as farther and hence larger. This account will also apply to other illusions, like (C), but it is strained or inapplicable to others, like (D).

(C) Ponzo illusion.

(D) Hering illusion.

Although they are often dismissed as curiosities, specific to artificial arrangements like lines on paper, the illusions occur in profusion in the real world. Architects since the ancient Greeks have learned what curves and compensations are needed to make horizontal stairs and vertical columns look straight, fashion designers devise shoes and dresses that make the wearer's feet and body look slimmer, and the vast industry of moving picture communication (film and television) rests on illusory movement and space. Illusions are important, therefore, not only because they tell us something about perception, but also because of their practical importance for such disciplines as architecture and graphic arts. For surveys of research and theories of the illusions, see Hochberg, 1971; Coren and Girgus, 1978.

perceptions and ideas about the objects and events of the world.

What I am calling the classical theory of perception thus had wide and deep connections with the mainstream of Western thought, and it remained the dominant theory in neurophysiology and psychology until the 1950s.

The Opposition and the Issues

The classical theory was dominant, but not without substantial opposition. The opposition to the classical theory rested (and still rests) on the question of what aspects of perception depend on the innate structure of the nervous

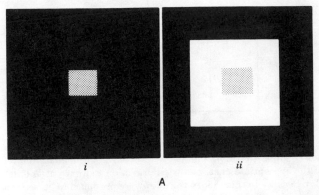

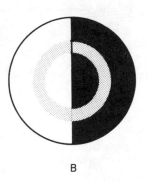

Figure 4.14. *Misperceptions of lightness: contrast.* As illusions of size are the counterpart of size constancy, illusions of color are the counterpart of color constancy. (A) The central targets in (i) and (ii) are equal in reflectance and in luminance, but (ii) is normally judged as darker. The effect is called *contrast*, a term which is also used to refer to the ratio of bright to dark (see Figure 4.7Biv). Another example, a modification of the Benussi figure (Hochberg, 1971) at (B), may work better on the printed page. The two halves of the gray ring, which is in fact homogeneous in reflectance (as may be seen by looking at the bottom), appear of unequal lightness if you look at the top.

Helmholt'z explanation of contrast is as we would now expect from the discussion in Figures 4.11 to 4.13. We base our estimate of illumination E on the luminance Ls, provided by the surround; when the surround is light (has a high reflectance) we overestimate E and therefore underestimate L, in deriving our perception of the reflectance of target Rt from the luminance Lt it provides. For discussion of literature on contrast, see Kaufman 1974, Hochberg, 1971 and Hurvich, 1981. We are further concerned with contrast, and its relationship to constancy, in pp. 223ff.

system and what is acquired through perceptual learning. The theory was opposed because it failed to account for the way the world looks (as distinct from what stimuli are indistinguishable); and it was criticized as being uneconomical. We consider these criticisms in turn.

Nativism versus Empiricism

The classical empiricist position rests on two arguments, closely related to each other in philosophy and theology but quite unrelated in psychology and physiology. The first argument was that proximal stimulation is inherently ambiguous (as we have seen it must be: see Figure 4.1), that is, that it could not give information about the world that we must accept with absolute certainty. Now this point is important to any philosophical inquiry into the question of what we can know for certain (in particular, to that branch of philosophy called *epistemology*, which is concerned with the criteria for knowing that something is true). In these terms, proximal stimulation simply *cannot* provide infallible information about the world. But that does not mean that it would be useless or harmful if an infant were born already "prewired" to respond to some of the features of

proximal stimulation. A depth cue has "high ecological validity" (Brunswik, 1956); that is, the cue is correct in most cases, and would be wrong only very infrequently. If any specific depth cue such as linear perspective (Figure 4.2) or motion perspective (Figure 4.4A) had a high but not perfect ecological validity, there would be an evolutionary advantage if the species were natively endowed to perceive depth directly in response to that proximal stimulus pattern. Some of the time the cue would be wrong (e.g., Figures 4.13A, C), and by relying on it one would be making a perceptual error, *but the same would be true of such reliance on the cue even if it were learned and not innate.*

Some cues are almost certainly not innate. Consider *familiar size* as a cue to an object's distance (as in Figures 4.15A and 4.15B). Or imagine that you recognize the sphere in Figure 4.1A to be some ball with which you are familiar: Because a ball might be almost any size, and only your experience with this one allows you to use that size to judge its distance, the cue could not be innate. Similarly, the *familiar color* of some object, such as an orange, might act as a cue to its illumination, or the *familiar shape* of some object like a tennis racquet might act as a

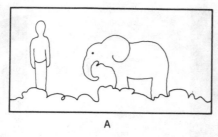
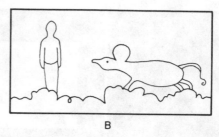

A   B

Figure 4.15. *Familiar size: a pure case of the classical model.* In the characteristic classical explanation for both perception (Figures 4.11, 4.12) and misperception (Figures 4.13, 4.14), one perception (e.g., of illumination or of distance), based on the learned significance of the appropriate cues, has been drawn on to arrive at another perception (e.g., reflectance or size, respectively). Because in this theory the cues were presumed to be learned by their association with other consequences of depth, the theory is called *associationist.* Because the viewer is not aware of perceiving the intermediate property (e.g., distance in Figure 4.13B, or illumination in Figure 4.14), or of making the calculations that are implied in those examples, this kind of explanation is termed *unconscious inference.*

Other explanations are available for all of these phenomena, as we will see. Only one class of cues actually *demands* an explanation in terms of associative learning: those cues based on familiar size, familiar color, and so on. In order to work, the depth cue of familiar size requires that the viewer *must* be basing depth perceptions on associative memories of the sizes of elephants, mice and so on. In pictures, the results are weak at best: is the man nearer or farther in (A)? in (B)?

The effect has been under dispute for years. See Gogel, 1977, and Hochberg, 1978, for reviews of this literature. The effect appears to be greater the more lifelike the presentation (Epstein, 1961). To the degree that this cue participates in normal depth perceptions, an irreducible minimum of associative learning and inference is involved in the perceptual process.

cue to an object's orientation or its continuation behind some other occluding surface (see Figures 4.32 and 4.33). Because their association with other object properties are arbitrary, these cues, if they are effective at all, can only result from the individual's experience with the world.

But most other cues are not arbitrary in this way: They do not depend on knowing the *particular* distal stimulus object. They can therefore be defined in ways that do not inherently involve any associative learning by the individual. And they can therefore be attributed to innate responses to the proximal stimulus patterns just as easily as to learned responses. *Phylogenetic* adaptation to the information in the sensory environment may have occurred through evolution, making unnecessary any *ontogenetic* adaptation (within the individual's development and learning).

This is the nativist—as opposed to the empiricist—position. Lest it seem mystical, consider the following argument. The perceptual learning that is supposed to occur according to empiricist theories must, after all, consist of specific changes in the nervous system. Whatever those changes might be, the resulting struc-

tures (or functionally equivalent ones) could just as well have been provided by inheritance.

This is an old argument, and it seems valid, but the mere fact that nativism is defensible does not make it true in any given case—nor even useful, unless we can specify what aspects of proximal information are innately used as the bases for the perception of the distal properties, and what the general consequences of those facts are. The fact is that the cue of familiar size does work, as noted in the caption of Figure 4.15 (Epstein, 1965; Dinnerstein, 1967; Ono, 1969; Eriksson and Zetterberg, 1975), and that fact means that learning of an associationist sort must also participate in the perceptual process. We will see that some of the structure found in perception is almost certainly due to the innate structure of the nervous system, as nativists would have it, but that this does not mean that associative learning plays no part in perception.

The Need to Account for Appearances: Deriving Physiology from Phenomenology

Some of the opposition to the classical theory was based on a cluster of purely psychological inadequacies: For example, although the theory tells us which different objects will produce the same perceptual experience—what wavelength mixtures, for example, will appear indistinguishable in color—it does not predict the experience itelf, that is, how that color seems similar to and different from other colors. As we will see, alternative theories, almost as old as the Young-Helmholtz theory (Figure 4.6), account much better for appearance.

The close study of appearances as such, as distinct from knowledge about the thing being perceived, is known as *phenomenology*. Notable among early proposals based on phenomenology were those offered by Hering and by Mach.

Hering (1878) argued that the colors we perceive consist of red *or* green, yellow *or* blue, and black *or* white, organized into opponent pairs so that only one of each pair can be experienced at any point. The appearance of each mixture is then given by those of its components (e.g., a red and a yellow yield a red- yellow, or orange). He also proposed that the connections between cells of the two retinas provided for a direct and innate sense of depth. And he held that lightness contrast and constancy are not the results of judgmental processes, but are direct sensory experiences that result from lateral inhibition between adjacent regions of the visual system (see Figure 4.16, and Chapter 2, for discussions and definitions of lateral inhibition).

In 1886, basing his discussions on what the boundaries between abrupt and less abrupt changes in brightness look like (Figure 4.16C), Mach proposed (among other things) that lateral connections between neurons in the retina provide networks that are sensitive to contours and not merely to incident energy, and argued that networks of such connections would respond directly to simple patterns in the retinal image. We now know that our visual systems are fundamentally responsive to change and differences (Figure 4.16A, B) and Mach's speculation about pattern-sensitive networks has been vindicated in the last few decades by the discovery of complex networks at various levels of the nervous system that respond to patterns and movements of many kinds (for recent reviews, see Braddick, Campbell, & Atkinson, 1978; Graham, 1981; Olzak & Thomas, 1986; see also Chapter 3).

These speculations about lateral inhibition, hue, and contrast, which have proved to be remarkably prophetic, are particularly interesting for two reasons: (1) their views of physiology were designed to fit the more evident phenomenological facts of perception, that is, what things look like, and (2) in order to do this, they proposed specific physiological mechanisms that by their construction make direct comparisons and calculations from the relations within the proximal stimulation, instead of leaving the computations to be done by general processes of association and computation.

Is Mental Structure Necessary?

Because of the nonsensory components in the classical explanation, it has been called an *indirect* theory of perception. Because the explanation assumes that a form of inference or problem-solving is inherent in perception, it has been called a *cognitive* theory of perception. Because the perceiver is unaware of any of the components, it has been characterized as unconscious inference from unnoticed sensations (Koffka, 1935). And because in this explanation, one percept, such as size, is explained as being caused by a process involving another percept, such as distance, which is itself a subjective or mental variable, the explanation has been called *mentalistic*. That term was meant as a condemnation during the long period in which Behaviorism dominated psychological theory, and such indictments have been given as reasons to abandon this class of explanation. Above all, the general classical theory often seems cumbersome and uneconomical when applied to individual cases. We must keep in mind, however, that it may seem considerably more economical than its individual competitors when offered as an overall explanation for a wide variety of phenomena.

The Gestaltist Alternative: Forms as Invariants

Both Mach and Hering were phenomenologists in the restricted sense in which I have used this term. A much more concerted effort to base our understanding of neurophysiology on phenomenology was made by the Gestalt psychologists, starting with the work of Wertheimer in 1923.

Gestalt theory was specifically opposed to the classical view that the direct responses (or fundamental sensations) of the nervous system occur independently to each small region of stimulation, and that perception is built up from

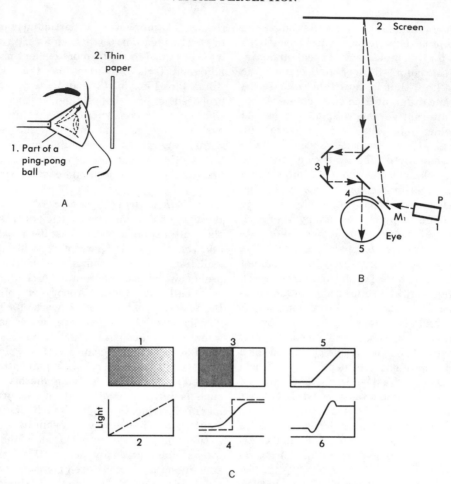

Figure 4.16. *Contours, inhibition and the importance of change.* In the classical analysis, the pattern of photic energy in the proximal stimulus is analyzed by independent sensory elements, and the resulting sensations reflect only local luminance and wavelength (spectral luminance) at each point in the retinal image. We now know that is false. There are lateral connections between the neurons, not merely a transmission chain to the brain; some of those connections are inhibitory; and the resulting networks are responsive more to change over time and space than to the local physical properties per se.

(A) A homogeneous optic array and retinal image (or *Ganzfeld*) of some uniform hue and luminance, as is most simply achieved by placing halved ping-pong balls over the eyes, quickly fades to dark gray; when the eyes are closed and reopened, the color reappears briefly, as it does with contours (shadows) in the field of view (Hochberg, Triebel, & Seaman, 1951).

(B) Contours too will disappear if their image is held stationary on the retina. Retinal images can be stabilized, or made independent of eye movements, in various ways. One way, is to provide an afterimage; in another a beam is projected through a mirror (M) mounted on a contact lens (4) that casts an image on the screen (2), which moves to compensate exactly any eye movement, as shown here (Riggs et al., 1953).

(C) Contours are not merely a transition from dark to light: they are positive responses that reveal the operation of lateral connections. A gradient from dark to light is shown at (1), and a graph of that gradient is shown at (2). An abrupt change in the reflectance of the printed area is shown at (3), graphed by the dotted line at (4). Because of the imperfect optics of the eye, that abrupt change is blurred and softened in the retinal image, as shown by the solid line in (4). The visual response to (5) is shown at (6). The gradient is sharpened and the contour is enhanced. Notice, however, that as part of this enhancement, a dark band appears on the dark side, a light band on the light side. These are *Mach bands*, illusory stripes that Mach explained in 1865 (see Mach, 1906; Ratliff, 1965) as being part of a process of lateral inhibition to which he attributed contour formation. If we imagine several receptors straddling the contour, each of which inhibits the other as well as transmitting these fundamental sensations by associative learning. Instead of such *punctiform* response, the nervous system is so structured or organized as to respond directly to the configuration (or *Gestalt*, in German) of the stimulus pattern impinging on the sense organ. According to the views of this theory's founder, Max Wertheimer (1923), and of its two most prominent advocates, Kurt Koffka (1935) and Wolfgang Köhler (1929), our nervous system responds directly to the *form* of patterns found in proximal stimulation. A melody transposed remains the same effective stimulus, even though every note is different, because its form is unchanged (von Hornbostel, 1926; Wertheimer, 1923). A particular shape—say, a square—remains a square, even when it falls on a different part of the retina (as when it or the eye moves; Figure 4.17A); or when its size on the retina changes because its distance changes (Figure 4.17B); or when it is presented in different colors—which are presumably the fundamental elements in the classical theory that Gestaltists opposed—and outlines (Figure 4.17C) or by no colors or outlines at all (Figures 4.17D). We will consider the main features of this theory and of its physiological speculations in the next section. Most of the Gestaltists' formulations, however, were in fact concerned only with the *patterning* of stimulation, and we consider those formulations here.

The central formulation was that the whole form, rather than its individual component points or patches, are the fundamental elements of neural response and perceptual experience. The form of the square remains *invariant* as it undergoes the transformations in Figures 4.17A to D, so both the neural response and the perceived form also remain invariant. (Note that

according to this view slant or shape constancy follows without any appeal to past experience.) Nor should we equate "form" with proximal stimulus pattern. In Figures 4.17Fii and iii, the same patterned line is perceived as bounding a vase and two faces, respectively, even though it stimulates exactly the same set of receptors and (according to the classical theory) provides the same set of fundamental visual elements.

Figure 4.17F also illustrates the *figure-ground* phenomenon, studied by Rubin (1921) and taken by the Gestalt theorists as a fundamental distinction in perception. In Figure 17Fii the vase is figure; in iii, the faces are figure. Any part of a contour can serve to give shape to (belong to) one of the areas it bounds, or the other, but not both simultaneously. The *figure* has shape, is normally perceived in front, and has surface quality; the *ground* has no recognizable shape, appearing to continue to some indefinite extent behind the figure, and is softer or more amorphous in surface quality. In order for some shape to be seen or some object to be recognized, it must be organized as figure, and that was said to depend on the total configuration. The whole organization determines the appearance of its parts (sometimes paraphrased as the whole is more than the sum of its parts). We will see later that neither of these supposedly factual assertions can be accepted as stated (p. 239).

Movement, figure-ground differentiation, and spatial form are, to the Gestaltists, all fundamental perceptual properties, not derived from sensations of color, and indeed more basic than the latter. These properties were held to result directly from the way in which the nervous system responds to the total pattern of

---

impulses to higher centers, the Mach bands are generated appropriately. The effects of a number of different assumptions about underlying networks are explored by Ratliff, 1965.

Mach proposed that contours occur only when the rate of change in luminance is steep enough, and then the more intensely stimulated region inhibits its neighbor more than it is inhibited, thus accentuating the difference, or contrast, between them. These effects do not extend very far (Leibowitz, Mote, & Thurlow, 1953), but the differences in response at the contour are especially important in determining the overall appearance of two regions, and more gradual changes in luminance within the contours that bound a region have little effect on its apparent lightness. Further treatment appears in Chapter 2, Goldstein, 1984, Kaufman, 1974, and Olzak & Thomas (1986).

Contours are obviously crucial to the perception of a definite shape, and their study therefore comprises a first step toward the understanding of shape and object perception, but we should note that contours can be perceived where no luminance differences are present, revealing the operation of higher processes that are still not understood, but that appear to be related to the completion phenomena described in connection with Figures 4.32 and 4.33.

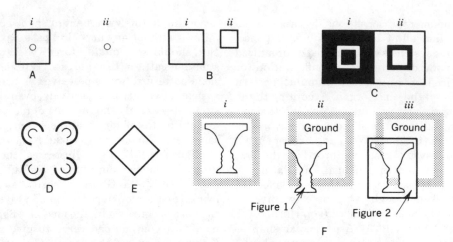

Figure 4.17. *Gestalt properties: invariance of form under transformation; figure versus ground.* A vigorous opposition to the classical model was based on its failure to account for perceived qualities. To Gestalt psychology, *form* is a direct response to the configuration or overall pattern of the contours in the proximal stimulus pattern. The first point is that the perceived form remains invariant, regardless of what receptors are stimulated, so long as the configuration is the same. At (A), the square looks unchanged as you switch your gaze from (i) to (ii), even though totally different receptors are involved. Likewise at (B) and (C), the square remains the same form at (i) and (ii), although very different sets of receptors are involved. At (D), not even the same contours are present, yet the square remains a square.

The invariance of form under transformation is a central problem for the study of perception, but for just that reason we should not misstate the problem by assuming more invariance than obtains; at (E), for example, the square when rotated has become something quite different in appearance—a diamond.

Gestalt theorists took as their primary perceptual quality the distinction between Figure and Ground, which does not even appear among the object properties describe in Figures 4.6 to 4.10. The "figure" has recognizable shape, the "ground" does not; figure extends to the contour, which belongs to it, whereas ground extends behind the contour to some indeterminate extent; figure has surface quality, ground is more amorphous. In general, we cannot recognize a shape if it was ground when seen previously (Rubin, 1921). In (F), the goblet (1) is figure at (ii); faces (2) are figure at (iii); and the two are free to alternate in *figure-ground reversal* at (i). (The figure is taken from Hochberg, 1978.)

Because what is not figure tends to be unrecognizable, and because in general two adjacent areas cannot both be figure at the same time, it is obvious that these Gestalt qualities are important in recognizing real and represented objects, and that their absence from the classical theory is a serious deficiency.

sensory stimulation. The nervous system is viewed as a self-organizing or self-equilibrating (*homeostatic*) structure, like a system of current flows and fields of force in a complex network of conductors and impedances, or like the bioelectrical potentials developed in living colloidal systems. Because such *brain fields* were thought to extend over substantial parts of the visual sections of the brain, they provide for extended spatial interactions between regions corresponding to different parts of the proximal stimulus.

This explanation was neither fully developed nor applied to the many kinds of constancy (size, color, motion), which, in addition to form constancy, must be explained. But it is clearly different in kind both from the classical explanation and from such specific mechanisms of direct perception as those proposed by Mach and Hering. It contains within it a notion that has been of great influence. We consider the element shortly.

Where the Theoretical Issues Stood at the End of the Classical Period

The Helmholtzian idea—that our perceptions of objects rest on computational or inferential process—was, like the failure to predict appearances, roundly criticized over the years as being uneconomical, mentalistic, and unparsimonious. Gestalt theory, which had a significant impact in psychology and art theory between the two World Wars, was particularly vocal in this regard. But the criticisms of the classical theory did not amount to much until the end of World

War II. Then the needs of new technology (flight training, radar and sonar displays, etc.), the development of new instrumentation (notably, direct amplifiers that made the measurement of very small bioelectrical tissue responses common and reliable), and the effects of governmental research grants that made the research career a viable occupation, all combined to turn the tables. As we will see, Helmholtz was right about the three cones; and, at the other end of the simplified flow chart in Figure 4.10, Helmholtz was right in some sense about the existence of mental structure and computation. Most of what lay between those points was wrong, however, and most of the alternative direct proposals that had been made by the critics of that dominant approach, especially those made by Hering and Mach, were quite remarkably vindicated within a very short period, after having been largely ignored for many decades.

THE 1950s AND AFTER: "DIRECT" SENSITIVITY TO OBJECT ATTRIBUTES VERSUS COMPUTATIONAL THEORIES AND MENTAL STRUCTURES

The classical theory rested mainly on two major arguments: first, that it was the simplest way of analyzing the world of sensory stimulation; and second, that it agreed with neurophysiological observation. In the 1950s, both of these supports were withdrawn.

Hering had proposed the existence of neural structures organized into *opponent pairs*—for example, structures that provide either red *or* green sensations but not both, and others that provide blue *or* yellow (and black or white response pairs as well). Unlike the Young-Helmholtz theory, this account of hue reflects the basic facts of color appearances: yellow is not a red-green mixture, as Figure 4.6 suggests, but a pure sensation; a reddish green and a yellowish blue are excluded experiences because wavelengths that stimulate both members of each pair equally simply appear gray; and the appearances and similarities of the various colors are given directly by how the wavelengths in the retinal image stimulate the opponent pairs: for example, red + yellow = reddish yellow (orange); blue + green = bluish green, and so on.

The three fundamental sensations of the Young-Helmholtz theory rested on the many decades of research since the time of Helmholtz and Maxwell, and used psychophysical methods that seemed to require no phenomenology: they measured only the point at which different spectral mixtures are indistinguishable. How could merely subjective opinions about appearances compete with such quantitative and supposedly objective bodies of data? Why should we imagine anything as complex as the opponent-process structures when neurophysiology provided neither evidence nor need for them? This was the dominant view before the 1950s, and before that Hering's theory received only marginal attention. What happened in the 1950s contains lessons for our science that have not yet been fully worked out, but that are important in any attempt to assess the contemporary search for alternative sensory analyzing systems.

The first major step in gaining acceptance for Hering's views was provided by Hurvich and Jameson's development of a way of quantifying the phenomenology of color appearances. Their procedure was simple. They presented a single wavelength of light and then determined how much of either member of an opponent pair (e.g., of light that appears to be subjectively pure red or subjectively pure green, subjectively pure blue or subjectively pure yellow) is needed to remove all traces of the other hue from this wavelength. This was done over the spectrum of wavelengths. By this procedure of titration they provided the quantitative response curves that the hypothesized opponent processes should have (1957). Informed by opponent-process theory, microelectrode research identified cells in the visual system of the goldfish (Svaetichin, 1956) and of the *Rhesus macaque* (DeValois, 1968) that responded to wavelength in just these ways, and it is now clear that simple networks could act as opponent pairs (Figure 4.18; Hurvich & Jameson, 1974). Recent reviews of color vision in systematic and historical context are offered by Boynton (1979), Hurvich (1981).

The setting was right. Psychologists had long used psychophysical procedures to construct scales of appearance and opinion. With the improved electronic apparatus available after World War II, neurophysiologists had shown that neurons are interconnected in organized networks, not in simple linear chains leading from the sense organ to the sensory cortex of the

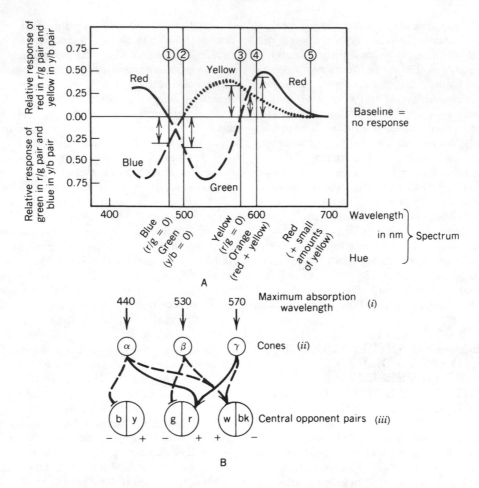

Figure 4.18. *Opponent-process pairs: an alternative to the Young-Helmholtz theory that accounts for the appearances of colors.* The theory of color vision sketched in Figure 4.6 summarizes and accounts for the matches that are obtained between different mixes of wavelength, but does not deal with the resulting appearances. Thus, in the example considered there, a red-appearing light and a green-appearing light yield a yellow-appearing mixture. Hering proposed instead a system of opposed pairs: red and green are opposite responses of one kind of neural structure; blue and yellow are opposite responses of another kind of neural structure.

(A) To measure the response made by each of these *opponent pairs* to each wavelength in the spectrum, Hurvich and Jameson asked their subjects (1) to add just enough of a light that was pure red (for that observer) to each point in the spectrum to remove all greenishness, measuring thereby the strength of the green response at that spectral wavelength; (2) to measure the red response by admixing a light that looked pure green; and (3) correspondingly to measure the strength of the yellow and blue responses of the other opponent process. These data are plotted as though they were the magnitudes (on the *y*-axis) of the two opposed responses of a red-green and a yellow-blue pair at each point in the spectrum (the *x*-axis). The appearance of each spectral wavelength, on the *x*-axis, is predictable by adding the two response curves at that wavelength, and is shown for each of five wavelengths.

(B) To explain these functions, Hurvich and Jameson proposed the networks shown here that would function as needed for Hering's theory. The three cones function much as they do in Figure 4.6, but their output is not independent, being linked by excitatory connections (arrows) and inhibitory connections (bars) to the opponent-pair cells shown at (iii). When inhibition just balances excitation for any of the cells at (iii), that cell fires at some baseline level. Considering the hues alone (the two cells on the left), when excitation exceeds inhibition for either the red-green or the yellow-blue cell, it fires above its baseline of activity, and provides signals for red and yellow, respectively; when inhibition exceeeds excitation, they fire below their baseline, and thereby signal green or blue, respectively.

brain and from there to the association areas in which learning had been presumed to occur. The most important single advance in instrumentation was the microelectrode, which made it possible to record the activity of individual nerve cells within the visual system and brain of an essentially intact animal as it is exposed to various sensory displays. It quickly became evident that most cells that had been observed in this way do not respond to individual points of local stimulus energy, but to extended spatial and temporal patterns—to adjacent differences in intensity, to specific features, and to movements in one rather than another direction (see Ch. 3). And they appear to accomplish this by means of networks of lateral connections, which were precisely what Mach and Hering had argued.

Using microelectrodes in the visual system, researchers found that cells respond to lines and edges at particular orientations, both moving and stationary (Hubel & Wiesel, 1962), to sine-wave gratings of a particular frequency (Blakemore & Campbell, 1969), and to disparities in the two eyes' views (Barlow, Blakemore, & Pettigrew, 1964). Even though the Helmholtzian model (Figure 4.10) may be the simplest, we must conclude that it does not accord with the neurophysiological facts.

These new structures raise two questions: how do they themselves work, and what perceptual functions do they serve?

With respect to how they work, they are widely believed to result from the activities of suitably interconnected networks of lateral inhibition and excitation (von Békésy, 1960; Ratliff, 1965). This was very much what Mach and Hering had speculated to be the case.

With respect to their possible perceptual functions, such pattern-sensitive networks open the way to very different kinds of explanation of the perceptual process. Primary among those are the proposals that lateral inhibition provides for the direct perception of reflectance and that detectors of binocular disparity provide the

stimulus for a direct perception of depth. Both of these have gained a much more tolerant hearing than they once received.

Reflectance Perception

The proposal made by Mach and Hering—that lateral inhibition occurs between adjacent neurons in the sensory system—has now received direct support and general acceptance inasmuch as a brightly illuminated patch on the retina lowers the response of neurons in adjacent retinal regions (Hering, 1878; Hartline, 1949). The inhibition of one group of neurons by an adjacent group would provide one mechanism for lightness constancy: As the intensity of the surround's retinal image increases, the inhibition it provides to the region that receives the object's image also increases. Depending on precisely how inhibition varies with the amount of light in the retinal image, the visual response to the object might then remain constant despite changes in illumination, so long as the reflectances of the objects and surroundings remained invariant (Figure 4.19). Moreover, the same theory explains (at least qualitatively) the illusion of simultaneous lightness *contrast* (Figure 4.14), in which a bright surround makes a gray object look darker, and it relates both contrast and constancy to a number of phenomena involving *contours*, the sharp boundaries that are perceived at abrupt changes in luminance (Figure 4.16).

Considered alone, this theory is far more economical than the classical one. It identifies a sensory channel in the visual nervous system which responds directly to a feature of the retinal image (i.e., adjacent luminance ratios) that varies directly with objects' reflectances under many conditions of viewing. And indeed cells have been found, for example, in the frog retina, whose output varies with the ratio (thus with the reflectances) of moving patches (Campbell, Hartwell, & Hood, 1978). This is the closest we can now come to a specific physiological

---

Although it includes components of the Young-Helmholtz theory (Figure 4.6), these proposals differ in two very important ways: (1) Unlike the former, they account directly for the similarities and differences between the hues, and (2) the physiological unit of response is not an independent receptor but an interrelated network. This kind of explanation has been attempted for other properties as well, as we will see in Figure 4.19. For recent reviews of the status of this approach to color vision, see Boynton (1979), Hurvich (1981), Pokorny & Smith (1986), Wyszecki (1986), and Chapter 2.

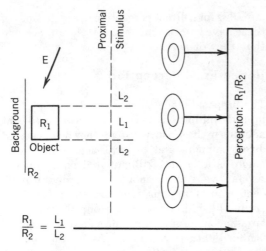

$$\frac{R_1}{R_2} = \frac{L_1}{L_2}$$

Figure 4.19. *A possible mechanism that responds directly to objects' reflectances.* We have seen that visual neurons are organized into networks (Figures 4.16, 4.18), which makes it possible to consider very different kinds of explanations from the classical theory of Figure 4.10. If our visual system contains networks that respond directly to adjacent ratios of luminance *L1:L2*, in Figure 4.12, their response to the reflectance of an object and its background (*R1:R2*) would remain constant despite changes in illumination *E* because the ratio of the target luminance to surround luminance *L1:L2* would remain unchanged. That is, the ratios of luminances remain invariant with changes in illumination, so this aspect of the proximal stimulation varies directly with the distal stimulus property (reflectances).

A mechanism like this one would make reflectance-perception direct, and would eliminate the need for the viewer to take illumination into account.

mechanism that would respond directly to a distal stimulus and would thereby make inference processes unnessary. We must answer several critical questions before trying to assess any such proposed reflectance receptor.

The first question is whether the quantitative effects expected from lateral inhibition account for the degree of the constancy or of the contrast that is in fact obtained. As noted in Figure 4.11, with constant reflectances, and with changing but equal illumination the ratio of adjacent luminances in the retinal image will remain constant, and there is evidence (Wallach, 1948) that viewers judge objects to be of equal lightness if the ratios of their luminances to their surround luminances are equal, regardless of what the luminances themselves may be.

The effects that lateral inhibition should have under different configurations and ranges of illumination have not yet been fully worked out and tested, but the inhibition theory does not lead us to expect that lightness responses are always determined by ratios per se (which is what an invariance theory must predict (see p. 210)). In fact, subjects' judgments of brightness do depart systematically from an equal-ratio function (Hess & Pretori, 1894; Heinemann, 1955; Jameson & Hurvich, 1961, 1964; Stevens & Stevens, 1960). Jameson and Hurvich made a start at working out this model (1964), but much physiological modeling must still be done, especially for the complex patterns that prevail in normal scenes.

Then there is the question of whether the degree of constancy found in constancy experiments is quantitatively just what it should be in terms of this model, and in terms of empirical studies of the effects of neighboring regions on their mutual brightness. For a review of this point, see Hochberg (1971). In fact, Flock reports that the most significant departures from the strict ratio formula disappear when subjects are asked to make lightness (reflectance) judgments rather than brightness judgments (Flock, 1970; see however Jameson & Hurvich, 1970). This issue is important with respect to what we will describe later as a generalized invariance theory, inasmuch as the ratio (other things being equal) remains invariant in the optic array despite changes in luminance levels.

Finally, we must recognize that lateral inhibition simply cannot be the sole cause of reflectance perception and constancy, as Hering was quite aware (cf. Hurvich & Jameson, 1964; Hurvich, 1981). Two stimulus patterns may have equal luminance ratios for their targets and surrounds and yet look unequal in apparent lightness, depending on how the perception is organized. Figure 4.20 reviews a set of studies in which the same patch may be seen as belonging to one surface or another, being in light or shade, receiving direct or slanting illumination. In all of these, the luminances of adjacent regions in the retinal image are constant, but relatively small changes in the configuration of the pattern provide for large changes in the perception of spatial arrangement, and therefore provide different bases for taking illumination into account, *if* inferential processes are

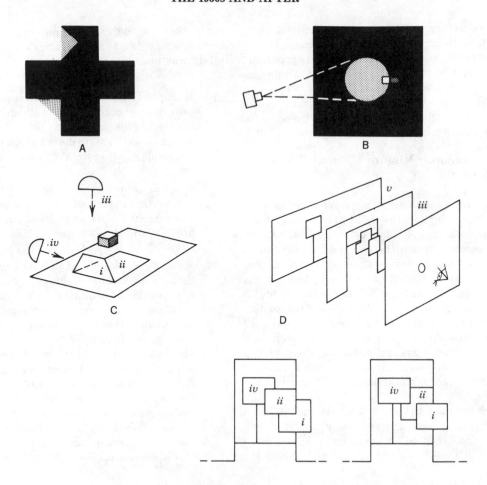

Figure 4.20. *Limitations of a ratio theory of reflectance perception.* There are many cases in which luminance ratios are the same but perceived lightness or reflectance differ. Five classes of such cases are shown here.

(A) The Benary cross: The two triangles are of equal reflectance, and therefore the ratios of their luminances to those of their surrounds are equal, but the upper one looks somewhat lighter. Presumably this is so because it is judged against the background of the black cross, whereas the lower one is judged against the white surround.

(B) In this demonstration by Gelb (1929), a black disk, hanging in the doorway of a black room, is so illuminated that only the disk is lit. As the lightest part of the field, the disk appears white. Only when a small scrap of white paper is placed against the surface of the disk, is the disk perceived as black. This effect is not merely a function of knowledge, because as soon as the white scrap is removed, the disk again looks white. It seems implausible to attribute this change to lateral inhibition, because the white scrap is small (but we should note that the effect does in fact decrease when the scrap is made smaller: Stewart, 1959).

(C) Viewed monocularly, an upright trapezoidal target (i) will look like a rectangle lying flat on the surface (ii) if it is cut so as to match the outline of that rectangle in the optic array. When viewed binocularly, the target will appear upright. Nearby objects provide cues as to the direction of illumination. If illuminated from above (iii), the target will, when viewed monocularly, appear to lie flat on the table and appears darker than when it is viewed binocularly, and it therefore appears upright, in its true orientation. If illuminated from in front (iv), it appears lighter monocularly than binocularly (Hochberg and Beck, 1954). The differences between monocular and binocular perceptions in each case are qualitatively consistent with what we would expect if the apparent illumination were being taken into account: When illuminated from above, and the target appears flat, it appears to be receiving more illumination than it actually is; when illuminated from in front, it appears to be getting less.

really involved. The precise interpretation of such demonstrations remains in dispute, that is, whether there is some component of appearance that must be incontestably assigned to a process of unconscious inference (Epstein, 1977; Rock, 1977; Hochberg, 1981). We will return to this question in the last section, when we discuss the evidence for mental structure (p. 253f).

Stereoscopic Vision: Current Theory and Fact

When the two eyes are converged to bring some fixation point (Figure 4.3) to the center of the fovea in each eye, binocular parallax (i.e., the difference between the two eyes' views) causes objects that lie nearer to or further from that fixation point to fall on different places in the two eyes. That difference is called the binocular disparity (Figure 4.3). With disparities of less than about 15 min of arc (known as *Panum's limit*), the disparity is not seen as such, and single objects are perceived in their proper spatial relationship, that is, in depth relative to the plane of the fixation point and to each other.

Helmholtz believed that sensations from each eye's view are separately analyzed and then combined in an act of unconscious inference. Although an argument for that position

could then be made, there are important facts of stereovision that comprise strong (but not absolutely conclusive) objections to it:

1. A disparity of about 2 sec of visual angle provides a detectible depth difference (Berry, 1948), although that disparity would be too small to detect as a minimum separable gap (Figure 4.7B) within a single eye.

2. Subjects cannot consciously detect which eye is the source of each image when external cues, such as sight of one's nose, are controlled (Pickersgill, 1961; Smith, 1946).

3. A *stereogram* is formed of a pair of views that are devised to provide each eye with a separate view, usually the pair of views that would be provided by some scene or layout in three-dimensional space. If a stereogram is prepared in which one eye's view is a random dot pattern and the other is identical except that some region within it has been displaced (Figure 4.21), the displaced region is not detectable as such in the single view. Binocularly, it is clearly visible, nearer or farther than the surrounding dots, depending on the direction of displacement. Because no objects or

---

(D) Viewers see two test cards (i, ii), presented in the opening of a dimly lit chamber (iii), so placed as to be seen adjacent to a card (iv) on the back wall of a brightly lit chamber (v). When card (ii) is cut so that it appears to be in front of card (i), and to be within the dim chamber, it is seen as brighter than when it is cut so as to appear behind the far card (iv) (Gilchrist, 1977), presumably because in the latter situation it is seen as being more brightly illuminated and therefore must be of lower reflectance.

Because of phenomena like these, known for many years, color perception cannot be explained completely by the proximal stimulus pattern (e.g., ratios, invariances, lateral inhibition, etc.). But on the other hand, these phenomena do not prove Helmholtzian inference, either. In all of the displays except for (C), the visual stimulus pattern has itself been changed by whatever means were used to change the apparent spatial arrangement. The resulting differences might be due to those changes per se, therefore, rather than to any process of taking illumination into account, although in some examples (e.g., B, C) the effects seem large compared with the small changes that are made. Moreover, it is likely that in arriving at the lightness judgment, the viewer attends to different aspects of the scene when the apparent spatial arrangement is different. For example, the target may be compared with other vertical surfaces when it looks upright, and with horizontal surfaces when it looks horizontal (Hochberg, 1971); any method that works to separate the target from its adjacent surround, such as binocular disparity (Gogel & Mershon, 1969) and causing the target to appear as ground rather than figure (Coren, 1969; Koffka, 1935), reduces the contrast effect between surround and target; and even the course of the eye movements that viewers make when comparing the target and its surroundings is different (Flock et al., 1966), which means that the response of the retina will then differ as a result of successive contrast (Hering, 1878).

For a more detailed introductory treatment of this issue, see Goldstein, 1984; for more complete discussion of the literature see Beck, 1972b, and Hochberg, 1971.

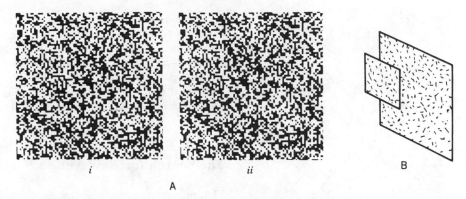

Figure 4.21. *Forms that can be seen only in stereoscopic viewing.*

(A) Although you probably cannot see how they differ, these two displays comprise a *random-dot stereogram*, in which the central part of the left view is displaced slightly to the right, relative to the corresponding region in the other view. When viewed in a stereoscope, therefore, in which the left and right eyes are shown fields (i) and (ii), respectively, the viewer perceives a square surface of random dots floating in space in front of a field of random dots, as visualized at (B).

Such displays, devised by Julesz in 1962, are remarkably useful tools for stereoscopic research, and have been offered as disproofs of both Hering's and Helmholtz's theories of stereopsis (Julesz, 1971). However, they do not address Hering's theory, which rests not on recognition of the individual views but on binocular local signs (see p. 217), and they do not absolutely refute Helmholtz because he did not in general mean that recognition of sensory components is a conscious process (see p. 212).

There is now an enormous literature using random-dot stereograms, with no single review able to do it justice. A general review of the literature of stereopsis and the use of such displays is found in Kaufman, 1974; a fair proportion of the research with random-dot displays is reviewed by Julesz (1971, 1981).

their contours are visible in each eye's view when considered separately, no simple version of Helmholtz's proposal—that we perceive the contents of each eye's view and then infer the layout in space that would provide them—can be sustained. Such dot-matrix figures were devised by Julesz in 1962, and have since been extremely useful in a wide variety of inquiries on stereopsis, grouping, and motion perception (see p. 244).

It is now known that the bulk of the cells in the visual system respond to binocular stimulation and indeed there are cells that respond to specific degrees of disparity (Barlow et al., 1967). Hering's specific theory of stereopsis or binocular depth perception (see Hochberg, 1962) has not been pursued. In agreement with his belief that innate connections between the two retinas underlie stereopsis, however, it is now widely held that stereopsis responses to disparity are indeed innate (although stereopsis can be permanently disrupted if vision is

interfered with at an early age; see Held *et al.*, 1983).

The most popular theory of stereopsis is essentially an internal reflection of Johannes Kepler's analysis of binocular geometry in Figure 4.3. This model, which has been repeatedly proposed over the years, is shown in Figure 4.22. Lines from (a), (a) can fuse only at cell (a′), lines from (b), (b) can fuse only at (b′) (Boring, 1933; Charnwood, 1951; Linkz, 1952; Dodwell & Engel, 1963; Sperling, 1970; Marr & Poggio, 1976). There are difficulties with this class of model, the chief one being the question of why spurious intersections are not activated; for example, why do aL and bR not fuse, or aR and bL? Context, and not merely individual points, must somehow go into determining which possible points are fused (Koffka, 1935). Sperling's solution (1970), a plausible one with applications that go beyond stereopsis (Sperling, Pavel, Cohen, Landy, & Schwartz, 1983), is that the binocular neural field is so wired that adjacent neurons reinforce or cooperate and inhibit more distant ones. This principle has been adopted by

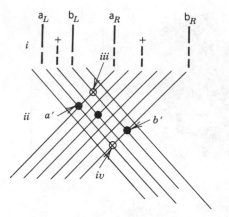

Figure 4.22. *A persistent model of the binocular neural field.* The geometry of Kepler's analysis in Figure 4.3, if turned inward, furnishes a model for the neural process underlying stereopsis—one that has been offered repeatedly and is still current. The left and right eyes' views of rods (a), (b), and a fixation point (+) (see Figure 4.3) are shown at (i). If neurons from each point on the retina project to a "binocular neural field" (ii), the points of intersection of corresponding points from each eye occur at a level that reflects the objects' loci in space.

This model is convenient for application to the dot-matrix stereograms of Figure 4.21A, and to the point-by-point analysis of scene that is most natural for computers. A problem with which all versions of this model must deal is that of "ghost point": how does the network know that points (iii) and (iv) do not represent real objects, whereas points (a′) and (b′) do? This is not much of a problem with an uncluttered field like this one, but it is a critical issue when dealing with stimuli like those in the real world or in Figure 4.21. A solution by Sperling (1970), subsequently adopted by Julesz (1971) and by Marr and Poggio (1976), is that nearby nodes with equal disparities in the neural field reinforce each others' activity, whereas more distant neurons inhibit each other.

A thorough review of stereopsis up to 1974 may be found in Kaufman (1974). Recent work attempting to devise computer models of stereopsis, for reasons we discuss on p. 251 is reviewed in Mayhew and Frisbie (1980), and in Marr (1980), but the reader should be warned that the value of the work rests on computer programs that are not actually there described, and is limited further by the facts considered in connection with Figure 4.23.

Julesz (1971), and by Marr and Poggio (1976), and has been successfully modeled in computer formulations (see p. 251).

None of these facts or models offers conclusive refutation of Helmholtz's theory, and in any case binocular information does not make the monocular cues irrelevant. But the fact that central cells have been found that respond to patterns and to binocular disparities, regardless of what their function turns out to be, has fostered the idea that we have mechanisms that respond directly to object properties, as we now see.

The Search for New Analytic Units

The microelectrode has revealed cells that respond to a wide range of different types of features, and the end is not yet in sight. Two lines of research seem most directly related to the problems of perception, as distinct from analyses of visual neurophysiology.

In 1863, Helmholtz proposed that the ear performs a Fourier analysis on the pressure waves that enter it, reducing all patterns of sound to a spectrum of sine waves at different frequencies, amplitudes, and phases. One can analyze a visual display, similarly, into a spectrum of spatial frequencies on a given axis, or in a bidimensional array. Engineers have long used such measures to characterize the effects of lenses, films, and so forth, on each stage of the transmission of visual information (Schade, 1964; Roufs & Bouma, 1981). In neurophysiological terms, it has been proposed that channels which are maximally sensitive to a sine wave of a particular spacing, or *spatial frequency*, perform what approximates in some ways a two-dimensional Fourier analysis on the retinal image (Campbell et al., 1968). Such channels, it has been argued, might be responsible for many of the phenomena of pattern vision and motion perception, including the geometrical illusions (Ginsberg, 1971), constancy (Campbell et al, 1968), and apparent motion (Adelson & Bergen, 1984; Morgan, 1980; Watson & Ahumada, 1983); and physiological units that respond to gratings of different spatial frequency and orientation have been identified in the cortex of the primate brain. See Braddick et al., 1978; Graham, 1979, 1981; and DeValois and Jacobs, 1984, for recent reviews. A Fourier analysis cannot actually provide the sufficient visual analysis of the extended visual scene, however. Spatial frequency channels do not take account of phase, so far as is now known. Moreover, an overall analysis would not work in any case,

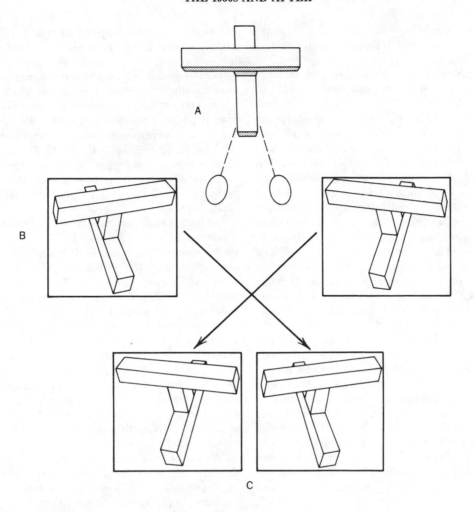

Figure 4.23. *Disparity versus monocular depth cues: The interaction of multiple determinants.* Where pictorial depth cues and binocular information are in conflict, the latter does not automatically prevail. The two eyes' views of the object at (A) are shown at (B) (in order to make clear what was done, the disparity is here exaggerated greatly). These views are interchanged at (C), so that the disparities in the stereogram have then been reversed, and parts that appear nearer in the monocular view should appear farther in binocular viewing. That does not happen. Instead, the monocular cue of interposition prevails, so that the depth that you see in the stereogram is essentially the same as that in the monocular view (Schriever, 1925). Similarly, the reversed views of a face look normally convex, not concave (for a recent discussion of this, see Gregory, 1980).

Although it is clear that many factors and cues interact to determine what we see, there has been very little research directed to exploring the nature and lawfulness of that interaction. Where the various cues agree (and it seems plausible that they usually do so), there is no problem. Where they do not agree (and they cannot always do so: see Figure 4.30), we cannot predict the outcome without such research. In addition to that of Schriever, and similar work with stereograms by Washburn and Wright (1938), Jameson and Hurvich reported work in 1959 showing that subjects' sensitives to small changes in distance under common-place conditions when all cues are available is close to the arithmetic sum of the sensitivities obtained with each cue alone. Dosher et al. (1984), using computer-generated rotating skeletal cubes in which relative brightness was varied independently of disparity, found that the contributions of luminance and disparity were summed according to a weighted linear model.

because we would have to think rather in terms of local analyses into different spatial frequencies at many parts of the retinal image and it is not clear how more local analyses would combine in the perceptions of extended objects and scenes.

Experimental evidence that large-scale and complex units of sensory analysis exist was offered long before the microelectrode was developed. The logic of the main method that was—and still is—used is as follows. After gazing at a red light for a few moments, the eye is less sensitive to red light, and neutral light (gray or white) then looks green. These after-image phenomena have long been attributed to the fatigue of receptor processes. For example, if the "red receptors" are made less sensitive, our blue and green response to light of the same energy will be stronger. Similarly, after gazing for a few minutes at a waterfall, one is less sensitive to downward motion (adaptation), and stationary objects appear to move upward (aftereffect). The research paradigm is precisely the one with which Helmholtz and subsequent psychologists had thought to prove that some attribute is a learned response, but here it is being used as evidence that sensory receptors exist for some attribute. Thus, the waterfall phenomenon has long been taken as evidence of sensory receptors which detect motion (Wohlgemuth, 1911). And there is now more direct and indirect evidence of such mechanisms (Grüsser & Grüsser-Cornehls, 1973; Sekuler & Ganz, 1963; see Chapter 3, and Anstis, 1986 for recent review.)

By showing that prolonged exposure to a particular stimulus event provides the kind of after effect that one would expect to find if a receptor were depleted or fatigued by that exposure, one could argue for the sensory nature of the response to the event.

This method has proliferated in recent years (see Graham, 1981; Harris, 1980), and has been used for quite different purposes. The paradigm has been used to argue that a particular perceptual attribute must be learned during perceptual development, because the perceptual response to some attribute like tilt, curvature, or even uprightness changes after exposure to a rearranged environment (Figure 4.24A, B; see Helmholtz, 1856; Held & Hein, 1963; Harris, 1980; for recent review, see Welch, 1986; for review, see Welch, 1986). It has also been used in demonstrations of *contingent aftereffects* (Figure 24C), in which, for example, the results of inspection of diagonal orange and black stripes alternating with opposite blue and black stripes cause a test figure of horizontal black and white stripes to look orange, while vertical test stripes look blue (McCullough, 1965); a variety of similar contingent effects are now known (Held & Shattuck, 1971; Riggs, 1973; Harris & Gibson, 1968), and they have been interpreted both as evidence of innate mechanisms and as examples of learning or plasticity (Harris, 1980).

Although such findings can be interpreted in a number of ways, the search for new sensory units received greater legitimacy from the neurophysiological findings and microelectrode research. Using the aftereffects paradigm, therefore, other channels, each responsive to some complex property of stimulation, have been proposed in recent years. These include what may be termed "edge detectors," "looming detectors," and detectors of sine wave gratings of a particular separation (*spatial frequency channels*) by which the visual system presumably performs a Fourier analysis upon the retinal image. For reviews of these, see Braddick et al., 1978; N. Graham, 1981; and Olzak & Thomas, 1986.

We do not yet know whether such pattern-sensitive and event-sensitive neural networks in fact contribute in any way to the constancies, illusions, and organizational phenomena. One of the strongest arguments against Hering's color theory, however, was that opponent-pairs ran counter to known physiology; similarly, lateral interactions, originally proposed to explain contrast and contour phenomena, were long regarded as mere speculation, logically unnecessary to explain the perceptual phenomena that had suggested them. The fact that suitable networks have been shown to exist makes it more plausible that many of the properties of the physical world are perceived directly as responses of specific sensory mechanisms.

On the other hand, because Hering and Mach tailored their neurophysiological speculations to fit the phenomena of object perception that needed explaining, *the perceptual consequences of accepting any of their models were built into the model.* That is simply not the case with current attempts at new units. No one proposes that we perceive sine gratings as such, and

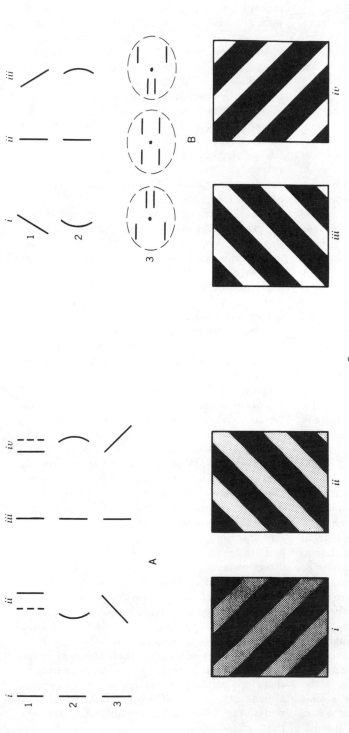

Figure 4.24. *Perceptual adaptation and aftereffects.*

(A) In column (i), we have the appearance of a straight line viewed normally. In column (ii), we have the appearance of that line when first wearing a prism that (1) displaces the image to the right, (2) curves the image to the right, or (3) tilts the image clockwise. In column (iii), we have the appearance toward which the stimulus tends (but does not reach), as adaptation to the prism continues. In column (iv), we have the appearance toward which the straight line tends after adaptation has occurred and the prism is removed (Helmholtz, 1856; Wundt, 1902). In all of these effects, active looking and touching are necessary or at least helpful to the effects (Held, Dichgans & Bauer, 1975; Held & Hein, 1958, 1963; Held & Rekosh, 1963).

(B) Similar effects can be obtained without prisms. In column (i) are shown adaptation or *inspection* stimuli, at which the subject stares for some time, and in column (ii) a subsequently presented test stimulus. In column (iii) we see the appearance of the test stimuli, demonstrating the aftereffects (Gibson, 1933; Gibson and Radner, 1937). Row (3) displays a form of contour-repulsion, in that the general effects can be summarized as the apparent displacement of contours from regions previously satiated by the contours of the inspection figures (Köhler and Wallach, 1944).

(C) Contingent aftereffects: (1) in 1965, McCullough discovered that after prolonged exposure to two alternating views in which stripes of one orientation and color, for example, orange (i) were replaced by stripes of opposite orientation and complementary color, for example, blue (ii), achromatic stripes of black and white in the first orientation (iv) and in the second orientation (iii) appear tinged with the blue and orange, respectively.

Similar contingent aftereffects have been found for a wide variety of coupled properties (e.g., Held and Shattuck, 1971; Riggs 1973). The explanation for these phenomena is not clear; it is tempting to think that they result from differential fatigue, during adaptation, of specific feature-detecting networks that are most sensitive to, say, edges of a particular slant and wavelength. Given the profusion of such effects, however, some form of calibration or learning also suggests itself. Research in the area has slowed down substantially in the past few years. For reviews of the field, see Harris, 1980, and Held, 1980.

phenomenology is virtually completely ignored in these formulations.

This is probably neither merely accidental nor perverse. The problem is that we do not have a workable prescription that tells us when we can make physiological inferences from perceptual appearances. Nor indeed do we have any simple procedures by which we can be sure that a subject "really" perceives what he reports perceiving. But the historical facts seem clear: *phenomenology has predicted more of recent neurophysiology than vice versa, and indeed if we wish eventually to be able to predict perceptual experience, then some explicit relationship between appearances and physiology must be provided.* This is not a matter for dismissal as "the old metaphysical mind-body problem," nor can attention to the problem be dismissed as "mere subjectivism." The issue is not a philosophical one, but an empirical one of some consequence.

At any event, so far as sensory analysis is concerned, the field is wide open. We do not know the fundamental vocabulary of the visual analytic system. If we have separate channels of processing (for color, for size, for shape, and so forth), we need some explanation of how the various attributes and features are assigned appropriately when there is (as is usual) more than one object in the field of view: Is it (for example) a large red cube and a small green sphere or a small green cube and a large red sphere? The problem is made salient by the finding of *illusory conjunctions* (Treisman, 1986) of separable object properties (Lawrence, 1971; Treisman & Schmidt, 1982) when presentation is brief and attention cannot be focused on each object. If we change what we take to be the units of sensory analysis, then what we attribute to more central processes must in general change as well. This is why I said at the beginning of this section that the field remains in ferment.

Of greatest theoretical significance are those sensory mechanisms that remain invariant even though the local stimulation at each point on the retina may vary, that is, those mechanisms that respond to aspects of the stimulation that covary directly with the physical properties of objects and events. Thus, as we noted above, the frog's retina does in fact contain cells that respond not to the intensity of light in some part of the retinal image, but to the *ratio* of intensities of surrounded and surrounding regions (Campbell et al., 1978), but we cannot say that

such cells (if they were present in the human) explain our perceptions of reflectance in the normal world. At most, we might say that if these cells serve as peripheral input to the visual system, we need postulate no additional process of inference (and we have seen in Figure 4.20 that not even that is true). In a similar fashion, the other analyzing mechanisms cannot themselves be taken as explanations, but they make it possible in principle that very different explanations might be developed of how a given object attribute (color, size, form, distance, velocity) is perceived, explanations that need not draw on speculations either about learning or about inference.

Faced with such proposals, perception psychologists must ask in each instance whether the distal property in question—depth, reflectance, form—can also be perceived under conditions that simply could not plausibly be explained by the channel being proposed. In many situations, we will see that such is indeed true. Furthermore, if by direct we mean immediate and automatic, at least some distal attributes appear to be less directly perceived than their proximal counterparts. For example, when viewing an object at a slant, at short exposures (Leibowitz & Bourne, 1956) and without specific attention to shape (Epstein & Lovitts, 1985), its foreshortened proximal shape is perceived rather than its invariant distal shape (see also Epstein & Broota, 1986). Therefore, the classical theory can then at least be maintained *in addition to* the proposed new channel, and the claim for greater theoretical economy has withered. This does not make such proposals false; it merely reduces their potential elegance and strongly circumscribes their predictive value.

Because such proposals about mechanisms of direct response to distal properties are useful as perceptual theories only insofar as they identify some aspect of stimulation that specifies some object property (i.e., some aspect of peripheral stimulation that is highly correlated with that property), there is no need even to be concerned with neurophysiology. In fact, the search for such *directly informative variables of stimulation* therefore actually antedates the neurophysiological discoveries (Gibson, 1950, 1979), and remains an influential approach that is actively pursued today.

The direct theories rest on a general criticism of the classical theory. Before we consider the theories we should discuss the general criticism of the classical theory, namely, that the latter was poorly equipped to deal with *relations* within the field of stimulation.

Do we Perceive According to Rules rather than Look-up Tables?

So far as explicit theories of association are concerned, perceptual learning by association would provide what we might now call look-up tables in which specific patterns of stimulation would be given specific perceptual meanings, that is, the associations acquired through experience. No specific associative theory of perceptual learning has been spelled out, to my knowledge, that accounts for how abstract rules might be learned (although recent attempts, which we note on p. 249, now make the prospect less implausible). Criticisms of the classical theory are often aimed at this point, and are only demonstrations intended to show that perception is determined by rules rather than by specific associations. The major systematic attempt at such criticisms was that of Gestalt theory, introduced in the last section, to which we now return.

Gestalt Demonstrations and Theory

The major effect of Gestalt theory, which mounted the most serious systematic challenge to Helmholtzian theory between the two World Wars, was to find perceptual rules, and from them to deduce the nature of the underlying brain processes. The patterns in Figure 4.25 are adapted from Wertheimer (1923), and Kopfermann (1930), and Metzger (1953). These rules, or "laws of organization," were held to determine whether we will perceive some object at all. In Figure 4.25A, which is a demonstration of the law of good continuation, a familiar number is concealed at (i), but not at (ii), because in order to see the number in (i), the configuration there requires us to break the unfamiliar but smoothly-continuing shape. Such rules, alien and unexpected within the classical theory, therefore determine whether we will perceive a given object, regardless of the state of the rods and cones. These rules also seem to determine whether an object appears flat or tridimensional, with no evident reference to the depth cues of

Figure 4.2. In Figure 4.25Bi) the pattern looks flat because the good continuation must be broken to perceive (1) and (2) as dihedrals at different distances, whereas Figure 4.25Bii, looks tridimensional because the dihedrals would have to be broken at (1), (2), and so on, for the pattern to look like a set of closed polyhedrons.

On a practical level, it would seem that these "laws" could be extremely useful in concealing real and pictured objects (camouflage and puzzle pictures: cf. Metzger, 1953; Hochberg, 1980), and in ensuring that pictured objects are correctly perceived. Because there is a large number of such proposed "laws" (Helson, 1926), and because they are not quantitatively framed, the outcome of conflicts between them is not predictable, making their application problematical. Moreover, in the past the problem of making pictures comprehensible was not as serious a practical problem as it has now become. Pictures and graphic displays were made by people who could correct any inadvertent violations of the so-called laws.

Today, pictures and graphs are increasingly being computer generated as needed (p. 251) by the user, with no human editor to prescreen them. The computer scientists who write the programs must know the rules that will automatically generate comprehensible pictures, therefore, and that is just what the laws of organization were intended to be. Moreover, as computer scientists try to devise machines that act in response to the same visual information that humans use (i.e., programs that "read" and that "perceive" pictures and scenes), the laws of organization, if they were available in more specific and quantitative form, would now be extremely useful. They are not, but that is not because efforts to develop them have been made and failed. It is simply uninformed to say that the attempts "dissolved into the fog of subjectivism" (Marr, 1982, p. 8). Gestalt theory had barely come to this country from Germany before World War II. German psychology had been effectively destroyed, and as American psychology emerged from the paralyzing effects that the behavioristic doctrine had exerted on perceptual research, a few attempts were made at objective and quantitative study of the laws of organization (Figure 4.25). But little was done along these lines because, as we will see (p. 237ff), alternative approaches which appeared more

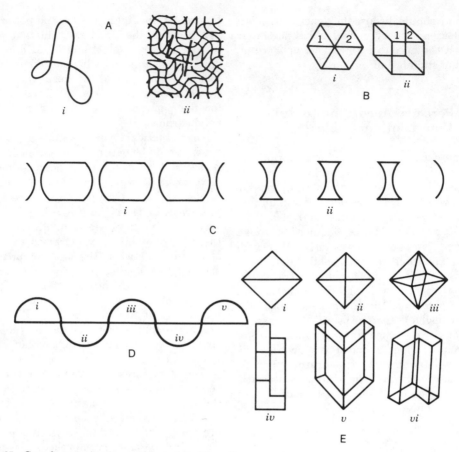

Figure 4.25. *Gestalt organization and two of its "laws."*

(A) *Good continuation*: A number is concealed at (i); the fact that it is difficult to see is not merely a matter of additional lines having been added, because even more lines are added at (ii), yet the number is perfectly visible. This "law" states that we so organize our perceptions as to break as few smoothly continuing lines as possible.

(B) Two views of the same cube are given. Good continuation determines whether it looks flat or three dimensional.

(C) *Closedness*: The closed region tends to be figure; compare (i) and (ii).

(D) *Good continuation* versus *closedness*: In accordance with the factor of closedness, we should see a set of five half-disks (i) to (v); in accordance with good continuation, we should see a sine wave crossing a straight line, and that is what is in fact predominantly perceived.

(E) In Gestalt theory, organization and not depth cues provide for the perception of space. As with (Bi) and (Bii), (Ei) and (Eiv) look flat, but (Eiii) and (Evi) look tridimensional, because the former are simpler as flat shapes (Hochberg & Brooks, 1960; Kopfermann, 1930).

general or economical led research along other paths.

On a theoretical level, the Gestalt demonstrations have been used to argue that organizing principles—inherent in the structure of our nervous systems—and not associative learning determines our perceptions. For example, in Figure 4.25Ai, specific familiarity is overcome by what seems to be an abstract configurational rule. In Gestalt theory, the structure of perceptual experience stands in *psychophysiological isomorphism* to the brain processes elicited by the proximal stimulation; that is, some property of the brain processes must stand in correspondence to each property of experience. (That a figure is enclosed by a ground in Figure 4.17F implies that something corresponding to figuredness and enclosedness exists in the underlying brain process.) The study of perceptual experience should therefore, it was held, provide the means by which we can study the nature of neural organization.

Few attempts were made to specify what this system and its rules would be (cf. Köhler, 1920, 1958; Köhler & Wallach, 1944; Brown & Voth, 1937), and still less research was conducted to that end, except for the study of the figural aftereffects, or FAE. After fixating a curve, a tilted line, or a shape of some given size (the *inspection figure*), a subsequent pattern (the *test figure*) appears with the opposite curve or tilt, respectively (Gibson, 1933, 1937; Gibson and Radner, 1937); and a slightly larger or smaller shape looks still larger or smaller (Köhler & Wallach, 1944; see Figure 4.24B3). Gibson had argued that such effects showed the direct or sensory nature of these attributes (see p. 230) Köhler (Köhler & Wallach, 1944; Köhler & Emergy, 1947) argued that the physiological correlate of figural perception consists of direct current flows within the brain as a volume conductor, and the aftereffects result from an increase in the resistance to these currents—a *satiation* of the cortical medium. We should remember that the general method of demonstrating aftereffects has been used to support quite different, and sometimes opposed, arguments (p. 230; see Figure 4.24A,B). The facts do not provide compelling support for the field processes proposed, although they remain incompletely explained (see Hochberg, 1971, for a review).

Such neurophysiological processes as were proposed are implausible, given present neurophysiological knowledge. But while present neurophysiological knowledge surely must be taken into account, we must also remember that the shape of that knowledge was anticipated by the phenomenologically based speculations, like those of Hering and Mach, that had been rejected on the grounds of earlier "present neurophysiological knowledge". Such knowledge depends entirely on the measurement instruments *and on what one looks for in the data they provide*. The microelectrode is suited for research on individual cells and centers, and is not well suited to the study of spatially extended cortical processes, such as those proposed by the Gestalt psychologists, except as those processes might be reflected in the activity of single cells on which they converge.

Moreover, because microelectrodes cannot be inserted into the brains of intact human observers, we cannot relate microelectrode research to perceptual phenomena in any reasonably direct way. We can measure some aspects of the electrical activity of the brain through the skull and scalp. Only the effects of stimuli that are presented repeatedly at precisely known times can be studied (this is necessary in order to separate the weak signals from the great amount of random noise that accompanies them). Moreover, until recently, only *evoked potentials* could be measured—for example, voltage changes on the scalp which probably reflect current flow through some region of the brain and skin. Because separate sources of such flow can add their effects, and because the actual flow distribution is affected by conductivity differences in the tissue of the head, the spatial patterning of underlying brain processes cannot confidently be retrieved from evoked potentials.

It has recently become possible to measure the *evoked neuromagnetic responses*, those weak magnetic fields whose sources may be the current flow within active neural tissue, and it seems to be possible that we will soon be able to separate and locate these sources with much more assurance and precision (Kaufman & Williamson, 1982). The study of patterns of brain activity in conjunction with perceptual study of the rules of perceptual organization remains, however, in the future.

The Gestalt rules need not be innate (though logically they could be). Thus, the viewer might learn to perceive the simplest alternative, or might learn to perceive the rigid alternative, because they are more likely to prove valid in dealing with the world (Brunswik, 1956; Hochberg, 1971, 1981). It should be remembered however that the apparent crispness of the notion of associative perceptual learning is more apparent than real (p. 212), and that in any case the classical Helmholtzian position, to which these proposals presumably stand in opposition, includes what amounts to rule learning, as well (p. 212; Figures 4.11–4.14).

Attempts to Reconcile Traditional and Gestalt Physiological Models.

An alternative model of extended cortical process was presented by Lashley (1942) in which waves of neural activity produce patterns of reinforcement and interference in the cortical medium; this view has not gained appreciable acceptance. More influential was Hebb's attempt in 1949 to meet the Gestaltists' criticisms within what was then known of neurophysiology. He proposed that cortical response to those features of proximal stimulation that occur very frequently (edges, corners, etc.) would come to act as single cortical units, or *cell assemblies*, by neural growth (*neurobiotaxis*) at the junctions of *synapses* between any nerves that are simultaneously active. Which cell assemblies actually respond to a particular pattern of stimulation depends, in his model, not only on the sensory stimulation of that moment, but also on what patterns of cell assemblies are already firing. Frequent successions of sensory-motor events, like glances at recurrent shapes or patterns in the world, produce *phase sequences*. These are cell assemblies linked in a sequence that provides a mechanism by which the effects of previous glances determine the response to the next one.

This model of the physiological process incorporates the classical tradition that culminated in Helmholtz and Mill (p. 212) in that it rests upon the buildup of complex sensory responses through learning. It provides a theoretical framework for units of sensory response (i.e., cell assemblies) that are much larger than points of color, so it might in principle explain the Gestalt phenomena. It also provides for the effects of learning and attention on the integration of the information in successive glances, in terms of the notion of combining adjacent and successive cell assemblies into phase sequences. Some research was done within this point of view, primarily directed to the following phenomenon: when the retinal image is stabilized (by optical methods) so that it does not change with changes in gaze direction, the shapes that one looks at break up and disappear (Riggs, Ratliff, & Cornsweet, 1953; see Figure 4.16B). In Hebbian terms, this occurs in part because interfering with the normal change in sensory patterns disrupts the phase sequences, and the fact that shapes are then reported to break up into organized or meaningful subunits rather than disappear in random fragments or all at once (Pritchard, Heron, & Hebb, 1960; Donderi and Kane, 1965) was taken as evidence of the constituent cell assemblies (for a review, see Hochberg, 1971). Two major factors deflected the straightforward development of this approach.

1. As noted on p. 223, microelectrode studies have revealed innate, prewired networks of neurons that respond to patterns or features, such as edges, adjacent luminance ratios, binocular disparities, and so on. Such feature analyzers fill at least some of the functions that were to be served by cell assemblies. Many feature analyzers respond to a particular feature wherever it occurs over an extended region of the retina, so that some degree of transformation constancy (invariance under transformation) may be innately built into the system. Further, if analyzing mechanisms that respond to a feature of a particular kind (e.g., an edge having some size or orientation) in one part of the retina are duplicated by similar *local spatial analyzers* in other parts of the retina, it is clear that with the appropriate wiring between them many of the Gestalt phenomena of transformation and part-whole determination (Figure 4.17A, B) could be explained (Palmer, 1977, 1982). What then should be attributed to cell assemblies created by perceptual learning, and what should be attributed to structures of spatial analyzers, is now a completely open question. The repertory of such preexisting units must be determined before the notion of acquired cell assemblies can serve any useful function.

2. Assertions about what learned cell assemblies—or about innate local spatial analyzers for that matter—would account for cannot simply be taken for granted. Such assertions are only an advance over previous Gestaltists' speculations if they are made specific enough to be tested. Given the immense number of elements involved, the only plausible way to test such a proposed explanation is by simulating the assumed nervous system as a computer program, if possible, and by showing that it performs as it is supposed to. The possibilities of such perceptual learning in a Hebbian network has received increasing atttention over the years (see p. 249), and more effort has gone toward the simulation of specific sensory networks, which we cite in the same section (see p. 249).

Attempts continue to devise physiological explanations of the Gestalt phenomena that are consistent with known physiology (Palmer, 1982, 1983; Ginsburg, 1971). To the present, however, none of these has addressed the major contribution of Gestalt psychology—the so-called laws of organization. Those rules, themselves, need far better study than they have received.

In part, the study of the Gestalt rules was suspended because a more general principle beckoned, one that could be expressed in terms of stimulation alone, with no reference either to exotic brain fields or to more orthodox physiological models. We consider that general principle next.

Simplicity Principle: From Organizational Laws to Coding Theories

It has long been speculated that we tend to perceive the simplest arrangement of surfaces and motions that we can (Mach, 1906) and that the Gestalt rules can be subsumed under such a principle (Koffka, 1935; Musatti, 1931; Hochberg & MacAlister, 1953). For recent reviews of the simplicity principle, see Pomerantz and Kubovy (1986), Hatfield and Epstein (1985), and Hochberg (1981a, 1986b). There is good reason to seek some unifying method for dealing with the various Gestalt factors. Because more than one Gestalt rule will usually apply in any real case, and because these rules are likely to work against each other (Figure 4.25C, D), they are not of much use in their present state. We have little or no quantitative measurement of their relative strengths, and no combinatorial rules of any kind. This does not mean that these deficiencies could not be remedied. The rules were neglected rather than rejected. The fact is that, until recently, only a handful of scientists were concerned with the problem of organization, and those few were diverted by three approaches to the problem that were offered in the 1950s and that continue to be pursued today.

The Promise of a Minimum Principle or Simplicity Rule: A Stimulus-Analysis Approach to Gestalt Organization

If the insights of Gestalt psychology are to have any predictive power, either we need quantitative measures of the strengths of the different rules, together with an appropriate combinatorial principle which predicts the consequences of combining two or more such rules (since the rules may work against each other), or we need instead some overarching or superordinate rule which supplants the group of individual rules and is itself quantitative and objective. Gestalt psychologists offered as an overarching rule the *minimum principle*—namely, that we perceive the simplest organization (the simplest alternative object or arrangement) that fits the stimulus pattern (Koffka, 1935).

How are we to decide in any case which alternative is simplest? At the time when the minimum principle was proposed, the Gestaltist picture of brain fields and current flows was at least marginally plausible, and it was hoped that our eventual understanding of those processes would provide a physiological basis for a minimum principle.

Alternatively, we might rely on appearances, and phrase the rule thus: we perceive that organization which *appears* the simplest. This would provide a mentalistic explanation, similar to Helmholtz's rule (p. 212), in that we must draw on perceptions themselves to predict what will be perceived. We then face the problem of measuring and predicting perceived simplicity.

A substantial effort was made between 1956 and 1970 at a psychophysics of form, relating subjects' judgements of such qualities as complexity, simplicity, and goodness to the measurable features of shapes, like those in Figure 4.26A, that had been generated according to arbitrary statistical procedures. Such forms were used in order to avoid specific associations and to provide a population to which the results could be generalized, that is, to all other shapes generated according to the same rules (Attneave and Arnoult, 1956). Reliable agreements between subjects were found about some properties (Zusne, 1970), but the choice of forms made it impossible to do anything further with such data. Flat, irregular, and unfamiliar polygonal silhouettes, and shapes with no indications of depth or layout, all provided data that had no known relation to the perception of three-dimensional objects and events or even to the perception of pictures of them. Procedures for generating more theoretically interesting figures were developed (Figure 4.26B), but their use quickly revealed insurmountable difficulties for the minimum principle, as we will see.

With apparently greater success, researchers

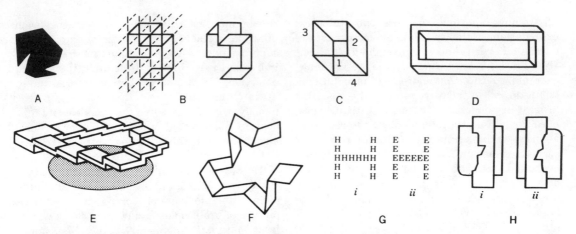

Figure 4.26. *Forms and objects: wholes and parts.* (A) an Attneave-Arnoult shape, for use in form research, is presented here. A sample is drawn randomly from a population of such shapes, which are obtained by following arbitrary procedures of construction, so that the results can be generalized with known reliability to other shapes drawn from that population (Attneave and Arnoult, 1956).

(B) This is a randomly-generated reversible-perspective shape and one of its two nonreversible alternatives (Hochberg, 1971), which permits more extensive testing of such simplicity rules as that in Figure 4.25E. One of the important results of such testing is illustrated in shapes C and F.

(C) The whole configuration does not determine the appearance of its parts. With your gaze fixed at intersection (1), perspective reversals will occur, and the vertical line will appear the nearer, even though that reading of the form is inconsistent with a simple figure, which is fixed in orientation at intersection (2) (Hochberg, 1978). This is true even with real, moving tridimensional objects, not only with such simple pictures (Hochberg & Peterson, 1987; Peterson and Hochberg, 1983), a fact that will be important to us when we discuss recent direct theories of object perception (pp. 240–241).

(D) In 1958, Penrose and Penrose discovered "impossible figures," pictures of objects that would be physically inconsistent if they existed in their casual reading. The "frame" (Hochberg, 1968) falls within one of the classes they found; note that it appears three dimensional even though its corners are then inconsistent, although the inconsistency is not immediately evident. It was originally thought that the inconsistency is tolerated because when one corner falls in foveal vision the other cannot be seen clearly (Hochberg, 1968), but because variations in overall size have little effect on the phenomenon, or on the related phenomenon in Figure 4.26C, it probably does not depend on retinal distance per se.

(E) A version of another class of Penrose figure is given here. Note that the "stairs" can either ascend or descend endlessly.

(F) Are the two ends of the ribbon the same or opposite face? One must deliberately "parse" the figure, fold by fold, in order to decide correctly, and the time that it takes to do so is a function of the number of folds (Klopfer and Hochberg, 1981). The perceived orientations of the surfaces are not automatically given by the overall configuration. In connection with attempts at direct theories of surface perception, it is important to note that similar uncertainties occur if the objects are in fact three-dimensional constructions viewed by a freely moving observer, and are not merely outline drawings of such objects.

(G) It is not that the more general context of a display has *no* effect on the perception of its parts. Subjects are faster at detecting the small letters of (i) than of (ii) (Navon, 1977), and better at identifying an object at some place in a briefly-flashed picture when both the object's setting and its place within that setting are what one would normally expect to be the case (Palmer, 1975; Biederman, 1981, respectively).

The whole-part relationship, which is fundamental to any understanding of the perception of objects, requires a great deal of thinking as well as research. We will consider part of what must go into such thinking in pp. 239, 256, 259.

(H) In the pattern at (i), the perceptual organization in which the irregular center strip appears in front of a square-like background is simpler than one in which the irregular leftmost region is nearest. When the pattern is inverted (ii), the irregular rightmost region becomes a face, and is readily seen as the nearest shape. The formal pattern has not changed, but its meaning has.

More detailed introductory treatment of the earlier work on these problems can be found in Hochberg, 1978; more recent work is reviewed in Goldstein, 1984. Collections of more advanced reviews can be found in Beck, 1982; Dodwell and Caelli, 1984; Kubovy and Pomerantz, 1981; Pomerantz and Kubovy, 1986.

initiated attempts in the 1950s (Attneave, 1954; Hochberg and MacAlister, 1953) to formulate an objective minimum principle, one which would require no intuitive judgments but which would rest instead on measurable features of the stimulus pattern. One formulation that has proved reasonably predictive analyzes each of the likely alternative distal objects that will fit the stimulus pattern being considered and uses some objective measure of those objects in deciding which alternative is simpler (e.g., the number of different lines, dihedrals or edges, the number of inflection points, etc.; Hochberg and Brooks, 1960). With an objective and quantitative rule of this sort, no intuitions would be needed. This is thus an attempt to account for the perception of objects in terms only of physical stimulus properties. Ideally, a computer could *in principle* assess any picture before showing it, and then select for display only those views for which the object to be represented is in fact the simplest alternative (e.g., Figure 4.25Eiii,vi rather than 4.25Ei, iv).

Although so far as I know no computer programs that would apply these principles to image generation have actually been attempted, variations on this approach continue today (Butler, 1982; Buffart, Leeuwenberg, & Restle, 1981; Leeuwenberg, 1971; Restle, 1982), and it has recently been applied to the perception of simple ambiguous patterns of moving dots (Restle, 1979). Such research would be theoretically important and practically useful if a minimum principle based only on objective measures of the stimulus pattern, and not on the theorist's intuitions, or on the viewer's individual knowledge or intentions, were in fact a feasible prospect, but both the theoretical and practical value of the minimum principle must be questioned in view of a set of facts that have been known to perceptual psychologists for several decades.

One of the facts is exemplified in Figure 4.26C. Note that the place that you attend determines how the object is perceived: When you attend intersection (2), the perceived orientation of the cube is such that the vertical edge is the nearer, in accordance both with the rule of good continuation and with any simplicity principle. To be consistent with that organization, the horizontal line at intersection (1) should appear nearer than the vertical. When you attend intersection (1), the perspective soon

reverses, and the vertical appears nearer (Hochberg, 1978, 1981a; Hochberg & Peterson, 1987; Peterson & Hochberg, 1983). This is inconsistent with the arrangement at (2), unless that intersection were perceived with the horizontal line there as nearer and as broken off just at the point at which it intersects the vertical in the drawing. It is not clear that that is what you see happen at (2) while you look at (1), and even if it were, this alternative is less simple (has more line segments of different length, etc.) than a cube by any accounting method.

This is not an isolated phenomenon, confined to some special class of outline drawings. It was clearly implied by discovery of the famous "impossible figures" by Penrose and Penrose (1958) in the 1950s, and by their widespread use in the popular graphic art of Maurice Escher (Figure 4.26E). It has been demonstrated with real cubes (three dimensional and moving), as well as with pictured versions of the cube in Figure 4.26C (Hochberg & Peterson, 1987; Peterson and Hochberg, 1983), and it has been known for some time that parts of coherent rotating objects may appear to turn in opposite directions (Gillam, 1972; see Figure 4.30E). No advocate of the minimum principle has, to date, dealt adequately with this problem.

It has been argued (Attneave, 1981; Boselie & Leeuwenberg, 1986) that the broken cube in Figure 26C is only slightly less simple than the unbroken version, but this argument overlooks the fact that with this procedure one can construct figures in which the difference in simplicity can be increased as desired. More important, it fails to address the fact that where you look, even within a single object, helps determine which parts contribute to the perceptual organization. Formal stimulus measures alone do not include such factors. This is a serious deficiency in view of the fact, introduced by the demonstrations in Figure 4.26C to H, that the viewer's attention and what is familiar (H), and not merely the measurable pattern of stimulation, helps determine what is perceived; we will return to this point shortly, and we will also consider other difficulties with simplicity formulations in connection with Figures 4.30 and 4.31.

Before we do so, we should consider the other factor that deflected attention from the objective study of organizational principles, namely, the opinion, now often asserted, that the Gestalt principles apply only to static drawings, and that the perception of the real world by moving viewers follows very different principles.

Ecological Realism: The Doctrine that Event Perception is both Fundamental and Veridical. An Account in Terms of Physical Measure

We have been considering various theories of perception that are direct, as distinct from inferential or cognitive. The most sweeping and radical of such direct theories, proposed for *all* aspects of perception by J.J. Gibson (1966, 1979), is that *our nervous systems "resonate" directly to the invariants that underlie the transformations of the proximal stimulus pattern that are received by the normally moving perceiver.*

Let us call this the *invariance theory*. It is the tenet of a broad approach to perception, called ecological realism, which tries to undertake research with events that are in some sense more natural than those events that have been studied thus far—events that Brunswik (1956) would have called "ecologically representative" (although it should be noted that he offered a prescription for identifying such events, and thus far there has been no attempt within this new approach to provide an explicit criterion). The advantage of such a theory is that at one stroke it accounts for our perception of the distal attributes of objects and layouts, inasmuch as those invariants in stimulation reflect the invariant structure of the physical world. That should be true wherever constant properties such as reflectance, rigidity, and so on, are found in the distal situation. This theoretical simplicity has appealed recently to many writers (Gibson, 1979; Johansson, 1982; Michaels & Carello, 1981; Shaw & Turvey, 1981).

As a particularly simple illustration of what that explanation might mean (which is not, however, one that was actually offered by any of those writers), consider what happens when the viewer moves towards the right in the three-dimensional layout in Figure 4.4A. Within the optic array provided by that layout, the objects' projections are displaced leftward. Motion parallax will displace the objects in proportion to their distances, as shown by the arrows, providing a form of motion perspective (Gibson, 1950, 1979). It we could respond directly to the ratio of the size of any object in the array divided by its parallax vector, we would be responding to a variable of stimulation that

itself remains invariant in the transformations of the optic array that are provided by the viewer's motions, and size constancy would be explained with no need for mental structures or unconscious inference.

This is of course very different from both the classical theory and the earlier direct theories. In the classical theory, what we perceive results from a process of problem solving, with the answer inferred or computed from various sources. The explanation of how we perceive size draws on perceptions of distance, regardless of the source of the information; the explanation of perceived lightness draws on perceived illumination. The computations underlying our perceptions therefore are not in general phrased only in terms of the information in the stimulation that is present at the time. More direct theories, like those of Hering and Mach, aimed at explaining specific perceptual abilities, being phrased in terms of mechanisms so constructed that they respond to an aspect of proximal stimulation that corresponds directly to some distal property. If we imagine the perceptual problem solver as a *homunculus* (a little person in the head), the homunculus need not base its computations on illumination at all in arriving at perceptions of reflectance because the input it receives from the sense organs already corresponds to that objects' reflectance. The computation is done by specifiable neural structures acting on specified aspects of proximal stimulation (e.g., luminance ratios). A large part of the problem of perception lies in successively reducing the task that confronts this imaginary homunculus (Attneave, 1961). The newer direct theories seek a general principle, which is to be expressed only by measurable physical stimulation and is not to be identified with some specific physiological mechanism. They are intended to replace the Helmholtzian notion of inferences or computations of one distal property based on perceptions of another.

The invariance principle is the most general explanation of this kind to have been offered. For such objects and parts of the environment as are themselves rigid and invariant in form, this principle means that we perceive those unchanging, rigid shapes and layouts in the world that project the changing, nonrigid two-dimensional patterns of light to the eye. That is, our nervous systems perform the required "reverse projective geometry" (Johansson, 1982) that will cause us to perceive a rigid distal object wherever that is permitted by the proximal stimulation at the eye. Given this principle (it is held), visual stimulation is not ambiguous, as it was (they say) mistakenly held to be since Berkeley; the optic array of the moving viewer fully specifies the tridimensional layout of the world (although we should note that Berkeley would instantly reject this argument; see p. 198).

By this account, normal perception occurs only when a viewer moves about in a natural environment. Research done in other situations is artificial and therefore supposedly misleading with respect to the nature of our perceptual systems. Because such invariance theories can of course only account for perception by moving observers, they take the perception of still objects and pictures to be a special case, governed by special and largely unknown principles (Gibson, 1954, 1979; Johansson, 1982). Indeed, the study of the perception of still objects is often dismissed as irrelevant to real perception; we will see that where such claims have been tested, they seem to be false (Figures 4.27D, 4.30).

The importance of motion in perception has been acknowledged for centuries. In the classical theory, Helmholtz placed knowing what one would see when moving around an object—that is, perceptual exploration—at the heart of what it means to perceive the object (p. 212). And motion parallax has long been known to be a potential source of information about spatial layout that is unavailable in the still image: As Leonardo Da Vinci knew, nearer objects are displaced more in the visual field of a moving viewer than are more distant ones, whereas the spatial relation between the parts of the flat picture, of course, all remain fixed. The picture is no longer a surrogate for the scene, therefore, if the viewer moves (Figure 4.4). The relative motions produced in the field of view by a given relative motion of the viewer are—with certain constraints or assumptions—specific to the layout of the points and surfaces of the scene in space. Mathematically, therefore, the differential motions within the stimulus pattern offered by the scene provides the moving observer with a rich source of information about the structure of the world. A critical question on which the viability of this approch depends is how much of that information is actually used, and in what form (Cutting, 1986; Hochberg, 1982, 1984a). To

examine that issue, let us turn from still pictures to moving patterns of stimulation.

It is surely true that most perceptual research has been done with still displays, but that has been a matter more of research feasibility than because psychologists have stubbornly avoided moving stimuli. Motion was not easy or cheap to use in a controlled and flexible manner. This situation, as we now see, has changed.

The Perception of Moving Displays

Until the early 1950s, only simple mechanical and electrical devices were generally available with which to study viewers' responses to moving patterns and to other stimuli that change over time. Since then, the study of patterns that change with time has been revolutionized by the introduction of relatively inexpensive 16 mm motion picture cameras capable of producing controlled motion through animation, and of even cheaper video equipment; and, above all, by the availability of computer-generated displays. Research on the topic has increased enormously, carried out as much by computer scientists, physicists, and neurophysiologists as by perception psychologists.

We will first consider the main facts of motion perception, and then return to the claims made by invariance theories or direct theories of perception that the perception of moving displays is primary, direct, and unambiguous.

MOTION THRESHOLDS

Absolute motions (Figure 4.27Ai), in order to be detected, must be faster than relative motions (4.27Aii). Much may follow from that. Research had been directed to the question of whether (and how well) our nervous system responds to the stimulus changes that carry information about depth and motion. Our visual system is extremely sensitive to motion parallax; even a slight difference in distance (Figure 4.27B) between two aligned or nearby rods can be detected (Berry, 1948). A small head movement on the part of the viewer will provide a displacement in the retinal image that should therefore be detectible (Wheatstone, 1839; Helmholtz, 1866). Two objects at different distances that happen to line up by chance, and provide for a misperception (as in Figure 4.27Ci), should be perceived as separate, given even a slight head movement to provide a detectible break in the good continuation (Figure 4.27Cii).

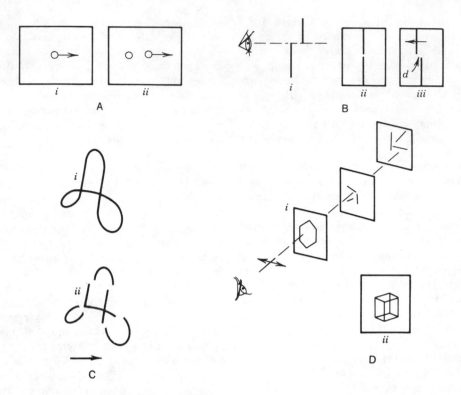

Figure 4.27. *The perception of motion.*

(A) Absolute motion: a single moving point relative to the viewer in an otherwise-dark room. Relative motion: two or more points moving at different velocities. Here, one is stationary and the other is moving rightward.

(B) Sensitivity for motion parallax: At (i) is shown a viewer looking at two aligned rods at different distances; at (ii) the optic array provided by (i). At (iii) a leftward movement of the viewer disturbs the alignment. We are extremely sensitive to such displacements, detecting as little as two sec of visual angle (Berry, 1948).

(C) If the contours of different objects should by chance line up in the environment (i), even slight head motions should provide displacements that disrupt the alignment; see (B).

(D) For this reason, many theorists assume that the Gestalt "laws," such as good continuation (Figure 4.25), are irrelevant to object perception in the real world. However, as Kopfermann reported in 1930, when the parts of a reversible-perspective cube are drawn on planes of glass so as to place adjacent parts at different distances (i), the cube not only appears as a continuous structure (ii) from the appropriate viewpoint, but slight head movements apparently fail to break the figure up into its component planes. The Gestalt factors are not artifacts of static drawings, nor are the pictorial depth cues, as we will see in connection with Figure 4.30.

This is why the Gestalt rule of good continuation may be a good cue to coplanarity and also an indication that the regions in question belong to a single object. It is also the main reason why direct theorists frequently assert that the phenomena of static pictorial perception, like the Gestalt rules and the geometrical illusions, are to be found only under such artificial conditions. But such arguments are in fact merely unsupported assertions. In 1930, Kopfermann reported that if the fragments of a cube were presented, torn out of spatial coherence, on panes of glass at different distances (Figure 4.27D), they would nevertheless look like a coherent cube. What is important here is that the cube continues to look coherent (although somewhat nonrigid) despite slight but detectable parallax that occurs owing to small motions of the viewer. So far as our present knowledge goes, such Gestalt factors as good continuation can within some limits overcome information about discontinuity and depth that is above the detection threshold for motion parallax.

Motions need not be continuous during the displacement in order to be perceived as such. Much of the earlier research studied the

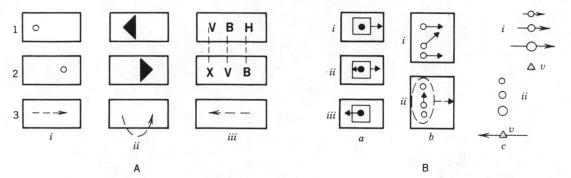

Figure 4.28. *Different stimuli can produce the same perceptions of motion, and the same stimuli can produce different perceptions of motion.*

(A) Perceived movement from successive stills (*stroboscopic movement*). With an appropriate duration and interval between the successive stimuli (ISI, or *interstimulus interval*) in (i), the successive still pictures (1, 2) are seen as rightward movement (3). Variously called stroboscopic movement, apparent movement, and beta movement, this clearly is related to phenomena on which motion pictures and television depend.

In the sequence of views 1, 2 in (ii), the form appears to rotate out of the plane, moving through the third dimension (3). This phenomenon is frequently explained as resulting from a perceptual tendency to maintain the identity of the object, but such cognitively phrased explanations cannot be taken too seriously. At (iii), the sequence of letters moves to the right, but leftward motion (3) is perceived, irresistibly, against the clear dictates of identity (Hochberg and Brooks, 1978a).

It now seems clear that stroboscopic motion is determined by factors that operate at quite different levels, and that these have different strengths and speeds. Recent research reviews to this point are Braddick, 1981 and Anstis, 1986. An earlier review by Kolers (1972) addresses the point made by (iii), and a review of perceptual factors of motion pictures is given by Hochberg (1986a). Even though the letters are displaced rightward in successive views, apparent movement occurs between the nearest contours of *non*corresponding objects, thus providing a leftward apparent movement in (3). The same effect will be provided by such clearly recognizable objects as people, words in sentences, and so on (Hochberg, 1986a).

(B) The same motion display may be seen in very different ways. At (a), for example, we have a stationary dot and a moving square (i), which may indeed be seen as such, but the relative motion may be perceived as split or partitioned between the two (ii); or, most commonly, the enclosing and moving square will appear to be stationary and the enclosed and stationary dot will appear as moving (iii), in what is called *induced movement* (Duncker, 1929; Wallach, 1982). The rules that govern how motion is partitioned provide a fertile field of research. Johansson reported in 1950 that a set of lights moving with the vectors shown at (b) in (i) are not perceived in that way at all but instead the center light appears to move on a line between the two outer lights and (much less prominently) the whole assembly moves rightward. From such demonstrations, he argued that the perceptual system extracts the common vector as a framework, against which the residual motion (in this case, that of the middle light) is seen.

In fact, he argues that the vector-extraction occurs by applying projective geometry to the stimulus motion (i), and that we perceive just that rigid structure in three-dimensional space (ii) which fits that pattern (Johansson, 1982). This proposal has not yet been spelled out clearly enough to assess, but it intersects an even more general problem which we consider in connection with Figure 4.29. For a recent review of the partitioning of motion, see Mack, 1986.

(C) If a significant area of the visual field moves coherently (i), the viewer (v) experiences self-movement (ii) (Held et al., 1975).

conditions that yield apparent movement with successive simple static stimuli (Korte, 1915; Kolers, 1972; Braddick, 1980; Morgan, 1980). *Apparent movement* or *stroboscopic movement* are names that are applied to smooth motion that is, under certain conditions, perceived in response to a succession of static stimuli. Examples are

shown and discussed in Figure 4.28A. A review of recent work may be found in Anstis, 1986.

INDUCED AND PARTITIONED MOTION

As might be expected from the differences between absolute and relative thresholds (Figure 4.27A), the display in Figure 4.28Ba may be seen

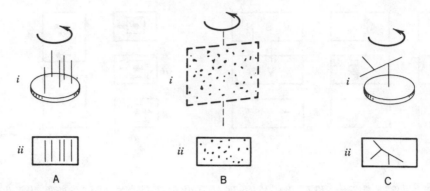

Figure 4.29. *Structure through motion.* All of the following procedures provide perceptions of space from two-dimensional moving patterns, which may themselves look flat when stationary (cf. Figures 4.28Aii and 4.28Bc).

(A) The shadows of rods mounted on a rotating turntable (i) are viewed through an aperture (Metzger, 1934; White and Mueser, 1960).

(B) Shadows of a field of dots on a moving pane of glass (i) are projected on a screen (ii) (Gibson and Gibson, 1957). These displays are now most readily produced by computer generation (Green, 1961; Lappin, Doneer, & Kottas, 1980). If displays consist of a few lights that move as though they were at the joints (wrist, elbows, knee, etc.) of human figures, the patterns may be totally unrecognizable when stationary, but are seen as humans in action, with recognizable characteristics (e.g., gender) as soon as they begin to move. (Cutting, 1978; Cutting & Proffitt, 1982; Johansson, 1977a; Todd, 1983).

(C) Unfamiliar 3D wire forms, mounted on a turntable, appear flat when static, and appear tridimensional when in motion (Wallach & O'Connell, 1953).

Such demonstrations have been used as evidence by those theorists (see text) who hold that we perceive spatial layout directly by drawing on an invariance or rigidity principle. Figure 4.30 argues against such generalizations.

---

as that in (ii) or as that in (iii). In general, visual movement may be partitioned in various ways (4.28B). Most important for any evaluation of the invariance theory (and of the related rigidity principle, see below) are studies on what has come to be called *structure through motion*: the two-dimensional shadows or projections of unfamiliar objects in irregular 3D arrangements are seen as flat patterns when stationary, but are typically seen as three-dimensional layouts when they are set into motion (Figure 4.29A, C; Metzger, 1934; Wallach & O'Connell, 1953 Green, 1961), and cause the stationary patterns to appear three dimensional on subsequent viewing (Wallach & O'Connell, 1953).

These phenomena are difficult to explain in terms of the classical empiricist theory, if by that we mean a set of specific associations between patterns of proximal stimulation—and the sensory responses made to them by independent receptors—on the one hand, and learned meanings or memories of prior clusters of sensory responses on the other. Even more than the static Gestalt demonstrations, these phenomena

seem difficult to explain as the results of using a look-up table. How plausible is it that the viewer has encountered the particular pattern of moving, randomly arrayed dots (shown in Figure 4.29B) so often that by familiarity it has become a recognizable tridimensional arrangement? It seems far more plausible that the phenomenon is the expression of a perceptual rule.

That still leaves open the question of what the rule is. The most simple and general solution is the *rigidity principle*: *we perceive that rigid object or layout—if one exists—that will fit the moving stimulation.* That rule would account for the perception of rigid objects and surfaces, without additional rules or constraints, in a very powerful way.

Moreover, some form of the rigidity principle is compatible with and indeed follows from virtually every other attempt at a general perceptual principle. It is not surprising, therefore, that the rigidity principle has been so widely held, directly or indirectly, by a full spectrum of perceptual psychologists (Gibson, 1966, 1979;

Johansson, 1977, 1982; Rock, 1983; Shepard, 1981; Todd, 1982) and computer scientists (Marr, 1982; Ullman, 1979).

In fact, however, *the rigidity principle will not work as a general and sufficient rule, either for the perception of objects in space or for the perception of their representations*, and the evidence to that effect has been known to perception psychologists for many years. It may be that a tendency to see the rigid alternative contributes to what we perceive (although it is not a well-established factor in any event), but it is not a *sufficient* principle; it will not account for what we perceive in a way that makes the other factors (depth cues, laws of organization, etc.) unnecessary or irrelevant, for reasons we consider next.

Why General Rigidity, Invariance, and Veridicality Principles must all be Rejected: Shapes and Scenes that cannot be Correctly Depicted or Perceived.

The strongest evidence for rejecting rigidity, invariance or simplicity as a sufficient principle is this: even when the geometry of the stimulus conditions should permit rigid shapes to be seen, and even when the stimulus is in fact a rigid object in motion, we may strongly and unambiguously perceive instead quite different shapes undergoing nonrigid deformation. This has been known at least since 1922, when von Hornbostel described how a real, rotating wire cube spontanteously appears to reverse front and back, and rotate in the opposite direction, even though it must then appear to stretch and bend. A remarkably robust illusion known as the Ames "window" has been widely described since 1951. A trapezoid (often cut and painted to suggest a window in perspective view) rotates continuously in one direction, in full view, as shown in Figure 4.30A. Instead of being seen to rotate, it appears to oscillate, reversing direction twice each cycle, so that the larger end (1) always appears to be the nearer.

In descriptive terms, it is as though the viewer first assigns depth on the basis of the static depth cue of linear perspective (Figure 4.2), overcoming motion derived stimulus information (presumably primary, according to Gibson and Johannson; see p. 241) to do so, and then unconsciously infers the direction of movement from the erroneously assigned depth. It must be added here that there is no experimental evidence that inference plays any part in explaining this class of illusion—that an inference explanation is difficult to reconcile with the phenomena that we discuss in connection with Figure 4.30B, D and E. In D, the argument that the effect occurs because the figure looks like a familiar rectangular window, is refuted: a perfectly normal letter A appears to be moving toward the viewer at its base when it is in fact moving away. Despite a considerable amount of research (most recently, by Braunstein, 1983), there is no single generally accepted explanation for this class of phenomena. What appears here to be a response resulting from inference or computation may instead be one of several alternative direct responses to the changing pattern (cf. Hochberg, 1974); specifically, once the large side is perceived as being nearer by some amount, the changing pattern that is provided by the object's rotation specifies a motion that is in the wrong direction. Another possible noninferential explanation (Braunstein, 1976) is that as interior corner angles decrease and increase, we perceive rotational motions of approach and recession, respectively. And a third possible direct or noninferential basis for the illusion is sketched in Figure 4.30C.

This illusion is difficult to overcome even when the viewer is confronting a real object, although then on close viewing one eye must be kept covered, and at closer distances even monocular viewing will reveal the true shape and rotation. When the viewer is shown not the object itself, but a moving picture of it, the illusion is almost irresistible. The point that is presently important to us is this: the virtual shape which fits the stimulus pattern when the erroneous orientation and movement are perceived must then be a nonrigid one, with stretching and shrinking parts (Figure 4.30C).

The trapezoid undergoes these illusory oscillations even if a rigid rod is rigidly affixed to the trapezoid. The rod appears to rotate, correctly, rather than to oscillate with the trapezoid. It cannot then appear rigidily fixed, of course, but appears to pass *through* the trapezoid like a phantom each time the large end of the trapezoid is erroneously perceived to be rotating nearer the viewer but is actually further (Ittelson and Kilpatrick, 1952). Knowledge of the true situation cannot dispel the illusion: it occurs even if the viewer is simultaneously shown the arrangement from above in a mirror. In the mirror, the

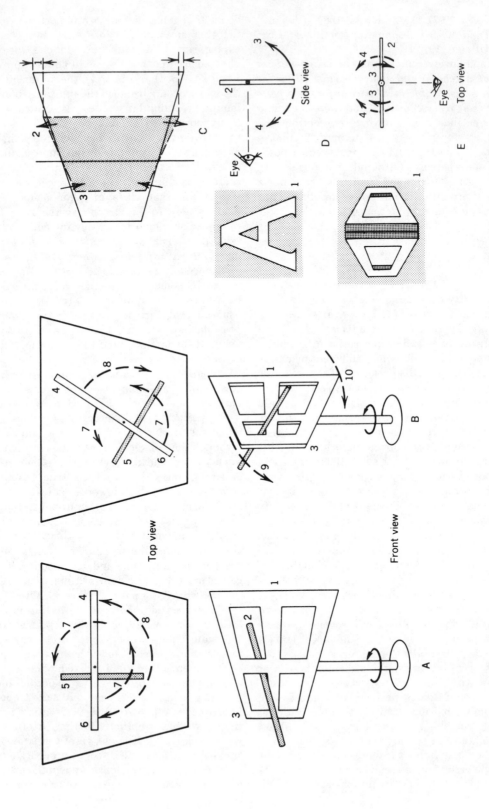

Figure 4.30. *The Ames "window" and its implications.*

(A) At (1, 3) a trapezoid, cut out of a flat sheet, painted as shown, and mounted on a turntable is seen in the frontal plane, with edges (1) and (3) equidistant from the viewer. Ames (1951) showed that when *rotated*, as shown by the arrow, it appears instead to *oscillate* back and forth. A rod (2) fixed rigidly to the trapezoid is perceived nonrigidly, rotating a full 360 degrees and therefore *passing through* the trapezoid when the latter appears to reverse (see 9, in B). The display is shown reflected from above in a mirror, where the true rotation is shown by the arrows marked (7) and the apparent oscillation is shown by the arrow marked (8). Even when the mirror and the trapezoid are seen at the same time, and the top view shows the true rotation, the trapezoid is seen directly and appears to oscillate.

(B) The trapezoid is here rotated so that the small end (3) is nearer the viewer.

(C) Although the rod is rigidly fixed to the trapezoid, that rigidity is not perceived (Ittelson & Kilpatrick, 1952). But in any case, the trapezoid itself cannot be perceived as rigid if it undergoes these illusory motions. The solid outline is the shape of the trapezoid as projected in the optic array when its edges are equidistant (as at A); the dotted line and shaded region show the shape of the figure in the optic array when edge (3) is nearer. If the right edge is incorrectly perceived as being nearer, then it must also appear to shrink by the amount shown here as (1), because of its greater distance (see Figure 4.1). In order to appear as oscillating, the right edge must appear to approach when it is actually receding, and the perceived object must appear to be changing its shape, nonrigidly, as shown here.

Because the object's upper edges are not perpendicular to the axis of rotation, the contours of the upper right edge move outward in the array (and in the retinal image), as at (2), and the upper left edge moves inward as at (3). Given the strong tendency for apparent movement between adjacent contours, regardless of whether they correspond (Figure 4.27C), this provides the stimulus pattern for expansion and approach, on the right, and contraction and recession, on the left—a "direct" basis for the illusion that is therefore given in the stimulus pattern, so that the illusion may not depend at all on inference processes.

(D) The effect described in (A) and (B) is not owing to the viewer's familiarity with windows. A cutout of the letter "A", with its lower edge moving away from the viewer as shown from the side (2) by arrow (3), appears instead to approach (arrow 4).

(E) The flat, rigid hexagon shown from in front at (1) and shown from the top at (2), appears to *fold* away from the viewers, according to the arrows marked (4), when it is in fact simply rotating; see the arrows marked (3). We do not perceive the rigid solution. Here, as in the other examples, that would be to see the object moving as it really is. And it is therefore not true in general that we will see the true disposition of surfaces in the world, if only they are in motion relative to the viewer (see Hochberg, 1987).

rod and trapezoid are seen to rotate 360 degrees as a single rigid unit, while to direct gaze they move as separate parts (Figure 4.30B), despite the viewer's efforts to see the true, rigid motion (Hochberg, Amira, & Peterson, 1984).

Finally, a perfectly rigid shape, as shown in Figure 4.30E, pivoting around the vertical axis so that the left side approaches the viewer, is seen as breaking in the middle, with both sides flapping away (Hochberg and Spiron, 1985). In short, the real, rigid and invariant object, moving in a simple and invariant orbit, is not perceived; instead, the object is seen as nonrigid and deformed, moving in a complex and variable path. Failures of rigidity in the perception of rigid objects are also reported and discussed by Braunstein & Andersen (1986), Hochberg (1987), Pomerantz (1983), Schwartz & Sperling (1983), Todd (1984), and Ullman (1986), among others.

In the one case in which a direct theoreist addresses this problem, Gibson (1979, p. 167) claims that the illusion occurs only when no information is provided as to trapezoid's true motion, and that when that happens the illusion occurs because the viewer presupposes that the object is a rectangle. This assertion leaves much unexplained. If moving surfaces provide optical information about depth, as in Figures 4.4 and 4.27, then there needs to be some explanation by direct theorists as to why that information should be available (or above threshold) in some cases, such as Figures 4.4 and 4.27, and unavailable (or below threshold) in the trapezoid. Furthermore, to explain the apparent motion of the trapezoid by appealing to the viewer's presupposition that the object is rectangular is to explain that motion as an unconscious inference. In invoking unconscious inference at all, this account of the illusion destroys the direct theory's claim to parsimony, and raises serious questions about when the unconscious inference that is then used could have been acquired in the first place, and about when else it will intrude into what appears to be normal perception (Hochberg, 1981, 1982). Motion similarly fails to dispel completely other illusions that appear to depend on static perspective misinformation (Gehringer & Engel, 1986).

In the third place, however, the Gibsonian account of the illusion is wrong. The motion information that should dispel the illusion, in terms of a rigidity or invariant theory, is clearly above threshold. This is made evident if we replace the trapezoid by a computer generated rotating row of rigid rods (Hochberg et al., 1984); as in the trapezoid it emulates, the large side always looks the nearer, but during the half of the cycle on which it is actually farther, it clearly appears to change size (see 1, Figure 4.30C).

Claims by direct theorists that stimulus information determines perception in accordance with an invariance principle or a rigidity principle have therefore not been sustained. Taken by itself, this might merely mean that we have not yet found the appropriate principle. However, there are other grounds for believing that the measurable stimulation is not in general sufficient to explain perception, and that we need to bring in what behaviorist psychologists rejected as mentalistic notions. We discuss this kind of explanation in the next section.

THE RETURN OF "MENTALISMS"/ THE EFFECTS OF COMPUTERS ON PERCEPTUAL PSYCHOLOGY

The introduction of the computer has affected perceptual psychology in many ways; it has radically changed the methodology of measurement and analysis, as it has in virtually every field of science. Computers make it possible, for example, to change the display of picture or text during the brief period of the saccadic eye movement (when the eye is quite insensitive), and to study how what is seen in peripheral vision in one glance contributes to the initiation and interpretation of the next. For example, when reading text while their gaze direction is monitored, subjects notice if letters are changed within a distance of four letter spaces ahead of where the eye is pointed, or if the shape of the word is changed within 14 letter spaces; their eyes pause longer subsequent to such changes, thus revealing the distance at which those informative features are picked up in peripheral vision while reading (McConkie & Rayner, 1975).

And of course the computer makes it possible to handle and analyze data in ways that were previously impractical. Physiological signals that are normally not strong enough to be distinguished from bioelectrical background noise that accompanies them can be cumulated over many occurrences, making it possible to measure the electrical potentials at the scalp that accompany perceptual events and that presumably reflect relevant brain activities (Donchin, Ritter, & McCallum, 1978; Sutton, Braren, Zubin, & John, 1965) and even to measure magnetic fields at the scalp which may reflect the underlying neural processes more directly (Kaufman & Williamson, 1982; Reite & Zimmerman, 1978).

Computers make it possible to model theoretical proposals that otherwise would be too laborious or even impossible to evaluate. Theories that are too complex to assess directly can often be tested by computer simulation to determine whether some hypothesized process would in fact account for the phenomena that are to be explained.

One cannot tell with any confidence from the verbal description of some hypothetical neural network whether it would in fact display, for example, the perceptual learning that Hebb was seeking to explain (p. 236f), or the stereoscopic depth organization toward which various versions of Figure 22 have been directed. With respect to perceptual learning: After some isolated work (Rosenblatt, 1962) and some negative prognoses (Minsky & Papert, 1969), a great deal of attention is being paid to how parallel networks of elements, connected by excitatory and inhibitory links, can change or learn (the rubric is PDP, for parallel distributed processing; McClelland, Rumelhart & Hinton, 1986; Rumelhart & McClelland, 1986) as part of a more general interest in the computational characteristics of such networks (e.g., Feldman & Ballard, 1983; Grossberg, 1987). Far more work has been done on models of specific sensory processing, with comprehensive recent reviews by Marr (1982) and Witkin & Tenenbaum (1983). One purpose for such models is to build machines that can replace humans at tasks that require interaction with the environment, that is, that require the performance of what might be termed perceptual tasks. In general, however, for these purposes there is no need to perform each task by the same means that humans use. Human perceptual functions thus serve only to show that the task can indeed be done.

But the computer also serves as an important source of analogies in our thinking about human perceptual processes. Psychologists are inherently vulnerable to entanglement in the mind-body problem and are therefore often tempted to deal only with variables that are conceived and measured in physical terms. Behaviorism exerted a strong hold on psychology in this country for some 30 years, and perceptual psychology was all but abandoned as a discipline until in the late 1950s what can only be called mental conceptions and measures again became generally scientifically respectable. I think that the fact that computer programs can in principle be transported between machines that are different physically, and can therefore be discussed in abstract functional terms without reference to specific hardware, was the major agent in this change of intellectual climate. With computer terminology and flow charts, it became possible to describe what the mind might be doing in ways that could, in principle, be instantiated in a program and embodied in a machine (Miller, Galanter, & Pribram, 1960; Rosenblatt, 1962; Selfridge, 1959).

Machine models of psychology in general, and of perception in particular, were attempted many times since Descartes in 1650, or even Democritus in ca. 400 B.C. The general purpose computer and transportable programs are far more flexible and plausible, however, than such machine models could ever be, and cognitive psychology is now couched in language very close to that used in computer science. If such a model can in fact be written or run as a computer program, it may then be convicted of being wrong or inconsistent, but not of being unacceptable because it is mentalistic.

At the extreme edge of this enterprise stand the attempts to write programs for performing perceptual tasks that work by simulating the functioning of the human nervous system and brain. This undertaking must necessarily start with empirical knowledge of how humans perceive, which is precisely the task of perceptual psychology. The two disciplines therefore now overlap greatly, and a considerable proportion of perceptual and cognitive psychology is currently done in computer science departments. (For conferences in which psychologists and computer scientists address related problems, see Beck, Hope & Rosenfeld, 1983, and Longuet-Higgins & Sutherland, 1980. Particularly comprehensive and critical overviews are provided by Haber (1983), a perception psychologist, and by Witkin & Tenenbaum, (1983), computer scientists.)

This is a very welcome development, both

because the ranks of researchers are increased, and because the computer is so important to the study of perception. But with the welcome must go some caution. Publications in this new field have often been hailed as breakthroughs, but we should not overestimate what has been accomplished so far. If strictly adhered to, the effort to simulate human perception in computer programs forces precise theories, testable by objective data, in a way that mere good resolutions toward the same goals do not. But the efforts at computer vision do not by themselves provide either new theories or new facts about human perception. In its first surge of activity, computer vision has had over a century of previous perceptual research and theory to draw upon. The point is worth spelling out in a brief examination of the field.

To begin with, any perceiving machine must be able to separate objects from their cluttered surroundings: to decide what parts of the visual field belong to the same objects. This problem is very difficult to deal with in still pictures, and indeed once we step beyond artificially simple outline drawing, it is even difficult to decide where an edge lies. In the retinal images that are provided by the world to the eye, gradations of light and shade arise for many reasons, such as cast shadows, modeling, reflectance differences, objects' edges, and so on. The transitions between dark and light at objects' edges (to take the simplest case) are not abrupt, and some decision must be made as to when and where to assign them. In 1886, Mach proposed that contours are a function of the second derivative of the intensity; in the form of "zero crossings" these have been taken as a first stage of image processing (Marr, 1982). That is not enough, however. In the two-dimensional image, whether a contour will occur at one place depends on the distribution at other places as well, which can to some extent be modeled by sampling over different sizes (or with different spatial frequencies: see p. 228, Roberts, 1965; Oately, 1978; Marr & Hildreth, 1980). Such attempts at explaining edge perception are complicated by the fact that we perceive edges between regions that have the same overall luminance, if they differ sufficiently in their texture. To define what comprises "sufficiently different texture," and to measure it, is not a simple matter. Using dot-matrix textures like those in Figure 4.21A, Julesz (1962, 1975) had proposed that the shapes of the texture elements

are not important to this problem, but that certain statistical properties determine whether an edge will, without special scrutiny, be perceived between the two regions. A rule like this about how texture elements are grouped by the nervous system would be relatively amenable to quantitative models and to incorporation in devices for machine vision. However, as Beck argued in 1972, and Julesz now also maintains (1981), the elementary shape features of the texture elements (*textons*) can be critically important (see Beck, Prazdny & Rosenfeld, 1983), and thus a problem of detecting primitive shape similarities exists even before the edges are extracted that provide the shape of the larger regions bounded by those edges.

In any case, these algorithms will not suffice to decide which edges belong together and bound the same object. For that, additional constraints, or assumptions about the world, are needed. We have discussed some of these in connection with the Gestalt rules (Figures 4.17, 4.25). Given enough constraints on the nature of the objects in the world, one can write rules by which to parse the scene into its component objects, and attempts by Guzman (1968) and Waltz (1975) have received attention in psychology texts. But we should stress that we do not know how far such schemes can be extended, nor do we know how well human visual perception conforms to any of them. The kinds of tolerance in Figure 4.26D, F and the effects of familiarity and expectation that we will discuss in connection with Figures 4.32, and 4.33 provide ready exceptions for which a more general formulation must provide. Other systems for describing shapes or for generating visual objects, and for deciding how to parse more complex objects into their simpler components, have been developed in recent years (Binford, 1981; Brady, 1983; Hoffman & Richards, 1984; Marr, 1982), and Biederman proposed in 1985 that the earliest stages of object recognition proceed very rapidly by analyzing any object into a small set of primitive components, as all printed words are analyzed into a small set of letters and all spoken words are analyzed into a small set of phonemes. According to Biederman's estimate, approximately 40 different primitive shapes or *geons* would, in combinations of from two to seven per object, suffice to describe and recognize some 2 million different objects, and that this is enough to account for the early stages of object recognition.

Because motion parallax and binocular parallax could serve in principle to sidestep so many perceptual problems, segregating objects in space without drawing on the myriad depth cues (Figure 4.2) and organizational rules (Figure 4.25), it is understandable that computer scientists have recently turned to models of binocular stereopsis (Marr and Poggio, 1976; Marr, 1982) and the perception of structure through motion (Ullman, 1979; Marr, 1982). These computational models are totally within the mainstream of perceptual psychology (it seems that this fact is not always clear to their proponents or their readers). For example, the computational models of binocular stereopsis devised and tested by Marr and his colleagues are relatively slight variations of Sperling's theory, described on p. 228. Similarly, Ullman (1979) undertook a mathematical analysis of successive views of a moving rigid 3D pattern of dots, to determine the minimum number of views and dots needed to determine their layout. Although there are unique and interesting features in his proposal—it proceeds by local regions, and discards the information given by perspective—and it has been tested as a computer simulation program, it is also conceptually well within the long tradition of such analyses and research (pp. 244). We should remember that computational theories that attempt to avoid dealing with the pictorial depth cues by concentrating on binocular or motion parallax are presently no better than the equivalent main-line theories at dealing with cases in which unimpeded binocular parallax is overcome by interposition—as in Figure 4.23C (Schriever, 1925)—or in which static cues interfere with the information in unimpeded motion parallax—as we have seen in Figure 4.30, in which at least some rigid objects are perceived as nonrigid and with the wrong slants and movements. In proposing a model that can tolerate some nonrigidity, Ullman (1984) does say in effect that static cues in conflict with the motion based information cause an erroneous and therefore nonrigid structure to be fitted to the motion. That discussion is purely verbal (as distinct from a computer simulation), however, and returns us in any event to the perceptual problem with which we started: how can we cope theoretically with all the depth cues and organi-

zational factors that must participate in any real perceptual situation?

Combining the depth cues and organizational determinants in different ways, and learning how they act when so combined, is a massive task. In principle, computer models can deal with the kind of multi-variable messiness of such a task, which may well yield data that cannot be summarized in a single rule or principle. Only a small amount of research work has actually been done on cue combination so far (Schriever, 1925; Jameson & Hurvich, 1959; Dosher, Sperling, & Wurst, 1984; see Figure 4.23); and the two later studies show what appears to be orderly, linear combination rules.

In any case, regardless of the philosophical merits of computer simulation and of the attempt to devise perceiving machines, there is a strong practical need, which has interesting theoretical aspects, to develop theories of human perception to the point that they can be embodied in computer programs. Computers are increasingly used specifically to *generate* pictures for a wide range of purposes: to provide a medium of communication with humans; to present some part of the world which would otherwise be impossible to view; to show the viewer what particular designs of buildings, machine parts, molecules, chromosomes, or cellular processes would look like; to replace human artists and animators in advertising and entertainment; to serve as simulators in aircraft trainers. Such use is great, and growing. Increasingly, the pictures (or pictorial sequences) shown have not themselves been programmed, or previewed in any sense, since they are generated in response to some question that the user asks or in reaction to something the viewer does (e.g., a display shows that what an architectural layout will look like from any point of view, or a low-altitude flight simulator in which the pilot's steering determines the display, respectively).

Because in such cases no human editor intervenes between computer and user, we must be able to specify, in terms that can be used by a computer, how humans will perceive any picture or a sequence, if we are to avoid misleading or uninterpretable pictures. The cases in which we misperceive (Figures 4.13, 4.14, and 4.30), which are often regarded merely as embarrassments in attempting general theories of perception, are then just those cases that must be the focus of our inquiry (Haber & Wilkinson, 1982; Hochberg, 1987).

There are practical limits, moreover, to the pictorial information that we can count on. One can see detail in a closeup, or an entire object or scene in a long shot, but not both. Picture quality is limited, and the techniques that motion picture and television film makers have developed (Hochberg & Brooks, 1978a; Hochberg, 1986a) to cope with those limits—surveying or scanning an object or scene by successive partial views or closeups—require the viewer to go beyond the momentary sensory input and to enter and store the successive partial views in some mental or *perceptual structure* of the object.

The term, perceptual or mental structure, has been used in different ways (see Garner, 1962). Here, it refers to the relationships *within* what one perceives, that is, to the information about the object that can be retrieved from the viewer. For example, that the sides of a cube look equal and parallel, and the vertical line at 1 in Figure 4.26C looks nearer than the horizontal line at 2, when 3 looks nearer than 4. To the degree that perceptual structure reflects the structure of the stimulus, physical analyses of optical information will serve to model the perceptual process. Obviously, *so long as we stipulate that a particular wire cube is perceived correctly, the layout of the physical cube itself will serve to predict the relative apparent nearnesses of its parts*. The simplicity of this task is of course what makes the more extreme direct theories so attractive. To the degree that perceptual structure reflects known (or hypothetical) neurological structure, the latter must also be taken into account. Thus, what we know about the distribution of acuity over the retina, or what we think we know about spatial frequency channels, must be used in attempting to predict the effects of the information that could otherwise be provided by the optical structure. Computer models of perception can incorporate both kinds of structure with very little input from psychological research.

However, to the degree that perceptual structure expresses what we may call mental structure, perceptual research must provide the facts that are needed *before* any computer models can be undertaken. We next consider very briefly the current state of research on mental structure in the perception of real and represented objects.

Research on Mental Structure as a Perceptual Component

What one perceives can to some degree be predicted from the distal or proximal stimulation provided by the world. That is necessarily true by *any* account of the perceptual process, given that our perceptions must guide our behaviors in the world. In some cases, the perceptual response reveals a set of relationships, or *structure*, that cannot be attributed to relationships within the stimulus pattern itself, and that therefore can be termed mental structure. But not all such cases absolutely require us to consider mental structure as a component of perception per se.

Because of the difficulties inherent in the notion of mental structure, and because of the controversy concerning its very existence, we should not draw on it unnecessarily. First, we consider some perceptual phenomena which, although they reveal the effects of factors other than sensory stimulation, can be plausibly explained without recourse to mental structure, and we consider what makes such phenomena suceptible to such explanation. Then we consider phenomena in which some account in terms of mental structure appears unavoidable.

When Alternatives to Mental Structure are Plausible.

According to the classical account of the perceptual constancies, relationships that we have learned from the physical world (i.e., our mental structures) are taken into account in arriving at perceptions of distal attributes from proximal stimulation (Figure 4.10). With the same patch of luminance, objects of different reflectance may be perceived, depending on the apparent illumination (Figure 4.11); with the same visual angle, objects of different size may be perceived, depending on the apparent distance (Figure 4.12); with a stationary retinal image, an object will appear to move if the viewer perceives himself to be moving relative to the field of view (Figure 31A,B; see also Rock and Ebenholtz, 1962). Our perceptions of reflectance and illumination are *coupled* to each other, as are those of size and distance, and of self-motion and object-motion. The mere fact that these couplings occur, however, does not necessarily implicate mental structure. If the subject learns of the change in illumination, or distance, or motion, by physical changes in stimulation (depth cues, illumination cues, etc.), those changes in stimulation might themselves *directly* cause the changes in appearance of the object (see Figure 4.20D caption; p. 240).

It is often very difficult, therefore, to rule out the possibility that what we take as perceptual effects of knowledge about the world are instead directly mediated by informative variables of stimulation. Moreover, even when the stimulus situation is apparently unchanged, the effects of the subject's knowledge (or of other extra-stimulus variables such as attention or instructions) may lead to a change in sensory behavior, such as where the eyes are directed, and that in turn may result in a change in stimulation which itself exerts direct effects on perception. For example, the knowledge that the trapezoid is upright in Figure 4.20C probably leads to a different set of eye movements in comparing it to its surroundings (Hochberg, 1971), and we know that the path that the eye takes through a field of different luminances affects its response to each of them (Flock, Wilson, & Poizner, 1966).

Before we can undertake to examine the existence and nature of mental structure, therefore, we should assemble an array of experimental situations in which alternative explanations are not so plausible.

Where no Plausible Alternatives to Mental Structure are Evident

There are at least three classes of phenomena that seem to demand explanation in terms of mental structure. In all three, the visual stimulus pattern is either constant, or is unable to account for the perceptual responses that are reliably obtained. Although these phenomena are all discussed in relation to the evidence of mental structure that they provide, there is presently no reason to believe that they are otherwise related to each other, or that they draw on the same processes.

COUPLING OF SELF-MOTION AND PERCEIVED OBJECT CHANGE

There is a certain class of demonstrations in which the *absence* of change in the visual stimulus, taken with the motion of the viewer, elicits perceptions of visual change that are hard to talk about without introducing notions equivalent to what has here been called mental structure. For example, when the viewer moves while looking at a picture, the spatial relations on the picture itself of course remain unchanged, and the optic array undergoes only a uniform translation and compression. Given the structure provided by the geometry of space (but not however present in the stimulation), because the viewer has moved the picture can no longer represent the same three-dimensional scene, and the spatial layout in the picture should appear to change (Figure 4.31Ai). With careful research, it has been shown that objects appear to change the direction in which they point when the viewer changes position (Figure 31Aii; Goldstein, 1979). Paradoxically, however, the spatial layout within the scene appears to remain relatively constant, as though two different and partially independent kinds of space are perceived in response to pictured depth.

Another example is shown in Figure 4.31B. When a moving subject views a stereogram in which both views are superimposed in space and separated optically by appropriate filters (e.g., polarized spectacles), the parallax that should occur between the surfaces that appear to lie at different distances in stereoscopic space, were they in fact at different distances in real space, does not of course occur. The only arrangement in real space that would fit this situation is one in which the surfaces so move as to cancel the parallax, as in Figure 4.31Bi,ii. This is what subjects in fact see; for discussion of such phenomena, see Gogel (1979, 1981, 1982, 1983) and Shebilske and Proffitt (1981, 1983). When ambiguous stereograms are used, which can be perceived in either of two spatial arrangements with the identical physical display, the direction of movement that is perceived is appropriate to the spatial arrangement that the subject has been instructed to try to perceive (Peterson, 1986).

It is not evident how these phenomena, or similar effects that have been obtained with reversible 3D cubes as in Figure 26C (Hochberg & Peterson, 1987), might be explained without attributing to the viewer some set of internal rules that relate perceived movement and perceived spatial arrangement, in other words, some *coupling* of apparent distance and movement. But although such couplings have often been treated as examples of mental structure, the rules themselves are simply formulated, and might reflect the occurrence of coupled responses (Hochberg, 1974); they might even be innate.

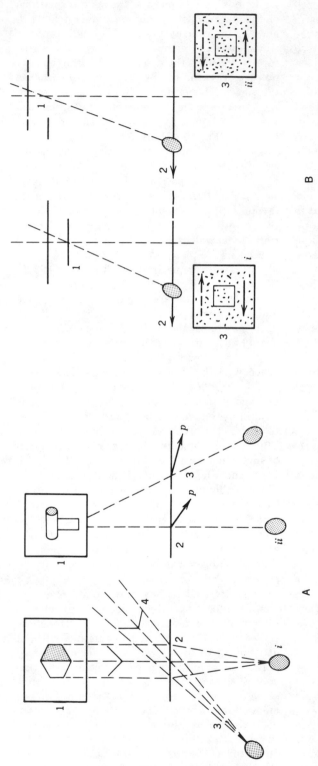

Figure 4.31. *"Inferred" movement.*

(A) Apparent changes in a still picture. At (1) there is a picture of an object. When viewed head on, as at (2), the object fits a symmetrical corner (e.g., of a building or a box). If the viewer were looking at a real box, the projection would change when he or she moved to (3). Because it is a picture, and does not change, an object of a slightly different (and slightly asymmetrical) shape—and different orientation (4)—would then be needed to fit the array provided by the picture, so that the change which does *not* occur in the picture demands a change in the object represented. Under proper conditions, such change is in fact perceived. In (ii), when viewers indicate the apparent direction of the pictured rod (1), as seen from different viewing angles (2, 3), by setting a pointer (p) the objects' orientations do appear to change with viewing angle (but not, paradoxically enough, the apparent layout within the picture; Goldstein, 1979).

(B) Apparent motion in a still stereogram. Dot-matrix stereograms (see Figure 4.21) can be made ambiguous so that by fusing different subsets of dots the viewer can see the depth in more than one way (Julesz, 1971; Kaufman & Pitblado, 1965). In an ambiguous dot-matrix stereogram in which the viewer sees a square in front (as in Bi), or a recessed surface (as in Bii), spontaneous reversals occur between the two alternatives, and which alternative will predominantly be seen depends partly on instructions, that is, on which the viewer *intends* to see. Peterson (1986) showed that compensatory (and illusory) motion will be seen which depends on the viewer's intentions: If the viewer (2) moves leftward while seeing the square in front, a rightward motion of the square would occur *if it really were in front*, as shown by the dotted arrow in Bi (3). Because the stereogram is in fact stationary, the reverse movement is seen when, in following instructions, the viewer sees the square to the rear, as in (ii). Using the identical stereogram, these relationships are reversed, and the opposite movement is seen when, in following instructions, the viewer sees the square to the rear, as in (ii). This phenomenon does not seem to be mediated by a difference in convergence (see Figure 4.3) sufficient to bring the two alternative sets of dots into registration (Peterson, 1985); it appears to be a strong and striking form of inferred movement, an example of the effect of the viewer's perceptual intentions on the structure of what is perceived. Similar effects can be obtained with a reversible 3D object (Figure 26C): Hochberg & Peterson (1987).

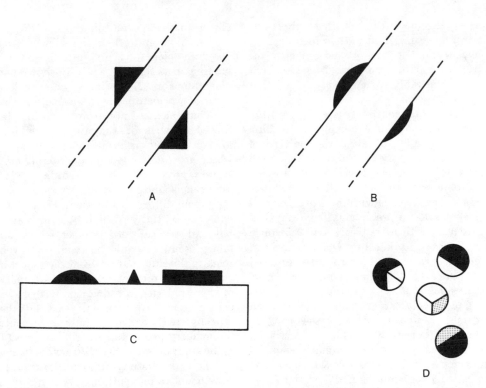

Figure 4.32. *Completion phenomena.* Four interrupted geometrical shapes are given: (A) square, (B) disk, (C) the word CAT, (D) cube. Of course, none of the fragments of shape shown actually *specify* any single object: for example, the partially hidden shapes at (C) might be a disk, triangle, and square.

Such completion figures and puzzle pictures have mostly been studied in reference to their organization (for a recent paper, see Kanizsa & Gerbino, 1982), but a strong demonstration of the effect of knowledge appears in the next figure (Figure 4.33).

A demonstration that some such coupling is innate would provide a strong impetus to further theoretical analysis.

It is also possible to demonstrate mental structures that are almost certainly the result of specific learning, and we consider these next.

COMPLETION PHENOMENA

Although the completion phenomena exemplified in Figures 4.32 and 4.33 have been known for a long time and are at least sometimes recognized as aspects of object perception that challenge computer modeling (Oatley, 1978; Marr, 1982), they have thus far not been addressed at all by the direct theorists. Yet by their nature they demand some explanation that goes beyond any stimulus measures and that draws on some notion of mental structure.

I know of no reason why these demonstrations can be ignored. They cannot be dismissed as artificial examples. In a world that is nor-

mally as cluttered as the average urban, forest, or home environment, *the visual interruption of one object by another must be the overwhelming rule rather than the exception.* The examples in Figures 4.32C and 4.33 cannot be ascribed to complex physiological units (such as receptive fields and frequency channels), as has been attempted with related figures. Nor can they be assimilated within the body of direct theory by declaring that those patterns in some sense specify the object that is only partly presented. In these examples, in order to perceive one object rather than separate fragments depends on the viewer's having specific knowledge of what that object normally looks like, and on his or her being ready to perceive that object.

That combination of knowledge about the object, and a readiness to test that knowledge against the momentary sensations, is precisely what Mill and Helmholtz meant by perception in the first place (see p. 212). A particularly impressive demonstration of this process is shown in Figure 4.33: Left to their own devices, few viewers can discern any clear object in the picture. After looking at Figure 4.34, however, it becomes remarkably difficult *not* to see that object in Figure 4.33.

Within the classical theory (see Figure 4.10), such demonstrations were simple to explain. They were thought to reveal the pattern of associations or sensory expectations that each viewer has learned from experience with specific kinds of objects in the world. Given that it is learned from experience with the world, mental structure should be predictable from physical structure (e.g., Brunswik, 1956; see p. 235), once sensory limits are taken into account. And in some circumstances mental structure is indeed at least approximately that of physical structure, for example, in the couplings of perceived layout and perceived reflectance, and between viewer motion and perceived movement, as described in Figures 4.20 and 4.31, respectively. But we have also known of dramatic counterexamples for at least the past 30 years, such as the so-called impossible figures and the Ames illusions of Figures 4.26D, E and 4.30A, B, respectively.

Although some psychologists still adhere to unconscious inference explanations (cf. Rock, 1983), these counterexamples make the conception of unconscious inference, as it now stands, an empty one. If that conception is to mean anything at all, the premises that determine such supposed inferences must be investigated and not simply taken to be the same as the structure of the physical world.

We must therefore undertake to study mental structure, and to devise objective measures of its characteristics. Having said this, one must agree that the very topic has an air of paradox and insubstantiality. Until the last few years, most psychologists, anxious to keep their science free of subjectivity and mentalism, would have considered this area of inquiry inherently unscientific. But the methods of inquiry do exist and have been used in a related area of research for a long time, namely, the study of mental imagery, which we next consider briefly.

If we are to study how someone perceives some object, we must in one way or another question him or her about that object; we must retrieve information from the subject about the object. In phenomena like those of Figures 4.32 and 4.33, we must ask the viewer questions about an object for which only those few stimulus fragments that are actually shown (e.g., the black blobs in 32) can be confidently described by the experimenter in physical terms. That fact is a challenge, but not an insuperable obstacle. Indeed, methods for studying how well individuals can retrieve information about objects for which *absolutely no stimulus information whatsoever is present* have been used since 1883, when Sir Francis Galton first undertook the study of individual differences in mental imagery. They consist essentially of such questions about the physical structure of an object, which is not in fact present, as could be readily answered by reading the information from the object as if it were actually present. Objective tests of imagery of this kind (see Woodworth, 1938) have been used a great deal in recent years, but they are now directed more at examining the nature of the imagery process itself (Kosslyn, 1980) than at the study of individual differences in imagery.

The task of studying mental structure as a component in perception, in which *some* stimulus information is present, is similar methodologically to the task of studying imagery, in which no stimulus at all is present. We do not yet know, however, whether imagery is related in any simple way to the mental structure that is involved in the perception of objects that are at least partially present. That can only be answered by research on the process by which mental structure gives meaning to, and serves to integrate, fragmentary sensory information.

The need to fit fragments of sensory information into some mental structure is pervasive in normal perception. In addition to the completions that are demanded by a cluttered environment, our perceptions of any moderately large or complex object or scene must be assembled over time by means of successive partial views, and we must be able both to keep track of objects even when they move behind nearer ones, and to recognize them when they reappear. These functions—integrating successive partial views, and keeping track of objects that are temporarily out of sight—which must be heavily practiced in our perceptions of real objects in the world, are required as well by all but the most primitive film and video presentations. Normally, in these media, cameras cut from one scene to another, and both functions suggest

Figure 4.33. *A puzzle picture.* The solution is in Figure 4.34. Once you see what it is, it will be difficult to avoid seeing it that way in Figure 4.33 (Dallenbach, 1951).

methods by which mental structure may be studied. We consider them in turn.

First we consider the question of how the information from successive glances is combined. In the normal process of directing our gaze around at different parts of some scene or object, each glimpse offers detailed vision only in a small central part of the retina (Figure 4.8). The information gained by the successive fragmentary glimpses (as many as four per second) must therefore be integrated by some nonsensory process into a single perception. To Helmholtz and to J. S. Mill, the usual description applies: We perceive whatever layout in space would under normal seeing conditions be most likely to provide the sequence of views that we actually receive. Moreover, because one's eyes have been moved in order to ask sensory questions, one of course knows how the resulting glimpses fit together. This explanation draws on cognitive processes rather than on peripheral encoding mechanisms. The question of how successive glances are integrated can be phrased in terms of physiology. As discussed in pp. 236f, Hebb speculated in 1949 about what neurophysiological structures and events might underlie the cognitive processes, but those speculations are essentially a rephrasing of the way the psychological phenomena are being described, not any neurophysiological reality. Let us review the problem.

Eye movements that are made in order to bring different parts of the optic array to foveal vision—ballistic saccades—take approximately one twentieth of a second to execute, but about one fifth of a second to initiate (Figure 4.9). The fastest rate at which glances can be sustained is about 250 msec per glance, or about one second per four glances. It takes significant time, therefore, to integrate the information from a series of successive glances at some object or scene. Because the glances are elective, and because the viewer may spend much longer than 250 msec looking at some of the more informative places in an optic array, substantial periods of time may elapse between looking at the different parts of the environment.

The ability to integrate successive glimpses cannot be fully explained by the eye movements that bring them about, inasmuch as we can combine glimpses of change that occurs independent of eye movements. Motion picture and video sequences routinely proceed by successive views or *shots*. These shots may be unrelated, or may provide partial views of some large scene. At very fast rates, the views simply superimpose through inadequate temporal resolution or through visible persistence (Eriksen, 1966). A briefly flashed view may persist for an additional 100–150 msec (for a general review, see Coltheart, 1980); subsequent views suppress the persistence (DiLollo & Hogben, 1985; Hogben & DiLollo, 1984), depending on adjacent contours in the successive images. If meaningful pictures are used, a sequence of different views (called *montage* in film terms) can be shown at a rate as high as 9 sec without one picture superimposing or intruding on another (Intraub, 1981, 1985; Potter, 1975, 1976), but unrelated or unintegrated parts of the picture may migrate, appearing to have occurred in an earlier or later view (Intraub, 1985). No such intrusions have been reported to occur with durations greater than 250 msec.

Most often, the shots used in moving pictures comprise partial views, called *close-ups* and *medium shots*. These provide detailed views of selected sections of a larger layout or scene. The latter may be revealed in a *long shot*. The procedure may work as well as it does because it mimics the viewer's allocation of attention (Hochberg & Brooks, 1978a, b; Jonides, 1980, 1983). The long shot provides a spatial framework to the mind's eye within which the partial views take their place. Or the long shot may never be shown in its entirety, and the layout being depicted may not in fact exist as a single

Figure 4.34. *The solution to the puzzle in Figure 4.33.* A cow, head at the left and looking rightward.

place at all, being assembled only in the perceptual space that bridges the successive views, that is, in the mind's eye of the viewer. This phenomenon represents in concrete and practical form one aspect of the problem of mental structure, as a kind of completion over time that should be of central importance to perceptual theory. It could not really be studied at all in the laboratory until motion pictures and high-speed computer graphics became practical tools in perceptual research.

Although a great deal of research has been devoted to the question of why the scene itself does not appear to be displaced whenever a saccadic eye movement displaces the retinal image (Figure 4.9), little more has been done about the question of how information is integrated across successive glances than to show that such research is possible (Hochberg & Brooks, 1978a, b; Brooks, 1984). An example to that point is summarized in Figure 4.35. The row of circles represents a sequence of views which simulate a stationary circular aperture through which the individual corners of some object (in this case, a cross) are successively visible, as the object is moved about behind the aperture. If the motions of the object are clearly visible within the aperture (as indicated by the small arrows in A), the viewer can perceive the shape of the entire object that lies behind the screen. That shape, never present as a whole, exists only in the mind's eye, like a scene presented only through close-ups.

Whenever we are confronted with the question of whether some non-sensory processes, like judgment or motivation, contribute directly to what we perceive, we need some criterion for asserting that the viewer's report indeed reflects his or her perceptual experience. That is especially true in connection with all the research discussed in this section. Introspection alone is not a good enough criterion because it misses too much of what goes by too rapidly. But even introspection tells us that the forms perceived in Figures 4.32, 4.33, and 4.35 are not identical to the forms of objects that are normally viewed. We know that we are not seeing the entire shape at once; what assurance can we have that a shape is in fact perceived at all, and not merely *named*?

Suggested solutions draw upon what have been called convergent definitions (Postman, 1952; Garner, Hake, & Eriksen, 1956; Hochberg, 1956), but no automatic prescription has emerged. Indeed, because the question's significance depends on the use to which the answer is to be put (Hochberg, 1956), it seems likely that there is no general prescription that will work for all purposes. One approach applicable to the present issue is that we ask questions that we would expect the viewer to be able to answer if a real object were completely present and the entire form spread out in space, questions we would not expect the viewer to be able to answer if he perceived only the succession of fragments at the same place in space. One such question is about the perception of short cuts—whether, for example, the right arm of the cross has been skipped within the sequence in Figure 4.35A9 (Hochberg, 1968). To tell that, for example, the right arm was skipped requires access to something like a two-dimensional map of the figure, and not merely a record of the sequence of views as such. Another task is to pick the piecemeal shape from among some set of shapes that are normally presented. Given the motion information symbolized by the arrows in Figure 4.35A, adults can identify such figures with ease (Hochberg, 1968; Murphy, 1973), but children cannot (Girgus, 1973).

The perception of shapes that have been presented piecemeal by moving them behind an aperture has a long history. When the aperture is narrow and the shape moves fairly rapidly for a short distance, there is a compelling impression that the entire shape has been perceived,

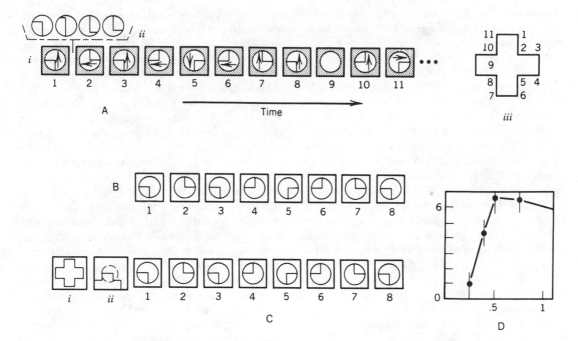

Figure 4.35. *Completion over time.*

(A) A sequence of views in which a geometric figure (here, a cross) is moved about behind an aperture, exposing the perimeter piecemeal. Motion is provided from one view to the next as indicated by the small arrow within each view. The frames by which that motion is provided between the first two views shown are shown at (ii). Subjects recognize when a shortcut has been taken (here, views 8 to 10). See Hochberg, 1968.

(B) A sequence of static right angles, presented at different durations per view (the X-axis in (D)). If shown two such sequences which may or may not differ near the middle of the sequences, subjects can tell no better than chance, which is shown by the baseline in (D), whether they are identical, because the number of *independent* views exceeds their memory span.

(C) In the experiment summarized in the graph (D), at least one member of each pair of sequences is a systematic succession of the corners of a cross. In this graph, the *y*-axis represents the subjects' responses as to whether the two sequences are identical, subtracting wrong responses from right responses. The *x*-axis represents the duration with which each successive view is shown. If both sequences are introduced by a pair of views, for example, views (i) and (ii) in C, which establish what the object is and where the sequence starts (a "long shot" and a "medium shot"), then the viewer can place each view in the structure thus brought to mind, and can distinguish the two sequences when they are different, within the range of view durations shown at (D) in seconds: Hochberg, 1978c.

albeit somewhat compressed along the axis of motion. The phenomenon has been explained as some form of mental construction or integration by Zöllner (1862), followed by Vierordt (1868) Hecht (1924), Parks (1965), Hochberg (1968, 1984a), Rock (1981), and Fendrich (1982). It has also been explained as the result of retinal painting, in which the eye moves in the same direction as the shape, and the successive parts of the shape that are shown through the aperture remain as an afterimage that has been laid down over an expanse of the retina because of the eye movement; this was the position taken by Helm-

holtz (1911), and by Anstis and Atkinson (who rediscovered the history of the problem in 1967), Haber and Nathanson (1968), and Morgan (1981). In fact, both processes must normally be at work when simple shapes are moved behind narrow slits, as argued by Fendrich (1982), Fendrich and Mack (1981), Hochberg (1968, 1971) and Morgan (1981).

We can rule out peripheral explanations of this ability (and indeed, rule out all direct explanations of the phenomenon) by constructing our stimulus sequences from *static* views (row B). In that case, the sequence is usually uninterpretable, and cannot be kept in mind as a single event; accordingly, the viewer cannot tell whether two such sequences are the same or different. However, if the viewer is shown a long shot of the object before the sequence is presented (as in row C), the long shot provides for a mental structure within which the subsequent views can take their place. The viewer now has available a schema of the object against which to check the successive static views behind the aperture (Hochberg, 1978c), and can now distinguish one sequence from another (Figure 4.35D). In a recent extension of this kind of question, using a method that seems a more general and flexible tool than the aperture viewing of Figure 4.33C, Klopfer (1985) has shown that when viewers are shown successive slices of three dimensional objects, like those in Figure 4.36A, they can construct, transform and compare mental representations of those objects. This method seems quite resistant to any peripheral explanation such as retinal painting.

MENTAL ROTATION RESEARCH

In the world outside the laboratory, viewer and objects are normally moving with respect to each other, so that objects are temporarily lost to sight as one passes before another and obscures it in the optic array. The perceptual system must be prepared, whether by evolution or by learning, to deal with invisible but continuing events, that is, a form of motion-completion over time. If this ability exists, it must draw on some mental structure that corresponds to motion through space, but that occurs only in the mind's eye of the viewer, and not in stimulation from the world. Events in the world that draw on this ability must be ubiquitous. And in terms of visual communication, the filmmaker or graphics programmer who provides a *cutaway* from one moving object or person to another, and back again, necessarily makes assumptions about how well the viewer keeps track of the motion that is not in the stimulus but is only in the viewer's mind during the cutaway.

Mental motion has been most convincingly investigated in the context of research on *mental rotation*. In a wide range of experiments, Shepard and his colleagues had shown that the time required by subjects to judge whether two objects (Figure 4.36A) are the same is proportional to the angle ϕ at which the objects are oriented to each other (Figure 4.36B). The data are linear, as though it were necessary to rotate one object, mentally, at some constant rate, bringing the two objects to the same orientation before they can be compared (Shepard & Metzler, 1971; Shepard & Cooper, 1982).

On pp. 217ff we noted the Gestaltists' claim that shape constancy requires no cognitive process (e.g., of taking orientation or slant into account) but occurs instead because shapes are direct responses to the configurations that remain invariant under transformation. As Attneave pointed out in 1981, the mental rotation data are clear demonstrations that shapes are not effectively invariant under rotation, and are not identical when in different orientations. If the shapes were in fact picked up directly from stimulus configurations that are invariant despite the rotation, one would not expect orientation to affect the time required to compare them. Indeed, the Gestalt theory and other holistic explanations of perception (e.g., direct theory, neural theories that provide for automatic shape constancy, etc.) seek to explain more perceptual constancy than in fact obtains (Hochberg, 1971), and this is easy to show. Although it is true that some transformations leave some shapes largely unchanged in appearance, most shapes change greatly when they are transformed. A square continues to look square as it is changed in size, shape, and—within limits—orientation; rotated 45 degrees, however, it becomes a diamond, and very different in appearance (Figure 4.17E). With more complex shapes, this fact is even more evident: faces are difficult to recognize when they are inverted (Hochberg & Galper, 1967; Köhler, 1929), as are letters and words. Some indirect cognitive process clearly must be involved in the comparison of shapes at different orientations.

That does not mean, of course, that mental motion is the only component in the data of Figure 4.36 (e.g., Carpenter & Just, 1978; Hochberg & Gellman, 1977), but a direct and compelling experiment shows that we can in fact predict the subject's response by assuming that motion of a (nonexistent) object had really occurred. Cooper first determined each subject's mental rotation rate. The subjects had memorized each of a set of polygons (Figure 4.37A), and were then asked to imagine some specified shape rotating, starting when a blank field was given. After a random interval, the

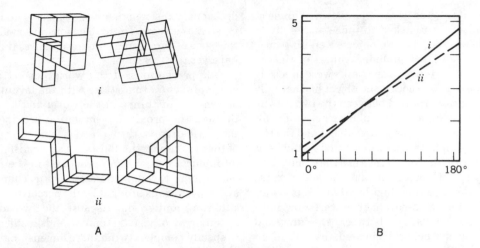

Figure 4.36. *Mental rotation 1: Shapes are not invariant under rotation.*
(A) Using pairs of shapes like those at (i) and (ii), Shepard and his colleagues have shown that viewers cannot instantly perceive whether two shapes that are at different orientations are the same or are instead mirror images. Instead, the time required to make that decision, as shown in seconds on the y-axis in (B), is a neatly linear function of the angle ϕ between their orientations, as shown on the x-axis in degrees. The solid line summarizes reaction times for two-dimensional rotations in the picture plane, as at (Ai), and the dotted line represents three-dimensional rotations, into the picture plane, as at (Aii). It is as though the subject must rotate the objects into the same mental orientations before they can be compared (Shepard and Metzler, 1971; Shepard and Cooper, 1982).

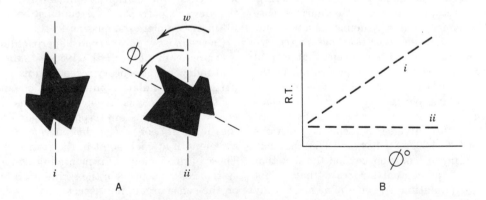

Figure 4.37. *Mental rotation 2: Probing the course of the rotation.* The metaphor of "mental motion" that is embodied in the graph in Figure 4.36B is given more compelling operational meaning in this experiment by Cooper (1976). We have seen in Figure 4.36B that subjects' reaction times (R.T.) for deciding whether two shapes are the same or different increases with the angle (ϕ) between their orientations (also shown here as Bi). Subjects first memorized each of a set of polygons (A), and were tested to determine their normal rate of mental rotation, ω. They were then asked to imagine one of the shapes as rotating, and a probe shape was presented for comparison with it after an interval, t. When $t = \phi/\omega$, R.T. did not increase with the angle (this is indicated by the graph (Bii). This is one concrete consequence of what one could mean by mental rotation. It is as though the subjects had actually rotated the tilted shape at rate ω for time t, so that the remembered shape was then at the same orientation as the probe shape—except that in fact no physical rotation was performed.

shape or its mirror image was shown at angle ϕ, and subjects were asked to judge as rapidly as possible whether the two objects were the same. The intervals used included values of time, t, such that $w \times t = \phi$. The results were precisely what one would expect if the object had actually been physically rotated between the two presentations, i and ii, at an angular velocity of w for a time t. Because the original object and the test object to which it is to be compared would be at the same orientation by the time the comparison was called, judgment times no longer increase with angle ϕ, as they had in all of the previous mental rotation research; they were now *independent* of the angle between the first and second object being compared, as shown in Figure 4.37Bii (Cooper, 1976).

These findings reveal a relation between perceived time and perceived distance that amounts to a mental structure, one which cannot be attributed to physical stimulus information alone, and they make mental rotation more than a metaphor for the fact that judgment time is a function of angle ϕ in Figure 4.36.

But Mental Structures are not the Things Themselves

The phenomena discussed in this section can be used to argue that mental processes in perception can be studied and are in that narrow sense real. The conception is by no means a new one, however, so that the assertion alone is no contribution today. Even if we accept that mental structure is involved in the perception of the world, we need to discover the precise role such structure plays. We need to determine the varieties of mental structure, since we have used that term for diverse perceptual functions (Figures 4.20, 4.30, 4.31, 4.34, and 4.35) that may have nothing in common beyond the fact that they reveal perceptual structure that is not given in stimulation. Above all, we must study the properties of mental structure, since we can be certain (Figures 4.26C, D; 4.30) that those properties are not simply those of the physical world. A schema is not a thing, or even a faithful mental picture or model of a thing. Given the theoretical functions that schemas must serve, and the kinds of tolerance of inconsistency or of missing detail that seem to characterize many perceptual phenomena (Figure 4.26), a better metaphor would appear to be a network of

decisions about whether some object is actually present and seen. Those decisions are made on the basis of perceptual rules or premises that we have yet to determine.

Our perceptions of the world depend on a chain of factors that starts with the layout and movements of things in the world and extends through the proximal stimulation provided to the sense organs; through such limited aspects of that proximal stimulation as are transformed into neural activity and processed in the nervous system; through the selective mechanisms and expectations brought by the perceiver to the situation, and so on. Because the two-dimensional array of visual stimulation is insufficient to specify completely the three-dimensional layout and movements of objects in the world, any given pattern or sequence of stimulation may have been provided by an indefinitely large set of events (even if the stimulation theoretically available to the sense organs were to be all processed effectively, which is generally not true), and the viewer's perceptual system must impose some constraints on those alternative events if the viewer is to emerge with any definite perception. Because only a small part of the information provided by the scene is in fact processed effectively at any time, and because the world is normally so cluttered that essential features of information are hidden from view, the viewer's perceptual system must be able to fill in or complete the missing features.

In the most widely accepted approach, which was predominant until the 1950s, it was held that independent sensory receptors analyze the pattern of stimulation into local elements; in vision, that means receptor neurons (rods, cones) that vary their response depending on the intensity of the light energy at each wavelength at each point in the retinal image. These basic elements of response in the nervous system reflect aspects of the stimulation falling on the sense organ, not aspects of the world of things and objects. Explanations of our perceptions of the latter, therefore, were phrased in terms of learned responses to those patterns of stimulation, or cues, that more often than not arose from particular situations in the world (characteristic signs of distance, of illumination, etc.), and in terms of further psychological processes, much like problem solving or inference, that take those cues into account and thereby arrive at the attributes or the properties of objects and events (size, reflectance, movements, etc.).

A great deal of research has been done within, or in opposition to, this general theoretical framework, amassing information about how well we achieve correct perceptions of object properties (the perceptual *constancies*); about what kinds of systematic perceptual errors prevail (the *illusions*); and about how the flux of stimulation is parsed into objects and events (perceptual *organization*). Thanks to such perceptual research, and more recent physiological findings, we now realize that the initial neural response to stimulation is not by way of independent points but by way of more extended patterns. Such patterned sensory responses are surely smaller than the extended configurations proposed by the Gestalt psychologists (who were the most vocal opponents of the traditional approach), but larger than the individual receptor response to points of light.

We do not now know the entire range of stimulus patterns by which sensory response analyzes the flux of energies on the sense organ, but the knowledge that such complex analyzing mechanisms exist necessarily changes our picture of the perceptual process and of what there is to be explained. Some of those patterns are usually correlated with the properties of objects in the world (e.g., with their reflectance or their objective size). We must work to discover whether each such informative variable of stimulation is in fact used in the perceptual process and if so whether and how it interacts with learned cues and with the inference-like processes that also seem to be at work. The task is a formidable one, but one that is necessary not only to our understanding of the psychology and physiology of the perceptual process, but to modern technology which relies ever more heavily on communication through artificially generated pictorial displays.

Given the magnitude of the task, it is natural that ambitious simplifications have been proposed from time to time. In recent years, two such theories have become very popular. One is the *invariance theory*, or the strong form of a rigidity constraint, which takes the perception of objects and events to be a direct and veridical (correct) response to properties of stimulation. This theory, it is claimed, makes it unnecessary, and in fact wrong, to think of cues or inferential processes as playing any significant role in perception. Explanations are phrased in terms of those abstract aspects of stimulation, confronting the sense organ, which correspond to (specify) the important properties of the things and events in the world.

The other theory is a revival of the notion that perception consists of a kind of problem solving or inference, to which both cues and mental structure are essential, and which reflects in internal representations the properties of events in the physical world.

In the course of this chapter, I have tried to show that the strong form of the invariance or rigidity theory is untenable on the basis of facts, some of which have been known for over half a century, and that its recommendations for film, video, and computer generated imagery, are misleading. The notion of perceptual problem solving, on the other hand, is vacuous unless we can specify what the premises of the inferences are. These premises are usually taken to mirror the structure of the real world, and we know enough about mental structure by now to know that this is untrue except as a rough approximation.

Strong formulations like these are useful in sharpening issues and considering alternatives, but if they are to be more than repeated declarations of faith, they must focus on the troubling examples—the illusions, the unrepresentable events, the phenomena that do not fit. These are the areas that are of urgent practical importance; where no perceptual anomalies exist, explanations are a luxury that can be deferred. They are also the areas in which the differences between perception and the world are laid bare, and in which the nature of the underlying mechanisms may be revealed. It is necessary above all to maintain a broad base of our knowledge of perceptual findings, and to evaluate general proposals against that base, rather than against some selected set of data.

REFERENCES

Adelson, E.H. & Bergen, J.R. (1984). Spatio-temporal energy models for the perception of motion. *Journal of the Optical Society of America*, *73*, 1861–1862.

Ames, A., Jr. (1925). Illusion of depth from single pictures. *Journal of the Optical Society of America*, *10*, 137–148.

Ames, A. (1951). Visual perception and the rotating trapezoidal window. *Psychological Monographs*, *65*: whole no. 324.

Anstis, S.M. (1980). The perception of apparent movement. In H.C. Longuet–Higgens & N.S. Sutherland (Eds.), *The psychology of vision* (pp. 153–167). London: The Royal Society.

Anstis, S. (1986). Motion perception in the frontal plane. In K.R. Boff, L. Kaufman and J.P. Thomas (Eds.), *Handbook of Perception and Human Performance. Vol. I: Sensory Processes and Perception* (pp. 16-1–16-27).

Anstis, S.M. & Atkinson, J. (1967). Distortions in moving figures viewed through a stationary slit. *American Journal of Psychology, 80,* 572–585.

Anstis, S.M. & Gregory, R. (1964). The after-effect of seen motion: The role of retinal stimulation and of eye movements, *Quarterly Journal of Experimental Psychology, 17,* 173–174.

Attneave, F. (1954). Some informational aspect of visual perception. *Psychological Review, 61,* 183–193.

Attneave, F. (1961). In defense of homunculi. In W.A. Rosenblith (Ed.), *Sensory communication* (pp. 777–782). New York: Wiley.

Attneave, F. (1981). Three approaches to perceptual organization: Comments on views of Hochberg, Shepard and Shaw and Turvey. In M. Kubovy & J. Pomerantz (Eds.), *Perceptual organization* (pp. 417–421). Hillsdale, NJ: Erlbaum.

Attneave, F. (1982). Pragnanz and soap bubble systems: A theoretical exploration. In J. Beck (Ed.), *Organization and representation in perception.* (pp. 11–29). Hillsdale, NJ: Erlbaum.

Attneave, F. & Arnoult, M.D. (1956). The quantitative study of shape and pattern perception. *Psychological Bulletin, 53,* 452–471.

Attneave, F. & Block, G. (1973). Apparent movement in tridimensional space. *Perception and Psychophysics, 13,* 301–307.

Attneave, F. & Frost, R. (1969). The discrimination of perceived tridimensional orientation by minimum criteria. *Perception and Psychophysics, 6,* 391–396.

Barlow, H., Blackemore, C., & Pettigrew, J. (1964). The neural mechanism of binocular depth discrimination. *Journal of Physiology, 193,* 327–342.

Beck, J. (1965). Apparent spatial position and the perception of lightness. *Journal of Experimental Psychology, 69,* 170–179.

Beck, J. (1972a). Similarity grouping and peripheral discriminability under uncertainty. *American Journal of Psychology, 85,* 1–19.

Beck, J. (1972b). *Surface color perception.* Ithaca: Cornell University Press.

Beck, J. (Ed.). (1982). *Organization and representation in perception.* Hillsdale, NJ: Erlbaum.

Beck, J., Hope, B., & Rosenfeld, A. (Eds.) (1983). *Human and Machine Vision.* New York: Academic Press.

Beck, J., Prazdny, K., & Rosenfeld, A. (1983). In J. Beck, B. Hope, and A. Rosenfeld (Eds.), *Human and Machine Vision.* (pp. 1–38). New York: Academic Press.

Békésy, G. von (1960). Neural inhibitory units of eye and skin: Quantitative description of contrast phenomena. *Journal of the Optical Society of America, 50,* 1060–1070.

Berkeley, G. (1709). Essay toward a new theory of vision. In A.A. Luce & T.E. Jessop (Eds.), *The works of George Berkeley Bishop of Cloyne* (1948, pp. 143–239). Toronto: Nelson.

Berry, R.N. (1948). Quantitative relations among vernier, real depth, and stereoscopic depth acuities. *Journal of Experimental Psychology, 75,* 708–721.

Biederman, I. (1981). On the semantics of a glance at a scene. In M. Kubovy & J. Pomerantz (Eds.), *Perceptual organization* (pp. 213–253). Hillsdale, NJ: Erlbaum.

Biederman, I. (1985). Human image understanding: Recent research and a theory. *Computer Vision, Graphics and Image Processing, 32,* 29–73.

Binford, T. O. (1981). Inferring surfaces from images. *Artificial Intelligence, 17,* 205–244.

Blakemore, C. & Campbell, F.W. (1969). On the existence of neurons in the human visual system selectively sensitive to the orientation and size of retinal images. *Journal of Physiology, 203,* 237–260.

Bonnet, C. (1982). Thresholds of motion perception. In A.H. Wertheim, W.A. Wagenaar, & H.W. Leibowitz (Eds.), *Tutorials on motion perception* (pp. 41–79). New York: Plenum Press.

Boring, E.G. (1933). *The physical dimensions of consciousness.* New York: Century.

Boselie, F. & Leeuwenberg, E. (1986). A test of the minimum principle requires a perceptual coding system. *Perception, 15,* 331–354.

Boynton, R.M. (1979). *Human color vision.* New York: Holt, Rinehart & Winston.

Braddick, O.J. (1974). A short-range process in apparent motion. *Vision Research, 14,* 519–527.

Braddick, O.J. (1980). Low-level and high-level processes in apparent motion. In H.C. Longuet-Higgins & N.S. Sutherland (Eds.), *The psychology of vision* (pp. 137–149). London: The Royal Society.

Braddick, O., Campbell, R.W., & Atkinson, J. (1978). Channels in vision: Basic aspect. In R. Held, H.W. Leibowitz, & H.L. Teuber (Eds.), *Handbook of sensory physiology,* Vol. 8 (pp. 3–38). New York: Springer.

Brady, M. (1983). Criteria for representation of shape. In J. Beck, B. Hope and A. Rosenfeld (Eds.), *Human and Machine Vision.* (pp. 39–84). New York: Academic Press.

Braunstein, M.L. (1976). *Depth Perception Through Motion*. New York: Academic Press.

Braunstein, M.L. (1983). Perception of rotation in depth: The psychophysical evidence. In *Motion: representation and perception* (pp. 242–247). Baltimore, MD: The Association for Computing Machinery.

Braunstein, M.L. & Andersen, G.J. (1986). Testing the rigidity assumption: A reply to Ullman. *Perception, 15,* 641–644.

Brooks, V. (1984). Why dance films do not look right: A study in the nature of the documentary of movement as visual communication. *Studies in Visual Communication, 10/2,* 44–67.

Brown, J.F. & Voth, A.C. (1937). The path of seen movement as a function of the vector field. *American Journal of Psychology, 49,* 543–563.

Brunswik, E. (1956). *Perception and the representative design of psychological experiments.* Berkeley: University of California Press.

Brunswik, E. & Kamiya, J. (1953). Ecological cue-validity of "proximity" and other Gestalt factors. *American Journal of Psychology, 66,* 20–32.

Buffart, H., Leeuwenberg E., & Restle, F. (1981). Coding theory of visual pattern completion. *Journal of Experimental Psychology: Human Perception and Performance, 7,* 241–274.

Buswell, G.T. (1935) *How people look at pictures.* Chicago: University of Chicago Press.

Butler, D.L. (1982). Predicting the perception of three-dimensional objects from the geometrical information in drawings. *Journal of Experimental Psychology: Human Perception and Performance, 8,* 674–692.

Campbell, A.G., Hartwell, R., & Hood, D.C. (1978). Lightness constancy at the level of the frog's optic nerve fiber. (Abstract) *Proceedings of the Eastern Psychological Association, 49,* 47.

Campbell, R.W. & Robson, J.G. (1964). Application of Fourier analysis to the visibility of gratings. *Journal of Physiology, 197,* 551–566.

Carpenter, R.A. & Just, M.A. (1978). Eye fixations during mental rotation. In J.W. Senders, D.F. Fisher, & R.A. Monty (Eds.), *Eye movements and the higher psychological functions* (pp. 115–133). Hillsdale, NJ: Erlbaum.

Cassirer, E. (1944). The concept of group and the theory of perception. *Psychologia, 5,* 1–35.

Charnwood, J.R.B. (1951). *Essay on binocular vision.* London: Halton Press.

Coltheart, M. (1980). Iconic memory and visible persistence. *Perception and Psychophysics, 27,* 183–228.

Cooper, L.A. (1976). Demonstration of a mental analog of an external rotation. *Perception and Psychophysics, 19,* 296–302.

Cooper, L.A. & Shepard, R.M. (1973). Chronometric studies of the rotation of mental images. In W.G. Chase (Ed.), *Visual information processing* (pp. 75–176). New York: Academic Press.

Corbin, H.H. (1942). The perception of grouping and apparent movement in visual depth. *Archives of Psychology,* No. 273, 1–50.

Coren, S. (1969). Brightness contrast as a function of figure-ground relations. *Journal of Experimental Psychology, 80,* 517–524.

Coren, S. & Girgus, J.S. (1978). *Seeing is deceiving: The psychology of visual illusions.* Hillsdale, NJ: Erlbaum.

Cutting, J.E. (1978). Generation of synthetic male and female walkers through manipulation of a biomechanical invariant. *Perception, 7,* 393–405.

Cutting, J.E. (1982). Blowing in the wind: Perceiving structure in trees and bushes. *Cognition, 12,* 25–44.

Cutting, J.E. (1986). *Perception with an Eye to Motion.* Cambridge, Mass: MIT Press.

Cutting, J. & Proffitt, D.R. (1982). The minimum principle and the perception of absolute, common, and relative motions. *Cognitive psychology, 14,* 211–246.

Dallenbach, K.M. (1951). A puzzle picture with a new principle of concealment. *American Journal of Psychology, 54,* 431–433.

Day, R.H. (1972). Visual spatial illusions: a general explanation. *Science, 175,* 1335–1340.

Descartes, R. (1650). *Les passions de l'ame,* Amsterdam. In: *The philosophical works of Descartes* (Trans. by E.S. Haldane & G.R.T. Rose) (pp. 330–427). Cambridge: Cambridge University Press.

De Valois, R.L. (1965). Behavioral and electrophysiological studies of primate vision. In W.D. Neff (Ed.), *Contributions to sensory physiology* (Vol. 1, pp. 138–178). New York: Academic Press.

De Valois, R.L. & Jacobs, G.H. (1968). Primate color vision. *Science, 162,* 533–540.

De Valois, R.L. & Jacobs, G.H. (1984). Neural mechanisms of color vision. In I. Darian-Smith (Ed.), *Handbook of physiology. Section 1: The nervous system. Vol. III: Sensory processes. Part I* (pp. 425–456). Bethesda, MD: American Physiological Society.

DiLollo, V. & Hogben, J.H. (1985). Suppression of visible persistence. *Journal of Experimental Psychology: Human Perception and Performance, 11,* 304–316.

Dinnerstein, A.J. (1967). Image size and instructions in the perception of depth. *Journal of Experimental Psychology, 25,* 525–528.

Dodwell, P.C. & Caelli, T. (Eds.). (1984). *Figural synthesis.* Hillsdale, NJ: Erlbaum.

Dodwell, P.C. & Engel, G.R. (1963). A theory of binocular fusion. *Nature, 198,* 39–40, 73–74.

Donchin, E., Ritter, W., & McCallum, W.C. (1978). Cognitive psychophysiology: The endogenous components of the ERP. In E. Callaway, P. Tueting, & S.H. Keslow (Eds.), *Event-related potentials in man* (pp. 349–411). New York: Academic Press.

Donderi, D.C. & Kane, E. (1965). Perceptual learning produced by common responses to different stimuli. *Canadian Journal of Psychology, 19,* 15–30.

Dosher, B.A., Sperling, G., & Wurst, S. (1984). Stereopsis vs. proximity-luminance covariance as determinants of perceived three-dimensional structure. *Proceedings of the 1984 Annual Meeting of the Optical Society of America,* p. 44 (Abstract).

Duncker, K. (1929). Ueber induzierte Bewegung. *Psychologische Forschung, 12,* 180–259. (Trans. and repr. in W.D. Ellis, Ed., *A sourcebook of Gestalt psychology.* London: Routledge and Keegan Paul, 1937.)

Eggert, L.A. (1985). The perception of rigid and nonrigid motion. *Proceedings and abstracts of the annual meeting of the Eastern Psychological Association, 56,* 38 (Abstract).

Epstein, W. (1961). Phenomenal orientation and perceived achromatic color. *Journal of Psychology, 52,* 51–53.

Epstein, W. (1963). The influence of assumed size on apparent distance. *American Journal of Psychology, 78,* 120–123.

Epstein, W. (1965). Nonrelational judgment of size and distance. *American Journal of Psychology, 78,* 120–123.

Epstein, W. (Ed.) (1977a). *Stability and constancy in visual perception.* New York: Wiley.

Epstein, W. (1977b). Historical introduction to the constancies. In Epstein, W. (Ed.) *Stability and constancy in visual perception* (pp. 1–22). New York: Wiley.

Epstein, W. & Broota, K.D. (1986). Automatic and attentional components in perception of size-at-a-distance. *Perception and Psychophysics, 40,* 256–262.

Epstein, W. & Lovitts, B.E. (1985). Automatic and attentional components in perception of shape-at-a-slant. *Journal of Experimental Psychology: Human Perception and Performance, 11,* 355–366.

Eriksen, C.W. (1966). Temporal luminance summation effects in backward and forward masking. *Perception and Psychophysics, 1,* 87–92.

Eriksson, S. & Zetterberg, P. (1975) *Experience and veridical space perception.* Report 169, Department of Psychology, Sweden: University of Uppsala.

Feldman, J.A. & Ballard, D.H. (1983). Computing with connections. In J. Beck, B. Hope and A.

Rosenfeld, *Human and Machine Vision* (pp. 107–155). New York: Academic Press.

Fendrich, R. (1982). *Anorthoscopic figure perception: The role of retinal painting produced by observer eye motions.* Ph. D. Dissertation, New School.

Fendrich, R. & Mack, A. (1980). Anorthoscopic perception occurs with a retinally stabilized image. *Supplement to Investigative Ophthalmology and Visual Science, 19,* 166 (Absract).

Fieandt, K. von. & Gibson, J.J. (1959). The sensitivity of the eye to the kinds of continuous transformation of a shadow-pattern. *Journal of Experimental Psychology, 57,* 344–347.

Flock, H.R. (1970). Jameson and Hurvich's theory of brightness contrast. *Perception and Psychophysics, 8,* 118–124.

Flock, H.R., Wilson, A., & Poizner, S. (1966). Lightness matching for different visual routes through a compound scene. *Perception and Psychophysics, 1,* 382–384.

Frisby, J.P. & Mayhew, J.E.W. (1980). Spatial frequency tuned channels: implications for structure and function from psychophysical and computational studies of stereopsis. In N.S. Sutherland & H.C. Longuet-Higgins (Eds.), *The psychology of vision* (pp. 95–113). London: The Royal Society.

Garner, W. (1962). *Uncertainty and structure of psychological concepts.* New York: Wiley.

Garner, W. (1970). Good patterns have few alternatives. *American Scientist, 58,* 34–42.

Garner, W.R., Hake, H.W., & Eriksen, C.W. (1956). Operationism and the concept of perception. *Psychological Review, 63,* 149–159.

Gehringer, W.L. & Engel, E. (1986). The effect of ecological viewing conditions on the Ames' distorted room illusion. *Journal of Experimental Psychology: Human Perception and Performance, 12,* 181–185.

Gelb, A. (1929). Die "Farbenkonstanz" der Sehdinge. In A. Bethe (Ed.), *Handbuch der normalen und pathologischen Physiologie* (12: pp. 594–678). Berlin: Springer-Verlag.

Gibson, J.J. (1933). Adaptation, aftereffect and contrast in the perception of curved lines. *Journal of Experimental Psychology, 16,* 1–31.

Gibson, J.J. (1937). Adaptation, after-effect and contrast in the perception of tilted lines: II. Simultaneous contrast and the areal restriction of the after-effect. *Journal of Experimental Psychology, 20,* 553–569.

Gibson, J.J. (1950). *The perception of the visual world.* Boston: Houghton Mifflin.

Gibson, J.J. (1954). A theory of pictorial perception. *Audio-Visual Communications Review, 1,* 3–23.

Gibson, J.J. (1959). Perception as a function of stimulation. In S. Koch (Ed.), *Psychology: A study of a science. Vol. 1* (pp. 456–501). New York: McGraw-Hill.

Gibson, J.J. (1966). *The senses considered as perceptual systems.* Boston: Houghton Mifflin.

Gibson, J.J. (1968). What gives rise to the perception of motion? *Psychological Review, 75,* 335–346.

Gibson, J.J. (1974). A note on ecological optics. In E.C. Carterette & M.P. Friedman (Eds.), *Handbook of Perception, Vol. I* (pp. 309–312). New York: Academic Press.

Gibson, J.J. (1979). *The ecological approach to visual perception.* Boston: Houghton Mifflin.

Gibson, J.J. & Gibson, E.J. (1957). Continuous perspective transformations and the perception of rigid motion. *Journal of Experimental psychology, 54,* 129–138.

Gibson, J.J., Kaplan, G.A., Reynolds, H.N., & Wheeler, K. (1969). The change from visible to invisible: A study of optical transitions. *Perception and Psychophysics, 5,* 113–116.

Gibson, J., Olum, P., & Rosenblatt, F. (1955). Parallax and perspective during aircraft landings. *American Journal of Psychology, 68,* 372–385.

Gibson, J.J. & Radner, M. (1937). Adaptation, aftereffect and contrast in the perception of tilted lines: I. Quantitative studies. *Journal of Experimental Psychology, 20,* 453–467.

Gilchrist, A.L. (1977). Perceived lightness depends on perceived spatial arrangement. *Science, 195,* 185–187.

Gillam, B. (1972). A depth processing theory of the Poggendorff illusion. *Perception and Psychophysics, 10,* 211–216.

Gillam, B. (1972). Perceived common rotary motion of ambiguous stimuli as a criterion for perceptual grouping. *Perception and Psychophysics, 11,* 99–101.

Ginsburg, A. (1971). Psychological correlates of a model of the human visual system. Wright-Patterson Air Force base, Ohio: Air Force Institute of Technology, Master's Thesis.

Ginsburg, A. (1980). Specifying relevant spatial information for image evaluation and display design: An explanation of how we see objects. *Proceedings of the Society for Information Display, 21,* 219–228.

Girgus, J. (1973). A developmental approach to the study of shape processing. *Journal of Experimental Child Psychology, 16,* 363–374.

Gogel, W.C. (1969). The effect of familiarity on the perception of size and distance. *Quarterly Journal of Experimental Psychology, 21,* 239–247.

Gogel, W.C. (1969b). The sensing of retinal size. *Vision research, 9,* 1079–1094.

Gogel, W.C. (1977). The metric of visual space. In W. Epstein (Ed.), *Stability and constancy in visual perception* (pp. 129–181). New York: Wiley.

Gogel, W.C. (1979). The common occurrence of errors of perceived distance. *Perception and Psychophysics, 25,* 2–11.

Gogel, W.C. (1981). Perceived depth is a necessary factor in apparent motion concomitant with head movement: A reply to Shebilske and Proffitt. *Perception and Psychophysics, 29,* 173–177.

Gogel, W.C. (1982). Analysis of the perception of motion concomitant with a lateral motion of the head. *Perception and Psychophysics, 32,* 241–250.

Gogel, W.C. (1983). An illusory motion of a stationary target during head motions unaffected by paradoxical retinal motion: A reply to Shebilske and Proffitt (1983). *Perception and Psychophysics, 34,* 482–487.

Gogel, W.C., Gregg, J.M., & Wainright, A. (1961). *Convergence as a cue to absolute distance.* U.S. Army Medical Research Laboratory (For Knox, KY), Report No. 467, 1–16.

Gogel, W.C. & Mershon, D.H. (1967). Depth adjacency in simultaneous contrast. *Perception and Psychophysics, 5,* 13–17.

Goldstein, E.B. (1979). Rotation of objects in pictures viewed at an angle: Evidence for different properties of two types of pictorial space. *Journal of Experimental Psychology: Human Perception and Performance, 5,* 78–87.

Goldstein, E.B. (1984). *Sensation and perception* (2nd ed.). Belmont, CA: Wadsworth Publishing Company.

Gordon, D. (1965). Static and dynamic visual fields in human space perception. *Journal of the Optical Society of America, 55,* 1296–1303.

Graham, N. (1981). Psychophysical evidence for spatial-frequency channels. In M. Kubovy & J. Pomerantz (Eds.), *Perceptual organization* (pp. 1–25). Hillsdale, NJ: Erlbaum.

Graham, N. (1981, August). Does the brain perform a Fourier analysis of the visual scene? *Trends in Neurosciences.*

Green, B.F. (1961). Figure coherence in the kinetic depth effect. *Journal of Experimental Psychology, 62,* 272–282.

Gregory, R.L. (1963). Distortion of visual space as inappropriate constancy scaling. *Nature, 199,* 678–680.

Gregory, R.L. (1970). *The intelligent eye.* London: Weidenfeld.

Gregory, R.L. (1980). Perceptions as hypotheses. In H.C. Longuet-Higgins & N.S. Sutherland (Eds.), *The psychology of vision* (pp. 137–149). London: The Royal Society.

Grossberg, S. (1987). Competitive learning: From interactive activation to adaptive resonance, *Cognitive Science, 11,* 23–63.

Grüsser, O.J. & Grüsser-Cornehls, U. (1973). Neuronal mechanisms of visual movement perception and some psychophysical and behavioral correlations. In R. Jung (Ed.), *Handbook of sensory physiology, Vol. 7 (3a): Central processing of information* (pp. 333–430).

Guzman, A. (1969). Decomposition of a visual scene into three-dimensional bodies. In A. Graselli (Ed.), *Automatic interpretation and classification of images* (pp. 243–276). New York: Academic Press.

Haber, R.N. (1983). Stimulus information and processing mechanisms in visual space perception. In J. Beck, B. Hope, and A. Rosenfeld (Eds.), *Human and machine vision* (pp. 157–237). New York: Academic Press.

Haber, R.N. & Nathanson, L.S. (1968). Post-retinal storage? Some further observations on Parks' camel as seen through the eye of a needle. *Perception and Psychophysics, 3,* 349–355.

Haber, R.N. & Wilkinson, L. (1982). The perceptual components of graphic displays. *Computer Graphics and Applications, 2,* 23–25.

Hallett, P.E. (1986). Eye movements. In K.R. Boff, L. Kaufman, and J.P. Thomas (Eds.), *Handbook of perception and human performance. Vol. I: Sensory processes and perception.* (10-1–10-112). New York: Wiley.

Harris, C.S. (Ed.) (1980). *Visual coding and adaptability.* Hillsdale, NJ: Erlbaum.

Harris, C.S. & Gibson, A. (1968). Is orientation-specific color adaptation in human vision due to edge detectors, afterimages, or "dipoles"? *Science, 162,* 1056–1057.

Hartley, D. (1791). *Observations on man, his frame, his duty and his expectations. Vol. 1,* pp. 1–12, 103–110. London: Johnson. Reprinted in W. Dennis (Ed.), *Readings in the history of psychology* (pp. 81–92). New York: Appleton (1948).

Hartline, H.K. (1949). Inhibition of activity of visual receptors by illuminating nearby retinal elements in the *Limulus* eye. *Federation Proceedings, 8,* 69.

Hay, J.C. (1966). Optical motions and space perception: an extension of Gibson's analysis. *Psychological Review, 73,* 550–565.

Hebb, D.O. (1949). *The organization of behavior.* New York: Wiley.

Hecht, H. (1924). Die simultane Erfassung der Figuren. *Zeitschrift für Psychologie, 94,* 153–194.

Heider, G.M. (1932). New studies in transparency, form and color. *Psychologische Forschung, 17,* 13–55.

Heider, F. and Simmel, M. (1944). An experimental study of apparent behavior. *American Journal of Psychology, 57,* 243–259.

Heinemann, E.G. (1955). Simultaneous brightness induction as a function of inducing- and test-field luminances. *Journal of Experimental Psychology, 50,* 89–95.

Held, R., Dichgans, J., & Bauer, J. (1975). Characteristics of moving visual scenes influencing spatial orientation. *Vision Research, 15,* 357–365.

Held, R. & Hein, A. (1958). Adaptation of hand-eye coordination contingent upon re-afferent stimulation. *Perceptual and Motor Skills, 8,* 87–90.

Held, R. & Hein, A. (1963). Movement-produced stimulation in the development of visually-guided behavior. *Journal of Comparative Psychology, 566,* 872–876.

Held, R. & Rekosh, J. (1963). Motor-sensory feedback and the geometry of visual space. *Science, 141,* 772–723.

Held, R. & Shattuck, S. (1971). Color and edge-sensitive channels in the human visual system: Tuning for orientation. *Science, 174,* 314–316.

Helmholtz, H.L.F. von. (1856/1962). *Treatise on physiological optics. Vols. II and III* (Trans. from the 3rd German ed., 1909–1911, J.P.C. Southall, ed. and trans.). Rochester, N.Y.: Optical Society of America, 1924–1925.

Helmholtz, H.L.F. von. (1863/1885). *On the sensation of tone* (Transl. A.J. Ellis), 2nd Engl. Ed. reprinted in 1954. New York: Dover.

Helson, H. (1926). The psychology of *Gestalt. American Journal of Psychology, 37,* 25–62.

Hering, E. (1861). *Beiträge zur Physiologie. Heft 1* (pp. 304 ff.). Leipzig: Englemann.

Hering, E. (1878/1964). *Outlines of a theory of the light sense.* L.M. Hurvich & D. Jameson (Transl.). Cambridge, MA: Harvard University Press.

Hershberger, W.A., Stewart, M.R., & Laughlin, N.K. (1976). Conflicting motion perspective simulating simultaneous clockwise and counterclockwise rotation in depth. *Journal of Experimental Psychology: Human Perception and Performance, 2,* 174–178.

Hess, C. & Pretori, H. (1894). Messende Untersuchungen über die Gesetzmässigkeit des simultanen Helligkeit-Contrastes. *Albrecht von Graefes Archive. Ophthalm., 40,* 1–27. H.R. Flock & J.H. Tenney (Transl.) *Technical report FLP-1.* Toronto: York University (1969).

Hobbes, T. (1651, chapter 2). *Human nature.* Reprinted in W. Dennis (Ed.), *Readings in the history of psychology,* New York: Appleton (1948).

Hochberg, C.B. & Hochberg, J. (1952). Familiar size and the perception of depth. *Journal of Psychology, 34,* 107–114.

Hochberg, J. (1956a). Perception: Toward the recovery of a definition. *Psychological Review, 63,* 400–405.

Hochberg, J. (1956b). The psychophysics of pictorial

perception. *Audio-Visual Communication Review*, *10*, 22–54.

Hochberg, J. (1962). Nativism and empiricism in perception. In L. Postman (Ed.), *Psychology in the making* (pp. 255–330). New York: Knopf.

Hochberg, J. (1968). In the mind's eye. Invited address, Div. 3, American Philological Association, 1966. In R.N. Haber (Ed.), *Contemporary theory and research in visual perception* (pp. 304–331). New York: Appleton-Century-Crofts.

Hochberg, J. (1970). Attention, organization and consciousness. In D.I. Mostofsky (Ed.), *Attention: Contemporary theory and analysis* (pp. 99–124). New York: Appleton-Century-Crofts.

Hochberg, J. (1971). Ch. 12. Perception: color and shape. Ch. 13. Perception: space and movement. In J.A. Kling & L.A. Riggs (Eds.), *Woodworth and Schlosberg's Experimental Psychology* (pp. 395–550). New York: Holt, Rinehart & Winston.

Hochberg, J. (1974). Higher-order stimuli and inter-response coupling in the perception of the visual world. In R.B. MacLeod & H.L. Pick (Eds.), *Perception: Essays in honor of James J. Gibson* (pp. 17–39). Ithaca: Cornell University Press.

Hochberg, J. (1978a). *Perception* (2nd ed.). Englewood Cliffs, NJ: Prentice-Hall.

Hochberg, J. (1978b). Art and Perception. In E.C. Carterette & M.P. Friedman (Eds.), *Handbook of Perception, X* (pp. 225–258). New York: Academic Press.

Hochberg, J. (1978c). Motion pictures of mental structures. Presidential Address of the Eastern Psychological Association.

Hochberg, J. (1979). Sensation and perception. In E. Hearst (Ed.), *The first century of experimental psychology* (pp. 89–142). Hillsdale, NJ: Erlbaum.

Hochberg, J. (1980). Pictorial functions and perceptual structures. In M.A. Hagen (Ed.), *The perception of pictures, Vol. 2* (pp. 47–93). New York: Academic Press.

Hochberg, J. (1981a). Levels of perceptual organization. In M. Kubovy & J. Pomerantz (Eds.), *Perceptual organization* (pp. 255–278). Hillsdale, N.J: Erlbaum.

Hochberg, J. (1981b). On cognition in perception: Perceptual coupling and unconscious inference. *Cognition, 10*, 127–134.

Hochberg, J. (1982). How big is a stimulus? in J. Beck (Ed.), *Organization and representation in perception* (pp. 191–217). Hillsdale, NJ: Erlbaum.

Hochberg, J. (1984a). Form perception: experience and explanation. In P. Dodwell & T. Caelli (Eds.), *Figural synthesis* (pp. 1–30). Hillsdale, NJ: Erlbaum.

Hochberg, J. (1984b). Perception. In I. Darien-Smith (Ed.), *Handbook of physiology. Sect. 1, Vol. III. Part I* (pp. 75–102). Bethesda, MD: American Physiological Society.

Hochberg, J. (1984c) Visual worlds in collision: invariances and premises, theories vs. facts. Presidential Address, Division of Experimental Psychology of the American Psychological Association. Toronto.

Hochberg, J. (1986a) The representation of space and events in video and cinematic display. In K. Boff, J. Thomas, & L. Kaufman (Eds.), *Handbook of perception and human performance. Vol. I* (pp. 22.1–22.64). New York: Wiley.

Hochberg, J. (1986b). Parts and wholes: A response to Arnheim. *New Ideas in Psychology, 4*, 285–293.

Hochberg, J. (1987). Machines should not see as people do, but must know how people see. *Computer vision, Graphics, and Image Processing, 37*, 221–237.

Hochberg, J., Amira, L., & Peterson, M. (1984, April). Extensions of the Schwartz/Sperling phenomenon: Invariance under transformation fails in the perception of objects' moving pictures. *Proceedings of the Eastern Psychological Association*, p. 44 (Abstract).

Hochberg, J. & Beck, J. (1954). Apparent spatial arrangement and perceived brightness. *Journal of Experimental Psychology, 47*, 263–266.

Hochberg, J. & Brooks, V. (1960). The psychophysics of form: Reversible-perspective drawings of spatial objects. *American Journal of Psychology, 73*, 337–354.

Hochberg, J. & Brooks, V. (1978a). The perception of motion pictures. In E.C. Carterette & M. Friedman (Eds.), *Handbook of perception. Vol. 10* (pp. 259–304). New York: Academic Press.

Hochberg, J. & Brooks, V. (1978b). Film cutting and visual momentum. In J.W. Senders, D.F. Fisher, & R.A. Monty (Eds.), *Eye movements and the higher psychological functions* (pp. 293–314). Hillsdale, NJ: Erlbaum.

Hochberg, J. & Galper, R.E. (1967). Recognition of faces: I. An exploratory study. *Psychonomic Science, 7*, 619–620.

Hochberg, J. & Gellman, L. (1977). The effect of landmark features on mental rotation times. *Memory and Cognition, 5*, 23–26.

Hochberg, J. & McAlister, E. (1953). A quantitative approach to figural "goodness," *Journal of Experimental Psychology, 46*, 361–364.

Hochberg, J. & Peterson, M.A. (1987). Piecemeal organization and cognitive components in object perception: Perceptually coupled responses to moving objects. *Journal of Experimental Psychology: General, 116*, 370–380.

Hochberg, J. & Spiron, J. (1985). The Ames window: unveridical "direct" perception and not perceptual inference? *Proceedings and abstracts of the annual meeting of the Eastern Psychological Association, 56*, 38 (Abstract).

Hochberg, J., Triebel, W., & Seaman, G. (1951). Color adaptation under conditions of homogeneous stimulation (Ganzfeld). *Journal of Experimental Psychology, 41*, 153–159.

Hoffman, D.D. & Richards, W.A. (1984). Parts of recognition. *Cognition, 18*, 65–96.

Hogben, J.H. & DiLollo, V. (1984). Practice reduces suppression in metacontrast and in apparent motion. *Perception and Psychophysics, 35*, 441–445.

Holzt, E. von. (1954). Relations between the central nervous system and the peripheral organs. *British Journal of Animal Behavior, 2*, 89–94.

Hornbostel, E.M. von. (1922). Ueber optische Inversion. *Psychologische Forschung, 1*, 130–156.

Hornbostel, E.M. von. (1926). The unit of the senses. *Psyche, 7*, 83–89.

Hubel, D. & Wiesel, T. (1962). Receptive fields, binocular interaction, and functional architecture in the cat's visual cortex. *Journal of Physiology, 160*, 106–154.

Hurvich, L. (1981). *Color vision.* Sunderland, MA: Sinauer Associates.

Hurvich, L. & Jameson, D. (1957). An opponent-process theory of color vision. *Psychological Review, 64*, 384–404.

Hurvich, L. & Jameson, D. (1974). Opponent processes as a model of neural organization. *American Psychologist, 29*, 88–102.

Intraub, H. (1981). Rapid conceptual identification of sequentially presented pictures. *Journal of Experimental Psychology: Human Perception and Performance, 7*, 604–610.

Intraub, H. (1985). Visual dissociation: An illusory conjunction of pictures and forms. *Journal of Experimental Psychology: Human Perception and Performance, 11*, 431–442.

Ittelson, W. & Kilpatrick, F. (1952). Experiments in perception. *Scientific American, 185*, 50–55.

Jahoda, G. (1966). Geometric illusions and environment: A study in Ghana. *British Journal of Psychology, 57*, 193–199.

Jameson, D. & Hurvich, L.M. (1959). Note on factors influencing the relation between stereoscopic acuity and observation distance. *Journal of the Optical Society of America, 49*, 639.

Jameson, D. & Hurvich, L.M. (1961). Complexities of perceived brightness. *Science, 133*, 174–179.

Jameson, D. & Hurvich, L.M. (1964). Theory of brightness and color contrast in human vision. *Vision Research, 4*, 135–154.

Jameson, D. & Hurvich, L.M. (1970). Improvable, yes;

insoluble, no: a reply to Flock. *Perception and Psychophysics, 8*, 125–128.

Jansson, G. (1977) Perceived bending and stretching motions from a line of points. *Scandinavian Journal of Psychology, 18*, 209–215.

Johansson, G. (1950). *Configurations in event perception.* Uppsala, Sweden: Almqvist and Wiksell.

Johansson, G. (1977a). Studies on visual perception of locomotion. *Perception, 6*, 365–376.

Johansson, G. (1977b). Spatial constancy and motion in visual perception. In W. Epstein (Ed.), *Stability and constancy in visual perception* (pp. 375–419). New York: Wiley.

Johansson, G. (1982). Visual space perception through motion. In A.H. Wertheim, W.A. Wagenaar, & H.W. Leibowitz (Eds.), *Tutorials on motion perception* (19–39). New York: Plenum Press.

Johnston, I.R. (1972). *Visual judgments in locomotion.* Doctoral dissertation, University of Melbourne.

Jonides, J. (1980). Toward a model of the mind's eye. *Canadian Journal of Psychology, 34*, 103–112.

Jonides, J. (1983). Further toward a model of the mind's eye's movement. *Bulletin of the Psychonomic Society, 21*, 247–250.

Julesz, B. (1962). Visual pattern discrimination. *IRE transactions on information theory, 8*, 84–92.

Julesz, B. (1964). Binocular depth perception without familiarity cues. *Science, 45*, 356–362.

Julesz, B. (1971). *Foundations of cyclopean perception.* Chicago: University of Chicago Press.

Julesz, B. (1975). Experiments in the visual perception of texture. *Scientific American, 232*, 34–43.

Julesz, B. (1981). Figure and ground perception in briefly presented isodipole textures. In M. Kubovy & J.R. Pomerantz (Eds.), *Perceptual organization* (pp. 27–54). Hillsdale, NJ: Erlbaum.

Kanizsa, G. & Gerbino, W. (1982). Amodal completion: Seeing or thinking. In J. Beck (Ed.), *Organization and representation in perception* (pp. 167–190). Hillsdale, NJ: Erlbaum.

Kardos, L. (1934). Ding und Schatten. *Zeitschrift für Psychologische Ergebnisse (23)*, X-184.

Kaufman, L. (1965). Some new stereoscopic phenomena and their implications for theories of stereopsis. *American Journal of Psychology, 78*, 1–20.

Kaufman, L. (1974). *Sight and mind.* New York: Oxford University Press.

Kaufman, L. & Pitblado, C.B. (1965). Further observations on the nature of effective binocular disparities. *American Journal of Psychology, 78*, 379–391.

Kaufman, L. & Rock, I. (1962). The moon illusion: I. *Science, 136*, 953–961.

Kaufman, L. & Williamson, S.J. (1982). Magnetic

location of cortical activity. *Annals of the New York Academy of Science, 388,* 197–213.

Kepler, J. (1611). *Dioptrice.* Augsburg, Germany: Frank. In W. von Dyk and M. Caspar (Eds.), *Gesammelte Werke, Vol. 4* (1937–1963) (pp. 330–414).

Klopfer, D.S. (1985). Constructing mental representations of objects from successive views. *Journal of Experimental Psychology: Human Perception and Performance, 11,* 566–582.

Koenderink, J.J. & van Doorn, A.J. (1981). Exterospecific component of the motion parallax field. *Journal of the Optical Society of America, 71,* 953–957.

Koffka, K. (1935). *Principles of Gestalt psychology.* New York: Harcourt, Brace & World.

Köhler, W. (1920). *Die physischen Gestalten in Ruhe und im stationaren Zustland.* Braunschweig: Vieweg.

Köhler, W. (1929). *Gestalt psychology.* New York: Liveright.

Köhler, W. (1958). The present situation in brain psychology. *American Psychologist, 13,* 150–154.

Köhler, W. & Emery, D.A. (1947). Figural after-effects in the third dimension of visual space. *American Journal of Psychology, 60,* 159–201.

Köhler, W. & Wallach, H. (1944). Figural after-effects: An investigation of visual processes. *Proceedings of the American Philosophical Society, 88,* 269–357.

Kolers, P.A. (1972). *Aspects of motion perception.* Oxford: Pergamon.

Kolers, P.A. & Pomerantz, J.R. (1971). Figural change in apparent motion. *Journal of Experimental Psychology, 87,* 99–108.

Kopfermann, H. (1930). Psychologische Untersuchungen über die Wirkung zweidimensionaler Darstellung korperlicher Gebilde. *Psychologische Forschung, 13,* 293–364.

Korte, A. (1915). Kinematoskopsiche Untersuchungen. *Zeitschrift für Psychologie, 72,* 193–296.

Kosslyn, S.M. (1980). *Image and mind.* Cambridge, MA: Harvard University Press.

Krauskopf, J. (1963). Effect of retinal image stabilization on the appearance of heterochromatic targets. *Journal of the Optical Society of America, 153,* 741–743.

Kubovy, M. & Pomerantz, J.R. (1981). *Perceptual organization.* Hillsdale, NJ: Erlbaum.

Lappin, J.S., Doneer, J.F. & Kottas, B. (1980). Minimal conditions for the visual detection of structure and motion in three dimensions. *Science, 209,* 717–719.

Lashley, K.S. (1942). The problem of cerebral organization in vision. In H. Kluver (Ed.), *Biological symposia 7,* pp. 301–322.

Lawrence, D.H. (1971). Two studies of visual search for word targets with controlled rates of presentation. *Perception and Psychophysics, 10,* 85–89.

Lee, D.N. (1974). Visual information during locomotion. In R.B. MacLeod & H. Pick (Eds.), *Perception: Essays in honor of James Gibson* (pp. 250–267). Ithaca, NY: Cornell University Press.

Leeuwenberg, E. (1971). A perceptual coding language for visual and auditory patterns. *American Journal of Psychology, 84,* 307–349.

Leeuwenberg, E. (1982). Metrical aspects of patterns and structural information theory. In J. Beck (Ed.), *Organization and representation in perception* (pp. 57–71). Hillsdale, NJ: Erlbaum.

Leibowitz, H. & Bourne, L. (1956). Time and intensity as determiners of perceived shape. *Journal of Experimental Psychology, 51,* 277–281.

Leibowitz, H.W. & Harvey, L.O., Jr. (1967). Size matching as a function of instructions in a naturalistic environment. *Journal of Experimental Psychology, 74,* 378–382.

Leibowitz, H.W., Mote, F.A., & Thurlow, W.R. (1953). Simultaneous contrast as a function of separation between test and inducing field. *Journal of Experimental Psychology, 46,* 453–456.

Leibowitz, H.W. & Pick, H. (1972). Cross-cultural and educational aspects of the Ponzo illusion. *Perception and Psychophysics, 12,* 403–432.

Linkz, A. (1952). *Physiology of the eye. Vol. 2: Vision.* New York: Grune and Stratton.

Longuet-Higgins, H.C. & Sutherland, N.S. (Eds.), (1980). *The Psychology of Vision.* London: The Royal Society.

Mach, E. (1906). *The analysis of sensations and the relation of the physical to the psychical.* (Trans. by S. Waterlow from the 5th German Ed.). New York: Dover, 1959.

Marr, D. (1980). Visual information processing: The structure and creation of visual representations. In H.C. Longuet-Higgins & N.S. Sutherland (Eds.), *The psychology of vision* (pp. 199–217). London: The Royal Society.

Marr, D. (1982). *Vision.* San Francisco: Freeman.

Marr, D. & Hildreth, E. (1980). Theory of edge detection. *Proceedings of the Royal Society (London), B207,* 187–217.

Marr, D. & Poggio, T. (1976). Cooperative computation of stereo disparity. *Science, 194,* 283–287.

Matin, L. (1982). Visual location and eye movements. In A.H. Wertheim, W.A. Wagenaar, & H.W. Leibowitz (Eds.), *Tutorials on motion perception* (pp. 101–156). New York: Plenum Press.

Matin, L. (1986). Visual localization and eye movements. In K.R. Boff, L. Kaufman, and J.P. Thomas (Eds.), *Handbook of Perception and Human*

Performance, Vol. I: Sensory Processes and Perception. (pp. 20-1–20-45) New York: Wiley.

Maxwell, J.C. (1861). On colour vision. In W.D. Niven (Ed.), *The scientific papers of James Clerk Maxwell* (pp. 267–279). London: Cambridge University Press (1890).

McClelland, J.L., Rumelhart, D.E., & Hinton, G.E. (1986). The appeal of parallel distributed processing. In *Parallel Distributed Processing. Vol. I: Foundations* (pp. 1–44). Cambridge, Mass: MIT Press.

McConkie, G.W. & Rayner, K. (1975). The span of effective stimulus during a fixation in reading. *Perception and Psychophysics, 17,* 578–586.

McConkie, G.W. & Zola, D. (1984). Eye movement control during reading. In W. Prinz & A.F. Sanders (Eds.), *Cognition and motor processes.* Berlin: Springer-Verlag.

McCullogh, C. (1965). Color adaptation of edge-detectors in the human visual system. *Science, 149,* 1115–1116.

Metzger, W. (1934). Tiefenerscheinungen in optischen Bewegungsfeldern. *Psychologische Forschung, 20,* 195–260.

Metzger, W. (1953). *Gesetze des Sehens.* Frankfurt- am-Main: Kramer.

Michaels, C.F. & Carello, C. (1981). *Direct perception.* Englewood Cliffs, NJ: Prentice-Hall.

Mill, J. (1829). *Analysis of the phenomena of the human mind.* In R.J. Herrnstein & E.G. Boring (Eds.), *A source book in the history of psychology* (pp. 363–377). Cambridge, MA: Harvard University Press (1965).

Mill, J.S. (1865). *An examination of Sir William Hamilton's philosophy.* In R.J. Herrnstein & E.G. Boring (Eds.), *A source book in the history of psychology* (pp. 377–380). Cambridge, MA: Harvard University Press (1965).

Miller, G.A., Galanter, E., & Pribram, K. (1960). *Plans and the structure of behavior.* New York: Holt, Rinehart & Winston.

Minsky, M. (1975). A framework for representing knowledge. In P.H. Winston (Ed.), *The psychology of computer vision.* New York: McGraw-Hill.

Minsky, M. & Papert, S. (1969). *Perceptrons.* Cambridge, MA: MIT Press.

Morgan, M.J. (1980). Analogue models of motion perception. In H.C. Longuet-Higgins & N.S. Sutherland (Eds.), *The psychology of vision* (pp. 117–134). London: The Royal Society.

Morgan, M.J. (1981). How pursuit eye motions can convert temporal into spatial information. In D.F. Fisher, R.A. Monty, & J.W. Senders (Eds.), *Eye movements: Cognition and visual perception* (pp. 111–133). Hillsdale, NJ: Erlbaum.

Mueller, J. (1838). *Handbuch der Physiologie des Menschen,* W. Baly (Transl.) (1842). In R.J. Herrnstein & E.G. Boring (Eds.), *A source book in the history of psychology* (pp. 26–39). Cambridge, MA: Harvard University Press (1965).

Murphy, R. (1973). Recognition memory for sequentially presented pictorial and verbal spatial information. *Journal of Experimental Psychology, 100,* 327–334.

Musatti, C.L. (1931). Forma e assimilazioni. *Archivio Italiano di Psicologia, 9,* 61–156.

Navon, D. (1976). Irrelevance of figural identity for resolving ambiguities in apparent motion. *Journal of Experimental Psychology: Human Perception and Performance, 2,* 130–138.

Navon, D. (1977). Forest before trees: The precedence of global features in perception. *Journal of experimental psychology: General, 9,* 353–383.

Newton, I. (1672). A new theory of light and colors. *Philosophical transactions of the Royal Society.* Reprinted in W. Dennis (Eds.), *Readings in the history of psychology* (pp. 44–54). Appleton-Century-Crofts (1948).

Oatley, K. (1978). *Perceptions and representations.* New York: Free Press.

Olzak, L.A. & Thomas, J.P. (1986). Seeing spatial patterns. In K.R. Boff, L. Kaufman, and J.P. Thomas (Eds.), *Handbook of Perception and Human Performance. Vol. I: Sensory Processes and Perception.* (pp. 7-1–7-56), New York: Wiley.

Ono, H. (1969). Apparent distance as a function of familiar size. *Journal of experimental psychology, 79,* 109–115.

Orlansky, J. (1940). The effect of similarity and difference in form on apparent visual movement. *Archive of Psychology, 246,* 85.

Owens, D.A., & Leibowitz, H.W. (1976). Oculomotor adjustments in darkness and the specific distance tendency. *Perception and Psychophysics, 20,* 2–9.

Palmer, S.E. (1975). Visual perception and world knowledge. Notes on a model of sensory-cognitive interaction. In D.A. Norman & D.E. Rumelhart (Eds.), *Explorations in cognition* (pp. 279–309). San Francisco: Freeman.

Palmer, S.E. (1977). Hierarchical structure in perceptual representation. *Cognitive Psychology, 9,* 441–474.

Palmer, S.E. (1982). Symmetry, transformation, and the structure of perceptual systems. In J.Beck (Ed.), *Organization and representation in perception* (pp. 95–144). Hillsdale, NJ: Erlbaum.

Palmer, S.E. (1983). The psychology of perceptual organization: A transformational approach. In J. Beck, B. Hope and A. Rosenfeld (Eds.), *Human and Machine Vision* (pp. 269–339), New York: Academic Press.

Pantle, A.J. & Picciano, L. (1976). A multistable movement display: evidence for two separate systems in human vision. *Science, 193*, 500–502.

Parks, T.E. (1965). Post-retinal storage. *American Journal of Psychology, 246*, 85.

Penrose, L. & Penrose, R. (1958). Impossible objects: A special type of visual illusion. *British Journal of Psychology, 49*, 31–33.

Peterson, M.A. (1986). Illustory concomitant motion in ambiguous stereograms: Evidence for non-stimulus contributions to perceptual organization. *Journal of Experimental Psychology: Human Perception and Performance, 12*, 50–60.

Peterson, M.A. (1985) How does elective intention affect perceptual organization? *Proceedings and abstracts of the annual meeting of the Eastern Psychological Association, 56*, 3 (Abstract).

Peterson, M.A. & Hochberg, J. (1983). The opposed-set measurement procedure: The role of local cues and intention in form perception. *Journal of Experimental Psychology: Human Perception and Performance, 9*, 183–193.

Pickersgill, M. (1961). On knowing with which eye one is seeing. *Quarterly Journal of Experimental Psychology, 13*, 168–172.

Pokorny, J. & Smith, V.C. (1986). Colorimetry and color discrimination. In K.R. Boff, L. Kaufman, and J.P. Thomas (Eds), *Handbook of Perception and Human Performance. Vol. I: Sensory Processes and Perception.* (pp. 8-1–8-51) New York: Wiley.

Pomerantz, J.R. (1983). The rubber pencil illusion. *Perception and Psychophysics, 33*, 365–368.

Pomerantz, J.R. & Kubovy, M. (1986). Theoretical approaches to perceptual organization. In K.R. Boff, L. Kaufman, and J.P. Thomas (Eds.), *Handbook of Perception and Human Performance. Vol. II: Cognitive Processes and Performance* (pp. 36-1–36-46). New York: Wiley.

Postman, L. (1954). The experimental analysis of motivational factors in perception. In J.S. Brown et al. (Eds.), *Current theory and research in motivation, 28*, 59–108.

Potter, M.C. (1975). Meaning in visual search. *Science, 187*, 965–966.

Potter, M.C. (1976). Short-term conceptual memory for pictures. *Journal of Experimental Psychology: Human Perception and Performance, 2*, 509–522.

Prazdny, K. (1980). Egomotion and relative depth from optical flow. *Biological Cybernetics, 36*, 87–102.

Prazdny, K. (1983). On the information in optic flows. *Computer Vision, Graphics, and Image Processing, 22*, 235–259.

Pritchard, R.M., Heron, W., & Hebb, D.O. (1960). Visual perception approached by the method of stabilized images. *Canadian Journal of Psychology, 14*, 67–77.

Proffit, D.R. & Cutting, J.E. (1980). Perceiving the centroid of curvilinearly bounded rolling shapes. *Perception and Psychophysics, 28*, 484–487.

Purdy, W.C. (1958). The hypothesis of psychophysical correspondence in space perception (Doctoral dissertation, Cornell University, 1958). University microfilms, No. 58–5594.

Rashevsky, N. (1948). *Mathematical biophysics.* Chicago: University of Chicago Press.

Ratliff, F. (1965). *Mach bands: Quantitative studies on neural networks in the retina.* San Francisco: Holden-Day.

Reite, M. & Zimmerman, J. (1978). Magnetic phenomena of the central nervous system. *Annual review of biophysics and bioengineering, 7*, 167–188.

Restle, F. (1979). Coding theory and the perception of motion configuration. *Phychological Review, 86*, 1–24.

Restle, F. (1982). Coding theory as an integration of Gestalt psychology and information processing theory. In J. Beck (Ed.), *Organization and representation in perception* (pp. 31–56). Hillsdale, NJ: Erlbaum.

Riggs, L. (1964). Visual acuity. In C.H. Graham (Ed.), *Vision and visual perception* (pp. 321–349). New York: Wiley.

Riggs, L. (1973). Curvature as a feature of pattern vision. *Science, 181*, 1070–1072.

Riggs, L., Ratliff, F., & Cornsweet, T. (1953). The disappearance of steadily fixated visual test objects. *Journal of the Optical Society of America, 43*, 493–501.

Roberts, L.G. (1965). Machine perception of three-dimensional solids. In I.J. Tippett, et al. (Eds.), *Optical and electro-optical information processing* (pp. 159–197). Cambridge, MA: MIT Press.

Rock, I. (1977). In defense of unconscious inference. In W. Epstein (Ed.), *Stability and constancy in visual perception* (pp. 321–373). New York: Wiley.

Rock, I. (1981). Anorthoscopic perception. *Scientific American, 244*, 145–153.

Rock, I. (1983). *The logic of perception.* Cambridge, MA: MIT Press.

Rock, I. & Ebenholz, S. (1962). Stroboscopic movement based on changes of phenomenal rather than retinal locus. *American Journal of Psychology, 75*, 193–207.

Rosenblatt, F. (1962). *Principles of neurodynamics*, New York: Spartan Books.

Roufs, J.A.J. & Bouma, H. (1980). Toward linking perception research and image quality. *Proceedings of the Society for Information Displays, 21 (3)*, 247–270.

Rubin, E. (1921). *Visuell wahrgenommene Figuren.* Copenhagen: Glydendalske.

Rumelhart, D.E., & McClelland, J.L. (1986). *Parallel Distributed Processing* (2 Vols.). Cambridge, Mass.: MIT Press.

Schade, O. (1964). Modern image evaluation and television (the influence of electronic television on the method of image evaluation). *Applied Optics, 3*, 17–21.

Schriever, W. (1925). Experimentelle Studien über das stereoskopische Sehen. *Zeitschrift für Psychologie, 96*, 113–170.

Schwartz, B.J. & Sperling, G. (1983). Non-rigid 3 D percepts from 2D representations of rigid objects. *Investigative ophthalmology and visual science.* ARVO supplement, *24*, 239. (Abstract).

Sedgwick, H.A. (1980). The geometry of spatial layout in pictorial representation. In M.A. Hagen (Ed.), *The perception of pictures Vol. I.* New York: Academic Press.

Sedgwick, H.A. (1986). Space perception. In K.R. Boff, L. Kaufman, and J.P. Thomas (Eds.), *Handbook of Perception and Human Performance. Vol. I: Sensory Processes and Perception* (pp. 21-1–21-57). New York: Wiley.

Segall, M., Campbell, D., & Herskovitz, M. (1966). *The influence of culture on visual perceptions.* Indiana: Bobbs-Merrill.

Sekuler, R. & Ganz, L. (1963). Aftereffect of seen motion with a stabilized retinal image. *Science, 139*, 419–420.

Selfridge, O.G. (1959). Pandemonium: A paradigm for learning. In *The mechanization of thought processes* (pp. 511–531). London: Her Majesty's Stationery Office.

Shaw, R. & Turvey, M.T. (1981). Coalitions as models for ecosystems: A realist perspective on perceptual organization. In M. Kubovy & J. Pomerantz (Eds.), *Perceptual organization* (pp. 343–415). Hillsdale, NJ: Erlbaum.

Shebilski, W.L. & Proffitt, D.R. (1981). The priority of perceived distance for perceived motion has not been demonstrated: Critical comments on Gogel's "The sensing of retinal motion." *Perception and Psychophysics, 29*, 170–172.

Shebilske, W.L. & Proffitt, D.R. (1983). Paradoxical retinal motion during head movements: Apparent motion without equivalent apparent displacement. *Perception and Psychophysics, 34*, 476–481.

Shepard, R. (1981). Psychophysical complementarity. In M. Kubovy & J. Pomerantz (Eds.), *Perceptual organization* (pp. 279–341). Hillsdale, NJ: Erlbaum.

Shepard, R.N. & Cooper, L.A. (1982). *Mental images and their transformations.* Cambridge, MA: MIT Press.

Shepard, R.N. & Judd, S.A. (1976). Perceptual illusion of rotation of three-dimensional objects. *Science, 191*, 952–954.

Shepard, R.M. & Metzler, J. (1971). Mental rotation of three dimensional objects. *Science, 171*, 701–703.

Smith, S. (1946). The essential stimuli in stereoscopic depth perception. *Journal of Experimental Psychology, 36*, 518–521.

Sperling, G. (1970). Binocular vision: a physical and neural theory. *American Journal of Psychology, 83*, 461–534.

Sperling, G. (1980). Bandwidth requirements for video transmission of American sign language and finger spelling. *Science, 210*, 797–799.

Sperling, G., Pavel, M., Cohen, Y., Landy, M.S., & Schwartz, B.J. (1983). Image processing in perception and cognition. In O.J. Braddick & A.C. Sleigh (Eds.), *Physical and biological processing of images* (pp. 359–378). Berlin: Springer-Verlag.

Sperling, G. & Speelman, R. (1965). Visual spatial localization during object motion, apparent object motion and image motion produced by eye movements. *Journal of the Optical Society of America, 55*, 1576 (Abstract).

Stevens, K.A. (1981). The information content of texture gradients. *Biological Cybernetics, 42*, 95–105.

Stevens, S.S. (1961) To honor Fechner and repeal his law. *Science, 133*, 80–86.

Stevens, S.S. & Stevens, J.C. (1960). Brightness function: Parametric effects of adaptation and contrast. *Journal of the Optical Society of America, 50*, 1139.

Stewart, E.C. (1959). The Gelb effect. *Journal of Experimental Psychology, 52*, 235–242.

Sutherland, N.S. (1959). Stimulus analyzing mechanisms. In *Proceedings of a symposium on the mechanization of thought processes* (pp. 575–609). London: Her Majesty's Stationery Office.

Sutton, S., Braren, M., Zubin, J., & John, E.R. (1965). Evoked potential correlates of stimulus uncertainty. *Science, 150*, 1187–1188.

Svaetichin, G. (1956). Spectral response curves from single cones. *Acta physiologica Scandinavica, 39*, (Suppl. 134), 17–46.

Tausch, R. (1954). Optische Taushungen als artifizielle Effekte der Gestaltungsprozesse von grossen und Formenkonstanz in der natürlichen Raumwahrnehmung. *Psychologische Forschung, 24*, 299–348.

Ternus, J. (1938). The problem of phenomenal identity. In W.D. Ellis (Trans. and Ed.), *A source-book of Gestalt psychology* (pp. 149–161). London: Routledge and Kegan Paul.

Thiery, A. (1896). Ueber geometrisch-optische Taushungen. *Philosophisches Studien, 12*, 67–126.

Titchener, E.B. (1910). *A text-book of psychology*. New York: Macmillan.

Todd, J.T. (1982). Visual information about rigid and nonrigid motion: A geometric analysis. *Journal of experimental psychology: Human perception and performance, 8*, 238–252.

Todd, J.T. (1983). Perception of gait. *Journal of Experimental Psychology: Human Perception and Performance, 9*, 31–42.

Todd, J.T. (1982). The perception of three-dimensional structure from rigid and nonrigid motion. *Perception and Psychophysics, 36*, 97–103.

Tolman, E.C. & Brunswik, E. (1935). The organism and the causal texture of the environment. *Psychological Review, 42*, 43–77.

Treisman, A. (1986). Properties, parts, and objects. In K.R. Boff, L. Kaufman, and J.P. Thomas (Eds.), *Handbook of Perception and Human Performance. Vol. I: Sensory Processes and Perception*. (pp. 10-1–10-112). New York: Wiley.

Treisman, A.M. & Schmidt, H. (1982). Illusory conjunctions in the perception of objects. *Cognitive Psychology, 14*, 107–141.

Turvey, M.T. (1977). Contrasting orientations to the theory of visual information processing. *Psychological Review, 84*, 67–88.

Ullman, S. (1979). *The interretation of visual motion*. Cambridge, MA: MIT Press.

Ullman, S. (1984). Maximizing rigidity: The incremental recovery of 3-D structure from rigid and nonrigid motion. *Perception, 13*, 255–274.

Ullman, S. (1986). Competence, performance, and the rigidity assumption. *Perception, 15*, 644–646.

Vierordt, K. (1868). *Der Seitsinn nach Versuchen*. Tübingen: Laup.

Wallach, H. (1948). Brightness constancy and the nature of achromatic colors. *Journal of Experimental Psychology, 38*, 310–324.

Wallach, H. (1959). The perception of motion. *Scientific American, 201*, 56–60.

Wallach, H. (1982). Eye movement and motion perception. In A.H. Wertheim, W.A. Wagenaar, & H.W. Leibowitz (Eds.), *Tutorials on motion perception* (pp. 1–18). New York: Plenum Press.

Wallach, H. & Bacon, J. (1976). The constancy of the orientation of the visual field. *Perception and Psychophysics, 19*, 492–498.

Wallach, H. & Floor, L. (1971). The use of size matching to demonstrate the effectiveness of accommodation and convergence as cues for distance. *Perception and Psychophysics, 10*, 423–428.

Wallach, H. & Lewis, C. (1966). The effect of abnormal displacement of the retinal image during eye movements. *Perception and Psychophysics, 1*, 25–29.

Wallach, H. & O'Connell, D.N. (1953). The kinetic depth effect. *Journal of Experimental Psychology, 45*, 205–217.

Waltz, D. (1975). Understanding line drawings of scenes with shadows. In P.A. Winston (Ed.), *The Psychology of Computer Vision* (pp. 19–91). New York: McGraw Hill.

Warren, R. (1976). The perception of egomotion. *Journal of Experimental Psychology: Human Perception and Performance, 2*, 448–456.

Washburn, M.F. & Wright, C. (1938). The comparative efficiency of intensity, perspective, and the stereoscopic factor in producing the perception of depth. *American Journal of Psychology, 51*, 151–155.

Watson, A.B. & Ahumada, A.J., Jr. (1983). A look at motion in the frequency domain. *NASA Technical Memorandum*, TM-84352.

Welch, R.B. (1986). Adaptation of space perception. In K.R. Boff, L. Kaufman and J.P. Thomas (Eds.), *Handbook of Perception and Human Performance. Vol. I: Sensory Processes and Perception* (pp. 24-1–24-45). New York: Wiley.

Wertheimer, M. (1912). Experimentelle Studien über das Sehen von Bewegung. *Zeitschrift für Psychologie, 61*, 161–265.

Wertheimer, M. (1923). Principles of perceptual organization. In D.C. Beardslee & M. Wertheimer (Eds.), *Readings in perception* (pp. 115–135). Princeton, NJ: Van Nostrand-Reinhold, 1958. (Originally published in German, 1923).

Wheatstone, C. (1839). On some remarkable and hitherto unobserved phenomena of binocular vision: Part 2. *Philosophical magazine, 4*, 504–523.

White, B. & Mueser, G. (1960). Accuracy of reconstructing the arrangement of elements generating kinetic depth displays. *Journal of Experimental Psychology, 60*, 1–11.

White, J. (1951). *The birth and rebirth of pictorial space*. London: Faber and Faber.

Williamson, S.J., Kaufman, L., & Brenner, D. (1977). Biomagnetism. In B.B. Schwartz & S. Foner (Eds.), *Superconductor applications: SQUIDS and machines* (pp. 355–402). New York: Plenum Press.

Witkin, A.P., & Tenenbaum, J.M. (1983). On the role of structure in vision. In J. Beck, B. Hope, and A. Rosenfeld, *Human and Machine Vision* (pp. 481–543). New York: Academic Press.

Wohlgemuth, A. (1911). On the aftereffect of seen movement. *British Journal of Psychology Monographs, 1*, 1–117.

Woodworth, R.S. (1938). *Experimental psychology*, New York: Holt, Rinehart & Winston.

Wundt, W. (1902). *Outlines of psychology* (4th German ed., trans. by C.H. Judd). Leipzig: Englemann.

Wyszecki, G. (1986). Color appearance. In K.R. Boff, L. Kaufman and J.P. Thomas (Eds.), *Handbook of Perception and Performance. Vol. I: Sensory Processes and Perception* (pp. 9-1–9-57), New York: Wiley.

Young, T. (1802). On the theory of light and colours. *Philosophical Transactions of the Royal Society (Lond.)*, *92*, 18–21.

Zöllner, F. (1862). Ueber eine neue Art anorthoskopischer Zerrbilder. *Ann. der Physik und Chemie*, *117*, 477–484.

Zusne, L. (1970). *Visual perception of form*. New York: Academic Press.

Chapter 5

PHYSICS AND PHYSIOLOGY OF HEARING

Nelson Yuan-sheng Kiang, *Massachusetts Institute of Technology, Harvard Medical School, Massachusetts General Hospital and Massachusetts Eye and Ear Infirmary*

William T. Peake, *Massachusetts Institute of Technology, Massachusetts Eye and Ear Infirmary*

INTRODUCTION

The study of hearing has as its goal an understanding of how acoustic stimuli interact with responsive organisms. Inspection of the physiological mechanisms for audition found in the animal kingdom reveals a wide assortment of specializations for processing acoustic information (Layon & Tavolga, 1960; Busnel, 1963; De Reuck & Knight, 1968; Sebeok, 1968; Sales & Pye, 1974; Bench, Pye, & Pye, 1975; Bullock, 1977; Lewis, 1983). Each organism responds to sounds in ways appropriate for survival in its ecological niche. Humans use hearing to monitor the environment, to locate sound sources, to identify sound generators, and, most importantly for a social animal, to communicate with others (National Advisory Neurological Diseases and Stroke Council, 1969; David & Denes, 1972; Schubert, 1980; Warren, 1982). In this chapter,

we describe how a generalized mammalian auditory system supposedly functions. Most of the principles are derived from studies of rodents, carnivores, and primates but the emphasis here is on presentation of general ideas rather than recitation of specific details.

We begin with a discussion of acoustics and some concepts basic to the understanding of signals and systems. A review of the main anatomical features of mammalian auditory systems is then followed by a short description of physiological mechanisms based on these structural considerations. In the final section a few selected topics serve as examples of the way knowledge from physics, anatomy, and physiology can be integrated in analysis of the physiological basis of auditory behavior. This way of thinking should enable the reader to examine other issues on auditory behavior in a like manner.

BASIC PHYSICAL CONCEPTS

Acoustics

Sound Variables

Sound signals are generated whenever the mechanical equilibrium of a medium is perturbed. Sound *sources* are objects that vibrate, such as strings, bells, loudspeaker diaphragms, or vocal cords. Sound *media* are materials that are moved and compressed by sound sources. For instance, when a source vibrates in air, it alternately compresses and rarefies the adjacent gaseous medium. The resulting changes in local pressure cause motion of the air, which in turn produces pressure changes further away from the source. This reciprocal coupling of pressure changes and motion leads to propagation of sound waves through the medium. To understand how airborne sounds are "heard" we first need to understand how sound depends on the medium and interacts with objects in the sound field.[1]

The variables used to describe sounds are the sound pressure, p, and the velocity of the medium, $\bar{v}$. Sound pressure is a scalar; it is the difference between the actual pressure and the equilibrium atmospheric pressure, P_0. Thus, p can be either positive or negative. The magnitude of the sound pressure is normally much smaller than atmospheric pressure; sounds are painful if the sound-pressure magnitude is as much as 100 Pascals (Pa), which is only about a thousandth of the atmospheric pressure. The pressure in any small region results from collisions of the gas molecules in the medium with the walls of the region. In acoustics we normally deal with a macroscopic description in which a large number of collisions occurs over any time interval or spatial region of interest. Thus we need be concerned only with average effects.

The velocity of the medium (sometimes called particle velocity), $\bar{v}$, is a vector quantity; it is an average of molecular velocities over a *region*. The velocities associated with acoustic disturbances are small perturbations on the random thermal motion of the molecules. For nitrogen gas (the main component of air) the root-mean-square velocity associated with thermal motion at 27°C is about 500 m/s (the mean velocity is zero). For a uniform, unidirectional, plane acous-

tic wave with a very high sound pressure of 200 Pa the particle velocity is about 5 m/s, and for sounds near the threshold of hearing the particle velocity is only 0.5 μm/s. The propagation velocity for sound waves is 343 m/s, so it is clear that sound propagation does not involve bulk movement of the medium from the sound source to the receiver.

Sounds convey mechanical energy from one location to another. Sound intensity, $I = p\bar{v}$, is the acoustic power density (energy per unit time per unit area). Energy is conveyed in the same direction as the velocity, which is also the direction of propagation of the sound wave. The mechanical properties of the medium determine its behavior as a sound carrier. If the viscosity of the medium is small enough (as it is in air for many purposes), only the mass density, ϱ, and the compressibility, $K = (\delta\varrho/\varrho)/\delta p$, are of primary importance. The mass density is the average mass of the medium per unit volume; the compressibility is the fractional change in density $(\delta\varrho/\varrho)$ per unit change in pressure (δp) for a volume containing a large number of molecules. These considerations become important when, for instance, helium is used to replace nitrogen in underwater artificial environments. Under these conditions speech signals are transformed so as to be virtually unintelligible without preprocessing (Fant & Lindquist, 1968).

Fundamental Equations of Acoustics

Most of theoretical acoustics is derivable from three physical laws: (a) Newton's second law ($\bar{f} = m\bar{a}$), which relates the force, $\bar{f}$, on a mass (m) to its acceleration, $\bar{a}$; (b) the conservation of matter ($\nabla \cdot \varrho\bar{v} = -\partial\varrho/\partial t$), which relates the mass-flow density of the medium, $\varrho\bar{v}$, to the time rate-of-change of the density, $\partial\varrho/\partial t$; and (c) the relationship between pressure and density as determined by the inherent compressibility of the medium ($K = \varrho^{-1}\partial\varrho/\partial p$). An additional constraint imposed in "linear" acoustics is that the acoustic perturbation represents only a small change from equilibrium conditions: i.e. the sound pressure, p, is small compared to atmospheric pressure. Combining these relations, we obtain the fundamental equations of acoustics:

$$\nabla p \;=\; -\varrho\, \frac{\partial\bar{v}}{\partial t} \tag{5.1}$$

$$\nabla \cdot \bar{v} \;=\; -K\, \frac{\partial p}{\partial t} \tag{5.2}$$

[1]Standard textbooks in acoustics include Beranek (1954), Kinsler and Frey (1962), Stephens and Bate (1966), Morse and Ingard (1968), Smith (1971) and Pierce (1981).

where ϱ is the equilibrium value of the mass density of the medium,[1] K is the compressibility,[2] and ∇ is the vector operator that in Cartesian coordinates is $\nabla = \bar{i}_x \partial/\partial x + \bar{i}_y \partial/\partial y + \bar{i}_z \partial/\partial z$, where $\bar{i}_x$, $\bar{i}_y$, and $\bar{i}_z$, are unit vectors in the x, y, and z directions. In these equations it is understood that the variables, p and $\bar{v}$, are functions of spatial coordinates and time. Equation 5.1 relates the net force (∇p) on a unit volume of the medium to its acceleration ($\partial\bar{v}/\partial t$): it is Newton's second law applied to acoustics.[3] Equation 5.2 is derived from the conservation of mass *and* the pressure-density relation for the medium: it states that if there is a net flow away from a point (i.e., $\nabla \cdot \bar{v} > 0$), the density, and therefore the pressure, at that point must decrease.

Equations 5.1 and 5.2 describe the relations of the acoustic variables *in* the acoustic medium. To determine the acoustic signals in a particular situation, the effects of other structures that form boundaries on the medium, such as sound sources and other acoustically reactive objects (e.g. reflectors and absorbers, such as bodies, heads and ears of animals) must be described. That the acoustic "boundaries" in the environment can be important is dramatically illustrated with echoes, where our estimation of the location of the original sound source can be grossly mistaken. Solutions of Equations 5.1 and 5.2 subject to these "boundary conditions," provide a complete description of the sound pressure and velocity in the medium as functions of the space and time variables.

Uniform Plane Waves

We now consider solutions of Equations 5.1 and 5.2 for situations with simple spatial depend-

ence. These solutions help develop an understanding of spatial relationships among acoustic variables and are significant for hearing since in many situations it is convenient to approximate more complicated acoustic solutions by a uniform plane wave, which can be simply described.

It is possible to drive an acoustic system so that the acoustic variables vary only along one spatial dimension. For instance, if an infinite rigid plane that is perpendicular to the x coordinate vibrates in the x direction in a space with no other objects, p and $\bar{v}$ will be dependent only on x, and time, t. In this case $p = p(x, t)$ and $\bar{v} = v(x, t)\bar{i}_x$, where $\bar{i}_x$ is a unit vector in the x direction: Equations 5.1 and 5.2 can be simplified and combined to yield

$$\frac{\partial^2 p(x, t)}{\partial x^2} = \varrho K \frac{\partial^2 p(x, t)}{\partial t^2}. \tag{5.3}$$

This is a one-dimensional wave equation which has a general solution of the form

$$p(x, t) = p_+(t - x/c) + p_-(t + x/c), \tag{5.4}$$

where $p_+(\cdot)$ and $p_-(\cdot)$ are arbitrary functions that represent waves propagating in the $+x$ and $-x$ directions respectively; $c = 1/\sqrt{\varrho K}$ is the speed of propagation of the sound waves. For air at 20°C and $P_0 = 1$ atmosphere, $\varrho = 1.2\,\mathrm{kg/m^3}$, $K = 7.1 \times 10^{-6}\,\mathrm{m^2/N}$, and $c = 343\,\mathrm{m/s}$.

The velocity, $v(x, t)$, satisfies an equation of the same form as Equation 5.4 and has a similar solution:

$$v(x, t) = v_+(t - x/c) + v_-(t + x/c). \tag{5.5}$$

This solution is independent of the spatial coordinates y and z and is therefore uniform in any yz plane. The velocity and pressure are related through Equations 5.1 and 5.2 so the solutions given in Equations 5.4 and 5.5 are not independent. The velocity can be written in terms of the pressure components as

$$v(x, t) = \frac{1}{\varrho c}[p_+(t - x/c) - p_-(t + x/c)]. \tag{5.6}$$

The factor $\varrho c = \sqrt{\varrho/K}$, which is the ratio of the pressure in each wave to the velocity magnitude of that wave, is called the *specific acoustic impedance*. For air $\varrho c = 41\,\mathrm{Pa\text{-}s/m}$. Notice that, although the relation between the velocity and pressure of each of the component waves is very simple, i.e., $p_+ = (\varrho c)v_+$; $p_- = -(\varrho c)v_-$, knowledge of the net pressure (or velocity) at one loca-

---

[1] During acoustic perturbations the density varies around this equilibrium.

[2] For most of the situations of interest in acoustics little heat transfer takes place and the partial derivative should be evaluated at constant entropy, i.e., K is the *adiabatic* compressibility. For an ideal gas, $K = (\gamma P_0)^{-1}$, where P_0 is the equilibrium atmospheric pressure, and γ, the ratio of the specific heat at constant pressure to the specific heat at constant volume, is equal to 1.4 for air.

[3] The acceleration is actually the total derivative of the velocity with respect to time,

$$\frac{d\bar{v}}{dt} = \frac{\partial\bar{v}}{\partial t} + \frac{\partial\bar{v}}{\partial x}\frac{dx}{dt} + \frac{\partial\bar{v}}{\partial y}\frac{dy}{dt} + \frac{\partial\bar{v}}{\partial z}\frac{dz}{dt},$$

but the assumption of small perturbations makes the last three terms negligible, because they are all products of small quantities.

tion does not determine the velocity (or pressure) at that location: in general, $p(z, t) \neq (\varrho c)v(z, t)$.

The intensity of this uniform plane wave, which is in the x direction with a magnitude

$$I(t, x) = p(t, x)v(t, x) = \frac{1}{\varrho c}[p_+^2 - p_-^2], \quad (5.7)$$

is the difference between components from the positive going and negative going waves.

Even more special is the case in which only the wave traveling in the $+x$ direction exists (i.e. $p_- \equiv 0$) so that

$$p(x, t) = p_+(t - x/c) = \varrho c \, v(t - x/c) \quad (5.8)$$

is a "unidirectional," uniform plane wave. The pressure and velocity have exactly the same spatial and temporal variations: the intensity $I(x, t) = pv = (\varrho c)v^2 = (\varrho c)^{-1}p^2$. In this case measurement of any variable at one location is enough to define the sound wave everywhere. Because this situation is simple to describe quantitatively, in those behavioral experiments in which the use of earphones is impractical, one often tries to produce a uniform unidirectional sound field. For a wave of this kind in air, when the sound-pressure magnitude approaches 200 Pa, which is near the human threshold of pain, the average power density is approximately 100 watts/m², whereas at the threshold of hearing (20 μPa) it is 10^{-12} watts/m². Thus, one must vary the sound intensity by a factor of 10^{14} to cover the entire behavioral range of most mammals.

Sinusoidal Time Functions

A further simplification of the solutions can be made by assuming that the variables all have a sinusoidal dependence on time, in which case these steady-state solutions are called "tones" in acoustics. Since all the variables are sinusoidal functions of time with the same frequency, the time dependence can be removed from the equations. It is convenient to represent these sinusoidal signals by complex numbers. For instance, a sound pressure that is a function of spatial coordinates, represented by $\bar{r}$, and time, t, can be written as:

$$p(\bar{r}, t) = |P(\bar{r})| \cos[\omega t + \theta(\bar{r})]$$
$$= \text{Re}[P(\bar{r})e^{j\omega t}], \quad (5.9)$$

where $\omega = 2\pi f$ is the radian frequency and $j = \sqrt{-1}$. $P(\bar{r})$ is a complex number that depends only on the spatial coordinates and has a mag-

nitude $|P(\bar{r})|$ and angle $\theta(\bar{r})$. That is, $P(\bar{r}) = |P(\bar{r})|e^{j\theta(\bar{r})} = |P(\bar{r})|[\cos \theta(\bar{r}) + j \sin \theta(\bar{r})]$. $\text{Re}(\cdot)$ is an operator that takes the real part of its complex argument. Thus, if the frequency, ω, is known, the sinusoidal time-function can be found from $P(\bar{r})$, which is called the "complex amplitude." The simplifying feature of the complex amplitude is that, although it represents a time-varying quantity, it is *not* a function of time.

The intensity in the sinusoidal steady state is the product of two sinusoids: it has both a constant component and a component that is sinusoidal at twice the frequency of the pressure and velocity. The average value of the intensity

$$I_{AV} = \left(\frac{|P|}{\sqrt{2}}\right)\left(\frac{|V|}{\sqrt{2}}\right)\cos \phi \quad (5.10)$$

where ϕ is the angle between P and V. Thus, if P and V are 90° "out of phase" (i.e., $\phi = \pm\pi/2$), $I_{AV} = 0$ and no average energy is transferred.

The sound pressure of a sinusoidal unidirectional uniform plane wave propagating in the $+x$ direction can be written as

$$p(t - x/c) = \text{Re}[P_+ e^{j\omega(t - x/c)}]$$
$$= \text{Re}[P_+ e^{-jkx} e^{j\omega t}]$$
$$= \text{Re}[P(x)e^{j\omega t}], \quad (5.11)$$

where $P(x) = P_+ e^{-jkx}$ is the complex amplitude of this spatially varying wave, with P_+ a complex constant and $k = \omega/c = 2\pi/\lambda$. The wavelength, $\lambda = c/f = cT$, is the distance that the wave travels in one period, T. k, which plays the same role for spatial variations that ω plays for time variations, is called the wave number or the propagation constant. A sinusoid is heard as a tone whose qualities (e.g. pitch and loudness) depend on both the frequency and amplitude of the sound. Differences in the phase angle, θ, between the sound signals at the two ears can play an important role in the perceived direction of the sound source.

Acoustic Impedance and Admittance

In many situations one need not be concerned with the details of the spatial variations of an acoustic signal so it is convenient to use volume velocity, $\bar{u}$, which is the integral of $\bar{v}$ over a surface. One useful feature of this variable is that the product of the sound pressure and the volume velocity is the acoustic power. The ratio of the complex amplitudes of sound pressure and volume velocity is defined as the *acoustic*

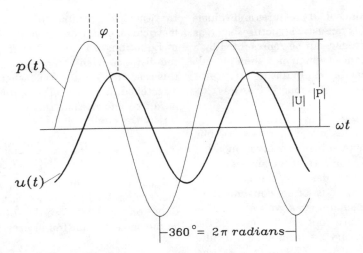

Figure 5.1. Acoustic impedance is a complex number that represents the relation between two sinusoids. This figure shows sinusoidal waveforms of sound pressure, $p(t) = \text{Re}(Pe^{j\omega t})$, and volume velocity, $u(t) = \text{Re}(Ue^{j\omega t})$. The acoustic impedance, $Z = P/U$, has a magnitude $|Z| = |P|/|U|$ and an angle, ϕ, so that $Z = |P|/|U|e^{j\phi}$. The angle of the acoustic impedance, ϕ, is the angle by which the pressure waveform leads the volume-velocity waveform.

impedance, $Z = P/U = |Z|e^{j\phi}$. The inverse of this ratio is called the *acoustic admittance,* $Y = 1/Z = U/P = |Y|e^{-j\phi}$. If an acoustic structure allows large velocity for a given pressure magnitude, it has a low impedance magnitude; that is, it "impedes" the motion little. The angle of the acoustic impedance, ϕ, is the angle of P minus the angle of U (Figure 5.1).

Consider some examples of impedances that result from simple relations between pressure and velocity. If inertial (mass) forces are dominant for a particular structure, the pressure will be proportional to the acceleration, and therefore

$$Z = \frac{P}{U} = j\omega M_A = \omega M_A e^{j\frac{\pi}{2}}, \quad (5.12)$$

where M_A, the *acoustic mass,* has the dimensions of mass/(area)^2. In this case pressure leads velocity by $\pi/2$ radians ($= 90°$), so the angle of the impedance of an acoustic mass is $90°$. Alternatively, if the pressure is proportional to the displacement, as in the case of a spring obeying Hooke's Law, the impedance is

$$Z = \frac{P}{U} = \frac{1}{j\omega C_A} = \frac{1}{\omega C_A} e^{-j\frac{\pi}{2}}, \quad (5.13)$$

so pressure lags velocity by $90°$. C_A, which is the volume displacement per unit pressure, is called the *acoustic compliance.* If the pressure is proportional to the velocity, as might be the case

for sound in a small tube where viscous forces dominate, the impedance, $Z = P/U = R$, has an angle of 0 and is called an *acoustic resistance.*

Acoustic impedance can be defined at any location where the sound pressure and volume velocity can be determined. Thus the acoustic effects of the middle ear on the external ear can be described in terms of the acoustic impedance at the tympanic membrane. The sound pressure that is generated under an earphone is determined by the earphone and the acoustic impedances of the ear and the air under the earphone.

The time-average power associated with sinusoidal time variations of acoustic variables can be expressed in a variety of ways:

$$P_{AV} = \frac{|U|}{\sqrt{2}} \frac{|P|}{\sqrt{2}} \cos\phi = \left(\frac{|U|}{\sqrt{2}}\right)^2 |Z| \cos\phi$$

$$= \left(\frac{|U|}{\sqrt{2}}\right)^2 \text{Re}[Z] = \left(\frac{|P|}{\sqrt{2}}\right)^2 \text{Re}[Y].$$

$$(5.14)$$

If the impedance (or admittance), Z, is associated with a passive device, $P_{AV} \geq 0$. Thus, the angle of the impedance (or admittance) of a passive device is always between $+90°$ and $-90°$. and $\text{Re}(Z) \geq 0$ (and $\text{Re}(Y) \geq 0$).

The concept of acoustic impedance is useful because it provides a simple description of the relation between sinusoidal pressures and volume velocities. Complex acoustic structures such as an earphone on an ear can be represented by a network of impedances which may then provide an analytical basis for manipulating structures so as to generate desired acoustic features.

Measures of Acoustic Variables

The acoustic variables, p and $\bar{v}$, are always time varying and average values at a given location are usually zero regardless of the size of amplitude fluctuations. To describe the size of an acoustic waveform, it is often convenient to use the *root-mean-square (rms)* value, which is defined as the square root of the mean of the square of the time varying variable. For a sinusoidal waveform, $p(t) = |P| \cos(\omega t + \theta)$, the rms value is the peak value divided by $\sqrt{2}$, i.e., $P_{rms} = |P|/\sqrt{2}$.

It is customary to specify sound-pressure magnitude with a logarithmic measure, the sound pressure level,

$$L = 20 \log_{10} \frac{P_{rms}}{P_{ref}} \qquad (5.15)$$

where L is identified in dimensionless units of decibels (dB). The usual reference pressure in studies of audition is $P_{ref} = 20\,\mu Pa$. This pressure is approximately the average human threshold of hearing for tones near 3 kHz. With this reference pressure the sound-pressure level is specified in "dB SPL." For example, if a 3 kHz tone has a level of 20 dB SPL, its sound-pressure magnitude is 10 times larger than a tone at threshold.

Decibels are used more generally for ratios of any quantities. Thus we may speak of a 20 dB voltage gain, if an amplifier increases voltages by a factor of 10. If the sound pressure magnitude at one ear it 10 times the sound pressure at the other ear, we say the interaural level difference is 20 dB. If the insertion of an ear plug reduces the sound pressure magnitude in the ear canal by a factor of 100, we say that the plug provides 40 dB of attenuation.

Spherical Waves

A one-dimensional wave that differs from the uniform plane wave can be obtained with spherical symmetry. If we assume that a sound source exists that is symmetrical about the origin of a spherical coordinate system (e.g., a pulsating spherical balloon centered at the origin), and

that the space around the source has no asymmetrical boundaries, then we expect solutions of Equations 5.1 and 5.2 that depend only on the distance from the origin, r, and time, t. In this case $\bar{v}(r, t) = v(r, t)\,\bar{i}_r$, where $\bar{i}_r$ is a radially directed unit vector. From these assumptions it can be shown that the sound pressure must satisfy the equation

$$\frac{\partial^2(rp)}{\partial r^2} = \frac{1}{c^2} \frac{\partial^2(rp)}{\partial t^2}. \qquad (5.16)$$

This equation is identical to Equation 5.3 except thar rp appears in Equation 5.16 in place of p in Equation 5.3. Therefore the solution for rp will be the same as that found previously for p:

$$p(r, t) = \frac{1}{r} [f_+(t - r/c) + f_-(t + r/c)], \qquad (5.17)$$

where $f_+(\cdot)$ and $f_-(\cdot)$ are arbitrary functions. Thus, we again have a superposition of two waves with one traveling in the $+r$ (outward) direction and another in the $-r$ (inward) direction.

If there are no sources or reflective surfaces at large values of r, there will be no reason for the inward wave to be nonzero. If we also restrict our attention to sinusoidal time dependence, $p(t, r) = \text{Re}[P(r)e^{j\omega t}]$, the complex amplitudes of the pressure and velocity are

$$P(r) = \frac{C}{r} e^{-jkr} \qquad (5.18)$$

and

$$V(r) = \frac{C}{\varrho c} \frac{e^{-jkr}}{r} \left(1 + \frac{1}{jkr}\right), \qquad (5.19)$$

where C is an arbitrary complex constant. In this case the pressure magnitude decreases as r increases and the angle of the pressure becomes more and more negative as r increases. Note that the velocity, $V(r)$, contains two terms; the magnitude of one is proportional to r^{-1} and the other is proportional to r^{-2}. For $kr \gg 1$, i.e., $r \gg \lambda/2\pi$, the first velocity term is dominant. This is called the "far field" condition. In the far field $p(r, t) \approx (\varrho c)\,v(r, t)$; that is, the velocity and pressure are related approximately as they are in a unidirectional uniform plane wave with both decreasing in magnitude as r increases. The intensity I in the far field is proportional to r^{-2}. This result is a consequence of the conservation of energy: as the energy propagates to larger radii it is spread over a larger area and the intensity, which is power *per unit area,* decreases accordingly. The net average power at any radius is independent of r. Thus, this condition of a unidirectional, spherically symmetric wave leads to the "inverse-square law" for acoustic intensity, $I \approx r^{-2}$.

In the "near field," the dependence of v on position is more complicated. The specific acoustic impedance is

$$\frac{P(r)}{V(r)} = \frac{\varrho c}{1 + \frac{1}{jkr}}, \qquad (5.20)$$

which shows that the impedance becomes dominated by an imaginary, mass-like term at small values of kr. Thus, although spherically symmetric sources can produce a far field which is, over a limited region, approximately a unidirectional uniform plane wave, in the near field the pressure and velocity are not in phase and have different spatial dependence.

More General Situations

In reality sound waves are rarely uniform plane waves or spherical waves. Sound sources can have irregular shapes, and miscellaneous objects in the environment can reflect or absorb some of the acoustic energy. The sound that reaches our ears in a particular listening situation is a complex function of the sound source, the other objects in the environment, and the location of the ears with respect to both. These factors are demonstrably important in determining everyday auditory perceptions. For instance, the appreciation of music is critically influenced by the "acoustics" of the concert hall and expensive revisions of buildings have had to be made when the acoustic properties do not conform to certain perceptual standards. The acoustic properties of an empty room create a different psychological environment from that after the room is furnished.

In conducting experiments one often uses earphones to control the sound reaching the ears. If earphones are not practical, loudspeakers are sometimes used to create a sound field that is approximately a unidirectional, uniform plane wave in the region that the subject occupies. Of course, when the subject is in this space the sound field around the subject is altered by the acoustic properties of the subject's head and body. "Sound proofed" rooms are needed to prevent extraneous sounds from reaching experimental subjects. For many purposes the monaural acoustic stimulus is completely specified by the pressure waveforms at the entrance to the ear canal. A binaural acoustic stimulus is then specified by the pressure waveforms at both ears. Standardization of stimulus generating and monitoring equipment has made possible audiological assessment of hearing capabilities (Fletcher, 1953; Beagley, 1981) and control of environmental noise (Kryter, 1970; Harris, 1979).

Representation of Signals and Systems

We define a signal as a quantity that varies in time and a system as a collection of elements capable of receiving and processing signals (Pfeiffer, 1961; Lathi, 1965; Papoulis, 1977; Oppenheim et al., 1983; Siebert, 1986).

Signals

The acoustic signal that enters the ear canal can be expressed as a sound presure (or velocity) that varies in time. The fact that such waveforms can be easily converted into an electrical waveform which can be changed back into an acoustic waveform has made possible such applications as electronic communication, musical recordings, and hearing aids.

A central idea in signal theory is that such time-varying signals, $s(t)$, can be alternatively described as functions of another variable, frequency (Pfeiffer, 1974). The frequency description, $S(f)$, called the spectrum of the signal, can be determined by mathematical operations from the time description. The mathematical transformations that relate a signal's time and frequency descriptions are dependent on the nature of the signal. For a particular purpose, the behavior of a system may be more convenient to describe in one "domain" than in the other. For instance, when we say that a system's output is the time derivative of its input, we are using a time-domain description. On the other hand, if we say that a system resonates at 2 kHz, we are using a frequency domain description. Both temporal and spectral features of signals are useful in analyzing the auditory system. When we measure the latency of a response after a sound is turned on, we are describing a temporal feature. When we measure the range of frequencies over which a response can be elicited, we are describing a spectral feature.

DETERMINISTIC PERIODIC SIGNALS

The value of a deterministic signal can be specified for all values of time, t. Waveforms in which a pattern is repeated over and over are called "periodic." A waveform, $s(t)$, is periodic with period T if

$$s(t) = s(t + nT), \quad n = \text{an integer.} \quad (5.21)$$

Sustained sounds produced by whistles, sirens, musical instruments, voices, and ticking watches have acoustic waveforms that are nearly periodic. (A precisely periodic waveform would satisfy Equation 5.21 for all time, $-\infty < t < +\infty$.) A periodic waveform can be expressed as a sum of sinusoids that have frequencies equal to integer multiples of the fundamental frequency, $f_0 = 1/T$:

$$s(t) = \sum_{k=0}^{k=\infty} A_k \cos (2\pi k f_0 t + \psi_k),$$

$$k = \text{a positive integer,} \quad (5.22)$$

where A_k and ψ_k are the magnitude and phase angle of the component at frequency kf_0. This sum, called the Fourier series, is more conveniently written in terms of exponentials as

$$s(t) = \sum_{n=-\infty}^{+\infty} S(nf_0) e^{j2\pi n f_0 t}, \quad n = \text{integer}$$

$$(5.23)$$

where $S(nf_0) = |S(nf_0)|e^{j\theta(nf_0)}$ is a complex number that can be determined from $s(t)$ as

$$S(nf_0) = \frac{1}{T} \int_0^T s(t) e^{-j2\pi n f_0 t} dt. \quad (5.24)$$

That the sum of exponentials in Equation 5.23 is equivalent to the sum of sinusoids in Equation 5.22 can be seen by pairing the terms for $n = +k$ and $n = -k$ in Equation 5.23. It can be shown that

$$S(kf_0)e^{j2\pi k f_0 t} + S(-kf_0)e^{-j2\pi k f_0 t}$$

$$= 2|S(kf_0)| \cos [2\pi k f_0 t + \theta(kf_0)], \quad (5.25)$$

which allows the terms of the two series to be equated if $S(kf_0) = (1/2)A_k e^{j\psi_k}$. Thus, sinusoidal (or exponential) signals can be used to represent any periodic waveform.

Equations 5.23 and 5.24 are the rules for transforming back and forth between the time domain description of a periodic signal, $s(t)$, and the frequency domain description, in which the spectrum, $S(f)$, exists only for the values of $f = nf_0$, which are the harmonics of the fundamental frequency. Thus, the spectrum of a periodic waveform is a set of magnitudes and angles (i.e., complex numbers that represent sinusoids) at each harmonic frequency. These spectral terms, $S(nf_0)$, have the same dimensions as $s(t)$.

Another representation in the frequency domain is the *power spectrum* $\Phi(nf_0) = |S(nf_0)|^2$. At each harmonic frequency, nf_0, this real quantity is proportional to the power that this signal can deliver. Note that, although $\Phi(nf_0)$ can be determined from $S(nf_0)$, in general, the reverse is *not* possible because knowledge of the angle of $S(nf_0)$ is lost in $\Phi(nf_0)$. Thus, the power spectrum alone does not uniquely determine a waveform.

DETERMINISTIC NONREPEATING (APERIODIC) SIGNALS

We shall now consider signals that are nonzero only over a restricted (although possibly very long) interval. Examples of such "aperiodic" signals are a click, a scream, a spoken sentence, or a recording of the sound outside the Great Pyramid of Cheops over the 5000 years of its existence. Such signals can be represented by an integral

$$s(t) = \int_{-\infty}^{\infty} S(f) e^{j2\pi ft} df, \quad (5.26)$$

where

$$S(f) = \int_{-\infty}^{\infty} s(t) e^{-j2\pi ft} dt. \quad (5.27)$$

$S(f)$ is called the Fourier transform (or Fourier integral) of $s(t)$. Notice the similarity of Equations 5.26 and 5.27 to Equations 5.23 and 5.24. The primary difference is that for aperiodic signals there is no fundamental frequency. One can imagine that the period, T, approaches infinity and the fundamental frequency, $f_0 = 1/T$, approaches zero so that the Fourier series of Equation 5.23 now has terms for all values of f and the sum becomes the Fourier integral of Equation 5.26. This integral can then be thought of as a sum of sinusoids of all frequencies, each having a complex amplitude $S(f)df$. Note that the dimensions of $S(nf_0)$ for the periodic signal are different from those of $S(f)$ for the aperiodic signal.

$\Phi(f) = |S(f)|^2$ for an aperiodic signal is the *energy density* spectrum: that is, the energy per unit frequency. Because these signals exist only for a finite time, their average *power* over all time is zero, but their *energy* is finite. At any frequency the energy in the signal is 0, but in the frequency band between f_a and f_b the energy is

$$W_{ab} = \int_{f_a}^{f_b} \Phi(f)\, df. \qquad (5.28)$$

Probabilistically Definable (Random) Signals

Some signals result from processes that cannot be described deterministically, but can be described in probabilistic terms. Examples of such acoustic signals are the sounds made by air turbulence from wind blowing in trees or by the air stream from the lungs flowing through constrictions in the vocal tract, as in speech segments such as /f/, /v/, /s/, and /sh/. Another source of random signals is the thermal motion of molecules in acoustic media. Random waveforms are often called "noise."

The waveforms of random signals can only be drawn as sample waveforms from the set of possible waveforms. Measures of random signals must be based on averages. A useful average is the autocorrelation function:

$$\phi(\tau) = \lim_{T \to \infty} \frac{1}{2T} \int_{-T}^{T} s(t)\, s(t + \tau)\, dt. \quad (5.29)$$

$\phi(\tau)$ is a determinsitic function of the time variable τ; its Fourier transform

$$\Phi(f) = \int_{-\infty}^{\infty} \phi(\tau)\, e^{-j\,2\pi f \tau}\, d\tau \qquad (5.30)$$

is the *power density* spectrum of the random signal. A random signal that continues for all time can deliver finite power. The power at any frequency is 0, but the power in a frequency band from f_a to f_b is

$$P_{ab} = \int_{f_a}^{f_b} \Phi(f)\, df. \qquad (5.31)$$

To summarize, periodic, aperiodic, and random signals can be represented as functions of time or frequency. There are some differences in these representations. For periodic signals the spectrum exists only at the harmonics of the fundamental frequency. Each of these harmonic terms can deliver a finite power. Aperiodic signals have spectra that are continuous functions of frequency; they can have a finite energy value only within a finite band of frequency components. Random signals have continuous power spectra and can deliver a finite power within finite frequency bands. Thus, to compare the strengths of a tone and a masking noise the intensity of the tone can be compared to the noise power in a specified frequency band.

Spectrograms

For many purposes specification of the overall spectral content of signals is sufficient, but such an analysis does not show, in the most convenient form, some of the signal features that are of most interest for complex acoustic stimuli. If one computes a Fourier transform of the sound-pressure waveform of a spoken sentence, this spectrum would describe the distribution of energy along the frequency dimension averaged over the whole sentence. However, features of the speech segments that are important in determining the speech information are lost in this transformation. It is clear that the spectral features of different speech segments are important in conveying their identities. Vowels, for instance, are primarily distinguished on the basis of differences in their spectra. Thus, a method is needed that provides an indication of the spectrum of the speech waveform for time intervals of the duration of speech segments. Such a procedure is called a short-time spectral analysis (Flanagan, 1972). The basic method is to multiply the (speech) waveform by a "window" function that has the desired "duration." The energy spectrum is then computed for the product signal. Since the window can be moved to different times in the waveform, this process gives a spectrum that is a continuous function of frequency and time. The result will, of course, depend on the specific window function that is chosen so that a "short-time spectrum" is not unique. Standard spectrograms (also known as sonograms or voice prints) used to display time-varying spectra of speech sounds are examples of short-time spectral analysis.

Spike Trains as Signals

Responses of the auditory system have been recorded in many ways. Many responses consist of waveforms that are deterministic transformations of the stimulus waveform. Examples are motion of the stapes or cochlear-microphonic potentials. A second class of responses is exemplified by action potentials (spikes) from individual nerve cells or their processes. It is generally assumed that (since the spikes are nearly identical in shape) the waveform of the spike is not of great importance in determining the information transmitted; the information is carried in the time *patterns* of spike occurrences. Instantaneous spike rate is assumed to code all features of interest and recorded spike trains are processed so as to give an estimate of the instantaneous rate as a function of time, $\lambda(t)$ (e.g. Johnson, 1978). It is important to emphasize that signals must be considered within the context of specific systems to be functionally meaningful.

Of primary importance is the fact that spike trains are, in general, probabilistic. For instance, the pattern of spikes that appears in response to a particular acoustic stimulus is not identical to that which occurs in response to a repetition of the same stimulus. However, a stable average is obtained when responses are averaged over many stimulus repetitions. The averaging process provides an estimate of a waveform, $\lambda(t)$, which can then be analyzed as a deterministic signal (Snyder, 1975).

Systems
Signal-processing systems are often described by block diagrams, in which a signal $x(t)$ is the input (stimulus) to a block and another signal, $y(t)$, is the output (response). The description of the block must specify the "process" that is performed. For example, the equations $y(t) = x^2(t)$ and $y(t) = dx/dt$ describe the processes of a "squarer" and a "differentiator" respectively.

Linear Time-invariant Systems
Many physical systems behave almost as if they were linear and time-invariant systems. A linear and time-invariant system has the very useful property that knowledge of its response to certain stimuli makes possible the determination of responses for all possible stimuli. A linear time-variant system can be defined by three properties:

1. If a particular input $x_1(t)$ produces an output $y_1(t)$, then the input $ax_1(t)$ (where a is a constant) will produce the output $ay_1(t)$. This is called the proportionality property: if the amplitude of the input waveform is changed, the output changes proportionately.

2. If the input $x_1(t)$ produces an output $y_1(t)$ and the input $x_2(t)$ produces an output $y_2(t)$, then the input $x(t) = x_1(t) + x_2(t)$ will produce the output $y(t) = y_1(t) + y_2(t)$. This is called the superposition property. If the input is a superposition of components, then the net output can be represented as a superposition of output components, each of which is associated with a particular input component.

3. If an input $x_1(t)$ produces an output $y_1(t)$, then the input $x_1(t - t_0)$ will produce the output $y(t) = y_1(t - t_0)$. This is called the time invariance property. The system is invariant in that a given stimulus will produce the "same" response no matter when the stimulus appears.

An important property of linear systems is that, if the input is a sinusoidal (or exponential) function of time, $x(t) = \mathrm{Re}[Xe^{j2\pi ft}] = |X|\cos(2\pi ft + \theta)$, where $X = |X|e^{j\theta}$, then the output is also sinusoidal (or exponential) with the same frequency, $y(t) = \mathrm{Re}[Ye^{j2\pi ft}] = |Y|\cos(2\pi ft + \beta)$, where $Y = |Y|e^{j\beta}$. Thus, in this case, if one thinks of the complex numbers X and Y as the signals, the "signal processing" of the block can be simply described as multiplication by a complex number H, because $Y = HX$. The ratio, $H = Y/X$, is called the transfer ratio. In general, this complex quantity is a function of frequency. If $H(f)$, called the transfer function, is known for all f, the system is completely described; that is, the response to any stimulus can be found.

The basis for this conclusion can be appreciated from the Fourier analysis discussed in the preceeding section. If we think of an input signal, $x(t)$, as a sum of exponentials each of whose amplitudes is given by the spectrum, $X(f)$, the amplitudes of the output exponentials are determined by the transfer function, so that $Y(f) = X(f)H(f)$. Because of the superposition property, the response to a sum of exponentials is the sum (or integral) of the responses to the individual exponentials. Thus,

$$y(t) = \int_{-\infty}^{\infty} Y(f)e^{j2\pi ft}df$$

$$= \int_{-\infty}^{\infty} H(f)X(F)e^{j2\pi ft}df. \qquad (5.31)$$

This equation says that the output waveform can be determined from the spectrum of the input waveform and the transfer function. It applies to any input waveform. The power of this approach lies in the use of frequency spectra and transfer functions to find the response, a method which is valid for any linear time-invariant system.

Non-linear Systems

Some aspects of auditory system response are nearly linear, such as the acoustic and mechanical responses of the external, middle, and inner ear. On the other hand, it is clear that the responses of the auditory nervous system are generally *not* linearly related to the acoustic stimuli. For instance, if the stimulus is two tones the instantaneous spike rate of cochlear nerve fibres can have components at many frequencies other than the stimulus-tone frequencies (Kiang & Moxon, 1972). Althought there are some theoretical approaches to general descriptions of nonlinear systems, they have had limited success in studies of the auditory system thus far (Johnson, 1980a). Descriptions of nonlinear signal processing by the auditory system have been restricted to selected classes of stimuli for which empirical data are available (Allen, Hall, Hubbard et al., 1986).

Complexes of Systems

Complex systems can be built by concatenating "blocks" so that the outputs of blocks (or their sums) are inputs to other blocks. If the system is linear, the transfer functions of the individual boxes can be combined to find the transfer function of the combination (Lathi, 1965; Pfeiffer, 1968). If part of the system is nonlinear, description of the signal processing is more complicated, but it can sometimes be conveniently done by compartmentalizing the nonlinear processes into blocks that are separate from the linear processes. For instance, if the nonlinear behavior results from a component block in the system which has an output y that is the cube of the input x, then the linear system preceeding this block can be analyzed to find x. The spectrum of the output can then be found from y. It will contain frequencies that were not present in the input, but the transmission of these components of y can be determined from the transfer function of the rest of the system. This approach has been used in the study of combination tones generated in the inner ear (Allen, Hall, Hubbard et al., 1986).

The method of analyzing a complex system by breaking it up into a set of concatenated blocks is generally useful. Such models need *not* be "physiological" in the sense that blocks may not correspond to easily identifiable physiological processes. For example all the frequency-selective properties of the system could be collected into one block in such a "functional" model even if, in the real system, the frequency selectivity were distributed throughout many physiological stages. Similarly, some adaptation may be introduced at each stage in the system but an overall adaptation function could be collected into one block in generating models. Such models may be useful in formulating functional descriptions of the system, but do not do well when the system is altered at specific stages (such as when hair cells are damaged by high intensity sound [Liberman & Kiang, 1978]) or when signals are inserted into an unusual place (such as when electrical stimuli are delivered to the auditory nerve [Parkins & Anderson, 1983; Kiang et al., 1984; Schindler & Merzenich, 1985]). Under such circumstances a true physiological model in which the concatenated blocks represent physiological stages in the system will be more useful. In the development of auditory models, physiological data allow truly physiological models to be developed. However, functional models can still be useful in constructing signal-processing machinery for applications in fields such as robotics or artificial intelligence.

THE ANATOMY OF THE AUDITORY SYSTEM

The basic plan of a typical mammalian auditory system is depicted in Figure 5.2. Sound is collected by each of the external ears, led to the tympanic membrane, and transmitted through a chain of three ossicles to the cochlear portion of the inner ear where the mechanical signals are transduced into neural signals. In the neural parts of the system these signals are processed by both parallel and serial networks, eventually leading to activity in effector organs (Whitfield, 1984).

External, Middle, and Inner Ear

In many mammals, the external ears are elaborately contoured and the animal can change their orientation or distort them to occlude the external auditory meatus, which is usually a tapered tube that terminates at the tympanic membrane (Pye & Hinchcliffe, 1976; Fleischer, 1978; Nicol & Chao-Charia, 1981). The tympanic membrane varies in appearance among species (Kirikae, 1960; Békésy, 1960), but it is generally attached to the handle of the malleus, the first of

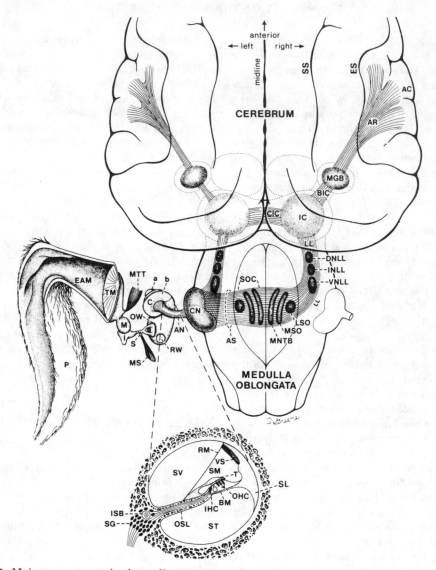

Figure 5.2. Major components in the auditory systems of a generalized mammal. The spatial relations are based on the cat as a model. The ossicles and muscles of the middle ear are shown as well as the cochlea and auditory nerve. An expanded cross-section of the cochlea is shown in the lower inset drawing. The open space between the inner and outer hair cells is the tunnel of Corti. The medulla oblongata is shown from a dorsal view. The mid- and fore-brain structures are seen through a transparent superimposed cerebrum. The major nuclei (stipples) that have connections with the left ear are indicated along with the major fiber tracts (solid lines). The distance from the lateral edge of one cochlear nucleus to the other is approximately 14 mm. The distances shown between various other structures are only roughly to scale and are not meant to be exact. AC = auditory cortex; AN = auditory nerve; AR = auditory radiations; AS = acoustic striae; BIC = brachium of the inferior colliculus; BM = basilar membrane; C(a) = cochlea (apical); C(b) = cochlea (basal); CIC = commissure of the IC; CN = cochlear nucleus; DNLL = dorsal nucleus of the lateral lemniscus; EAM = external auditory meatus; ES = ectosylvian sulcus; I = incus; IC = inferior colliculus; IHC = inner hair cell; INLL = intermediate nucleus of the lateral lemniscus; ISB = intraganglionic spiral bundle; LL = lateral lemniscus; LSO = lateral superior olive; M = malleus; MGB = medial geniculate body; MNTB = medial nucleus of the trapezoid body; MS = stapedius muscle; MSO = medial superior olive; MTT = tensor tympani muscle; OHC = outer hair cells; OSL = osseus spiral lamina; OW = oval window; P = pinna; RM = Reissner's membrane; RW = round window; S = stapes; SG = spiral ganglion; SL = spiral ligament; SM = scala media; SOC = superior olivary complex; SS = suprasylvian sulcus; ST = scala tympani; SV = scala vestibuli; T = tectorial membrane; TM = tympanic membrane; VNLL = ventral nucleus of the lateral lemniscus; VS = stria vascularis.

the three ossicles. In some species the tympanic membrane is stiff but attached flexibly around its perimeter, resembling a loudspeaker cone. In other species large portions of the membrane are flaccid, the movements of these portions presumably being less well coupled to those of the ossicular chain (Kohllöffel, 1984). Cetaceans lack a pinna and the tympanic membrane is considerably modified from that of terrestrial mammals (Reysenback de Haan, 1956; Stebbins, 1983).

The three ossicles are suspended by ligaments (Henson, 1974). In general, the malleus is coupled to the incus and the incus to the stapes by synovial joints. Motion of the ossicles can be modified by contractions of two middle-ear muscles, the tensor tympani, which inserts onto the malleus, and the stapedius, which inserts onto the stapes. The stapes footplate fits into the oval window of the cochlea and is suspended by the annular ligament. A mobile ossicular chain is required for normal hearing sensitivity, but when the ossicles are immobilized through disease, functional hearing can be established through conduction of amplified sound signals to the cochlea through alternate acoustic pathways lumped under the term, "bone conduction" (Tonndorf, 1972).

The inner ear is filled with two kinds of fluids separated into compartments by sheets of cells connected by tight junctions. In the cochlear part of the inner ear, the scala media, a space enclosed by Reissner's membrane, basilar membrane, the stria vascularis and the spiral ligament, is filled with endolymph, a unique extracellular fluid with a high potassium concentration and a low sodium concentration. The endolymphatic space is connected through the endolymphatic duct to the endolymphatic sac, which is located within the cranial cavity adjacent to the duramater. The rest of the intracochlear space consists of the scala vestibuli and the confluent scala tympani, which are filled with perilymph, a fluid more like most extracellular fluids, low in potassium and high in sodium. The perilymph is confluent with cerebrospinal fluid through the cochlear aqueduct. The relationships of the various spaces and the differing compositions of the fluids may be functionally important in maintaining the specialized chemical and electrical environment necessary for the sensory cells to perform transduction at competitive levels of sensitivity (Iurato, 1967; Schuknecht,

1974; Kimura, 1975; Smith, 1978; Brown & Daigneault, 1981; Katsuki, 1982).

When the stapes pushes into the scala vestibuli, perilymph is displaced so that the basilar membrane moves towards scala tympani and the round window moves outward into the middle-ear airspace. At the apical end of the cochlea, scala vestibuli and scala tympani are connected by a passage, the helicotrema, which, for stimulation at infrasonic frequencies, allows perilymph to flow from oval window to round window with little displacement of the basilar membrane.

The sensory cells (hair cells) are positioned within a framework of supporting cells; the entire complex forms the organ of Corti which lies on the basilar membrane (Retzius, 1884; Lim, 1969; Ades & Engstrom, 1972, 1974; Angelborg & Engstrom, 1973; Ades, 1974; Lim 1986). The hair cells are specialized so that at one end they have stiffened modified microvilli called stereocilia, often inserted into an acellular structure known as the tectorial membrane (Kimura, 1966, 1975; Hoshino, 1976; Lim, 1977); at the other end the hair cells make contact with nerve endings. These anatomical relations point to the key role played by these cells in converting movement into neuronal activity (Retzius, 1884; Engstrom, Ades, & Andersson, 1966; Smith, Cameron, & Richter, 1976). In a typical mammalian cochlea, there is one row of inner hair cells (IHC) and three or four rows of outer hair cells (OHC) arranged in a regular mosaic pattern (Figures 5.2 and 5.3). The two types of hair cells are separated by supporting cells which form an intercellular space called the tunnel of Corti.

One can regard the elaborately specialized structure of the cochlea as providing, at an organ level, means for increasing sensitivity of the system that is constrained at a cellular level to using transducer mechanisms with inherent limitations in sensitivity and frequency range. Mechanical transduction by sensory cells seems to be a very early specialization already existing in primitive invertebrates (Lentz, 1968), whereas the arrangement of cells and tissues into a special sense organ, the cochlea, is a relatively recent development in vertebrate evolution (Romer, 1949; van Bergeijk, 1967).

The Auditory Nervous System

The afferent innervation of hair cells arises from primary sensory neurons whose cell bodies

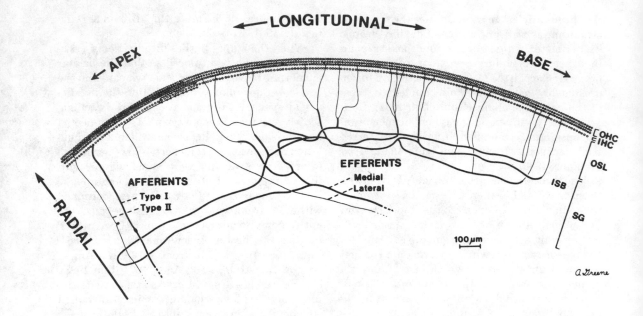

Figure 5.3. Semi-schematic illustration in the plane of the hair-cell sheet (i.e., parallel to the basilar membrane) of the afferent and efferent innervation of a small portion of the mammalian organ of Corti, based on cat and guinea pig. (Data on efferents were supplied by M.C. Liberman and M.C. Brown.) Hair cells are represented by circles. In the representation of nerve fibers, the thicker lines represent portions of nerve fibers that are myelinated. Filled circles represent hair cells innervated by the indicated fibers. The type-I afferent neuron typically contacts one inner hair cell (IHC) via a myelinated peripheral process emanating from a relatively large cell body in the spiral ganglion (SG); its myelinated central process contacts many neuronal structures within the ipsilateral cochlear nucleus (CN). The type-II afferent neuron contacts from 10 to 100 outer hair cells (OHC) via an unmyelinated peripheral process. The central course of the type-II axon is unknown except that it does enter the ipsilateral CN. The efferent neurons are also of two types. They are classified on the basis of the location of the cell body in the superior olivary complex (SOC). "Medial efferents" arise from cell bodies near the medial nucleus of the trapezoid body (MNTB) and form a predominantly contralateral projection to the OHCs. For most of their course (including the portion in the intraganglionic spiral bundle (ISB) these neurons are myelinated. However, they appear to become unmyelinated deep within the osseus spiral lamina (OSL). As shown here, one medial efferent can branch to contact OHCs spanning as much as 3 mm of the organ of Corti, corresponding to roughly an octave of characteristic frequency (CF). The "lateral efferent" fibers arise from cell bodies near the lateral superior olivary nucleus (LSO) and form a predominantly ipsilateral projection, via unmyelinated axons, to the neuropil in the IHC area, where they branch profusely and contact primarily the dendrites of type-I afferent neurons. In the cat the total number of neurons per ear in each category is approximately: Type-I afferents, 45,000-50,000; Type-II afferents, 2500-3500; Medial efferents, 450; Lateral efferents, 750 (Spoendlin, 1972; Warr, Guinan, & White, 1986.)

are located in the spiral ganglion (Spoendlin, 1966, 1974; Kiang et al., 1982). As indicated in Figure 5.3 the larger type-I ganglion cells innervate IHCs; their unbranched myelinated fibers rarely innervate more than one IHC but each IHC is innervated by many myelinated fibers, the exact number (5–20) depending upon the species and the longitudinal cochlear location (Spoendlin, 1972). Type-II spiral ganglion neurons are smaller and send unmyelinated fibers that run radially, bypassing the IHCs, then longitudinally basalward in spiral bundles under outer hair cells to eventually innervate many OHCs

within a row. Each OHC in cats receives up to 8 afferent endings.

The cochlea is also innervated by efferent fibers that originate from cell bodies in the brain stem (Guinan, Warr, & Norris, 1984). Efferent innervation of the cochlea provides mechanisms by which the central nervous system can influence cochlear activity (Fex, 1974; Gifford & Guinan, 1983; Brown & Nuttall, 1984). Although the anatomy of the efferent olivocochlear neurons has been extensively studied with older methods (Rasmussen, 1953, 1960; Smith & Rasmussen, 1963, 1965; Terayama & Yamamoto, 1971; Smith

& Haglan, 1973; Perkins & Morest, 1975; Iurato et al., 1978), much of the following description is based on recent work in which individual neurons were labelled (Liberman & Brown, 1986). Peripheral courses of efferent fibers in the cochlea are shown in Figure 5.3 with the afferent fibers. The "medial" efferent fibers, which are relatively large (2-5 μm in diameter) originate from cells in the region of the medial nucleus of the trapezoid body (MNTB) (Guinan, Warr & Norris, 1983). Most of these fibers cross the brainstem to travel in the contralateral vestibular branch of the eighth nerve, shift to the cochlea in a separate bundle (Bundle of Oort) (Arnesen & Osen, 1984), travel longitudinally in the intraganglionic spiral bundles (ISB) in the spiral ganglion, branch profusely, lose their myelin sheaths, become smaller in diameter, and cross the tunnel of Corti to form large vesiculated endings on OHCs (Smith & Sjostrand, 1961; Kimura & Wersall, 1962; Ades & Engstrom, 1972; Smith, 1973). A small number of these medial efferents innervate the ipsilateral cochlea (Warr, 1975). The field innervated by the large efferent fibres is variable, but can cover a few millimeters (Liberman & Brown, 1986). Each fiber does not innervate every OHC in its span, the distribution being irregular with large gaps between radial branches (Figure 5.3). Individual medial efferent fibers have the most widespread innervation pattern of any cochlear fibers. Most of the smaller (0.5–1 μm) lateral efferents begin as unmyelinated axons of cells in the region of the lateral superior olive, travel in the ipsilateral vestibular nerve, cross to the cochlea via the Bundle of Oort (Arnesen & Osen, 1984), travel longitudinally in the spiral ganglion, and turn either basally or apically to innervate afferent fibers under the IHCs (Iurato, 1967; Brown, 1987). A minority of the small efferents innervate the contralateral cochlea.

The axons of spiral ganglion cells form the auditory nerve and enter the cochlear nucleus which lies on the lateral surface of the posterior brainstem. As shown in Figure 5.4, each myelinated axon from a type-I neuron bifurcates in the nucleus to form an ascending and a descending branch (Ramon y Cajal, 1909; Lorente de Nó, 1933; Osen, 1970; Fekete, Rouiller, Liberman & Ryugo, 1984). The points of bifurcation are distributed so that fibers from neurons innervating more basal parts of the cochlea systematically project to more dorsomedial parts of the nucleus. Some such cochleotopic projection pattern is found in all the main nuclei in the classically defined auditory system (Clopton, Winfield, &

Flamino, 1974). Collaterals and swellings of the main branches of auditory nerve fibers form endings on a wide variety of cell bodies or processes of cells in the cochlear nucleus. Fibers from other cells of the cochlear nucleus or other parts of the brain also terminate in the nucleus (Lorente de Nó, 1933; Rasmussen, 1967; McDonald & Rasmussen, 1971; Cant & Morest, 1978).

As seen in Figure 5.5 some of the output fibers of cochlear-nucleus cells travel medially in well-defined fiber tracts, the dorsal, intermediate, and ventral acoustic stria (Papez, 1967; Kiang, 1975; Warr, 1982). It appears that no primary neuron projects beyond the cochlear nucleus so these tracts are made up of fibres from cochlear nucleus neurons or efferent fibres to the cochlear nucleus from more central nuclei or the other cochlear nucleus (Adams & Warr, 1976; Cant & Gaston, 1982).

A cluster of nuclei on each side of the lower medulla forms the core of the superior olivary complex (Figure 5.5). The cells in and around these nuclei receive projections from combinations of fibers from the two cochlear nuclei, other parts of the superior olivary complex and more central regions of the brain (Stotler, 1953; van Noort, 1969; Borg, 1973a, b; Brugge & Geisler, 1978; Harrison, 1978).

Some branches of axons from the cochlear nucleus along with axons from the superior olivary complexes proceed cranially in laterally placed tracts, the lateral lemnisci (Figure 5.2). Some of these fibers terminate on cells in the nuclei of the lateral lemnisci; others proceed dorsocranially to the inferior colliculi, two prominent bumps on the dorsal surface of the midbrain (Papez, 1967; Morest & Oliver, 1984). Each inferior colliculus has a central or core portion where most of the afferent projections are represented in topographic order and a "rind" which receives some ascending but more descending projections. With a few exceptions the inferior colliculus is an obligatory synaptic station (Van Noort, 1969). Fibers connecting the two colliculi course in the commissure of the inferior colliculi (Masterton, Glendenning, & Nudo, 1982). The cells of each inferior colliculus provide the major ascending axons to the ipsilateral medial geniculate body (Calford & Aitkin, 1983), a complex assortment of cells (Morest, 1964, 1965; Calford, 1983), many of which provide inputs to the primary auditory projection areas of the cortex (AC in Figure 5.2). The medial geniculate bodies and inferior colliculus also receive projections from the cortex

(Colwell, 1975; Ravizza, Straw, & Long, 1976). The primary auditory cortices on the two sides have connections not only with each other through the corpus callosum, but also with other cortical areas and non-cortical regions (Imig, Reale, & Brugge, 1982). There also appear to be very orderly connections between the many distinct auditory cortical projection areas. One caveat for the non-specialist in reading the literature on auditory neuroanatomy is that many of the descriptions are method dependent. Even such standard methods as the Nissl and Golgi have generated descriptions that are surprisingly difficult to correlate (Brawer, Morest, & Kane, 1974). An additional problem is that many of the classic descriptions (e.g., Ramon y Cajal, 1909; Lorente de Nó, 1933) rely heavily on data from neonates and the mature forms may differ significantly (Ryugo & Fekete, 1982).

A great many regions of the brain such as hippocampus, cerebellum, pulvinar, superior colliculus, and reticular formation also have auditory inputs but are not generally considered to be part of the auditory system per se because their functional roles are presumably better described in a more general context where auditory input is but one among many input modalities. The major components of the auditory system as shown in Figure 5.2 are almost uniformly present in mammals although relative

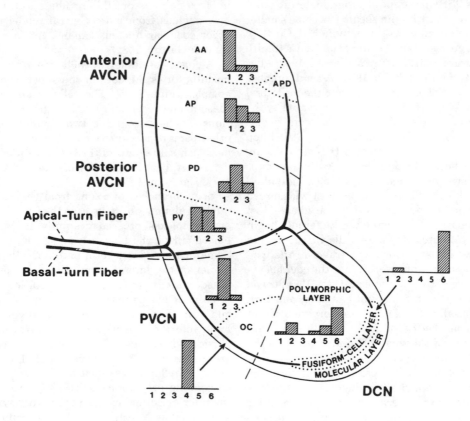

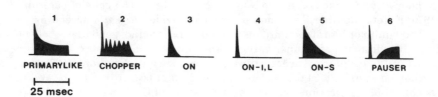

sizes of specific components may vary considerably as functional elaboration is dictated by survival needs in different ecological niches (Harrison & Howe, 1974; Willard & Ryugo, 1983). For example, animals specialized for high frequency hearing (such as bats or dolphins) have virtually no MSO but prominent LSOs (Irving & Harrison, 1967), whereas low frequency animals, such as man, barely have a definable LSO or MNTB but have prominent MSOs (Richter et al., 1983).

The possible existence of a centrifugal or efferent system in addition to the centripetal afferent system has been recognized for some time. The anatomy of the efferent neural supply to the cochlea is complex but orderly (Warr, Guinan, & White, 1986). More generally, probably most neurons in the auditory system receive inputs from multiple sources with many of these inputs being from more central locations (Rossi & Cortesina, 1965; Filogamo, Candiollo, & Rossi, 1967; Borg, 1973b). Whether there are chains of efferent neurons that are activated sequentially, thus forming an organized descending *system*

under central control is not yet clear. There do appear to be many neurons lying in the classically defined auditory nuclei whose axons are directed peripherally rather than centrally (Adams & Warr, 1976). At the moment, only anatomical data are available for these cells since physiological recordings do not generally indicate the direction in which the impulses travel (Adams, 1976) and labeled units have not been studied.

PHYSIOLOGY OF THE AUDITORY SYSTEM

External Ear

The "external ear" couples sound stimuli from the environment into the middle ear (Shaw, 1974). The head is an acoustically hard body that is large compared to a wavelength for high audiofrequencies and small for low frequencies. The head itself has a significant effect on the sound pressure at the ear, and could be considered

---

Figure 5.4. Types of response patterns recorded from cells of the cochlear nucleus (based on one series of studies on cat). The cochlear nucleus (CN) is represented as a single section with auditory-nerve fibers entering laterally from the left. The fibers bifurcate, distributing their daughter branches systematically so that the more apical fibers innervate cochlear nucleus cells in the lateral part of the nucleus while the more basal fibers innervate cells in the more medial part of the nucleus. The major divisions of the nucleus are anteroventral (AVCN), posteroventral (PVCN) and dorsal (DCN) cochlear nucleus. The AVCN is subdivided on the basis of cytoarchitectonic criteria into an anterior portion with an anterior (AA) and a posterior (AP) part and a posterior portion with anterior (PD) and posterior (PV) parts. A part of the dorsal AP is designated APD which lies anterior to a small-cell cap (not shown). The PVCN is also divided into an anterior part adjacent to the nerve root and a posterior part called the octopus-cell region (OC). The dorsal cochlear nucleus (DCN) is a layered structure in most mammals with an outer molecular layer (just below an outer granule cell layer), a fusiform (or pyramidal) cell layer below which is a polymorphic layer with many cell types.

Neuron response types are characterized by the postimulus time (PST) histograms shown at the bottom of the figure. Each PST histogram depicts a category of response pattern (instantaneous spike rate vs. time after stimulus onset) to short (25 msec) tone bursts and is assigned a name and a number. The numbers are used as the abscissa in the upper histograms that illustrate the relative frequency of occurence of particular response types in different CN regions. (Based on unpublished data from D.A. Godfrey and T.R. Bourk.)

The PST response pattern labeled 1 is characterized as "primarylike" because of its similarity to that of auditory-nerve fibers. The "chopper" pattern (2) has a characteristic series of maxima and minima with the interpeak times being not only variable across units but also with tone level. Varieties of "on" units (3, 4, and 5) are all characterized by a transient increase in rate at the onset of the tone burst with adaptation to the spontaneous level after the tone is maintained a while. The time course of adaptation is different for the three "on" categories. Pattern 4 shows the sharpest transient peak and can be separated into two different types, the On-I and the On-L, which differ only in that the On-I units have no spontaneous activity. Histogram 6 shows a typical "pauser" pattern which is characterized by a sharp peak at the onset of the tone burst, followed by a reduction in response rate that lasts many msec, followed by a gradual increase to a steady discharge rate above spontaneous level. If the tone burst repetition rate or duty cycle is increased, the initial peak may decrease or even disappear.

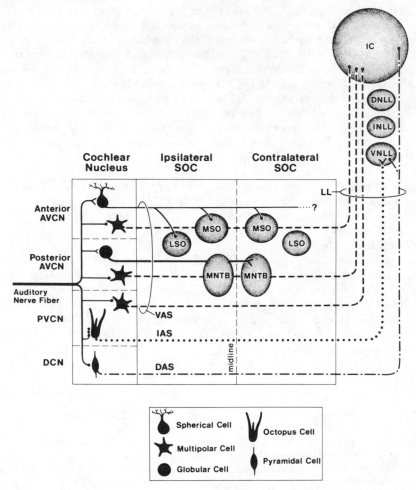

Figure 5.5. Sample types of cell morphology in the cochlear nucleus (CN) with some of the probable output projections. A schematized myelinated auditory nerve fiber is shown entering the CN from the left. The cell types, named in the key at the bottom of the figure are based on the appearance of the somata in Nissl material. The location of the region in which each cell type is predominantly found is indicated on the left. The output axons are shown by heavy lines (solid, dashed, dotted and dash-dot) that run in three fiber tracts the ventral, intermediate and dorsal acoustic strias (VAS, IAS, and DAS). The brainstem nuclei are shown as shaded blobs labeled as in Figure 5.1. Output axons that are rostrally directed in the ipsilateral lateral lemniscus are not portrayed in this figure.

functionally as a part of the external ear. A listener's body also has some effect on the sound pressure input into the ear.

Sound pressures in the external ear are approximately linearly related to the free-field stimulus. For a uniform plane wave stimulus, signal processing by the external ear can be described by a transfer function, made up of two stages (Figure 5.6). The more peripheral stage is affected primarily by the head, the pinna flange, and the concha: that is, the parts of the ear that are outside of the ear canal. The second stage is affected primarily by the geometry of the ear canal and the acoustic impedance of the middle ear.

Because of acoustic "shadows" produced by the head and the pinna (among other things), the pressure at the entrance to the canal is dependent on direction of sound propagation relative to the orientation of the head (Butler, 1975; Shaw, 1982; Blauert, 1983). One important effect of the directional dependence of the external ear transfer function is that the two ears receive different acoustic signals. Interaural dif-

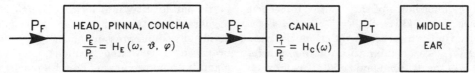

Figure 5.6. A model for signals in the external ear. P_F is the pressure in the free-field uniform plane wave, P_E is the pressure at the entrance to the ear canal, P_T is the pressure in the ear canal just outside the tympanic membrane. The transfer function of the more peripheral part, $H_E(\omega, \theta, \phi)$ depends on the frequency, ω, *and* the direction of propagation of the incident plane wave as specified by the direction angles, θ and ϕ. The second block represents the ear canal. Because the cross-sectional dimensions of the ear canal are small compared to the acoustic wavelengths (except for the highest audio frequencies), the acoustic waves in the canal are uniform plane waves. Because of reflections at the tympanic membrane, waves propagate in both directions. Summation of the incident and reflected waves produces standing waves in the ear canal; at the resonant frequency where the canal is $\lambda/4$ long (near 4 kHz for the human ear), the sound pressure at the tympanic membrane, $|P_T|$, is about 15 dB larger than the sound pressure at the entrance to the canal, $|P_E|$ (Shaw, 1974).

ferences in the sound pressures can be used by the nervous system in "localizing" the sound source. Also the spectrum of the sound that reaches each ear depends on the sound direction; if the central processor is able to compare monaural spectra with a standard, then the dependence of the spectrum on source direction will also provide a "monaural" localization cue' (Durlach & Colburn, 1978).

Middle Ear

The middle ear responds to sound pressure in the ear canal with motion of the tympanic membrane and the ossicles. Movement of the stapes into the cochlea produces pressure changes in the cochlear fluids. The motion of the tympanic membrane is rather complex with the spatial patterns depending on frequency (Khanna & Tonndorf, 1972). The malleus and incus apparently rotate about an axis through the bodies of these ossicles. The stapes motion, in-and-out of the oval window, is piston-like (Guinan & Peake, 1967; Dankbaar, 1970). The mechanical responses of the middle ear are, throughout much of its range, almost linearly related to the sound pressure at the tympanic membrane, so the middle ear's overall signal-transmission properties can be characterized by a transfer function. The curve in Figure 5.7 shows a transfer function for the cat middle ear.

The structures that influence the middle-ear transfer function include those of the middle and inner ear and the transfer function reflects their mechanical interactions (Møller, 1974). For instance, the air-filled cavities in the middle ear are important for the mobility of the system. At low frequencies the cavities behave as an

acoustic compliance, and the prominence of their effects varies among species: in cats, this compliance is approximately equal to that contributed by the tympanic membrane and ossicles (Møller, 1965; Guinan & Peake, 1967), whereas in guinea pigs the cavity impedance is so large that the motion of the ossicles is essentially controlled by the cavity (Mundie, 1963). At higher frequencies the acoustic effect of the cavities varies with frequency. In the cat a resonance between the two coupled cavities in each ear

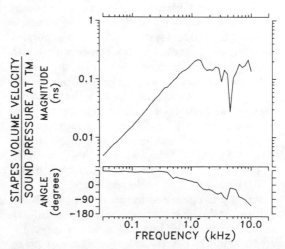

Figure 5.7. A transfer function of the cat middle ear defined as the ratio of the complex amplitude of the stapes volume-velocity divided by the complex amplitude of the sound pressure at the tympanic membrane. The sharp dip in the magnitude near 4 kHz results from a resonance in the middle-ear cavities. The vertical axis has the dimensions of an acoustic admittance [1 nanoSiemen = 10^{-9} m^3(Pa·s)$^{-1}$]. (From Rosowski et al., 1986.)

causes the impedance of the cavities to become very large near 4 kHz. This effect produces a sharp drop in the magnitude of the transfer ratio (Figure 5.7). The combination of the transfer functions of the external and middle ears provides filtering at the input of the system that can have rather complex frequency dependences. The fact that we are not generally aware of these variations in sensitivity indicates that the central processor has "adapted" to the "coloration" of the sounds introduced at the periphery of the system.

It is a common experience that one's hearing is decreased in sensitivity when the static pressure in the environment changes suddenly (e.g. during an abrupt change of altitude in an airplane). This is clearly a nonlinear effect, since superposition does not apply (addition of the low-frequency [static] pressure signal changes the response to an audiofrequency stimulus). It is instructive to consider the relative size of the pressures involved. A change in altitude of 100 meters from sea level produces a pressure change of 1000 Pascals or 154 dB re 20 μPa. This pressure change is very large compared to the sound pressures normally encountered in hearing. This comparison should make clear the benefits of having inner ears that are relatively insensitive to low frequency pressure changes. Although the mechanical system of the middle ear responds linearly for the pressures encountered in normal hearing, it is nonlinear for these large static pressures. The changes in sensitivity occur because the large displacements of the middle ear caused by static pressure drive the tympanic membrane and ligaments beyond their linear region: such large mechanical strains in the membrane and ligaments make them stiffer. The Eustachian tube, which allows pressure differences between the environment and the middle-ear cavities to be equalized, is essential to avoid operation in this nonlinear region. Failure of the Eustachian tube to open regularly leads to the "build-up" of negative pressure in the middle ear because the enclosed gases are absorbed by the tissues lining the cavity (Guinan & Peake, 1967).

Mechanical Responses of the Cochlea

Measurements of the motion of structures in the cochlea by Békésy (1960) demonstrated that even the dead cochlea has some of the properties of a mechanical frequency analyzer. That is, for a particular longitudinal location on the basilar membrane, the transfer function of displacement divided by sound pressure at the tympanic membrane has a particular frequency at which the magnitude is maximum. This frequency varies systematically with location along the length of the basilar membrane. The apical end of the cochlea, where the basilar membrane is broad, responds best to low frequencies, whereas more basally the basilar membrane is narrow and responds better to higher frequencies. Most of Békésy's measurements were limited to the apical parts of the cochlea that responded best to frequencies below a few kHz.

In recent decades, newer methods have provided more sensitive measurements of cochlear motion for more basal parts of the cochlea (Johnstone & Boyle, 1967; Rhode, 1984). These studies support Békésy's general finding of a spatial frequency analyzer, but differ in two important ways. Firstly, the frequency selectivity exhibited by the basilar-membrane motion (for basal regions) is much sharper than Békésy reported (for apical regions). Secondly, the basilar-membrane motion is nonlinearly related to the sound pressure stimulus even at low sound pressure levels. These differences apparently result from postmortem or injury effects in Békésy's experiments. Still, no one has been successful in making measurements of basilar membrane motion in a living mammalian preparation that are stable over sufficient time to permit the collection of definitive measurements in the normal state (Robles, Ruggero, & Rich, 1986.)

The nonlinear mechanical characteristics of the cochlea have effects that are detectable from noninvasive acoustic measurements in the ear canal (Zurek, 1985). Apparently distortion products can be generated in the cochlea and delivered through the middle ear to the tympanic membrane thus producing acoustic distortion products detectable in the sound pressure of the ear canal. Although these distortion components tend to be small compared to the delivered stimuli, they are measurable with sensitive equipment. The possibility of studying cochlear mechanical properties with measurements in the ear canal has advantages from an experimental point of view, as the measurements are relatively easy to make and no surgery compromising the cochlea is required. However, measurements in the ear canal can be interpreted in terms of cochlear mechanisms with confidence only if the intervening mechanisms are known and no other nonlinear mechanisms are significant. Because acoustic distortion products in the canal can be influenced by stimulation of the olivocochlear nerve bundle (Siegel & Kim, 1982; Mountain, 1980; Guinan, 1986) which forms endings on the outer hair cells (OHCs), it has been suggested that the mechanical properties of hair cells are involved in cochlear non-linear behavior. Perhaps the most dramatic of these "acoustic emissions" are narrowband noises that are measurable in about half of the tested human ears *with no externally delivered stimulus* (Kemp, 1979; Zurek, 1985). Although these emissions might be considered a possible source of tinnitus, they are unlikely to be the basis for most clinically important forms of this complaint (McFadden, 1982).

One issue concerning cochlear mechanics has been addressed repeatedly: Is the frequency selectivity of the basilar-membrane motion adequate to explain the observed frequency selectivity of cochlear nerve fibers? Many of the mechanical measurements show relatively broad tuning of the basilar membrane. On the other hand, measurements in mammals have indicated that the mechanical frequency selectivity (and nonlinear behavior) diminishes as a function of deterioration of the experimental preparation. It now seems possible that the answer to the above question is affirmative (Khanna & Leonard, 1982; Robles, Ruggero, & Rich, 1986). To further complicate the picture, measurements in two reptilian species have indicated that mechanisms other than the mechanical system of the basilar membrane can contribute to frequency selectivity in these cochleas. The mechanical and electrical characteristics of hair cells themselves may well be the prime determinants of sharp tuning in these species. (Crawford & Fettiplace, 1981; Weiss, 1984). Thus, it is possible that the mechanisms of sharp tuning differ among species. For example, the sharp tuning in mammals may result from the special organization of cochlear structures including the separation of hair cells into inner and outer hair cells, their relationship to the tectorial membrane and their electrochemical environment (Liberman & Kiang, 1984). It also appears possible that in mammals the sharp tuning detectable at the basilar membrane level results from back coupling of hair cell responses, in which case sharp tuning would involve active participation of electromechanical mechanisms

at the hair cell level (see, e.g., Allen et al., 1986; Moore, 1986).

Cochlear Transduction

The sequence of events that results from the motion of the basilar membrane and leads to the generation of action potentials in cochlear-nerve fibers can now be pictured, although quantitative descriptions of these processes are just emerging (Dallos, 1981; Weiss, 1984; Weiss, Peake, & Rosowski, 1985; Hudspeth, 1985). Motion of the basilar membrane causes the stereociliary tufts on the hair cells to bend through a mechanical linkage probably involving the tectorial membrane. The displacement of the cilia somehow results in a change in the electrical resistance of the hair cell membrane in the region of the cilia. This resistance change leads to a flow of ions though the cell membrane and a change in the electric potential across the membrane (Figure 5.8). This receptor potential results in the release of an unknown chemical transmitter from the base of the hair cells into the synaptic cleft opposite the terminals of the afferent nerve fibers. The transmitter produces an electric change in the postsynaptic membrane of the afferent terminals which leads to a depolarization of the nerve fiber and the triggering of action potentials in the afferent nerve fibers exiting from the cochlea.

The characteristics of the receptor potential in hair cells are clearly nonlinear (Russell, 1981). A steady (dc) depolarization of the hair cells is seen when the stimulus is sinusoidal, and the ac component generally has components at harmonics of the tone frequency. The prominence of the ac component relative to the dc component decreases as the frequency is increased.

The role of IHCs in mammals is clear. They secrete the chemical transmitter that triggers spike discharges in the type I afferent neurons. The role of OHCs is more difficult to describe simply. Although evidence from several directions indicates that the OHCs play a role in the excitation of the IHCs (Dallos, 1984; Liberman & Kiang, 1984; Kiang, Liberman, Sewell, & Guinan, 1986), the mechanism of this interaction has yet to be determined. It does appear that IHC responses are sharply tuned (Sellick & Russell, 1978) and that the OHCs are necessary for this sharp tuning, which is then reflected in the sharp tuning of Type I afferent neurons as

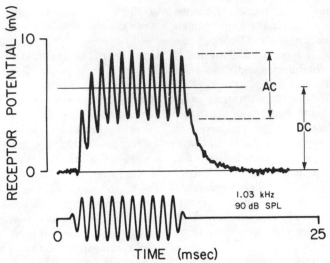

Figure 5.8. Receptor potential recorded from a hair cell in the cochlea of alligator lizard. In response to a tone burst (lower trace) the intracellular potential has a "steady" depolarizing (DC) component as well as an AC component with a fundamental frequency equal to that of the stimulus tone. The receptor potential is the deviation from the intracellular resting potential of about $-70\,\text{mV}$. (From the work of T. Holton and T.F. Weiss.)

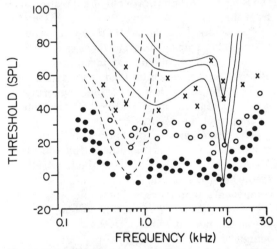

Figure 5.9. Idealized tuning curves for auditory nerve fibers of a typical mammal (based on cat). Solid curves are for fibers innervating inner-hair cells in the basal turn of the cochlea. Dashed curves are for fibers innervating a more apical region of the cochlea. The filled circles indicate the tips of tuning curves of the most sensitive population of fibers; the opened circles of tips of tuning curves of the intermediately sensitive population and the X's the tips of tuning curves for the least sensitive population. The threshold values (expressed as SPL measured at the tympanic membrane), of course, depend upon the criterion for threshold (Geisler, Deng, and Greenberg, 1985). For these idealized examples threshold was defined as a fixed increase (20/sec) in the spike rate above spontaneous rate (Liberman, 1978).

shown in Figure 5.9 (Kiang, Liberman, Sewell, & Guinan, 1986). The function of the Type II afferent neurons that innervate OHCs (Figure 5.3) is unknown. These neurons have axons so small that their action potentials would arrive at the cochlear nucleus many milliseconds after the first responses to sound appear in middle-ear muscle motoneurons or olivocochlear neurons (Kiang, Keithley, & Liberman, 1983). Thus, the fast components of these reflexes cannot involve type II neurons. One speculation is that these small afferents from OHCs mediate pain or other nociceptive sensations that result from release of chemical substance from HCs or supporting cells when damaged. This idea is consistent with all known evidence and would effectively remove this class of inputs from participation in acoustic information processing except as indicators of overstimulation or injury.

Auditory Nerve Discharges

The signal output of the cochlea is activity in auditory-nerve fibers which, with the possible exception of activity in saccular fibers (Cazals, Aran, & Erre, 1983), forms the totality of auditory inputs to the nervous system. Quantitative knowledge of auditory-nerve fiber responses in mammals is exclusively based on recordings from type-I ganglion cells (Liberman,

1982; Liberman & Oliver, 1984). For normal anesthetized animals, spike discharge patterns in response to "simple" stimuli such as clicks, tones or noise and complex stimuli such as speech have been studied extensively (Kiang, 1984). It appears that knowledge of a fiber's "tuning curve" allows many predictions to be made about its responses to more complex stimuli. The tuning curve is the threshold of responses to tones (Geisler, Deng, & Greenberg, 1985) plotted as a function of frequency (Figure 5.9). The tips of tuning curves indicate the characteristic frequency, CF (the frequency of tone to which the fiber is maximally sensitive). For normal cats, fibers have also been divided into three groups based on their spike rate in the absence of acoustic stimuli ("spontaneous rate") (Kiang, Liberman, & Levine, 1976; Liberman, 1978). In any particular CF range fibers with high spontaneous rates (> 18 spikes/sec) tend, as a group, to be the most sensitive in their responses to tones, those with low spontaneous rates (< 0.5 spikes/sec) include the least sensitive and those with intermediate spontaneous rates tend to be intermediate in sensitivity.

It is possible to first record from a fiber and then inject a marker, so that after histological processing one can identify the cell's projections both peripherally and centrally (Liberman, 1982; Fekete, Rouiller, Liberman, & Ryugo, 1984). All marked fibers have been shown to terminate peripherally on IHCs, none on OHCs. Fibers with high spontaneous activity represent approximately 60 percent of sampled units in cats and have thick terminal segments with endings that contact an IHC on the side facing the tunnel of Corti and away from the spiral ganglion. Both the medium spontaneous (30 percent) and low spontaneous (10 percent) neurons have thin terminal segments with endings that contact the IHCs on the side nearest the spiral ganglion. Thus it appears that the spontaneous activity and the average sensitivity (as measured by Kiang, Moxon, & Levine, 1970; Liberman, 1978) have some correlation with the ultrastructure of the terminations on the IHCs. The central projections of high-spontaneous neurons have patterns of swellings and terminals that are quantitatively different from low and medium spontaneous neurons (Rouiller, Cronin Schreiber, Fekete, & Ryugo, 1983). Thus here is a distinct possibility that the central processing of signals differs among these subgroups of auditory nerve fibers.

By and large, the response properties of normal auditory-nerve fibers are predictable from their tuning curves and are quantitatively distinguishable for the different spontaneous-activity subgroups. For example, discharge rates tend to saturate at a maximum value for high- and medium-spontaneous fibers, but perhaps not for the low-spontaneous group, which often continues to show increases in spike rate even at sound levels that cause acoustic trauma. At any stimulus level, the rates for the low-spontaneous fibers usually remain much lower than for other fibers (Shofner & Sachs, 1986).

The responses of auditory-nerve fibers to tones have been measured in two ways, the average discharge rate, based on rates measured over times longer than a period of the stimulus, and "synchrony," based on spike rates measured over the time interval within a stimulus period (usually averaged over many stimulus cycles). A measure of synchrony is the "synchronization index," which is obtained from the Fourier series representation of the instantaneous spike rate (see, e.g., Johnson, 1980b). As the tone level increases, both synchrony and average rate increase over a level range of about 30 dB and then saturate at a maximum value. These changes are approximately parallel for the two rate measures but the synchrony changes occur at levels about 10–15 dB lower than the average rate changes (Johnson, 1980b). At very high stimulus levels, there are dramatically nonmonotonic changes in average discharge rate which suggest interactions of multiple excitatory mechanisms (Kiang & Moxon, 1972; Kiang, 1984; Gifford & Guinan, 1983; Kiang, Liberman, Sewell, & Guinan, 1986). If the tone frequency is increased, synchrony falls rapidly as frequency rises above 1 kHz and is difficult to detect for frequencies above 7 kHz (Johnson, 1980b).

Systematic serial recording of responses from large numbers of auditory-nerve fibers can be used to depict the instantaneous activity patterns along the entire array of myelinated fibers so long as the preparation is stable (Kiang, 1975; Sachs & Young, 1979; Kim, Molnar, & Matthews, 1980). In response to clicks, fibers with CF greater than 2 kHz discharge with short latencies, whereas fibers with lower CF discharge with longer latencies (the lower the CF the longer the latency). Histograms for low CF fibers display multiple peaks separated by 1/CF (Kiang, Watanabe, Thomas, & Clark, 1965; Kiang, 1975;

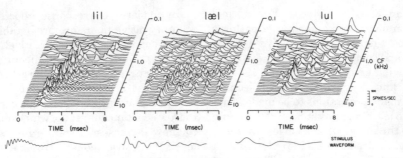

Figure 5.10. Neurograms of auditory-nerve-fiber responses to three sustained two-formant synthetic vowels, /i/, /ae/, /u/. One period of each stimulus waveform is shown below. The formant frequencies are for:

/i/,   0.25 & 3.2 kHz;
/ae/, 0.80 & 1.8 kHz;
/u/,   0.30 & 0.7 kHz.

Stimulus levels were 75 dB SPL. Each trace in the neurograms represents the instantaneous spike rate (with a bin width of 50 μsec and averaged over 5000-10,000 stimulus repetitions) for a fiber with a particular CF. One axis is characteristic frequency (CF) on a logarithmic frequency scale. Some CFs have been slightly adjusted ($\pm$ 10%) to achieve equal spacing. The second axis is time within the fundamental period of the vowel. All fibers had spontaneous activity greater than 10 spikes/sec. (Figure produced with the help of B. Delgutte and I. Stefanov-Wagner.)

Antoli-Candela & Kiang, 1978). These patterns can be effectively displayed in "neurograms," which are three dimensional plots of instantaneous spike rate as a function of time and CF (Kiang, 1975). Examples of "neurograms" are shown in Figure 5.10. One can think of a neurogram as an "internal representation" of the sound stimulus at the level of the auditory nerve (Delgutte & Kiang, 1984a). Using such a display, one can demonstrate the cues available at this level for further processing by the central nervous system (Delgutte & Kiang, 1984b). Such statistical descriptions can help to define the theoretical limits of performance by an ideal central processor operating on the neural information available from the periphery (Siebert, 1970; Colburn & Durlach, 1978).

Cochlear Nucleus Activity

As auditory-nerve fibers ramify in the cochlear nucleus, the information carried by each fiber is presumably distributed to all the neurons with which it synapses. The cochleotopic arrangement of auditory nerve fibers (Figure 5.4) is reflected in the spatial distribution of characteristic frequencies for cochlear nucleus neurons (Rose, 1960; Bourk, Mielcarz, & Norris, 1981). Although the fibers appear to be arranged in a modular way (Ramon y Cajal, 1909; Lorente de Nó, 1933) an inventory of cells innervated by auditory nerve components has never been completely described

for even *one* fiber. Thus, it is not yet known how similar the central projections of all the fibers are. Moreover, there is little known about the central projections of type II ganglion cells except that they do enter the cochlear nucleus and project to various regions running apparently close to the type I fibers originating in the same part of the spiral ganglion (Brown, Berglund, & Ryugo, 1987).

Even without a complete anatomical description of auditory-nerve inputs to cochlear nucleus cells, one can approach the problem of signal processing in the cochlear nucleus by gathering physiological data for populations of single units. ("Units" are physiological entities and "cells," "neurons," "fibers," etc. are anatomical entities.) Assuming that the activity arriving at auditory nerve terminals is the same as that recorded in auditory-nerve recordings, one can then formulate input-output relations for individual cochlear nucleus cells. With sufficient data one can then try to match the distribution of single units having various signal-processing characteristics with the distribution of cells having specific morphological features. By this process physiological response patterns might eventually be matched with cell morphology as defining criteria for both are refined. In Figure 5.4, the distributions of physiologically characterized response types (as defined by responses to short tone bursts) are shown for cytoarchitechtonically   determined   divisions   of   the cochlear nucleus. At this gross regional level, a cytoarchitectonic division usually contains a mixture of unit types (Godfrey, Kiang, & Norris, 1975a, b; Bourk, 1976). This observation is consistent with the anatomical observation that these cytoarchitectonic divisions are generally occupied by a mixture of morphologically distinct cell types (Osen, 1969; Brawer, Morest, & Kane, 1974). A reasonable hypothesis is that the relative proportions of various types of units might correspond to the relative proportions of cell types (Kiang, Pfeiffer, Warr, & Backus, 1965; Pfeiffer, 1966), particularly if the unit distributions across subdivisions match those of cell distributions. At present, although several correspondences appear to be established (Kiang, 1975), the conclusions based on population studies have not always been confirmed by single-unit recordings from marked cells (Rhode, Oertel, & Smith, 1983; Rouiller & Ryugo, 1984). Using Figures 5.4 and 5.5, we now examine some of these correspondences between unit types classified using short tone bursts at the CF as a test stimulus and morphological categories based on features seen either in Nissl or Golgi preparations.

As can be seen in Figure 5.4, there are regions in the cochlear nucleus where "primarylike" units (response pattern exemplified by histogram type 1 in Figure 5.4) are the predominant type. These units are so named because their response characteristics resemble those of auditory-nerve fibers. The preponderance of "primarylike" units in the rostral pole of the AVCN (region AA) suggests strongly that these units correspond to those cells that are designated either as spherical cells in Nissl material or bushy cells in Golgi material (Fig. 5.5.) This conclusion is supported by the observation that the relative number of "primarylike" units decreases as one moves posteriorly into AP and PD where multipolar (Nissl) or stellate (Golgi) cells become more dominant. In this view, the "chopper" units (histogram type 2 in Figure 5.4) would be multipolar (stellate) cells. Multipolar cells do not form a morphologically homogeneous group so some may be "on" units. Proceeding more posteriorly into PV, the proportion of "primarylike" units again increases. This is the main region where globular cells (Nissl) are found. In Golgi material this is another type of bushy cell (Fig 5.5). In the anterior part of the PVCN the number of "primarylike" units decreases abruptly

and "chopper" units dominate. Globular cells are sparse in the PVCN so their distribution *does* match that of posterior "primarylike" units. In the posterior part of the PVCN there is a region called the octopus cell area (OC in Fig. 5.4). Here one finds only certain types of "on" units which are unique in having a very abrupt increase and decline in spike rate at the onset of tone bursts (Godfrey, Kiang, & Norris, 1975a). These units are only found in OC and can be further separated into two groups. One group (On-I in Figure 5.4) has no spontaneous discharges and does not fire in the presence of steady-state high-frequency tones. The second (On-L in Figure 5.4) has a similar pattern except that there is a low level of steady discharge during the presence of high-frequency tones after the initial "on" response. These two groups of "on" units are found almost exclusively in OC. Thus, the correspondence between octopus cells and "on" units (both I and L) is convincing. Finally, Figure 5.4. shows that the most frequent response pattern in the DCN is a "pauser" pattern (histogram 6 in Figure 5.4) characterized by an onset peak, followed by a period of no response, followed by a gradual increase in discharge rate to a steady level that lasts as long as the tone burst. The DCN is a layered structure and one of the layers which is characterized by the presence of fusiform (pyramidal) cells is dominated by "pauser" units. There are some special "On-S" units (histogram 5 in Figure 5.4) as well as "choppers" and a smattering of other unit types in the DCN.

Comparison of the relative distributions of units and cells does not by itself provide convincing proof of correspondences because factors such as biases of recording electrodes or selective effects of anesthesia are difficult to assess. It is interesting therefore to consider how the suggested correspondences might relate to mechanisms that could produce such a variety of patterns from auditory-nerve inputs. If plausible mechanisms can be proposed to account for the empirically described input-output functions, belief in the apparent correspondences would be strengthened.

In AA there are many extraordinarily large endings of auditory nerve fibers called end bulbs of Held which embrace spherical cells. An extracellular, low-impedance electrode placed in this region very often records a positive spike followed a fraction of a millisecond later by a negative spike. These have been interpreted as the pre- and postsynaptic action potentials, respectively, of these synapses (Pfeiffer, 1968; Bourk, 1976). In standard anesthetized preparations these two spikes normally are always paired and the spike discharge patterns are similar to those recorded from fibers in the auditory nerve (i.e., "primarylike"). The cells receiving end bulbs also receive endings that are not from the auditory nerve, so presumably under some conditions activity can be modulated by inputs from other sources. The postsynaptic spherical cells presumably have "primarylike" response pattern because each end bulb contains numerous synaptic regions that are all activated simultaneously so that, unless overridden by other inputs, each spike in the incoming auditory-nerve terminal will elicit a spike from the postsynaptic cell. Globular cells in PV, on the other hand, have "primarylike" patterns presumably because the effects of many convergent endings from different auditory-nerve fibers are integrated by the postsynaptic cell to yield patterns that resemble the averaged activity in auditory-nerve fibers from a particular cochlear region. It is somewhat reassuring that the response patterns of globular cells to bursts of sound are usually distinguishable from those of spherical cells in that for globulars, the probability of discharge is much greater at the sound onset with a short refractory effect immediately afterwards, giving a so-called "primarylike with notch" pattern, a subgroup of the primarylike pattern illustrated in Figure 5.4 (Kiang et al., 1973).

"Chopper units" are found throughout the cochlear nucleus but are more prevalent around the cochlear nerve root, a distribution very much like that of multipolar cells. Their response patterns to tone bursts show regular oscillations that decline to a steady level of discharge higher than spontaneous so long as the stimulus is on. This pattern is achieved presumably through the interaction of a steady excitatory input (Kiang, 1975; Romand, 1978) with a postsynaptic membrane that having discharged, becomes refractory, then recovers with a well-defined time course. There are apparently at least two kinds of multipolar cells, one with terminals on cell bodies as well as on dendrites and another with terminals only on cell bodies (Cant & Morest, 1978). The latter kind may correspond

to "choppers" and the former with units having certain types of "on" patterns (histogram 3 in Figure 5.4).

The octopus cells are unique, with long dendrites oriented across the incoming auditory-nerve fibers from different parts of the cochlea (Osen, 1969; Kane, 1973). Unlike most cochlear-nucleus cells, which receive projections from a narrow region in the cochlea and have sharp tuning curves, the octopus cells have broad tuning curves often with a very sharp small tip (Godfrey, Kiang, & Norris, 1975a). These cells are located in a region of the posteroventral cochlear nucleus occupied by two types of "on" units (histogram 4 in Figure 5.4) which show abrupt increases in discharge rate at the onset of sound stimuli. One type of "on" unit (On-I) has no spontaneous discharges and may respond with only a single spike at the onset of tone or noise bursts; the other (On-L) has a low level of spontaneous activity and shows a large transitory increase in rate at the onset of tone bursts, with a low steady level of responses throughout the duration of tone bursts. For continuous tones of frequencies below a few hundred Hertz, these units have discharges synchronized with each cycle of the tone as if each cycle were a separate stimulus. These "on" units will respond with regular discharges synchronized to the fundamental frequency of periodic stimuli such as sustained vowels. They also respond asymmetrically when tones are swept in frequency in different directions. Thus the problem of characterizing the functional significance of these units is not simple and illustrates an inherent difficulty in assigning simple feature-detection terms at the single unit level.

The "pauser" units in the DCN have complex response patterns (Mast, 1970; Young, 1984) almost certainly derived from the complicated nature of the inputs to the cells in this region (Osen & Mugnaini, 1981). The fusiform cells found concentrated in a definable layer in the cat have at least a half dozen different sources of innervation.

What is the significance of having these different types of response patterns (among others) in the cochlear nucleus? One answer is that different aspects of the stimulus are coded by different cells and distributed via their axonal outputs to specific locations in the brain specialized for particular functions. Consistent with this view, the axons of specific cell types should be segregated as to destination, and indeed there is evidence that they are (Figure 5.5). As data accumulate, one expects that certain cell groups in the central nervous system will be seen to receive projections from specific types of cells. Given present techniques it seems only a matter of time before wiring diagrams at the level of cell types will reveal the nature of the circuitry available for information processing. At the same time, physiological studies can demonstrate the nature of the signals in the various pathways so that functional arguments can be generated.

An example of how the available data can lead to speculations about function is shown by examining the following line of thought. One can conjecture that cues based on fine (cycle by cycle) synchrony information will not be preserved in elements receiving inputs from "chopper" units, whose responses exhibit much less synchrony than "primarylike" units. On this basis, binaural cells in the brainstem that receive inputs from multipolar neurons might not be able to detect accurately interaural phase differences, whereas binaural units receiving inputs from primarylike units could. A functional organization of this nature is actually suggested by work on birds, where cochlear nucleus cell types appear to be more completely segregated in the nucleus (Sullivan & Konishi, 1984). Thus, knowing the response characteristics of cells and their connections enables one to propose how these cells might be involved in carrying information necessary for certain calculations made at higher levels in the brain. By recording activity at these higher levels, one might establish whether such calculations are indeed made. These data would then provide a concrete basis for analyzing how the brain is organized to accomplish perceptual tasks (Carterette & Friedman, 1978).

Clearly these last remarks apply not only to the cochlear nucleus but also to more central levels of the system. Space does not permit us to describe the present state of physiological knowledge for the higher auditory regions in this chapter; some reviews and textbooks provide an introduction to this subject (e.g., Whitfield, 1967; Boudreau & Tsuchitani, 1973; Syka & Aitkin, 1981; Pickles, 1982; Keidel, Kallert, & Korth, 1983; Møller,

1983; Aitkin, Irvine, & Webster, 1984; Irvine, 1986).

Efferent Pathways and Their Role

At every stage in the auditory system pathways are provided for feedback control. We review here the mechanisms involved in these efferent systems at the peripheral stages and suggest some possible roles that can be assigned to these systems.

At the level of the external ear, efferent control is generally achieved in humans through a motor system that can change the position of the head with respect to the sound field or to close the opening of the external ear canal (e.g., by inserting a finger or covering the pinnas). Some mammals can change the orientation of their pinnas voluntarily or reflexly. Especially for high frequencies, the pinnas act as directionally selective filters so that the whole system can make use of an ability to control the way these filters are directed towards the space that is monitored. At the level of the middle ear, efferent neural signals are represented by activity in motoneurons of the middle-ear muscles. The acoustic reflexes are consensual in that high-level sounds delivered to only one ear can elicit reflex contraction on both sides. Contractions of these muscles reduce stapes motion so as to selectively attenuate low-frequency components of sounds. Thus efferent inputs to the middle ear produce effects that resemble insertions of bilateral high-pass filters into the acoustic pathway.

The mechanism of action for the olivocochlear efferents is a subject of considerable current speculation. When effective, electrical stimulation of the crossed olivocochlear bundle generally reduces auditory-nerve fiber discharges (Fex, 1962; Wiederhold & Kiang, 1970; Teas, Konishi, & Nielsen, 1972; Gifford & Guinan, 1983). Since the crossed bundle is mainly made up of medial efferents that innervate only OHCs (Warr, 1975) and auditory-nerve recordings are thus far exclusively from fibers that innervate IHCs (Kiang, 1984; Liberman & Oliver, 1984), the reduction of activity most likely is achieved through some functional coupling between outer and inner hair cells (Brown & Nuttall, 1984; Liberman & Kiang, 1984). Both sets of hair cells have stereocilia embedded in the tectorial membrane so that there is a possibility for mechanical coupling (Zwislocki & Kletsky, 1979). Thus efferent inputs to OHCs could affect the OHCs (Brownell et al., 1985; Ashmore, 1987) so as to change the mechanical properties of the organ of Corti, ultimately affecting the IHCs and thereby Type I auditory nerve fibers.

Little is known about situations that normally activate the olivocochlear efferents. The available evidence (Fex, 1965; Cody & Johnstone, 1982; Robertson, 1984; Liberman & Brown, 1986; Brown, 1987) indicates that in response to sound: (1) some olivocochlear neurons respond predominantly to ipsilateral ear stimulation, some to contralateral stimulation and a few to either ear, (2) responses can be elicited at low sound pressure levels (within 20 dB of afferent thresholds), (3) their tuning cures are comparable to those of auditory-nerve fibers with the efferent CF being close to that of the cochlear region innervated by the efferent fiber, (4) the latency of responses to acoustic stimuli can be as short as 5–6 msec, (5) responses to sound are present in animals given barbiturates; olivocochlear activity is present in "standard" preparations for electrophysiological experiments.

We may now try to relate these findings on the olivocochlear efferents to stimulus coding in the cochlea.

At the hair cell level, the acoustic stimulus has undergone spectral analysis and different hair cells are maximally sensitive to different frequencies. The information in the sound waveform is now distributed over an array of sharply tuned elements. Given the distribution of endings from a single efferent fiber (Figure 5.3) one may presume that it is possible to affect a smattering of OHCs within a local region in the cochlea by stimulating a single medial efferent fiber, thereby selectively attenuating components within particular CF bands. Complex patterns of attenuation should be achievable. From the data currently available, the filter characteristics introduced by cochlear efferents should be those of narrow band-reject filters operating over frequency regions covering about an octave. However, much is yet to be learned about the anatomical and physiological characteristics of efferent inputs as a function of location within the cochlea. In addition, little is known about the physiology of lateral efferents. These neurons with small unmyelinated fibers are distributed to the afferent Type I dendrites under the IHCs, in fact predominantly to the thinner afferents (Liberman, 1980). Whatever their role, it is unlikely that the lateral efferents have fast action. Taken altogether, it may be that the cochlear efferents provide the system with channel-specific gain controls that overcome the natural limitations in dynamic range imposed at cellular levels so that at the organ level a broad dynamic range is achievable. Thus the system may be brought to bear within its most effective sound-intensity range as far as is possible. Protection from the damaging effects of overstimulation would automatically derive from keeping the effective mechanical stimulus within limits. To some extent, this latter idea may also be applicable to middle-ear muscle activity.

In the cochlear nucleus, there is probably no neuron innervated exclusively by auditory-nerve fibers; all may receive efferent inputs either from the central nervous system or from other parts of the cochlear nuclei. Preliminary results suggest that electric stimulation of some trapezoid body (ventral acoustic stria, Figure 5.5) fibers can selectively reduce responses of chopper units without reducing those of primarylike units even when both types of units are encountered in the same electrode pass through the AVCN (T.R. Bourk, personal communication). If it is true that there are efferent inputs from the trapezoid body (ventral acoustic stria) to the cochlear nucleus that affect specific unit types, then the distribution of efferents will segregate units that were originally distinguished solely on the basis of response patterns to sounds. Obviously, thoughts about the functional significance of specific neuronal types will have to take the efferent inputs into consideration.

One might speculate that at each level of the system, local feedback signals help to control afferent activity in accordance with the organizational structure for that level. Upon these local systems more global higher level controls can be superimposed. Such a system then would not be merely a passive responder to physical stimuli but could control its own responsiveness according to the experiences and needs of the central processor (Powers, 1973). With the demonstration that very complex control mechanisms might be available, our theoretical conception of the auditory system becomes more compatible with the flexible, goal-oriented behavior we all take for granted.

AUDITORY BEHAVIOR

Threshold of Audibility for Tones

The most basic auditory behavior is detection. The most widely used measure for auditory detection is the *monaural* absolute threshold for tonal stimulation determined as a function of tone frequency. The measurement involves a simple stimulus, a tone, and a simple behavioral response, a motor output indicating "heard" or "not heard."

One methodological problem arises from the choice of the stimulus delivery system. Many behavioral measurements are made using loudspeakers to deliver a free-field acoustic wave that approximates a uniform plane-wave in the region that the subject is to occupy; to achieve monaural stimulation one ear-canal is plugged. The sound pressure of the plane wave at the threshold of detectability is called the minimum audible field (MAF). An alternative stimulus system uses earphones with stimuli delivered only through one earphone. In this method the sound pressure under the earphone at the threshold of detectability is called the minimum audible pressure, MAP. A well-known experimental result is that for low-frequency tones the MAP is approximately 6 dB higher than the MAF. This was, for some time, a puzzling result because at low frequencies acoustic wavelengths are much larger than the head and body so with a free-field stimulus the sound pressure in the "field" should be very nearly the same as that at the entrance to the ear canal. (This puzzle was sometimes known as "The Case of the Missing 6 dB"). It appears now that, if one takes into account physiological noise that is generated under an earphone, the two methods lead to the same results for the threshold sound-pressure level at the entrance to the ear canal (Anderson & Whittle, 1971). This conclusion suggests that the threshold sound-pressure level at the ear-canal entrance is independent of the configuration of the sound source. (Although this inference may be true for sources that generate airborne sound, it is probably *not* true for sources that deliver vibrations directly to the head, e.g., bone-conduction receivers.) Thus comparisons of physiological and behavioral data can be made by relating both kinds of responses to the sound-pressure at the ear-canal entrance. Alternatively, if the transfer function of the ear canal, $H_C(\omega)$

(Figure 5.6), is known, the sound pressure at the tympanic membrane can be used.

For clinical assessments of hearing, measurements of threshold sound pressure for tones plotted as deviations from population norms (and called audiograms) are standardly used as the primary determination of hearing capability (Beagley, 1981). Measurements are generally made at seven frequencies one octave apart (0.125 to 8 kHz). Thresholds for various animal species have also been determined (Masterton, Heffner, & Ravizza, 1969; Heffner & Heffner, 1980; Popper & Fay, 1980; Stebbins, 1980). In most cases the curve of threshold sound pressure vs. frequency is U-shaped: in a middle-frequency region the thresholds are a minimum and at higher and lower frequencies they rise more-or-less monotonically. Because measurements are usually made at octave intervals, the detailed shapes are not usually known. In cases where thresholds have been determined with greater frequency resolution, considerable "fine structure" in the threshold curve can be seen (e.g., Zwicker & Schloth, 1983).

A goal for auditory physiology is to associate features of the threshold-frequency curve with physiological properties of particular stages of the system. There are some general problems that arise in making comparisons of behavioral and physiological measurements. One such problem results from the fact that the "states" of subjects during physiological and behavioral measurements are not generally comparable. Most physiological studies are conducted on anesthetized, surgically prepared animals, whereas behavioral studies usually involve subjects that are highly motivated (e.g., to obtain food or other rewards) and free to use any tactic that can help, such as moving the head or changing activity in feedback pathways. Thus, to make comparisons one must assume (or demonstrate) that the physiological data apply to the "behavioral state." Another kind of complication arises from the fact that both physiological and behavioral thresholds are somewhat arbitrarily defined. The behavioral "threshold value" depends on the choice of "criterion level" (e.g., a percentage-correct level for a psychometric function). The physiological measure also involves the choice of a "threshold value." Changing the criterion for either measure can obviously alter the relationship between the two thresholds.

To address the issue of how activity at a

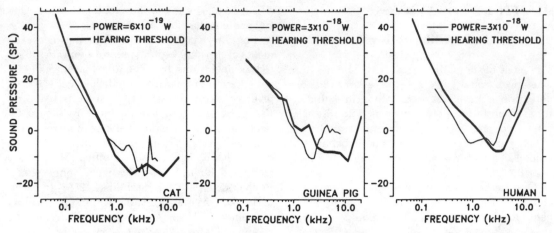

Figure 5.11. A comparison (for three species) of behavioral threshold for tones (minimum-audible field, MAF) with contours of constant acoustic power into the cochlea. The power level for the iso-power contours was chosen to minimize the mean difference between the curves. (From Rosowski et al. 1986.)

particular level of the auditory system relates to the behavioral threshold curve one can define a physiological measure of response to tones, $R(f)$, that can be assessed across tone frequencies. Typical measures might be the rms velocity at the tympanic membrane, the maximum spike-rate found among cochlear nerve fibers, or spike counts in the central nucleus of the inferior colliculus averaged over all cells with CFs within one-half octave of the tone frequency. If such measures, determined at threshold sound pressure, $R_{TH}(f)$, are shown to be independent of f, several conclusions are suggested: (a) the system central to the level where $R(f)$ is measured acts as a detector of $R(f)$, (b) the constant value, $R_{TH}(f)$, is the value that the central system can just detect, (c) other measures that behave very differently are probably not the determining factors for the threshold curve, and (d) the more peripheral parts of the system determine the shape of the threshold curve.

It has often been suggested that the normal threshold-frequency curve is determined by the external and middle ears (e.g., Dallos, 1973; Rosowski et al., 1986). Data are available for cats, guinea pigs and (to a lesser extent) humans to test specific hypotheses. The curves in Figure 5.11 are intended to test the idea that the average acoustic *power* $P_{AV}(f)$, into the cochlea at threshold is independent of frequency. For each of the three species a curve of hearing threshold expressed in terms of the free-field sound-pressure is plotted with a calculated contour of the free-field sound-pressure required to obtain a particular level of acoustic power to the cochlea. The calculations use physiological measurements of the performance of the external and middle ears to determine the average power into the cochlea:

$$P_{AV}(f) = \tfrac{1}{2}[H_{EE}(f, \phi, \theta)\ H_{ME}(f)\ P_F(f)]^2$$
$$\times\ \mathrm{Re}[Z_C(f)],$$

where $H_{EE} = H_E \times H_C$ is the external-ear transfer function as defined in Figure 5.6, H_{ME} is the middle-ear transfer function defined in Figure 5.7, P_F is the sound pressure in the free-field plane wave, and Z_C is the acoustic input impedance of the cochlea.

In examining the three pairs of curves in Figure 5.11 we see in each pair, rapid variations with frequency that differ between the two curves. The reasons for these particular differences are thought to be methodological; let us focus here on the general trends of the frequency dependence. For the highest frequencies the physiological data are unavailable; for cat and guinea pig no curve is shown and for human an extrapolation has been assumed, so it is difficult to make comparisons in the frequency regions where the threshold sound pressure rises. On the other hand at low frequencies we see that the two curves generally rise in the same frequency ranges by roughly the same amount. This observation is consistent with the hypothesis that *for this task* the system central to the cochlear input functions as a "power detector."

These observations also suggest an answer to the question: Why does the threshold rise at low frequencies? At frequencies below 1 kHz the external ear alters the sound pressure of a plane wave very little, i.e., $H_{EE}(f, \phi, \theta) \approx 1$ (Shaw, 1974). Also the real part of the cochlear input impedance, $\text{Re}[Z_C(f)]$, is approximately independent of frequency in the range $0.1 < f < 1$ kHz (Lynch et al., 1982). However, the magnitude of the middle-ear transfer function grows approximately proportionally with frequency in this range (see Figure 5.7). Thus, to maintain constant power into the cochlea as frequency is lowered from 1 to 0.1 kHz the sound pressure, $P_F(f)$, must be increased by a factor of 10 (20 dB). One might say that the threshold rises at low frequencies because the volume-velocity output of the middle ear decreases. At frequencies below 0.1 kHz additional mechanisms may be involved (Lynch et al., 1982).

What is the relation of behavioral tone-thresholds to responses in auditory nerve fibers? Comparison of neural responses and behavioral threshold can place some constraints on the cues that the CNS uses. Since the output of the cochlea is a spatial array of signals, any single measure of the output must take into account the spatial dimension. Two very simple possibilities can be considered: (1) The CNS might perform a logical "AND" operation on the neural spike trains. In this case the tone would be heard if all of the neurons responded. (2) The CNS might perform a logical "OR" operation on the neural spike trains. In this case the tone would be heard if any of the neurons responded. From the known behavior of cochlear neural responses (Figure 5.9) we can rule out the AND possibility; neurons with low characteristic frequencies (CF) do not respond to high-frequency tones even at very high sound-pressure levels. Therefore, at the tone threshold for a 10 kHz tone most cochlear neurons will *not* be responding. If, on the other hand, the CNS performed an OR operation, behavioral threshold for a particular frequency should correspond to the threshold of those neurons that are most sensitive at that frequency, so the behavioral threshold should have the shape of the lower limit of the solid dots in Figure 5.9. This seems to be true, so the CNS could be performing a logical OR operation on auditory nerve responses in threshold detection.

This idea can be tested by measurements in which lesions are made in the cochlea in particular CF regions. In monkeys it has been shown that if drugs are used that destroy all hair cells in the basal portion of the cochlea, the monkeys do not respond to high-frequency tones even when they are 110 dB above the normal threshold (Stebbins et al., 1979), whereas for low frequencies the behavioral thresholds are normal. In chinchillas with high-CF regions where only the outer hair-cells are destroyed, the thresholds are elevated by about 60 dB for tones in that CF region, which is equivalent to the increase in auditory-nerve-fiber thresholds for the same CF region (Dallos and Harris, 1977). In cats with partial lesions in the auditory nerve, the thresholds are consistent with removal of specific frequency-selective channels (Kiang, 1981).

All of these results fit with the idea that the CNS can detect responses in a small number of fibers. A natural next question is: What measure of auditory-nerve activity does the central processor use? Two measures that have been considered are the average spike-rate and the synchrony of spike occurences relative to the tone. In the Dallos and Harris (1977) study, an average-rate measure was used and the frequency dependence of the behavioral and cochlear-nerve thresholds was found to be similar in both normal and abnormal chinchillas. However, the behavioral thresholds were about 15 dB lower than the *mean* neural thresholds. Several possibilities can be suggested to account for this difference: (1) The neural measure used was the *mean* fiber threshold; the difference would be smaller if the most sensitive fiber thresholds had been used. (2) If different criteria for both neural and behavioral thresholds had been used, the difference could be further reduced. (3) The central processor might detect synchrony in the spike trains even when the average rate is not appreciably increased.

The possible use of synchrony in the spike trains by the CNS is of particular interest because it has been suggested that this ability is important in pitch perception for some kinds of signals or in speech discrimination (Kiang & Moxon, 1974; Sachs & Young, 1979). It has been shown that synchrony can be detected (in PST histograms) at levels that are 15–20 dB below those at which average-rate increases are easily detected (Johnson, 1980b). It has also been suggested (from studies on fish) that synchrony cues are available at stimulus levels below behavioral threshold (Fay & Coombs, 1983). If the CNS could extract a measure of synchrony similar to that found in PST histograms, it presumably would be capable of detecting stimuli 15–20 dB lower than it could by using average-rate criteria. However, this improvement would not be uniform across frequency, because synchrony decreases as frequency increases above 1 kHz and is difficult to measure above 7 kHz. Thus, since this mechanism might be expected to lower thresholds more at low frequencies than at high, it is not by itself an explanation for the reported difference between behavioral and neural thresholds, which are approximately constant across frequency. It remains possible that different neural cues are used for detecting stimuli in different frequency ranges or even that different species depend on different neural cues. Thus, we see that even for the simplest kind of auditory behavior questions remain about *how* the auditory system achieves its performance.

Acoustic Reflex

The middle ear is not just a passive transmitter of sound; its response characteristics can be altered by activity in the brain. Each of the muscles of the middle ear, the tensor tympani and the stapedius, affects signal transmission through the middle ear when it contracts. Contractions occur under many circumstances and can be produced voluntarily by some people (Reger, 1960). One stimulus that produces contractions is an intense sound. Because this "acoustic reflex" can occur with a very short latency (as little as 6 msec from stimulus onset to stapedius muscle activity) and it requires only the lower parts of the brainstem, it is an attractive example of motor response to acoustic stimulation that can be studied without necessarily involving large portions of the higher central nervous system.

The acoustic reflex has been studied extensively in both humans and laboratory mammals (Anderson, 1976; Silman, 1984). When the middle-ear muscles contract, they change the acoustic impedance of the middle ear. This change is detectable with measurements in the ear canal in intact subjects. Because the reflex is an involuntary response, it has been used clinically as an objective test for the intactness of peripheral auditory functions. It has been demonstrated

in many mammalian species that the stapedius muscle contributes to the acoustic reflex. In humans, it is thought that the stapedius might be entirely responsible for the acoustic reflex when one ear is stimulated (Møller, 1984). Therefore we will focus on the stapedius muscle in the remainder of this discussion.

When the stapedius contracts it pulls the stapes in a direction perpendicular to its movement in response to sound (Figure 5.1). As a result the impedance of the mobile structures increases and their motion in response to a given sound is reduced. That is, the magnitude of the middle-ear transfer-function is reduced. The attenuation introduced by the muscle contractions is largest for low frequencies, where it can be as much as 30 dB for electrical stimulation of the stapedius muscle (Pang & Peake, 1986). At higher frequencies moderate contractions produce little change in transmission, but large contractions can attenuate transmission appreciably.

Some features of the acoustic reflex have been reliably reported and appear to be common to different mammalian species:

1. The reflex is consensual: that is, a monaural acoustic stimulus can evoke muscle contractions in both ears. The ipsilateral reflex is stronger than the contralateral (Guinan & McCue, 1987).
2. The threshold sound pressure required for a tone to elicit the reflex is generally rather high (80 ± 10 dB SPL) and is relatively independent of tone frequency.
3. If several tones are presented, less sound power in each is required to reach the reflex threshold than when a single tone is used.
4. The threshold can be lower with a binaural tone than with a monaural tone.
5. The strength of the reflex increases with stimulus strength over a range of at least 30 dB.
6. If the stimulus tone is maintained, the contraction builds up to a steady level within a few hundred msec after the tone onset and may be maintained for minutes, although it usually decays gradually.
7. Barbiturates in doses used in most animal experiments abolish or greatly reduce the reflex.
8. The attenuation introduced by the reflex is

approximately independent of frequency for frequencies below 0.5 kHz and has a maximum value of 10–15 dB for contralateral stimuli. At frequencies above 2 kHz the attenuation is generally less than 5 dB.

The identification of anatomical structures involved in the acoustic reflex is incomplete. It has been demonstrated that the reflex can occur when the brain is sectioned transversely anterior to the colliculi (Carmel & Starr, 1963). Thus, although the higher parts of the brain can affect the contractions, they are not necessary for the reflex. Lesions in the brain stem have demonstrated that interruption of the ventral acoustic stria (Figure 5.5) greatly diminished the contralateral reflex, whereas lesions in the dorsal and intermediate stria do not (Borg, 1973c). Similarly lesions in the dorsal cochlear nucleus do not affect the reflex, whereas lesions in the ventral cochlear nucleus do (Borg, 1973c, 1977). Axons of the stapedius motoneurons leave the brain in the facial nerve. Reflex measurements after lesions in subgroups (Joseph et al., 1985) of the motoneurons of the stapedius indicate that the ipsilateral and contralateral reflexes can be altered somewhat independently (McCue & Guinan, 1983). It appears that different motoneurons may be involved under different situations and that a maximal contraction might be elicitable only when all pathways (including non-acoustic) are activated simultaneously.

The combination of these physiological and anatomical features of the reflex with our knowledge of the response properties of the cochlea and cochlear nucleus provides a basis for constructing physiological models for the stapedius reflex (Møller, 1984). It is possible to suggest a structure for the reflex pathway which is consistent both with the behavior of the reflex and the elements known to be involved. As we describe the hypothetical system we will point out how the system characteristics result from the features of the components.

The shortest latency of the earliest auditory response recordable in stapedius motoneurons is about 5 msec, so the small afferents from OHCs cannot be involved in the early response because their conduction velocities are too slow. Thus some subset of the Type I neurons must be involved in the reflex. These first-order neurons must provide an input to the system that signals the existence of a suprathreshold acoustic stimulus at about 80 dB SPL and continues to signal changes as the stimulus is increased up to levels of 120 dB SPL. The responses of these neurons cannot saturate at high stimulus levels as many cochlear neurons having high or medium rates of spontaneous activity do (Kiang, 1968; Sachs & Abbas, 1974; Liberman, 1978; Johnson, 1980b; Sachs & Young, 1980). Responses of cochlear neurons with low-spontaneous rates often continue to increase at very high stimulus levels (Sachs & Abbas, 1974). Thus, they are likely candidates to play a role in the sensory arm of the reflex. The second-order (cochlear nucleus) cells (as well as the first-order cells) must have a maintained response during prolonged tone stimulation in order to sustain a steady contraction of the muscle. Thus, none of the "On" varieties of CN units (Figure 5.4) would be appropriate. The most likely candidates are the "primarylike" or "chopper" units of the VCN, since DCN cells are eliminated by the lesion experiments. "Chopper" units in particular have a large dynamic range. Both "primarylike" and "chopper" units have tuning curves not unlike those of auditory nerve fibers so the summation of reflex activity for widely separated tones must be introduced at a later level. Since most of these cochlear nucleus units are monaural (at least for short latency responses), the consensual properties of the reflex also require a third order neuron. At present the location of third order neurons in the reflex chain is unknown. It is possible that they are the stapedius motoneurons themselves. The location where barbiturate anesthesia blocks the reflex is also unknown but is presumably after the cochlear nucleus. It is a distinct possibility that there are many parallel pathways for acoustic reflexes, some of which could involve substantially different chains of neurons than do the short latency components of the reflex.

Speculations about the functional importance of middle-ear muscles have not led to simple answers. The acoustic reflex produces only a modest reduction in transmission which is primarily in the low-frequency range; people without a functioning stapedius (for instance after stapedectomy surgery) do not report gross deficits in hearing. It may be that the stapedius is not very important for humans. On the other hand, contractions of the middle-ear muscles occur under a variety of other conditions including vocalization, chewing, head movement, swallowing, and Rapid Eye Movement sleep (Baust, Berlucchi, & Moruzzi, 1964; Anderson, 1976). It is possible that the muscles help the system to maintain its sensitivity to high frequencies in the presence of high-intensity, low-frequency masking noise (Kiang & Moxon, 1974), a situation that occurs in self-vocalization and chewing. The role of these muscles in reducing the effects of acoustic trauma is still being assessed. It is possible that the most important functional role of the middle-ear muscles has yet to be identified.

Since the acoustic reflex alters the input of the cochlear nerve to the CNS, it allows tests of a general question: Does the perception of auditory inputs take into account the modifications in the peripheral system that have been generated by the CNS? If, when the stapedius contracts during an acoustic reflex, the CNS takes the effects of the contraction precisely into account in its processing of the cochlear-nerve signals, then perceptual responses should be unaltered by the reflex. A simple perceptual response is a "loudness judgment." During stapedius contractions loudness *is* reduced (Morgan & Dirks, 1975). Furthermore, the magnitude of the loudness reduction is consistent with the known changes in middle-ear transmission: the reduction in loudness of a 0.5 kHz tone is equivalent to about a 10 dB stimulus reduction and the loudness of a 1.5 kHz tone is not significantly changed. These results would be expected if the loudness judgment were based on the output of the cochlea *without* consideration of the state of contraction of the muscle. Thus, for this perceptual task, the sensory system seems to ignore the effects of its motor outputs.

Another behavioral consequence of the stapedius reflex is that the temporary loss of hearing sensitivity that follows high-intensity sound stimulation (known as temporary threshold shift, TTS) can be reduced by the reflex. This has been dramatically demonstrated (Zakrisson & Borg, 1974) in measurements with subjects who have unilateral facial nerve paralysis (Bell's palsy), which abolishes the stapedius reflex. After a 5 minute exposure to high-intensity, narrow-band noise centered at 0.5 kHz the ear with the non-functioning stapedius reflex showed a threshold increase of 23 dB, whereas the normal ear's threshold increased only 3 dB. After the subject recovered from the paralysis, the same noise exposure produced equally small threshold increases in both ears. When the high-intensity noise was centered at 2 kHz, no difference was apparent between the normal and paralyzed ears. These results are consistent with the measured changes in middle-ear transmission and the observation that the sensitivity of cochlear-nerve fibers is reduced following high-intensity stimulation. Presumably the temporary threshold shift is a cochlear effect and the extent of the TTS is determined by the input to the cochlea.

Yet another behavioral effect of the reflex has been demonstrated with speech discrimination tests given to subjects with Bell's palsy (Borg & Zakrisson, 1973). Nonsense monosyllables (consonant-vowel-consonant) were delivered monaurally at varying sound levels and subjects were required to identify each syllable. The test was run while one stapedius was paralyzed and repeated after the subject recovered. The articulation score (percentage of words correctly identified) was above 90 percent for moderate stimulus levels, but decreased at very high stimulus levels in both cases. However, the level at which the score dropped when the stapedius was not functioning was 20 dB lower than when the stapedius was functioning. One possible physiological explanation is that the low-frequency components of the high-level speech stimuli produce large responses in high-CF cochlear-nerve fibers making it difficult for the high-frequency components of the speech (which are crucial for consonant distinctions) to produce distinctive temporal-spatial patterns of response in the cochlear nerve (Kiang & Moxon, 1974). More recently another study has demonstrated in normal subjects an improvement brought about by the acoustic reflex in the identification of vowels at high stimulus levels (Dorman et al., 1987).

The foregoing discussions illustrate how the known acoustic, anatomical, and physiological features of the auditory system can help to generate conceptual pictures of possible mechanisms underlying the behavioral characteristics and consequences of the acoustic reflex.

Localization of Sound Sources

If the most basic function of an auditory system is the *detection* of sounds, next in importance for an animal's survival may be the ability to *locate* sound sources. The auditory system has multiple cues available for "localization" and in a normal environment many of these are probably used simultaneously (Mills, 1972; Colburn & Durlach, 1978; Durlach & Colburn, 1978; Gatehouse, 1982; Blauert, 1983; Hausler, Colburn & Marr, 1983). As the next example of how knowledge of acoustics, anatomy and physiology can combine to enhance our understanding of auditory behavior, we shall consider the localization of a tone source as the source is moved in a horizontal plane (Rayleigh, 1886). Two cues are available based on differences between the waveforms at the two ears: the difference in phase (or timing) of the tone, called the interaural time difference (ITD), and the difference in sound pressure level called the interaural level difference (ILD), also often loosely called the interaural intensity difference (IID). (If the source is *not* a single tone, then the differences between the sound-pressure waveforms at the two ears cannot, in general, be described completely by two numbers.) Since both cues are based on a comparison of the acoustic signals at the two ears, we must consider how the neural signals from the opposite ears are combined within the CNS.

The differences between the sound signals at the two ears are determined primarily by the locations of the ears on the surface of the acoustically rigid head and the orientation of the head with respect to the sound source. If a sound source radiates uniformly in all directions (a spherically symmetric source), the listener is many wavelengths away from the source (in the far field), and no other surfaces interfere, then the sound wave that impinges on a listener is approximately a uniform plane wave. One can compute the sound pressures at the ears by considering the acoustical problem of a rigid sphere immersed in a uniform, unidirectional plane wave, where we wish to know the sound pressure on the surface of the sphere. The answer is obtained by finding a solution to the equations of acoustics that satisfies the boundary conditions of (1) a uniform, unidirectional plane wave incident on a region, and (2) a velocity at the surface of the rigid sphere whose component normal to the sphere is zero. The resulting solution includes two components, one of which is the incident uniform plane wave, and the other is a non-uniform, non-plane wave representing the sound "scattered" by the sphere. The general mathematical solution for the sinusoidal steady state is straightforward, but the result is a relatively complicated expression (Skudrzyk, 1971;

Kuhn, 1977). For our purposes, some important gross features can be stated in words.

Assume that the radius of the head (sphere) is a. For low frequencies such that $ka \ll 1$, (i.e., $\lambda \gg 2\pi a$ = the circumference of the head) the magnitude of the sound pressure is approximately constant over the surface of the head. For dimensions approximating a human head ($a = 8.75$ cm) at 62 Hz ($ka = 0.1$), the maximum variations are about 0.1 dB, which is well below the JND for interaural level difference measured with earphones (Mills, 1972). Thus, when the head is small compared to a wavelength, it has only a small effect on the incident field; i.e., the "shadow" it casts is hard to detect. The time difference between the ear locations, at these low frequencies, is approximately $ITD = 3(a/c)\sin\theta$, where θ is the azimuth of the source. (Azimuth is the angle measured in the horizontal plane between straight ahead and the source direction.) Measurements indicate that for frequencies below 0.5 kHz the ITD with a non-spherical head is in rough agreement with this analysis (Kuhn, 1977). For a sound incident from one side (i.e., $\theta = 90°$) $ITD = 0.76$ msec, and for a source that deviates from straight ahead by the "minimum audible angle" of about 1° (Mills, 1972), $ITD = 0.027$ msec, which is close to the behavioral JND measured for interaural time. Thus, the physical properties of the head alone indicate that *for low frequency tones* ITD is a usable cue for localization, whereas ILDs are too small to be very useful.

For high frequencies, (i.e., $ka \gg 1$ or $\lambda \ll 2\pi a$) the spherical head solution yields rather different results (Kuhn, 1977). When the head is much larger than a wavelength (e.g., at 6.2 kHz where $ka = 10$ for a human head), the head introduces large changes in the sound field so that variations in the sound pressure magnitude around the head can be 10 dB or more (Shaw, 1974) and may vary rapidly with f and θ, i.e., the head clearly casts an acoustic shadow. The interaural time delay is approximately $ITD = (a/c)(\theta + \sin\theta)$. For a high frequency tone with $\theta = 90°$ a maximum delay of 0.65 msec occurs. For $f = 6.2$ kHz this time corresponds to an interaural phase difference of $2\pi f \times ITD = 2\pi \times 4$ radians $= 4 \times 360°$, which is identical to 0, 1, 2, or 3 $\times$ 360°. At this frequency then, there are 5 values of θ in the range $0 \leq \theta \leq 90°$ which produce *the same* interaural angle difference in the sound pressure at the ears. Thus, for high-frequency tones, interaural time difference, which must be inferred from interaural angle difference in the sinusoidal steady state, is an ambiguous cue for source azimuth, whereas interaural level differences are large enough to be helpful.

These acoustical interactions of the head and sound field suggest that to localize the source of a low-frequency tone the CNS has to use ITD cues, whereas for a high-frequency tone ILD cues must be used. Since the synchrony of auditory-nerve responses to tones is minimal at high frequencies, the timing cues in the neural signals will be difficult to detect in any case. Thus, one might expect that ILD alone would be used at high frequencies and ITD alone at low frequencies. At intermediate frequencies both could be helpful, especially if the results of the two neural calculations agree. This picture of different mechanisms operating in different frequency ranges is consistent with many psychophysical results (Mills, 1972). Note that for tone *bursts* the high frequencies do carry time cues in the arrival time of the burst at the two ears.

What neural structures might be involved in combining neural signals from the two ears to generate estimates of ITD and ILD? There are many possibilities (Masterton, Glendenning, & Nudo, 1982; Yin and Kuwada, 1984). In every major nucleus along the auditory pathway, including the cochlear nucleus, one can find cells whose responses are influenced by the acoustic input to *both* ears; the most extensively studied nuclei are in the lower brainstem (Guinan, Guinan, & Norris, 1972; Tsuchitani, 1978). Some neurons in the medial superior olivary nucleus (MSO, Figure 5.2) are excited by monaural stimuli to either ear (Goldberg & Brown, 1968, 1969; Guinan, Norris, & Guinan, 1972), and their CFs are about the same for stimulation of either ear. Also these neurons preserve the synchrony of responses to tones that is seen in cochlear nerve-fiber responses. Let us consider how these neurons can signal ITD. If the "latency" of response of a cell is equal for monaural stimulation of either ear, and if the tones at the two ears are identical (i.e., the sound source is directly ahead, $\theta = 0$), then with a low frequency tone the excitatory inputs from the two ears will be in phase and the net response will have maximal variations in rate during a cycle of stimulation. However, if the source moves off the midline to an azimuth where a phase difference of 180° exists between the two ears, the excitatory half-period from one ear will overlap with the nonexcitatory

half-period of the other and the fluctuation in rate will be small. Thus, the size of the fluctuation in rate will be an indication of ITD. If the latencies of the neuron for monaural stimulation of each ear were not identical, then that neuron might have its maximum rate fluctuations for an ITD different from zero. Thus, two features of the responses of such a population can signal ITD: the size of the rate fluctuation in individual neurons and the particular neurons that have the maximum fluctuations. Presumably at some higher stages (e.g., the colliculus or cortex) the outputs of the MSO could be processed so as to extract a measure related to the ITD. A further feature of the MSO (in cat, at least) that is consistent with its involvement in ITD detection, is its relative dedication to low frequencies: about 2/3 of the space in MSO is taken up with cells whose CF's are *below* 4 kHz. This is distinctly different from the neighboring lateral superior olivary nucleus (LSO), where 2/3 of the volume is cells with CF's *above* 4 kHz (Guinan, Norris, & Guinan, 1972).

The LSO contains cells whose binaural response properties suggest that they could be involved in detecting ILD (Boudreau & Tsuchitani, 1970; Guinan, Norris, & Guinan, 1972). They are exicted by monaural ipsilateral stimuli and *inhibited* by monaural contralateral stimuli. The excitatory input comes through ventral cochlear nucleus cells; the inhibitory input through cells from the ipsilateral medial nucleus of the trapezoid body (MNTB, Figure 5.2), which receive their inputs from the contralateral cochlear nucleus probably though globular cells (Figure 5.5; Kiang, 1975). Despite the greater distance and the extra synapse, the activity from the contralateral side reaches the LSO cells with about the same latency as the ipsilateral signals, presumably because the output fibers from the MNTB are very large and fast conducting. The response features of LSO neurons can provide an indication of ILD for high frequency stimuli. Suppose that the sound source is toward the left side. The sound pressure at the left ear will be larger than at the right ear and the excitatory input to the left LSO will be large and the inhibitory input small, thereby producing a large response. In the right LSO the situation will be reversed, thereby producing little response. If at a higher stage the outputs of the left and right LSO cells are compared, a reliable indication of ILD could be obtained which would be relatively independent of the overall stimulus level. The relationship between ILD and azimuth depends on frequency so that the CNS will have to take into account the CF of the cells that indicate a particular ILD and somehow integrate across CF to arrive at a judgment of azimuth. The fact that the LSO consists mainly of cells with high CFs is consistent with its involvement in high-frequency localization. It should be noted that at higher stimulus levels, high CF neurons respond to frequencies below their CF so that in theory the LSO could also be involved in phase comparisons between the two ears for low-frequency stimuli.

Psychophysical measurements for humans with multiple sclerosis have shown that it is possible to have normal ability at detecting ILD with large deficits in ITD detection. Those patients who have a large ITD deficit often have abnormal or absent electric responses of the brainstem as recorded from the scalp (Hausler & Levine, 1980). The failure to record evoked brainstem responses suggests a disruption of synchronization produced by altered conduction times resulting from abnormal myelinization. These observations on neurological patients are generally consistent with the existence of separate structures for processing ITD and ILD at a relatively low level of the central nervous system. A similar conclusion has been reached from extensive work with barn owls (Konishi, 1986).

For realistic localization situations in which the stimulus is neither a tone nor a uniform plane wave, and the head is neither spherical nor stationary, the CNS has a much richer selection of localization cues (Searle, Braida, Davis, & Colburn, 1976), and can use more than one in most situations. Among these cues are those based on spectral directional asymmetries, head and ear movements, efferent control of sensory inputs, and cues from other sensory modalities. Nevertheless, multiple and even conflicting cues normally lead to a unitary estimate of source location. Some hierarchy of decision-making levels must exist in the system so that in any behavioral situation, the most appropriate cues are weighted favorably (Middlebrooks & Knudsen, 1987). With the variety of possibilities and with the fact that the usefulness of different cues depends on the acoustic properties of the stimulus as well as the listener's previous experience, there is probably considerable variety and even plasticity in the way the CNS arrives at localization judgments.

It may eventually be possible to show that significant individual differences in the ability to localize sounds under various conditions can be attributed to variations in strategy chosen by the central processor as well as simple differences in the peripheral structures.

Speech Discrimination

The special role of the auditory system in the normal development of speech and language functions is acknowledged. That these functions reach a unique level in man is commonly associated with the enormous expansion of the cerebral cortex in areas closely associated with auditory regions. The anatomical asymmetry of these cortical regions (Geschwind & Galaburda, 1984) is thought to be the basis for the asymmetrical vulnerability of speech and language functions to unilateral brain damage (Geschwind & Galaburda, 1985a, b, c). For right-handed individuals the left cortex is supposedly essential for normal language functions, whereas the situation is more complex for left-handed individuals. Very little is known about auditory processing at these levels of the system, but, even if the cortex is of overwhelming importance in speech perception, our understanding of speech processing must take account of events at the periphery (Kiang, 1980).

Analysis of speech stimuli traditionally uses the speech spectrogram, which is a visual display of a short-time spectrum as a function of time (Potter, Kapp, & Kapp, 1966). Spectrograms show rapid fluctuations in spectral components that are consistent with alterations in the physical characteristics of the speech production apparatus during vocalization (Ainsworth, 1976; Carlson & Granstrom, 1982). For instance, during a vowel the spectrum has peaks at frequencies that are the resonant frequencies of the vocal-tract configuration used to generate that vowel. The values of these "formant" frequencies, particularly the two lowest, which are in the 0.2 to 3.5 kHz range, are thought to be of primary importance in discriminating vowels (Peterson & Barney, 1952).

Speech stimuli are modified by the external and middle ears in ways that are describable by transfer functions whose amplitudes do not vary rapidly in the frequency range of the speech formants. Thus, although the waveform may be changed considerably by relative attenuation and phase shifting of frequency components, the formant peaks in the spectrum are usually preserved.

In the cochlea, mechanical frequency analysis is performed so that each inner hair cell (IHC) and its associated cochlear-nerve fibers respond most sensitively to spectral components near the CF (Kiang & Moxon, 1972). The response of the entire array of nerve fibers can be represented in three dimensions in a display similar to a spectrogram, which has been called a "neurogram" (Kiang, Eddington, & Delgutte, 1979). From the neurograms shown in Figure 5.10 one can roughly see how formant frequencies might be represented. In the vowel /i/ the two formants, at 0.25 and 3.2 kHz, are clearly discernable in the stimulus waveform. It can be seen that fibers with CFs near these frequencies respond quite vigorously to /i/, as do many fibers at other CFs. A possible scheme for vowel identification is that the central processor scans across the array of fibers to find peaks in the activity pattern that indicate the formant frequencies. In the /i/ neurogram another possibility can also be seen. The low CF fibers clearly respond with a temporal periodicity equal to the period of the first formant (4 msec). In addition, for fibers with CFs near 3.5 kHz the periodicity of the second formant is detectable in the time variations of the spike rate. Thus, the central processor could also determine formant frequencies by assessing periodicities in the spike rates for neurons of particular CFs. Similar conclusions can be reached by examining the other neurograms.

The issue of formant representation for vowels has been studied by Sachs and Young (Sachs & Young, 1979; Young & Sachs, 1979), who showed that in anesthetized cats the formants are detectable in the average discharge rate vs. CF display for low and moderate levels of acoustic stimulation. However, at higher stimulation levels, where speech discrimination is still good, the spike rates of the cochlear nerve fibers tend to be saturated and it is more difficult to discern a maximum in the rate vs. CF display.

Several possibilities exist for processes that the central processor might use in overcoming this limitation in dynamic range. First, many of the high threshold (low-spontaneous rate) fibers (not portrayed in Figure 5.10) still operate within their dynamic range at high levels and they are represented over the entire CF range. If the central processor selected these fibers at high levels they could convey the formant information (Shofner & Sachs, 1986). Secondly, feedback mechanisms (middle-ear muscles and medial olivocochlear efferents acting on OHCs) could act to reduce the input to cochlear neurons so as to avoid saturation of their spike rate (Borg & Zakrisson, 1973, 1975). Finally, the synchronization of the discharge patterns of individual fibers to the formant frequencies is detectable even when the average rate is saturated (Young & Sachs, 1979). Much the same lines of argument would apply to the perception of any signal in noisy backgrounds (Delgutte & Kiang, 1984c; Miller et al., 1987).

It should be noted that speech discrimination is a robust phenomenon and that discrimination is maintained in the presence of considerable distortion in the speech waveforms. This resistance to distortion is at least partially a result of the redundant cues that are differentially affected as listening conditions vary in level, background noise, or motion of the source. The possibility of multiple cues creates difficulties for simple theories of speech discrimination but is a boon to organisms that have to face a variety of different listening conditions. A common error is to suppose that because a particular cue is the only one available under a specific experimental conditions it is one that is being used under more general conditions.

In theory, one could construct neurograms for any group of neurons that have CFs (e.g., middle or low spontaneous units in the auditory nerve, octopus cells in the cochlear nucleus, principle cells in the MNTB, etc.) or that can be ordered along some other dimension. Data for a complete collection of neurons implicated in any behavior would give a panoramic picture of signal processing towards a given end. We are only at the beginning of such an undertaking and data on responses of neurons in the central nervous system to speech sounds are still sparse (Watanabe & Sakai, 1973; Keidel, 1974; Kiang, 1975).

Perceptual Aspects of Hearing

Human beings are endowed at birth with an auditory system capable of receiving and responding to sounds (Kidd & Kidd, 1966). Much of this system is essentially genetically determined (Rubel, 1978; Romand, 1983) requiring only a reasonably normal environment to be expressed. The anatomical descriptions that have been presented here probably reflect hardwired (although not necessarily unalterable) portions of the system with well-defined elements located and connected in stereotypic fashion. It seems likely that the more central parts of the auditory system require regular activation to develop their full potential, and that the structure of the mature system is determined by interactions between genetics, learning, and usage (Nottebohm, 1980). The physiological machinery that operates for perceptual tasks (Garner, 1974) is less well understood than some of the reflex mechanisms.

Ideally, a sensory system should be organized so as to retain as much stimulus information as possible in a form that can be accessed when needed. In contrast, motor systems need to be organized so as to act quickly, decisively, and efficiently. The central nervous system has to reconcile these two sets of disparate goals, while minimizing costs such as processing time, size of components, and energy usage. In a real sense the function of the brain in the struggle for survival is to select those aspects of stimuli that require attention and to activate the most appropriate responses at the correct time. Man's capacity for "Selective Hearing" has been demonstrated through such phenomena as the "cocktail party effect" (Broadbent, 1958; Moray, 1969), but without current state of knowledge it is difficult to formulate testable hypotheses about the physiological bases for this level of behavior (Sanders, 1967; Oatman, 1971, 1976; Picton & Hillyard, 1974). It may be that selective hearing and other cognitive functions use many functional subunits that operate at reflex levels, in which case the study of simple reflex organization is by no means irrelevant to the study of "higher mental processes." There are a few hints that efferent systems may be involved (Lukas, 1980, 1981) in selective hearing. We lack knowledge of the role of efferent pathways in behavior because there are few observations of efferent activity in behaviorally interesting conditions. Such observations are technically difficult at present. Studies of the effects of electric stimulation of the efferent pathways can only indicate some properties of the efferents as effector neurons (Wiederhold & Kiang, 1970; Klinke & Galley, 1974; Gifford & Guinan, 1983). These physiological ideas together with the data on anatomical organization currently provide some constraints on speculations about function, but they can only lay the groundwork for more realistic studies.

Consider the task of discrimination of monaural signals in noise. It has been suggested that lesions of the olivocochlear bundle affect the discrimination of speechlike sounds in a noisy background (Dewson, 1968). One can conceive a possible mechanism through which the medial OCB could contribute to this task. With a noise spectrum that is constant in time but not flat in frequency, a maximum in the spectrum would evoke a large response in cells in a particular CF range. These cells would activate medial OCB efferents thus reducing responses of the cochlear neurons at these CFs and preventing their being driven into saturation by the speech sounds. Moreover, if the noise has a flat spectrum, the medial OCB might be controlled so as to reduce responsiveness in particular CF ranges. Thus the important spectral components of the speech would become more discriminable. Any such speculations must be guarded because the existence of the *lateral* olivocochlear system could introduce physiological factors as yet unknown. It is likely that any hypothetical picture proposable now would be far from complete. At the moment, then, our lack of knowledge of the response properties of the efferent neurons in behavioral situations limits constructive thinking and better methods of study are needed.

What approaches will help us to understand the complexities of the operation of the central nervous system in sensory behavior? A few possibilities can be discussed. As the auditory pathway is followed from cochlea to cortex it appears to expand into a network of highly organized subunits (Merzenich, Jenkins, & Middlebrooks, 1984). Some subunits are definable in terms of cell morphology, some in terms of nuclei or pathways, some in terms of connections, some in terms of chemical properties, and some in terms of response characteristics. To make progress in understanding this complex system, we need to determine principles for relating these organizational features to each other and to behavior. For example, particular cell morphologies occur at different points in the auditory system, such as the very large axonal endings found on cell bodies in AVCN, MNTB, and VNLL. In this case it is clear that these neurons of similar morphology are not connected in a chain, but this specialization certainly has some significance for the input-output function of these cells. If it becomes possible to infer signal-processing functions from knowledge of cell morphology, we will have a helpful short cut in relating structure to behavior. We are now trying to understand what the cellular components of the nervous system might do, but have as yet only a glimpse of what complex circuits involving these elements might accomplish.

To deal with the questions of the functional role of the more central parts of the system, one would like to determine some organizational principles that govern the operation of large parts of the system. For instance, the inferior colliculi are crucially placed; almost all ascending fibers and all known descending fibers in the classical auditory pathways form synapses there. Thus, there probably is some basis for thinking about a collicular level of control, which can interact with but need not require the corticogeniculate machinery. It would be of great interest to determine whether this brainstem processing is unconscious or preconscious (Dixon, 1981), if such terms can be unambiguously defined, but such questions are not now formulatable, to say nothing of resolvable. Progress in understanding the CNS and its organization for higher level behavioral functions must await more complete physiological and anatomical knowledge. Until the technical ability to monitor activity in large numbers of neurons under behaviorally "natural" conditions is made routine, the goal of relating behavior to physiology, not only for audition but for other functions as well, will remain largely a program for the future (Desmedt, 1975; Phelps, Maziotta, & Huang, 1982; Williamson, Romani, Kaufman, & Modeno, 1983).

REFERENCES

Adams, J.C. (1976). Single unit studies on the dorsal and intermediate acoustic striae. *Journal of Comparative Neurology, 170*, 97–106.

Adams, J.C. & Warr, W.B. (1976). Origins of axons in the cat's acoustic striae determined by injection of horseradish peroxidase into severed tracts. *Journal of Comparative Neurology, 170*, 107–121.

Ades, H.W. (1974). Anatomy of the inner ear. In W.D. Keidel & W.D. Neff (Eds.), *Auditory system. Anatomy. Physiology (Ear), Vol. V/1, Handbook of sensory physiology,* pp. 125–158 Berlin: Springer-Verlag.

Ades, H.W. & Engstrom, H. (Eds.). (1972). Inner ear studies. *Acta Otolaryngologica,* supplement 301.

Ades, H.W. & Engstrom, H. (Eds.). (1974). Inner ear studies II. *Acta Otolaryngologica* supplement 319.

Ainsworth, W.A. (1976). *Mechanisms of speech recognition.* Oxford: Pergamon.

Aitkin, L.M., Irvine, D.R.F., & Webster, W.R. (1984). Central neural mechanisms of hearing. In I. Darian-Smith, (Ed.), *Handbook of physiology Section 1. The nervous system Vol. III. Sensory processes, part 2,* (pp. 675–737). Bethesda MD: American Physiological Society.

Allen, J.B., Hall, J.L., Hubbard, A., Neely, S.T., & Tubis, A. (Eds.) (1986). *Peripheral auditory mechanisms. Lecture notes in biomathematics,* 64, Berlin: Springer-Verlag.

Anderson, C.M.B. & Whittle, L.S. (1971). Physiological noise and the missing 6 dB. *Acustica, 24,* 261–272.

Anderson, S.D. (1976). The intratympanic muscles. In R. Hinchcliffe & D. Harrison (Eds.), *Scientific foundations of otolaryngology* (pp. 257–280). Chicago: Year Book.

Angelborg, C. & Engstrom, H. (1973). The normal organ of Corti. In A.R. Møller, (Ed.), *Basic mechanisms in hearing* (pp. 125–182). New York: Academic Press.

Antoli-Candela, F. & Kiang, N.Y.S. (1978). Unit activity underlying the N1 potential. In R.F. Naunton & C. Fernandez (Eds.), *Evoked electrical activity in the auditory nervous system* (pp. 165–191). New York: Academic Press.

Arnesen, A.R. & Osen, K.K. (1984). Fibre population of the vestibulocochlear anastomosis in the cat *Acta Otolaryngologica, 98,* 255–269.

Ashmore, J.F. (1987). A fast motile response in guinea-pig outer hair cells: The cellular basis of the cochlear amplifier. *Journal of Physiology, 388,* 323–347.

Baust, W., Berlucchi, G., & Moruzzi, G. (1964). Changes in the auditory input in wakefulness and during the synchronized and desynchronized stages of sleep. *Archives Italiennes de Biologie, 102,* 657–674.

Beagley, H.A. (1981). *Audiology and audiological medicine vols. 1 and 2,* Oxford: Oxford U. Press.

Békésy, G. von (1960). *Experiments in hearing,* New York: McGraw-Hill.

Bench, R.J., Pye, A., & Pye, J.D. (Eds.). (1975). *Sound reception in mammals.* London: Academic Press, Inc. (Symposium of the Zoological Society of London).

Beranek, L.L. (1954). *Acoustics.* New York: McGraw-Hill.

Blauert, J. (1983). *Spatial hearing: The psychophysics of human sound localization* (J.S. Allen, trans.). Cambridge, MA: The MIT Press (Original work published 1974).

Borg, E. (1973a). A neuroanatomical study of the brainstem auditory system of the rabbit. Part I. Ascending connections. *Acta Morphologica Neerlando-Scandinavica, 11,* 31–48.

Borg, E.A. (1973b). A neuroanatomical study of the brain stem auditory system of the rabbit, Part II. Descending connections. *Acta Morphologica Neerlando-Scandinavica, 11,* 49–62.

Borg, E.A. (1973c). On the neuronal organization of the acoustic middle ear reflex. A physiological and anatomical study. *Brain Research, 49,* 101–123.

Borg, E. (1977). The intra-aural muscle reflex in retrocochlear pathology: a model study in the rabbit. *Audiology, 16,* 316–330.

Borg, E. & Zakrisson, J.E. (1973). Stapedius reflex and speech features. *Journal of the Acoustical Society of America, 54,* 525–527.

Borg, E. & Zakrisson, J.E. (1975). The stapedius muscle and speech perception. *Symposia of the Zoological Society London, 37,* 51–68.

Boudreau, J.C. & Tsuchitani, C. (1970). Cat superior olive S-segment cell discharge to tonal stimulation. In W.D. Neff (Ed.), *Contributions to sensory physiology* (Vol. 4). New York: Academic Press.

Boudreau, J.C. & Tsuchitani, C. (1973). *Sensory neurophysiology,* New York: Van Nostrand Reinhold.

Bourk, T.R. (1976). *Electrical responses of neural units in the anteroventral cochlear nucleus of the cat.* Doctoral dissertation, Massachusetts Institute of Technology, Cambridge.

Bourk, T.R., Mielcarz, J.P., & Norris, B.E. (1981). Tonotopic organization of the anteroventral cochlear nucleus of the cat. *Hearing Research, 4,* 215–241.

Brawer, J.R., Morest, D.K., & Kane, E.C. (1974). The neuronal architecture of the cochlear nucleus of the cat. *Journal of Comparative Neurology, 155,* 251–299.

Broadbent, D. (1958). *Perception and communication,* New York: Pergamon.

Brown, M.C. (1987). Morphology of labeled efferent fibers in the guinea pig cochlea. *Journal of Comparative Neurology, 260,* 605–618.

Brown, M.C., Berglund, A.M., & Ryugo, D.K. (1987). The central projections of type-II spiral ganglion cells in rodents. *Society Neuroscience Abstracts* 13:, 1258.

Brown, M.C. & Nuttall, A.L. (1984). Efferent control of cochlear inner hair cell responses in the guinea-pig. *Journal of Physiology, 354,* 625–646.

Brown, R.D. & Diagneault, E.A. (Eds.). (1981). *Pharmacology of hearing: Experimental and clinical bases.* New York: Wiley.

Brownell, W.E., Bader, C.R., Bertrand, D., & de Ribaupierre, Y. (1985). Evoked mechanical responses of isolated cochlear outer hair cells. *Science, 227,* 194–196.

Brugge, J.F. & Geisler, C.D. (1978). Auditory mechanisms of the lower brainstem. *Annual Review of Neuroscience, 1,* 363–394.

Bullock, T.H. (Ed.). (1977). *Recognition of complex acoustic signals.* Berlin: Abakon Verlagsgesellschaft.

Busnel, R.G. (Ed.). (1963). *Acoustic behaviour of animals.* Amsterdam: Elsevier.

Butler, R.A. (1975). The pinna's influence on the localization of sound. In W.F. Reidel & W.D. Neff (Eds.). *Handbook of sensory physiology, Volume V/2, Auditory system. Physiology (CNS). Behavioral studies. Psychoacoustics* (pp. 249–259). Heidelberg: Springer-Verlag.

Calford, M.B. (1983). The parcellation of the medial geniculate body of the cat defined by the auditory response properties of single units. *Journal of Neuroscience, 3,* 2350–2364.

Calford, M.B. & Aitkin, L.M. (1983). Ascending projections to the medial geniculate body of the cat: evidence for multiple, parallel auditory pathways through thalamus. *Journal of Neuroscience, 3,* 2365–2380.

Cant, N.B. & Gaston, K.C. (1982). Pathways connecting the right and left cochlear nuclei. *Journal of Comparative Neurology, 212,* 313–326.

Cant, N.B. & Morest, D.K. (1978). Axons from noncochlear sources in the anteroventral cochlear nucleus of the cat. A study with the rapid Golgi method. *Neuroscience, 3,* 1003–1029.

Carlson, R. & Granstrom, B. (Eds.). (1982). *The representation of speech in the peripheral auditory system.* New York: Elsevier Biomedical Press.

Carmel, P.W. & Starr, A. (1963). Acoustic and non-acoustic factors modifying middle-ear muscle activity in waking cats. *Journal of Neurophysiology, 26,* 598–616.

Carterette, E.C. & Friedman, M.P. (Eds.). (1978). *Handbook of perception: Hearing (Vol. IV).* New York: Academic Press.

Cazals, Y., Aran, J.-M., & Erre, J.-P. (1983). Intensity difference thresholds assessed with eighth nerve and auditory cortex potentials: Compared values from cochlear and saccular responses. *Hearing Research, 10,* 263–268.

Clopton, B.M., Winfield, J.A., & Flamino, F.J. (1974). Tonotopic organization: Reviews and analysis. *Brain Research, 76,* 1–20.

Cody, A.R. & Johnstone, B.M. (1982). Acoustically evoked activity of single efferent neurons in the guinea pig cochlea. *Journal of the Acoustical Society of America, 72,* 280–282.

Colburn, H.S. & Durlach, N.I. (1978). Models of binaural interaction. In E.C. Carterette, & M.P. Friedman, (Eds.), *Hearing: Vol. IV, Handbook of perception,* (pp. 467–518). New York: Academic Press.

Colwell, S.A. (1975). Thalamocortical-corticothalmic reciprocity: a combined anterograde-retrograde tracer technique. *Brain Research, 92,* 443–449.

Crawford, A.C. & Fettiplace, R. (1981). Non-linearities in the responses of turtle hair cells. *Journal of Physiology, 315,* 317–338.

Dallos, P. (1973). *The auditory periphery: Biophysics and physiology.* New York: Academic Press.

Dallos, P. (1981). Cochlear physiology, *Annual Review of Psychology, 32,* 153–190.

Dallos, P. (1984). Peripheral mechanisms of hearing. In I. Darian-Smith, (Ed.), *Handbook of physiology. Section 1: The nervous system. Vol. III. Sensory processes Part 2* (pp. 595–637). Bethesda MD: American Physiological Society.

Dallos, P. & Harris, D.M. (1977). Properties of auditory nerve responses in the absence of outer hair cells. *Journal of Neurophysiology, 41,* 365–383.

Dankbaar, W.A. (1970). The pattern of stapedial vibration. *Journal of the Acoustical Society of America, 48,* 1021–1022.

David, E.E., Jr. & Denes, P.B. (Eds.). (1972). *Human communication: A unified view.* New York: McGraw-Hill.

Delgutte, B. & Kiang, N.Y.S. (1984a). Speech coding in the auditory nerve: I. Vowel-like sounds. *Journal of the Acoustical Society of America, 75,* 866–878.

Delgutte, B. & Kiang, N.Y.S. (1984b). Speech coding in the auditory nerve: IV. Sounds with consonant-like dynamic characteristics. *Journal of the Acoustical Society of America, 75,* 897–907.

Delgutte, B. & Kiang, N.Y.S. (1984c). Speech coding in the auditory nerve: V. Vowels in background noise. *Journal of the Acoustical Society of America, 75,* 908–918.

De Reuck, A.V.S. & Knight, J. (Eds.). (1968). *Hearing mechanisms in vertebrates.* Boston: Little, Brown.

Desmedt, J.E. (1975). Physiological studies of the efferent recurrent auditory system. In W.D. Keidel, & W.D. Neff, (Eds.). *Handbook of sensory physiology, Volume V/2, Auditory system. Physiology (CNS). Behavioral studies. Psychoacoustics.* (pp. 219–246). Berlin: Springer-Verlag.

Dewson, J.H. (1968). Efferent olivocochlear bundle: Some relationships to stimulus discrimination in noise. *Journal of Neurophysiology, 31,* 122–130.

Dixon, N.F. (1981). *Preconscious processing.* New York: Wiley.

Dorman, M.F., Lindholm, J.M., Hannley, M.T., & Leek, M.R. (1987). Vowel intelligibility in the absence of the acoustic reflex: Performance-intensity characteristics. *Journal of the Acoustical Society of America, 81,* 562–564.

Durlach, N.I. & Colburn, H.S. (1978). Binaural phenomena. In E.C. Carterette, & M.P. Friedman (Eds.), *Hearing, Vol. IV, Handbook of perception* (pp. 365–466). New York: Academic Press.

Engstrom, H., Ades, H.W., & Andersson, A. (1966).

Structural pattern of the organ of Corti. Baltimore: Williams and Wilkins.

Fant, G. & Lindquist, J. (1968). Pressure and gas mixture effects on diver's speech. *Speech transmission laboratory quarterly progress and status report 1,* Royal Institute of Technology, Stockholm.

Fay, R.R. & Coombs, S. (1983). Neural mechanisms in sound detection and temporal summation. *Hearing Research, 10,* 69–92.

Fekete, D.M., Rouiller, E.M., Liberman, M.C., & Ryugo, D.K. (1984). The central projections of intracellularly labeled auditory nerve fibers in cats. *Journal of Comparative Neurology, 222,* 432–450.

Fex, J. (1962). Auditory activity in centrifugal and centripetal cochlear fibers in cat. A study of a feedback system. *Acta Physiologica Scandinavica, 55,* (Suppl. 189), 1–68.

Fex, J. (1965). Auditory activity in uncrossed centrifugal cochlear fibres in cat. A study of a feedback system, II. *Acta Physiologica Scandinavica, 64,* 43–57.

Fex, J. (1974). Neural excitatory processes of the inner ear. In W.D. Keidel & W.D. Neff (Eds.). *Handbook of sensory physiology (Volume V/1) Auditory system. Anatomy. Physiology (Ear).* (pp. 586–646). New York: Springer-Verlag.

Filogamo, G., Candiollo, L., & Rossi, G. (1967). The morphology and function of auditory input control. *Hearing Research, 20,* 1–153.

Flanagan, J.L. (1972). *Speech analysis, synthesis and perception.* Berlin: Springer-Verlag.

Fleischer, G. (1978). *Evolutionary principles of the mammalian middle ear. Advances in anatomy, embryology and cell biology.* Berlin: Springer-Verlag.

Fletcher, H. (1953). *Speech and hearing in communication.* Princeton, NJ: D. Van Nostrand.

Garner, W.R. (1974). *The processing of information and structure.* New York: Wiley.

Gatehouse, R.W. (Ed.). (1982). *Localization of sound: Theory and applications.* Groton, CT: Amphora Press.

Geisler, C.D., Deng, L., & Greenberg, S.R. (1985). Thresholds for primary auditory fibers using statistically defined criteria. *Journal of the Acoustical Society of America, 77,* 1102–1109.

Geschwind, N. & Galaburda, A.M. (Eds.) (1984). *Cerebral dominance. The biological foundations.* Cambridge, MA: Harvard University Press.

Geschwind, N. & Galaburda, A.M. (1985a). Cerebral lateralization. Biological mechanisms, associations, and pathology: I. A hypothesis and a program for research. *Archives of Neurology, 42,* 428–459.

Geschwind, N. & Galaburda, A.M. (1985b). Cerebral lateralization. Biological mechanisms, associations, and pathology: II. A hypothesis and a program for research. *Archives of Neurology, 42,* 521–552.

Geschwind, N. & Galaburda, A.M. (1985c). Cerebral lateralization. Biological mechanisms, associations, and pathology: III. A hypothesis and a program for research. *Archives of Neurology, 42,* 634–654.

Gifford, M.L. & Guinan, J.J. (1983). Effects of crossed-olivocochlear-bundle stimulation on cat auditory nerve fiber responses to tones. *Journal of the Acoustical Society of America, 74,* 115–123.

Godfrey, D.A., Kiang, N.Y.S., & Norris, B.E. (1975a). Single unit activity in the posteroventral cochlear nucleus. *Journal of Comparative Neurology, 162,* 247–268.

Godfrey, D.A., Kiang, N.Y.S., & Norris, B.E. (1975b). Single unit activity in the dorsal cochlear nucleus. *Journal of Comparative Neurology, 162,* 269–284.

Goldberg, J.M. & Brown, P.B. (1968). Functional organization of the dog superior olivary complex: an atomical and electrophysiological study. *Journal of Neurophysiology, 31,* 639–656.

Goldberg, J.M. & Brown, P.B. (1969). Response of binaural neurons of dog superior olivary complex to dichotic tonal stimuli: some physiological mechanisms of sound localization. *Journal of Neurophysiology, 32,* 613–636.

Guinan, J.J., Jr. (1986). Effect of efferent neural activity on cochlear mechanics. *Scandinavian Audiology Supplement, 25,* 53–62.

Guinan, J.J. Jr. & Peake, W.T. (1967). Middle-ear characteristics of anesthetized cats. *Journal of the Acoustical Society of America, 41,* 1237–1261.

Guinan, J.J. Jr., Guinan, S.S., & Norris, B.E. (1972). Single auditory units in the superior olivary complex, I: Responses to sounds and classifications based on physiological properties. *International Journal of Neuroscience, 4,* 101–120.

Guinan, J.J. Jr. & McCue, M.P. (1987). Asymmetries in the acoustic reflexes of the cat stapedius muscle. *Hearing Research, 26,* 1–10.

Guinan, J.J. Jr., Norris, B.E., & Guinan, S.S. (1972). Single auditory units in the superior olivary complex, II. Locations of unit categories and tonotopic organization. *International Journal of Neuroscience, 4,* 147–166.

Guinan, J.J. Jr., Warr, W.B., & Norris, B.E. (1983). Differential olivocochlear projections from lateral vs. medial zones of the superior olivary complex. *Journal of Comparative Neurology, 221,* 358–370.

Guinan, J.J. Jr., Warr, W.B., & Norris, B.E. (1984). Topographic organization of the olivocochlear projections from the lateral and medial zones of the superior olivary complex. *Journal of Comparative Neurology, 226,* 21–27.

Harris, C.M. (Ed.). (1979). *Handbook of noise control.* New York: McGraw-Hill.

Harrison, J.M. (1978). The auditory system of the brain stem. In R.F. Naunton & C. Fernández (Eds.). *Evoked electrical activity in the auditory nervous system* (pp. 353–368). New York: Academic Press.

Harrison, J.M. & Howe, M.E. (1974). Anatomy of the afferent auditory nervous system of mammals. In W.D. Keidel, & W.D. Neff (Eds.). *Handbook of sensory physiology. Volume V/1. Auditory system. Anatomy. Physiology (Ear)* (pp. 283–336). Berlin: Springer-Verlag.

Hausler, R., Colburn, S., & Marr, E. (1983). Sound localization in subjects with impaired hearing. Spatial-discrimination and interaural-discrimination tests. *Acta Oto-laryngologica* (Suppl 400), 1–62.

Hausler, R. & Levine, R.A. (1980). Brain stem auditory evoked potentials are related to interaural time discrimination in patients with multiple sclerosis. *Brain Research, 191,* 589–594.

Heffner, R. & Heffner, H. (1980). Hearing in the elephant (*Elephas maximus*). *Science, 208,* 518–520.

Henson, O.W. (1974). Comparative anatomy of the middle ear. In W.D. Keidel & W.D. Neff, (Eds.). *Handbook of sensory physiology, Vol. V/1, Auditory system. Anatomy. Physiology (Ear),* (pp. 39–110). New York: Springer-Verlag.

Hoshino, T. (1976). Attachment of the inner sensory hairs to the tectorial membrane. A scanning electron microscopic study. *Annals of Otology, Rhinology and Laryngology, 38,* 11–18.

Hudspeth, A.J. (1985). The cellular basis of hearing: the biophysics of hair cells. *Science 230,* 745–752.

Imig, T.J., Reale, R.A., & Brugge, J.F. (1982). The auditory cortex. Patterns of corticocortical projections related to physiological maps in the cat. In C.N. Woolsey (Ed.). *Cortical sensory organization, Vol. 3, Multiple auditory areas* (pp. 3–41). Clifton NJ: Humana.

Irvine, D.R.F. (1986). *The auditory brainstem,* Berlin: Springer-Verlag, 279 pp.

Irving, R. & Harrison, J.M. (1967). The superior olivary complex and audition: A comparative study. *Journal of Comparative Neurology, 130,* 77–86.

Iurato, S. (1967). *Submicroscopic structure of the inner ear.* London: Pergamon Press.

Iurato, S., Smith, C.A., Eldredge, D.H., Henderson, D., Carr, C., Ueno, Y., Cameron, S., & Richter, R. (1978). Distribution of the crossed olivocochlear bundle in the chinchilla's cochlea. *Journal of Comparative Neurology, 182,* 57–76.

Johnson, D.H. (1978). The relationship of post-stimulus time and interval histograms to the timing characteristics of spike trains. *Biophysics Journal, 22,* 413–430.

Johnson, D.H. (1980a). Applicability of white-noise nonlinear system analysis to the peripheral auditory system. *Journal of the Acoustical Society of America, 68,* 876–884.

Johnson, D.H. (1980b). The relationship between spike rate and synchrony in responses of auditory-nerve fibers to single tones. *Journal of the Acoustical Society of America, 68,* 1115–1122.

Johnstone, B.M. & Boyle, A.J.F. (1967). Basilar membrane vibration examined with the Mössbauer technique. *Science, 158,* 389–390.

Joseph, M.P., Guinan, J.J., Fullerton, B.C., Norris, B.E., & Kiang, N.Y.S. (1985). Number and distribution of stapedius motoneurons in cats. *Journal of Comparative Neurology, 232,* 43–54.

Kane, E.C. (1973). Octopus cells in the cochlear nucleus of the cat: heterotypic synapses upon homeotypic neurons. *International Journal of Neuroscience, 5,* 251–279.

Katsuki, Y. (1982). *Receptive mechanisms of sound in the ear.* Cambridge Eng.: Cambridge University Press.

Keidel, W.D. (1974). Information processing in the higher parts of the auditory pathway, In E. Zwicker, & E. Terhardt (Eds.). *Psychophysical models and physiological facts in hearing.* Berlin: Springer-Verlag.

Keidel, W.D., Kallert, S., & Korth, M. (1983). *The physiological basis of hearing: A review.* New York: Thieme-Stratton.

Kemp, D.T. (1979) Evidence of mechanical nonlinearity and frequency selective wave amplification in the cochlea. *Archives of Otorhinolaryngology, 224,* 37–45.

Khanna, S.M. & Leonard, D.G.B. (1982). Basilar membrane tuning in the cat cochlea. *Science, 215,* 305–306.

Khanna, S.M. & Tonndorf, J. (1972). Tympanic membrane vibrations in cats studied by time-averaged holography. *Journal of the Acoustical Society of America, 51,* 1904–1920.

Kiang, N.Y.S. (1968). A survey of recent developments in the study of auditory physiology. *Annals of Otology, Rhinology and Laryngology, 77,* 656–675.

Kiang, N.Y.S. (1975). Stimulus representation in the discharge patterns of auditory neurons, In D.B. Tower (Ed.). *The nervous system vol. 3, Human communication and its disorders* (pp. 81–96). New York: Raven.

Kiang, N.Y.S. (1980). Processing of speech by the auditory nervous system. *Journal of the Acoustical Society of America, 68,* 830–835.

Kiang, N.Y.S. (1981). A re-examination of "The effects of partial section of the auditory nerve." *Perspectives in Biology and Medicine. Winter:* 254–269.

Kiang, N.Y.S. (1984). Peripheral neural processing of auditory information. In I. Darian-Smith (Volume Ed.). *Handbook of Physiology.* (*Section I The nervous system. Vol. III, Sensory processes. Part 2*). Bethesda, MD: American Physiological Society.

Kiang, N.Y.S., Eddington, D.K., & Delgutte, B. (1979). Fundamental considerations in designing auditory implants. *Acta Otolaryngologica, 87,* 203–218.

Kiang, N.Y.S., Fullerton, B.C., Richter, E.A., Levine, R.A., & Norris, B.E. (1984). Artificial stimulation of the auditory system. *Advances in Audiology, 1,* 6–17.

Kiang, N.Y.S., Keithley, E.M., & Liberman, M.C. (1983). The impact of auditory nerve experiments on cochlear implant design. In C.W. Parkins & S.W. Anderson (Eds.). *Cochlear prostheses, an international Symposium* (pp. 114–121). New York: The New York Academy of Sciences.

Kiang, N.Y.S., Liberman, M.C., & Levine, R.A. (1976). Auditory-nerve activity in cats exposed to ototoxic drugs and high-intensity sounds. *Annals of Otology, Rhinology and Laryngology, 75,* 1–17.

Kiang, N.Y.S., Liberman, M.C., Sewell, W.F., & Guinan, J.J. Jr. (1986). Single unit clues to cochlear mechanisms. *Hearing Research, 22,* 171–182.

Kiang, N.Y.S., Morest, D.K., Godfrey, D.A., Guinan, J.J., & Kane, E.C. (1973). Stimulus coding at caudal levels of the cat's auditory nervous system: Response characteristics of single units. In A. Møller (Ed.). *Basic mechanisms in hearing,* (pp. 455–478). New York: Academic Press.

Kiang, N.Y.S. & Moxon, E.C. (1972). Physiological considerations in artificial stimulation of the inner ear. *Annals of Otology, Rhinology and Laryngology, 81,* 714–730.

Kiang, N.Y.S. & Moxon, E.C. (1974). Tails of tuning curves of auditory-nerve fibers. *Journal of the Acoustical Society of America, 55,* 620–630.

Kiang, N.Y.S. & Moxon, E.C., & Levine, R.A. (1970). Auditory-nerve activity in cats with normal and abnormal cochleas. In B.E.W. Wolstenholme & J. Knight (Eds.). *Sensorineural hearing loss,* (pp. 241–273). London: J. and A. Churchill.

Kiang, N.Y.S., Pfeiffer, R.R., Warr, W.B., & Backus, A.S.N. (1965). Stimulus coding in the cochlear nucleus. *Annals of Otology, Rhinology and Laryngology, 74,* 463–485.

Kiang, N.Y.S., Rho, J.M., Northrop, C.C., Liberman, M.C., & Ryugo, D.K. (1982). Hair-cell innervation by spiral ganglion cells in adult cats. *Science, 217,* 175–177.

Kiang, N.Y.S., Watanabe, T., Thomas, E.C., & Clark, L.F. (1965). *Discharge patterns of single fibers in the cat's auditory nerve.* Research Monograph No. 35, Cambridge MA: M.I.T. Press.

Kidd, A.H. & Kidd, R.M. (1966). The development of

auditory perception in children. In A.H. Kidd, & J.L. Rivoire (Eds.). *Perceptual development in children* (pp. 113–142). New York: International Universities Press.

Kim, D.O., Molnar, C.E., & Matthews, J.W. (1980). Cochlear mechanics: nonlinear behavior in two-tone responses as reflected in cochlear-nerve-fiber responses and in ear-canal sound pressure. *Journal of the Acoustical Society of America, 67,* 1704–1721.

Kimura, R.S. (1966). Hairs of the cochlear sensory cells and their attachments to the tectorial membrane. *Acta Otolaryngologica, 61,* 55–72.

Kimura, R.S. (1975). The ultrastructure of the organ of Corti. *International Review of Cytology, 42,* 173–222.

Kimura, R. & Wersall, J. (1962). Termination of the olivo-cochlear bundle in relation to the outer hair cells of the organ of Corti in guinea pig. *Acta Otolaryngologica, 55,* 11–32.

Kinsler, L.E. & Frey, A.R. (1962). *Fundamentals of acoustics.* New York: Wiley.

Kirikae, I. (1960). *The structure and function of the middle ear.* Tokyo: University of Tokyo Press.

Klinke, R. & Galley, N. (1974). Efferent innervation of vestibular and auditory receptors. *Physiological Review, 54,* 316–357.

Kohllöffel, L.U.E. (1984). Notes on the comparative mechanics of hearing. *Hearing Research, 13,* 83–88.

Konishi, M. (1986). Centrally synthesized maps of sensory space. *Trends in Neurosciences, 9,* 163–168.

Kryter, K.D. (1970). *The effects of noise on man,* New York: Academic Press.

Kuhn, G.F. (1977). Model for interaural time differences in the azimuthal plane. *Journal of the Acoustical Society of America, 62,* 157–167.

Lanyon, W.E. and Tavolga, W.N. (Eds.). (1960). *Animal sounds and communication.* Washington, D.C.: American Institute of Biological Sciences.

Lathi, B.P. (1965). *Signals, systems and communication.* New York: Wiley.

Lentz, T.L. (1968). *Primitive nervous systems.* New Haven: Yale University Press.

Lewis, B. (Ed.). (1983). *Bioacoustics: A comparative approach.* New York: Academic Press.

Liberman, M.C. (1978). Auditory-nerve response from cats raised in a low-noise chamber. *Journal of the Acoustical Society of America, 63,* 442–445.

Liberman, M.C. (1980). Efferent synapses in the inner hair cell area of the cat cochlea: An electron microscopic study of serial sections. *Hearing Research, 3,* 189–204.

Liberman, M.C. (1982). Single-neuron labeling in the cat auditory nerve. *Science, 216,* 1239–1241.

Liberman, M.C. & Brown, M.C. (1986). Physiology and anatomy of single olivocochlear neurons in the cat, *Hearing Research, 24,* 17–36.

Liberman, M.C. & Kiang, N.Y.S. (1978). Acoustic trauma in cats. Cochlear pathology and auditory-nerve activity. *Acta Otolaryngologica,* Suppl. 358, 63 pp.

Liberman, M.C. & Kiang, N.Y.S. (1984). Single-neuron labeling and chronic cochlear pathology. IV. Stereocilia damage and alterations in rate- and phase-level functions, *Hearing Research, 16,* 75–90.

Liberman, M.C. & Oliver, M.E. (1984). Morphometry of intracellularly labeled neurons of the auditory nerve: correlations with functional properties, *Journal of Comparative Neurology, 223,* 163–176.

Lim, D.J. (1969). Three dimensional observation of the inner ear with the scanning electron microscope, *Acta Otolaryngologica,* supplement 255.

Lim, D.J. (1977). Current review of SEM techniques for inner ear sensory organs. O. Johari (Ed.). *Scanning Electron Microscopy Vol. II: Proceedings of the Workshop on Biomedical Applications—SEM studies of sensory organs.* (pp. 401–408). Chicago: ITT Research Institute.

Lim, D.J. (1986). Functional structure of the organ of Corti: a review, In: *Cellular mechanisms in hearing,* Flock, A. & Wersäll, J., Elsevier, pp. 117–146.

Lorente de Nó, R. (1933). Anatomy of the eighth nerve III, general plans of structure of the primary cochlear nuclei, *Laryngoscope, 43,* 327–350.

Lukas, J.H. (1980). Human auditory attention: the olivocochlear bundle may function as a peripheral filter, *Psychophysiology, 17,* 444–452.

Lukas, J.H. (1981). The role of efferent inhibition in human auditory attention: an examination of the auditory brainstem potentials. *International Journal of Neuroscience, 12,* 137–145.

Lynch, T.J., III, Nedzelnitsky, V., & Peake, W.T. (1982). Input impedance of the cochlea in cat. *Journal of the Acoustical Society of America, 72,* 108–130.

Mast, T.E. (1970). Binaural interaction and contralateral inhibition in dorsal cochlear nucleus of the chinchilla. *Journal of Neurophysiology, 33,* 108–115.

Masterton, R.B., Glendenning, K.K., & Nudo, R.J. (1982). Anatomical pathways subserving the contralateral representation of a sound source. In R.W. Gatehouse (Ed.). *Localization of Sound: Theory and Applications,* (pp. 113–125). Groton: Amphora.

Masterton, B., Heffner, H., & Ravizza, R. (1969). The evolution of human hearing. *Journal of the Acoustical Society of America, 45,* 966–985.

McCue, M.P. & Guinan, J.J. (1983). Functional segregation within the stapedius motoneuron pool. *Society for Neuroscience Abstracts, 9,* 1085.

McDonald, D.M. & Rasmussen, G.L. (1971). Ultrastructural characteristics of synaptic endings in the cochlear nucleus having acetylcholinesterase activity. *Brain Research, 28,* 1–18.

McFadden, D. (1982). *Tinnitus: Facts, theories, and treatment.* Washington, D.C.: National Academy Press.

Merzenich, M.M., Jenkins, W.M., & Middlebrooks, J.C. (1984). Observations and hypotheses on special organizational features of the central auditory nervous system. In G.M. Edelman, W.E. Gall, & W.M. Cowan (Eds.). *Dynamic aspects of neocortical function* (pp. 397–424). New York: Wiley.

Middlebrooks, J.C. & Knudsen, E.I. (1987). Changes in external ear position modify the spatial tuning of auditory units in the cat's superior colliculus, *Journal of Neurophysiology, 57,* 672–687.

Miller, M.I., Barta, P.E., & Sachs, M.B. (1987). Strategies for the representation of a tone in background noise in the temporal aspects of the discharge patterns of auditory-nerve fibers. *Journal of the Acoustical Society of America, 81,* 665–679.

Mills, A.W. (1972). Auditory localization. In J.V. Tobias (Ed.). *Foundations of modern auditory theory, Vol. II* (pp. 303–345). New York: Academic Press.

Møller, A.R. (1965). An experimental study of the acoustic impedance of the middle ear and its transmission properties. *Acta Otolaryngologica, 60,* 129–149.

Møller, A.R. (1974). Function of the middle ear. In W.D. Keidel and W.D. Neff (Eds.). *Handbook of sensory physiology, Volume V/1, Auditory system, Anatomy, Physiology (Ear).* (pp. 491–517). Berlin: Springer-Verlag.

Møller, A.R. (1983). *Auditory physiology.* New York: Academic Press.

Møller, A.R. (1984). Neurophysiological basis of the acoustic middle-ear reflex. In S. Silman (Ed.). *The acoustic reflex*(pp. 1–34). New York: Academic Press.

Moore, B.C.J. (1986). *Frequency selectivity in hearing.* London: Academic Press.

Moray, N. (1969). *Listening and attention.* Baltimore, MD: Penguin Books.

Morest, D.K. (1964). The neuronal architecture of the medial geniculate body of the cat. *Journal of Anatomy, 98,* 611–630.

Morest, D.K. (1965). The laminar structure of the medial geniculate body of the cat. *Journal of Anatomy, 99,* 143–160.

Morest, D.K. & Oliver, D.L. (1984). The neuronal architecture of the inferior colliculus in the cat: Defining the functional anatomy of the auditory midbrain. *Journal of Comparative Neurology, 222,* 209–236.

Morgan, D.E. & Dirks, D.D. (1975). Influence of middle-ear muscle contraction on pure-tone suprathresh-

old loudness judgments. *Journal of the Acoustical Society of America, 57,* 411–420.

Morse, P.M. & Ingard, K.U. (1968). *Theoretical acoustics.* New York: McGraw-Hill.

Mountain, D.C. (1980). Changes in endolymphatic potential and crossed olivocochlear bundle stimulation alter cochlear mechanics. *Science, 210,* 71–72.

Mundie, J.R. (1963). The impedance of the ear—a variable quantity. U.S. Army Medical Research Laboratory Report No. 576, 63–85.

National Advisory Neurological Diseases and Stroke Council. (1969). *Human communication and its disorders—an overview,* Bethesda MD: National Institutes of Health, Public Health Service.

Nicol, T. & Chao-Charia, K.K. (1981). Clinical anatomy of the auditory part of the human ear. In H.A. Beagley, (Ed.). *Audiology and audiological medicine,* Vol. 2 (pp. 3–49). Oxford: Oxford University Press.

Nottebohm, F. (1980). Brain pathways for vocal learning in birds: a review of the first 10 years. In J.M.S. Sprague & A.N.E. Epstein (Eds.). *Progress in psychobiology and physiological psychology. Vol. 9* (pp. 85–124). New York: New York Academy Press.

Oatman, L.C. (1971). Role of visual attention on auditory evoked potentials in unanesthetized cats. *Experimental Neurology, 10,* 341–356.

Oatman, L.C. (1976). Effects of visual attention on the intensity of auditory evoked potentials. *Experimental Neurology, 51,* 41–53.

Oppenheim, A.V., Willsky, A.S., & Young, I.T. (1983). *Signals and systems.* Englewood Cliffs, NJ: Prentice-Hall.

Osen, K.K. (1969). Cytoarchitecture of the cochlear nuclei in the cat. *Journal of Comparative Neurology, 136,* 453–478.

Osen, K.K. (1970). Course and terminations of the primary afferents in the cochlear nuclei of the cat. An experimental anatomical study, *Archives Italiennes de Biologie, 108,* 21–51.

Osen, K.K., & Mugnaini, E. (1981). Neuronal circuits in the dorsal cochlear nucleus. In J. Syka & L. Aitkin (Eds.). *Neuronal mechanisms of hearing.* (pp. 119–125). New York: Plenum.

Pang, X.D. & Peake, W.T. (1986). How do contractions of the stapedius muscle alter the acoustic properties of the ear? In J.B. Allen, J.L. Hall, A. Hubbard, S.T. Neely, & A. Tubis (Eds.). *Peripheral auditory mechanisms, Lecture notes in mathematics, Vol. 64* (pp. 36–43). New York: Springer-Verlag.

Papez, J.W. (1967). *Comparative neurology. A manual and text for the study of the nervous system of vertebrates.* New York: Hafner.

Papoulis, A. (1977). *Signal analysis.* New York: McGraw-Hill.

Parkins, C.W. & Anderson, S.W. (Eds.). (1983). *Cochlear prostheses. An international symposium.* New York: New York Academy of Sciences.

Perkins, R.E. & Morest, D.K. (1975). A study of cochlear innervation patterns in cats and rats with the Golgi method and Normarski optics. *Journal of Comparative Neurology, 163,* 129–158.

Peterson, G.E. & Barney, H.L. (1952). Control methods used in a study of the vowels. *Journal of the Acoustical Society of America, 24,* 175–184.

Pfeiffer, P.E. (1961). *Linear systems analysis.* New York: McGraw-Hill.

Pfeiffer, R.R. (1966). Classification of response patterns of spike discharges from units in the cochlear nucleus: tone-burst stimulation. *Experimental Brain Research, 1,* 220–235.

Pfeiffer, R.R. (1968). Anteroventral cochlear nucleus: waveforms of extracellularly recorded spike potentials. *Science, 154,* 667–668.

Pfeiffer, R.R. (1974). Consideration of the acoustic stimulus. In W.D. Keidel & W.D. Neff (Eds.). *Handbook of sensory physiology, Vol. V/1 Auditory system, anatomy physiology (ear).* Berlin: Springer-Verlag.

Phelps, M.E., Mazziotta, J.C., & Huang, S.-C. (1982). Study of cerebral function with positron computed tomography. *Journal of Cerebral Blood Flow and Metabolism, 2,* 113–162.

Pickles, J.O. (1982). *An introduction to the physiology of hearing.* London: Academic Press.

Picton, T.W. & Hillyard, S.A. (1974). Human auditory evoked potentials II: effects of attention. *Journal of Electroencephalography and Clinical Neurophysiology, 36,* 191–199.

Pierce, A.D. (1981). *Acoustics: An introduction to its physical principles and applications.* New York: McGraw-Hill.

Popper, A.N. & Fay, R.R. (Eds.), (1980). *Comparative studies of hearing in vertebrates.* New York: Springer-Verlag.

Potter, R.K., Kopp, G.A., & Kopp, H.G. (1966). *Visible speech.* New York: Dover.

Powers, W.T. (1973). *Behavior: The control of perception.* New York: Aldine.

Pye, A. & Hinchcliffe, R. (1976). Comparative anatomy of the ear. In *Scientific foundations of otolaryngology* (pp. 184–202). Chicago: Year Book Medical Publications.

Ramon y Cajal, S. (1909). *Histologie du systèm nerveux de l'homme et des vertébrés.* Paris: Maloine.

Rasmussen, G.L. (1953). Further observations of the afferent cochlear bundle. *Journal of Comparative Neurology, 99,* 61–74.

Rasmussen, G.L. (1960). Efferent fibers of the cochlear nerve and cochlear nucleus. In G.L. Rasmussen & W.F. Windle (Eds.). *Neural mechanisms of the audi-*tory and vestibular systems* (pp. 105–115). Springfield, IL: Charles C. Thomas.

Rasmussen, G.L. (1967). Efferent connections of the cochlear nucleus. In A.B. Graham. *Sensorineural hearing processes and disorders* (pp. 61–75). Boston: Little Brown.

Ravizza, R.J., Straw, R.B., & Long, P.D. (1976). Laminar origin of efferent projections from auditory cortex in the golden Syrian hamster. *Brain Research, 114,* 497–500.

Rayleigh, Lord (J.W. Strutt), (1886). *The theory of sound. Vol. 2.* London: Macmillan.

Reger, S.N. (1960). Effect of middle ear muscle action on certain psycho-physical measurements. *Annals of Otology, Rhinology and Laryngology, 48,* 498–503.

Retzius, G. (1884). *Das Gehörorgan der Wirbelteire, Vol. II, das Gehörorgan der Reptilien, der Vogel, und der Saugetiere.* Stockholm: Samson & Wallin.

Reysenbach de Haan, F.W. (1956). *De Ceti Auditu. Over de Gehoorzin Bij de Walvissen.* Utrecht: Drukkerif Fa. Schotanus & Jens.

Rhode, W.S. (1984). Cochlear mechanics. *Annual Review of Physiology, 46,* 231–246.

Rhode, W.S., Oertel, D., & Smith, P.H. (1983). Physiological response properties of cells labeled intracelullarly with horseradish peroxidase in cat ventral cochlear nucleus. *Journal of Comparative Neurology, 213,* 448–463.

Richter, E.A., Norris, B.E., Fullerton, B.F., Levine, R.A., & Kiang, N.Y.S. (1983). Is there a medial nucleus of the trapezoid body in humans? *American Journal of Anatomy, 168,* 157–166.

Robertson, D. (1984). Horseradish peroxidase injection of physiologically characterized afferent and efferent neurones in the guinea pig spiral ganglion. *Hearing Research, 15,* 113–121.

Robles, L., Ruggero, M.A., & Rich, N.C. (1986). Basilar membrane mechanics at the base of the chinchilla cochlea. I. Input-output functions, tuning curves, and response phases. *Journal of the Acoustical Society of America, 80,* 1364–1374.

Romand, R. (1978). Survey of intracellular recording in the cochlear nucleus of the cat. *Brain Research, 148,* 43–65.

Romand, R. (Ed.). (1983). *Development of auditory and vestibular systems.* New York: Academic Press.

Romer, A.S. (1949). *The vertebrate body.* Philadelphia: Saunders.

Rose, J.E. (1960). Organization of frequency sensitive neurons in the cochlear nuclear complex of the cat. In G.L. Rasmussen & W.F. Windle (Eds.). *Neuronal mechanisms of the auditory and vestibular systems* (pp. 116–136). Springfield, IL: Charles, C. Thomas.

Rosowski, J.J., Carney, L. H., Lynch, T.J. III & Peake, W.T. (1986). The effectiveness of the external and middle ears in coupling acoustic power into the cochlea. In J.B. Allen, J.L. Hall, A. Hubbard, S.T. Neely, & A. Tubis, (Eds.). *Peripheral auditory mechanisms. Lecture Notes in Biomathematics, 64,* Berlin: Springer-Verlag.

Rossi, G. & Cortesina, G. (1965). The efferent innervation of the inner ear. *Laryngoscope, 75,* 212–235.

Rouiller, E.M. & Ryugo, D.K. (1984). Intracellular marking of physiologically characterized neurons in the ventral cochlear nucleus of the cat. *Journal of Comparative Neurology, 225,* 167–186.

Rouiller, E.M., Cronin Schreiber, R., Fekete, D.M., & Ryugo, D.K. (1983). Morphology of auditory nerve fiber innervation of the cat cochlear nucleus in relation to spontaneous rate activity, *Society for Neuroscience Abstracts, 9,* 495.

Rubel, E.W. (1978). Ontogeny of structure and function in the vertebrate auditory system. In M. Jacobson, (Ed.). *Handbook of sensory physiology. Vol. IX. Development of sensory systems* (pp. 135–237). Berlin: Springer-Verlag.

Russell, I. (1981). Properties of hair cells in the mammalian cochlea. In M.S. Laverack and D.J. Cosens (Eds.). *Sense organs.* (pp. 64–85). Glasgow: Blackie and Son Ltd.

Ryugo, D.K. & Fekete, D.M. (1982). Morphology of primary axosomatic endings in the anteroventral cochlear nucleus of the cat: A study of the endbulbs of Held. *Journal of Comparative Neurology, 210,* 239–257.

Sachs, M.B. & Abbas, P.J. (1974). Rate versus level functions for auditory-nerve fibers in cats: tone burst stimuli. *Journal of the Acoustical Society of America, 56,* 1835–1847.

Sachs, M.B. & Young, E.D. (1979). Encoding of steady-state vowels in the auditory nerve: Representation in terms of discharge rate. *Journal of the Acoustical Society of America, 66,* 470–479.

Sachs, M.B. & Young, E.D. (1980). Effects of nonlinearities on speech encoding in the auditory nerve. *Journal of the Acoustical Society of America, 68,* 858–875.

Sales, G. & Pye, D. (1974). *Ultrasonic communication by animals.* New York: Wiley.

Sanders, A.F. (Ed.) (1967). *Attention and performance.* Amsterdam: North-Holland.

Schindler, R.A. & Merzenich, M.M. (Eds.). (1985). *Cochlear implants,* New York: Raven.

Schubert, E.D. (1980). *Hearing: Its function and dysfunction.* New York: Springer-Verlag.

Schucknecht, H.F. (1974). *Pathology of the ear.* Cambridge, MA: Harvard University Press.

Searle, C.L., Braida, L., Davis, M.F., & Colburn, H.S. (1976). Model for auditory localization. *Journal of the Acoustical Society of America, 60,* 1164–1175.

Sebeok, T.A. (Ed.). (1968) *Animal communication.* Bloomington: Indiana University Press.

Sellick, P.M. & Russell, I.J. (1978). Intracellular studies of cochlear hair cells: Filling the gap between basilar membrane mechanics and neural excitation, in R.F. Naunton & C. Fernández, (Eds.). *Evoked electrical activity in the auditory nervous system.* Academic Press.

Shaw, E.A.G. (1974). The external ear. In W.D. Keidel & W.D. Neff, (Eds.). *Handbook of sensory physiology, Vol. V/1, Auditory system. Anatomy. Physiology. (Ear)* (pp. 455–490). Berlin: Springer-Verlag.

Shaw, E.A.G. (1982). The 1979 Rayleigh Medal Lecture: The elusive connection. In R.W. Gatehouse, (Ed.). *Localization of sound: Theory and applications* (pp. 13–29). Groton: Amphora.

Shofner, W.P. & Sachs, M.B. (1986). Representation of a low-frequency tone in the discharge rate of populations of auditory nerve fibers. *Hearing Research, 21,* 91–95.

Siebert, W.M. (1986). *Circuits, signals, and systems.* Cambridge, MA: M.I.T. Press: McGraw-Hill.

Siebert, W.M. (1970). Frequency discrimination in the auditory system: Place or periodicity mechanisms. *Proceedings of the Institute of Electrical and Electronics Engineers, 58,* 723–730.

Siegel, J.H. & Kim, D.O. (1982). Efferent neural control of cochlear mechanics? Olivocochlear bundle stimulation affects cochlear biomechanical nonlinearity. *Hearing Research, 6,* 171–182.

Silman, S. (Ed.). (1984). *The acoustic reflex.* Orlando: Academic Press.

Skudrzyk, E. (1971). *The foundations of acoustics.* New York: Springer-Verlag.

Smith, B.J. (1971). *Environmental physics: Acoustics.* London: Longman.

Smith, C.A. (1973). The efferent neural supply to the vertebrate ear. *Advances in Oto-Rhino-Laryngology, Vol. 20* (pp. 296–310). Basel: Karger.

Smith, C.A. (1978). Structure of the cochlear duct. In R.F. Naunton & C. Fernández (Eds.). *Evoked electrical activity in the auditory nervous system* (pp. 3–19). New York: Academic Press.

Smith, C.A., Cameron, S., & Richter, R. (1976). Cochlear innervation: current status and new findings by use of the Golgi stain. In S.K. Hirsh, D.H. Eldredge, I.J. Hirsh, & S.R. Silverman (Eds.). *Hearing and Davis* (pp. 11–24). St. Louis: Washington University Press.

Smith, C.A. & Haglan, B.J. (1973). Golgi stains on the guinea pig organ of Corti. *Acta Otolaryngologica, 75,* 203–210.

Smith, C.A. & Rasmussen, G.L. (1965). Degeneration in the efferent nerve endings in the cochlea after axonal section. *Journal of Cell Biology, 26,* 63–77.

Smith, C.A. & Rasmussen, G.L. (1963). Recent observations on the olivo-cochlear bundle. *Annals of Otology, Rhinology and Laryngology, 72,* 1–18.

Smith, C.A. & Sjostrand, F.S. (1961). Structure of the nerve endings on the external hair cells of the guinea pig cochlea as studied by serial sections. *Journal of Ultrastructure Research, 5,* 523–556.

Snyder, D.L. (1975). *Random point processes.* New York: Wiley.

Spoendlin, H. (1966). *The organization of the cochlear receptor. Advances in otolaryngology. Vol. 13.* 227p. Basel: Karger.

Spoendlin, H. (1972). Innervation densities of the cochlea. *Acta otolaryngologica, 73,* 235–248.

Spoendlin, H. (1974). Neuroanatomy of the Cochlea. In E. Zwicker, & E. Terhardt (Eds.). *Facts and models in hearing* (pp. 18–36). New York: Springer-Verlag.

Stebbins, W.C. (1980). The evolution of hearing in mammals. In A.N. Popper & R.R. Fay (Eds.). *Comparative studies of hearing in vertebrates* (pp. 421–436). New York: Springer-Verlag.

Stebbins, W.C. (1983). *The acoustical sense of animals.* Cambridge MA: Harvard University Press.

Stebbins, W.C. Hawkins, J.E. Jr., Johnson, L.-G., & Moody, D.B. (1979). Hearing thresholds with outer and inner hair cell loss. *American Journal of Otolaryngology, 1,* 15–27.

Stephens, R.W.B. & Bate, A.E. (1966). *Acoustics and vibrational physics.* London: Edward Arnold.

Stotler, W.A. (1953). An experimental study of the cells and connections of the superior olivary complex of the cat. *Journal of Comparative Neurology, 98,* 401–431.

Sullivan, W.E. & Konishi, M. (1984). Segregation of stimulus phase and intensity coding in the cochlear nucleus of the barn owl. *Journal of Neuroscience, 4,* 1787–1799.

Syka, J. & Aitkin, L. (Eds.). (1981). *Neuronal mechanisms of hearing.* New York: Plenum Press.

Teas, D.C., Konishi, T., & Nielsen, D.W. (1972). Electrophysiological studies on the spatial distribution of the crossed olivocochlear bundle along the guinea pig cochlea. *Journal of the Acoustical Society of America, 51,* 1256–1264.

Terayama, Y. & Yamamoto, K. (1971). Olivo-cochlear bundle in the guinea pig cochlea after central transsections of the crossed bundle. *Acta Otolaryngologica, 72,* 385–396.

Tonndorf, J. (1972). Bone conduction. In J.V. Tobias, (Ed.). *Foundations of modern auditory theory (Vol. II)* (pp. 197–237). New York: Academic Press.

Tsuchitani, C. (1978). Lower auditory brain stem structures of the cat. In R.F. Naunton & C. Fernández (Eds.). *Evoked electrical activity in the auditory nervous system* (pp. 373–401). New York: Academic Press.

van Beregijk, W.A. (1967). The evolution of vertebrate hearing. In W.D. Neff (Ed.). *Contributions to sensory physiology (Volume 2).* (pp. 1–49). New York: Academic Press.

Van Noort, J. (1969). *The structure and connections of the inferior colliculus. An investigation of the lower auditory system,* Assen, Netherlands: Van Gorcum.

Warr, W.B. (1975). Olivocochlear and vestibular efferent neurons of the feline brain stem: their location, morphology and number determined by retrograde axonal transport and acetylcholinesterase histochemistry. *Journal of Comparative Neurology, 161,* 159–182.

Warr, W.B. (1982). Parallel ascending pathways from the cochlear nucleus: Neuroanatomical evidence of functional specialization. *Contributions to Sensory Physiology, 7,* 1–38.

Warr, W.B., Guinan, J.J. Jr., & White, J.S. (1986). Organization of the efferent fibers: The lateral and medial olivocochlear systems, In R.A. Altschuler, D.W. Hoffman & R.P. Bobbin (Eds.). *Neurobiology of hearing: The cochlea* (pp. 333–348). New York: Raven.

Warren, R.M. (1982). *Auditory perception: A new synthesis.* New York: Pergamon Press.

Watanabe, T. & Sakai, H. (1973). Responses of the collicular auditory neurons to human speech. I. Responses to monosyllable, /ta/. *Proceedings of the Japanese Academy, 49,* 291–296.

Weiss, T.F. (1984). Relation of receptor potentials of cochlear hair cells to spike discharges of cochlear neurons. *Annual Review of Physiology, 46,* 247–259.

Weiss, T.F., Peake, W.T., & Rosowski, J.J. (1985). A model for signal transmission in an ear having hair cells with free-standing stereocilia. I. Empirical basis for model structure. *Hearing Research, 20,* 131–138.

Whitfield, I.C. (1967). *The auditory pathway.* Baltimore: Williams & Wilkins.

Whitfield, I.C. (1984). *Neurocommunications: An introduction.* Chichester, England: Wiley.

Wiederhold, M.L. & Kiang, N.Y.S. (1970). Variations in the effects of electric stimulation of the crossed olivocochlear bundle on cat single auditory-nerve-fiber responses to tone bursts. *Journal of the Acoustical Society of America, 48,* 966–977.

Willard, F.H. & Ryugo, D.K. (1983). Anatomy of the central auditory system. In J.F. Willott (Ed.). *The auditory psychobiology of the mouse.* (pp. 201–304). Springfield IL: Charles C. Thomas.

Williamson, S.J., Romani, G.-L. Kaufman, L., & Modeno, I. (Eds.). (1983). *Biomagnetism: An interdisciplinary approach.* New York: Plenum Press.

Yin, T.C.T. & Kuwada, S. (1984). Neuronal mechanisms of binaural interaction. In G.M. Edelman, W.E. Gall, & W.M. Cowan (Eds.). *Dynamic aspects of neocortical function* (pp. 263–313). New York: Wiley.

Young, E.D. (1984). Response characteristics of neurons of the cochlear nucleus. In C.I. Berlin (Ed.). *Hearing science* (pp. 423–460). San Diego: College-Hill.

Young, E.D. & Sachs, M.B. (1979). Representation of steady-state vowels in the temporal aspects of the discharge patterns of populations of auditory-nerve fibers. *Journal of the Acoustical Society of America, 66*, 1381–1403.

Zakrisson, J.-E. & Borg, E. (1974). Stapedius reflex and auditory fatigue. *Audiology, 13*, 231–235.

Zurek, P.M. (1985). Acoustic emissions from the ear: A summary of results from humans and animals. *Journal of the Acoustical Society of America, 78*, 340–344.

Zwicker, E. & Schloth, E. (1983). Interrelation of different oto-acoustic emissions. *Journal of the Acoustical Society of America, 75*, 1148–1154.

Zwislocki, J.J. & Kletsky, E.J. (1979). Tectorial membrane: A possible effect on frequency analysis in the cochlea. *Science, 204*, 639–641.

Chapter 6

AUDITION: PSYCHOPHYSICS AND PERCEPTION

David M. Green, *University of Florida*

INTRODUCTION

This chapter reviews the inferences that can be made about the process of hearing based on psychophysical, that is, behavioral evidence. The previous chapter outlined the physics of the stimulus and how that stimulus is transformed in the various neural stations between cochlea and the auditory areas. Here we will consider experiments in which we study the reaction of human observers to various kinds of sounds. We commonly describe these reactions as the observer's auditory perceptions. Auditory perception includes, among other topics, the topics of speech, space, pitch, and musical perception. Some of those topics are treated by Hirsh in Chapter 7, Vol. I. In this chapter we discuss space and pitch perception.

We begin with a brief discussion of methods used in current auditory experiments and a brief

The preparation of this chapter was supported, in part, by the National Institute of Health and by the National Science Foundation. A first draft was prepared in the spring of 1981; it was revised in 1983. I wish to thank F.L. Wightman for his extensive comments on the first draft and A. Pippin for her help.

history of the field. This is followed by a review of the substantive topics of (1) intensity discrimination, (2) loudness, (3) nonlinearity phenomena, (4) pitch perception, and finally, (5) space perception.

Methods

Auditory psychophysics, commonly called psychoacoustics, is the study of the relation between the physical stimulus, sound, and the observer's reaction to that sound. One should recognize that there are basically three methods used in behavioral research to make inferences about how the hearing mechanism operates. These are (1) discrimination, (2) equality, and (3) sensory scaling.

Discrimination

In its simplest form, the method of discrimination determines the smallest difference between two sounds that can be reliably distinguished—the just noticeable difference, or jnd. The observer, in making such discriminations, need not state how the sounds differ; the observer must only be able to distinguish reliably one sound from the other. We can evaluate this process in a completely objective fashion, and since we know which stimulus was presented, we can determine if the observer is able to discriminate correctly between them. Ordinarily, the stimuli differ only on a single physical dimension, for example, a difference in intensity between two sinusoidal signals of the same frequency. One could also reduce the intensity of a single signal to determine if the signal could be discriminated from silence or detected in the presence of some other sound. Such a task is called a detection experiment.

The basic strengths of the discrimination tasks are their objectivity and precision—often the measurements can be made with two- and sometimes three-digit accuracy. The weakness is that all measurements are local. Any large change in the stimulus is clearly discriminable, and hence beyond the scope of this method.

Equality

The method of equality if used to determine when two stimuli are equal on some subjective dimension despite being clearly unequal on some other subjective dimension. Unlike the successful application of this method in color vision, where two lights of dissimilar physical spectra (called metamers) appear exactly equal—they are in fact indiscriminable—there are no useful auditory metamers. Sounds with different physical spectra are generally easy to distinguish, and we must instruct the observer to equate some single dimension, such as the loudness of the two sounds, while ignoring an obvious second dimension of the sounds, such as its pitch. Thus, one must first carefully define the subjective dimension to be equated. To the degree that the dimension `is clear, that is, when it generates substantial agreement among different observers, then regular and consistent data can be obtained. The equal-loudness contours, for example, relate how the intensities of different sinusoidal frequencies must be changed to produce judgments of equal loudness.

The strengths of this method are two. First, it can be used for quite varied and easily discriminated stimuli. Second, it requires no numerical estimation on the part of the observer. Its weakness is that, unless the subjective dimension is very clear, one can expect considerable variance caused by differences among individual observers, and discrepancies among different sets of data are likely to be sizable.

Scaling

In addition to the determination of equality, one would also like to know how much the change in some physical attribute has altered the subjective dimension. Does raising the physical intensity by a factor of ten increase the loudness by a similar amount? Sensory scaling is the method used to answer such questions. To begin, one must define the subjective dimension, and furthermore, assume that the observer can use numbers in a reliable and consistent manner.

There are some techniques that attempt to construct scales from discrimination data, Thurstone (1927a, b) and Torgerson (1958), but they are less in vogue now than in earlier times. The degree of numerical sophistication required of the observer differs according to method. Some only require the observer to change some physical parameter of the stimulus so that the sensed quality is doubled or halved. Others, such as magnitude estimation, require the observers to report any number they desire, asking only that the ratios of the reported numbers reflect the ratios of the sensed changes along the appropriate sensory dimension (see Chapter 1 above by Luce and Krumhansl).

The advantage of these scaling methods is that their range of applicability is virtually unlimited. Stevens (1975) pioneered the application of the method to a variety of conditions for a number of modalities. One can ask the observer to give numerical estimates of any stimulus dimension imaginable. The disadvantage is that, as with equality, there must be consensus among the observers on the exact definition of the subjective dimension. In addition, individual differences in the use of numbers contribute an unwanted source of variance. Watson (1973) has written a careful discussion of the different kinds of information one can obtain from these different methods. He states that the method of discrimination is largely used to study what he calls "sensory capacity"; the other methods are used to study "response proclivity," since there is no way to score the response as correct or incorrect, but some judgments generate wide consensus among different observers.

History

The modern era of psychoacoustic research began during the second quarter of this century when developments in electronics and electro-mechanical devices allowed investigators to control and measure the stimulus with precision. Without such technology, the control of the major physical variables of the stimulus, especially intensity, was far from satisfactory. Only a century ago, Lord Rayleigh (1882) provided the first method for determining the absolute intensity of a sound source, using the torque produced on a disc suspended on a fine thread in the acoustic field (Rayleigh's disc). With electromechanical transducers such as earphones it is comparatively easy to specify the absolute intensity of the pressure produced in an average ear canal, at least for frequencies below 6000 Hz where, because of the sound's long wavelength, standing waves are not present. Oscillators make it easy to control and vary sinusoidal frequency. The specification of the frequency of a sinusoidal stimulus can be made to within about one part in a thousand.

The digital computer also allows one to compute a given waveform, store the successive values of the waveform in the computer, and play the stored value through a digital-to-analog converter. Thus, practically any sound waveform, having whatever properties the investigator desires, can be closely approximated. The degree of approximation is determined by the number of samples generated per time unit (the sampling rate) and the number of different numbers used to express each sample (the quantizing level).

Many of the waveforms used in psychoacoustics are now either digitally generated, using the process just described, or digitally controlled. Digital control means the computer controls some peripheral device such as an attenuator, or an oscillator, which, in turn, generates the electric signal that is finally transformed into the sound wave.

All of these changes have occurred largely within the last 50 years. Early psychoacoustic research began at the Bell Telephone Laboratory where it was led by Harvey Fletcher. The earliest investigators were Wegel and Lane (1924) who studied the detection of one sinusoid in the presence of another. This was followed by two classic studies on the discrimination of a change in the two major parameters of a sinusoid, a change in intensity (Riesz, 1928), or a change in frequency (Shower & Biddulph, 1931). At about the same time, Stevens and Newman (1936) at Harvard conducted one of the first carefully controlled studies of binaural localization. They used special chairs mounted above the roof of the Biology building as their approximation of an anechoic (echoless) acoustic field and, to ensure a relatively noise-free environment, conducted their experiments in the small hours of the morning. In those days, Cambridge was a quieter and less congested town.

Prior to the First World War, there were a few individual investigators, but no major laboratories existed outside the United States. In the Netherlands in 1940 J.F. Schouten, a physicist, completed a series of brilliant studies on pitch perception. After the war, Schouten established a laboratory devoted to the investigation of subjective phenomena at the Philips Laboratory at Eindhoven. In addition, following the war, the defense establishment at Soesterberg developed an impressive psychoacoustic laboratory with R. Plomp as its head. In Germany, E. Zwicker, first in collaboration with Feldkeller, and later independently, contributed a number of impressive studies on a wide range of topics. In England, the Medical Research Council unit in Cambridge and the Sound and Vibration Institute of Southampton became major centers for psychoacoustic research, especially in the applied area.

In the United States, the advent of the Second World War stimulated the need for objective data on how well one could hear under high levels of noise, such as occurs in the cockpit of an airplane. To study such matters, the Psycho-Acoustic Laboratory (PAL) was established at Harvard under S.S. Stevens' direction in 1940. More than 50 professional investigators worked in this laboratory, and more than 200 articles and reports were issued between 1945 and 1960. Among its more distinguished investigators was Georg von Békésy, who joined the Psycho-Acoustic Laboratory in 1947 and won the Nobel Prize in 1961 for his earlier work on cochlear mechanics.

Meanwhile, researchers at the Bell Laboratories continued their efforts and a number of influential papers were published in the next twenty years. Among them was a means of evaluating the quality of a voice communication system, that is, how well did the system preserve the intelligibility of the speech signal, based only on physical measurements of the communication system (French & Steinberg, 1947). Fletcher and Munson's experiments on the critical band (Fletcher, 1940) were another milestone.

Three books dominated the field. The first was Fletcher's *Speech and Hearing* (1929) (later revised as *Speech and Hearing in Communication*, 1953). The second, by Stevens and Davis, *Hearing* (1938) provided good substantive summaries of both psychological and physiological facts. The third book, Wever's *Theories of Hearing* (1949), provided a fine historical perspective for the current theories.

The continued development of the electronics industry made psychoacoustic equipment inexpensive and widely available. Following the war, a number of other laboratories became active. Many were headed by people who had worked at Stevens' PAL during the war.

The applied characteristic of psychoacoustic research developed along with the basic science. In addition to the concern with noise control and better speech communication systems, there has also been interest in hearing pathology. Measuring how well people hear is called audiometry, and there has been an active interest in this topic on the part of psychoacousticians. The combination of interests in voice communication systems and deafness has led to a considerable effort to improve hearing aids for the partially deaf.

In addition to this applied characteristic, there has been continued interest in theory. Classical auditory theory was essentially a theory of pitch perception. Since Helmholtz's time, the basic theoretical question was how the auditory system encodes frequency and performs the frequency resolution that is apparent to anyone listening to combinations of sinusoidal signals, such as a musical tone. Helmholtz's answer was physical resonance (Helmholtz, 1954). He likened the ear to a stringed instrument such as a harp. A musical tone would then produce vibrations of the strings tuned to the appropriate frequency. Pitch was then place, each nerve encoded a different quality (pitch), and the degree of activity signaled the amplitude or intensity of the particular frequency.

Opposed to this view was the temporal theory. It has had many advocates, but the views of Rutherford (1886) and Seebeck (1841) were prominent. They believed the auditory system might encode frequency as repetition of neural impulses and intensity as the total number of active nerve fibers. The absolute refractory period of the nerve fiber, about 1 msec, would restrict the upper limits that such repetition might follow and thus Weber's volley principle (Wever, 1949), which suggested the group of fibers fired in alternation, became a necessary corollary to any temporal theory of pitch.

Lively interest in the topic of pitch perception continues, and we will report on the recent developments in detail later in the chapter. But a modern theory of hearing also encompasses a number of other topics. How does the binaural system permit us to localize sources of sound in space? How can one best characterize the process of discriminating or distinguishing between two sounds that differ in intensity? How and why does one sound make another sound difficult or impossible to hear? To what extent does the ear distort the acoustic waveform and hence introduce frequency components not present in the original waveform?

Obviously, these questions are more quantitative and detailed than the earlier question of pitch perception. The earlier classic question of pitch perception was essentially a question of how the two predominant physical dimensions, frequency and intensity, are coded in the nervous system. The modern questions reflect the increase in quantitative knowledge that has been acquired in the last half century. Modern psychoacoustic theory, however, is also sensitive to physiological data, and most theories attempt to incorporate the recent physiological findings, such as those discussed in the preceding chapter. While one can treat psychoacoustic data in a black box manner, that is, as the description of the relation between the physical stimulus, the input, and the observed responses, the output, only a minority do so. Most theories attempt to present the presumed stimulus transformation terms of established physiological mechanisms. This often makes the evaluation of competitive theories difficult, since the ability to make exact quantitative predictions of the psychoacoustic data is only one of several objectives.

INTENSITY DISCRIMINATION AND MASKING

Introduction

This area is one of the most active topics of

psychoacoustic research at present. The ability to detect one sinusoid, the signal, in the presence of others, called maskers, is of particular interest, since the psychophysical results have been associated with neural suppression and the general form of the results strongly resembles the tuning curves measured in the peripheral auditory system. In addition to this topic, we will also deal with the absolute threshold of auditory signals, that is, the minimal intensity needed to detect a sinusoidal signal in quiet. This minimal intensity as a function of frequency defines a baseline of hearing. Departures from this average hearing level imply some degree of deafness or loss of normal hearing acuity. We will also review the discrimination of an increment in the intensity of a sinusoidal signal, a relation that is close to, but systematically different from, Weber's law, which says that the size of a just detectable increment in a sinusoid is a constant proportion of the initial sinusoid. Finally, we will also review the ability to discriminate a sinusoidal signal in white Gaussian noise. Because noise is so widely used in masking and discrimination experiments, we begin our review with this stimulus.

Detection of Signals in Noise

A combination of a sufficient number of unrelated acoustic sources produces a sound that we call noise. If no single source is much more intense than any other, then, by the central limit theorem, the instantaneous pressure distribution of noise will be Gaussian. If there is equal energy at all frequencies, we call the noise "white". Noise is frequently used in psychoacoustic experiments as a masking stimulus, that is, as a sound to make another sound difficult or impossible to hear.

The detectability of a pulsed signal in noise is determined by the ratio of signal energy to noise power density. For noise of equal energy over a band of frequences W, the noise density N_0 is the total noise power N (watts), divided by the bandwidth W (cycles per second): N_0 has the units of energy, that is, power multiplied by time. Signal energy is proportional to the integral of the pressure waveform squared. For a rectangularly gated sinusoid of duration T, the signal energy is simply the steady-state power of the sinusoid P times the duration T. It is often convenient to work in decibels,

$$\tilde{E} = 10 \log E \qquad \tilde{N}_0 = 10 \log N_0.$$

The quantity $\tilde{N}_0$ is also called the spectrum level of the noise if the reference pressure is 0.0002 dyne/cm^2. One of the most important and fundamental properties of the detection of a signal in a noise background is that only the signal-to-noise ratio is important. This basic fact has been appreciated since serious quantitative work on this topic was undertaken (Fletcher, 1953; Hawkins & Stevens, 1950). Thus, to a very good first approximation, if the signal is just detectable in some noise background and the level of the noise is raised 10 dB, the signal must be raised by 10 dB to restore the same degree of detectability. Reed and Bilger (1973) have reported a small departure from that rule. They find a small but reliable increase in the just detectable signal-to-noise ratio as a function of noise level. The increase is about 0.75 dB per 10 dB increase in noise level. Weber (1977) has measured a similar mean increase, but in his measurements we cannot statistically reject the hypothesis that the true value is zero. Of course these rules fail at very low noise levels; the noise may be inaudible and the signal's detectability is then determined by the minimal energy, as discussed earlier. But even at these low levels, we can view the threshold as determined by some small, constant level of internal noise. As we increase the external noise level, the internal noise is eventually overwhelmed, and the signal's threshold then becomes nearly proportional to the external noise intensity.

For a signal frequency of 1000 Hz and a signal duration of about 1/10 second, the signal threshold will be $\tilde{E} - \tilde{N}_0 = 10$ dB ± 1 dB. This fact has been verified by so many laboratories on so many occasions that it is a benchmark in the field. There are essentially no individual differences (Kerkhof, van der Schaaf, & Korving, 1980). Even rather hard-of-hearing observers achieve this value. If the frequency is changed, a good approximation for the threshold values at different frequences is given by the following approximation (Green, McKey, & Licklider, 1959),

$$\tilde{E} - \tilde{N}_0 = 2(f/F) + 8 \quad (250 < f < 4000 \text{ Hz})$$

where f is the signal frequency and F is 1000 Hz. This approximation was obtained with a signal duration of 1/10 sec and is probably valid in the range from about 10 to 200 msec. At very short durations, the energy is not only at the signal frequency, but is smeared to other, nearby, frequencies and more energy is required (Garner,

1947). Beyond about 200 msec, the ear can no longer integrate efficiently and more energy is then required. For signals of arbitrary duration, the signal energy is also arbitrary, but one can calculate the signal power to noise power density, 10 log P/N_0. That function is about 8 dB at 1000 Hz and varies with frequency in about the same way as the approximation expressed above (Fletcher, 1953; Hawkins & Stevens, 1950).

The detectability of a *noise* signal in noise depends on the signal's bandwidth, its duration and the signal-to-noise ratio. For a just detectable signal (about 76 percent correct in two-alternative forced-choice tasks), Green (1960) has derived the following equation based on the analysis of a simple energy detector

$$d' = \tfrac{1}{3}\sqrt{W_s T}\,\frac{S_o}{N_o}$$

where S_o is the signal power density, N_o is the noise power density, W_s is the signal bandwidth and T is the signal duration. The factor 1/3 represents the relative efficiency of the human observer.

This equation has been shown to give a reasonable approximation to empirical data (Green, 1960). Schacknow and Raab (1976) have presented a recent review of all available evidence. They show that the power spectrum of the signal must fall off at a faster rate than the spectrum of the noise for the equation to be valid. If the signal spectrum and the noise spectrum are the same, for example, if both are passed through the same filter, then the observer can listen over a noise band much larger than the nominal bandwidth of the filter. The threshold signal intensity is then almost independent of the signal's bandwidth.

Next, we consider the faintest sound level that one can hear in quiet, that is, without an externally generated noise. Since this minimal energy defines what we call average or normal hearing acuity, deviations from the norm may imply hearing pathology. It is, thus, an extremely important measurement, both practically and theoretically. Our struggle to define this standard has been arduous and somewhat halting. It is important to review the history carefully, and to consider the technical aspects of this topic in some detail.

Absolute Threshold

By the absolute threshold of a sinusoid, we mean the minimum energy or intensity needed to detect the signal in quiet, that is, without another sound present. Early measurements of this function were discrepant from one another for a variety of reasons that we have come to understand—the major variable being individual differences among observers of different ages and the exact way in which the stimulus is presented to the observer, that is, in a free field via a loudspeaker or with earphones placed over the ears.

In 1933, Sivian and White of the Bell Telephone Laboratories published an extensive investigation of the absolute threshold for a group of relatively young observers. Actually, two types of measurement conditions were used in their research. The first, a minimum audible field (MAF), measured the minimal pressure that could be detected by an observer positioned in front of a sound source in an anechoic (echoless) environment. Since no reflections occur, there are no standing waves in such an environment and the minimal pressure is measured with the observers absent, by simply measuring the sound pressure near the position formerly occupied by the observer's head. Data were obtained from five men and four women ranging in age from 18 to 26, all having hearing rated as normal or better.

In addition, they measured how the azimuth, the angle between the speaker and the observer, influenced this minimal audible field pressure when the subject was listening with a single ear. As might be expected from physical considerations, there was little change in this minimum audible presence as a function of azimuth for low frequencies, because the wavelength of the sound is long compared with the size of the head. When the source is opposite the listening ear, however, this minimal pressure changes by 25 dB or more for frequencies over 6000 Hz where the wavelength is 5 cm or less.

The investigators compared their data with a number of prior studies and concluded that most of the discrepancies, some as large as 20 dB, can be explained on the basis of azimuth or the age of the observers. They quoted two contemporary studies indicating that hearing acuity diminishes with age, a finding that is now well established (Hinchcliffe, 1959).

Sivian and White also considered the absolute threshold when it was measured with earphones. They call this latter measurement a minimum

Table 6.1. Entries are minimum audible pressure re 0.0002 dynes/cm^2

| | Sivian & White (1933) | | Earphone (MAP) | | |
| | MAF | MAP | Anderson & Whittle (1971) | Watson et al. (1972) | ISO |
Frequency	0° azimith		Sharpe HA-10	TDH-49	WE-750-A
100	32	46	37		
125				46	46
200	19	29			
250			24	25	25
300	14	22			
400	10	16			
500			13	13	11
600	7	14			
800	4	10			
1000	4	8	8	9	6.5
1500	−1	6			6.5
2000	−1	5		11	8.5
3000	−6	6			7.5
4000	6	9		15	9.5
6000	4	14			8
8000	10	9			9.5
10000	14	26			
20000	27	44			

audible pressure (MAP). Measurement of this pressure is straightforward at lower frequencies, since the pressure at any point in the ear canal is nearly the same. At higher frequencies, standing waves are present, and it is important to measure very close to the eardrum. Table 6.1 presents the two sets of data: the MAP entries are from the smooth curve of Figure 10 from Sivian and White; the MAF curve is the zero incidence curve of Figure 3 from Sivian and White.

The difference between these two sets of data is well known. Within the limits of experimental error, the differences above 1000 Hz are to be expected on purely physical grounds. There are, after all, a number of reflecting objects in the free field when the observer is present and the external meatus and the ear canal act as resonant objects. Shaw (1974) has presented an extensive summary of these factors and their quantitative influence. In general, they are of such a magnitude as to explain accurately the MAF, MAP differences above 1000 Hz. Below 1000 Hz, however, the reason for the difference is less obvious, and the difference of more than 10 dB at 100 Hz is particularly perplexing.

The most likely explanation for the differ-

ence, according to Sivian and White, was that enclosing the ear with the phone might introduce masking noise that would make the sinusoidal signal harder to hear. The most plausible mechanism is that pressure fluctuations occur because of the relative motion between the side of the head and the earphone. These motions are induced by the pump action of the heart. This hypothesis was supported by later studies of Brogden and Miller (1947) and Rudmose (1950). Munson and Wiener (1952), who called the discrepancy the "missing 6 dB," cast some doubt on the physiological noise hypothesis, however, since they found that loudness balances displayed the same discrepancy even with high level signals. However, these results using a loudness balance could not be replicated by Anderson and Whittle (1971), who instead found that pressure and field measurements converge as the level of the tone is raised—a result to be expected if the masking noise hypothesis is correct. These authors also made extensive physical measurements of the noise level under the earphone, measurements that replicated Shaw and Piercy's (1962) earlier measurements almost exactly.

Our best opinion is that enclosing the ear

produces appreciable low frequency noise that is of sufficient magnitude to elevate the absolute threshold for these low (below 1000 Hz) frequencies. Furthermore, as the volume of the enclosed acoustic cavity increases, the intensity of the noise diminishes (Shaw & Piercy, 1962; Brogden & Miller, 1947). This fact would explain why Tillman, Johnson, and Olsen (1966) obtained an even larger MAF–MAP discrepancy with ear insert phones than with conventional headphones. Rudmose (1962) showed that the MAF–MAP difference was virtually eliminated if a small rubber tube conducted the sound to the head. Killion (1978) and Rudmose (1982) have recently published extensive reviews of this entire topic and both authors have concluded that the case of the missing 6 dB can be considered closed.

The resolution of these discrepancies means that we need only obtain a sufficiently large sample of measurements from young observers with good ears to establish the normal hearing threshold for the population. This effort went on for some time, both in the United States and elsewhere. We will not recount the particular studies and the various disputes. Finally, in 1963 the International Standards Organization adopted a recommendation for normal hearing levels. These are listed in Table 6.1 along with the values obtained by Anderson and Whittle at low frequencies and by Watson, Franks, and Hood (1972) at the audiometric frequencies. Watson et al. used a two-alternative forced-choice task, generally considered the most sensitive psychophysical method. Their thresholds are slightly higher than ISO recommendations, but the Watson et al. signal was only 125 msec in duration as opposed to the 500 msec or longer duration commonly used in audiometric tests. In general, one can see that there is remarkable consistency among the various estimates.

Differential Intensity Thresholds

In addition to knowing the minimal audible intensity at each frequency, we can gain insight into the auditory mechanism if we understand the smallest change in intensity that can be reliably detected. The experimental paradigm is as follows: there is a standard stimulus of intensity I and that that we add an increment ΔI. When we have adjusted the value of the increment ΔI to be just detectable or discrimi-

nable from the standard, then we have established what is called the *difference limen* or DL. An important theoretical issue is how this difference limen varies with the intensity I of the standard.

Terminology is far from standard in this area, so a brief digression is necessary. The two most commonly used measures of the difference limen are the simple ratio of intensities, $\Delta I/I$, and $10 \log (1 + \Delta I/I) = 10 \log [(I + \Delta I)/I]$, called the ΔI in decibels. A value of $\Delta I/I = .2$ means the increment needs to be 20 percent of the standard in order to detect it; this would correspond to $10 \log (1 + \Delta I/I) = .791$. Note that since $10 \log [(I + \Delta I)/I] = 10 \log (I + \Delta I) - 10 \log I$, the latter measure is simply the decibel difference between the standard plus increment and the standard. One should also know that since intensity is proportional to pressure squared and because $\log (1 + x) \cong .434x$ for small x, the following approximations are valid.

$$\Delta I/I = 2\Delta p/p + (\Delta p/p)^2$$

$$= 2\Delta p/p \text{ for small } \Delta p/p$$

$$10 \log (I + \Delta I/I) \cong 10 \log [1 + 2\Delta p/p]$$

$$\cong 8.69 (\Delta p/p)$$

where p refers to pressure (see Jesteadt, Wier, & Green, 1977).

Sometimes one or the other of the preceding measures is termed *the* Weber fraction, after the German physiologist Ernst H. Weber (1795–1878). In fact, all these measures and some others have been used at various times and no consensus is evident. A recent paper by Grantham and Yost (1982) discusses the relative merits of the different measures.

Weber's law states that $\Delta I/I$ is constant and independent of I. In hearing, as in many other senses, this is a fair approximation, but it is not exactly correct. In audition, there is general agreement that $\Delta I/I$ diminishes slowly as I increases. Figure 6.1 shows some representative data from Riesz's (1928) study along with a summary of a recent study by Jesteadt et al. (1977). The recent study used two pulsed sinusoids in a two-alternative forced-choice task; one sinusoid was the standard, the other the increment plus standard. Riesz's study employed a slow beating between two sinusoids, which is equivalent to the detection of a slow modulation of the amplitude of a single sinusoid (Rayleigh, 1894, Vol. I, pp. 21–24).

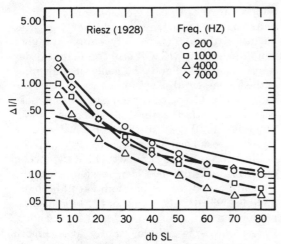

Figure 6.1. The Weber fraction for a sinusoid as a function of the level of the sinusoid at several different frequencies. The data is from Riesz (1928) using a modulation technique. The solid line is from Jesteadt, Wier, and Green (1977) using pulsed sinusoids. From "Intensity Discrimination as a Function of Frequency and Sensation Level" by W. Jesteadt, C.C. Wier, and D.M. Green, 1977, *Journal of the Acoustical Society of America*, p. 174. Copyright 1977 by the American Institute of Physics. Reprinted by permission.

The most striking feature of the recent measurements of Jesteadt et al. is that they found $\Delta I/I$ to be the same function of I at all frequencies tested (200 to 8000 Hz). All other modern studies using pulsed sinusoids and studying two or more frequencies have also found no significant changes in the Weber fraction with signal frequency (Dimmick & Olsen, 1941; Harris, 1963; Schacknow & Raab, 1973; Penner, Leshowitz, Cudahy, & Richard, 1974). The following equation used to summarize Jesteadt et al. data is

$$\Delta I/I = .463(I/I_0)^{-0.072}$$

where I_0 is the minimal audible intensity at that frequency (10 log I/I_0 is the sensation level of the sinusoid). The Jesteadt et al. data suggest that the difference limens for sounds of equal sensation level are equal. Regrettably, there is not much agreement on the exact size of the difference limen. For example, at 40 dB sensation level the following values of $\Delta I/I$ were determined by the indicated investigator: $\Delta I/I = 1.034$ [sic], Dimmick and Olson (1941); $\Delta I/I = 0.168$, Harris (1963); $\Delta I/I = 0.334$, Schacknow and Raab (1973); $\Delta I/I = 0.667$, Penner, Leshowitz, Cudahy, and Richard (1974); $\Delta I/I = 0.239$,

Jesteadt et al. (1977). Because differences among observers in the same experiment are generally small, this variability presumably rests on procedural differences. Note that the Weber fraction for noise was given previously (see above, Detection of Signals in Noise). Like sinusoids, it is independent of frequency (Green, 1960), but proportional to the square root of the bandwidth of the noise signal.

Theoretical interest in the difference limen has been stimulated by a number of models of the detection process that liken it to the process of detecting weak signals in a noisy communication channel. Siebert (1968, 1970) likens the neural impulses to a nonhomogeneous Poisson* process and the brain to an optimum statistical tester determining whether I or $I + \Delta I$ was presented. McGill and Goldberg (1968a, 1968b) assume a Poisson process but with a non-linear, compressive mapping of the number of neural counts and the intensity of the stimulus. Luce and Green (1974) assume the neural activity can be modeled by a renewal process and consider a decision rule based on the interarrival time between pulses. All models predict a decline in $\Delta I/I$ with I, but Siebert predicts the decline will be as the square root of I, whereas McGill and Goldberg and Luce and Green predict a slower decline because they assume a compressive relation between the number of counts and the stimulus intensity.

The McGill and Goldberg model is the simplest to derive and is a good example of this general approach. The number of neural impulses generated in response to a signal of intensity I is assumed to be Poisson distributed with mean and variance N, where the number of counts N follows Stevens' power law

$$N = K(I/I_0)^\gamma$$

for $I > I_0$, where I_0 is absolute threshold, and the power law exponent, γ, is about 0.3. Thus, using the binomial expansion,

$$\frac{N + \Delta N}{N} = \frac{K(I + \Delta I/I_0)^\gamma}{K(I/I_0)^\gamma}$$

$$= \left(\frac{I + \Delta I}{I}\right)^\gamma = 1 + \gamma \frac{\Delta I}{I}$$

*A Poisson process is one in which events occur randomly in time. Roughly, it could be constructed by dividing time into very small intervals, and determining whether or not an event occurs with a fixed probability independent of all other intervals. A nonhomogeneous Poisson process allows this probability to vary with time.

or

$$\Delta N = \gamma N (\Delta I / I)$$

The detectability index d' is the change in count rate divided by the standard deviation of the distribution of counts. Therefore,

$$d' = (\Delta N / N)^{1/2}$$

For $d' = 1.00$, which is 76 percent correct in two-alternative forced-choice,

$$\Delta I / I = \gamma^{-1} K^{-1/2} (I/I_o)^{-\gamma/2}$$

Assume $\gamma = .3$, the ratio $\Delta I / I$ should decline with an exponent of about 0.15, about twice what Jesteadt et al. observed empirically.

Interestingly, if we assume that the relation between N and I is governed by Fechner's law rather than Stevens' law, then

$$\Delta N = K \log_{10}(I/I_o)$$

and

$$\Delta N = K \log_{10} I + \Delta I / I \cong 0.434 K \Delta I / I$$

for $\Delta I \ll I$. Hence

$$d' = 0.434 (\Delta I / I) K^{1/2} [\log(I/I_o)]^{-1/2}$$

or,

$$\Delta I / I \propto [\log(I/I_o)]^{1/2}$$

This asserts that $\Delta I / I$ increases with I which is clearly inconsistent with all of the data. The potential linkage between McGill and Goldberg's "the near miss to Weber's law" and Stevens' "power law" has stimulated considerable interest in this topic. Investigators have seen the potential to link discrimination data to judgments of loudness. Since discrimination data are considerably more precise than direct estimates of loudness and show considerably less variability among observers, there are strong practical as well as theoretical reasons for pursuing this potential linkage.

Another quite different account of the near miss to Weber's law has been proposed by Viemeister (1972). Briefly, he notes that nonlinearity in the mechanical transduction process could possibly generate the slow decline in $\Delta I / I$ with I. Suppose, for example, that the proximal or effective pressure p' can be represented by a power series in the distal or measured pressure p

$$p' = \sum_{i=1}^{n} a_i p^i$$

Suppose further that the coefficients a_1, a_2, a_3, and so on, are of such magnitude that quantities such as $p^2(t)$ and $p^3(t)$ are only audible at higher signal levels. As we will see, the higher order terms, such as $p^2(t)$ and $p^3(t)$, generate harmonics of the fundamental. Therefore, if we increase the fundamental f by one dB, then a two dB increase occurs at $2f$ and a three dB increase at $3f$. Suppose the Weber fraction is constant and roughly the same at all frequencies. For purposes of illustration, let us assume that a difference of one dB is just audible. Then, as we increase the standard pressure, the harmonic at $2f$ becomes audible and a $1/2$ dB change at the fundamental produces a 1 dB change at $2f$, and that change, by hypothesis, is audible. Finally, at still more intense levels the next harmonic becomes audible and then a $1/3$ dB change at the fundamental produces a 1 dB change at the frequency $3f$. Viemeister (1972) has argued that this change with level in the Weber fraction is in general agreement with what we know about the amount of nonlinear distortion present in the auditory system.

A simple and effective test of Viemeister's hypothesis consists of determining the relation of $\Delta I / I$ and I in the presence of some masking noise that makes the higher harmonics of the fundamental inaudible. If the harmonics are inaudible, then Weber's law should be exactly true. Unfortunately, the empirical evidence is not entirely clear. Viemeister found that adding high-pass or band-pass noise about the signal frequency made $\Delta I / I$ largely independent of I.

Schacknow and Raab (1973) studied pure tone intensity discrimination at 250, 1000, 4000, and 7000 Hz. The change in $\Delta I / I$ with I was much the same at all frequencies. They argue that more distortion should be audible at 250 Hz than at 7000 Hz, and thus reject Viemeister's distortion hypothesis.

Penner et al. (1974) found that the change of $\Delta I / I$ with I is largely independent of frequency and evident even at 12,000 and 9000 Hz where the second harmonic's distortion should be inaudible. Moore and Raab (1974) also found that neither high nor band-pass noise eliminated the change of $\Delta I / I$ with I, only band-stop noise—a sinusoid presented with the noise gap—yields the result that $\Delta I / I$ was independent of I. Such results are inconsistent with the distortion hypothesis.

Theoretical Implications of Masking Data

Frequency Characteristics/Excitation Patterns

Masking or discrimination is the opposite of frequency analysis. If the auditory system can filter the masker from the signal, then masking should not occur. In the earliest quantitative study of pure tone masking, Wegel and Lane (1924) used the data to make inferences about the filtering properties of the auditory mechanism. More recent studies of masking are being used for the same purpose (Zwicker, 1970). In this section, we briefly review this effort and comment on the most recent topics, namely, psychophysical tuning curves and two-tone suppression.

Noise Masking-Critical Bands

Among the earliest inferences made from the data on sinusoidal signals masked by noise was that only a narrow band of noise surrounding the signal was effective in masking the signal. Fletcher (1940) was the first to suggest this hypothesis, and it was supported by data in which he systematically filtered the noise in different bands about the signal frequency and measured the signal threshold. For example, at 1000 Hz, as long as the noise width was larger than about 60 Hz, the signal threshold was independent of bandwidth. If the width was narrower than 60 Hz, the signal became easier to hear. This suggested that the hearing system has a "critical band" of frequencies, and that

Table 6.2. Extrapolated estimates of the width of the critical band at about 1000 Hz

Schafer, Gales, Shewmaker, and Thompson (1950)	62 Hz
Hamilton (1957)	140 Hz
Greenwood (1961) [see Patterson (1974) reinterpretation]	175 Hz or 66 Hz
Swets, Green, and Tanner (1962)	95 Hz
Bos and de Boer (1966)	124 Hz
Margolis and Small (1975)	57 Hz
Patterson (1976)	140 Hz
Small and Tyler (1978)	110 Hz
Spiegel (1979)	82 Hz

only those components are really effective in masking the signal.

Fletcher performed this experiment at several different signal frequencies and found that the critical bandwidth changed systematically, increasing the width at the higher frequencies. Fletcher also suggested another way to estimate the critical band. This method rests on two assumptions: (1) that the band is essentially rectangular, and (2) that the signal reaches threshold when the signal power equals the total noise power, that is, when

$$P = WN_o$$

where P is the signal power at threshold, W is the critical bandwidth in cycles per second and N_o is the noise power density of the noise. Zwicker, Flottorp, and Stevens (1957) have dubbed this method of determining a critical band the *critical ratio* method, since W is the ratio of P/N_o. Obviously, this latter method makes two assumptions, but it provides an extremely easy way of estimating W, and results from the critical-ratio method used by Fletcher to construct his estimates of the critical band.

Fletcher's original experiment has been repeated with minor variations by a number of other investigators. The extrapolated estimate of the width of the critical band at about 1000 Hz is listed in Table 6.2. Fletcher's original estimate of 60 Hz is probably small and Zwicker's (1961) proposal of 160 Hz, based largely on nonmasking data, is clearly too large. Recent research on this topic has explored both experimental and theoretical methods to determine the shape of the auditory filter (Patterson, 1974; Patterson, 1976; Patterson & Henning, 1977; Patterson & Nimmo-Smith, 1980; Glasberg, Moore, & Nimmo-Smith, 1984).

Psychophysical Tuning Curves

In the previous chapter, the authors described the tuning curve associated with each auditory fiber. Recently, a psychophysical procedure has been proposed that produces curves closely resembling the physiological ones. These new curves are called psychophysical tuning curves (Zwicker, 1974). Let us briefly review the rationale of this procedure.

Consider a weak sinusoidal signal presented only 5 to 10 dB above absolute threshold. The only fibers capable of responding to that signal must be restricted to a narrow patch along the

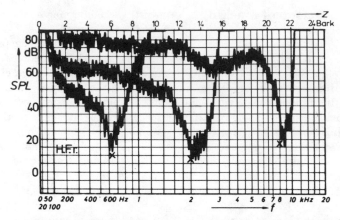

Figure 6.2. Three psychophysical tuning curves, from E. Zwicker (1974). The level of the masker is plotted on the ordinate. The signal frequency is either 630 Hz, 2 kHz, or 8 kHz. From "On a Psychoacoustical Equivalent of Tuning Curves" in *Facts and Models in Hearing* (p. 134) by E. Zwicker and E. Terhardt (eds.), 1974, New York: Springer-Verlag. Copyright 1974 by Springer-Verlag. Reprinted by permission.

basilar membrane, where the fibers have a characteristic frequency very near the frequency of the signal. Other fibers with different characteristic frequencies cannot detect the signal, because they will only respond to that frequency at much larger amplitudes. Now we select other sinusoidal frequencies as maskers, and vary their level until they interfere with the detection of the signal. At these other frequencies and levels, the masker must be producing sufficient excitation at a characteristic frequency equal to the signal to interfere with its perception. Thus, the resulting curve must strongly resemble the physiological tuning curve. Zwicker (1974) fixed the signal in level and frequency but adjusted the level and frequency of the masker and produced the data shown in Figure 6.2. The strong resemblance to physiological tuning curves is apparent.

In the following years, many other investigators have explored this procedure. Moore (1978) has systematically compared the tuning curves obtained with a simultaneous procedure (signal and masker both on at the same time) with a forward masking procedure (a brief signal is presented after the masker is terminated). He confirmed an earlier suggestion by Wightman, McGee, and Kramer (1977) that the tuning curve is sharper in forward masking than in simultaneous masking. The forward masking procedure has the advantage of avoiding the beats and other interactions of signal and masker.

An important practical and theoretical problem is how and why the shape of the psychophysical tuning curve changes with signal level. The practical reason relates to the desire to compare tuning curves taken from normal and hard-of-hearing observers. The abnormal observer will by necessity require a more intense signal. The theoretical reason is that we wish to understand in detail the process that generates the original curve so we can understand why it changes shape with level. Vogten (1974) demonstrated that the slope of the high frequency side of the curve changed little with level while on the low frequency side the slope decreased as the signal level was raised. This confirmed other previous studies of tone-on-tone masking (Egan & Hake, 1950; Ehmer, 1959; Small, 1959; Wegel & Lane, 1924; Zwicker, 1958; Greenwood, 1971). Vogten (1974) also noted a small progressive shift in the tip of the tuning curve to lower frequencies with increased signal level, a result still not fully understood.

Johnson-Davies and Patterson (1979) have clearly demonstrated the reasons for the general changes in the shape of the tuning curve with signal level. As signal level is increased, a wider patch along the basilar membrane is stimulated by the signal. In the presence of a low frequency masker, the higher frequency fibers are used to detect the signal, for a high frequency masker the lower frequency fibers are used to detect the signal. Fibers remote from the signal frequency and, of course, farthest in frequency from those stimulated by the masker are the ones effective in detecting the signal. This general hypothesis has been called *off-frequency listening*. Johnson-Davies and Patterson (1979) present a general means to test whether this has occurred. They first find the level of two maskers, one on each side of the signal, that just masks the signal when used separately. They then turn one masker on at a constant level about 10 dB below this determined level, and redetermine the level of the opposite mask that just obscures the signal. If no off-frequency listening occurs, then the level should be the same as previously determined. If that level has changed, we have evidence for off-frequency listening.

One means of determining if the tuning curves are similar in shape as a function of level is to use a constant noise background. The signal can then be set at a constant sensation level, say 5 to 10 dB. Tuning curves can then be determined by varying the frequency and level of a sinusoidal masker. Green, Shelton, Picardi, and Hafter (1981), Nelson (1980) and Wightman (1981) found that the tuning curves were nearly the same shape and independent of absolute signal level when noise was used to hold sensation level constant.

Two-Tone Suppression

While the preceding discussion of the critical band likens the auditory system to a simple resonance filter, physiological studies of the auditory periphery have found directly inhibitory actions of one tone on another (Sachs & Kiang, 1968). Such findings are of considerable interest because they raise the specter of lateral inhibition, a process ubiquitous in other sensory modalities, especially vision.

Briefly, what Sachs and Kiang found was that if one tone is adjusted to produce a small but reliable response on an auditory fiber, one could find other tones that would appear to block or inhibit the action of the first tone. These secondary or suppressing tones need to be greater in level than the first tone and close in frequency. The physiological picture is that each fiber is excited by a range of frequencies with a high degree of tuning. Surrounding that area of excitation there are other inhibitory areas, that is, where combinations of frequency and intensity act to inhibit the fiber. Early attempts to demonstrate such areas of inhibition psychophysically were unsuccessful (Carterette,

Friedman, & Lovell, 1969; Small, 1975). Houtgast (1972) was the first to demonstrate what has become known as psychophysical suppression, and the topic has become a lively one in recent times.

Psychophysical suppression experiments typically employ (1) a masker, (2) a signal, often of the same frequency as the masker, and (3) a suppressor, usually slightly higher or lower in frequency than the masker. Application of the suppressor is successful if it makes the signal easier to hear, that is, if it suppresses the masker. Houtgast believed that any attempt to demonstrate suppression would fail if the signal and suppressor were simultaneously present. He reasoned that the suppressor would act on both the masker and the signal leaving the signal-to-masker ratio unchanged, and hence, the signal threshold would not be measurably different in the two conditions—masker alone or masker with suppressor. He, therefore, devised a non-simultaneous masking technique called the pulsation method. With this method, he could successfully demonstrate suppression-like effects. We need not concern ourselves with his technique; a forward masking paradigm will work as well, as Houtgast also demonstrated. In a forward masking procedure, a brief signal is presented shortly after the masker is terminated. The suppressor, when applied, is simultaneous with the masker, but terminated when the signal is presented. Thus, presumably, the suppressor acts only on the masker, not on the signal. Application of the suppressor in this way can make the signal 10 to 20 dB easier to hear. Many experiments have explored various parameters of this paradigm: Houtgast (1972, 1973, 1974); Shannon (1976); Duifhuis (1976); Tyler and Small (1977); and Abbas (1978). Similar results will be obtained if one uses a narrow band of noise as the masker and a tone as the suppressor. Alternatively, one can simply broaden the noise; the flanks of the noise presumably become suppressors, and the signal becomes easier to hear as the noise is widened (Houtgast, 1972, 1973, 1974; Terry & Moore, 1977; Weber, 1978; O'Malley & Feth, 1978; Jesteadt & Javel, 1978; Weber & Green, 1978, 1979).

Theoretical accounts of the suppression effects are also being studied. Duifhuis (1976) has proposed an explicit physiological model of the suppression effects, which we discuss in detail elsewhere (see Nonlinearity phenomena).

Others, in particular Terry and Moore (1977), have described suppression in terms of more central mechanisms. They believe that the addition of the suppressor to the masker produces some new "qualitative difference between masker and probe" that makes the signal (probe) easier to hear. One possible phenomenal cue is a pitch shift. Since the signal and masker frequency are often the same, the addition of the suppressor changes the pitch of the masking complex, and the presentation of the signal causes a slight pitch shift.

One should appreciate that suppressionlike effects can be observed in both forward and backward masking experiments (Weber & Green, 1979). Stimulus manipulations often affect the results quite differently in forward and backward masking. In backward masking, suppression of nearly 30 dB can be obtained by placing the suppression stimulus in the contralateral ear, that is, masker and signal in left ear and suppressor in the right (Weber & Green, 1979). Such a result is clearly inconsistent with a peripheral suppression mechanism and consistent with a more central explanation. In the same study, they found that a contralateral suppressor was only slightly effective (3 dB) in forward masking. They cite a number of other differences to support their conclusion that suppression observed in forward masking is largely determined by peripheral processes, whereas suppression observed in backward masking is dominated by other central factors.

NONLINEARITY PHENOMENA

Nonlinear phenomena are a topic of major interest in current auditory thinking for two reasons. First, they alter and modify the distal or external stimulus and generate a new proximal stimulus or internal spectrum. Knowledge of this internal spectrum may allow us to understand psychophysical results that appear mysterious and unfathomable when only the external stimulus is known. Second, nonlinear phenomena may be an inherent property of cochlear mechanics. Understanding this nonlinearity would materially advance our knowledge of cochlear filtering, neural transduction, and, perhaps, even later aspects of neural processing such as two-tone suppression. Although the original observations in this area are very old, for many

years the topic languished. Some recent studies have revitalized the subject and illuminated the topic in a new and important manner. As one might expect, given such a difficult and complex topic, our understanding is far from complete. But recent progress gives considerable reason for optimism.

This review will stress the methods used to study nonlinear phenomena and will begin with a description of how nonlinear processes are studied and measured. Next, we will summarize the major theoretical positions, and review some of the more salient findings. Finally, we will briefly describe some implications of these nonlinear phenomena for other substantive areas of psychoacoustic research.

More emphasis will be devoted to theoretical ideas than to empirical fact. This asymmetry is intentional because of the complicated nature of nonlinear phenomena. First, interactions abound, and empirical relations that are true under one set of conditions may be completely different under other conditions. Some theoretical structure is needed to indicate the range over which this relation may be expected to hold and to identify the critical nature of the other experimental parameters. Second, individual differences are the rule rather than the exception in this area; contradictory results are common. Again, theory is needed to suggest how these differences can be reconciled.

Let us begin by considering some properties of a *linear* system. Sinusoids are eigenvectors of a linear time-invariant system. A sinusoid in passing through such a linear system may be altered in amplitude and phase, but the frequency remains the same. Therefore, a linear time-invariant system guarantees that a sinusoid of some frequency at its output arises from a sinusoid with the same frequency at the input. For a nonlinear system, that implication does not necessarily, or even usually, hold. A component of some frequency at the output may mean that the same frequency component is present at the input, or it may be produced by an interaction of other input components with different frequencies. Thus, the basic frequency composition of the stimulus may be completely altered by a nonlinear process. Since frequency analysis is a pervasive and central property of practically all auditory phenomena, it is important to understand how these new frequency components arise. The search for such newly created components was, in fact, the basis of the earliest studies of nonlinear aspects of hearing.

Methods

Tartini (1754) is usually credited with first reporting a third tone that was audible during a simultaneous sounding of two other tones. Other investigators, including Weber (1829) and König (1876), have also investigated what became known as *combination* or *distortion* tones. Helmholtz (1862) begins Part II of his *Sensations of Tone* with a chapter on "Combination Tones," and their importance in matters of musical consonance and disonance is also pursued in subsequent chapters. This early history is reviewed by Plomp (1965). In the report of Plomp's experimental work, we find the levels and frequencies at which different observers are able to detect the presence of these combination tones. In his technique, Plomp presented two sinusoids called *primary* tones. The intensity of these tones is varied and the observer is asked at what level the combination tone becomes evident. As we will discuss shortly, the frequency of potential distortion components can be predicted from the frequencies of the primaries. Sometimes other auxiliary oscillators are employed. Plomp used one oscillator at the frequency of the combination tone to direct the observer's attention to a given frequency. The second one was slightly mistuned and would beat with the distortion component once it was audible. By successively listening to the primaries and then one of the two auxiliary oscillators, the observer could determine the level at which the new tone is, in fact, evident. Thresholds for the levels of the primaries at which these combination tones appear are greatly different for different observers. In one of Plomp's conditions, the standard deviation, over 18 observers, is 12 dB and the range 28.5 dB.

Plomp's procedure establishes the existence or presence of certain combination tones. Some inferences about the nature of the nonlinear process can be deduced solely on the basis of the frequencies of these combination tones. But more could be learned if the amplitude and phase of these combination tones were also known. Obviously, the preceding technique is inadequate to provide this information, and hence other methods must be devised. Loudness judgment could be used to estimate the combination tone's amplitude, but such judgments are highly variable, and they would be affected by masking from the primary tones that produce the distortion product.

The method of best beats was one technique used in an attempt to quantify the amplitude of these distortion products. In this method, the observer varied the amplitude of an external sinusoid tuned near the frequency of the internal combination tone. Two ordinary tones produce the loudest beats when their amplitudes are equal. The amplitude of the external sinusoid producing the loudest beats was, therefore, used as an estimate of the combination tone amplitude. The method of best beats was first used by Wegel and Lane (1924), but the results obtained with this method have been subjected to two quite different interpretations (see Green, 1976, pp. 241–243). As a result Wegel and Lane's method is seldom used nowadays. Today, the best available technique is the cancellation method.

The cancellation technique and the related terminology can most easily be understood through an example. Suppose we present as *primary* tones sinusoids at 1300 and 1500 Hz. At high levels (e.g., 90 dB SPL), they produce many distortion products, one component of which is at 200 Hz. We estimate the magnitude of the 200 Hz combination tone with a third tone, called the *cancellation* tone. By adjusting the amplitude and phase of this cancellation tone, we attempt to remove any audible 200 Hz component. As one can imagine, this is a judgment of some subtlety. To help us determine if the cancellation is complete, we introduce a fourth tone with a frequency a few cycles away from the tone we are trying to cancel. If a beat is heard when the fourth tone is sounded, then we infer that the cancellation is not complete, and continue to adjust the phase and amplitude of the cancellation tone. If no beat is evident, then apparently the cancellation is complete. The amplitude of the cancellation tone is an estimate of the amplitude of the distortion product. Its phase is assumed to be directly (180 degrees) opposite that of the cancellation tone. Zwicker (1955) was the first to use this technique, and it has become standard procedure with modern investigators.

The technique is reasonably precise if the

distortion products are clearly audible. If the distortion products are near threshold, however, then the nulling adjustments are more difficult, and the adjusted amplitude is, relatively, more variable. The major drawback of the technique is that it is extremely slow and requires sophisticated and very patient listeners. Another procedure for measuring the amplitude of a distortion product is the pulsation technique of Houtgast (1974). It has not been widely used and we postpone its description until the relevant substantive material has been introduced. As we shall see, interpreting the results of cancellation or pulsation experiments depends on the assumptions one makes concerning the nature of the nonlinear process. Nonlinear systems have no simple taxonomy; they are many and varied, and only a handful have been explored with any degree of thoroughness.

Classical Power-Series Nonlinearity

In this discussion, we shall consider only nonlinear systems that have no memory; that is, the present value of the output can be predicted if we know only the present value of the input. Although the input pressure is a function of time, as is output, we will express the output, y, as a function of the input, x, and ignore the time variable, t, because the relation between y and x is true at any time. Probably the best known nonlinearity is the finite power-series or polynomial nonlinearity (Helmholtz, 1862; Fletcher, 1929),

$$y = a_0 + a_1x^1 + a_2x^2 + a_3x^3 + a_4x^4 \ldots$$

$$+ a_nx^n = \sum_{i=0}^{n} a_ix^i$$

where a_i are constants. Since only variations in pressure are audible, we can ignore the constant a_0. The usual assumption is that the values of the other constants, a_i, are such that for small variation in pressure level, where the range of x is small, only the linear term a_1x is important and the higher order terms can be ignored. This state of affairs is sometimes called *small-signal linearity*. At high pressure levels, the higher-order terms become increasingly important. In practice, however, only the first three terms, x, x^2, and x^3 have received much attention.

One advantage of this particular model of a nonlinear system is that it is relatively easy to calculate how each of the terms affects a sinusoidal signal or combinations of two or more sinusoids. Consider first how each term of the power series affects a single sinusoidal input of frequency, f. The term x^1 produces a component with frequency, f, since it is a linear term. The term x^2 produces a component with frequency, $2f$, since $\sin^2 \alpha = 1/2 - 1/2 \cos 2\alpha$. The term x^3 produces two components with frequencies f and $3f$, since $\sin^3 \alpha = 3/4 \cos \alpha + 1/4 \cos 3\alpha$. The frequencies of the components produced by the higher order terms can be determined by repeated applications of these two identities. For example, the term $x^5 = (x^2)^3 = (1/2 - 1/2 \cos 2\alpha)^3$ produces components of frequency $2f$, $4f$, and $6f$.

Consider next how the terms of the polynomial generate combination tones when the input consists of a pair of sinusoids of frequency, f_1 and f_2; we assume $f_2 > f_1$. Here the rule can be summarized fairly simply because the x^i term generates components having the frequencies

$$k_1f_1 \pm k_2f_2$$

for all $k_j = 0, 1, 2, \ldots, i$ such that $k_1 + k_2 = i$. A pure cubic distortion, then, produces components of $3f_1$, $3f_2$ and $2f_1 \pm f_2$ and $2f_2 \pm f_1$.

The amplitude of the distortion produced at any of these components will obviously depend on the constants a_i of the power series and the amplitude of the input signals. The constants a_i determine the level at which the various distortion components can be detected. The growth of these distortion components as a function of the level of the primary components is also determined by the exact values of the constants. Molnar (1974) has shown that by judicious selection of the constants a_i the growth of the distortion product as a function of the level of the primaries can be almost any value one wishes, at least over some finite range. Considerable effort has been devoted to treating the series as if it were truncated and contained no terms larger than x^2 and x^3. This effort has been expended because two distortion components, each produced by one of these nonlinearities, are most evident under a variety of conditions. These two components are the simple difference frequency, $f_2 - f_1$, and the cubic distortion product, $2f_1 - f_2$. The other distortion products have frequencies higher than those of the primaries and hence are subjected to considerable masking. Little is known of the amplitude

Table 6.3. Asymptotic slope of level of distortion product versus level of primary or primaries*

		$L_1 = L_2$	L_1 Varied		L_2 Varied	
			$L_1 < L_2$	$L_1 > L_2$	$L_2 < L_1$	$L_2 > L_1$
Classical	$2f_1 - f_2$	3	2	1	2	1
power series	$f_2 - f_1$	2	1	1	1	1
Normalized	$2f_1 - f_2$	1	2	0	1	-1
power series	$f_2 - f_1$	1	1	0	1	0
vth Law	$2f_1 - f_2$	v	2	$v - 1$	1	$v - 2$
component amplitude	$f_2 - f_1$	v	1	$v - 1$	1	$v - 1$
vth Law	$2f_1 - f_2$	1	2	0	1	-1
cancellation prediction	$f_2 - f_1$	1	1	0	1	0
vth Law	$2f_1 - f_2$	1	$2/v$	$1 - 1/v$	$1/v$	$1 - 2/v$
pulsation technique	$f_2 - f_1$	1	$1/v$	$1 - 1/v$	$1/v$	$1 - 1/v$

*Both coordinates logarithmic, i.e. decibels

behavior of these higher frequency distortion components.

The classical power-series theory predicts how the $f_2 - f_1$ and $2f_1 - f_2$ components should grow as a function of the level of the primaries. The first and second rows of Table 6.3, marked classical power series, show these predictions. The three major columns of Table 6.3 show how the distortion products change when the primary level is varied. Three cases are considered: both primaries are increased together, $L_1 = L_2$; or the lower frequency primary L_1 varies while the higher is fixed; or the higher frequency primary L_2 varies while the lower is fixed. The table gives the expected asymptotic slope of the change in level of the distortion product versus the level of the primary or primaries—and both coordinates are assumed to be logarithmic, for example, decibels. For example, a 10 dB increase in the level of both primaries should increase the cubic difference tone $2f_1 - f_2$ by 30 dB. If $L_1 < L_2$, and it is varied with L_2 fixed in level, then the cubic difference tone should grow 20 dB for each 10 dB increase in L_1. Such disproportionate change in the distortion products with changes in the primary should be easily noted. The bulk of experimental evidence shows a very different result (Zwicker, 1968). In a recent summary by Humes (1980), the measured slope for the $L_1 = L_2$ condition is about one or slightly less, given that $f_2/f_1 < 1.2$. The range of measured values, over seven independent determinations,

is 0.6 to 1.1. Support for the classical theory is also lacking if we consider the empirical results obtained with the simple difference tone $f_2 - f_1$. A 10 dB change in two equal amplitude primaries should produce a 20 dB change in the level of the difference tone. The average of seven determinations, again for $f_2/f_1 < 1.2$, is 12.6 dB. Clearly, something is amiss with the classical power-series hypothesis.

Normalized Power Series

Goldstein (1967) has suggested a simple modification of the power-series hypothesis that produced more acceptable predictions concerning the growth of distortion components. He suggested that each term in the power series was normalized by the peak amplitude of the input signal, that is, the ith term in the series was divided by the peak amplitude raised to the $i - 1$ power. The amplitude of the cubic difference tone would then vary as $(A_1^2 A_2)/(A_1 + A_2)^2$, where A_1 is the amplitude of f_1 and A_2 is the amplitude of f_2. For $A_1 = A_2$, the cubic difference tone should grow linearly with the amplitude of the primaries. This result is strikingly confirmed in Goldstein's own data and is certainly close to the results obtained by other investigators.

The slope predictions for the normalized power-series hypothesis are shown as the third and fourth rows of Table 6.3. Goldstein used the phrase "essential" nonlinearity to describe these predictions, remarking that this was not a hypothesis, but rather that for equal amplitude primaries "the relative level of the cubic combination tone is almost independent of the stimulus level." For $f_2/f_1 = 1.2$, he found the cubic difference tone to be about 20 dB below the level of the primaries over a range of nearly 50 dB! In some cases the level of the distortion product should be independent of the level of the primaries (0 entry in the table) and such data have been observed.

It must be pointed out that in all of the preceding discussion an unstated premise of the analysis is the assumption of small-signal linearity. The force of this assumption is that the level of the cancellation tone provides a direct measure of the level of the distortion product. The cancellation tone is assumed to pass through the process in a linear manner because it is small relative to the level of the primary tones, and only the primary tones are subjected to the nonlinear operator. The assumption is plausible; almost all physical systems will distort at extreme amplitudes, even if they are linear for moderate signals. But the assumption becomes strained when coupled with a normalization assumption. Consider two equal amplitude primaries of say 60 dB producing a 40 dB distortion product. Now raise the primary level to 80 dB, and the distortion product will be 60 dB. The cancellation tone is treated linearly, even when its level is the same as the primary that formerly caused distortion. Perhaps dissatisfaction with this state of affairs led Smoorenburg to explore another hypothesis about aural nonlinearity.

Smoorenburg's Power Law of Nonlinearity

Smoorenburg (1972 a and b) introduced the idea of a pure power-law nonlinearity and reinterpreted the results of the cancellation experiment. Consider a pure power-law nonlinearity such as

$$y = \text{sign}(x)[x]^v$$

where v is an exponent, not necessarily integer, and sign (x) maintains the same sign at the output as is present at the input. Other versions of this same hypothesis assume that the output is zero for all negative input values. Note that there is no small-signal linearity. All signals are distorted no matter how small the value of x.

Exact analysis of such systems is difficult, but some work has been done by Feuerstein (1957), Smoorenburg (1972 a and b), and Duifhuis (1976). We will simply use their results in this discussion, but a few points can be derived from very simple considerations. A pure power-law device will introduce new frequency components when stimulated by a sinusoid or a combination of two sinusoids, unless the exponent, v, is equal to 1. Since the transfer function is monotonic, the output waveform will repeat only when the input does. For this reason, the output wave must have the same period as the input wave. All the distortion products will be integer multiples of the fundamental, because of Fourier theorem. Suppose we stimulate with two frequencies, f_1 and f_2. If the amplitudes of the two primaries are scaled by the same constant k, then the output changes by k^v. Since we can express the output as a sum of sinusoids, each component of the summation will also be scaled by k^v, and, in particular, any distortion components will change by k^v. Thus, if we change the input by 10 dB, then all output components will be changed by the same amount, v times 10 dB.

The asymptotic behavior for such distortion products is presented in the fifth and sixth rows of Table 6.3. Unlike the previous hypothesis which assumed small-signal linearity, the component amplitudes do not give a sufficient description of the experimental outcomes, because the prediction of the experimental results is more complicated for the vth law device. This occurs because the test tone, the sinusoid used to estimate the amplitude of the distortion component, is also subjected to distortion.

Consideration of this hypothesis means that we must reinterpret the cancellation method to estimate the amplitude of the distortion component. According to this theory, the primaries create some internal component at the distortion frequency, say $2f_1 - f_2$. We set our external cancellation component at this same frequency and vary the amplitude and phase to null the distortion component. We next increase both primaries by 10 dB and repeat the process. If the levels of the primaries are equal ($L_1 = L_2$), then the internal distortion should increase $10v$ dB (see rows 5 and 6 of Table 6.3). But how much must we increase the level of the external cancellation tone to increase its level by v times 10 dB? The answer, of course, is 10 dB, because the cancellation tone must pass through the vth-law nonlinearity just as the primaries do. Thus, when the primaries increase 10 dB in level, we will need to increase the level of the cancellation tone by 10 dB to achieve the null. Our cancellation procedure makes it seem as if the nonlinearity were self-normalizing.

The predictions for the vth-law device, as taken from Duifhuis, are shown in Table 6.3 as the seventh and eighth rows. The predictions are exactly the same as the normalized power series hypothesis.

At this point, we will describe the pulsation technique that we referred to earlier. The rationale for this method is quite simple. Suppose we alternate the primaries with a pure tone whose frequency is equal to that of the distortion component. A 4 Hz rate of alternation is typical. The listener adjusts the level of the pure tone until there is no apparent fluctuation in loudness at that frequency. Presumably the lack of fluctuation means that the level of the pure tone and the level of the distortion component are nearly equal. When the two are unequal, the loudness fluctuates or pulses, hence the name pulsation technique or pulsation threshold.

What will the vth-law device predict if we use the pulsation technique to estimate the level of the distortion product? Since the effective level of the pulsation tone changes by v dB for every 1 dB of change in the actual (external) level, the estimated growth of the distortion product will be altered by a factor of $1/v$. The last two rows of Table 6.3 show these predictions; they are simply the expected growth of the internal distortion component, the factors given in rows five and six of the table, multiplied by $1/v$.

But what is the value of v, and how do we measure it? Note that if $v = 1$ then the component amplitudes and the predicted experimental results are all the same, and indeed the same as the normalized power series of Goldstein (see Table 6.3). But if $v = 1$, the device would be linear. Given that $v \neq 1$, the differences in the predictions of the vth-law model for the cancellation and pulsation results present a possible way to estimate the parameter v. This approach has been taken by Smoorenburg, but with only limited success. Suppose we fix L_1 and vary L_2. Qualitatively, the results are in rough agreement with the predictions if we

assume v is somewhat less than 1, say 0.6 to 0.8. This value for the exponent is near that obtained with magnitude estimation, about 0.6. The problem is that the slope for the growth of the distortion product is smaller for the pulsation method than for the cancellation method when $L_1 = L_2$, especially so when f_2/f_1 is small. For both conditions, the slope should be unity (see Table 6.3). Duifhuis (1976) has discussed this issue and proposed a tentative hypothesis to resolve the discrepancy. He suggests that the nonlinearity generated at the site of the primaries acts as an additional input component. Consequently, it is analyzed at the place along the membrane corresponding to that distortion frequency.* For example, f_1 and f_2 generate a component $2f_1 - f_2$ analyzed at the place corresponding to that frequency. The force of this hypothesis is to suggest that the distortion product undergoes two nonlinearities, one at the site of the primaries where it is generated, and the second at the site corresponding to the frequency at which it is detected. Duifhuis shows how this hypothesis is in rough agreement with all of Smoorenburg's results.

Experimental Results

While the preceding theory is extremely speculative, it is consistent with an increasing body of evidence to suggest that there are two types of nonlinearity. The first nonlinearity operates when the two primary frequencies are far apart and obeys the classical model. The second nonlinearity operates when f_2/f_1 is less than 1.2 or 1.3 and obeys a vth law nonlinearity. This suggestion is consistent with a great deal of previous theoretical work including that of Goldstein (1967), Pfeiffer (1970), Engebretson and Eldredge (1968), and Duifhuis (1976). It is also forcefully stated in a recent review by Humes (1980), who argues that the failure to recognize the importance of the f_2/f_1 ratio may well account for most of the discrepant claims found in the literature on distortion products. It has long been recognized (Zwicker, 1955; Goldstein, 1967) that the f_2/f_1 ratio has a

---

*Formby and Sachs (1980) have shown that the tuning curve for a distortion component is the same as it is for a real component. Thus, it is probable that the distortion component is detected at the same cochlear site as a real component of the same frequency.

pronounced effect on the size of the distortion product. Humes suggests the ratio also affects the growth rate, that is, the exponent v.

But to anyone who has reviewed the experimental evidence in this area, it is also clear that there are large individual differences among observers. This fact was confirmed in Plomp's (1965) investigation of the detection of combination tones and can be seen in other data on the growth of distortion products. Smoorenburg (1974) shows some data on cancellation level of the cubic difference tone as a function of L_2 level with L_1 fixed. According to Table 6.3, the cancellation tone should increase with slope one until the level of L_1 is reached and then decrease with a slope of -1. One observer shows data almost exactly in accord with that prediction; the second observer shows the slope one increase, but at the level of L_1 the increase stops and the distortion component remains roughly constant in level. Minor adjustments of individual parameters can change the level and amount of distortion to fit individual observers, but it is difficult to believe that the nonlinear process itself is different for different observers. Duifhuis (1980) has recently studied a number of observers in a suppression paradigm, and the results of that study may well be explained in terms of a distortion hypothesis. He fails to find any general trend that is true for all observers. This failure to understand individual differences, or to have theories that can account for them, is a major impediment to our further understanding of this area.

Summary

Recent experiments suggest that nonlinear phenomena play a major role in a number of auditory processes. The classical power-series approach is clearly inadequate to explain any of the combination tones produced by primaries located near each other in frequency, $f_2/f_1 < 1.2$. For more widely spaced primaries, a power series approach may be valid, but these distortion products are probably less interesting, since they play a minor role in most auditory processing. The vth law nonlinearity or the normalized power series predicts reasonably well the data obtained with $f_2/f_1 < 1/2$. The vth law nonlinearity is very difficult to analyze analytically, however, and to calculate its predictions in all but the simplest case is nearly

impossible. Unfortunately, large individual differences are seen in practically any empirical study and, as yet, the theoretical accounts provide no very convenient means of accounting for such individual differences.

We should stress that the study of the amplitude and frequency of distortion tones is simply one means of studying the nature of the nonlinearity in the hearing process. The importance of this topic is that understanding this nonlinearity may permit us to understand other important hearing phenomena. Generally, the distortion products themselves are fairly small, relative to the primaries, and their existence may only be important in understanding certain second-order effects. A good example of this application will occur when we discuss the results of pitch-shift experiments. Here the distortion components supplement the multi-tonal complexes and extend the spectrum to include successive harmonic components above and below those present in the original experiment. Understanding this augmented spectrum allow us to predict correctly the pitch of the shifted primaries.

But understanding the nonlinear process may also provide us with a means of understanding other psychoacoustic effects that initially seem unrelated. A good example of this is Duifhuis's compressive nonlinearity theory. Duifhuis (1976) proposes a three-stage process: (1) a first filter, probably the mechanical filtering observed in the amplitude of motion as a function of position along the basilar membrane, (2) a compressive nonlinearity, such as the vth law device, and (3) a hair cell sensitivity that depends on the direction of the radial component of motion. With this model, he attempts to explain both psychophysical suppression and the suppression observed with two tones in physiological experiments (Duifhuis, 1980).

PITCH PERCEPTION

Introduction

At one time, the topic of pitch perception was the central topic of auditory theory. Since the middle of the 19th century, when Helmholtz set forth the resonance theory of hearing, the dominant view was that different neural elements code differences in frequency by virtue of their place along the cochlea and that the vigor of the neural response codes intensity. The observation of von Békésy, in the early 20th century, confirmed that the mechanisms of resonance caused different frequencies to vibrate at a different place along the basilar membrane, and thereby established a condition that is necessary but not sufficient for any place theory. But temporal theory was not completely abandoned and certain nagging problems, such as the missing fundamental, continued to require special explanation. Schouten (1938–40) took hold of these issues in a series of brilliant experiments, and reshaped the entire field. For a time, place theory was clearly on the defensive. In the last two decades, however, place theory has been reestablished but in a way that is completely different from its former, simpler self. Auditory nonlinear distortion, always necessary in the earlier place theory, has also undergone enormous conceptual change. This section will recount these developments and try to outline the main empirical facts, as well as the major theoretical issues.

While the major question is in essence physiological—how is a physical dimension of the stimulus encoded—the basic evidence has come almost entirely from psychophysical experiments. These proceed by having the observer compare one or more stimulus complexes. The manipulations of the stimulus and particularly the spectrum of the stimulus are often involved and intricate. To appreciate the force of these experiments will require some knowledge of signal specification and Fourier analysis. We will briefly review some of the crucial background and terminology here. For a more extended discussion of this material, E. de Boer's (1976) review of residue pitch is highly recommended.

Fourier Analysis and Synthesis

Almost all the stimuli that produce a clear perception of pitch are periodic; that is, they repeat themselves after an interval called the period of the waveform. Thus, periodic stimuli of period T are of the form

$$p(t) = p(t + T) \quad \text{for all } t.$$

One simple periodic stimulus is the sinusoid

$$s_i(t) = a_i \sin (2f_i t + \theta_i)$$

where the reciprocal of the period, $1/T = f_i$ is

the frequency of the sinusoid, usually expressed in cycles per second or Hz, a_i is the amplitude of the sinusoid and θ_i the phase, that is, the initial amplitude when $t = 0$. By changing θ the waveform can be shifted in time, for example if θ is such that the amplitude is maximum, a_i, at $t = 0$ we have what is called a cosine wave.

For periodic stimuli, $p(t)$ with period T, Fourier's theorem essentially asserts that the stimulus $p(t)$ can be represented by a sum of sinusoids where the frequencies of the sinusoids have definite properties, i.e.

$$p(t) = \sum_{i=0} s_i(t)$$

and the frequencies of the sinusoids present in the waveform $p(t)$ have a definite relation to its period, T. Specifically when f_o is called the *fundamental* frequency.

$$f_o = \frac{1}{T} \text{ and } f_i = if_o$$

Hence if the period of the wave is 5 msec, the *fundamental* frequency $f_o = 200$ Hz and the only other frequencies present in the periodic wave are multiples of 200 Hz. The first multiple, 400 Hz, is called the second harmonic, 600 Hz the third harmonic, and so on. Naturally some of the harmonics may be missing, that is, any a_i may be zero, including a_o, the amplitude of the fundamental. However, no other frequency can be present; for example, no component at a frequency of 325 Hz is present in a wave with a period of 5 msec. Only the reciprocal of the period and multiples of that fundamental frequency can comprise a periodic waveform. We call a periodic wave with two or more sinusoids present a complex wave; the individual sinusoids are called components.

Fourier analysis and Fourier synthesis are simply different ways of viewing the basic identity. If we start with the components and add them together, this is synthesis; if we begin with the complex wave and determine the amplitude and phase of the components, this is analysis. Figure 6.3 shows some examples of complex periodic waveforms. In part (a) we have ten sinusoids of equal amplitude. The fundamental is 200 Hz. That component and all nine harmonics are at maximum amplitude for $t = 0$; i.e., θ_1 has been chosen to make them all cosine waves. The amplitude of that peak is exactly equal to the sum of the amplitudes of the

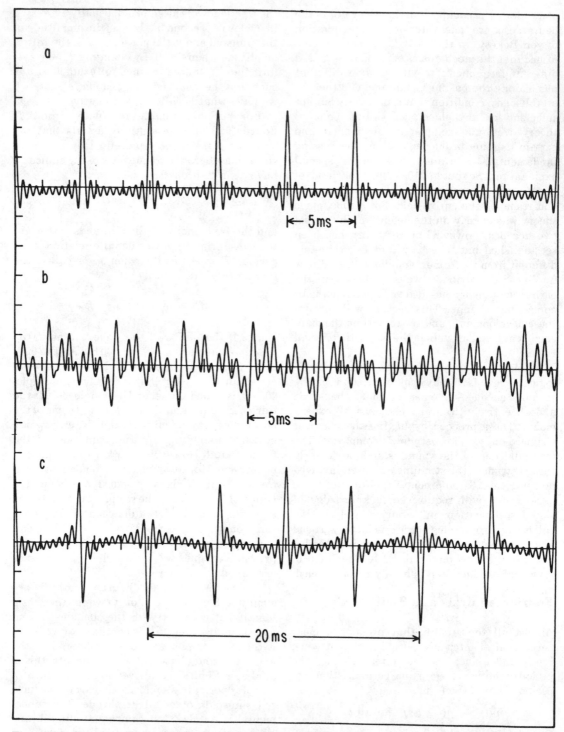

Figure 6.3. Waveforms (pressure versus time) of ten sinusoids of equal amplitude. In panels (a) and (b) the fundamental is 200 Hz and the nine successive harmonics, 400, 600 . . . 2000 Hz. The components are all in cosine phase in panel (a) and random phase in panel (b). In panel (c) the components have all been shifted upward in frequency by 50 Hz. The periods of the waveforms are indicated in the figure.

individual components. The duration of the period is noted in the figure. In part (b) the same components with the same amplitude are shown, only the phase of the components differ. As is evident, the resultant waveform is quite different. At no time are all the components exactly in phase and hence the peak value of the complex wave is less than that of part (a). Again the period of the wave is noted. Examples (a) and (b) show that the phase of the components is important in specifying the shape of the complex pressure wave. In many cases the relative phase of the components may be inaudible, and hence we tend to emphasize the amplitude and frequency of the component more than the phase. Nevertheless the shape of the complex wave clearly does depend on the relative phase of the components.

In part (c) of the figure we again show ten equal-amplitude components, all in cosine phase, but each component frequency is shifted upward by 50 Hz. The resulting waveform has a period of 20 msec and two periods of the waveform are shown in the figure. The period or fundamental of a complex wave can be determined from the frequencies of the components that make up the periodic waveform. The period can be computed by determining the greatest common divisor of all the component frequencies. In this case 50 Hz divides 250 Hz, 450 Hz, 650 Hz . . . 2050 Hz, so that the period is 20 msec. This waveform is called *inharmonic* because successive components are not successive integer multiples of the fundamental. Waves of this type have made important contributions to our understanding of pitch perception.

Linearity

A major reason for the use of Fourier theory is the importance of sinusoids in linear systems. A *linear* system is one in which the response of the system to a given input is independent of any other input. Thus if input $x_1(t)$ produces output $y_1(t)$ and input $x_2(t)$ produces $y_2(t)$, then response to the combined inputs $x_1(t) + x_2(t)$ is simply the sum of each response, $y_1(t) + y_2(t)$. A *time-invariant* system has the property that any delay in the input is reflected by an equal delay in the output. A *linear, time-invariant* system has the property that a certain frequency of sinusoidal input produces the same frequency of sinusoidal output, where the amplitude and

phase of the sinusoid may be different but not the frequency. Thus if the input to a system is the set of components shown in Figure 6.3, we know that the same set of components must appear at the output. Perhaps the phase and amplitude of the components will be changed, and hence the waveform altered in shape, but the period will be the same and hence the fundamental frequency. Many parts of the auditory system, especially the initial filtering of the waveform, can be treated as linear systems.

Nonlinear systems are complex and aspects of that topic were treated earlier. For our present purposes their most important property is that nonlinear distortion produces additional frequencies at their output not present at the input. For example, a 200 Hz input might produce an output of 200 Hz and 600 Hz—such a device is said to produce *harmonic distortion*. Of special relevance here is the output of a device when the input consists of a pair of sinusoids f_1 and f_2. The output might consist of sinusoids of frequency f_1 and f_2, but in addition other sinusoids may be produced having frequencies of $f_1 + f_2$ and $f_2 - f_1$, so called *sum* and *difference* tones. For pitch perception the difference tone has occupied an especially important role in theoretical accounts of pitch. Note that in Figure 6.3 the most common difference frequency is 200 Hz for all the waves, and that for the waves of part (a) and (b) this frequency is also the fundamental frequency.

Operational Definition of Pitch

When a musical instrument plays a given note, the resulting waveform is often periodic with a fundamental frequency equal to what we call the pitch of the note. Technically we define the pitch of a periodic wave as the frequency of a sinusoid set to match the wave.

Since the waveform is periodic, we also know that the Fourier decomposition is the harmonic sequence of components. The higher harmonics are usually called *overtones*. Although many sinusoids are present in the waveform they are not all equally audible. It is clear that the first few overtones are widely separated perceptually, whereas the later ones are crowded closer and closer together. After all, the first two tones are separated by an octave. Plomp (1964) measured the ability of observers to resolve components in a complex periodic wave. He asked them to listen to three stimuli: either a complex of fundamental f_o, or two sinusoidal frequencies. One of the sinusoids was an overtone of the complex, nf_o, the other sinusoid was halfway between two overtones, $(n + 1/2)f_o$ where n is an integer. The observer's task was to say which of the two single sinusoids, nf_o or $(n + 1/2)f_o$, was a harmonic of the complex. The percentage of correct discriminations was perfect for low values of n and dropped to chance in the region between 4 and 9 depending on f_o. The frequency difference required to hear the overtones was roughly a constant fraction of the central frequency region above about 500 Hz. The fraction was about 20 percent. This result should not be surprising. The resolving power of the auditory system as measured in other experiments (e.g., critical band) is roughly a constant percentage of the center frequency. In 12 tones of the musical scale successive notes are separated by about 6 percent ($2^{1/12} = 1.059463$). Thus the successive overtones of a harmonic series, since all are spaced by an equal difference in frequency f_o, become perceptually more and more difficult to resolve.

The dominant method used in the study of pitch perception is the pitch match. In the simplest case there is some stimulus under question (the unknown) and some reference stimulus. The observer is asked to adjust the reference stimulus until its pitch matches that of the unknown stimulus. Ideally the reference stimulus would be a sinusoid, in which case the frequency of the sinusoid would be used to measure the pitch. Unfortunately a sinusoid has a timbre or quality so unlike the unknown stimulus, which is often a complex periodic wave, that some other stimulus is often used as a reference instead of the sinusoid. A pulse train is frequently used. It has a number of components all of roughly equal amplitude (the next section contains a detailed discussion of its spectrum) and there is the possibility that the observer may match the reference to the unknown so that one component of the reference is equal to one of the components of the unknown stimulus. To avoid this problem one often filters the reference stimulus so that no components of the reference stimulus overlap with any components in the unknown stimulus. This avoids the problem of matching single components but makes the timbre of the two sounds different and hence makes the judgment more

difficult. There is no completely satisfactory way to avoid all these problems.

Everyone would probably agree that a musical tune or melody is composed of a sequence of sounds that change pitch in a certain manner. Thus, an acid test of whether a particular type of sound has pitch is whether one can play a melody with this type of sound (Burns & Viemeister, 1981). If this is possible, then obviously successive pairs of sounds are related by some musical interval, that is, by a third, a fifth, and so on. One procedure to determine the pitch of some unknown sounds might be to have the observer identify the interval produced by a pair of sounds played in succession. Houstma and Goldstein (1972) used exactly this technique with musically trained observers. This neatly avoids one of the basic problems of the matching procedure, namely, trying to equate two stimuli along a single dimension when they clearly differ on other dimensions. But Houstma and Goldstein's procedure has not been widely copied as a general procedure in this area, probably because extensive pretraining is needed.

A brief word about the selection of observers in pitch experiments. Often one selects observers that have some musical background. Musical subjects can presumably appreciate the dimension of the sound to be judged and make matches more easily than nonmusically trained observers. Their judgments will be made more quickly and with less variability. There is no evidence that nonmusical observers will produce results different, on average, from musical observers, although this issue has not been extensively explored. Patterson (1973) used a naive observer along with two musically trained observers in an extensive series of pitch matches for inharmonic complexes. He found the average data to be the same but the variability of the naive observer was somewhat greater than for the other two observers.

Classical Theory

One must appreciate that during the middle half of the last century, when the classical views were formulated, there were only a few ways to generate complex sounds. The tuning fork was convenient for generating sinusoids, and musical instruments of various kinds would produce harmonic complexes. Filtering the resulting spectra to attenuate or accentuate a particular component was accomplished by listening through a pipe of a given length or a certain size cavity such as a Helmholtz resonator. Control of relative intensity was difficult and specification of absolute intensity was impossible until Rayleigh's disc of 1882. Fourier's theorem was known and the decomposition of certain idealized waveforms was understood; but the convenient and efficient analysis of the acoustic stimulus with wave analyzers and Fast Fourier transforms was nearly a century away.

Seebeck (1841) used a very simple acoustic device, the siren, to produce a set of stimuli that severely taxed the simple resonance-place theory of Ohm and Helmholtz. Seebeck's siren had many holes, but the one drawn in part (a) of Figure 6.4 has only one. If this siren is rotated at a uniform speed in front of an air source, then each time the hole is in front of the source a puff of air pressure occurs. We have idealized the sequence of pressure pulses by the train of thin rectangles illustrated next to the siren. The pressure pulse is repeated each T seconds so we have produced a complex periodic waveform of period T.

The decomposition of this wave is a harmonic sequence with fundamental frequency $f_o = 1/T$ and multiples of that frequency as shown in the right hand side of Figure 6.4, part (a). The amplitudes of the first few harmonics are nearly equal to the fundamental. The amplitudes gradually decrease and reach zero for the first time at $f = 1/\tau$, where τ is the duration of the pressure pulse, which, in turn, is clearly proportional to the size of the hole. Thus we could increase the relative amplitude of the higher harmonics by making the hole smaller and smaller, but this occurs at the expense of less energy per pulse. Thus we compromise on a hole of sufficient size to make the siren both audible and able to produce a few components of nearly equal amplitude.

Next consider the pulse sequence produced

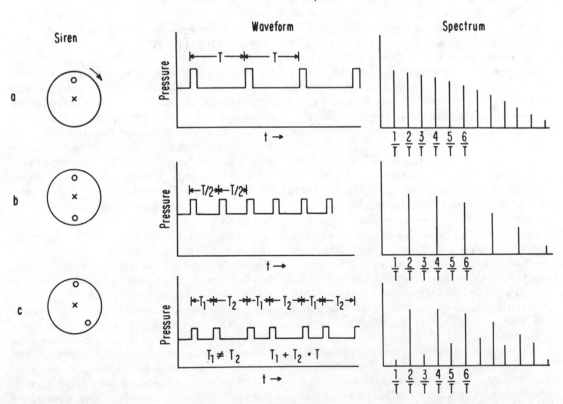

Figure 6.4. Seebeck's siren experiment. The sirens, the waveforms, and the spectra of the sounds are shown in columns of the figure. See text for a discussion of the experiment.

by the second siren, Figure 6.4, part (b). The speed of rotation is assumed to be the same as with the first siren. Consequently, since there are twice as many holes and the intervals between the two pulses are equal, the frequency of the pulses, and their period is doubled. The fundamental is $2/T$, an octave above $1/T$ and if we listened to siren a and then siren b, we would hear that sound b is higher in pitch than sound a by an octave.

The interesting stimulus is that produced by siren c. As can be seen, this produces a pair of pulses that repeat each T seconds, but the interval between successive pulses is unequal. Because the period of repetition is T, the fundamental is $1/T$, but as the spectrum shows, the amplitude of this component is very small. In many respects there is great similarity between the low frequency portion of the spectra produced by siren b and siren c. Thus Seebeck argued that, according to frequency or place theory, sirens b and c should produce a pitch that should be heard as nearly equal.

Seebeck himself argued that the frequency content of the sound was not critical in determining the pitch; he believed rather that the periodicity of the waveform was crucial. In his view, siren a and siren c should be matched in pitch because the periodicity is the same. And he was correct—once the second pulse is moved a few microseconds away from the point equal distant from the first pulse, the pitch drops an octave and the pitch of siren c matches the pitch of siren a.

In siren c the energy at the fundamental frequency $f_o = 1/T$ is some 10 to 15 dB below the amplitude of the component at $2/T$. It is hard to believe that a component so small can have such a profound effect on the pitch of the complex, yet siren c clearly has a pitch an octave below that of siren b. Further, if the place theory were really correct, and the ear were analyzing a complex sound into components, one component at each place, why then was there so little correlation between the subjective loudness of the low harmonics and their actual physical amplitude?

This ingenious demonstration caused considerable consternation in the place-resonance camp. Ohm was so disturbed that he suggested it was caused by "auditory illusions," a suggestion unworthy of the general level of debate. A more satisfactory way to avoid the difficulties produced by this demonstration is to introduce the idea of nonlinear distortion. Such distortion may produce a difference tone, and, since all pairs of consecutive components are spaced $f_o = 1/T$ apart, the accumulation of such distortion produces considerable energy at the fundamental frequency, even though not much energy is evident in the original physical spectrum.

In any event the views of Helmholtz and Ohm prevailed, perhaps because Helmholtz suggested a simple physiological model of how the analysis proceeded. He suggested that different parts of the basilar membrane were tuned or resonant to different frequencies. Thus the various components of a complex wave stimulated different parts of the basilar membrane, and frequency is coded by place, while the vigor of the response codes intensity. The distribution of amplitudes over the components controlled the timbre of the sound. Nonlinear distortion could be invoked to handle the awkward problem of periodic complexes with weak or missing fundamentals.

Modern Era—The Ascendancy of Periodicity Theory

Seebeck's siren is a relatively contrived way of producing a complex sound with a missing fundamental and certainly an unusual stimulus to encounter in the 19th century. One could almost dismiss the missing fundamental waveform as a rare and abnormal stimulus. In the 20th century, however, the modern era of electronic technology produced this type of signal in abundance, because the telephone only reproduces frequencies in the range from about 300 to 4000 Hz. Human voices, for example, with a fundamental frequency of about 125 Hz for men and 225 Hz for women, when heard on the telephone are all waveforms with missing fundamentals! Following Helmholtz, Fletcher (1929) also believed that distortion products were sufficient to account for the perceived pitch, at least at the relatively high levels of intensity used in telephone conversations. Curiously, Fletcher (1924) also described how the pitch of a missing fundamental stimulus did not change as one progressively diminished its intensity. Even near threshold such a waveform retained a pitch equal to the missing fundamental, a finding at variance with the then current view on the nature of the nonlinear distortion.

J.F. Schouten reported a series of observations that were extremely damaging to the classical resonance theory. The initial publications were just prior to the outbreak of the Second World War and their full impact was not felt until almost two decades after the war. But Schouten's original investigations contained the germ for several major experimental programs as well as for the theoretical statements of what would become the central tenets of modern periodicity pitch.

Schouten used an optical means of generating his stimuli. While this technique is hardly as convenient as those presently available, it did permit him to generate a wide class of arbitrary, periodic waveforms, and still maintain separate control of each component. He could, for example, cancel exactly the fundamental frequency of a pulse train—the purest form of "the missing fundamental." Even at the lowest overall intensity level, he found that the pitch of the pulse train was the same whether or not the fundamental was present; only the timbre changes. He could also cancel other components of the pulse train. When the fundamental and the successive lower harmonics were canceled, the timbre became increasingly "bright," but this stimulus still had a pitch equal to that of the fundamental. This sensation of pitch caused by the higher harmonics, which are individually unresolved, Schouten called a *residue*. Clearly, some relation among unresolved higher harmonics led to the perception of the low pitch. Two candidates were evident, either the frequency separation between successive harmonics or the periodicity of the waveform. Schouten generated a second pulse train, similar to the one shown in Figure 6.4a, but with every other pulse of opposite polarity. Such a waveform is periodic and of the form,

$$g(t) = -g(t - T/2).$$

Because of this feature only odd harmonics are present in the spectrum (a fundamental, third, fifth, etc., harmonics are present but no second, fourth, sixth, etc., harmonics). If we set an ordinary pulse train to have a fundamental of 400 Hz and the alternating-pulse train to have a fundamental of 200 Hz, then the periods are an octave different but the spacing between successive components is the same—the regular

pulse train has components 400, 800, 1200, 1600 Hz, and so on; the alternating pulse train has components 200, 600, 1000, 1400 Hz, and so on. Schouten found that the pitches were in agreement with the period, not the difference frequency, and therefore concluded that periodicity of the residue determined its pitch.

To understand how Schouten believed residue pitch was generated we must consider how the basilar membrane will respond to a pulse train and what the filtering action of the peripheral auditory system will do to modify the input waveform. Figure 6.5, taken from Plomp (1966), is an attempt to depict this situation for a pulse train stimulus of 200 Hz fundamental. Arrayed along the left side of the figure are the bandpass filters of the first stage of the auditory system. They are assumed to have the same shape when plotted on a logarithmic frequency scale, such as the one used in this figure. Note that the successive lines in the diagram represent approximately 20 percent changes in frequency. Because the spacing between successive harmonics is 200 Hz, the lower harmonics are resolved and produce nearly sinusoidal outputs from the filters. The higher harmonics are not independently resolved and their combinations produce the beating patterns seen in the upper time lines. For example, at 5000 Hz the bandpass is approximately 4600 to 5400 Hz and thus five harmonics, 4600, 4800, 5000, 5200, 5400 Hz are combined in the output of this filter. This interaction among the unresolved harmonics produces clear epochs every 5 msec. The detection of these epochs was, for Schouten, the basis of residue pitch.

Note that this view accepts the indisputable fact that the auditory periphery analyzes components into different places depending on their frequencies. What is heretical from a classical, place point of view is that the rate of firing can transmit both *quality* and *quantity*. Variation in firing rate can signal a change in pitch or in loudness, depending on how the change in rate occurs.

Two Recent Experiments

Although all the experiments undertaken by Schouten were persuasive, they often required considerable experience and introspective sophistication on the part of the observer. Licklider (1954) presented a convincing demonstration at

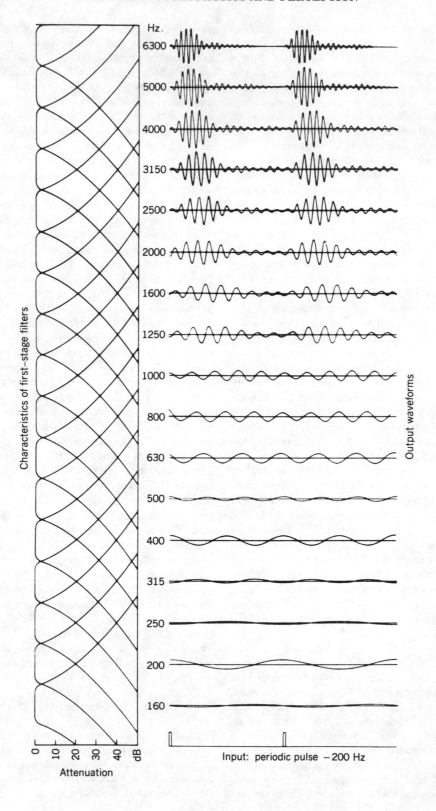

Characteristics of first-stage filters

Attenuation

Output waveforms

Input: periodic pulse −200 Hz

a meeting of the Acoustical Society of America that something was seriously wrong with classical place theory. Licklider played a simple scale using a pure tone and a pulse train. He alternately used each type of stimulus to play the successive notes of the scale. Once he had completed a sequence up and down the scale, he turned on a low-pass noise with a cutoff frequency higher than any of the frequencies in the scale. As the noise increased in intensity, the pure tones became masked and one could no longer hear the musical scale generated by the pure tones. The pulse train was still evident by virtue of the higher components of the pulse train and the pitch produced by these higher components still continued to present the musical scale. One could not appeal to nonlinear distortion since even if distortion generated energy at the fundamental frequency, the noise should obscure it, as it did the sinusoidal stimulus. No special training or introspection was needed, and the demonstration was clear to all in attendance. A version of this demonstration is contained in a set of audio tapes often used in classroom demonstrations. It is always a clear and compelling demonstration. The inescapable conclusion is that higher frequency channels are capable of generating the perception of low-frequency pitch.

A second experiment was the so-called pitch-shift experiment carried out by de Boer (1956) in Holland. Using a modulation technique, de Boer generated a sequence of six or seven components having a constant difference between the frequency of successive components. The exact frequency of the components could be adjusted, but the difference frequency remained constant. One could set the components so as to form a harmonic sequence, that is, so components were successive integer multiples of the fundamental. When this is done, a clear residue pitch is heard equal to the pitch of the fundamental frequency. For example, if the difference frequency is 200 Hz, he could generate a wave containing

components at 1200, 1400, 1600, 1800, 2000 and 2200 Hz; the pitch would equal that of a 200 Hz sinusoid. If he raised or lowered the frequency of each component in the sequence by a small amount, then an inharmonic wave would result, for example 1250, 1450, 1650, 1850, 2050, 2250 Hz. What is the pitch of the inharmonic wave? The answer is that the pitch matches about 208 Hz, and although other pitch matches can be made, none are at 200 Hz, the common frequency difference. This experiment is particularly damaging to place theory because it demolishes the crutch of place theory, namely, the appeal to a nonlinear distortion producing a difference tone at the missing fundamental frequency. At a moderate intensity level (below 70 dB SPL), a pitch equal to the difference frequency of 200 Hz is simply not evident in these inharmonic complexes. This demonstration of pitch shift with inharmonic complexes was first reported by Schouten (1938–40), but he used only three components in his stimulus and the resulting pitch perception is relatively weak compared with that heard when more components are present. Musically trained observers are needed to make the judgment of pitch shifts containing fewer than four or five components.

To see why more than one pitch may be present in these stimuli, consider the following sequences of complex waveforms listed by their constituent components in Table 6.4. Clearly, Waves A and E are harmonic and will have a pitch equal to a tone set to the fundamental frequency of 200 Hz. The fundamental of Waves B and D is 50 Hz. Wave B will generally have a pitch somewhat higher than 200 Hz, and Wave D will often be judged somewhat lower. In the middle of the sequence there is great ambiguity. Wave C might be judged to have a pitch of 215 or 185 Hz. The actual fundamental of 100 Hz is seldom, if ever, judged to be equal to its pitch. If the sequence is presented in the order A to E, the higher pitch match is likely; if the order is reversed, the lower pitch match is more probable.

Figure 6.5. Illustrative waveforms at the output of a bank of filters similar to the ear's critical bands, after Plomp (1966). The input to the bank of filters is an impulse repeated 200 times per second. The response of the filters is shown in the right side of the figure. The frequency characteristic of the filters is shown in the left side of the figure. The center frequency of the filter increase from the bottom of the figure to the top. The bandwidth is proportional to the center frequency (constant Q). At low frequencies the output is essentially a single sinusoid; at higher frequencies the output is a combination of several sinusoids and the periodicity of the input is evident. From *Experiments on Tone Perception* (p. 128) by R. Plomp, 1966. Unpublished dissertation. Reprinted by permission.

Table 6.4.

Wave	Components
A	1600, 1800, 2000, 2200, 2400
B	1650, 1850, 2050, 2250, 2450
C	1700, 1900, 2100, 2300, 2500
D	1750, 1950, 2150, 2350, 2550
E	1800, 2000, 2200, 2400, 2600

Figure 6.6 shows some results of a pitch-shift experiment. The data are those of Schouten, Ritsma and Cardozo (1962), and uses a three component complex with 200 Hz spacing between the signals. The center frequency of the complex is plotted along the abscissa, and the ordinate is the pitch match. The number n appearing near the curve gives the rank of the center component of the complex, that is, the harmonic number minus one, when the complex is a harmonic sequence. The data can be approximated to the first order by taking the center frequency of the complex and by dividing by this rank number,

thus for $n = 7$ the complex consisting of 1250, 1450 and 1650 has a pitch of approximately 207 Hz (1450/7). This approximation will be called the *pseudo-period calculation*. There are known to be systematic deviations from this calculation, but it is clearly a very simple and reasonably accurate approximation.

We next consider how a periodicity theory might try to explain the pitch shift results. This exercise will also reveal the Achilles' heel of periodicity theory. Let us consider the waveforms generated by the complex Waves A, B, and C of Table 6.4 at the output of a peripheral filter centered at 2000 Hz (see Figure 6.7). Since the bandwidth of the filter is about 400 Hz, we will assume that the three middle components are passed by the filter (1800, 2000 and 2200 for Wave A; 1850, 2050 and 2250 for Wave B; and 1900, 2100 and 2300 Hz for Wave C). In fact, the situation is slightly more complicated, but our example will illustrate the main issues.

The output of the filter for Wave A is shown

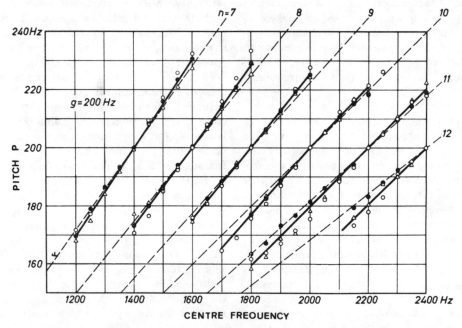

Figure 6.6 The results of the pitch-shift experiment, from Schouten, Ritsma, and Cardozo (1962). The ordinate of the figure is the center frequency of a three-component complex. The two other components are always 200 Hz above and below the central component. The abscissa is the apparent pitch. For example, take the line labeled $n = 7$; when the center frequency is 1400 Hz, the pitch is 200 Hz. When the three components have been increased by 50 Hz, the components are 1250, 1450, and 1650 Hz, and the pitch is about 210 Hz. One can arrive at the same set of components by starting with a center frequency of 1600 Hz, the line labeled $n = 8$, and shifting all the components down 150 Hz. In that case, the resulting pitch is about 180 Hz. From "Pitch of the Residue" by J.F. Schouten, R.J. Ritsma, and B.L. Cardozo, 1962, *Journal of the Acoustical Society of America*, p. 1422. Copyright 1962 by the American Institute of Physics. Reprinted by permission.

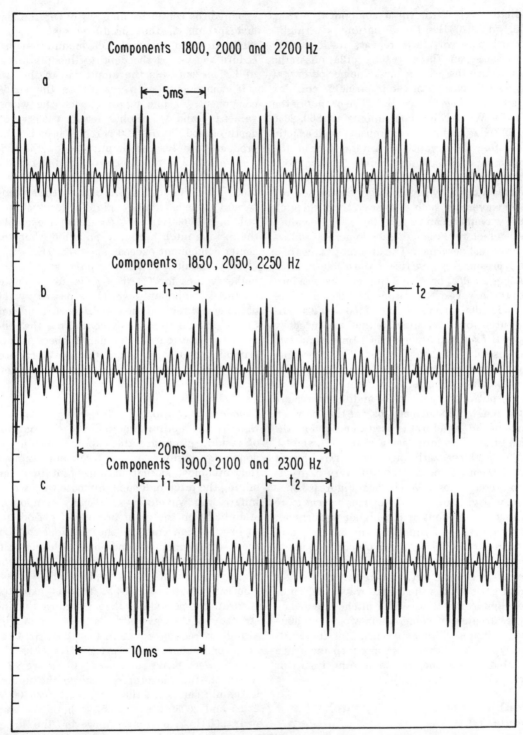

Figure 6.7. The waveforms produced by the three components in typical pitch-shift experiments. The frequencies of the components are indicated in the panels of the figure, the periods of the successive panels are 5, 10, and 20 msec as indicated. The pseudo periods marked t_1 and t_2 are used in some theoretical account to explain the pitch-shift results.

in Figure 6.7. With these components—1800, 2000, and 2200 Hz—the situation is straightforward. The waveform repeats itself exactly every 5 msec, and there are ten oscillations in the wave before the peak recurs. The periodicity of this wave is clear. For the inharmonic complex the situation is more complex. The output of the filter for Wave B has components at 1850, 2050 and 2250 Hz. This waveform repeats itself exactly only after 20 ms, but the interaction of the components causes discernible epochs four times within each period. If within these epochs one measures between peaks of "fine-structure" of the waveform, such as t_1 or t_2, then the pitch of the waveform can be calculated. These values lead, in fact, to the same "pseudo-period" values we have just described. The different values of t_1 and t_2 presumably give rise to the different pitch matches 2050/10 or 2050/9 that can be obtained with these waves. The output produced by Wave C yields components at 1900, 2100 and 2300 Hz. The situation is similar to that produced by Wave B except the period is 10 msec and two clear pseudoperiods are evident. The preceding is an account of how pitch is determined according to orthodox periodicity theory. Epochs in the output of the peripheral auditory filter are noted and, within such epochs, the time between peaks of the waveform is used to determine the pitch of the waveform (see Figure 6.7, t_1 and t_2).

The problem with this account is that it makes incorrect predictions for very high frequency complexes. If you inspect Figure 6.5 once more, you will note that the epochs become more distinct and evident at the higher frequencies, because at those frequencies the bandwidth of the filter, which is a fixed proportion of the center frequency, allows more and more components to interact and thus to generate larger and larger peaks in the output waveform. Thus, one might expect that residue pitches created by higher frequency components would produce better pitches. Two experiments of the 1960s clearly indicated that this was not so and hence initiated a decline in the enthusiasm for periodicity pitch mechanisms.

Troubles with Periodicity Pitch Mechanisms

Existence Region

In 1962 Risma, a student of Schouten, used three-component complexes and systematically explored the center frequency f of the complex and spacing Δf that produced good residue pitch. He used an amplitude modulation procedure and varied the depth of modulation as well. This controls the amplitude of the two side components with respect to the center component. As one might expect, the widest values of f and Δf are obtained for the greatest depth of modulation (100 percent) because this produces the largest amplitude for the side components. For no choices of f and Δf could a residue pitch be heard when f exceeded about 5000 Hz. Further, unless one chooses the spacing carefully, the existence region for residue pitch falls below 4000 Hz. At $\Delta f = 200$, for example, the residue pitch becomes inaudible when the center component exceeds about 3800 Hz.

Why should the residue pitch stop at the higher values for f? At 5000 Hz, for example, all three components would be passed by the peripheral filter and the epochs, occurring each 5 msec, should then be evident. Note that the refractory period of the nerve fibers is not critical because, although the waveform frequency is high, the periodic information is low frequency.

Dominance Region

Equally disquieting to periodicity explanations of residue pitch are the experiments on the dominant regions—those frequency regions that are most salient or important in determining the pitch judgment. Suppose we have an inharmonic waveform with many component stimuli. From the point of view of periodicity theory, we can compute the pseudopitch from the lower components and obtain a larger shift in pitch value than if we compute it from the higher components, for example, 1250/6 = 208.3, whereas 2050/11 = 204.5. This is expected according to periodicity theory because the fine structure of the waveform changes more rapidly at higher frequency regions (e.g., 2050 Hz) than at lower frequency regions (1250 Hz). Thus, the time between peaks such as t_1, t_2 in Figure 6.7 is nearer the fundamental frequency of the highest harmonic series. In the extreme, 20050/100 = 200.5 and 20050/101 = 198.5, so both are very near 200 Hz. Apparently however, the lower components are the ones used to determine the pitch match, since the data are best fit if we assume that the pseudoperiod is computed from these lower components. In fact, this tendency is so strong that Walliser (1969) and Patterson (1973) suggest that the pitch of an inharmonic series be computed from the *lowest* component divided by its rank number. But why should this be so when the epochs of the filtered waveform are much clearer at the higher frequencies?

In 1967, both Plomp and Ritsma made a direct test of this proposition that the lower frequency components are more important or dominant in determining pitch. Basically, they generated ambiguous stimuli having one pitch below a certain frequency and a different pitch above that frequency. To make the judgment task more convenient, they actually used pairs of such stimuli. The components were arranged so that the pitch of the successive pairs moved in one direction above the critical frequency and moved in the opposite direction below it. By determining whether the pitch judgment moved up or down, one could infer which frequency region was perceptually most important or dominant in the pitch judgment. The value of the critical frequency, f_c, where half the judgments go in one direction and half in the other direction, marks the center of this dominant region. The value of f_c increases somewhat with increasing value of the judged pitch. If the judged pitch is near 100 Hz, the value of f_c was between 400 and 700 Hz; if 200 Hz, then f_c was between 800 and 1400 Hz; if 400 Hz, then f_c was between 800 and 2000 Hz. These ranges for f_c represent the scatter obtained with different listeners.

Ritsma also explored how the dominant region depended on the relative amplitude of the components. Given a fixed value of f_c, he attenuated the components in the dominant region to determine how large they needed to be, relative to the nondominant components, to continue to exercise their dominance. The answer is that if the lower components are 10 to 15 dB above their own thresholds, they are dominant, largely independent of the amplitude of the other nondominant components.

Such a pattern of results hardly reflects a putative detector of pseudoperiodicity. Few components can win over many, and peaks in a waveform cannot be crucial if the pitch is almost independent of the relative amplitude of the components. Rather, it appears that the low frequency *resolved* components are critical in determining residue pitch. Before turning to an alternative to periodicity theory let us review two more experiments that are important to our understanding of residue pitch.

Dichotic Pitch

Houtsma and Goldstein (1972) used twelve musically trained observers and measured their accuracy in judging one of eight possible musical intervals produced by presenting two successive stimuli. Each of the successive stimuli consisted of two sinusoidal components that were adjacent integer multiples n, $n + 1$, of two different fundamentals a and b. To prevent the judgment from being based on the change in frequency of a single component, the lowest harmonic used on any trial for either a or b fundamental was chosen from a limited set. Thus, presumably the subject's judgment reflected the change in pitch from a to b, independent of the particular overtones used to generate the low pitch. The experiment consisted in measuring the percentage of correct judgments of the musical interval as a function of the lowest fundamental frequency a and the harmonic numbers n and $n + 1$.

As might be expected, performance was good for low values of n and lower fundamental frequencies. Perfect performance was obtained for $n \leq 3$ and all fundamentals from 200 to 1000 Hz. Less accurate performance occurs if n is increased or if the fundamental frequency is increased.

The unexpected results were those obtained when the two components of the harmonic sequence were presented to different ears, what is called the dichotic condition. In this condition, for example, the first stimulus could consist of $n(a)$ presented to the left ear, and $(n + 1)a$ to the right ear. In the second interval, $(n + 1)b$ might be presented to the left ear and $n(b)$ to the right ear. Surprisingly, the judgment of the musical interval, $a:b$, was nearly as good as when both components of the stimulus were presented to the same ear! Clearly the peripheral interaction of the waveforms from such stimuli is impossible in this dichotic condition. The residue pitch mechanism must be located after the information from the two ears is combined.

Smoorenburg's Results

Smoorenburg (1970) studied the pitch of two-tone complexes in the pitch-shift paradigm. Well-trained subjects were used and the reference stimulus was another two-tone harmonic complex.

Special controls, similar to those employed by Houtsma and Goldstein, were used to avoid the problem of basing judgments on single components of the complex. The difference in frequency between the two components was always 200 Hz. Since only two components are available, there is not much room for argument about the rank number that should be used in the calculation of the pseudoperiod. It should be easy to compute the pseudoperiod and predict the shift in pitch produced by these inharmonic complexes. Nevertheless, the measured pitch shifts, especially those obtained by the higher frequencies, were much greater than expected from the pseudoperiod calculation. For example, two components at 2850 and 3050 Hz were judged to have a pitch equal to 205 Hz. The value based on a pseudoperiod calculation is $2850/14 = 203.6$ or $3050/15 = 203$. How can a value of 205 Hz be obtained? One way is to use much lower rank numbers, for example, $2050/10 = 205$, but 2050 Hz is a component not present in the physical stimulus. How can such nonexistent components contribute to the pitch match? It is now clear that the components responsible for the anomalous results were the cubic and higher-order distortion products. The remainder of Smoorenburg's paper is a careful marshaling of evidence that such lower-frequency components were generated in the ear via distortion.

Also, we know from Ritsma's work on dominance that the lower component pairs are dominant so long as they are 10 to 15 dB above their thresholds. In Smoorenburg's experiment, then, the external components are joined by a set of internally generated distortion products. These components extend the spectrum, the so-called internal spectrum, that determined the pitch match. Smoorenburg also demonstrated that such components are audible. For example, he fixed f_1 and gradually lowered the frequency of f_2 while the observer was instructed to listen for a component in the vicinity of $2f_1 - f_2$. Since the component with frequency $2f_1 - f_2$ moved up when f_2 moved down, its detection was easy. Smoorenburg also confirmed the frequency of this distortion product by having his listeners match its pitch to that of a pure tone.

Modern Residue Pitch Theories

It is a remarkable fact that all modern theories of residue pitch are what may be called modi-

fied place theories. The theories of Terhardt, Wightman, and Goldstein all begin by assuming that some mechanism attempts to identify the frequencies of individual components of a complex stimuli. These frequencies serve as the basic data for further processing by a pitch computer. All of the theories were suggested about a decade ago and have remained the dominant theories in this area. No crucial experimental tests have been proposed to choose among the theories, in part, because they agree on many of the basic assumptions. Let us begin with Terhardt's theory.

Terhardt's Theory

Terhardt (1974) proposed a very general theory of musical perception, including pitch, consonance, and harmony. Essentially pitch perception is an example of holistic or gestalt principles. In many respects, the basic ideas are similar to those presented by Thurlow (1963), who had described residue pitch as a result of a mediation mechanism. Complex sounds are often assigned a pitch by matching them to a vocal hum. Through learning and past associations, we learn that certain patterns of frequencies for complex stimuli correspond to a low pitch, the residue pitch. Terhardt calls this low pitch a virtual pitch and distinguishes it from spectral pitch. In two recent papers, he has presented an algorithm for how this virtual pitch is computed (Terhardt, Stoll, & Seewann, 1982a) and has provided several examples of its application (Terhardt, Stoll, & Seewann, 1982b).

Wightman's Theory

Wightman (1973a, b) proposes that pitch arises from a Fourier transform of the power spectrum on the stimulus, as it is determined by the first stage peripheral filtering of the auditory system. This first-stage processing calculates a power spectrum and, hence, phase information is ignored. Wightman (1973a) argues that while phase information may, in certain circumstances, be audible, it does not affect the pitch match. The important aspect of this first process is that the spectrum is computed with limited resolution. Thus, the lower frequency components are resolved and separated, whereas the higher components are not.

This first stage of processing provides the input to the second stage which computes a Fourier transform of this first-stage spectrum, that is, it determines what oscillatory components are present in this approximation to a power spectrum. If the input is a harmonic sequence and the components are low enough in frequency to be resolved, then the second stage will detect the components that repeat at the fundamental frequency. Actually, if the sequence is inharmonic, then more than a single component will be present and the third stage of Wightman's pitch perception mechanism is a device that searches the second-stage output and computes a *strength* value of each potential *pitch*. A potential pitch is simply the frequency of the oscillatory component, and its amplitude a measure of its strength.

Making reasonable assumptions about the first-stage filter, namely, a bandwidth proportional to center frequency, Wightman is able to predict the pitch-shift data to within the limits of experimental error. Also, the strength measure is high on harmonic complexes and lower on inharmonic complexes. The existence region and dominance data are predicted because only the lower components tend to be resolved and hence only these components produce clear peaks in the spectrum that in turn generate clear periodicities in the second stage transform. The theory is a remarkably concise account of a large amount of data with a theory containing practically no parameters.

Yost and Hill (1978) have extended Wightman's models by suggesting a weighting function that modifies the peripheral spectrum prior to the Fourier transform. This weighting function contains an inhibiting side lobe that slightly improves the pitch matches made to rippled noise (Yost & Hill, 1978; Yost, Hill, & Perez-Falcon, 1978).

Goldstein's Theory

Goldstein (1973) also begins with the assumption that only the power spectrum of the stimulus is important, and that phase information is ignored. Despite this common assumption, practically all other aspects of the theory differ from Wightman's. The first stage in Goldstein's theory is the determination of the *frequency* of all the *resolved* components computed from the spectrum. Thus, the first stage output is a set of numbers. The amplitude of the components is ignored, and only those that can be resolved are reported. Finally, it is assumed that these numbers, representing component frequencies,

are subject to error, that is, the frequencies reported are somewhat inaccurate.

The next stage in Goldstein's theory is a central processor. This device tries to determine a fundamental frequency of f_0 and *successive* integers i, $i + 1$, $i + 2$, and so on, that best fit the set of numbers computed by the first stage. A maximum likelihood procedure is used to estimate the unknown parameters f_0 and i. If this fit between the measured frequencies and the computed frequencies is good, for instance if the least squared error is low, then the pitch percept is strong. If the fit is poor, the pitch percept is less strong and the pitch match ambiguous. In a more recent paper, Gerson and Goldstein (1978) relax the requirement that the components need to be *successive* integers.

Poor fits occur for inharmonic complexes. If the components are 2050, 2250, and 2450, then a fundamental of 204.5 produces a sequence of 2045, 2250, and 2454 Hz. The low component is a bit low and the high component a bit high, and this deviation will persist independent of the error involved in determining the component frequencies in the first stage.

The central empirical assumption of this theory is the function relating error and frequency. Goldstein uses the data of Houtsma and himself (1972) to estimate how the standard deviation $\sigma(f)$ of the frequency estimates depend on frequency. This function is quite unlike the critical bandwidth or other similar measures of frequency resolution. The relative standard deviation, $\sigma(f)/f$, diminishes from a value of 0.03 at 100 Hz to a value of about 0.007 in the region of 1000 to 3000 Hz and then accelerates rapidly above 3000 Hz.

This function predicts that the middle frequencies rather than the very lowest will be given more weight in the calculation of pitch, a result consistent with data on pitch dominance. Wightman's theory couples dominance with resolvability and hence suggests that the lowest tone should be most important.

Goldstein's theory handles the pitch-shift data well. The theory predicts that the effective rank is the average of the highest and lowest rank values, for moderate- and low-frequency complexes. It uses the combination tones to extend the components present in the physical (external) spectrum, on the low-frequency side.

This empirically derived error function is peculiar in that its variance is much larger than the just discriminable change in the frequency of a pure tone. Just why this should be is unclear. Goldstein, Gerson, Srulovicz, and Furst (1978) suggest that the discrepancy may occur because "aural measurement at component frequencies is subject to uncertain bias, [and hence] we have no reason to expect agreement between frequency discrimination and estimation" (p. 496, Goldstein et al., 1978). Moore, Glasberg, and Shailer (1984) have suggested another explanation for the discrepancy between $\sigma(f)$ and other data on frequency discrimination. They point out that estimates of the difference limen for a pure tone are made in isolation, whereas estimates of the spectral components of a complex pitch stimulus are made in the presence of other components. They found that the frequency difference limen for a complex was better than the most discriminable component, as Goldstein's theory would predict. Their data on the difference limen as a function of frequency, however, did not resemble the $\sigma(f)$ function. This still remains a perplexing puzzle.

In summary, Goldstein's theory also provides an excellent prediction of pitch matches in a wide variety of experimental procedures.

LOUDNESS

Psychophysical Measures of Loudness

If the physical intensity of a sound is varied, then clearly a psychological attribute of the sound, namely, the loudness, also varies. Because different sounds can have quite different frequency spectra, it is also clear that sounds of equal physical intensity need not be equally loud. For this reason, it is desirable to develop some means of assessing the loudness of sounds so that their psychological magnitudes can be compared. This enterprise is usually called constructing a scale of loudness, just as the meter stick is a scale of length.

Scales of loudness are relatively recent developments in the field of psychoacoustics. The development of such an auditory scale seems slow when contrasted with the analogous scale in the field of vision. The development of measures that assessed the apparent magnitude of visual sources actually preceded the specification of light sources in terms of physical measurements. The standard candle existed

long before radiometer specification was convenient or even possible. One reason for this difference is that only about ten percent of the physical energy of a typical incandescent radiator is effective in stimulating the sense of sight. In addition, changes in the physical intensity, since they change the color temperature of the source, change the proportion of energy that is visually effective. Also, in vision, it is easy to achieve a visual environment where the inverse square law is true. Therefore, distance can be used to change the physical intensity of the source in an accurate and convenient manner. For all these reasons, scales of the visual effect of light sources have been available for well over a century. The standard candle is a product of the middle of the 19th century and, although its standardization has moved from a process of visual matching to a calculation based upon radiometric units, it is nevertheless a psychological scale of the apparent magnitude of a visual source.

The situation is quite different in the auditory sense. Common auditory sources, while differing somewhat in their relative efficiency, are all highly effective in stimulating the sense of hearing. Physical measures of sound intensity developed around the turn of the century, became standardized, and, with the advent of modern electronic instrumentation, were convenient and easy to use. There was never any standard auditory sound, such as a "pin-drop," analogous to a standard candle, partly because nearly all acoustic environments produce sizable reflections at their borders, and thereby produce standing wave patterns. Even if a standard sound were available, it could not be varied easily in level in order to permit comparisons with other acoustic sources. Thus, the physical specification of the stimulus with regard to its intensity ran far ahead of the corresponding specification in terms of its psychological effect.

A major stimulus for the development of psychological scales of loudness was the increased mechanization of society and the generation of more intense physical sources associated with this machinery. Most notable in its generation of very loud and annoying acoustic emissions was the airplane. Specification of the loudness or, what is highly correlated, the annoyance of an airplane flyover became a major objective of psychoacoustic research starting as early as the mid-1930s.

A-Weighted Sound Level

Again, it is of interest to note the similarity between one of the earliest scales of acoustic magnitude, the sound level scale, and a comparable scale in the field of vision. Visual luminance measured in foot candles is now specified for the physical intensity of the source using the following equation:

$$L_m = K_n \int y(\lambda) E(\lambda) d\lambda$$

where $E(\lambda)$ is the intensity of the light source measured in some physical units, $y(\lambda)$ is the relative visibility of energy at that wavelength, and K_n is a dimensional constant that converts the physical quantity obtained by the integral to the psychological counterpart, for example, to lumens or foot-candles. Thus, luminance is assessed by simply weighting the energy at different regions in the spectrum according to the function $y(\lambda)$ and by adding up the contributions for all regions of the spectrum.

In audition, a similar quantity is calculated in the scale of A-weighted sound level. As with most acoustic scales, the fundamental quantities are convereted to logarithms, but the argument of the logarithmic function is analogous to the visual counterpart.

$$A \text{ level } = 10 \log c \int P(f) A(f) df$$

where $P(f)$ is the power at frequency f, $A(f)$ is the weighting function, and c is a dimensional quantity that adjusts the origin of the decibel scale. The integral, therefore, adds up all the physical intensity at various regions of the spectrum according to the weighting function $A(f)$. The function, $A(f)$, when plotted in decibels is shown in Figure 6.8 as the curve marked A in the figure. It was derived by measuring the reciprocal of the power needed to equate the loudness of two sinusoids of different frequencies at very low listening levels—the reciprocal of equal-loudness contours. Thus, the ear is maximally sensitive to acoustic energy in the region between 2000 and 3000 Hz and the A level gives maximum weight to those frequency regions.

The advantage of such a scale of loudness is the ease with which it can be determined, given any arbitrary source. It is fairly easy to make a physical filter that corresponds to the function $A(f)$. The output of that filter is then squared to obtain a quantity proportional to power. Again, electronics is used to perform the integration of the equation. In fact, the situation is somewhat more complicated than we have indicated, since the sound pressure or power is evaluated only

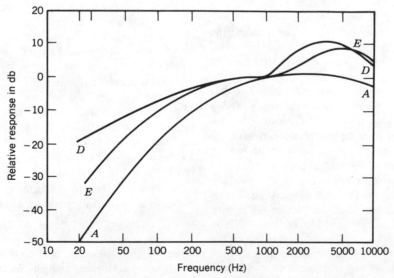

Figure 6.8. Frequency weighting functions [20 log $A(f)$] used in A, D, and E, level meters, after Green (1976). All scales give relatively little weight to the lower frequencies. The maximum contribution is in the region between 2000 and 5000 Hz and is consistent with the results obtained measuring equal loudness contours. From *An Introduction to Hearing* (p. 294) by D.M. Green, 1976, New York: Lawrence Erlbaum Associates, Inc. Reprinted by permission.

over some finite interval of time called the time-constant of the sound-level meter. In the present instrumentation, two time-constants called slow and fast respectively are used. The fast time-constant is about 35 msec and the slow time-constant is about 1000 msec. Roughly, one may regard the quantity calculated by the equation as a sample of sound lasting about 1000 or 35 msec, depending upon whether slow or fast time-constant is used in assessing the loudness.

While measures such as A level are convenient and easy to obtain, they are unsatisfactory to some psychoacoustic investigators for the following two reasons. First, while they may reflect accurately the relative loudness of two sources, they do not provide us with any direct indication of how different these sources are in actual loudness. By their very construction, both the visual and auditory calculation are linear with respect to changes in the overall intensity of the source. To some, this is a serious flaw. It is clear to most observers that if one raises the physical intensity by an order of magnitude, then the psychological counterpart does not change by a similar amount. In both vision and hearing, it is usually conceded that there is considerable compression of the physical quantity. In both senses, to double the brightness of a large source in a dark room or to double the loudness of a sound source requires a change in intensity of nearly a factor of ten. Thus, to compare two sources of unequal magnitude, one must find a separate way to relate the psychological quantity and the physical quantity over the entire scale.

Second, a more fundamental problem is that one can easily demonstrate that the auditory integral is wrong in detail. Consider the following thought experiment. Suppose we have a very loud source (X) with most of its energy concentrated in a 2000 Hz band. As we reviewed in a previous chapter, this sound will produce considerable upward spread of masking. Therefore, sound from another source (Y) with energy located above the 2000 Hz region will be inaudible, unless it is almost as intense as the original source. If Y is less intense than X, then it will be inaudible and hence cannot contribute to the apparent loudness of the total sound stimulus $(X + Y)$. Yet, because of the linearity of the integral, Y makes the same contribution to the total loudness whether or not X is present. Admittedly, the difference between the calcu-

lated loudness of X and $X + Y$ might be comparatively slight. Unless stimulus Y is nearly as intense as stimulus X, the difference between X and Y will be small and taking the logarithm of each will further minimize the discrepancy. Even in the most contrived examples, the error caused by ignoring this upward spread of masking might amount to only a few decibels. Nevertheless, the calculation is flawed and one might try to construct other scales of loudness that will avoid this anomaly.

Loudness Scales

Two such procedures have been developed, and both are presently used as international standards of loudness. One plan, suggested by Stevens (1956), is international standard ISOR532, Method A. The steps in calculating loudness according to this scheme are as follows:

1. First, one determines the sound pressure level in various frequency bands; either octave or one-third octave bands may be used.

2. A constant is added or subtracted from each band level according to an equal-loudness contour so that a corrected level is obtained. This corrected quantity is called the phon. If two bands are equal in phons, they should be equal in loudness. For the 1000 Hz band, the phon is equal to the sound pressure level in that band, that is, the correction constant is zero. At other frequencies the constant varies according to the equal-loudness contour.

3. The level in phons for each band is converted to the loudness in sones according to a power law transformation that maps from phons to sones. At the end of this step, the sound is represented by a series of numbers corresponding to the loudness in sones at each band. Denote the loudness in band i by s_i.

4. Finally, the total loudness is computed according to the following formula

$$S = s_{max} + F \sum_{i \neq max} s_i$$

where s_{max} represents the largest s_i and the summation is the sum over the remainder, and F is a constant equal to 0.3 if octave band analysis is used or 0.13 if one-third octave bands are used.

This peculiar combination rule allows for the effects of masking, since in general the band with the highest loudness or sone level will partially mask the remaining bands, and hence the remainder will contribute to the total loudness with a considerably reduced weight. In addition, since the summation has the units of sones, the quantity represents the loudness of the sound directly. If two sounds differ by a factor of 2 in sones then, in principle, one will be judged twice as loud as the other, at least by the majority of observers.

The second method of analyzing loudness is the so-called Zwicker method; this is ISO recommendation 532, Method B. In Zwicker's procedure, one first obtains the sound-pressure level in a series of third-octave bands. These band levels are plotted on a special chart which has frequency along the abscissa and level along the ordinate. A series of special lines represent the upward spread of masking at each band level. One uses these lines to construct a loudness profile for the sound. For each level, one enters the graph with that loudness, and following the special lines, one extrapolates the spread of masking produced by that band to the higher frequencies. For example, one establishes the level in the band at a center frequency of 1000 Hz. One then extrapolates along the special line to predict the masking at the next band centered at 1250 Hz. Should the level in this adjacent band be lower than the extrapolated upward spread of masking, then that band contributes nothing to the calculation of loudness. When this extrapolation procedure is complete, one has a profile either of the sound level in each band or, if masking occurs, the spread of masking created by a lower band. The area under this overall profile then determines the total loudness of the sound.

In addition to the graphic method just described, a commercial firm has built a small computer that carries out this calculation automatically in a few seconds. The Zwicker method obviously incorporates upward spread of masking, and the chart is constructed so that loudness grows nonlinearly with sound intensity, according to the same function used in Stevens' method. Both methods have received extensive testing and do reasonably well on a majority of common sound sources.

Basic Assumptions in Loudness Scales

All of the major scales share a common set of assumptions. They agree that loudness is composed of elementary loudnesses associated with each frequency region, and that total loudness is the combination of these elementary contributions. By virtue of the upward spread of masking, the combination rule cannot be simply linear. Stevens uses a special nonlinear formula, and Zwicker uses a nonlinear geometric construction.

Beyond this combination rule, two other sets of assumptions are critical: first, how sounds of different frequencies may be equated in intensity to produce equal loudness—the equal-loudness contours; and second, how loudness changes as a function of physical intensity—the growth of loudness function.

Stevens was a pioneer in trying to arrive at consensus on the equal-loudness contours. In 1972, he reviewed several dozen studies concerning the equal-loudness contour, and presented a mean and median loudness contour as obtained from the average of all these studies. One should be aware that the equal loudness contour changes somewhat with overall sound level. Above 40 dB sound pressure level, however, the curves are roughly parallel, and this is the region of most practical interest. Naturally, at very low sound pressure levels the curves must change. In fact, they must converge on the absolute threshold curve at the lowest sound pressure levels. One should also be aware that the contours at very low frequencies, under 1000 Hz, are still a matter of considerable dispute.

The problem of how loudness grows with physical intensity is a very old one in the field. It has been the subject of numerous experimental attacks. On this subject too Stevens (1955) published a thorough summary of all the available data. In that paper, he pointed out that there had been considerable consensus for a power-law relation between loudness and intensity level. If we express intensity in watts per square centimeter of acoustic power, then the relation between loudness and intensity is

$$L = aI^{0.3},$$

where L is the loudness, I is the intensity measured in power or energy terms, and a is a scale constant.

For a fixed acoustic impedance, acoustic power is proportional to acoustic pressure squared. We can therefore express the relation between loudness L and pressure p,

$$L = cp^{0.6},$$

where c is a scale constant. This power-law relation says, in effect, that if we raise the sound level by 10 dB, we will double the sound's loudness. There are, of course, slight deviations from this rule if we consider a wide range of overall intensities. At very low intensities, there may be some slight deviation from this rule. Also, the available data seem to indicate that at very high intensities there is a further compression of loudness, so that an increment of 20 dB is needed to double the loudness if the initial sound is very loud (100 dB or more).

This review has touched the essential features needed to assess the apparent magnitude of acoustic intensity and has discussed two international standards used to calculate the loudness of an arbitrary spectrum.

LOCALIZING AND UNDERSTANDING SOUND SOURCES

We conclude this chapter with a brief review of binaural phenomena. We will also discuss a topic that von Békésy (1960) called echo suppression. Our review of binaural phenomena will cover the traditional topics; it will be brief because this material is well covered in several other sources and because the binaural area of most current interest, masking level differences, has recently been the topic of an extensive review (Colburn & Durlach, 1978). The phenomenon of echo suppression is often ignored in discussions of psychoacoustic material because our understanding of this phenomenon is slight. Its general importance and potential interest to psychologists, however, cause us to review this topic even if we are unable to elucidate the sensory mechanisms responsible for this remarkable ability in any detail.

Binaural Localization

Sinusoidal of Periodic Stimuli
The earliest systematic work on sound localization was carried out in anechoic (echo-free) environments. One of the pioneer investigators was Lord Rayleigh who carried out the research, in part, in the open fields at the family estate at Terling. He summarized his findings in 1907 in the Sidgwick lecture given in Cambridge, England. Rayleigh (1907) suggested that low-frequency sinusoids are localized on the basis of interaural temporal differences between the two ears. Above about 1500 Hz, however, interaural phase or time differences do not affect the apparent location of a sinusoidal source. At higher frequencies, interaural intensity differences are the effective localization cue. The premise that the cue responsible for localization is different for high and low frequencies is the essential premise of the duplex theory of sound localization. For the next half century a number of more detailed and controlled investigations have elaborated this basic position and generated quantitative data on the physical differences at the two ears and how well observers could use these cues. There were many physical studies that carefully measured the difference in interaural time or interaural intensity that would be present for the two ears of a human observer in an anechoic field (Firestone, 1930; Hartley & Fry, 1921; Sandel, Teas, Feddersen, & Jeffress, 1955; Stewart, 1920; Wiener, 1947). An excellent summary of the physics and measurement of interaural time differences is Kuhn (1977); and of interaural intensity factors is, Shaw (1974).

Many psychophysical studies have measured how well a source can be localized in an anechoic environment. One of the earliest was the study of Stevens and Newman (1936). Later work, especially by Mills (1958, 1960), provided more detailed measurements of the just detectable change in localization as a function of initial azimuth and frequency.

In addition to these free-field studies, binaural experiments using earphones began in earnest. With earphones one can independently regulate and control the sounds presented at the two ears. One can, therefore, achieve a separation of the potential cues to localization that is impossible in the free field. For example, one can vary interaural intensity, holding interaural time constant, or the reverse. With headphone listening, the phenomenal image is within the head. We say the image is *lateralized* rather than localized. Of course changing the interaural parameters may move the lateralized image toward one ear or the other. The studies, though artificial and "unnatural", confirmed the earlier hypotheses about the usefulness of certain cues in the localization of real sources. Thus, Mills

(1960) was able to use Zwislocki and Feldman's (1956) data on discrimination of binaural stimuli using earphones to predict his data on the discrimination of sources in the free field.

The physical fact that diffraction by the head generates quite different interaural time and intensity cues as a function of frequency and the continued interest in the duplex theory maintained a constant interest in localization of sinusoidal stimuli.

The duplex theory, which claims the interaural *time* is the critical low-frequency cue and interaural *intensity* is the critical high-frequency cue, has provided a convenient integrative framework for organizing many facts of localization. One should note, however, that is was developed largely on the basis of localizing *sinusoidal* sources. For such simple stimuli, interaural temporal information becomes ineffective above about 1500 Hz. But as a series of recent papers has shown, this does not mean that the ear is deaf to interaural temporal differences at high frequencies. Henning (1974), McFadden and Pasanen (1976), and Nuetzel and Hafter (1976) have demonstrated that complex signals consisting of several high-frequency tones can be lateralized with as good accuracy as low-frequency tones. While a variety of different stimuli have been used, they generally consist of high-frequency carrier signals being modified in some way by a low-frequency signal. For example, Henning (1974) used an amplitude modulated signal. The carrier frequency was 3900 Hz and it was amplitude modulated at 300 Hz. Delaying either the entire waveform, the 300 Hz envelope, or a pure tone at 300 Hz produced about 75 percent correct lateralization judgments at an interaural delay of 70 μsec. All investigators have ruled out a low-frequency difference tone as the basis for discrimination by showing that the ability to lateralize the high-frequency complex is unaffected by a low-frequency masking noise. Moreover, Henning (1980) in a series of clever experiments has also demonstrated that this ability is not simply an envelope detector (square-law with low-pass filter), since quasi-frequency modulated signals can also be lateralized and such signals show no fluctuation at the envelope frequency. Using amplitude modulated signals with a 300 Hz modulation and a carrier of either 600 or 4000 Hz, he also showed that the lateralization judgments are different for low- and high-frequency complexes.

At high frequencies, a delay of the modulation waveform produced good lateralization; moving the carrier alone produced no change in the image. At low frequencies, the results were reversed: a delay of the carrier waveform produced good lateralization; moving the modulating waveform did not. The result is understandable if we realize that a simple amplitude modulated signal can be constructed with three sinusoidal components—one at the carrier frequency, f_o, and two side-band components at $f + f_o$ and $f_o - f$, where f is the rate of modulation. The failure to appreciate the modulation delay at low frequencies undoubtedly occurs because all three components, the carrier and both side bands, are resolved at low frequencies. The lack of lateralization is understandable if one considers the interaural phase relation of the three components of an amplitude modulated waveform. With modulation delay the carrier frequency has zero interaural delay, but the high frequency side band is delayed in one ear and the low frequency side band is advanced in that same ear. Thus, an ambiguous stimulus is created if the components of the complex wave can be resolved, as they probably are at low frequencies. At high frequencies, the side bands are probably not resolved and the entire complex contributes to the lateralization judgment.

There is no general agreement on the precise mechanism responsible for the use of these interaural temporal differences at high frequencies, but there is no doubt that these cues can be utilized by the binaural system.

Transient Stimuli

When using sinusoidal stimuli in binaural experiments, one takes extreme care to avoid any transient sounds associated with the presentation of the sinusoids, since the localization system is very sensitive to such cues. If a brief click is used as a stimulus, one can detect an interaural time difference of about 20 to 30μsec, although well-trained observers might be able to detect a difference of only 10μsec. The frequency composition of the transient is critical however. If the click is filtered to provide only high frequency information, say 4000 Hz and above, then the interaural time difference must be increased to 100 to 200μsec to maintain the same level of detectability that is required for a 30μsec low-frequency click (Yost, Wightman, & Green, 1971). This difference is surprising, especially when one considers the duration of the stimuli presented in the two cases. For the low-pass click, filtered at say 500 Hz, the stimulus duration is about 2000μsec, yet a difference of 30μsec between the waveform at the two ears is detectable. For the high-pass click the duration is only 200 to 300μsec, yet a time difference nearly equal to this duration is needed to detect the interaural time difference. Indeed, McFadden and Pasanen (1976) argue that it is exactly this difference in duration that makes the low-frequency transient easier to lateralize.

The largest time difference ever encountered in a natural environment depends somewhat on frequency and is about 800μsec for frequencies below 500 Hz for an average head size. If one listens with headphones to interaural time differences less than this amount, the phenomenal image moves towards the leading ear, as one might expect. If the interaural time difference exceeds about 600 to 800μsec, the image splits, so that, for example, two clicks arriving beyond this time difference sound as if two acoustic transients had occurred; one at one ear, the next at the opposite ear. In this case, we say that binaural image is not fused.

Median Sagittal Plane

For many years, almost all localization studies concerned themselves with objects located in a horizontal plane, a plane roughly determined by the observer's ear canals and the tip of the nose. Except for sources located straight ahead, all other sources will produce a stimulus with some interaural intensity or interaural time difference at the two ears.

But what of sources located straight ahead at various elevations, that is, in the plane midway between the two ears and perpendicular to the line connecting the two ears—the median-sagittal plane? To the extent that the head and ears are symmetric, there are no interaural time or intensity cues for any source located in this plane. Is localization possible? Surprisingly, localization is possible in the median-sagittal plane, although it is poorer by a factor of about five than localization in the horizontal plane.

Recent experimental work has very carefully isolated the cues responsible for our ability to localize sources in the median-sagittal plane. Part of the ability is based on the fact that the convolutions of the pinna exert a strong filtering action on the stimulus, and the form of the filter-

ing changes markedly with elevation (Shaw, 1966; Searle, Braida, Cuddy, & Davis, 1975). One observer in the latter study showed a notch of nearly 35 dB at 10 kHz for a source at 165° elevation; the value at 90° or 0° elevation was nearly 0 dB. Such filtering is most pronounced only at the higher frequencies (above 6 kHz). These facts would nicely account for Gardner's (1973) and Butler's (1969) finding that sagittal localization is noticeably poorer for low-pass than for high-pass noise. It is also consistent with the Gardner and Gardner (1973) finding that progressive occlusion of the pinna leads to poorer and poorer localization performance. Clearly, one must have some general information about the shape of the stimulus spectrum to make use of the changes produced by this filtering.

In addition to this essentially monaural cue, there are slight asymmetries between the ears and these asymmetries produce slight differences between the stimulus at the two ears, even if the source is located in the median-sagittal plane. As the measurements of Searle et al. show, the asymmetries produce palpable physical differences at the two ears. These "binaural" cues supplement the filtering cues and account for the improvement in judgments in the median-sagittal plane when the observers use both ears as opposed to monaural listening (Gardner, 1973; Butler, 1969). Searle et al. also scramble the spectrum to confuse any judgments based on spectral shape. They show that binaural listening can tolerate such scrambling better than monaural listening. In short it appears that binaural and monaural cues contribute about equally to localization judgments in the median-sagittal plane.

Searle, Braida, Davis, and Colburn (1976) have advanced an analytic model of sound localization based on an optimum statistical combination of six cues. They assess the relative contribution of each cue and suggest a way to incorporate the effects of stimulus range (potential number and extent of physical sources one might be asked to localize) to predict the errors of judgment found in a localization experiment. Their treatment of nearly 50 localization experiments with this integrative model provides a valuable summary of localization work over the past two decades.

Echo Suppression

We conclude this chapter with a brief discussion

of an auditory phenomenon usually called *echo suppression*. As we shall see, the term is not very apt, but since no other substitute has wide currency we will use it here. The phenomenon often receives scant attention from psychologists, although it is one of the most remarkable of auditory abilities. The phenomenon will be clear if we consider some elementary physical properties of the sound wave. Sound, unlike light, has a wavelength that is often comparable to the size of objects in the environment. Thus, an ordinary wooden or plaster wall reflects 95 to 97 percent of the incident acoustic energy. Also, the speed of sound compared with light is very slow, covering only about 35 cm per msec. Let us consider how these facts are manifest when we make a brief sound in a typical room. Suppose you are seated near the center of a small room, say 4 by 4 meters. There is a rug on the floor, one wall has large windows, the other walls are plaster, and the ceiling is acoustic tiles. You are facing the windows and a friend standing 1/2 meter from the windows makes a transient sound, say a hand clap, about one meter away. Approximately 3 msec after the clap, a nearly plane wave reaches your head; this is the direct path of the sound. For the next 100 to 200 msec, echoes from that transient bounce around the room and sweep over your head with intensities rivaling, if not surpassing, the first direct wave. For example, in addition to the direct path, the acoustic transient also sends a wave towards the window that is reflected with practically no attenuation, and this reaches your head only 3 msec after the original direct wave. Waves also travel towards the wall to your right and left richoceting towards you and reaching your head perhaps 10 to 12 msec after the original hand clap. If these waves reinforce each other, they may be 6 dB more intense than the sound of the hand clap as contained in the direct wave.

Consider next what happens when your friend says, "Oh, I hope I didn't startle you." The exclamation, like the hand clap, undergoes the same process of reflection and echoes and leaves an acoustic disturbance that is probably less attenuated than the sounds of the initial sentence arriving by their direct path. These later sounds also undergo reflections, but one is scarcely aware of any echo in this small environment.

The term echo suppression suggests that the echoes are not heard. This is not entirely correct because the quality of the sound is definitely affected by the acoustic environment in which it is heard. One immediately notices if the acoustic absorption in a room is excessive—the room sounds "dead." So the echoes in a typical room are appreciated, but they are not heard as distinctive echoes. In fact, we seldom notice echoes until the delays approach 1000 msec or more.

From a common-sense point of view, we might say that echoes are not perceived unless the delays are long and the intensity of the echo is appreciable. That certainly describes the situation well, but it hides the essential mystery. Why are these reverberations not heard with the short delays encountered in a typical room, and how is the ear able to suppress the echoes arriving within the first 50 to 100 msec so that they do not confuse the first arriving information? While the ear is suppressing the echoes from "I hope," how can it possibly listen and attend to the rest of the words of the sentence, especially when they are often arriving during the time that the echoes of the previous words are being suppressed?

This entire process is one of the most intriguing and interesting of auditory skills. With it, we could scarcely localize a sound source except in the most open and barren acoustic environments. Localizing an acoustic source in a typical, hard-wall room is like trying to locate a candle in a room whose four walls are covered with mirrors. There are literally hundreds of reasonable candidates as to the true location of the source.

Similarly, the perception of speech or music, which is so effortless we are hardly aware of it, is possible in intimate environments only because this process of echo suppression is at work. One immediately becomes aware of this process when one uses electronic devices to amplify or transform the acoustic information. The typical broadcast studio is made as echoless as possible, with great quantities of sound-absorbing material. Also, the broadcasters speak directly into their microphones at a close distance so that the direct path reaches the microphone earlier than any of the reflections and with greater intensity. Without these precautions, the listener would complain that the broadcast sounds peculiar and "hollow". The same listener has no trouble suppressing echoes produced in the room where the radio is playing, but he cannot ignore the echoes produced in the broadcast studio even if all these echoes occur in roughly the same time span. If nothing else, this example proves we are not inherently echo deaf.

In a very large auditorium or hall, a potential problem is that the source, whether a speaker or performer, cannot produce sufficient energy to be heard throughout the enclosure. If the walls of the enclosure are acoustically hard, then the acoustic intensity can be maintained, but at the price of very long delays which finally the ear notices and dislikes. If the hall absorbs the energy and thereby avoids the long echoes, the source intensity must be very great to compensate for this absorption.

The solution, of course, is to provide amplification. As has been appreciated for the past 30 or 40 years, this amplification must be accompanied with delays. If the delay is sufficient to allow the direct path to reach the listener's ears before the amplified wave arrives, then as much as 10 dB amplification from a secondary source will be tolerated. Indeed, the loudspeaker producing the delayed reinforced sound will be unnoticed by the naive listener. Without this delay, the listener would complain that the source was coming from the loudspeaker rather than the original source and perhaps comment on the echoes of the hall. Clearly, some echoes are not bad, only unnatural echoes create annoyance. But many of the phenomena described in the preceding paragraphs can be heard with a single ear. Localization of a sound source is clearly more difficult with one rather than with both ears, but still not impossible. Echo suppression is certainly present in the monaural system. One is not aware of excessive echoes in typical rooms if one closes one ear. Nevertheless, we have followed tradition and include this topic in our brief discussion of binaural localization.

The topic of echo suppression is little discussed in typical chapters on psychoacoustics because so little is known about the process. Two studies remain the source of practically all the experimental evidence available on this topic and, since one study is a binaural localization task, it is commonly assumed that processes involving the binaural system must be intimately involved.

The two classic studies in this area are the precedence experiment of Wallach, Newman, and Rosenzweig (1949) and the "law of the first waveform" by Haas (1949).

Haas published a doctoral dissertation in 1949 from the University of Göttingen. A translation by Ehrenberg of that now-famous work appeared in 1972. Haas used two loudspeakers and could independently control the delay and the ratio of intensity coming from the two sources. He measured the influence of these two parameters under a variety of listening conditions. For delays between 1 and 30 msec, so long as the delayed sound was 10 dB below the primary sound, the effect of the echo produced "a pleasant modification of the sound impression in the sense of a broadening of the primary sound source, while the echo source is not perceived acoustically." The direction from which the echo originates is not important. If greater delays or greater reinforcement are used, the delayed source is noticeable and, for example, interference with speech intelligibility will occur. So long as the delayed source occurs within this 30 msec and 10 dB intensity level, the effect of sound reinforcement is tolerated and indeed appreciated. As Muncey, Nickson, and Dubout (1953) have shown, in a reverberant room the sound reinforcement system can produce longer delays and louder echoes and still be tolerated more than a sound reinforcement system can in a dead room. More delay is also tolerated for music than for speech. In more recent studies, Lochner and Burger (1958) have confirmed Haas' original findings; they report, for example, that a second source delayed by 20 msec, but 8–10 dB more intense than a primary source, will not be heard as a "separate" source. They also measure the improvement in the subject's ability to recognize speech and show that perfect energy integration extends to a secondary source of equal amplitude for delays as long as 30 msec. Outside these limits, the reinforcement becomes disturbing.

The precedence experiment by Wallach, Newman, and Rosenzweig (1949) employed pairs of clicks occurring in rapid succession at the two ears. A critical feature of this experiment is that two clicks delivered to the same ear are fused if the clicks occur within about $1000\mu sec$, that is, the two clicks are heard as a single event. Pairs of clicks are delivered to both ears with different delays between the first and second click of the pairs. One can demonstrate that the delay between the first click is considerably more important than any delay between the trailing clicks in establishing the location of the fused image. For example, a delay of 50μsec (left leading right) between the first click may determine a fused image heard on the left even if the second pair of clicks has a delay of 500μsec (right leading left). The clear rule is that the first information on the locus of the source is given more weight or precedence than any information arriving later.

Although the precedence experiment has been widely replicated, and although the use of the Haas principle is widely used in the design of sound-reinforcing systems, there is little further work to elucidate the mechanisms responsible for this amazing ability.

REFERENCES

Abbas, P.J. (1978). Effects of stimulus frequency on two-tone suppression: A comparison of physiological and psychological results. *Journal of the Acoustical Society of America, 63*, 1878–1886.

Anderson, C.M.B. & Whittle, L.S. (1971). Physiological noise and the missing 6 dB. *Acustica, 24*, 261–272.

Békésy, G. von. (1966). *Experiments in hearing.* New York: McGraw-Hill.

Bos, C.E. & de Boer, E. (1966). Masking and discrimination. *Journal of the Acoustical Society of America, 39*, 708–715.

Brogden, W.J. & Miller, G.A. (1947). Physiological noise generated under earphone cushions. *Journal of the Acoustical Society of America, 19*, 620–623.

Burns, E.M. & Viemeister, N.F. (1981). Played-again SAM: Further observations on the pitch of amplitude-modulated noise. *Journal of the Acoustical Society of America, 70*, 1655–1660.

Butler, R.A. (1969). Monaural and binaural localization of noise bursts vertically in the median sagittal plane. *Journal of Auditory Research, 9*, 230–235.

Carterette, E.C., Friedman, M.P., & Lovell, J.D. (1969). Mach bands in hearing. *Journal of the Acoustical Society of America, 45*, 986–998.

Colburn, H.S. & Durlach, N.I. (1978). Models of binaural interaction. In E.C. Carterette & M.P. Friedman (Eds.), *Handbook of perception*, vol. IV, pp. 467–518. New York: Academic Press.

de Boer, E. (1956). On the "residue" in hearing. Doctoral dissertation, University of Amsterdam.

de Boer, E. (1976). On the "residue" and auditory pitch perception. In W.D. Keidel & W.D. Neff (Eds.), *Handbook of sensory physiology*, Vol. V/3, pp. 479–583. New York: Springer-Verlag.

Dimmick, F.L. & Olson, R.M. (1941). The intensive difference limen in audition. *Journal of the Acoustical Society of America, 12*, 517–525.

Duifhuis, H. (1976). Cochlear nonlinearity and second filter: Possible mechanisms and implications. *Journal of the Acoustical Society of America, 59*, 408–423.

Duifhuis, H. (1980). Level effects in psychophysical two-tone suppression. *Journal of the Acoustical Society of America, 67*, 914–927.

Durlach, N.I. & Colburn, H.S. (1978). Binaural phenomena. In E.C. Carterette & M.P. Friedman (Eds.), *Handbook of perception*, Vol. IV, pp. 365–466. New York: Academic Press.

Egan, J.P. & Hake, H.W. (1950). On the masking pattern of a simple auditory stimulus. *Journal of the Acoustical Society of America, 22*, 622–630.

Ehmer, R.H. (1959). Masking patterns of tones. *Journal of the Acoustical Society of America, 31*, 1115–1120.

Engebretson, A.M. & Eldredge, D.H. (1968). Model for nonlinear characteristics of cochlear potentials. *Journal of the Acoustical Society of America, 44*, 548–554.

Feuerstein, E. (1957). Intermodulation products for v-law biased wave rectifier for multiple frequency input. *Quarterly of Applied Mathematics, 15*, 183–192.

Firestone, F.A. (1930). The phase difference and amplitude ratio at the ears due to a source of a pure tone. *Journal of the Acoustical Society of America, 2*, 260–270.

Fletcher, H. (1924). The physical criterion for determining the pitch of a musical tone. *Physical Review, 23*, 427–437.

Fletcher, H. (1929). *Speech and hearing.* London: Macmillan.

Fletcher, H. (1940). Auditory patterns. *Review of Modern Physics, 12*, 47–65.

Fletcher, H. (1953). *Speech and hearing in communication.* New York: Van Nostrand.

Formby, C. & Sachs, R.M. (1980). Psychophysical tuning curves for combination tones 2f1-f2 and f2-f1. *Journal of the Acoustical Society of America, 67*, 1754–1758.

French, N.R. & Steinberg, J.C. (1947). Factors governing the intelligibility of speech sounds. *Journal of the Acoustical Society of America, 19*, 90–119.

Gardner, M.B. (1973). Some monaural and binaural facets of median plane localization. *Journal of the Acoustical Society of America, 54*, 1489–1495.

Gardner, M.B. & Gardner, R.S. (1973). Problem of localization in the median plane: Effect of pinnae cavity occlusion. *Journal of the Acoustical Society of America, 53*, 400–408.

Garner, W.R. (1947). Auditory thresholds of short tones as a function of repetition rates. *Journal of the Acoustical Society of America, 19*, 600–608.

Gerson, A. & Goldstein, J.L. (1978). Evidence for a general template in central optimal processing for pitch of complex tones. *Journal of the Acoustical Society of America, 63,* 498–510.

Glasberg, B.R., Moore, B.C.J., Patterson, R.D., & Nimmo-Smith, I. (1984). Dynamic range and asymmetry of the auditory filter. Submitted to *Journal of the Acoustical Society of America, 76,* 419–427.

Goldstein, J.L. (1967). Auditory nonlinearity. *Journal of the Acoustical Society of America, 41,* 676–689.

Goldstein, J.L. (1973). An optimum processor theory for the central formation of the pitch of complex tones. *Journal of the Acoustical Society of America, 54,* 1496–1516.

Goldstein, J.L., Gerson, A., Srulovicz, P., & Furst, M. (1978). Verification of the optimal probabilistic basis of aural processing in pitch of complex tones. *Journal of the Acoustical Society of America, 63,* 486–497.

Grantham, D.W. & Yost, W.A. (1982). Measures of intensity discrimination. *Journal of the Acoustical Society of America, 72,* 406–410.

Green, D.M. (1960). Auditory detection of a noise signal. *Journal of the Acoustical Society of America, 32,* 121–131.

Green, D.M. (1976). *An introduction to hearing.* Hillsdale, NJ: Erlbaum.

Green, D.M., McKay, M.J., & Licklider, J.C.R. (1959). Detection of a pulsed sinusoid in noise as a function of frequency. *Journal of the Acoustical Society of America, 31,* 1446–1452.

Green, D.M., Shelton, B.R., Picardi, M.C., & Hafter, E.R. (1981). Psychophysical tuning curves independent of signal level. *Journal of the Acoustical Society of America, 69,* 1758–1762.

Greenwood, D.D. (1961). Auditory masking and the critical band. *Journal of the Acoustical Society of America, 33,* 484–502.

Greenwood, D.D. (1971). Aural combination tones and auditory masking. *Journal of the Acoustical Society of America, 50,* 502–543.

Haas, H. (1972). The influence of a single echo on the audibility of speech. *Journal of the Audio Engineering Society, 20,* 146–159 (translated by K.P.R. Ehrenberg from Haas's 1949 doctoral dissertation).

Hamilton, P.M. (1957). Noise masked thresholds as a function of tonal duration and masking noise band width. *Journal of the Acoustical Society of America, 29,* 506–511.

Harris, J.D. (1963). Loudness discrimination. *Journal of Speech and Hearing Disorders,* Monogr. Suppl. II, 1–63.

Hartley, R.V.L. & Fry, T.C. (1921). The binaural localization of pure tones. *Physical Review, 18,* 431–442.

Hawkins, J.E., Jr. & Stevens, S.S. (1950). The masking of pure tones and of speech by white noise. *Journal of the Acoustical Society of America, 22,* 6–13.

Helmholtz, H.L.F. von. (1862). *Die Lehre von den Tonempfindungen als physiologische Grundlage für die Theorie der Musik,* Braunschweig: Vieweg. Transl., A.J. Ellis *On the sensations of tone as a physiological basis for the theory of music,* New York: Dover, 1954.

Henning, G.B. (1974). Detectability of interaural delay in high-frequency complex waveforms. *Journal of the Acoustical Society of America, 55,* 84–90.

Henning, G.B. (1980). Some observations on the lateralization of complex waveforms. *Journal of the Acoustical Society of America, 68,* 446–454.

Hinchcliffe, R. (1959). The threshold of hearing as a function of age. *Acustica, 9,* 303–308.

Houtgast, T. (1972). Psychophysical evidence for lateral inhibition in hearing. *Journal of the Acoustical Society of America, 51,* 1885–1894.

Houtgast, T. (1973). Psychophysical experiments on "tuning curves" and "two-tone inhibition." *Acustica, 29,* 168–179.

Houtgast, T. (1974). *Lateral suppression in hearing. A psychophysical study on the ear's capability to preserve and enhance spectral contrasts.* Doctoral dissertation, Soesterberg, The Netherlands: Institute for Perception.

Houtsma, A.J.M. & Goldstein, J.L. (1972). The central origin of the pitch of complex tones: Evidence from musical interval recognition. *Journal of the Acoustical Society of America, 51,* 520–529.

Humes, L.E. (1980). On the nature of two-tone aural nonlinearity. *Journal of the Acoustical Society of America, 67,* 2073–2083.

Jesteadt, W. & Javel, E. (1978). Measurement of suppression in a simultaneous masking paradigm. *Journal of the Acoustical Society of America, 63,* S44. Abstract.

Jesteadt, W., Wier, C.C., & Green, D.M. (1977). Intensity discrimination as a function of frequency and sensation level. *Journal of the Acoustical Society of America, 61,* 169–177.

Johnson-Davies, D. & Patterson, R.D. (1979). Psychophysical tuning curves: Restricting the listening band to the signal region. *Journal of the Acoustical Society of America, 65,* 765–770.

Kerkhof, G.A., van der Shaaf, T.W., & Korving, H.J. (1980). Auditory signal detection: Effects of long-term practice and time on task. *Perception & Psychophysics, 28,* 79–81.

Killion, M.C. (1978). Revised estimate of minimum audible pressure: Where is the missing 6 dB? *Journal of the Acoustical Society of America, 63,* 1501–1508.

König, R. (1876). Ueber den Zusammenklang z'weier Töne. *Annalen der Physik und Chemie, 157*, 177–237. (Trans., On the simultaneous sounding of two notes. *Philosophical Magazine I.* 1876, 5th ser., *1*, 417–446, 511–525.)

Kuhn, G.F. (1977). Model for the interaural time differences in the azimuthal plane. *Journal of the Acoustical Society of America, 62*, 157–167.

Licklider, J.C.R. (1954). "Periodicity" pitch and "place" pitch. *Journal of the Acoustical Society of America, 26*, 945. Abstract.

Lochner, J.P.A. & Burger, J.F. (1958). The subjective masking of short time delayed echoes by their primary sounds and their contribution to the intelligibility of speech. *Acustica, 8*, 1–10.

Luce, R.D. & Green, D.M. (1974). Neural coding and psychophysical discrimination data. *Journal of the Acoustical Society of America, 56*, 1554–1564.

Margolis, R.H. & Small, A.M. (1975). The measurement of critical masking bands. *Journal of Speech and Hearing Research, 18*, 571–587.

McFadden, D. & Pasanen, E. (1976). Lateralization at high frequencies based on interaural time differences. *Journal of the Acoustical Society of America, 59*, 634–639.

McGill, W.J. & Goldberg, J.P. (1968a). Pure-tone intensity discrimination and energy detection. *Journal of the Acoustical Society of America, 44*, 576–581.

McGill, W.J. & Goldberg, J.P. (1968b). A study of the near-miss involving Weber's law and pure-tone intensity discrimination. *Perception & Psychophysics, 4*, 105–109.

Mills, A.W. (1958). On the minimum audible angle. *Journal of the Acoustical Society of America, 30*, 237–246.

Mills, A.W. (1960). Lateralization of high-frequency tones. *Journal of the Acoustical Society of America, 32*, 132–134.

Molnar, C.E. (1974). Analysis of memoryless polynomial nonlinearities. *Journal of the Acoustical Society of America, 56*, S21. Abstract.

Moore, B.C.J. (1978). Psychophysical tuning curves measured in simultaneous and forward masking. *Journal of the Acoustical Society of America, 63*, 524–532.

Moore, B.C.J., Glasberg, B.R., & Shailer, M.J. (1984). Frequency and intensity difference limens for harmonics within complex tones. *Journal of the Acoustical Society of America, 25*, 550–561.

Moore, B.C.J. & Raab, D.H. (1974). Pure-tone intensity discrimination: Some experiments relating the "near-miss" to Weber's law. *Journal of the Acoustical Society of America, 55*, 1049–1054.

Muncey, R.W., Nickson, A.F.B., & Dubout, P. (1953). The acceptability of speech and music with a single artificial echo. *Acustica, 3*, 168–173.

Munson, W.A. & Wiener, F.M. (1952). In search of the missing 6 dB. *Journal of the Acoustical Society of America, 24*, 498–501.

Nelson, D.A. (1980). Comment on: The use of psychophysical tuning curves to measure frequency selectivity. In G. van den Brink & F.A. Bilsen (Eds.), *Psychophysical, physiological and behavioural studies in hearing,* Proceedings of the 5th International Symposium on Hearing, pp. 116–117. Delft: Delft University Press.

Nuetzel, J.M. & Hafter, E.R. (1976). Lateralization of complex waveforms: Effects of fine structure, amplitude, and duration. *Journal of the Acoustical Society of America, 60*, 1339–1346.

Ohm, G.S. (1843). Ueber die Definition des Tones, nebst daran geknüpfter Theorie der Sirene und ähnlicher tonbildender Vorrichtungen. *Annalen der Physik und Chemie, 59*, 497–565.

O'Malley, H. & Feth, L. (1978). Relationship between auditory frequency selectivity and two-tone suppression. *Journal of the Acoustical Society of America, 63*, S30. Abstract.

Patterson, R.D. (1973). The effects of relative phase and the number of components on residue pitch. *Journal of the Acoustical Society of America, 53*, 1565–1572.

Patterson, R.D. (1974). Auditory filter shape. *Journal of the Acoustical Society of America, 55*, 802–809.

Patterson, R.D. (1976). Auditory filter shapes derived with noise stimuli. *Journal of the Acoustical Society of America, 59*, 640–654.

Patterson, R.D. & Henning, G.B. (1977). Stimulus variability and auditory filter shape. *Journal of the Acoustical Society of America, 62*, 649–664.

Patterson, R.D. & Nimmo-Smith, I. (1980). Off-frequency listening and auditory-filter asymmetry. *Journal of the Acoustical Society of America, 67*, 229–245.

Penner, M.J., Leshowitz, B., Cudahy, E., & Richard, G. (1974). Intensity discrimination for pulsed sinusoids of various frequencies. *Perception & Psychophysics, 15*, 568–570.

Pfeiffer, R.R. (1970). A model for two-tone inhibition of single cochlear nerve fibers. *Journal of the Acoustical Society of America, 48*, 1373–1378.

Plomp, R. (1964). The ear as a frequency analyzer. *Journal of the Acoustical Society of America, 36*, 1628–1636.

Plomp, R. (1965). Detectability threshold for combination tones. *Journal of the Acoustical Society of America, 37*, 1110–1123.

Plomp, R. (1966). Experiments on tone perception. Doctoral dissertation, Soesterberg, The Netherlands: Institute for Perception.

Plomp, R. (1967). Pitch of complex tones. *Journal of Acoustical Society of America, 41*, 1526–1533.

Rayleigh, Lord. (1882). An instrument capable of measuring the intensity of aerial vibrations. *Philosophical Magazine, 14*, 186–187.

Rayleigh, Lord. (1894). *The theory of sound.* 2nd ed., New York: Dover, 1945, vol. 1, pp. 20–24.

Rayleigh, Lord. (1907). On our perception of sound direction. *Philosophical Magazine, 13*, 214–232.

Reed, C.M. & Bilger, R.C. (1973). A comparison study of S/N_0 and E/N_0. *Journal of the Acoustical Society of America, 53*, 1039–1044.

Riesz, R.R. (1928). Differential intensity sensitivity of the ear for pure tones. *Physical Review, 31*, 867–875.

Ritsma, R.J. (1962). Existence region of the tonal residue: I. *Journal of the Acoustical Society of America, 34*, 1224–1229.

Ritsma, R.J. (1967). Frequencies dominant in the perception of the pitch of complex sounds. *Journal of the Acoustical Society of America, 42*, 191–198.

Rudmose, W. (1950). Free-field thresholds vs. pressure thresholds at low frequencies. *Journal of the Acoustical Society of America, 22*, 674. Abstract.

Rudmose, W. (1962). Pressure vs. free field thresholds at low frequencies. *Proceedings of the 4th International Congress on Acoustics*, Copenhagen, 1962, Paper H52.

Rudmose, W. (1982). The case of the missing 6 dB. *Journal of the Acoustical Society of America, 71*, 650–659.

Rutherford, W. (1888). A new theory of the sense of hearing. *Journal of Anatomy (Lond.), 1886, 21*, 166–168.

Sachs, M.B. & Kiang, N.Y.S. (1968). Two-tone inhibition in auditory nerve fibers. *Journal of the Acoustical Society of America, 43*, 1120–1128.

Sandel, T.T., Teas, D.C., Feddersen, W.E., & Jeffress, L.A. (1955). Localization of sound from single and paired sources. *Journal of the Acoustical Society of America, 27*, 842–852.

Schacknow, P.N. & Raab, D.H. (1973). Intensity discrimination of tone bursts and the form of the Weber function. *Perception & Psychophysics, 14*, 449–450.

Schacknow, P.N. & Raab, D.H. (1976). Noise-intensity discrimination: Effects of bandwidth conditions and mode of masker presentation. *Journal of the Acoustical Society of America, 60*, 893–905.

Schafer, T.H., Gales, R.S., Shewmaker, C.A., & Thompson, P.O. (1950). The frequency selectivity of the ear as determined by masking experiments. *Journal of the Acoustical Society of America, 22*, 490–496.

Schouten, J.F. (1938–1940). *Five articles on the perception of sound.* Eindhoven, The Netherlands: Institute for Perception.

Schouten, J.F., Ritsma, R.J., & Cardozo, B.L. (1962). Pitch of the residue. *Journal of the Acoustical Society of America, 34*, 1418–1424.

Searle, C.L., Braida, L.D., Cuddy, D.R., & Davis, M.F. (1975). Binaural pinna disparity: Another auditory localization cue. *Journal of the Acoustical Society of America, 57*, 448–455.

Searle, C.L., Braida, L.D., Davis, M.F., & Colburn, H.S. (1976). Model for auditory localization. *Journal of the Acoustical Society of America, 60*, 1164–1175.

Seebeck, A. (1841). Beobachtungen über einige Bedingungen der Entstehung von Tönen. *Annalen der Physik und Chemie, 53*, 417–436.

Seebeck, A. (1843). Ueber die Sirene. *Annalen der Physik und Chemie, 60*, 449–481.

Shannon, R.V. (1976). Two-tone unmasking and suppression in a forward masking situation. *Journal of the Acoustical Society of America, 59*, 1460–1470.

Shaw, E.A.G. (1966). Ear canal pressure generated by a free sound field. *Journal of the Acoustical Society of America, 39*, 465–470.

Shaw, E.A.G. (1974). The external ear. In W.D. Keidel & W.D. Neff (Eds.), *Handbook of sensory physiology*, Vol. V/1, pp. 455–490. New York: Springer-Verlag.

Shaw, E.A.G. & Piercy, J.E. (1962). Physiological noise in relation to audiometry. *Journal of the Acoustical Society of America, 34*, 745. Abstract.

Shower, E.G. & Biddulph, R. (1931). Differential pitch sensitivity of the ear. *Journal of the Acoustical Society of America, 3*, 275–287.

Siebert, W.M. (1968). Stimulus transformations in the peripheral auditory system. In P.A. Kolers & M. Eden (Eds.), *Recognizing patterns*, pp. 104–133. Cambridge, MA: MIT Press.

Siebert, W.M. (1970). Frequency discrimination in the auditory system: Place or periodicity mechanisms? *Proceedings of the IEEE, 58*, 723–730.

Sivian, L.J. & White, S.D. (1933). On minimum audible sound fields. *Journal of the Acoustical Society of America, 4*, 288–321.

Small, A.M., Jr. (1959). Pure-tone masking. *Journal of the Acoustical Society of America, 31*, 1619–1625.

Small, A.M. (1975). Mach bands in auditory masking revisited. *Journal of the Acoustical Society of America, 57*, 251–252.

Small, A.M. & Tyler, R.S. (1978). Additive masking effects of noise bands of different levels. *Journal of the Acoustical Society of America, 63*, 894–904.

Smoorenburg, G.F. (1970). Pitch perception of two-frequency stimuli. *Journal of the Acoustical Society of America, 48*, 924–942.

Smoorenburg, G.F. (1972a). Audibility region of combination tones. *Journal of the Acoustical Society of America, 52*, 603–614.

Smoorenburg, G.F. (1972b). Combination tones and

their origin. *Journal of the Acoustical Society of America*, 52, 615–632.

Smoorenburg, G.F. (1974). On the mechanisms of combination tone generation and lateral inhibition in hearing. In E. Zwicken & E. Terhardt (Eds.), *Facts and models in hearing*, pp. 332–343. New York: Springer-Verlag.

Spiegel, M.F. (1979). The range of spectral integration. *Journal of the Acoustical Society of America*, 66, 1356–1363.

Stevens, S.S. (1955). The measurement of loudness. *Journal of the Acoustical Society of America*, 27, 815–829.

Stevens, S.S. (1956). Calculation of the loudness of complex noise. *Journal of the Acoustical Society of America*, 28, 807–832.

Stevens, S.S. (1972). Perceived level of noise by Mark VII and decibels (E). *Journal of the Acoustical Society of America*, 51, 575–601.

Stevens, S.S. (1975). *Psychophysics: Introduction to its perceptual, neural, and social prospects*. New York: Wiley.

Stevens, S.S. & Davis, H. (1938). *Hearing: Its psychology and physiology*. New York: Wiley.

Stevens, S.S. & Newman, E.B. (1936). The localization of actual sources of sound. *American Journal of Psychology*, 48, 297–306.

Stewart, G.W. (1920). The function of intensity and phase in the binaural location of pure tones. I. Intensity. *Physical Review*, 15, 425–431.

Swets, J.A., Green, D.M., & Tanner, W.P., Jr. (1962). On the width of critical bands. *Journal of the Acoustical Society of America*, 34, 108–113.

Tartini, G. (1751). Trattato di musica secondo la vera scienza dell' armonia. *Padova*, 1754, 10–19.

Terhardt, E. (1974). Pitch, consonance, and harmony. *Journal of the Acoustical Society of America*, 55, 1061–1069.

Terhardt, E., Stoll, G., & Seewann, M. (1982a). Pitch of complex signals according to virtual-pitch theory: tests, examples, and predictions. *Journal of the Acoustical Society of America*, 71, 671–678.

Terhardt, E., Stoll, G., & Seewann, M. (1982b). Algorithm for extraction of pitch salience from complex tonal signals. *Journal of the Acoustical Society of America*, 71, 679–688.

Terry, M. & Moore, B.C.J. (1977). "Suppression" effects in forward masking. *Journal of the Acoustical Society of America*, 62, 781–784.

Thurlow, W.R. (1963). Perception of low auditory pitch: A multicue mediation theory. *Psychological Review*, 70, 461–470.

Thurstone, L.L. (1927a). A law of comparative judgment. *Psychological Review*, 34, 273–286.

Thurstone, L.L. (1927b). Psychophysical analysis. *American Journal of Psychology*, 38, 368–389.

Tillman, T.W., Johnson, R.M., & Olsen, W.O. (1966). Earphone versus sound-field threshold sound-pressure levels for spondee words. *Journal of the Acoustical Society of America*, 39, 125–133.

Torgerson, W.S. (1958). *Theory and methods of scaling*. New York: Wiley.

Tyler, R.S. & Small, A.M. (1977). Two-tone suppression in backward masking. *Journal of the Acoustical Society of America*, 62, 215–218.

Viemeister, N.F. (1972). Intensity discrimination of pulsed sinusoids: The effects of filtered noise. *Journal of the Acoustical Society of America*, 51, 1265–1269.

Vogten, L.L.M. (1974). Pure-tone masking: A new result from a new method. In E. Zwicker & E. Terhardt (Eds.), *Facts and models in hearing*, pp. 142–155. New York: Springer-Verlag.

Wallach, H., Newman, E.B., & Rosenzweig, M.R. (1949). The precedence effect in sound localization. *American Journal of Psychology*, 62, 315–336.

Walliser, K. (1969). Zusammenhänge zwischen dem Schallreiz und der Periodenhöhe. *Acustica*, 21, 319–329.

Watson, C.S. (1973). Psychophysics. In B.B. Wolman (Ed.), *Handbook of general psychology*, pp. 275–306. Englewood Cliffs, NJ: Prentice-Hall.

Watson, C.S., Franks, J.R., & Hood, D.C. (1972). Detection of tones in the absence of external masking noise. I. Effects of signal intensity and signal frequency. *Journal of the Acoustical Society of America*, 52, 633–643.

Weber, D.L. (1977). Growth of masking and auditory filter. *Journal of the Acoustical Society of America*, 62, 424–429.

Weber, D.L. (1978). Suppression and critical bands in band-limiting experiments. *Journal of the Acoustical Society of America*, 64, 141–150.

Weber, D.L. & Green, D.M. (1978). Temporal factors and suppression effects in backward and forward masking. *Journal of the Acoustical Society of America*, 64, 1392–1399.

Weber, D.L. & Green, D.M. (1979). Suppression effects in backward and forward masking. *Journal of the Acoustical Society of America*, 65, 1258–1267.

Weber, W. (1829). Ueber die Tartinischen Töne. *Annalen der Physik und Chemie*, 15, 216–222.

Wegel, R.L. & Lane, C.E. (1924). The auditory masking of one pure tone by another and its probable relation to the dynamics of the inner ear. *Physical Review*, 23, 266–285.

Wever, E.G. (1949). *Theory of hearing*. New York: Wiley.

Wiener, F.M. (1947). On the diffraction of a progressive

sound wave by the human head. *Journal of the Acoustical Society of America, 19,* 143–146.

Wightman, F.L. (1973a). The pattern-transformation model of pitch. *Journal of the Acoustical Society of America, 54,* 407–416.

Wightman, F.L. (1973b). Pitch and stimulus fine structure. *Journal of the Acoustical Society of America, 54,* 397–406.

Wightman, F.L. (1981). Personal communication.

Wightman, F., McGee, T., & Kramer, M. (1977). Factors influencing frequency selectivity in normal and hearing-impaired listeners. In E.F. Evans & J.P. Wilson (Eds.), *Psychophysics and physiology of hearing,* pp. 295–306. New York: Academic Press.

Yost, W.A. (1979). Models of the pitch and pitch strength of ripple noise. *Journal of the Acoustical Society of America, 66,* 400–410.

Yost, W.A. & Hill, R. (1978). Strength of the pitches associated with ripple noise. *Journal of the Acoustical Society of America, 64,* 485–492.

Yost, W.A., Hill, R., & Perez-Falcon, T. (1978). Pitch and pitch discrimination of broadband signals with rippled power spectra. *Journal of the Acoustical Society of America, 63,* 1166–1173.

Yost, W.A., Wightman, F.L., & Green, D.M. (1971). Lateralization of filtered clicks. *Journal of the Acoustical Society of America, 50,* 1526–1531.

Zwicker, E. (1955). Der ungewöhnliche Amplitudengang der nichtlinearen Verzerrungen des Ohres. *Acustica, 5,* 67–74.

Zwicker, E. (1958). Ueber psychologische und methodische Grundlagen der Lautheit. *Acustica, 8,* 237–258.

Zwicker, E. (1961). Subdivision of the audible frequency range into critical bands (Frequenzgruppen). *Journal of the Acoustical Society of America, 33,* 248.

Zwicker, E. (1968). Der kubische Differenzton und die Erregung des Gehörs. *Acustica, 20,* 206–209.

Zwicker, E. (1970). Masking and psychological excitation as consequences of the ear's frequency analysis. In R. Plomp & G.F. Smoorenburg (Eds.), *Frequency analysis and periodicity detection in hearing,* pp. 376–396. Leiden: A.W. Sijthoff.

Zwicker, E. (1974). On a psychoacoustical equivalent of a tuning curve. In E. Zwicker & E. Terhardt (Eds.), *Facts and models in hearing,* pp. 132–141. New York: Springer-Verlag.

Zwicker, E., Flottorp, G., & Stevens, S.S. (1957). Critical band width in loudness summation. *Journal of the Acoustical Society of America, 29,* 548–557.

Zwislocki, J. & Feldman, R.S. (1956). Just noticeable differences in dichotic phase. *Journal of the Acoustical Society of America, 28,* 860–864.

Chapter 7

Auditory Perception and Speech

Ira J. Hirsh, *Washington University and Central Institute for the Deaf*

INTRODUCTION

Knowledge of hearing as a sensory process has come from a long series of laboratory studies in psychophysics and physiology. Theory and experiments have elucidated the relations between traditional acoustic properties of sounds and (1) psychological responses, for example, detection, discrimination, identification, sensory-magnitude scaling, (2) biomechanical behavior of the ear, and (3) physiological responses in the cochlea and auditory nervous system. These laboratory studies have, naturally enough, utilized sounds that can be controlled and specified acoustically. Results are treated by Green (Chapter 6) and by Kiang and Peake (Chapter 5) in this volume.

Those results concern what would be called *sensation* in the traditional dichotomy of sensation and perception. The emphasis in this chapter will be on *perception*, by which we mean

Acknowledgments—Preparation of this chapter was partially supported under a Program Project Grant (NS-03856) from the National Institute for Neurological and Communicative Disorders and Stroke and a Research Grant from the USAF Office of Scientific Research to the Central Institute for the Deaf. Dr. Judith Lauter and two anonymous reviewers read and offered important comments and suggestions on earlier drafts.

those auditory phenomena associated with sounds and sound patterns that yield information about the acoustical environment. While the distinction between sensory and perceptual processes is not always clear, we shall find that the emphasis on perception forces us to go beyond classical acoustical dimensions, which for the most part describe single sounds, to more holistic properties of sound patterns.

One can describe a hierarchical typology of sounds from single, simple sounds through single, complex ones, to strings or sequences of both simple and complex sound patterns, to entire bird calls, sentences, and musical refrains.

We begin with a physical approach to patterns, mainly because little is known about the appropriate dimensions for sound patterns. Thus, we begin with the stimulus. While this approach may be arbitrary, it is no more so than one that is based upon a supposed parallelism between the dimensions of sound patterns and either those of music theory or of phonological systems in human language. Our focus will be on patterns that differ from each other, so that they can be used in ensembles, vocabularies or sets of alternatives for transmission of acoustic information.

Types of sound patterns

Single Sounds, Steady State

From the point of view of a physical stimulus, the simplest set of sounds is one in which each sound retains its properties in a steady state. For example, in a set of musical notes the sounds differ from each other in only one dimension—fundamental frequency. Another example of a set of only two sounds is found in the short and long tones of the Morse Code. Examples of other sets are the sounds of orchestral instruments or the vowel sounds of a language. In the sounds of both orchestral instruments and vowels, the fundamental frequency may be constant, while the pattern of harmonics—their relative amplitudes and phases (and resulting timbre or vowel color) —varies.

Single Sounds, Changing State

Somewhat more complex than single sounds in steady state are those whose acoustical properties change within the duration of the sound. When the intensity grows or fades as in a brief crescendo or diminuendo, or when the frequency changes as in a glide or glissando, or when the spectral composition changes as in a spoken diphthong (see below), the sound must be described not merely as an instantaneous or a long-term spectrum, but also as one that changes as a function of time. Although such changes will normally characterize sequences or patterns of sound elements, even short, single sounds may include some element of change. A further degree of complexity in such sounds is shown by the change in more than one acoustical property over time, for example, in the second syllable of "oh no!" where the vowel (/o/ to /u/) is marked by a change in the relative amplitudes of the harmonics, and also the intensity and fundamental frequency fall to indicate a downward inflection.

Sound Sequences

Almost all sound patterns that serve to provide acoustical information consist not of single sounds, but of strings or sequences of single-sound elements or events. Variation among such patterns may be related to (1) the number of elements, (2) the number of ways in which the elements differ from each other, and (3) the order and timing of the elements within the sequence (Hirsh, 1959). If we were limited to single sounds only, the stimulus information in any ensemble of such sounds would be proportional to the number of such sounds. With patterns, information for any given pattern may be increased beyond information for a given sound when the pattern consists of chains of two or more sounds. Thus with only two sounds, a tone and a noise, the set of possible sequential patterns of the two elements would be: tone-noise, noise-tone, tone-tone, and noise-noise.

The number of dimensions of variation used in constructing sound sequences form an interesting hierarchy. Such a sequence may consist entirely of homogeneous elements, for example, the beats of a monotone drum, where changes are made only in the intervals between successive sounds. Or the elements may differ in only one dimension, such as duration, in which event we have the sequences that comprise the alphabet in Morse Code. The elements may also differ in two dimensions, such as duration and frequency, in which event we now have the beginnings of melody. In running speech, many dimensions of the acoustic signal may vary to produce the elements of the message.

Concurrent Sound Sequences

A sound sequence as complicated as a whole sentence or a symphonic movement is not, however, the most complex pattern to which a listener may be exposed. There can be several sources of individual sounds or of sound sequences acting concurrently. Sometimes two or more sound patterns are highly correlated, while at other times they are virtually independent. In a concert hall, for example, the musical sounds traveling directly from the orchestra to the listener comprise one sound pattern (we neglect for the moment the differences between the sounds at the two ears of the listener), while another set of sounds is reflected from the walls and ceiling. As a result, the listener receives a group of sounds, all formed from a single, combined pressure wave that has arisen from different sources at slightly different times. At another extreme, a patterned sound sequence may be accompanied by a background noise. Speech in a room of noisy machines gives rise to a combined, complex pressure wave at the ears, and yet the listener seems to be able to separate the two sources so that the speech is perceived and recognized. An intermediate situation is one in which two sound streams are to be perceived, for example, music on the stage and the conversation of your neighbor, or speech from one person and perhaps a conversation between two others. An oscilloscope or spectrum analyzer displays the complex combinations of such multiple sounds, which the listener is able to separate with remarkable ability. We do not understand all the rules of coherence, context, and perceptual grouping that apply to this example of figure-ground separation.

Perception of Sound Patterns

In the following sections, we will review some of the research that deals with the processing of auditory information in the different kinds of sounds mentioned above. Most of this research of an empirical and phenomenological nature has not yet been systematized in such a way as to yield a quantitative theory.

Pitch and loudness of single simple sounds are the perceptual attributes that have been most studied (see Green, Chapter 6 this volume). To pitch and loudness we must add other dimensions that have received much less attention. Nevertheless listeners seem to use more than those two attributes to describe and categorize sounds. We must consider, for example, duration and some additional dimensions related to the notion of *timbre*, which either can be restricted to musical sounds or complex tones, or can be considered more generally as sound quality that can be extended to all sounds including noises.

For single sounds with changing state, we will find that most of the studies concern either the discrimination of a change or the effect of a change on some attribute such as pitch. Research on sound sequences has applied a great variety of psychophysical tasks to elucidate both pattern properties and the influence of certain aspects of pattern on more fundamental psychoacoustic dimensions.

AUDITORY ATTRIBUTES OF SINGLE SOUNDS

Pitch, loudness, and apparent duration are the principal unidimensional auditory attributes; they can be scaled respectively from low to high, weak to strong, or short to long. Pitch and loudness are most often studied both because the related physical dimensions of frequency and

intensity can be controlled and also because they have been shown to be useful in describing basic mechanisms of the peripheral auditory system. Apparent duration is not peculiarly auditory, but as one of John Locke's "primary" sensory attributes it has been studied as part of more general time perception (Woodrow, 1951; Fraisse, 1963).

In view of the great variety of sounds that human listeners can discriminate and identify, it is apparent that those three attributes alone are not sufficient to characterize a particular sound sensation. Another more complex characteristic is often referred to as *sound quality*. In the sections below we will try to cover several of the aspects that contribute to judgments of sound quality. Chief among them, at least for musical sounds or complex tones, is *timbre*. While some use quality and timbre interchangeably, we will restrict the use of timbre to refer to complex tones.

Duration

Perceived duration has been studied as an attribute that applies to all senses. In important reviews (Woodrow, 1951; Fraisse, 1963), measures of apparent duration of visual or auditory stimuli or both were made by asking observers to press a key to match the stimulus just observed (method of reproduction), or to name the duration (in seconds or minutes) of the stimulus just observed (method of estimation).

There is a second approach that concerns the effect of physical duration on psychoacoustic phenomena. For example, Doughty and Garner (1947) studied the effect of the duration of a tone on its tonality (see below under *pitch strength*). Pitch matching and pitch discrimination are both affected by the duration of tonal signals, according to observations made by Békésy (as cited in Stevens & Davis, 1938) and Turnbull (1944). As tonal duration increases, the difference limen for frequency diminishes (Liang & Chistovich, 1960). Both loudness and loudness discrimination have been found to be related to tonal (physical) duration (Garner & Miller, 1947). Duration also interacts with intensity, an effect shown for the absolute and masked thresholds and for judgments of constant loudness (Licklider, 1951; Zwislocki, 1969). The effects of duration both on frequency discrimination and on intensity discrimination

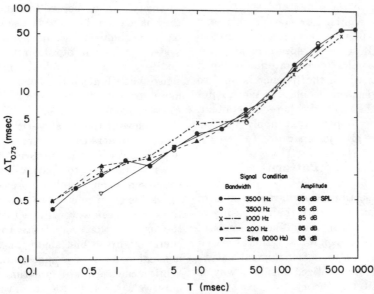

Figure 7.1. Duration discrimination as a function of the duration to which the increment is added. The just-discriminable increment (ΔT) is shown for different noise bandwidths, waveforms, and amplitudes. (From "Duration Discrimination of Noise and Tone Bursts" by S. Abel, 1972, *Journal of the Acoustical Society of America, 51*, p. 1221. Copyright 1972 by the American Institute of Physics. Reprinted by permission.)

have been compared directly by Henning (1971). (See also Luce and Krumhansl, Chapter 1 this volume, Figure 1.29). Although it is difficult to summarize the many experiments pertaining to the effects of sound duration on psychoacoustic phenomena, the results in general show that when a tone has a duration of greater than approximately 100 msec, most measurements are about the same as they would be for longer tones. Durations shorter than 100 msec yield increased variability in matching pitch or loudness.

A third experimental approach is specifically concerned with perceived duration of sounds and temporal discrimination. Even though we cannot compare two successive sounds simultaneously, there are data on the ability of listeners to discriminate the durations of simple sounds (Figure 7.1; see also Small & Campbell, 1962; Creelman, 1962; Abel, 1972). In speech the apparent duration of syllables contributes to the perception of stress (Fry, 1958); and the apparent duration of vowels signals whether the subsequent consonants are voiced or voiceless, e.g., /d/ or /v/ as opposed to /t/ or /f/ (Denes, 1955; Raphael, 1972). In music, different durations— symbolized musical notation marked by different dots and flags—give rise to different rhythms.

Sound Quality

Out of the many sound attributes gathered under the notion of *quality*, we can distinguish two categories of acoustical characteristics. First, there are those characteristics that can be described by the steady-state spectrum of a sound, whether a line spectrum with discrete tonal components or a continuous spectrum in which individual frequencies are not apparent. The line spectrum is characteristic of complex tones while continuous spectrum is used to describe noises. The spectrum alone accounts for a great variety of qualities, as illustrated in Figure 7.2, taken from Fastl and Stoll (1979) Complex tones yield line spectra (e.g., numbers 1, 2, 3, 5, 6 and 12), described by the number of harmonic components, the fundamental or lowest frequency of the components, the bandwidth of a filter through which the complex tone has passed, or the rate at which the amplitude of the components falls off as a function of frequency, or a combination of all of these. Such spectral differences underlie our recognition of different vowels and of different musical instruments. Individual frequency (line) components are not seen in the noises illustrated under numbers 4, 7, 8, 9 and 11. Continuous spectra of

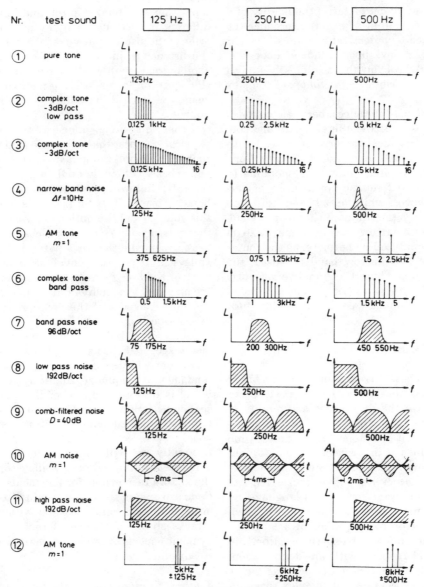

Figure 7.2. Acoustical spectra of a variety of sounds that differ in predominant or fundamental frequency (columns), or in spectral character (rows). (From "Scaling of Pitch Strength" by H. Fastl and G. Stoll, 1979, *Hearing Research*, *1*, p. 294. Copyright 1979 by Elsevier Science Publishers B.V. (Biomedical Division). Reprinted by permission.)

noises may show differences in bandwidth and also in the number of peaks in the noise spectra (e.g., number 9).

Falling into the second group of acoustical characteristics are those signals that are more fittingly described by temporal than by spectral analysis. These include frequency modulation, amplitude modulation (Figure 7.2, number 10), the amount and rate of interruption, abruptness of onset or decay, and similar factors than cannot be described by the spectrum alone.

Unlike the unidimensional scales of pitch, loudness, and duration, the perceptual dimensions that are used to describe sound quality are more abstract. While there are some dimensions that appear to be scalar (for example, sounds can be rated *sharp* to *dull*, *consonant* to *dissonant*, *tonal* to *noisy*), a large number of the adjectives used to characterize the quality of a sound refer to familiar objects that produce the sound, suffixed by adjectival endings of "-y" or "-like" (e.g., raspy, boomy, noisy, oboe-like, machine-like). Probably the most closely studied sound-quality attribute is the *timbre* of complex tones.

The physical differences between complex tones and noises, between line spectra and continuous spectra, seem to correspond well with judgments of "tonal" and "noisy" quality. Complex tones have pitch, often corresponding to the fundamental frequency of a series of harmonics. However, while broad-band noises do not have such pitch, we note that as the bandwidth of a noise narrows, the noise may take on a pitch-like quality. Furthermore, as the center frequency of this narrow band is raised, the pitch goes up. Thus the tonal-versus-noisy dimension of quality may not be a dichotomy, but rather a continuum (see below under *pitch strength*).

Timbre of Complex Tones

The fullest classical treatment of the timbre of complex tones appears in Helmholtz (1912), in chapter 5, "On the differences and quality of musical tones," and chapter 6, "On the apprehension of qualities of tone." In that discussion timbre is defined as that aspect of complex tones according to which the listener can identify sounds that characterize a given musical instrument or the different vowels of a language. So long as the natural sounds produced by such an instrument or by a speaker of a language remained the subject of experimentation, the listener could respond with an identification. However, experimenters going back as far as Helmholtz have synthesized complex tones, in order to vary the amplitudes and phases of individual harmonic components. For such tones, the resulting sound may not be characteristic of any one instrument or of any particular vowel, and accordingly the responses of listeners have shown greater diversity.

In the following sections we will review briefly the adjectives used for different timbres in descriptions that are both numerous and difficult to interpret. Factor analysis (von Bismarck, 1974) has led to a reduction in the number of response categories that are required to cover a timbral space. One can also simplify responses by asking listeners to distinguish between two tones that are equal in pitch and loudness but different in spectrum. A more advanced utilization of the discriminative response may require the listener to judge pairs of similar and dissimilar tones within a triad of complex tones (Plomp, 1970; for underlying methods and concepts, see Luce & Krumhansl, Chapter 1 this volume).

Other questions concern the particular physical factors that underlie judgments of timbre. Helmholtz emphasized the amplitudes and phases of individual harmonics. More recently, following developments of critical-band theory in hearing (see Green, Chapter 6 this volume) and the notion of *formant* in vowel theory (see below), complex tones have come to be represented either by a pattern of peaks and valleys in a spectrum envelope or by a profile (Green, Kidd, & Picardi, 1983), rather than by the amplitudes of individual components.

Another aspect of the appropriate stimulus description concerns the relative-versus-absolute role of harmonic frequencies. It is commonly accepted that a saxophone sounds like a saxophone whether it is playing a low or a high fundamental frequency. Similarly, a particular vowel is uniformly apprehended whether it is spoken by a man, woman or child with different fundamental frequencies and differently sized vocal tracts.

Finally we will consider the limitation of using steady-state properties alone to represent the factors responsible for judgments of timbre. Comparisons of listeners' ability to identify musical instruments with and without initial attacks show how much of timbre resides in dynamic aspects of the sounds, as opposed to the steady-state spectrum.

Timbre: Components of the Spectrum

Through an ingenious arrangement of electrically-driven tuning forks, resonator enclosures, and distances between source and receiver, Helmholtz was able to control the relative amplitudes and phases of components in a harmonic series. He concluded that timbre was determined by the relative amplitudes of the individual component. "The quality of the musical portion of a compound tone depends solely on the number and relative strength of its partial simple tones, and in no respect on their differences of phase" (Helmholtz, 1912, p. 126). About a hundred years after the publication of Helmholtz's first edition of 1863, Plomp and

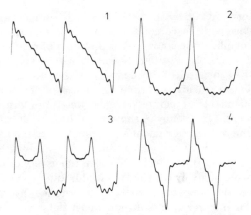

Figure 7.3. Waveforms of four complex tones. Numbers 1 and 2 consist of harmonics, all in sine or cosine phase. In Numbers 3 and 4, successive harmonics are of different phase (e.g. in (3) harmonics 1, 3, 5, 7 and 9 are in sine phase, while 2, 4, 6, 8, and 10 are in cosine phase; in (4) the reverse is true). (From *Aspects of Tone Sensation* (p. 69) by R. Plomp, 1976, Orlando, FL: Academic Press. Copyright 1976 by Academic Press. Reprinted by permission.)

Steeneken (1969) showed that phase could contribute to timbre even though its role was secondary to amplitude. Using modern synthesis techniques with electronic and computer controls, they demonstrated that although two tones in which all the harmonic components were in sine phase did not sound different from a tone in which all components were in cosine phase, nevertheless both those tones sounded different from one in which successively higher harmonic components had alternately sine and cosine phase, or the reverse. Although one is tempted to suspect that the phase changes produced waveform differences that were sufficient to produce timbre differences, this suspicion is not supported by Figure 7.3, taken from their paper. All four waveforms are quite distinct to the eye but 1 and 2 are judged similar by the ear, as are 3 and 4. Either 1 or 2 sounds dissimilar to 3 or 4.

Timbre and Formants
As noted above, studies attempting to relate timbre judgments to aspects of the spectrum have gradually shifted from a description of the stimulus as a series of individual harmonic components toward more holistic descriptions of the spectrum. In particular, research on the vowels of speech and conceptions of the peripheral

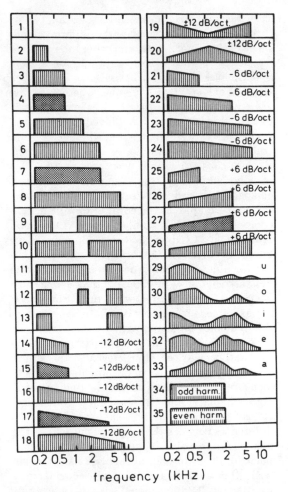

frequency (kHz)

Figure 7.4. Spectral envelopes of a variety of experimental sounds, including complex tones (line-hatched areas) and noises (cross-hatched areas). See text. (From "Timbre of Steady Sounds: A Factorial Investigation of Its Verbal Attributes" by G. von Bismarck, 1974, *Acustica, 30*, p. 150. Copyright 1974 by Acustica. Reprinted by permission.)

auditory system as a set of filters have given rise to emphasis on frequency regions, or "formants," where components are high in amplitude relative to the rest of the spectrum. Consider, for example, Figure 7.4, taken from a study by von Bismark (1974). Different spectra are shown, all describing tones with a common fundamental frequency. Among vowel sounds, as shown in numbers 29 to 33, are peak regions where the amplitudes are higher than in the spectral valleys. Spectra numbers 1 to 8 do not show formants since, within the bandwidth of the stimulus, the amplitudes of the several components are the same. Numbers 9 to 13, however, show formant structures where there are two or three frequency regions with uniform amplitudes of the components, and other intermediate frequency regions where the amplitude is zero. Spectra may also be characterized by an average slope of the spectral envelope, whether falling as in numbers 14 to 18, or rising as in numbers 25 to 28. A third dimension displayed by these spectra is the center of gravity, whether concentrated in the low, middle, or high frequencies. Each of these 35 sounds was rated on 30 scales of polar adjectives—for example, weak-strong, compact-scattered, and so on. Responses on these scales were analyzed according to a principal-components factor analysis (see Luce and Krumhansl, Chapter 1 this volume). Three groups of adjectives (factors) emerge as accounting for almost 80 per cent of the variance, the first associated with "sharp," the second with "compact," and the third with "full." Sharpness, for example, increases with the upper limit of the frequency band and with the slope (rising or positive aspect) of the overall spectrum.

Another way of characterizing the differences among the spectra of complex tones is to measure the spectrum of each sound in third-octave bands (Plomp, 1970). If each band is considered a dimension of complexity, then the differences between the sounds of musical instruments, for example, could be given as a composite of the difference at each of 15 such bands, with the overall result being considered a position in 15-dimensional space. In keeping with this physical representation, a related psychoacoustic experiment consisted of the presentation of different sounds in groups of three, where a listener was asked to judge which two of the three were most similar, and which two were most dissimilar. The two matrices thus obtained are then treated mathematically according to a multi-dimensional scaling technique (see Luce & Krumhansl, Chapter 1 this volume). This method was used for synthetic sounds, as well as for the sounds of musical instruments and vowels. Correlations between the dissimilarity matrix and the sound-spectrum matrix were high. A further step is to reduce the spectral dimensions to a more manageable few, a task that seems simpler for vowel sounds than for other sounds (Plomp, 1976).

Timbre and Vowel Quality

The earliest studies of the timbre of complex tones dealt with both musical sounds and vowels, the two classes being similar in that a complex-tone source feeds a system of resonant cavities. They differ, however, with respect to the sharpness of tuning, or Q, of the resonators. Those musical instruments whose pitch corresponds to a coincidence between the fundamental frequency of the source (lips, reeds) and one of the instrument's resonances are characterized by very sharp tuning of hard-walled cavities. But vowels, whose pitch is governed exclusively by the fundamental frequency of the vocal cords, have spectra determined by the much lower Q of soft, mucous-membrane-lined cavities of the throat and mouth.

In a study designed to show the dependence of vowel quality and musical timbre on spectra, Slawson (1968) had listeners estimate the magnitude of the difference in quality between a standard and a comparison sound, both produced synthetically. Slawson's vowel synthesizer permitted control of the fundamental frequency (F_0) and four formant frequencies (the lower formants F_1 and F_2, and the higher formants F_3 and F_4). The standard sounds used formant values from Peterson and Barney (1952) for six vowels of American English. Comparison sounds differed in fundamental frequency, in the lower two formants, or in the higher two formants. The same sounds were presented to listeners under two sets of instructions: (1) to judge on the basis of "vowel quality," or (2) to judge "instrumental color." Results were expressed in the magnitude of the apparent difference between the two sounds of a pair. The two kinds of judgments yielded similar results with respect to the greater effect of changing the first two formants as compared with changing the upper two formants. It is not clear whether this result can be generalized to more truly musical tones than those made with the low-Q spectra of an apparatus designed to synthesize vowels.

Timbre and pitch

If one plays a complex tone, keeping F_0 steady, while at the same time changing the resonant frequency of a filter through which it passes, one can hear a change in a pitch-like aspect of timbre, even though the fundamental pitch remains the same. J.-C. Risset (1978) distinguished *tonal pitch* from this *spectral pitch*; the latter is associated with a peak or peak-group in the spectrum.

It is tonal pitch that carries melody in music and appears to have two components (Revesz, 1913): a *tone height* that moves between low and high continuously, and a *chroma* which is the within-octave pitch of musical scales. Thus Revesz proposed that, as frequency increases, the pitch increases in spiral fashion, coming back on itself in a similar chroma as successive octaves are passed. Spectral pitch is more linear than circular, and is that aspect of timbre that is judged as ranging from low to high. Tonal pitch seems to correspond to Schouten's (1940) *periodicity pitch*, and also to Davis, Silverman, and McAuliffe's (1951) *buzz pitch* (as opposed to their *body pitch*). The dichotomy is referred to by Terhardt (1979) as *virtual pitch* versus *spectral pitch*.

Other Attributes of Sound Quality

There are some general attributes of the quality of sound that cannot easily be brought into the context of timbre. At one extreme, all the polar adjectives used in von Bismarck's (1974) study would represent a list of such attributes. We can single out a few on which experimental work has been done, while limiting our description to those aspects related to properties of the steady state.

Consonance and Dissonance
When two (usually complex) tones are sounded together, the resulting dyadic chord is said, by music theorists and by musical listeners to be consonant or dissonant, depending on the ratio or difference in fundamental frequencies. On one hand, consonance and dissonance are assumed to be properties of certain frequency ratios. The musical intervals that comprise the Western musical scale were founded on notions of consonance related to the ratio of frequencies of the two notes defining a musical interval. Two notes that stand an octave apart—a frequency ratio of $2:1$—are said to be most consonant. Successively smaller frequency ratios of $3:2$, $4:3$, and so on are less and less consonant. The least consonant intervals on the musical scale, the whole tone and the semitone, involve the smallest frequency ratios—$9:8$ and $16:15$. While it is not our purpose to delve deeply into the theory of musical scales (see Burns and Ward, 1982), we should note that it is this tonal background, dating at least from the time of

Pythagoras, that captured the interest of auditory theorists such as Helmholtz. Listeners judge "consonance" and "dissonance" according to these predicted intervals. Helmholtz suggested that intervals judged to be dissonant were those in which some pair of the harmonics of the two complex tones sounding together involved frequencies that were only 20 to 30 Hz apart, and therefore produced a beating sensation that was unpleasant and rough. Thus, on the psychological side, consonant and dissonant qualities bear similarities to qualities of timbre. In fact, of all the adjectives to describe tones in connection with timbre, "roughness" is the one most often used for dissonance.

A newer conception of a model underlying judgments of dissonance, as suggested by Plomp and Levelt (1965), is the filter bandwidth. The critical bandwidth describes peripheral auditory processing (Green, Chapter 6 this volume). Figure 7.5, taken from Plomp (1976), compares information on judgments of roughness and maximum dissonance. It also includes details regarding the auditory critical band. According to Plomp and Levelt (1965) dissonance arises when two components lie within a narrow bandwidth. This more general view differs from

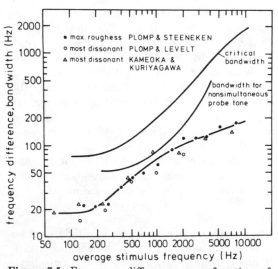

Figure 7.5. Frequency difference, as a function of average frequency, of pairs of tones for maximal roughness (solid circles), and maximal dissonance (open symbols). Curves for auditory bandwidth are superimposed for comparison. (From *Aspects of Tone Sensation* (p. 89) by R. Plomp, 1976, Orlando, FL: Academic Press. Copyright 1976 by Academic Press. Reprinted by permission.)

the older one held by Helmholtz (1912) that argued for an absolute difference in frequency —corresponding to rough beats—between two components.

It is still not clear to what degree judgments of consonance and dissonance depend on a general auditory capability, or to what degree such judgments reflect the training of musical listeners. What is clear is that there is a strong correlation between judgments of dissonance and roughness.

Roughness

Roughness, as a separate psychological attribute of tones, has been studied systematically by Guirao and Garavilla (1976) and by Terhardt (1977), who varied the degree of amplitude modulation of tones at different frequencies. Terhardt's measurements included scaling techniques whereby listeners indicated the amount of roughness associated with different waveform envelopes. In general, roughness increases with the degree of amplitude modulation and appears also to be at a maximum for modulation frequencies between approximately 60 and 80 Hz. These results approximate those of Kameoka and Kuriyagawa (1969) for judgments of consonance (see Figure 7.5). It is clear that both dissonance and roughness involve frequency components that lie within the critical bandwidth, and such judgments have contributed to auditory-filter theories about the ear. However, the description of these phenomena in terms of auditory-filter bandwidths may be secondary to the effect of another characteristic of the physical stimulus. For example, if waveforms with sharp discontinuities were more likely to be judged rough than waveforms with smoother contours, then roughness may well be the isomorphic feature—both in the waveform and in the listener's judgment.

Pitch Strength

There are four broad classes of single sounds: pure tones, complex tones, noises, and transients. Both pure tones and complex tones have clear pitch, related most directly to the single frequency of pure tones or to the fundamental frequency of complex tones. Noises and transients have a less clear pitch; however, when those sounds are passed through bandpass filters, a change in the center frequency of the band also produces a change in some aspect of the

sound that can vary from low to high. We may assume that there is a continuum from the regularly recurring waveforms of tones to the more random waveforms of noise that corresponds inversely to the degree of tonality or pitch. Fastl and Stoll (1979) have called this degree of tonality *pitch strength*. The sounds whose spectra were schematized in Figure 7.2 are the ones used by those authors to explore the acoustical factors on which the magnitude of pitch strength depends. The sounds in Figure 7.2 are in fact ordered according to the degree of pitch strength, with the pure tone representing the maximum strength. In a situation where 500 Hz marks the center or critical frequency for the array of sounds, a decrease in the magnitude of pitch strength occurs as we move from a pure tone to a low-pass complex tone through a gradually falling spectrum to a narrow band of noise (bandwidth = 10 Hz). In this last position (sound 4) the waveform resembles a noise less than it does a fluctuating tone. The results show a rather abrupt downward change in the amount of pitch strength as we approach the noises beginning with sound 7, all of which involve passbands wider than the 10 Hz. The extremes of the scale of pitch strength are best described by adjectives such as "noisy" at one end and "tonal" or "smooth" at the other.

Something similar to this scale of pitch strength was applied to transient sounds by Doughty and Garner (1947). Although unfiltered click has very little pitch strength in itself, when passed through a bandpass filter such a click takes on more of a pitch-like character as the passband is made narrower. That pitch can then rise or fall depending on the center frequency of the filter (as any player of musical temple blocks knows). Instead of using filters, Doughty and Garner manipulated the number of individual periods of a sound wave that comprised the signal. In general, they found that for frequencies above 1000 Hz approximately 10 msec was required for tonal pitch, and that minimum duration increased as the frequency decreased below 1000 Hz. Although such a short duration will yield a "pitchy" quality, the variability in pitch matching—as mentioned earlier —will still be high relative to longer tones.

When we refer to pitch in complex sounds such as those of speech, we must remember that there are at least two dimensions: one that moves from low to high, and another —aspect of quality—that describes the tonality, pitchiness, or pitch strength of a sound. These two dimensions seem to be analogous, respectively, to hue and saturation in color.

Qualities of a Changing State

The attributes of timbre and other sound qualities discussed above were associated with steady-state properties of sounds. As explained in the introduction, it is also useful to consider single sounds in which the acoustical state changes within the duration of the sound. Of particular interest, because of their implications for speech perception and music, are (1) frequency glides, and (2) onset or attack characteristics.

Frequency Glides

Glissandi in music or frequency transitions in speech are examples of frequency glides. We will use this term to refer to a unidirectional, continuous change in frequency, sometimes called a frequency-modulation (FM) ramp. Frequency modulation and amplitude modulation were used early on as the principal method for stimulus control in the study of long-term frequency and amplitude discrimination. In those studies, periodic modulation persisted over time, whereas here our emphasis is on singular transition. One exercise concerns the ability of listeners to discriminate between an upward or downward changing pitch and a steady pitch in a tone that may last anywhere from 10 msec to 100 sec. Although such a discriminative ability has been studied more often in bats (Suga, 1981) than in man, Sergeant and Harris (1962) observed a listener's ability to distinguish a rising pitch from a falling pitch, both starting at 1500 Hz. They found an interaction between the rate of frequency change (df/dt), and the duration of tone, the interaction indicating an almost constant value of frequency change that was necessary to distinguish up from down independent of the tonal duration. In order to be certain that listeners were not basing their judgments of up or down on terminal frequencies, Pollack (1968) extended these studies and introduced two new controls. First, on successive trials he changed the initial frequency. Second, he did not present the FM-glide alone, but rather presented the glide as a middle segment in a three-segment stimulus, in which the first and last segments

were steady tones at the initial and final frequencies. In addition to the first exercise of having listeners distinguish between a changing and a steady pitch, Pollack further sought to determine the smallest discriminable change in rate of transition that the listeners could detect. He observed that for relatively long transitions of the order of 1/2 to 1 sec, the transition change required for discriminability (75 percent correct) is independent of the frequency interval between the initial and final frequencies. For very brief transitions of less than 100 msec, the change in transition time required decreased as the frequency separation increased. As for the discrimination between rising and falling frequency change, results qualitatively corroborated those of Sergeant and Harris (1962), showing a reciprocal relation between the rate of frequency change and the transition duration. These findings indicate that the amount of frequency change required for glide discriminations is constant over durations from 0.5 to 4 sec and for several base frequencies.

A similar stimulus configuration was used by Nabelek and Hirsh (1969) in their study on the discrimination of frequency transitions. Since one of the cues for discriminating consonants appears to be what Liberman, Delattre, Gerstman, and Cooper (1956) call *tempo of frequency change* (as in the syllables /be/ and /we/), it was of interest to try to determine the listener's ability to discriminate rate of frequency change. Nabelek and Hirsh (1969) generated sounds consisting of a transition between an initial and a final frequency (both variable) at different rates (also variable), followed by a steady-state portion at the final frequency so as to keep the duration and apparent loudness of the total sound constant. Results indicated that at three different base frequencies, the difference limen (DL) for rate of transition was smallest for high standard rates of transition (change of an octave), intermediate for the change of a musical fifth (ratio 3:2), and largest for the smallest frequency change of a major second (9:8). Of more general interest was the finding that the optimal transition duration for rate discrimination, for all base frequencies, and for all frequency changes lay between 20 and 30 msec, a value that appears to coincide with what has been thought to be a critical transition duration when this kind of discrimination is called for in speech (Liberman et al., 1956).

Onset or Attack Characteristics

A second dynamic attribute of sounds that contributes to their judged quality is the initiation or onset of a sound. Quality judgments are governed far more by the initiation of a sound than by its termination. This principle is especially valid for the timbre of musical sounds, and has been a matter of common observation in the recognition of the qualities of different musical instruments.

The initiation of a natural musical sound is not described merely by the overall amplitude envelope; it must also be described more fully in terms of the different rates in which the amplitudes of the several harmonics build up, since they do not all increase at the same rate. If one removes the initial attack from recordings of instrumental sounds, the problem of recognition becomes increasingly difficult (Berger, 1964). It has also been observed that piano tones no longer resemble piano tones when a recording is reversed (see Schaeffer, 1966).

In a series of quantitative observations, Grey (1975, 1978) presented synthetic versions of three different musical instruments (bassoon, clarinet, and trumpet), either as isolated sounds, in the context of a single-voice melody, or in the more complicated context of multi-voice patterns. The isolated versions, which included the normal onset characteristics, were best discriminated, while the fuller versions showed a decrease in discrimination except for the bassoon. These experiments illustrate that the timbral quality of a sound cannot be predicted completely by the spectrum, but requires also the kinds of temporal information available to the listener in the isolated tones (Kendall, 1987).

SOUND SEQUENCES

Only rarely does a listener have an opportunity to recognize what we have described as a single sound in an acoustical environment. To be sure, single-sound characteristics such as timbre, pitch and duration do permit identification of a snapping twig, a barking dog, a smoothly running machine, and even the cough of a familiar person. More generally, however, auditory information resides in auditory figures or patterns of sequences of single sounds. These auditory patterns are articulated or evolve in time in a manner analogous to the articulation of steady visual patterns in space (Julesz & Hirsh, 1972).

Time plays several roles in auditory patterns (Hirsh, 1959, 1974). Duration of single events is a single-sound attribute, like intensity or frequency or spectral complexity. Durations involved in successive sounds, however, give rise to rhythmic patterns. Even with a string of constant-duration sounds (e.g., beats on a drum), pattern properties of rhythmic form (the 3/4 time of a waltz or the 4/4 time of a foxtrot) can emerge from manipulation of inter-stimulus intervals.

Time also serves as a unidirectional dimension for such perceptual properties as the order of events or, as controlled by the physical order of events, particularly pattern qualities. One can easily observe which aspects of auditory perception depend upon temporal ordering by noting which aspects are destroyed or severely changed when a tape recording of the patterns is reversed. Steady-state event properties are least affected, whereas transitional, ordered, and rhythmic aspects are drastically changed.

Temporal patterns also serve to illustrate some principles of figure-ground perception in hearing—from the intertwining of concurrent melodies to the phenomena of message competition and interference in speech.

Two-Event Patterns

The simplest case of an auditory sequential pattern composed of single events is the two-event sequence. The time interval between onsets will determine whether the two sounds are heard as one fused, complex sound, or as two separate sounds. The critical point at which the shift occurs has been investigated since the time of Exner (1875, cited in Hirsh & Sherrick, 1961), with rather general agreement placing the value at approximately 2 msec.

Only if two sounds are different in some attribute can we ask questions about temporal order —whether the louder, the higher, the longer, or the noisier sound came first. Even in this simplest sequence of events, results depend on the task. If, for example, one presents two brief sounds or clicks differing in loudness to a listener and asks for a discrimination response comparing a sequence of loud-soft with the reverse, soft-loud, Patterson and Green (1970) reported that about 10 msec difference sufficed for statistically significant discrimination. If one asks the listener successfully to identify whether a particular sequence is loud-soft or soft-loud, in other words, to identify whether the loud or soft click came first, the separation must be greater—about 18–20 msec (Hirsh, 1959).

The underlying psychological processes in the judgment "A came first" or "B came first" are not clear. As Broadbent and Ladefoged (1959) pointed out, the sequence A–B, even if not heard as two separate sounds (A and B), may have an overall quality different from that of B–A. If the experimenter provides feedback about correctness of order judgments—note that Hirsh, 1959, did not—the listener soon learns to apply correctly verbal labels to those qualities. Even though the labels contain words such as "A first," it is not clear that decisions about "apparent" sequential aspects are being made.

Melodic Perception

Information about sequences of tones has application in recognition of musical melodies. Much of our information about good or bad, easy or difficult melodies has come from music theory and composition. But in the last 10 to 15 years, there have also been experiments on the processing of melodic information that yield some important concepts (Bregman, 1981), some of which are quite in accord with older notions from the study of music itself (Dowling, 1982).

Kinds of Information
There is a hierarchy of units or kinds of information to be considered (Jones, 1978). Listeners may identify the pitch of individual tones and their succession or order, or listeners may identify a succession of pitch intervals (i.e., the frequency relations in successive pairs of tones that comprise a melody). Listeners seem able to identify a melody in spite of transposition, where the individual frequencies are changed but the successive intervals, as frequency ratios, are maintained. Listeners may also judge as similar, but not identical, melodic contours in which the rises and falls in pitch are similar but the intervals are changed. Such apparent similarity is lessened when the successive pitches are atonal, that is, when melodies are not organized in a particular key that is readily recognized in the listener's musical culture. If the melodic contour itself is changed (e.g., if a mirror image is created in the realm of frequency or time), the contour is no longer judged to be similar (Dowling, 1972, 1982).

Psychophysics of Melodic Fragments
If one conceives of melody perception as depending on the recognition of pitches and the order in which they occur (but see also Dowling, 1972, and Jones, 1978, for alternative views), then one is led to examine at a more microscopic level the cues that might be relevant. Where two tones of different pitches are used, Hirsh (1959) reported that approximately 20 msec had to intevene between the onsets of the two if their order was to be reported correctly. This interval appeared to be independent of the frequencies used, at least for trained observers. When inexperienced listeners were faced with the same task, they required approximately 60 msec between tone onsets for correct recognition of order (Hirsh & Fraisse, 1964); however, the required time decreased from about 60 to a minimum of 20 msec over a period of training (Gengel & Hirsh, 1970).

When a third tone is added so that the possible different orderings are six (do-re-mi, re-do-mi, mi-do-re, etc.), trained listeners can recognize those six melodic fragments even when the onsets are separated by as little as 10 msec (Divenyi & Hirsh, 1974). The results show that the particular frequencies and even the relations among the frequencies are not critical, since performance remains approximately constant when the frequency values have changed from those in a musical do-re-mi (frequency ratios of 9 : 8) to wider frequency intervals up to a range (between the lowest and highest frequency) of two octaves. What appear to be more critical are certain features of the ordered sequences themselves. For example, the easiest pattern of three notes was one in which the frequency changed in the same direction from tone to tone, either upward (do-re-mi) or downward (mi-re-do).

In a subsequent study frequencies were adjusted in successive blocks of trials to test the proposition that transposition would not affect performance (Divenyi & Hirsh, 1978). Transposition-like modifications were made in three different ways. First, ordinary transposition was made simply by changing the three frequencies into different frequency ranges, while maintaining the same frequency relations among them. Second, the frequency ratios were enlarged or decreased symmetrically; that is, the upper frequency ratio (f_3/f_2) was changed but kept equal to the lower frequency ratio

(f_2/f_1). Third, asymmetrical frequency-ratio change was accomplished by placing a greater interval between the upper two frequencies than the lower, or vice versa. For these observations, a recognition response was made immediately after each presentation of three tones. In a musical context, what was interesting about the frequency changes was that performance remained the same whether the frequency intervals were part of the traditional western musical scale, or were different. This result agrees with the suggestion of Dowling (1972), that the importance of common frequency intervals is greater for tasks that depend on long-term memory, but less for those that rely on short-term memory.

If one adds a fourth tone to this sequence of three, while requiring recognition of only the first three, one finds that the "blanking" role of the fourth tone (i.e., in affecting identification performance) is strong only when the frequency of the fourth tone lies within the frequency range of the preceding pattern (Divenyi & Hirsh, 1975). When the frequency of the fourth tone is removed from the three frequencies comprising the pattern, there is very little effect.

This observation is consistent with other experiments on pitch segregation or stream segregation (Bregman & Campbell, 1971). Miller and Heise (1950) had earlier reported that a rapid alternation between two pitches is perceived as an alternation so long as the frequencies involved are within approximately 1 to 1.5 critical bands, but if the frequency separation is greater, the listener reports hearing two pulsing trains of tones simultaneously—one high and one low—without any sense of alternation between the two. Bregman and Campbell (1971) observed that the order in a sequence of some half-dozen tones ranging widely in frequency is not reported correctly by listeners, although the temporal order of pitches within an upper range and those within a lower range can be recognized correctly. The temporal relations between the high and low frequency ranges cannot be retained. Such stream segregation can be avoided, that is, the order among all the tones can be maintained, if FM-glides or transitions are inserted from one tone to the next, or if some cue for continuity is provided (Bregman & Dannenbring, 1973).

The experiments cited above required listeners to recognize frequency order within short melodies or melodic fragments. In other tasks, listeners have been required to judge whether a particular melody or melodic fragment is identical to or different from one previously presented. In these experiments, more drastic changes can be made in the stimulus pattern by such transformations as (1) transposing all the frequencies while preserving the frequency ratios, (2) changing the frequencies and the frequency ratios so that only the up-and-down contour is the same, and (3) reversing the temporal order of the entire sequence (Dowling, 1972; Idson & Massaro, 1976). If a particular melody serves as a target, the likelihood that another transformed melody will be judged similar (recognized as having been heard before) is highest for the original target, next highest for ordinary transpositions, still good for changes in frequency ratio that preserve the contour, and poorest for reversal in order or reversal in rise and fall of pitch (Dowling & Fujitani, 1971; Dowling, 1972).

At a more detailed level one can ask questions about the factors upon which discrimination of two successive patterns are based. Watson and his colleagues (Watson, Wroton, Kelly, & Benbassat, 1975; Watson, Kelly, & Wroton, 1976; Spiegel & Watson, 1981) have studied the discrimination of sequences of 10 tones, one at a time, in frequency, intensity or duration, where each tone is 40 msec in duration and potentially variable. These studies have yielded information on the dependence of discrimination of such tone patterns on degree of uncertainty (whether the pattern is one of a large or small catalogue), degree of training of the listener, position in the sequence where the change is made, and the frequency of the tones that are changed. It is from these studies, for example, that we learn that changes made very late in the sequences are more noticeable than those made early, and that changes in high frequencies are more noticeable than changes in low. It is not yet clear that all the relations discovered will hold for more slowly occurring tones that are more characteristic of musical melodies.

Auditory Sequences and Patterns

It has been argued that time (Julesz & Hirsh, 1972) and spectrum (Kubovy, 1981) serve auditory patterns as space does for visual patterns. Nevertheless, although auditory patterns consist of successions of acoustic events, we still have no sufficient framework for talking about pattern structures in these sequences. If a series of events is completely homogeneous, that is, if the events are identical one to another, can we say more than that the sequence is a sequence? Clearly, variations in the inter-event interval (IEI) will produce different groupings and perception of rhythmic patterns (Fraisse, 1956, 1974, 1978; Povel & Essens, 1985). More interesting and complex auditory patterns are generated when the events are made perceptually different one from another. These differences can be determined on an ordinal scale, as in duration, frequency or intensity, or they may be merely nominal as in a sequence of many different timbres (although, as shown above, some aspects of timbre can also be considered in scalar terms).

The dimensions of pattern structure that have been studied appear in part to be related to the dimensions that differentiate the events in a pattern. Sounds that differ from each other along several dimensions simultaneously are difficult for the listener to organize into an ordered sequence. In a series of early experiments recently summarized, Warren (1982) and his colleagues found that sounds as different as a tone, a buzz, a hiss, and a click, had to be separated by several hundred milliseconds before listeners could report correctly their order. Here a verbal encoding appeared to be necessary, probably because the sounds were so dissimilar as to prevent organizational, sequential properties from operating. Pitch similarities, for example, enhance the formation of sequential streams (Bregman & Campbell, 1971).

Garner (1974) has developed concepts such as sequences of similar elements, or gaps between such sequences, to define some basic dimensions of auditory patterns. In the experiments that he and his collaborators carried out, however, the events were of only two natures: (1) two different timbres of sounds, each in a different location, and (2) sounds of two different frequencies in different locations. It is not clear how Garner's notions about auditory-pattern structure can be extended to sequences in which there are more than two kind of events.

Similarly, the organization of patterns according to an accent structure as suggested by Martin (1972) requires the sort of general structures that is found in music and speech. Here accent is provided by changes in one of the attributes of single elements (e.g., duration, intensity, or frequency) and co-occurs with variations among events in those sequences that also include dimensions unrelated to accent.

Perhaps the broadest attempt to characterize the dimensions of auditory-temporal patterns is that of Jones (1978), who takes into account not only temporal structure but also the relation between temporal structure and perceptual processes. In particular, Jones attempts to show that the pattern properties are attributes of a sequential ensemble. She also comments on the kinds of processing that lead to recognition—elemental associations within the sequence, gestalt-like configurations of the pattern to be discovered by the listener, and a more cognitive plan in which listeners synthesize structure as they listen. Such a theory of perception common enough in visual research, now holds promise for helping us to understand the processing of auditory patterns.

SPEECH

In accordance with general usage, we here define *speech* as those activities that produce an outgoing acoustic message. Later we will discuss *speech perception* as the processes that deal with messages as they are received by a listener. In the present chapter we do not attempt to describe in detail either speech production or speech acoustics, preferring rather to outline those aspects most relevant to speech perception, or, more particularly, to general auditory perception.

Accordingly, our discussion of speech production and speech perception—both as behavioral aspects of language communication—will be brief. The study of language and language behavior includes syntactic, semantic, and phonological aspects. Our present concern is with the phonological aspect of language and its representation in the speech-production and speech-perception activities of speakers and listeners. We first present some basic facts about speech production and the consequent acoustical aspects of speech as it emanates from the mouths of talkers. Although our description of the sounds of speech will include previously outlined acoustical concepts, there are some further acoustical properties that need to be emphasized. These properties are associated with the particular devices that affect sound production in speech, such as the larynx, and certain physical structures in the vocal tract.

Speech From a Linguistic Point of View

Until recently, studies in speech were largely subsumed under the broader heading of linguistics. Indeed much of our present phonological knowledge of speech has arisen from the work of linguistic phoneticians. One of the major goals of the descriptive linguist has been to characterize speech productions in terms of a language system. The syntactic and phonological components of such a system extend through a hierarchy that begins with whole sentences then descends through phrases, word components, and syllables to phonemes—the smallest unit in the system. A phoneme is defined linguistically as the smallest unit that is capable of producing a difference in meaning, on the basis of what is termed the *minimal pair*. For example, in the word "bill," a change in one of the sounds corresponding to the three orthographic elements can result in pair changes such as bill/pill, bill/bull, bill/bin. Although the phoneme has this unitary status in the linguistic system, we shall see presently that there are no invariant and segmentable temporal stretches in the acoustic signal that can be related unambiguously to the phonemes, or their observed representation in speech, the *phones*. In short, while the phoneme forms a unit in a linguistic system, it is not likely to be a unitary event in the speech sequence.

In considering the interactions between speech perception and speech production, we must remember that the users of a language—both speakers and listeners—give evidence that they have acquired rules about the language at different levels in the linguistic hierarchy. Thus we must acknowledge that both the motor activities on the output side and the perceptual activities on the input side represent an interaction not only between motor and perceptual processes but also between the motor-perceptual processes and the linguistic knowledge that has accumulated in the memory from the beginning of life within the context of a language environment. The rules that take shape are concerned not only with the order of words in sentences but also with more elemental structures or word components called morphemes. For example, in

forming the third persion of regular verbs in English, one must add s to the first person form; thus, "I laugh, she laughs; I kick, he kicks; I love, she loves; I dig, it digs." While the s in all these words is the same on the printed page, the sound is pronounced as /s/ in the first two examples, where it follows the sounds /f/ and /k/; but it is pronounced as /z/, where it follows the sounds /v/ and /g/. It is possible to develop a rule for such properties of English. The rule may be expressed as follows: "If the first person singular ends in a voiceless sound, the s ending is voiceless; if the first person ends in a voiced sound, the s will be voiced." The voicing properties of phonemes determine the pronunciation. The desire to express these simple rules has led some linguists to break phonemes down into still more elemental or distinctive features (Chomsky & Halle, 1968). It should be noted that, while the description of the distinctive feature is related to the phonetic description of speech sounds which will concern us in the remainder of this chapter, the description itself was developed for abstract use in writing rules for linguistic systems.

Listeners are able to detect the sounds of an unknown language; they are also able to discriminate sounds one from another, though not as well as users of that language. What they cannot do is process the speech sounds as parts of the sequential patterns that form the phrases and sentences of the unknown language. These matters are more properly dealt with in psycholinguistics, a study directed at a more cognitive level of speech behavior than represented in this chapter. Here our emphasis will center on perceptual processes and those rules that define an auditory perceptual domain that includes both speech and nonspeech sounds.

The Physiology of Speech Production

Obviously a great deal of planning, organization, and memory recall precedes speech production; however, our emphasis here will be on the output process itself, and the roles of the three physical parts of the mechanism—the lungs, the larynx, and the oral-nasal region of the vocal tract. These parts are linked to each other in the manner shown roughly in Figure 7.6. Excellent reviews of speech production are given by Borden and Harris (1984), by Ladefoged (1982) and by MacNeilage and Ladefoged (1976).

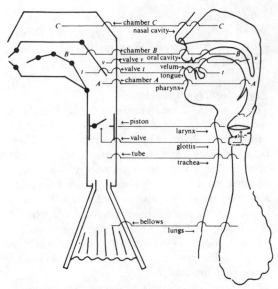

Figure 7.6. A sketch of the main vocal mechanisms (at the right) along with a functional, mechanical diagram (at the left). As the air stream moves up from the lungs the larynx (valve) interrupts, producing the vocal tone, which is modified by the upper cavities of the vocal tract. (From From *Fundamental Problems in Phonetics* (p. 18) by J.C. Catford, 1977, Bloomington IN: Indiana University Press. Copyright 1977 Indiana University Press. Reprinted by permission.)

THE LUNGS

The human sound-producing system uses a moving air stream in order to produce mechanically complex periodic sounds, noises, and transients. This moving air stream is normally provided by the exhalation phase of breathing. In normal (tidal) breathing, we draw air into the lungs for about 40 percent of the cycle, and exhale for about 60 percent. In speech, however, we change the cycle by imposing voluntary control on vegetative function so that we inhale 10 percent of the time and devote 90 percent of the cycle to exhalation.

The lungs, elastic structures located in the thoracic cavity, operate rather like an accordian. When the thorax is enlarged either by flattening the diaphragm, and hence the floor of the thorax, or by raising the ribs, thereby enlarging the thoracic circumference, the lungs expand, and, since air pressure is then lower outside the lungs than inside, air will flow in, causing the lungs to expand. Exhalation is caused by the combination of passive and active forces. Since the lungs are composed of elastic tissue, they

have an increasing tendency to collapse the more they are stretched outward; the active forces are generated by the muscles themselves to reduce the size of the thoracic cavity. Thus the air pressure for phonation develops differently in different phases of exhalation. A good review of breathing during speech may be found in Hixon (1973).

THE LARYNX

The vocal folds of the larynx and the space between them, known as the glottis, act as a valve across the trachea or the exit from the lungs. Without going into detail about laryngeal structure, we merely note that the laryngeal cartilages support the vocal folds, a pair of fleshy shelves that can be moved in and out of the path of the exhaled air stream from the lungs. When the folds are adducted by muscle activity, the air stream acts to push them apart. A cyclical activity results: increased air pressure against the under surface of the vocal folds blows them apart; decreased air pressure caused by the dynamics of air flow assists in an elastic return to the closed position. This periodic opening and closing creates pressure pulses in the air of the vocal tract. The size of the pressure pulses, and hence the intensity of the sound they create depend in large part on the pressure generated by the lungs. The repetition frequency of the glottal pulses—the *fundamental frequency* of the voice—depends largely on the mass and tension of the fleshy shelves that form the vocal folds. Changes in mass and tension are caused by the complex musculature of the larynx. The sound generated by this complicated laryngeal mechanism is a complex tone with a sawtoothed waveform. Thus, the larynx serves a similar function to the reed in a clarinet: a complex-tone source feeds a system of resonant cavities. Changes in the fundamental frequency of the source are perceived as melodies of song or as intonation of speech.

THE UPPER VOCAL TRACT

Above the glottis lies the upper vocal tract (Figure 7.7), a bent tube extending from the vocal cords to the lips. It also includes an optional branching tube, the nasal cavity, which is opened and closed by the muscles of the velum, but remains closed for most speech sounds. The shape of the oral vocal tract is controlled by the muscles of the pharynx, tongue, jaw, and lips. In

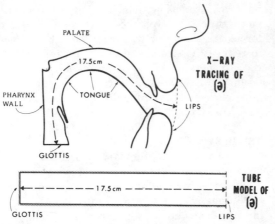

Figure 7.7. Sketch of an x-ray tracing of the shape of the vocal tract, and an idealized simple tube model of the tract, for the neutral of "shwa" vowel. (From *The Sounds of Speech Communication* (p. 42) by J.M. Pickett, 1980, Austin, TX: PRO-ED, Inc. Copyright 1980 by PRO-ED, Inc. Reprinted by permission.)

the process of articulation in speech, we may distinguish three degrees or kinds of oral articulation, according to whether the vocal tract is relatively open (as for vowels) constricted (as for fricative consonants like /s/ or /f/), or momentarily closed (as for plosives like /p/ or /t/). For the vowels, the upper vocal tract serves as a filter of the glottal source. In the case of all noisy consonants, the role of the upper vocal tract is twofold: (1) by means of an oral constriction or the release of a momentary stoppage of exhaled air it provides a noise source for some consonant sounds, and (2) by the shape of the vocal tract it filters the noise just as happens for the laryngeal tone. The situation is especially complicated for voiced consonants like /z/ and /b/. Here, there are two sound sources. One

sound source is provided when the vocal folds are adducted and hence vibrate, while a second source is provided by constriction or stoppage in the upper vocal tract.

Phonetic Classification

The phonetic classification of the sounds of speech is based on a set of three distinctions. First, and most important, we differentiate between vowels and consonants—or between an open versus a not-completely-open vocal tract. Second, we distinguish between nasal and oral sounds, that is, sounds created when the nasal branch of the tract is open versus those when it is closed. The third contrast pertains to voiced versus voiceless sounds, that is, sounds produced by the vibration of the vocal folds versus those that are not.

In American English, vowels are normally voiced and oral, that is, they are produced with a vibrating larynx and a closed nasal branch. However, in many languages nasal and voiceless (whispered) vowels are part of the phonemic structure.

The classification of consonants is more complicated than that of vowels. In English there are some 30 consonants that differ from each other in three dimensions of speech production: (1) voicing (whether the sound source is produced by laryngeal tone alone, or by turbulence created alone, or by a combination or the two), (2) manner (whether the vocal tract is completely stopped or whether it is only partially closed at the point of articulation), and (3) place (whether the place of articulation is at the lips, between the tongue and the teeth, between the tongue and the palate, etc.). These relations are illustrated in Table 7.1.

Table 7.1. Classification of American English consonants

Manner of production	Place of articulation						
	Bilabial v* u*	Labiodental v u	Linguadental v u	Lingualveolar v u	Palatal v u	Velar v u	Glottal v u
Plosive (Stop)	b p			d t		g k	
Fricative	hw (where)	v f	th th (the-thin)	z s	zh sh		h
Affricate					j ch		
Oral Resonant	w			l, r	y		
Nasal Resonant	m			n		ng (ring)	

*v = voiced, u = unvoiced

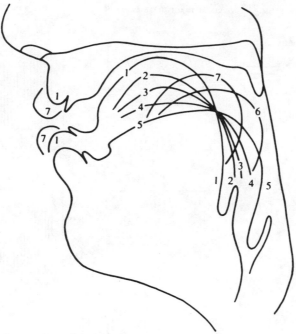

Figure 7.8. The vocal-tract shape for 7 vowels, as in the words: (1) heed, (2) hid, (3) head, (4) had, (5) father, (6) good, (7) food. (After Ladefoged, 1982. From *Speech Science Primer*, 2nd Ed. (p. 106) by G. Borden and K. Harris, 1984, Baltimore, MD: The Williams & Wilkins, Co. Copyright © 1984 by The Williams & Wilkins, Co. Reprinted by permission.)

The Vowels

Within the class of vowels, the tongue, jaw, and lips produce different shapes of the vocal tract —the jaw by being more or less open, the lips by being more or less protruded, and, most important, the tongue by humping and flattening, and moving back and forth in the mouth. Figure 7.8 (after Ladefoged) shows typical tongue and lip shapes for some important vowels. Within this group /i/ and /u/ are high vowels, in that the tongue is high and the vocal tract is relatively closed during their production; of these two /i/ is called a front vowel, because the front of the tongue is raised at the front of the mouth, while /u/, a back vowel, is made by raising the back of the tongue toward the velum. Note that /u/ is also a rounded vowel, in that the lips are protruded. In English, only back vowels are rounded, but languages such as Swedish and Dutch have rounded front vowels. There are also speech sounds that form compound vowels, or *diphthongs*; these are produced by a continuous transition from one vowel target to another. Thus, we have "boy" /bɔɪ/ and "cone" /koʊn/.

Acoustic Phonetics

It has been recognized since the time of Helmholtz that the acoustic spectrum of vowel sounds can be predicted from a consideration of the shape of the vocal tract and a knowledge of the properties of resonant cavities. A classical modern treatment is provided by Fant (1960, 1973) and, at a more elementary level, by Pickett (1980) and Stevens and House (1972).

The glottal sound produced in the larynx has a complex waveform, whose spectrum is shown in the upper left of the diagram in Figure 7.9. This spectrum is filtered by the transfer function shown in the middle panel of Figure 7.9, to produce the spectrum shown in the righthand panel.

When the vocal tract is positioned for making the neutral or "shwa" vowel, the cross-sectional area along its length is fairly uniform. An idealized tube of that uniform shape with a length of 17.5 cm would have resonances, as shown in Figure 7.10, at frequencies of 500, 1500, 2500 Hz, and so on—that is, in odd multiples of the first peak or first formant. Since the vocal tract of the infant is approximately half the

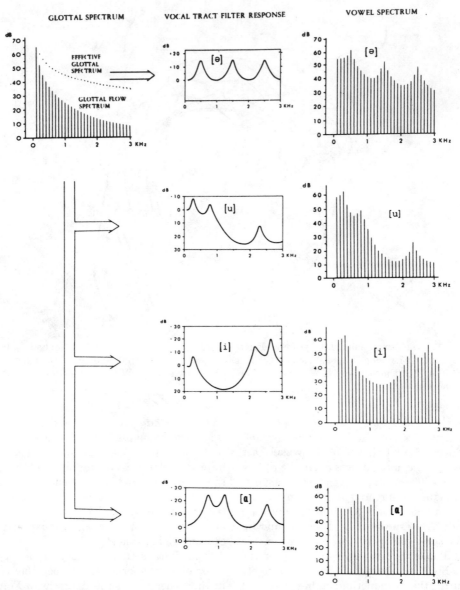

Figure 7.9. Production of model vowels according to a source-and-filter theory. The basic glottal spectrum is shown at the upper left. In the center, the filter response of the vocal tract is shown and, at the right, the resulting vowel spectrum, for the neutral vowel. (From *The Sounds of Speech Communication* (p. 48) by J.M. Pickett, 1980, Austin, TX: PRO-ED, Inc. Copyright 1980 by PRO-ED, Inc. Reprinted by permission.)

length of that of a man, in the middle panel of Figure 7.10 one sees a higher set of formants for a child's "shwa" at 1000, 3000, 5000, and so on. The bottom panel represents an ideal model of the adult female vocal tract where the first formant is at approximately 600, the second at 1800, and the third at 3000 kHz.

Of course the actual vocal-tract "tube" is not

always uniform; movements of the tongue bring different points on the tongue's surface closer to the teeth, the palate, or the velum. The result is no longer a simple tube but one whose formants are not simple multiples of the first formant. These are illustrated in Figure 7.9 (from Pickett, 1980). It should be emphasized that (1) the peaks in the spectrum, or formants, are characteristics

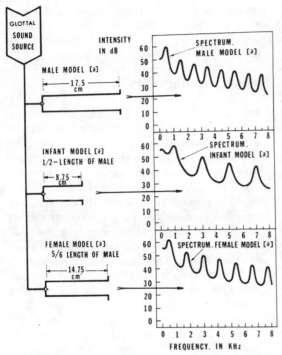

Figure 7.10. Tube models of the vocal tracts of an adult male, infant, and adult female and the consequent spectrum envelope. The neutral or "shwa" vowel is being produced. Note that the formant frequencies and the spacings between them are inversely related to tube length. (From *The Sounds of Speech Communication* (p. 66) by J.M. Pickett, 1980, Austin, TX: PRO-ED, Inc. Copyright 1980 by PRO-ED, Inc. Reprinted by permission.)

of the vocal tract and not of the vocal source and (2) the pitch in which one sings or intones these vowels is not related to the frequency location of the formants, except indirectly by virtue of the correlation between the length of the vocal cords and the size of the vocal tract.

Noisy Speech Sounds

The spectra of the vowels shown in Figure 7.9 are line spectra, that is, they represent complex tones with harmonics at multiples of a fundamental frequency. The speech mechanism is also capable of producing noises, either by creating a narrow constriction which through the air stream is blown, with the result that turbulence (noise) in the air flow is created, or by completely stopping the air stream in the vocal tract at any of several places. When the closure is released, a puff or small explosion is produced which is heard as a brief noise. The continuous noise spectra for the fricative consonants show differences among these, for example, a relatively narrow band of noise in the frequency range from 6 to 8 kHz for /s/, and a somewhat broader band of noise extending down to 2 or 3 kHz for the sound /sh/. Another important dimension in describing consonant sounds, however, consists of changes in time, somewhat analogous to frequency glides and attack times noted above as qualities of a changing state. The spectrogram provides an illustration of such factors, as shown in Figure 7.11.

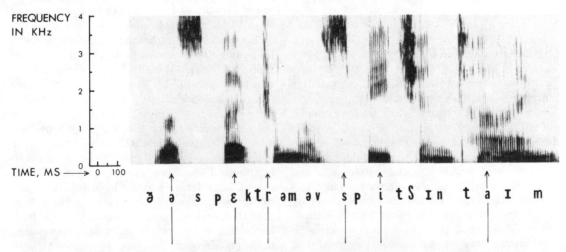

Figure 7.11. Speech spectrogram of the phrase "the spectrum of speech in time." Frequency is shown on the vertical scale, and time on the horizontal. (From *The Sounds of Speech Communication* (p. 38) by J.M. Pickett, 1980, Austin, TX: PRO-ED, Inc. Copyright 1980 by PRO-ED, Inc. Reprinted by permission.)

This spectogram shows many of the acoustical features of speech discussed so far. In the phrase "the spectrum of speech in time" we can observe the high-frequency noise that is /s/ at the beginning of "spectrum" and "speech," and the somewhat broader bandwidth associated with /sh/ at the end "speech." The /t/ in the middle of "spectrum" and at the beginning of "time" is characterized by a very brief burst of noise with a fairly wide bandwidth. In the vowel segments, the fundamental frequency of this talker is sufficiently low that the vertical striations appear, representing individual glottal pulses. Note also the formant transition that characterizes the diphthong in the vowel segment of "time."

With our tools of acoustical description we should be able to return to Table 7.1 and describe the acoustical dimensions that correspond to the articulatory dimensions displayed there: voiced versus unvoiced, nasal versus non-nasal, place of articulation, manner of articulation. Attempts have been made at categorizing speech sounds to match articulatory and acoustic characteristics (Jakobson, Fant, & Halle, 1967). Such attempts demonstrate that the match is not a simple one-to-one relation between articulatory gestures and acoustical properties. However, acoustical characteristics are associated with each articulatory class of sounds. Acoustical analysis of speech sounds does not itself predict what will be the most critical dimensions for accurate perception of the sounds by native listeners.

SPEECH PERCEPTION

Even in the limited sample of the approximately forty speech sounds that comprise the phonemic repertoire of American English, we see examples of all the sound categories of the nonspeech sounds and sound sequences discussed earlier. The sounds of speech are remarkable, however, in two perceptual respects. First, as sound makers and talkers, humans have been monitoring the acoustic outputs of their speech mechanisms since the first gurglings in the crib. It is probable that a very close connection is established between certain auditory properties and the kinesthetic and somesthetic feedback involved in speaking. Second, the sound patterns of speech may be "privileged" in relation to other sounds, particularly in perceptual memory, since they are heard and manipulated so frequently in the context of reinforcement in communicative exchange.

Speech Intelligibility

Early studies of speech perception were motivated by the need for designing telephone and radio communications systems. Quantitative evaluation of the intelligibility of speech transmitted through systems in which acoustical variables could be manipulated was achieved through a procedure in which lists of syllables or words or sentences were spoken by one or more speakers, and their identification was recorded by crews of listeners who wrote down what they heard. The basic procedures used in this pioneering work are summarized in Fletcher (1929), Licklider and Miller (1951), Miller (1951), and Hirsh (1952).

These same references contain summaries of the results of manipulating some of the variables associated with transmission systems. We know, for example, that in a quiet environment, speech levels must exceed approximately 20 dB sound-pressure level (SPL) for any intelligibility at all. Further, intelligibility, measured as a percentage of items identified correctly, increases with level to about 40 dB SPL. If the speech is heard against a background of broad-spectrum noise, intelligibility begins to increase from 0 percent at approximately -10 dB speech-to-noise ratio, to reach nearly perfect scores at 10 to 15 dB speech-to-noise ratio.

Because of its importance in design criteria, frequency distortion, in particular the effect of reducing the bandwidth of a transmission system, has been studied. The definitive early study (French and Steinberg, 1947) showed that, in spite of the predominance of speech power in the frequencies below 1000 Hz, the frequencies between 1000 Hz and 6000 Hz seemed to be more important for intelligibility. Although no testing techniques were available in that early period for relating specific bandwidths to particular speech sounds or even to acoustic features of speech sounds, one could surmise from knowledge of speech acoustics that the absence of high frequencies would interfere most with the identification of voiceless consonants and, further, that the absence of frequencies in the middle range between 500 and

2000 Hz would reduce the intelligibility of vowels.

One of the goals of early work, which investigated the dependence of speech intelligibility on speech level, system noise, and frequency distortion, was to produce a scheme whereby design engineers could predict speech intelligibility from such system variables when they were planning telephone or radio systems to be used in particular environments. The most widely used of such schemes, the *articulation index* (French and Steinberg, 1947; Kryter, 1956), gives a value between 0 and 1.0, depending on the signal-to-noise ratio in each of 20 frequency bands distributed across a frequency region from 200 to 6500 Hz, where each of the bands is selected to be equal to each of the other bands in contributing to speech intelligibility. The index thus designates an area whose height corresponds to speech-to-noise ratio, and whose width corresponds to the bandwidth of the transmission system. The index does not predict speech intelligibility directly, but is related to the intelligibility of different kinds of speech items, such as syllables, words, and sentences. It has already been of practical use, and has further implications for speech processing and thus for auditory theory (Licklider, 1959).

Still another variable, addressed in those early studies, was the amount of information transmitted by a single item. The relative intelligibility of a word is related inversely to the number of alternatives from which the identification response might be chosen. Miller, Heise, and Lichten (1951) showed that the intelligibility of the words depended on the size of the vocabulary (known beforehand to the listener). They also showed that intelligibility was lower for words in a list than for the same words imbedded in sentences. In another study, Hirsh, Reynolds, and Joseph (1954) showed that the effect of masking noise and frequency distortion on intelligibility was more severe as the type of item changed from a polysyllabic word, to a monosyllabic word, or to a nonsense syllable.

The correlation between intelligibility and the size of vocabulary or the number of alternatives from which a listener could choose an identification response led to an important methodological development. The dependent variable in all early studies was a global performance measure—the percentage of items identified correctly. None of the system variables studied could be related to particular types of confusions between pairs of speech sounds or between families or categories of speech sounds. Such information, while perhaps not so important when applied to telephone or radio communication, could be very valuable for measuring the effects of hearing disorders. Knowledge of particular problems might guide auditory rehabilitation. Modifications of tests for speech intelligibility that limited the number of response alternatives clarified particular confusions associated with particular phonetic dimensions.

Closed Message Sets

One approach to understanding the pattern of speech confusions was to reduce the number of alternatives to a few that were still somehow related (i.e., a reduction not merely in number). Thus Miller and Nicely (1955) asked listeners, in a test of only 16 consonant-vowel (CV) syllables, to identify which syllable was spoken. The vowel was always /a/, the only difference being in the initial consonant—either one of six voiced or unvoiced plosives, one of eight voiced or unvoiced fricatives, or one of two nasals.

The chief advantage of thus constraining or limiting the response set was that one phonetic feature at a time would be affected by manipulation of acoustical factors (e.g., speech-to-noise ratio and bandwidth of filter). As opposed to the global percentage score used in the traditional intelligibility tests with their open response sets, this particular test employed a matrix of confusions that could reveal which consonant sound was heard in each condition when a particular consonant sound had been presented. Three tables from Miller and Nicely (1955) are reproduced here (Tables 7.2, 7.3, and 7.4) to show examples of (1) a "good" transmission system (Table 7.2), (2) one that is restricted in bandwidth (Table 7.3), and (3) one that is characterized by a poor speech-to-noise ratio (Table 7.4). From a much larger number of similar matrices, Miller and Nicely could conclude that such articulatory features as place of articulation, affrication, and duration require higher speech-to-noise ratios than features associated with voicing or nasality. We also know that elimination of high frequencies has a more deleterious effect on the recognition of place of articulation, affrication, and duration than on voicing or nasality. Note that in these experiments speech itself was not a subject for experimental manipulation; the independent

Table 7.2. Confusion matrix for identification of consonants, under favourable conditions of transmission: speech-to-noise ratio of $+6\,\mathrm{dB}$, bandwidth 200–6500 Hz. The spoken consonants are listed across the top, and the listeners' responses along the vertical column. (From Miller and Nicely, 1955, p. 341.)

	p	t	k	f	θ	s	ʃ	b	d	g	v	ð	z	ʒ	m	n
p	162	10	55	5	3							1				
t	8	270	14													
k	38	6	171	1												
f	5	1	2	207	57			3				1				
θ	5	1	2	71	142	3					2	2				
s		1		1	7	232	2			1						
ʃ						1	239									
b				1	2			214			31	12				
d									206	14		9	1	2		
g								11	64	194		4	2	1		
v				1	1			14	2		205	39	5			1
ð								2	4		55	179	22	2		
z									3	10	2	20	198	3		
ʒ									3	4			2	215		
m															217	3
n										1					2	285

Note: From "An Analysis of Perceptual Confusions among some English Consonants" by G. Miller and P. Nicely, 1955, *Journal of the Acoustical Society of America, 27*, p. 341. Copyright 1955 by the American Institute of Physics. Reprinted by permission.

Table 7.3. Confusion matrix for identification of consonants, under favorable speech-to-noise ratio $(+12\,\mathrm{dB})$, but limited bandwidth (200–1200 Hz). (From Miller and Nicely, 1955, p. 343.)

	p	t	k	f	θ	s	ʃ	b	d	g	v	ð	z	ʒ	m	n
p	165	46	31	3	1			1					1			
t	91	83	68	4	1	2		1				2				
k	48	55	147	2	3							1				
f	16	4	3	146	60	3	2	11			1	2				
θ	4	3		109	76	17	2	12	1			2	1	1		
s	2	1	1	43	83	83	11	3		1	1	7				
ʃ	1	6	2	12	41	86	90		6	4		4				
b				14	5			223	4		5	1				
d	1				1	3	4	4	173	37		2	1	2		
g	1					1			102	107	1	2	7	7		
v	2	2		2	1			23	1	2	163	62	14	3	1	
ð				1		3	2	27	6	32	87	107	36	7		
z	1							4	12	48	10	15	114	39		1
ʒ							1	3	35		1	16	60	134	2	
m	1							1							229	9
n															5	247

Note: From "An Analysis of Perceptual Confusions among some English Consonants" by G. Miller and P. Nicely, 1955, *Journal of the Acoustical Society of America, 27*, p. 343. Copyright 1955 by the American Institute of Physics. Reprinted by permission.

Table 7.4. Confusion matrix for identification of consonants, under conditions of wide bandwidth (200–6500 Hz), but poor speech-to-noise ratio (−12 dB). (From Miller and Nicely, 1955, p. 340.)

	p	t	k	f	θ	s	ʃ	b	d	g	v	ð	z	ʒ	m	n
p	51	53	65	22	19	6	11	2		2	3	3	1	5	8	5
t	64	57	74	20	24	22	14	2	3	1	1	2	1	1	5	1
k	50	42	62	22	18	16	11	4	1	1	1	2			4	2
f	31	22	28	85	34	15	11	3	5		8	8	3		3	
θ	26	22	25	63	45	27	12	6	9	3	11	9	3	2	7	2
s	16	15	16	33	24	53	48	3	5	6	3	1	6	2		1
ʃ	23	32	20	14	27	25	115	1	4	5	3		6	3	4	2
b	4	2	2	18	7	7	1	60	18	18	44	25	14	6	20	10
d	3		1	4	7	4	11	18	48	35	16	24	26	14	9	12
g	3	1	1	1	4	5	7	20	38	29	16	29	29	38	10	9
v		1	1	12	5	4	5	37	20	23	71	16	14	4	14	6
ð		1	4	17	2	3	2	53	31	25	50	33	23	5	13	9
z	6	1	2	2	6	14	8	23	29	27	24	19	40	26	3	16
ʒ	3	2	2	1		6	7	7	30	23	9	7	39	77	5	14
m		1			1	1		11	3	6	8	11		1	109	60
n	1			1		1		2	2	6	7	1	1	9	84	145

Note: From "An Analysis of Perceptual Confusions among some English Consonants" by G. Miller and P. Nicely, 1955, *Journal of the Acoustical Society of America, 27*, p. 340. Copyright 1955 by the American Institute of Physics. Reprinted by permission.

variables here (relative noise level, filtering characteristics) were those that pertain to the characteristics of transmission systems.

Message Competition and Interference

Early studies on the intelligibility of speech in noise employed various kinds of white noise, bands of noise, or more realistic machinery noise. Other interfering sounds opened up new variables besides the spectral relations between speech and background. One such interference was the phenomenon of multiple echoes encountered in rooms and concert halls (see Green, Chapter 6 this volume, for a discussion of echo suppression in auditory localization). Still another was competing speech. Much has been written on message competition, especially in the practical context of, for example, airport control towers where a listener must monitor many speech sources simultaneously but attend to only one for particular messages (Broadbent, 1958; Webster, 1983). A useful discovery was that the intelligibility of one source of speech could be enhanced by using filters that gave different voices different qualities. Again, if the sources were processed in such a way as to appear to be coming from different places, intelligibility was improved. While we cannot detail this group of studies here, we can point to a similarity between them and the perception and segregation of auditory streams mentioned above in connection with multiple sound sequences. Segregation for speech and non-speech sounds delivered separately to the two ears (dichotic listening) has been reviewed by Lauter (1983).

Phonetic Cues

A further step forward was taken with the invention of a device that permitted manipulation of some of the acoustical characteristics of speech. Just as the development of the spectrograph (Potter, Kopp, & Green, 1947) aided in the acoustical description of speech sounds, so the development of the pattern-playback speech-synthesizer (Cooper, Delattre, Liberman, & Borst, 1952) opened an important era in our understanding of the role played by dynamic acoustical variables in the recognition of speech sounds. The first pattern playback was an optical-acoustical device that permitted the conversion of the spatial patterns of spectrograms back into sound, in a manner somewhat analogous to that of the player piano. The type of manipulation of speech signals provided by the pattern playback is today available through speech synthesis on a computer.

Vowels

Although acoustic theory and analysis show that vowels have many formants, synthetic vowels satisfactory for recognition by listeners can be generated with only two or three lowest formants (Delattre, Liberman, Cooper, & Gerstman, 1952). As already discussed, the formant structure of the different vowels is very like a set of timbres for complex tones. This aspect of vowel perception, therefore, brings the vowels under the notion of steady-state single sounds. If one looks at the spectrum of a sample of natural speech, however, it turns out that the formants of the vowels are rarely in a steady state. They fluctuate and are influenced by neighboring consonant sounds. Although vowels can be identified in steady state, in natural speech their formants are influenced by consonant environment, with the result that the dynamic aspects of the vowel may be important in perception (Verbrugge, Strange, Shankweiler, & Edman, 1976).

Stop Consonants

Spectrograms show us those features associated with stop consonants in running speech: (1) a brief silence, preceding (2) a burst of energy, most often spread over a wide frequency range, and (3) a transition or ramp in the formants, especially in the second formant, from the burst to the following vowel. Of course, the initial silence is not obvious if the stop is at the beginning. Many experiments have been conducted within the stop-consonant category on the cues that are used to distinguish both voiced from unvoiced stops and among sounds within each of those categories as to place of articulation (Borden & Harris, 1984, pp. 176–181). When the stop consonant begins a syllable, a sufficient cue for distinguishing voiced /bdg/ from unvoiced /ptk/ stops lies in the time interval between the consonant burst and the onset of phonation for the following vowel. This is referred to as voice-onset time (VOT). When the time interval is imperceptible (zero msec) voiced stops are heard, and when it is about 20 or 30 msec, unvoiced stops are heard (Lisker & Abramson, 1967). In fact, the insertion of a silent interval in a word like "slit," between the s and the l will result in listeners' reporting that "split" is heard (Fitch, Halwes, Erickson, & Liberman, 1980). If the silent interval between a burst and a following vowel is increased, a word like

"rabid" sounds like "rapid" (Lisker & Abramson, 1967). While this crucial difference of about 20 to 30 msec for identification of voiceless plosives has been described as a feature unique to speech, it appears to be similar to a phenomenon involving judged order in nonspeech sounds (Hirsh, 1959; Miller, Wier, Pastore, Kelly, & Dooling, 1976; Pastore, 1976).

Perhaps even more studied are the acoustical cues for the place of articulation of initial stops. Inspection of spectrograms will show that bursts are located in different parts of the frequency range for /ptk/, and also that there are different directions of transitions from the burst to the formants of the following vowels. There is a problem here concerning the most appropriate cue for identification, whether the absolute location in frequency of the burst or the magnitude and direction of the frequency transition for the burst to the following vowel formants. One of the earliest studies with synthetic speech on the problem (Liberman, Delattre, & Cooper, 1952) used artificial bursts of noise at different locations in the frequency spectrum and followed each of these by a pair of formants, synthesizing each of seven English vowels. While high-frequency bursts always resulted in a judgment of /t/ by listeners for all vowels, bursts in the mid-frequency range around 1500 Hz were heard as /p/, before front vowels like /i, e/ or with the four back vowels /o, u/, but as /k/ when preceding middle vowels. There was also a range of low-frequency bursts, around 500 kHz, that sounded like /p/ with all vowels. The burst that most often gave rise to the judgment /k/ was a burst whose frequency approximated that of the second formant of the following vowel. The interaction between burst frequency and the formants of the following vowels gives rise to an emphasis on the degree and direction of transition from burst to the second formant of the following vowel and a deemphasis on the frequency location of the initial burst (Liberman et al. 1956; but see also Stevens & Blumstein, 1981). Here is a case in which the cue (for place of articulation) did not appear to reside in the spectral feature of any steady-state sound, but rather in the transition between two such states. Here was also an example of a perceptual cue based on the discrimination of glide rate or glide extent, where the gliding was of a formant rather than a fundamental frequency.

There are other examples of cues for classes

of consonant sounds that have been illuminated by listening tasks and synthesized patterns (see Borden & Harris, 1984; Darwin, 1976; Studdert-Kennedy, 1975). In the next section we will comment on the influence of such studies on theories of speech perception. Here an additional comment on the experiments themselves is in order. Most of the studies that have sought to define the acoustic cues associated with phonetic recognition have manipulated the acoustic stimulus in various ways and sought the listener's response in a highly constrained set of two or three possibilities. From a psychophysical point of view, such studies may have emphasized too strongly stimulus-response associations developed over a long period of language learning, which in turn were interpreted to yield information about the auditory perceptual system.

Theories of Speech Perception

The effect of certain acoustical variables on speech intelligibility does not give rise to a theory of speech perception in the sense of addressing how human listeners accomplish the speech-understanding tasks that they do. Nor, for that matter, does the rich experimental literature that is based on the recognition of phonetic cues associated with segments of speech address the larger task. Instead, speech-perception theory has incorporated aspects of more general perceptual and cognitive theory with only limited success. It is clear that a listener recognizes a speech segment, syllable, word, or sentence by combining information from memory with that of the incoming stimulus. What just preceded the stimulus? What phonological and syntactic rules of language apply? What is the present context? There is great disagreement among contemporary theorists both about the nature of the processing of the incoming stimulus and about the processes of memory based upon information not specified in the incoming stimulus.

Several levels of processing are appealed to in accounting for speech perception (Pisoni, 1977). First, there is an acoustical analysis in which representations in the auditory nervous system specify correlates of fundamental frequency, intensity, spectrum, and duration. Second, there is a stage of phonetic analysis in which recognition of particular segments is based upon a catalogue of speech sounds, for example, those speech sounds that the listener can make with his speech mechanism. A third stage is more phonological than phonetic; namely, that the processing for recognition is influenced by learned rules about the particular language being spoken. A fourth stage involves additional levels of processing that include lexical search, syntactic analysis, and semantic interpretation of the original utterance. Definition of these levels of processing depend on the particular kinds of experiments that are done. Contemporary theories about speech perception emphasize one or another model of perceptual activity but an overall theory involving all such levels has yet to appear. Even if it turns out that this distinction of the four levels is useful, it is not yet clear whether there is a serial relation among the levels or whether they represent different parallel aspects of an overall process.

One approach to the problem of speech recognition is an extension of general theories of pattern recognition. This approach emphasizes stored templates or targets that are defined by features of the incoming stimulus patterns (Fant, 1973; Stevens and Blumstein, 1981; Miller, 1984). The memory load implied by such a theory will be determined by the unit of analysis or by the nature of the pattern that is assumed. Even though there are only forty-plus phonemes in American English, there are many more syllables, and still more individual words. The theoretical notions that have been based on experiments of acoustic cues have focused on small segmental units, like phonemes, but the fact that spoken utterances appear to stream into relatively long phraselike sound sequences has called for descriptions of a more active, continuous process. One such approach to a study of longer sequences is analysis-by-synthesis, an example of which is given by Stevens and House (1972). Here reception of the incoming stream of speech events is accompanied by concurrent hypothesis making, with immediate confirmations or rejections as the next unit of the speech message is received. A recent extension of these concepts at several levels is given in McLelland and Elman (1986).

Categorical Perception

There still remains a problem about the unit that is actually addressed by the listener's hypothesis. Although a small set of phonemes characterize American English, the representation of those phonemes acoustically consists of a much greater variety of sounds when spoken by the same individual on different occasions or when spoken by different individuals. Many studies on contemporary speech perception have dealt with the ability of the listener to collapse this very large array of sounds into a relatively small set of phonemic categories. This literature is reviewed by Strange and Jenkins (1978), Borden and Harris (1984), Darwin (1976) and Repp (1984). The majority of the studies are concerned with voice-onset time. What has been observed is that presentation of a series of synthetic stimuli with gradually increasing voice-onset time results in a sharp discontinuity in recognition performance if listeners switch suddenly between two steps in the series from a voiced-consonant judgment to a voiceless-consonant judgment. It was further observed that temporal discrimination of VOT is very sharp at those values that define a boundary between the phonemic categories. Some authors have associated this phenomenon of categorical perception with a unique aspect of speech perception, peculiar to human users of language (Liberman & Studdert-Kennedy, 1978; Studdert-Kennedy, 1975). Others have asked whether such categorical perception can be shown to be a general property of auditory systems in animals other than human and with stimuli other than speech (Kuhl & Miller, 1975; Miller et al., 1976; Pastore, 1976; Darwin, 1976).

Theoretical arguments concerning categorical perception have been extended to the possibility that "detectors" of features critical in the recognition of speech sounds are stored in the human processing system (Diehl, 1975). Evidence for such feature detectors, analogous to those found for the visual system (Hubel & Wiesel, 1968), may be sought in repeated presentation of the appropriate stimulus, thereby shifting the point on a stimulus-series continuum where judgments shift from one category to another (Eimas and Corbit, 1973; Darwin, 1976). Again it appears that the phenomenon may be as demonstrable for nonspeech sounds as for the sounds of speech.

Motor Theory of Speech Perception

Although the interaction between speech production and speech perception has long been discussed, a "motor theory" of speech perception has more recently been advanced by Liberman, Cooper, Harris, and MacNeilage (1963) and criticized by Lane (1965). At the experimental level, it has been shown that the points of discontinuity in stimulus dimensions that gave rise to the notion of categorical perception corresponded, in many cases, to genuine discontinuities in the articulation process. It has further been suggested that the motor patterns of speech, or the remembered images of them, might serve better than auditory images in collapsing a variety of acoustic signals into a few phonemic categories. Moreover, such internal motor processes might well serve as the imagery for any perception theory based upon analysis-by-synthesis. For primary sources see especially reviews by Strange and Jenkins (1978), Pisoni (1977), and Liberman and Studdert-Kennedy (1978).

In the context of the present chapter it must be noted that these two special groups of phenomena (categorical perception and postulated motor processes of speech perception) are extremely important, especially in that area of speech-perception theory that emphasizes them as special and unique to the processing of speech. Perhaps the sharpest difference between the picture of speech perception based on the general characteristics of auditory perception emphasized in this chapter and the view that speech perception is special for speech signals (Liberman & Studdert-Kennedy, 1978) concerns the earliest level of processing. If indeed the perceiver calls into play a system that is specifically designed to process speech, and holds for other uses an auditory system that deals with nonspeech and speech of a foreign language, there must at some early level be sufficient auditory analysis (with some stored characteristics of speech stimuli) to permit the listener to know when to "turn on" his speech system. The crucial experiments to decide this point have not yet been devised.

CONCLUSION

This chapter attempts to assemble some topics that do not normally go together. Students of speech and speech perception show an impatience with traditional psychophysical research on hearing, which has, admittedly, emphasized those phenomena of detection, masking, and frequency resolution that appear to illuminate our understanding of basic auditory mechanisms. Psychoacoustic reasearch has, however, included some areas of more direct interest to the perceptual processes that underlie speech and music. By emphasizing properties of brief acoustic events—duration and quality, properties of changing acoustic events, and certain properties of sequences of such sounds—we have attempted here to extend psychoacoustics in the direction of more general auditory perception.

Our review of matters related to speech and speech perception has been sketchy and has omitted many topics of great, current interest. Our omission of the cognitive aspects of language processing is not meant to belittle the obviously important role of memory, coding, transformation, and knowledge of rules. However, the chief reason for this omission has been one of emphasis; we have sought rather to concentrate on neglected areas of auditory perception that bear more directly on speech, music, and the acoustical environment than has been done in the past.

Listeners process sequences and streams. Those sequences not only have gestaltlike properties of their own, they also have properties of unitary sound events that can be isolated for study under assumptions that are based on acoustical or linguistic analysis. The understanding of auditory perception must be based on the study of both.

REFERENCES

Abel, S.M. (1972). Duration discrimination of noise and tone bursts. *J. Acoust. Soc. Amer.*, *51*, 1219–1223.

Berger, K.W., (1964) Some factors in the recognition of timbre, *J. Acoust. Soc. Amer.*, *36*, 1888–1891.

Bismarck, G. von. (1974). Timbre of steady sounds: a factorial investigation of its verbal attributes. *Acustica*, *30*, 146–159.

Borden, G.J., & Harris, K.S. (1984). *Speech science primer* (2nd ed.). Baltimore: Williams and Wilkins.

Bregman, A.S. (1981). Asking the "what for?" question in auditory perception. In M. Kubovy and J.R. Pomerantz (Eds.), *Perceptual organization*. Hillsdale, NJ: Erlbaum.

Bregman, A.S., & Campbell, J. (1971). Primary auditory stream segregation and perception of order in rapid sequences. *J. Exp. Psychol*, *89*, 244–249.

Bregman, A.S., & Dannenbring, G.L. (1973). The effect of continuity on auditory stream segregation. *Perception and Psychophysics*, *13*, 308–312.

Broadbent, D.E. (1958). *Perception and communication*. Oxford: Pergamon.

Broadbent, D.E., & Ladefoged, P. (1959). Auditory perception and temporal order. *J. Acoust. Soc. Amer.*, *31*, 1539–1540.

Burns, E.M., & Ward, W.D. (1982). Invervals, scales and tuning. In D. Deutsch (Ed.), *The psychology of music*. New York: Academic Press.

Catford, J.C. (1977). *Fundamental problems in phonetics*. Bloomington: Indiana University Press.

Chomsky, N., & Halle, M. (1968). *The sound pattern of English*. New York: Harper & Row.

Cooper, F.S., Delattre, P.C., Liberman, A.M., Borst, J.M., & Gerstman, L.J. (1952). Some experiments on the perception of synthetic speech sounds. *J. Acoust. Soc. Amer.*, *24*, 597–606.

Creelman, C.D. (1962). Human discrimination of auditory duration. *J. Acoust. Soc. Amer.*, *34*, 582–593.

Darwin, C.J. (1976). The perception of speech. In E.C. Carterette & M.P. Friedman (Eds.), *Handbook of perception*. Vol. VII, *Language and speech*. New York: Academic Press.

Davis, H., Silverman, S.R., McAuliffe, D.R. (1951). Some observations on pitch and frequency. *J. Acoust. Soc. Amer.*, *23*, 40–42.

Delattre, P., Liberman, A.M., Cooper, F.S., & Gerstman, L.J. (1952). An experimental study of the acoustic determinants of vowel color. *Word*, *8*, 195–210.

Denes, P. (1955). Effect of duration on the perception of voicing. *J. Acoust. Soc. Amer.*, *27*, 761–764.

Diehl, R.L. (1975). The effect of selective adaptation on the identification of speech sounds. *Perception and Psychophysics*, *17*, 48–52.

Divenyi, P.L., & Hirsh, I.J. (1974). Identification of temporal order in three-tone sequences. *J. Acoust. Soc. Amer.*, *56*, 144–151.

Divenyi, P.L., & Hirsh, I.J. (1975). The effect of blanking on the identification of temporal order in three-tone sequences. *Perception and Psychophysics*, *17*, 246–252.

Divenyi, P.L., & Hirsh, I.J. (1978). Some figural properties of auditory patterns. *J. Acoust. Soc. Amer.*, *64*, 1369–1385.

Doughty, J.M., & Garner, W.R. (1947). Pitch characteristics of short tones. *J. Exp. Psychol.*, *37*, 351–365.

Dowling, W.J. (1972). Recognition of melodic transformations: Inversion, retrograde, and retrograde inversion. *Perception and Psychophysics*, *12*, 417–421.

Dowling, W.J. (1982). Melodic information processing and its development. In D. Deutsch (Ed.), *The psychology of music*. New York: Academic Press.

Dowling, W.J., & Fujitani, W.S. (1971). Contour, interval and pitch recognition in memory for melodies. *J. Acoust. Soc. Amer.*, *49*, 524–531.

Eimas, P.D., & Corbit, J.D. (1973). Selective adaptation of linguistic feature detectors. *Cognitive Psychology*, *4*, 99–109.

Fant, G. (1960). *Acoustic theory of speech production*, s'Gravenhage, Netherlands: Mouton.

Fant, G. (1973). *Speech sounds and features*. Cambridge, MA: M.I.T. Press.

Fastl, H., & Stoll, G. (1979). Scaling of pitch strength. *Hearing Research*, *1*, 239–301.

Fitch, H.L., Halwes, T., Erickson, D.M., & Liberman, A.M. (1980). Perceptual equivalence of two acoustic cues for stop consonant manner. *Perception and Psychophysics*, *27*, 343–350.

Fletcher, H. (1929). *Speech and hearing*. New York: van Nostrand.

Fraisse, P. (1956). *Les structures rythmiques*. Louvain: Editions Universitaire.

Fraisse, P. (1963). *The psychology of time*. New York: Harper.

Fraisse, P. (1974). *Psychologie du rythme*. Paris: Presses Universitaire de France.

Fraisse, P. (1978). Time and rhythm perception. In E.C. Carterette & M.P. Friedman, (Eds.), *Handbook of perception*, Vol. VIII: *Perceptual coding*. New York: Academic Press.

French, N.R., & Steinberg, J.C. (1947). Factors governing the intelligibility of speech sounds. *J. Acoust. Soc. Amer.*, *19*, 90–119.

Fry, D.B. (1958). Experiments in the perception of stress. *Language and Speech*, *1*, 126–152.

Garner, W.R. (1974). *The processing of information and structure*. New York: Wiley.

Garner, W.R., & Miller, G.A. (1947). The masked threshold of pure tones as a function of duration. *J. Exp. Psychol.*, *37*, 293–303.

Gengel, R.W., & Hirsh, I.J. (1970). Temporal order: The effect of single versus repeated presentations, practice and verbal feedback. *Perception and Psychophysics*, *7*, 209–211.

Green, D.M., Kidd, G., Jr., & Picardi, M.C. (1983). Successive vs. simultaneous comparison in auditory discrimination. *J. Acoust. Soc. Amer.*, *73*, 639–643.

Grey, J.M. (1975). An Exploration of Musical Timbre. Report No. STAN-M2, Stanford University, Department of Music.

Grey, J.M. (1978). Timbre discrimination in musical patterns. *J. Acoust. Soc. Amer.*, *64*, 467–472.

Guirao, M., & Garavilla, J.M. (1976). Perceived roughness of amplitude-modulated tones and noise. *J. Acoust. Soc. Amer.*, *60*, 1335–1338.

Helmholtz, H.L.F. von. (1912). *Sensations of tone* (A.J. Ellis, Trans. of Helmholtz, *Die Lehre von dem Tonempfindungen* (4th Ed., 1877). London: Longmans, Green.

Henning, G.B. (1971). A comparison of the effects of signal duration on frequency and amplitude discrimination. In R. Plomp & G. Smoorenburg (Eds.), *Frequency analysis and periodicity detection in Hearing* (pp. 350–359). Leiden, Netherlands: Sijthoff.

Hirsh, I.J. (1952). *The measurement of hearing*. New York: McGraw-Hill.

Hirsh, I.J. (1959). Auditory perception of temporal order. *J. Acoust. Soc. Amer.*, *31*, 759–767.

Hirsh, I.J. (1974). Temporal order and auditory perception. In H.R. Moskowitz, B. Scharf & J.C. Stevens (Eds.), *Sensation and measurement* (pp. 251–258). Dordrecht, Holland: Reidel.

Hirsh, I.J., & Fraisse, P. (1964). Simultanéité et succession de stimuli hétérogènes. *L'année Psychologique*, *64*, 1–19.

Hirsh, I.J., Reynolds, E.G., & Joseph, M. (1954). Intelligibility of different speech materials. *J. Acoust. Soc. Amer.*, *26*, 530–538.

Hirsh, I.J., & Sherrick, C.E. (1961). Perceived order in different sense modalities. *J. Exp. Psychol.*, *62*, 423–432.

Hixon, T.J. (1973). Respiratory function in speech. In F.D. Minifie, T.J. Hixon, & F. Williams (Eds.), *Normal aspects of speech, hearing, and language* (pp. 73–125). Englewood Cliffs, NJ: Prentice-Hall.

Hubel, D.H., & Wiesel, T.N. (1968). Receptive fields and functional architecture of monkey striate cortex. *Journal of Physiology*, *195*, 215–243.

Idson, W.L., & Massaro, D.W. (1976). Cross-octave masking of single tones and musical sequences. *Perception and Psychophysics*, *19*, 155–175.

Jakobson, R., Fant, C.G.M., & Halle, M. (Eds.). (1967). *Preliminaries to speech analysis; The distinctive features and their correlates*. Cambridge, MA: M.I.T. Press.

Jones, M.R. (1978). Auditory patterns: Studies in the perception of structure. In E.C. Carterette & M.P. Friedman (Eds.), *Handbook of perception*, Vol. VIII, *Perceptual coding*. New York: Academic Press.

Julesz, B., & Hirsh, I.J. (1972). Visual and auditory perception: An essay of comparison. In E.E. David & P.B. Denes (Eds.), *Human communication: A unified view* (pp. 283–340). New York: McGraw-Hill.

Kameoka, A., & Kuriyagawa, M. (1969). Consonance Theory Part I: Consonance of Dyads. *J. Acoust. Soc. Amer.*, *45*, 1451–1459.

Kendall, R.A. (1987). The role of acoustic signal partitions in listener categorization of musical phrases. *Music Perception*, *4*, 185–213.

Kryter, K.D. (1965). On predicting the intelligibility of speech from acoustical measures. *J. Speech Hear. Disord.*, *21*, 208–217.

Kubovy, M. (1981). Concurrent-pitch segregation and the theory of indispensable attributes. In M. Kubovy & J.R. Pomerantz (Eds.), *Perceptual organization*. Hillsdale, NJ: Erlbaum.

Kuhl, P.A., & Miller, J.D. (1975). Speech perception by the chinchilla. *Science*, *190*, 69–72.

Ladefoged, P. (1982). *A course in phonetics* (2nd ed). New York: Harcourt, Brace, Jovanovich.

Lane, H. (1965). The motor theory of speech perception: A critical review. *Psychol. Rev.*, *72*, 275–309.

Lauter, J.L. (1983). Stimulus characteristics and ear advantages: a new look at old data. *J. Acoust. Soc. Amer.*, *74*, 1–17.

Liang, C., & Chistovich, L.A. (1960). Frequency difference limens as a function of tonal duration. *Sov. Phys. Acoustics*, *6*, 75–80.

Liberman, A.M., Cooper, F.S., Harris, K.S., & MacNeilage, P.F. (1963). A motor theory of speech perception. In C.G.M. Fant (Ed.), *Proceedings of the Speech Communication Seminar*. Stockholm: Royal Institute of Technology.

Liberman, A.M., Delattre, P.C., & Cooper, F.S. (1952). The role of selected stimulus variables in the perception of unvoiced stop consonants. *Amer. J. Psychol.*, *65*, 497–516.

Liberman, A.M., Delattre, P.C., Gerstman, L.J., & Cooper, F.S. (1956). Tempo of frequency change as a cue for distinguishing classes of speech sounds. *J. Exp. Psychol.*, *52*, 127–137.

Liberman, A.M., & Studdert-Kennedy, M.M. (1978). Phonetic perception. In R. Held, W.R. Leibowitz, & H.-L. Teuber (Eds.), *Perception*: Vol. VIII. *Handbook of sensory physiology*. Berlin: Springer.

Licklider, J.C.R. (1951). Basic correlates of the auditory stimulus. In S.S. Stevens (Ed.), *Handbook of experimental psychology*. New York: Wiley.

Licklider, J.C.R. (1959). Three auditory theories. In S. Koch (Ed.), *Psychology: A study of a science*: Vol. I (pp. 76–94). New York: McGraw-Hill.

Licklider, J.C.R., & Miller, G.A. (1951). The perception of speech. In S.S. Stevens (Ed.), *Handbook of experimental psychology*. New York: Wiley.

Lisker, L., & Abramson, A. (1967). Some effects of context on voice-onset time in English stops. *Language and Speech*, *10*, 1–28.

MacNeilage, P., & Ladefoged, P. (1976). The production of speech and language. In E.C. Carterette & M.P. Friedman (Eds.), *Handbook of perception*: Vol. VII. *Language and speech*. New York: Academic Press.

McLelland, J.L., & Elman, J.L. (1986). The TRACE model of speech perception. *Cognitive Psychology*, *18*, 1–86.

Martin, J.G. (1972). Rhythmic (hierarchical) versus serial structure in speech and other behavior. *Psychol. Rev.*, *79*, 487–509.

Miller, G.A. (1951). *Language and communication*. New York: McGraw-Hill.

Miller, G.A., & Heise, G. (1950). The trill threshold. *J. Acoust. Soc. Amer.*, *22*, 637–638.

Miller, G.A., Heise, G., & Lichten, W. (1951). The intelligibility of speech as a function of the context of the test materials. *J. Exp. Psychol.*, *41*, 329–345.

Miller, G.A., & Nicely, P.A. (1955). An analysis of perceptual confusions among some English consonants. *J. Acoust. Soc. Amer.*, *27*, 338–352.

Miller, J.D. (1984). Auditory processing of the acoustic patterns of speech. *Arch. Otolaryngol.*, *110*, 154–159.

Miller, J.D., Wier, C.C., Pastore, R.E., Kelly, W.J., & Dooling, R.J. (1976). Discrimination and labeling of noise-buzz sequences with varying noise-lead times: An example of categorical perception. *J. Acoust. Soc. Amer.*, *60*, 410–417.

Nabelek, I., & Hirsh, I.J. (1969). On the discrimination of frequency transitions. *J. Acoust. Soc. Amer.*, *45*, 1510–1519.

Pastore, R.E. (1976). Categorical perception: a critical re-evaluation. In S.K. Hirsh, D.H. Eldredge, I.J. Hirsh, & S.R. Silverman (Eds.), *Hearing and Davis, Essays honoring Hallowell Davis* (pp. 253–264). St. Louis: Washington University Press.

Patterson, J.H., & Green, D.M. (1970). Discrimination of transient signals having identical energy spectra. *J. Acoust. Soc. Amer.*, *48*, 894–905.

Peterson, G.E., & Barney, H.L. (1952). Control methods used in a study of the vowels. *J. Acoust. Soc. Amer.*, *24*, 175–184.

Pickett, J.M. (1980). *The sounds of speech communication*. Baltimore: University Park Press.

Pisoni, D.B. (1977). Speech perception. In W.K. Estes (Ed.), *Handbook of learning and cognitive processes*. Hillsdale, NJ: Erlbaum.

Plomp, R. (1970). Timbre as a multidimensional attribute of complex tones. In R. Plomp and G.F. Smoorenburg (Eds.), *Frequency analysis and periodicity detection in hearing* (pp. 397–410). Leiden, Netherlands: Sijthoff.

Plomp, R. (1976). *Aspects of tone sensation*. London: Academic Press.

Plomp, R., & Levelt, W.J.M. (1965). Tonal consonance and critical bandwidth. *J. Acoust. Soc. Amer.*, *38*, 548–560.

Plomp, R., & Steeneken, H.J. (1969). Effect of phase on the timbre of complex tones. *J. Acoust. Soc. Amer.*, *46*, 409–421.

Pollack, I. (1953). Information of elementary auditory displays. *J. Acoust. Soc. Amer.*, *25*, 765–769.

Pollack, I. (1968). Detection of rate of change of auditory frequency. *J. Exp. Psychol.*, *77*, 535–541.

Pollack, I., & Ficks, L. (1954). Information of elementary multi-dimensional auditory displays. *J. Acoust. Soc. Amer.*, *26*, 155–158.

Potter, R.K., Kopp, G.A., & Green, H.C. (1947). *Visible speech*. New York: D. van Nostrand.

Povel, D.-J., & Essens, P. (1985). Perception of temporal patterns. *Music Perception*, *2*, 411–440.

Raphael, L.J. (1972). Preceding vowel duration as a cue to the perception of the voicing characteristic of word-final consonants in American English. *J. Acoust. Soc. Amer.*, *51*, 1296–1303.

Repp, B.H. (1984). Categorical perception: issues, methods, findings. In H.J. Lass (Ed.), *Speech and language: Advances in basic research and practice*: Vol. 10. New York: Academic Press.

Revesz, G. (1913). *Zur Grundlegung der Tonpsychologie*. Leipzig: Veit.

Risset, J.-C. (1978). Musical Acoustics. In E.C. Carterette & M.P. Friedman (Eds.), *Handbook of perception*: Vol. IV, *Hearing* (pp. 521–564). New York: Academic Press.

Schaeffer, P. (1966). *Traité des objets musicaux*. Paris: Editions du Seuil.

Schouten, J.F. (1940). The perception of pitch. *Philips Tech. Rev.*, *5*, 286–294.

Sergeant, R.L., & Harris, J.D. (1962). Sensitivity to unidirectional frequency modulation. *J. Acoust. Soc. Amer,*, *34*, 1625–1628.

Slawson, A.W. (1968). Vowel quality and musical timbre as functions of spectrum envelope and fundamental frequency. *J. Acoust. Soc. Amer.*, *43*, 87–101.

Small, A.M., & Campbell, R.A. (1962). Temporal differential sensitivity for auditory stimuli. *Amer. J. Psychol.*, *75*, 401–410.

Spiegel, M.F., & Watson, C.S. (1981). Factors in the discrimination of tonal patterns. III. Frequency discrimination with components of well-learned patterns. *J. Acoust. Soc. Amer.*, *69*, 223–230.

Stevens, K.N., & Blumstein, S.E. (1981). The search for invariant acoustic correlates of phonetic features. In P.D. Eimas & J.L. Miller (Eds.), *Perspectives on the study of speech*. Hillsdale, NJ: Erlbaum.

Stevens, K.N., & House, A.S. (1972). Speech Perception. In J.V. Tobias (Ed.), *Foundations of modern auditory theory*: Vol. II. New York: Academic Press.

Stevens, S.S., & Davis, H. (1938). *Hearing*. New York: Wiley.

Strange, W., & Jenkins, J.J. (1978). Role of linguistic experience in the perception of speech. In R.D. Walk & H.L. Pick (Eds.), *Perception and experience*. New York: Plenum Press.

Studdert-Kennedy, M. (1975). Speech Perception. In N.J. Lass (Ed.), *Contemporary issues in experimental phonetics*. Springfield, IL: C.C. Thomas.

Suga, N. (1981). Neuroethology of the auditory system of echolocating bats. In Katsuki, Norgren & Sato (Eds.), *Brain mechanism of sensation*. New York: Wiley.

Terhardt, E. (1977). The two-component theory of musical consonance. In E.F. Evans and J.P. Wilson (Eds.), *Psychophysics and physiology of hearing* (pp. 381–390). London: Academic Press.

Terhardt, E. (1979). Calculating virtual pitch. *Hearing Research*, *1*, 155–182.

Turnbull, W. (1944). Pitch discrimination as a function of tonal duration. *J. Exp. Psychol.*, *34*, 302–316.

Verbrugge, R.R., Strange, W., Shankweiler, D.P., & Edman, T.R. (1976). What information enables a listener to map a talker's vowel space? *J. Acoust. Soc. Amer.*, *60*, 198–212.

Warren, R.H. (1982). *Auditory perception*, New York: Pergamon.

Watson, C.S., Kelly, W.J., & Wroton, H.W. (1976). Factors in the discrimination of tonal patterns. II. Selective attention and learning under various levels of stimulus uncertainty. *J. Acoust. Soc. Amer.*, *60*, 1176–1186.

Watson, C.S., Wroton, W.H., Kelly, W.J., & Benbassat, C.A. (1975). Factors in the discrimination of tonal patterns. I. Component frequency, temporal position, and silent intervals. *J. Acoust. Soc. Amer.*, *57*, 1175–1185.

Webster, J.C. (1983). Applied research on competing messages. In E. Schubert & J.V. Tobias (Eds.), *Hearing research and theory*. New York: Academic Press.

Woodrow, H. (1951). Time perception. In S.S. Stevens (Ed.), *Handbook of experimental psychology*. New York: Wiley.

Zwislocki, J.J. (1969). Temporal summation of loudness: an analysis. *J. Acoust. Soc. Amer.*, *46*, 431–441.

Chapter **8**

OLFACTION

William S. Cain, *John B. Pierce Foundation Laboratory and Yale University*

INTRODUCTION

The sense of smell comprises an extraordinarily sensitive channel for the detection and discrimination of airborne molecules. The modality seems blind to most inorganic compounds, with hydrogen sulfide, ammonia, and ozone notable exceptions. Single organic compounds that form potential stimuli for olfaction probably equal about half a million. Odor experts such as perfumers and flavorists would expect that in direct comparisons the nose could discriminate among almost all half million. In order to understand discriminative capacity, it becomes necessary to understand the steps that lead to olfactory sensations. The steps include conduction of stimulus to the receptors, molecular recognition by receptors, and neural coding.

Somewhat aside from the question of how the nose discriminates among different odorants, there are issues concerning dynamic, functional

properties of olfaction. These concern intensity discrimination, perceived odor magnitude, adaptation, masking, processing of mixtures, and interactions with other chemoreceptive modalities. Such issues determine how an organism might use olfactory information productively.

A discussion of olfaction also demands some consideration of affective reactions. Research on this topic ranges from simple cataloging of perceived pleasantness to complex issues of odors and motivation. The topic of how odor pleasantness develops in the young organism will offer a focal point for consideration of affective consequences.

In its treatment of discrimination capacity, functional properties, and affective reactions this chapter will focus primarily on human olfaction. A rapidly expanding corpus of knowledge on animal olfaction, including olfactory-guided behavior, olfaction-induced motivation, and the role of olfaction in physiological regulation will receive only brief mention in this short, and hence selective, summary.

I wish to thank Drs. Janneane Gent, Joseph C. Stevens, and Charles J. Wysocki for helpful advice and criticism.

FUNCTIONAL ANATOMY

Nasal Cavity

The nose of mammals has evolved from a simple sac-like olfactory organ into a complex structure with various roles (Eccles, 1982). It functions as an air conditioning system to heat or cool and moisten air destined for the sensitive epithelium of the lungs. The nonolfactory or respiratory epithelium in the nasal cavity exhibits considerable vasomotor and secretory lability regulated by autonomic innervation of blood vessels and mucus glands. Activity in the autonomic nerves often represents the motor component of sensory reflexes. Inhalation of an irritant, for example, will cause increased mucus secretion, engorgement of the epithelium, and even potent respiratory and cardiovascular reflexes.

The tortuous internal structure of the mammalian nose promotes rapid heat and moisture exchange and efficient dust collection. After air enters the relatively wide circular bore at the external nares of the human nose, it becomes flattened into a ribbon-like flow distributed vertically through the region of the turbinate bones. This configuration favors contact between the inhaled air and the nasal epithelium, which in the posterior two-thirds of the nasal cavity comprises ciliated cells. The cilia beat with a biphasic motion, a rapid effective stroke and a slow recovery stroke. Undulations of 10 to 20 per second transport a blanket of mucus lying above the cilia toward the nasopharynx where the mucus is swallowed. Gases and particles captured by the mucus are thereby cleared.

The process of molecular recognition takes place in unique bipolar neurons that comprise the olfactory receptor cells. About five million cells exist in a small patch of mucosa located primarily in the lateral wall of each human nasal cavity (Figure 8.1). Whereas the area of the patch equals about 2 to 4 cm^2 per nasal cavity in human beings, it equals larger values in other species such as the cat (20 cm^2) and dog (20–200 cm^2). The number of receptor cells is roughly proportional to areal extent.

The position of the olfactory mucosa in the nasal cavity may play a strategic role in species

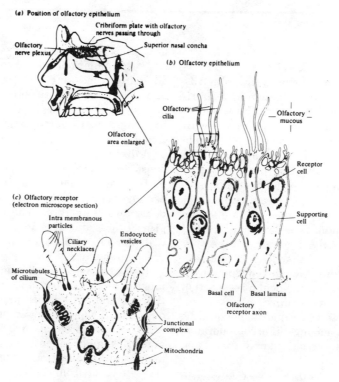

Figure 8.1. The peripheral olfactory system. From Keverne (1982).

differences in sensitivity. In many mammals the olfactory mucosa sits in the main airstream, whereas in human beings it sits out of the path. Calculations have indicated that during quiet breathing only five to ten percent of inspired air reaches the vicinity of the human olfactory receptors and about two percent contacts the receptors (Stuiver, 1958). In order to increase the amount of contact, a person will sniff. This act creates eddy currents and increases the amount of contact by about an order of magnitude. On average, a human sniff lasts about 400 msec, has a volume of 200 cm³, and an instantaneous flow rate of 30 liters per min (Laing, 1982). Bigger sniffs do not lead to notably more detectable or stronger smells, or vice versa (Laing, 1983). The size or vigor of a sniff matters less than that it is a sniff.

Olfactory Receptors

A typical vertebrate olfactory receptor comprises: (1) a terminal knob of about 2 μm diameter, (2) a dendritic midsection of 10 to 100 μm length (1 μm diameter in its apical portion and 5 μm in the region of the nucleus), and (3) an axon of 0.2 μm diameter. Unlike all other sensory systems, no synapse intervenes between the receptor cell and the axon that forms a fiber of the first cranial nerve.

The olfactory knob (or vesicle) gives rise to ten or more slender cilia (0.1 to 0.2 μm diam.) up to 200 μm in length. The cilia may exceed the cell body itself (about 100 μm) in length. Although they have a characteristic internal structure of typical cilia, they do not beat in undulating manner as do the cilia in the neighboring respiratory epithelium (Vinnikov, 1975). Human olfactory cilia apparently lack inherent motility, although air currents may lead to irregular motility that may perhaps merely stir the mucus (Moran & Rowley, 1983). The process could serve for local clearing and cleansing. (In some vertebrate species, cilia may have motility at first, but may then lose it.)

The membranes of olfactory cilia have more protein particles than do the cilia of adjacent respiratory epithelial cells. The most likely candidates for actual receptor sites are intramembraneous particles to which odorant molecules may bind. Chen and Lancet (1984) identified four olfactory-specific ciliary membrane glycoproteins, one or more of which may serve as the receptor molecules with the others serving roles in transduction. The relative densities of certain intramembraneous proteins may play a role in species or strain differences in sensitivity (Menco, Laing, & Panhuber, 1980).

Studies of odorant binding on receptor material have given functional evidence that the cilia contain the active sites for olfactory reception (Cagan & Rhein, 1980). Selective removal of the cilia accordingly destroys reception (Adamek, Gesteland, Mair, & Oakley, 1984). It is not yet established whether the entire surface of each cilium has chemoreceptive properties, but if so then the actual olfactory surface area in mammals would equal hundreds of square centimeters (Beidler, 1961).

In addition to receptors, the olfactory epithelium contains supporting (or sustentacular) cells and basal cells. The supporting cells form tight juctions with receptor cells. A collar of supporting cells around a receptor apparently seals off the surface from migration of odorous molecules to underlying spaces. (Respiratory epithelium presents no such tight junctions.) The supporting cells also ensure anatomical and functional isolation of one olfactory receptor from another. In the intracellular region just below the apical microvilli of the sustentacular cells, granules secrete materials that contribute to the mucus. Bowman's glands situated below the lamina propria and with ducts that reach the epithelial surfaces are, however, the primary source of mucus.

Mucus, which consists of an outer watery layer and an inner mucoid layer, can be viewed as a relevant morphological feature of the olfactory system (Figure 8.2) (Getchell & Getchell, 1977). In some respects it serves as a selective attenuator. The water-air partition coefficient predicts accurately how many molecules of water soluble substances will be deposited. This coefficient underestimates the number of lipid soluble molecules that will be deposited, presumably because the lipid membrane of the mucosa of the mucoid layer participates in the partitioning (Hornung, Mozell, & Serio, 1980). The mucus also serves as a leaky capacitor that slows down migration of molecules to the receptor membrane. Its constituents may even change the conformation of molecules. Since olfaction behaves in part as a molecular shape detector, any influence of mucus on conformation and orientation can translate into an influence on quality discrimination.

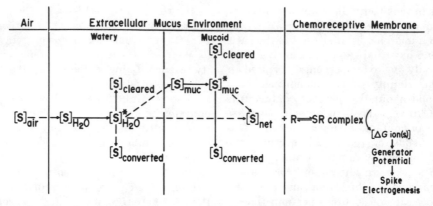

Figure 8.2. A schema to describe the likely progression of stimulus from the air phase to the chemoreceptive membrane. As the stimulus passes through the watery and mucoid layers of the mucus, there is some attenuation of concentration via clearance and possible conversion to other products. Modified from Getchell and Getchell (1977).

Olfactory receptor cells derive from the basal cells of the olfactory epithelium both in developing and mature organisms (Graziadei, 1977). The birth and death of a receptor cell takes about 60 days in primates and somewhat less time in lower organisms (e.g., 30 days in mice) (Moulton, 1975). Hence, normal olfactory mucosa contains cells of all the various possible ages. Any attempt to uncover morphologically distinct types of receptor cells must reckon with cell age.

The unique property for the olfactory receptor/neuron to generate spontaneously makes it possible to discover how sensitivity varies in the developing cell. When a cell begins to sprout cilia, it first shows little chemosensitivity. When the cilia reach about one quarter their mature length, the cell shows generalized sensitivity (Gesteland, Yancey, Mair, Adamek, & Farbman, 1980). At this point, a material known as olfactory marker protein has appeared within the cell (Farbman, Scholz, Emanuel, & Margolis, 1980). Its presence just anticipates the formation of the synapse at the olfactory bulb. As the cilia grow to about half their mature length, the cells abruptly reduce their generalized sensitivity and show narrower tuning. Instead of responding to 90 percent of odorants presented, they respond to fewer than 50 percent (Gesteland et al., 1980). Further growth yields no further reduction in breadth of tuning.

As a receptor develops, it sprouts an axon from its proximal end and that axon must find its way to the olfactory bulb. It does so by joining one or another bundle of about 1000 fibers. Such bundles, wrapped in myelin sheaths, course

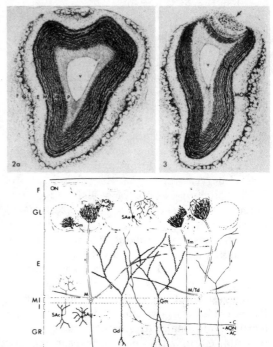

Figure 8.3. Top: Nissl-stained frontal section through the main olfactory bulb of the rabbit. F, olfactory nerve fiber layer; GL, glomerular layer; E, external plexiform layer; MI, mitral cell layer; GR, granule cell layer; P, periventricular layer; v, ventricle. Arrow indicates the location of the accessory olfactory bulb. Bottom: Diagram depicting the neuronal organization of the mammalian main olfactory bulb based on Golgi impregnation (from Shepherd, 1979). PG, periglomerular cells; SA, short-axon cells; G, granule cells; M, mitral cells; T, tufted cells. From Broadwell (1977).

through the perforations of the cribriform plate of the ethmoid bone. The bundles then reach the olfactory bulb where the individual fibers, which have had no previous opportunity to interact, enter glomeruli (Figure 8.3). Here, the possibility for interaction is great. Each glomerulus receives thousands of fibers.

Central Neuroanatomy

The connections within a glomerulus invite the conclusion that it must behave as a functional unit. The number of glomeruli falls below about 10,000, which makes the scale of functional olfactory units actually seem relatively modest. The glomerular layer of the bulb is the second of seven arranged around the extension of the lateral cerebral ventricle: (1) olfactory nerve fiber layer, (2) glomerular layer, including periglomerular and short-axon interneurons, (3) external plexiform layer containing fibers from various types of cells, as well as the cell bodies of second-order tufted cells, (4) mitral cell body layer, (5) internal plexiform layer (not always apparent), (6) granule cell layer (granule cells inhibit mitral and tufted cells), and (7) afferent and efferent fiber tracts (Broadwell, 1977; Shepherd, 1972). The circuitry in the vicinity of a glomerulus is reminiscent of that in the retina (Shepherd, 1979). It contains a direct pathway from the primary receptor fiber to the second order cell with two strata of horizontal connections. Mitral cells, with axons that form the lateral olfactory tract, comprise the major second order cells. Granule and periglomerular cells in the vicinity of the synapse between olfactory nerve (first order) fibers and the mitral (second order) dendrites function as interneurons and as sources of lateral and backward inhibition. The dendrites of periglomerular cells are apparently inhibitory to the apical dendrite of the mitral cell. This linkage permits information from one or another glomerulus to influence the flow of information passed on by the mitral cell. Granule cells synapse with mitral cells in the external plexiform layer. The granule cell, also apparently inhibitory, is postsynaptic to collaterals of mitral cell axons and to centrifugal fibers from other parts of the brain. It forms a linkage whereby one mitral cell may influence another and centrifugal fibers may influence mitral cells (Keverne, 1982).

The olfactory mucosa projects to the olfactory bulb with reasonable topographic fidelity (Land & Shepherd, 1974; Costanzo & Mozell, 1976). That is, a fiber from a cell in a particular part of the mucosa has a rather good chance of being found in a predictable part of the bulb. Functional evidence suggests that a given area of mucosa projects heavily to one area of the bulb, but rather diffusely to many areas (Kauer, 1980). If the bulb is removed, then the olfactory nerve fibers will continue to grow beyond their normal length and will form glomeruli in tissue where none would ever occur otherwise. Such ectopic glomeruli will even form in brain tissue placed into the space vacated by an excised olfactory bulb (Graziadei & Monti Graziadei, 1980). These glomeruli may exhibit some neural activity, but may be devoid of olfactory properties (Goldberg, Graziadei, & Nemitz, 1980).

The normal olfactory bulb has been found to contain numerous neuroactive substances (e.g., taurine, carnosine), but one in particular, olfactory marker protein, distinguishes this tissue from others (Margolis, 1977). Although its presence seems to have importance, its special function among the many neurotransmitters and neuromodulators found in the bulb is obscure.

Because a septum isolates the right from the left nasal cavity, bilateral functional interaction in olfaction occurs only in the brain, primarily via the anterior limb of the anterior commissure. This fiber tract, known as the medial olfactory tract and made up of the axons of second order mitral or tufted cells, connects one bulb to another via the anterior olfactory nucleus. The number of such fibers varies from species to species and is especially small in primates. Mitral cell fibers that run more laterally in the lateral olfactory tract comprise the main afferent pathway. This courses to the pyriform cortex, a region of paleocortex on the ventral temporal lobe.

Third order fibers that leave the pyriform cortex exceed the number of entering second order fibers by about 100-fold. Hence, the convergence seen in the bulb has its complement in divergence more centrally. The central anatomy of the olfactory system can be seen as forming two circuits, one primarily just sensory and another possibly regulatory. The former comprises a path through the thalamus and to the cortex and the latter comprises a path through the hypothalamus. Whereas this duality is drawn along olfactory versus vomeronasal lines

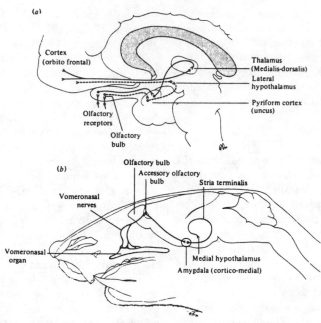

Figure 8.4. a: Central olfactory projections characteristic of higher primates. There are two parallel paths, one passing through the hypothalamus and one passing through the thalamus. b: The transhypothalamic pathway of higher primates has its equivalent in accessory olfactory projections in many lower species. The peripheral receptors of this pathway lie in the vomeronasal organ. From Keverne (1982).

in infraprimates, it apparently exists at the strictly olfactory level in primates (Takagi, 1980) (Figure 8.4). Both transhypothalamic and transthalamic olfactory pathways project to orbitofrontal cortex where, according to Takagi (1980), the transhypothalamic terminations exhibit fine-grained sensitivity and the transthalamic exhibit diffuse sensitivity.

As with most sensory systems, efferent projections have received less attention than afferent projections. Efferent projections in the olfactory system course distally primarily through the pyriform cortex to the olfactory bulb (Kerr, 1977). These may play a substantial role in the modulation of behavior. For example, Pager (1977a) found that the mitral cells exhibited more activity and longer lasting activity in hungry than in satiated free-moving rats. The extent of such hunger-induced activation depended upon the food rewarding character of the odor. Efferent innervation of the bulb must almost certainly mediate such modulations in activity.

Other Chemosensory Systems in the Nose

In addition to olfaction, the nasal cavity contains receptors of up to four other chemosensory systems. The trigeminal nerve, which endows the face with cutaneous sensitivity (touch, warmth/cold, pain), sends branches to the nasal cavity from two of its three divisions: the maxillary division and the ethmoid branch of the ophthalmic division. The distal ends of trigeminal fibers in the nasal mucosa comprise free, unmyelinated endings. Their sensitivity allows chemically induced sensations of pungency, irritation, and warmth and cold. The term common chemical sense refers generally to the "modality" that mediates such sensations arising from mucosal areas. Hence, the eyes, pharynx, oral cavity, and trachea all have common chemical sensitivity. In the eyes, anterior oral cavity, and rostral pharynx, the trigeminal nerve mediates the sensations, whereas in the other areas, the glossopharyngeal and vagus nerves serve.

It seems prudent to resist any temptation to consider the common chemical sense in the nasal cavity as simply a pain sense. The modality does indeed respond to noxious stimuli, such as caustic agents (acids, anhydrides, unsaturated aldehydes, ammonia, the halogens), and chemical reactivity of the sort that will denature proteins does account for much of the activity of common chemical stimuli. Nevertheless, many relatively nonreactive substances also stimulate the common chemical sense at environmentally realistic concentrations (Doty, Brugger, Jurs, Orndorff, Snyder, & Lowrey, 1978; Cain, 1981). The appreciation of carbonated beverages and cigarettes, for example, depends heavily on common chemical sensations (Cain, 1980).

The vomeronasal chemosensory system, which exists widely among reptiles and among the mammals excluding old world primates, has received growing attention for its primacy in reptilian chemoreception and its role in behavior relevant to mating in mammals (Wysocki, 1979). The vomeronasal organ, or organ of Jacobson, forms a lined, tubular cul-de-sac, accessory to the rostral nasal cavity and with an opening to the nasal cavity (e.g., rodents), the nasopalatine duct (e.g., carnivores and primates), or the oral cavity (e.g., cows, snakes) (Figure 8.5). The lateral hemisphere of the vomeronasal lining contains nonneural epithelium whereas the medial hemisphere contains sensory epithelium. Like olfactory mucosa, vomeronasal sensory epithelium contains bipolar sensory neurons and supporting cells. The sensory neurons differentiate from staminal cells at the interface between the sensory and nonsensory epithelium (Graziadei, 1977). Like olfactory cells, they regenerate continuously and have a life of mere weeks. Unlike olfactory cells, they lack cilia and possess microvilli instead. The axons of the receptors form the vomeronasal nerve, which runs along the medial surface of the main olfactory bulb and terminates in a structure known as the accessory olfactory bulb embedded within the main bulb (Figure 8.3).

Second order neurons from the accessory olfactory bulb neither communicate with those of the main bulb nor project to the same central areas. After reaching the nucleus of the stria terminalis and amygdala, third order fibers of the vomeronasal system reach various parts of the hypothalamus and the mammillary bodies. The system may have no specific neocortical representation.

Although the vomeronasal system may respond to some stimuli in common with olfaction, its threshold differs. More importantly, the vomeronasal system can respond to stimuli of much higher molecular weight than olfaction. Nonvolatile stimuli in urine and various secretions become available when an animal places its

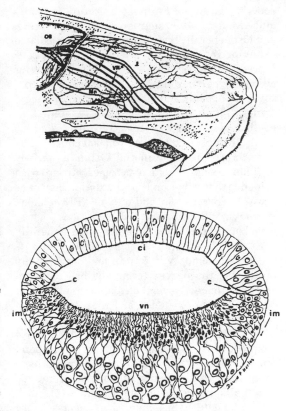

Figure 8.5. Upper portion: Sagittal section through the nose of the rat at the level of the septum (s) and showing five neural systems. OB, olfactory bulb; nT, terminal nerve; VN, vomeronasal nerve; t, branches of the trigeminal nerve; Mn, nerves of the septal organ of Masera. The region of the septum close to the olfactory bulb and lamina cribrosa (cr) represents the olfactory region proper. Lower portion: Cross section through the vomeronasal organ to show the common ciliated (ci) and vomeronasal (vn) epithelia which are in contact at regions denoted C. Immature elements (im) eventually mature and travel downwards to become mature neurons (r). Supporting cells shown by s. From Graziadei (1977).

nose or tongue on the material. (Elephants use their trunks (Rasmussen, Schmidt, Henneous, Groves, & Daves, 1982).) Depending on the species, the tongue may flick into the aperture of the organ (Meredith & Burghardt, 1978) or a vascular pump under sympathetic control via the nasopalatine nerve may draw liquid into the lumen (Meredith & O'Connell, 1979).

Elimination of vomeronasal functioning will disrupt courtship and mating behavior in male rodents, alter sex hormone secretion in males and females, alter aggression and mothering, and just generally disable chemosensory mediated behavior in certain invertebrates (Wysocki & Meredith, 1987). The catalogue of behavior guided by vomeronasal functioning will continue to expand as research on the topic continues. Much behavior previously viewed as exclusively under olfactory control now seems in whole or part under vomeronasal control. The urge to see the vomeronasal system as largely a "pheromonal" system becomes strong with evidence that vomeronasal stimulation may have reward properties in and of itself (Beauchamp, Wysocki, & Wellington, 1985).

Whereas the vomeronasal system generally does not exist in human beings (some claim its presence commonly in fetuses and occasionally in adults), the nervus terminalis has indisputable existence. Nevertheless, anatomists first overlooked its existence and then failed for a time to appreciate that it had an afferent, as well as an efferent (autonomic) role. The precise stimuli to which its free nerve endings respond remain obscure, although thermal stimuli have been suggested. Noting the origin of nervus terminalis neurons in the olfactory placode, Graziadei (1977) has favored a chemosensory role. Indeed, Demski and Northcutt (1983) demonstrated that the terminal nerve, rather than the accepted olfactory system, mediated the response to sex attractant in the goldfish.

The fifth system in the nasal cavity comprises the septal organ of Masera and its nerves, which enter the olfactory bulb. The organ, which forms an island of sensory mucosa in the epithelial tissue of the septum, contains olfactory-like receptors. These differ, however, in their ultrastructure. Any functional differences between the two systems remain unspecified.

Neural Measures

Figure 8.6 depicts various ways to read neurophysiological information from the olfactory system (Gesteland, 1978). The measures include: (1) the electro-olfactogram (EOG), a graded potential that reflects the activity of many receptor cells; (2) action potentials recorded, usually extracellularly, from single receptor cells in the mucosa; (3) multiunit (typically integrated) activity from olfactory nerve branches; (4) surface potentials from the bulb; and (5)

single unit recordings from the bulb. Multiunit and single unit recording can also take place at third order and other higher order loci.

In general, gross potentials and multiunit recordings offer useful indicators of intensive functional properties, such as adaptation or temporal integration. Comparisons of such indicators with psychophysical data often prove valuable. Single unit recordings have more use in the exploration of the quality code, a subject treated later.

The EOG, occasionally termed the Ottoson potential, deserves special mention primarily because of its usefulness and secondarily because of controversy regarding its origin. This particularly convenient measure is a predominantly negative, easily recordable potential with a peak amplitude in the millivolt range. Its amplitude rises to a peak shortly after the onset of stimulation, then falls to a lower level for the duration of stimulation. Ottoson's (1956) early experiments established the plausibility of the EOG as a receptor potential. Nevertheless, experiments by Shibuya (1964) and Mozell (1962) implied a dissociation between the EOG and activity in the olfactory nerve. These experiments left open the possibility of the EOG as artifact or epiphenomenon. Subsequent research on current flow in the mucosa reestablished the plausibility of the receptor potential interpretation (Getchell, 1974; see also Ottoson & Shepherd, 1967).

SENSITIVITY

Absolute Sensitivity

The ability to stimulate olfaction varies from odorant to odorant over many orders of magnitude (Table 8.1) (Amoore, 1982). Particularly potent stimuli, such as some mercaptans and amines, α-ionone, and vanillin, require on the order of a part per trillion of air. Stuiver (1958) estimated that, after losses due to stimulus transmission, concentrations of that magnitude would stimulate between about five and 40 human olfactory receptor cells (one molecule per cell). If correct, Stuiver's calculations reveal that human olfactory sensitivity falls near its theoretical limit. Furthermore, the calculation suggests that species differences in sensitivity may be reducible to the biophysical question of

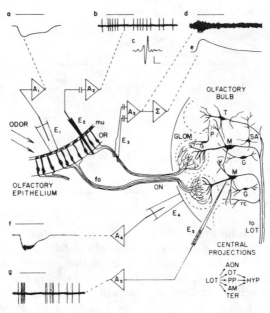

Figure 8.6. A schematic representation of the cellular anatomy of the peripheral olfactory system of vertebrates and of its odor-evoked electrical activity. Olfactory receptor neurons (OR) lie in the olfactory epithelium, the cilia on their dendrites bathed by mucus (mu). Saline electrode E_1 measures the electro-olfactogram (shown in inset a). Electrode E_2, a metal microelectrode, measures extracellular spike activity in single receptor cells (shown in insets b and c). Bundles of axons form the fila olfactoria (fo), which coalesce as the olfactory nerve (ON). Bipolar wire electrodes E_3 record asynchronous spike activity from a bundle of axons or the whole nerve (shown in inset d). The signal can be rectified and summated with a decay (Σ) to give a smoothed measure of evoked activity (shown in inset e). Axon terminals branch at the olfactory bulb in spherical concentrations of neuropil called glomeruli (GLOM), in which they synapse with processes of second-order neurons. Extrinsic neurons of the bulb include mitral cells (M) and tufted cells (T), whose axons project centrally as the lateral olfactory tract (LOT). Neurons intrinsic to the bulb are periglomerular cells (P), which form lateral connections between glomeruli, granule cells (G) and short axon cells (SA). Mitral cells send recurrent collaterals (rc) toward the glomeruli. Electrode E_4 is a saline pipette that records bulb surface potentials (shown in inset f). A microelectrode, E_5, records extracellular activity of single second-order neurons (shown in inset g). The lateral olfactory tract projects to the anterior olfactory nucleus (AON), olfactory turbercle (OT), prepyriform cortex (PP), amygdaloid complex (AM), and the transitional entorhinal cortex (TER). Projections from the olfactory tubercle, prepyriform cortex, and amygdaloid complex go to the hypothalamus (HYP). Other central connections and centrifugal pathways to the bulb have been omitted. The horizontal lines in insets a, b, d, f, and g represent the stimulus delivery period, 5 sec. All responses are drawn with positive voltages upward. Inset c shows the waveform of an extracellularly recorded receptor action potential seen with an expanded sweep. For this the calibration marks represent $200\,\mu V$ and 5 msec. Amplifiers are all single-ended except A_3, which is differential. From Gesteland (1978).

how many molecules can reach the receptors. (In the male silk moth, a single molecule of the female sex attractant can evoke a detectable response in a receptor neuron and activity in about 200 receptors will evoke behavior (Schneider, 1969; Shorey, 1976). There exists some possibility that Stuiver's calculations underestimate the concentration of odorant in mucus, a matter that would probably not alter

comparisons among land dwelling vertebrates (Price, 1984).)

A slight change in the size or shape of a molecule may increase the threshold by one or more orders of magnitude. Indeed, virtually any change in a molecule may change the threshold. The question is whether the change can be seen as part of an understandable pattern. In aliphatic series, absolute sensitivity often changes

Table 8.1. Odor detection thresholds of selected compounds[a]

Compound	Odor threshold concn. in air	
	(mg/m^3)	(ppm, v/v)
Ethane	1.5×10^5	120,000
Methanol	6.6×10^2	500
Chloroform	3.2×10^2	65
Benzene	1.7×10^1	5.2
Camphor	1.1×10^0	0.17
Furfural	2.3×10^{-1}	0.059
Isoamyl acetate	3.8×10^{-2}	0.0071
5α-Androst-16-en-3-one	2.1×10^{-3}	0.00019
2-Methoxy-3-isobutylpyrazine	3.6×10^{-6}	0.00000054

[a]From a literature survey by Amoore and Hautala (1981).

progressively (Figure 8.7). In the aliphatic alcohol series, for instance, the threshold decreases from methanol (wood alcohol), to ethanol (grain alcohol), to propanol (rubbing alcohol), to the higher molecular weight species up to about octanol. This kind of progression also holds true for aliphatic esters, ketones, hydrocarbons, mercaptans, acids, and other series although the point of minimum threshold varies from one series to another (Laffort, 1969).

The progressive change in threshold with carbon chain length suggests a possible relation between threshold and solubility. Attempts to account for or predict threshold usually take this more or less for granted. In a predictive formula derived by Davies and Taylor (1959), solubility shows up in a term that combines air-water and water-oil partition coefficients.

The other important term in the formula was an index of the cross-sectional area of the molecule oriented along its hydrophilic-hydrophobic axis. In a more elaborate and more accurate model, certain parameters of solubility (molecular volume, ability to accept and donate protons, and local polarizability) are determined via gas chromatographic measurements and combined into a predictive formula (Laffort, 1977). In principle, the formula describes both the filtering effect of the mucus as molecules approach it from the gas phase and the affinity of the molecules for the phospholipid bilayer that comprises the bulk of the receptor cell membrane.

Although correlations between Laffort's theoretical and obtained values in a given data set reach values as high as 0.8, the predicted value may overestimate or underestimate the threshold

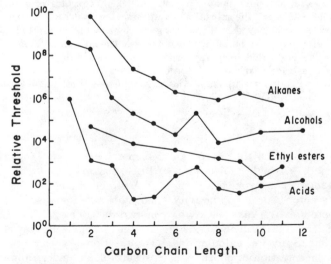

Figure 8.7. Odor thresholds measured in human subjects for four aliphatic series. Data from Laffort (1969).

by an order of magnitude or more. An apparent irony between a high correlation and a large error arises because the total span of theoretical and measured values equals many orders of magnitude.

It is unfortunate that the models of threshold lack high accuracy, since various applications exist for an accurate formula. There are many applications in food chemistry and atmospheric pollution in which an accurate odor threshold formula would have value, but the existing formulas have too high a margin of error. Hence, compilations of thresholds measured through the decades are used instead (e.g., Fazzalari, 1978; van Gemert & Nettenbreijer, 1977). These tables also have serious limitations since such factors as psychophysical methodology, precision of stimulus control, and mode of stimulus presentation have varied from study to study, often for justifiable reasons (see Punter, 1983, for discussion). These factors often introduce enough systematic or random variation to nullify any benefit. However, Amoore and Hautala (1983) have sought to produce a tabulation purged of grossly deviant values. This tabulation for 214 industrial materials is at present the most useful.

The question often arises "Are animals more sensitive than human beings?" It appears that dogs are more sensitive by a factor of about 1000 and that their sensitivity may be the keenest of all (Marshall & Moulton, 1981; Moulton &

Marshall, 1976). (There are of course psychophysical and instrumental considerations to keep in mind in any species comparison.) Is this three orders of magnitude advantage constant across compounds? That is, do the dog and other species with sensitivities between human beings and dogs show the same relative sensitivity across compounds? Some data suggest so (see Laing, 1975).

Figure 8.8 show the relation between log threshold and log chain length for aliphatic alcohols and acetates in the rat (Moulton, 1960; Moulton & Eayrs, 1960). These results on relative sensitivity are similar to those obtained from human beings, frogs, dogs, and even blowflies. In the case of the frog, the measure was the amplitude of the EOG (Ottoson, 1958). Such data as these reinforce the conclusion that absolute sensitivity derives largely from biophysical factors (see also Schmidt, 1978). Nevertheless, in this instance, as in so much of olfactory research, the conclusion comes mainly from circumstantial evidence. Biophysical factors may account for some of the variance, but just enough to make the similarity appealing and perhaps to prompt an oversimplified answer.

Differential Sensitivity

The ability to resolve small differences in concentration of odorant has traditionally seemed poor. The Weber fraction, that is, the fractional

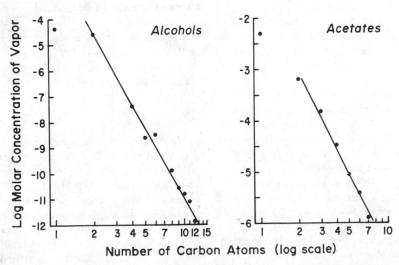

Figure 8.8. Odor thresholds in rats versus carbon chain-length of aliphatic alcohols (from Moulton & Eayrs, 1960) and acetates (from Moulton, 1960).

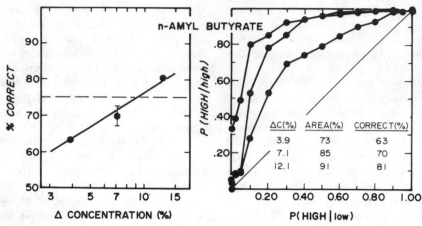

Figure 8.9. Left side shows a psychometric function for odor intensity discrimination (two-alternative forced-choice). The x-axis shows the average difference in vapor-phase concentration between the high and low members of each pair of test concentrations. Right side shows receiver operating characteristic (ROC) curves derived from chromatographic measurement of the pairs of test concentrations. They characterize trial-to-trial fluctuations in concentration. Each curve represents a given average ΔC from the psychophysical experiment. The area under these curves defines the maximum possible performance achievable in the two-alternative forced-choice test. The inset on the right portrays the comparison of psychophysical performance (percent correct) with predictions of optimum performance (percent area under the ROC curves). From Cain (1977c).

change in concentration necessary to perceive a difference half the time, has commonly been reported as about 0.30, with some values as high as 0.58 (Hainer, Emslie, & Jacobson, 1954; Stone, 1964). This implies that a chemosensory system with extraordinary ability to detect very small amounts of material cannot reliably register small changes in amount. The system has ironically seemed to have low apparent noise for one task and high noise for the other.

Could the high noise apparent in differential sensitivity possibly arise from sources outside the organism, specifically from fluctuations in the stimulus? In an effort to answer this question, Cain (1977a) presented pairs of concentrations for intensity resolution of human subjects and to a gas chromatograph. The chromatograph, with a known low level of internal noise, indicated substantial random fluctuations in the concentrations presented for resolution (Figure 8.9). Interestingly, human subjects performed the task of intensity resolution almost as well as the chromatograph. It turned out that internal noise in the human subject was actually not very substantial and that fluctuations in the stimulus played a large role in limiting intensity resolution. Values of the Weber fraction corrected for the physical fluctuations averaged slightly less than 0.10, about the same as for

loudness discrimination by the ear and brightness discrimination by the eye for stimuli presented in succession. Hence, olfaction no longer seems dull when it comes to intensity discrimination.

FUNCTIONAL RELATIONS

Suprathreshold Magnitude

Perceived odor magnitude increases with concentration in negatively accelerated fashion. Direct ratio scaling techniques, such as magnitude estimation, have commonly led to the outcome

$$\psi = k\phi^\beta,$$

in which ψ represents perceived magnitude and ϕ concentration. The value of β almost always falls below 1.0, commonly to a considerable degree. This compression of output relative to input seems to have a largely peripheral origin. Both the EOG and integrated neural recordings imply much compression at the periphery (Drake, Johansson, von Sydow, & Døving, 1969; Mozell, Sheehe, Swieck, Kurtz, & Hornung, 1984; Ottoson, 1970) (Figure 8.10). A comparison of the EOG and the slow bulbar potential implies

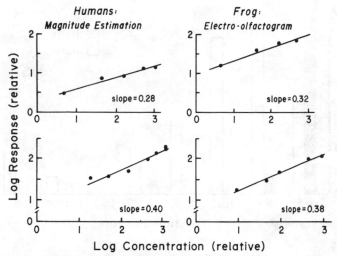

Figure 8.10. Psychophysical and neurophysiological odor intensity functions for methyl benzoate (upper functions) (from von Sydow, 1968) and 1-butanol (lower functions) (left, from Jones, 1958; right, from Ottoson, 1956).

proportionality, that is, no further compression, from first order to second order cells (Ottoson, 1970). Transformations at higher levels of the nervous system have not been studied, but seem unlikely to yield surprises.

The degree of compression seen psychophysically varies from odorant to odorant and can be summarized in terms of exponents of psychophysical power functions. These range from about 0.10 to about 0.80 (Berglund, Berglund, Ekman, & Engen, 1971; Cain, 1969; Engen, 1965; Patte, Etcheto, & Laffort, 1975). The lower exponent implies that a tenfold (1000 percent) increase in concentration will lead to a mere 26 percent increase in perceived magnitude.

Differences in steepness show up just as readily in odor intensity judgements made via category rating scales: zero (no odor) to five (very strong). A U.S. Bureau of Mines study collected 69 odor intensity functions in this manner (Katz & Talbert, 1930). Typically, the data proved describable by logarithmic functions (Fechner's Law) (Figure 8.11). Katz and Talbert summarized the steepness of the functions by the parameter f in the formula:

$$f = (C_5/C_0)^{1/5}$$

in which C_0 and C_5 equal the concentrations that led to ratings of zero and five, respectively. The f factor, called the dilution factor, specifies the attenuation necessary to drop one scale step. Hence, a dilution factor of 10 indicates the need for a tenfold attenuation to reduce rated

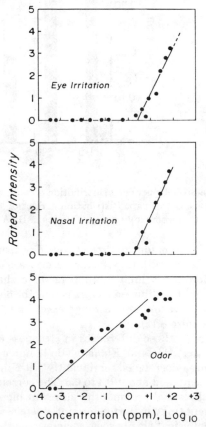

Figure 8.11. Psychophysical functions for eye irritation, nasal irritation, and odor of benzyl mercaptan. The dilution factor (see text) for odor equalled 15 and those for nasal and eye irritation equalled 2.8 and 3.1, respectively. From Katz and Talbert (1930).

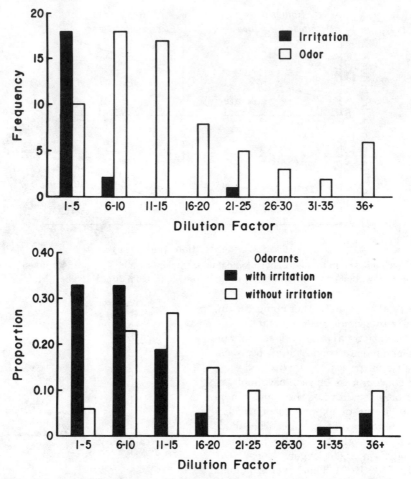

Figure 8.12. Upper part: Distribution of dilution factors for 69 odor intensity functions and 21 nasal irritation functions. Lower part: Distribution of dilution factors for odor intensity functions of odorants that did or did not evoke accompanying nasal irritation. Data from Katz and Talbert (1930).

intensity from four to three, three to two, and so forth. A low dilution factor describes a steep function and a high dilution factor a shallow function. The dilution factors among the 69 odor functions varied over a range exceeding ten to one (Figure 8.12).

Why do these differences in steepness exist? Laffort, Patte, and Etcheto (1974) noted that steepness correlates significantly with threshold; r^2 equalled about 0.4 to 0.5. The correlation with threshold prompts the idea that biophysical events may in part determine steepness, just as biophysical events seem to determine threshold. For instance, a given change in incident concentration at the nose could be altered nonlinearly by filtration in nonolfactory mucus (i.e., as odorized air courses through the nasal cavity), by migration through olfactory mucus, or by other biophysically relevant factors. One factor or more than one may account for the general degree of compression that EOG measurements imply is peripheral in origin (Figure 8.10).

Irritation offers another correlate of steepness. Unlike most others who have scaled odor intensity, Katz and Talbert required their participants to resolve odor and irritation perceptually. The judgments led to erection of 21 irritation functions. In the other 48 cases, irritation proved insufficient to lead to a function. Had Katz and Talbert allowed participants simply to judge a composite odor-irritation attribute, they would probably have yielded a higher proportion of low dilution factors for, as Figure 8.12

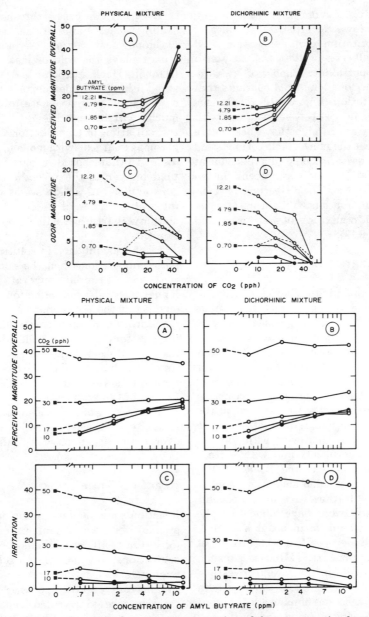

Figure 8.13. Top: A. Perceived magnitude versus concentration of the pungent stimulus carbon dioxide for carbon dioxide presented alone (filled circles), the odorant amyl butyrate presented alone (filled squares), and mixtures of carbon dioxide and amyl butyrate. Parameter is concentration of amyl butyrate. B. Same as A, but combinations of carbon dioxide and amyl butyrate presented dichorhinically, that is, irritant (carbon dioxide) to one nostril and odorant (amyl butyrate) to the other. C. Perceived odor component (denoted odor magnitude) of amyl butyrate alone (filled squares), carbon dioxide alone (filled circles), and physical mixtures. The nonmonotonic function formed by the thin dashes depicts how odor magnitude would change in a case where concentration of odorant and irritant changed jointly. D. Same as C, but dichorhinic mixtures. Bottom: A. Same psychophysical data as in top portion, but plotted here against concentration and amyl butyrate: amyl butyrate alone (filled circles), carbon dioxide alone (filled squares), and physical mixtures. Parameter is the concentration of carbon dioxide. A noteworthy feature is the flatness of the psychophysical functions. B. Same as A, but dichorhinic mixtures. C. Perceived irritating component of carbon dioxide alone (filled squares), amyl butyrate alone (filled circles), and physical mixtures. D. Same as C, but dichorhinic mixtures. From Cain and Murphy (1980).

illustrates, dilution factors for irritation typically came out low. Nevertheless, in spite of whatever odor-irritation resolution was achieved by Katz and Talbert's participants, they still yielded a disproportionate number of low dilution factors for odor alone from odorants that did produce irritation (Figure 8.12). The segregation of dilution factors between odorants with and without irritation might have been more impressive without the unavoidable complicating factor that high irritation may suppress odor at higher concentrations and may thereby flatten the odor function. Katz and Talbert made reference to this, an observation that Cain and Murphy (1980) confirmed in mixtures of an odorant and irritant (Figure 8.13).

Temporal Integration

For short durations of stimulation, concentration may be traded with time in such a way as to maintain the response magnitude constant. DeVries and Stuiver (1961) reported nearly perfect trading at threshold only for durations below about 20 msec, with imperfect trading for durations up to about 100 msec. Trading over such short durations could probably have arisen simply from the concentration gradient of the impinging wave of stimulation. That threshold experiment contrasts, however, with various suprathreshold experiments and with certain neural data. Kobal (1981) and Békésy (1964) found that perceived odor magnitude continued to grow for durations exceeding a second. Numerous investigations have found that the EOG rises to a maximum in about a second. Such slow growth seems quite unlikely to reflect an artifact of stimulus arrival. Indeed, no such artifact played a role in the careful investigation of Mozell et al. (1984) who explored both how the primary variables of number of odorant molecules, volume, and duration, and the derived variables of concentration, flow rate, and delivery rate altered integrated activity in the olfactory nerve of the frog. The number of molecules and duration had a positive influence on activity whereas volume had a negative influence. As other suprathreshold experiments had implied, concentration could be traded with time to maintain a constant response. The data of Mozell et al., however, permitted a quantitative statement: Concentration could be traded with duration raised to the 2/3 power, up to their maximum duration of 0.7 sec.

Here, as in the case of threshold and intensity scaling, we must at least consider the operation of biophysical factors. As noted above, the mucus plays the role of leaky capacitor (see Getchell, Heck, DeSimone, & Price, 1980). As stimulating molecules deposit themselves into mucus from the gas phase, diffusion through mucus will become the rate limiting step in the initiation of transduction. The mucus will become "charged" with molecules and will then dissipate that charge in part on the phospholipid bilayer of the receptor cells. The time-constant of this action seems consistent with integration times of a second or more. This matter will arise again in connection with reaction time.

Insofar as diffusion in solution governs temporal integration, then the common chemical sense should exhibit temporal integration over longer intervals than olfaction. The free nerve endings of the trigeminal nerve lie within the respiratory mucosa, deeper than do the cilia of the olfactory receptors. Molecules actually may need to diffuse through a portion of the respiratory epithelium to reach the free nerve endings. Longer intervals of integration do indeed occur. Cometto-Muniz and Cain (1984) found nearly perfect trading of time and mass for durations as long as 4 sec. Some integration may even occur over a time span of many minutes (Elsberg, Levy, & Brewer, 1935).

Reaction Time

Reaction time to odors in human beings is surprisingly long, with a minimum of about 500 msec for virtually all odors (Wells, 1929). At low concentrations, reaction time exceeds a second. Such values clearly exceed the combined duration necessary to transport molecules from the external nares to the mucosa and to conduct the neural message within the nervous system. Some other latency must account for the length of reaction time. Getchell and Shepherd (1978) also made the observation that neural membrane events could hardly account for latencies seen in single unit recordings in the olfactory mucosa (see Kauer & Shepherd, 1977, for bulbar unit latencies, 200 to 300 msec). Getchell et al. (1980) subsequently demonstrated that a model of mass transfer of odorous molecules through mucus could account for the latency. The model makes the reasonable assumption that a neuron will fire when a critical concentration of odorant

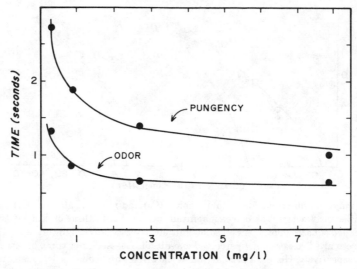

Figure 8.14. Reaction time to the odor and pungency of n-butyl alcohol. From Cain (1981).

diffuses through mucus to the depth of what we might term the receptor compartment, approximately 10 to 70 μm beneath the surface. Single unit data for various substances and from various labs implied that the average depth equalled 46 μm.

Figure 8.14 shows reaction time functions for the odor and pungency of n-butyl alcohol perceived by humans (Cain, 1976, 1981). Two functions resulted because subjects had to respond on some trials to odor and on others to irritation. At any given concentration, the latency of pungency exceeded that of odor. The temporal disparity between the attributes could well have arisen from differences in depth between olfactory receptors (estimated here as 70 μm) and free nerve endings of the trigeminal nerve (estimated as 110 μm).

Adaptation

After an initial phase of integration, the olfactory sensation will begin to wane. Psychophysical investigations of the time-course of adaptation imply an exponential decay. After a few minutes of constant stimulation, sensation magnitude falls to steady state of about 30 to 40 percent of initial magnitude (Figure 8.15). Existing studies imply little odorant-to-odorant variation in the rate of decline or in the steady state reached, but such lack of variation could have resulted from choice of stimuli (see Schafer, Criswell, Fracek, & Brower, 1984). Some stimuli,

such as various musks and anisoles, are reputed to show very rapid adaptation (Griffiths & Fenwick, 1977). This could reflect the strong tendency of musks to adsorb strongly on surfaces, including the tissue. Repeated sniffs of musk may cause a particularly large accumulation of odorant in the mucus and at the receptors. For stimuli that adsorb less strongly, desorption or clearance between sniffs may prevent steady accumulation (compare with Hornung

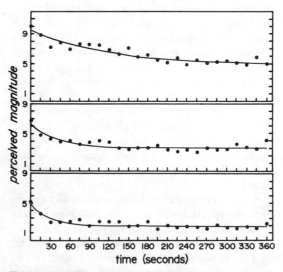

Figure 8.15. The time-course of adaptation to n-butyl acetate at concentrations of 0.8 mg per liter of air (bottom function), 2.7 mg per liter (middle function), and 18.6 mg per liter (top function). From Cain (1974).

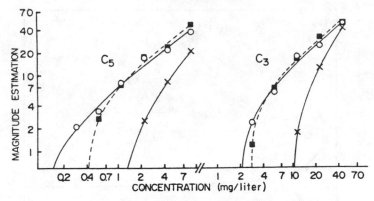

Figure 8.16. Psychophysical functions for n-amyl alcohol (C$_5$) and n-propyl alcohol (C$_3$) under conditions of self-adaptation. Unfilled circles depict perceived magnitude assessed after three breaths of 0.5 mg per liter C$_5$ or 2.0 mg per liter C$_3$. Filled squares depict perceived magnitude assessed after eight breaths of 0.5 and 2.0 mg per liter C$_5$ and C$_3$, respectively. Crosses depict perceived magnitude assessed after three breaths of 9.2 and 21.6 mg per liter C$_5$ and C$_3$, respectively. Hence, a comparison of the circles and squares demonstrates the influence of the duration of adaptation and a comparison of the circles and crosses demonstrates the influence of concentration of the adapting stimulus. From Cain and Engen (1969).

& Mozell, 1977). For the substances studied, the rate of decay has also shown little systematic variation with concentration except at levels high enough to evoke pungency (Cain, 1974). An odor with accompanying pungency will tend to show less rapid adaptation (see top function in Figure 8.15).

The absolute threshold will increase over the time of exposure to a suprathreshold adapting concentration. Stuiver's (1958) measurements implied that the threshold would eventually rise to the level of the adapting concentration. Such a dramatic rise probably overstates the situation. Nevertheless, exposure to a given adapting concentration will have a greater depressing effect on the perceived magnitude of lower concentrations than on higher concentrations (Figure 8.16). In this respect, olfaction resembles vision, taste, and vibrotaction. Olfactory psychophysical functions obtained under conditions of adaptation imply that duration of an adapting stimulus has a somewhat weaker influence than concentration.

Olfactory adapation exhibits generally unpredictable specificity. Two stimuli with relatively similar odors and similar molecular structures will often show considerable cross-adaptation; that is, exposure to one will alter sensitivity to or perceived magnitude of the other. It would seem likely that similar stimuli would show greater cross-adaptation than dissimilar stimuli and hence that the study of cross-adaptation

would unlock the secrets of receptor specificity or, depending on the locus of adaptation, quality coding. Such simplicity has not prevailed. Two quite dissimilar stimuli may show considerable cross-adaptation and two similar stimuli may show little. Furthermore, cross-adaptation is commonly asymmetric, that is, stimulus A may have more of an effect on stimulus B than B has on A (Köster, 1971). Occasionally, cross-adaptation seen when one stimulus precedes another may even become cross-facilitation with a reverse order of presentation (Berglund, Berglund, & Lindvall, 1978; Corbit & Engen, 1971; Laing & Mackay-Sim, 1975; Mair, 1982).

Although cross-adaptation has yet to reveal desired underlying principles, two additional observations have some relevance. First, prior exposure to one stimulus invariably has some depresssing effect on the perception of another, irrespective of the qualities or molecular structures of the molecules (Köster, 1971). This implies either the existence of a subpopulation of receptors relatively nonspecific to quality or the existence of very broad tuning in general. Second, cross-adaptation with one stimulus rarely seems to alter the quality of another. That is, cross-adaptation with one stimulus does not selectively depress sensitivity of just a specific set of receptors (other than some hypothetical nonspecific receptors). If it did, then we would routinely expect an alteration in the quality of the test stimulus.

At the receptor cell level, Baylin and Moulton (1979) found both clear self-adaptation and clear cross-adaptation. Some units, however, showed neither type or adaptation and some showed greater cross-adaptation than self-adaptation. (The latter finding has never showed up psychophysically.) Cross-adaptation rarely proved reciprocal. The pattern of results led the investigators to conclude that a given receptor cell contained more than one kind of "receptive site types" and that the number of sites of any given type varied from one receptor cell to another. Although difficult to dispute on specific grounds, the argument only stands for lack of anything better. Acceptance of the argument forecloses any possibility for cross-adapatation to unlock secrets of stimulus similarity or olfactory coding.

Where in the nervous system does adaptation occur? The receptors would seem the likely locus, but they account for only part of the effect. The EOG measured at the mucosa has shown about a 40 percent decrement with repeated stimulation (Ottoson, 1956). Multiunit recordings in the olfactory bulb have also shown only relatively small decrements with time. Adrian (1950) noted that repeated stimulation would at first disrupt normal oscillations of electrical potentials in the bulb but that these would eventually reappear. He concluded that adapta-

tion occurred largely in the bulb and entailed a shifting neural signal-to-noise ratio among various sets of neurons.

The neurophysiological data point to the existence of both a peripheral and a central neural locus of adaptation. Psychophysical data obtained with dichorhinic stimulation support the duality of the process. When an adapting stimulus and test stimulus presented to the same nostril succeed each other rapidly, the test stimulus is depressed in intensity. When the test stimulus is presented to the other nostril, intensity is still depressed, but to a smaller degree (Figure 8.17).

Bilateral Integration and Localization

The experiment on adaptation "across the midline" implied some interaction between the two sides of the olfactory system (Cain, 1977a). The two sides also exhibit bilateral additivity: the perceived magnitude of concentrations smelled bilaterally exceeds the magnitude of those smelled unilaterally. The additivity is less than complete and its nature suggests some possible inhibitory interaction between the two sides.

Evidence for interaction across the midline also emerged in an ablation study by Bennett (1968). In that case, transection of the anterior limb of the anterior commissure disinhibited

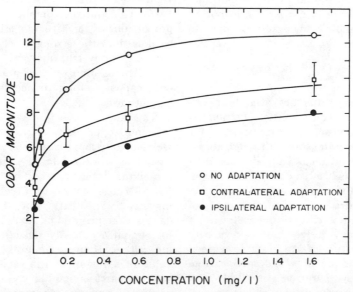

Figure 8.17. Psychophysical functions for linalyl acetate obtained when test concentrations succeeded a diluent (unfilled circles, no adaptation) and when they succeeded an adapting stimulus (0.53 mg per liter of air) on the same side (filled circles, ipsilateral adaptation) or on the opposite side (squares, contralateral adaptation). From Cain (1977a).

adaptation. Hence, one side of the system seemed to hold the other under some degree of tonic control. A neurophysiological study by Leveteau and MacLeod (1969) gave evidence that inhibitory interaction between the olfactory bulbs had temporal properties compatible with some observations on lateralization of odors.

Békésy's (1967) experiments in various modalities have established an important role for inhibition in the lateralization of stimulation. So far, however, Békésy (1964) has been the only investigator to find reliable odor lateralization due to bilateral temporal disparity or concentration disparity (see Schneider & Schmidt, 1967). Internasal differences of just a few milliseconds or a few percent in concentration permitted lateralization. Leveteau and MacLeod (1969) and Daval and Leveteau (1975) found interbulb inhibition when stimulation of one bulb lagged that of the other by a few milliseconds.

There is little doubt that most organisms can localize odors in real life situations. This may occur through sniffing separate points in space in rapid succession and registering differences in intensity from one sniff to another. If the organism moves in the direction of the higher perceived intensity, successful localization will occur. Whether the rate of success would be greater with dirhinic than with monorhinic sampling is unknown, but seems relevant to whether internasal differences actually operate in the environment.

Mixtures

Naturally occurring olfactory stimuli invariably comprise many constituents. The number of identifiable constituents in essential oils, for instance, usually equals scores, although not all with have odor relevance. The odors of such common products as brewed coffee, fried bacon, perfumes, wine, and cigarettes similarly comprise scores, hundreds, or even thousands of constituents. In a few exceptional instances, a natural product may derive its odor primarily from only one constituent. An example is green bell pepper, the odor of which arises from 3-methoxy-3-isobutyl pyrazine (see Table 8.1). The threshold for this constituent equals approximately one part per trillion, placing it in the class of the most potent odorants. If even a trace of this odorant or another with a similar threshold ever appeared in almost any mixture, it would tend to dominate. As a general matter, it seems worthwhile to note that even an odorant with 99 percent purity is actually a mixture. The 1 percent residual could readily dominate the olfactory effect if it contains potent contaminants.

The complexity of natural stimuli makes the perception of mixtures central to olfactory psychophysics. One simple rule that has emerged so far is that a mixture will smell less intense than the sum of the perceived intensities of its unmixed constituents (Jones & Woskow, 1964; Köster, 1969). In binary (two-component) mixtures, intensity has proven describable by vector addition of psychological quantities:

$$\psi_{ab} = (\psi_a^2 + \psi_b^2 + 2\psi_a\psi_b \cos \alpha)^{1/2},$$

in which ψ_a and ψ_b equal the perceived intensities of the unmixed components, and ψ_{ab} equals the intensity of the mixture (Berglund, Berglund, & Lindvall, 1971). The model implies complete symmetry in the contribution of components to the perceived intensity of the mixture.

The vector addition model has had more practical than theoretical importance. The parameter α has commonly turned out greater than 90°, typically 105 to 130° (Berglund, Berglund, Lindvall, & Svensson, 1973; Cain, 1978b; Laing, Panhuber, Willcox, & Pittman, 1984; Moskowitz & Barbe, 1977). This outcome implies that, for certain proportions of constituents, mixtures will smell weaker than the stronger constituent smelled alone. The physical addition of a second component to an atmosphere containing an existing odor can, therefore, reduce the net perceived magnitude.

The relative invariance of α tends to thwart attempts to understand its origin. At first it seemed likely that α would vary with the similarity of the odors in a binary mixture. If so, then the mixture intensity might have revealed underlying features of receptor functioning. The finding that α varies little, if at all, with similarity dashes that prior hope. It appears reasonably likely that α actually reflects central processing rather than peripheral processing. The value of α remained the same irrespective of whether participants judged presented physical mixtures (components comingled in same air) or dichorhinic mixtures (one component in one nostril and the other component in the other nostril) (Figure 8.18). Any variation in α with

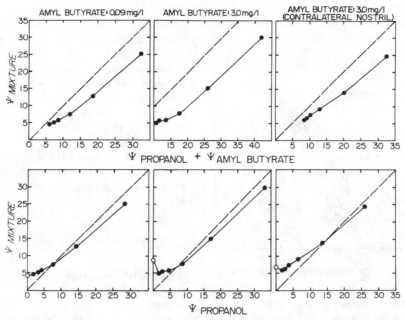

Figure 8.18. Perceived magnitude of mixtures of various concentrations of 1-propanol and 0.09 or 3.0 mg per liter amyl butyrate. Results in the top row show the magnitude of the mixtures versus the magnitude of the unmixed components. Results in the bottom row show the magnitude of the mixtures versus the magnitude of propanol alone. The "mixture" in the right hand column was dichorhinic, that is, amyl butyrate in one nostril and propanol in the other nostril. Note that the mixtures characteristically smelled less intense than the sum of the unmixed components and sometimes smelled less intense than the stronger component smelled alone. From Cain (1975).

perceptual or physical similarity of components will probably show itself only in small variations in α around an average value greater than 90 degrees.

Despite the uniformity of the outcome for binary mixtures, only a few pairs of odorants have received attention and, as in the case of adaptation, generalizations are undoubtedly premature. Attempts to apply the vector addition model or some variant of it to mixtures of more than two components have met with only limited success and variants of the model have been proposed in part to deal with this problem (Laffort & Dravnieks, 1982). Consistent underestimation of predicted perceived intensity for four and five components casts some doubt on the long-term prospects of the vector model (Berglund, 1974). In any case, a quantitative description of the intensity of mixtures with the degree of complexity of most naturally occurring odorous stimuli seems only a distant prospect.

The phenomenon of masking, long recognized as a feature of olfactory functioning, has always provided a clear indication that mixtures display

less than complete additivity. In the extreme case, masking represents obliteration of one odor by the presence of another. Hence, the smell of some malodor will disappear after a spray of a strongly odorous "counteractant" such as evergreen. Masking can occur to various degrees. That is, the addition of some evergreen can cause some attenuation of the malodor and the addition of more evergreen will cause larger attenuation. Laing and Willcox (1983) and Laing et al. (1984) have found that the range of concentrations that define the zone between no masking and complete masking is surprisingly small, less than an order of magnitude. The range seems likely to vary, however, for different pairs of odors. Insofar as masking depends on the relative perceived intensities of the constituents, then the range between no masking and complete masking should relate to the steepness of the psychophysical function.

The psychophysical function for a test odor smelled in the presence of a masking odor of fixed concentration is steeper than normal (Cain & Drexler, 1974). Stimuli weaker in intensity

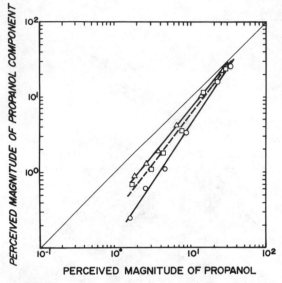

Figure 8.19. Perceived magnitude of the propanol component in the mixtures shown in Figure 8.18. The departures from the diagonal represent masking of propanol by amyl butyrate. The mixtures were: physical mixtures of propanol and 0.09 mg per liter amyl butyrate (squares, dashed line), physical mixtures of propanol and 3.0 mg per liter amyl butyrate (circles), and dichorhinic mixtures of propanol and 3.0 mg per liter amyl butyrate (triangles). From Cain (1975).

than the masker will tend to be depressed more than stimuli stronger than the masker (Cain, 1975). This occurs in both physical and dichorhinic mixtures (Figure 8.19).

Smell-Taste Mixtures

Solutions of tastants and odorants taken in the mouth and judged for overall perceived intensity have shown almost perfect algebraic additivity of sensation. Murphy and Cain (1980) and others have reported a "near miss" to perfect additivity. That is, the mixtures have fallen just short of perfect additivity (Gillan, 1983; Murphy, Cain, & Bartoshuk, 1977). Whether this near miss represents a minor version of the kind of hypoadditivity seen in odor mixtures remains unclear, but at the very least we can state that odors cause no serious inhibition of taste magnitude nor vice versa. That is, there is here nothing akin to the powerful phenomenon of odor masking (Cometto-Muniz, 1981; Garciá-Medina, 1981; Hornung & Enns, 1984). Nevertheless, a certain categorical phenomenon still awaits explanation: Even sophisticated observers

tend to misperceive odors as tastes. Hence, a tasteless odorous solution taken into the mouth will seem to have some odor and some taste. This illusion of taste is compelling even when the observer alternates between nose closed and nose open and therefore has the opportunity to discover the absence of true taste. As Hollingworth and Poffenberger (1917) stated: "Why should it be the rule that, since the taste and smell qualities are to be confused, smell should so commonly sacrifice its claim, so that odors are called tastes rather than vice versa?" (p. 14). The cause of the illusion deserves further attention.

COGNITIVE PROPERTIES

Odor Identification

Although there exists little formal evidence on the matter, olfaction is generally believed to allow very keen quality discrimination. Such keenness reveals itself in the appreciation of nuances in fine fragrances, of the bouquet of wine, and even of subtle off-odors in leftovers. Keen discrimination does not necessarily imply an excellent ability to identify odors. Indeed, the first efforts to determine the *channel capacity* for odor quality implied that lay persons could transmit only about four bits of information; that is, they could identify 16 odors without error (Engen & Pfaffmann, 1960). Although perfumers exhibited better talent for identification, even then there was a striking contrast between measured ability to identify and presumed ability to discriminate (Jones, 1968).

Of course, side-by-side discrimination makes fewer demands on memory than does identification. The latter requires existence of an association between an odor and its label. A disparity between discrimination and identification could arise either because of the absence of a learned association between an odor and its name or because of failure to retrieve the label from memory (Cain, 1979b).

Learning to associate labels with smells does occur slowly (Davis, 1977). The reason may lie in how odors are encoded in memory. Like human faces, they appear to be encoded essentially holistically rather than as sets of features (Cain & Gent, 1986). To the lay person at least, lemon smell, maple smell, rose smell, and so forth,

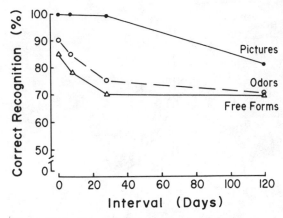

Figure 8.20. Recognition memory for familiar odors (O), pictures from travel magazines (P), and free-form contours (FF) without redundant features. The free forms and odors, which were apparently encoded mainly holistically, displayed a different pattern of forgetting in the two-alternative forced-choice memory task than did the pictures from travel magazines. From Lawless (1978).

appear phenomenologically unanalyzable. In this regard, odors differ greatly from tastes, which are readily perceived in more analytic fashion (e.g., salty-sour, bittersweet). Holistic encoding precludes utilization of redunancy in the stimulus. A scene from a magazine, for instance, will have many independent and redundant features, and one or more of which may possibly serve to aid retrieval of a label taught as a response to the picture. Even recognition memory for such scenes differ from that for odors, presumably because of differences in encoding (Figure 8.20) (Lawless, 1978). Once an odor has achieved long-term storage, it tends to endure remarkably well (Engen & Ross, 1973; Lawless & Cain, 1975; Rabin & Cain, 1984).

Although it may take relatively long to attach a label to a new odor, the labels attached to the ordinary odors of life have become attached over periods of years. Hence, it should pose less difficulty for a person to identify everyday smells with their correct names than to identify uncommon smells with names just supplied by an experimenter. Early experiments on odor identification paid little attention to the important variable of the name used for identification (Cain, 1977d). Recent experiments with up to 80 odors have shown that simple identification of well-known odors (e.g., beer, bubble gum, cigar butts, cinnamon, rubber, wood) equals about 50 percent on the first trial. Substances not identi-

fied exactly, however, are often identified with moderate precision (e.g., wine for beer, candy for bubble gum, cigarette butts for cigar butts). If given feedback with veridical names for all items, participants can eventually (within about five trials) identify the vast majority of 80 odors (Cain, 1979b). In a test with female college students, performance equalled 94 percent by the fifth trial. A separate test indicated 95 percent discrimination among the items. Hence, odor identification does indeed seem limited in the long run mainly by discrimination. Given the time and the interest, a person could therefore add indefinitely to his or her personal repertoire of identifiable odors.

Odor identification has become a useful way to uncover group differences in olfactory information processing. Short-term tests have shown that women outperform men with everyday odors, including those predicted by both men and women to be more identifiable to men (Cain, 1982). (Whether women discriminate better than men remains unknown.) Similarly, younger persons outperform the elderly, even when both young and old have demonstrated at least adequate discrimination (Schemper, Voss, & Cain, 1981; Schiffman, 1977). The large disparity between young and elderly and the smaller disparity between males and females could arise from differences in degree of previous experience or interest in odors, adequacy of verbal encoding of the odors, or facility of retrieval of labels in memory. Encoding and retrieval generally deteriorate with age. Whatever the cause of the deterioration with age, however, it does not begin only in old age, but in middle age (Figure 8.21) (Doty, Shaman, Applebaum, Giberson, Sikorski, & Rosenberg, 1984).

Even though the process of odor identification remains only incompletely understood, the task has proven useful for clinical assessment of olfactory functioning (Cain, Gent, Catalanotto, & Goodspeed, 1983; Doty, Shaman, & Dann, 1984). An essential ingredient in its use is minimization of cognitive demands. Tests that give the patient a list of odor names to draw upon have yielded good agreement with clinical assessments performed by other means, such as thresholds.

ODOR PLEASANTNESS

The pleasantness of an odor commonly seems its

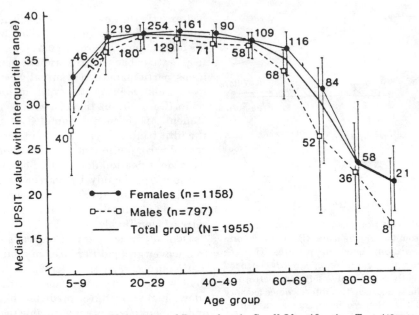

Figure 8.21. Performance on the University of Pennsylvania Smell Identification Test (40 scratch and sniff labels with four verbal choices per label) as a function of age and gender. Numbers next to the data points indicate number of participants. From Doty, Shaman, Applebaum, Giberson, Sikorski, and Rosenberg (1984).

most salient immediate characteristic (Engen & McBurney, 1964). Of course, pleasantness does not exist separately from quality. Certain qualities (putrid, skunky, fecal) seem quite unpleasant whereas others seem neutral or pleasant. Nevertheless, persons will remark on pleasantness even when at a complete loss to describe quality or identify the source of odor. One question often posed by the layman concerns whether odor pleasantness somehow represents an innate characteristic or is an acquired one (Laing & Clark, 1983). There are many ways to refine this question (e.g., Is the reaction to unpleasant odors fixed at birth and that to neutral and pleasant odors acquired afterwards?), but we will ignore such refinements here.

The temptation to consider hedonic reactions as "hard wired" probably stems in part from knowledge that olfaction plays a vital role in various regulatory functions (feeding, drinking, sex) in various species and, more specifically, from the appealing simplicity of the pheromone concept. As Engen (1982) remarked, "The provocative thought is that such chemical messengers may exist in humans; it has probably been the single most important factor in renewing interest in the sense of smell, illustrated by emphasis on sexually arousing perfumes" (p. 125).

Although the forceful nature of biological semiochemicals (signaling chemicals) on conspecifics had long been known to animal breeders, only in the 1950s did the techniques of analytical chemistry permit precise identification of specific odor-active ingredients in such natural secretions. Early experiments dealt with secretions of Bombyx moths (Shorey, 1976). A substance termed Bombykol was isolated from female secretions. When synthesized and presented to males, it elicited sensory responses and sexual behavior normally elicited by the actual female secretions. The Bombyx story has been repeated again and again in other insects, though inevitably with variations. For instance, the active fraction in the natural secretion may be a mixture rather than just a single ingredient; the presence of the active fraction may depend on the diet of the donor (Shorey, 1976). It has become increasingly clear that even in insects pheromone-induced activity occurs within a biological and behavioral context. The male winter moth responds to sex attractant only at temperatures between six and 16 degrees C, when mating can occur (Roelofs, Hill, Linn, Meinwald, Jain, Herbert, & Smith, 1982).

The coining of the term pheromone and the increasing availability of techniques to analyze chemical secretions rapidly led to the investigation of putative pheromones in many species, including rodents and primates. (Although the generalization of the pheromone concept to higher orders has particular interest within the present context, we should note that all animal orders including bacteria (e.g., Suzuki, Mori, Sakagami, Isogai, Fujino, Kitada, Craig, & Clewell, 1984) utilize pheromones.) The terms trail pheromone, alarm pheromone, maternal pheromone, primer pheromone, releaser pheromone all joined sex pheromone in the vocabulary of biobehavioral scientists. Unless viewed critically, it could appear that the olfactory-guided behavior, and certain features of reproductive physiology, generally came about from playing a preprogrammed chemical code. This uncritical view led some investigators to question the application of the term pheromone to any instance where the organism might have simply learned to associate a certain smell with a rewarding event, such as the willingness of a female to copulate (Beauchamp, Doty, Moulton, & Mugford, 1976). Other investigators continued to use the term pheromone to signify any olfactory-mediated response to a conspecific (e.g., Goodwin, Gooding, & Regnier, 1979). Within this context, there arose the issue of whether human beings may employ pheromones, perhaps unconsciously and as vestigial remnants. Such speculation has a distinctly nativist ring.

Only one line of evidence implies that pleasantness reactions in human beings may exist at birth. Photographs of the facial expressions of neonates during olfactory stimulation led Steiner (1974) to conclude that odors considered unpleasant by adults generally give rise to facial expressions interpretable as aversive and odors considered pleasant by adults give rise to facial expressions interpretable as contented. Engen's (1982) observation on the expressions of neonates led to a different conclusion: "All the facial and bodily responses to the odors, whether pleasant or unpleasant to adults, looked like mild startle and escape reactions" (p. 131).

An experiment in older children revealed that the range of odor pleasantness increases with age (Engen, 1974b). When asked to decide which of a pair of odors they "liked best" or "liked least," children at four years showed little pattern, whereas older children did. The data agreed with the interpretation made in observational work that young children feel relatively indifferent about the pleasantness or unpleasantness of odors (e.g., feces and vomitus). The indifference shown by one to two year olds in an investigation in which the children sat on their mothers' laps even alarmed some mothers, who questioned whether their children could smell at all (Engen, 1982). Only when children reach about ten years of age does their range of preference apparently approximate that of adults. Engen noted that a progressive broadening of the hedonic range could indicate progressive learning about pleasantness/unpleasantness or progressive biological (neural) maturation (Engen, 1974a).

Despite the results on hedonic range, it hardly seems likely that the young human being develops no strong preferences. Within two weeks, nursing infants will turn selectively toward pads worn next to the breasts of their mothers (Russell & Mendelson, cited in Engen, 1982). Presumably such a feeding cue will be preferred over what would otherwise comprise an uninteresting array of odors. The ability to learn about "good" and "bad" odors occurs remarkably early in rodents, and perhaps in humans, also. Two day old rats, for instance, will learn to avoid odors associated with illness (Rudy & Cheatle, 1977). A neonatal rat exposed to an experimental odor in utero will selectively suckle only from nipples with that odor (Pedersen & Blass, 1982). There is, of course, no incompatability between a general indifference to odors of no particular biological or behavioral significance and specific preferences or aversions for significant odors.

If innate, pleasantness reactions would presumably prove difficult to modify. Conditioned aversions to particular food odors in persons (or animals) who became ill after ingesting that food provide one instance of the modifiability of odor preference (e.g., Bernstein & Webster, 1980). Nausea following overindulgence with beer, for example, causes many cases of conditioned aversion to alcoholic beverages and disgust with the mere odor of such beverages. There now exists a large literature on conditioned food aversions and on the relative roles of taste and odor in the conditioning of the aversions. Such research not only demonstrates the possibilities for altering the hedonic tone of chemosensory stimuli, but can provide a way to study quality discrimination in animals (Nowlis, Frank, & Pfaffmann, 1980).

Could odor pleasantness be innately determined in spite of the modifiability shown in conditioned aversion studies? Such aversions, because of their potential biological usefulness to prevent poisoning, might override the innate reaction. Far less drastic means, however, may also alter pleasantness. Mere exposure to an odorant suffices (Cain & Johnson, 1978). Repeated exposure to an unpleasant odor causes its unpleasantness to wane and repeated exposure to a pleasant odor causes its pleasantness to wane. Habituation to unpleasant odors occurs commonly in everyday experience, particularly in occupational settings where the rankest smells (tannery odors, rendering odors, feedlot odors) cease to bother employees rather rapidly (Cain, 1979a).

Another observation relevant to the modification of odor pleasantness arises from the well known context dependence of pleasantness. A cheesy smell may evoke pleasure in one context and disgust in another. The personal products and soap/detergent industries have long recognized the potent influence of odors in context to signal the beneficial attributes of their products (gentleness, cleaning power, ability to disinfect, etc.). A pleasant, but inappropriate, fragrance may send an otherwise perfectly acceptable product to oblivion.

The context-dependence of odor acceptability can limit the usefulness of pleasantness judgments obtained in the sterile surroundings of the psychophysical laboratory. Nevertheless, data obtained in that way can address some gross questions, such as whether odors change drastically in pleasantness with concentration. Surprisingly, they do not. An unpleasant odor will get more unpleasant at increasing concentrations, neutral ordors will stay neutral and then gravitate toward unpleasantness, and pleasant odors may increase in pleasantness or level off before gravitating toward unpleasantness (Moskowitz, 1977). The concentration dependence of these changes is, however, surprisingly weak. In this respect, odor contrasts with taste which exhibits strong concentration dependence. Conceivably, this difference between modalities lies in how perceived intensity changes with concentration (Lawless, 1977). Psychophysical functions for taste usually have much greater steepness than those for smell.

Cabanac's (1971) notion of alliesthesia offers another instance of the modifiability of odor pleasantness. (Alliesthesia refers to how a given sensory stimulus can induce a pleasant or unpleasant sensation depending on the organism's internal state.) Indeed, Aristotle remarked how the pleasantness of food odors depended on whether a person was hungry or sated (Cain, 1978a). Modern evidence supports that conclusion, although it must come to grips with some idiosyncratic behavior (Mowrer, Mair, & Engen, 1977). Pager's (1977a, 1977b) findings of differential activity in mitral cells in hungry and satiated rats seems to offer the beginning of a neural basis for odor alliesthesia (see also Chaput & Holley, 1976).

ODOR QUALITY

The search to understand odor quality led historically to the erection of classification schemes (Cain, 1978a). The hope was that some natural order would drop out of a scheme. It never did. Such schemes can, however, serve a strictly practical purpose. For example, botanists need a reasonably precise but exhaustive classification scheme for descriptions of plant odors. On a more limited level, brewers, distillers, and other manufacturers can derive benefits from a classification of the odor characteristics of their products.

The most recent general classification scheme, that of John Amoore (1962a, b), was intended more as the basis for a theory than as a classification scheme *per se*. In an effort to elucidate the chemical basis for odor quality, Amoore searched the existing literature on the qualities of more than six hundred odoriferous materials and found that 14 descriptors occurred with the highest frequency. He decided that the seven most frequent names probably represented "primary" odors and that the less frequently used names represented "complex" odors. He recognized the primaries ethereal, fruity, floral, camphoraceous, minty, putrid, and pungent. He offered no subcategories nor any geometric representation, for this scheme had less pretention as an exhaustive categorization of experience than did previous schemes of Zwaardemaker (1895, 1925) and Henning (1916). It did, however, offer an important suggestion regarding a molecular correlate of odor quality, specifically that the size and shape of the molecule determined quality in five of the seven classes. The notion

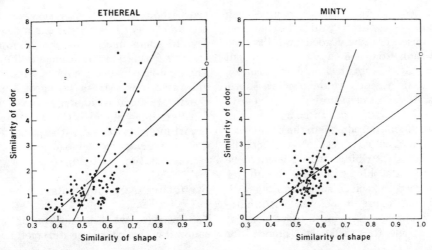

Figure 8.22. Perceived odor similarity of 106 test odors to an ethereal prototype, 1,2-dichloroethane, and a camphoraceous prototype, 1,8-cineole, versus similarity of molecular shape to the prototypes. From Amoore and Venstrom (1967).

that stereochemistry governed quality was not exactly new (Moncrieff, 1967). Nevertheless, Amoore took the bold step of proposing receptor types of specific dimensions for five odor categories. These types comprised geometric complementaries of a stereochemical least-common-denominator of molecules in a class. Like Henning's (1916) odor prism before it, Amoore's geometric theory aroused considerable interest at first (see Cain, 1978a). It stimulated some experiments on mixtures and on cross-adaptation, but general lack of success dampened enthusiasm.

Amoore chose to test the relation between quality and stereochemistry via psychophysical estimates of odor similarity and comparison of such estimates with a derived index of shape and size (Figure 8.22). The outcome of these experiments caused him to abandon the theory as stated. ("The site-fitting model for olfaction is evidently of rather limited value" (Amoore, 1970, p. 138).) He nevertheless retained the position that stereochemical properties played a role in odor quality. Regarding this, there is now little dispute.

In recent times, the exercise of creating classification schemes has been replaced by the derivation of multiple factors (via factor analysis) or dimensions (via multidimensional scaling) that will presumably account for odor quality as assessed by human subjects (e.g., Berglund, Berglund, Engen, & Ekman, 1973; Schiffman,

1974; Schiffman & Leffingwell, 1981; Yoshida, 1975). Typically, direct estimates of similarity serve as the input for multidimensional solutions (Schiffman, Reynolds, & Young, 1981).

Aside from direct estimates of similarity of odor pairs, a profile of odor quality is obtainable from judging the similarity of a test odor to certain fixed attributes. Crocker and Henderson (Boring, 1928) used a set of four attributes (fragrant, acid, burnt, caprylic). An odor was judged for its applicability to each on a zero to nine category scale. Four numbers therefore "described" any test odor. Recognizing the need for finer resolution among profiles, Harper, Bate-Smith, Land, and Griffiths (1968) proposed attribute rating using 44 attributes. These included only names any layman should feel comfortable with. In an even more ambitious effort to obtain resolution, the Committee on Sensory Evaluation of the American Society for Testing and Materials (ASTM) expanded and modified Harper's list to include 146 descriptors (Dravnieks, 1982, 1983; Dravnieks, Masurat, & Lamm, 1984). The descriptors almost invariably refer to odoriferous *objects*, for example, lavender, dill, crushed grass, beer, fresh tobacco smoke, new rubber, sauerkraut. When a person uses the list to describe any given odor, he or she will employ only a small fraction of the 146. That is, the person will find all but certain key descriptors inapplicable in any given case.

Are 146 descriptors adequate to give each odor a unique signature? Profiles derived over groups of observers show good stability and good resolution from one odor to another, but there seems little doubt that random variation in the attribute ratings would obscure subtle differences. And, yes, there probably is a need to expand the number of terms in comparisons of qualitatively similar products. In the evaluation of floral fragrances for soaps, for instance, the number of floral attributes would need to be expanded considerably, although the judges would also need to receive some training with respect to the odors associated with more obscure attributes (e.g., jonquil, tuberose). For such applications, the ASTM list, intended for use without training, may serve as a starting point and may be edited and expanded as necessary. In some industries, the terminology for sensory evaluation has become well established. The Scotch whiskey wheel in Figure 8.23 provides an example (Hose & Piggott, 1980; Swan & Burtles, 1980). Most likely, however, individual distillers have modified the wheel (e.g., added terms) in order to deal with special features of their product or to increase sensitivity to very minor variations in the product.

Structure-Activity Relations

The issue of what properties of a molecule endow it with a characteristic smell has spawned

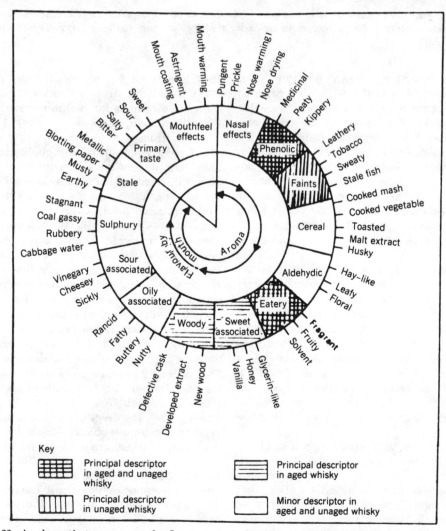

Figure 8.23. A schematic to represent the flavor notes in Scotch whisky. From Swan and Burtles (1980).

Table 8.2. Proposals regarding the molecular basis for olfaction

Author	Date	General class	Salient features
Ogle	1870	Vibrational	Vibrations affected nasal pigment, which gave out heat which excited the olfactory cells
Woker	1906	Chemical	Unsaturation main cause of odor, but not essential if substance very volatile
Fabre	1911	Vibrational	Limited to insects. Not known by man. Human olfaction due to material particles
Marchand	1915	Chemical	Unsaturation (including $>C=O$). Two points of unsaturation reduces odor
Henning	1916	Chemical	Osmosphore groups are important, but their relative position determines the type of odor
Heyninx	1917	Vibrational	Vibrations causing absorption in the ultra-violet band also caused odor
Backman	1917	Chemical	Water solubility and lipoid solubility essential
Teudt	1919	Vibrational	Electronic vibrations of sensory nerves increased by resonance with similar vibrations of odorants
Durrans	1920	Chemical	Residual affinity. Addition reaction on the olfactory epithelium
Heller	1920	Chemical	Direct chemical action on nerve-ending
Ruzicka	1920	Chemical	Osmophore and osmoceptor
Tschirch	1921	Chemical	Substance must be soluble in air. Loose compound formed with plasma of the olfactory cell
Zwaardemaker	1922	Chemical-vibrational	Possess odoriphore, be volatile, lower surface tension, lipid soluble. Odoriphore depends on variations in molecule
Ungerer and Stoddard	1922	Vibrational	Intramolecular vibrations within definite frequency range. Unsaturation helpful. Interference and resonance effects
Delange	1922	Chemical	Unsaturation
Missenden	1926	Chemical	Intensity depends on number of molecules making contact with nose. Quality depends on nature of reaction between odorous molecules and lipoid tissues
Nicol	1926		Function of sinuses
Pirrone	1929	Chemical	Two osmophore groups, one determines type of odor, the other the variety
Niccolini	1933	Chemical	Volatility. Solubility in nasal mucosa. Oxidizability
Krisch	1934	Vibrational	Insects
Müller	1936	Physical	Odorous substances are dipolar. Irritate the molecular fields of the osmoceptor in nose
Dyson	1937	Vibrational	Volatility. Lipoid solubility. Raman shift between 1,400 and $3,500 \, \mathrm{cm}^{-1}$
Beck and Miles	1947	Vibrational	Infra-red radiation from receptors absorbed by odorants
McCord and Witheridge	1939	Electro-chemical	Change in bonding angle of odorant molecules on solution in mucosa
Baradi and Bourne	1951	Enzyme	Inhibition of enzyme action by odorants
Hainer	1953	Information	Thirty levels of intensity; 24 kinds of primary odor
Wright	1954	Vibrational	Raman shift of frequency lower than $800–1000 \, \mathrm{cm}^{-1}$.
Davies	1954	Physico-chemical	Puncturing of olfactory cell membrane and exchange of Na^+ and K^+
Moncrieff	1961	Physical	Volatility, adsorbability and customary absence from olfactory region

From Moncrieff (1967).

many so-called theories of olfaction. These have included chemical theories, vibrational theories, enzyme theories, stereochemical theories, and so forth (see Table 8.2).

For instance, Wright (1954, 1964) proposed that odor quality derives from low-frequency intramolecular oscillations measurable via infra-red spectroscopy. Molecules with overlapping frequencies have indeed often proven categorically similar in assays performed either with expert human panelists or, interestingly, with insects (Wright, 1981). Wright (1976) saw the infrared signature not only as a correlate of quality, but as indicative of the olfactory mechanism, that is to say, the transfer of quanta of vibrational energy from an excited receptor to an unexcited stimulus. As with most olfactory theories, the infrared theory derives virtually all its support from correlations between the quality and the molecular property of interest (here the IR spectrum), rather than from functional properties of olfaction. Two apparent exceptions to the theory are: (1) the ability of observers to resolve enantiomers or optical isomeric pairs qualitatively (e.g., d-carvone smells of caraway and l-carvone of spearmint), and (2) the presence of odor in hydrogen sulfide (it lacks vibration in the "correct" region). Regarding the former, Wright (1982) proposed that the identical frequency-pattern of two enantiomers might become nonidentical at the moment of interaction with an acceptor side. Regarding the latter, he proposed that hydrogen sulfide either contains higher homologues (e.g., H_2S_2, H_2S_3 which have vibrational frequencies in the correct range) as trace contaminants or that such contaminants are created en route to the receptors. Hence, tension between fact and theory led to no alteration in the theory.

As noted above, Amoore's stereochemical theory postulated seven categories of "primary" odors. Five of the seven had hypothetical receptor sites of fixed dimensions into which the proper stimuli would presumably fit, although loosely. The process of appropriately occupying a site would presumably trigger transduction. Amoore's stereochemical theorizing, sans receptor types, is generally accepted as compatible with the known facts, particularly for molecules above about 100 daltons. For such molecules, shape and size measured with the molecule oriented with respect to its primary functional group offer some predictive power, but not enough to justify much theorizing, such as erection of categorical boundaries between odors or of hypothetical receptor types.

For molecules below about 100 daltons, the identity of the functional group has an importance that it lacks in larger molecules. Molecules with hydroxyl groups smell like alcohol, those with amino groups like fish or urine, those with

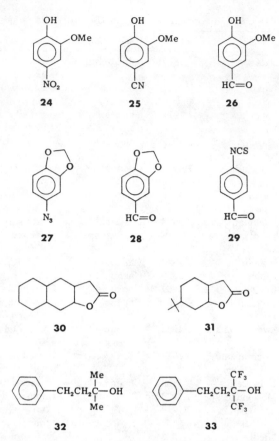

Figure 8.24. Examples of molecules with different functional groups but similar odors. 4-Nitroguaiacol (24) and 4-cyanoguaiacol (25) have weak odors similar to vanillin (26). 1-Azido-3,1-methylenedioxybenzene (27) and the isothiocyanate (29) have similar odors to heliotropin (28). Compounds (30) and (31) have sandalwood odors and dimethylphenylethylcarbinol (32) and its hexafluoro derivate (33) have similar floral odors. From Beets (1982).

thiol groups like skunk, those with acetate groups like fruit, and so forth (Polak, 1973; Schafer & Brower, 1975). In larger molecules, one group may prove interchangeable with another and a substitution may therefore induce little or no detectable change in quality, depending on such matters as the polarity induced by such substitutions (Figure 8.24). Beets (1978) articulated stereochemical determinants of stimulation as follows:

> This efficiency [of stimulation] may be assumed to depend primarily on two factors, the mutual steric complementarity of the two patterns and the mutual compatibility of their polar features.

Nothing will happen when steric barriers prevent the interaction between the relevant structural details of molecule and host site. If an interaction is permitted more or less readily for steric reasons, it will be most effective when two mutually compatible polar groups or combinations of such groups are available in favorable configurations and least effective when one of the patterns has no polar feature to be accommodated by the host site and when any interaction depends entirely upon weak dispersion forces. . . .For flexible molecules, an extra degree of freedom contributes the steric complementarity between molecule and site. During the alignment of such a molecule at a host site, its conformation may change in order to maximize its adaptation to the steric requirements of the membrane feature. [pp. 85–86]

The idea that conformational changes may play a role in the accommodation of stimulus and receptor adds considerable complexity to the stereochemical argument. It implies that molecules may not stimulate in their lowest energy state or statistically most common conformation. It also leaves considerable room for one odorant to mimic another through a conformational change.

After abandoning his site-fitting scheme, Amoore (1970) began a new theoretical tack based on observations of what is called specific anosmia. This term actually refers to a *relative*, rather than *absolute*, insensitivity to an odorant and its structural relatives. In various cases, the distribution of sensitivity is bimodal. The number of reputed specific anosmias equals about 70 but may prove greatly reducible upon testing. Amoore (1982) argued that each true specific anosmia represents the loss of a receptor type for a "primary odor." He and his colleagues have cataloged various "primaries" by extensive threshold testing. There is virtually no converging evidence at present to support either the notion of primaries or the relation of any such entities to actual receptors. However, there exists evidence that specific anosmia to at least one odorant, 5α-androst-16-en-3-one is genetically determined (Wysocki & Beauchamp, 1984). This may offer the opening wedge for thorough understanding of the biological basis of an important olfactory phenomenon.

In general, theorizing about odor quality goes on now at a more refined level than in the past. Specific groups of compounds rather than the whole spectrum of odorants have become the focus. This arises from the commercial origins of the work. The search for more stable, less expensive, or more interesting fragrance materials has led to extensive explorations of structure versus activity in musks (more than half a dozen structurally different families are called musks, mainly because of their smell), ambergris, and certain flowers (jasmine, violet) and other botanicals (vetiver grass, sandalwood). The question is asked: Is there a common molecular feature in all musky smelling compounds, all amber smelling compounds, and so forth? In the case of musks, Jurs, Ham, and Brügger (1981) found a common substructural unit in steroid and polynitroaromatic musks (Figure 8.25). Computer-assisted pattern recognition and feature detection performed on the structures of the molecules led to this extraction of commonality. The techniques also helped to specify a set of 13 molecular structural descriptors that could discriminate substances with musk odors from those without. The kind of descriptors used in such an effort included fragment descriptors (e.g., number of bonds of a given type), substructure descriptors such as shown in Figure 8.25, environment descriptors to reflect connections of subunits with other parts of the molecule, molecular connectivity descriptors to reflect branching, and more. Despite the advantage

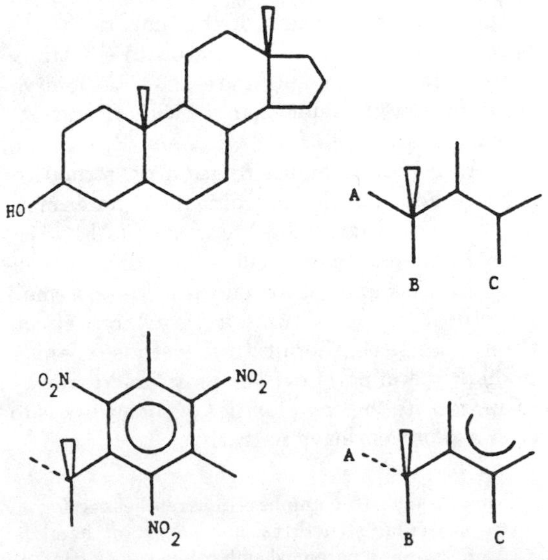

Figure 8.25. Right side shows a computer-derived common substructural unit for steroid musk (upper example) and polynitroaromatic musk (lower example). From Jurs, Ham, and Brügger (1981).

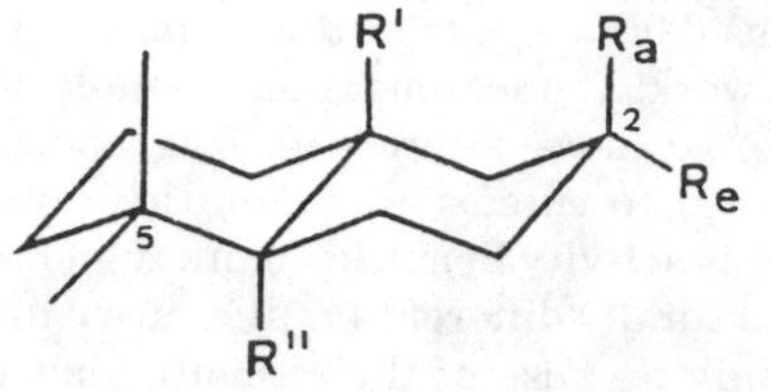

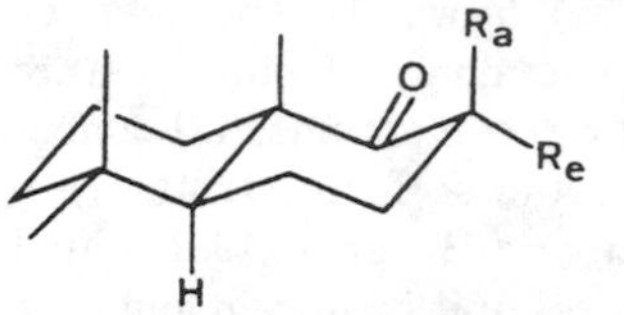

Figure 8.26. Upper part shows the transfused decalin skeleton proposed as essential for ambergris odorants by Ohloff. Lower part shows how small structural changes can have a large olfactory effect. Compounds 134, 136, and 139 have an amber odor while their diastereoisomers have no odor. From Ohloff (1982).

derived from the computer techniques, the statistical separation of substances into musky smelling versus nonmusky smelling by a set of descriptors still yields only rather crude information.

Ohloff's (1982) triaxial rule of odor sensation provides another example of what we might call the commonality approach to structure-activity. Through observations on almost two hundred variations of amber smelling compounds, he proposed that odorants of the ambergris type bore a strong structural relation to the trans-fused decalin skeleton (Figure 8.26). His observations on how the odor changes with alterations in the substituents R', R", R_a, and R_e form an elaborate corpus of information on structure-activity. For example, regarding the 11-nordriman-9-one series (Figure 8.26), compounds 134, 136, and 139 have an amber odor, their diasteresisomers 135, 137, and 138 are odorless. Here, a small structural change causes a very large effect. Often, changes in the substituents cause changes in quality and potency. The most practical way to appreciate the complexities of such work is to read a representative narrative:

Lactone (162) [the numbers in parentheses refer to particular structures, not important here] . . . possesses a balanced amber-like woody odor with a weak fecal note vaguely recalling civet. Lactone (163) has a sandalwood-like fecal odor with moldy undertones. Its oxa analog in the trans series (176) possesses an amber fragrance

that is close to that of (14). . . . The two acetals (177) and (178) lack all the amber characters that are so convincingly expressed in compound (176). The basic odor of the pair of acetals (177)/(178) can be described as flowery-woody. Thus (177) has a fresh camphoraceous tonality, while compound (178) is dominated by a phenolic leathery note with a strong smell of horse stables. [Ohloff, 1982, pp. 557–559.]

Such descriptions resist scientific analysis and hence remain isolated from other olfactory data. Nevertheless, such narratives also highlight qualitative complexities given no attention in global olfactory theorizing. How far these seem from a scheme comprising just ethereal, fruity, floral, and so forth.

Will the search for structural commonality in various similar smelling compounds ever help to understand olfaction? Perhaps yes and perhaps no. The search arises from certain aspects of categorical perception that may actually mislead. In the case of a family of chemicals with similar smells, structure-activity researchers commonly tend to view each material as comprising a fundamental odor quality with accompanying overtones. Such descriptions foster the illusion of, for example, an amber-smelling core to a molecule and certain accompanying non-amber molecular features. Any anticipated isomorphism between phenomenological properties and molecular properties is gratuitous. There is, in addition, the practical matter that no two experts will describe an unfamiliar odor in the same way. One expert may perceive one fundamental and the other may find another. This then raises the question of what exactly is to be explained. The two experts could probably agree on a description if given the chance to collaborate, but will rarely agree when working independently. It is not a matter of who is correct, but of point of view. Instead of asking what molecular properties will make a substance smell lemony, almondy, or floral, we should probably ask which molecular properties enable discrimination of one substance from another. A scale of discriminability would provide the way to quantify the importance of any given change.

Even in those extremely rare instances in which one odor proves qualitatively indistinguishable from another, it is not clear whether the equivalence can arise only via identical peripheral messages or whether it can arise centrally. If peripherally distinguishable messages do sometimes lead to perceptual equivalence, then it would seem advisable to add functional tests (e.g., cross-adaptation) to psychophysical investigations of structure versus activity. Difficult-to-distinguish substances with similar peripheral messages may show more cross-adaptation than substances with only similar central activity. Another possibility would be to use a neurophysiological assay, principally recordings from single olfactory receptors.

Beginning in the early 1960s, it became feasible to record from single units in the olfactory mucosa (Gesteland, Lettvin, Pitts, & Rojas, 1963). A stimulus battery commonly contained ten to twenty odorants of rather diverse properties. That is, the investigators did not explore the kind of subtle structural changes explored psychophysically by Ohloff, for instance. Nevertheless, the primary question invariably concerned the relation between molecular structure and the single-unit response, irrespective of the odorants explored.

The largest data set on single units was collected on the frog by a team of French investigators, for example, Duchamp, Revial, Holley, and MacLeod (1974); and Revial, Duchamp, and Holley (1978). The experiments entailed monitoring both the EOG and single units. The amplitude of the EOG was used to choose concentrations of stimuli more or less matched in physiological effectiveness. Without some such procedure, a difference in firing rate could simply reflect gross differences in intensity. Unfortunately, in the single-unit experiment with many odorants it is not even remotely possible to obtain a concentration-response function for every odorant from every unit. If this were possible, it would reveal whether a unit that responded to odorant A, but not to odorant B, at a given test concentration might respond to B at a somewhat higher concentration. Before we inspect the outcome of the work, we should also note that it was not guided by any theory nor was it intended to test any hypothesis. Such features would probably have yielded a somewhat more satisfying outcome.

Figure 8.27 presents an odorant-by-unit array for 65 units (Revial, Sicard, Duchamp, & Holley, 1982). Odorants in this battery included the enantiomers d-carvone (DCA) and l-carvone (LCA) which smell to humans like caraway and spearmint, respectively, and d-citronellol (DCI) and l-citronellol (LCI) which smell like citronella

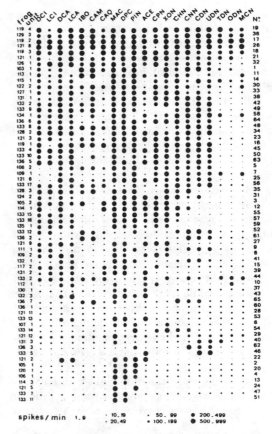

Figure 8.27. Odorant by receptor unit array of 20 odorants and 65 units. The size of a dot represents the activity evoked by odor stimulation. The odorants were: (1) DCI, d-citronellol; (2) LCI, l-citronellol; (3) DCA, d-carvone; (4) LCA, l-carvone; (5) IBO, isoborneol; (6) CAM, dl-camphor; (7) CAQ, camphorquinone; (8) MAC, methylamylketone; (9) DPC, dipropylketone; (10) PIN, pinacolone; (11) ACE, acetophenone; (12) CPN, cyclopentanone; (13) XON, cyclohexanone; (14) CHN, cycloheptanone; (15) CNN, cyclononanone; (16) CDN, cyclodecanone; (17) UDN, cycloundecanone; (18) TDN, cyclotetradecanone; (19) ODN, cyclooctadecanone; and (20) MCN, musk ketone. From Revial, Sicard, Duchamp, and Holley (1982).

and Bulgarian rose, respectively. The overall picture presented by the array is of relative nonspecificity. The majority of odorants stimulated more than half the receptors and some odorants stimulated almost all. Those few units that seemed to exhibit reasonable specificity actually responded to those nearly universal stimuli. This array would give little encouragement to any suggestion that vertebrates, like some invertebrates, may have two classes of cells, generalists and specialists (see Boeckh, 1980). Although the number of units and the number of odorants in the present study is well above average, the outcome represents a tiny sample of the behavior of the mucosa. We must bear this in mind in any attempt to generalize the results.

Discrimination between enantiomers proved surprisingly poor. Of 45 units responsive to carvone, only two resolved the d-forms and the l-forms clearly and of the 38 responsive to citronellol only three resolved its d-forms and l-forms clearly.

The pattern shown here is similar to that shown in many other single unit studies. A prime difference was that the level of stimulation was high, up to about one-half saturated vapor, which probably decreased selectivity. Within the context of this investigation, Revial et al. (1982) showed that relatively minor reductions in concentration could increase selectivity. This means that concentration matching can become crucial: "It is evident that our findings do not allow us to state that our findings are completely independent of odorant concentration" (Revial et al., 1983, p. 194).

Accepting the data of Revial et al. (1982) at face value, we can ask whether there is order in the array. Pairwise correlation of the activity of

odorants across units revealed considerable order, some of it intuitively reasonable (e.g., high correlations among the smaller cycloketones and between enantiomers) and some of it not (e.g., moderate correlation between d-citronellol and d-carvone) (Figure 8.28). A joint analysis of both receptor-relatedness and odorant-relatedness revealed no classes of either, although the idea of receptor classes was not rejected entirely.

The apparent absence of types, it should be noted, can be interpreted in various ways: (1) individual cells could have vastly different absolute sensitivities, such that a given odorant could fall subthreshold for one unit and suprathreshold for another; (2) conditions of recording could damage or otherwise alter the specificity of cells; (3) cells could be relatively specific at just barely suprathreshold levels and nonspecific well above threshold levels; (4) the more narrowly tuned cells may not spontaneously discharge and therefore may be bypassed when the microelectrode is driven through the mucosa; (5) the number of types could be too large (e.g., 40) to be uncovered with only 10 to 20 arbitrarily chosen stimuli; (6) the number of types could be relatively small, but the picture could be complicated by the existence of a population of generalist cells that respond to virtually everything; (7) the

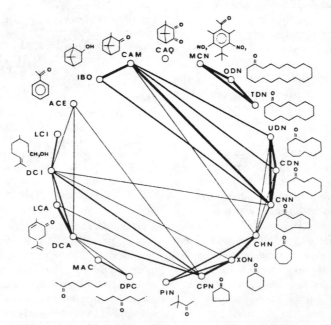

Figure 8.28. Intercorrelations among odorants based on their stimulating effects on receptor units (Figure 8.27). Three classes of significant correlations are represented: $0.55 < r \leq 0.60$, thin lines; $0.61 < r \leq 0.70$, medium lines; and $r > 0.70$, thick lines. From Revial, Sicard, Duchamp, and Holley (1983).

receptors could be sensitive to molecular features not readily apparent when the unit of analysis is the *odorant*; and (8) the mucosa could be devoid of types. This list is not exhaustive. The absence of apparent cell types could also derive from the existence of more than one type of receptor site or, more appropriately, acceptor site on the cell membrane. Acceptor types have typically been thought to be protein molecules in the cell membrane. Although it might seem unlikely that a given cell would give rise to more than one kind of acceptor site, this is a possibility. Moreover, it is possible that not all acceptor sites are proteins and hence lack some of the specificity expected of proteins (Price, 1984). Finally, it must be recalled that the various cells are in various stages of development.

All in all, it is not clear whether neural data enjoy a categorical advantage over carefully obtained psychophysical data in the exploration of structure-activity relations. Presumably, advances in techniques of neurophysical recording will eliminate some of the sources of random or systematic noise that now exist. Whether advances in psychophysical data collection will also occur seems less certain. A combined neurophysiological-psychophysical approach would seem ideal if species differences would not preclude such an effort. On more than one occasion, a correspondence between human perceptual similarity and similarity of frog neural responses has been found (Døving & Lange, 1967). After making some of their own perceptual observations, Revial, Sicard, Duchamp, and Holley (1983) commented, "A remarkable parallelism can therefore be established between the data provided by frog receptor cells and those pertaining to the human experience of odor qualities" (p. 193).

SENSORY CODING

Two decades prior to any single unit recording from the olfactory mucosa, Adrian (1942) had commented:

> For a smell to produce a specific pattern of excitation in the olfactory epithelium we need only suppose that the different receptors are not all equally sensitive to different chemical stimuli. Such a differential sensitivity might depend on the intrinsic properties of the recep-

tors, and it might also be due to extrinsic factors such as the amount of mucus in different regions, the rate of diffusion of the active molecules, etc. In this way an endless variety of smells might be distinguished because the process would be comparable not to the discrimination of colours but to that of visual patterns. It is to be hoped that further experiments will show whether this view can be confirmed. (p. 472.)

This comment came after Adrian had recorded from the olfactory bulb at which he uncovered no evidence of types. He had noted, however, that some odorants (water soluble) tended to stimulate the anterior part of the bulb whereas others (lipid soluble) tended to stimulate the posterior. He clearly recognized that such an outcome could have arisen from "intrinsic properties of receptors" mapped onto the bulb, or from "extrinsic factors."

The notion that extrinsic factors may create a pattern on the olfactory mucosa received definitive support in a series of studies by Mozell and colleagues. Mozell's (1964) recordings from spatially separated nerve branches first established a spatial and temporal discharge pattern across the mucosa. The nerve branch innervating the anterior mucosa always discharged before the branch innervating the posterior mucosa, but the difference in latency and the ratio of response between branches varied with the stimulus. This effect proved generally independent of concentration and reversed itself when the flow of stimulating air was reversed. Hence, the pattern appeared to depend on extrinsic factors, such as the affinity of airborne odorant for the mucus-covered receptor sheet.

The idea that the sorptive properties of the mucosa governed the pattern of molecular deposition led Mozell to view the mucosa as essentially the liquid phase of a gas-liquid chromatograph, a matter he demonstrated in direct comparisons of the frog olfactory sac with a polar stationary phase (Mozell & Jagodowicz, 1974). (The primary variable of interest in gas chromatography is the retention time of materials injected into a column packed or lined with an adsorbent material known generically as the stationary phase. The physicochemical properties of the adsorbent material *vis à vis* those of the injected sample will determine how long a given constituent will take to reach the end of the column when propelled by an inert gas.) The range of

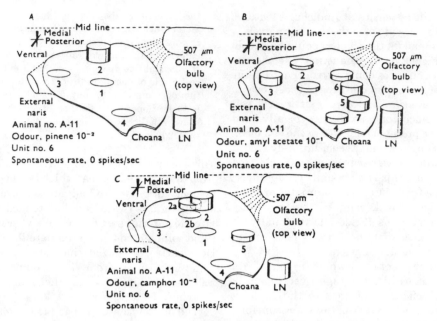

Figure 8.29. Responses of a single olfactory bulb unit (507 μm deep) to punctate stimulation at various positions on the salamander olfactory mucosa. Upper left shows that a medial position was most effective (cylinder 2 is highest) for stimulation with pinene. Upper right shows that both ventral and posterior positions were somewhat effective for stimulation with amyl acetate. Lower portion shows that the medial position was most effective for stimulation with camphor. Responses to overall stimulation are shown by the heights of the cylinders depicted to the right of each schematic mucosa. From Kauer and Moulton (1974).

variation in retention time in either the polar column or the frog sac left little doubt that many resolvable temporal patterns could occur. Supplementary to this, Hornung and Mozell (1977) demonstrated via the autoradiographic patterns set up with tritiated odorants that many spatial patterns could undoubtedly occur.

Although extrinsic factors do indeed set up *imposed patterns* on the mucosa, intrinsic factors may set up *inherent patterns*. Kauer and Moulton (1974) addressed the issue by recording from olfactory bulb units in the tiger salamander upon stimulation with a punctate delivery system that stimulated only about 50,000 receptors. They found that a given unit would repond to the stimulation of widely scattered areas of the mucosa, but that from unit to unit certain spatial nonuniformities recurred (Figure 8.29). The nonuniformities formed an apparent spatial pattern characteristic for an odorant. Typically one or two areas dominated others in the pattern. The patterns in Figure 8.29 show only excitation, but some units responded by excitation to one odorant and suppression to another. The spatial pattern of suppression was usually

uniform rather than characteristic. This led Kauer and Moulton to conclude, as have others on the basis of other evidence, that inhibitory responses carry much less information about odor quality than do excitatory responses.

In addition to the interest aroused by Kauer and Moulton's discovery of inherent spatial patterning, interest in spatial encoding of odors was sparked further by olfactory analogues of "restricted environment" studies well known in vision. With the vision experimental model in mind, Døving and Pinching (1973) placed two-week-old rats into an environment odorized with cyclo-octanone or an environment with clean room air. Insofar as possible, customary odors (e.g., from cage litter) were swept away by appropriate air currents. After exposures of two weeks to 11 months, the animals were sacrificed and their olfactory bulbs inspected in coronal section. The group exposed to cyclo-octanone (as opposed to room air) exhibited regular changes, particularly in the mitral cell layer: shrinkage of the nucleus and cytoplasm and heavy uptake of stain (methylene blue; Azure II) typical of transneural degeneration seen in mitral cells when the mucosa is destroyed. But the investigators found no sign of peripheral damage and decided that the apparent degeneration arose from a functional rather than an anatomical cause. Rats in the control group also showed slight degeneration, far less than seen in the experimental group. In both groups, however, the locus within the coronal section was characteristic: mainly ventromedial in the experimental group and dorsomedial in the controls. These sectors of change ran a considerable distance in the anterior-posterior direction.

The possibility that the spatial distribution of such degeneration may carry meaning led Pinching and Døving (1974) to explore patterns for 44 different odorants. Each odorant did

indeed lead to a characteristic zone of change (two degrees of severity were used in this analysis). As Pinching and Døving concluded "The patterns observed in the olfactory bulb must represent, in some way, the functional topology of this system. The degree of overlap between different patterns may represent the distribution of neurones affected by, but not specific to, a particular odour. On the other hand, it may represent properties shared by different odours" (p. 203). In the second investigation, as in the first, the patterns maintained the same spatial character for a considrable distance along the anterior-posterior axis, but varied in severity along that axis.

Did the alterations in the mitral cells result

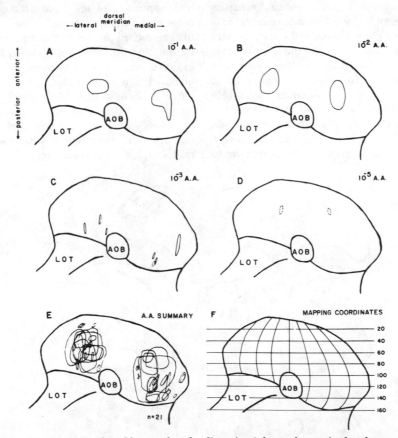

Figure 8.30. Density patterns produced by uptake of radioactive 2-deoxyglucose in the glomerular layer of the olfactory bulb of the rat after stimulation with amyl acetate. Patterns are plotted on a two-dimensional representation of the unfolded glomerular layer oriented as shown in lower right (F). A-D. Individual experiments at four different concentrations. Increased densities in glomerular layer are indicated by enclosed areas. Left olfactory bulb uptake shown by solid lines; right olfactory bulb uptake shown by dashed lines. E Summary map for 21 experiments at various concentrations; right and left bulbs. From Stewart, Kauer, and Shepherd (1979).

from deprivation or from overstimulation? Do animals reared in a one-odorant environment exhibit altered sensitivity to that odorant or to other odorants? Laing and Panhuber (1978) concluded that the selectively degenerated cells were those deprived of stimulation. This would therefore make the degeneration pattern equivalent to a photographic negative rather than a photographic positive. Evidence for this conclusion came from: (1) a finding of diffuse degeneration in rats raised in charcoal-filtered air (as opposed to unfiltered room air), and (2) a finding of higher preference and better detection of the exposure odors in the odorant-exposed rats. Hence, rats exposed to a given odorant hardly lost sensitivity to it (Laing & Panhuber, 1980). Rather, it appeared that sensitivity to the exposed odor was maintained and that sensitivity to others may be lost. Not surprisingly, rats exposed only to charcoal-filtered air were more uniformly insensitive in comparison to rats reared normally. It must be noted, however, that animals exposed to just room air delivered in such a way as to prevent other odors from reaching the animal had no apparent loss of sensitivity (Dalland & Døving, 1981; Laing & Panhuber, 1978, 1980). Although this might appear to be a less severe form of deprivation than exposure to

charcoal filtered air, it is noteworthy that charcoal filtered air, although seemingly chemically "pure," has an odor (Brisk, Turk, & Cain, 1983).

From the early experiments of Døving and Pinching (1973) to the later experiments of Laing and Panhuber (1980), there was an increasing focus on exposure during just an early portion of the organism's life. The as yet unrealized hope was that evidence of a critical period might arise. In some recent experiments that have entailed early exposure, patterns of degeneration have differed considerably from those seen previously (van As, Smit, & Köster, 1980; Cunzeman & Slotnick, 1984).

Difficulties of interpretation of long-term exposure studies will probably not disappear readily and will probably only very slowly add to our understanding of any spatial code. However, other techniques, principally the 2-deoxyglucose uptake technique, have also contributed useful information. Radioactively labeled 2-deoxyglucose injected into the bloodstream will behave like glucose but, because of its incomplete metabolism, will remain at sites of high energy metabolism. Hence, injection into an animal during odor exposure will leave an imprint of where in the olfactory bulb the stimulus was processed. Autoradiography of coronal sections of the bulb

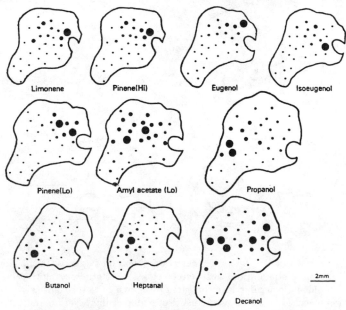

Figure 8.31. Patterns of EOG amplitude at various points on the salamander olfactory mucosa upon punctate stimulation with various odorants. Size of dot represents EOG amplitude at that site. From Mackay-Sim, Shaman, and Moulton (1982).

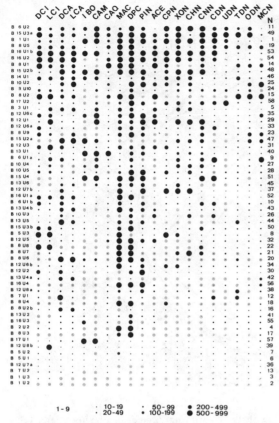

Figure 8.32. Odorant by mitral cell unit array for 20 odorants and 58 units. The size of the filled circles represents magnitude of odor-evoked excitation. Circles with inner points represent inhibitory responses. The odorants are the same as shown in Figure 8.27. From Duchamp (1982).

showed that the glomerular layer of the bulb had the highest uptake of 2-deoxyglucose and that the spatial distribution of uptake varied with the odorant (Sharp, Kauer, & Shepherd, 1977). Nevertheless, any given odorant-generated activity occurred over a wide area, and the distribution of activity showed considerable overlap among odorants. Figure 8.30 illustrates patterns for amyl acetate in an unfolded schematic of the glomerular layer (Stewart, Kauer, & Shepherd, 1979). The focal nature of 2-deoxyglucose uptake has become an issue of increasing interest (Jourdan, Duveau, Astic, & Holley, 1980), particularly since the development of a high-resolution technique has made it possible to investigate uptake in individual glomeruli (Lancet, Greer, Kauer, & Shepherd, 1982). It has now become evident that even in areas of sizable uptake, there

are large differences from one glomerulus to another. Hence, the spatial pattern seen with low resolution increases in complexity with higher resolution.

Did the patterns of degeneration or those of 2-deoxyglucose arise from inherent patterning or from imposed patterning? No definitive answer exists, but research in Moulton's laboratory suggested that the two may play supplementary roles. Moulton (1976), who saw many limitations of imposed patterning, felt that this kind of pattern might enhance inherent patterning. Hence, receptors could be located in places at which their peak sensitivities would match a high probability of deposition, a kind of hand-in-glove notion. Conversely, receptors could be situated in locations that may sharpen the detection of gradients. Mackay-Sim, Shaman, and Moulton (1982) found mainly the former in an investigation of EOGs recorded in restricted regions under punctate stimulation (see also Kubie, Mackay-Sim, & Moulton, 1980). That is, the pattern seen with punctate stimulation had surprising similarities to what would have been seen with whole-mucosa stimulation (Figure 8.31).

Despite the mounting circumstantial evidence for some type of spatial encoding, there remains considerable evidence that individual units chosen without respect to position carry the important afferent information (Kauer, 1980). In an effort to make his bulbar recordings as comparable as possible to the olfactory receptor recordings of Revial et al. (1982), Duchamp (1982) used the same species (Rana ridibunda), odorants, and concentrations to record from mitral cells. One anticipated difference between the two studies was the evocation of inhibitory responses in the bulb. (Kauer, 1974, defined three types of excitatory and two types of suppressive responses. Any given bulbar unit could exhibit any of the responses depending on the odorant presented. Excitatory responses were often concentration dependent over a relatively narrow range, which led Kauer to coin the term concentration tuning.) If we ignore whether the response was inhibitory or excitatory and compare Figure 8.32 with Figure 8.27, we find decided similarities. Most odorants caused a response in half or more of the bulbar units and some odorants (DPC, MAC) caused a response in almost all. Degree of selectivity was slightly greater among bulbar units (note

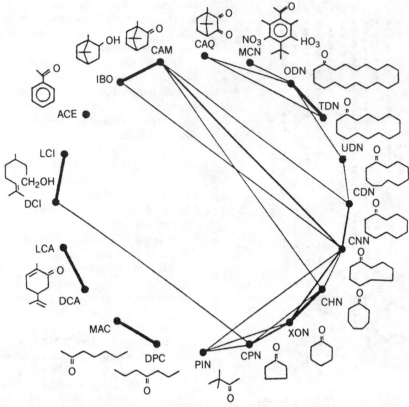

Figure 8.33. Intercorrelations among odorants based on their stimulating effects on olfactory bulb units (Figure 8.32). Three classes of significant correlations are represented: $0.48 \leqslant r < 0.60$, thin lines; $0.60 \leqslant r < 0.70$, medium lines; and $r \geqslant 0.70$, thick lines. From Duchamp and Sicard (1984).

the discrimination between d-forms and l-forms) and the existence of both inhibitory and excitatory responses implies that more complex processing has begun, but the superficial picture is still one of considerable similarity between the two loci. The correlation between the periphery and bulb in terms of the percentage of responding cells across odorants equalled $+0.75$.

Interodorant correlations reinforce the conclusion of similarity between periphery and bulb, but with some sharpening at the bulb (Figure 8.33). Since second order neurons are still reasonably distal in the olfactory nervous system, there is still a theoretical opportunity for further sharpening of neural tuning at higher levels. Do we have reason to believe that this is necessary? The answer is no. Any seeming fuzziness in the pattern of neural data seen in the bulb results in large measure from the small sample of units. A larger sample would assuredly enhance discrimination.

Recordings from third order units in the pyri-

form cortex generate a picture much like that seen in the bulb. However, recordings from the frontal cortex appear to be more narrowly tuned (Tanabe, Iino, Oshima, & Takagi, 1975). The case for sharpening is only circumstantial, however, since the same odorants, concentrations, stimulus delivery techniques, and so forth, have not been used to compare different central levels.

SUMMARY AND CONCLUSIONS

Functional Anatomy

1. The olfactory system comprises an ever-changing population of receptor neurons each of which must grow to an appropriate point of termination in the olfactory bulb. In view of this flux and in the absence of clear morphological differences in receptor cells, it would seem that olfaction must maintain its functional afferent stability

statistically. Neurophysiological data tend always to confirm and never to contradict this conclusion.

2. Mucus acts as a selective filter to olfactory stimulation. Mucus may even alter the structure of odorous materials.

3. Olfactory transduction most likely takes place on the proximal segments of the protein-rich receptor cilia.

4. Millions of receptor cells in the olfactory periphery converge on a few thousand glomeruli in the olfactory bulb. This situation suggests that the glomerulus behaves as a functional unit, but no data have yet proven the point.

5. The olfactory bulb possesses a unique profile of neurotransmitters and neuro-modulators.

6. The olfactory central projections bifurcate into transthalamic and transhypothalamic pathways. The transhypothalamic pathway may represent a regulatory pathway.

7. The vomeronasal system seems to rival olfaction in chemosensory importance in many species. It seems particularly important in sexual and maternal behavior in rodents. Stimulation of the vomeronasal system may be pleasurable in itself.

8. In addition to the olfactory and vomero-nasal organs, the nasal cavity contains three other chemoreceptive systems: (1) the terminal nerve, (2) the septal organ, and (3) the trigeminal nerve. The trigeminal nerve mediates common chemical sensations of pungency that often accompany olfactory stimulation.

9. Among the various neural measures of olfactory functioning, the receptor potential called the electro-olfactogram (EOG) has proven particularly useful.

Sensitivity

1. Odor thresholds vary across 12 orders of magnitude. For the most potent·stimuli, olfaction seems to function at about its theoretical limit, that is, a sensitivity of one molecule per cell, after subtraction of putative transmission losses.

2. Minor changes in a molecule will most likely change its threshold. Such changes

may reflect primarily alterations in solubility. Models to compute threshold give heavy weight to solubility and to the filtering effect of mucus.

3. The likelihood that threshold sensitivity is governed both by solubility and by the number and location of olfactory receptors in the nasal cavity raises the possibility that different species have the same relative sensitivity across compounds. Some data support this notion.

4. Humans can resolve differences in concentration of about 10 percent or better. Previous findings of much poorer resolution failed to take into account the physical noise added by fluctuations in vapor phase concentration.

Functional Relations (Intensity, Time, Adaptation, Mixtures)

1. Psychophysical functions for odor intensity reveal strong compression of output relative to input. The degree of compression, that is, steepness of the functions, varies over a wide range. Odorants with steep odor functions tend to have high odor thresholds and to evoke some irritation.

2. The compression seen in psychophysical functions also occurs in EOG recordings. Hence, the compression has a peripheral locus in whole or in part.

3. Psychophysical functions for irritation have much greater steepness than those for odor. Irritation can suppress odor.

4. Suprathreshold olfactory responses exhibit temporal integration up to durations greater than a second. Trigeminal responses show temporal integration over much longer durations. No critical durations have been specified.

5. Reaction time to olfactory stimulation in humans equals 500 msec or more depending upon concentration. Reaction time to an irritant or to the irritating component of an odorant typically exceeds olfactory reaction time considerably. The relative depths of the olfactory cilia and free nerve endings of the trigeminal nerve may determine relative reaction times.

6. During constant exposure to an odorant, perceived magnitude decays exponentially over about four minutes to an asymptote at 30 to 40 percent of the initial magnitude. The perceived magnitude of concentrations that evoke common chemical sensations decays more slowly.

7. Exposure to one stimulus will depress sensitivity to virtually any other subsequent stimulus to at least some degree. The degree of such cross-adaptation varies from one stimulus pair to another in unpredictable ways. Commonly, the cross-adapting effect of one stimulus on another will be unsymmetric for the two members of a pair. This occurs in neurophysiological recordings of receptor cells and in psychophysical experiments.

8. Olfactory adaptation has in part a peripheral neural locus and in part a central locus.

9. Olfaction exhibits partial bilateral addition.

10. The issue of whether humans can localize (or lateralize) odors from internostril time and intensity cues remains unsettled. Nevertheless, a neural basis for such localization has been uncovered.

11. Most natural products derive their odors from many chemical constituents. Only occasionally will just one constituent endow a product with its characteristic quality.

12. Mixtures invariably smell less intense than the sum of the intensities of their unmixed constituents. Vector addition applied to the perceived intensities of the constituents offers an adequate practical description of the intensity of simple mixtures.

13. The hypoaddition that characterizes physical mixtures also occurs with dichorhinic "mixtures."

14. Commercial odor counteraction takes advantage of the way in which the olfactory system processes mixtures. Hypoaddition ensures that a mixture of malodor and counteractant will smell less intense than their sum and, given the appropriate odor proportions, less intense than the stronger component smelled alone. Another factor at work in odor counteraction is masking. In a binary mixture, the stronger component will tend to make a disproportionate contribution to odor quality.

15. Taste and smell commonly operate as a single perceptual system. The psychophysical observer (and the ordinary person) will tend to ascribe to taste some portion of olfactory sensations produced from odorous solutions in the mouth. Nevertheless, taste has no masking influence on smell or vice versa.

Cognitive Properties (Memory, Identification)

1. Odor recognition memory displays characteristics of holistic encoding, like memory for amorphous shapes.

2. The ability to retrieve labels for familiar odors from memory plays a major role in performance in odor identification. When the problems of such retrieval are circumvented or solved, odor identification is seen to be limited primarily by discrimination. The number of substances that a person can identify can therefore be very large (probably thousands).

3. Women outperform men in the identification of everyday odors. Young people outperform older people.

4. Given appropriate test design, odor identification can be used to test the sense of smell rapidly in the clinic.

Pleasantness

1. Odor pleasantness and unpleasantness seem so compelling as to motivate the question of whether they are innate or acquired. For humans and most mammals, the data support the conclusion that pleasantness and unpleasantness are acquired. Important observations on this topic include the expansion of hedonic reactions during the first decade of life and the modifiability of odor pleasantness through conditioned aversions or mere experience with an odor.

2. Odor learning is very rapid in young organisms. Some pheromone-mediated behavior probably occurs because of rapid early learning whereby an odor cue from a conspecific becomes associated with some reinforcing event.

3. Odor pleasantness will depend heavily on context and, perhaps, on biological needs (alliesthesia).

Odor Quality (Theories, Structure-activity)

1. Odor classification systems can serve a useful practical purpose to describe products, but have added little to understanding the mechanism of olfaction.

2. Amoore's odor classification system and his postulation of "primary" odors of stereochemical similarity have been abandoned, but the idea that the shape and size of a molecule (its stereochemical features) determine odor quality lives on.

3. The most complete and accurate way to "measure" the quality of an odor entails matching with attributes. A current ASTM procedure for such profiling employs 146 descriptors. This number is probably insufficient to give every odor a unique signature.

4. Among the numerous global "theories" of olfaction, only Wright's infrared absorption theory remains intact.

5. Amoore has proposed a theory that the key to the olfactory code will be found in mapping specific anosmia to various compounds. A given specific anosmia could arise from the absence of a particular receptor type. No evidence has either confirmed or denied this assertion.

6. Current work on structure-activity relations focuses on well-defined groups of commercially interesting fragrances, such as ambergris and musks. The work illustrates how very minor changes in molecular structure may cause large changes in odor quality and intensity.

7. The search for structural least-common-denominators for a given odor quality or quality note seems quite unlikely to give insight into the nature of olfaction.

Coding of Quality

1. Electrophysiological recordings from receptor cells imply that odor quality emerges statistically across millions of receptors rather than from labeled lines or a small number of cell types. It is conceivable, however, that technical and conceptual limitations have obscured the existence of types.

2. Whenever human psychophysical data on the relations among odors have been compared to neurophysiological data from lower organisms, the agreement has been impressive.

3. Inhaled odorants distribute themselves onto the mucosa in a spatial and temporal pattern. To some degree, the pattern depends upon biophysical factors. The polar properties of mucus, for example, allow the nasal mucosa to behave similarly to a polar chromatographic column.

4. Imposed spatio-temporal patterns set up by the sorptive properties of the mucus-receptor compartment coexist with inherent spatial patterns derived, perhaps, from receptor affinities.

5. The study of the possible spatial code for odor quality has included chronic exposures of young, developing rats to only one odor and a search for how this exposure has altered olfactory bulb (mitral cell) morphology. Animals raised in such environments exhibit spatially characteristic patterns of what has been called selective degeneration in the mitral cell layer. Some data suggest that the degenerated areas represent zones of stimulus deprivation.

6. The uptake of radioactive 2-deoxyglucose in the glomerular layer during olfactory stimulation also reveals characteristic spatial patterns.

7. Despite evidence for a spatial code at the level of the olfactory bulb, recordings of bulbar units chosen without respect to spatial location imply that an across-fiber pattern explanation has as much, if not more, relevance to functioning in the bulb as it does to the receptor cells.

REFERENCES

Adamek, G.D., Gesteland, R.C., Mair, R.G., & Oakley, B. (1984). Transduction physiology of olfactory receptor cilia. *Brain Research, 310,* 87–97.

Adrian, E.D. (1942). Olfactory reactions in the brain of the hedgehog. *Journal of Physiology, 100,* 459–473.

Adrian, E.D. (1950). The electrical activity of the mammalian olfactory bulb. *Electroencephalography and Clinical Neurophysiology, 2,* 377–388.

Amoore, J.E. (1962a). The stereochemical theory of olfaction. 1. Identification of the seven primary odours. *Proceedings of the Scientific Section, Toilet Goods Associations, 37* (Suppl.), 1–12.

Amoore, J.E. (1962b). The stereochemical theory of olfaction. 2. Elucidation of the stereochemical properties of the olfactory receptor sites. *Proceedings of the Scientific Section, Toilet Goods Association, 37* (Suppl.), 13–23.

Amoore, J.E. (1970). *Molecular basis of odor.* Springfield, IL: Charles C. Thomas.

Amoore, J.E. (1982). Odor theory and odor classification. In E. T. Theimer (Ed.), *Fragrance chemistry: The science of the sense of smell* (pp. 27–76). New York: Academic Press.

Amoore, J.E. & Hautala, E. (1983). Odor as an aid to chemical safety: Odor thresholds compared with threshold limit values and volatilities for 214 industrial chemicals in air and water dilution. *Journal of Applied Toxicology, 3,* 272–290.

Amoore, J.E. & Venstrom, D. (1967) Correlations between stereochemical assessments and organoleptic analysis of odorous compounds. In T. Hayashi (Ed.), *Olfaction and taste II* (pp. 3–17). Oxford: Pergamon Press.

Baylin, F. & Moulton, D.G. (1979). Adaptation and cross-adaptation to odor stimulation of olfactory receptors in the tiger salamander. *Journal of General Physiology, 74,* 37–55.

Beauchamp, G.K., Doty, R.L., Moulton, D.G., & Mugford, R.A. (1976). The pheromone concept in mammalian chemical communication: A critique. In R. L. Doty (Ed.), *Mammalian olfaction, reproductive processes and behavior* (pp. 143–160). New York: Academic Press.

Beauchamp, G.K., Wysocki, C.J., & Wellington, J.L. (1985). Extinction of response to urine odor as a consequence of vomeronasal organ removal in male guinea pigs. *Behavioral Neuroscience, 99,* 950–955.

Beck, L.H. & Miles, W.R. (1947). Some theoretical and experimental relationships between infrared absorption and olfaction. *Science, 106,* 511.

Beets, M.G.J. (1978). *Structure-activity relationships in human chemoreception.* London: Applied Science Publishers.

Beets, M.G.J. (1982). Odor and stimulant structure. In E.T. Theimer (Ed.), *Fragrance chemistry: The science of the sense of smell* (pp. 77–122). New York: Academic Press.

Beidler, L.M. (1961). Mechanisms of gustatory and olfactory receptor stimulation. In W.A. Rosenblith (Ed.), *Sensory communication* (pp. 143–157). Cambridge, MA: M.I.T. Press.

Békésy, G. von (1964). Olfactory analogue to directional hearing. *Journal of Applied Physiology, 19,* 369–373.

Békésy, G.von (1967). *Sensory inhibition.* Princeton, NJ: Princeton University Press.

Bennett, M.H. (1968). The role of the anterior limb of the anterior commissure in olfaction. *Physiology & Behavior, 3,* 507–515.

Berglund, B. (1974). Quantitative and qualitative analysis of industrial odors with human observers. *Annals of the New York Academy of Sciences, 237,* 35–51.

Berglund, B., Berglund, U., Ekman, G., & Engen, T. (1971). Individual psychophysical functions for 28 odorants. *Perception & Psychophysics, 9,* 379–384.

Berglund, B., Berglund, U., Engen, T., & Ekman, G. (1973). Multidimensional analysis of twenty-one odors. *Scandanavian Journal of Psychology, 14,* 131–137.

Berglund, B., Berglund, U., & Lindvall, T. (1971). On the principle of odor interaction. *Acta Psychologica, 35,* 255–268.

Berglund, B., Berglund, U., & Lindvall, T. (1978). Olfactory self- and cross-adaptation: Effects of time of adaptation on perceived odor intensity. *Sensory Processes, 2,* 191–197.

Berglund, B., Beglund, U., Lindvall, T., & Svensson, L.T. (1973). A quantitative principle of perceived intensity summation in odor mixtures. *Journal of Experimental Psychology, 100,* 29–38.

Bernstein, I.L. & Webster, M.M. (1980). Learned taste aversions in humans. *Phsyiology & Behavior, 25,* 363–366.

Boeckh, J. (1980). Neural basis of coding of chemosensory quality at the receptor cell level. In H. van der Starre (Ed.), *Olfaction and taste VII* (pp. 113–122). London: IRL Press.

Boring, G. (1928). A new system for the classification of odors. *American Journal of Psychology, 40,* 345–349.

Broadwell, R.D. (1977). Neurotransmitter pathways in the olfactory system. In J.A. Ferrendelli (Ed.), *Society for neuroscience symposia: Vol. 3: Aspects of behavioral neurobiology* (pp. 131–166). Bethesda, MD: Society for Neuroscience.

Brisk, M.A., Turk, A., & Cain, W.S. (1983). Influence

of carbon-treated air on odor perception. *Atmospheric Environment, 17,* 1023–1024.

Cabanac, M. (1971). Physiological role of pleasure. *Science, 173,* 1103–1107.

Cagan, R.H. & Rhein, L.D. (1980). Biochemical basis of recognition of taste and olfactory stimuli. In H. van der Starre (Ed.), *Olfaction and taste VII* (pp. 35–44). London: IRL Press.

Cain, W.S. (1969). Odor intensity: Differences in the exponent of the psychophysical function. *Perception & Psychophysics, 6,* 349–354.

Cain, W.S. (1974). Perception of odor intensity and the time-course of olfactory adaptation. *ASHRAE Transactions, 80,* 53–75.

Cain, W.S. (1975). Odor intensity: Mixtures and masking. *Chemical Senses and Flavor, 1,* 339–352.

Cain, W.S. (1976). Olfaction and the common chemical sense: Some psychophysical contrasts. *Sensory Processes, 1,* 57–67.

Cain, W.S. (1977a). Bilateral interaction in olfaction. *Nature, 268,* 50–52.

Cain, W.S. (1977b). Differential sensitivity for smell: "Noise" at the nose. *Science, 195,* 796–798.

Cain, W.S. (1977c). Odor magnitude: Coarse versus fine grain. *Perception & Psychophysics, 22,* 545–549.

Cain, W.S. (1977d). Physical and cognitive limitations on olfactory processing in human beings. In D. Müller-Schwarze & M.M. Mozell (Eds.), *Chemical signals in vertebrates* (pp. 287–301). New York: Plenum Press.

Cain, W.S. (1978a). History of research on smell. In E.C. Carterette & M.P. Friedman (Eds.), *Handbook of perception: Vol. 6A: Tasting and smelling* (pp. 197–229). New York: Academic Press.

Cain, W.S. (1978b). The odoriferous environment and the application of olfactory research. In E.C. Carterette & M.P. Friedman (Eds.), *Handbook of perception: Vol. 6A: Tasting and smelling* (pp. 277–304). New York: Academic Press.

Cain, W.S. (1979a). Lability of odor pleasantness. In J.H.A. Kroeze (Ed.), *Preference behavior and chemoreception* (pp. 303–315). London: Information Retrieval.

Cain, W.S. (1979b). To know with the nose: Keys to odor identification. *Science, 203,* 467–470.

Cain, W.S. (1980). Sensory attributes of cigarette smoking. In G.B. Gori & F.G. Bock (Eds.), *Banbury Report* (pp. 239–249). New York: Cold Spring Harbor Laboratory.

Cain, W.S. (1981). Olfaction and the common chemical sense: Similarities, differences, and interactions. In H.R. Moskowitz & C. Warren (Eds.), *Odor quality and intensity as a function of chemical structure* (pp. 109–121). Washington DC: American Chemical Society.

Cain, W.S. (1982). Odor identification by males and females: Predictions versus performance. *Chemical Senses, 7,* 129–142.

Cain, W.S. & Drexler, M. (1974). Scope and evaluation of odor counteraction and masking. *Annals of the New York Academy of Sciences, 237,* 427–439.

Cain, W.S. & Engen, T. (1969). Olfactory adaptation and the scaling of odor intensity. In C. Pfaffmann (Ed.), *Olfaction and taste: Proceedings of the third international symposium* (pp. 127–141). New York: Rockefeller University Press.

Cain, W.S. & Gent, J.F. (1986). Use of odor identification in clinical testing of olfaction. In H.L. Meiselman & R.S. Rivlin (Eds.), *Clinical measurement of taste and smell* (pp. 170–186). New York: Macmillan.

Cain, W.S., Gent, J., Catalanotto, F.A., & Goodspeed, R.B. (1983). Clinical evaluation of olfaction. *American Journal of Otolaryngology, 4,* 252–256.

Cain, W.S. & Johnson, F., Jr. (1978). Lability of odor pleasantness: Influence of mere exposure. *Perception, 7,* 459–465.

Cain, W.S. & Murphy, C.L. (1980). Interaction between chemoreceptive modalities of odour and irritation. *Nature, 284,* 255–257.

Chaput, M. & Holley, A. (1976). Olfactory bulb responsiveness to food odor during stomach distension in the rat. *Chemical Senses and Flavor, 2,* 189–201.

Chen, Z. & Lancet, D. (1984). Membrane proteins unique to vertebrate olfactory cilia: Candidates for sensory receptor molecules. *Proceedings of the National Academy of Sciences, 81,* 1859–1863.

Cometto-Muniz, J.E. (1981). Odor, taste, and flavor perception of some flavoring agents. *Chemical Senses, 6,* 215–223.

Cometto-Muniz, J.E. & Cain, W.S. (1984). Temporal integration of pungency. *Chemical Senses, 8,* 315–327.

Corbit, T.E. & Engen, T. (1971). Facilitation of olfactory detection. *Perception & Psychophysics, 10,* 433–436.

Costanzo, R.M. & Mozell, M.M. (1976). Electrophysiological evidence for a topographical projection of the nasal mucosa onto the olfactory bulb of the frog. *The Journal of General Physiology, 68,* 297–312.

Cunzeman, P.J. & Slotnick, B.M. (1984). Prolonged exposure to odors in the rat: effects on odor detection and on mitral cells. *Chemical Senses, 9,* 229–239.

Dalland, T. & Døving, K.B. (1981). Reaction of olfactory stimuli in odor-exposed rats. *Behavioral and Neural Biology, 32,* 79–88.

Daval, G. & Leveteau, J. (1975). Multiple function of the anterior olfactory nucleus (A.O.N.): Lateral discrimination and centrifugal control. In D.A.

Denton & J.P. Coghlan (Eds.), *Olfaction and taste V* (pp. 297–301). New York: Academic Press.

Davies, J.T. & Taylor, F.H. (1959). The role of adsorption and molecular morphology in olfaction: The calculation of olfactory thresholds. *Biological Bulletin, 117*, 222–228.

Davis, R.G. (1977). Acquisition and retention of verbal associations to olfactory and abstract visual stimuli of varying similarity. *Journal of Experimental Psychology: Human Learning and Memory, 3*, 37–51.

Demski, L.S. & Northcutt, R.G. (1983). The terminal nerve: A new chemosensory system in vertebrates. *Science, 220*, 435–437.

DeVries, H. & Stuiver, M. (1961). The absolute sensitivity of the human sense of smell. In W.A. Rosenblith (Ed.), *Sensory communication* (pp. 159–167). Cambridge MA: M.I.T. Press.

Doty, R.L., Brugger, W.E., Jurs, P.C., Orndorff, M.A., Snyder, P.J., & Lowry, L.D. (1978). Intranasal trigeminal stimulation from odorous volatiles: Psychometric responses from anosmic and normal humans. *Physiology & Behavior, 20*, 175–185.

Doty, R.L., Shaman, P., Applebaum, S.L., Giberson, R., Sikorski, L., & Rosenberg, L. (1984). Smell identification ability: Changes with age. *Science, 226*, 1441–1443.

Doty, R.L., Shaman, P., & Dann, M. (1984). Development of the University of Pennsylvania Smell Identification Test: A standardized microencapsulated test of olfactory function. *Physiology & Behavior, 32*, 489–502.

Døving, K.B. & Lange, A.L. (1967). Comparative studies of sensory relatedness of odours. *Scandanavian Journal of Psychology, 8*, 47–51.

Døving, K.B. & Pinching, A.J. (1973). Selective degeneration of neurones in the olfactory bulb following prolonged odour exposure. *Brain Research, 52*, 115–129.

Drake, B., Johansson, B., von Sydow, E., & Døving, K.B. (1969). Quantitative psychophysical and electrophysiological data on some odorous compounds. *Scandanavian Journal of Psychology, 10*, 89–96.

Dravnieks, A. (1982). Odor quality: Semantically generated multidimensional profiles are stable. *Science, 218*, 799–801.

Dravnieks, A. (1983). Odor character profiling. *Journal of the Air Pollution Control Association, 33*, 775–778.

Dravnieks, A., Masurat, T., & Lamm, R.A. (1984). Hedonics of odors and odor descriptors. *Journal of the Air Pollution Control Association, 34*, 752–755.

Duchamp, A. (1982). Electrophysiological responses of olfactory bulb neurons to odour stimuli in the frog. A comparison with receptor cells. *Chemical Senses, 7*, 191–210.

Duchamp, A., Revial, M.F., Holley, A., & MacLeod, P.

(1974). Odor discrimination by frog olfactory receptors. *Chemical Senses and Flavor, 1*, 213–233.

Duchamp, A. & Sicard, G. (1984). Odour discrimination by olfactory bulb neurons: Statistical analysis of electrophysiological responses and comparison with odour discrimination by receptor cells. *Chemical Senses, 9*, 1–14.

Eccles, R. (1982). Neurological and pharmacological considerations. In D.F. Proctor & I.B. Andersen (Eds.), *The nose: Upper airway physiology and the atmospheric environment* (pp. 191–214). The Netherlands: Elsevier Biomedical Press.

Elsberg, C.A., Levy, I., & Brewer, E.D. (1935). The trigeminal effects of odorous substances. *Bulletin of the Neurological Institute of New York, 4*, 270–285.

Engen, T. (1965). Psychophysical analysis of the odor intensity of homologous alcohols. *Journal of Experimental Psychology, 70*, 611–616.

Engen, T. (1974a). Method and theory in the study of odor preferences. In A. Turk, J.W. Johnston, Jr., & D.G. Moulton (Eds.), *Human responses to environmental odors* (pp. 121–141). New York: Academic Press.

Engen, T. (1974b). The potential usefulness of sensations of odor and taste in keeping children away from harmful substances. *Annals of the New York Academy of Sciences, 237*, 224–228.

Engen, T. (1982). *The perception of odors*. New York: Academic Press.

Engen, T. & McBurney, D.H. (1964). Magnitude and category scales of the pleasantness of odors. *Journal of Experimental Psychology, 68*, 435–440.

Engen, T. & Pfaffmann, C. (1960). Absolute judgments of odor quality. *Journal of Experimental Psychology, 59*, 214–219.

Engen, T. & Ross, B.M. (1973). Long-term memory of odors with and without verbal descriptions. *Journal of Experimental Psychology, 100*, 221–227.

Farbman, A., Scholz, D., Emanuel, D., & Margolis, F. (1980). Maturation of olfactory receptor cell terminals. In H. van der Starre (Ed.), *Olfaction and taste VII* (pp. 147–150). London: IRL Press.

Fazzalari, F.A. (Ed.) (1978). *Compilation of odor and taste threshold values data*. Philadelphia: American Society for Testing and Materials.

García-Medina, M.R. (1981). Flavor-odor taste interactions in solutions of acetic acid and coffee. *Chemical Senses, 6*, 13–22.

Gesteland, R.C. (1978). The neural code: Integrative neural mechanisms. In E.C. Carterette & M.P. Friedman (Eds.), *Handbook of perception: Vol. 6A: Tasting and smelling* (pp. 259–276). New York: Academic Press.

Gesteland, R.C., Lettvin, J.Y., Pitts, W.H. & Rojas, A. (1963). Odor specificities of the frog's olfactory receptors. In Y. Zotterman (Ed.), *Olfaction and taste* (pp. 19–34). Oxford, Eng.: Pergamon Press.

Gesteland, R.C., Yancy, R.A., Mair, R.G., Adamek, G.D., & Farbman, A.I. (1980). Ontogeny of olfactory receptor specificity. In H. van der Starre (Ed.), *Olfaction and taste VII* (pp. 143–146). London: IRL Press.

Getchell, T.V. (1974). Electrogenic sources of slow voltage transients recorded from frog olfactory epithelium. *Journal of Neurophysiology, 37,* 1115–1130.

Getchell, T.V. & Getchell, M.L. (1977). Early events in vertebrate olfaction. *Chemical Senses and Flavor, 2,* 313–326.

Getchell, T.V., Heck, G.L., DeSimone, J.A., & Price, S. (1980). The location of olfactory receptor sites inferences from latency measurements. *Biophysical Journal, 29,* 397–412.

Getchell, T.V. & Shepherd, G.M. (1978). Responses of olfactory receptor cells to step pulses of odour at different concentrations in the salamander. *Journal of Physiology, 282,* 521–540.

Gillan, D.G. (1983). Taste-taste, odor-odor, and taste-odor mixtures: Greater suppression within than between modalities. *Perception and Psychophysics, 33,* 183–185.

Goodwin, M., Gooding, K.M., & Regnier, F. (1979). Sex pheromone in the dog. *Science, 203,* 559–561.

Graziadei, P.P.C. (1977). Functional anatomy of the mammalian chemoreceptor system. In D. Müller-Schwarze & M.M. Mozell (Eds.), *Chemical signals in vertebrates* (pp. 435–454). New York: Plenum Press.

Graziadei, P.P.C. & Monti Graziadei, G.A. (1980). Plasticity of connections in the olfactory sensory pathway: Transplantation studies. In H. van der Starre (Ed.), *Olfaction and taste VII* (pp. 155–158). London: IRL Press.

Griffiths, N.M. & Fenwick, R. (1977). Odour properties of chloroanisoles—Effects of replacing chloro- by methyl groups. *Chemical Senses and Flavor, 2,* 487–491.

Hainer, R.M., Emslie, A.G., & Jacobson, A. (1954). An information theory of olfaction. *Annals of the New York Academy of Sciences, 58,* 158–174.

Harper, R., Bate-Smith, E.C., Land, D.G., & Griffiths, N.M. (1968). A glossary of odor stimuli and their qualities. *Perfumery and Essential Oil Record, 59,* 22.

Henning, H. (1916). *Der Geruch* (The sense of smell). Leipzig: Barth.

Hollingworth, H.L. & Poffenberger, A.T. (1917). *The sense of taste.* New York: Moffat, Yard.

Hornung, D.E. & Enns, M.P. (1984). The independence and integration of olfaction and taste. *Chemical Senses, 9,* 97–106.

Hornung, D.E. & Mozell, M.M. (1977). Factors influencing the differential sorption of odorant molecules across the olfactory mucosa. *Journal of General Physiology, 69,* 343–361.

Hornung, D.E., Mozell, M.M., & Serio, J.A. (1980). Olfactory mucosa/air partitioning of odorants. In H. van der Starre (Ed.), *Olfaction and taste VII* (pp. 167–170). London: IRL Press.

Hose, L.P., & Piggott, J.R. (1980). Descriptive sensory analysis of Scotch whisky. In H. van der Starre (Ed.), *Olfaction and taste VII* (pp. 449–450). London: IRL Press.

Jones, F.N. (1958). Scales of subjective intensity for odors of diverse chemical nature. *American Journal of Psychology, 71,* 305–310.

Jones, F.N. (1968). The informational content of olfactory quality. In N.N. Tanyolaç (Ed.), *Theories of odor and odor measurement* (pp. 133–146). Istanbul: N.N. Tanyolaç.

Jones, F.N. & Woskow, M.H. (1964). On the intensity of odor mixtures. *Annals of the New York Academy of Sciences, 116,* 484–494.

Jourdan, F., Duveau, A., Astic, L., & Holley, A. (1980). Spatial distribution of [^{14}C]2-deoxyglucose uptake in the olfactory bulbs of rats stimulated with two different odours. *Brain Research, 188,* 139–154.

Jurs, P.C., Ham, C.L., & Brügger, W. (1981). Computer-assisted studies of chemical structure and olfactory quality using pattern recognition techniques. In H.R. Moskowitz & C. Warren (Eds.), *Odor quality and intensity as a function of chemical structure* (pp. 143–160). Washington DC: American Chemical Society.

Katz, S.H. & Talbert, E.J. (1930). *Intensities of odors and irritating effects of warning agents for inflammable and poisonous gases* (Technical Paper 480). Washington DC: U.S. Department of Commerce.

Kauer, J.S. (1974). Response patterns of amphibian olfactory bulb neurones to odour stimulation. *Journal of Physiology, 243,* 695–715.

Kauer, J.S. (1980). Some spatial characteristics of central information processing in the vertebrate olfactory pathway. In H. van der Starre (Ed.), *Olfaction and taste VII* (pp. 227–236). London: IRL Press.

Kauer, J.S. & Moulton, D.G. (1974). Responses of olfactory bulb neurones to odour stimulation of small nasal areas in the salamander. *Journal of Physiology, 243,* 717–737.

Kauer, J.S. & Shepherd, G.M. (1977). Analysis of the onset phase of olfactory bulb unit responses to odour pulses in the salamander. *Journal of Physiology, 272,* 495–516.

Kerr, D.L.B. (1977). Olfactory centrifugal pathways. In J. LeMagnen & P. MacLeod (Eds.), *Olfaction and taste VI* (pp. 97–103). London: Information Retrieval.

Keverne, E.P. (1982). Chemical senses: Smell. In H.B. Barlow & J.D. Mollon (Eds.), *The senses* (pp. 409–427). Cambridge, Eng.: Cambridge University.

Kobal, G. (1981). *Elektrophysiologische Untersuchungen des menschlichen Geruchsinns (Electrophysiological investigation of the human sense of smell)*. New York: Thieme-Copythek.

Köster, E.P. (1969). Intensity in mixtures of odorous substances. In C. Pfaffmann (Ed.), *Olfaction and taste*, Proceedings of the third international symposium (pp. 142–149). New York: Rockefeller University Press.

Köster, E.P. (1971). Adaptation and cross-adaptation in olfaction. Unpublished doctoral dissertation, University of Utrecht.

Kubie, J., Mackay-Sim, A., & Moulton, D. (1980). Inherent spatial patterning of responses to odorants in the salamander olfactory epithelium. In H. van der Starre (Ed.), *Olfaction and taste VII* (pp. 163–166). London: IRL Press.

Laffort, P. (1969). A linear relationship between olfactory effectiveness and identified molecular characteristics, extended to fifty pure substances. In C. Pfaffmann (Ed.), *Olfaction and taste: Proceedings of the third international symposium* (pp. 150–157). New York: Rockefeller University Press.

Laffort, P. (1977). Some aspects of molecular recognition by chemoreceptors. In J. LeMagnen & P. MacLeod (Eds.), *Olfaction and taste VI* (pp. 17–25). London: Information Retrieval.

Laffort, P. & Dravnieks, A. (1982). Several models of suprathreshold quantitative olfactory interaction in humans applied to binary, ternary and quaternary mixtures. *Chemical Senses, 7*, 153–174.

Laffort, P., Patte, F., & Etcheto, M. (1974). Olfactory coding on the basis of physicochemical properties. *Annals of the New York Academy of Sciences, 237*, 193–208.

Laing, D.G. (1975). A comparative study of the olfactory sensitivity of humans and rats. *Chemical Senses and Flavor, 1*, 257–269.

Laing, D.G. (1982). Characterization of human behavior during odour perception. *Perception, 11*, 221–230.

Laing, D.G. (1983). Natural sniffing gives optimum odour perception for humans. *Perception, 12*, 99–117.

Laing, D.G. & Clark, P.J. (1983). Puberty and olfactory preferences of males. *Physiology & Behavior, 30*, 591–597.

Laing, D.G. & Mackay-Sim, A. (1975). Olfactory adaptation in the rat. In D.A. Denton & J.P. Coghlan (Eds.), *Olfaction and taste V* (pp. 291–295). New York: Academic Press.

Laing, D.G. & Panhuber, H. (1978). Neural and behavioral changes in rats following continuous exposure to an odor. *Journal of Comparative Physiology, 124*, 259–265.

Laing, D.G. & Panhuber, H. (1980). Olfactory sensitivity of rats reared in an odorous or deodorized environment. *Physiology & Behavior, 25*, 555–558.

Laing, D.G., Panhuber, H., Wilcox, M.E., & Pittmann, E.A. (1984). Quality and intensity of binary odor mixtures. *Physiology & Behavior, 33*, 309–319.

Laing, D.G. & Willcox, M.E. (1983). Perception of components in binary odor mixtures. *Chemical Senses, 7*, 249–264.

Lancet, D., Greer, C.A., Kauer, J.S., & Shepherd, G.M. (1982). Mapping of odor-related neuronal activity in the olfactory bulb by high-resolution 2-deoxyglucose autoradiography. *Proceedings of the National Academy of Sciences, 79*, 670–674.

Land, L.J. & Shepherd, G.M. (1974). Autoradiographic analysis of olfactory receptor projections in the rabbit. *Brain Research, 70*, 506–510.

Lawless, H.T. (1977). The pleasantness of mixtures in taste and olfaction. *Sensory Processes, 1*, 227–237.

Lawless, H.T. (1978). Recognition of common odors, pictures, and simple shapes. *Perception & Psychophysics, 24*, 493–495.

Lawless, H.T. & Cain, W.S. (1975). Recognition memory for odors. *Chemical Senses and Flavor, 1*, 331–337.

Leveteau, J. & MacLeod, P. (1969). Reciprocal inhibition at glomerular level during bilateral olfactory stimulation. In C. Pfaffmann (Ed.), *Olfaction and taste: Proceedings of the third international symposium* (pp. 212–215). New York: Rockefeller University Press.

Mackay-Sim, A., Shaman, P., & Moulton, D.G. (1982). Topographic coding of olfactory quality: Odorant-specific patterns of epithelial responsivity in the salamander. *Journal of Neurophysiology, 48*, 584–596.

Mair, R.G. (1982). Adaptation of rat olfactory bulb neurones. *Journal of Physiology, 236*, 361–369.

Margolis, F.L. (1977). Biochemical studies of the primary olfactory pathway. In J.A. Ferrendelli (Ed.), *Society for neuroscience symposia: Vol. 3: Aspects of behavioral neurobiology* (pp. 167–188). Bethesda, MD: Society for Neuroscience.

Marshall, D.A. & Moulton, D.G. (1981). Olfactory sensitivity to α-ionone in humans and dogs. *Chemical Senses, 6*, 53–61.

Menco, B.Ph.M., Laing, D.G., & Panhuber, H. (1980). Strain- or sample-dependent variations in intramembranous particle densities using freeze-fracturing on aldehyde-fixed, cryoprotected olfactory and nasal respiratory epithelium surface structures of the rat. In H. van der Starre (Ed.), *Olfaction and taste VII* (p. 93). London: IRL Press.

Meredith, M. & Burghardt, G.M. (1978). Electrophysiological studies of the tongue and accessory olfactory bulb in garter snakes. *Physiology & Behavior*, *21*, 1001–1008.

Meredith, M. & O'Connell, R.J. (1979). Efferent control of stimulus access to the hamster vomeronasal organ. *Journal of Physiology*, *286*, 301–316.

Moncrieff, R.W. (1967). *The chemical senses* (3rd ed.). London: Leonard Hill.

Moran, D.T. & Rowley, J.C., III. (1983). The structure and function of sensory cilia. *Journal of Submicroscopic Cytology*, *15*, 157–162.

Moskowitz, H.R. (1977). Intensity and hedonic functions for chemosensory stimuli. In M.R. Kare & O. Maller (Eds.), *The chemical senses and nutrition* (pp. 71–101). New York: Academic Press.

Moskowitz, H.R. & Barbe, C.D. (1977). Profiling of odor components and their mixtures. *Sensory Processes*, *1*, 212–226.

Moulton, D.G. (1960). Studies in olfactory acuity. III. Relative detectability of n-aliphatic acetates by the rat. *Quarterly Journal of Experimental Psychology*, *12*, 203–213.

Moulton, D.G. (1975). Cell renewal in the olfactory epithelium of the mouse. In D.A. Denton & J.P. Coghlan (Eds.), *Olfaction and taste V* (pp. 111–114). New York: Academic Press.

Moulton, D.G. (1976). Spatial patterning of response to odors in the peripheral olfactory system. *Physiological Reviews*, *56*, 578–593.

Moulton, D.G. & Eayrs, J.T. (1960). Studies in olfactory acuity. II. Relative detectability of n-aliphatic alcohols by the rat. *Quarterly Journal of Experimental Psychology*, *12*, 99–109.

Moulton, D.G. & Marshall, D.A. (1976). The performance of dogs in detecting α-ionone in the vapor phase. *Journal of Comparative Physiology*, *110*, 287–306.

Mowrer, G.D., Mair, R.G., & Engen, T. (1977). Influence of internal factors on the perceived intensity and pleasantness of gustatory and olfactory stimuli. In M.R. Kare & O. Maller (Eds.), *The chemical senses and nutrition* (pp. 103–121). New York: Academic Press.

Mozell, M.M. (1962). Olfactory mucosal and neural responses in the frog. *American Journal of Physiology*, *203*, 353–358.

Mozell, M.M. (1964). Olfactory discrimination: Electrophysiological spatiotemporal basis. *Science*, *143*, 1336–1337.

Mozell, M.M. & Jagodowicz, M. (1974). Mechanisms underlying the analysis of odorant quality. *Annals of the New York Academy of Sciences*, *237*, 76–90.

Mozell, M.M. Sheehe, P.R., Swieck, S.W., Jr., Kurtz, D.B., & Hornung, D.E. (1984). A parametric study of the stimulation variables affecting the magnitude of the olfactory nerve response. *Journal of General Physiology*, *83*, 233–267.

Murphy, C.L. & Cain, W.S. (1980). Taste and olfaction: Independence versus interaction. *Physiology and Behavior*, *24*, 601–605.

Murphy, C.L., Cain, W.S., & Bartoshuk, L.M. (1977). Mutual action of taste and olfaction. *Sensory Processes*, *1*, 204–211.

Nowlis, G.H., Frank, M.E., & Pfaffmann, C. (1980). Specificity of acquired aversions to taste qualities in hamsters and rats. *Journal of Comparative and Physiological Psychology*, *94*, 932–942.

Ohloff, G. (1982). The fragrance of ambergris. In E.T. Theimer (Ed.), *Fragrance chemistry: The science of the sense of smell* (pp. 535–573). Academic Press: New York.

Ottoson, D. (1956). Analysis of the electrical activity of the olfactory epithelium. *Acta Physiologica Scandinavica*, *35* (Suppl. 122).

Ottoson, D. (1958). Studies on the relationship between olfactory stimulating effectiveness and physicochemical properties of odorous compounds. *Acta Physiologica Scandinavica*, *43*, 167–181.

Ottoson, D. (1970). Electrical signs of olfactory transducer action. In G.E.W. Wolstenholme & J. Knight (Eds.), *Taste and smell in vertebrates* (pp. 343–356). London: Churchill.

Ottoson, D. & Shepherd, G.M. (1967). Experiments and concepts in olfactory physiology. In Y. Zotterman (Ed.), *Progress in brain research* (pp. 83–138). Amsterdam: Elsevier.

Pager, J. (1977a). Nutritional states, food odors, and olfactory function. In M.R. Kare & O. Maller (Eds.), *The chemical senses and nutrition* (pp. 51–68). New York: Academic Press.

Pager, J. (1977b). The regulatory food intake behavior: Some olfactory central correlates. In J. LeMagnen & P. MacLeod (Eds.). *Olfaction and taste VI* (pp. 135–142). London: Information Retrieval.

Patte, F., Etcheto, M., & Laffort, P. (1975). Selected and standardized values of suprathreshold odor intensities for 110 substances. *Chemical Senses and Flavor*, *1*, 283–305.

Pedersen, P.A. & Blass, E.M. (1982). Prenatal and postnatal determinants of the first suckling episode in albino rats. *Developmental Psychobiology*, *15*, 349–355.

Pinching, A.J. & Døving, K.B. (1974). Selective degeneration in the rat olfactory bulb following exposure to different odours. *Brain Research*, *82*, 195–204.

Polak, E.H. (1973). Multiple profile-multiple receptor site model for vertebrate olfaction. *Journal of Theoretical Biology*, *40*, 469–484.

Price, S. (1984). Mechanisms of stimulation of olfactory neurons: An essay. *Chemical Senses*, *8*, 341–354.

Punter, P.H. (1983). Measurement of human olfactory thresholds for several groups of structurally related compounds. *Chemical Senses*, *7*, 215–235.

Rabin, M.D. & Cain, W.S. (1984). Odor recognition: Familiarity, identifiability, and encoding consistency. *Journal of Experimental Psychology: Learning, Memory, and Cognition*, *10*, 316–325.

Rasmussen, L.E., Schmidt, M.J., Henneous, R., Groves, D., & Daves, G.D., Jr. (1982). Asian bull elephants: Flehmen-like responses to extractable components in female elephant estrous urine. *Science*, *217*, 159–162.

Revial, M.F., Duchamp, A., & Holley, A. (1978). Odour discrimination by frog olfactory receptors: A second study. *Chemical Senses and Flavor*, *3*, 7–21.

Revial, M.F., Sicard, G., Duchamp, A., & Holley, A. (1982). New studies on odour discrimination in the frog's olfactory receptor cells. I. Experimental results. *Chemical Senses*, *7*, 175–190.

Revial, M.F., Sicard, G., Duchamp, A., & Holley, A. (1983). New studies on odour discrimination in the frog's olfactory receptor cells. II. Mathematical analysis in electrophysiological responses. *Chemical Senses*, *8*, 179–194.

Roelofs, W.L., Hill, A.S., Linn, C.E., Meinwald, J., Jain, S.C., Herbert, H.J., & Smith, R.F. (1982). Sex pheromone of the winter moth, a geometrid with unusually low temperature precopulatory responses. *Science*, *217*, 657–658.

Rudy, J.W. & Cheatle, M.D. (1977). Odor-aversion learning in neonatal rats. *Science*, *198*, 845–846.

Schafer, R. & Brower, K.R. (1975). Psychophysical recognition of functional groups on odorant molecules. In D.A. Denton & J.P. Coghlan (Eds.), *Olfaction and taste V* (pp. 313–316). New York: Academic Press.

Schafer, R., Criswell, D.W., Fracek, S.P., Jr., & Brower, K.R. (1984). Olfactory studies using ethyl bromoacetate and other chemically active odorants. *Chemical Senses*, *9*, 31–52.

Schemper, T., Voss, S., & Cain, W.S. (1981). Odor identification in young and elderly persons: Sensory and cognitive limitations. *Journal of Gerontology*, *36*, 446–452.

Schiffman, S.S. (1974). Contributions to the physicochemical dimensions of odor: A psychophysical approach. *Annals of the New York Academy of Sciences*, *237*, 164–183.

Schiffman, S. (1977). Food recognition by the elderly. *Journal of Gerontology*, *32*, 586–592.

Schiffman, S. & Leffingwell, J.C. (1981). Perception of odors and simple pyrazines by young and elderly subjects: A multidimensional analysis. *Pharmacology, Biochemistry, and Behavior*, *14*, 787–798.

Schiffman, S.S., Reynolds, M.L., & Young, F.W. (1981). *Introduction to multidimensional scaling*. New York: Academic Press.

Schmidt, U. (1978). Evoked-potential measurement of olfactory thresholds of laboratory mice (Mus musculus) to carboxylic acids. *Chemical Senses and Flavour*, *3*, 177–182.

Schneider, D. (1969). Insect olfaction: Deciphering system for chemical messages. *Science*, *163*, 1031–1037.

Schneider, R.A. & Schmidt, C.E. (1967). Dependency of olfactory localization on non-olfactory cues. *Physiology and Behavior*, *2*, 305–309.

Sharp, F.R., Kauer, J.S., & Shepherd, G.M. (1977). Laminar analysis of 2-deoxyglucose uptake in olfactory bulb and olfactory cortex of rabbit and rat. *Journal of Neurophysiology*, *40*, 800–813.

Shepherd, G.M. (1972). Synaptic organization of the mammalian olfactory bulb. *Physiological Reviews*, *52*, 864–917.

Shibuya, T. (1964). Dissociation of olfactory neural response and mucosal potential. *Science*, *143*, 1338–1339.

Shorey, H.H. (1976). *Animal communication by pheromones*. New York: Academic Press.

Steiner, J.E. (1974). Discussion paper: Innate, discriminative human facial expressions to taste and smell stimulation. *Annals of the New York Academy of Sciences*, *237*, 229–233.

Stewart, W.B., Kauer, J.S., & Shepherd, G.M. (1979). Functional organization of rat olfactory bulb analysed by the 2-deoxyglucose method. *Journal of Comparative Neurology*, *185*, 715–734.

Stone, H. (1964). Behavioral aspects of absolute and differential olfactory sensitivity. *Annals of the New York Academy of Sciences*, *116*, 527–534.

Stuiver, M. (1958). *Biophysics of the sense of smell*. The Hague: Excelsior.

Suzuki, A., Mori, M., Sakagami, Y., Isogai, A., Fujino, M., Kitada, C., Craig, R.A., & Clewell, D.B. (1984). Isolation and structure of bacterial sex pheromone, cPDI. *Science*, *226*, 849–850.

Swan, J.S. & Burtles, S.M. (1980). Quality control of flavour by the use of integrated sensory analytical methods at various stages of Scotch whisky production. In H. van der Starre (Ed.), *Olfaction and taste VII* (pp. 451–452). London: IRL Press.

Takagi, S.F. (1980). Dual nervous systems for olfactory functions in mammals. In H. van der Starre (Ed.), *Olfaction and taste VII* (pp. 275–278). London: IRL Press.

Tanabe, T., Iino, M., Oshima, Y., & Takagi, S. (1975). Neurophysiological studies on the prefrontal olfactory center in the monkey. In D.A. Denton & J.P. Coghlan (Eds.), *Olfaction and taste V* (pp. 309–312). New York: Academic Press.

van As, W., Smit, J.G.J., & Köster, E.P. (1980). Effects of long-term odour exposure on mitral cells of the olfactory bulb in rats. In H. van der Starre (Ed.), *Olfaction and taste VII* (p. 296). London: IRL Press.

van Gemert, L.J. & Nettenbreijer, A.H. (Eds.) (1977). *Compilation of odour threshold values in air and water*. Voorburg, Netherlands: National Institute for Water Supply.

Vinnikov, Y.A. (1975). The evolution of olfaction and taste. In D.A. Denton & J.P. Coghlan (Eds.), *Olfaction and taste V* (pp. 175–187). New York: Academic Press.

Wells, F.L. (1929). Reaction times to affects accompanying smell stimuli. *American Journal of Psychology, 41*, 83–86.

Wright, R.H. (1954). Odour and chemical constitution. *Nature, 173*, 831.

Wright, R.H. (1964). *The science of smell*. New York: Basic Books.

Wright, R.H. (1976). Odour and molecular vibration: A possible membrane interaction mechanism. *Chemical Senses and Flavor, 2*, 203–206.

Wright, R.H. (1981). Odor and molecular vibration: Redundancy in the olfactory code. In H.R. Moskowitz & C. Warren (Eds.), *Odor quality and intensity as a function of chemical structure* (pp. 123–141). Washington DC: American Chemical Society.

Wright, R.H. (1982). *The sense of smell*. Boca Raton, FL: CRC Press.

Wysocki, C.J. (1979). Neurobehavioral evidence of the involvement of the vomeronasal system in mammalian reproduction. *Neuroscience & Biobehavioral Reviews, 3*, 301–341.

Wysocki, C.J. & Beauchamp, G.K. (1984). Ability to smell androstenone is genetically determined. *Proceedings of the National Academy of Sciences, 81*, 4599–4902.

Wysocki, C.J. & Meredith, M. (1987). The vomeronasal system. In T.E. Finger & W.L. Silver (Eds.), *Neurobiology of taste and smell* (pp. 125–150). New York: Wiley.

Yoshida, M. (1975). Psychometric classification of odors. *Chemical Senses and Flavor, 1*, 443–464.

Zwaardemaker, H. (1895). *Die Physiologie des Geruchs (The physiology of smell)*. Leipzig: Engelmann.

Zwaardemaker, H. (1925). *L'Odorat (The sense of smell)*. Paris: Doin.

TASTE

Linda M. Bartoshuk, *John B. Pierce Foundation Laboratory and Yale University*

TASTE ANATOMY AND PHYSIOLOGY

Papillae

The human tongue gets its bumpy appearance from four kinds of small papillae embedded in its surface. Taste buds are found in the surface epithelium of three of the four kinds of papillae. The fourth kind, filiform papillae, are distributed the most widely over the tongue surface and contain no taste buds. The fungiform papillae (named after the button mushrooms they resemble) appear primarily on the tip and along the edges of the front of the tongue. The foliate papillae consist of a set of parallel folds on the rear edges of the tongue. The circumvallate papillae, flat mounds surrounded by trenches, form an inverted V on the rear of the tongue. Taste buds are buried in the surfaces of the fungiform and foliate papillae and are buried in the tissues that form the inner surfaces of the trench surrounding the circumvallate papillae. These three papillae show variation across species but are found in all mammals (Bradley, 1971).

The number of taste buds in a papilla varies with the type of papilla and the species. A single human fungiform papilla has been observed to contain as many as 27 taste buds (Arvidson, 1979, 1980). Those of sheep contain up to 8 and those of rat contain 1 each (Mistretta, 1981). Figure 9.1 shows a single human fungiform papilla. The openings into three taste buds are visible.

Taste buds are also found on the soft palate (the soft part of the roof of the mouth), the pharynx (throat), the larynx, the esophagus, and the laryngeal surface of the epiglottis, which closes off the larynx to prevent food and fluids from entering the lungs during swallowing (Bradley, 1971). The function of these latter taste buds is intriguing since they face the lungs during swallowing and would not normally be stimulated by food. If these receptors are stimulated with water in the lamb, a sudden cessation of breathing (i.e., apnea) results (Storey & Johnson, 1975). This apnea may be involved in Sudden Infant Death Syndrome (SIDS). If this is so, then taste buds can have quite different functions in different loci (Bradley, Cheal, & Kim, 1980).

Taste Buds

The taste bud is a globular cluster of cells arranged something like the segments of an orange (see Figure 9.2). The opening through these cells, linking the taste bud to the tongue

461

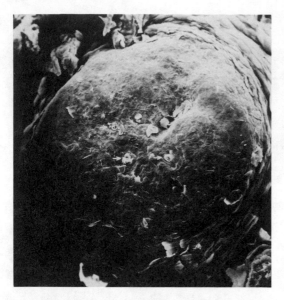

Figure 9.1. Scanning electron micrograph of the top of a human fungiform papilla. The openings of three taste buds are visible. The tissue was fixed in formaldehyde. SEM, × 220. From "Scanning Electron Microscopy of Fungiform Papillae on the Tongue of Man and Monkey" by K. Arvidson, 1976, *Acta Otolaryngol.*, *81*, p. 498. Copyright 1976 by Acta Otolaryngol. Reprinted by permission.

surface, is called the taste pore. The tops of some cells in the taste bud taper to a thin extension of the cell membrane and project into the taste pore.

The cells in the taste bud are not all identical. By electron microscopy some of them appear darker than others because they have electron-dense cytoplasm. This led to a light cell–dark cell distinction. Morphological characteristics have also been used to differentiate the cells.

Some investigators (e.g., Delay, Kinnamon, & Roper, 1983) believe that the variations reflect developmental stages of a single cell type. Others (e.g., Farbman, Hellekant, & Nelson, 1985; Murray, 1973) argue that there are distinct cell types. The types suggested by Murray (as studied in rabbit foliate papillae) are illustrated in Figure 9.2. In this view, the type 3 cell is believed to be the taste receptor cell since it synapses with taste neurons.

Kinnamon and his colleagues (Kinnamon, Taylor, Delay, & Roper, 1985) have used computer generated three-dimensional reconstructions of serial sections to study the nature of

synapses in mouse taste buds (see Figure 9.3). Some synapses were flat (e.g., S_1 and S_2) while others (finger-like) projected into the taste cell (e.g., top of S_3). In this study the synapses were not associated with any particular cell type. Resolution of these issues will be critical to an understanding of peripheral processing in taste.

The cells making up the taste bud have limited life spans. Radioactive labeling shows that they die and are replaced by new cells (Beidler & Smallman, 1965). Farbman (1980) found that rat taste bud cells could be divided into two groups. One group had a life span of about 9 days while the second group lived significantly longer. As a cell goes through its life cycle, it appears to move from the edge to the center of the taste bud. Since the nerve fibers do not move, receptor cells are presumably innervated by different nerve fibers as they change location. This poses a problem for stable quality perception. The population of receptor cells that synapse with a single fiber at various times should have the same sensitivities in order to ensure that a given stimulus always evokes the same neural signal.

Taste buds remain even when the nerve is cut although they need innervation to achieve their mature form (Whitehead, Frank, Hettinger, Hou, & Nah, 1987). In the rat, Oakley (1967) cut the chorda tympani nerve which innervates the front of the tongue and the glossopharyngeal nerve which innervates the back of the tongue and then crossed them. Each nerve regrew into the area previously innervated by the other nerve. After cross-regeneration was complete, the nerves had exchanged sensitivities. That is, each nerve had come to show the sensitivity characteristic of the new tongue area in which it was located. This might mean that the sensitivities of the taste buds survive the changes resulting from denervation. Yet the specific tissue innervated cannot be the sole determinant of the sensitivities of a neuron because the sensitivities of each of the individual tongue areas innervated by branches from a single neuron seem to be remarkably similar (Oakley, 1975). This suggests that a neuron might select receptor cells from those available so as to insure that it always connects to receptor cells of equivalent sensitivities.

In sheep, as in humans, taste buds develop in utero. This makes the sheep an excellent species for the study of the early development of the taste bud. Bradley and Mistretta (1975) pioneered

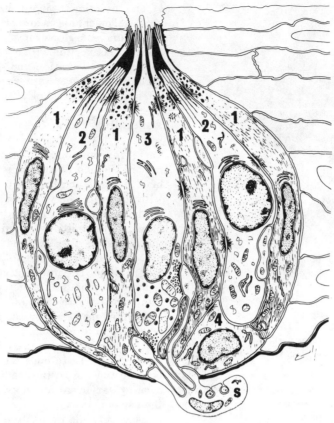

Figure 9.2. Longitudinal section through a taste bud from a rabbit foliate papilla. Type 3 cells form synapses with neurons (n) and may be the taste receptor cells. Type 1 cells may have a supportive function. The function of type 2 cells is unknown but their extensive contact with nerve fibers suggests the possibility that they may play a role in the generation of neural signals. Type 4 cells may provide replacement cells. A Schwann cell(s) surrounds the neuron synapsing with the type 3 cell. From "The Ultrastructure of Sensory Organs" by R. G. Murray, 1973, in *The Ultrastructure of Sensory Organs* (p. 43), I. Friedmann (ed.), New York: Elsevier North Holland Publishing Co. Copyright 1973 by Elsevier Science Publishers B.V. (Biomedical Division). Reprinted by permission.

the procedures for recording from taste nerves and the taste central nervous system (CNS) of fetal sheep. They found an important taste change that correlated with development (see Mistretta, 1981, for a review). Neurons in younger fetuses were less responsive to NaCl. Rats showed a similar developmental change but it occurred postnatally. Such changes raise the issue of plasticity in the taste system.

The early development of taste buds suggests that the fetus may taste substances in amniotic fluid. This is especially important for the evaluation of the effects of early experience on taste preferences. At birth, an organism already may have had a considerable amount of taste experience (Bradley & Mistretta, 1973).

Peripheral Integration in Taste

Taste fibers branch several times before innervating taste receptor cells so that a single neuron can innervate more than one receptor cell, (Beidler, 1961). The branching pattern provides a possible mechanism for lateral interactions in taste. When a taste receptor cell is stimulated, impulses are sent toward the CNS. When these impulses reach a branch point, they travel antidromically back along the other branches toward the receptor cell as well as on toward the CNS. The antidromic impulses inhibit the receptor cells innervated by those branches (Filin & Esakov, 1968; Rapuzzi & Casella, 1965). A second mechanism for peripheral integration in taste

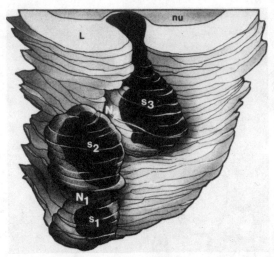

Figure 9.3. Computer generated three-dimensional reconstruction of synaptic complexes (S_1, S_2, and S_3) between neurons (N_1, and N_2) and a light cell (L). From "Ultrastructure of Mouse Vallate Taste Buds: I. Tase Cells and Their Associated Synapses" by J. C. Kinnamon, B. J. Taylor, R. J. Delay, and S. D. Roper, 1985, *Journal of Comparative Neurology*, p. 58. Copyright 1985 by Alan R. Liss Inc. Publishers. Reprinted by permission.

involves summation of generator potentials along unmyelinated terminals of single taste nerve fibers (Miller, 1971).

The functional significance of these two potential mechanisms for peripheral integration is still unclear. However, they have been mentioned in connection with quality coding (Miller, 1971), cross-adaptation and enhancement (Bernard, 1971; Wang & Bernard, 1969), and mixture interactions (Bartoshuk, 1975; Wang, 1983).

Ascending Taste System

Taste information is transmitted via three nerves: the chorda tympani and greater superficial petrosal (both branches of the facial or VIIth cranial nerve), the glossopharyngeal (IXth cranial nerve), and the vagus (Xth cranial nerve). The chorda tympani nerve innervates the fungiform papillae and the glossopharyngeal nerve innervates the foliate and circumvallate papillae. The innervation of the taste buds found on other oral structures is not as well established. Taste buds on the soft palate are innervated primarily by the greater superficial petrosal nerve although the glossopharyngeal and vagus nerves may also play a role (Cleaton-Jones, 1976). Taste buds on the laryngeal surface of the epiglottis are innervated by the superior laryngeal nerve (which is a branch of the vagus nerve).

The central projections (primarily ipso-

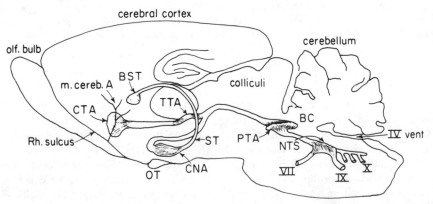

Figure 9.4. Projections of taste in the central nervous system of the rat. NTS, nucleus of the solitary tract; PTA, pontine taste area; BC, brachium conjunctivum; TTA, thalamic taste area; CTA, cortical taste area; CNA, central nucleus of the amygdala; ST, stria terminalis; BST, bed nucleus of the stria terminalis; OT, optic tract; IV vent., fourth ventricle; VII, IX, X, seventh, ninth, and tenth cranial nerves; RH. sulcus, rhinal sulcus; m. cereb. A., middle cerebral artery. From "A Synposis of Gustatory Neuroanatomy" by R. Norgren, 1977, in *Olfaction and Taste, VI* (p. 229), J. LaMagnen (ed.), New York: Information Retrieval, Ltd., Copyright 1977 by IRL Press, Ltd. Reprinted by permission.

lateral) of the rat taste system are shown in Figure 9.4 (see Norgren, 1984, and Hamilton & Norgren, 1984). The three nerves mediating taste project to the solitary nucleus of the medulla (NTS in Figure 9.4). Although the areas to which they project overlap to some extent, the two branches of the facial (VII) nerve, the chorda tympani, and the greater superficial petrossal nerves terminate in the rostral end of the nucleus; the vagus (X) terminates in the caudal end, and the glossopharyngeal (IX), in an area between these two (Burton & Benjamin, 1971; Norgren, 1984).

Some pontine neurons (PTA in Figure 9.4) project to the dorsal thalamus (TTA in Figure 9.4), but others project to the central nucleus of the amygdala (CNA in Figure 9.4), an area that may be important for the regulation of feeding and drinking (Norgren, 1976). Neurons of a third group project to both areas (Norgren, 1974; Norgren & Leonard, 1973).

The thalamic taste area (TTA in Figure 9.4) is located near the tip of the area which responds to tongue touch (Burton & Benjamin, 1971). The small amount of crossing that exists, occurs at this level. The cortical taste area (CTA in Figure 9.4) for the rat has been located in the agranular-insular cortex (Kosar, Norgren, & Grill, 1985).

The central projections in other species are generally similar to those of the rat with two exceptions. Primate taste systems do not synapse at the pons (Beckstead, Morse, & Norgren, 1980; Goto, Yamamoto, Kaneko, & Tomita, 1983), and primates (as well as other species, like cat) have two rather than one cortical taste area (Burton & Benjamin, 1971; Ganchrow & Erickson, 1972). One of these is in the tongue portion of the somatotopic projection of the body surface in somatic sensory area 1. The second area is in the anterior opercular-insular cortex.

Transduction

Taste *transduction* refers to the initial events in taste: the interactions of stimulus and receptor that ultimately give rise to a neural signal. Before transduction can occur, the taste stimulus must get to the receptor membrane. This involves the physics of convection (e.g., flowing the stimulus to the vicinity of the receptor molecules) and diffusion (DeSimone & Heck, 1980). The properties of the actual interactions between receptor and stimulus molecules are elusive because they must be studied indirectly. Stimulus molecules are believed to interact with molecules in the membranes of the parts of the receptor cells that project into the taste pore; these reactive molecules are called *receptor sites*. However, even the locus of the stimulus–receptor interaction has been questioned for some bitter stimuli.

The specificity of the stimulus–receptor interaction is obviously important for quality perception. A variety of models have been proposed to explain the selectivity of receptors (DeSimone & Price, 1976, for a comprehensive review). Models of the stimulus–receptor interaction tend to be based on physical or chemical characteristics that are common to stimuli with similar taste qualities. Since human taste experience is usually described as salty, sour, sweet, and bitter, most models have been constructed to deal with classes of substances which have one of these qualities in common.

Salty

The salty taste is produced primarily by inorganic salts dissolved in water to produce a solution of positive ions (cations) and negative ions (anions). The salt with the purest salty taste is sodium chloride (NaCl). Other salts tend to taste sour, bitter, or sweet as well as salty. The tastes of a variety of these salts can be duplicated by a mixture of NaCl, quinine hydrochloride, tartaric acid, and glucose (von Skramlik, 1922). In general, as the anion and cation get larger, salts taste increasingly bitter (Moncrieff, 1967). One salt, monosodium glutamate, is sometimes said to have a taste quality that cannot be described by sweet, salty, sour, and bitter. Salts of some other amino acids (monosodium glutamate is the sodium salt of glutamic acid), as well as the amino acids themselves, produce unusually persistent tastes as well as nontaste sensations (e.g., tactile sensations). Whether or not the taste quality itself is unique is unclear.

About a decade after the discovery that strong acids and salts dissociate into cations and anions in water (Arrhenius, 1887), two laboratories published studies on the origin of the salty taste (Höber & Kiesow, 1898; Kahlenberg, 1898). Both pursued the same kind of logic: they compared the saltiness of equimolar concentrations of salts with different anions. For example, .04 M NaCl is slightly salty but .04 M Na acetate is essentially tasteless. Since the two solutions contain equal numbers of sodium cations, differences in saltiness would seem to be due to the anions. Thus investigators of that day concluded that the chloride anion must be the source of saltiness.

The work of Beidler uncovered a logical flaw in this argument. The nineteenth century scientists had not considered the possibility of inhibitory effects of ions on taste. Beidler (1954, 1967) argued that cations are excitatory and anions inhibitory in taste. Thus, saltiness is produced by the sodium cation of NaCl. Anions vary in their inhibitory power; large anions tend to produce more inhibition than small anions. Since acetate is a larger anion than chloride, sodium acetate is less salty than sodium chloride.

Although the entire physiological sequence of events leading to saltiness is not known, recent work on the physical chemistry of the taste membrane suggests the following possible events (DeSimone & Price, 1976; Heck, Mierson, & DeSimone, 1984). The taste receptor membrane sensitive to NaCl is seen as a phospholipid layer with a negative surface charge. When positively charged cations (e.g., Na^+) are attracted to the membrane, they neutralize the charge. This causes a local change in the surface tension (normally maintained by the mutual repulsion of the negatively charged phospholipid molecules). Ultimately, ion channels that selectively admit sodium ions are opened. This view is supported by the observation that amiloride, which blocks sodium channels, reduces reponses to NaCl in dog (DeSimone, Heck, & DeSimone, 1981), rat, and man (DeSimone, Heck, Mierson, & DeSimone, 1984; Schiffman, Lockhead, & Maes, 1983). The human data are especially noteworthy because the taste of KCl was reported to be unaffected. This leads to the conclusion that the salty tastes of NaCl and KCl are mediated by different receptor mechanisms, a conclusion that conflicts with the results of cross-adaptation studies to be discussed later.

Anions can have tastes of their own in addition to any possible effects they may have on the action of cations. For example, the sweet taste of Na saccharin results from interactions between the saccharin anion and the sweet receptor site. Thus, the taste of a salt depends on its ability to stimulate all taste receptors and not just those sensitive to cations.

Sour

The sour taste has long been believed to result from the dissociated hydrogen ion (H^+) in acids (Beidler, 1967). Acids do not all dissociate to an equal extent. One puzzle concerning acids is that weak organic acids (e.g., acetic acid) tend to taste more sour than strong acids (e.g., HCl) of the same pH. Boudreau and Nelson (1977) suggested that this puzzle would be solved if the sour taste were to result from proton donating molecules. Boudreau and Nelson argue that the undissociated molecules of weak acids are proton donors and thus are sour.

The anions of acids and/or the undissociated molecules can apparently stimulate sweet and bitter tastes just as the anions of salts can. For example, saccharin is available in soluble or insoluble form. The soluble saccharin is the sodium salt of saccharin and the insoluble saccharin is the acid containing the saccharin anion. Both forms are sweet. Another example, picric acid, is bitter. This probably results from the presence of NO_2 groups in the anion of picric acid that produce a bitter taste intense enough to suppress the sour taste of the acid (Moncrief, 1967).

Sweet

The prototypical sweet stimuli are the sugars sucrose (common table sugar), glucose (blood sugar), and fructose. Fructose and glucose are monosaccharides (e.g., simple molecules made up of multiples of the CH_2O group). Sucrose is a disaccharide made up of the monosaccharides fructose and glucose. A few inorganic compounds are sweet (e.g., beryllium chloride), but sweetness is associated more typically with organic compounds. A variety of these are well known because they have been or are in use as nonnutritive sweeteners. These include dulcin (ultimately discovered to be toxic), cyclamate salts (now banned in the U.S. but legal in Canada), saccharine salts (now banned in Canada but legal in the U.S.), neohesperidine and naringen dihydrochalocone (derived from citrus fruits by scientists of the USDA), and aspartame (a dipeptide only recently approved by FDA).

Shallenberger and Acree (1967) identified an AH, B system common to many sweet substances. AH refers to an electronegative atom A, like oxygen or nitrogen, convalently bonded to a hydrogen atom, H, and B refers to a second

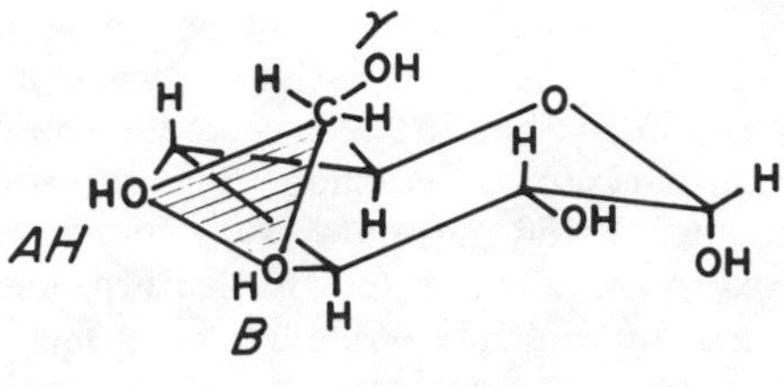

D-GLUCOSE

Figure 9.5. D-glucose in the "chair" conformation. The AH, B, γ triangle is shaded. From "Chemical Clues to the Perception of Sweetness" by R. S. Shallenberger, 1977, in *Sensory Properties of Foods*, G. G. Birch, J. C. Brennan, and K. J. Parker (eds.), London: Applied Science Publishers. Adapted by permission.

electronegative atom (or an electronegative center; see Shallenberger and Acree, 1971, for details). AH and B must be separated by about 3 Å. For sugars, the AH, B system consists of two OH units positioned so that one OH could be the AH group, and the oxygen atom of the other OH group could be B. A third binding site (Kier, 1972; Shallenberger & Lindley, 1977) transformed the bipartite AH, B system into an AH, B, γ triangle (see Figure 9.5).

The possibility that sweet substances all share a common structure suggests that the receptor site for sweet might be a complementary structure (Shallenberger & Acree, 1971). However, there are several lines of evidence that suggest that more than one type of receptor is required to account for sweetness. One line of evidence comes from recordings from taste nerves. If the sweetnesses of all sugars were mediated by a single receptor type, then all sweet-sensitive neurons would order sugars the same way. Yet in the squirrel monkey, some neurons are more sensitive to sucrose than fructose and some are the reverse (Pfaffmann, 1969; Pfaffmann, Frank, Bartoshuk, & Snell, 1976). Another argument notes that if the sweetness of sucrose and saccharin were mediated by a single receptor type, then mixtures of the two would be equivalent to higher concentrations of either sweetener. Jakinovich (1982) showed that in the gerbil, this is not the case. Rather, the mixtures produced larger responses than they would have if the components had been effectively the same sweet stimulus.

In the rat, Zawalich (1973) reversibly inhibited neural responses to glucose by treating the tongue with alloxan, a compound that induces

diabetes by destroying beta cells in the pancreas. Alloxan did not affect the response to sodium saccharin. This suggests that in the rat as well as the gerbil, saccharin does not stimulate the same receptors as sugars do.

Dastoli and Price (1966) were the first to isolate a protein fraction from cow tongues that complexed with sugars. The identification of protein as a part of the receptor for sweet is supported by studies using certain proteolytic enzymes (substances that digest proteins). For example, Hiji (1975) applied Pronase E to rat and human tongues. In the rat the neural response to sucrose was suppressed but those to NaCl, HCl, and QHCl were unaffected. In human subjects, the threshold for sucrose was elevated and those for NaCl, HCl, and QHCl were unaffected.

Species differences with regard to the effectiveness of sweeteners are consistent with the idea that sweet receptors are not identical across species. For example, Hellekant (1976) showed that hamsters, pigs, and rabbits are not responsive to monellin (a protein, sweet to humans, from the African plant *Dioscoreophyllum Cumminsii*) and thaumatin (a protein, sweet to humans, from the African plant *Thaumatococcus danielli*), and Jackinovich (1981) showed that gerbils are not responsive to dihydrochalcone.

Gymnema sylvestre, the Indian herb that suppresses sweetness in human subjects, is not effective on most other mammals (see detailed discussion below). This difference also supports the idea that sweet receptors are not identical across species. Similarly, miracle fruit, which induces sweet taste in human subjects (see below) also fails on most other mammals. One limitation of interpreting species differences with modifiers as evidence that sweet receptors differ across mammals is that the mechanisms of these modifiers may involve more than simple competition with sweet sites.

Jakinovich (1983) and Jakinovich and Ulahopoulos (1984) discovered compounds that compete with sucrose for receptor sites. These compounds do not stimulate a sweet taste themselves but when mixed with sucrose, prevent the sucrose response. These sweet inhibitors offer a new and very important tool for the study of sweet receptor mechanisms. If inhibitors with different structures prove to be differentially effective across species or across sweeteners within a species, then these inhibitors will not only provide powerful evidence for multiple sweet receptor mechanisms but will also help elucidate the nature of those receptor mechanisms.

Cross-adaptation studies provide evidence for multiple sweet receptor mechanisms in human subjects. McBurney (1972) was the first to show that adapting to sucrose, also cross-adapted a variety of other sweeteners including other sugars (e.g., fructose and glucose) as well as artificial sweeteners (e.g., saccharin and cyclamate). Adapting to saccharin produced less cross-adaptation among the same group of sweeteners. However, McBurney noted that while the occurrence of cross-adaptation is evidence for common receptor sites, the absence of cross-adaptation does not necessarily imply multiple receptors because there are a variety of artifacts that are hard to eliminate. For example, if the sweetnesses of the two stimuli are not matched precisely, then adaptation to the weaker will not completely cross-adapt the stronger. In addition, failure to completely adapt to the first stimulus will result in incomplete cross-adaptation of the second. Finally, adaptation to some sweeteners produces a sweet water taste (Van der Wel, 1972) that can add to the second stimulus and produce apparent failures to cross-adapt.

Schiffman, Cahn, and Lindley (1981) examined cross-adaptation among a variety of sugars and artificial sweeteners and concluded that cross-adaptation failed in many cases. They also found cross-enhancement in some cases.

Lawless and Stevens (1983) noted that the study of Schiffman et al. (1981) failed to eliminate some of the artifacts described by McBurney. Lawless and Stevens tested sucrose, dihydrochalcone (DHC), aspartame, and saccharin with an improved experimental design. They found no cases of cross-enhancement but did find some clear failures of cross-adaptation. For example, DHC and saccharin failed to cross-adapt sucrose (although both were cross-adapted by sucrose).

A variety of other psychophysical studies also provide evidence that a single type of receptor site cannot explain all sweetness in human subjects. Van der Wel and Arvidson (1978) noted that the protein sweeteners thaumatin and monellin produced the most sweetness on the lateral edges of the tongue while sucrose did so on the tip of the tongue.

Faurion, Saito, and MacLeod (1980) meas-

ured the thresholds and the slopes of psychophysical functions for a variety of sweeteners. They reasoned that if two sweeteners bind to common receptor sites, then their thresholds and slopes should correlate. They found many failures to correlate which they interpreted as evidence for multiple sweet receptor mechanisms.

The association between the intensity of sweetness of some compounds and genetic status for testing PTC/PROP (see below) provided another kind of evidence for multiple sweets (Gent & Bartoshuk, 1983). Sucrose and DHC, while both sweeter to tasters of PTC/PROP than to nontasters, had significantly different ratios. Sucrose was twice and DHC was three times as sweet to tasters.

Bitter

Bitterness, like sweetness, is produced by some inorganic and a variety of organic compounds. There is no single generalization for bitter substances as inclusive as the AH, B, γ system for sweet substances, however, some observations about the relation between structure and taste are possible.

Alkaloids are found naturally in plants; some examples are caffeine, nicotine, solanine, cocaine, strychnine, and frucine (Shallenberger & Acree, 1971). The toxicity of these substances may have provided environmental pressure that promoted the evolution of the aversion to bitterness found in so many species (Garcia & Hankins, 1975). Species that avoided alkaloids would have had a selective advantage over those that did not.

Glycosides are derived from certain sugars and are also found in plants (Shallenberger & Acree, 1971). Some of the glycosides have been studied in detail to determine the effect of substitutions at various sites on the molecules (Horowitz & Gentili, 1969). These studies are very important to the development of any comprehensive theory of bitterness, however, they have also had a more practical impact. Certain substitutions produce compounds that are intensely sweet at low concentrations and may be useful as nonnutritive sweeteners, such as neohespridine and naringin dihydrochalcone.

Another group of organic compounds found in plants, diterpenes, has also been analyzed for structure-bitterness relations (Kubota & Kubo, 1969). An AH, B system similar to that of Shallenberger was suggested as the common link.

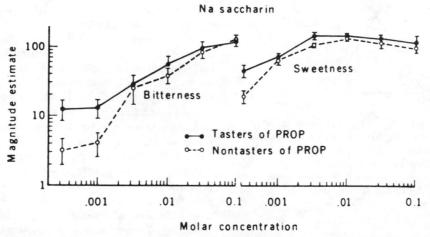

Figure 9.6. Magnitude estimates (± 1 standard error of the mean, SEM) of the bitterness and sweetness of sodium saccharin for tasters and nontasters of PROP. The left-most portions of the bitterness and sweetness functions were significantly different for tasters and nontasters. The concentrations of saccharin once used in diet sodas ranged from .0010 to .0015 M. From "Bitter Taste of Saccharin: Related to the Genetic Ability to Taste the Bitter Substance of 6-*n*-propylthiouracil" by L. M. Bartoshuk, 1979, *Science, 205,* p. 934. Copyright 1979 by the AAAS. Reprinted by permission.

PTC (phenylthiorcarbamide or phenylthiourea) and other compounds containing the H–N–C=S grouping (e.g., 6-*n*-propylthiouracil or PROP) are of special interest because sensitivity to their bitter taste is genetically mediated. That is, an individual with two recessive genes has a high threshold for PTC or PROP leading to the classification *nontaster* or *taste blind* while an individual with one or both dominant genes has a low threshold leading to the classification *taster*. The bitter tastes of some common substances (KCl, caffeine, Na and K benzoate, and saccharin) are associated with PTC/PROP status in a strange way that is not yet understood. These molecules do not contain a chemical group like that contained by PTC or PROP yet they tend to be more bitter to tasters than to nontasters (Bartoshuk, 1979a; Bartoshuk, Rifkin, & Speers, 1980; Hall, Bartoshuk, Cain, & Stevens, 1975; Rifkin & Bartoshuk, 1980). Certain sweet substances tend to taste sweeter to tasters as well (Bartoshuk, 1979a; Gent & Bartoshuk, 1983). Figure 9.6 shows how the taste of saccharin differs for tasters and nontasters of PTC/PROP.

Since there is no overall generalization about properties common to all bitter substances, there can be no general model of the bitter receptor, however some specific hypotheses have been formulated. One suggestion for a

bitter mechanism is especially interesting because it departs from the conventional view that taste receptor sites are located in the receptor membrane. Rather, bitter substances are seen as entering the receptor and affecting intracellular processes (Kurihara & Koyama, 1972; Price, 1973, 1974). The ease with which a compound can enter the cell may be related to its lipid solubility so that those compounds of the greatest lipid solubility would be the most bitter (Kurihara & Koyama, 1972).

The evidence cited above suggests that many sweet molecules and bitter molecules probably contain more than one site that is capable of producing the molecule's characteristic taste. Multiple receptor sites (potentially under independent genetic control) plus multiple stimulus sites even on a single molecule permit a great deal of variability across subjects for the perceptions of sweetness and bitterness.

TASTE PSYCHOPHYSICS AND THE FOUR BASIC TASTES

History

Henning's tetrahedron (1927) (see Figure 9.7) was an early attempt to formalize the four basic tastes. He placed substances that tasted sweet, salty, sour, and bitter at the four corners of the

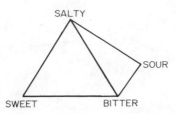

Figure 9.7. Henning's Taste Tetrahedron. Modified from Henning (1927). From "Psychologische studien am Beschmackssinn" by H. Henning, 1927, in *Handbuch der Biologischen Arbeitsmethoder* (p. 34), F. Aberholden (ed.) Berlin: Urban & Schwarzenberg. Copyright (c) 1927 by Urban & Schwarzenberg. Reprinted by permission.

tetrahedron, substances with two taste qualities along the appropriate edge, and those with three taste qualities on a face. He left the tetrahedron hollow because he did not believe that there were any substances that had all four basic tastes. Henning did not intend to place mixtures on the tetrahedron because he did not believe that the tastes of complex substances could be duplicated by a mixture of simple substances. However, Von Skramlik (1922) did duplicate complex tastes with mixtures of the four basic tastes. For example, KCl was duplicated by a mixture of quinine and NaCl. According to Von Skramlik's view, the taste tetrahedron reflected the analytic nature of taste quality: that complex tastes can be analyzed into their component qualities by introspection.

The four basic tastes were accepted by both of the giants in the 19th century world of taste psychophysics, Hjalmar Öhrwall and Friedrich Kiesow, but did not mean quite the same things to them. These two men were educated during an era of explosive development of the physiology and psychology of the senses. Johannes Müller's doctrine of specific nerve energies (1838) and its extensions to individual nerve fibers (Natanson, 1844) led the investigators of that day to look for the units of sensation and the specific receptors that mediated them. Müller's student, Hermann Helmholtz, clarified *modality* and *quality* used as psychological terms. Sensations so different that no transitions exist between them belong to different modalities (e.g., blue, sweet, warm, and high pitched). On the other hand, sensations that can be described as more similar than others (e.g., red and orange are more similar than red and

blue) represent different qualities within one modality (Helmholtz, 1879).

Wundt, credited with founding the first laboratory of experimental psychology in Leipzig, and Holmgren, a physiologist studying color vision, were both students of Helmholtz. Öhrwall, who studied with Holmgren, concluded that no transitions exist between taste qualities and thus there are really four modalities of taste: sweet, salty, sour, and bitter (Öhrwall, 1891, 1901). Kiesow, who studied with Wundt followed a different path: he set out to search for possible analogies between taste quality and color in a systematic way (Kiesow, 1894a, 1894b, 1896). Colored afterimages and color mixing were well known to the group working with Wundt. Kiesow found a taste analogy to colored afterimages: exposing the tongue to a solution of one quality caused solutions of certain other qualities to taste stronger. Kiesow also found an analogy for cancellation of opponent colors. A mixture of weak sucrose and salt lacked both sweetness and saltiness and tasted flat. Öhrwall disputed Kiesow's interpretations of these studies. He compared the independence of the four tastes to the independence of the touch, temperature, and pain senses in the skin. Kiesow's point of view was widely cited in U.S. texts of the early twentieth century, perhaps in part because Wundt trained a number of American psychologists who, with their students, wrote some of the early textbooks. Yet the argument between these two giants in taste research was never resolved. Echoes from it can still be heard in modern arguments about the nature of taste quality.

A dramatic experiment on the physiology of taste changed the course of taste research. Pfaffmann (1941) recorded from single fibers of the chorda tympani taste nerve of the cat. A single fiber responded to more than one of the four basic tastes. The expectation of both Öhrwall and Kiesow that a single nerve fiber would be highly specific to one of the four basic tastes was not confirmed. The emphasis in taste research turned away from the classic psychophysical studies of human taste and toward comparative studies of the taste quality coding made possible by the new electrophysiological recording technique.

The direct scaling methods of S.S. Stevens and his colleagues at Harvard (Stevens, 1958, 1969, 1975) stimulated renewed interest in taste psychophysics. These methods were simple, fast, and permitted direct assessments of supra-threshold intensities. For example, magnitude estimation (a popular direct method) instructs subjects to assign numbers to the intensity of the sensation evoked by a stimulus. The assigned numbers are to be proportional to the perceived sensations, so that a stimulus that produces a sensation judged to be twice as large as the preceding sensation should be given a number twice as large. This procedure is reliable and efficient. A scale, showing how perceived intensity varies from near threshold to very strong, can be produced for a particular taste substance with one individual subject in half an hour. Using the indirect Fechnerian techniques, a half hour was required to obtain a single threshold value.

Modern Psychophysical Studies

Two divergent philosophies dominate modern taste psychophysics. One of these (Bartoshuk, 1978; McBurney, 1974; McBurney & Gent, 1979) retains the four basic tastes. The taste phenomena which Kiesow believed to be analogous to color vision, have been reinterpreted (see discussions below) and now appear consistent with the independence of the four basic tastes as seen by Öhrwall. Taste intensities can be modified in a variety of ways (e.g., adaptation, mixtures) but taste qualities can still be recognized. Tastes not easily described in terms of the four basic tastes, if they exist at all, are the exception, not the rule.

The second philosophy (Erickson, 1968; 1975; 1977; Erickson & Covey, 1980) challenges the special status of the four basic tastes and maintains that taste experience cannot be analyzed into sweet, salty, sour, and bitter components but rather that tastes fuse in mixtures such that new unitary qualities result. One of the difficulties with this latter position is that it does not lead easily to generalizations about taste experience. Thus, most of the research on taste uses the descriptive terms sweet, salty, sour, and bitter.

Adaptation
After a taste substance is on the tongue for a few seconds, it begins to fade. If the tongue is undisturbed and the stimulus is not diluted (i.e., by saliva) the taste may disappear altogether. This is called *adaptation*. In the 1930s and 1940s,

Hahn and his colleagues measured nearly 15,000 absolute thresholds for 108 taste substances on 43 subjects (Hahn & Ulbrich, 1948) before and after adaptation. They found that after adaptation, the concentration that could barely be detected (i.e., the absolute threshold) was just above that of the adapting solution (Hahn, 1934; Hahn, Kuckulies, & Taeger, 1938).

Incidentally, the tongue is usually adapted to saliva, which contains NaCl. McBurney and Pfaffmann (1963) removed saliva with a water rinse and the NaCl threshold dropped from around .01 M to about 0.0001 M NaCl.

The Taste of Water
The intrinsic taste of water is related to adaptation. Several early authors expressed doubts about the tastelessness of distilled water (Henle, 1880; Öhrwall, 1891). Some investigators (Camerer, 1870; Kiesow, 1894b; von Skramlik, 1922) even found individuals to whom distilled water tasted bitter. We now know that water takes on tastes that vary depending on what precedes the water on the tongue (Bartoshuk, 1968; Bartoshuk, McBurney, & Pfaffmann, 1964; McBurney & Shick, 1971). Figure 9.8 shows the effects of exposing (i.e., adapting) the tongue to NaCl. On the left, the taste of water and NaCl are shown after adaptation to water. Note that water after water was virtually tasteless. Weak NaCl after water tasted sweet, an observation made first by Renqvist (1919), and stronger NaCl tasted salty. The right part of Figure 9.8 shows the same solutions tasted after adaptation to 0.01 M NaCl (about the concentration of NaCl in unstimulated saliva). Note that adaptation to 0.01 M NaCl rendered it virtually tasteless. Solutions more concentrated than 0.01 M tasted salty, while those less concentrated tasted bitter–sour; water produced the strongest bitter–sour taste. Variation in the descrptions of the taste of water may be related at least in part to the normal variation that occurs in salivary electrolytes. High electrolyte concentrations would be expected to make water taste bitter–sour while low electrolyte concentrations would be expected to make water tasteless. *Flat* might refer to a taste that is detected but not recognized.

The globe artichoke produces a particularly dramatic water taste (Bartoshuk, Lee, & Scarpellino, 1972). For those sensitive to it (sensitivity may be genetic), all liquids taste sweetened

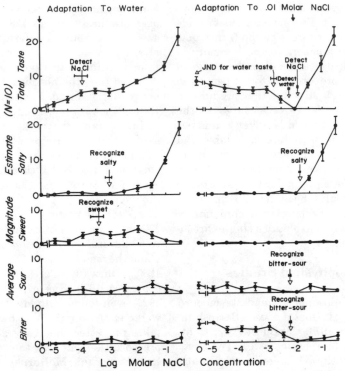

Figure 9.8. Magnitude estimates (± 1 SEM) of water and NaCl under adaptation to water (left) and .01 M NaCl (right). The top functions show the total taste intensity. The lower functions show the salty, sweet, sour, and bitter components. From "NaCl Thresholds in Man: Thresholds for Water Taste or NaCl Taste?" by L. M. Bartoshuk, 1974, *Journal of Comparative and Physiological Psychology, 87,* p. 313. Copyright 1974 by the American Psychological Association. Reprinted by permission of the author.

after eating artichokes. Figure 9.9 compares the sweet taste imparted to water after exposure of the tongue to various concentrations of an artichoke extract.

Cross-Adaptation among Substances with Similar Tastes

After adaptation to one substance, the taste intensity of another substance may be reduced. If so, we say that cross-adaptation has occurred. Cross-adaptation has played an important role in taste because substances that cross-adapt one another are believed to stimulate the same receptor mechanisms (e.g., see discussion under "Sweet"). Hahn did a series of studies on cross-adaptation before WW II (Hahn, 1949). His most famous result occurred among 24 salts; no cross-adaptation occurred. At the time, these results seemed to mean that at least 24 receptor mechanisms would be required to mediate the tastes of the salts alone.

McBurney and his students (McBurney &

Lucas, 1966; Smith & McBurney, 1969; McBurney et al., 1972; McBurney, 1972) measured perceived saltiness of suprathreshold concentrations rather than thresholds and came to very different conclusions about cross-adaptation among salts. Adaptation to NaCl reduced the salty taste of all salts tested but did not reduce the other taste qualities that were present. Hahn may have mistakenly measured the presence of those other qualities. For example, NaCl is predominantly salty and KCl is salty and bitter. Figures 9.10 and 9.11 show cross adaptation between NaCl and KCl. Note that adaptation to NaCl reduced the saltiness of KCl but not the bitterness. Hahn appears to have measured the detection threshold for the bitterness of KCl after adaptation to NaCl.

The cross-adaptation of saltiness plays a role in a current controversy about how saltiness is mediated in the nervous system. Recordings from single neurons suggest that the neurons optimally sensitive to NaCl do not respond to

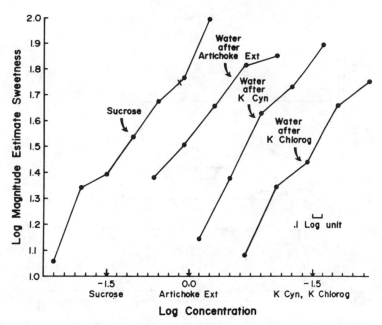

Figure 9.9. The magnitude estimates of the sweetness of sucrose, and the sweetness of water after exposure of the tongue to artichoke extract (purified, freeze-dried, then reconstituted into a concentration series) and to potassium salts of cynarin (K Cyn) and chlorogenic acid (K Chlorog). The abscissa shows the concentration of sucrose when it was the stimulus solution, and the inducing concentration of artichoke extract or constituents when water was the stimulus solution. The amount of artichoke extract is expressed as the log of the percent powder by weight. The sucrose and the potassium salts of cynarin and chlorogenic acid are expressed as the log of the molar concentration. The X on the sucrose function indicates the sweetness of 2 teaspoons of sucrose in 6-ounces of water (.16 M). The plots of sucrose and of water after artichoke extract are arbitrarily placed on the abscissa. For example, − 1.7 log molar sucrose is located 2 units to the left of the sucrose arrow on the abscissa. From "Sweet Taste of Water Induced by Artichoke (*Cynara scolymus*)" by L. M. Bartoshuk, C. H. Lee, and R. Scarpellino, 1972, *Science, 178*, p. 989. Copyright 1972 by the AAAS. Reprinted by permission.

KCl (Boudreau, Hoang, Oravec, & Do, 1983; Frank, Contreras, & Hettinger, 1983). Further, the effects of amiloride (Schiffman, Lockhead, & Maes, 1983) suggest that the receptor mechanisms of NaCl and KCl differ. Yet the cross-adaptation results (Figures 9.10 and 9.11) suggest that the salty tastes of NaCl and KCl are mediated by a common mechanism. These conclusions are unreconciled at present.

Sourness like saltiness, cross-adapts (McBurney, Smith, & Shick, 1972). This is consistent with the generally accepted idea that there is a unitary stimulus for sour.

Some bitter compounds cross-adapt but others do not (McBurney & Bartoshuk, 1973; McBurney et al., 1972). This fits well with the belief that there is no single chemical structure mediating bitterness.

Some sweet compounds cross-adapt, but others do not (McBurney, 1972; Lawless and

Stevens, 1983; Schiffman, Cahn, and Lindley, 1981; van der Wel and Arvidson, 1978). Cross-adaptation failures are consistent with multiple stimuli for sweetness. One interesting feature in both the sweet and bitter cross-adaptation data is that it is not always symmetric. This is consistent with the possibility discussed above that molecules can possess one or more of the several chemical structures that give rise to sweetness.

Cross-Adaptation among Substances with Different Tastes

Kiesow's (1894a) demonstration that tasting one substance caused another substance to taste more intense was an example of *successive contrast* to him. Today we would call it *cross-enhancement*, the opposite of cross-adaptation.

Kiesow observed cross-enhancement long before the work on water tastes, so controls for

TASTE

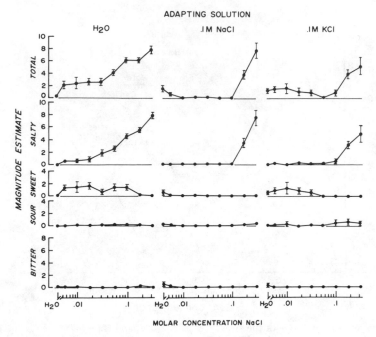

Figure 9.10. Magnitude estimates (± 1 SEM) of the taste of NaCl under three adapting solutions: water, 0.1 M NaCl, and 0.1 M KCl (N = 8). Solutions were warmed to body temperature and flowed (4 ml/sec) across the tongue through a "Hahn Geschmacksluppe." Data collect by B. Bierer as part of her senior thesis at Yale University. From "Sensory Analysis of the Taste of NaCl" by L. M. Bartoshuk, 1980, in *Biological and Behavioral Aspects of Salt Intake* (p. 93), M. R. Kare, M. J. Fregley, and R. A. Bernard (eds.), Orlando, FL: Academic Press. Copyright 1980 by Academic Press. Reprinted by permission.

water taste are obviously absent in his studies. Kiesow's apparent cross-enhancement now looks like the addition of a water taste (McBurney & Bartoshuk, 1973). For example, adaptation to acid seemed to enhance the sweetness of sucrose. However, since adaptation to HCl makes water taste sweet, the apparent enhancement may simply reflect summation of the sweetnesses of the sucrose and the water solvent. When water tastes are taken into account, cross-enhancement disappears with one exception. Kuznicki and McCutcheon (1979) found that sugar genuinely enhanced the sourness of acid on single papillae. But for the most part, cross-adaptation among sweet, salty, sour, and bitter is minimal or does not occur at all.

Regional Sensitivity of the Tongue

A tongue map showing that sweet sensitivity is greatest on the tip, sour on the sides, and bitter on the back of the tongue (Hänig, 1901) is widely cited but incorrect. Collings (1974) noted that a careful reading of Hänig shows that the differ-

ences that he originally reported were small and have been exaggerated in secondary sources. Collings's reexamination of regional sensitivity with improved methods generally confirmed Hänig; regional differences do occur but they are small.

Collings went on to examine the way in which taste intensity increased with concentration (i.e., the psychophysical function) for taste stimuli on different tongue loci. The bitterness of quinine increased with concentration faster on the back of the tongue than it did on the front. This result explains the common observation that bitter substances like medicines taste particularly strong on the back of the tongue.

Mixtures

When substances are mixed, the taste qualities of the components are identifiable but the perception of the intensities of those qualities are often suppressed. However, experiments on the same mixtures produced conflicting results about the amount of the suppression (Moskowitz,

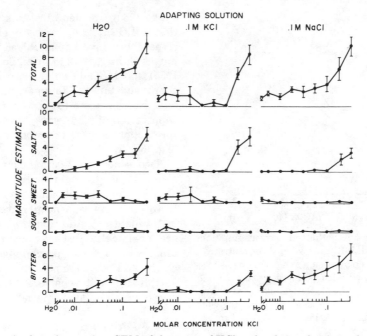

Figure 9.11. Magnitude estimates ($\pm$ 1 SEM of the taste of KCl under three adapting solutions: water, 0.1 M KCl, and 0.1 M NaCl (N = 8). Solutions were warmed to body temperature and flowed (4 ml/sec) across the tongue through a "Hahn Geschmacksluppe." Data collected by B. Bierer as part of her senior thesis at Yale University. From "Sensory Analysis of the Taste of NaCl" by L. M. Bartoshuk, 1980, in *Biological and Behavioral Aspects of Salt Intake* (p. 92), M. R. Kare, M. J. Fregley, and R. A. Bernard (eds.), Orlando, FL: Academic Press. Copyright 1980 by Academic Press. Reprinted by permission.

1972; Pangborn, 1960). General theories devised to try to predict the exact degree of suppression in mixtures (Bartosuk, 1975; Moskowitz, 1972) have been remarkably unsuccessful. One reason may be that mixture suppression is actually a composite phenomenon. Some mixture interactions appear to occur on the tongue surface. For example, NaCl suppresses the bitterness of quinine, perhaps by interfering with the normal binding of quinine to its receptors (Bartoshuk, 1979b; Bartoshuk & Seibyl, 1982). Sucrose suppresses the bitterness of quinine also, but an ingenious study by Lawless (1979) suggests that this suppression is central. Lawless put sucrose on one side of the tongue and quinine on the other. The taste intensities of both substances were reduced. Since the taste system projects ipsolaterally to the thalamus in the central nervous system, the suppression must have occurred at or above the thalamus. The different suppression mechanisms may be sensitive to different procedural variables. Thus, contradictions across studies could result

from procedural variations that are not understood as yet.

Experiments with mixtures of substances with similar taste qualities, usually sweet (Cameron, 1947; Stone & Oliver, 1969; Yamaguchi, Yoshikawa, Ikeda, & Ninomiya, 1970) produced occasional reports of *synergism*: the perceived intensity of the mixture was actually greater than the simple sum of the components.

The concept of synergism requires some kind of *normal* additivity rules because synergism means that those rules have been violated; that is, we seem to have gotten something for nothing. Thus, the key point is the definition of normal. The usual definition of normal has been simple addition. However, neurophysiological studies suggest that this is wrong (Beidler, 1961; Pfaffmann, 1959). Both Pfaffmann and Beidler noted that taste responses are not linear functions of concentration. Their logic can be extended to the psychophysical functions in Figure 9.12. The three power functions represent the kinds of functions found for taste. The

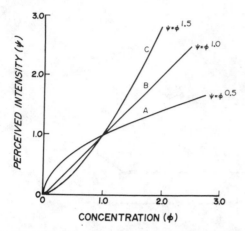

Figure 9.12. Three hypothetical power functions showing perceived intensity versus concentration. Function A shows compression and function C shows expansion. Reprinted with permission from *Physiological Behavior*, *14*, L. M. Bartoshuk, "Taste Mixtures: Is Mixture Suppression Related to Compression?" Copyright 1975, Pergamon Press, Ltd.

simplest kind of addition of two substances of similar taste is the addition of a substance to itself. Consider adding concentration 1.0 of A to itself. The perceived intensity of the sum—that is, of concentration 2.0, is 1.4. Adding the same concentration to itself along functions B and C would produce perceived intensities of 2.0 and 2.8, respectively. Function A is said to show *compression* and function C is said to show *expansion* (Stevens, 1958). The only time a substance would add to itself such that the mixture is equal to the simple sum of the components would be when its perceived intensity is directly proportional to its concentration (e.g., the power function with an exponent equal to one in Figure 9.12). This suggests that the definition of normal additivity should be based on the psychophysical function. Synergism should reflect something greater than additivity along that function. If we examine the mixture studies in this light, almost all of the cases of apparent synergism turn out to be cases where substances have psychophysical functions like C in Figure 9.12. That is, the synergism is an artifact of the false assumption that simple addition is normal in taste. The only exception to this occurs with mixtures of MSG (monosodium glutamate, the so-called taste enhancer) and certain ribonucleotides (sodium inosinate and guanylate). These mixtures show true synergism (Rifkin and Barto-

shuk, 1980). Incidentally, this does not mean that MSG is truly a taste enhancer. Taste researchers have known for many years (Lockhart & Gainer, 1950; Pilgrim, Schutz, & Peryam, 1955) that MSG does not intensify the tastes of simple substances like sugar, salt, etc. Rather, it adds its own taste to food. It may cause some suppression of food tastes, but this kind of mixture suppression is common to any condiment (e.g., NaCl).

Two issues complicate the mixtures discussed above. First, the logic applies only to mixtures of substances which are chemically identical. However, all sweets and all bitters are not chemically identical. Addition laws for stimuli that are chemically distinct but taste alike are unknown. Second, psychophysical functions can be altered by temperature (Bartoshuk, Rennart, Rodin, & Stevens, 1982), flow rate, and area of tongue stimulated (Meiselman, 1971; Meiselman, Bose, & Nykvist, 1972) among other factors. Additivity seems to change as the psychophysical function does (Bartoshuk & Cleveland, 1977) but the causes for the changes in the function are not all known.

Taste mixtures are very different from color mixtures. When colors are mixed, they fuse into a new color. The components of the mixture cannot be identified in the new color. When taste qualities are mixed, the qualities of the components can be identified (see the discussion on coding for further discussion of mixtures).

Taste Modifiers

Plant substances that can modify taste have been known for centuries. The two plant species most studied are *Gymnema sylvestre* and *Synesepalum dulicificum*.

Gymnema sylvestre is a woody climbing plant that runs over the tops of high trees in southern India, Ceylon, and tropical West Africa. Captain Edgeworth, a British officer stationed in India, reported more than a century ago that chewing the leaves of this plant abolished the sweetness of the sugar in his tea. Several investigators in the nineteenth century concluded that *Gymnema sylvestre* suppressed sweetness and, to a lesser extent, bitterness (Hooper, 1887; Kiesow, 1894c; Shore, 1892). The effects on bitterness are now attributed to cross-adaptation produced by the bitter taste of the leaves. When the bitter taste of *Gymnema sylvestre* is removed with a rinse, the taste of sucrose is suppressed but the tastes of QHCl as well as NaCl, citric acid, and HCl are unaffected.

Gymnema sylvestre suppresses the sweetness of a variety of sweet substances, with the possible exception of chloroform (Kurihara, 1969). Although *Gymnema sylvestre* does not affect the saltiness and bitterness of stimuli like NaCl and quinine (Bartoshuk, Dateo, Vanderbelt, Buttrick, & Long, 1969), it does affect the saltiness and bitterness of some stimuli, like alanine, which are sweet as well as salty and bitter (Meiselman & Halpern, 1970). This may simply reflect the effects of mixture interactions since the removal of one component in a mixture removes its own taste and also removes its effects on the other taste qualities (Meiselman & Halpern, 1970).

Synsepalum dulcificum described in Western literature as early as 1725, was named miracle fruit by Europeans who experienced its taste-modifying effects while traveling in tropical West Africa more than 100 years ago (Daniell, 1852). After the tongue is exposed to berries from this plant, sour substances taste as if they have been sweetened and also taste less sour than normal. For example, lemons taste like lemonade and can be eaten like oranges. Figure 9.13 shows how citric acid tasted after the tongue was exposed to miracle fruit.

David Fairchild (1931), an explorer working for the U.S. Department of Agriculture, introduced this plant to Americans and offered an explanation for its mechanism. He suggested that miracle fruit inhibits sourness, thus permitting any sweet taste present to be more noticeable. An experiment with *Gymnema sylvestre* proves that his explanation was wrong. Sourness returned to normal when the sweetness induced by miracle fruit was abolished by *Gymnema sylvestre* (Bartoshuk et al., 1969; Bartoshuk, Gentile, Moskowitz, & Meiselman, 1974). Miracle fruit appears to reduce the sourness of acids the same way that adding sugar does: through mixture suppression (Bartoshuk et al., 1974).

The active component of miracle fruit is a glycoprotein which has sugar molecules attached to it. Kurihara and Beidler (1969) suggested that this glycoprotein may have two binding sites. One of these binds to the receptor membrane, and the other (one of the sugar molecules) binds to the sweet receptor site in the usual fashion. Normally, the sugar molecule is held on the glycoprotein in a position that prevents its binding to the sweet receptor. Acid is assumed to change the conformation of the sweet receptor site (or the glycoprotein) so that the sugar molecule and receptor can come into contact.

Taste modifiers have potential practical importance. For example, miracle fruit offers a novel way to produce a non-caloric sweetener. In the early 1970s, miracle fruit was actually marketed as a sweetener (Tripp, 1985) but was banned by FDA apparently on the grounds that it had not been proved to be safe. Modifiers are also useful in the laboratory to study taste; however, this use is limited because the effects are species specific (see below).

CODE FOR QUALITY: PATTERNING VERSUS LABELED-LINES

Patterning

Early Fiber Types

In 1941 Pfaffmann discovered that single fibers in the cat chorda tympani were not specific to a single quality. He classified these fibers into three types: those responsive to acid only, those responsive to acid and NaCl, and those responsive to acid and quinine. Pfaffmann concluded, "In such a system, sensory quality does not depend simply on the 'all or nothing' activation

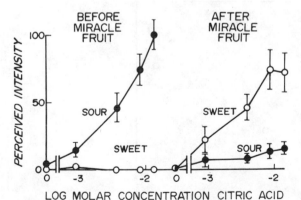

Figure 9.13. Magnitude estimates (± 1 SEM) of citric acid before and after miracle fruit. The total taste is divided into its sour, bitter, salty, and sweet components. Reprinted with permission from *Physiological Behavior, 12*, L. M. Bartoshuk, R. L. Gentile, H. R. Moskowitz, and H. L. Meiselman, "Sweet Taste Induced by Miracle Fruit (*Synsepalum dulcificum*)," Copyright 1974, Pergamon Press, Ltd.

Table 9.1

Stimulus	"Water" fiber	"Salt" fiber	"Acid" fiber	"Quinine" fiber	Sensations evoked
H_2O (salt $< .03$ M)	+	0	0	0	Water
NaCl ($> .05$ M)	0	+	0	0	Salt
HCl (pH 2.5)	+	+	+	0	Sour
Quinine	+	0	0	+	Bitter

of some particular fiber group alone, but on the pattern of other fibers active." When all fibers responded, the message was *acid*. When only the acid–NaCl fibers responded, the message was *NaCl*. When only the acid–quinine fibers responded, the message was *quinine*.

Cohen, Hagiwara, & Zotterman (1955) accepted the same logic for the sensory coding of taste quality but proposed somewhat different fiber types. Table 9.1 shows the stimuli to which each type responded and the sensation that was assumed to result. Two of the fiber types are the same in both studies (the type responsive to HCl and NaCl and the type responsive to HCl only) but the fiber type that was specific to quinine was not observed in Pfaffmann's study. However, the most dramatic difference between the studies concerned the water fibers. These will be discussed more fully in a later section.

Later Views of Nonspecificity of Taste Neurons

Technical difficulties limited the number of neurons studied in the early years. As data accumulated, Pfaffmann (1955) began to question the existence of fiber types. Each taste neuron seemed to be unique. It seemed reasonable that the code for quality would be the pattern of activity across a population of neurons each with its own set of sensitivities.

Erickson (1963), a student of Pfaffmann, compared the patterns of activity across neurons for ammonium chloride (NH_4Cl), potassium chloride (KCl), and sodium chloride (NaCl) (see Figure 9.14). The patterns for KCl and NH_4Cl (both taste salty-bitter to humans) were similar, but both were different from that for NaCl. Erickson then devised a behavioral test based on generalization of shock avoidance. Rats

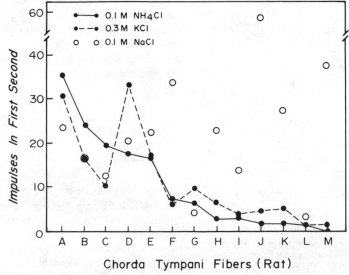

Figure 9.14. A cross-fiber patterns for three salts: NH_4Cl, KCl, and NaCl. Single fibers are arranged along the abscissa in order of responsiveness to NH_4Cl. The KCl pattern is similar to the NH_4Cl pattern. Neither of these is similar to the NaCl pattern. From Erickson (1963).

shocked for drinking KCl avoided NH₄Cl and vice versa. Neither group generalized as much to NaCl, and rats shocked for drinking NaCl generalized slightly but equally to KCl and NH₄Cl. The salts with similar neural patterns appeared to taste similar to the rat.

Frank's Classification of Taste Fiber Types

The rejection of fiber types, based largely on the early rat studies (Pfaffmann, 1955; Erickson, 1963), was subsequently challenged by the work of Frank (1973) on the hamster. In Frank's study, hamster chorda tympani fibers were classified according to the stimulus that produced the largest response. Some were stimulated best by sucrose, some by NaCl, and some

by HCl. Frank subsequently classified fiber types in the rat from both the chorda tympani nerve that innervates fungiform papilla (data from Ogawa, Sato, & Yamashita, 1968) and the glossopharyngeal nerve that innervates both the foliate and circumvallate papillae (data from Frank, 1975). She found the same types as those found in the hamster as well as a QHCl-best type (see Figure 9.15). The absence of the QHCl-best type in the chorda tympani reflects the fact that the anterior tongues of rat and hamster are relatively insensitive to this bitter.

The least specific fiber types in Frank's system, and thus the hardest to classify, were NaCl-best and HCl-best. Further study suggested that these are distinct populations (Frank et al.,

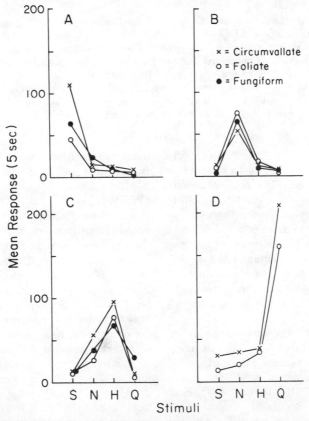

Figure 9.15. Neural responses to sucrose (S), NaCl (N), HCl (H), and QHCl (Q) from the circumvallate papillae (X's), foliate papillae (open circles), and fungiform papillae (filled circles). The circumvallate data came originally from Frank (1975); the fungiform data came originally from Ogawa (1968); the foliate data were not published prior to 1981. From "Quality Coding in Gustatory Systems of Rats and Hamsters" by G. H. Nowlis and M. E. Frank, 1981, in *Perception of Behavioral Chemicals* (p. 63), D. M. Norris (ed.), Amsterdam: Elsevier Biomedical Press. Copyright 1981 by Elsevier Science Publishers B.V. (Biomedical Division). Reprinted by permission.

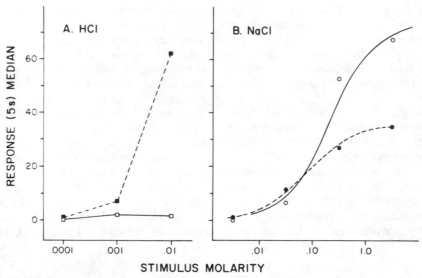

Figure 9.16. Concentration functions for HCl (panel A on the left) and NaCl (panel B on the right) for NaCl-best neurons (open symbols) and HCl-best neurons (filled symbols). Responses are the median numbers of impulses above base-line activity elicited during seconds 6–10 of stimulation. Points on the HCl functions are connected by straight lines. NaCl functions represent Beidler's (1953) taste equation. Note that HCl-best neurons are stimulated by NaCl (filled symbols in panel B) while NaCl-best neurons are not stimulated by HCl (open symbols in panel A). From "Nerve Fibers Sensitive to Ionic Stimuli in Chorda Tympani of the Rat" by M. E. Frank, R. J. Contreras, and T. P. Hettinger, 1983, *Journal of Neurophysiology, 50,* p. 951. Copyright 1983 by The American Physiological Society. Reprinted by permission.

1983). The NaCl-best fibers were specifically tuned to sodium salts and failed to respond to non-sodium salts like KCl. The HCl-best fibers were responsive to many electrolytes including acids and salts. However, their responses to salts were different from those of the NaCl-best fibers (see Figure 9.16). The existence of neurons tuned quite specifically to sodium salts suggests the possibility that these fibers code saltiness. If so, then how can we explain the saltiness of KCl? We will return to this issue in the discussion below.

Boudreau and his colleagues have approached the classification of taste fibers by utilizing stimuli chosen from substances commonly found in foods and also using measures of latency and spontaneous activity (Boudreau, 1974; Boudreau & Alev, 1973; Boudreau, Anderson, & Oravec, 1975; Boudreau & Nelson, 1977). Another innovation in this work is the use of recordings from the geniculate ganglion (the cell bodies of the axons in the chorda tympani nerve). Their work supports discrete fiber types just as that of Frank and her co-workers does. In addition, they have identified several species with

neurons specifically tuned to sodium salts (e.g., Boudreau et al., 1983).

CNS Studies

In recordings from hamster taste neurons in the chorda tympani nerve, the solitary nucleus, and the parabrachial nucleus (Smith, Van Buskirk, Travers, & Bieber, 1983a, 1983b; Travers & Smith, 1979; Van Buskirk & Smith, 1981), Frank's fiber types were in evidence at all three levels. The CNS neurons appeared to be more broadly tuned than neurons in the periphery. On the other hand, neurons in the opercular cortex of awake cynomolgous monkeys proved to be more narrowly tuned than those in the solitary nucleus (Scott, Yaxley, Sienkiewicz, & Rolls, in press). In macaque monkeys, in a secondary cortical taste area (orbitofrontal cortex), some neurons appear to be even more sharply tuned and to respond predominantly to sweet substances. These neurons appear to be involved with satiety since the responses varied with the deprivation of the monkey.

There are species differences in taste CNS neurons. For example, the firing rate of the NTS is much higher than that of the chorda tympani for the rat (Doetsch & Erickson, 1970; Ganchrow & Erickson, 1970) but not the hamster (Travers & Smith, 1979). In addition, the hamster CNS shows more inhibitory responses than the rat (Perotto & Scott, 1976; Scott & Erickson, 1971; Travers & Smith, 1979).

Spatial codes play important roles in several modalities. Evidence for sorting of CNS taste units by taste quality (chemotopic mapping) has been found in the medulla of the rat (Halpern, 1967), the thalamus of the cat (Ishiko, Amatusu, & Sato, 1967), and the cortex of the dog, rat (Funakoshi, Kashahara, Yamamoto, & Kawamura, 1972), and cat (Ishiko & Akagi, 1972). However, some of these maps might reflect only differential sensitivity to qualities on the tongue that topographically project to higher levels of the nervous system.

Incidentally, just as in the periphery, some CNS neurons respond to temperature and/or touch as well as taste (Sato, 1967). These neurons provide one means by which temperature and touch can influence taste.

Labeled-Lines

Frank's Fiber Types and Labeled-Lines

On the basis of Frank's fiber types, Pfaffmann reverted to a theory of quality coding in which the four basic tastes play a role (Pfaffmann, 1974; Pfaffmann et al., 1976). This theoretical shift was stimulated by the fiber types sensitive to sweeteners found in the squirrel monkey (Frank, 1974). Sucrose-best fibers (i.e., those that were more sensitive to sucrose than to salts, HCl, or quinine) responded more to sucrose than fructose while salt-best fibers (i.e., those that were more sensitive to salts than to sugars, HCl, or quinine) responded more to fructose than to sucrose. Pfaffmann related these results to a puzzling preference phenomenon. In whole nerve recordings, fructose produced a larger response than sucrose, yet, sucrose was preferred to fructose in preference experiments. Suppose that the sucrose-best fibers code sweetness and the NaCl-best fibers code saltiness. Fructose would taste sweet-salty because it stimulates two sets of fibers: sucrose-best and NaCl-best. However, fructose would not be the most preferred sugar because it produces a complex taste, sweet and salty, and the sweetness in the complex taste would be less intense than the

sweetness of sucrose (note that the sucrose must also produce a complex sweet-salty taste but it would be more sweet and less salty).

The *labeled-line theory* predicts a number of side tastes for simple chemicals. For example, in Figure 9.15 the fibers responding best to HCl also responded to NaCl. The labeled-line theory says that when NaCl stimulates these fibers the taste quality evoked is sour. The complete taste of a stimulus is determined by the responses of all four types to that stimulus. Thus the taste of NaCl on the circumvallate papillae of the rat tongue can be derived from Figure 9.15 by noting the responses to NaCl from each fiber type (the Xs show the circumvallate papillae). NaCl evokes a modest salty taste from the NaCl-best fibers (B in Figure 9.15), a sour taste of greater magnitude from the HCl-best fibers (C in Figure 9.15), a small sweet taste from the sucrose-best fibers (A in Figure 9.15), and a small bitter-taste from the quinine-best fibers (D in Figure 9.15). In fact, simple chemicals do tend to have the complex tastes predicted by the labeled-line theory. For example, salts tend to taste sour and acids tend to taste salty, just as the labeled-line theory predicts.

Incidentally, Smith et al. (1983a) analyzed data from 31 neurons in the parabrachial nuclei in the hamster CNS to 18 taste stimuli. They classified the neurons according to their best stimuli: Frank's four types. They also examined cross-fiber patterns by applying multidimensional scaling to the correlations among all pairs of the 18 taste substances: this produced a *similarity space* in which the distance between two taste substances represented the degree to which they stimulated neurons in a similar fashion. To evaluate the contribution of the fiber types, restricted similarity spaces were constructed omitting each of the fiber types. The results showed that the major part of the pattern for a given substance was contributed by the fibers responding best to that substance. For example, panel A in Figure 9.17 shows a two-dimensional representation of the similarity space for all 31 neurons. Note that the sweet stimuli (sucrose, fructose, d-glucose, Na-saccharin, and dl-alanine form one group, the sodium salts (NaCl and $NaNO_3$) form a secondary group, and the acids and non-Na-salts form a third group. These groups can be verified with cluster analysis. The bitter stimuli (urea and QHCl) are distant from the others. Panel B in

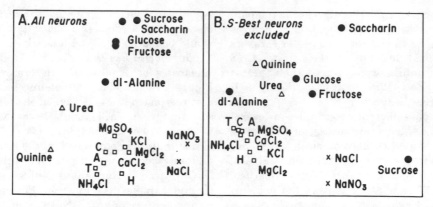

Figure 9.17. Two-dimensional representations of the stimulus relationships obtained from multidimensional scaling. A: all 31 neurons were used to generate the across-neuron correlations represented by this space. B: across-neuron correlations were calculated without responses of the sucrose-best neurons. Stimuli are named in the figure except for the acids. These are HCl (H), tartaric (T), citric (C), and acetic (A) acids. From Smith et al. (1983a).

Figure 9.17 shows the similarity space that resulted when the 10 sucrose-best neurons were removed. Note that the group formed by the sweet substances is scattered. The other groups remain. The sweet-best neurons are necessary to give these substances their common identity, i.e., sweetness.

Patterning vs Labeled-Lines
Pfaffmann proposed the *across-fiber pattern theory* in an effort to explain how quality discriminations could take place in the absence of taste neurons specifically tuned to sweet, salty, sour, and bitter. Had he seen Frank's fiber types in 1941, the pattern theory might never have been born.

Now clusters of fiber types are widely accepted (Scott & Chang, 1984). However, there are still nagging concerns about why the specificity of taste neurons is not complete, if the neurons are really labeled-lines. Perhaps we can get some perspective by asking an even broader question. Why are some neurons that appear to be taste neurons also responsive to temperature and touch? We might conclude that these neurons have roles in all three sensory continua but the more common conclusion (see Sato, 1967) is that these are taste neurons and that the taste message transmitted is modulated by the thermal and touch sensitivities. For example, a quinine-best neuron sensitive to cooling would produce a greater bitter sensation to cool quinine than to warm quinine.

The dilemma of patterning versus labeled-lines has been faced in the skin senses as well as taste. Early faith in specificity was replaced by pattern theories (Stevens & Green, 1978) but these withered as the receptor and neuron specificities that eluded early neurophysiologists were slowly revealed. In taste, neither theory can be proved to be correct as of now. The critical experiment, could it be done, would be to stimulate single taste fibers and see if each produces one and only one of the four basic taste sensations.

Coding Theories and Human Taste Experience
Erickson has linked the neurophysiological controversy between patterning and labeled-lines to the nature of taste mixtures in human experience (Erickson & Covey, 1980). As discussed above, the mixture literature historically has accepted the analytic character of mixtures as a given. Erickson and his co-workers have challenged this. They reasoned that if taste qualities produce unique patterns of activity across a population of neurons that give rise to unitary qualities, then a mixture should produce a pattern that gives rise to an equally unitary quality. In experiments using single stimuli and mixtures, they found some mixtures that were reported to be *unitary*. Unfortunately, this analysis ignored the large literature on mixture suppression. If one mixture component is greater than the other or has greater

suppressive power, then the other component may disappear in the mixture. Needless to say, such a mixture is "unitary."

Another psychophysical spin-off from the pattern theory is the use of *multidimensional scaling* (MDS) to search for alternatives to the four basic tastes. Schiffman and Erickson (1971) used MDS to construct a similarity space in which distance between stimuli reflected the degree of their perceived similarity. They selected three dimensions for their space: molecular weight, pH, and hedonic value. Since the location of any stimulus in the taste space can theoretically be specified by giving its coordinates in terms of axes, its taste can be said to be described by these coordinates. However, this is not a psychological description since molecular weight, pH, and hedonic value cannot be used to describe qualitative taste experiences.

Similarity spaces have also been used to challenge the classic taste tetrahedron (see also Yoshida and Saito, 1969). A tetrahedron can usually be drawn within a gustatory similarity space such that substances that taste sweet, salty, sour, and bitter fall at its corners. Some stimuli fall outside the tetrahedron. This has been interpreted to mean that these tastants have attributes that the four basic tastes do not describe. Any such attributes might represent a failure of the four basic tastes to adequately describe taste quality; however, it may also simply reflect the effects of modalities other than taste (e.g., touch or odor).

Are There Four Basic Tastes?

Scott and Chang (1984) summarized the debates over this issue in a review of taste coding theories. They concluded, "As long as the definition is kept unimposing, the answer is a prompt and inexpensive 'yes'." The most important concern that prevents this from being a more costly 'yes' is valid and should be addressed. Some substances seem to have tastes that cannot be described exhaustively by sweet, sour, salty, and bitter (e.g., monosodium glutamate and alkalis) this suggests that the four basic tastes are not exhaustive and that other taste quality names are necessary.

This issue has ancient historical roots. One of the earliest approaches to a study of the senses was to classify sensations. Thus, we have lists of basic tastes as far back as Aristotle (see Table 9.2). Aristotle's list (see Beare, 1906) dominated until the Renaissance. Fernel (1581), a French physiologist, for the most part accepted Aristotle's list but added insipid (a name for the absence of taste probably originally contributed by Arabian physicians). Haller (1786), a physiologist, offered even more extensive additions (see Table 9.2).

The search for a proper set of taste quality names changed dramatically in the nineteenth century. Horn (1825) assessed the lists provided by his predecessors and found them wanting. He argued that earlier authors had included terms that described nongustatory sensations in their lists. These included olfactory sensations (e.g., spiritous), and touch sensations (e.g., rough). By the turn of the century, the taste quality names that were generally accepted as representative of pure taste sensations were the familiar four basic tastes: sweet, salty, sour, and bitter.

Concern that these quality names fail to

Table 9.2 Lists of basic tastes

Aristotle (384–322 B.C.)	Fernel (1581)	Haller (1786)	Horn (1825)	Örhwall (1891)	Kiesow (1896)
sweet	sweet	sweet	sweet	sweet	sweet
bitter	bitter	bitter	bitter	bitter	bitter
sour	sour	sour	sour	sour	sour
salty	salty	salty	salty	salty	salty
astringent	astringent	rough	alkaline		
pungent	pungent	urinous			
harsh	harsh	spiritous			
	fatty	aromatic			
	insipid	acrid			
		putrid			
		insipid			

encompass all taste experience has motivated modern reexaminations of this old issue. O'Mahony and his colleagues have examined taste names in other languages (O'Mahony & Alba, 1980; O'Mahony & Muhiudeen, 1977) as well as taste descriptions generated by a variety of psychophysical settings. O'Mahoney and Thompson (1977) found that subjects will use novel descriptive terms if they are not restricted to the use of sweet, sour, salty, and bitter. At first glance, this might seem to support the idea that the four basic tastes are not exhaustive. However, the nature of the novel terms brings to mind Horn's arguments. O'Mahoney's novel terms suggest object names (e.g. seawater, aspirin, onion crisps), tactile sensations (e.g., tangy, soapy) and olfactory sensations (e.g., fishy, plastic). That is, the novel terms suggest that the subjects are either describing non-taste attributes of the stimuli or are naming the substances.

In sum, the possibility that we have somehow overlooked relevant taste qualities cannot be totally dismissed. But proponents of this view have yet to propose even a single new basic taste that does not suggest nongustatory sensations.

The four basic tastes have proved useful for describing taste experience and for organizing psychophysical data (e.g., the laws of cross-adaptation) and will almost certainly continue to dominate taste psychophysics unless a more useful system comes along.

TASTE WORLDS OF OTHER SPECIES

Sensitivity and Quality

With the advent of neural recordings, a wealth of cross-species comparisons were possible. These were followed by ingenious behavioral studies that were initially aimed at thresholds but later addressed even the fascinating question of qualitative experience in other species. Although there are important differences across species, the similarities have turned out to be more impressive.

Taste Thresholds: The Adrenalectomy Controversy

The earliest rat threshold experiments were designed to resolve a controversy over the role

of taste in the specific hunger for sodium, induced by removal of the adrenal glands (adrenalectomy), but the value of the techniques developed goes far beyond this one problem. Adrenalectomy causes a loss of body sodium which dramatically increases the consumption of suprathreshold NaCl and also decreases the preference threshold for NaCl in the rat. Richter (1936, 1939) concluded that "rats ingest more salt . . . because of chemical changes in the taste mechanisms in the oral cavity, giving rise to an enhanced salt discrimination." Pfaffmann and Bare (1950) recorded from the chorda tympani taste nerves of adrenalectomized and normal rats and found the same thresholds (about 0.001 M NaCl). This agreed with the preference threshold of adrenalectomized rats (about 0.001 M NaCl) but did not agree with the preference threshold of normal rats (about 0.01 NaCl). The obvious conclusion seemed to be that normal rats were able to taste NaCl at 0.001 M but were indifferent to the concentrations between 0.001 and 0.01 M, while the adrenalectomized rats, because of increased preference for NaCl, were not indifferent to these concentrations. As we shall see below, there is a better explanation.

The *two-bottle preference technique* is extremely simple. An animal is given access to two solutions: water and a taste substance dissolved in water. The concentration of the taste substance is varied and the concentration at which preference or rejection fails is the threshold. Figure 9.18 shows preference and rejection functions for adrenalectomized and normal rats as well as for normal rats with extra NaCl added to the diet. The two-bottle procedure has been widely used with suitable modifications for other species (e.g., see Bell, 1959 for the two-bucket procedure used with cattle). Its one major drawback is that the hedonic properties of the substance provide the motivation for the behavior. The preference threshold is not a true sensory threshold if an animal can taste a weak substance but is indifferent to it.

To avoid this dilemma, new threshold procedures were designed to motivate the animals in other ways. The earliest of these studies used shock avoidance. Deprived rats were shocked for drinking NaCl (Harriman & MacLeod, 1953) or water (Carr, 1952) and subsequently avoided those substances. The concentration of NaCl was decreased until discrimination failed. The

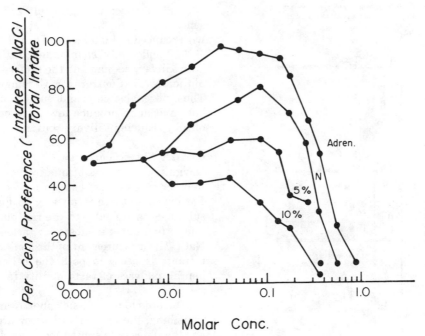

Figure 9.18. NaCl preference-rejection functions for four groups of rats: adrenalectomized (Adren.), normal (N), and those whose diets were supplemented by 5% or 10% NaCl. From "Taste Mechanisms in Preference Behavior" by C. Pfaffmann, 1957, *American Journal of Clinical Nutrition, 5*, p. 145. Copyright (c) 1957 by the American Journal of Clinical Nutrition, American Society for Clinical Nutrition. Reprinted by permission.

resulting thresholds were as low as the neural threshold which seemed to confirm the suggestion that the preference threshold for normal rats was not a true sensory threshold.

Later threshold studies (Koh & Teitelbaum, 1961; Morrison & Norrison, 1966; Shaber, Brent, & Rumsey, 1970) developed even more ingenious psychophysical methods that did not depend on preference to motivate the animal. These studies also produced thresholds that were lower than the preference threshold, reinforcing the idea that the preference threshold was in error.

If the NaCl in rat saliva is taken into consideration, then the various NaCl thresholds can be reinterpreted (Bartoshuk, 1974). Resting rat saliva contains 0.005 to 0.01 M sodium (Hainsworth & Stricker, 1971). Since the absolute threshold for the taste of a salt is determined by the concentration of its cation in the adapting solution, experiments in which the rat is adapted to its saliva cannot produce NaCl thresholds lower than 0.005 to 0.01 M. The preference threshold (0.01 NaCl) is probably a true sensory threshold based on adaptation to saliva. The neural thresholds were obtained

with water rinses that removed saliva so the low values are to be expected. The puzzling results are the low behavioral thresholds. They appear to be lower than the salivary sodium level, which is impossible. The answer to this dilemma concerns the water taste. Remember that we discussed the observation that water following NaCl tastes bitter to humans. Neural studies show that some of the QHCl-best fibers in the rat respond to water if the tongue was previously adapted to NaCl (see Figure 9.19). Thus, the rat tastes water after NaCl much like the human does. In a two bottle preference experiment, a rat can first sample the water (in the process rinsing its tongue) and then taste the saltiness of dilute NaCl in the other bottle or it can first sample the NaCl (in the process adapting to it) and then taste the bitterness of the water in the other bottle. Either scenario permits discrimination between the two bottles.

The low preference threshold for adrenalectomized rats appears to be related to salivary sodium (Thrasher & Fregly, 1980). Adrenalectomy in rats (like adrenal insufficiency or Addison's disease in humans) causes the body to

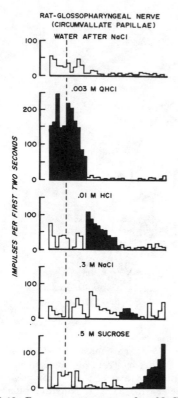

Figure 9.19. Responses to water after NaCl, QHCl, HCl, NaCl and sucrose from fibers in the rat glosso-pharyngeal nerve. These fibers innervated the circumvallate papillae. The 5 fibers to the left of the dashed line are arranged (left to right) in order of decreasing response to water after NaCl. The 29 fibers to the right of the dashed line are arranged to group fibers that respond best to QHCl, HCl, NaCl, or sucrose (the bars showing the best response are filled). Further the HCl-best and NaCl-best fibers are arranged as follows. The NaCl-best fibers that respond more to sucrose than HCl were placed (left to right) in order of descending response to NaCl. The NaCl-best fibers responding more to HCl than sucrose were placed (right to left) in order of descending response to NaCl. In the case of the HCl-best fibers, all 10 fibers responded better to NaCl than to QHCl and so were placed (left to right) in order of descending response to NaCl. Unpublished data, discussed in Bartoshuk, Frank, and Pfaffmann (1978).

lose sodium. However, when this loss is made up by providing NaCl, salivary sodium is actually higher than normal (rat: Sweeney & Catalanotto, 1976; Thrasher & Fregly, 1980; human: Frawley & Thorn, 1951). When the sodium loss is not made up (e.g., during the NaCl preference testing), the salivary sodium drops rapidly. Thus, the low preference threshold for NaCl in

adrenalectomized rats probably reflects a true sensory threshold based on adaptation to saliva with reduced sodium levels (Thrasher & Fregly, 1980). Incidentally, sodium deprivation reduces both salivary sodium and the preference threshold for NaCl (Contreras & Catalanotto, 1980). Thus, adrenalectomy and sodium deprivation both appear to produce low preference thresholds by reducing salivary sodium.

Quality Classifications

Obviously, questions of qualitative experience in other species must be approached indirectly. For example, there is no way to find out if a substance tastes salty to the rat, but it is possible to find out if a substance tastes similar to NaCl. The measurement of the similarity of two tastants is basic to both the behavioral and neural analyses of taste quality in nonhuman species.

If an animal is made sick shortly after tasting something, the animal will associate the taste and the illness and subsequently avoid that substance as well as others with a similar taste. The illness can be produced by chemicals like LiCl (Nachman, 1963) or apomorphine (Garcia & Ervin, 1968), or by radiation (Smith, 1971). Figure 9.20 shows the results of a conditioned aversion study with hamsters (Nowlis & Frank, 1981). For the most part, the hamsters grouped stimuli much as human subjects do. For example, sucrose, fructose, and saccharin tasted alike. The most impressive difference resulted for KCl. Human subjects find KCl to taste both bitter and salty but the hamsters treated KCl as if it tasted like quinine.

Taste similarity data from the rat suggest KCl tastes like QHCl and not like NaCl to the rat as well. These data were obtained with an ingenious design based on generalization, but using a food reward rather than conditioned aversion (Morrison, 1967).

These results are relevant to the discussion above concerning taste neurons in the rat that respond to NaCl (and other sodium salts) but do not respond to KCl. The behavioral data suggest that KCl tastes like QHCl and not like NaCl to the rat. To human subjects, KCl tastes like NaCl as well as like QHCl (i.e., KCl is salty-bitter). Why does KCl fail to taste like NaCl to the rat? Perhaps the saltinesses of KCl and NaCl are mediated by different receptor mechanisms. On the other hand, perhaps rats are more sensitive

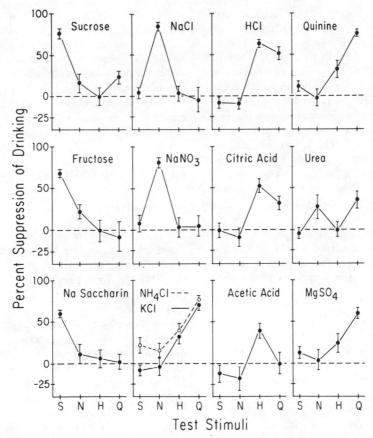

Figure 9.20. Suppression of drinking across four test stimuli: 0.1 M sucrose (S), 0.1 M NaCl (N), 0.01 M HCl (H), and 0.001 M quinine hydrochloride (Q) after aversions were conditioned in hamsters to one of 13 solutions: four identical to the test stimuli; 0.3 M fructose; 0.1 M $NaNO_3$; 0.003 M citric acid; 3 M urea; 0.001 M sodium saccharin; 0.3 M NH_4Cl; 0.3 M KCl; 0.01 M acetic acid; 0.1 M $MgSO_4$. Data points are means of groups of 12 animals ($\pm$ SE). From "Quality Coding in Gustatory Systems of Rats and Hamsters" by G. H. Nowlis and M. E. Frank, 1981, in *Perception of Behavioral Chemicals* (p. 65), D. M. Norris (ed.), Amsterdam: Elsevier Biomedical Press. Copyright 1981 by Elsevier Science Publishers B.V. (Biomedical Division). Reprinted by permission.

to the bitterness of KCl and perhaps the bitterness inhibits the saltiness. We know very little about the mechanisms mediating the taste of KCl. The mysteries surrounding KCl are among the most fascinating in taste.

Neural Responses to Water

Zotterman (1949) discovered that the frog had taste fibers that responded to water. He and his colleagues went on to discover water fibers in the cat, dog, pig, and monkey (Gordon, Kitchell, Ström, & Zotterman, 1959; Liljestrand & Zotterman, 1954; Zotterman, 1956). Zotterman was able to obtain recordings from human subjects because of a unique collaboration with col-

leagues performing stapedectomies to restore hearing. This surgery restores hearing by permitting the small bones in the middle ear (stapes) to move properly in response to movements of the ear drum. Since the chorda tympani taste nerve crosses the ear drum, it can be exposed for recordings during surgery. When recordings from human taste nerves (Borg et al., 1967) failed to show water fibers, Zotterman concluded that water taste might be a category of taste quality important in the taste worlds of some other species but lacking in man's.

Later experiments (Bartoshuk, Frank, & Pfaffmann, 1978; Bartoshuk & Pfaffmann, 1965; Bartoshuk et al., 1971; Ogawa et al., 1972; Smith

& Frank, 1972; Pfaffmann et al., 1976; Yamamoto & Kawamura, 1974) suggest a different conclusion. Many taste neurons will respond to water but only if the water follows certain other substances. For example, as we noted above, some QHCl-best fibers are sensitive to water following NaCl (see Figure 9.19) and water following NaCl tastes bitter to human subjects. Some fibers are sensitive to water following sucrose, some to water following HCl, and so forth. Neural responses to water depend on the nature of the adapting solution just as the taste of water to human subjects depends on the nature of the adapting solution. The original experiments on water fibers did not test a variety of adapting solutions but rather used Ringer's solution (a solution of approximately 0.15 M NaCl) as a rinse between stimuli. The responses to water probably were actually responses to water following NaCl.

Taste Modifiers

Gymnema sylvestre (an Indian herb) and *Synsepalum dulcificum* (a tropical fruit) both modify human taste experience but have variable effects on other species.

A water extract (i.e., tea) prepared from the leaves of the plant *Gymnema sylvestre* selectively suppresses and may even totally abolish sweet tastes in humans (Bartoshuk et al., 1969; Borg, Diamont, Oakley, Ström, & Zotterman, 1967; Warren and Pfaffmann, 1959). The higher the concentration of the extract, the greater the suppression. It has similar effects on chimpanzees (Hellekant, 1985). It may have similar effects on the dog (Andersson, Langren, Olsson, & Zotterman, 1950) although its effects have been less extensively tested on that species. It has been shown to have some effects on the hamster (Faull & Halpern, 1971; Hellekant & Gopal, 1976; Pfaffmann, 1969; Pfaffmann & Hagstrom, 1955; Yackzan, 1969), rat (Hellekant & Gopal, 1976; Oakley, 1962), and the housefly (Kennedy, Sturckow, & Waller, 1975) but the effects are not as selective as those on humans. It does not affect a variety of monkeys at all (Glaser, Hellekant, Brouwer, & van der Wel, 1984; Snell, 1965).

Miracle fruit adds a sweet taste to the taste of acids in man and certain species of monkeys (Bartoshuk, Gentile, & Moskowitz, 1974; Hellekant, 1983; Hellekant, Hagstrom, Kasahara, & Zotterman, 1974) but not in lower species (Hellekant et al., 1974; Harvey, 1970).

The meaning of the failure of these taste modifiers to work across species is not clear. The effects of the modifiers might vary because the sweet receptor sites in other species differ from those in humans. However, as noted earlier, the receptor sites could be identical and the modifiers could fail for other reasons.

CLINICAL PROBLEMS

Taste Loss

Total Taste Loss is Rare
Total loss of taste is called *ageusia*. Its rarity is not surprising considering that taste travels to the CNS via eight nerves (the chorda tympani, greater superficial petrosal, glossopharyngeal, and vagus nerves on both sides of the body). These innervate separate areas of the oral cavity and travel by separate routes to (for the most part) separate areas of the brain. In theory, taste could be totally destroyed by destroying all taste receptors, severing all of the nerves, or by destroying central representation of taste. Total loss of taste can in fact occur with radiation therapy (Bartoshuk, 1978; Conger, 1973; Mossman & Henkin, 1978), which may kill receptor cells; and head trauma (Sumner, 1967; Schechter & Henkin, 1974), which may damage CNS taste areas. With time, partial recovery often occurs with both sources of loss.

The more common taste losses are partial ones (*hypogeusia*). These can result from the total loss of part of the sensory field (e.g., severing of nerves) or from partial loss over the whole sensory field, or a combination of the two. Incidentally, taste loss can occur for some qualities (especially bitter) and not others, and for some concentrations and not others.

Total Loss Over Restricted Areas
The taste system is organized to maintain constancy of perceived taste intensities even when relatively large areas are lost. For example, at one time the chorda tympani taste nerve was sometimes cut during stapedectomy, the surgery that allowed Zotterman to obtain neural recordings from humans. This abolished taste permanently on the front of the tongue on the side on which the nerve was cut. Out of 126 cases

evaluated (Bull, 1965), 20 percent reported no symptoms at all. In the remaining 80 percent, the major complaints were of metallic phantom sensations or dry mouth. The phantom sensations may have been caused by irritation of the cut end of the nerve and the dry mouth resulted from disturbance of salivation. Even in 32 individuals in whom the chorda tympanies were cut on both sides, the most common complaint was dry mouth. Only 7 noticed that taste sensations occurred exclusively from the back of the mouth.

The seeming unimportance of total taste losses over sizable areas to overall taste experience is a consequence of the way in which taste is spatially organized across the tongue. Taste shows some spatial summation over small areas (Smith, 1971). This means that for a given concentration, taste intensity grows as the area stimulated grows. However, spatial summation is limited. Even over small areas, doubling area does not double intensity. In fact, taste solutions painted on a small portion of the tongue with a Q-tip taste almost as strong as when they are sipped and tasted in the normal manner (Bartoshuk, Desnoyers, O'Brien, Gent, & Catalanotto, 1985). We might think of taste much like we think of the skin senses. We can perceive taste quality and intensity on restricted areas of the tongue just as we can perceive temperature and touch on restricted areas of the skin.

Stimulation of one tongue location has the ability to inhibit input from other locations. Such inhibitory interactions among tongue loci also contribute to the ability of a small tongue area to produce strong sensations. Halpern and Nelson (1965) were the first to demonstrate this inhibition. They recorded from an area in the rat medulla that receives input from both the front and back of the tongue. When they anesthetized the chorda tympani nerve (which innervates the front) the response from the back increased in magnitude. This suggests that input from the front normally inhibits the back. Anesthetizing the chorda tympani released that inhibition.

Release of inhibition can also be demonstrated psychophysically. After anesthetization of the human chorda tympani (with dental anesthesia) some taste solutions (especially sucrose) tasted more intense than normal (Ostrom, Catalanotto, Gent, & Bartoshuk, 1985).

Release of inhibition also appears to have occurred with a rare case of a CNS-induced taste phantom. A patient at the Connecticut Taste and Smell Center compained of a salty taste continually present on the tip of her tongue. Rinsing with water had no effect on the taste. When a topical anesthetic was applied to the tongue area from which the salty taste seemed to come, the taste was unaffected. When the anesthetic was applied to the whole tongue surface, the salty taste doubled in intensity.

Taste Loss over Restricted Concentrations

Psychophysical functions show the way in which perceived intensity grows with the concentration of a taste stimulus. A large body of data exists on the forms of the psychophysical functions for normal individuals (see Meiselman et al., 1972). Thus, theoretically, we can detect departures from normal.

Figure 9.21 shows examples of how taste functions can be altered. Note that these examples underline the peril of relying on thresholds to characterize taste function. For example, panels A, B, and C depict elevated thresholds. However, note that the threshold elevation does not necessarily predict what will happen at suprathreshold concentrations.

In panel A, perceived intensity is reduced by a constant proportion across all concentrations by *Gymnema sylvestre*. This kind of taste loss is also induced temporarily by exposing the tongue to detergents like the sodium lauryl sulfate found in many toothpastes and mouthwashes (DeSimone, Heck, & Bartoshuk, 1980). Panel B shows the addition of a sweet water taste to the sweet taste of sucrose (McBurney & Bartoshuk, 1973). This is similar to an abnormality found in some patients with dysgeusia. A chronic background taste adds onto the weakest stimuli (elevating the psychophysical function at the lower end) and acts as a masking taste for the threshold task (i.e., the patient must detect an increment above the background taste).

Panel C shows the effects of adaptation to sucrose. Adaptation to NaCl has similar effects on the salty taste of NaCl. Consider a patient with elevated Na^+ levels in saliva (as in Addison's disease). The threshold is increased (to a value just above the salivary Na^+ level) but the consequences of the elevated adaptation level are quickly overridden as concentration rises. Thus, at moderate to high NaCl concentrations, perceived saltiness is normal. Incidentally, this situation can lead to a peculiar set of detection

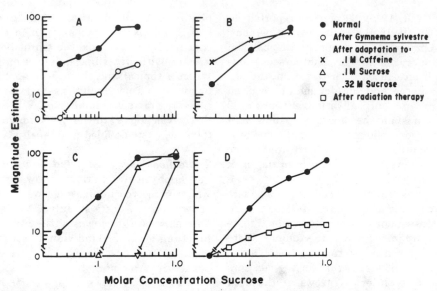

Figure 9.21. Examples of alterations in the taste psychophysical function for the sweetness of sucrose. From "Ratio Scaling" by L. M. Bartoshuk and L. E. Marks, 1986, in *Clinical Measurement of Taste and Smell* (p. 56), New York: MacMillan Publishers. Copyright 1986 by MacMillan Publishers. Reprinted by permission.

threshold values because of the water taste discussed above.

Panel D reflects the kind of change we observed from a patient undergoing radiation therapy for cancer of the neck (Bartoshuk, 1978). Shortly after therapy began, the patient's thresholds became severely elevated and her psychophysical functions flattened. Two months after therapy ended, her thresholds had returned to normal but her psychophysical functions remained flattened. She lived in a pastel taste world in spite of her normal thresholds.

Taste Loss for Individual Qualities

When taste losses occur they are not equivalent for all qualities. Sweet and bitter provide dramatic examples. A rare total lack of the ability to taste sweet has been associated with hypoparathroidism (Henkin & Shallenberger, 1970) and the ability to taste bitter appears to be especially vulnerable to head injury (Sumner, 1967). Specific loss of sweet or bitter is consistent with the independence (e.g., separate receptors, separate neurons) of sweet and bitter from each other and from salty and sour. Since both sweet and bitter appear to have more than one kind of receptor mechanism, there may well exist taste pathologies that are specific to certain sweet or bitter stimuli.

The salty taste of NaCl has been of special

interest because of the importance of low sodium diets to health. Contreras and Frank (1979) found that the rat's chorda tympani response to NaCl diminished as a result of sodium deprivation. Similarly, Bertino, Beauchamp, and Engleman (1983) showed that human subjects deprived of sodium perceived a highly salted soup to taste less salty. In a study on long-term sodium deprivation, the effect reversed: Subjects reported that NaCl tasted saltier.

The fact that the sensitivity to NaCl can change with dietary manipulations suggests that much more attention should be given to possible sensory changes in eating disorders.

Dysgeusia (Presence of a Persistent, Often Unpleasant, Taste)

This is the most debilitating taste disorder. There are at least two different origins for the symptoms: the actual presence of molecules with noxious taste in the mouth and disturbances in the nervous system.

Routes by which Noxious Molecules can Enter the Mouth

Bad tastes can get into the mouth by a variety of routes. Infected teeth or gums are obvious sources. Adjacent teeth filled with different metals can produce small electric currents (the metals act as the poles of a battery) that induce taste. Saliva can introduce abnormal substances into the mouth. In particular, some medications get secreted with saliva. Crevicular fluid (the fluid in gums near the teeth) may also be a source of noxious molecules. The permeability of the gum tissue increases when the tissue is inflamed (Alfano, 1974) making this a source that might be especially troublesome during certain disease states. Some dysgeusias may even result from *venous taste*: taste sensations resulting from the diffusion of taste substances from blood into the tissue surrounding the taste bud (Bradley, 1973). In all of these cases, the dysgeusia is produced by a normal taste system perceiving stimuli that have bad tastes.

Taste Phantoms Originating from Nerve Injury

The metallic taste reported by some patients in whom the chorda tympani was severed during ear surgery (discussed above) is an example of a taste phantom induced by nerve injury. These metallic phantoms are localized to the tongue area innervated by the nerve.

Taste Phantoms Originating in the CNS

Dysgeusia can also be produced by abnormal activity in the central nervous system. Hughlings Jackson (see Taylor, 1931) described *uncinate fits* as epileptic seizures which began with a sensation of smell or taste. These have subsequently been observed by a variety of others including Daly (1958) who reported 16 patients with taste, but no olfactory, hallucinations. The taste quality involved was usually unpleasant (sour, bitter, metallic) but one patient reported a salty sensation. In some of the reports, patients localized the sensation to a particular tongue area.

Taste phantoms originating from the CNS need not be associated with obvious seizures. The patient at the Connecticut Taste and Smell Center (discussed above) that perceived a salty taste coming from the tip of her tongue did not experience seizures and an EEG did not reveal any seizure activity. However, an anticonvulsive medication abolished the phantom. Two phenomena appear to be useful to distinguish local from central origins for dysgeusia: localization of the taste and its susceptibility to topical anesthesia. A central origin is suggested if the dysgeusia seems to be coming from a specific tongue area. A local origin is suggested if topical anesthesia reduces or abolishes dysgeusia.

REFERENCES

Alfano, M.C. (1974). The origin of gingival fluid. *Journal of Theoretical Biology, 47*, 127–136.

Andersson, B., Langren, S., Olsson, L., & Zotterman, Y. (1950). The sweet taste fibres of the dog. *Acta Physiologica Scandinavica., 21*, 105–119.

Arrhenius, S. (1929). *The foundations of the theory of dilute solutions* (Trans.). Edinburgh: Oliver and Boyd. (Original work published 1887).

Arvidson, K. (1976). Scanning electron microscopy of fungiform papillae on the tongue of man and monkey. *Acta Oto-Laryngologica., 81*, 496–502.

Arvidson, K. (1979). Location and variation in number of taste buds in human fungiform papillae. *Scandinavian Journal of Dental Research, 87*, 435–442.

Arvidson, K. (1980). Human taste: Response and taste bud number in fungiform papillae. *Science, 209*, 807–808.

Bare, J.K. (1949). The specific hunger for sodium chloride in normal and adrenalectomized rats. *Journal of Comparative and Physiological Psychology, 42*, 242–253.

Bartoshuk, L.M. (1968). Water taste in man. *Perception and Psychophysics, 3*, 68–72.

Bartoshuk, L.M. (1974). NaCl thresholds in man: Thresholds for water taste or NaCl taste? *Journal of Comparative and Physiological Psychology, 87*, 310–325.

Bartoshuk, L.M. (1975). Taste mixtures: Is mixture suppression related to compression? *Physiology and Behavior, 14*, 643–649.

Bartoshuk, L.M. (1978). The psychophysics of taste. *American Journal of Clinical Nutrition, 31*, 1068–1077.

Bartoshuk, L.M. (1979a). Bitter taste of saccharin: Related to the genetic ability to taste the bitter substance 6-*n*-propylthiouracil (PROP). *Science, 205*, 934–935.

Bartoshuk, L.M. (1979b, November). Taste interactions in mixtures of NaCl with QHCl and sucrose with QHCl. Poster presented at the 9th Annual Meeting of the Society for Neuroscience, Atlanta GA.

Bartoshuk, L.M. and Cleveland, C.T. (1977). Mixtures of substances with similar tastes: A test of a new model of taste mixture interactions. *Sensory Processes, 1*, 177–186.

Bartoshuk, L.M., Dateo, G.P., Vanderbelt, D.J., Buttrick, R.L., & Long, L. (1969). Effects of *Gymnema silvestre* and *Synsepalum dulcificum* on taste in man. In C. Pfaffmann (ed.), *Olfaction and taste: III*. New York: Rockefeller University Press, pp. 436–444.

Bartoshuk, L.M., Desnoyers, S., O'Brien, M., Gent, J.F., & Catalanotto, F.C. (1985). Taste stimulation of localized tongue areas: The Q-tip test. *Chemical Senses, 10*, 453.

Bartoshuk, L.M., Frank, M., & Pfaffmann, C. (1978, November). Gustatory responses to water. Paper presented at the 8th Annual Meeting of the Society for Neuroscience, St. Louis, MO.

Bartoshuk, L.M., Gentile, R.L., Moskowitz, H.R., & Meiselman, H.L. (1979). Sweet taste induced by miracle fruit (*Synsepalum dulcificum*). *Physiology and Behavior, 12*, 449–456.

Bartoshuk, L.M., Harned, M.A., & Parks, L.H. (1971). Taste of water in the cat: Effects on sucrose preference. *Science, 171*, 699–701.

Bartoshuk, L.M., Lee, C.H., & Scarpellino, R. (1972). Sweet taste of water induced by artichoke (*Cynara scolymus*). *Science, 178*, 988–990.

Bartoshuk, L.M. & Marks, L.E. (in press). Ratio Scaling. In *Clinical measurement of taste and smell*. New York: Macmillan. pp. 50–65.

Bartoshuk, L.M., McBurney, D.H., & Pfaffmann, C. (1964). Taste of sodium chloride solutions after adaptation to sodium chloride: Implications of the "water taste". *Science, 143*, 967–968.

Bartoshuk, L.M. & Pfaffmann, C. (1965). Effects of pre-treatment on the water taste response in cat and rat. *Federation Proceedings, 24*, 207.

Bartoshuk, L.M., Rennert, K., Rodin, J., & Stevens, J.C. (1982). The effects of temperature on the perceived sweetness of sucrose. *Physiology and Behavior, 28*, 905–910.

Bartoshuk, L.M., Rifkin, B., & Speers, M. (1980). Tastes of salts. In H. Van der Starre (ed.), *Olfaction and taste: VII* (pp. 367–370). London: IRL Press.

Bartoshuk, L.M. & Seibyl, J.P. (1982, April). Suppressions of bitterness of QHCl in mixtures: Possible mechanisms. Poster presented at the 4th Annual Meeting of the Association of Chemoreception Sciences, Sarasota, FL.

Beare, J.I. (1906). Greek theories of elementary cognition from Alcmaeon to Aristotle. Oxford: Clarendon Press.

Beckstead, R.M., Morse, J.R., & Norgren, R. (1980). The nucleus of the solitary tract in the monkey: Projections to the thalamus and brain stem nuclei. *Journal of Comparative Neurology, 190*, 259–282.

Beidler, L.M. (1959). A theory of taste stimulation. *Journal of General Physiology, 38*, 133–139.

Beidler, L.M. (1961). Taste receptor stimulation. In *Progress in Biophysics and Biophysical Chemistry* (pp. 107–151). New York: Pergamon Press.

Beidler, L.M. (1967). Anion influences on taste receptor response. In T. Hayashi (ed.), *Olfaction and taste: II* (pp. 509–534). New York: Pergamon Press.

Beidler, L.M. & Smallman, R.L. (1965). Renewal of cells within taste of buds. *Journal of Cell Biology, 27*, 263–272.

Bell, F.R. (1959). The sense of taste in domesticated animals. *Veternary Record, 71*, 1071–1079.

Bernard, R.A. (1971). Antidromic inhibition: A new theory to account for taste interactions. In F.F. Kao, K. Koizumi, & M. Vasselle (eds.), *Research in Physiology* (pp. 431–439). Bologna: Aulo Gaggi.

Bertino, M., Beauchamp, G.K., & Engelman, K. (1983). Increased dietary salt increases preferred level of salt. Presented at the fifth annual meeting of the Association for Chemoreception Sciences, Sarasota, FA.

Birch, G.G. (1976). Structural relationships of sugars to taste. *Critical Review of Food Science Nutrition, 8*, 57–95.

Borg, G., Diamant, H., Oakley, B., Ström, L., & Zotterman, Y. (1967). A comparative study of neural and psychophysical responses to gustatory stimuli. In T. Hayashi (ed.), *Olfaction and taste: II* (pp. 253–264). New York: Pergamon Press.

Boudreau, J.C. (1974). Neural encoding in cat geniculate ganglion tongue units. *Chemical Senses and Flavor, 1*, 41–51.

Boudreau, J.C. & Alev, N. (1973). Classification of chemoresponsive tongue units of the cat geniculate ganglion, *Brain Research, 54*, 157–175.

Boudreau, J.C., Anderson, W., & Oravec, J. (1975). Chemical stimulus determinants of cat geniculate ganglion chemoresponsive group II unit discharge. *Chemical Senses and Flavor, 1*, 495–518.

Boudreau, J.C., Hoang, N.K., Oravec, J., & Do, L.T. (1983). Rat neurophysiological taste responses to salt solutions. *Chemical Senses, 8*, 131–150.

Boudreau, J.C. & Nelson, T.E. (1977). Chemical stimulus determinants of cat geniculate ganglion chemoresponsive group I unit discharge. *Chemical Senses and Flavor, 2*, 353–374.

Bradley, R.M. (1971). Tongue topography. In L.M. Beidler (ed.), *Handbook of sensory physiology: Vol. IV. Chemical Senses: Section 2. Taste* (pp. 1–30). New York: Springer-Verlag.

Bradley, R.M. (1973). Electrophysiological investigations of intravascular taste using perfused rat tongue. *American Journal of Physiology, 224*, 300–304.

Bradley, R.M., Cheal, M.L., & Kim, Y.H. (1980). Quantitative analysis of developing epiglottal taste buds in sheep. *Journal of Anatomy, 130*, 25–32.

Bradley, R.M. & Mistretta, C.M. (1975). The developing sense of taste. In D.A. Denton & J.P. Coghlan (eds.), *Olfaction and taste: V* (pp. 91–98). New York: Academic Press.

Bull, T.R. (1965). Taste and chorda tympani. *Journal of Laryngology and Otology, 79,* 479–493.

Burton, H. & Benjamin, R.M. (1971). Central projections of the gustatory system. In L.M. Beidler (ed.), *Handbook of sensory physiology: Vol. IV. Chemical Senses: Section 2. Taste* (pp. 148–164). New York: Springer-Verlag.

Camerer, W. (1870). Ueber die Abhängigkeit des Geschmacksinns von der gereizten stelle der Mundhöhle. *Zeitschrift fur Biologie, 6,* 440–452.

Cameron, A.T. (1947). The taste sense and the relative sweetness of sugars and other sweet substances. *Scientific Reports of the Sugar Research Foundation; No. 9,* New York.

Carr, W.J. (1952). The effect of adrenelectomy upon the NaCl taste threshold in rat. *Journal of Comparative and Physiological Psychology, 45,* 377–380.

Cleaton-Jones, P. (1976). A denervation study of taste buds in the soft palate of the albino rat. *Archives of Oral Biology, 21,* 79–82.

Cohen, M.J., Hagiwara, S., & Zotterman, Y. (1955). The response spectrum of taste fibers in the cat: A single fibre analysis. *Acta Physiologica Scandinavica, 33,* 316–332.

Collings, V.B. (1974). Human taste response as a function of stimulation on the tongue and soft palate. *Perception and Psychophysics, 16,* 169–174.

Conger, A.D. (1973). Loss and recovery of taste acuity in patients irradiated to the oral cavity. *Radiation Research, 53,* 338–347.

Contreras, R.J. & Catalanotto, F.A. (1980). Sodium deprivation in rats: Salt thresholds are related to salivary sodium concentrations. *Behavioral and Neural Biology, 29,* 303–314.

Contreras, R.J. & Frank, M. (1979). Sodium deprivation alters neural responses to gustatory stimuli. *Journal of General Physiology, 73,* 569–594.

Daly, D. (1958). Uncinate fits. *Neurology, 8,* 250–260.

Daniell, W.F. (1852). On the *Synsepalum dulcificum, de Cand.*; or miraculous berry of western Africa. *Pharmaceutical Journal, 11,* 445–448.

Dastoli, F.R. & Price, S. (1966). Sweet-sensitive protein from bovine taste buds: Isolation and assay. *Science, 154,* 905–907.

Davy, D. (1958). Uncinate fits. *Neurology, 8,* 250–260.

Delay, R.J., Kinnamon, J.C., & Roper, S.D. (1983). Stereo HVEM Autoradiography of mouse taste buds. *Proceedings of the 41st Annual Meeting of the Electron Microscopy Society of America,* San Francisco Press: San Francisco.

DeSimone, J.A. & Heck, G.L. (1980). An analysis of the effects of stimulus transport and membrane charge on the salt, acid and water-response of mammals. *Chemical Senses, 5,* 295–316.

DeSimone, J.A., Heck, G.L., & Bartoshuk, L.M. (1980). Surface active taste modifiers: A comparison of the physical and psychophysical properties of gymnemic acid and sodium lauryl sulfate. *Chemical senses, 5,* 317–330.

DeSimone, J.A., Heck, G.L., & DeSimone, S.K. (1981). Active ion transport in dog tongue: A possible role in taste. *Science, 214,* 1039–1041.

DeSimone, J.A. & Price, S. (1976). A model of the stimulation of taste receptor cells by salt. *Biophysical Journal, 16,* 869–880.

DeSimone, J.A., Heck, G.L., Mierson, S., & DeSimone, S. (1984). The active ion transport properties of canine Lingual Epithelia in vitro. *Journal of General Physiology, 83,* 633–656.

Doetsch, G.S. & Erickson, R.P. (1970). Synaptic processing of taste-quality information in the nucleus tractus solilarius of the rat. *Journal of Neurophysiology, 33,* 490–507.

Erickson, R.P. (1963). Sensory neural patterns and gustation. In Y. Zotterman (ed.), *Olfaction and taste: I* (pp. 205–213). New York: Pergamon Press.

Erickson, R.P. (1968). Stimulus coding in topographic and nontopographic afferent modalities: On the significance of the activity of individual sensory neurons. *Psychological Review, 75,* 447–465.

Erickson, R.P. (1975). Parallel "population" neural coding in feature extraction. In G. Warner (ed.), *Feature extraction by neurons and behavior* (pp. 155–169). Cambridge, MA: MIT Press.

Erickson, R.P. (1977). The role of "primaries" in taste research. In J. LeMagnen & P. MacLeod (Eds.), *Olfaction and taste: VI* (pp. 369–376). London: Information Retrieval.

Erickson, R.P. & Covey, E. (1980). On the singularity of taste sensations: What is a taste primary? *Physiology and Behavior, 25,* 79–110.

Fairchild, D. (1931). *Exploring for plants.* New York: Macmillan.

Farbman, A.I. (1980). Renewal of taste bud cells in rat circumvallate papillae. *Cell Tissue Kinetics, 13,* 349–357.

Farbman, A.I., Hellekant, G., & Nelson, A. (1985). Structure of taste buds in foliate papillae of the rhesus monkey *Macaca mulatta. American Journal of Anatomy, 172,* 42–56.

Faull, J.R. & Halpern, B. (1971). Reduction of sucrose preference in the hamster by gymnemic acid. *Physiology and Behavior, 7,* 903–907.

Faurion, A., Saito, S., & MacLeond, P. (1980). Sweet taste involves several distinct receptor mechanisms. *Chemical Senses, 5,* 107–121.

Fernel, J. (1581). *Therapeutices universalis*. Frankfurt: Andream Wechelum.

Filin, V.A. & Esakov, A.I. (1968). Interaction between taste receptors. *Byulletin' Eksperimental'noi Biologii i Meditsiny*, 65, 12–15.

Frank, M. (1973). An analysis of hamster afferent taste nerve response functions. *Journal of General Physiology*, 61, 588–618.

Frank, M. (1974). The classification of mammalian afferent taste nerve fibers. *Chemical Senses and Flavor*, 1, 53–73.

Frank, M. (1975). Response patterns of rat glossopharyngeal taste neurons. In D.A. Denton & J.P. Coghlan (Eds.), *Olfaction and taste V:* (pp. 59–69). New York: Academic Press.

Frank, M.E., Contreras, R.J., & Hettinger, T.P. (1983). Nerve fibers sensitive to ionic taste stimuli in chorda tympani of the rat. *Journal of Neurophysiology*, 50, 941–960.

Frawley, T.F. & Thorn, G.W. (1951). The relation of the salivary sodium-potassium ratio to adrenal cortical activity. In J.R. Mote (Ed.), *Proceedings of the second clinical ACTH conference: Vol 1*. New York: Balkiston.

Funakoshi, M., Kashahara, Y., Yamamoto, T., & Kawamura, Y. (1971). Taste coding and central perception. In D. Schneider (ed.), *Olfaction and taste: IV* (pp. 336–342). Stuttgard: Wissenschaftliche Verlagsgesellschaft MBII.

Ganchrow, D. & Erickson, R.P. (1972). Thalamocortical relations in gustation. *Brain Research*, 36, 289–305.

Ganchrow, J.R. & Erickson, R.P. (1970). Neural correlates of gustatory intensity and quality. *Journal of Neurophysiology*, 33, 768–783.

Garcia, J. & Ervin, F.R. (1968). Appetites, aversions, and addictions: A model for visceral memory. In J. Wortis (Ed.), *Recent Advances in Biological Psychiatry*, 10, 284–293.

Garcia, J. & Hankins, W. (1975). The evolution of bitter and the acquisition of toxiphobia. In D.A. Denton & J.P. Coghlan (Eds.), *Olfaction and taste: V* (pp. 39–45). New York: Academic Press.

Gent, J.F. & Bartoshuk, L.M. (1983). Sweetness of sucrose, neohesperidin dihydrochalcone, and saccharin is related to genetic ability to taste the bitter substance 6-*n*-propylthiouracil. *Chemical Senses*, 7, 265–272.

Glaser, D., Hellekant, G., Brouwer, J.N., & van der Wel, H. (1984). Effects of gymnemic acid on sweet taste perception in primates. *Chemical Senses*, 8, 367–374.

Gordon, G., Kitchell, R., Ström, L., & Zotterman, Y. (1959). The response pattern of taste fibers in the chorda tympani of the monkey. *Acta Physiologica Scandinavica*, 46, 119–132.

Goto, N., Yamamoto, T., Kaneko, M., & Tomita, H. (1983). Primary pontine hemorrhage and gustatory disturbance: Clinicoanatomic study. *Stroke*, 14, 507–511.

Guth, L. (1971). Degeneration and regeneration of taste buds. In L.M. Beidler (ed.), *Handbook of Sensory Physiology: Vol. IV. Chemical Senses: Section 2. Taste* (pp. 63–74). New York: Springer-Verlag.

Hagstrom, E.C. (1957). Nature of taste stimulation by sugar. Unpublished doctoral dissertation, Brown University. Providence, R.I.

Hagstrom, E.C. & Pfaffmann, C. (1959). The relative taste effectiveness of different sugars for the rat. *Journal of Comparative and Physiological Psychology*, 52, 259–262.

Hahn, H. (1934). Die Adaptation des geschmackssinnes. *Zeitschrift für Sinnesphysiologie*, 65, 105–145.

Hahn, H. (1949). *Beiträge zur Reizphysiologie*. Heidelberg: Scherer.

Hainsworth, F.R. & Stricker, E.M. (1971). Evaporation cooling in the rat: Differences between salivary glands as thermoregulatory effectors. *Canadian Journal of Physiology and Pharmacology*, 49, 573–580.

Hall, M.J., Bartoshuk, L.M., Cain, W.S., & Stevens, J.C. (1975). PTC taste blindness and the taste of caffeine. *Nature* (London), 253, 442–443.

Haller, A. von. (1966). First lines of physiology. New York: Johnson Reprint Corp. (Original work published, 1786).

Halpern, B.P. (1967). Chemotopic coding for sucrose and quinine hydrochloride in the nucleus of the fasciculos solitarius. In T. Hayashi (ed.), *Olfaction and taste: III* (pp. 549–562). New York: Pergamon Press.

Halpern, B.P. & Nelson, L.M. (1965). Bulbar gustatory responses to anterior and to posterior tongue stimulation in the rat. *American Journal of Physiology*, 209, 105–110.

Hamilton, R.B. & Norgren, R. (1984). Central projections of gustatory nerves in the rat. *Journal of Comparative Neurology*, 222, 560–577.

Hänig, D.P. (1901). Zur Psychophysik des Geschmackssinnes. *Philosophische Studien*, 17, 576–623.

Harriman, A.E. & MacLeod, R.B. (1953). Discriminative thresholds of salt for normal and adrenalectomized rats. *American Journal of Psychology*, 66, 465–471.

Harvey, R.J. (1970). Gustatory studies relating to *Synsepalum dulcificum* (miracle fruit) and neural coding. Unpublished doctoral dissertation, Worcester Polytechnic Institute, Worcester, MA.

Heck, G.L., Mierson, S., & DeSimone, J.A. (1984). Salt taste transduction occurs through an amiloride-sensitive sodium transport pathway. *Science*, 223, 403–404.

Hellekant, G. (1976). On the gustatory effects of Monellin and thaumatin in dog, hamster, pig, and rabbit. *Chemical Senses and Flavor, 2,* 97–105.

Hellekant, G. (1983). Sweetness-inducing effect of miraculin in the Rhesus monkey. 5th annual meeting of the Association for Chemoreception Sciences, Sarasota, Florida.

Hellekant, G. & Gopal, V. (1976). On the effects of gymnemic acid in hamster and rat. *Acta Physiologica Scandinavica, 98,* 136–142.

Hellekant, G., Hagstrom, E.C., Kasahara, Y., & Zotterman, Y. (1974). On the gustatory effects of miraculin and gymnemic acid in the monkey. *Chemical Senses and Flavor, 1,* 137–145.

Hellekant, G., Hard, C., Segerstad, A.F., & Roberts, T. (1985). Effects of gymemic acid on the chorda tympani proper nerve responses to sweet, sour, salty and bitter taste stimuli in the chimpanzee, Presented at the Seventh Annual Meeting of the Association for Chemoreception Sciences, Sarasota, FA.

Helmholtz, H. (1968). Die Thatsachen in der Wahrnehmung [the facts of perception]. In R.M. Warren and R.P. Warren (transl.), *Helmholtz on perception: Its physiology and development.* (p. 210). Wiley, New York: (Original work published 1879).

Henkin, R.I. & Shallenberger, R.S. (1970). Aglycogeusia: The inability to recognize sweetness and its possible molecular basis. *Nature, 227,* 965–966.

Henle, J. (1880). Ueber den Geschmackssinn. *Anthropologische Vorträge, 2,* 3–24.

Henning, H. (1927). Psychologische Studien am Geschmackssinn. In F. Aberholden (ed.), *Handbuch der biologischen arbeitsmethoden.* Berlin: Urban and Schwarzenberg, pp. 627–740.

Hiji, Y. (1975). Selective elimination of taste responses to sugars by proteolytic enzymes. *Nature, 256,* 427–429.

Hiji, Y. & Ito, H. (1977). Removal of "sweetness" by proteases and its recovery mechanism in rat taste cells. *Comparative Biochemistry and Physiology, 58,* 109–113.

Höber, R. & Kiesow, F. (1898). Über den geschmack von Salzen und Laugen. *Zeitschrift für Physikalische chemie, 27,* 601–616.

Hooper, D. (1887). An examination of the leaves of *Gymnema sylvestre. Nature* (London), *35,* 565–567.

Horn, W. (1825). Ueber den geschmackssinn des menschen. Heidelberg: Karl Groos.

Horowitz, R.M. & Gentili, B. (1969). Taste and structure in phenolic glycosides. *Journal of Agricultural and Food Chemistry, 17,* 696–700.

Ishiko, N. & Akagi, T. (1972). Topographical organization of gustatory nervous system. In D. Schneider (ed.), *Olfaction and taste: IV* (pp. 343–349). Stuttgart: Wissenschaftliche Verlagsgesellschaft MBH.

Ishiko, N., Amatusu, M., & Sato, Y. (1967). Thalamic representation of taste qualities and temperature change in the cat. In T. Hayashi (ed.), *Olfaction and taste: II* (pp. 563–572). New York: Pergamon Press.

Jakinovich, W. (1982). Stimulation of the gerbil's gustatory receptors by saccharin. *The Journal of Neuroscience, 2,* 49–56.

Jakinovich, W. (1983). Methyl 4,6-dichloro-4,6-dideoxy-α-D-galactophranoside: An inhibitor of sweet taste responses in gerbils. *Science, 219,* 408–410.

Jakinovich, W. (1982). Stimulation of the gerbil's gustatory receptors by saccharin. *Journal of Neuroscience, 2,* 49–56.

Jakinovich, W. & Vlahopoulos, U. (1984, April). Inhibition of the gerbil's electrophysiological sucrose taste response by para-phenyl-α-D-glucopyranoside and chloramphenicol. Paper presented at the 6th Annual Meeting of the Association for Chemoreception Sciences. Sarasota, FL.

Kahlenberg, L. (1898). The action of solutions on the sense of taste. *Bulletin of the University of Wisconsin, 2,* 3–31.

Kennedy, L.M., Sturckow, B., & Waller, F.J. (1975). Effect of gymnemic acid on single taste hairs of the housefly, *Musca domestica. Physiology and Behavior, 14,* 755–765.

Kier, C.V. (1972). A molecular theory of sweet taste. *Journal of Pharmaceutical Sciences, 61,* 1394–1397.

Kiesow, F. (1894a). Beiträge zur physiologischen Psychologie des Geschmackssinnes. *Philosophische Studien, 10,* 329–368.

Kiesow, F. (1894b). Uber die Wirkung des Cocain und der Gymnemasäure auf die Schleimhaut der Zunge und des Mundraums. *Philosophische Studien, 9,* 510–527.

Kiesow, F. (1896). Beiträge zur physiologischen Psychologie des Geschmackssinnes. *Philosophische Studien, 12,* 255–278.

Kinnamon, J.C., Taylor, B.J., Delay, R.J., & Roper, S.D. (1985). Ultrastructure of mouse vallate taste buds: I. Taste cells and their associated synapses. *Journal of Comparative Neurology, 235,* 48–60.

Koh, S.D. & Teitelbaum, P. (1961). Absolute behavioral taste thresholds in the rat. *Journal of Comparative and Physiological Psychology, 54,* 223–229.

Kosar, E., Norgren, R., & Grill, H.J. (in press). Delimination of rat gustatory cortex. Presented at the 7th Annual Meeting of the Association for Chemoreception Sciences, Sarasota, FL, 1985.

Kubota, T. & Kubo, I. (1969). Bitterness and chemical structure. *Nature* (London) *223,* 97–99.

Kurihara, K. & Beidler, L.M. (1969). Mechanism of the action of taste-modifying protein. *Nature* (London), *222,* 1176–1179.

Kurihara, K. & Koyama, N. (1972). High activity of adenyl cyclase in olfactory and gustatory organs. *Biochemical and Biophysical Research Communications*, *48*, 30–34.

Kurihara, Y. (1969). Antisweet activity of gymnemic acid A_1 and its derivatives. *Life Sciences*, *8*, 537–543.

Kuznicki, J.T. & McCutcheon, N.B. (1979). Cross enhancement of the sour taste on single human taste papillae. *Journal of Experimental Psychology: General*, *108*, 68–89.

Lawless, H.T. (1979). Evidence for neural inhibition in bittersweet taste mixtures. *Journal of Comparative and Physiological Psychology*, *93*, 538–547.

Lawless, H.T. & Stevens, D.A. (1983). Cross adaptation of sucrose and intensive sweeteners. *Chemical Senses*, *7*, 309–315.

Liljestrand, G. & Zottermann, Y. (1954). The water taste in mammals. *Acta Physiologica Scandinavica*, *32*, 291–303.

Lockhart, E.E. & Gainer, J.M. (1950). Effect of monosodium glutamate on taste of pure sucrose and sodium chloride. *Food Research*, *15*, 459.

Makous, W., Nord, S., Oakley, B., & Pfaffmann, C. (1963). The gustatory rely in the medulla. In Y. Zotterman (ed.), *Olfaction and taste: I* (pp. 381–393). New York: Pergamon Press.

McBurney, D.H. (1972). Gustatory cross-adaptation between sweet tasting compounds. *Perception and Psychophysics*, *11*, 225–227.

McBurney, D.H. (1979). Are there primary tastes for man? *Chemical Senses and Flavor*, *1*, 17–28.

McBurney, D.H. (1977). Temporal properties of the human taste system. *Sensory Processes*, *1*, 150–162.

McBurney, D.H. & Bartoshuk, L.M. (1973). Interaction between stimuli with different taste qualities. *Physiology and Behavior*, *10*, 1101–1106.

McBurney, D.H. & Gent, J.F. (1979). On the matter of taste qualities. *Psychological Bulletin*, *86*, 151–167.

McBurney, D.H. & Lucas, J.A. (1966). Gustatory cross adaptation between salts. *Psychonomic Science*, *4*, 301–302.

McBurney, D.H. & Pfaffmann, C. (1963). Gustatory adaptation to saliva and sodium chloride. *Journal of Experimental Psychology*, *65*, 523–529.

McBurney, D.H. & Shick, T.R. (1971). Taste and water taste of twenty-six compounds for man. *Perception and Psychophysics*, *10*, 249–252.

McBurney, D.H., Smith, D.V., & Shick, T.R. (1972). Gustatory cross adaptation: sourness and bitterness. *Perception and Psychophysics*, *11*, 228–232.

Meiselman, H.L. (1971). Effect of presentation procedure on taste intensity functions. *Perception and Psychophysics*, *10*, 15–18.

Meiselman, H.L., Bose, H.E., & Nykvist, W.E. (1972). Effect of flow rate on taste intensity responses in humans. *Physiology and Behavior*, *9*, 35–38.

Meiselman, H.L. & Halpern, B.P. (1970). Effects of Gymnema sylvestre on complex tastes elicited by amino acids and sucrose. *Physiology and Behavior*, *5*, 1379–1384.

Miller, I.J. (1971). Peripheral interactions among single papilla inputs to gustatory nerve fibers. *Journal of General Physiology*, *57*, 1–25.

Mistretta, C.M. (1981). Neurophysiological and anatomical aspects of taste development. In *Development of perception: Vol. I.* (pp. 433–455). New York: Academic Press.

Moncrieff, R.W. (1967). *The Chemical Senses*. London: Leonard Hill.

Morrison, G.R. (1967). Behavioral response patterns to salt stimuli in the rat. *Canadian Journal of Psychology*, *21*, 141–152.

Morrison, G.R. & Norrison, W. (1966). Taste detection in the rat. *Canadian Journal of Psychology*, *20*, 208–217.

Moskowitz, H.R. (1972). Perceptual changes in taste mixtures. *Perception and Psychophysics*, *11*, 257–262.

Mossman, K.L. & Henkin, R.I. (1978). Radiation-induced changes in taste acuity in cancer patients. *International Journal of Radiation Oncology, Biology, Physics*, *4*, 663–667.

Müller, J. (1938). *Handbuch der Physiologie des Menschen*. Coblenz: J. Hölscher.

Murray, R.G. (1973). The ultrastructure of taste buds. In I. Friedmenn (ed.), *The Ultra structure of sensory organs* (pp. 1–81). New York: American Elsevier.

Nachman, M. (1963). Learned aversion to the taste of lithium chloride and generalization to other salts. *Journal of Comparative and Physiological Psychology*, *56*, 343–349.

Natanson, L. (1844). Analyse der Funktionen des Nervensystems. *Archiv für Physiologische Heilkunde*, *3*, 515–535.

Norgren, R. (1974). Gustatory afferents to ventral forebrain. *Brain Research*, *81*, 285–295.

Norgren, R. (1976). Taste pathways to hypothalamus and amygdala. *Journal of Comparative Neurology*, *166*, 17–30.

Norgren, R. (1977). A synopsis of gustatory neuroanatomy. In J. LeMagnen (ed.), *Olfaction and taste: VI* (pp. 225–248). New York: Information Retrieval, Ltd.

Norgren, R. (1984). Central neural mechanisms of taste. In J.B. Brookhart & U.B. Mountcastle (eds.), *Handbook of physiology: Vol. III. Sensory process: part 2* (pp. 1087–1128). Bethesda, MD: American Physiological Society.

Norgren, R. & Leonard, C.M. (1973). Ascending central gustatory pathways. *Journal of Comparative Neurology, 150,* 217–238.

Nowlis, G.H. & Frank, M.E. (1981). Quality coding in gustatory systems of rats and hamsters. In D.M. Norris (Ed.), *Perception of behavioral chemicals* (pp. 58–80). Amsterdam: Elsevier Biomedical Press.

Oakley, B. (1962). Microelectrode analysis of second order gustatory neurons in the albino rat. Doctoral dissertation, Brown University. University Microfilms, Ann Arbor, Michigan, No. 63-1045.

Oakley, B. (1967). Altered temperature and taste responses from cross-regenerated sensory nerves in the rat's tongue. *Journal of Physiology* (London), *188,* 353–371.

Oakley, B. (1975). Receptive fields of cat taste fibers. *Chemical Senses and Flavor, 1,* 431–442.

Ogawa, H., Sato, M., & Yamashito, S. (1968). Multiple sensitivity of chorda tympani fibers of the rat and hamster to gustatory and thermal stimuli. *Journal of Physiology, 17,* 243–258.

Ogawa, H., Yamashita, S., Noma, A., & Sato, M. (1972). Taste responses in the macaque monkey chorda tympani. *Physiology and Behavior, 9,* 325–331.

Öhrwall, H. (1891). Untersuchungen über den Geschmackssinn. *Skandinavian Archiv für Physiologie, 2,* 1–69.

Öhrwall, H. (1901). Die Modalitäts- und Qualitätsbegriffe in der Sinnesphysiologie and deren Bedeutung. *Skandinavian Archiv für Physiologie, 11,* 245–272.

Ostrum, K.M., Catalanotto, F.A., Gent, J., & Bartoshuk, L.M. (in press). Effects of oral sensory field loss on taste scaling ability. *Chemical Senses,* in press.

O'Mahoney, M. & Alba, M. d. C.M. (1980). Taste descriptions in Spanish and English. *Chemical Senses, 5,* 47–61.

O'Mahoney, M. & Muhiudeen, H. (1977). A preliminary study of alternative taste languages using qualitative description of sodium chloride solutions: Malay versus English. *British Journal of Psychology, 68,* 275–278.

O'Mahoney, M. & Thompson, B. (1977). Taste quality descriptions: Can the subject's response be affected by mentioning taste words in the instructions? *Chemical Senses and Flavor, 2,* 283–298.

Pangborn, R.M. (1960). Taste interrelationships. *Food Research, 25,* 245–256.

Perotto, R.S. & Scott, T.R. (1976). Gustatory neural coding in the pons. *Brain Research, 110,* 283–300.

Pfaffmann, C. (1941). Gustatory afferent impulses. *Journal of Cellular and Comparative Physiology, 17,* 243–258.

Pfaffmann, C. (1955). Gustatory nerve impulses in rat, cat and rabbit. *Journal of Neurophysiology, 18,* 429–440.

Pfaffmann, C. (1957). Taste mechanisms in preference behavior. *American Journal of Clinical Nutrition, 5,* 142–147.

Pfaffmann, C. (1959). The sense of taste. In J. Field (ed.), *Handbook of physiology: section I. neurophysiology: Vol. I* (pp. 507–533). Washington, DC: American Physiological Society.

Pfaffmann, C. (1969). Taste preference and reinforcement. In J.T. Tapp (ed.), *Reinforcement and behavior* (pp. 215–241). New York: Academic Press.

Pfaffmann, C. (1974). Specificity of the sweet receptors of the squirrel monkey. *Chemical Senses and Flavor, 1,* 61–67.

Pfaffmann, C. & Bare, J.K. (1950). Gustatory nerve discharges in normal and adrenalectomized rats. *Journal of Comparative and Physiological Psychology, 43,* 320–324.

Pfaffmann, C., Frank, M., Bartoshuk, L.M., & Snell, T.C. (1976). Coding gustatory information in the squirrel monkey chorda tympani. In J.M. Sprague & A.N. Epstein (eds.), *Progress in psychobiology and physiological psychology* (pp. 1–27). New York: Academic Press.

Pfaffmann, C. & Hagstrom, E.C. (1955). Factors influencing taste sensitivity to sugar. *American Journal of Physiology, 183,* 651.

Pfaffmann, C., Norgren, R., & Grill, H.J. (1977). Sensory affect and motivation. *Annals of the New York Academy of Sciences, 290,* 18–34.

Pilgrim, F.J., Schutz, H.G., & Peryam, D.R. (1955). Influence of monosodium glutamate on taste perception. *Food Research, 20,* 310–314.

Price, S. (1973). Phosphodiesterase in tongue epithelium activation by bitter taste stimuli. *Nature* (London), *241,* 54.

Price, S. (1974). Chemoreceptor proteins in taste cell stimulation. I.T.M. Poynder (ed.), *Transduction mechanisms in chemoreception* (pp. 177–184). London: Information Retrieval.

Price, S. & Hogan, R.M. (1969). Glucose dehydrogenase activity of a sweet-sensitive protein from bovine tongues. In C. Pfaffmann (ed.), *Olfaction and taste: III* (pp. 397–403). New York: Rockefeller University Press.

Rapuzzi, G. & Casella, C. (1965). Innervation of the fungiform papillae in the frog tongue. *Journal of Neurophysiology, 28,* 154–165.

Renqvist, Y. (1919). Ueber den Geschmack. *Skandinavian Archiv für Physiologie, 38,* 97–201.

Richter, C.P. (1936). Increased salt appetite in adrenalectomized rats. *American Journal of Physiology, 115,* 155–161.

Richter, C.P. (1939). Salt taste thresholds of normal

and adrenalectomized rats. *Endocrinology, 24,* 367–371.

Rifkin, B. & Bartoshuk, L.M. (1980). Taste synergism between monosodium glutamate and disodium 5′-guanylate. *Physiology and Behavior, 24,* 1169–1172.

Rolls, E.T. (1985). Gustatory responses of single neurons in the orbitofrontal cortex of the macaque monkey. *Chemical Senses,* in press.

Sato, M. (1967). Gustatory response as a temperature-dependent process. In W.D. Neff (ed.), *Contributions to Sensory Physiology* (pp. 223–251). New York: Academic Press.

Schechter, P.J. & Henkin, R.I. (1974). Abnormalities of taste and smell after head trauma. *Journal of Neurology, Neurosurgery, and Psychiatry, 37,* 802–810.

Schiffman, S.S., Cahn, H., & Lindley, M.G. (1981). Multiple receptor sites mediate sweetness: Evidence from cross-adaptation. *Pharmacology, Biochemistry & Behavior, 15,* 377–388.

Schiffman, S.S. & Erickson, R.P. (1971). A theoretical review: A psychophysical model for gustatory quality. *Physiology and Behavior, 1,* 617–633.

Schiffman, S.S., Lockhead, E., & Maes, F.W. (1983). Amiloride reduces the taste intensity of Na$^+$ and Li$^+$ salts and sweeteners. *Proceedings of the National Academy of Sciences, 80,* 6136–6140.

Scott, T.R. & Chang, F.-C.T. (1984). The state of gustatory neural coding. *Chemical Senses, 8,* 297–314.

Scott, T.R. & Erickson, R.P. (1971). Synaptic processing of taste-quality information in thalamus of the rat. *Journal of Neurophysiology, 34,* 868–884.

Scott, T.R., Yaxley, S., Sienkiewicz, Z.J., & Rolls, E.T. (in press). Gustatory responses in opercular cortex of the alert cynomolgous monkey. *Chemical Senses.*

Shaber, G.S., Brent, R.I., & Rumsey, J.A. (1970). Conditioned suppression taste thresholds in the rat. *Journal of Comparative and Physiological Psychology, 73,* 193–201.

Shallenberger, R.S. (1977). Chemical clues to the perception of sweetness. In G.G. Birch, J.C. Brennan & K.J. Parker (Eds.), *Sensory properties of foods* (pp. 91–100). London: Applied Science Publishers.

Shallenberger, R.S. & Acree, T.E. (1967). Molecular theory of sweet taste. *Nature* (London), *216,* 480–482.

Shallenberger, R.S. & Acree, T.E. (1971). Chemical structure of compounds and their sweet and bitter taste. In L.M. Beidler (ed.), *Handbook of sensory physiology: Vol. IV. chemical senses: section 2. taste* (pp. 221–277). New York: Springer-Verlag.

Shallenberger, R.S. & Lindley, M.G. (1977). A lipophilic-hydrophobic attribute and component in the stereochemistry of sweetness. *Food Chemistry, 2,* 145–153.

Shenkin, H.A. & Lewey, F.H. (1944). Taste aura preceding convulsions in a lesion of the parietal operculum. *Journal of Nervous and Mental Disease, 100,* 352–354.

Shore, L.E. (1892). A contribution to our knowledge of taste sensations. *Journal of Physiology* (London), *13,* 191–217.

Smith, D.V. (1971). Taste intensity as a function of area and concentration: Differentiation between compounds. *Journal of Experimental Pschology, 87,* 163–171.

Smith, D.V. & Frank, M. (1972). Cross-adaptation between salts in the chorda tympani nerve of the rat. *Physiology and Behavior, 8,* 213–220.

Smith, D.V. & McBurney, D.H. (1969). Gustatory cross-adaptation: Does a single mechanism code the salty taste? *Journal of Experimental Psychology, 80,* 101–105.

Smith, D.V., Van Buskirk, R.L., Travers, J.B., & Bieber, S.L. (1983a). Coding of taste stimuli by hamster brain stem neurons. *Journal of Neurophysiology, 50,* 541–558.

Smith, D.V., Van Buskirk, R.L., Travers, J.B., & Bieber, S.L. (1983b). Gustatory neuron types in hamster brain stem. *Journal of Neurophysiology, 50,* 522–540.

Smith, J. (1971). Radiation: its detection and its effects on preferences. In *Progress in physiological psychology* (pp. 53–118). New York: Academic Press.

Snell, T.C. (1965). The response of the squirrel monkey chorda tympani to a variety of taste stimuli. Unpublished Master's thesis, Brown University. Providence, R.I.

Stevens, J.C. & Green, B.G. (1978). History of research on feeling. In E.C. Carterette & M.P. Friedman (Eds.), *Handbook of perception: vol. 6b. feeling and hurting* (pp. 3–25). New York: Academic Press.

Stevens, S.S. (1958). Measurement and Man. *Science, 127,* 383–389.

Stevens, S.S. (1969). Sensory scales of taste intensity. *Perception and Psychophysics, 6,* 302–308.

Stevens, S.S. (1975). *Psychophysics,* New York: Wiley.

Stone, H. & Oliver, S.M. (1969). Measurement of the relative sweetness of selected sweeteners and sweetener mixtures. *Journal of Food Science, 34,* 215–222.

Storey, A.T. & Johnson, P. (1975). Laryngeal receptors initiating apnea in lambs. In J.F. Bosma & J. Showacre (eds.), *Development of upper respiratory anatomy and function* (pp. 184–198). Bethesda, MD: U.S. DHEW.

Sweeney, E.A. & Catalanotto, F.A. (1976). Salivary sodium and potassium concentrations in adrenalectomized rats. Presented at the International Association of Dental Research.

Sumner, D. (1967). Post-traumatic ageusia. *Brain, 90,* 187–202.

Taylor, J. (1931). *Selected writings of John Hughlings Jackson: Vol. One. On epilepsy and epileptiform convulsions.* London: Hodder and Stoughton.

Teeter, J. & Kare, M.R. (1974). Passive electrical properties and responses to chemical stimulation of cutaneous taste bud cells and surrounding surface cells of the catfish. *Federation Proceedings, 33,* 416.

Thrasher, T.N. & Fregly, M.J. (1980). Factors affecting salivary sodium concentration, NaCl intake, and preference thresholds and their interrelationships. In M.R. Kare, M.J. Fregley, & R.A. Bernard (Eds.), *Biological and Behavioral Aspects of Salt Intake* (pp. 145–165). New York: Academic Press.

Travers, J.B. & Smith, D.V. (1979). Gustatory sensitivies in neurons of the hamster nucleus tractus solitarius. *Sensory Processes, 3,* 1–26.

Tripp, N. (1985). The miracle berry. *Horticulture, The Magazine of American Gardening, 63,* 58–72.

Van Buskirk, R.L. & Smith, D.V. (1981). Taste sensitivity of hamster parabrachial pontine neurons. *Journal of Neurophysiology, 45,* 144–171.

Van der Wel, H. & Arvidson, K. (1978). Quantitative psychophysical studies on the gustatory effects of the sweet tasting proteins thaumatin and monellin. *Chemical Senses and Flavor, 3,* 291–297.

Von Stramlik, E. (1922). Mischungsgleichungen im Gebiete des Geschmackssines. *Zeitschrift für Sinnes-Physiologie, 53,* 36–78.

Wang, M.B. (1973). Analysis of taste receptor properties derived from chorda tympani nerve firing patterns. *Brain Research, 54,* 314–317.

Wang, M.B. & Bernard, R.A. (1969). Characterization and interaction of taste receptors in chorda tympani fibers of the cat. *Brain Research, 15,* 567–570.

Warren, R.M. & Fraffmann, C. (1959). Suppression of sweet sensitivity by potassium gymnemate. *Journal of Applied Physiology, 14,* 40–42.

Whitehead, M.C., Frank, M.E., Hettinger, T.P., Hou, L.T., & Nah, H.D. (1987). Persistence of taste buds in denervated fungiform papillae. *Brain Research, 405,* 192–195.

Yackzan, K.S. (1969). Biological effects of Gymnema sylvestre fractions: II. Electrophysiology-effect of gymnemic acid on taste receptor response. *Alabama Journal of Medical Sciences, 6,* 455–463.

Yamaguchi, S., Yoshikawa, T., Ikeda, S., & Ninomiya, T. (1970). Studies on the taste of some sweet substances: II. Interrelationships among them, *Agricultural and Biological Chemistry, 34,* 187–197.

Yamamoto, T. & Kawamura, Y. (1974). An off-type response of the chorda tympani nerve in the rat. *Physiology and Behavior, 13,* 239–243.

Yoshida, M. & Saito, S. (1969). Multidimensional scaling of the taste of amino acids. *Japanese Psychological Research, 11,* 149–166.

Zawalich, W.S. (1973). Depression of gustatory sweet response by alloxan. *Comparative and Biochemical Physiology, 44A,* 903–909.

Zotterman, Y. (1949). The responses of the frog's taste fibres to the application of pure water. *Acta Physiologica Scandinavica, 18,* 181–189.

Zotterman, Y. (1956). Species differences in the water taste. *Acta Physiologica Scandinavica, 37,* 60–70.

PART 2

MOTIVATION

Chapter 10

THE ADAPTIVE-EVOLUTIONARY POINT OF VIEW IN EXPERIMENTAL PSYCHOLOGY

Paul Rozin, *University of Pennsylvania*

Jonathan Schull, *Haverford College*

INTRODUCTION

Charles Darwin and Psychology

Charles Darwin is undoubtedly one of the most influential figures in the history of experimental psychology. Boring (1950) ranks him with Helmholtz, Freud, and James. Darwin made two great contributions of relevance to psychology, but only one had a significant

This manuscript dates from August, 1984 when the final MS was submitted, in accordance with the publication plans at that time. It does not cover materials published subsequent to that date.

We thank W. John Smith for invaluable discussions and a critical reading of the manuscript. He could well be a third author. We also thank Ruth Colwill, Michael Domjan, Paula Durlach, Henry Gleitman, Robert Rescorla, Sara Shettleworth, and Sidney Perloe for critical comments.

influence on the field; his insight into the historical continuity of animals and men. Expressed most clearly in *The Descent of Man* (1871), this idea influenced the growth of comparative psychology and the psychology of animal learning (Jenkins, 1979; Lockard, 1971). Because it emphasized the similarity of structure among organisms, it implied that mechanisms and principles of animal psychology might apply as well to human behavior and mental life.

Darwin's (1859) more fundamental insight dealt with the diversity of biological species and their remarkably adaptive fit with their environment. To explain this, he combined the principle of heritable variation with the principle of differential reproductive success of more fit variants, and formulated the theory of evolution by natural selection. These principles and the simple fact that environments vary greatly highlight the adaptive diversity of living things, whereas the principle of continuity emphasizes the similarity among organisms.

In psychology, the lure of continuity has overshadowed the draw of diversity. At best, these two perspectives made little contact with each other; often they were seen as antagonistic. However, the last few decades have seen some reconciliation. A major goal of this chapter is to chronicle the confrontation and reconciliation of these two perspectives in a number of areas of psychology, especially animal learning, where the historical and contemporary issues are most clearly drawn (see Boakes's *From Darwin to Behaviorism* [1984] for a history of the period).

Behavior Theory

An early response to the principle of continuity was the collation of anecdotes alleged to demonstrate human-like intelligence and cognition in animals (Romanes, 1882). Inspired by the ideal of objectivity, later researchers eschewed the imputation of "higher mental processes" to animals and humans and sought to show that human performance could be explained by the same basic principles operative in animals (Morgan, 1894; Thorndike, 1898; reviewed in Gottlieb, 1979). From the turn of the century, animal models of human learning were a prime concern. Although it was launched and justified by the principle of continuity, this enterprise was modeled on physics and physiology, rather than evolutionary biology. Species differences, especially in receptors and effectors, were acknowledged, but psychologists were primarily interested in just those reflexive and associational mechanisms which "lower" animals shared with that most versatile species, man. They emphasized the arbitrariness of the components of associations, and their procedures were designed to eliminate those species-specific traits of their subjects which might interfere with the extraction of general principles. Thus, Thorndike designed his apparatus to be arbitrary, so that it "could not have been previously experienced or provided for by heredity" (1898, pp. 7–8) (Jenkins, 1979; Timberlake, 1983). The study of learning became the dominant enterprise in experimental psychology, and its proponents included many of the leading psy

chologists of the century: Watson, Tolman, Hull, and Skinner. It was rigorous and it was vigorous.

The principles of association and continuity, and strong views on the nature of science as an objective enterprise (Jenkins, 1979) contributed to a general set of attitudes toward research, known as *behavior theory* or *general process theory* (Logue, 1985a, 1985b; Rachlin, 1976; Schwartz & Lacey, 1982). Its major tenets were linked by history more than by logic. We offer here a distillation, closest to the position held by Skinner (1938, 1953).

1. (a) The underlying principles of learning are the same across species. (b) The underlying principles of learning are the same across domains (e.g., reproduction, feeding, different perceptual systems) within a species. These comprise the general process assumption.

2. Learning is decomposable into one or a few basic associative processes.

3. Most behavior is acquired ("environmentalism" or "empiricism").

4. Behavior, and only behavior, can be the proper basis for an objective experimental psychology.

These four assumptions each have their own roots: the general process assumption traces to Darwin, and yet ironically it is the only one that conflicts with the full expression of Darwin's views. The second and third assumptions derive from the British empiricist philosophers, and the fourth stems from the reaction against introspectionism, psychoanalysis and overly-mentalistic interpretations of animal behavior.

The first and second assumptions are the most relevant for this chapter, for they spawned the associationist "principle of equipotentiality": "The most important characteristic of a learned response (R) is that it can be associated with any arbitrarily selected stimulus (S) within the animal's repertoire" (Miller, 1967). This widely held principle figures centrally in the reevaluation of behavior theory in the last 15 years.

While embracing Darwin's principle of continuity, behavior theory ignored the *raison d'etre* of Darwin's theory of evolution: variation and adaptive fit. Uniformity in species, environments, and demands made by different types of life problems (feeding, avoiding predation, mating) was assumed, and species differences were relegated to natural history unless they happened to be exploited as useful model systems (the convenient laboratory rat, the all-cone bird retina). However, in the last two decades adaptive-evolutionary perspectives have emerged in psychology, and in particular in the study of learning.

The Adaptive-Evolutionary Approach

What has happened? Most notable, the science of ethology, developed primarily by the European zoologists Lorenz (1981) and N. Tinbergen (1951), provided an alternative approach to the study of animal behavior (see chapter by Baerends). Ethologists studied the evolutionary origins and adaptive value of behavior, as well as its development and mechanisms, and demonstrated that species-typical behaviors were appropriate objects of scientific attention. They could be treated, for example, as symptoms of taxonomic relatedness (Lorenz, 1971) and as products of studiable selection pressures operative in each species' ecological niche (N. Tinbergen, 1963b).

The approaches of ethology and behavior theory were complementary. While ethologists focussed on innate, species-specific behaviors in natural settings, behavior theorists studied acquired, arbitrary behaviors in the laboratory. However, this complementarity led to mutual disinterest instead of cross-fertilization. Imprinting (Lorenz, 1937), for example, had virtually no impact on the psychology of learning because it did not fit into the associative framework; it was passively acknowledged as a special mechanism for species recognition that wasn't really "learning."

Lorenz, in turn, thought the American emphasis on learning and experience was hopelessly naive (see Lorenz, 1981; Lehrman, 1970). The distance between these two approaches was increased by the shared assumption that behaviors were *either* learned *or* innate and is exemplified by Skinner's (1938) derogation of "botanizing"—the unedifying cataloging of species-specific reflexes.

The adaptive-evolutionary approach presented in this chapter adopts the ethological focus on selection pressures and adaptive functions. It acknowledges that just as botanizing is appropriate in a world of plants, so is the study of adaptive diversity appropriate in the world of animals. However, the ethologist's emphasis on innate behaviors is not essential to such an approach. Learning and plasticity are products of evolution by natural selection. Behaviors are not learned *or* innate; they are more or less influenced by experience.

Thus the goal of the adaptive-evolutionary approach is to understand how animals represent the world and act effectively upon it. It is committed to explaining the full range of behaviors and to the consideration of natural contexts before theory construction. Finally, for ecological and empirical reasons, it anticipates that explanations of behavior will involve both general processes and specific adaptations.

There are two approaches to the rigorous investigation of the adaptiveness of behavior. The older is a comparative approach, recently recommended to psychologists by Domjan and Galef (1983). Functions and phylogenies of behaviors are analyzed through comparison of related species occupying differing habitats and unrelated species occupying similar niches (e.g., Cullen, 1957). A different approach, more congenial to psychologists, involves modeling the forces directing adaptation and testing the predictions of the model against the animal's behavior. Optimality theory in foraging, which we shall discuss, does just this. The critical point about both approaches is that they make predictions that can be shown to be right or wrong in any specific case.

Cognition, Language, and Perception

Although the adaptive-evolutionary approach is applicable to all psychological phenomena, it has been notably absent from the area of cognition, as well as learning. Since the study of cognition has focused on human beings, the general process claim has asserted generality across domains (different perceptual or conceptual systems or different motivational systems such as feeding and reproduction) rather than across species. Two of the major approaches to cognition—verbal learning and psycholinguistics—correspond in some ways to the general process and ethological approaches. Like behavior theory, the verbal-learning approach: (1) adopted an empiricist and associative account of human memory and thinking (but was markedly less behavioristic); (2) emphasized general processes that span all domains of human information processing; (3) acknowledged specificity in sensory systems but tended to ignore it elsewhere; and (4) emphasized laboratory studies, with only limited forays into natural settings (see Neisser, 1976). The more recent information processing approach, although quite different from verbal learning, still shares to some degree all but the first attitude.

Like ethology, psycholinguistics challenged some of these assumptions. One major claim was that domain-general processes could not account for what animals and people actually do. Chomsky (1975) argued that there must be innate "constraints" on language learning that render tractable a task that would otherwise be hopelessly difficult for a child endowed only with a "general process" inductive system (Wexler & Cullicover, 1980). These constraints are assumed to be embodied in specialized neurological mechanisms (Lenneberg, 1967), as part of out (human) species-typical endowment. Within this framework the study of language has prospered, developing, for example, models of speech perception that assume special phonological processing modes (Liberman & Studdert-Kennedy, 1978).

The case for species-specific and domain-specific innate predispositions or constraints has been made for other areas of cognition. Fodor (1983) and Rozin (1976a; Rozin & Kalat, 1971) call attention to modules or adaptive specializations in animals (e.g., bee navigation) and humans (e.g., language, spatial representation), whose inputs, outputs, and interconnections to other systems are limited. These are theoretically required, because the world underdetermines the possible interpretations of experience (as with language) and because an unconstrained general inductive system would be too slow. These considerations, along with neuropsychological work on language and lateralization, helped move cognitive science towards recognition of some degree of specialization (Posner & Shulman, 1979).

In perception, specializations related to ecological factors have long been acknowledged, along with the coexistence of both general and specific adaptations. General principles of optics and neural processing (e.g., lateral inhibition) are involved in all complex eyes, and yet, within vertebrates, there are many specific adaptations that relate to ecological niches,

such as the relative number of rods and cones (Walls, 1947) or the "bug detectors" of the frog retina (Lettvin, Maturana, McCullock, & Pitts, 1959). The "bug detectors" are clearly food detectors, or stimuli for eating. In line with this type of finding, J.J. Gibson's (1966, 1977) ecological approach asserts that the adaptive function of perception is to mediate the recognition of affordances—meaningful aspects of the environment (objects, surfaces, etc.) that provide opportunities for adaptive action.

Students of perception also recognize that the physical environment underdetermines the kinds of perceptual construals which might be arrived at, which has led to the identification of innate predispositions that facilitate development of a useful model of the world. For example, infants seem to connect intermodal stimuli (e.g., flashing lights with synchronized sounds) that correspond to one another and perceive the unity of partly occluded moving objects (E. Gibson, 1984; Spelke, 1982).

Historically it is not clear whether these developments in ethology, cognition, language, and perception had any direct influence on the subsequent course of events in animal learning, which was, after all, concerned with a different set of phenomena. They probably encouraged concern for more naturalistic settings, greater acceptance of the idea of innate constraints, and the development of the field of animal cognition.

Constraints

This historical review provides a context for critically evaluating a term which has, perhaps unfortunately, come to stand for the study of specialized psychological processes.

Although many specializations are species-specific, most interest in "constraints" centers on within-organism specializations in particular domains (e.g., phonological processing in audition/language; conditioned taste aversions in food selection).

This cross-domain, within-species emphasis has not always predominated. Comparative psychology in the United States has always been centered on human beings as the reference organism and has sought to discover the rudiments of mind in lesser creatures (Gottlieb, 1979). In the 1950s and 1960s, these comparative psychologists assumed that psychological abilities were domain general and sought to document their species-specific limitations. This approach, exemplified by the work of Bitterman (1975), adopted as a standard certain *general process learning abilities* present in humans and rats (e.g., the partial reinforcement effect). These abilities were assayed in a number of widely separated vertebrate species in an attempt to identify the point in phylogeny at which these abilities appeared. Although this approach did uncover interesting species differences in abilities to perform in arbitrary situations, it did not take into account the branching nature of evolutionary lineages (Hodos & Campbell, 1969) or the possibility that an ability might appear only in limited domains. From this anthropocentric perspective, it was natural to think of other species as more or less limited, or "constrained" variations on the human standard.

As we have seen, "constraints" first emerged in the context of general process assumptions, and amidst recognition of the adaptive need to constrain perceptual and linguistic inputs. But the term also has the negative connotation of limitation. And it is in this sense that the term is regarded by many in animal learning.

A specialized system can be described either in terms of constraint or predisposition. Although both descriptions are logically equivalent, they stress different aspects and suggest different origins and research approaches. "Constraint" focuses on limitations of the domain of action and often implies that the system was in some sense carved out of a preexisting general process system. On the other hand, "predisposition" highlights the superior accomplishments of the system within the domain in which it is an evolved adaptation and implies that the specialized system arose as such, rather than being derived from a general process system. In at least some cases, "constraints" is misleading and unhelpful. Are birds constrained to fly? Was Mozart constrained to be a great composer? (If so, the investigation of his genius should concentrate on what his parents *didn't* expose him to.) For these reasons, we prefer relatively neutral terms like "modules" or "specializations." Specialized systems are *both* limited in domain and impressive in their accomplishments. Whether they evolve or develop from more general systems is an empirical question.

General Process and Adaptive-Evolutionary Approaches: Complementarity and Cooperation

The general process and adaptive-evolutionary approaches aim at different types of explanation. The general process approach seeks mechanistic accounts of ongoing behavior as well as historical accounts that date from conception. The adaptive-evolutionary approach seeks explanation in terms of adaptive function and historical events that occurred before conception, in evolutionary time.

While these two approaches are complementary, they are not independent. We will illustrate this in a later section on the study of foraging, in which precise optimization predictions based on functional-adaptive considerations are tested using operant technology, theories of response allocation that arise from the laboratory are applied in natural contexts, and foraging tasks engaging general principles as well as specific adaptations are studied. However foraging still represents the exception, rather than the rule, because each approach persists in holding serious reservations about the other.

One criticism of behavior theory by adaptive-evolutionary theorists holds that it has dealt with only one aspect of learning, at best. The argument is that while behavior theorists claimed to study all of learning, they in fact neglected what had originally spurred Darwin's theorizing: the widespread occurrence, in species after species, of specific adaptations to diverse environments. Behavior theorists failed to test or question the limits or sufficiency of their general principles and defined too narrowly the range of the plastic phenomena they studied. The behavior of animals in the Skinner Box, T-maze, and shuttle-box only scratches the surface of "The Behavior of Organisms." Many eminently studiable plastic phenomena (i.e., experimentally induced modifications of behavior) remain unrecognized and untouched.

Behavior theory is also criticized for focussing on arbitrary (unrelated to natural context) situations. While there is merit in this criticism, there is a positive side to this focus. For behavior theory has, in fact, produced a body of data of interest from the adaptive-evolutionary perspective. One of its basic accomplishments is to show us what some animals *can* do in a strange environment (Jenkins, 1979). Strange (unanticipated) environments do occur in the world, and it is of interest to know how a system selected for a particular niche can perform in others. Furthermore, arbitrary environments can be considered natural for humans. Hence examination of an animal's behavior in such environments is of comparative interest and might serve as a model for human learning (if not for animal learning) (Schwartz, 1974, 1981). In addition, exploration of an animal's capabilities, whether in a forest or a Skinner box, might be expected to reveal some fundamental general adaptive features, perhaps adapted to universal features of environments. The law of effect is an example. Another is the fact that contingency is critical for association formation (Rescorla, 1967), since (as opposed to contiguity) it relates to the *prediction* of the occurrence of events.

Adaptive principles have emerged from general process research in part because behavior theorists have often been concerned with accounting for adaptation in general to the environment in general, sometimes quite explicitly, as in the work of Hull (1929) and Skinner (1981). (The Darwinian principle of adaptation by selection has played a central role. Instrumental learning was explicitly conceived by its proponents to be analogous to natural selection: In the life of the individual organism, the principle of reinforcement selects those behaviors which produce beneficial consequences, just as in the evolution of species, the principle of natural selection selects those behaviors which increase survival [Skinner, 1981; Staddon & Simmelhag, 1971; Thorndike, 1899, as cited by Gleitman, 1981, p. 110]).

Behavior theorists, in turn, have two criticisms of the adaptive-evolutionary approach. One is that it is irrelevant to their interests, a claim we try to refute in this chapter. A second is that adaptive explanations are speculative, *ad hoc*, and not subject to the type of experimental analysis and control characteristic of the animal learning laboratory. There is no question that adaptive explanations have been offered with little thought and evidence and that standards of proof are necessarily less satisfactory in cases of adaptive-evolutionary explanation. However, in recent years the theory and empirical methodology of behavioral adaptation has risen to new levels of precision, as will be discussed later.

Organization of This Chapter

We begin with a detailed discussion of the narrow arena in which the adaptive-evolutionary and behavior theory perspectives met head on: the study of selective associations. We first review the anomalous findings that caused a rethinking of some aspects of general process theory and the theoretical responses they provoked. We then consider the evidence on whether associations are really selective. In the next sections, we attempt to clarify the adaptive-evolutionary position by showing how it relates to other approaches in psychology. We examine three fundamental conceptual issues, on which the adaptive and general process perspectives differ: the relations between (1) general laws and specific adaptations, (2) function (adaptation) and mechanism, and (3) nature and nurture. In the next section, we examine one domain of activity, food selection and foraging, to illustrate the operation of the adaptive-evolutionary approach. We then consider specializations in other domains, to expose the diversity of phenomena of potential interest to psychologists and to introduce some recent lines of research within this broader frame. Finally, we discuss the current status of "constraints" and the prospects for the future.

SELECTIVE ASSOCIATION: THE CHALLENGE TO BEHAVIOR THEORY

The Anomalies of the 1960s and 1970s

The major impetus for a reconsideration of general process theory came from within the field, in empirical and theoretical papers dating from the 1960s and early 1970s. The empirical work challenged the generality of some accepted basic laws of learning and prompted consideration of the evolutionary histories of the behaviors and organisms under study.

The most direct challenge came from research on learned taste aversions by John Garcia and his colleagues. In the classic "belongingness" (selective association) study, Garcia and Koelling (1966) showed that rats would avoid tastes but not audio-visual cues when these were paired with illness, but would avoid audio-visual cues and not tastes when these were paired with electric shock. This finding directly challenged the principle of equipotentiality.

In the same year, Garcia, Ervin, and Koelling (1966) reported that taste aversion learning could bridge taste-illness intervals of over one hour (long delay learning), a finding grossly out of line with results from traditional learning procedures and contradicting the principle of temporal contiguity. They suggest that

> . . . mammalian learning mechanisms do not operate randomly, associating stimuli and reinforcers only as a function of recency, frequency and intensity. The omnivorous rat displays a bias, probably established by natural selection, to associate gustatory and olfactory cues with internal malaise even when these stimuli are separated by long time periods (p. 122).

These experiments were stark demonstrations of abilities that were less salient in prior or simultaneous research on poison avoidance (Barnett, 1963; Richter, 1950; Rzoska, 1953), avoidance of tastes associated with X-radiation (Garcia, Kimeldorf, & Hunt, 1961; McLaurin, 1964; Smith, 1971), and specific hungers and the acquisition of food preferences (Capretta, 1961; Harris, Clay, Hargreaves, & Ward, 1933; Richter, 1943; Rozin, 1967; Scott & Verney, 1947). They directly challenged fundamental general process principles and they fit well within an adaptive framework: the taste-illness specificity and long delay learning capability are particularly suited to the problem of avoiding poisons and learning about nutritious foods (Garcia & Ervin, 1968; Rozin & Kalat, 1971).

Another basic tenet, the law of effect, was challenged at about the same time. In 1961, Keller and Marion Breland, former students of Skinner's who had been using the technology of reinforcement to train animals for commercial exhibits, reported that animals given food reinforcement for arbitrary behaviors began to perform species-typical ingestive behaviors so vigorously that these responses interfered with the original operant. In one case, a pig which had been trained to deposit oversize coins in a piggy bank eventually became loath to part with the coin, chewing it and rooting with it instead, despite the fact that the pig thereby forfeited the food reward. The Brelands noted that this violated the law of effect and gave their paper the provocative title "The Misbehavior of

Organisms." In more controlled experimental situations, Bolles (1970) demonstrated that avoidance learning was much more rapid, and perhaps qualitatively different, if a species-specific defensive response was used as the response. Brown and Jenkins (1968) and Williams and Williams (1969) showed that the paradigmatically arbitrary operant, the pigeon's key peck, could be elicited by response-independent pairings of food with the brief illumination of the response key ("autoshaping"), with such vigor as to override reward contingencies. These studies suggested that Pavlovian processes and species-specific behaviors could intrude into arbitrary instrumental situations.

Thus, all of these studies argue for nonarbitrary relations among stimuli, responses, and reinforcers. They provoked a variety of theoretical and empirical responses.

Theoretical Responses to the Anomalies

The phenomena described in the 1960s are now generally accepted, but this was not always so. Garcia had great difficulty publishing his original findings, and they were ignored for some years, except by "prepared" workers involved with related problems (Revusky & Bedarf, 1967; Rozin, 1967; Smith & Roll, 1967). At least one general process theorist (Bitterman, 1976) claimed that the results were artifactual (cf. Revusky, 1977b). This position is now behind us. Most work on conditioned taste aversions today is done by animal learning researchers working within some kind of general process framework.

Our review will progress from views that sought to preserve the core of general process theory to those that departed most radically from it.

Preserving the Core of General Process Theory

Three positions had this goal. First, many textbooks of the 1970s characterized conditioned taste aversions as an anomalous exception to otherwise general principles. Second, many learning theorists tried to assimilate the findings as parametric variations in general laws; by this view, the anomalous results represent quantitative rather than qualitative departures from basic general principles (Logue, 1979). This is true to some extent, though some aspects of conditioned taste aversions, such as one trial learning with long delays, arguably stretch the meaning of "quantitative" excessively (Logue, 1979). A third view is that, qualitative or quantitative, the differences are not produced by differences in associative processes *per se*, but rather by restriction of inputs or variations in "response rules" (Rescorla & Holland, 1976). We shall see that at least some anomalous results probably can be accounted for in this manner.

Accepting Limited Modifications of General Process Theory

Seligman (1970; Seligman & Hager, 1972) and Revusky (1971, 1977a) explicitly invoked a selective association principle to bolster general process theories. Seligman rejected associative equipotentiality and suggested that traditional laws of learning hold only for arbitrary events. He postulated a dimension, "preparedness," which ranges from the most readily learned (prepared) associations (specific evolutionary adaptations such as conditioned taste aversions) to the least readily learned (contraprepared) associations. Seligman operationalized preparedness as the "amount of input" (e.g., number of trials, amount of information) necessary to produce a given level of conditioning. He also suggested that prepared associations might have different physiological substrates and be less influenced by cognitive factors. Preparedness provided an explicit and testable alternative to equipotentiality.

Seligman's credentials in animal learning, the straightforward simplicity of his formulation, and its compatibility with much of general process theory all made preparedness the most influential approach arising from the anomalous findings. In their book, *Biological Boundaries of Learning*, Seligman and Hager (1972) emphasized the importance of ecological variables and adaptation, calling attention to a wide range of plastic adaptations—from navigation to traditional learning situations to language.

Seligman's theory has two weaknesses. First preparedness applies only to associative learning and cannot encompass other forms of plasticity (e.g., some navigational learning). Second, preparedness was linked to a package of other characteristics, such as resistance to extinction. But why should one package apply universally? In imprinting, relatively rapid acquisition does

go with great resistance to extinction, as it should, adaptively. But a bee must quickly exploit a particular clump of flowers when it blooms and abandon it quickly when it goes out of bloom. Here rapid learning and rapid extinction should go together. Thus, preparedness does not allow for a tight fit between abilities and the problem at hand.

Revusky (1971; 1977a; Revusky & Garcia, 1970) proposed that the selective association principle be incorporated into general process theory. He then used this principle to account for the other major anomaly of contitioned taste aversions: long delay learning. He claimed that long delay learning is usually prevented by interference from competing stimuli that occur during the delay interval. However long delay learning of taste-illness associations is possible because selective association limits the range of possible interfering stimuli to tastes. Revusky attributed broad similarities of learning in different situations to universal features of the causal structure of the world. Like Testa (1974), Revusky (1977a) argued for the value and correctness of general process theory, but not the "standard" version that was generally accepted through the 1960s.

Linking Adaptive Perspectives with the Study of Learning

While the theorists just considered sought to preserve major features of the traditional positions, other theorists considered the concept of adaptation to be central and related it to learning, more broadly conceived. They emphasized the diversity as well as the commonality of organisms.

The classical ethologists viewed learning as just another adaptive feature of behavior. Their focus was on the variety of situations in which learning occurred, the context of learning, and the interplay of prestructured and acquired components:

> The student of innate behavior, accustomed to studying a number of different species and the entire behavior pattern, is repeatedly confronted with the fact that an animal may learn some things much more readily than others . . . . . In other words, there seem to be more or less strictly localized "dispositions to learn." Different species are predisposed to learn different parts of the pattern. So far as we know,

these differences between species have adaptive significance (N. Tinbergen, 1951, p. 145).

. . . . . innumerable observations and experiments tend to show that modifiability occurs, if at all, only in those preformed places where built-in learning mechanisms are phylogenetically programmed to perform just that function. How specifically these mechanisms are differentiated for one particular function is borne out by the fact that they are very often quite unable to modify any but one strictly determined system of behavior mechanisms (Lorenz, 1967, p. 47).

Bolles (1970) claimed that learning in the laboratory could be better understood if related to the animal's behavior in the natural environment: "The prevailing theories of avoidance learning and the procedures that are usually used to study it seem to be totally out of touch with what is known about how animals defend themselves in nature" (p. 32). His alternative was to interpret the facility with which various avoidance responses are learned in terms of their similarity to natural species-specific defensive responses.

Garcia and his colleagues (Garcia & Ervin, 1968) stressed the adaptiveness of learning and the issues of selective association. They distinguished between interoceptive (taste and visceral [malaise]) and exteroceptive (vision, hearing, and skin [peripheral pain]) systems and suggested that associations were selectively made within (but not between) these systems. They posited that the interoceptive system is more sluggish, less accurate, and localized lower in the brain (Garcia, Hankins, & Rusiniak, 1974). They differed from other theorists in stressing differences in the neurological substrates for different types of learning. But like other adaptively oriented theorists, they explicitly recognized species-specific adaptations and advocated a more naturalistic approach to learning:

Criticism should be directed at constricted experimental paradigms designed to control the animal. Such paradigms cannot lead to comprehensive behavioral laws, for so long as the plastic capacity of the test organism far exceeds the demands of the test conditions, the data will reflect the limits of apparatus and experimental schedule rather than the nature of the beast (Garcia, McGowen, & Green, 1972, p. 20).

Rozin and Kalat (1971, 1972; Rozin, 1976a), Shettleworth (1972), and Hinde (1973) similarly emphasized adaptive aspects of learning. They did not rule out the possibility of general laws but emphasized that such laws would be the product of general features of environments.

Shettleworth (1972) first used the term "constraint" to describe specialization in learning, classifying and analyzing them by considering how behavior in traditional learning situations may be influenced by the nature of the stimulus, the response or the reinforcer. She then concentrated on constraints in learning about relations among these elements. Rozin and Kalat (1971, 1972) made a detailed case for learning specializations in food choice and then argued that the feeding system is not unique: ". . . laws or mechanisms of learning are adapted to deal with particular types of problems and can be fully understood only in a naturalistic context" (1971, p. 459). Shettleworth and Rozin and Kalat call attention to the wide range of plastic adaptations in nature. Their claim that mechanisms of association may differ across situations remains tenable but unproven.

Starting Over: Extreme Ecological Positions

Lockard (1971) and Johnston (1981; Johnston & Turvey, 1980) shared the adaptive and ecological perspectives already discussed. But whereas Shettleworth and Rozin and Kalat appreciated both adaptive and general process approaches, including the study of behavior in arbitrary situations, Lockard and Johnston doubted that much of value could come from the study of animals outside of their natural context. They called for a new start. Johnston and Turvey (1980) take a Gibsonian ecological perspective. They view the reception of information (invariances) from the environment as transactional and insist that organism and environment must be studied together because they are part of the same system. Johnston differs from most other researchers in that he is interested exclusively in functional-adaptive (and not mechanistic) principles (Hinde, 1981). In our opinion, he undervalues information gained from the study of animal learning in arbitrary situations (Schwartz, 1974, 1981; see Introduction). Johnston also criticizes the "biological boundaries" approaches for failing to provide an alternative paradigm for research on learning, and proposes that organism-environment transactions be studied in nature, building up from descriptions of local adaptations to statements relating ecological situations to types of learning. (For example, the greater the chance for confusion of young, the better developed will be individual recognition abilities; see also Lockard, 1971.)

Selective Associations: A Case Study

Because behavior theorists have paid special attention to the anomalous findings on selective association, we will now consider the evidence on the existence and nature of selective associations. Since there is dispute as to whether selectivity resides in associations themselves, as opposed to inputs or outputs, we will use the term "selective association" in quotes, to refer to the *outcome* of the anomalous studies, as opposed to their interpretation. The literature is vast, and our review is relatively brief (see Domjan, 1980, 1983; Riley & Baril, 1976). We will first discuss evidence for the existence and extent of "selective associations," then consider whether the associative process itself is selective, and finally consider the related phenomenon of potentiation.

The Existence and Extent of "Selective Associations"

Garcia and Koelling's (1966) original bright-noisy-tasty water experiment illustrates the now paradigmatic "cross-over" design for demonstrating "selective associations." One group of animals receives pairing of two conditioned stimuli (CS1, CS2) with unconditioned stimulus (US1), and another group receives pairing of the same two CSs with a different US (US2). The critical result is that with US1 (illness) the animal's reaction to CS1 (taste) changes more, whereas with US2 (peripheral shock) the animal's reaction to CS2 (audio-visual cues) changes more. Differences between the two groups in responses to the various CSs cannot be attributed to CS or US properties *per se*, and must therefore be due to CS–US relations (although Garcia's original studies did not control for non-associative CS–US relations; see LoLordo, 1979; Rescorla & Holland, 1976; Schwartz, 1974 for discussions of this and related designs).

In reviewing instances of selective association, we will follow Shettleworth (1972) in examining relations among stimuli, responses, and reinforcers.

SELECTIVITY IN STIMULUS-REINFORCER RELATIONS

The "selective associability" of exteroceptive cues with shock, and of tastes with visceral malaise has been reported many times by many investigators (Domjan, 1980, 1982). While non-associative factors may contribute to "selective association," it is generally recognized as associative (see Domjan, 1980, for alternative interpretations), since it obeys many of the laws of associative learning (e.g., contingency sensitivity and extinction) (Logue, 1979). There are a few other examples of this type. Pigeons were exposed to audiovisual compound stimuli paired with food or shock; with food, light elicited more pecks than did sound; with shock, sound elicited more conditioned prancing than did light (LoLordo, 1979). There is also evidence for "selective association" based upon stimulus modalities and submodalities (e.g., color) in higher order conditioning (Rescorla & Cunningham, 1979; Rescorla & Furrow, 1977).

SELECTIVITY IN STIMULUS-RESPONSE RELATIONS

The first (crossover design) evidence for selective stimulus-response associations also appeared in 1966 (Dobrzecka, Szwejkowska, & Konorski, 1966; Konorski, 1967; see Shettleworth, 1979). In a food reward discrimination paradigm, different frequencies of sound produced better learning of a "go, no go" discrimination than did differences in the location of the same stimulus. When the response to be learned was flexion of the left versus right leg, location differences in the stimuli were more effective.

SELECTIVITY IN RESPONSE-REINFORCER RELATIONS

Subsequent to Breland and Breland's report (1961), Bolles and Seelbach (1964) showed that punishment with, and escape from, loud noises operate differently as reinforcers of various responses (grooming, rearing, investigating a window in the chamber). Similarly, Sevenster (1973) showed that while sticklebacks (*Gasterosteus aculeatus*) learn equally well to swim through a ring for either a courtship or an aggressive display reward, they learn to bite a rod much more slowly with courtship than with aggressive display reward.

Shettleworth (1975) studied the modifiability of a variety of responses of hamsters in conjunction with different reinforcers. She found that responses differ in susceptibility to reinforcement or punishment. Some responses even *decrease* in duration when they are rewarded by food or brain stimulation. Other responses are differentially susceptible to reward or punishment (Shettleworth, 1978; Timberlake, 1983; see Domjan, 1982, for a review). Nonetheless, the basic parameters of acquisition are surprisingly similar across reinforcements (Hogan & Roper, 1978).

Is Selective Association Learned or Innate?

If "selective association" were itself learned, then it might not present a special problem to learning theory. Some "selective association" may be due to dimensional learning or learned relevance and irrelevance (Mackintosh, 1973; Testa & Ternes, 1977), but this cannot provide a complete explanation, since one-day-old rats show the phenomenon (Gemberling & Domjan, 1982).

The Locus of "Selective Association"

General process learning theorists have been reluctant to concede that the mechanism(s) of "selective association" lie in the process of association formation *per se*. They have investigated the possibility of selectivity at inputs and outputs of a hypothetical associative process.

SELECTIVITY IN INPUT: ORIENTATION AND ATTENTION

The presentation of a US can induce selective attention or behavioral orientation to certain classes of CSs, which might in turn affect associations on subsequent trials (Rescorla & Holland, 1976, suggest an appropriate control). While this kind of mechanism may well contribute to "selective associations" in multiple trial situations (Gillette, Martin, & Bellingham, 1980), it cannot account for one-trial learning, a salient and robust feature of conditioned taste aversions. In a recent critical experiment, a crossover design was used to demonstrate "selective association" with only one presentation of each US (Miller & Domjan, 1981).

SELECTIVITY IN OUTPUT: LEARNING VERSUS PERFORMANCE

The possibility that selective association can result from performance limitations or response rules is the most plausible alternative to selectivity in the associative process itself (Rescorla & Holland, 1976; Shettleworth, 1983). By such accounts the animal might be *learning* about all CS–US pairings without bias, but *responding* in a detectable way to only some combinations of CS and US (the learning-performance distinction).

Although it is impossible to prove that learning has *not* occurred, it is sometimes possible to unmask covert learning with sensitive performance measures. For example, Rescorla (1980) has used the second order conditioning paradigm to show that potential conditioned stimuli that had no measurable effect on responses could effectively "transmit" measurable changes to a previously neutral stimulus. Similarly, LoLordo and Jacobs (1983) showed that while a tone paired with food produced no apparent conditioned response (CR), the tone could operate as a conditioned reinforcer. Also, illness-paired exteroceptive cues can block conditioning of tastes, implying that such cues can in fact be associated with illness (Rudy, Iwens, & Best, 1977).

Motivational factors, both unconditioned and conditioned, can also prevent the expression of existing associations in performance. Reward-induced sexual motivation made it difficult for sticklebacks to learn to bite a rod for courtship opportunities (Sevenster, 1973; see also Shettleworth, 1975). Also, multiple conditioned responses may interact so as to spuriously suggest selective association: Through Pavlovian conditioning, the rod came to elicit courting gestures that intefered with biting (Sevenster, 1973).

Conditioned taste aversions exemplify a number of learning/performance problems. Humans develop aversions to foods that are followed by illness; typically the taste and smell become unpleasant, while stimuli from other modalities do not change in affective value (Garb & Stunkard, 1974; Logue, Ophir, & Strauss, 1981). However, associations may nonetheless be made between illness and the appearance of the food or the context. If one gets sick hours after eating enchiladas at a restaurant, one might well develop a dislike only for enchiladas, but one might also remember the pattern and color of the tablecloth. One way to describe this result is that taste-illness "belongingness" is confined to an affective expression system, while causal attributions in the same context might show a different bias. This raises the unexamined possibility that learning and/or performance may be specialized and constrained differently in different "response systems."

Some claim that conditioned taste aversions involve hedonic changes in the taste CS, whereas in taste-shock pairings the taste serves as a signal for shock but does not change in hedonic (affective) value (Garcia, Kovner, & Green, 1970; Gleitman, 1974; Rozin & Kalat, 1971). Questionnaire data on human food avoidances indicate that when food ingestion is followed by nausea, there is a strong tendency for the food to become disliked, whereas most other postingestional symptoms (e.g., heartburn, gas pains, respiratory distress) usually produce avoidance without negative hedonic change (Pelchat & Rozin, 1982).

Comparable results have been obtained with rats, using tastes as CSs, and nausea (LiCl) versus a variety of other negative effects as USs (Parker, 1982; Pelchat, Grill, Rozin, & Jacobs, 1983). While animals learn to avoid tastes paired with any of the USs, they show negative facial responses (Grill & Norgren, 1978) of the sort shown only to bitter tastes to tastes paired with nausea. Thus, in rats and humans, affective food rejection responses are apparently selective to taste-nausea associations.

In summary, it is clear that performance factors play a significant role in selective associations, although they may not be sufficient to explain the phenomena.

SELECTIVITY IN ASSOCIATIVE PROCESSES
Since we do not have detailed formulations of the associative process at physiological or psychological levels, it is not clear how one would know that "selective association" did operate at the very mechanism of asociation, rather than at inputs or outputs. Defining the domain of association *per se* as epsilon, there is always an epsilon small enough that any demonstrated site of specificity falls on either side of it.

The difficulty is illustrated by the *response potentiation* interpretation of "selective association" (Shettleworth, 1975, 1983; Timberlake, 1983). By this account, motivational or situational stimuli activate certain appropriate response systems and make them more available for association. (Responses which increase with

food deprivation are generally those that are effectively increased by food reinforcement [Shettleworth, 1975]. It is easier to increase ear scratching in dogs with food reinforcement if cotton, a subthreshold elicitor of ear scratching, is placed in the ear [Konorski, 1967].) If these biases operate only at the performance level, they represent selectivity in outputs. If they heighten reactivity to stimuli that elicit the behaviors, they are input biases. But if the associative process itself preferentially incorporates these activated responses, the selectivity would be in the associative process.

A similar problem arises with Konorski's (1967) suggestion that there are pre-existing subthreshold connections between certain inputs and outputs. LoLordo and Jacobs (1983) have carefully scrutinized CSs for any tendency to produce the relevant responses. Their findings favor selectivity in the associative process itself.

The only other explicit attempt to account for "selective association" is the neurological proximity theory of Garcia et al. (1974). They point to the close apposition of taste and gastrointestinal inputs involved in conditioned taste aversions in the medulla and argue that only neighbors can meet. Unavailability of non-taste and non-illness inputs to certain integrators or associative devices could indeed lead to "selective association," as would constrained outputs from these loci. But here, too, one could argue that the selectivity occurs at the input or output stages.

Selective Association: Summary and Evaluation
We conclude that "selective association" is a genuine and probably widespread phenomenon (Domjan, 1983; LoLordo, 1979; LoLordo & Jacobs, 1983). The case for predispositions in the associative process itself remains open (Domjan, 1983; Shettleworth, 1983). The demonstration of selectivity at one locus does not preclude the existence of selectivity at others. The appeal of parsimony notwithstanding, multiple, somewhat redundant mechanisms are common in biology. Furthermore, while selectivity in the associative process is the behavior theorist's explanation of last resort, an adaptive perspective gives no special priority to the associative process. From an ecological point of view, the essential outcome is that the animal avoid those

objects which are most likely to have poisoned it, and this is probably achieved by multiple input, output, and association mechanisms. There is no compelling reason why the burden of proof should lie with those who favor selectivity in the association process.

Potentiation and "Selective Association"

A well-established feature of associative learning is the overshadowing effect (Pavlov, 1927). When two stimuli are simultaneously paired with an event, the more salient stimulus detracts from, or overshadows, conditioning of the other. Work on taste aversions in animals has uncovered the reverse phenomenon: potentiation. The presence of a taste (a particularly salient CS) during the pairing of olfactory or visual stimuli with illness can enhance conditioning of this other less readily conditionable stimulus (Clarke, Westbrook, & Irwin, 1979; Domjan, 1973; Durlach & Rescorla, 1980; Galef & Osborne, 1978; Rusiniak, Hankins, Garcia, & Brett, 1979; see Garcia & Rusiniak, 1980, and Domjan, 1980, for reviews). A similar phenomenon has been reported in an autoshaping experiment in which a keylight was paired with injections of water into a pigeon's crop. The keylight came to elicit pecking only if the injections were accompanied by oral stimulation (Woodruff & Williams, 1976).

From an ecological point of view, animals must learn about objects and events in the world, not isolated inputs in particular modalities (Gibson, 1966). For feeding, the relevant stimuli are potentially edible objects, and the critical event is ingestion—that is, the experience of the object in the mouth. Such "mouth objects" produce stimulation in a number of modalities (taste, olfaction, temperature, touch, pain) but are perceived as unitary entities, which we describe in common speech as "taste." The salience of taste as a CS related to gastrointestinal events is highly adaptive, since the great majority of gastrointestinal disturbances are caused by ingested items, and the system seems to be predisposed accordingly: stronger aversions result from tastes which are actually ingested and not just placed in the mouth (Domjan, 1980; Domjan & Wilson, 1972). However, it would also be adaptive to associate more distal aspects of the object (appearance, smell) with postingestional events, if the object in question were something actually ingested. In this context, potentiation makes sense; taste could flag these nonoral stimuli as food related. In keeping with this idea, odors that emanate from food are potentiated more readily than ambient odors merely present at the time of ingestion (Domjan, 1973; Garcia & Rusiniak, 1980; see Galef & Dalrymple, 1981; Logue, 1980; and Rescorla & Cunningham, 1979, for comparable demonstrations involving vision).

We do not yet know whether potentiation is limited to ingestion learning systems, whether it is a property of the associative process *per se*, nor what the underlying mechanisms are (although there is some evidence that it can be understood within the framework of higher-order conditioning (Durlach & Rescorla, 1980). Whatever the underlying mechanisms, they seem to be tuned to ecological features.

Principles of "Selective Association"

We now ask about the psychological and ecological organizing principles of selective association. Shettleworth (1983) and Timberlake (1983) suggest that situationally relevant responses are more readily acquired as operants. Interpreted ecologically, "relevant" refers to those responses which are effective in the real world for obtaining the reinforcer. Interpreted psychologically, "relevant" refers to those responses facilitated by the current motivational state. (Interpreted adaptively, these two senses should overlap.)

"Related" or "similar" stimuli may be selectively associated. Testa and Ternes (1977) suggested that taste and illness go together because they have similar temporal patterns. There is evidence for other determinants of similarity, including common modality (e.g., two visual stimuli) or submodality (e.g., two colors or two shapes) (Rescorla & Furrow, 1977) and similarity in spatial location (Rescorla & Cunningham, 1979; Testa & Ternes, 1977). From a psychological perspective, "relatedness" corresponds to common perceptual features.

However, "ecological relatedness" could also be due to common origin (as suggested for potentiation) or causal relationship. Common locus in space and time are ecological markers for objects and events. The acquisition of object representations would often be based on simultaneous associations, as opposed to the successive associations traditionally studied in conditioning. Simultaneous associations have only recently come under investigation and are robust and interestingly different from successive associations (Rescorla, 1981). For causally related stimuli we might expect different principles of selective association based on *successive* conditioning.

Ultimately, the mechanisms of selective association and potentiation have been shaped by the causal structure of the species' niche. Therefore, consideration of the structure of the environment may help in the investigation of the structure of the organism.

GENERALITY AND SPECIFICITY

General Processes and Specific Adaptations

The pursuit of laws of the greatest generality is a major goal of natural science. In this spirit, behavior theory assumes generality across species and across domains within individuals. Our concern in this section is to examine the conditions under which this assumption holds.

Natural selection directs attention to both general processes *and* specific adaptations. A general-specific antagonism arises only if one believes that everything falls into only one of these categories, a proposition for which there is no basis in the facts of biology or the principles of evolution. We will examine the reasons for specificity first, and then those for general processes.

Forces for Specificity

Fish swim, birds fly, lions pursue antelopes, antelopes eat grass. Diversity is such a fundamental feature of life that it must be explained. It results from diversity in environments and selection pressures, diversity in the mutations and genetic combinations upon which selection acts, diversity of phylogenetic histories, and from accidents of history, Habitat differences make specific demands on organisms, which are reflected in sensory, perceptual, motor, and other capacities. Within-organism diversity is, in turn, produced by the different types of interactions organisms have with their environments in various domains. Predator avoidance, nutrient procurement, and parenting all require different abilities. Similarly, the different sources of information (e.g., contact; audition; or vision,

and within the visual domain, color, objects, etc.) have some specific or unique properties (e.g., the importance of spatial mapping in vision but not gravity reception). It would be perverse to assume that in the particular areas of plasticity and cognition the forces for diversity were suspended.

Forces for Generality

General process approaches in biology (from molecular genetics to body fluid physiology) have been very successful; this approach should succeed in psychology as well. Why should we expect general principles?

UNIVERSAL PROPERTIES OF ENVIRONMENTS
The laws of physics testify to the operation of many general conditions of relevance to animals across all earthly environments: the operation of gravity, the laws of mechanics (relevant to any animal tracking prey or actively avoiding predators), the validity of Euclidean geometry as a metric, the existence and integrity of objects, the laws of optics. On ecological grounds alone we would expect (analogous or homologous) adaptations to these universal features of the world to hold across species and across domains. The existence of such highly general features as similarities in design of the vertebrate and cephalopod eye (analogy) or contour exaggeration in vision speak to these general conditions. Particularly relevant for plasticity are such universals as: (1) the importance of spatial and temporal contiguity in mechanical causation, (2) the temporal direction of causation (presumably related to the prepotency of forward over backward conditioning), and (3) the consistency of events and the coherence of objects (providing the grounds for conditioning processes which generalize from past occurrences to future events and from parts to wholes).

UNIVERSAL PREREQUISITES FOR LIFE
Organisms must maintain essential physiological processes. Homeostatic mechanisms are universal. Other universal goals, such as nutrient location and consumption and reproduction, constrain or direct similar adaptations across species.

COMMONALITIES DUE TO COMMON ANCESTRY (HOMOLOGIES)
Just as common environmental factors tend to

promote common adaptations, so does the common ancestry of organisms. For example, the universality of the neuron as a unit and the control of behavior by networks of these units constrains possible adaptations; the temporal properties of action potentials prevent individual neurons from tracking high frequency stimuli. Common ancestry can produce widespread (although not universal) commonalities within taxonomic groups, such as the design of the eye throughout the vertebrates (Walls, 1942). The fact that animal displays can be used as indicators of phylogenetic relatedness demonstrates the relevance of common ancestry to behavior (Brown, 1975; Lorenz, 1971).

CONSTRAINTS ON ADAPTATION

DEVELOPMENTAL CONSTRAINTS. The necessity for an orderly and precisely timed process of development, especially of a structure as complex as the nervous system, makes many types of reorganization practically impossible. Simon (1967) argues that construction of complex multicomponent systems must be based on assembly of stable subsystems in a hierarchical structure. As a consequence, viable changes are likely to involve either modest changes in individual components or in the pattern of assembly of components. In addition, the path of development is buffered in such a way as to resist a wide variety of perturbations (this is Waddington's, 1966, concept of developmental homeostasis).

CONSTRAINTS FROM COMMON COMPONENTS AND THEIR INTERACTION. Common components —whether derived from common ancestry (homology), similar selection pressures (analogy), or both—lead one to expect general principles to apply across species and across domains. This is true both because the components offer certain opportunities for adaptation while precluding others and because they constitute part of the environment to which new genes must adapt. Thus the internal physiological environment, which is very similar in most animals, must give rise to a set of selection pressures that constrain the range of viable physiological mechanisms. One such constraint, for example, would resist evolutionary changes that disturb homeostasis. Pavlovian conditioning mechanisms based on response generalization (in which the CR resembles the UR) would often be selected

against in homeostatic systems, since it would be adaptive to generate a response capable of neutralizing the anticipated disturbance (Hollis, 1982; Schull, 1979; Siegel, 1979).

The constraints we have discussed in this section suggest that if a given mechanism has evolved to instantiate a particular principle, then there is a greater likelihood that it will evolve again in a different domain or species. This is simply because its existence indicates that it has a higher probability of occurring than other solutions. Within a species, a mechanism present in one domain is more likely to appear in other domains both for the reasons mentioned above, and because the physical presence of the solution in a particular animal allows for direct utilization (access) of the mechanism in other domains (Rozin, 1976a).

UNIVERSAL MODES OF PROBLEM SOLVING

There may be only one generic way to increase knowledge or competence: the generation of alternatives (behaviors, hypotheses, etc.) and the retention or rejection of them based on feedback from the environment (rewards, data, etc.) (Campbell, 1974; Dennett, 1975; the TOTE of Miller, Galanter, & Pribram, 1960). Something of this sort is seen even in the Protozoan, *Stentor coeruleus*, which responds to noxious stimulation by sequencing gradually through up to four different avoidance responses until the noxious stimulus is removed (Jennings, 1906). Such mechanisms are present in behaviors as diverse as instrumental learning (described as trial and error), construction of the perceptual world, and problem solving in primates. In humans, the process is often conscious and voluntary. The universal value of this procedure explains its generality.

In sum, the factors discussed often work in concert to produce similarities among all animals, among groups of animals, and across domains within species. Thus the structural and behavioral similarities of kangaroo rats and desert rats reflect selection pressures produced by the common desert environment, common ancestry, and conservative constraints on evolution and development.

The Existence of Domain-Specific Adaptations

There are many examples of plastic adaptations

that are both species-specific and domain-specific (Griffin, 1982; Hinde & Stevenson-Hinde, 1973; Rozin, 1976a; Seligman and Hager, 1972; Shettleworth, 1972). These include the many astronomical specializations used by navigating animals such as bees, landmark memory and geometrical representations in some of the same species, constraints to learn songs that fit specific genetically determined templates in some songbirds (Marler, 1970), the ability of salmon to remember the odor of their home stream after years at sea (Hasler, 1966), and other varieties of imprinting (Hess, 1973). The domain of these adaptive specializations may be an input channel, an output system, or a motivational system.

Similarly, there is much evidence for domain-specific abilities in humans, variously described as adaptive specializations (Rozin, 1976a), multiple intelligences (Gardner, 1983) or modules (Fodor, 1983). These include a variety of "intelligent" or "interference making" perceptual systems (Rock, 1983), a constrained system involved in the acquisition of conceptions of the basic categories of existence (ontological knowledge; Keil, 1981), and the isolated and impressive intellectual accomplishments of idiot savants (Anastasi & Levee, 1959). The existence of such capacities in animals and humans argues against the traditional quest to determine whether a species possesses a particular ability. The question should be whether the ability appears in any or all domains.

The idea of human domain-specific specialized systems is elaborated in Fodor's (1983) book, *The Modularity of the Mind* (see Schwartz & Schwartz, 1984, for a critical summary). Fodor's modules are specialized perceptual and linguistic input systems which serve to "represent the world so as to make it accessible to thought" (Fodor, 1983, p. 40). Their outputs feed into a central general process system which accounts for fixation of belief, general problem solving, rational decision making, analogical reasoning, and so forth. Domain-specific modules include the color identification system within vision and the phonological system within audition and language, among others. Their operations are limited, or constrained, in order to perform rapid and appropriate operations on the inputs. Fodor characterizes the modules as: (1) computationally elaborated (the work they do is complex), (2) domain specific (they receive a limited set of inputs), and (3) informationally encapsulated (they have limited access to other systems, are limited in the set of hypotheses by which they interpret their inputs, and are accessible to subsequent systems only at their final output). Modules are also mandatory (they operate involuntarily and automatically), fast, and typically have a fixed neural circuitry and a characteristic developmental pace and sequence. Fodor holds that these features of modules are adaptive because of the underdetermination of the world and the necessity of fast action (cf. Introduction of this chapter). With respect to all of these features, modules differ from the open-ended general central system. Fodor holds that because of their predispositions or constraints, modules are much easier to study than the central system, with its multiple inputs and outputs, and unconstrained operation (which he takes to be similar to the process of scientific confirmation). His claim that the rich collection of features listed above tends to co-occur in systems that analyze sensory input and language is unconfirmed, though there is suggestive evidence.

Degrees of Generality and Specificity

The arguments for generality and specificity reviewed at the beginning of this section suggest that the module/general-system dichotomy actually represents a continuum along a dimension of accessibility (Rozin, 1976a). Like Fodor's (1983) general system, highly accessible adaptations span all domains and environments and are available to all systems, including consciousness. Moderately accessible adaptions operate in a narrower range of domains (e.g., spatial arrays in audition, vision, and touch; scanning in memory and perceptual arrays). Inaccessible adaptations operate in single domains (analogously to some of Fodor's modules).

From Specificity to Generality: Evolution and Development of Intelligent Systems

Evolution and development may proceed either from the general to the specific or *vice versa*. On the one hand, modules or inaccessible adaptations could be carved out of relatively unstructured general systems, in keeping with the general embryological process of differentiation. With respect to the nervous system, a general initial state might be a network of multiconnected neurons which are winnowed to achieve constrained systems. This is known to occur in development (e.g., programmed cell death), but there is no evidence that the earlier systems have the competence of a general process system. A clearer example is the automatization of motor routines, which are mediated by a general (conscious, voluntary) system at first, but which become progressively less accessible as they become more routinized. In the evolutionary frame, the prior appearance of a general system would require mutations that produce adaptive systemwide changes, as for example, if a single change in all neurons (or all of a certain class) could endow them with more plastic properties. (In skin pigmentation, for example, a mutation might affect melanin regulation so as to make all the skin darker.)

On the other hand, the facts of evolution and development suggest that, in many cases, specialized adaptations appear first and then become more accessible over time. Thus, in many invertebrate species, Pavlovian conditioning is present only in very well-defined domains, whereas in some mammals it is a widely accessible adaptation, which functions to connect arbitrary events.

According to accessibility theory, the evolution and development of intelligence involves an increase in accessibility of initially domain-specific adaptations (Rozin, 1976a; Rozin & Kalat, 1972; see also Gelman & Gallistel, 1978). With respect to many capacities, the child begins as "a bundle of relatively special purpose computational systems . . . which are quite restricted in their range of application" (Fodor, 1972, p. 93) and which become integrated and more accessible over time. This scheme fits with the developmental phenomenon of *decalage* (sequenced appearance of the same ability in different domains) (Flavell, 1963; Piaget, 1955) and with aspects of the development of number concepts (Gelman, 1982; Gelman & Gallistel, 1978), and language (Gleitman & Gleitman, 1979). Increased accessibility has also been reported in output linkages. In infants, habituation techniques are required to demonstrate a number of abilities, including perception of occluded parts of objects. Later in development these abilities become linked to other output systems and can be detected with other behavioral measures (E. Gibson, 1984; Spelke, 1982). At

advanced stages of development, the child becomes aware of some of his or her own processes; this metacognitive ability may be the highest level of accessibility (Brown, 1980; Flavell & Wellman, 1977; Gleitman & Gleitman, 1979; Gleitman & Rozin, 1977).

Processes of acquisition may differ depending on whether an inaccessible, modular system or a general system is involved. In comparison to the acquisition of new, arbitrary material such as, most school subjects, acquisition of material that fits into a module (e.g., language, many types of perceptual and skill learning) occurs rapidly, effortlessly, without formal instruction, with opaqueness to introspection, and, when acquisition is complete, with a sense of certainty and insight (like linguistic intuition) (Fodor, 1983; Keil, 1981; Rozin, 1976a).

This formulation suggests a type of learning that has not previously been considered: extension, through learning, of access to domain-limited programs (Rozin, 1976a). Whereas language is a long-established biological adaptation in our species, reading is a recent cultural invention. To read alphabets, one must become aware of the speech units (phonemes) used by one's own domain-limited phonological segmentation system. With practice, this becomes completely obvious and intuitive, perhaps because access to the phonological system has been gained (Rozin & Gleitman, 1977).

However, the notion of accessibility, as currently developed, is vague. First, failure to show a capacity in a particular domain might reflect lack of access or merely disinclination to utilize it. Second, extension of access (in development or evolution) might mean extension of a specialization to more inputs or outputs and/or the connection of separate systems. For example, Jerison (1973) suggests that when the primates moved into a diurnal niche, vision was reestablished as a primary sensory system at a cortical level and connected to the auditory-spatial specializations evolved in nocturnal mammals; this putatively allowed for multimodal maps of the world. Third, the mechanism of extension of access is unclear. Accessibility might be gained by establishing a physical connection of one system to another (shared circuitry). Alternatively, accessibility could result from duplication of one system's circuitry in another part of the brain (Rozin, 1976a).

Summary

Systems and capacities vary in the extent to which they are domain-limited, modular, or accessible. Both domain-general and domain-specific systems are worthy of study, as is the evolutionary or development transition from one degree of domain specificity (accessibility) to another. Their study will reveal some principles shared by both and others unique to each.

FUNCTION, PRINCIPLES, AND MECHANISMS

In this section, we try to show that mechanistic and adaptive approaches are complementary and can enrich each other. Our presentation owes much to a stimulating and thorough paper by Shettleworth (1983).

Integration of adaptive and mechanistic approaches would enhance understanding of the phenomena and principles of psychology in two ways. First, it would extend the psychologist's traditional mode of explanation (determination of principles and mechanisms), which is simply incomplete. Second, the adaptive-evolutionary perspective interacts with, and can enlighten the type of understanding psychologists normally seek. This latter point will lead us into discussions of the relation between function and mechanism.

Biopsychological Explanation

Research usually begins with the selection and characterization of a phenomenon to be explained, a reference phenonemon. This can be described at different levels of integration, depending largely on the researcher's discipline. Thus, psychologists might describe predator avoidance as a group of behaviors, or the avoidance of a specific predator, or in terms of the releasers for identification of the predator. A neurophysiologist might describe the same phenomenon in terms of the neural circuits that mediate the recognition. We refer to the level at which a phenomenon is described as its reference level and define principles as statements about relations or regularities *at that level*. For most psychologists, principles would be statements of some generality relating environments to behaviors or mental events, or relating behav-

iors (or mental events) to each other (Shettleworth, 1983). A first goal in the investigation of learning, for example, is the discovery of principles such as extinction, higher order conditioning, and the like.

The second goal of psychologists is typically analysis of underlying *mechanisms* that account either for reference phenomena or principles (Shettleworth, 1983). (As a starting point for analysis of mechanisms, we will take reference phenomena and principles to be equivalent.) The immediate precursors (causes) and consequences of the reference phenomenon are investigated, and/or it is analyzed into simpler units, or "mechanisms", that are usually both smaller (involving less behavior or neural circuitry) and briefer than the reference phenomenon (or principle). Thus, avoidance behaviors might be studied with regard to their immediate environmental causes and consequences or analyzed into component learning processes, reflexes, or neural programs.

As N. Tinbergen (1951, 1963a) pointed out, a *complete* understanding of a behavioral phenomenon requires an answer to four questions, of which "What are the mechanisms?" is only one. The others are: "How does it develop in the life of the individual?"; "What is its evolutionary history?"; and "What is its adaptive function?"

Rozin and Adler (in preparation) define two dimensions of explanation. The analytic-synthetic dimension spans levels of organization and relates to the analysis of phenomena or principles into smaller units (the search for mechanisms) or the synthesis of larger units from smaller ones (Teitelbaum, 1967; Tinbergen's first question). The temporal-historical dimension places the reference phenomenon in time and includes Tinbergen's other three questions, dealing with development, evolution, and adaptation (function). These two dimensions of explanation are orthogonal: Each type of temporal explanation can be applied to phenomena at different levels of organization, and every explanation occurs at a particular level of integration and includes a particular time frame. (Even mechanistic explanations include a brief time frame—from immediate cause to immediate consequence).

We believe that by limiting themselves to mechanistic and developmental (ontogenetic) explanations, psychologists have limited the breadth of their understanding. But even if the psychologist's search for mechanistic (analytic-synthetic) explanations is accepted as *the* goal of research, adaptive-evolutionary perspectives can be helpful. To develop this point, we first discuss the relations among mechanisms, adaptive functions, and principles.

Relations Among Functions, Principles, and Mechanisms

Psychologists frequently suggest alternative physiological or psychological mechanisms to account for a principle. Thus, for the principle of habituation, three alternative physiological mechanisms are: (1) sensory adaptation (e.g., depletion of photoreceptor pigments); (2) transmitter depletion at a specified synapse; or (3) active presynaptic inhibition at a specified synapse. In nature, redundant mechanisms may underlie the same principle in a single organism, and, as Lehrman (1970) and Shettleworth (1983) have noted, even closely related species often achieve the same adaptive function by very different mechanisms. Therefore, they conclude, what matters about a behavior, from the point of view of natural selection, is how it functions, not how it is achieved (its mechanism). Lehrman (1970) holds that "nature selects for *outcomes*" not mechanisms (p. 28). Shettleworth (1983) concludes that function makes contact with principles of learning at the level of principles, not behavioral mechanisms *per se*, and examines the claim that "considerations of learning as an adaptive phenomenon have no relevance at all to the traditional concerns of learning theory" (p. 13). However, the negation of this claim is a central theme of her paper and of this chapter.

Functional and mechanistic concerns would be independent and irrelevant to each other if two dubious assumptions were true: (1) there are multiple mechanisms that are truly equivalent and (2) the psychologist's principles have a priviliged relation to function.

The Problem of Equivalent Mechanisms

Two different mechanisms very rarely generate exactly the same principle. Indeed, finding different behavioral consquences which follow from alternative hypothetical mechanisms is the experimental psychologist's bread and butter. For example, different possible mechanisms of long delay learning—interference, trace decay,

learned safety, and aftertaste—make different predictions about the effect of frequency and type of taste experiences in the interval between ingesting the target substance and the occurrence of the negative US (Domjan, 1983; Rozin & Kalat, 1971). Since these different behavioral outcomes can be discriminated by psychologists, they could also be "discriminated" by natural selection (except in the unlikely case that the alternative outcomes are of equal net adaptive value, and, even then, they would likely produce differences in other behaviors). Nor is the actual evolution of a particular mechanism based solely on its consequences (functions). Which mechanism ultimately appears is also constrained by genetic accidents (mutations, recombinations, etc.); environmental events (some of which may be unpredictable and unique); and the feasibility of evolving, developing, and executing the mechanism. Mechanisms may differ in the amount of genetic material, neural tissue, and attentional resources that they require and, hence, in the extent to which they cause abandonment or postponement of other potentially valuable activities.

Because of the rarity of truly equivalent mechanisms and different costs and likelihoods of evolving different mechanisms, it seems unlikely that evolution is indifferent to mechanism.

Function and Mechanism as Different Aspects of the Same Principle

The claim that function is linked to principles but may be unrelated to mechanisms (Shettleworth, 1983) depends on the distinction between principles and mechanisms. But this distinction is epistemological, not ontological. It depends on the investigator's perspective or discipline. Put most simply, one researcher's principle may be another's mechanism. Pavlovian conditioning is both a mechanism of avoidance learning and a principle whose mechanism is sought. It follows that functions can be assigned to mechanisms as well as to principles, since principles and mechanisms are often interchangeable. Temporal (adaptive, evolutionary, or ontogenetic) explanations can be posited for any level of analysis.

Similarly, the same activity or principle can often be described as a mechanism or function. When an activity is viewed as a component of some more molar (higher level) activity, it is a mechanism. When the activity is viewed as a fitness-promoting trait, it is called a function. Species recognition is a function of imprinting and a mechanism of mate selection. Thus, one cannot even hold the view that evolution acts on functions but not mechanisms, because many activities are simultaneously functions *and* mechanisms. (In some cases, a principle or mechanism may not have a function. For example, the principle that the time required for a serial search through memory is *linearly* related to the size of the set being searched is a by-product of the particular search mechanism. It is unlikely that there was selection for linearity.)

This conception and its implications can be made more concrete with an illustration which depicts an individual organism as a hierarchy of interacting, fitness-promoting activities (a functional hierarchy) (Figure 10.1). At the top of the hierarchy is the activity which is the ultimate function of all adaptations, behavioral or otherwise: the promotion of inclusive fitness. (At the same time, this highest *node* spans all of the behavioral systems of the organism.) As we move

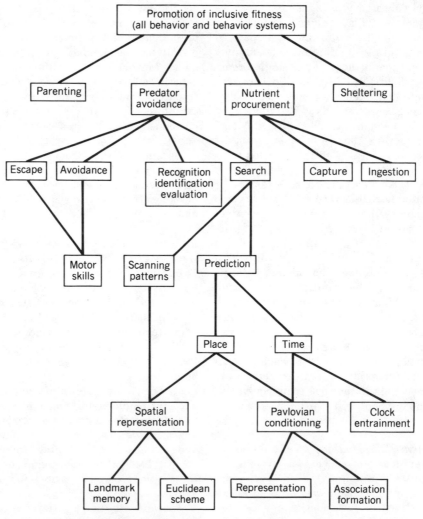

Figure 10.1. A preliminary functional hierarchy of behavior. Specificity increases as one moves down the hierarchy. In many cases, an activity is a mechanism of the superordinate activities to which it is connected and a function of the activities that are subordinate to it.

down the hierarchy we encounter functional activities which are more and more molecular, and of decreasing duration. (Figure 10.1). For the organisms psychologists typically study, certain broad categories of fitness-promoting activities can be recognized, such as parenting, reproduction, nutrient procurement, predator avoidance, sheltering, and so forth (Figure 10.1). The next level of activities would include, in nutrient procurement for example, detection of energy or nutrient deficits, food search patterns, food recognition, food capture, and so forth. These subactivities are built up of yet smaller activity "units" such as feature detectors, specific motor skills, and long delay learning. Obviously, this hierarchy can be extended downwards for many more levels and will vary from species to species. But we believe that all animals are organized in lattice hierarchies of this sort (Gallistel, 1980), in which an activity at any level may appear under more than one node at the next higher level. An item at any level of this hierarchy is usually, at one and the same time, both a mechanism of the items above it and a proximal function of the items below it.

Thus, the claim that natural selection only acts upon functions (or principles) cannot be maintained because most of the traits on which natural selection acts are both functions *and* mechanisms. Perhaps the appeal of the idea that natural selection operates at the level of the psychologist's principles (e.g., the law of extinction) but not their mechanisms comes from the fact that function is more salient the higher one is in the hierarchy, because it is easier to relate it to the promotion of inclusive fitness. In this sense, mate selection is more functionlike than recognition of one's own species, which is in turn, more functionlike than the underlying recognition mechanisms (e.g., imprinting or feature detection). But we must remember that natural selection produces whole organisms whose adaptations can be described at many levels.

Using Function to Study Principles and Mechanisms

Given the intimate connection between functions and mechanisms, it is surprising that adaptive considerations are so rarely applied to mechanistic investigations. They could be of aid in the selection of problems, in the search for principles and in the exploration of mechanisms.

GETTING STARTED ON THE RIGHT PROBLEMS

Functional considerations can help identify meaningful principles and representative phenomena to be explained. They direct attention to what animals actually do in nature—their ecology and their relations to and transactions with their environment. This has a number of salutary effects.

1. It gives the investigator a general idea of what the system under study is about. A beginning student of football would be well advised to know the purpose of the game before delving into mechanisms. Consider the relation of conditional response (CR) to unconditional response (UR) in Pavlovian conditioning. According to Hollis (1982), conditioned responses are adaptive. Given that URs have evolved to improve the animal's adaptive commerce with the US, it will often (but not always) be adaptive for the animal to prepare for the US's arrival by beginning to emit the same response in advance of the US. If salivation helps one masticate and digest food, it may help even more if one has begun salivating before dry food has a chance to gum up the mouth. The virtue of this formulation is that it can account for (and even predict) situations in which CRs will fail to mimic URs, on the grounds that other responses constitute more adaptive alternatives. Thus chicks approach, peck, and snuggle up to visual CSs which signal warmth, whereas they twitter and crouch (UR) in response to the warmth US itself (Wasserman, 1981). Why? Because in the chick's natural environment, the warmth-producing event is the mother hen and approaching, pecking, and snuggling up to her elicits brooding behavior (Hogan, 1974). Twittering and crouching when exposed to distal visual CSs given off by the hen would honor the principle of stimulus substitution but would be maladaptive.

2. Function can help in the discovery of principles of behavior. Principles can be discovered by at least three routes: (a) observation of empirical relations; (b) working up from mechanisms (e.g., making assumptions about mechanisms and drawing implications from those

assumptions); (c) working down from presumed functions. An example of the latter is the principle that animals cooperate preferentially with close kin (Hamilton, 1964); this principle has recently received a number of striking confir- mations, and the mechanisms are now being investigated. Derivation of prin- ciples from functional considerations can also be done quantitatively. In optimiz- ation theory the characteristics of behav- ior are predicted on the basis of cost- benefit analysis, and confirmation of these predictions is sought (and often obtained) by observation or experiment (see section on foraging).

3. Although it is true that any principle or phenomenon has a mechanism, one reason for investigating a principle and pursuing its mechanism is that it has ecological validity. A number of confirmed principles of meal spacing generated by laboratory rats in highly impoverished laboratory environments are markedly altered when the animal is given a separate nesting area (Nicolaidis, Danguir, & Mather, 1985). In natural situations, animals almost always have more behavioral options than are typically offered in the laboratory. Prin- ciples obtained in the laboratory may therefore provide little insight into natural functions *or* mechanisms of behav- ior. Many of these problems can be avoided by careful selection of laboratory conditions.

4. Ecological thinking can help one select appropriate species and systems (nutrient procurement, reproduction) for exploring particular types of mechanisms. Those interested in nestlings' learning of species identification would be well advised to steer clear of cuckoos, cowbirds, and other nest parasites.

5. Adaptive-evolutionary perspectives bring together varieties of behavior that share common functions, but which may not be grouped together by experimental psy- chologists. Consider the concept of "plas- ticity" as opposed to "learning." The wide variety of naturally occurring plastic behaviors (navigation, skill acquisition, management of social relations) extends well beyond the narrow group tradition- ally studied in animal learning. These may provide new instances of traditional principles and mechanisms, prompt their modification, or reveal new principles and mechanisms.

From Function to Mechanism

6. Mechanism may instantiate function (McFarland, 1976). That is, a function may describe a mechanism. In the case of regu- lation of food intake, some proposed mech- anisms involve direct regulation of aspects of energy intake and expenditure (e.g., Friedman & Stricker, 1976), while others may employ rules of thumb (McFarland, 1976), such as monitoring taste correlates of nutritive value. Obviously, when mech- anism instantiates function, to understand the function (e.g., a cost-benefit balancing) is to describe the mechanism.

Determining the Adequacy of a Mechanistic Explanation

7. Functional considerations aid in evalu- ating the completeness of a mechanistic explanation of a reference phenomenon. The idea that multiple, sometimes redun- dant, mechanisms may exist in the same organism is typically rejected by psycholo- gists as unaesthetic and unparsimonious. Yet such redundancy is a common feature of biological systems. It provides for stable and reliable development in the face of a changing and often unpredictable environment (Waddington, 1966; Shettle- worth, 1983). Multiple mechanisms can be expected when: (a) even low chances of error cannot be tolerated; (b) single mech- anisms are unreliable (i.e., will lead to adaptive behavior only some of the time); or (c) individual mechanisms will only work in a subset of all possible conditions. The case of animal navigation illustrates this point. Effective performance requires integrating information from different environmental sources and modalities. Local conditions (e.g., cloud cover) render some mechanisms inoperable some of the time. Until recently, progress in this area has been impeded by attempts to iden- tify *the* critical navigational cue and by

acceptance of the notion that if orientation is possible when a particular channel of information is eliminated, then that channel is not normally used in navigation (see Keeton, 1974). Shettleworth (1983) discusses a number of systems (e.g., food recognition in young chicks [Hogan, 1977] or rats [Galef, 1977]) in which multiple mechanisms have been identified.

In closing, it also worth noting that other evolutionary considerations can also aid in the study of mechanisms. Knowledge of evolutionary lineages allows one to estimate the likelihood that common mechanisms underly the same principles or reference phenomena in different species.

NATURE, NURTURE, AND THE EVOLUTION OF PLASTICITY

Nature and Nurture

No issue has generated more controversy in psychology than the nature-nurture issue, and contemporary debate about sociobiology shows that the question is far from settled. It is still often assumed (1) that species-specific behaviors are necessarily innate, (2) that demonstrably learned behaviors are not naturally-selected adaptations, and (3) that the behaviors that genes code for are necessarily unlearned and immutable. Each of these assumptions is incorrect and worth examining briefly.

The first two assumptions were countered in Hailman's (1967) study of "how an instinct is learned." Hailman showed that learning plays an important role in the development of the species-typical bill-pecking response of young gulls. His conclusions in no way contradicted Tinbergen and Perdeck's (1950) findings that the response was triggered by very specific species-wide stimuli, nor that the specificity was adaptively tuned to the gull's way of life. But they did show that much of that specificity and adaptiveness was based upon experience, albeit experience which was a reliable aspect of the gull's niche (i.e., stimuli produced by the parent's head and movement). Similarly, human language is a quintessential species-specific adaptation that relies heavily on experience.

Contrary to the second assumption, the fact that learning is often adaptive is itself strong evidence for the importance of innate, naturally selected determinants of behavior. Just as the vast majority of mutations are disadvantageous, many effects of experience on development would be maladaptive, if not for adaptive constraints on plasticity. According to Lorenz (1981, p. 260), "an explanation is needed for the indubitable fact that learning practically always results in an improvement of the teleonomic function of behavior." That explanation certainly involves natural selection. If natural selection had made tissue damage rewarding or hunger-reduction punishing (rather than the reverse), the law of effect would often lead us astray.

With regard to the third assumption, innate behaviors are often easily modified (the rat's innate preference for sugar solutions can be reversed by one pairing of such a solution with nausea), and genetically programmed behaviors are often learned. The "genes for" a given behavior may cause that behavior to appear, for example, by predisposing the animal to learn it or by promoting other behaviors which induce conspecifics to teach the behavior in question.

Effects of Plasticity on Evolution

In the next section we will examine selection pressures favoring learned *vs* unlearned adaptations. However, it is often forgotten that plastic adaptations have important effects upon selection pressures and on the evolution of other characteristics. Learning can enable an individual with a novel mutation or characteristic to learn how to exploit new traits that might otherwise be maladaptive. Learning abilities can enable a species to invade new niches, thereby exposing it to new selection pressures (Baber & Morris, 1980; Partridge, 1978). By enabling subpopulations to develop adaptations to local circumstances, learning may promote diversity, racial variations, and speciation. This is especially true when cultural transmission of learned behaviors is involved. In birds, the learning of local song dialects may allow females to choose mates who are adapted to local circumstances (e.g., Tomback & Baker, 1984). In humans, the cultural practice of milk drinking led to the evolution of the ability of adults in some dairying cultures to digest milk sugar (lactose) (Simoons, 1979).

Learning can be a first stage in the programming of innate behaviors. If an organism is capable of a particular form of adaptive learning (e.g., associating X and Y), selection pressures would subsequently favor genes that would improve this learning (e.g., a predisposition to associate X and Y). As the evolutionary psychologist James Mark Baldwin (1896) pointed out, this could ultimately lead to hard wiring of this initially learned relation. Therefore, in species with general learning abilities, learning may be a multipurpose preadaptation that can steer evolution without the need for Lamarckian inheritance. If so, this would be an important and relatively uninvestigated benefit of plastic abilities (Baldwin, 1896; G. Bateson, 1963; Braestrup, 1971; Schull, in preparation).

The Evolution of Plasticity

In this section, we apply the adaptive-evolutionary approach to a central issue in the nature-nuture controversy: When will evolution promote behavioral adaptation which depends importantly on learning or experience, and when will it promote nonplastic adaptations? Our discussion combines our own thoughts with those of Johnston (1982), who has written the only systematic evaluation of the costs and benefits of learning (see also Pulliam & Dunford, 1980). Mayer (1974) observes:

"Considering the great advantage of learning, it is rather curious in how relatively few phyletic lines genetically fixed behavior patterns have been replaced by the capacity for the storage of individual acquired information" (p. 652).

Besides the obvious advantages that learning enables individuals to adapt to their particular environments, learning may have unique advanges in certain situations. P.P.G. Bateson (1978) suggested that imprinted birds learn the particular visual characteristics of their own parents, which would be difficult to program genetically. This allows the individual to choose mates that are sufficiently dissimilar to achieve optimal outbreeding.

In some other situations, behavior must be genetically programmed. Cuckoos and cowbirds are nest parasites. Since they are reared by other species, species recognition (required for mating) must be innate, and it is. Furthermore, learning carries costs. It tends to require a longer period of dependency, vulnerability, and incompetence while the young or naive organism acquires the appropriate information; it may also require more parental investment.

Learned solutions may also be more fallible than fixed solutions; environmental quirks can misguide overly plastic organisms. This consideration leads Plotkin and Odling-Smee (1979) to distinguish three temporal frames within which adaptations can occur. The phylogenetic frame involves adaptive change in the organization of the gene pool. The ontogenetic frame responds more rapidly to changed circumstances, and involves environmentally induced change in the developmental history of the organism. Finally, learning involves even more rapid (and often reversible) change in the organization of the individual's nervous system. Relatively rapid and unpredictable changes in the environment will promote more adaptive change at the level of learning. Unpredictable changes that occur several times in the individual's lifetime would promote plastic adaptations; relatively slow (e.g., geological) changes and predictable rapid changes (such as the diurnal cycle) would favor genes for adaptations which do not involve plasticity. In addition to unpredictable temporal variation, unpredictable spatial variation will also promote plastic adaptations.

Too little is known about the neurophysiology of plasticity to make detailed arguments about the relative costs of plastic versus nonplastic adaptations. But in different circumstances, one mode or the other will require more resources (more "space" in the nervous system, more genes in the genome). The assumption that simpler organisms are relatively lacking in plastic adaptations leads one to assume that plasticity requires more resources, but consider a species that eats 40 different kinds of prey. Even in a stable, predictable environment, the genetic and development cost of programming 40 innate neural templates might be larger than simply programming the directive "remember what your parents feed you." Given that the animal already possesses sensory-perceptual machinery to encode the different prey items, only a simple instruction need be added. (A similar argument justifies imprinting as opposed to genetic determination of species recognition.) The issue of preadaptation (Bock, 1959; Mayr,

1960) is thus of critical importance, because a major determinant of likelihood of evolution is what is available. Similarly, if an organism already has the neural mechanisms for plastic adaptations in one domain, it might then be applicable to new adaptive problems (see discussion of access).

We are obviously burdened by ignorance of the relative magnitudes of the costs and benefits we have reviewed. However, based on the extent of time (and space) over which events are predictable, certain types of solutions can be excluded. Forest-dwelling birds should have genetic programs for the recognition of trees, but not for the location of particular trees. Similarly, there are genetic programs for representing universal or highly stable features of astronomy (the sun arc, patterns of star movement), but not the particular arc of the particular pattern of stars, both of which vary with location and season (Emlen, 1970; Keeton, 1974, 1981). It generally appears that what is genetically determined is what is predictable. Returning to Mayr's point pertaining to the paucity of plasticity, we pause to ponder the possibility that our planet is probably a pretty predictable place.

FOOD SELECTION

The study of food selection provides the best example to date of how the study of plasticity can be integrated with the study of ecological factors and with rigorous and empirically fertile adaptive theorizing.

An Ecological Overview: Strategies of Food Selection

The food selection sequence (arousal of interest in food, search, identification, capture, processing-handling, ingestion, and evaluation) probably occupies more of the waking animal's (or human's) time than any other set of activities and may well be the most important cause of evolutionary diversity. Changes in food selection are associated with many major evolutionary transitions, including the critical human transition from forest to savanna dweller. Many major taxonomic groups are identified by their food habits (e.g., the Carnivora and Insectivora). Indeed, outside of taxonomic classifi-

cation, the most informative piece of information about an animal is often the type of food it eats.

For some species, such as the large mammalian carnivores, the most complex adaptations involve capture. For other species, such as grazing mammals, capture is less significant than identification. We will concentrate on identification and choice of appropriate foods, one portion of an integrated sequence.

The general problem in food selection is to obtain adequate amounts of energy and nutrients, while avoiding dangerous levels of (food-associated) toxins. This requires recognition and evaluation of objects in the environment and detection of internal metabolic states (ranging from negative energy balance to specific nutrient deficiency) (see Rozin, 1976b, for a review). A variety of strategies have evolved to deal with this problem; they can be arrayed along a dimension that varies from specialist (limited range of foods, with specific adaptations to recognize and obtain them, and a substantial degree of genetic preprogramming) to generalist (wide range of foods with a higher degree of plasticity).

The specialist strategy is often the least complex, psychologically. At its extreme are animals that consume only one type of food, such as many highly specialized insects and the Koala bear, which eats only a few species of eucalyptus leaves (Degabriele, 1980). In such "univores," food recognition is typically preprogrammed and based on unique stimulus properties of the food. Detecting the need for food is correspondingly simple: Since the single food must be adequate in nutrients, only an "eat" signal is required. Other animals consume a few types of food, with multiple preprogrammed recognition systems and one or a few internal nutrient-deficit detectors. The best studied example is the blowfly, *Phormia regina* (Dethier, 1976).

Carnivorous or insectivorous animals show many commonalities with the "univores" in food selection strategy. Since animal food is usually an adequate source of all nutrients, a single metabolic-state detector may suffice. And, at least in some cases, it is possible to preprogram recognition of the food category; thus, some species of insect-eating frogs code food as small moving objects.

The psychological aspects of food selection are of more interest for general herbivores and omnivores, whose broad range of acceptable food reduces the impact of blights, climatic changes, and more specialized competitors for particular foods. In such animals it would be almost impossible to genetically program recognition and acceptance of all potential foods and rejection of toxic substances. These generalists must deal with food via "open programs" (Mayr, 1974), which acquire information about the edibles and toxins in the environment. The wide range of potential foods carries a risk of nutrient imbalance or deficiency since few plant foods are nutritionally complete for most generalists and requires detection of multiple metabolic states. The wide range of foods also increases the chances of poisoning, since plants often evolve toxins as a defense against predators. For these reasons, food selection presents generalists with a complex and difficult problem.

Consider the large grazing mammals. Their food is easy to obtain but low in energy density, so they must spend much time consuming large quantities (Westoby, 1974). To minimize nutrient imbalance, they select appropriate proportions of various plant types (Belovksy, 1978). To cope with plant toxins, there are multiple mechanisms. Grazers may learn about toxic and nutritive consequences of eating different foods (Westoby, 1974; Zahorik & Haupt, 1977). Innate taste biases, such as avoidance of bitter, keep them from consuming too much of certain toxins. However, low levels of bitter toxins are so common in utilizable plant foods that general herbivores probably cannot afford to reject bitter foods completely. Many natural toxins can be tolerated at low level because detoxification occurs in the gut and/or liver and toxins can be excreted. In this context, the common general herbivore strategy of "spreading the risk" (Freeland & Janzen, 1974) by not consuming too much of any single food source makes adaptive sense.

The Rat: A Study in Omnivory

The laboratory rat and its wild progenitor (*Rattus norvegicus*) have been the subject of much research on food selection. The omnivore's nutritional requirements are very similar to the requirements for humans. Its ability to correct nutritional imbalances was demonstrated conclusively in the classic work of Curt Richter (1943) and others, as was its ability to avoid poisons, many of which were explicitly concocted with the rat in mind (Barnett, 1963; Richter, 1950; Rzoska, 1953). More recent work has elucidated some of the mechanisms underlying these abilities (Barker, Best, & Domjan, 1977; Barnett, 1963; Kalat, 1977; Milgram, Krames, & Alloway, 1977; Rozin, 1976b).

Until weaning, one totally adequate food, milk, is provided by the mother: This permits survival and growth while basic regulatory, selection, or other behavioral mechanisms mature (Blass & Teicher, 1980; Galef, 1981). However, even in the first few days of life, the rat pup can learn how and where milk is to be obtained (Blass & Teicher, 1980) and acquire aversions to odors (Rudy & Cheatle, 1979). The weaning period is a sequence of stages of coadaptation between parent and pup that effects the transition to independence (Galef, 1981).

The rat has innate equipment for dealing with the bewildering array of potential foods. It has an innate tendency to prefer sweet tastes (an ecological correlate of a particular natural energy source, sugars) and to avoid bitter tastes (correlated with toxins in nature). Furthermore, it reacts to at least three distinct internal states: energy, water, and sodium deficits. The sodium deficit state is innately linked to sensory and memory representations of the salty taste (Denton, 1982; Krieckhaus & Wolf, 1968; Richter, 1956; Schulkin, 1982). Thus a rat that has never tasted a salty food shows an immediate preference for sodium salts the first time it becomes sodium deficient (Nachman, 1962; Richter, 1956). There may be an equivalent recognition of water innately linked to the distinctive internal signal of water deficit (thirst) and an innate linkage between the sweet taste and the internal signal of energy deficit: that is, for sodium, and perhaps water and energy, there are prewired specialist subsystems within the generalist (Rozin, 1976b).

The generalist's dilemma is to explore new potential foods while avoiding poisons. This leads to a conflict between interest in, and avoidance of, new foods. The wild rat, and to a lesser extent the domestic rat, tends to avoid unfamiliar foods and then samples only small amounts in separate meals (Barnett, 1956; Rozin, 1976b; Rzoska, 1953). This neophobia contributes to a preference for familiar foods. Familiarization begins during nursing through exposure, by a set of redundant mechanisms, to the mother's food: (1) as particles on her body; (2) as tastes transmitted through her milk; and (3) directly, by feeding with (next to) her (Galef, 1977).

The major problem in evaluating potential foods is the inherent delay, due to digestion, between ingestion and its metabolic consequences. The long delay learning process neatly handles this serious problem, in conjunction with potentiation and the "selective associability" of food-related cues with certain gastrointestinal and other visceral effects (see earlier discussion).

Other adaptations—some specialized, others general—contribute to the evaluation of potential foods. First, interference from other foods is minimized by the way the rat spaces its meals. Second, when faced with a new food, the rat samples it in small amounts and then waits (Rzoska, 1953). Third, when faced with multiple new foods, the rat tends to sample them one at a time in separate meals (Rozin, 1976b). Thus the rat's natural sampling behavior dovetails with its learning abilities to facilitate the association of particular foods with their own consequences. Fourth, some general features of associative learning also play a role. For example, a new consequence will be attributed to a new food (the correct attribution in most cases). When illness is induced after ingestion of both a new and old food, the animal will primarily avoid the new food (Revusky & Bedarf, 1967). Also, when dealing with familiar foods, rats avoid concentrating on any one food (sensory specific satiety; LeMagnen, 1967; Rolls, Rolls, Rowe, & Sweeney, 1981). This spreads the risk of high levels of toxin ingestion and reduces the possibility of nutrient imbalance.

Fifth, there is an important social source of information about dangerous and beneficial foods. Weanling rats develop preferences for foods that adult rats consume, hence profiting from the experience of the older rats (reviewed in Galef, 1977). The information is transferred by a number of routes, all mediated by the rat's preference for familiar, safe foods. Weanlings prefer to eat at food sources where adults have eaten, tend to eat where adults are eating, and are exposed to some of the characteristics of adults' diets through mother's milk and the mere presence of an adult who has previously fed on a particular diet (Galef, 1977; Galef & Wigmore, 1983; Posadas-Andrews & Roper,

1983). Most of these effects seem to be mediated by olfactory cues.

The rat's well-documented ability to select foods that correct a variety of specific deficiencies was originally attributed to innate recognition of specific substances and/or the development of acquired preferences (Richter, 1943; Young, 1948). The discovery of learned taste aversions led to the suggestion that specific hungers were primarily aversions to deficient diets (Rozin & Kalat, 1971). While it is clear that aversion does play an important role in specific hungers, there is also evidence that animals can acquire positive preferences based on postingestional benefits; rapid satiety has been identified as the most potent US (Booth, Stoloff, & Nichols, 1974; see reviews by Booth, 1982; Zahorik, 1979; and section on autoshaping). Aversions seem to be learned much more readily than preferences (Rozin & Kalat, 1971; Zahorik, 1979; cf. Booth, 1982), perhaps because, due to the threat posed by many negative stimuli (e.g., poisons, predators), there may be only one opportunity to learn.

Thus, an ensemble of integrated behavioral, physiological, and psychological mechanisms helps the rat select an adequate and safe diet. For most nutrients, the rat's general ability to learn about the consequences of food obviates the need for innate recognition of every deficiency and of foods which cure those deficiencies. Rather, when ill (from any of a variety of deficiencies), it learns what foods relieve or accentuate its distress.

Why, then, is there a built-in system for sodium (reviewed by Denton, 1982; Rodgers, 1967; Rozin, 1976b; Rozin & Kalat, 1971)? Sodium is a major and essential constituent of body fluids, and its level is homeostatically regulated. In comparison to many other nutrient deficiencies, sodium deficiency is rather common in nature. The prior existence in many animals of taste receptors tuned to sodium reflects the importance of sodium and may have made the evolution of sodium hunger easier. Furthermore, because the initial phases of recovery from sodium deficiency may not be reinforcing, it may be that the preference acquisition processes discussed above will not work for sodium.

We cannot yet explain how rats successfully mix balanced diets in the cafeteria situation and how they avoid, rather than cure, nutrient deficiencies (Richter, 1943). Perhaps variety (spreading the risk) strategies account for much of their success. The quantitative aspects of rat food selection (e.g., regulating the amount of protein or energy intake) have not been fully explained, though it seems that some sort of calibrational learning is involved in assessing the amount of repletion produced by a fixed amount of food (Booth, 1982).

Food Selection in Other Generalists

We have selected one well-studied species to illustrate how plastic mechanisms fit with environmental demands. Humans manifest many of the same biological adaptations, but the primary determinant of food selection in humans is culture, which has itself been influenced by these biological adaptations (Rozin, 1982). There are informative studies of how other vertebrates come to distinguish nutritive from non-nutritive substances (Hogan, 1977; Hogan-Warburg & Hogan, 1981, with chickens; Reisbick, 1973, with guinea pigs). Among social animals, the problem is yet more complex, as there may be subspecialization in feeding within a social group. For example, herring gull pairs coordinate nutritional needs with shared duties in guarding the nest by developing complementary specializations for foods with different temporal availabilities (e.g., garbage dumps, low tide foods) (McFarland, 1985).

Autoshaping and Food Recognition

The special linkage between taste and post-ingestive consequences for rats stems from their reliance on chemical cues. Other species differ in the extent to which nonchemical cues are important in food recognition, although there is an inherent relation between oral sensation and eating (since the mouth is the final common path for ingestion). This led Rozin and Kalat (1971) to suggest that animals associate *food related* cues (rather than taste *per se*) with characteristic consequences of ingestion. Birds, which generally use vision to identify food, should tend to associate visual stimuli with consequences of ingestion. Wilcoxon, Dragoin, and Kral (1971) reported that quail (*Colinus virginianus*) preferentially associate the color of a liquid, rather than its taste, with subsequent illness.

Similarly, the tendency for birds to treat visual stimuli paired with nutritional consequences as if they were food is demonstrated in every autoshaping experiment.

The directed pecking responses which emerge in appetitive autoshaping can be considered a mechanism of food recognition (Williams, 1981), as illustrated in an experiment by Woodruff and Starr (1978). Newly hatched ducklings are exposed to pairings of a keylight with food introduced directly into the mouth. After a number of pairings, the ducklings approach and peck at the light. They have never been rewarded for pecking the light, so this cannot be explained instrumentally. The simplest interpretation is that the duckling comes to treat the light as if it were food, through a Pavlovian process. Such contingencies occur every time an animal perceives an object, ingests it, and experiences some sort of repletion, and whenever a parent bird dangles a worm in front of a nestling and then stuffs the worm down the nestling's gullet. The mechanisms underlying autoshaping play a role in the recognition of food and water (Williams, 1981; Woodruff & Williams, 1976; cf. Holman, 1968; Hunt & Smith, 1967) and in avian foraging (Hollis, 1982; Neuringer & Bullock, 1977; Rashotte, O'Connell, & Beidler, 1982; Wasserman, 1981; Williams, 1981).

In both autoshaping and conditioned taste aversions, an animal comes to treat a stimulus paired with a post-ingestional consequence as if it were the physical source of that consequence: A keylight paired with repletion is treated as if it were food, and a taste paired with illness is treated as if it were poison. Both autoshaping and taste aversion learning are best understood in the Pavlovian framework. Both phenomena involve food-related cues typical of the species involved, suggesting a major role for Pavlovian processes in food selection. Yet the two phenomena are often interpreted differently: In autoshaping it is said that the CS "elicits" the ingestion response, whereas in learned aversions it is said that the taste becomes aversive (implying that the ingestive response is voluntary). Whether these two phenomena are, in fact, evolutionary variations on the same mechanistic theme or whether there are fundamental differences between them is unclear at this time (Schull, 1984).

Adaptive-Optimization Approaches: Foraging

We presented a qualitative and functional approach to food selection. More quantitative analyses of function are possible through the application of optimality theory. This new approach has been applied most extensively to the analysis of food selection, in the form of optimal foraging theory. While it has developed independently of mechanism-oriented approaches, McFarland and his colleagues have studied both aspects of feeding (McFarland 1977a, 1977b), and the two approaches are currently converging.

Optimality Theory

Mechanistically oriented investigators often attempt to generate quantitative predictions of behavior by modeling underlying mechanisms. However, prediction-via-mechanism is very difficult to carry out in complex systems (McFarland, 1976). Optimality theory is an alternative: prediction-via-function. It *assumes* that natural selection has produced animals which behave in the most adaptive way possible when faced with the kinds of choice typical of their niche. This assumption encourages analysis of opportunities and constraints afforded by the environment and of the animal's capacities and limitations. One can then estimate costs and benefits of the various behavioral options facing the animal and determine the optimal behavior. If the prediction is not confirmed, one revises the model of costs and benefits. Optimality theory assumes, but does not test, the hypothesis of optimality (cf. Dawkins, 1982; Gould & Lewontin, 1978; Krebs & Davies, 1984). Rather, it is a disciplined program for identifying and quantifying selection pressures, organismic constraints, and behavior.

The advantages of foraging for optimality theory are many. Nutritional requirements are quantifiable and there are clear measures of success: intake, weight, growth, and so forth. In most species, feeding occurs frequently (unlike predator avoidance or copulation) and is easily observable. Finally, because operant psychologists have developed a sophisticated technology for the control and analysis of food-appetitive behavior, a large data base with which to test quantitative optimization predictions is rapidly accumulating. Here we will emphasize the programmatic implications for the psychologist (for

reviews of theory and data, see Collier, 1983; Commons, Herrnstein, & Rachlin, 1982; Kamil & Sargent, 1981; Krebs & Davies, 1981, 1984; Lea, 1981; Shettleworth, 1984; and Staddon, 1980, 1983).

A first problem is to decide upon a criterion of organismic success. Ultimately, natural selection's criterion is inclusive fitness, but the animal and the optimal foraging theorist may adopt a more proximal and measurable index of success, such as minimization of time spent foraging or maximization of energy intake or net rate of intake. Which index is appropriate depends to some extent upon circumstances, for example, whether time spent foraging increases the risk of predation (Schoener, 1971).

Four basic problems facing the forager have been investigated (Pyke, Pulliam, & Charnov, 1977). Which food items should it eat? Which foraging sites ("patches") should it choose? When should it abandon a patch? What path through a patch should it take? The detailed answer to these questions depends on the specific case under consideration and can frequently involve laborious computation. However, Lea (1981) points out that the first three questions have a general and simple solution: accept an encountered prey type (or enter a patch, or stay in your current patch) "so long as the return for doing so exceeds the 'opportunity cost,' the possible return for doing something else" (p. 361). Thus, when high quality prey are abundant, low quality prey should be rejected in favor of further foraging for finer foods, whereas when high quality prey are not abundant, the animal should be less selective. For example, rats prefer shelled to unshelled sunflower seeds, but when the ratio of shelled to unshelled drops below about one to five, they begin to consume unshelled seeds as well (Collier, 1983). More precisely, Charnov (1976) showed that if net food value is defined as the nutritional value of the food divided by the total time spent obtaining and ingesting it, then any specific food type should be included in the diet in an all-or-none fashion if its net food value is greater than that of the diet without it. Similar formulations hold for patch choice and abandonment of patches.

An Example

The optimal foraging approach has been applied to the selection of mussels by shore crabs (*Carcinus maenas*) (Elner & Hughes, 1978). The crabs must break the mussel shells. Calculations

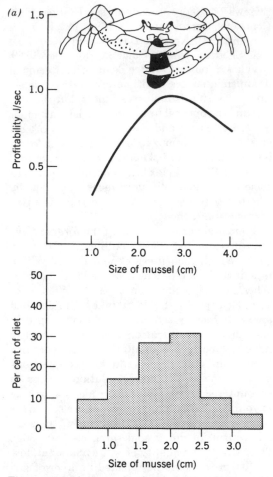

Figure 10.2. An example of optimization. Shore crabs (*Carcinus maenas*) prefer to eat the size of mussel that gives the highest rate of energy return. (a) The curve shows the calorie yield per second of time used by the crab in breaking open the shell. (b) The histogram shows the sizes eaten by crabs when offered a choice of equal numbers of each size in an aquarium. Source: Elner and Hughes, 1978. From *An Introduction to Behavioural Ecology* (p. 54) by J.R. Krebs and N.B. Davies, 1981, Oxford: Blackwell Scientific Publications Ltd. Copyright 1981 by Blackwell Scientific Publications Ltd. Reprinted by permission.

of the energy value of different sized mussels and the time spent breaking the shell indicate that the optimal behavior is to eat intermediate sized mussels—larger mussels take too long to break and smaller mussels don't have enough meat—(energy/handling time) is highest for intermediate size (Figure 10.2). Thus by assuming that the crab is an optimal forager, one can predict its preferences, and the predictions are

approximately correct (Figure 10.2), although crabs do consume sizes quite deviant from the optimal. As predicted, crabs are more likely to accept less than ideal mussels when the density of ideal mussels is lower.

A variety of mechanisms might account for this performance. The crab could learn about energy values, handling costs, and search costs for mussels of different sizes and make decisions based on this information. That is, it could be directly computing the optimal behavior, using estimates of costs and benefits. Or it could be using a "rule of thumb," a simpler procedure with approximately the same outcome (Krebs & Davies, 1981; Shettleworth, 1984). The data favor the latter alternative: acceptance of less than ideal mussels depends on the quality of the last few mussels encountered (Elner & Hughes, 1978; Charnov, 1976). This rule engages plastic mechanisms only minimally, in the "memory" of recent prey encounters. This may reflect an organismic constraint, or it may be an appropriate adaptation for a species in a highly variable and difficult-to-monitor environment, as Elner and Hughes suggest.

Optimality and Operant Approaches

There are major parallels between the optimal foraging approach and much of operant psychology. They both (1) deal primarily with steady-state performances; (2) are concerned with the economics of allocating behavior among alternative food-rewarded activities; (3) assume that the animal already "knows" about or has been exposed to all the relevant environmental contingencies; and (4) focus on environmental determinants of behavior. These parallels have not gone unnoticed and currently form the most fertile area of interaction between ecology and psychology. Behavioral ecologists have used the Skinnerian reinforcement technology to test their models, and operant psychologists are working on laboratory simulations of foraging problems (Collier, 1983; Kamil & Sargent, 1981; Kamil & Yoerg, 1982; Lea, 1981; Staddon, 1980, 1983).

The much-studied concurrent schedules of reinforcement may simulate situations in which an animal must choose between two patches of prey. Herrnstein's (1970) matching law states that the proportion of responses allocated to one of two options (e.g., response keys) is equal to the proportion of reinforcers available on that option. The law has an adaptive quality, and in many situations matching approaches the optimal solution (see Commons, Herrnstein, & Rachlin, 1982). On the other hand, the ecological relevance of the matching law is uncertain; it is most firmly established with concurrent variable interval schedules, which may be rare in nature. Also, since the decision to leave a patch is critical to the foraging animal, more attention must be paid to the fact that most foraging sites become depleted as the animal forages, while unforaged patches are replenished. The costs of switching must also be considered; (in the Skinner box the costs are minimal because the choices are two neighboring keys, but in nature the costs may include substantial energy expenditure and predator risk).

Mechanisms of Optimization

While the operant and optimality approaches emphasize the functional economics of steady-state behavior, underlying mechanisms and acquisition processes are of interest as well. Herrnstein and Vaughan (1980) have suggested that steady-state preferences develop through "melioration"—continuous preference shifts toward the alternative with the highest rate of reinforcement. Fantino (1981) and Abarca and Fantino (1982) argue that pigeons do not evaluate rates of reinforcement in terms of net energy intake *per se*, but in terms of reduction in time to the next reinforcer. In the laboratory this can sometimes result in choices which are far from optimal, as when animals choose immediate small rewards over delayed large rewards (Fantino, 1981). But in nature, this rule of thumb may, nonetheless, make adaptive sense for species whose prey are likely to become unavailable with delay (through escape or through predation by a competitor).

Optimality theory is of particular interest to psychology because optimal performances often engage plastic and complex mechanisms. Furthermore, how animals acquire the information on which optimal performance depends has yet to be explored. Plasticity will be involved in learning about densities, nutritive values, and the search and handling costs of different prey types. The animal's experience of the variability of the environment (over space or time) could influence the time spent gathering information to determine costs and benefits. Spatial representations of patches and associated travel times may be used to decide how and when to move between and within patches. Decision rules may themselves be learned (see Staddon, 1980, 1983, for a signal detection treatment of this problem). Furthermore, there may well be decisions about the costs and benefits of searching for one or more prey which depend upon constraints in cognition (see discussion of search images below).

Optimality theory may also help us understand why plastic abilities are as they are in various species. Over what time frames should animals be integrating the information they sample? Too broad a frame would make an animal insensitive to short term changes; too narrow a frame would produce erratic responses to random fluctuations. The answer should vary across species, environments, and prey types (see Shettleworth, 1984).

Thus optimality theory has profitted from the theories and technology of operant psychology, while operant psychology is gaining ecological validity and a new set of research problems from the applications to foraging. As Kamil and Yoerg (1982, p. 341) point out, "Once ecologists began examining invidual foraging behavior in detail, it was inevitable that they would become interested in learning." At the same time, psychologists, rather than ecologists, are probably best suited for the analysis of the mechanisms involved. The moral is that students of behavior in general and food selection in particular have much to gain and little to fear from the integration of adaptive and mechanistic viewpoints.

VARIETIES OF COMPLEX AND PLASTIC ADAPTATIONS

One of the virtues of a functional perspective is that it brings into view phenomena and mechanisms which might otherwise be overlooked in process-oriented or paradigm-oriented classifications (e.g., Rescorla & Holland, 1976). In this section we try to highlight the complexity and diversity of plastic adaptations in aspects of feeding other than food selection and foraging and in other domains.

Plastic and Complex Adaptations to Feeding

Search

Food search involves strategies (which may not

be learned), the ability to represent the spatio-temporal environment and its food sources, and memory for this representation. Olton's (1979) laboratory studies on rats illustrate all of these capacities. In an eight arm radial maze, with each arm baited only once, rats show a strong win-shift strategy, rarely revisiting an arm before sampling all of the others. Contrary to reinforcement theory, they do this more readily than learning to return to a previously baited arm. On reflection this makes sense: having depleted the food supply in one arm, the least likely place to expect to find food is in the same location. Even more impressive, chimpanzees, after watching an experimenter in an outdoor enclosure hide nine preferred food items, and nine less preferred items, visit the locations with the more preferred food first, in a path that minimizes the total distance traveled (Menzel, 1979).

Marsh tits (*Parus palustris*), who store food in the wild, have similar capacities (Shettle-worth & Krebs, 1982). The birds are allowed to cache 12 seeds in 97 sites on large twigs ("trees") in an experimental room. Later, they recover the seeds without exploring too many empty holes, and return to more recently cached sites first. This "recency" principle could either result from memory decay or be an adaptation to the fact that older stores are less likely to still be in place. In Clark's nutcracker (*Nucifraga columbiana*), memory for stored seeds may persist for months with hundreds to thousands of caches (Tomback, 1980; Vander Wall, 1982).

Search is organized in time as well as space, since some foods are available only at specific times (e.g., at night, or at low tide). Herring gulls (*Larus argentatus*) that feed at garbage dumps arrive shortly before the trucks which bring the day's fresh garbage; they do not come on week-ends (when no garbage is dumped). This involves complex learning and timing abilities, because they do come on weekday holidays, even though garbage is not dumped (the exception that proves the rule) (McFarland, 1985).

Identification
Identification involves perceptual learning to recognize significant biological entities and activation of search images. Using operant techniques, Pietrewicz and Kamil (1981) have confirmed L. Tinbergen's (1960) idea that foraging animals acquire "specific search images."

After establishing visual recognition of a set of natural prey (different moth species) in blue jays (*Cyanocitta cristata*), they show that experience of a few successive exemplars of one species enhances detection of that species. Furthermore, presumably because of limitations in attention or memory, prey detection rates decrease when jays search for more than one type of prey at the same time.

The classic work of von Frisch and his followers laid out the complex system used by bees to identify, evaluate, locate, and communicate about food sources (von Frisch, 1967; Gould & Gould, 1982; Lindauer, 1961; Manning, 1976; Menzel & Erber, 1978). Honey bees (*Apis sp.*) will learn to visit up to nine different dishes marked with scents at different times of the day (related to different flowering times). When the bee approaches a feeding source, it identifies and remembers the color for the period of some seconds leading up to and including landing on the flower, the scent while on the flower, and the location (landmarks) in the first few seconds after departing (Menzel & Erber, 1978; Opfinger, 1931). These are among the best examples of temporally constrained learning.

Capture and Handling
Skill acquisition is important in capturing and handling food. Inexperienced red squirrels (*Sciurus vulgaris*) open hazel nuts by gnawing a series of furrows, until the nut opens (Eibl-Eibesfeldt, 1970). Experienced squirrels gnaw one or two lengthwise furrows and then crack the nut by inserting their teeth. The acquisition is not typical instrumental learning, since the skill is acquired even if the kernels are removed from the nuts.

Skill acquisition can also lead to subspecialization within a species. Heinrich (1979) reports that individual bumblebees become experts at extracting nectar from particular types of flowers, becoming more specialized and more efficient with age. Individual oyster catchers (*Haematopus ostralegus*) have different acquired techniques for opening shells and these skills are transmitted from parents to young (Norton-Griffiths, 1969).

The Organization of Behavioral Adaptations in Other Domains

Our review of feeding was intended to indicate

the wide range of adaptations present in one domain. Many mechanisms, such as the spatial mapping abilities involved in food search and storage, also subserve other major functions, such as predator avoidance. This is true for some learning processes, as well, although other mechanisms, such as long-delay learning, may be unique to one domain. This illustrates two points made earlier: (1) Adaptations exist over a range from the highly specific to the very general and (2) they are organized in a lattice hierarchy (Figure 10-1), in which elements at any level can fall under a number of higher nodes and in which the same element may serve as a higher or lower node in different systems. Thus navigational abilities are subordinate to feeding, predator avoidance, and reproduction (e.g., search for mates), and motor and perceptual abilities are subordinate to all of these. At the same time, it must be recognized that the operation of systems and general processes subserving multiple domains will often be adaptively specialized for each domain. The rat's tendency to avoid sites in the radial arm maze where reward was recent obtained makes sense when the domain is feeding. If the reward were shelter, however, this tendency might well be reversed.

We now review some adaptations in domains other than feeding, with the aim of illustrating the richness of the phenomena awaiting investigation, as well as some promising starts.

Navigation

Getting around in the world is a problem faced by all animals in a number of domains. Specializations involving time are common in navigation and are often linked with special spatial representation abilities. For example, bees employ sun position in flying to and from food sources and are able to extrapolate the sun's path through the sky (the sun arc) based on limited exposure to the sun during only one part of the day (see von Frisch, 1967; Gould & Gould, 1982; Lindauer, 1961; Menzel & Erber, 1978, for reviews). They can also "adjust" this arc for the systematic changes that occur throughout the year. It appears that the basic features of the sun arc are genetically determined and must be either calibrated or selected by environmental input. This illustrates what is probably a common and little explored role of experience: calibration of systems that need an environmental

"setting" (Lorenz, 1967). This should be especially common in navigational systems. Comparable specializations have been described for homing and migration in a number of bird species, including learning of constellation patterns for night migration (Emlen, 1970), imprinting on magnetic cues, and use of sun position compensated for time of day and season (see Keeton, 1981).

The Social World

One of the most intriguing areas of animal (and human) learning and cognition is the management of social relations, including the memorial and communication skills this entails. The need to manage social relations may be the selective force most responsible for the cognitive abilities of humans (Humphrey, 1976). Important observations of primate behavior in the field (e.g., Kummer, 1982) and laboratory studies of social cognition in chimpanzees (e.g., Premack & Woodruff, 1978) now touch on such difficult problems as the perception of other selves, the "personalities" of conspecifics, and intentionality (imputing mental states to others).

Perception

Just as navigational and social competencies subserve both feeding and reproductive functions, so do many perceptual and motor abilities subserve adaptive behavior in virtually all domains. Universal features of environments should promote similar adaptations in perception in humans and other animals, including such sophisticated specializations as apparent movement, construction of three-dimensional representations, parsing the visual environment into objects, and so forth, all of which are established features of human visual perception (Hochberg, 1978; Rock, 1983). Many of these abilities in humans have been explained by mechanisms involving hypothesis formation and inference. Surprisingly, there are few if any studies attempting to show complex constructional abilities in perception in animals.

Animals should be able to learn to identify significant objects in their environment. Herrnstein and his collaborators (Herrnstein & deVilliers, 1980) have shown that pigeons acquire natural concepts such as "person" or "water" when reinforced for responding to pictures that contain exemplars of the concepts, and are beginning to analyze the mechanisms of concept formation. A single instance of a category (one oak leaf silhouette) along with some negative instances are sufficient for acquisition of a concept which will positively identify a variety of different oak leaves (Cerella, 1979). While these abilites may well have evolved as adaptations to natural objects in the animal's world, it seems that the categories animals can now acquire are not limited to those which are ecologically relevant: Pigeons have also learned to recognize letters of the alphabet and fish (Herrnstein & DeVilliers, 1980).

Along these same lines, Premack's (1976) work on teaching a plastic symbol vocabulary to chimpanzees is particularly impressive. After exposure to only a few instances of a concept associated with its symbol, chimps can often classify new stimuli correctly (with concepts such as apple, fruit, etc.). They seem to parse the world as we do.

Action

The study of the organization of action, like that of spatial representation, has been woefully neglected. One area of research is the development of skill and the automatization of action. Schwartz (1980) has studied the acquisition of a sequence of key pecking responses in pigeons. The pigeon must move from the lower left corner to the upper right corner of a five-by-five array of key lights, pecking at adjacent keys without reversing direction. Schwartz reports that each pigeon develops its own sequence, which then becomes stereotyped and resistant to modification. This seems to be an excellent model for the construction of higher-order motor units. More ethologically oriented research has also uncovered a number of instances of skill acquisition (see discussion above of food handling).

The Varieties of Plasticity

We have reviewed examples of plastic and complex adaptations in different domains. Our functional classification of plastic phenomena is orthogonal to, but compatible with, traditional classifications of learning processes (habituation, sensitization, instrumental and Pavlovian conditioning). The functional framework reveals that the processes studied by psychologists are but a subset of the extant plastic processes, which include imprinting; perceptual, skill, and calibration learning; construc-

tion of spatial representations; entrainment of biological rhythms; and general problem solving by hypothesis generation and testing. Interest in this wider range of plastic phenomena has increased among psychologists in recent years, probably because of the influence of biological perspectives, and a greater willingness to grant humans and animals mental representations and other cognitive capacities (Griffin, 1976, 1982).

CONCLUSIONS

It is ironic that by aspiring to account objectively for all behavior of all organisms in terms of a few all-encompassing principles, behavior theory *narrowed* its scope unnecessarily, in the belief that any organism and situation would suffice for the discovery of universal laws. Behavior theorists tended to avoid phenomena which did not emerge from within the established paradigms and so did not explore many important and tractable plastic phenomena. Their rejection of mental representations and other cognitive processes further limited their scope (see critique by Griffin, 1976). This was particularly unfortunate because the study of plasticity was not a major concern of any other subfield of psychology or any other discipline. Nonetheless, behavior theory did establish and explore at least some species' ability to perform well in arbitrary situations and did develop highly refined techniques to analyze behavior.

The study of animal learning and behavior could only be enriched if behavior theorists would bite off more than they eschew. Increased attention to diversity would not impede the pursuit of general laws of learning. On the contrary, truly general laws of learning will necessarily encompass principles of diversity. The generality of some associative laws has in fact been confirmed by taste aversion and autoshaping phenomena, which were initially seen as irreconcilable to general process premises.

Our basic point in this chapter is that the study of principles and mechanisms of behavior and mind is enriched and facilitated by adaptive and evolutionary considerations. It is enriched because a full understanding must include adaptive and evolutionary explanations and because ecological perspectives reveal a much wider range of plastic and complex behaviors than have been previously studied by psychologists. It is facilitated because knowledge of function (adaptive value) can directly and indirectly guide research on principles and mechanisms and make specific predictions about behavior. We discuss principled grounds on which one can predict the relative roles of genetic programming and experience in the determination of particular behaviors and the likelihood that a particular adaptation or principle will be general or limited to particular species or domains. Ecological perspectives reveal a much wider range of plastic and complex behaviors than have been previously studied by psychologists.

The evidence for adaptation and evolution in general is overwhelming, but at the same time the data explicitly supporting it in the domain of behavior are meager. It is a well justified act of faith that these principles are powerful determinants of behavior. Adaptive explanations are easy to abuse. With a modest amount of cleverness, one can concoct an adaptive explanation for anything. But this need not be confused with reasoned predictions, based on knowledge of evolution and ecology, as illustrated by research on foraging.

While espousing an adaptive-evolutionary approach, we do not mean to imply that this area of biology provides a completely firm foundation to be trusted uncritically. Evolutionary biology is itself in great ferment (King's College Sociobiology Group, 1982). While the facts of evolution are universally accepted, there is still debate about whether all characteristics are naturally-selected biological adaptations (Gould & Lewontin, 1978). There are also questions about the pace of evolution and the levels of selection: When are genes, individuals, groups, and/or species units of selection? These are questions to which psychologists have much to contribute, because these problems often hinge on the role of psychological phenomena such as kin recognition and altruism in mediating adaptation, social behavior. and evolution.

Furthermore, we suspect that some major questions of the future will concern the influence of behavioral and psychological phenomena on similarities and interactions between evolutionary and developmental processes of adaptation. This is already apparent in the study of that species which is the proper study of so many psychologists, *Homo sapiens*. Culture has effects on human biology, just as biology influences culture. Biocultural evolution is currently under study by anthropologists and biologists, and they frequently draw upon the psychological literature since psychological phenomena mediate the interaction of culture and biology (Lumsden & Wilson, 1981, 1983; Pulliam & Dunford, 1980).

Perhaps our major point is that psychology is a particularly interesting branch of biology. Thus, while this chapter has emphasized the contributions that biological perspectives can offer psychologists, the potential contribution of psychology to neighboring disciplines in the life sciences is very great, *if* psychologists recognize their kinship to those disciplines, and *if* they recognize that evolution necessarily gives rise to both themes and variations. Regularities in the world and constraints in the origins, structure and, development of organisms create a small number of recurring themes. Competition, diversity in environments and chance spawn diversity and variation on those themes. To quote from the last page of Darwin's *The Origin of Species*, "whilst this planet has gone on according to the fixed law of gravity, from so simple a beginning endless forms most beautiful and most wonderful have been, and are being evolved."

REFERENCES

Abarca, N., & Fantino, E. (1982). Choice and foraging. *Journal of the Experimental Analysis of Behavior, 38*, 117–123.

Anastasi, A., & Levee, R.F. (1959). Intellectual defect and musical talent. *American Journal of Mental Deficiency, 64*, 695–703.

Baber, D.W., & Morris, J.G. (1980). Florida scrub jays foraging from feral hogs. *Auk, 97*, 202.

Baldwin, J.M. (1896). A new factor in evolution. *American Naturalist, 30*, 441–451, 536–553.

Barker, L.M., Best, M.R., & Domjan, M. (1977). *Learning mechanisms in food selection*. Waco, TX: Baylor University Press.

Barnett, S.A. (1956). Behaviour components in the feeding of wild and laboratory rats. *Behaviour, 9*, 24–43.

Barnett, S.A. (1963). *The rat: A study in behavior*. Chicago: Aldine.

Bateson, G. (1963). The role of somatic change in evolution. *Evolution, 17*, 529–539.

Bateson, P.P.G. (1978). Sexual imprinting and optimal outbreeding. *Nature, 273,* 659–660.

Belovsky, G.E. (1978). Diet optimization in a generalist herbivore: the moose. *Theoretical Population Biology, 14,* 105–134.

Bitterman, M.E. (1975). The comparative analysis of learning. *Science, 188,* 699–709.

Bitterman, M.E. (1976). Flavor aversion studies. *Science, 192,* 266–267.

Blass, E.M., & Teicher, M.H. (1980). Suckling. *Science, 210,* 15–22.

Boakes, R.A. (1984). *From Darwin to Behaviourism: Psychology and the minds of animals.* Cambridge, England: Cambridge University Press.

Bock, W.J. (1959). Preadaptation and multiple evolutionary pathways. *Evolution, 13,* 194–211.

Bolles, R.C. (1970). Species-specific defense reactions and avoidance learning. *Psychological Review, 77,* 32–48.

Bolles, R.C., & Seelbach, S.E. (1964). Punishing and reinforcing effects of noise onset and termination for different responses. *Journal of Comparative and Physiological Psychology, 58,* 127–131.

Booth, D.A. (1982). Normal control of omnivore intake by taste and smell. In J. Steiner & J. Ganchrow (Eds.), *The determination of behavior by chemical stimuli. ECRO Symposium* (pp. 233–243). London: Information Retrieval.

Booth, D.A., Stoloff, R., & Nicholls, J. (1974). Dietary flavor acceptance in infant rats established by association with effects of nutrient composition. *Physiological Psychology, 2,* 313–319.

Boring, E.G. (1950). *A history of experimental psychology* (2nd ed.). New York: Appleton-Century-Crofts.

Braestrup, F.W. (1971). The evolutionary significance of learning. *Vidensk. Meddr. dansk naturh. Foren., 134,* 89–102.

Breland, K., & Breland, M. (1961). The misbehavior of organisms. *American Psychologist, 16,* 681–684.

Brown, A. (1980). Learning and development: The problems of compatibility, access and induction. *Human Development, 25,* 89–115.

Brown, J. (1975). *The evolution of behavior.* New York: Norton.

Brown, P.L., & Jenkins, H.M. (1968). Autoshaping of the pigeon's keypeck. *Journal of the Experimental Analysis of Behavior, 11,* 1–8.

Campbell, D.T. (1974). Evolutionary epistemology. In P.A. Schilpp (Ed.), *The philosophy of Karl R. Popper.* LaSalle, IL: Open Court Publishing.

Capretta, P.J. (1961). An experimental modification of food preferences in chickens. *Journal of Comparative and Physiological Psychology, 54,* 238–242.

Cerella, J. (1979). Visual classes and natural categories in the pigeon. *Journal of Experimental Psychology: Human Perception and Performance, 5,* 68–77.

Charnov, E.L. (1976). Optimal foraging: Attack strategy of a mantid. *American Naturalist, 110,* 141–151.

Chomsky, N. (1975). *Reflections on language.* New York: Pantheon Books.

Clarke, J.C., Westbrook, R.F., & Irwin, J. (1979). Potentiation instead of overshadowing in the pigeon. *Behavioral and Neural Biology, 25,* 18–29.

Collier, G. (1983). Life in a closed economy: The ecology of learning and motivation. In M.D. Zeiler & P. Harzem (Eds.), *Advances in analysis of behavior: Vol. 3. Biological factors in learning.* Chichester, England: John Wiley.

Commons, M.L., Herrnstein, R.J., & Rachlin, H. (Eds.). (1982). *Quantitative analysis of behavior: Vol. 2. Matching and maximizing accounts.* Cambridge, MA: Bullinger.

Cullen, E. (1957). Adaptations in the Kittiwake to cliff nesting. *Ibis, 99,* 275–302.

Darwin, C.R. (1859). *On the origin of species by means of natural selection, or the preservation of favoured races in the struggle for life.* London: John Murray.

Darwin, C.R. (1871). *The descent of man, and selection in relation to sex.* London: John Murray.

Dawkins, R. (1982). *The extended phenotype.* San Francisco: W.H. Freeman.

Degabriele, R. (1980). The physiology of the Koala. *Scientific American, 243,* (July) 110–117.

Dennett, D.C. (1975). Why the law of effect will not go away. *Journal of the Theory of Social Behavior, 5,* 169–187.

Denton, D. (1982). *The hunger for salt.* New York: Springer-Verlag.

Dethier, V.G. (1976). *The hungry fly.* Cambridge, MA: Harvard.

Dobrzecka, C., Szwejkowska, G., & Konorski, J. (1966). Qualitative versus directional cues in two forms of differentiation. *Science, 153,* 87–89.

Domjan, M. (1973). Role of ingestion in odor-toxicosis learning in the rat. *Journal of Comparative and Physiological Psychology, 84,* 507–521.

Domjan, M. (1980). Ingestional aversion learning: Unique and general process, In J.S. Rosenblatt, R.A. Hinde, C. Beer, & M. Busnel (Eds.), *Advances in the study of behavior: Vol. 11.* New York: Academic Press.

Domjan, M. (1983). Biological constraints on instrumental and classical conditioning: Implications for general process learning theory. In G.H. Bower (Ed.), *Psychology of learning and motivation: Vol. 17.* New York: Academic Press.

Domjan, M., & Galef, B.G., Jr. (1983). Biological constraints on instrumental and classical conditioning: Retrospect and prospect. *Animal Learning and Behavior, 11,* 151–161.

Domjan, M., & Wilson, N.E. (1972). Contribution of ingestive behaviors to taste-aversion learning in the rat. *Journal of Comparative and Physiological Psychology, 80,* 403–412.

Durlach, P.J., & Rescorla, R.A. (1980). Potentiation rather than overshadowing in flavor-aversion learning: An analysis in terms of within compound associations. *Journal of Experimental Psychology: Animal Behavior Processes, 6,* 175–187.

Eibl-Eibesfeldt, I. (1963). Angegorenes und Erworbenes im Verhalten einiger Sauger. *Zeitschrift fur Tierpsychologie, 20,* 705–754; described in Eibl-Eibesfeldt, I. *Ethology: The biology of behavior.* New York: Holt, Rinehart, & Winston, 1970.

Elner, R.W., & Hughes, R.N. (1978). Energy maximization in the diet of the shore crab, *Carcinus maenas. Journal of Animal Ecology, 47,* 103–116.

Emlen, S.T. (1970). Celestial rotation: Its importance in the development of migratory orientation. *Science, 170,* 1198–1201.

Fantino, E. (1981). Contiguity, response strength and the delay-reduction hypothesis. In P. Harzem & M.D. Zeiler (Eds.), *Advances in Analysis of Behavior: Vol. 3. Predictability, correlation, and contiguity.* New York: John Wiley.

Flavell, J.H. (1963). *The developmental psychology of Jean Piaget.* Princeton, NJ: Van Nostrand-Reinhold.

Flavell, J.H., & Wellman, H.M. (1977). Metamemory. In R.V. Kail, Jr., & J.W. Hagen (Eds.), *Perspectives on the development of memory and cognition.* Hillsdale, NJ: Erlbaum.

Fodor, J.A. (1972). Some reflections on L.S. Vygotsky's thought and language. *Cognition, 1,* 83–95.

Fodor, J.A. (1983). *The modularity of mind.* Cambridge, MA: M.I.T. Press.

Freeland, W.J., & Janzen, D.H. (1974). Strategies of herbivory by mammals: The role of plant secondary compounds. *American Naturalist, 108,* 269–289.

Friedman, M.I., & Stricker, E.M. (1976). The physiological psychology of hunger: A physiological perspective. *Psychological Review, 83,* 409–431.

Frisch, K. von. (1967). The dance language and orientation of bees. Cambridge, MA: Harvard University Press.

Galef, B.G., Jr. (1977). Mechanisms for the social transmission of acquired food preferences from adults to weanling rats. In L.M. Barker, M.R. Best, & M. Domjan (Eds.), *Learning mechanisms in food selection* (pp. 123–148). Waco, TX: Baylor University Press.

Galef, B.G., Jr. (1981). The ecology of weaning: Parasitism and the achievement of independence by altricial mammals. In D.J. Gubernick & P.H. Klopfer (Eds.), *Parental care in mammals* (pp. 211–241). New York: Plenum.

Galef, B.G., Jr., & Dalrymple, A.J. (1981). Toxicosis-based aversions to visual cues in rats: A test of the Testa and Ternes hypothesis. *Animal Learning and Behavior, 9,* 332–334.

Galef, B.G., Jr., & Osborne, B. (1978). Novel taste facilitation of the association of visual cues with toxicosis in rats. *Journal of Comparative Physiological Psychology, 92,* 907–916.

Galef, B.G. Jr., & Wigmore, S.W. (1983). Transfer of information concerning distant food in rats: A laboratory investigation of the "information centre" hypothesis. *Animal Behaviour, 31,* 748–758.

Gallistel, C.R. (1980). *The organization of action.* Hillsdale, NJ: Erlbaum.

Garb, J., & Stunkard, A.J. (1974). Taste aversions in man. *American Journal of Psychiatry, 131,* 1204–1207.

Garcia, J., & Ervin, F.R. (1968). Gustatory-visceral and telereceptor-cutaneous conditioning—Adaptation in internal and external milieus. *Communications in Behavioral Biology, Part A, 1,* 389–415.

Garcia, J., Ervin, F.R., & Koelling, R.A. (1966). Learning with prolonged delay of reinforcement. *Psychonomic Science, 5,* 121–122.

Garcia, J., Hankins, W.G., & Rusiniak, K.W. (1974). Behavioral regulation of the milieu interne in man and rat. *Science, 185,* 824–831.

Garcia, J., Kimeldorf, D.J., & Hunt, E.L. (1961). The use of ionizing radiation as a motivating stimulus. *Psychological Review, 68,* 383–385.

Garcia, J., & Koelling, R.A. (1966). Relation of cue to consequence in avoidance learning. *Psychonomic Science, 4,* 123–124.

Garcia, J., Kovner, R., & Green, K.F. (1970). Cue properties versus palatability of flavors in avoidance learning. *Psychonomic Science, 20,* 313 314.

Garcia, J., McGowan, B.K., & Green, K.F. (1972). Biological constraints on conditioning. In A.H. Black & W.F. Prokasy (Eds.), *Classical conditioning II: Current research and theory* (pp. 3–27). New York: Appleton-Century-Crofts.

Garcia, J., & Rusiniak, K.W. (1980). What the nose learns from the mouth. In D. Muller-Schwarze & R.M. Silverstein (Eds.), *Chemical signals.* New York: Plenum.

Gardner, H. (1983). *Frames of mind: The theory of multiple intelligences.* New York: Basic Books.

Gelman, R. (1982). Recent trends in cognitive development. In J. Schierer & A. Rogers (Eds.), *The G. Stanley Hall Lecture Series: Vol. 3.* Washington, DC: American Psychological Association.

Gelman, R., & Gallistel, C.R. (1978). *The child's understanding of number*. Cambridge, MA: Harvard University Press.

Gemberling, G.A., & Domjan, M. (1982). Selective associations in one-day-old rats: Taste-toxicosis and texture-shock aversion learning. *Journal of Comparative and Physiological Psychology, 96*, 95–113.

Gibson, E.J. (1969). *Principles of perceptual learning and development*. New York: Appleton-Century-Crofts.

Gibson, E.J. (1984). Perceptual development from the ecological approach. In M.E. Lamb, A.L. Brown, & B. Rogoff (Eds.), *Advances in Developmental Psychology Vol. 3* (pp. 243–286). Hillsdale, NJ: Erlbaum.

Gibson, J.J. (1966). *The senses considered as perceptual systems*. New York: Houghton Mifflin.

Gibson, J.J. (1977). The theory of affordances. In R. Shaw & J. Bransford (Eds.), *Perceiving, acting and knowing. Towards an ecological psychology*. Hillsdale, NJ: Erlbaum.

Gillette, K., Martin, G.M., & Bellingham, W.P. (1980). Differential use of food and water cues in the formation of conditioned aversions by domestic chicks (*Gallus gallus*). *Journal of Experimental Psychology: Animal Behavior Processes, 6*, 99–111.

Gleitman, H. (1974). Getting animals to understand the experimentor's instructions. *Animal Learning and Behavior, 2*, 1–5.

Gleitman, H. (1981). *Psychology*. New York: Norton.

Gleitman, H., & Gleitman, L.R. (1979). Language use and language judgment. In C.J. Fillmore, D. Kempler, & W.S.Y. Wang (Eds.), *Individual differences in language ability and language behavior* (pp. 123–126). New York: Academic Press.

Gleitman, L.R., & Rozin, P. (1977). The structure and acquisition of reading. I. Relations between orthographies and the structure of language. In A.S. Reber & D. Scarborough (Eds.), *Toward a psychology of reading* (pp. 1–53). Potomac, MA: Erlbaum.

Gottlieb, G. (1979). Comparative psychology and ethology. In E. Hearst (Ed.), *The first century of experimental psychology* (pp. 147–173). Hillsdale, NJ: Erlbaum.

Gould, J.J., & Gould, C.G. (1982). The insect mind: Physics or metaphysics. In D.R. Griffin (Ed.), *Animal mind, human mind* (pp. 269–298). Dahlem Konferenzen. New York: Springer.

Gould, S.J., & Lewontin, R.C. (1978). The spandrels of San Marco and the Panglossian paradigm: A critique of the adaptationist program. *Proceedings of the Royal Society, London, 205*, 581–598.

Griffin, D.R. (1976). *The question of animal awareness*. New York: Rockefeller University Press.

Griffin, D.R. (Ed.). (1982). *Animal mind, human mind*. Dahlem Konferenzen. New York: Springer.

Grill, H.J., & Norgren, R. (1978). The taste-reactivity test I. Oro-facial responses to gustatory stimuli in neurologically normal rats. *Brain Research, 143*, 263–279.

Hailman, J.P. (1967). Ontogeny of an instinct. *Behavior, Suppl. 15*.

Hamilton, W.D. (1964). The genetic evolution of social behavior. I, II. *Journal of Theoretical Biology, 7*, 1–52.

Harris, L.J., Clay, J., Hargreaves, F., & Ward, A. (1933). Appetite and choice of diet. The ability of the vitamin B deficient rat to discriminate between diets containing and lacking the vitamin. *Proceedings of the Royal Society, London, Series B, 113*, 161–190.

Hasler, A. (1966). Underwater guideposts: Homing of salmon. Madison, WI: University of Wisconsin Press.

Heinrich, B. (1979). Majoring and minoring by foraging bumblebees. *Bombus vagans*: An experimental analysis. *Ecology, 60*, 245–255.

Herrnstein, R.J. (1970). On the law of effect. *Journal of the Experimental Analysis of Behavior, 13*, 243–266.

Herrnstein, R.J. (1982). Melioration as behavioral dynamism. In Commons, M.L., Herrnstein, R.J., & Rachlin, H. (Eds.), *Quantitative analysis of behavior: Vol. 2. Matching and maximizing accounts*. Cambridge. MA: Bullinger.

Herrnstein, R.J., & de Villiers, P.A. (1980). Fish as a natural category for people and pigeons. In G.H. Bower (Ed.), *The psychology of learning and motivation: Vol. 14* (pp. 59–95). New York: Academic Press.

Herrnstein, R.J., & Vaughan, W. (1980). Melioration and behavioral allocation. In J.E.R. Staddon (Ed.), *Limits to action: The allocation of individual behavior* (pp. 143–176). New York: Academic Press.

Hess, E.H. (1973). *Imprinting: Early experience and the developmental psychobiology of attachment*. New York: Van Nostrand Reinhold.

Hinde, R.A. (1973). Constraints on learning—An introduction to the problems. In R.A. Hinde & J. Stevenson-Hinde (Eds.), *Constraints on learning: Limitations and predispositions* (pp. 1–19). New York: Academic Press.

Hinde, R.A. (1981). Biological approaches to the study of learning: Does Johnston provide a new alternative? *The Behavioral and Brain Sciences, 4*, 146–147.

Hinde, R.A., & Stevenson-Hinde, J. (1973). *Constraints on learning: Limitations and predispositions*. New York: Academic Press.

Hochberg, J.E. (1978). *Perception* (2nd ed.). Englewood Cliffs, NJ: Prentice-Hall.

Hodos, W., & Campbell, C.B.G. (1969). *Scala Naturae:* Why there is no theory in comparative psychology. *Psychological Review, 76,* 337–350.

Hogan, J.A. (1974). Responses in Pavlovian conditioning studies. *Science, 186,* 156–157.

Hogan, J.A. (1977). The ontogeny of food preferences in chicks and other animals. In L.M. Barker, M. Best, & M. Domjan (Eds.), *Learning mechanisms in food selection* (pp. 71–97). Waco, TX: Baylor University Press.

Hogan, J.A., & Roper, T.J. (1978). A comparison of the properties of different reinforcers. In J.S. Rosenblatt, R.A. Hinde, C. Beer, & M. Busnel (Eds.), *Advances in the study of behavior: Vol. 8* (pp. 155–255). New York: Academic Press.

Hogan-Warburg, A.J., & Hogan, J.A. (1981). Feeding strategies in the development of food recognition in young chicks. *Animal Behavior, 29,* 143–154.

Hollis, K.L. (1982). Pavlovian conditioning of signal-centered action patterns and autonomic behavior: A biological analysis of function. In J.S. Rosenblatt, R.A. Hinde, C. Beer, & M. Busnell (Eds.), *Advances in the study of behavior Vol. 12* (pp. 1–64). New York: Academic Press.

Holman, G.L. (1968). Intragastric reinforcement effect. *Journal of Comparative and Physiological Psychology, 69,* 432–441.

Hull, C. (1929). A functional interpretation of the conditioned reflex. *Psychological Review, 36,* 498–511.

Humphrey, N.K. (1976). The social function of intellect. In P.P.G. Bateson, & R.A. Hinde (Eds.), *Growing points in ethology* (pp. 303–317). Cambridge, England: Cambridge University Press.

Hunt, G.L., & Smith, W.J. (1967). Pecking and initial drinking responses in young domestic fowl. *Journal of Comparative and Physiological Psychology, 64,* 230–236.

Jenkins, H.M. (1979). Animal learning and behavior theory. In E. Hearst (Ed.), *The first century of experimental psychology* (pp. 177–228). Hillsdale, NJ: Erlbaum.

Jennings, H.S. (1906). *The behavior of lower organisms.* New York: Columbia University Press.

Jerison, H.J. (1973). *Evolution of the brain and intelligence.* New York: Academic Press.

Johnston, T.D. (1981). Contrasting approaches to a theory of learning. *Behavioral and Brain Sciences, 4,* 125–173.

Johnston, T.D. (1982). Selective costs and benefits in the evolution of learning. In J.S. Rosenblatt, R.A. Hinde, C. Beer, & M. Busnel (Eds.), *Advances in the study of behavior: Vol. 12* (pp. 65–106). New York: Academic Press.

Johnston, T.D., & Turvey, M.T. (1980). A sketch of an ecological metatheory for theories of learning. In G.H. Bower (Ed.), *The psychology of learning and memory: Vol. 14* (pp. 147–205). New York: Academic Press.

Kalat, J.W. (1977). Biological significance of food aversion learning. In N.W. Milgram, L. Krames, & T.M. Alloway (Eds.), *Food aversion learning* (pp. 73–103). New York: Plenum.

Kamil, A.C., & Sargent, T.D. (Eds.). (1981). *Foraging behaviour: Ecological, ethological, and psychological approaches.* New York: Garland Press.

Kamil, A.C., & Yoerg, S.I. (1982). Learning and foraging behavior. In P.P.G. Bateson & P.H. Klopfer (Eds.), *Perspectives in ethology: Vol. 5. Ontogeny* (pp. 325–364). New York: Plenum.

Keeton, W.T. (1974). The orientation and navigational basis of homing in birds. In D.S. Lehrman, J.S. Rosenblatt, R.A. Hinde, & E. Shaw (Eds.), *Advances in the study of behavior: Vol. 5* (pp. 47–132). New York: Academic Press.

Keeton, W.T. (1981). The ontogeny of bird orientation. In G.W. Barlow, L. Petrinovich, & M. Main (Eds.), *Behavioral Development* (pp. 509–517). New York: Cambridge University Press.

Keil, F. (1981). Constraints on knowledge and cognitive development. *Psychological Review, 88,* 197–227.

King's College Sociobiology Group. (1982). Current problems in sociobiology. Cambridge, England: Cambridge University Press.

Konorski, J. (1967). *Integrative activity of the brain.* Chicago: University of Chicago Press.

Krebs, J.R., & Davies, N.B. (1981). *An introduction to behavioural ecology.* Oxford, England: Blackwell Scientific Publications.

Krebs, J.R., & Davies, N.B. (Eds.). (1984). *Behavioral ecology* (2nd ed.). Oxford, England: Blackwell Scientific Publications.

Krieckhaus, E.E., & Wolf, G. (1968). Acquisition of sodium by rats: Interaction of innate mechanisms and latent learning. *Journal of Comparative and Physiological Psychology, 64,* 197–201.

Kummer, H. (1982). Social knowledge in free ranging primates. In D.R. Griffin (Ed.), *Animal mind, human mind.* Dahlem Konferenzen. New York: Springer.

Lea, S.E.G. (1981). Correlation and contiguity in foraging behavior. In P. Harzem, & M.D. Zeiler (Eds.), *Advances in Analysis of Behavior: Vol. 2. Predictability, correlation, and contiguity.* New York: John Wiley.

Lehrman, D.S. (1970). Semantic and conceptual issues in the nature-nurture problem. In L.R. Aronson, E. Tobach, D.S. Lehrman, & J.S. Rosenblatt (Eds.), *Development and evolution of behavior* (pp. 17–52). San Francisco: Freeman.

LeMagnen, J. (1967). Habits and food intake. In C.F. Code (Ed.), *Handbook of Physiology, Section 6, Alimentary Canal: Vol. 1. Control of Food and Water Intake*. Washington, DC: American Physiological Society.

Lenneberg, E.H. (1967). *Biological foundations of language*. New York: Wiley.

Lettvin, J.Y., Maturana, H.R., McCullock, W.S., & Pitts, W.H. (1959). What the frog's eye tells the frog's brain. *Proceedings of the Institute of Radio Engineers, 47*, 1940–1951.

Liberman, A.M., & Studdert-Kennedy, M. (1978). Phonetic perception. In R. Held, H. Leibowitz, & H.L. Teuber (Eds.), *Handbook of Sensory Physiology: Vol. VIII. Perception*. Heidelberg: Springer-Verlag.

Lindauer, M. (1961). *Communication among social bees*. Cambridge, MA: Harvard University Press.

Lockard, R.B. (1971). Reflections on the fall of comparative psychology: Is there a message for us all? *American Psychologist, 26*, 168–179.

Logue, A.W. (1979). Taste aversion and the generality of the laws of learning. *Psychological Bulletin, 86*, 276–296.

Logue, A.W. (1980). Visual clues for illness-induced aversions in the pigeon. *Behavioral and Neural Biology, 28*, 372–377.

Logue, A.W. (1985a). The origins of behaviorism. In C. Buxton (Ed.), *Points of View in the Modern History of Psychology*. New York: Academic Press.

Logue, A.W. (1985b). The growth of behaviorism. In C. Buxton (Ed.), *Points of View in the Modern History of Psychology*. New York: Academic Press.

Logue, A.W., Ophir, I., & Strauss, K.E. (1981). The acquisition of taste aversions in humans. *Behavior Research and Therapy, 19*, 319–331.

LoLordo, V.M. (1979). Selective associations. In A. Dickinson & R.A. Boakes (Eds.), *Mechanisms of learning and motivation* (pp. 367–398). Hillsdale, NJ: Erlbaum.

LoLordo, V.M. & Jacobs, W.J. (1983). Constraints on aversive conditioning in the rat: Some theoretical accounts. In M.D. Zeiler & P. Harzem (Eds.), *Advances in the analysis of behavior: Vol. 3*. New York: John Wiley.

Lorenz, K.Z. (1937). The companion in the bird's world. *Auk, 54*, 245–273. Originally published in German in 1935 (*J. Orn. Lpz., 83*, 137–213, 289–394.)

Lorenz, K.Z. (1971). Comparative studies of the motor patterns of Anatinae. In Lorenz, K.S., *Studies in animal and human behavior: Vol. II*. Cambridge, MA: Harvard University Press. (Original work published 1941).

Lorenz, K.Z. (1967). *Evolution and the modification of behavior*. Chicago: University of Chicago Press.

Lorenz, K.Z. (1981). *The foundations of ethology*. New York: Springer-Verlag.

Lumsden, C.J., & Wilson, E.O. (1981). *Genes, mind and culture*. Cambridge, MA: Harvard University Press.

Lumsden, C.J., & Wilson, E.O. (1983). *Promethean fire*. Cambridge, MA: Harvard University Press.

Mackintosh, N.J. (1973). Stimulus selection: Learning to ignore stimuli that predict no change in reinforcement. In R.A. Hinde & J. Stevenson-Hinde (Eds.), *Constraints on Learning*. London: Academic Press.

Manning, A. (1976). Animal learning: Ethological approaches. In M.R. Rozenzweig, & E.L. Bennett (Eds.), *Neural mechanisms of learning and memory* (pp. 147–158). Cambridge, MA: M.I.T. Press.

Marler, P.A. (1970). Comparative approach to vocal learning: Song development in white crowned sparrows. *Journal of Comparative and Physiological Psychology, Monograph 71(2)*, 1–25.

Mayr, E. (1960). The emergence of evolutionary novelties. In S. Tax (Ed.), *Evolution after Darwin: Vol. 1. The evolution of life* (pp. 349–380). Chicago: University of Chicago Press.

Mayr, E. (1974). Behavior programs and evolutionary strategies. *American Scientist, 62*, 650–659.

McFarland, D.J. (1976). Form and function in the temporal organisation of behavior. In P.P.G. Bateson, & R.A. Hinde (Eds.), *Growing points in ethology* (pp. 54–94). Cambridge, England: Cambridge University Press.

McFarland, D.J. (1977a). Decision making in animals. *Nature, 269*, 15–21.

McFarland, D.J. (1977b). *Feedback mechanisms in animal behavior*. London: Academic Press.

McFarland, D.J. (1985). Food selection and time sharing in the Herring Gull. Unpublished manuscript.

McLaurin, W.A. (1964). Postirradiation saccharin avoidance in rats as a function of the interval between ingestion and exposure. *Journal of Comparative and Physiological Psychology, 57*, 316–317.

Menzel, E. (1979). Cognitive mapping in chimpanzees. In S.H. Hulse, H. Fowler, & W.K. Honig (Eds.), *Cognitive processes in animal behavior*. Hillsdale, NJ: Erlbaum, 375–422.

Menzel, R., & Erber, J. (1978). Learning and memory in bees. *Scientific American, 239(1)*, 102–110.

Milgram, N.W., Krames, L., & Alloway, T.M. (Eds.) (1977). *Food aversion learning*. New York: Plenum.

Miller, G.A., Galanter, E., & Pribram, K.H. (1960). *Plans and the structure of behavior*. New York: Holt, Rinehart, & Winston.

Miller, N. (1967). Laws of learning relevant to its biological basis. *Proceedings of the American Philosophical Society, 111*, 315–325.

Morgan, C.L. (1894). *An introduction to comparative psychology.* London: Scott.

Nachman, M. (1962). Taste preference for sodium salts by adrenalectomized rats. *Journal of Comparative and Physiological Psychology, 55,* 1124–1129.

Neisser, U. (1976). *Cognition and reality.* San Francisco: Freeman.

Neuringer, A., & Bullock, D. (1977). Social learning by following: An analysis. *Journal of the Experimental Analysis of Behavior, 27,* 127–135.

Nicolaidis, S., Danguir, J., & Mather, P. (1985). Effect of a niche on rat's feeding and sleep: A biobehavioral correlation. Unpublished manuscript.

Norton-Griffiths, N.N. (1969). The organization, control and development of parental feeding in the oyster catcher (*Haematopus ostralegus*). *Behaviour, 34(2),* 55–114.

Olton, D.S. (1979). Characteristics of spatial memory. In S.H. Hulse, H. Fowler & W.K. Honig (Eds.), *Cognitive Processes in Animal Behavior* (pp. 341–373). Hillsdale, NJ: Erlbaum.

Opfinger, E. (1931). Uber die Orientierung der Biene an der Futerquelle. *Zeitschrift fur Vergleichende Physiologie, 15,* 431–487.

Parker, L.A. (1982). Nonconsummatory and consummatory behavioral CRs elicited by lithium- and amphetamine-paired flavors. *Learning and Motivation, 13,* 281–303.

Partridge, L. (1978). Habitat selection. In J.R. Krebs & N.B. Davies (Eds.), *Behavioural ecology: An evolutionary approach* (pp. 351–376). Oxford, England: Blackwell Scientific.

Pavlov, I.P. (1927). *Conditioned reflexes.* Oxford: Oxford University Press.

Pelchat, M.L., Grill, H.J., Rozin, P., & Jacobs, J. (1983). Quality of acquired response to taste depends on type of associated discomfort. *Journal of Comparative Psychology, 97,* 140–153.

Pelchat, M.L., & Rozin, P. (1982). The special role of nausea in the acquisition of food dislikes by humans. *Appetite, 3,* 341–351.

Piaget, J. (1955). Les stades du developpement intellectuel de l'enfant et de l'adolescent. In P. Osterrieth et al. (Eds.), *Le Probleme des Stades en Psychologie de l'Enfant* (pp. 33–133). Paris: Presses Universite France.

Pietrewicz, A.T., & Kamil, A.C. (1981). Search images and the detection of cryptic prey: An operant approach. In A.C. Kamil & T.D. Sargent (Eds.), *Foraging behavior: Ecological, ethological, and psychological approaches.* New York: Garland Press.

Plotkin, H.C., & Odling-Smee, F.J. (1979). Learning, change, and evolution: An enquiry into the teleonomy of learning. In J.S. Rosenblatt, R.A. Hinde, C.G. Beer, & M. Busnel (Eds.), *Advances in the Study of Behavior, 10* (pp. 1–41). New York: Academic Press.

Posadas-Andrews, A., & Roper, T.J. (1983). Social transmission of food preferences in adult rats. *Animal Behaviour, 31,* 265–271.

Posner, M.I., & Shulman, G.L. (1979). Cognitive science. In E. Hearst (Ed.), *The first century of experimental psychology* (pp. 371–405). Hillsdale, NJ: Erlbaum.

Premack, D. (1976). *Intelligence in ape and man.* Hillsdale, NJ: Erlbaum.

Premack, D., & Woodruff, G. (1978). Does the chimpanzee have a theory of mind? *The Behavioral and Brain Sciences, 4,* 515–526.

Pulliam, H.R., & Dunford, C. (1980). *Programmed to learn.* New York: Columbia University Press.

Pyke, G.H., Pulliam, H.R., & Charnov, E.L. (1977). Optimal foraging: A selective review of theories and facts. *Quarterly Review of Biology, 52,* 137–154.

Rachlin, H. (1976). *Behavior and learning.* San Francisco: W.H. Freeman.

Rashotte, M.E., O'Connel, J.M., & Beidler, D.L. (1982). Associative influences on the foraging behavior of pigeons (*Columba livia*). *Journal of Experimental Psychology: Animal Behavior Processes, 8,* 142–153.

Reisbick, S.H. (1973). Development of food preferences in newborn guinea pigs. *Journal of Comparative and Physiological Psychology, 85,* 427–442.

Rescorla, R.A. (1967). Pavlovian conditioning and its proper control procedures. *Psychological Review, 74,* 71–80.

Rescorla, R.A. (1980). *Pavlovian Second-Order Conditioning.* Hillsdale, N.J.: Erlbaum.

Rescorla, R.A. (1981). Simultaneous associations. In P. Harzem, & M.D. Zeiler (Eds.), *Advances in Analysis of Behavior: Vol. 2. Predictability, correlation and contiguity.* New York: John Wiley.

Rescorla, R.A., & Cunningham, C.L. (1979). Spatial contiguity facilitates Pavlovian second-order conditioning. *Journal of Experimental Psychology: Animal Behavior Processes, 5,* 152–161.

Rescorla, R.A., & Furrow, D.R. (1977). Stimulus similarity as a determinant of Pavlovian conditioning. *Journal of Experimental Psychology: Animal Behavior Processes, 3,* 203–215.

Rescorla, R.A., & Holland, P.C. (1976). Some behavioral approaches to the study of learning. In M.R. Rosenzweig, & E.L. Bennett (Eds.), *Neural mechanisms of learning and memory* (pp. 165–192). Cambridge, MA: M.I.T. Press.

Revusky, S. (1971). The role of interference in association over a delay. In W.K. Honig & P.H.R. James (Eds.), *Animal Memory* (pp. 155–213). New York: Academic Press.

Revusky, S. (1977a). Learning as a general process with an emphasis on data from feeding experiments. In N.W. Milgram, L. Krames, & T.H. Alloway (Eds.), *Food aversion learning* (pp. 1–51). New York: Plenum Press.

Revusky, S. (1977b). Interference with progress by the scientific establishment: Examples from flavor aversion learning. (Appendix to Chapter 1). In N.W. Milgram, L. Krames, & T.H. Alloway (Eds.), *Food aversion learning* (pp. 53–71). New York: Plenum Press.

Revusky, S., & Bedarf, E.W. (1967). Association of illness with prior ingestion of novel foods. *Science*, *155*, 219–220.

Revusky, S., & Garcia, J. (1970). Learned associations over long delays. In G.H. Bower (Ed.), *The psychology of learning and motivation: Vol. 4.* (pp. 1–84). New York: Academic Press.

Richter, C.P. (1943). Total self-regulatory functions in animals and human beings. *Harvey Lecture Series*, *38*, 63–103.

Richter, C.P. (1950). Taste and solubility of toxic compounds in poisoning of rats and man. *Journal of Comparative and Physiological Psychology*, *43*, 358–374.

Richter, C.P. (1956). Salt appetite of mammals: Its dependence on instinct and metabolism. In Fondation Singer Polignac (Ed.), *L'Instinct dans le Comportement des Animaux et de l'Homme* (pp. 577–629). Paris: Masson.

Riley, A.L., & Baril, L.L. (1976). Conditioned taste aversions: A bibliography. *Animal Learning and Behavior*, *4*, 15–135.

Rock, I. (1983). *The logic of perception*. Cambridge, MA: M.I.T. Press.

Rodgers, W.L. (1967). Specificity of specific hungers. *Journal of Comparative and Physiological Psychology*, *64*, 49–58.

Rolls, B.J., Rolls, E.T., Rowe, E.A., & Sweeney, K. (1981). Sensory specific satiety in man. *Physiology and behavior. 27*, 137–142.

Romanes, G.J. (1882). *Animal intelligence*. London: Kegan Paul.

Rozin, P. (1967). Thiamine specific hunger. In C.F. Code (Ed.), *Handbook of Physiology, Section 6, Alimentary Canal: Vol. 1. Control of Food and Water Intake* (pp. 411–432). Washington, DC: American Physiological Society.

Rozin, P. (1976a). The evolution of intelligence and access to the cognitive unconscious. In J.A. Sprague, & A.N. Epstein (Eds.), *Progress in Psychobiology and Physiological Psychology: Vol. 6* (pp. 245–280). New York: Academic Press.

Rozin, P. (1976b). The selection of food by rats, humans and other animals. In J. Rosenblatt,

R.A. Hinde, C. Beer, & E. Shaw (Eds.), *Advances in the Study of Behavior: Vol. 6* (pp. 21–76). New York: Academic Press.

Rozin, P. (1982). Human food selection: The interaction of biology, culture and individual experience. In L.M. Barker (Ed.). *The Psychobiology of Human Food Selection*. Bridgeport, CT: AVI, 225–254.

Rozin, P., & Adler, N.T. (in preparation). Biopsychological explanation. Unpublished manuscript.

Rozin, P., & Gleitman, L.R. (1977). The structure and acquisition of reading. II. The reading process and the acquisition of the alphabetic principle. In A.S. Reber & D. Scarborough (Eds.), *Toward a Psychology of Reading* (pp. 55–141). Potomac, MD: Erlbaum.

Rozin, P., & Kalat, J.W. (1971). Specific hungers and poison avoidance as adaptive specializations of learning. *Psychological Review*, *78*, 459–486.

Rozin, P. and Kalat, J.W. (1972). Learning as a situation-specific adaptation. In M.E.P. Seligman & J.L. Hager (Eds.), *Biological Boundaries of Learning* (pp. 66–96). New York: Appleton-Century-Crofts.

Rudy, J., & Cheatle, M.D. (1979). Ontogeny of associative learning: Acquisition of odor aversions by neonatal rats. In N.E. Spear & B.A. Campbell (Eds.), *Ontogeny of learning and memory*. Hillsdale, NJ: Erlbaum.

Rudy, J., Iwens, J., & Best, P.J. (1977). Pairing novel exteroceptive cues and illness reduces illness-induced taste aversions. *Journal of Experimental Psychology: Animal Behavior Processes*, *3*, 14–25.

Rusiniak, K.W., Hankins, W.G., Garcia, J., & Brett, L.P. (1979). Flavor-illness aversions: Potentiation of odor by taste in rats. *Behavioral and Neural Biology*, *25*, 1–17.

Rzoska, J. (1953). Bait shyness, a study in rat behavior. *British Journal of Animal Behavior*, *1*, 128–135.

Schoener, T.W. (1971). Theory of feeding strategies. *Annual review of ecology and systematics*, *2*, 369–404.

Schulkin, J. (1982). Behavior of sodium-deficient rats: The search for a salty taste. *Journal of Comparative and Physiological Psychology*, *96*, 628–634.

Schull, J. (1979). A conditioned opponent theory of Pavlovian conditioning and habituation. In G. Bower (Ed.), *The Psychology of Learning and Motivation: Vol. 13*. New York: Academic Press.

Schull, J. (1984). The significance of signals and the importance of portents. Unpublished manuscript.

Schull, J. (in preparation). Evolution and learning: Analogies and interactions. In E. Laszlo (Ed.). *The evolution paradigm*.

Schwartz, B. (1974). On going back to nature: A review of Seligman and Hager's *Biological boundaries of learning. Journal of the Experimental Analysis of Behavior, 21,* 183–198.

Schwartz, B. (1980). Development of complex, stereotyped behavior in pigeons. *Journal of the Experimental Analysis of Behavior, 33,* 153–166.

Schwartz, B. (1981). The ecology of learning: The right answer to the wrong question. *The Behavioral and Brain Sciences, 4,* 159–160.

Schwartz, B., & Lacey, H. (1982). *Behaviorism, science and human nature.* New York: W.W. Norton.

Schwarts, M.F., & Schwartz, B. (1984). In defence of organology. *Cognitive Neuropsychology, 1,* 25–42.

Scott, E.M., & Verney, E.L. (1947). Self selection of diet: VI. The nature of appetites for B vitamins. *Journal of Nutrition, 34,* 471–480.

Seligman, M.E.P. (1970). On the generality of the laws of learning. *Psychological Review, 77,* 406–418.

Seligman, M.E.P., & Hager, J.L. (Eds.) (1972). *Biological boundaries of learning.* New York: Appleton-Century-Crofts.

Sevenster, P. (1973). Incompatibility of response and reward. In R.A. Hinde & J. Stevenson-Hinde (Eds.), *Constraints on learning: Limitations and predispositions.* London: Academic Press.

Shettleworth, S.J. (1972). Constraints on learning. In D.S. Lehrman, R.A. Hinde, & E. Shaw (Eds.), *Advances in the study of behavior: Vol. 4.* New York: Academic Press.

Shettleworth, S.J. (1975). Reinforcement and the organization of behavior in golden hamsters: Hunger, environment, and food reinforcement. *Journal of Experimental Psychology: Animal Behavior Processes, 1,* 56–87.

Shettleworth, S.J. (1978). Reinforcement and the organization of behavior in golden hamsters: Punishment of three action patterns. *Learning and Motivation, 9,* 99–123.

Shettleworth, S.J. (1979). Constraints on conditioning in the writings of Konorski. In A. Dickinson & R.A. Boakes (Eds.), *Mechanisms of learning and motivation: A memorial volume to Jerzy Konorski* (pp. 399–416). Hillsdale, NJ: Erlbaum.

Shettleworth, S.J. (1983). Function and mechanism in learning. M. Zeiler, & P. Harzem (Eds.), *Advances in Analysis of Behavior: Vol. 3. Biological factors in learning* (pp. 1–39). New York: John Wiley.

Shettleworth, S.J. (1984). Learning and behavioral ecology. In J.R. Krebs & N.B. Davies (Eds.), *Behavioral Ecology, Second Edition* (pp. 170–194). Oxford, England: Blackwell Scientific Publications.

Shettleworth, S.J., & Krebs, J.R. (1982). How marsh tits find their hoards: The roles of site preference and spatial memory. *Journal of Experimental Psychology: Animal Behavior Processes, 8(4),* 354–375.

Siegel, S. (1979). The role of conditioning in drug tolerance and addiction. In J.D. Keehn (Ed.), *Psychopathology in animals,* New York: Academic Press.

Simon, H.A. (1967). The architecture of complexity. *Proceedings of the American Philosophical Society, 106,* 467–482.

Simoons, F.J. (1979). Dairying, milk use, and lactose malabsorption in Eurasia: A problem in culture history. *Anthropos, 74,* 61–80.

Skinner, B.F. (1938). *The behavior of organisms: An experimental analysis.* New York: Appleton-Century-Crofts.

Skinner, B.F. (1953). *Science and human behavior.* New York: Macmillan.

Skinner, B.F. (1981). Selection by consequence. *Science, 213,* 501–504.

Smith, J.C. (1971). Radiation: its detection and its effects on taste preferences. In E. Stellar, & J.M. Sprague (Eds.), *Progress in Physiological Psychology* (53–118). New York: Academic Press.

Smith, J.C., & Roll, D.L. (1967). Trace conditioning with X-rays as an aversive stimulus. *Psychonomic Science, 9,* 11–12.

Spelke, E. (1982). Perceptual knowledge of objects in infancy. In J. Mehler, M. Garrett & E. Walker (Eds.), *Perspectives on mental representation.* Hillsdale, NJ: Erlbaum.

Staddon, J.E.R. (1980). Optimality analyses of operant behavior and their relation to optimal foraging. In J.E.R. Staddon (Ed.), *Limits to action. The allocation of individual behavior.* London: Academic Press.

Staddon, J.E.R. (1983). *Adaptive behavior and learning.* Cambridge, England: Cambridge University Press.

Staddon, J.E.R., & Simmelhag, V.L. (1971). The "superstition" experiment: A reexamination of its implications for the principles of adaptive behavior. *Psychological Review, 78,* 3–43.

Teitelbaum, P. (1967). *Physiological psychology.* Englewood Cliffs, NJ: Prentice-Hall.

Testa, T.J. (1974). Causal relationships and the acquisition of avoidance responses. *Psychological Review, 81,* 491–505.

Testa, T.J., & Ternes, J.W. (1977). Specificity of conditioning mechanisms in the modification of food preferences. In L.M. Barker, M.R. Best, & M. Domjan (Eds.), *Learning mechanisms in food selection* (pp. 229–253). Waco, TX: Baylor University Press.

Thorndike, E.L. (1898). Animal intelligence: An experimental study of the associative processes in animals. *The Psychological Review Monograph Supplements, 2, whole No. 8.*

Thorndike, E.L. (1899). The associative processes in animals. *Biological lectures from the Marine Biological Laboratory at Woods Hole.* Boston: Atheneum.

Thorpe, W.H. (1963). *Learning and instinct in animals* (2nd edition). London: Metheun.

Timberlake, W. (1983). The functional organization of appetitive behavior: Behavior systems and learning. In M.D. Zeiler, & P. Harzem (Eds.), *Advances in analysis of behavior: Vol. 3. Biological factors in learning.* New York: John Wiley.

Tinbergen, N. (1951). *The study of instinct.* Oxford, England: Clarendon Press.

Tinbergen, L. (1960). The natural control of insects in pinewoods. I. Factors influencing the intensity of predation by songbirds. *Archives Neerlandaises de Zoologie, 13,* 265–343.

Tinbergen, N. (1963a). On aims and methods of ethology. *Zeitschrift fur Tierpsychologie, 20,* 410–429.

Tinbergen, N. (1963b). Egg shell removal by the black-headed gull (*Larus r. ridibundus L.*); a behaviour component of camouflage. *Behaviour, 19,* 74–117.

Tinbergen, N., & Perdeck, A.C. (1950). On the stimulus situation releasing the begging response in the newly hatched Herring Gull chick (*Larus a. argentatus*). *Behaviour, 3,* 1–38.

Tomback, D.F. (1980). How nutcrackers find their seed stores. *Condor, 82,* 10–19.

Tomback, D.F., & Baker, M.C. (1984). Assortative mating by white-crowned sparrows at song dialect boundaries. *Animal Behavior, 32,* 465–469.

Vander Wall, S.B. (1982). An experimental analysis of cache recovery in Clark's nutcracker. *Animal Behavior, 30,* 84–94.

Waddington, C.H. (1966). *Principles of development and differentiation.* New York: Macmillan.

Walls, G.L. (1942). *The vertebrate eye and its adaptive radiation.* Bloomfield Hills, MI: Cranbrook Institute of Science. [Reprinted in 1963: Hafner Publishing Company, N.Y.]

Wasserman, E.A. (1981). Response evocation in autoshaping: Contributions of cognitive and comparative-evolutionary analyses to an understanding of directed action. In C.M. Locurto, H.S. Terrace, & J. Gibbon (Eds.), *Autoshaping and conditioning theory.* New York: Academic Press.

Westoby, M. (1974). An analysis of diet selection by large generalist herbivores. *American Naturalist, 108,* 290–304.

Wexler, K., & Culicover, P. (1980). *Formal principles of language acquisition.* Cambridge, MA: M.I.T. Press.

Wilcoxon, H.C., Dragoin, W.B. & Kral, P.A. (1971). Illness-induced aversions in rat and quail: Relative salience of visual and gustatory cues. *Science, 171,* 826–828.

Williams, D.R. (1981). Biconditional behavior: Conditioning without constraint. In C.M. Locurto, H.S. Terrace, & J. Gibbon (Eds.), *Autoshaping and conditioning theory.* New York: Academic Press.

Williams, D.R., & Williams, H. (1969). Auto-maintenance in the pigeon: Sustained pecking despite contingent nonreinforcement. *Journal of the Experimental Analysis of Behavior, 12,* 511–520.

Woodruff, G., & Starr, M.D. (1978). Autoshaping of initial feeding and drinking reactions in newly hatched chicks. *Animal Learning and Behavior, 6,* 265–272.

Woodruff, G., & Williams, D.R. (1976). The associative relation underlying autoshaping in the pigeon. *Journal of the Experimental Analysis of Behavior, 26, 26, 1–13.*

Young, P.T. (1948). Appetite, palatability and feeding habit: A critical review. *Psychological Bulletin, 45,* 289–320.

Zahorik, D.M. (1979). Learned changes in preferences for chemical stimuli: Asymmetrical effects of positive and negative consequences, and species differences in learning. In J.H.A. Kroeze (Ed.), *Preference behavior and chemoreception* (pp. 233–243). London: Information Retrieval.

Zahorik, D.M., & Haupt, K. (1977). The concept of nutritional wisdom: Applicability of laboratory learning models to large herbivores. In Barker, L.M., Best, M.R., & Domjan, M. (Eds.), *Learning mechanisms in food selection* (pp. 45–67). Waco, TX: Baylor University Press.

Chapter 11

NEUROSCIENCE AND MOTIVATION: PATHWAYS AND PEPTIDES THAT DEFINE MOTIVATIONAL SYSTEMS

Bartley G. Hoebel, *Princeton University*

INTRODUCTION

In this chapter motivation will be studied from the point of view of both neuroscience and psychology. Given that psychology is the dual study of behavior and mental processes, this chapter is designed to meld three traditions: the study of the nervous system, the study of behavior, and the study of mental processes. A dominant theme in this field has been the effort to understand drive and reinforcement in neural terms. This research is becoming more cognitive

For classroom use, slide sets on this topic by Hoebel, Leibowitz, Teitelbaum, Stein, Valenstein, and others are available from Life Science Associates, Fenimore Road, Bayport, NY 11705, and a film (Hoebel, Rosenquist, & Caggiula, 1969) from Psychological Cinema Register, Pennsylvania State University, College Park, PA. Word-processing was done expertly by Kathleen B. McGeady. Sabbatical and research support was provided by Princeton University, the Salk Institute, and USPHS Grant MH35740 and DA03597. The author would also like to thank colleagues who reviewed sections of this manuscript: Alan Gelperin, George Koob, John Morley, Gorden Mogenson, Charles Nemeroff, Klaudiusz Weiss, and Roy Wise. This chapter was written in 1984 and corrected in 1987.

and more clinical as the neurotransmitters we are studying—for example, monoamines, opiates, and brain-gut peptides—are proving to be involved in both specific behavior categories, such as feeding, drinking, mating and aggression, and in general categories, such as stress, drug seeking, depression and psychosis. These categories involve both motivation and cognition, and many of the neurotransmitters seem to play similar roles in animals and humans.

The neurochemical correspondence between animals and people was the discovery of the century. Human specialization seems to lie in the complexity of brain anatomy more than in brain chemistry. Most human neurotransmitters have been found in animals and even in microorganisms as primitive as the amoeba. Opiates induce feeding in rats and amoeba. The human of today is the result of a chemical inheritance that is relatively unchanged in spite of an extraordinary anatomical evolution. There seem to be only dozens, or perhaps hundreds, of transmitters for billions of neurons. Evidence will be presented to suggest that certain neurotransmitter chemicals play identifiable roles in motivation throughout much of evolution. In particular this chapter will search for clues hidden in the brain-gut peptides which may provide organizational principles for the neuroscience of motivation. There is evidence that some of these peptides serve the same overall function in the periphery and in the brain. The recent ability of neuroanatomists to trace central and peripheral nerves according to their neurotransmitters is allowing us to create a new psychological taxonomy based on chemical neuroanatomy.

In sum, motivational neuroscience encompasses the study of the peripheral and central nervous sytems as they work together to integrate information from the internal and external environments to create both the behavioral and mental events in normal and abnormal motivation.

Motivation

The Strategy

The hypothetical constructs that have been developed for the study of motivation are embodied in concepts such as instinct, drive, incentive, and desire. The usefulness of these concepts is still debated (Deutsch, 1979; Morgane, 1979; Stellar & Stellar, 1985). Other concepts such as homeostasis, hierarchical control, operant responding, and optimal foraging have become so useful that they have gradually metamorphosed from hypotheses into principles that are taken for granted. The question is not whether they are true, but under what conditions they matter. The accepted principles are the ones built on variables that can be measured physiologically (e.g., homeostasis), anatomically (e.g., encephalization), behaviorally (e.g., operant responding), or ecologically (e.g., optimal foraging). The accepted principles of the near future will be based on variables measured by chemical neuroanatomy. Therefore the plan of this chapter is to elucidate such principles by labeling real neural mechanisms, not hypothetical ones. Hopefully this new taxonomy of motivation will have greater heuristic value than the old.

The strategy is to use operationally defined descriptions of neural function until a given pathway has been stimulated, lesioned, drugged, and recorded in so many physiological, anatomical, behavioral, and ecological contexts that a general, overall description of its function is obvious and unambiguous. As a specific example, the function of certain lateral hypothalamic cells will not be described in terms of feeding incentive or drive, but rather with the following description.

1) Lateral hypothalamic (LH) lesions disrupt feeding, and LH stimulation elicits it. 2) Animals will stimulate the LH themselves. 3) LH self-stimulation in certain cases is increased by the taste of food or by food deprivation. 4) LH self-stimulation electrodes can be used to record from single cells that fire in response to the sight or taste of a food that the animal chooses at a given time. Moreover these cells respond to preferred tastes with a frequency change that depends on the degree of food deprivation. 5) Injection of catecholamine agonists such as amphetamine cause anorexia and inhibit an LH system for feeding and self-stimulation; protein —as opposed to carbohydrate—intake is selectively inhibited. 6) A radioactively labeled catecholaminergic drug has been shown to bind to LH receptors as a function of deprivation and refeeding. The source of endogenous catecholamines that suppress feeding is known. Putting all these results together, there appears to be an LH system that can be operationally labeled a *feeding-reward* system, and it is modulated by catecholamines from known pathways.

References for this statement will be given later. The point now is that the ideas of hunger, drive, or incentive are replaced with specific response preferences on the part of the animal, by deprivation conditions imposed by the experimenter, by the firing rate of neural elements, by response to locally applied drugs, by receptor affinity for a radioactively labeled compound, and by selective depletion of chemically defined pathways. Some of these results are controversial as explained later; therefore the idea of an LH feeding-reward system is also controversial, but it is eminently testable. Several controversial, testable, anatomically labeled elements of motivation will be presented in this chapter.

Some cellular responses that make up elements of motivation are subconscious just as the responses of edge detectors in the visual cortex are subconscious. The responses of edge detector cells are combined to produce complex feature detectors, and these visual outputs are further combined until at some place in the brain the animal perceives a completed feature of the environment (Gross, Desimone, Albright, & Schwartz, 1984). I assume by analogy that the same is true of motivation. The completed motivational feature is encoded by cells that receive inputs from other elements. We need to know which motivational feature detectors are directly experienced by the animal, just as we need to know which visual feature detectors are directly experienced. That is one of the questions which makes neuropsychology interesting.

The experience of reward has long been described as pleasurable or hedonic and the search for this experience as pleasure-seeking or hedonism. Wise (1982) has suggested that a particular dopamine pathway is necessary for reinforcing behavior and for sensing pleasure, that is, its destruction or blockade causes *anhedonia* leading to response extinction. To establish this in animals it is necessary to talk to conscious humans with a similar neural deficit. At the present time it is a matter of faith and judgment whether to generalize from human hedonism to animal hedonism. If, for example, we associate pleasure with opiates, then fallacious, slippery-slide logic suggests that monkeys, rats, slugs, amoebae and poppies all feel pleasure because they all have endogenous opiates. Clearly this is nonsense. On the other hand, it is obvious to most people that monkeys do feel pleasure. Rats elicit less empathy, but they too seek many of the same things, including opiates, that are pleasurable to people and monkeys. This chapter will show how it is possible to study pleasure-seeking in rats, but the endeavor will be treated as three problems. The functions of opioids and other neurochemicals will be divided into the study of sensations, responses, and the decision-making interface between the two.

The techniques used most often to measure responses, such as operant feeding, operant self-stimulation, and operant self-injection, do not lend themselves to the measurement of sensation except through the measurement of response threshold and the fine-grain analyses of responses on various schedules.

Sensations can be studied independent of responses by holding responses constant. For example, it is possible to study sensations independent of motor requirements by using a stimulus generalization task in which an animal learns to emit identical responses on one of two levers as a function of how the animal feels. Just as rats can use lights or sounds as stimulus cues, they can also use cues that are introspective. Given a highly trained rat, an experimenter can systematically vary the neural or chemical activity in the rat's brain, and the animal will report whether a sensation during the test feels like the sensation that was used as a training stimulus. An example of such an introspective cue is the sensation created by brain injections of amphetamine. In well-trained rats, amphetamine injected in the nucleus accumbens feels like amphetamine injected peripherally (Nielsen & Scheel-Kruger, 1984). This approach is similar to classical conditioning in that it tests stimulus substitution, but it is different because it uses operant response output as a criterion and therefore guarantees that the sensory mechanism involved is linked to somatic output which we consider motivated.

New jargon has not been avoided entirely in these studies; the key word is *reward*. In deference to behaviorist tradition we usually reserve *reinforcer* for a stimulus that increases response performance (Skinner, 1953) and reserve *pleasure* for the human experience. Thus the thing in the brain that is the stimulus sensation part of a reinforcer, independent of performance, is often alluded to as reward. This chapter is, in part, a review of the efforts to define operationally that thing called reward. We start with the premise that reward is a thing. Since I do not know what it looks like, I do not propose to look for it. Instead we will study neurochemicals, neural pathways, and neural potentials that seem to lead in interesting directions. They are signposts for information flow in the field of motivation.

The Guides

Gallistel (1980) reviews and integrates the literature on reflexes underlying motivation. He suggests that motivation is the potentiation of behavioral units made up of (1) reflex arcs, (2) pacemaker oscillators, and (3) servomechanism feedback loops. The problem is then to explain how these units are linked and selectively potentiated.

Pfaff (1982) defines motivation as an intervening variable necessary to explain why an animal performs a given act at one time and not at another when the environmental stimuli are the same both times. This is the behavioral manifestation of *chronobiology* (Halberg, 1969). From this perspective Pfaff phrases the question:

What reward or hormonal changes explain variations in responsiveness to environmental stimuli available in constant form? The mechanisms include factors such as time-variant hormonal surges, and physiological deprivations that modulate central control systems as part of homeostasis. This definition rules out responses that are invariant. Unfortunately there are very few invariant responses so little is ruled out. For example, the gull that behaves like an egg-rolling robot does so only when hormonally motivated. Thus the chronobiological definition of motivation is extremely broad; it includes virtually all behavior at one time or another.

Dethier (1982) argued that when a fly is spontaneously aroused to fly randomly and then to turn upwind when encountering food odors, it is performing a series of reflexive motor programs which needs no verbal adornment, but if one insists on talking about motivation then this may be it. The beginnings of motivation are seen as arousal and orientation.

Teitelbaum (1977) proposed that all the basic elements of motivation have come into play when an animal performs an operant response arbitrarily chosen within its capabilities. The arbitrariness of the response, such as a lever press, guarantees that the animal was not born with the response as a reflexive motor program. The program had to be learned, and thus the animal had to be motivated. Recently Teitelbaum (1982b) has been struck by the observation that each step toward an operant response can be measured as a sensorimotor reflex. Thus the question becomes how, when, and where do the reflexes get chained together to form an operant.

The latest version of the Dethier-Teitelbaum debate is given in the contrasting views of Weiss, Koch, Koester, Rosen, and Kupfermann (1982) and Epstein (1982a). Weiss et al. study the limited repertoire of the sea snail, *Aplysia*, and note Hinde's five characteristics of motivated behavior: (1) activity during arousal, (2) spontaneous behavior such as head waving, or searching, (3) motor variety in orienting, (4) behaviors grouped together in time leading to food that is a goal object, and (5) behavior consummation, or satiation. However, in Epstein's (1982a) categorization, Hinde's five elements of motivation are all treated as instinctive behaviors that lack the essence of motivation. Epstein starts with Teitelbaum's requirement of operant behavior, and then adds two more requirements, anticipation and affect: (1) the behavior must

show more than motor variety, more than species-typical response to releasing stimuli, more than behaviors clustered in time; it also must show behavior individuation, that is, response substitution or *operant behavior*; (2) the behavior must show more than goal-oriented appetitive behavior; it must be modified by prior experience to display *anticipation* of an outcome, such as changes in response vigor based on the memory of reward potency; and (3) the behavior must be accompanied by *affect* which is defined as an integrated pattern of somatic and autonomic responses typical of individuals of that species when they engage in the behavior, for example, smiles and adrenal responses. Neural concomitants also count. Electroencephalogram or depth electrodes can pick up correlates of expectancy and affect.

Epstein's categorization does not hinge on learned versus unlearned behavior, because he defines both instinct and motivation to include acquired components. For anyone who believes that instincts are genetically programmed, Epstein's view creates the conundrum of genetically programmed learning. For Epstein the main distinguishing characteristic of instinct is that both the releasing stimulus and the behavioral output are species specific, which means typical of the species and all individuals in it. Moreover the individuals displaying an instinct do not act as if they expected any reward, because there is no sign of elation or disappointment, and no sign of affect such as purring, chortling, or crying. Epstein argues the distinction between instinct and motivation with ethological data encapsulated in examples and provocative questions. Can a cricket cry? To know whether crickets have affect, and thus motivation, Epstein says it would be necessary to demonstrate a distinctive pattern of responding that includes visceral and glandular effects. The distinction hinges on a pattern of autonomic as well as the more obvious somatic responses. Epstein's guidelines form a triangle: (1) before the motivated response there is expectancy behavior, (2) the response itself must be capable of substitution, and (3) after the response there is an affective, somatic-autonomic pattern which is the basis for future expectancy.

In summary, the components of motivation that will be our guides are Hinde's five basic tenets which include the reflex potentiation theories of Gallistel, Pfaff and Weiss, plus Teitelbaum's operant criterion to which Epstein added two more, and a ninth which is Olds' legacy. These nine points may be summarized as follows:

1. Responsiveness (arousal)
2. Response spontaneity (time-variant reflexes)
3. Response variety (chaining different reflexes to achieve directedness)
4. Response grouping (consummatory acts)
5. Response stopping (satiation)
6. Response substitution (operant conditioning)
7. Reinforcing stimulus anticipation (expectancy, which includes stimulus substitution, i.e., secondary reinforcement and classical conditioning)
8. Affective concomitants (autonomic and glandular response patterns, signs of emotion)
9. Motivational concomitants in the brain (such as brain signs of reward and aversion, selective sensory attention, premotor responses, central autonomic components, or coded neurochemicals such as drive peptides, Olds, 1977; gratifying peptides, Stein, 1980; or reward peptides, Hoebel et al., 1982; Glimcher, Margolin, Giovino, & Hoebel, 1984).

These nine features of motivation drawn from various definitions are our guides, not our goals. They are guides based on reflexes in the ethological tradition, environmental features in the behaviorist tradition, autonomic features in the tradition of physiological psychology and psychophysiology, and mental features in the tradition of cognitive psychology.

The Goal
I want to define motivation, including its mental aspects, in terms of neural systems. This is based on the belief that what we feel is nerve impulses, not glandular secretion. A secretory response pattern, like an operant response, is a legitimate basis for ascribing motivation; it is not, however, a full definition, because it glosses over the mental processing that leads to the response. If we can learn to measure the relevant mental processes in terms of neurochemistry, neuroanatomy, and neurophysiology, we can define motivational elements in neural terms alone.

When the key central circuits for the various bits and pieces of motivation have been identified, we may then be able to detect activity in these central systems even when the output to the peripheral muscles and glands is blocked. When we have identified the systems for motivation, we will be able to record motivation happening in the brain without either glandular or muscular behavior occurring. Thus aspects of motivation will be recorded during paralysis, dreaming, or just thinking, and from isolated pieces of the central nervous system (CNS) containing the relevant circuits.

This reductionist approach runs the risk that we will lose sight of the motivated behavior with which we started. However, if done well, it should be possible to resynthesize conceptually the isolated neural parts to recreate the whole behavior. Along with this ability will come new understanding.

Perhaps the reader is thinking that there is no way to define neural activity as being part of motivation without some end point such as an operant or glandular response. This is no longer a problem. We can define the neural aspects of motivation by the release of specified neurotransmitters, neural activity in specified pathways, activity in CNS subcircuits that generate a specific evoked potential, or activity in systems that bind to a specific antibody (Levitt, 1984). In summary, the goal is to find the relevant neural mechanisms and to begin redefining motivation accordingly.

The Chapter Plan
In accordance with the stated goal, we will study elements of motivated behavior and their neural bases, then declare that activity in a specified neural system is itself an element of motivation independent of behavior. This will give us a neural taxonomy for further study of mental process used in planning motivated behavior with or without performance. It goes beyond Hinde's ethological description or Weiss's neuro-ethological description of reflexes, beyond Teitelbaum's operant criterion, and a step beyond Epstein's somatic-autonomic description, to reach the neural correlates involved in priming, planning, and conducting motivated behavior. We are trying to reach the neural correlates of reward and aversion on the one hand, and approach and escape on the other, so that we can study the systems that modulate, evaluate and create behavior. It is hoped that

this exploration will eventually lead us to predict if and when a response will be performed based on an understanding of how the brain makes such a decision.

For psychologists not versed in neurophysiology or neurochemistry, the next section on Elements of Motivation in Simpler Preparations is written in a way to introduce concepts needed to follow later discussions of brain mechanisms in more complex preparations. Some essentials of physiology and endocrinology are included in the third section dealing with homeostasis and neuropeptides. Homeostasis is traditionally the depletion-repletion teeter-totter on which psychologists build their science of motivation. However, that enterprise is gradually changing to include the study of anticipation of homeostatic needs that can maintain a balance with hardly a tilt (Collier & Rovee-Collier, 1983). The function of integrative peptides in homeostatic behavior will be discussed as a possible new organizing principle. In the fourth section, laboratory models of motivation are presented. These models externalize motivation by letting an animal directly control the electrical activity or chemistry of its own brain through self-stimulation or self-injection. These informative models of self-control are also models of drug abuse and motivational psychopathology that result from related neurochemical disturbances. Drug discrimination techniques will be proposed as a way to ask an animal how a brain chemical feels. The fifth section discusses sensory feature detectors, motor command neurons, and three cortical-subcortical loops that appear to be involved in motivation, associations, and premotor instructions. A motivational map of the brain, albeit fragmentary, is drawn based on the information in all five sections. It is a synthesis of neural mechanisms labeled according to some of their functions as we currently know them.

ELEMENTS OF MOTIVATION IN SIMPLER PREPARATIONS

Unicellular Animals

Chemical Communication
Social interaction is often considered the most complex motive, but single-celled animals reduce the problem to manageable, chemical proportions. They use chemical messages that diffuse through the environment to interact with receptor molecules on their neighbors. These chemicals are often the same as those found in higher forms of life, including people. For example the bacterium *E. coli* makes insulin. Bacteria can also synthesize thyroid stimulating hormone (TSH) and other hormones released from the human pituitary. Somatostatin is a peptide in the brain that inhibits pituitary release of growth hormone. Protozoan somatostatin does it just as well. Thus the cells in our bodies communicate using many of the same chemicals that unicellular animals use in their liquid environment. We have evolved tremendously in anatomical structure, but our chemistry is noticeably protozoan (Acher, 1983).

Peptides with a Behavioral Purpose
Certain yeast secrete a mating factor which is the same as mammalian leutinizing hormone releasing hormone (LHRH) which triggers ovulation in women and induces sexual receptivity. This does not mean that we can deduce the function of a human hormone by finding its function in single-celled animals. It does suggest, however, that some hormones have a behavioral function that has evolved using a genetic code that is millions of years old.

The hormones mentioned above are all peptides, that is, pieces of protein made up of a sequence of amino acids. The sequence is the genetically coded message. Peptide hormones seem to affect a concatenation of related biochemical processes and thereby imbue behavior with a recognizable purpose, such as reproduction. Genes have outdone themselves by creating nervous systems that can transmit information from brain to brain in the form of ideas and culture. Dethier (1982) suggests that the nervous system is selfish, in the same sense that genes are selfish, and that good ideas fight out evolutionary battles with bad ideas. To understand the workings of the nervous system, however, he has chosen a simple animal in which cultural purposes do not confuse the issue. Simplicity is a virtue, he argues, because it allows us to see the basis for emergent properties of the nervous system. This is the persuasive argument for comparative psychology, the field in which evolution is the ruler. To know where the human species is going, and what our current purposes are, we need to know where we are coming from. Simpler animals are the answer.

Flies

Arousal as a Central Excitatory State

How a blowfly forages, feeds, and finally stops lest it burst, is a classic in the annals of neurobiology (Dethier, 1976). In brief, the fly first becomes randomly active. Then when a food odor is detected it flies upwind. Activity is one sign of what is often called arousal. Dethier prefers not to call this motivation, but labeled this process of the nervous system a *central excitatory state* which is operationally defined in terms of random behavior. After homing in on the odor, the fly walks about until it tastes the food with taste hairs on its feet. Neural recordings made by inserting an electrode through a tiny hole drilled in the side of a taste hair reveal four neurons: one sensitive to water, one to sugar, and the other two for salt. These neurons fire in proportion to stimulus concentrations and can trigger motor extension of the proboscis to adequate concentrations of sugar. Taste hairs on the tip of the proboscis also contain neurons with chemically coded receptors. Acceptance or rejection of the food depends on a number of factors.

A fly may taste water but not drink it at one moment, then change states and drink the same water immediately after a taste of sucrose. Thus sucrose can raise a specialized central excitatory state defined in terms of water intake.

Central Inhibitory State

An inhibitory process can be shown by interjecting a taste of strong salt between the taste of sucrose and the water. The inhibitory aftereffect of the salt cancels the excitatory effect of the sucrose with the result that the fly chooses not to drink water. Thus we see the principle of integration of excitatory and inhibitory signals in the decision-making process.

Satiety

The feeding process continues as long as time permits until internal physiological factors terminate feeding entirely. In the fly the signal to stop eating is generated by stomach distension. Flies have a food shortage crop with stretch receptors activated by expansion. When the fly is physically full, feeding stops (Figure 11.1). If this inhibitory information is cut off by severing the nerve from the stretch receptors to the brain then hyperphagia (overeating) results. In that case the fly spends a longer time eating meals and starts again sooner. A hyperphagic fly may binge until it bursts. Different patterns of hyperphagia, such as eating too often or eating too much at a time, can be produced by cutting different feedback nerves.

Aversion

There is more to ingestive behavior than arousal, starting, and stopping. Proboscis withdrawal can be a sign of an active escape response that is more than mere satiety, that is, more than a failure to start eating or cessation of eating after a big meal. Moderate concentrations of salt may cause extension of the proboscis or acceptance, while slightly higher concentrations of the same salt will cause withdrawal or rejection. A difference of only three sensory nerve impulses initiated during the first 100 msec can make the difference between acceptance and rejection. Thus a list of the elements of homeostatic behavior needs to include escape or aversion as well as approach.

Sliding Set Point

The shift from acceptance to rejection for a given stimulus concentration depends on the fly's level of deprivation. Thus the switch-over concentration is not fixed, but instead can vary with the energy stores in the animal. This variability or shift in the switch-over from acceptance to rejection is a function of the central nervous system, because the firing rate of the sensory receptors does not change before and after the switch. Therefore, some central mechanism must compare the sensory signal from the external world with internal sensory signals from stretch receptors in the stomach and then adjust motor output accordingly. This again illustrates integration of external and internal sensory signals.

Even though the fly has only a simple trigger system (three sensors: water, sugar, salt) and an even simpler brake system (stretch receptors), its homeostatic behavior is elegantly adjusted by the sliding threshold for palatability (Moss & Dethier, 1983). A machine with a fixed set point such as a locked thermostat, is not as useful as one with a set point that can slide within safe limits, such as the home thermostat with a

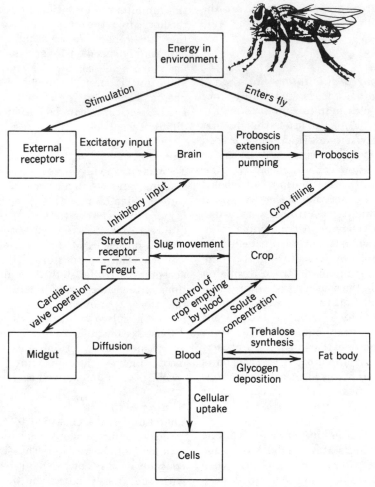

Figure 11.1. Homeostatic mechanism for regulation of energy flow in the blowfly. From "The Contribution of Insects to the Study of Motivation" by V.G. Dethier, 1982, in *Changing Concepts of the Nervous System*, (p. 451) A.R. Morrison and P.L. Strick (eds.), New York: Academic Press. Copyright 1982 by Academic Press. Reprinted by permission.

pointer that can be raised or lowered. Food is not all equally filling, caloric, nutritious, hydrated, or digestable. Therefore, it seems appropriate that an organism should be able to adjust the response to external sensors accordingly. The blowfly does it on the basis of taste, gut fullness and perhaps blood-borne factors. This shifting response to sensory stimuli based on CNS integration of internal and external sensory stimuli is one of the major elements of motivation. It begins to explain why an animal engages in a given behavior at one time, but not at another.

This principle applies to complex behaviors such as learning. Fruit flies can be trained to approach or avoid food, but only when they are empty (Quinn & Greenspan, 1984).

The Sea Slug, *Aplysia*

Two main components of arousal have been discerned in *Aplysia*: (1) a central arousal system similar to the central excitatory state described for the fly, but consisting of both locomotor and internal physiological arousal, and (2) an executive arousal system, similar to Dethier's example of a central state for water intake. Executive arousal controls particular types of behavior (Weiss et al., 1982).

Locomotor Arousal

An *Aplysia* that senses a seaweed salad, especially when food deprived, will locomote with periodic stops during which it moves its head as if to locate the food source. When it reaches the food, it bites into it using the muscles of its buccal mass (buccal refers to the mouth and is pronounced "buckle"). When the slug becomes physically full it will display a satiety response, marked by decreased spontaneous activity, decreased approach to food, and even a turning away from food that is proffered. In these respects the slug is just like the fly. Arousal starts as random locomotion and leads into locomotion with specified reference to approach, escape, and avoidance.

The entire appetitive pattern and each of its parts, including arousal movements, head scanning, bite latency, and bite strength, show circadian rhythmicity. The rhythm depends on an internal clock that is entrained in synchrony with the day-night cycle.

Autonomic Arousal

During the locomotor arousal that accompanies food intake there is a concomitant increase in heart rate and blood pressure (Weiss et al., 1982). Thus in addition to locomotive arousal there is a physiological arousal component to food approach. The total central arousal state can be induced by handling or tailpinch, and it contributes to the likelihood of feeding (Figure 11.2).

This slug has three different ganglia which are necessary for three different behavioral elements. Lesions of the posterior or *pedal-pleural* ganglion, eliminated approach to food, but not the actual eating if the food was brought to the mouth. Recording from the middle or *cerebral* ganglion revealed a role in arousal and orienting responses such as head waving. Lesions of the front or *buccal* ganglion, eliminated eating but not approach. Analogous observations in the rat will be described later.

Neural Modulation

The cerebral ganglion in *Aplysia* is perhaps the most interesting for psychologists because its location suggests it integrates and modulates diverse stimuli that contribute to a central excitatory state for appetitive behavior. Within the cerebral ganglion two very large cell bodies can be seen, identified and impaled on

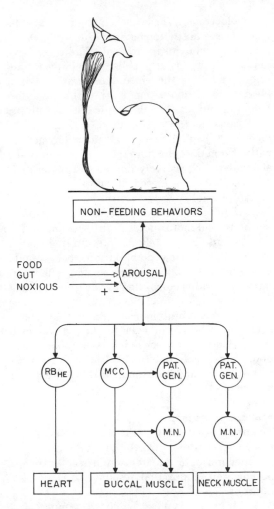

Figure 11.2. Hypothetical model of the organization of arousal in *Aplysia*. Food induces arousal and gut distension inhibits it. Noxious stimuli such as tail pinch excite or inhibit depending on their strength. This arousal system affects autonomic (heart) and somatic processes. Pattern generator cells (pat. gen.) activate buccal (mouth) muscles for eating. Pattern generators may use dopamine, and motor neurons (M.N.) use acetylcholine. Note that the metacerebral cell (MCC) can modulate the feeding system at four levels: the pattern generator, the motor neuron cell, presynaptic endings, and the muscle. The MCC cell is serotonergic but other interneurons may be involved. From "The Role of Arousal in Modulating Feeding Behavior of *Aplysia*: Neural and Behavioral Studies" by K.R. Weiss, U.T. Koch, J. Koester, S.C. Rosen, and I. Kupfermann, 1982, in *The Neural Basis of Feeding and Reward* (p. 52) by B.G. Hoebel and D. Novin (eds.), Brunswick, ME; Haer Institute for Electrophysiological Research. Reprinted by permission.

microelectrodes. These giant metacerebral cells (MCC) generate action potentials at a rate which parallels behavioral arousal. Their activity modulates the firing of cells in the buccal ganglion, and thus they modulate eating. It is a clear case of neural modulation that modifies behavior output. The mechanism is as follows.

Arousal at the beginning of a meal can be measured behaviorally and neurophysiologically. From the behavioral point of view, the sea slug bites progressively harder and faster as it tears off bits of seaweed. It can also be shown electrophysiologically that the buccal muscles receive progressively larger synaptic potentials as the buccal motor neurons fire with more frequent bursts. The short interburst interval allows long-lasting potentiation (post-tetanic potentiation) to build to a crescendo. The interburst interval is controlled by the giant cells in the cerebral ganglion (Weiss et al., 1982). These giant metacerebral neurons do not by themselves fire the motor cells for biting. Instead, they illustrate the principle that specialized neurons can modulate the likelihood that appropriate environmental stimuli will fire the motor neurons.

Muscle Modulation
The nerve labeled MCC (Figure 11.2) has axonal branches that go directly to the muscles to produce muscular modulation. These branches potentiate the muscular response to the motor neurons.

In *Aplysia* this effect on chewing muscles is mediated by cyclic adenosine monophosphate (cAMP). A muscle that is aroused by input from metacerebral cells produces more cAMP than control muscle. Evidence suggests that serotonin is the neurotransmitter that is released by the metacerebral cells. Serotonin crosses the neuromuscular junction (first messenger) where it interacts with serotonergic receptors in the cell membrane; this, in turn, activates the enzyme that produces cAMP (second messenger) which potentiates muscle contraction perhaps by acting on the contractile proteins.

Presynaptic Modulation
Figure 11.2 shows that the MCC also produces direct or indirect potentiation of motor neuron terminals. Serotonin has the effect of increasing the size of synaptic potentials produced by the motorneurons. This effect could result from increased release of transmitter from nerve terminals or sensitization of the postsynaptic receptors.

Pattern Generator
A third function of the MCC may be potention of a pattern generator cell, the output of which imposes a pattern of firing on several motor neurons for muscle coordination.

Multiple Arousal Functions of a Monoamine
The heart muscles, like the feeding muscles, are also controlled by a serotonergic cell. In humans the heart is accelerated by norepinephrine from sympathetic nerves and by epinephrine from the adrenal gland. In *Aplysia* serotonin does the job, but the principle is the same, and the intracellular mechanism is the same. Heart muscle is potentiated by cAMP in both species.

Given that the *Aplysia's* buccal muscles for biting and the heart muscles for blood circulation are potentiated during arousal, Weiss et al. (1982) postulate a system of arousal cells that stimulate both (Figure 11.2).

This simple mechanism illustrates the basic premise of psychophysiology. This is how a lie detector is supposed to work. One can measure a central excitatory state in *Aplysia* with an electromyogram (EMG) from the mouth muscles or with an electrocardiogram (EKG) from the heart muscles. Weiss, Kupfermann and colleagues have chosen to label the general, nonspecific function as a central arousal system or just *arousal* for short. Note that food stimuli can excite this; whereas gut distension inhibits it. Thus a little bit of food on the lips or even in the gut can potentiate feeding responses, that is, cause appetite; but a full gut causes satiety (Susswein, Weiss, & Kupfermann, 1984). Noxious stimuli such as tail pinch or shock have excitatory or inhibitory effects depending largely on stimulus strength.

The cell circuitry for withdrawal from food (food aversion) is not shown in this diagram. Gut fullness not only inhibits the arousal system and thereby calms the feeding system (i.e., kills the appetite), but can also cause the *Aplysia* to turn away from seaweed.

In the feeding story of *Aplysia* to date, Weiss points out all of Hinde's features of motivation (which Epstein calls instincts), arousal, searching, orientation, specific behavior potentiation, and satiation. Homing in on food and eating to satiation gives the appearance of purpose to the behavior. From a teleological perspective the behavior has a goal object. One might even say the *Aplysia* itself has a goal or purpose. Whether or not *Aplysia* has a goal in mind depends on whether you think ganglia can constitute a mind.

Aplysia has met two out of three of Epstein's criteria for motivation. They have been trained to wave their heads when reinforced with more water in which to live. They will also locomote to the vicinity where a food dish routinely appears and stop responding if the food is enclosed in a net that prevents swallowing (Susswein et al., 1984). So far nobody has suggested a pattern of glandular and somatic responses to signify emotion.

Sensitization

This is an increase in reflex response to one stimulus caused by another stimulus that is intense or noxious. For example, if one touches the skin of an *Aplysia*'s water siphon, the siphon and gill will retract to protect them from harm. This response decreases with repeated touches (habituation), but a blow to the head has the opposite effect. This rude awakening sensitizes the animal to touch (Hawkins & Kandel, 1984). All kinds of stimuli are sensitized, whether previously habituated or not. Habituation and sensitization are nonassociative forms of learning. These are in contrast to classical conditioning which requires the association of two stimuli with the result that a conditioned stimulus (CS) takes the place of the unconditioned stimulus (US). Sensitization is pseudoconditioning; some might say it is merely motivating.

It is a matter of definition whether we consider a blow to the head to motivate gill withdrawal. Given that gill withdrawal is an unconditioned, species-typical reflex, it exemplifies a primitive stimulus-response (S–R) linkage. Habituation is merely a decrement in reflex strength caused by stimulus repetition; dishabituation or sensitization of the reflex by another stimulus is more interesting.

Presynaptic Facilitation

Kandel and his co-workers have discovered that sensitization is the result of serotonergic modulation of a sensorimotor reflex. Serotonin (or a serotonin-like substance) is released onto the terminals of a sensory neuron; thus the effect is presynaptic facilitation. Serotonin causes neither the depolarization-excitation effect nor the hyperpolarization-inhibition effect characteristic of straightforward synapses. Instead serotonin or related transmitters alters the ionic flow in and out of the terminal (decreased potassium outflux and increased calcium influx), thereby increasing the duration of the action potential and increasing calcium available for binding vesicles to the terminal membrane. This in turn increases the number of vesicles that release their content of neurotransmitter in response to an action potential (Hawkins & Kandel, 1984).

Kandel's group has theorized that monoamines can alter S-R links semi-permanently. It is logical to suppose that microcircuits could exist in an *Aplysia* ganglion to sensitize impulse flow from neutral stimulus input to unconditioned response output so that the neutral stimulus becomes a conditioned stimulus. Classical conditioning has been demonstrated in *Aplysia* by tickling the siphon as a CS, shocking the tail as a US and observing the gill-syphon withdrawal reflex as the unconditioned response (UR) which becomes a conditioned response (CR). Unfortunately the neutral tickle produces a slight withdrawal reflex all by itself. Moreover shocking the tail can sensitize the response to the CS (pseudoconditioning). Thus sensitization, they suggest, may use some of the same circuitry as classical conditioning.

Garden Slug, *Limax Maximus*

Learned Taste Aversion

This is a special case of classical conditioning. Tastes that usually elicit approach can be conditioned to elicit avoidance. If a good taste is paired with gastric illness, or in some cases if a good taste is paired with a bad taste, the good taste becomes bad. Animals thereby learn to avoid certain foods. This is an example of learned motivation.

Gelperin (1983) has demonstrated learned aversion in *Limax maximus*, the terrestrial cousin of *Aplysia*. This garden slug sniffs its way home to sleep by day, and sallies forth on its slimy foot to forage by night. One taste of quinine or a bitter plant substance paired with the taste of a garden vegetable will create an aversion to that vegetable taste, or even to the odor of that vegetable.

To carry out experiments, *Limax* is first taught a taste aversion. For example an aversion to potato can be programmed into the slug's cerebral ganglion by pairing potato with bitter quinine. This training or programming phase can be done in the whole animal, or with the isolated nervous system that has intact neural connections to the lips. In this lip-brain preparation, the learned aversion is detected as selective inhibition of the feeding motor nerve when potato flavor is placed on the lips.

Cholinergic Motor Neuron, Dopamine Pattern Neuron and Serotonin Neuromodulator Neuron

As you might predict, acetylcholine is the transmitter for motor neurons that activate the feeding muscles. The motor nerve response for feeding can be elicited with dopamine. There are six dopamine neurons that project to the feeding motor neurons. Apparently dopamine triggers the motor program for eating. Serotonin potentiates the feeding motor program so that any palatable taste input elicits a more vigorous neural response; the frequency of firing in some feeding motor neurons can double, and the response duration is lengthened (Gelperin, 1986). Other neurons are inhibited by serotonin, even neurons with the same function. For example, one nerve for mouth opening might be facilitated, but another inhibited. Thus the precise functional role of serotonin is not clear except to say that it modulates the responsiveness of motor neurons. It does so at every level by altering the threshold for firing in sensory neurons, central neurons, salivary glands, gut muscles and motor neurons. Thus serotonin sets the level of activation in parts of the whole feeding system, from sensory input to response output. The mechanism for controlling specific learned aversions is still a mystery.

Higher Order Conditioning

We know how to write the software instructions

Limax logic

Before conditioning:	A, B, C are attractive (+) odors Q is a repellent (−) taste
1st order conditioning:	$A^+ + Q^- \rightarrow A^-, B^+$
2nd order conditioning:	$A^+ + Q^-; B^+ + A^- \rightarrow A^-, B^-, C^+$
Compound conditioning:	$A^+ + B^+ + Q^- \rightarrow A^-, B^-, C^+$
Block of conditioning:	$A^+ + Q^-; B^+ + A^- + Q^- \rightarrow A^-, B^+$

Figure 11.3. Summary of classical conditioning logic shown by experiments with *Limax*. From "Neuroethological Studies of Associative Learning in Feeding Control Systems" by A. Gelperin, 1983, in *Neuroethology and Behavioral Physiology* (pp. 198–205) by F. Huber and H. Markl (eds.), Berlin: Springer-Verlag. Copyright 1985 by Springer-Verlag. Reprinted by permission.

for the little computer in *Limax* (Figure 11.3). The system is capable of suppressing approach to apple paired with quinine (1st order conditioning), suppressing approach to banana paired with apple that was paired with quinine (2nd order conditioning), suppressing approach to apple and banana when both are simultaneously paired with quinine (compound conditioning), and suppressing approach to apple but not banana when quinine is paired first with apple and then with both (block of conditioning). Presumably the conditioned links are made between sensory input and the dopaminergic pattern generator output for approach.

Neurotransmitter Precursors in the Diet

In *Limax*, dietary choline boosts acetylcholine levels and prolongs performance of a learned aversion. The effect can last for days. Cholinergic motor neurons do not store memory because that is central. Here is proof. *Limax* can learn an aversion by sensing potato paired with quinine on its left half-lip and then display the same learned aversion to potato placed on the right half-lip; thus the association must be learned and stored centrally. The improved cholinergic motor performance with dietary choline may mean that there was an improved motor response to the CS. Perhaps behavior would be altered by dietary tryptophan which boosts serotonin levels, or tyrosine which might increase dopamine. The experiments have not been done yet in *Limax*.

Summary

Study of the fly has demonstrated motoric reflex patterns controlled by a central excitatory state (arousal) and sensory input that could adapt (habituate) or be inhibited centrally by gastric filling (satiety). The *Aplysia* story was basically the same, but in addition central arousal was monitored electrophysiologically and a specific feeding arousal system was found. It was serotonergic. *Aplysia* also demonstrated that habituation can occur in the presynaptic endings of a monosynaptic reflex where serotonin modulates another transmitter released at the S-R junction. The emerging view of presynaptic modulation raised hopes of understanding not only stimulus sensitization, but also stimulus substitution. In *Limax* there is every expectation that the same principles of neurophysiology will work. We seem to have come a few steps closer to a mechanism for motivation. Evidence points to the following conclusions: (1) arousing stimuli can activate a variety of motor and autonomic systems; appetite seems to be mediated by central serotonergic neurons with widely ramifying outputs which modulate taste, salivation, gastric function, dopaminergic feeding neurons, and motor neurons for eating; (2) feeding motor patterns are produced by dopaminergic neurons coordinating cholinergic motor outputs; and (3) this mini-brain is capable of first- and second-order conditioning, compound conditioning, and block of conditioning. In these details of the learned aversion paradigm the slug behaves as a rat does.

Brain-Transected Rats

Basic Feeding Motor Programs

In normal rats the basic feeding motor pattern consists of (1) mouth movements, (2) tongue protrusion, (3) lateral tongue movement, and (4) a gape response to bad-testing substances like quinine. The gape consists of retracting the lower lip as if to let the food drain out (Figure 11.4). An intact rat will gape and then rub its lower lip on the floor, shake its head, wipe its mouth off, shake its paws and then wipe them on the floor. Even a good-tasting food can switch over to elicit this food rejection reaction if it is paired with LiCl to induce a conditioned aversion (Norgren & Grill, 1982). This reaction is similar to *Limax* learning to reject potato paired with quinine. Excess satiety is sufficient to prime the aversion response. I have seen the rejection reaction caused in rats by the taste of food or self-stimulation after force feeding. This is analogous to *Aplysia* turning away from food when its stomach is full.

Decerebrate Rats

These animals are named for what they have lost, which is the cerebrum, including the thalamus, hypothalamus and the rest of the forebrain. They could also be called spinal cord-hindbrain-midbrain rats for what they retain. They seldom move, but will run in bursts of activity triggered by sudden stimuli such as a water spray. Decerebrates groom themselves almost normally. Thus a complete program for grooming exists in the midbrain and below. They do not seek food, but will swallow food placed in the mouth. They react to food tastes with normal facial expressions

Figure 11.4. Top: ingestive responses elicited by the taste of palatable sugar solutions. Bottom: the aversion sequence elicited by bitter quinine taste (from Berridge, Flynn, Schulkin, & Grill, 1984). Similar ingestive responses are seen during perifornical LH self-stimulation, but after the rat is force-fed, self-stimulation is slower and elicits the aversion responses such as chin rubbing. From "The Caudal Brainstem and the Integrated Control of Energy Balance" by F.W. Flynn and H.J. Grill, 1985, in *The Neural and Metabolic Bases of Feeding* (p. 526) by G. Bray and T. Castonquay (eds.), Syracuse, NY: Ankho International. Copyright 1985 by Ankho International. Reprinted by permission.

of acceptance or aversion. Thus the basic feeding motor patterns are intact. They shift from acceptance to aversion as they become satiated during a meal. They also show an increased preference for sucrose when made hypoglycemic with insulin injections (Flynn & Grill, In press). They do not learn a conditioned aversion. The decerebrate rat is worse off than an intact slug. Both animals have feeding motor programs, both respond to tastes, both react to internal stimuli, and both have intact satiety mechanisms, but the slug can arouse itself to locomote to food and learn to reject poisonous food. The decerebrate rat can eat if a friend helps by bringing safe food into the mouth. Apparently it is the job of the forebrain to be such a friend to the hindbrain and midbrain.

Brainstem-Hypothalamic Rats

These are decerebrates that retain all or part of the hypothalamus. They have the extraordinary capability to self-stimulate. Even when everything anterior to the hypothalamus has been removed, they will perform simple operant responses, such as head movements, to trigger electrical stimulation through a lateral hypothalamic electrode. Thus descending pathways from the hypothalamus are sufficient to reinforce operant behavior. Rats will even self-stimulate the brainstem, and do so when decerebrated on the same side. By a process of elimination, Huston (1982) concludes that an operant reinforcement mechanism exists between the hypothalamus and the brainstem.

Thalamic Rats

These have a hindbrain, midbrain, hypothalamus and thalamus. Everything else in front of it and above it, including the hippocampus, is removed. Sparing the thalamus does more harm than good in the sense that these rats behave as if everything tastes bad. Thus the normal taste responses of the brainstem are made abnormal by the addition of a higher structure. Even though thalamic rats refuse all food (Norgren & Grill, 1982), they will self-stimulate (Huston, 1982).

Decorticate Rats

These can respond to salt deprivation by remembering how and where to obtain salt (Norgren & Grill, 1982). Thus a specific hunger for salt does not require a neocortex.

Summary

The hindbrain and midbrain are sufficient to coordinate acceptance and rejection of fluids based on taste and blood sugar. The hindbrain and midbrain can also self-stimulate, even without the ipsilateral hypothalamus. The thalamus devoid of a hippocampus and cortex suppresses acceptence of any food. The forebrain without a cortex can express locomotion and learned responses for food. The whole brain, with its cortex, is the clever rat known to climb into the rafters of a warehouse, slide down a rope into a hanging basket of eggs, then hang over the edge of the basket to start a chain of rats so that the other rats can slide down to the floor carrying eggs in their armpits to feed the young. That is motivation.

Infant Rat

Like an insect or mollusk, an infant rat will ingest milk until its stomach is physically full. However, there is no sign of sensory adaptation that would divide the orgy into distinct meals. Instead the baby glutton, given an unlimited milk supply, drinks until it fills. In a more naturalistic setting when pups must compete for nipples, and nipples can run dry, rats as young as five days will display adult-like capability to control food intake. If they have to work for nipple attachment, they vary their rate of intake as a function of deprivation and gastric loading (Cramer & Blass, 1982).

Hypothalamic mechanisms play a role in this feeding behavior. A three-day-old rat pup, having no fur and unopened eyes, with an electrode in its hypothalamus will display elements of the feeding motor pattern for food acceptance during stimulation. At higher intensity, stimulation elicits the gape for food rejection (Figure 11.4). Mild stimulation induces feeding reflexes in the presence of a puddle of milk, and this leads to significant milk intake, thus showing orientation to the food stimulus and proper sequencing of the feeding reflexes (Moran & Blass, 1982). Rats do not have a functional amphetamine-sensitive arousal system until 15 days old (Campbell & Randall, 1977), but hypothalamic stimulation is sufficient to arouse three-day-olds to eat.

The forward-probing response so useful for reaching a nipple, can be used for pressing a lever in a small Skinner box. Imagine three-day-old rat pups lever pressing for hypothalamic self-stimulation (Moran & Blass, 1982). The key to training infant rats, like brainstem-hypothalamic rats, is in picking the operant to take advantage of the animal's intact motor capabilities. As the saying goes, "You cannot teach pigs to fly," but you can teach them to nose poke. The same is true of infants and brainstem-hypothalamics.

Brain Lesioned Rat

Teitelbaum and his colleagues have modernized the Jacksonian concept of hierarchy in the neural systems. In addition to viewing the brain as a series of increasing complex suprabrains that can be peeled off with maximal lesions to find the least tissue sufficient for motivated behavior (Huston, 1982), Teitelbaum considers the hierarchy as an interdigitated linkage of components that contribute to progressive encephalization. The analysis involves cutting the links to find the least damage sufficient to cause a recognizable deficit in motivated behavior.

Lateral Hypothalamic Syndrome

Behavior subsystems can be discerned by making lesions (Teitelbaum, 1982a, 1982b). For example, analysis of the well-known lateral hypothalamic (LH) lesion syndrome and its recovery revealed stages: aphagia with adipsia (neglect to take food or water), anorexia with adipsia (takes milk not water), adipsia, and recovery with regulation of dry food and water intake but with impaired responses to taste and glucostatic and osmotic challenges. Similar stages were seen in the development of the infant (Teitelbaum, 1967). Then it was discovered that LH lesions can cause general sensory neglect and akinesia contributing to starvation and death by overall indifference and immobility (Ungerstedt, 1971). Finer analysis demonstrated body weight regulation at lowered levels (Keesey & Corbett, 1984) and fragments or stages of akinesia which include deficits in righting, pivoting, head scanning, and forward movement. These parallel infant development three to five days after birth (Teitelbaum, Schallert, & Whishaw, 1983).

Sweet tastes can trigger reflexes that save the life of an otherwise aphagic rat; similarly cold water can trigger movement in an otherwise akinetic rat. An intact system of reflexes and the critical stimulus is all that is needed for these animals to rise from a comatose state, warm up their motor systems and spring to life. What Teitelbaum terms warm up, everyone else calls arousal. The new idea is that arousal consists of a predictable sequence of activity in a set of motor subsystems that are recruited one after another. Complex behavior thus results from a predictable sequence of stimuli impinging on the brain as the animal moves in its environment triggering one reflex after another to create a behavior pattern. The pattern is ipso facto typical of the animal in its ecological niche because the pattern is generated by the sequence of stimuli encountered in the niche.

Behavior Elicited on a Background of Suppression and Depotentiation

The next point is that some subsystems are actively suppressed. We saw one example from Norgren and Grill's (1982) work in which the thalamus suppressed food intake in decorticate rats. In another example, two-day-old rats move freely until the third day of life when their locomotion is suppressed; they recover in stages as encephalization develops a healthy balance. Similarly, lateral hypothalamic lesioned rats are functionally inhibited and must recover dominance over systems that suppress behavior. Within the hypothalamus, dominance seems to be a function of intact lateral tissue which facilitates behavior in competition with medial tissue which inhibits it (Ellison, 1968; Hoebel, 1984, Hoebel, 1985a). Lesion studies also suggest that within the amygdala there are regions for facilitation and suppression of behavior patterns (Fonberg, 1969).

For complex behavior, Gallistel (1981) suggests that reflex arcs, and servomechanisms can be combined in circuits that produce different walking and running gaits depending on the phase coupling of the oscillators that provide the rhythm for leg muscles. The same circuits acting in a different sequence may be used for righting or grooming. Thus the three elemental units of behavior combine into complex units to produce coordinated action patterns which can have variety depending on the timing of the units. Exhibition of the various action patterns theoretically depends on the selective potentiation, or depotentiation of the complex units. This is another way of saying that behavior patterns that are facilitated emerge against a background of behavior suppression. Ethologists Lorenz, Tinbergen and Von Friesch received the Nobel Prize for breaking the mold in which behavior was viewed in terms of either classical or operant conditioning. In their formulations fixed action patterns are under the control of central hormonal states and are triggered by releasing stimuli. This is similar to the idea that complex units of behavior can be selectively potentiated.

The invertebrate studies that have already been described suggest that dopamine and serotonin might be important in the facilitation and suppression of behavior. Lesion studies in vertebrates bear this out. For example, lesions that severely deplete dopamine in the striatum cause akinesia.

Neurochemically Impaired Rat

Akinesias

Drugs and selective neurotoxins have taken the place of lesions in most brain research. Dopamine systems can be blocked with neuroleptics such as haloperidol or pimozide (Coyle & Enna, 1983) or they can all be depleted with the selective neurotoxin, 6-hydroxydopamine, given into the ventricles. Either procedure can cause symptoms like those that result from lateral hypothalamic lesions. The animal is akinetic (immobile) and cataleptic (retains bizarre postures). Locomotion, scanning, orientation and mouthing can also be impaired. However, depending on the degree of dopamine block or depletion, a rat may be willing to swim to avoid drowning (Stricker, 1983b). Similarly, people immobilized with Parkinson's disease caused by loss of dopamine have been known to get up and miraculously move to flee a fire. Appropriate amounts of stress or therapy that boost dopaminergic function will improve their chances of responding. Therefore Stricker (1983b) describes this dopamine system as a central excitatory system. Gradual recovery of function is explained in terms of improved dopamine synthesis, increased release, receptor supersensitivity, and growth of nerve collaterals (Marshall, 1984; Stricker, 1983b).

It is important to apply these drug techniques locally in the brain whenever possible; otherwise they alter an entire monoamine system (dopamine, norepinephrine, epinephrine or serotonin) and thus may create the appearance of a general state where finer gradations exist. For example, norepinephrine depletion in one region may cause overeating and in another cause undereating (Hoebel & Leibowitz, 1981). The effect of monoamine manipulations also depends on the state of other systems. For example, sex steroids apparently are necessary for overeating after serotonin depletion in the medial hypothalamus (Waldbillig, Steel & Clemons, in prep.) and adrenal glucocorticoids are necessary for norepinephrine-induced feeding in the paraventricular hypothalamus (Leibowitz, 1980). The akinesia seen after dopamine block or depletion depends on impairment to the dopamine pathways that ascend from the midbrain to the basal ganglia (i.e., to the striatum, which includes the caudate and putamen, and the nucleus accumbens shown in Figures 11.5, 11.8, 11.9, and 11.11).

In akinetic rats, a blocker of the neurotransmitter gamma-aminobutyric acid (GABA) or a lesion in the reticular formation will help initiate movement. Otherwise the dopamine impaired animals just remain hunched on the floor or sink in water. Akinetic rats remain quietly upright, and sink quietly upright. But when dropped through the air, some akinetic rats can move fast enough to right themselves in mid-air and land on all four feet. Thus postural righting is intact even though locomotion reflexes for approach are turned off in dopamine depleted, Parkinsonian rats (Teitelbaum, 1982b).

The stiff, hunched, upright posture of a cataleptic, akinetic rat is transformed into prone, relaxed torpor by warming the animal (Teitelbaum et al., 1983). Therefore postural reflex elements of behavior interact strongly with temperature regulation. The evolutionary explanation of this is discussed by Satinoff (1983) in an article that explains how homeostatic behavior envolved so as to engage a wide variety of motor patterns. For example, the heat given off by postural muscles becomes a major factor in temperature homeostasis in animals that balance themselves in an upright posture. The synergism is so close that temperature can control posture in akinetic rats. In this example the animal is stuporous in a warm environment; righting and standing reflexes are recruited in a cool environment, and swimming or walking reflexes come into action in a cold environment. It appears that patterns of reflexes depend on dopaminergic facilitation which cold stress can provide if the dopamine system is sufficiently intact. Other stresses, such as tail pinch, can also have dopaminergic effects that facilitate action patterns. As you would expect, dopaminergic drugs such as amphetamine mimic the effect of ecological stress, and thus act as pharmacological stressors which activate behavior patterns in dopamine depleted animals (Antelman & Chiodo, 1983; Crese, 1983).

Systemic morphine in high doses causes immobility, and the rat will not right itself. This form of akinesia involves a different pattern of muscular abnormality and may give way to explosive running if the animal is lightly tapped. This is similar to death-feigning transformed into flight. Although akinetic, the animal is ready to run (DeRyck & Teitelbaum, 1983). It has also been suggested that endogenous opiates may induce analgesia as part of fighting for food

(Morely & Levine, 1985). These ideas remind us that drug induced abnormalities might be perfectly normal under certain conditions, provided that the drug mimics the actions of endogenous neurochemicals. Conversely, drugs that block or deplete endogenous neurochemicals give us a simplified animal whose behavior reflects the relative loss of a subsystem that is neurochemically defined (Teitelbaum, 1982a).

A combination of lesions and drugs can reveal the hierarchical levels and structures necessary for the drug action. Haloperidol and morphine akinesias were abolished by lesions of the brainstem reticular formation. These lesions induced forward galloping. Therefore, this brainstem region normally inhibits forward locomotion, and the drugs may cause akinesia by indirectly activating this locomotion-inhibitory region (Teitelbaum, 1982b). Neither the dopamine blocked rat nor the morphinized rat will perform tasks unless appropriately stressed or threatened. Haloperidol and morphine seem to alter the stimulus input needed to trigger certain motor action patterns which are nevertheless still intact.

Hyperkinesias

Behavioral stimulants are drugs that cause hyperkinesis. For example, it is well known that amphetamine induces exploring, walking, running, and stereotyped behavior in intact animals. What are stereotyped behaviors? They are the same simple responses we have been discussing; for example, head scanning, grooming, paw wiping and components of locomotion. In humans, amphetamine is not only a behavioral simulant and a stressor, it can also cause paranoia and thought patterns that are stereotyped or flitting. Thus hyperkinesia shades into amphetamine psychosis (other factors will be discussed later, Figure 11.9). Perhaps psychosis in the absence of amphetamine can be treated as a stress induced syndrome (Antelman & Chiodo, 1983).

Single Neurons in a Normal Brain

Dopamine Neurons

The epitome of simplification in the midst of complexity is to record from a single neuron in a mammal that is awake. It is possible to record from identified dopamine neurons in the midbrain of a freely moving cat or monkey by lowering a microelectrode until it makes contact with

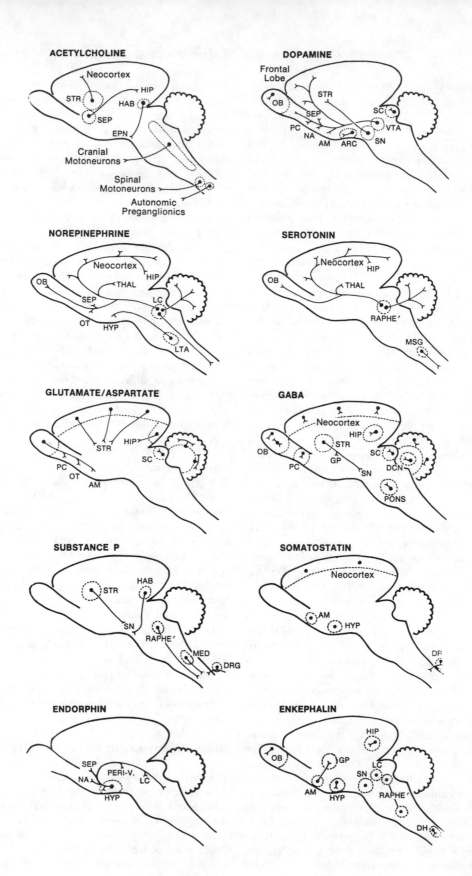

a cell body that can be recognized by its slow regular firing rate and its response to dopaminergic drugs. A dopaminergic cell responds to dopaminergic drugs if it has dopamine receptors called *autoreceptors* on its cell body and dendrites, or if it has a feedback pathway from its dopamine terminals back to its cell body (see dopamine and GABA paths to and from the striatum in Figure 11.5). Some spontaneously active dopamine cells fire almost continuously, slowing only 20 percent when the cat sleeps. However, such a cell does speed up when the cat is startled by a click or light, and stops briefly when the cat rivets its attention on something (Jacobs, 1986). In monkeys it is clear that these cells also speed up as a premotor function in anticipation of reaching out (Schultz, Ruffieux, & Aebischer, 1983). This could be interpreted to mean that dopamine cells in the nigrostriatal tract exert weak potentiation of motor circuits at all times, notably when awake and especially when startled; their firing may also potentiate premotor responses involved in generating behavior. Their slowing may depotentiate some motor circuits when the animal is sleeping or attending closely to a novel situation without moving. This function of nigrostriatal neurons can be summarized as activation and orientation (Figure 11.8).

Serotonin Neurons

Some serotonin cells fire in proportion to the animal's overall level of arousal or arousability. Their pace varies as you might expect for an overall central excitatory state, quickening when the cat is alert, slowing to a stop when the animal is drifting down through the stages of sleep, quickening again when it is dreaming (i.e., arousal without muscle tone), and going off like an alarm clock seconds before the animal awakes (Jacobs, Heym, & Steinfels, 1984).

Norepinephrine Neurons

Some norepinephrine cells also vary their firing rate with arousal level. Their response varies with noradrenergic drugs as a result of autoreceptors on the cell bodies or dendrites. This allows them to be identified in the locus coeruleus (LC) when an electrode is lowered in an awake cat. These cells fire when the cat is alarmed and are calmed by minor tranquilizers (Librium or Valium) or by sleep. Thus they may play a role in anxiety (Jacobs, 1986). These noradrenergic cells project throughout the forebrain where their terminals release norepinephrine to enhance sensory responsiveness (Figure 11.5). For example, a feature detector cell in the visual cortex gives an enhanced neural response if the ascending norepinephrine input to the visual cortex is stimulated (Figure 11.8). LC cells may be especially involved in attention to environmental stimuli (Aston-Jones & Bloom, 1981). Other norepinephrine cell

---

Figure 11.5. Highly simplified summary of major locations of neurons containing various neurotransmitters. Abbreviations as follows: AM, amygdala; ARC, arcuate nucleus; DCN, deep cerebellar nuclei; DH, dorsal horn; DRG, dorsal root ganglion; EPN, endopeduncular nucleus; GP, globus pallidus; HAB, habenula; HIP, hippocampus; HYP, hypothalamus; LC, locus coeruleus; LTA, lateral tegmental area; MED, medulla; MSG medullary serotonin group; NA, nucleus accumbens; OB, olfactory bulb; OT, olfactory tubercle; PB, parabrachial nucleus; PC, pyriform cortex; PERI-V., periventricular gray; SC, superior colliculus; SEP, septum; SN, substantia nigra; STR, striatum; THAL, thalamus; VTA, ventral tegmental area. (From Shephard, 1983, after Angevine & Cotman, 1981; for CCK paths, see text.)

Note for example: Acetylcholine: SEP-HIP path implicated in memory and Alzheimer's disease. Dopamine: SN-STR path, needed for activation and depleted in Parkinson's disease, also VTA-NA and VTA-frontal lobe paths implicated in schizophrenia. Norepinephrine: LC-neocortex path, attention, stress and anxiety. Serotonin: raphé-neocortex path, tends to counteract norepinephrine. Glutamate/aspartate: cortical input to STR. GABA: STR-SN path, extrapyramidal motor output and feedback loop in conjunction with dopamine paths. GABA AC-VTA path is not shown. Substance P: This is another STR-SN output (also to GP). Somatostatin: interneurons inhibit several hormone releasing factors in the HYP. Cholecystokinin: There is space on this diagram for you to draw in the newly discovered CCK path from PONS to HYP that may be involved in a satiety sequence. Endorphin: HYP-LC path discussed in the ACTH section in connection with stress. Enkephalin is mostly in short neurons; enkephalinergic reward and feeding has been shown in the HYP, VTA and AC. For additional details see also Nauta and Domesick (1982) and Smith and Lane (1983). From *Neurobiology* (pp. 219, 456, 460) by G.M. Shephard, 1983, New York: Oxford University Press. Copyright 1983 by Oxford University Press. Reprinted by permission.

groups seem to modulate internal states as described later.

Summary

Some norepinephrine cells permit or enhance sensory input, thereby contributing to attention. Some serotonin cells permit or enhance mental arousal in part by suppressing behavior when awake or dreaming, and some of the dopamine cells permit or enhance motor output. The point is that central excitatory and inhibitory states of the whole animal can be correlated with the nerve impulse rate in single, monoamine neurons in vertebrates, as in mollusks. Some of these states may be general, others may be executive arousal states for subroutines that favor certain sensory or motor programs.

The next objective is to discover factors which potentiate homeostatically-appropriate behavior. The simplified preparations described above have shown us some of the elements of motivation, notably monoamine arousal functions and motor action patterns. Next we need neural principles for organizing the patterns into recognizable proclivities for anticipatory homeostasis and survival.

PATTERNS IN MOTIVATION: INTEGRATIVE PEPTIDES AS AN ORGANIZING PRINCIPLE

Homeostasis: Physiological, Behavioral and Cognitive

Homeostasis refers to regulation of the body's internal environment. The chemicals within us must be maintained within appropriate ranges to provide the correct environment for cells to live and function. Our ancestors lived in seawater that provided much of the constancy needed to support life. When they crawled out of the ocean and adapted to an amphibian's life, a system for maintaining fluid composition had to develop (Smith, 1953). Safe at last from being eaten by a big fish, the little amphibious fish gradually developed the physiology for breathing air, digesting terrestrial foods, breeding on land, and retaining salty blood as we find it in mammals today. How did they do it? What stimuli do animals use to regulate their bodily functions and to integrate that regulation with behavior and mental processes? This section

will answer the question by organizing homeostatic functions according to the functions of *regulatory peptides*. These are peptides that regulate tissue function, including regulation of the pituitary and related neural and glandular tissues. Olds (1977) predicted that some peptides might be drive peptides because they induce motivation. I will go a step further, the point of this excercise being to show that some peptides have an effect on motivation that is integrated with their effect on physiology. Thus a subset of peptides will be designated as *integrative peptides* to emphasize their role in integrating physiology and psychology.

If a peptide controls a tissue function it is a regulatory peptide. If it controls a number of tissues with related homeostatic functions that becomes more interesting. If the same peptide controls related functions in both the periphery and in the brain (e.g. water reabsorption in the periphery and thirst in the brain), then it is a candidate for the title of integrative peptide. However, this parallelism is not enough. An integrative peptide, in the most powerful sense, would be a peptide that connects its central receptor field with its peripheral receptor field, thus uniting brain and body with its chemical code for a homeostatic purpose. The connection could be made (1) by having the peptides get through the blood-brain barrier to act both centrally and peripherally, or (2) by influencing a nerve such as the vagus that connects the peripheral and central receptor fields for the same peptide. It would be particularly exciting if the nerve that made the connection used the same peptide as a neurotransmitter.

Background

Peptides and Proteins as Messengers and Effectors

DNA is transcribed into RNA which acts through a number of stages to assemble amino acids in coded series to form peptides imbedded within longer chains. The long peptide chains are proteins. These proteins are later cleaved to liberate bioactive peptides. The liberated peptides take on a distinctive three-dimensional *conformation*. Some peptides are mobile and can drift in the blood stream, extracellular fluid or intracellular fluid as messengers. Others that are usually much larger have a tail that holds them to a membrane surface where they act as receptors. In many cases peptide messengers and receptors interact like a key and lock, unlocking a cascade of chemical reactions leading to a physiological response. The peptide messenger may also be taken into the recipient cell to act inside the cell (Kriger, Brownstein, & Martin, 1983; Szego, 1984).

Evolution of Peptides

Fifty animal species are known to have genes for an oxytocin-like peptide and a vasopressin-like peptide. One must go back 280 million years to the lamprey to find a vertebrate with just one such peptide gene. Whatever the functions of oxytocin and vasopressin, these peptides have been with us a long time. In general, genes produce peptides, and these peptides help produce behavior. Within vertebrates at least, certain ancestral peptides seem to correspond to certain functions. In this exmple, oxytocin is generally involved in reproduction as one of its major functions; whereas vasopressin is for water and mineral regulation (Acher, 1983). Thus vertebrate evolution can be traced in part to a genetic mutation giving rise to a new gene that manufactured a new peptide sequence which enhanced propagation and survival. In sum, peptides are genetically programmed information carrying molecules that are part of the survival code. Peptides can be neurotransmitters, neuromodulators, neurohormones or hormone-releasing factors. They can trigger, modulate or prime behavior because they act on a variety of control systems which presumably evolved in the presence of the peptide. As anatomical complexity increased over the eons, and the brains of animals were molded by evolutionary events, the neural control systems often became so entangled and adapted to a variety of purposes (Satinoff, 1983) that it is now difficult to discern what constitutes a system on anatomical grounds alone. In some cases, diverse parts of a system still respond to the ancestral peptides. I venture to say that what integrates some of the parts into the system is the peptide. The medium of communication is the peptide, and the medium is the message.

The 1951 *Handbook of Experimental Psychology* described neurons in terms of their electrical properties (Brink, 1951). Now it is more useful to think of them as secretory cells. Neurosecretion was the phylogenetic development that made possible coded communication between specialized cells. Coelenterates developed cells with two poles, one for reception and one for secretion. These neurosecretory cells were the forerunners of nerve cells and endocrine cells. Annelid worms developed neural ganglia, but still no endocrine glands. Arthropods developed endocrine cells specialized to store large amounts of hormone for release into the blood stream. Insects display the forerunner of our two-stage process in which neurons control endocrine cells (Rodriguez, 1984).

Dual Regulation of Pituitary and Brain

The neurosecretory cells in the hypothalamus often serve a dual function. Their axons branch out to influence both the endocrine system and the nervous system. These cells secrete peptides that serve as pituitary hormone-releasing factors. The same peptides are secreted as neurotransmitters from axonal branches which extend great distances into the brain. For example luteinizing hormone releasing hormone (LHRH) is secreted by hypothalamic cells which control ovulation through pituitary release of luteinizing hormone, and the *same* hypothalamic cells also modulate various neural circuits involved in sex and sexuality (Krieger et al., 1983).

Coexistence of Monoamines and Peptides

Some peptidergic neurons are short and contain more than one peptide. Others are long and ramifying, and some contain both a monoamine (serotonin, dopamine, norepinephrine, or epinephrine) and one or more peptides (Hokfelt et al., 1982). It has been proposed that the neurosecretory cells which synthesize both amines and peptides have a common embryonic origin. These cells may ramify widely, but most of their cell bodies have been found in the pineal gland, the hypothalamus, the anterior and intermediate lobes of the pituitary, midbrain, and hindbrain, and scattered diffusely in various glands and organs of the periphery (Pearse & Takor, 1979). Peptides that coexist with the monoamines are positioned to serve as cotransmitters with monoamines.

Cotransmitters

Coexistence does not prove cotransmission. To prove that a substance is a transmitter requires the traditional tests: (1) Cellular synthesis of the neurotransmitter, (2) release of the neurotransmitter by appropriate stimuli, (3) action mimicked by exogenous neurotransmitter, (4) a mechanism for termination of its synaptic action, and (5) pharmacological blockade of its postsynaptic receptor and other drug effects (Siggins, 1981; Krieger et al., 1983).

In summary, neurosecretory cells have developed phylogenetically into two additional cell types, endocrine cells and neurons. All three cell types and various intermediate forms may derive from the same cells of origin in the embryo, and all three types can use a given chemical messenger regardless whether the cell ends up in the cortex, hypothalamus, pituitary, adrenal gland, or pancreas. For example, brain neurons can contain messenger peptides that were formerly thought to act just as adrenal hormones, pituitary hormones, or hypothalamic releasing factors. Some neurons use more than one of these chemicals as transmitter substances. This may sound confusing, but it is actually a great opportunity to understand the brain by using the classical hormonal functions of these well-known messengers as clues to their brain function. This may be a way to find order amid the confusion.

Strategies for Studying Integrative Peptides

Five strategies will be used to sort out the functional signal in the chemical noise. The first is to look for matched functions of a given peptide in the body and brain. For example in response to blood loss, angiotensin acts both peripherally to increase cardiovascular tone and centrally to cause drinking. This relation of peripheral and central effects is not an irrelevant coincidence. The second strategy is to look for coordinated functions of peptides that release other peptides. For example, angiotensin in the brain releases vasopressin which promotes water reabsorption in the kidneys, again contributing to blood pressure. A third strategy is to determine the neuropeptide content of neurons that connect functionally related parts of the brain, such as different areas involved in thirst.

The fourth strategy is to measure the movement of neuropeptides through the blood-brain barrier. Given that some peptides are secreted into the gastrointestinal track, some into organs, some into the blood, some into the brain, some into the ventricles, it is crucial to know if a peptide can serve an integrative function by diffusing from one compartment to another.

Recent evidence suggests that parts of the blood-brain barrier can be viewed as a dialysis filter that lets small molecules pass through (Reid, 1984).

Fluid is secreted into the ventricles, leaving behind all the blood cells, monoamines, and most of the blood proteins and peptides. The cerebrospinal fluid in the ventricles (CSF) is on the brain side of the blood-brain barrier. The CSF contains less potassium and calcium than blood, but more NaCl; thus ionic balance appears to be independently regulated. The CSF provides a source of nutrition and information which augments the blood vasculature. Most peptides such as angiotensin circulate in the blood with rather little cross over under normal blood pressure conditions (M.I. Phillips, 1984). If this is correct, then angiotensin in the blood and angiotensin in the CSF may not mix. However some neuropeptides are secreted into CSF by neurosecretory neurons in the brain. The fluid within this canal flows from the lateral ventricles down through the third ventricle and out through the fourth ventricle where it flows over the area postrema (AP) and passes along to bathe the outer surface of the brain and to fill the spinal canal. Eventually it is taken into the venous blood return. Thus a spinal tap to sample the cerebrospinal fluid can give a doctor some idea of chemical functioning deep in the less-accessible reaches of the brain. The brain itself may sample some peptides in the CSF through the walls of the ventricles.

It was once thought that specialized circumventricular organs served this purpose because of their location in the walls of the ventricles, but new evidence suggests these specialized structures are better suited to monitor chemicals in the blood (Meisenberg & Simmons, 1983). The *circumventricular organs* are small regions of tissue on the borders of the ventricles where the blood capillaries are fenestrated to allow passage of materials from the blood directly into the brain tissue. The brain can react to blood-borne chemicals that come in through these porous filters (Simpson, 1981). Everywhere else in the brain the capillaries are surrounded by cells with such tight junctions that nothing can get across unless it can dissolve in the fatty memtrane or attach to a specific, metabolically-active, blood-to-brain carrier. In a similar way, the circumventricular organs are sealed off from the ventricles by a tight cellular layer

(M.I. Phillips, 1984). Clearly the circumventricular organs are ideal locations for chemosensory neurons to sample small molecules in the blood.

This example typifies a recurring problem. Which source of the peptide affects behavior: blood angiotensin, angiotensin secreted in the ventricles, or angiotensin secreted by neurons? These three are not mutually exclusive given that some peptides can move from blood into the circumventricular organs, and from neurosecretory cells into the blood and ventricles, and from ventricles directly into surrounding brain tissue; moreover the ventricles eventually empty into venous blood. Thus there may be chemical communication or leakage between the fluids on the two sides of the blood-brain barrier (Reid, 1984). Some peptides are degraded too fast to move very far, but others have a half-life measured in minutes or hours.

The fifth strategy for identifying integrative peptides is to examine the functions of cotransmitters on the theory that there is no such thing as strange bed fellows after millions of years in the same bed. For example, what does it mean that adrenocorticotropic hormone (ACTH), which stimulates the adrenals to secrete adrenalin in emergencies, is coreleased from the pituitary with beta-endorphin, one of the body's morphine-like compounds? The answer must lie in the physiological, behavioral and cognitive effects of ACTH and beta-endorphin during stress. Marathon running is a well known example of such a stress that requires adrenalin plus a pain killer.

Most of the answers concerning neuropeptide functions are not available yet. The writer will indulge in fantasies of coordinated neuropeptide function for the sake of demonstrating the strategy as much as to demonstrate the truth. Our perception of the truth is changing daily as new data come in. I have only enough data to explain what might be a general principle, and not enough data to show how often it might be wrong. We must be cautious because all cells in a given species have the same genome. Therefore all cells, including all nerve cells, contain the information to manufacture all the proteins and peptides. Obviously cells specialize and do not use all this information, but it is quite possible that some cells do use the information to make some peptides that are not functional. Even when a peptide is functional,

we are forewarned that CNS peptides do not necessarily have functions that parallel peripheral functions (Schneider, Alpert, & Iversen 1983). I am not suggesting that such a relationship is necessary, only that such relationships do exist, and when they do, there is heuristic value in a theory of integrative peptides.

Angiotensin and Fluid Pressure

Three hormones appear to have major influences on body fluids: angiotensin, vasopressin, and aldosterone. They interact with each other. Angiotensin appears to be most involved with maintaining adequate blood pressure through adequate blood volume. Logically, angiotensin is involved in maintaining both adequate water and salt. Vasopressin is the brain's response to hypertonicity; therefore this peptide seems to have the job of supplying water. Aldosterone is a steroid hormone that responds to lack of sodium and has the job of garnering salt. It should be clear that to understand fluid homeostasis, we cannot focus just on the physiology of circulation or on the psychology of drinking. Now it begins to look as if certain peptides and steroids do the holistic job of integrating fluid dynamics, from foraging for water and salt to controlling fluid and salt excretion (Figure 11.6).

A great deal is known about angiotensin's physiological and behavioral functions (Epstein, 1981, 1982b; Setler, 1977; Hatton & Armstrong, 1981; Reid, 1984; M.I. Phillips, 1984; Stricker, 1983a; Toates, 1979; Johnson, 1979; Ganten, Speck, Schelling, & Unger, 1981; Grossman, 1984).

The stimulus for angiotensin release is low blood pressure created by low blood volume, hypovolemia. A decrease in blood volume acts on receptors in the heart and kidney. The heart sends a neural signal to the brain. The kidney releases renin which frees angiotensin I, which is coverted to angiotensin II by an important angiotensin-converting enzyme (Horovitz, 1981). Angiotensin II increases blood pressure. The brain uses vasopressin to direct the kidney to reabsorb water; the adrenal medulla is directed to release adrenaline, and the adrenal cortex is directed to release aldosterone for sodium retention. The overall effect is coordinated, multifaceted reinstatement of blood pressure. If a person's blood pressure is regulated at too high a level, a drug to inhibit angiotensin-

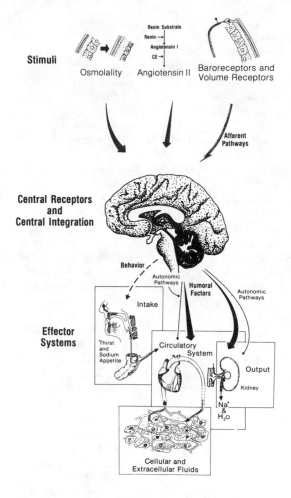

Stimuli

Osmolality   Angiotensin II   Baroreceptors and Volume Receptors

Afferent Pathways

Central Receptors and Central Integration

Behavior

Autonomic Pathways   Humoral Factors   Autonomic Pathways

Intake

Effector Systems

Thirst and Sodium Appetite

Circulatory System

Output

Kidney

Na$^+$ & H$_2$O

Cellular and Extracellular Fluids

Figure 11.6. Controls exerted by the brain as part of body fluid homeostasis. Behavior input is depicted at the left; excretion at the right. The organs shown and the brain are integrated through the action of neural connections, fluid-control peptides, and aldosterone (from Johnson, 1982). Angiotensin affects fluid intake and the circulatory system. By way of vasopressin it also controls fluid output, and with aldosterone it induces salt appetite. Angiotensin may function as a blood hormone, brain neuromodulator and neurotransmitter. If it crosses the blood-brain barrier in the subfornical organ so as to integrate physiological and behavioral functions, then it is an integrative peptide in the strongest sense of the term. Reprinted by permission of the publisher from "Neurobiology of the Periventricular Tissue Surrounding the Anteroventral Third Ventricle (AV3V) and Its Role in Behavior, Fluid Balance, and Cardiovascular Control," by A.K. Johnson, in O.A. Smith, R.A. Galosy, and S.M. Weiss (eds.), *Circulation, Neurobiology, and Behavior*, pp. 277–295. Copyright 1982 by Elsevier Science Publishing Co., Inc.

converting enzyme can be a life saver (Horovitz, 1981).

Research techniques

Pitfalls along the research route have made this beautiful angiotensin story difficult to construct. When injecting angiotensin into the brain, reflux up to the outside of a cannula shaft has always been a problem, especially when the cannula passes through a ventricle. The primary site of action was first thought to be the lateral hypothalamus, then the subfornical organ (Simpson & Routtenberg, 1973), and then the tissue at the anterior-ventral end of the third ventricle (Brody & Johnson, 1980). At each stage of progress someone had to be willing to believe in the alternative explanation enough to research it. All three sites may turn out to have angiotensin receptors as more becomes known about angiotensin circulation and circuitry.

Similarly, the lesion technique has been both helpful and risky—risky, because it has verified the cannulation research at each stage of progess. When lateral hypothalamic angiotensin induces drinking, lesions there block it. When subfornical injections induce drinking, lesions there block it. Now the the anterior ventricular tissue is known to be a site of angiotensin action, and lesions again back up the conclusion that this is a site necessary for angiotensin thirst. The reason for the perpetual success story with the lesion technique is that many brain structures are necessary for drinking, and some of them may be connected in a series (Brody & Johnson, 1980; Miselis, 1981).

Electrical stimulation has also had its trials and tribulations. Lateral hypothalamic stimulation induces drinking, and this can be potentiated by water deprivation (Mogenson, 1977). However, the rat may switch from drinking to eating or gnawing depending on individual propensities and stimuli available in the cage (Valenstein, 1974). Excitation of dopamine arousal systems may be at fault in this fickle behavior, or it may be that the stimulated systems are indeed coded and that an electrode stimulates several systems at once.

These behavioral—"top-down"—approaches to the brain have led the way. The lesion technique was started by Lashley, stimulation by Hess, and neurotransmitter injections by Grossman. With these approaches we measure behavior and guess about the neural substrate. Now psychologists are starting from the bottom up using neuroscience approaches too. We trace neural structures and monitor neural function and guess about behavior. These techniques are valuable because they study smaller populations of neurons and discern pre- and post-synaptic effects. Ideally, one would do both at once by measuring the electrical or chemical activity of a number of single nerves of a given type in a behaving animal (Olds, 1977; Jacobs, 1986; Hernandez, Stanley & Hoebel, 1986).

Another approach is to let the animal control its own angiotensin level. Strangely enough, rats will self-inject angiotensin into their brain and make themselves drink in the process (Nicolaidis, 1974). Thus angiotensin is a positive reinforcer of emitted behavior, as well as an inducer of drinking behavior.

Procedures which increase synaptic dopamine in the nucleus accumbens often reinforce behavior as explained later. Angiotensin injected intraventricularly releases dopamine measured with a microdialysis probe implanted in the accumbens (unpublished observation). This may explain why angiotensin is rewarding.

Neurotransmitter Status of Angiotensin

Neurotransmitter criteria can be demonstrated with a combination of top-down and bottom-up approaches. It requires that a brain chemical be localized in a neuron, released by natural input, deactivated by enzymes of reuptake, and blocked at its receptors by antagonists. Sensory input and motor output can be used as criteria as well as electrical or chemical input and output. Angiotensin is rapidly approaching neurotransmitter status. Precursors and enzymes for its manufacture have been discovered in the brain (Ganten, Hermann, Bayer, Unger, & Lang, 1983). Immunological stains reveal angiotensin containing cells in the subfornical organ (SFO) (Hokfelt et al., 1982), and angiotensin neurons project from the hypothalamus to the SFO and other sites (Lind, Swanson, & Ganten, 1984). Miselis (1981) injected radioactively labeled tracers into the SFO and traced neural projections down to the anterior third ventricle region which is sensitive to angiotensin in the production of drinking. Therefore angiotensin cells may project from one part of the thirst system to another! They may also go to the nearby medial preoptic nucleus (MPO) where osmoreceptors lie. The SFO also projects to the supraoptic

nucleus (SON) where cells control the secretion of vasopressin (Sgro, Ferguson, & Renaud, 1984). Thus a circuit has been proposed as follows: in the SFO with its fenestrated capillaries, blood-borne angiotensin leaks onto angiotensin receptive cells. SFO neurons then have information that blood pressure receptors in the kidneys or heart are activating blood-borne angiotensin, which means there is (or was) low blood pressure in the periphery. These informed neurons project to several hypothalamic regions where action potentials may release angiotensin from their terminals. If so, angiotensin, the neurotransmitter, carries information about angiotensin, the hormone. Meanwhile, any angiotensin secreted or injected into the ventricles could pass through the ventricular walls into the sensitive regions to mimic the neurotransmitter and affect the synapses for angiotensin induced changes in CNS output. As yet no one has actually collected angiotensin from a brain site in response to neural stimulation or hypovolemia.

An angiotensin blocker, saralasin, antagonized peripheral or central angiotensin-induced thirst when the saralasin was injected in the brain. This confirms that brain angiotensin receptors are necessary for angiotensin induced thirst (Epstein, 1982b). Angiotensin neurons might conceivably potentiate osmoreceptor circuits in the preoptic region to release vasopressin during hypotensive crisis. But saralasin did not block osmotically induced drinking. Therefore the osmoreceptor circuits must employ some neurotransmitter other than angiotensin. In summary, angiotensin has a coordinating function (Ganten et al., 1983) in cardiovascular regulation and thirst. It defends blood volume in a number of ways (Epstein, 1982b).

Vasopressin and Osmotic Balance

The stimulus for vasopressin release is generally believed to be loss of intracellular water. This is caused osmotically by a hypertonic environment in the neighborhood of osmoreceptors in the lateral preoptic nucleus (LPN). Anderson, who first proposed the osmotic mechanism now thinks that sodium ions may be a stimulus for vasopressin release (rev. by Epstein, 1982b). Osmotic effects could stimulate the cell by shrinking it or by increasing intracellular fluid concentration and increasing intracellular sodium. Extracellular sodium could have a synergistic effect by passing through sodium channels, thereby adding to intracellular sodium and further depolarizing the neuron. For example the taste of NaCl on the tongue is actually a response to sodium ions which pass through the membrane and depolarize it (Heck, Mierson, & DeSimone, 1984). Nicolaidis recorded from hypothalamic sodium receptors that were not osmotically sensitive, and Adachi (personal communication) finds them in the midbrain. Therefore osmolarity and sodium may have different detectors. Osmoreceptors or sodium receptors may be connected to cells in the SON and paraventricular hypothalamic nucleus (PVN) which secrete vasopressin (Hatton & Armstrong, 1981).

Vasopressin neurosecretory cells release their peptides not only into the blood stream in the posterior pituitary, but also into the ventricles (Rodriguez, 1984). This new finding suggests that the ventricles serve as a conduit for some of vasopressin's actions in the brain.

It is conceivable that vasopressin controls the osmolarity of fluid secreted into the CSF. It is well known that peripheral vasopressin causes vasoconstriction which increases circulatory resistance and increases blood pressure.

It also causes water reabsorption from the kidney; thus its other name is antidiuretic hormone. Neurosecretory vasopressin does all the same things in the brain; it controls cerebral vasoconstriction, cerebral blood pressure, and possibly absorption of CSF water.

Brain vasopressin neurons may stimulate the sympathetic innervation to the heart. There are connections from the hypothalamus to the brainstem autonomic nuclei which exert cardiac control. Conversely, stretch receptors in the heart and baroreceptors in the carotid and aortic arteries project back to the hypothalamus to release vasopressin following a drop in blood pressure. The degree to which angiotensin is an intermediary in this pressor effect is not known (Hatton & Armstrong, 1981).

In summary, angiotensin appears to mediate and integrate control systems for extracellular fluid dynamics. Vasopressin does it for intracellular or transmembrane fluid dynamics.

Aldosterone, Naturetic Factor and Sodium Balance

Sodium ions are important in generating neural potentials. Sodium is also a major factor in osmosis. Therefore sodium needs regulation.

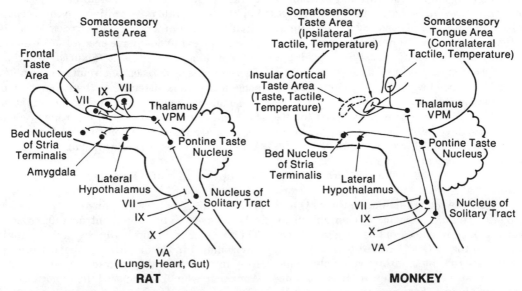

Figure 11.7. Side view of taste pathways of rat and monkey. Inputs from cranial nerves, VII, IX, X, and other visceral afferents (VA) project to the pontine taste nuclei which include the NST and parabrachial nucleus (see text). It projects directly to the lateral hypothalamus and amygdala (in the rat). Note multiple taste areas in the cortex of both species. From *Neurobiology* (pp. 219, 456, 460) by G.M. Shephard, 1983, New York: Oxford University Press. Copyright 1983 by Oxford University Press. Reprinted by permission.

Using the functions of angiotensin and vaso-pressin as our guide, we can predict an integrating peptide that is a hormone in the blood, a neurosecretory factor in the hypothalamus, and a neurotransmitter in brain circuits for salt control and salt appetite. Perhaps the peptide atrial naturetic factor (ANF) serves this purpose. Angiotensin in synergy with the steroid aldosterone plays an important role.

Reviews of sodium balance and sodium appetite give bits and pieces of an incomplete, but intriguing story (Hatton & Armstrong, 1981; Epstein, 1982b). Angiotensin in the blood releases aldosterone which mobilizes the animal's physiology and behavior to reclaim renal sodium and to eat sodium salt.

Aldosterone is secreted by the adrenal cortex both in response to angiotensin and perhaps in response to input from detectors of low sodium. Nerves that fire selectively to sodium chloride, not other equiosmotic challenges, have been described in the tongue, liver, nucleus of the solitary tract (NST) and hypothalamus. Sodium signals from the liver arrive at sodium receptors in the hindbrain NST (Kobashi & Adachi, 1984). This is a location where sodium taste inputs could also converge from the tongue (Figure 11.7). If so, then all three sodium signals from the NST, liver, and tongue could project over the same pathway to the hypothalamus for further integration. If sodium receptor inputs do converge, it could help explain the synergism of salt taste and salt deficit in the elicitation of salt appetite. During salt deprivation, the NST response to salt shifts in the direction of sugars. Aldosterone receptors may also exist in the brain if we judge by results in which intraventricular aldosterone induced permanent salt appetite in angiotensin primed rats (Fluharty & Epstein, 1983).

Atriopeptin is a newly discovered peptide that has opposite effects of angiotensin. Atriopeptin lowers blood pressure through loss of renal sodium and inhibition of drinking (Wardener & Clarkson, 1985).

Fluid Control Peptides and Learning
DeWied started a new line of research when he found that extinction of a conditioned emotional response was hastened by removing the pituitary (rev. by van Wimersma Greidanus & Versteeg, 1984). Escape behavior in a shuttle box was unaffected. He suggested that a pituitary

factor was involved in remembering the emotional response, but not in reacting to pain. The response was restored and made resistant to extinction by injections of vasopressin (VP). A single intraperitoneal injection could extend extinction far beyond the life of the peptide which is degraded relatively rapidly. VP also prolonged extinction of conditioned heart rate deceleration.

Other cognitive effects of VP are indicated by potentiation of passive avoidance in a step-through box and prevention of reversal of retrograde amnesia after electroconvulsive shock (Martinez, Jensen, Messing, Rigter, & McGaugh, 1981). Under some circumstances VP can even induce analgesia (Kordower & Bodnar, 1984). Appetitive tasks can be potentiated by VP given to hungry, thirsty, or sexually motivated rats (Koob & Bloom, 1983), but some tasks are impaired as if the animal were over-aroused (Sahgal, 1983).

On the theory that the arginine form of vasopressin (AVP) is what influences memory and retrieval of memory, picogram quantities of AVP were injected in the ventricles. This prolonged extinction of a pole-climb avoidance response. Similarly it improved passive avoidance training. As a control, oxytocin or antibody to VP had the opposite effect. Oxytocin and vasopressin generally have opposite effects on the memory involved in avoidance (van Wimersma, Greidanus & Versteeg, 1984). Stein, Belluzzi, and Wise (1976) showed that norepinephrine was necessary for memory in an avoidance task, and vasopressin may act in part by modulating norepinephrine. Various analogues and metabolites of VP have been reported to improve memory in rats (Burbach, Kovacs, & De Wied, 1983) and concept learning in humans (Beckwith, Petras, Kanaan-Beckwith, Couk, & Haug, 1982). In a dramatic new experiment it was found that osmotic stress prolonged active avoidance just as injections of AVP did, and the effect was prevented by a specific antagonist of AVP (Koob, Dantzer, Rodriguez, Bloom, & Le Moal, 1985). An active metabolite of VP can improve memory in passive avoidance tasks even though the metabolite has no effect on water balance (Burbach et al., 1983); therefore some of these cognitive effects may not be directly owing to whole AVP but to other breakdown products in sites where the appropriate enzymes exist (Martinez et al., 1981).

In summary, the peptide known for controlling water reabsorption and blood pressure in response to intracellular dehydration has been discovered to improve memory. At the moment there is almost nothing to suggest that VP has a cognitive function related to thinking about water. There are only anecdotal reports that fluid deprivation leads to thinking, craving, and dreaming about water (Hatton & Armstrong, 1981). No one has tested an antagonist of angiotensin or vasopressin to see if it blocks such visions. We have been alerted to the fact that some of a peptide's effects could be caused by its metabolites and thus be independent of the parent peptide's effects on homeostasis.

Angiotensin provided the foundation for the theory that some peptides have integrative roles in the periphery and in the brain; next we shall try out the theory in the realm of energy balance.

Cholecystokinin and Digestion

Cholecystokinin (CCK) is a prime candidate. To present the background on peripheral CCK, I can do little more than reflect the 50-year history documented by Smith's recent review (1984). However I will go on to present new results with CCK in the brain. Some of the new intracerebral results fit the view of CCK as a gut peptide for digestion and satiety, therefore as an integrative peptide (Hoebel, 1985b). Other results are radically different and suggest a role in locomotion and reinforcement. The implications are exciting, unverified, and testable.

CCK is a peptide secreted by cells in the upper small intestines. CCK stimulates secretion of gastric acid and pepsin and contracts the gall bladder to put bile into the intestines. It is released by substances such as the amino acid, phenylalanine, in food. Therefore, it might be involved in aspects of aminostasis.

CCK Satiety and Aversion
After considerable controversy (Smith, Gibbs, & Kulkosky, 1982; Deutsch, 1982) it appears that CCK has effects which can be quietly satiating or distressingly aversive depending on the dose and assay used. The aversive properties have been shown in learned aversion and place preference tests (Swerdlow, van der Kooy, Koob, & Wenger, 1983); the satiating properties in feeding tests. Smith, Gibbs and their colleagues have marshalled evidence that intra-

peritonel injection of CCK inhibits sham feeding. CCK infusion at the start of each meal suppressed meal size, but the animals ate more meals thus making up for the difference (West, Fey, & Woods, 1984). CCK-induced satiety includes a natural behavior sequence of grooming, sniffing, locomotion, and rearing, followed by withdrawal from the food site and resting or sleep.

People who were given phenylalanine to eat, on the theory that it would release CCK, reported increased satiety relative to a placebo. People given CCK to induce satiety did tend to eat less and did not report illness in some studies. It is fairly clear that peripheral CCK in natural amounts can shorten a meal, particularly when there is synergism with other satiating factors (Schallert, Pendergrass, & Farrar, 1982).

Satiety in the extreme becomes aversive. Most of us can testify to this after overeating a holiday dinner. On the other hand, Smith refers to the "intimate experience of pleasure, tranquilization, and satisfaction that follows a good meal." We can also testify to this. Thus we need to be alert for both the pleasure and the aversion that may accompany satiety under various circumstances. The question is whether CCK is a code that induces either one or both.

It is important to keep in mind that satiety is not all-or-none. Satiety, defined as cessation of eating, can be sensory specific. That is to say, the animal stops eating one food but will still eat another (Rolls, 1979; Mook, 1983).

Peripherally induced satiety with CCK depends on intact vagal sensory nerves. CCK-induced satiety was prevented by gastric vagotomy (Smith, 1984). The vagus ends in sensory relay nuclei of the hindbrain including the nucleus of the solitary tract (NST), which was discussed earlier in the context of hepatic afferents for sodium signals (Figure 11.7). The afferent input from the stomach could be necessary either for transmitting a CCK-initiated signal or for potentiating a hormonal effect of CCK that reaches the brain. Blood-borne CCK could theoretically pass the blood-brain barrier in some circumventricular organ and then activate a receptor by itself or in combination with brain CCK or other synergistic inputs from the gut.

A detective job is in order to pick out the CNS mechanisms of CCK satiety. Crawley and Schwaber (1984) used the decrease in locomotion which is part of the satiety sequence as a marker for CCK satiety and found that NST lesions prevented this CCK effect. Given that taste neurons also project to the NST, this is a logical place for interactions between gustatory input and gut CCK inputs. In an interesting study, peripheral CCK injections did not inhibit intake of plain water, but did inhibit intake of sweetened water (Bartness & Waldbillig, 1984), suggesting that CCK inputs and taste inputs interact.

In the rat, axons emanating from the NST project to a pontine taste nucleus, the parabrachial nucleus (Figure 11.7). Neurons there project to the LH, VMH and PVN (Smith & DeVito, 1984). CCK receptors are found within the vagus, the NST, the parabrachial nucleus, a path to the VMH, and the PVN (Zarbin, Wamsley, Innis, & Kuhar, 1981; Zaborsky, Beinfeld, Palkovitz, & Heimer, 1984). Perhaps CCK is a satiety transmitter as well as a peripheral satiety stimulus. Some studies found no feeding suppression with central injection of CCK; others were successful with ventricular injections (Morley, 1982). CCK injected in the PVN suppressed the feeding induced by norepinephrine (McCaleb and Myers, 1980).

One must be cautious when interpreting behavior after large amounts of exogenous peptide injected into the brain. Many techniques have been devised to cross-validate the results (Moss & Dudley, 1984; Myers, 1980). One way to find out if CCK satiety is a false clue is to find out if a CCK antibody injected in the brain induces feeding. It does. However this has only been shown in sheep (Balle & Della-Fera, 1984), and species differences for CCK effects are known to exist (Morley & Levine, 1985; Morley, 1982). Another way is to find out if a CCK blocker induces feeding. Proglumide is a weak but reasonably specific receptor blocker used in some countries to treat ulcers by blocking CCK-induced gastric acid secretion. It also appears to block satiety in sheep that eat proglumide with their meal (Baile & Della-Fera, 1984). We found that proglumide injected in the PVN caused rats to eat. The effect was counteracted by simultaneously applied CCK (Hoebel, 1985b). Injectors lowered 1.5 mm deeper in the hypothalamus failed to cause proglumide induced feeding, so we agree with McCaleb and Myers (1980) in thinking the relevant neurons are well localized. The effect has been mapped and replicated with another more potent CCK blocker

(Schwartz, Dorfman, Hernandez & Hoebel, In press). At this moment, it appears that CCK contributes both to intestinal satiety as a peptide hormone and to PVN satiety as a peptide neurotransmitter. Thus CCK will qualify as an integrative peptide if it can be shown that CCK neurons or CCK itself travels from one site to another.

Other Effects of CCK

We have found that rats will self-inject amphetamine in the nucleus accumbens (Hoebel et al., 1983) where it releases dopamine (Figure 11.5 and 11.8). Rats also self-inject dopamine in the accumbens (Guerin, Goeders, Dworkin, & Smith, 1984). CCK is a cotransmitter with dopamine in neurons that project to the posterior nucleus accumbens (Hokfelt et al., 1982). CCK injected into the posterior accumbens with dopamine can enhance dopamine-induced locomotion (Stivers & Crawley, 1984). Therefore CCK as a cotransmitter may amplify its partner's effects. At other sites, CCK can inhibit various activities depending on the dose and the test used (Schneider et al., 1983; Vaccarino & Koob, 1984; Van Ree, Gaffori, & De Wied, 1983). Clearly there is much more to be learned.

Della-Fera, Baile, Schneider, and Grinker (1981) suggest that CCK released into the ventricles during feeding can flow downstream to act at other brain sites. According to this theory, we might also suppose that CCK, which is released further upstream in the accumbens during operant behavior and locomotion, reaches the nearby lateral ventricles and flows down to the hypothalamus where it could conceivably contribute to satiety and lethargy if the appropriate taste or gastro-intestinal inputs were also present. Thus CCK could first be involved in accumbens functions and then contribute to satiety or lethargy. It is also possible that CCK released during dopaminergic reinforcement in the accumbens has something to do with reinforcing feeding. We do not know yet.

Neurotensin and Lipostasis

Neurotensin is like CCK in that it signals an energy surfeit. Neurotensin signals the presence of fat in the gut and tells the brain and body what to do about it.

Rosell (1982) reviews evidence that neurotensin reduces gastric acid secretion and alters intestinal peristalsis to accommodate the digestion and absorption of a fatty meal. Neurotensin is released from the walls of the distal small intestine, the ileum, which is about 12 feet long in people. A meal consisting of 40 ml whiskey, a white bread roll with 4 g of butter, fried potatoes, steak and bernaise sauce, wine, and coffee caused a significant rise in circulating neurotensin in plasma. Appropriately I first heard this scientific fact from Rosell while drinking wine after a large supper in the French Alps. Neurotensin in the blood stream selectively constricts capillary vessels in fatty tissue, not muscle, and does so in thin men more than in fat ones. In any case, Rosell (1982, p. 192) suggests that the physiological role of neurotensin might be "to *coordinate* blood flow, motility, and acid secretion in the gastrointestinal canal in order to, for example, optimize the digestion of fat."

Neurotensin Satiety
The theory that some peptides have coordinated physiological and psychological functions led us to inject neurotensin in the paraventricular hypothalamic (PVN) site where McCaleb and Myers (1980) had reported obtaining satiety with CCK. The result was satiety with neurotensin (Stanley, Hoebel, & Leibowitz, 1983). Neurotensin inhibited the eating induced by food deprivation or PVN norepinephrine injections. It suppressed eating induced by norepinephrine injected on the same side of the brain more than on the opposite side, so it did not seem to make rats ill, just unresponsive to norepinephrine or food deprivation. Neurotensin's effect was specific to feeding as opposed to drinking. Neurotensin blockers are unavailable as a test for local receptors, but we did find that the neurotensin satiety phenomenon failed to appear when small fragments of the neurotensin molecule were tested (Stanley et al., 1985). Thus neurotensin has the earmarks of a satiety peptide in the PVN; however, the effective dose is high enough to question the relevance of the effect to normal PVN function.

Neurotensin Trophotropism
Neurotensin's effects when injected ventricularly seem to be the opposite of thyrotropin releasing hormone (TRH). Neurotensin enhances the sedative effects of drugs, antagonizes stimulants, and lowers body temperature. It tends to reduce reaction to pain and to relax muscles. It

can even cause catalepsy. Prange and Nemeroff (1982) suggest the organizing principle here is a trophotropic response pattern. This encompasses withdrawal, recuperation, and anabolism with general insulation from the environment. This conclusion rests on neurotensin's tendency to reduce pain when hurt, reduce temperature when cold, and to reduce arousal when stimulated.

Other Effects of Neurotensin
Prange and Nemeroff (1982) have marshaled much work which suggests that neurotensin is a dopamine antagonist in the nucleus accumbens, like an antipsychotic drug. Hence it could be a natural antipsychotic. It antagonizes the locomotor stimulating effects of dopamine, amphetamine and cocaine. This implicates the mesolimbic dopamine system (VTA to nucleus accumbens path in Figures 11.5, 11.8 and 11.9). Neurotensin exists in large quantities both in the mesolimbic dopamine cell-body region (ventral tegmental area, VTA) and its terminal area (nucleus accumbens, ACC). The antipsychotic effects are attributed to neurotensin in the ACC.

In the VTA, neurotensin has the opposite effects; it induces behavioral activity and reward (Hoebel, 1984). This will be explained further in the section on self-injection.

In sum, neurotensin can be described as having something generally to do with vegetative, or trophotropic, responses—notably temperature regulation, fat absorption into the intestine, fat disposition in the body and behavioral satiety mediated by the PVN. Lipostasis may be the organizing principle for some of neurotensin's effects. Neurotensin also exists in places such as the thymus gland, adrenal medulla, VTA, ACC and cerebral cortex. What it is doing in these places, and whether this has anything to do with lipostasis, is not clear.

TRH and Calorigenesis

Thyrotropin-releasing hormone (TRH) from the hypothalamus releases thyroid-stimulating hormone (TSH) from the pituitary. Without going into details of thyroid function, we merely ask whether TRH organizes behavior concordant with its physiological effects and thereby defines another motivation system. Recall that angiotensin influences vasopressin and aldosterone in a cascade of effects restoring blood pressure. So also TSH can release prolactin and, in some conditions, can release growth hormone. Therefore TSH, prolactin, and growth hormone may be part of a cascade creating a physiological and psychological pattern. The physiological effects of TSH via the thyroid are increased oxygen consumption and heat production; TSH also facilitates new protein synthesis.

A great deal of evidence suggests that TRH is a neurotransmitter (Prange et al., 1979). It is found in extrahypothalamic as well as hypothalamic areas and can activate an animal even when pituitary TSH is removed. TRH antagonizes a variety of sedatives; TSH does not. TRH injected centrally increases body temperature, breathing, and spontaneous locomotion, and potentiates 1-DOPA induced behavioral stimulation. It also decreases food intake and operant responding for food without interfering with self-stimulation or active avoidance (Prange, Nemeroff, & Lipton, 1978; Andrews & Sahgal, 1983). Some effects are quite different in cats and rats, but in general TRH is an arousing and activating peptide that seems to turn up the body's heat-production mechanism through its direct actions in the brain and its actions via TSH in the body (Myers, 1980). In sum, it is calorigenic or ergotrophic. Thermal production seems to be a raison d'être.

Yarbrough (1983) proposes that many of TRH's functions have to do with regulating cholinergic neurons. This includes cholinergic nerves to the skeletal muscles, the gastrointestinal tract, the pupil, and the thyroid. There are also cholinergic neurons from the striatum to cortex, septum to hippocampus and other brain projections. Therefore in focusing on temperature regulation, I may be picking out a subset of TRH effects that happen to be involved in motivation, while ignoring other effects in the eye and brain. A far-fetched possibility is that all TSH-cholinergic interactions were at one time related to calorigenesis.

Insulin and the Absorptive State

The discovery of satiety-inducing peptides such as CCK, perhaps bombesin (Smith et al., 1982), and neurotensin (Stanley et al., 1983) has redoubled the search for appetite-inducing peptides. Such peptides should cause feeding and metabolic adjustments, just as angiotensin induces drinking and fluid adjustments. Insulin

is a logical candidate because of its role in metabolism and correlation with body weight (Smith, 1984; Le Magnen, 1983; Woods & Porte, 1978). Insulin is a long peptide, a protein. Its effects fit the model of brain-gut peptides, but its size does not. Insulin can induce both feeding and satiety depending on the circumstances. Some of its feeding effects are mediated through glucoprivation in the liver and brain (Smith, 1984). The vagus carries glucostatic information from the liver to the brain for integration (Niijima, 1977). Within the brain, insulin can affect the firing of hypothalamic cells (Oomura, 1980) and the release of norepinephrine (rev. by Hendricks, Roth, Rishi, & Becker, 1983).

Insulin causes a myriad of metabolic effects, almost all of which have to do with distribution, utilization, and storage of carbohydrate, protein, and fat in liver, muscle, and adipose tissue. Peripheral insulin secretion is controlled in part by glucose concentration in the pancreas. Glucose releases insulin which promptly stores away the glucose. Insulin also promotes intracellular metabolism of glucose and other energy-rich molecules. The mere taste or thought of palatable food can release insulin, which may be one of the causes of appetite whetting (Johnson & Wildman, 1983). This anticipatory effect is part of a cephalic-phase response analogous to anticipatory salivation and gastric secretion (Booth, 1980). Just as salivation and gastric secretion can be conditioned in Pavlovian experiments, so can insulin secretion (Woods, 1977).

Insulin's effects in feeding experiments can be confusing. Results depend on the site of injection, the dose, the metabolic state of the animal, and prior experience. In general, insulin first induces appetite and ingestion, then nutrient utilization leading to satiety. However, in diabetic animals insufficient insulin or insulin insensitivity can preclude utilization and lead to paradoxical appetite in the face of hyperglycemia. Conversely, excessive insulin, which causes excessive glucose transport out of the blood stream, can lead to hypoglycemia, feeding, and obesity (Hoebel & Teitelbaum, 1966). However, chronic, mild hyperinsulinemia can reduce body weight (Le Magnen, 1983). In sum, insulin can promote feeding, then make the ingested food satiating, but in the case of insulin-induced hypoglycemia it causes feeding again, and in the case of chronic hyperinsulinemia the brain may compensate leading to weight loss. Thus insulin can be considered a peptide for feeding (Smith, 1984) or for satiety (Stricker, 1982) depending on the metabolic state of the animal. Therefore it is better to look at it as an absorptive-state peptide, because its function is mainly to take in energy from the blood and environment for utilization and storage.

The hormones with the opposite metabolic effect of insulin are epinephrine from the adrenal glands, glucagon from the pancreas, and growth hormone from the pituitary. All three cause carbohydrate and protein to reenter the circulation, and all three are released by a variety of stresses. Insulin is the primary hormone for transporting fuel into cells, for synthesizing tissue (along with growth hormone), and for storing fat; whereas epinephrine is the primary hormone for burning (oxidizing) fuel; therefore Danquier, Nicolaidis, and Le Magnen suggest that insulin predominates during the photoperiod when animals eat and store energy, and epinephrine predominates when animals sleep and live off their stores (rev. by Le Magnen, 1983).

Woods and Porte (1978) point out that basal insulin level as measured in the CSF is directly proportional to body weight. Therefore the brain could receive information about fat stores by monitoring ventricular insulin. Insulin levels in the CSF do not fluctuate with blood levels but remain fairly stable. Therefore, if insulin receptors sample the CSF they could integrate this information into a set point for body weight. Blood-borne factors, on the other hand, may act on insulin receptive cells, glucose receptors, and cells sensitive to glucose utilization that have been described in the hypothalamus. Oomura, Shimizu, Miyahara, and Hattori (1980) cite indirect evidence that these cells also play a role in feeding behavior.

There is no compelling evidence that insulin has a neurotransmitter role, so pursuit of the theory stops here. One might ask, if there is a smaller neuropeptide that could be a neurotransmitter to induce feeding. Growth hormone releasing factor (GRF) is a new possibility (Vaccarino, Bloom, Rivier, Vale, & Koob, 1985). Neuropeptide Y is a sure thing.

Neuropeptide Y and Glucostasis

A recent discovery in the field of feeding research is the tremendous feeding effect of neuropeptide Y (NPY). This is a peptide which coexists with norepinephrine in the sympathetic nervous system (Polak & Bloom, 1984). Knowing that norepinephrine neurons which project to the PVN induce feeding by releasing norepinephrine (Leibowitz, 1980), researchers were led next to inject NPY in that brain region. Less of this peptide was required to induce feeding than any substance ever tested (Stanley & Leibowitz, 1984; Morley & Levine, 1985; Leibowitz & Stanley, 1985). It also made rats drink water.

Norepinephrine injected in the PVN causes a rat to choose high carbohydrate foods. Under natural conditions norepinephrine may be responsible for high carbohydrate intake at the beginning of the nighttime feeding period in rats (Leibowitz, In press a). Similarly, NPY causes rats to select a high carbohydrate diet. Thus NPY is a candidate for studies of carbohydrate metabolism in the periphery based on the integrative peptide theory. Instead of predicting brain function on the basis of gut function, the theory might be useful in reverse, from brain to gut.

ACTH and Stress

Hypothalamic corticotropin-releasing factor (CRF) releases adrenocorticotrophic hormone (ACTH), also called adrenocorticotropin or corticotropin, which is a neuropeptide with a global function in sympathetic arousal. ACTH-containing cells are found in the anterior pituitary, ventromedial hypothalamus, and adrenal medulla (Nemeroff & Dunn, 1984). ACTH travels from the anterior pituitary in the blood to the adrenal medulla where it releases the well-known stimulant epinephrine (adrenalin) and the adrenal corticoids, such as corticosterone. This steroid is called a *glucocorticoid* to distinguish it from the *mineralocorticoid*, aldosterone, which controls sodium level as described earlier. Glucocorticoids, such as cortisol and corticosterone, promote the breakdown of protein into amino acids and conversion to glucose. Cortisol promotes effects of pancreatic glucagon and inhibits the effects of insulin. Thus cortisol raises blood-sugar levels to feed the brain, and raises amino-acid levels for tissue repair and energy. CRF inhibits feeding (Koob & Bloom, 1985; Morley & Levine, 1985). These effects are appropriate for a stressful situation and are essential during migration, flights, or threats that force the animal to forgo eating. An animal that is injured releases cortisol which catabolizes (cannibalizes) body protein, and the animal lives in a state called *stress*.

Novel situations, conditioned emotional responses, social defeat, crowding and conflict situations have all been shown to raise epinephrine and cortisol levels. We can trace cortisol release back to ACTH release and note that beta-endorphin is coreleased with ACTH. Both are under the control of corticotropin releasing factor, CRF (Krieger et al., 1983).

Vasopressin (VP) also releases ACTH and beta-endorphin; VP acts synergistically with CRF and adrenergic agonists in the process. Thus one of the body-fluid integrating peptides can tap into the CRF-controlled system and thereby arouse the peripheral sympathetic system via adrenal stress hormones. VP and CRF gradually desensitize the CRF receptors in the pituitary, so their effects are self-limiting. In addition there is negative feedback from the adrenal hormones that are released (Axelrod & Reisine, 1984).

ACTH has been extensively studied in learning, memory, and motivation tasks including imprinting (Koob & Bloom, 1985; Martinez et al., 1981). The first 13 amino acids of the 39 in ACTH can be split off to form melanocyte-stimulating hormone (alpha-MSH). This and other shorter fragments of ACTH restore certain learning capabilities of rats even after removal of the pituitary with its store of ACTH (Nemeroff & Dunn, 1984). In normal rats ACTH 4-10 enhanced a conditioned taste aversion without causing an adrenal stress response (Smotherman & Levine, 1980). Unfortunately there is no proof that ACTH fragments act as neurotransmitters in brain mechanisms; however, it makes sense that peptides will be found which coordinate the ACTH and beta-endorphin response with an alert mind and behavioral readiness needed during stress.

Some of the same stress factors which release ACTH and beta-endorphin from the pituitary also activate the neural output that triggers epinephrine release from the adrenal medulla and norepinephrine from sympathetic nerves. The ratio of epinephrine to norepinephrine appearing in the blood has been correlated with various types of stress and the "A" versus "B" type person (Axelrod & Reisine, 1984). It is interesting that noradrenaline cells in the locus

coeruleus (LC) have been found to enhance the responsiveness of visual sensory cells in the cortex (Figure 11.8) and other neural mechanisms throughout the brain (Aston-Jones & Bloom, 1981). Attention and alertness are the terms sometimes used to describe this noradrenergic function. Jacobs (1986) suggests that their function might be better described as a response to noxious stimuli and stress. Activation of such a stress system may manifest itself as anxiety, and indeed Jacobs' group reports that minor tranquilizers quiet these noradrenergic cells in the LC. Cells in the ventromedial hypothalamus that contain endorphin and ACTH project to the LC, thereby unifying these stress related systems.

Learned Helplessness

Liebeskind (personal communication) reports that stress caused by footshock of a type that will cause learned helplessness will also cause immune suppression and increase the odds of losing a battle with cancer. These effects are naloxone blockable and therefore opiate in nature. Apparently some stresses leave the animal helpless and immunologically weak after strong sympathetic arousal.

In summary, the integrative function of ACTH seems to be a stress or alarm response that involves stimulation of both adrenal and brain catecholamines. Given that beta-endorphin is released along with ACTH it is logical to suppose that endorphinergic pain suppression and endorphinergic social attachment are part of this coping response (Panksepp, 1983).

Opioids in Stress and Feeding

One of the greatest discoveries in physiological psychology was that electrical stimulation of the midbrain central gray area suppresses pain. When psychologists discovered that this was reversed by the opiate blocker, naloxone, they concluded that brain stimulation releases opioids (Liebeskind & Paul, 1977). Demonstration of opiate receptors in the brain confirmed that there might be an endogenous opioid for the receptors. Biochemists reported the isolation of endogenous morphine-like factors. There appeared to be two pentapeptides, later given the names methionine enkephalin and leucine enkephalin, in addition to a larger 31 amino acid peptide, beta-endorphin. Then alpha-

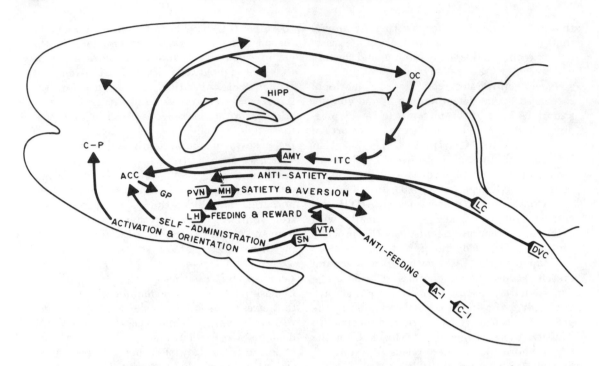

Figure 11.8. Some of the regions, pathways, and functions involved in feeding and its reinforcement as described in this chapter. (1) First is an unlabeled system for preparedness (attention, stress, anxiety): locus coeruleus (LC) to frontal cortex (FC), hippocampus (HIPP), and optic cortex (OC). (2) Sensory feature detection is illustrated: optic cortex to infratemporal cortex (ITC) to the amygdala (AMY). (3) The nigrostriatal path is labeled "activation and orientation"; substantia nigra (SN) to caudato-putamen (C-P) for response to stress and novelty and for disinhibiting premotor circuitry involved in stereotypy and warm up for recruiting locomotion and operant responses. The following additional sequence would theoretically be sufficient for feeding to occur. (4) Antisatiety: inhibition of satiety involving increased activity in the dorsal vagal complex (DVC) and other noradrenergic inputs to the paraventricular nucleus (PVN) and medial hypothalamus (MH). (5) Satiety and aversion: eating can be induced by decreased PVN and MH output. (6) Antifeeding: decreased activity in an ascending pathway from norepinephrine, e.g. (A-1), or epinephrine (C-1) cell groups disinhibits LH feeding and reward. (7) Feeding and reward: medial forebrain bundle, including lateral hypothalamic (LH) inputs to the ventral tegmental area (VTA) and other sites for enhancing food-related responses and their repetition. (8) Self-administration: VTA and other dopamine inputs to the nucleus accumbens (ACC) facilitate inputs such as the one shown from the AMY and outputs to the ventral globus pallidus (GP) for locomotion and reinforcement. Findings from this laboratory include: (a) 6-OHDA destruction of the antifeeding pathway increases feeding and self-stimulation; (b) neurotensin suppresses norepinephrine-induced feeding in the PVN; (c) the CCK blocker, proglumide, induces feeding in the PVN; (d) enkephalin also prolongs feeding in the PVN, presumably by suppression of satiety and aversion, but the effect is delayed; (e) enkephalin and neurotensin induce reward in the VTA; (f) rats self-inject amphetamine in the ACC, (g) LH self-stimulation varies with appetite, and (h) LH stimulation, feeding and stimulant drugs increase extracellular dopamine in the ACC. From "Neurotransmitters in the Control of Feeding and Its Rewards: Monoamines, Opiates and Brain-Gut Peptides" by B.G. Hoebel, 1984, in *Eating and Its Disorders, 62*, p. 17, Association for Research on Nervous and Mental Disease, New York: Raven Press. Copyright 1984 by Raven Press. Reprinted by permission.

neoendorphin, other fragments, and most recently, dynorphin were isolated (rev. by Koob, Le Moal, & Bloom, 1984). It is becoming the convention to refer to these endogenous compounds as 'opioids,' rather than 'opiates.'

Systemic injection of morphine first suppresses feeding, then increases it. With repeated injections and the development of tolerance to aversive effects, the feeding effect is enhanced and occurs sooner after the injection. Under the influence of morphine animals accept a wide range of tastes and eat for a long time once they start (Reid & Sivy, 1983). Conversely systemic injections of low doses of naloxone suppressed food intake of genetically obese rodents that had a natural excess of beta-endorphin and excess body fat (Margules, Moisset, Lewis, Shibuya, & Pert, 1978).

Studies using central injections also suggest a role for opioids in feeding. Intraventricular morphine or a long-lasting enkephalin analogue increased food intake (Belluzzi & Stein, 1982). Morphine injected into the VMH or PVN induced feeding (Grandison & Guidotti, 1977; Leibowitz & Hor, 1982; Tepperman, Hirst, & Gourdey, 1981). An enkephalin analogue, d-ala-met-enkephalinamide (DALA), injected into the PVN produced a dose-dependent increase in feeding after 45 minutes (McLean & Hoebel, 1983). Naloxone injected into the PVN reversed the effect. DALA increased water intake only when food was available, suggesting the primary effect was on feeding.

Several opiate-receptor types have been discovered; mu, delta, and kappa types are well characterized. All are blocked by naloxone, a fact used to good advantage in thousands of biochemical and behavioral tests. Naloxone may have other effects as well (Grevel & Sadee, 1983). The mu and delta agonists such as morphine, beta-endorphin and enkephalin all induce feeding (Cooper & Sanger, 1984; Mucha & Iverson, 1986). There is also evidence that kappa agonists can increase feeding when injected in the ventricles (Morley, Levine, Yim & Lowy, 1983), PVN, lateral hypothalamus or midbrain VTA. The endogenous kappa agonist is dynorphin. There is a good chance that the endogenous agonists, endorphins, enkephalins, and dynorphin play different roles in various aspects of feeding. The details remain a puzzle.

Reinforcing Effects of Opiates

An interesting problem for psychologists lies in the addictive nature of opiate reinforcers. We know that endorphin is coreleased with pituitary ACTH in response to CRF during stress, so perhaps certain kinds of stress are addictive. Witness the long-distance runner. It was also discovered that dynorphin coexists with vasopressin (Whitnall, Gainer, Cox, & Molineaux, 1983). Therefore it would appear that some of the homeostatic functions of vasopressin neurons may be addictive because an opiate peptide is coreleased with the nonopiate peptide.

Self-administration of opiates and nonopiate peptides will be described in the next section. Another way to show opioid reward is to block reinforcement with antagonists. Here are a few intriguing examples (from Cooper & Sanger, 1984; Hoebel & Novin, 1982; Morley et al., 1983). Naloxone can block a rat's preference for sweet tastes. When regular rat food was used, naloxone caused rapid termination of meals, that is, satiety. It also reduced stress induced avidity for salty tastes. Again, in the lateral hypothalamus where stimulation induces feeding and reward (Hoebel, 1976; 1979), naloxone diminished deprivation induced potentiation of feeding-reward (Carr & Simon, 1983). If these findings can be generalized to humans, we should not expect naloxone to suppress feeding unless the patients are deprived, or the test food is very palatable. This conclusion fits with the overall perception from pain studies that naloxone does nothing unless the endogenous opioid system is driven. Naloxone therapy for obesity has not been very successful except in rare diseases (Morley et al., 1983).

Exorphins

Opiates are found in food (rev. Morley et al., 1983). In addition to the infamous extract of poppy, opiate peptides have been found in milk and hydrolysates of casein, for example, beta-casomorphin. These food products could have analgesic potency if they were to escape digestion. Opiates injected into baby chicks calmed their distress at being separated from the mother hen (Panksepp et al., 1983). Therefore some foods may turn out to be rewards in part because they chemically reduce anxiety, stress, or discomfort.

Several interesting integrative theories of opioid function have been offered. The opiate-related combination of stress, analgesia, and feeding led Margules (1979) to suggest a role for opioids in preparation for famine or hibernation. Similarly, Reid and Siviy (1983) call it a global response to starvation including suppression of pain and distress for far-ranging foraging, intake of unpalatable food and gorging on palatable food. Margules suggests that an opposing set of naloxone-like peptides in the brain ready the animal for energy expenditure as in mating. Morley et al. (1983) suggest opioids might be involved in self-preservation and self-sacrifice for species preservation. The hypothesis that opioids are involved in altruistic behavior or any response that matches expectation to outcome has been discussed in the context of sociobiology and law (Hoebel, 1982). I suspect fewer functions will be attributed to opioids as we learn how other peptides can also reinforce behavior (Hoebel, 1984).

LHRH and Reproductive Functions

Angiotensin was the foundation of the integrative peptide theory; leutinizing hormone releasing hormone (LHRH) is the capstone. LHRH is a hypothalamic neuropeptide released into the anterior pituitary to liberate leutinizing hormone (LH) and trigger ovulation. Axonal branches containing LHRH extend to other parts of the brain where LHRH induces behavioral readiness in estrogen-primed females. Estrogen is a sex steroid accumulated by cells in the ventromedial hypothalamus which, as a result, become increasingly excitable and potentiate reflexes for sexual postures (Pfaff, 1982). LHRH induces the female sexual posture when injected into the ventromedial hypothalamus or midbrain. This is a clear case of coordinated physiological and behavioral readiness produced by a peptide.

This hormone of sex and sexuality may also work in males of some species. LHRH given subcutaneously to male rats with normal testosterone levels reduced the time needed to achieve ejaculation (Moss & Dudley, 1984; Shivers, Harland, & Pfaff, 1983). In sum, it might be the brain's aphrodisiac.

More Peptides
This section has been a selective review of neuropeptides chosen to explain the pros and cons of the integrative-peptide theory. There are more peptides and more studies than could possibly be incorporated into this section or this theory. For further reference some of the large collections of peptide research are listed (Hughes, 1978; Liebeskind et al., 1979; Costa & Trabucchi, 1980; Lombardini & Kenny, 1980; Martin, Reichlin, & Bick, 1981; Iversen et al., 1983; Krieger et al., 1983; Nemeroff & Dunn, 1984).

MODELS OF MOTIVATION: SELF-STIMULATION AND SELF-INJECTION IN SELF-CONTROL OF NEURAL PATHWAYS

Hypothalamic Stimulation

The new theory that some peptides link physiology to behavior should relate to the old theory that reward-aversion systems link physiology to behavior (Hoebel, 1976; 1979). If both theories are correct, integrative peptides should have predictable effects on reward-aversion systems.

Self-stimulation is a model of motivation in the sense that it is not natural motivation. Whatever we learn from electrically manipulating the brain will be a caricature based on the exaggerated features we draw from the data. Whereas lesions can happen naturally, brain stimulation cannot. Nevertheless, brain stimulation has proven to be a useful tool, first in the laboratory and then in the clinic. People use self-stimulation to suppress chronic pain. In animals the self-stimulation model has been used primarily to study reward.

For background reading on brain stimulation the reader is referred to three major collections of work, *Brain Stimulation Reward* (Wauquier & Rolls, 1976), *The Neural Basis of Feeding and Reward* (Hoebel & Novin, 1982) and *Brain Reward Systems and Abuse* (Engel & Oreland, 1987). Other pertinent books include those by Rolls (1975), Olds (1977), Valenstein (1974), Mogenson (1977) and Stellar and Stellar (1985). The field started with the discovery that brain stimulation could induce motivated behavior (Hess, 1954), reward (Olds & Milner, 1954) and aversion (Delgado, Roberts, & Miller, 1954). We found that a single electrode could produce all three (e.g., stimulation-induced feeding, self-stimulation and stimulation-escape), and all three could vary with physiological states (Hoebel, 1976, 1979). It is interesting to ask why one electrode can induce behavior, reward, and aversion. The simplest answer is still the best answer. Natural stimuli such as food or sexual stimuli can do all three, and brain stimulation can mimic those natural stimuli. For example, food induces feeding, food reinforces behavior and food becomes aversive when the animal is overfull or overweight. Hypothalamic stimulation and food probably have similar effects on the brain. If this is the case, then researchers can study motivation and reinforcement by studying hypothalamic stimulation.

Olds (1977) reviews his evidence that castrated male rats would self-stimulate more rapidly at certain electrodes on days when injected with androgen to create a sex drive, and they would prefer other electrodes on days when they were food deprived to make them hungry. Similarly, rats given a choice may choose one electrode for self-stimulation when food deprived and another electrode when water deprived (Gallistel & Beagley, 1971). Moreover injections of androgen or insulin affected different self-stimulation electrodes in the same rat (Hoebel, 1979; Hernandez & Hoebel, 1978). Thus it appears that different self-stimulation sites can be sensitive to different physiological needs.

Mating-Reward Hypothesis

A basic postulate of sex research is that mating behavior reflects the interplay of behavior, environment, and hormones as they change over time (Adler & Allen, 1983; Pfaff, 1982; Shivers et al., 1983). Sex hormones can alter the sensitivity of erogenous zones on the body (Adler & Allen, 1983) and also increase number, size, and functions of brain neurons for receiving and sending mating signals. Brain stimulation experiments in which we manipulated androgen level suggested that there can be an increase in the behavior reinforcement function of neurons excited by an electrode that elicits mating behavior (Caggiula & Hoebel, 1966). In the posterior hypothalamus self-stimulation decreased with castration and increased with testosterone-replacement therapy. During self-stimulation semen was released, and continuous stimulation in the presence of an estrous female induced copulation. The anatomical overlap of a site for testosterone-sensitive self-stimulation and stimulation-induced copulation suggested a copulation-reward hypothesis. This hypothesis states that the operant reward and respondent behavior systems for copulation are the same or closely linked when excited by the hypothalamic electrode. In other words, it appears as if a single neural system at the electrode tip reinforces operant behavior (lever pressing), and elicits both ejaculatory reflexes and mating behavior (on film: Hoebel, Rosenquist, & Caggiula, 1969). At the present time there is no proof that the electrode stimulates one type of neuron

that causes both self-stimulation and mating. A single electrode may stimulate a natural circuit at more than one place by exciting one system both antidromically and orthodromically or by exciting two adjacent system.

Feeding-Reward Hypothesis

In the case of feeding the argument is the same. It is axiomatic that feeding is coupled with environmental cues and internal processes, both metabolic and experiential (Booth, 1980; Bray & York, 1979; Hernandez & Hoebel, 1978, 1980). Therefore it is interesting that hypothalamic self-stimulation can be increased by food deprivation or good-tasting food and then decreased by a meal (Hoebel, 1979; Olds, 1977). This suggested that such electrodes stimulate a system that couples taste and internal chemoreceptive input with operant behavior output. The way to identify an electrode site where self-stimulation will vary with food intake is to find an electrode that induces feeding. The lateral hypothalamus near the fornix is a good place to obtain this effect. This is the same region where catecholaminergic appetite suppressants are known to act (Leibowitz, 1980). Apparently perifornical LH stimulation excites a feeding-reward system; the anorectic drugs inhibit it.

Self-Induced Obesity

It must be emphasized that electrical stimulation can both prod the animal into action and reinforce prior actions. The phenomenon is illustrated by the following example. Lateral hypothalamic stimulation which lasted 30 seconds provoked a rat to eat a 45 mg food pellet delivered automatically. The same stimulation reinforced bar pressing. Then by letting the rat press the lever for both stimulation and a pellet, the animal was voluntarily trapped in a bulimic binge of pressing for stimulation which induced eating and then pressing for more food, hence more stimulation and more eating. The result of this program 22 hours per day was twice normal food intake and self-induced obesity (Hoebel, 1979). Clearly the combination of hypothalamic stimulation, food and bar pressing can be extraordinarily motivating and rewarding, even when an animal is overweight. The effect is similar to obesity induced by very palatable diets (Sclafani, 1980). This led to the conclusion that perifornical lateral hypothalamic stimulation is like palatable food in inducing both appetite and reward (Figure 11.8).

Feeding Reward and Mating Reward in the Same Rat

Two male rats were trained to self-stimulate at both lateral hypothalamic and posterior hypothalamic electrodes that elicited feeding and mating, respectively. They were given experience eating during stimulation of one electrode and mating with the other, then were castrated. Self-stimulation showed a decrement at only the mating-linked electrode. The feeding related electrode was immune to the effects of castration in the same rat, even though precisely the same operant response was required on the same lever. Conversely, in other experiments a decrement in feeding reward, not mating reward, was caused by an over-the- counter appetite suppressant drug, phenylpropanolamine (Hoebel, 1980), or an anorectic dose of insulin (Hernandez & Hoebel, 1978). Clearly both electrodes reinforced the same motor programs for lever pressing, but the effects of stimulation at one electrode were modulated by feeding stimuli, and at the other electrode by sex stimuli.

Priming

In the tradition of Deutsch's (1976) two factor drive-reinforcement theory, Gallistel used a runway to separate priming in the start box as a measure of drive, from bar pressing in the goal box as a measure of reinforcement. Brain stimulation delivered in the start box accelerated subsequent running to reach a self-stimulation lever. Any self-stimulation electrode could be used to prime approach to any other self-stimulation electrode (Gallistel, Shizgal, & Yeomans, 1981). Thus stimulation primed the animal to work for more of the same stimulation a short time later. However, the same priming inhibited running to get food (Stellar & Stellar, 1985). A few seconds after the current went off, stimulation was still rewarding, but food was not.

Rebound Inhibition

Ongoing feeding, drinking, or mating can be inhibited, as if by rebound, when hypothalamic stimulation is turned off (Valenstein, 1974). This suggests that hypothalamic stimulation induces behavior in part by inhibiting satiety, because when current goes off satiety is disinhibited. In

spite of this, there is the enduring facilitation of approach behavior to get stimulation. This suggests there can be at least six response effects underlying hypothalamic self-stimulation: (1) arousal and approach tendencies, (2) response reinforcement, (3) consummatory behavior such as feeding, (4) inhibition of satiety, (5) post-stimulation disinhibition of satiety, and (6) residual arousal and approach tendencies.

Reward as Preference Induction and Memory Enhancement

It is not known how the reinforcement system determines which response is rewarded (Halperin & Pfaff, 1982). Routtenberg (1980) suggests that stimulation at some sites disrupts past learning and memory, but immediately prior events might be particularly well reinforced. Hypothalamic stimulation which follows a novel coffee taste can create a preference for the novel taste (Ettenberg & White, 1978). In a totally different setting, stimulation after avoidance learning can facilitate learning to avoid the pain (Huston et al., 1977). Therefore stimulation at various sites can make animals remember a novel taste as a preferred taste and remember how to avoid being shocked. Huston et al. (1977) suggest that a short-term memory trace is itself like an operant, and that conventional reinforcers or lateral hypothalamic stimulation reinforce the memory trace. However, in the case of the coffee taste, stimulation did more than reinforce the recent memory; it also gave it a positive valence so the rat came to prefer that flavor. Therefore it seems that rewarding stimulation can reinforce a memory and also associate sensory input with positive outcomes to create a preference. It follows that any natural food which had neural effects like hypothalamic electrodes in these experiments would be an arouser, an appetite whetter, an inhibitor of satiety, a preferred food, and a remembered food.

Stimulation Escape and its Relation to Satiety

In the MH self-stimulation is slow or lacking entirely; instead animals will work to turn the current off. MH stimulation caused monkeys to spit out food they were eating (Robinson & Mishkin, 1968). Rats given MH stimulation when satiated showed behavioral signs of food rejection, such as chin rubbing (Figure 11.4;

Hoebel, 1976). At some sites in between the LH and MH, rats both turn stimulation on and turn it off. The relative preponderance of self-stimulation relative to stimulation escape at a midhypothalamic (perifornical LH) site can be shifted by a large meal, phenylpropanolamine, or insulin (Hernandez & Hoebel, 1978). Thus metabolic variables modulate not only stimulation approach, but also escape behavior.

There are many physiological and endocrine changes which can be induced with brain stimulation (Wauquier & Rolls, 1976). Some of these changes such as insulin and glucose level will be signaled back to the hypothalamus by way of the vagus and blood-borne stimuli. This physiological feedback is surely an important factor in the behavioral results of hypothalamic stimulation.

Systemic CCK suppressed self-stimulation nonspecifically (Kornblith, Ervin, & King, 1978; Ettenberg & Koob, 1984), but this could be due to an effect in the nucleus accumbens (Vaccarino & Koob, 1984). CCK can also suppress stimulation-escape (Hoebel, unpublished). The same was true of the serotonergic appetite suppressant, d,l-fenfluramine; it suppressed both self-stimulation and escape (Hoebel, 1980). Amphetamine, on the other hand, increased both. This points up the disadvantage of response rate as a measure of reinforcement (Leibman, 1983), but it also illustrates that self-stimulation and escape rate can be used together to detect overall depression or overall hyperkinesis. When an appetite suppressant such as phenylpropanolamine or d-fenfluramine decreases self-stimulation rate, but not escape rate, this suggests a decrease in feeding reward independent of overall changes in arousal (Hoebel, Hernandez, McClelland & Schwartz, In press).

Behavior Switching

Valenstein (1974) reviews work showing that during LH stimulation rats will switch behaviors if there are a variety of things to catch their attention. They eat, drink, gnaw, mate, run in a wheel, hoard, kill mice, or do other things best predicted by past experience, the environment, or other individual and ecological idiosyncracies (Hoebel, 1976; Panksepp, 1982; Valenstein, 1980). There is a component of stimulation that is no more specific than pinching the rat's tail; these procedures produce an activated state in which animals learn to respond to objects in the environment (Fray, Koob, & Iversen, 1982)

Stimulated animals may switch from feeding to drinking, rather than switch from one food to another. Thus the stimulation can bypass or overwhelm homeostatic concerns. Moreover feeding is often obtained at many electrode sites in a single rat or monkey, which argues against localization of function (Valenstein, 1980). Response prepotency is the idea used to describe the nonspecific aspects of stimulation induced behaviors. Valenstein proposes that the elicited behaviors are not governed by the same rules that govern behavior employed in the homeostatic regulation of tissue needs; he suggests that elicited behavior is not motivated by a natural drive state. The behavior is in a sense schizophrenic (Valenstein, 1980). Antelman and Chiodo (1983) document that the physiological and stereotypic effects of electrical stimulation can be similar to those produced by a variety of drug and environmental stressors. In addition, priming is nonspecific (Gallistel et al., 1981), and animals are reinforced for anything they do during stimulation, which helps to explain why they do many things.

Other data, which were obtained in a different way, suggest that many of the homeostatic rules can apply. We found that intragastric intubation of water inhibited stimulation-induced drinking, but not eating (Devor, Wise, Milgram, & Hoebel, 1970); whereas intragastric feeding inhibited stimulation-induced feeding (Berthoud & Baettig, 1974), but not drinking. The findings of Valenstein's group and mine are reconciled by the suggestion that stimulation does not mimic a deprivation state; it mimics appetitive states that can be modulated by deprivation. In colloquial terms, stimulation does not induce hunger, it induces appetites (Hoebel, 1976). Collier and Rovee-Collier (1983) point out that animals are seldom deprived. They anticipate their needs and satisfy them before severe deprivation occurs. Stimulation-induced behaviors may mimic some of the animal's efforts at foraging (Toates & Halliday, 1980). Perhaps rats fed ad libitum eat during stimulation to meet the commands of a set of sensory, cognitive and behavior conditions determined by the pathways stimulated and their synaptic thresholds as modulated by circulating nutrients, peptides, monoamines, and other internal factors, including stimulation-induced memories and preferences.

As mentioned before, the problem with

stimulation is that it may activate cell bodies, descending paths, and ascending paths. To make matters worse it sends nerve impulses both orthodromically and antidromically, thus invading distant cell bodies as well as distant terminals. The fact that behavior occurs at all, and occurs under homeostatic modulation, is evidence that the brain imposes some order on the abnormal situation created by electricity. As illustrated in the first section we can begin to understand what the brain is doing by simplifying the situation. One approach is to record from single cells; another is to shut down some of the stimulated systems. This can be done with lesions such as MH lesions, neurotoxins such as 6-hydroxydopamine, or drugs such as pimozide. Each of these approaches to self-stimulation will be illustrated.

Effect of MH Lesions on LH Reward and Aversion

If electrodes are properly placed in the LH to elicit feeding as well as self-stimulation, then MH lesions cause the self-stimulation rate to change parallel to the time course of hyperphagia (Hernandez & Hoebel, 1978; Hoebel, 1979). MH lesions could augment self-stimulation in many ways, such as by (1) disinhibiting feeding-reward, (2) reducing satiety and aversion, (3) causing nonspecific arousal (Grossman, 1979), (4) increasing anticipatory feeding reflexes in the mouth and gut (Powley, Opsahl, Cox, & Weingarten, 1980), or (5) directly and indirectly altering insulin release and metabolism (Bray & York, 1979; Stricker, 1983b).

MH lesions that increase self-stimulation can decrease the rate of stimulation-escape from the same midlateral (perifornical) electrode. Therefore by definition, MH lesions increase reward and decrease aversion. Relatively little is known about the aversive component of LH stimulation. Shizgal and Matthews (1977) suggest that aversion builds up during prolonged stimulus trains. Our evidence shows that postingestional satiety factors can potentiate the aversion when train length is held constant, and MH lesions can markedly decrease satiety and aversion, at least until the animal becomes obese. I suspect this aversive component is normally involved in inhibiting feeding and setting body weight at a particular level. The aversive component of the neural system may be activated directly by the stimulating electrode,

or it may be an indirect opponent process (Solomon, 1982) which opposes the reward component. In any case, the behavioral manifestations of MH lesions are mediated in part by a shift in the reward-aversion interaction such that aversion is not sufficient to balance reward until the rat becomes fatter.

Presumably aversion is a function of neurochemical, hormonal, and metabolic inputs to the systems affected by the stimulation. We know that if a normal rat is forced to gain weight, then self-stimulation decreases and stimulation-escape can increase. Some correlate of being fat suppresses the reward and fosters aversion. It follows that mechanisms that control body weight can act by way of this reward-aversion system. There is a shift from reward to aversion as the animal gets full or fat. This appears to be a sliding set point analogous to the one discussed for feeding behavior in the blowfly. We suggest that MH lesions can elevate the body weight level (set point) at which this shift occurs. The MH-damaged rats overeat, just as they over self-stimulate and under-escape, until they become obese.

To summarize, hypothalamic stimulation near the fornix primes an animal to run to get more stimulation; it causes eating or other behaviors during stimulation, and halts eating afterwards; it also causes a reward and an aversion that vary directly with appetite and vary inversely with each other. To obtain these effects it is necessary to use low rates of responding, electrodes that induce feeding, and manipulations that do not cause overall hyperkinesis or hypokinesis. MH lesions appear to raise the body weight level at which feeding-reward and feeding-aversion come into balance.

A Prediction

On the basis of the prior discussion of integrative peptides, one could predict that some peptides will selectively affect stimulation-induced behavior and self-stimulation. We have already shown that this is the case for insulin (Hernandez & Hoebel, 1978), and it should also be true for some of the shorter peptides. For example, angiotensin should enhance electrically induced drinking, not eating. NPY should potentiate induced feeding and drinking, and LHRH mating. CCK should suppress stimulated eating, but not drinking, unless the dose causes overall lethargy. CRF or other sympathetic peptides might affect the nonspecific arousal component of elicited behaviors. Similarly, self-stimulation should be preferred and potentiated at drinking sites with angiotensin, at feeding and drinking sites with NPY, and at mating sites with LHRH.

Recording from Feeding-Reward Cells

Some lateral hypothalamic neurons in the unanesthetized monkey have electrical firing patterns congruent with the feeding-reward hypothesis (Rolls, Burton, & Mora, 1980). These neurons responded to the taste of food or a discriminative stimulus that had been paired with food. The cells were only responsive when the monkey was willing to eat the food. The neural response preceded and predicted behavioral feeding responses. Stimulation-induced eating was observed with trains of stimulation applied through the rewarding electrode. The monkeys would also self-stimulate, but when enough food was consumed to inhibit feeding, then self-stimulation was inhibited too (Rolls, 1975, 1981). Nishino, Ono, Fukuda, & Sasaki (1982) categorized three types of lateral hypothalamic feeding-related neurons in monkeys. One type responded to the sight of food, another to food in the mouth, and a third responded to food sight, food taste, and also bar pressing for food. Again satiation eliminated responsiveness. Similar results recording from LH cells during feeding and self-stimulation have been obtained in rats (Ono, Sasaki, Nakamura, & Norgren, 1985).

These cellular effects correspond to our behavioral data in rats. They suggest that LH cell bodies, not just fibers of passage, are involved in self-stimulation, and these same cells are sensitive to the animals' homeostatic state.

In monkeys, potent self-stimulation sites were found in parts of the frontal cortex (rev. Cooper, 1981), thalamus, nucleus accumbens, amygdala, and lateral hypothalamus. This agrees with rat self-stimulation maps (Clavier & Routtenberg, 1980). In addition, the trigeminal sensory system (Jacquin & Enfiejian, 1982) and motor system (Van Der Kooy & Phillips, 1977) may be a substrate for self-stimulation in rats. In some cases self-stimulation depends on an intact vagus (rev. Panksepp, 1983). Therefore some of the modulating influences observed in hypothalamic recording studies may arrive via cranial nerve systems as well as brain chemosensitive circuits. Of great importance was the

observation with monkeys that several of the self-stimulation sites were interconnected. Stimulating one could activate neurons in another. For example, the feeding-reward neurons in the hypothalamus (described above) could be influenced by stimulation of the nucleus accumbens (Rolls, 1981). Thus there is hope of finding an interconnected self-stimulation system (Wise & Bozarth, 1984). On the other hand, not all self-stimulation sites were interconnected, and many had no observed relation to feeding at all. These other systems are presumably somewhat separate (A.G. Phillips, 1984) and related to stimuli and behaviors other than cuisine and eating.

In sum, it is likely that some of the nutrient-sensitive cells in the hypothalamus are feeding-reward cells and have a role in both physiology and behavior (Oomura et al., 1982). The behavioral role seems to involve a change in the rate of firing when food is anticipated, seen, or tasted. Many of these cells stop their feeding-related activity during satiety.

Lesions and Stimulation in Light of Recording

Electricity stimulates thousands of lateral hypothalamic cells and axons passing through the region. We know from recording studies that there are cells in the LH that normally change their rate of firing when the animal sights food, tastes it, recalls prior experience with food-related discriminative stimuli, or engages in the act of bar pressing for food. Therefore it may be that stimulation is effective not just because it generates nerve impulses, but also because it generates an informational change in the rate of impulses. Whatever the cell's normal rate, it will change during electrical stimulation onset, and again at offgo. Both the English and Japanese monkey studies suggest that changes in firing rate tend to disappear as the animal becomes satiated. Clearly satiety depotentiates these cells. It decreases their responsiveness to rewarding or appetite whetting stimuli. Satiety may decrease their responsiveness to electrical stimulation. Perhaps that is the neural basis of what we report as homeostatic control of stimulation-induced feeding and self-stimulation.

The behaviorally nonspecific effects of stimulation may be due in part to the power of stimulation to overwhelm the mechanisms that normally depotentiate cellular responsiveness.

When many cells related to different behaviors are forced into activity at once, a rat may temporarily appear unsatiated for everything—food pellets, powdered food, water, running, and so on. Nevertheless, according to the recording studies there are in fact lateral hypothalamic cells that are tuned to specific food preferences and sensory specific satiety. Therefore the behavioral effects of hypothalamic stimulation are not entirely owing to non-specific mechanisms.

These findings also rule out the argument that all lesion-induced feeding deficits are due to fibers of passage. Fibers passing by, such as the dopaminergic neurons, may be necessary for the normal function of the cells recorded and for switching from one set to another, but there is no doubt that hypothalamic cell bodies related to feeding do exist, and would be damaged by hypothalamic lesions.

Another inference can be drawn from modern recording studies. Aversion, food rejection, and stimulation-escape may all be in a system different from reward and self-stimulation. Neither the groups in England nor in Japan reported cells that were affected one way during food acceptance and the other way during food rejection. Instead the cells just stopped responding. For example, a cell described in detail by Rolls responded to the taste of syrup as a direct function of the amount of syrup ingested during tube feeding, even though the monkey's behavior switched from avid ingestion to rejection halfway through the tube-fed meal. Thus the cells that mediate grimacing, food-escape and stimulation-escape might be somewhere else. Given Oomura's evidence for MH cells with properties opposite to LH cells, and the well-known evidence for MH and PVN satiety functions, I suspect that the aversion cells are in the MH-PVN region. If so, the shift from self-stimulation to stimulation escape which we saw in force-fed or overweight rats was a shift from a predominance of LH signals to MH-PVN signals (Figure 11.8).

Hedonic Ratings

We cannot tell if a fly that shifts from proboscis protrusion to retraction over the course of a sugar meal is giving a hedonic rating. We cannot judge jaundiced joy in an *Aplysia* that shifts from eating seaweed to rejecting it, nor in a decerebrate rat that shifts from a "smile" to a "grimace," nor in a wired rat that shifts from self-stimulation to stimulation-escape. Hedonic ratings might conceivably be attributed to the facial expressions and cellular responses of the monkey described above as it lost its appetite for sugar syrup. But to do it correctly one has to do it in people, and of course it works. Sugar switches from pleasant to unpleasant over the course of a meal of sucrose (Cabanac, 1971).

Psychophysical Studies of Self-stimulation Axons

What are the physical characteristics of a reward neuron? Just as one can use electrical stimulation and a motor response (muscle twitch) to determine neural refractory period and conduction velocity in a frog's sciatic nerve, these parameters can also be measured within the brain by stimulating a fiber bundle and by measuring the self-stimulation response (Gallistel, 1981). Shizgal, Kiss, & Bielajew (1982) placed two electrodes in the medial forebrain bundle at a lateral and a posterior hypothalamic site. Pairs of pulses were used for stimulation with one pulse applied to each electrode. Rats self-administered a train of pulse pairs under this condition. Conduction direction was determined by producing an anodal block with one of the two electrodes that stopped the action potentials coming towards it from the other electrode. When this happened the animal would self-stimulate at half its prior rate. This showed which electrode was downstream to the other. To measure conduction velocity, the interval between pulses at the two electrodes was varied. When the interpulse interval was long, two orthodromic action potentials, one from each electrode, reached downstream synapses where they would each release neurotransmitter. The interpulse interval was gradually reduced until antidromic action potentials from the downstream electrode collided with the orthodromic action potentials from the upstream electrode and eliminated them. As a result of eliminating half the nerve impulses by collision, half as much transmitter was released as indicated by the fact that rats self-stimulated at half the baseline rate. The conduction velocity was then calculated on the basis of the time taken for nerve impulses to traverse the intraelectrode distance without a collision. Recording electrodes in the midbrain ventral tegmental area (VTA, Figure 11.9) were used to detect the

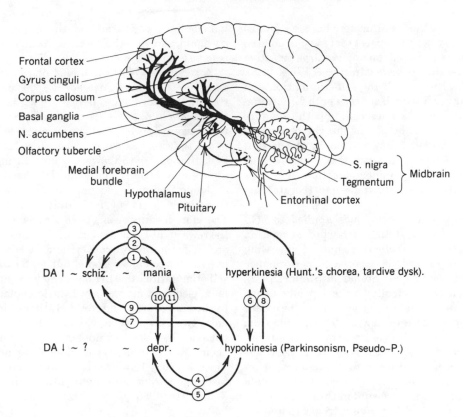

Figure 11.9. Upper drawing: Major dopamine pathways in the human brain. From "Dopamine Receptors" by I. Creese, 1981, in *Neurotransmitter Receptors: Part 2, Biogenic Amines* (p. 132) by H.I. Yamamura and S.J. Enna (eds.), London: Chapman & Hall, Ltd. Copyright 1981 by Chapman & Hall. Reprinted by permission. Lower drawing: The top line represents states of excessive dopamine (DA) functioning, and the bottom line DA hypo-functional states. Arrows indicate theoretical changes from one condition to another with time, drug therapy, or involvement of other unspecified neural systems. Note that neuroleptic drugs have an antidopaminergic effect. Antidepressants tend to increase dopaminergic activity in a variety of ways. Theoretical and descriptive changes are indicated by number: (1) Schizo-affective psychosis is a schizophrenia with affective symptoms. (2) Urstein psychosis is a schizophreniform state after many episodes of mania. (3) Huntington's chorea has been studied as a disease related to schizophrenia. (4) In endogenous depression motor (as well as psychomotor) inhibition is a typical symptom. (5) In Parkinson's disease a statistical overrepresentation of endogenous depressive states is found. (6) With neuroleptics it is possible to titrate from a hyperkinetic state to a hypokinetic state. (7) In the treatment of schizophrenia neuroleptics very often induce hypokinesia. (8) A common side effect of 1-dopa treatment in Parkinsonism is hyperkinetic movements. (9) Another side effect of 1-dopa treatment is paranoid state, sometimes with schizophreniform symptoms. (10) A prolonged neuroleptic (antimanic) treatment may induce a depression. (11) A prolonged antidepressant treatment may induce a manic state (from Randrup, Divac, Fog, & Munkvad, 1984). Hyperkinesis and hypokinesis are polar opposites. Mania and depression are also bipolar states. The opposite of schizophrenia is a question mark—perhaps compulsive one-track thinking, or type II schizophrenia. From personal communication with A. Randrup.

elicited nerve impulses and confirm these conclusions (Shizgal et al., 1982).

Note that behavior was used to infer internal transformations on a physical stimulus. S.S. Stevens would have appreciated this new internalized application of psychophysics.

To the question—what are the characteristics of reward neurons?—this technique gives the following answer. Reward neurons in the medial forebrain bundle are small, myelinated axons conducting from the forebrain toward the midbrain at the rate of about one to eight m/sec along axons several millimeters long. Estimates of refractory period suggest there are two nerve populations involved, one of which is sensitive to cholinergic blockade (Gratton & Wise, 1985).

On the basis of all the self-stimulation and recording studies cited above, a path for feeding-reward is shown as a descending path in Figure 11.8. This cannot be one of the catecholamine pathways because they ascend in the medial forebrain bundle. Instead this may be one of the descending connections that subserves self-stimulation in Huston's decerebrate rats described earlier.

Psychophysical techniques applied to self-stimulation suggest that a reward-summation function is an excellent means of assessing changes in reward, as opposed to performance (Gallistel et al., 1981; Stellar & Stellar, 1985). Running speed in an alley is the dependent variable. Approximately eight pulses are necessary and sufficient to reward a rat for running from the start box to the goal box to press a lever. More reward pulses in the goal box cause faster running. Any treatment that reduces performance ability does not change the *threshold* number of pulses for reward in the goal box, but does reduce speed of running to get there. For example, running is slowed down by marbles on the runway floor, by debilitating drugs, or by an uphill climb, but these factors do not necessarily change the threshold number of pulses needed for reward. Conversely, certain drugs such as dopamine blockers (neuroleptics) can increase the number of pulses the rats demand for a reward without altering running speed. Rats with mild dopamine dysfunction can run with maximum speed, but demand more pulses at the end. The neuroleptic drugs that reduce this measure of reward are used to treat schizophrenia which suggests that an aspect of psychosis is too much of this dopamine-mediated reward.

The next question is whether neuroleptics will also block stimulation-induced priming in the start box. Priming increases running speed. Pimozide did not block the priming effects of 1000 pulses given in the start box before the door was opened (Gallistel & Karras, 1984). The rats raced down the alley, but when they reached the goal box a 100 pulse reward was not felt if we may judge by the fact that the pimozide-treated animals quickly gave up running. Their self-stimulation in a Skinner box also extinguished.

If a cue light was turned on, the animals would try again, showing they were still capable of the response (Franklin & McCoy, 1979).

A reduction in the amount of priming, for example, 500 pulses instead of 1000, caused a running performance deficit, not a reward threshold change (Gallistel et al., 1981); therefore it again appears that the priming aftereffect is not the same as the reward effect. This suggests that part of the reward occurs during—not after—stimulation. The same is true of hypothalamic feeding; it occurs during stimulation. Sometimes it is even inhibited afterwards. Therefore feeding seems to *co-occur* with part of the reward. For this reason, and because feeding and self-stimulation *covary*, and because some hypothalamic cells respond during feeding and self-stimulation, the LH pathway in Figure 11.8 is labeled feeding and reward. As explained in the last part of this chapter, LH stimulation may have two reward components. One reinforces behavior by releasing dopamine in the nucleus accumbens (Hernandez & Hoebel, In press a). The other may reinforce behavior by mimicking taste input from the tongue (Murzi, Hernandez & Baptista, 1986).

Self-stimulation and Norepinephrine

The topic of self-stimulation neurotransmitters has been a perpetual source of controversy because the standard technique does not lend itself to neurochemical analysis. Electrical stimulation activates too many substrates at once. Stein and his colleagues collected pharmacological and anatomical evidence consistent with a norepinephrine theory of reward. Amphetamine releases both norepinephrine and dopamine, but it lost its rate-enhancing effect after norepinephrine depletion. Norepinephrine injections in the ventricle restored self-stimulation. Dopamine did not. Clonidine, which stimulates postsynaptic norepinephrine receptors, failed to restore bar-press work for self-stimulation. Stein (1980) explained that this could be the result of chronic reward; whereas behavior-contingent reward is needed for self-stimulation. Other work demonstrated that similar norepinephrine manipulations could influence memory (Stein et al., 1976). Recently norepinephrine has been shown to have a role as a neuromodulator that can improve the signal-to-noise ratio in hippocampal cells, in visual-feature detectors in the cortex and probably throughout most of the CNS (rev. Jacobs, 1986). Therefore it is quite possible that aspects of the reinforcement process are enhanced by norepinephrine.

Norepinephrine is not essential for reinforcement. Dopamine is essential if the rest of the brain is intact. A variety of lesions designed to interrupt norepinephrine pathways failed to interrupt self-stimulation (Wise, 1978; Panksepp, 1983; Routtenberg, 1980; Fibiger & Phillips, 1986). We found that rats depleted of forebrain norepineprine with 6-hydroxydopamine (6-OHDA) self-stimulated faster instead of slower (Hernandez & Hoebel, 1980, 1982). In this experiment, the 6-OHDA might have caused denervation supersensitivity to norepinephrine, but it is more likely that norepinephrine depletion disinhibited self-stimulation (Hoebel, 1979) and disinhibited feeding (Ahlskog & Hoebel, 1973). Stein (1980) reviews evidence for a joint action of norepinephrine and dopamine.

Modulation of Neuromodulation

The various catecholamine and serotonergic systems interact with each other at numerous hierarchical levels, and all of them may be neuromodulators rather than classical neurotransmitters. This means they enhance or diminish ongoing processes in nerve cells and terminals instead of inciting processes by themselves. To make matters more complicated, peptides and other cotransmitters released by some of the same monoamine neurons may modulate the modulation. For example, some dopamine neurons can release not only dopamine, but also CCK (Hokfelt et al., 1982) and ascorbic acid (Rebec & Bashore, 1984).

Self-stimulation and Dopamine

Numerous reviews discuss the ways dopamine may be necessary, sufficient, or merely involved in self-stimulation (Fibiger & Phillips, 1986; Simon et al., 1979; Wise, 1983). Dopamine blockers, such as pimozide, haloperidol, or flupenthixol block self-stimulation. These neuroleptic drugs can impair motor output and might prevent a rat from bar pressing with its paw even though it could still operate a lever with its nose (Ettenberg, Koob & Bloom, 1981; Simon et al., 1979). Wise has coped with this problem by observing that dopamine blockers can also prevent conditioned reward measured after the drug has worn off (Stewart, de Wit, & Eikelboom, 1984; Wise & Bozarth, 1984).

For further discussion of rate-free measures, see Liebman (1983), Stellar and Stellar (1985) and Stewart et al. (1984).

In summary, dopamine is necessary for ordinary hypothalamic self-stimulation, but if a rat is decerebrated (Huston, 1982), or if the operant response involves certain simple movements of the trunk, then dopamine neurons may not be necessary (Simon et al., 1979). Teitelbaum's work on motor subsystems suggests that dopamine is needed to disinhibit movement if the inhibitory systems are functioning. The same may be true for dopamine disinhibition of complex associational (cognitive) and limbic functions as described further on. The most intriguing clinical hypotheses suggest that enough dopamine is needed in the right places to disinhibit motor performance and limbic reward processes to prevent symptoms of depression, without disinhibiting cognitive processing to the point of disordered thinking (Figure 11.8).

In summary, it now appears that dopamine is necessary for operant behavior in a number of ways that we do not fully understand. Norepinephrine is not necessary, at least not in the forebrain. An animal may even learn operant behavior without dopamine, but only under unusual circumstances such as when decerebrate or very young. Thus the search for reward transmitters goes on.

Opiates and Self-stimulation

Peripheral morphine has biphasic effects on self-stimulation, first causing immobility and then increased responding. The debilitating or inhibitory effect gradually disappears. This unmasks the facilitatory effect. The reward-facilitating effect shows little or no tolerance. Peripheral morphine, like other drugs of abuse, lowers the threshold for self-stimulation, and naloxone blocks this effect (Kornetsky & Bain, 1983). Therefore brain opioids may be important for self-stimulation reward (Smith & Lane, 1983).

Opioids are involved in LH feeding-reward at sites that excite feeding. Carr and Simon (1983) found that systemic naloxone blocked the rate-increasing effect of deprivation, but did not block baseline self-stimulation. Therefore endogenous opioids appear to be involved in deprivation-induced increases in self-stimulation at feeding sites.

In summary, norepinephrine is not necessary for self-stimulation, but plays some role as a neuromodulator in memory, arousal, alertness, and stress. Dopamine is necessary for bar pressing, but not for some simpler operants. When dopamine is necessary, and when the animal has enough dopamine to perform the task, then one of its other roles seems to be the rewarding of the operant. The work involved in approaching has a dopaminergic component which may or may not be revealed depending on the test, the drug, the dose, and the site of injection. Opioids are involved, at least in deprivation-induced enhancement of the feeding-reward component of LH self-stimulation. An LH self-stimulation system projects, in part, to taste relay cells in the NST, and to the VTA where dopamine cells bodies lie. Faced with dopamine pathways to many forebrain regions including the caudate-putamen (striatum), the accumbens, the amygdala, and the frontal cortex, all passing through the LH, we have turned to chemical self-injection for greater specificity and a new perspective on the problem.

Intracerebral Self-Injection

Opiate Self-injection
The ventral tegmental area (VTA) is the crossroad reached by Shizgal et al. (1982) when following the descending axons of the medial forebrain bundle (MFB). The MFB descends further (Murzi et al., 1986), but we were stopped in our tracks by the discovery that this is a place where rats self-inject morphine, and naloxone partially blocks intravenous opiate self-administration (Bozarth, 1983; Wise, 1983).

It is known from intravenous self-injection studies that drugs are unusual as reinforcers. Giving more drug per injection usually causes less responding (Smith & Lane, 1983). This is because fewer operant responses are needed to achieve the optimal systemic dose. Rats will self-inject opiates intravenously, intraventricularly, or into a variety of limbic sites including the lateral hypothalamus and accumbens (Olds & Williams, 1980; Smith & Lane, 1983). By using opiate blockers that do not cross the blood brain barrier, Koob, Pettit, Ettenberg, & Bloom (1984) have shown that the acute reinforcing effects of intravenous heroin involve opiate receptors in the CNS, not in the periphery. When animals self-inject directly into brain tissue, drug leakage into the ventricles can make interpretation difficult. A mapping study

suggests that the VTA is the most sensitive site for morphine self-injection (Bozarth, 1983). Morphine is primarily a mu receptor agonist. A high concentration of delta opiate receptors in the nucleus accumbens led Goeders, Lane, and Smith (1984) to demonstrate enkephalin self-injection into that region. Naloxone will block all these effects.

Opiate Conditioned Place Preference
Opiate reward in the VTA has been confirmed with the conditioned place-preference technique. An injection of morphine or a long-acting enkephalin analogue, d-ala-met-enkephalin-amide (DALA), given repeatedly in a distinctive part of the cage can induce a preference for that part of the cage (Bozarth, 1987; Smith & Lane, 1983). We confirmed this conditioned place preference with thiorphan which inhibits the breakdown of enkephalin (Glimcher, Giovino, Margolin, and Hoebel, 1984). This enkephalin-ase inhibitor is thought to protect endogenous VTA enkephalin and some other peptides from degradation and thereby induce a place preference using the brain's own peptides. This effect was blocked by local naloxone, which suggests local opioid receptors were in fact involved.

Workers in this field are wondering what conditioned place preference actually measures. This technique appeared to have the great advantage that rats were tested drug-free so there would be no performance impairment (Rossi & Reid, 1967). Animals must use their memory of the drug stimulus effects and secondary reinforcement cues to know which side of the test cage was associated with drug injections on prior days. The question is whether the test measures conditioned reward, conditioned locomotion (Swerdlow & Koob, 1984), or antianxiety effects of drugs, especially if one side of the cage is brightly lit and makes the rats anxious (Bozarth, 1987). It is advisable to use several converging techniques before claiming to have measured reward. (Reviews in Engel & Oreland, 1987).

The Mesolimbic Dopamine System and Self-injection
Dopamine neurons respond to a variety of putative neurotransmitters. GABA is released in a path that directly or indirectly inhibits dopamine cells (Figure 11.5). CCK is excitatory and can even depolarize a dopamine cell body so

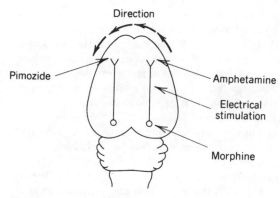

Direction

Pimozide

Amphetamine

Electrical
stimulation

Morphine

Figure 11.10. A simple example of identified neurochemical control of behavior in the vertebrate. The rotational model is used to assess functional asymmetries in activity of nigrostriatal and mesolimbic dopamine paths. The animal circles away from the side with the most active dopaminergic system due to body posture and/or sensory-motor reflexes. Morphine stimulates dopamine cell bodies; self-stimulation can stimulate axons or via a descending path to the cell bodies; amphetamine releases dopamine from nerve terminals. This model is useful in assessing potential therapeutic drugs (e.g. pimozide, a dopamine receptor blocker) and newly discovered peptides. For example, neurotensin injected in the cell body region (SN) was found to act like morphine in this diagram (Prange & Nemeroff, 1982). Rotation can help predict drug abuse liability in humans and self-injection in animals. From "Opiate Reward Mechanisms Mapped by Intracranial Self-Administration" by M.A. Bozarth, 1983, in *The Neurobiology of Opiate Reward Processes* (p. 346) by J.E. Smith and J.D. Lane (eds.), New York: Elsevier Biomedical Press. Copyright 1983 by Elsevier Biomedical Press B.V. Reprinted by permission.

severely that it stops repolarizing and therefore stops firing. This is called *depolarization block*. Bunney (1984) suggests that depolarization block may account for the effectiveness of neuroleptics by silencing dopamine cells in the treatment of schizophrenia (Figure 11.9).

Morphine excites dopamine cell bodies. Opiate agonists injected into the VTA are rewarding, as explained above, and induce locomotion including rotation to the side opposite a unilateral injection (Figure 11.10; Iversen, 1983; Bozarth, 1987). It is concluded that VTA opioids act, in part, by exciting the nigrostriatal dopamine path labeled *activation and orientation*, or the mesolimbic dopamine pathway which is involved in locomotion and reinforcement, labeled *self-administration* (Figure 11.8). Rats

will self-inject heroin intravenously after mesolimbic dopamine damage (Pettit, Ettenberg, Bloom, & Koob, 1984), and they will self-inject opiates directly into the accumbens (Goeders et al., 1984; Olds & Williams, 1980), which suggests that opiates not only act via the mesolimbic path by activating it in the VTA but also act directly in the accumbens.

Neurotensin, a Non-opiate Rewarding Peptide

Neurotensin applied iontophoretically excites dopamine cell bodies in a way similar, in some respects, to the effect of opiates. Anything that excites the mesolimbic dopamine system is a candidate for generating behavior such as locomotion, and for reinforcing behavior such as bar pressing. Therefore we predicted that VTA neurotensin would be rewarding. To be of more than pharmacological interest, the putative reinforcement transmitter must exist naturally in the VTA, and the dopamine cells must have receptors for it.

Neurotensin fulfills these requirements. It has been immunocytochemically identified in the VTA, and dopamine cell bodies have receptors that bind to labeled neurotensin. Cannula injection of neurotensin causes behavioral hyperactivity that depends on dopaminergic excitation (Prange & Nemeroff, 1982).

To see if neurotensin induces reinforcement we first used the conditioned place-preference paradigm in a half light, half dark cage, and then cross validated the results with direct self-injection. Rats kept in the bright side of a test cage under the influence of neurotensin in the VTA showed a conditioned preference for that side on a later day when injected with saline (Glimcher, Margolin et al., 1984). Significant preference shifts were obtained with the intact tridecapeptide, NT_{1-13}, but not neurotensin fragments 1 to 8, or 8 to 13. Rats also self-injected NT_{1-13} directly into the VTA by bar pressing for it, so this nonopiate peptide appears to satisfy the definition of a reinforcer.

The question, however, is whether the VTA ever receives such large quantities of neurotensin under normal circumstances. I doubt that we used too large a dose, because depolarization block would probably have reversed the neurotensin effect on dopamine cell bodies. The fact that shorter neurotensin fragments failed to generate a place preference supports the argument for a receptor interaction. This also rules out hydraulic pressure effects and other injection artifacts. We need a neurotensin receptor blocker to be certain of our conclusion, but none is available. In sum, it appears that nonopiate peptides that provide an excitatory input to VTA dopamine cells can be behavior reinforcers.

Where and What is Reinforcement?

Two 1984 papers illustrate the problem. One makes a case for "four circuit elements 'wired' in apparent series" (Wise & Bozart, 1984). The four circuit elements are the descending medial forebrain bundle (MFB) paths through the LH, an opiate connection in the VTA, the ascending mesolimbic dopamine path, and its next connection. The other paper makes the case for "separate systems" on the grounds that there are other independent reward systems (A.G. Phillips, 1984). We have already discussed the descending MFB reward system from the hypothalamus to the VTA (Figure 11.8). One of its neurotransmitters may be acetylcholine (Gratton & Wise, 1985). Then we discussed opiate reward receptors in the VTA which Wise and Bozarth suggest might be a second link. Britt and Wise (1983) report that naloxone injected into the VTA attenuates the reward of intravenous heroin self-injection, suggesting that VTA opiate receptors are essential for the full effect of heroin abuse. Heroin reward also seems to be blunted by dopamine blockers (Wise & Bozarth, 1984). It is a well-known fact that dopamine blockers (neuroleptics) can cause inanition and a variety of Parkinsonian side effects that sometimes interfere with behavior. This has caused controversy over the interpretation of neuroleptic effects (Ettenberg, Koob, & Bloom, 1981). Therefore it is important to note that some rats self-injecting some doses of cocaine accelerated their rate of pressing to compensate for the dopaminergic block. This rules out inanition or debilitating hypoactivity quite well in these particular animals (Wise & Bozarth, 1984). All told, it is clear that opiates act in part by way of dopamine neurons. Whether opiate cells link the descending hypothalamic self-stimulation neurons to the ascending dopamine neurons is still a moot point. Neurotensin could serve this role just as well. Neurotensin has the same general reward properties and receptor localization as opiates in the VTA,

and neurotensin-induced hyperactivity can be blocked with neuroleptics, but we do not claim that it is a link for lack of definitive evidence. Our evidence does suggest that any neurochemical which excites the appropriate dopamine cell bodies is going to have reinforcement properties, whether it is an opioid or not.

Where is reinforcement? To this question we can now give partial answers. One component of ment reinforcement could be in LH cells that enhance sweet taste input in the NST (Murzi et al., 1986); another is in the excitatory inputs to the VTA dopamine cell bodies; another is in the forebrain circuits that are potentiated by dopamine.

What is reinforcement? To this question we can now answer that one aspect of reinforcement could be taste-induced stimulation of LH cells which enhance the taste, i.e. taste positive feedback gated in the LH. Another aspect could be the release of VTA enkephalin and perhaps VTA neurotensin to increase the rate of firing or cause bursts of action potentials in dopamine cells active at the time. The reinforcer could also be the action of dopamine on forebrain circuits as proposed by Mogenson (1982), Fibiger and Phillips (1986) and others. It is unlikely that dopamine cells that fire slowly, regularly, and spontaneously could provide reinforcement by themselves (Jacobs, 1986) unless burst firing or facilitatory inputs to their terminals (presynaptic facilitation) increases their transmitter output as a function of some measure of success. Dopamine or its cotransmitter could then enhance neural activity in circuits operational at that time, analogous to the effect of monoamines on operational sensory-motor synapses during conditioning in *Aplysia* (Clark and Kandel, 1987). Therefore, the trail leads on to the dopamine terminals.

The Nucleus Accumbens, Hot Spot for Stimulant Abuse

This is the dopamine site most studied by reward researchers. It is here that we were able to train rats to self-inject amphetamine (Hoebel et al., 1983). Amphetamine is well known to induce stereotypy in the striatum, locomotion in the accumbens, and to enhance any low-rate operant response when given systemically (Caldwell, 1980; Creese, 1983); therefore it was essential to have good controls for these various forms of hyperkinesis. Amphetamine in the accumbens satisfied the criteria for a reinforcer because rats learned to switch from one lever to another depending on which lever delivered amphetamine. If automatic injections were programmed at half the rat's usual rate, then the animal responded half as often, thereby keeping its total dose the same across a four-hour session.

If amphetamine acts by releasing dopamine, then rats should also be willing to self-inject dopamine in the accumbens. They do (Guerin et al., 1984).

If dopamine terminals are necessary for the action of amphetamine or cocaine, then destruction of terminals in the crucial areas should eliminate intravenous self-injection. The catecholamine neurotoxin, 6-hydroxydopamine, injected into the nucleus accumbens decreased hypothalamic self-stimulation, decreased amphetamine potentiation of self-stimulation, and decreased intravenous self-injection of amphetamine and cocaine. Apomorphine, on the other hand, is a dopamine stimulant that acts postsynaptically, directly on dopamine receptors. It does not depend on intact dopamine terminals for systemic self-injection (Roberts, Koob, Klonoff, & Fibiger, 1980). Thus there is general agreement that the accumbens is a major focus of stimulant reinforcement effects (Wise & Bozarth, 1987).

Puzzlement and controversy swirl around the interpretation of reward in this context. Mogenson (1982) proposes that accumbens dopamine controls a gate between sensory input and motor output. Fibiger & Phillips (1986) propose that dopamine amplifies sensory inputs. Wise and Colle (1984) suggest dopamine is needed for motivational impact. Neill, Garr, Clark, and Britt (1982) see dopamine as providing willingness to work. Gallistel and Karras (1984) ally dopamine with reward as opposed to performance as explained earlier. Herberg, Stephans and Franklin (1980) propose the opposite, that is, dopaminergic motivation as opposed to reward. Koob, Riley, Smith, and Robbins (1978) point to dopaminergic involvement in motor output. Therefore I prefer an operational description for the time being and have labeled the mesolimbic dopamine path, *self-administration*, in Figure 11.8. Our working hypothesis is that dopamine causes self-administration of anything that releases more dopamine by enhancing the release of other neurotransmitters and facilitating structural changes in synapses of simultaneously active circuits involved in operant behavior. Simply put, dopamine in the accumbens can make the animal repeat itself by physically reinforcing active neural circuits.

Wise went so far as to suggest that dopamine released by amphetamine induces euphoria, and dopamine blockers cause anhedonia in rats as well as in people. This idea fits Epstein's definition of motivation as hedonic, as explained in the first section. Instead of measuring this feeling or emotion as patterns of somatic, autonomic and glandular responses as Epstein suggests, Wise (1982) has inferred anhedonia in rats that display response extinction under dopamine blockade. Most of these experiments rely on systemic administration of the dopamine blocker. Thus it is not necessarily acting in the accumbens, but could also act in the amygdala, hippocampus, frontal cortex or other DA terminal areas.

Self-injection in the Frontal Cortex

The learning and extinction of discriminative stimuli used in choice behavior seem to be coded in cells of the frontal cortex (Rolls, 1981). This region is modulated by dopamine input from the same general VTA cell group that serves the accumbens, but the path is now recognized to have two components, mesolimbic to the accumbens, and mesocortical to the frontal cortex. With cannulas in the frontal cortex monkeys will self-inject amphetamine (Fibiger & Phillips, 1986), and rats will self-inject cocaine (Goeders & Smith, 1983). It follows that dopamine might be a reinforcer here too.

Dopamine cells have a topographical organization which suggests that a functional homunculus for dopaminergic arousal and self-administration will eventually be found. Some mesolimbic neurons are unusual in that they lack inhibitory autoreceptors. Some are also different because they contain CCK as a cotransmitter. Perhpaps these differences will also reveal different functions for dopamine subsystems.

CCK: Cotransmitter with Dopamine

CCK has been discovered in the accumbens where it is co-released with dopamine. CCK-injected locally potentiated dopamine-induced locomotion in the accumbens, but not in the striatum (Stivers & Crawley, 1984). This disagreed with reports that CCK antagonized dopamine mediated behaviors (as cited earlier). Cell recording studies in the accumbens of anesthetized animals also contradict each other. Iontophoresis of CCK enhanced both excitatory and inhibitory processes going on in the accumbens during electrical stimulation of inputs from the hippocampus in anesthetized rabbits (DeFrance, Sikes, & Chronister, 1984). This could mean that CCK is a neuromodulator that amplifies many incoming signals. In anesthetized rats CCK depolarized cells and caused action potentials, unless the cells went into depolarization block (White & Wang, 1984). The crucial information from awake rats is not available. The technology is available for awake cats, but cats in their contrary way have CCK in dopamine neurons to the striatum instead of dopamine neurons to the accumbens as rats and people do.

Self-injection has the advantage as a research tool that there is always ongoing behavior, namely the self-injection bar press. Therefore a neuromodulator that amplifies ongoing signals will automatically be injected at the correct moment to reinforce the signals from bar pressing. To know what spontaneous behavior will be reinforced, we can look at the respondent behavior. In the case of dopamine self-injection in the accumbens, the reinforced operant is a bar press and the elicited respondent is locomotion. Locomotion is often considered an animal model of exploratory behavior. A low dose of CCK in the accumbens did not induce locomotion by itself, only in combination with dopamine injections (Stivers & Crawley, 1984). Therefore conditions that chronically release dopamine will lead to explorations as a respondent, and then specific acts which release additional dopamine or perhaps CCK in the accumbens might be reinforced as an operant.

Mesolimbic dopamine cells in anesthetized rats can fire in a bursting mode which may release extra dopamine or CCK (Grace & Bunney, 1984). In monkeys, some dopamine cells will fire as a forerunner to a reaching movement (Schultz et al., 1983).

Reinforcement of Premotor Plans

If dopamine cells fire a burst before a motor act, and if dopamine or CCK is somehow reinforcing, then it follows that the premotor anticipatory response, or plan, is what gets reinforced, not the motor act itself. Similarly, if a rat is given systemic amphetamine while responding for pellets, then the animal may respond again and again without eating the pellets. This suggests that the taste of the pellet is unnecessary to reinforce behavior in the drugged rat. Therefore the pellet is not the reinforcer when a rat is under the influence of amphetamine. This is similar to the concept of functional autonomy in which secondary reinforcers, premotor events, or other mental processes are sufficient to maintain the behavior output without the usual primary reinforcer.

Displacement, or Adjunctive Behavior

Typical external reinforcers such as food pellets delivered automatically once every minute arouse an animal and lead to extraneous behavior known as displacement responses or adjunctive behavior (Wayner, Barone, & Loullis 1981). In the case of schedule-induced drinking, it is called psychogenic polydipsia. Under these conditions a rat will drink, gnaw, run, or do some prepotent, ecologically possible act after every pellet. Drug and lesion studies suggest that the central excitatory state that causes this phenomenon depends on dopamine (Robbins & Koob, 1980; Singer, Wallace, & Hall, 1982). If so, adjunctive behavior may be an example of a dopamine-induced activity, and suggests that this dopaminergic effect can last for some time after eating a pellet in the absence of another pellet.

Cognitive Anatomy of Opiates and Stimulants

Where do opiates feel like opiates? Where do stimulants feel like stimulants? The drug discrimination paradigm is beginning to give answers. In this paradigm rats that are food deprived are trained to respond for food, but only one of two levers will deliver a pellet. During training no lights or buzzers are used to help the rat pick the correct lever. The cue is the effect of a drug injection (Appel, White, & Kuhn, 1978). For many drugs it can be shown that the cue only exists in the rat's brain. For example, rats can be trained to press the right-hand lever as the one that gives a pellet whenever they feel the effects of a systemic opiate injection. They also learn that the other, left-hand, lever will pay off with food whenever they do not feel the drug effects. Then they are tested with an opiate injected into the brain to find out where it feels like the training dose. The midbrain raphe is one site where beta-endorphin feels similar to a systemic opiate injection (Young, Woods, Herling, & Hein, 1983).

Rats trained with systemic amphetamine generalized to amphetamine injected in the accumbens (Nielsen & Scheel-Kruger, 1984). Thus accumbens amphetamine feels like wholebody amphetamine. The next step will be to find out if rats generalize from amphetamine to accumbens dopamine or CCK. That will tell us whether these two cotransmitters have similar cognitive cue effects generated by their action in the accumbens.

SYNTHESIS

Having discussed guidelines for motivation in the first section, simplified elements of motivation in the second, peptidergic organization of homeostatic behavior in the third, and models of brain self-control in the fourth, the next step is to integrate these findings with higher forebrain functions.

Sensory Input

Complex and Hypercomplex Sensory Detectors

The workings of visual feature detectors illustrate the way various aspects of a stimulus within one modality are refined, combined, and processed until at some point individual cells only fire to hypercomplex stimuli. A cell that only responds to the shape of a hand is an example of a feature detector (Gross et al., 1984). The taste system is particularly instructive because it serves as a model of chemical sensation which might apply not only to chemoreceptive organs in the tongue, but also in the body and brain. Glucoreceptors in the tongue may be similar to glucooreceptors in the pancreas, midbrain, or hypothalamus. Similarly, sodium receptors in the tongue may tell us about sodium receptors in the liver, hindrain and hypothalamus.

Is it interesting to note that animals can taste the molecule which is the primary source of energy for the brain and the ion which maintains membrane potentials. Taste information about glucose, sodium, and other molecules is sent to the NST in the brainstem via sensory neurons that respond to more than one type of taste receptor. Thus a given neuron might respond to both glucose and salt. To decode such a message the brain must reverse the process and extract an across-fiber pattern which represents a taste feature.

The Feature Detectors for Taste

People recognize more tastes than can be accounted for by a combination of four primary tastes—sweet, salty, bitter, and sour. The features decoded from across-fiber patterns could include other brainstem inputs that are combined with the pattern from the tongue. Chang and Scott (1984) have evidence that the pattern they record in the NST does not reflect just the tongue's expertise at analytical chemistry; it also reflects postingestional effects on prior occasions. The taste of a food that had made the rat ill can give a bitter-type pattern even if it started out originally with a sweet-type pattern. Thus the pattern may be coded for features of ecological safety, not just analytical chemistry. Learned taste aversion may be a feature coded, in part, in the first relay in the brainstem. Lesion data suggest the amygdala is an area needed to recognize the feature for purposes of rejecting the poisonous food. The taste of poison associated with illness is often called bitter. The importance of this lies in the idea that sensory meaning can be a combination of inputs from a variety of sensory inputs, even at the first relay center (Figure 11.7).

In the special case of salt sensibility, cells have been found in the rat's NST that respond not only to salt signals from the liver coming in over visceral afferents, but also to NaCl applied directly by iontophoresis (Kobashi & Adachi, 1984). Other hypertonic solutions or other salts do not activate these cells. Thus the liver and the NST respond to sodium per se. I imagine that the taste of hepatic sodium and NST sodium must be integrated with the taste of oral sodium. If it is true, as suggested above, that taste can carry physiological meaning as well as chemical meaning, then a mechanism is present through which the taste of salt in the mouth is going to depend on salt in the liver and salt in the brain. By the time this taste of mouth-gut-brain salt reaches the amygdala its meaning will also have access to the memory of salt in the animal's past experience. Mark and Scott (1987) discovered that salt deprivation changed the NST response to salt on the tongue, making it give a neural response more like a sweet substance. This is further evidence that the NST codes taste on the basis of need and safety.

Feature Detectors for Metabolism

Glucose receptors are known to exist in tongue, pancreas, midbrain, and forebrain. Again the evidence is fragmentary, but consistent with the possibility that many sources of a glucose signal are integrated in the brain. Learned glucose features are probably in the amygdala and frontal cortex. Glucose location in the environment is probably coded in the hippocampus. Blood glucose availability is probably detected in the hypothalamus and midbrain. Glucoreceptors in the medial hypothalamus are affected by insulin and free fatty acid; therefore they are better described as feature detectors with metabolic meaning. Hernandez (1976) and Oomura et al. (1982) suggest they play an important role in feeding behavior as well as in metabolic control.

Temperature receptors send converging information from the periphery and hypothalamic centers to neurons that integrate these two major sources of thermal information (Boulant, 1980; Myers, 1980). Satinoff (1983) makes the point that the site of physiological integration and behavioral output does not need to be the same for all thermoregulatory responses. A dissociation of physiological and behavioral output implies that not all temperature-related behavior need be homeostatic. Thus thermoregulation is a multiple-control system with sensors, integrators, and response-output systems each at different hierarchical levels. Many of the responses such as activity, cuddling, panting, salivation, and vasomotor reflexes are part of other behavior patterns. This leads Satinoff to conclude that most, if not all, thermoregulatory responses are used for other purposes as well. They were integrated into action patterns for thermoregulation during the course of evolutionary adaptations. For example, she suggests that muscular heat produced by the legs and body in maintaining an upright, walking posture created a new source of body heat. Thus, postural and locomotor responses are now used for thermoregulation.

Multimodal Feature Detectors

Amygdala recordings demonstrate that this is one place where neural responses to food stimuli incorporate more than one sensory modality, for example, the color, taste, and odor of a food (Rolls, 1981). The hypothalamus further modulates the sensory response according to physiological signals relating to homeostasis.

A challenge for neuroscientists is clear. On the one hand, evidence has been presented that sensory elements, such as glucose or sodium signals, funnel into the same brain regions, and even into the same brain cells, from different parts of the body. Moreover single cells respond as if they combined this input with learned associations from past experience and homeostatic needs. I also dedicated a section of this chapter to the possibility that some cells release coded peptides that might act at a number of sites in the brain and body with crossover so as to integrate related physiological and behavioral functions. On the other hand, according to Satinoff's cogent analysis of temperature regulation viewed from an evolutionary perspective, there is no necessity for a single central coordinator for behavior that to our eyes looks coordinated, "any more than Darwin required the existence of an 'adaptor' to explain adaptations." Her suggestion is that fractions of complex patterns started out as simpler behavioral entities; thus different wholes of behavior can be assembled from the same rudimentary parts. This is also the essence of Gallistel's (1981) analysis of behaviors assembled from basic reflexes, pacemakers and servomechanisms. It is also the direction Teitelbaum (1982a, 1982b) has taken in his analysis of motion subsystems. The challenge is to find out how, when, and where coded peptides or other chemicals are a strong organizing principle, and when and where the elemental neural wiring diagrams are sufficient explanations in themselves.

Studies of cortical sensory maps suggest that neural activity in various cortical fields contribute to evocation of perceptions. The number of cortical fields devoted to each modality has increased with phylogenetic development (Merzenich & Kaas, 1980). The task of defining connections from sensory-perceptual fields to motor output is an important part of motivational neuroscience.

Effector Output

Fixed Action Patterns

Fixed action patterns are complex motor acts

involving specific temporal sequences triggered in all-or-none fashion. Examples already mentioned include righting, walking, and bracing. Many fixed action patterns are programmed in the spinal cord to coordinate reflexes from one side of the body to the other and one segment to another. Others are programmed in the brain. Two structures appear to contain the primary machinery for triggering action patterns, the cerebellum and the basal ganglia. Neurons in these two regions fire in anticipation of predictable motor actions. They fire before the motor cortex, and they send a program via the thalamus to the motor cortex. This would be essential because cortico-spinal output cells are the final common path for motor instructions to the spinal segments.

Command Neurons and their Modulation

Command neurons control a fixed action pattern, or at least part of one (Davis & Kovac, 1981; Kupferman & Weiss, 1978; Panksepp, 1982). Hierarchies of command neurons contribute to the premotor outputs. Others facilitate the ongoing actions. Thus command neurons control or facilitate a pattern-generating network. For example, neurons descending from brainstem centers facilitate walking routines by modulating the output of cortico-spinal neurons. You will recall other examples from research on slugs showing serotonergic neuromodulatory neurons that potentiate an arousal pattern and dopaminergic neurons that trigger buccal motor programs.

In feeding, as in walking, we can expect to find various levels of command neurons to facilitate or inhibit various levels of the motor programs. Feeding programs exit from cranial motor neurons in the hindbrain, whereas walking motor neurons exit the spinal cord. Nevertheless there may be interaction between the two. Food approach usually involves walking, and food ingestion must depotentiate it. Thus feeding engages the walking program at times and disengages it at others.

Zeigler (1983) suggests that orosensory inputs are necessary for patterned feeding outputs and therefore the sensory and motor aspects of the trigeminal system may be necessary for, or identical to, central motivational mechanisms. Oral stimulation involving the trigeminal system can be a necessary stimulus for eating in response to deprivation. Trigeminal deaffer-

entation can even block operant bar pressing for food in rats capable of bar pressing for self-stimulation (Jacquin & Enfiejian, 1982). These authors explain this as elimination of preingestive jaw movements that act as anticipatory, fractional responses necessary to recruit the full-fledged feeding mechanism.

Panksepp (1982) has suggested that some of the command neurons for feeding are in the hypothalamus. One would expect them to influence locomotion and stereotyped feeding patterns of at least two types: approach-feeding-reward intake and escape-satiety-aversion expectorate (Figure 11.4). The same two types of neurons, or ones that are closely linked, might command the autonomic responses for digestion and nausea. Feeding and satiety neurons in rats and people seem to be modulated by monoamine neurons in a manner analogous to the slug (see anti-feeding and anti-satiety pathways that modulate feeding and satiety in Figure 11.8).

Integrative peptides such as angiotensin or CCK may play a dual role as neurotransmitters and as free-floating neuromodulators that enhance related functions at sites along the lattice of command neurons.

Dopaminergic Arousal of Striatal and Limbic Functions

Vanderwolf (1983) suggests that behavioral programs for feeding form two categories. One includes walking, running, swimming, rearing, jumping, digging, manipulation of objects with forelimbs, isolated movements of head or one limb, and shifts of posture. These are the movements used in approach behavior. This type is accompanied by a characteristic rhythmic activity (theta rhythm) in the hippocampus. The significance of theta rhythm is unknown, but he suggests that it generates exploratory behavior which, in turn, leads to operant behavior as the more successful responses are selected.

The other category includes alert immobility, licking, chewing, teeth chattering, sneezing, startle response, vocalization, grooming, and various reflexive postures. These he considers relatively automatic, reflexive, and respondent in character. During this type of behavior, another slower theta rhythm occurs. These simpler reflexive type behaviors have been described in great detail by Fentress (1983). Grooming, for example, is under the control of long sequences of motor programs that can be played out in the absence of normal sensory feedback. These programs also occur as displacement behaviors during stress of various kinds. Apparently these reflexive behaviors such as chewing and face grooming are triggered either by natural peripheral stimuli around the mouth or by central arousal. Centrally induced displacement grooming is even more stereotyped then the peripherally induced form. Both are linked to the slow theta thythm.

These two general categories of behavior correspond to the rough dichotomy often drawn between striatal and accumbens functions. The dorsal striatum seems to mediate more of the respondent, reflexive, or stereotyped behaviors; whereas the accumbens has more to do with operant, flexible, locomotor behaviors. There is a major dopamine projection to each of these two areas and also a third one to the septum, cingulate cortex and frontal cortex. These projections are called nigrostriatal, mesolimbic, and mesocortical, respectively.

Major Sensorimotor Interfaces

The foregoing paragraphs discussed sensory input as multimodal hypercomplex feature detection, and motor output in terms of command neurons for complex motor patterns. These are potentiated at several levels by monoamines and sometimes integrated by peptides. The next question is how the feature detectors and command neurons get together at sensorimotor interfaces.

The Hindbrain and Midbrain
The hindbrain and midbrain contain most of the sensory and motor nuclei of the cranial nerves. The optic tract sends inputs straight to optic motor nuclei. The trigeminal facial input connects to facial outputs; the vagus sensory input connects to the vagus motor output, and so forth. As described earlier, these S-R connections can accomplish a great deal. For example, decerebrates not only move their mouths appropriately for good and bad tastes; they also adjust this effect to homeostatic challenge by mouthing more avidly during hypoglycemia (Flynn & Grill, 1985). The brainstem may contain glucoreceptors involved in such functions, and physiological signals arrive in the hindbrain via axons from the GI tract and liver (Norgren, 1983;

Novin & Oomura, 1980; Roper & Atema, 1987). In addition, chemical stimuli in the ventricular fluid bathe the area postrema which overlies some of the NST and vagal nuclei. In the brainstem there is the possibility for a four-way interaction between gustatory input, visceral input, oral motor output, and visceral output.

The Hypothalamus

This region also contains cells that respond to both external and internal sensory signals. In rats, food deprivation increased the number of units that were sensitive to oral sucrose (Norgren, 1983). Similarly in the monkey, food deprivation enhanced the response of single units to taste stimuli as described earlier. Norgren, Rolls and Ono suggest that such units could be related functionally to the electrical self-stimulation phenomenon. This agrees with work cited earlier showing that lateral hypothalamic self-stimulation can vary with both oral and postingestional factors (reviews by Hoebel, 1969, 1976; Mogenson, 1977; Rolls, 1975).

The Dual-Center Hypothesis
According to the classic dual-center theory, the LH excites feeding and the MH exerts a satiety influence (Powley, Opsahl, Cox, & Weingarten, 1980; Teitelbaum 1982a; Stellar & Stellar, 1985). When it was discovered that the main reason rats starve after lateral hypothalamic (LH) lesions is that they have been deprived of ascending dopaminergic innervation of the striatum, many scientists rejected the idea of an LH feeding center. Stricker (1983b) suggests that changes in a dopaminergic central excitatory system and serotonergic central inhibition system account for most changes in feeding after LH and MH lesions, and that the dual center model of feeding and satiety be abandoned. Morgane (1979) summarized the center concept as a new phrenology, the problem being that a center based on lesion data does not do justice to the many anatomical and neurochemical inputs and outputs to the lesioned area. Nevertheless kainic acid lesions that kill cell bodies while sparing most axons of passage suggest that LH-cell bodies play a role in ingestive behaviors (Stricker, Swerdloff, & Zigmond, 1978; Grossman, Dacey, Halaris, Collier, & Kouttenberg, 1978). Hypothalamic recording studies prove the existence of LH cell bodies that fire in

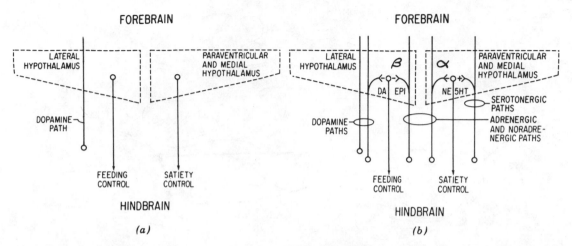

Figure 11.11. Part A. Summary of hypothalamic lesion data. The lateral hypothalamus contains nigrostriatal dopamine fibers of passage and a feeding control output. The paraventricular and medial hypothalamic regions contain a satiety control system. Part B. The diagram on the right is elaborated on the basis of findings from Leibowitz (1980) to include the beta-adrenergic (norepinephrine or epinephrine) and dopaminergic systems in the lateral hypothalamus. Note that epinephrine (EPI) and/or norepinephrine, and dopamine (DA) have an effect on feeding that is inhibitory (minus signs). Amphetamine curbs the appetite by releasing these catechol-amines. In the paraventricular and medial region (on right-hand side of the diagram), the alpha-adrenergic (norepinephrine, NE) and serotonergic (5HT) systems are added to the schema. Note that norepinephrine reduces satiety (minus sign), whereas the predominant effect of serotonin is seen as facilitating satiety (plus sign). Not shown is a newly discovered serotonin function in the LH to inhibit feeding (Schwartz, Kloekner, Hernandez & Hoebel, 1987). Noradrenergic drugs act in the PVN to cause feeding and obesity as a side effect of antidepressant therapy. Fenfluramine may induce satiety and weight loss by releasing serotonin. GABA, endorphin, enkephalin and the "gut peptides", neurotensin, CCK, and bombesin are not shown but may fit into this useful model. See text for details. From "Neurotransmitters in the Control of Feeding and Its Rewards: Monoamines, Opiates and Brain-Gut Peptides" by B.G. Hoebel, 1984, in *Eating and Its Disorders*, *62*, p. 16, Association for Research on Nervous and Mental Disease, New York: Raven Press. Copyright 1984 by Raven Press. Reprinted by permission.

harmony with feeding, and neurochemical injection studies prove the existence of receptors on neurons involved in feeding and satiety (Figure 11.11).

Medial Hypothalamus and PVN

In brief, hypothalmic injection of norepinephrine can induce eating, as discovered by Grossman (1962), and it acts most sensitively anterior to the MH in the PVN (Leibowitz, 1980). Chronic injection of norepinephrine, or a PVN lesion, leads to hyperphagia much like the classic MH lesions. Therefore norepinephrine in this region probably induces eating by inhibiting some aspect of the classical medial hypothalamic satiety system (Figure 11.11). The conclusion that PVN norepinephrine induces feeding is as close to established fact as you will find in neuropsychopharmacology. It meets the criteria for neurotransmitter function (Hoebel,

1984). Evidence comes from studies with local injection of adrenergic agonists, antagonists, synthesis inhibitors, releasers, reuptake blockers, radio labeled ligand binding as a function of fasting and refeeding (Leibowitz, 1980) and from push-pull cannula studies that recover endogenous norepinephrine released when a rat eats (Myers & McCaleb, 1980). The source of this norepinephrine input is, in part, a component of the dorsal noradrenergic bundle which arises in dorsal midbrain and hindbrain cell-body clusters. It is logical to guess that ascending catecholamine inputs to the hypothalamic interface provide some of the multimodal, oral-gastrointestinal and hepatic controls over feeding and satiety systems in the hypothalamus (Figure 11.12). Histofluorescent studies and axonal-tracing studies reveal norepinephrine inputs to the PVN from the locus coeruleus (LC), which may have the general arousal and stress function

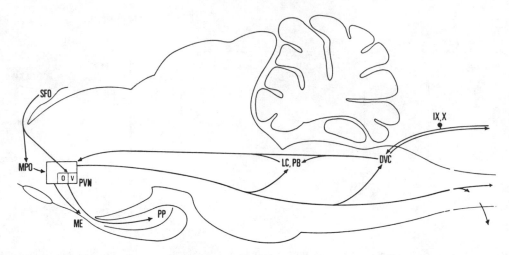

Figure 11.12. Some details of paraventricular nucleus (PVN) input and output. The ascending input contains norepinephrine fibers in the dorsal noradrenergic bundle. One function of these is to promote carbohydrate intake by inhibiting satiety. The effect depends on an intact vagus and cortisterone level (Leibowitz, 1980). The descending input from the subfornical organ (SFO) to the medial preoptic (MPO) and PVN may control vasopressin (V) release. A descending path from the PVN back to the locus coeruleus (LC), parabrachial nucleus (PB) and dorsal vagal complex (DVC) is also shown. Oxytocin (O) and vasopressin (V) neurons project to the posterior pituitary (PP) and elsewhere. Note that the PVN can communicate with the periphery via the SFO, the weak blood-brain barrier in the media eminence (ME), the vagus and the spinal cord. Some of these connections are shown in simplified form in Figures, 11.5, 11.6, and 11.10. From "Neural Mechanisms for the Functional Coupling of Autonomic, Endocrine and Somatomotor Responses in Adaptive Behavior" by L.W. Swanson and G.J. Mogenson, 1981, *Brain Research Review, 3*, p. 18. Copyright 1981 by Elsevier Biomedical Press B.V. Reprinted by permission.

discussed earlier (see ACTH section). Norepine-phrine also comes from the dorsal vagal complex (DVC) which could relay gut signals to the hypothalamus, and from a ventral noradren-ergic cell body group known as Al which also receives vagal input (Figure 11.12). The PVN sends fibers back to the LC and DVC (Swanson & Mogenson, 1981), and knife cuts anywhere along this path cause hyperphagia (Sclafani & Kirchgessner, 1986). Thus there appears to be a loop between some of the norepinephrine cell-body areas which inhibit the PVN satiety sys-tem and PVN output back to the same regions. The role of the PVN in responding to peptides and producing pituitary hormone-releasing fac-tors puts this hypothalamic interface at the crossroads of behavior and neuroendocrine functions (Swanson & Mogenson, 1981; Swan-son & Sawchenko, 1983).

Also in the PVN, serotonergic drugs inhibit feeding (Figure 11.8; Hoebel & Leibowitz, 1981). The serotonin neurotoxin 5,7-DHT given to deplete a medial system causes hyperphagia in female rats (Waldbillig et al., in prep.) The

evidence for opioid cell bodies, receptors and opiate-induced feeding in this area is also sug-gestive of an opioid inhibition of satiety as dis-cussed earlier, but feeding may be secondary to other changes that occur in the long delay after opiate injection before the animals overeat. Evidence has also been presented that the nonopiate peptides, CCK and neurotensin, inhibit feeding in the PVN. By strict standards we will not know this for sure until studies of pharmacological antagonism, peptide release, and receptor binding can be performed.

Diet selection studies provide excellent evidence that some of these putative neuro-transmitters play specific roles in feeding. In the PVN, norepinephrine induces carbohydrate intake, and serotonin inhibits it (Leibowitz, 1986a; Leibowitz & Stanley, 1986).

In sum, the demonstration that a variety of putative neurotransmitters act in the MH-PVN region to control various aspects of feeding and metabolism suggests that the midline region contains cells or dendrites involved in meal pat-tern, dietary selection, metabolic processing, and body weight (Blundell, 1983). No other brain region is known to do all this, so perhaps it will turn out to be a center after all, if these ischemetric (energy regulation) functions are interrelated.

Figure 11.8 goes beyond the data in assuming that VMH and PVN neurons that mediate satiety also mediate aversion (Hoebel, 1984). Something about this aversion increases during satiety, as defined by the increase in stimulation-escape in overfed or overweight rats. At the present time there is no evidence for a functional overlap of stimulation-escape and this descending satiety path.

Perifornical LH

Various electrode sites in the LH will affect different proportions of ascending monoamine fibers, different proportions of descending cholinergic and GABA fibers, and different proportions of the various cell types recorded by Hernandez, Norgren, Rolls, Oomura, Ono and others as cited earlier. Therefore a discussion of this LH region as a sensorimotor interface must make some distinction as to which region of the LH is under discussion. The LH region near the fornix is the spot that we found to be best for obtaining three behaviors: self-stimulation, stimulation-escape, and stimulation-induced feeding, all under the influence of postingestinal factors (Hernandez & Hoebel, 1978). Leibowitz (1980) found this to be the best place to obtain catecholamine induced satiety, a phenomenon originally observed by Margules (rev. by Hoebel, 1971). Locally injected dopamine, norepinephrine, or epinephrine all suppress feeding in this region (Figure 11.11). This is a primary site for amphetamine anorexia (Leibowitz, 1980; Parada, Hernandez, Schwartz & Hoebel, In press). The ascending adrenergic and dopaminergic inputs to the perifornical LH are apparently the substrates from which amphetamine releases the anorectic neurotransmitters (Ahlskog, Randall, Hernandez, & Hoebel, 1984; Hoebel & Leibowitz, 1981).

If one grants the following—(1) LH cells respond to taste inputs (Rolls, 1981; Norgren, 1983); (2) LH cells respond to products of metabolism (Oomura et al., 1982); (3) LH cells play a role in feeding output (Ono et al., 1985); (4) LH self-stimulation varies with many of the same taste, postingestinal, and catecholaminergic factors that control feeding (Hoebel, 1984); (5) part of the reward of self-stimulation is carried by a descending fiber system (Gratton & Wise, 1985; Shizgal et al., 1982). (6) This descending system enhances taste input (Murzi et al., 1986); and (7) part of the reward of feeding and LH self-stimulation comes from release of dopamine which reinforces active operant response circuits in the nucleus accumbens (Hernandez and Hoebel, In press a)—then we are led to the following conclusion. Cells in the LH respond to taste as a function of metabolic and hormonal factors and have descending axons that carry information involved in the induction of feeding and reinforcement of feeding. Therefore this is labeled as a feeding and reward pathway (Figure 11.8).

The LH interconnects with the hindbrain (Smith & DeVito, 1984), midbrain VTA, and amygdala, and it also has a direct line to the frontal cortex (Oomura, 1980). Almost everything a researcher can do to the lateral regions has the opposite effect when applied to the medial regions. In all likelihood some of the MH-PVN outputs and the LH outputs are reciprocally inhibited at various levels in the forebrain, midbrain, and hindbrain. Exceptions which we do not fathom are opiate-induced feeding (cited earlier) and stimulation-induced hyperglycemia (Le Magnen, 1983) which occur in both regions.

In summary, there are an enormous number of observations using a wide variety of stimulation, drug, and recording techniques which demonstrate that the hypothalamus is a dual sensorimotor interface that participates in the control of metabolism, feeding, and even diet selection. The latest exciting research shows that neurochemical anatomy will allow the dual system to be further subdivided according to metabolic and behavioral control of the macronutrients: carbohydrate, fat and protein (Leibowitz, In press a).

The Nucleus of the Diagonal Band (NDB)

This nucleus lies at the anterior end of the hypothalamus where the medial forebrain bundle starts its descent, picking up fibers from cell bodies in the LH along the way to the VTA, interpeduncular nucleus and dorsal midbrain (Nauta & Domesick, 1982). The NDB also sends output up to the septum, hippocampus, amygdala, and a structure sitting on top of the thalamus called the habenula. The lateral habenula projects down to the interpeduncular nucleus and dorsal midbrain. This is interesting because both the NDB and the habenula have been implicated in radioactive 2DG studies showing high neural activity during self-stimulation (Gallistel, 1983). The output of the NDB seems to be cholinergic and is in a position to excite much of the limbic system.

The Amygdala

Fonberg (1969) used lesions to show that the amygdala contains feeding and satiety functions analogous to the hypothalamus. Since that time, the amygdala has emerged as a major forebrain site for multimodal sensory integration as described earlier. Its access to motor programs presumably occurs through its connections to the medial and lateral hypothalamus and to parts of the striatum and accumbens (Figure 11.8). Thus the amygdala could be considered a sensory-motor interface, but it seems to be more on the sensory side. The amygdala projects to the hippocampus to contribute to spatial-place information and whatever else the hippocampus does, and to the parietal lobe for body space (lesions there cause body neglect), and to frontal cortex for complex discriminative decisions.

The Nucleus Accumbens

The accumbens receives sensory input from the amygdala, hippocampus, and limbic cortex. The accumbens is also the region described earlier as the dopamine terminal field necessary for some component of reinforcement (see Models of Motivation section). Therefore the accumbens is an interface that receives, in part, multimodal feature detection direct from the amygdala, plus feature location via hippocampus, plus feature choice via limbic cortex, and dopamine input from the midbrain VTA which seems to have the function of enhancing accumbens functions. There are other inputs, too, from the septum, olfactory tubercle, and cingulate gyrus which are all part of the Papez circuit of the limbic system (rev. by Mogenson & Yim, 1981; Chronister & DeFrance, 1981), but I have arbitrarily limited the discussion.

To this anatomical and behavioral description, one can now add some neurochemistry. The transmitter for the direct amygdala input to the accumbens is unknown, but input from the hippocampus probably enters the accumbens via

glutamate neurons. According to the model of Chronister and DeFrance (1981) these glutamate neurons end on many spine-covered GABA neurons that output to the globus pallidus (GP) and VTA. There are also smooth (aspiny) cholinergic interneurons. Glutamate is always excitatory. It accounts for depolarization of accumbens cells when stimulating the input from the hippocampus (DeFrance et al., 1984). Groves (1983) has elaborated this model to include a second type of spiny cell and three aspiny ones. The spiny type contains a peptide, substance P, and projects to the globus pallidus and midbrain like the GABA neurons.

The same cellular pattern seems to hold for both the striatum and the accumbens, although the inputs and outputs have different distributions. The dorsal striatum projects to its reciprocal dopamine circuit in the substantia nigra; the ventral striatum and accumbens project to the reciprocal dopamine circuit in the VTA.

Accumbens function is reviewed by Mogenson and Yim (1981) who subscribe to the sensory gate or sensory filter theory that originated with Stevens when she proposed that the accumbens fails to filter properly in schizophrenics. Yim and Mogenson (1983) demonstrated by recording in the ventral globus pallidus that injections of procaine or amphetamine into the accumbens attenuated neural responses to amygdala stimulation. The amphetamine effect was reduced if the dopaminergic input from the VTA was killed ahead of time with 6-hydroxydopamine.

Groves's (1983) neural network model explains the gating system. Glutamine neurons from the cortex play upon a matrix of spiny GABA cells, which sharpen the signal through lateral inhibition in a classical network of inhibitory collaterals. In addition the input ends on cells that make up a cluster around spiny-substance P cells. These are excited by the cholinergic interneurons and inhibited through a recurrent axon collateral connected to an interneuron. The massive GABA output from the ventral striatum and accumbens inhibits target cells of the ventral globus pallidus and VTA. The ventral GP cells, in turn, inhibit motor cells of the ventral thalamus. The striatal substance P output to the GP is excitatory and would therefore inhibit thalamic motor output. Dopamine, according to Groves's model has a weak excitatory effect on the spiny GABA-output neurons and a strong inhibitory influence on the aspiny cholinergic interneurons. The net result of both dopamine functions is to *disinhibit* motor behavior. (The reader who enjoys puzzles should try drawing the circuit.)

McGeer (1975) has stressed the importance of dopamine-ACh balance for healthy functioning of the striatum and accumbens. As seen in Figure 11.9 a deficiency of dopamine (or an excess of ACh) would lead to chronic hypokinesia. In this state, cortical hippocampal and amygdala inputs might come into play upon accumbens keys, but nothing would get out (like a pipe organ being played without opening any of the stops). Conversely, Huntington's disease and tardive dyskinesia are two diseases characterized by involuntary movements. Dopaminergic and cholinergic drugs have effects on these systems which are in accord with this model (Bannon & Roth, 1983; Groves, 1983). These neurochemicals, diseases, and drugs are usually discussed as a whole. However, in fact, the striatum has its own homunculus, representing body parts or movement patterns (Evarts, Kimura, Wurtz, & Hikosaka, 1984; DeLong, Georgopoulos, & Crutcher, 1983).

In sum, the striatum appears to receive cortical motor decisions for action and to respond by organizing the premotor commands to disinhibit thalamic projections to the motor cortex. If we assume that the accumbens acts in a similar fashion, then the accumbens receives limbic (prefrontal, amygdala and hippocampal) decisions and puts them into action. If a primary function of the limbic cortex is stimulus choice, and if the amygdala is for stimulus recognition and the hippocampus for stimulus location, we can see some sense in this arrangement. Locating, recognizing, and choosing stimuli such as food would come through the accumbens to trigger feeding responses. Performance of stereotyped feeding motor patterns would come through the dorsal striatum. Animals seldom search and eat at the same time, so I suppose these two systems may be mutually inhibitory at some level.

The Role of Dopamine

According to this model dopamine could be a behavior reinforcer if it could activate the GABA output and inhibit substance P output of selected cell assemblies at appropriate times. But if dopamine cells fire continuously, they can be reinforcers only if: (1) some other system ends

presynaptically on the dopamine terminals to facilitate dopamine release in response to successful acts, (2) the dopamine cells shift to a burst pattern of firing to release more dopamine or a cotransmitter, (3) dopamine reinforces only the cell assemblies that are active at the moment of success, or (4) a normally silent population of dopamine cells turn on during reward success. It is also possible that some other pathway helps reinforce this system. A post-response glutamate input could do it, or a post-response input to the ACh or substance P cells, or most likely a *presynaptic* facilitatory input that would cause successful circuits to be enhanced in the manner of the *Aplysia* learning model. The balance of behavioral evidence suggests that dopamine is normally necessary for reinforcement that involves limb movement. Self-injection of dopamine and dopamine agonists (Guerin et al., 1984; Hoebel et al., 1983) suggests dopamine is also sufficient for reinforcement in the accumbens. In short, it is normally necessary and sufficient. However the gate theory suggests that dopamine has these effects by allowing other circuits to function.

Three Parallel Cortical-Subcortical Circuits: Premotor Loop, Complex Association Loop and Limbic Loop

Figure 11.13 shows this idea in a nutshell. Across the top of the figure three cortical areas are listed in topographical order. Not shown is the primary motor area which projects directly to the spinal cord. Starting with the premotor cortex (PMC) note that it projects down to the striatum, which has two major outputs. Output to the substantia nigra (SN) was described above (Figure 11.5). Focus now on the one to the globus pallidus (Figure 11.13). It projects to the thalamus and back to the premotor cortex (DeLong et al., 1983; Evarts et al., 1984; Heimer, Switzer, & Van Hoesen, 1982). Further forward in the cortex is a region referred to as frontal cortex (FC) or complex associational area. Its descending projections go to a different part of the striatum and then circle back through the thalamus, thus forming a second, concentric loop. A third circle route is a distinct possibility. It starts in the limbic cortical region and follows a very similar path, down to the ventral striatum and adjacent ACC (Groenewegen, Room, Witter, & Lohman, 1982; Mogenson, Jones, & Yim,

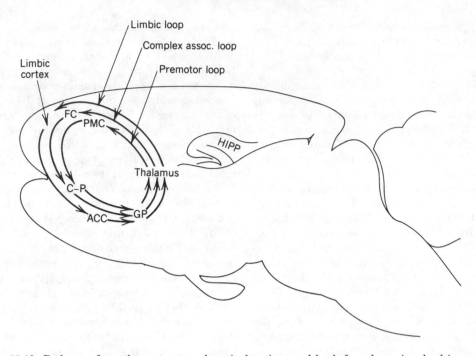

Figure 11.13. Pathways from the cortex to subcortical regions and back form loops involved in generating behavior. The *premotor loop* consists of the premotor cortex (PMC) which projects to the striatum, specifically the putamen (P) in primates, to the dorsal globus pallidus (GP), the thalamus, and back up to the premotor cortex. *Complex association loop*: frontal cortex (FC) to caudate (C), to GP, to thalamus and back to FC. *Limbic loop*: limbic cortex to nucleus accumbens (ACC) and ventral striatum, to ventral GP, to thalamus and back to the limbic cortex. These concentric wheels vary in function from extrapyramidal motor to limbic motivational if we judge by the sensory information that is fed into them. Thus they appear as a "grist mill" for thinking over plans before activating the pyramidal motor output to the spinal cord. Of particular interest are limbic system connections into the limbic loop. For example the hypothalamus connects to the limbic cortex, and the amygdala connects to the hypothalamus, accumbens and limbic cortex. Each loop projects out to the midbrain substantia nigra (SN) or ventral tegmental area (VTA) via GABA neurons. The SN and VTA modulate this output with ascending dopamine neurons (not shown, see Figures 11.5, 11.9 and 11.10). These midbrain regions also project to the thalamus (see text for references to rat, cat, and monkey research on which this figure is based). Compare the names of three loops with the three bipolar disorders in Figure 11.9.

1980), then to the ventral GP or subpallidal region (Swerdlow, Swanson, & Koob, 1984) and back (Heimer et al., 1982).

The inner loop, labeled *premotor*, is largely for initiating movement. The next one, labeled *complex associational*, seems to be responsible for memory-contingent responses. It is like the premotor loop in that neural activity precedes movement and does so only in certain behaviorally significant contexts (Evarts et al., 1984). The associational loop is more complex in the degree to which learning and memory are involved in the firing of cells that have been sampled. The third loop is designated *limbic* because of its association with limbic system

inputs from the amygdala and hippocampus (Levitt, 1984; Livingston & Hornykiewicz, 1976). It presumably is involved in affect-laden decisions. It uses the most ventral route through the basal ganglia by way of the ventral striatum and nucleus accumbens to the ventral GP (Domesick, 1981). Its projection to and from the midbrain involves the VTA more than the substantia nigra; thus it is linked to mesolimbic and mesocortical dopamine systems more than to the nigrostriatal dopamine system.

The function of the limbic loop system is further shown by experiments in which stimulation of the amygdala altered cellular discharges in the accumbens (Yim & Mogenson,

1983). The amygdala could reach the accumbens directly, or via the hippocampus, or via the limbic cortex. The response of the accumbens cells was modulated by stimulation of the VTA which releases dopamine in the accumbens and limbic cortex (Yim & Mogenson, 1983; DeFrance et al., 1984). For an overview of this limbic anatomy see Angevine and Cotman (1981) or Nauta and Domesick (1982), and for another discussion of its function see the review by Kelley & Stinus (1984). They suggest that the nucleus accumbens may be important for "the release of locomotion involved in goal-directed behaviors."

It is difficult to name the three loops without introducing the explanatory fictions and teleological attributions we eschewed at the outset. The inescapable fact, however, is that the brain thinks. The danger lies not in attributing goals, plans, and learned drives to the brain, but in attributing them to the wrong structures. It is the old mistakes of phrenology that one would like to avoid. The debate over the naming of extrapyramidal systems for movement, motor planning, and decision making is already in full swing (McKenzie, Kemm, & Wilcock, 1984; Oberg & Divac, 1981). The designations, premotor, complex associational, and limbic are reasonably conservative. It will be very interesting when we learn how thought processes move from one loop to another as limbic motivation interacts with complex memory-dependent associations and premotor plans finally to access the primary motor system.

Summary and Test of the Model

The first part of this chapter reviewed definitions of motivation that we could use as guidelines. Then elements of motivation were described in simpler invertebrate preparations and brain damaged or drugged rats. The conclusion from this review was that monoamines modulate sensory, motor, and sensorimotor functions in ways that researchers designate as states of warm-up, arousal, activation, and stress. The importance of presynaptic control of neurotransmitter release was emphasized as a mechanism for motivation and learning.

The third part reviewed physiology and behavior involved in homeostatis. An overall theory was presented suggesting that peptides are coded to receptors in ways that give certain peptides the ability to organize an animal's physiology and psychology. The integrative peptides helped to define subsets of motivation.

The fourth section focused on self-stimulation and self-injection as models of motivation in which animals control their own brain functions directly and artificially. Both monoamines and peptides seemed capable of important roles in an animal's own efforts to use electricity or chemicals to control brain circuitry. This demystified the drives and rewards of motivation by reducing them to motor actions aimed at modulating the neural activity in various brain sites. Self-stimulation in the perifornical LH seemed to work very much like the taste of food. Opiates and neurotensin were reinforcing in the VTA, and opiates and dopamine, in the accumbens. The role of CCK as a dopamine cotransmitter in the accumbens was presented as an important topic for basic and applied research.

The last section took a closer look at some characteristics of selected sensory systems to see where they might interface with respondent motor programs and operant motor acts. Anatomy, electrophysiology and neuropharmacology are combining forces to reveal how feature detectors meet command neurons. On the input side, it was interesting that salt taste input resembles sweet when salt is needed, and sweet paired with nausea gives an input like bitter. On the motor-output side, progress has been made in picking out the behavior drills that occur as units. Catecholamines play important roles as neuromodulators at the interface. Norepinephrine from locus coeruleus cells seems to amplify the signal and suppress the noise in sensory feature detectors during wakefulness. The hindbrain norepinephrine cell-body groups modulate internal sensory detectors, at least those for feeding and satiety. Nigrostriatal dopamine seems necessary to potentiate input to stereotyped behavior circuits. Mesolimbic dopamine potentiates and reinforces limbic input to locomotor, exploratory and operant behaviors. Mesocortical dopamine presumably enhances and helps reinforce complex learning. The neuromodulator role of serotonin in the limbic system is less clear, but its synaptic function may enhance circuits for suppression of pain and suppression of feeding. Serotonergic function increases during arousal and acts as an antidepressant.

At the beginning of this chapter it was

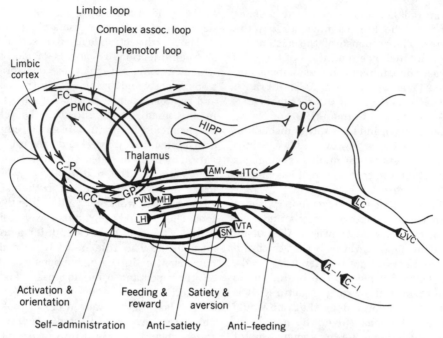

Figure 11.14. An amalgam of the prior figures to provide a complex, but still oversimplified, picture of some of the pathways involved in motivation. Functional labels are operationally defined and meant to be suggestive, not exclusive. The reader is challenged to enter this maze at taste and vagal inputs at the far right and emerge with a bar press for feeding and reward.

proposed that selected neural systems could be defined according to their behavioral functions. This would enable the researcher to record the electrical and chemical activity of these systems to study motivation with or without behavior. The challenge was to measure activity in brain circuits for motivation with criteria based on chemical anatomy. The question now is whether this model is good enough to meet the challenge.

According to the diagram in Figure 11.14, lateral hypothalamic (LH) stimulation activates a descending pathway for feeding and reward. A recent recording study shows the LH path descends all the way to the hindbrain NST that receives input from taste receptors on the tongue. LH stimulation has effects on NST cells that mimic palatable tastes in the mouth, even when the rat is anesthetized (Murzi, Hernandez, & Baptista, 1986). This taste effect helps to explain why LH stimulation induces feeding when the animal is awake; the stimulation probably whets the appetite as if it were food. The taste effect also helps to explain the phenomenon of self-stimulation which apparently gives the animal some of the electrophysiological effects

of taste without having to eat. This reaffirms that neural activity in this pathway is a component of the feeding reward process (Hoebel, 1971, 1974, 1979).

The diagram also suggests that the feeding-reward pathway excites the ascending meso-limbic dopamine pathway from the ventral tegmental area to the accumbens (see arrow pointing to the VTA and from the VTA to the ACC). If this dopamine path is involved in rewarding feeding, then measurements of dopamine release in the ACC should reveal an increase in extracellular dopamine when the animal eats. This has been shown by micro-dialysis.

Microdialysis is a valuable new technique for monitoring neural function (Hernandez, Paez, & Hamlin, 1983; Ungerstedt, 1984). It allows us to test the model by measuring neurotransmitter release in precise brain regions with or without behavior (Hernandez, Stanley, & Hoebel, 1986; Westerink, Dmasma, DeVries and Horn, 1987). The brain microdialysis probe we devised consists of two very narrow stainless steel tubes, one inside the other, with a hollow tip of permeable cellulose 0.2 mm wide by 2 mm long. A guide shaft is implanted in the brain by stereotaxic surgery. A week later when the animal has recovered, the probe tip is inserted through the guide shaft so that the cellulose tip is lodged in the brain site of interest. The microdialysis probe collects neurotransmitters and their metabolites from the adjacent extracellular space. The neurochemicals passively diffuse into the probe tip and are carried out by a slow stream of Ringer's solution circulating within the probe. A quantitative measure of several neurochemicals is obtained by injecting the sample into a high pressure liquid chromatograph (HPLC).

Microdialysis in the accumbens confirmed earlier techniques (rev. in Hernandez and Hoebel, in press, a) by revealing an increase in extracellular dopamine when animals ate food or self-stimulated. Dopamine increased when underweight rats ate a meal; when rats deprived of food for one day were allowed to bar press for pellets, and when satiated rats ate in response to LH stimulation (Hernandez and Hoebel, in press, b). In control studies, microdialysis showed that extracellular dopamine increased selectively in the ACC when rats were actually eating, not with the mere passage of time, and not in the nearby ventral striatum (Figure 11.15). In salt deprived rats given salty water to drink, there was a similar increase in ACC dopamine (Hernandez & Hoebel, unpublished). Therefore the effect extends to motivated behaviors other than eating food pellets. We conclude that components of the mesolimbic dopamine pathway are activated by free feeding, bar pressing for food, stimulation-induced feeding, self-stimulation and some other consummatory behaviors yet to be explored in detail.

The next question was whether or not stimulation of the LH feeding-reward system would release dopamine in the absence of feeding. Figure 11.16 shows the positive result. If one accepts the increase in extracellular dopamine in the ACC as a sign of reward, then LH stimulation is a rewarding event even though the rat is not performing any instrumental behavior that we measure. We hypothesize that dopamine released from the mesolimbic system in the ACC, and perhaps also from branches extending up to the frontal cortex, helps reinforce whatever circuits are active at the time.

If the LH feeding reward system is disinhibited

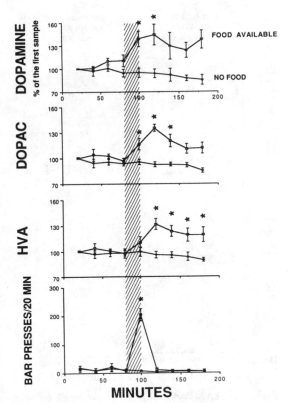

Figure 11.15. Responses for food pellets and eating were associated with an increase in extracellular dopamine and its metabolites, DOPAC and HVA, in the nucleus accumbens. Microdialysis samples taken when no food was available provide the control. The shaded area indicates when the pellet feeder was operative during the "food available" condition (*: $p < 0.05$).

so it can be stimulated by good tastes, then the LH stimulates the mesolimbic DA system to reinforce those circuits that are active in association with the taste. By analogy one can suppose that when the complex association loop is activated in association with good tastes then the relevant neurons can be physically reinforced by dopamine released in the frontal cortex. As mentioned earlier, the mechanism of dopamine's action could be similar to that recently shown in *Aplysia* in which serotonin selectively increased neural activity in active sensory circuits and not inactive ones (G. Clark, personal communication). This would also help explain the observation that dopamine in the mesolimbic system of rats seems to augment ongoing responses and prepotent responses with shifts from one response to another depending on the

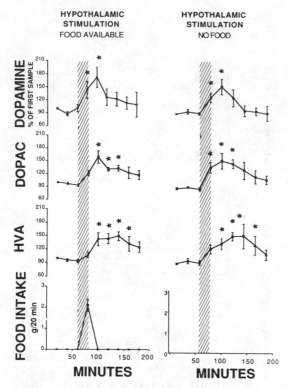

Figure 11.16. LH stimulation that induced feeding when food was available caused a significant increase in extracellular dopamine, DOPAC and HVA in the nucleus accumbens (left graphs). The LH stimulation had the same effect with no food present (right graph).

availability of stimuli in the environment and prior experience with the environment (Mittleman and Valenstein, 1984). Perhaps this is why ACC dopamine, or LH simulation which releases dopamine, facilitates warm-up leading to locomotion until the animal engages in operant responding that procures specific stimuli such as food taste. The new operant response is reinforced in part by the action of dopamine on the active neural inputs to the ACC. The circuit reinforcing action of dopamine does not necessarily stop there. That just happens to be the place we have measured dopamine release. It could serve similar circuit enhancement functions in the frontal cortex, amygdala or hippocampus. Stein and Belluzzi (1987) have evidence that dopamine iontophoresed onto hippocampal cells in temporal contiguity with their firing can reinforce their firing rate. The thing that makes dopamine special in the accumbens is its ability to reinforce an entire behavior pattern, includ-

ing operant behavior, such as bar-pressing for food.

Dopamine in the ACC is involved in addiction (Wise, 1983). As cited earlier, rats will self-inject dopamine or amphetamine directly into the nucleus accumbens. Presumably amphetamine is a reinforcer because it releases dopamine. If so, amphetamine should increase extracellular dopamine as measured by microdialysis. Amphetamine, cocaine, phenycycline and nicotine all have this effect (Hernandez, Auerbach and Hoebel, in press; Hernandez & Hoebel, in press, a; Hernandez, Lee and Hoebel, 1987); so do opiates, alcohol and barbiturates (DiChiara and Imperato, in press). When these drugs of abuse increase extracellular dopamine in the nucleus accumbens they are artificially affecting pathways that evolved over the millennia to reinforce feeding and related behavior. These drugs release dopamine indiscriminately in all the brain sites mentioned above; therefore an overdose has crazy effects on motor programs in the striatum, on cognition in the frontal cortex, and on limbic processes in the accumbens. These abnormal effects can mimic various aspects of schizophrenia.

In summary, our present data shows that extracellular dopamine in the ACC increases during and after eating. There is no evidence that dopamine increases during food deprivation alone. Thus dopamine may play a role in reinforcing at least those circuits which are active during and after feeding. Given the evidence that stimulation of the LH feeding-reward system both activates NST taste cells and releases ACC dopamine, it appears that there are LH cells that both potentiate specific feeding-related sensory input and potentiate forebrain circuits for cognitive processing and behavior output. Dopamine injected into the ACC induces warm-up, locomotion and operant reinforcement; when taste stimulates the LH feeding-reward system this is tantamount to a dopamine injection with the addition of a taste-like input. If the stimulation is not too intense, the animal stops locomoting long enough to eat. If there is no food, the animal may turn to something else. Feeding that releases dopamine leads to more feeding. Salt intake that releases dopamine presumably leads to more salt intake. The behavior we observe depends on the circuits that are opened by dopamine, stimulated by the internal or external environment, and reinforced by more dopamine, perhaps in synergy with cotransmitters such as CCK. As described in the section on integrative peptides, some circuits may be coded with peptide neurotransmitters. For example, angiotensin exists in a circuit for behavior that maintains blood pressure through the ingestion of water and salt. The observation that angiotensin, itself, can increase extracellular dopamine in the ACC (Hernandez, Mark and Hoebel, unpublished) suggests that such peptides can facilitate the release of dopamine thereby facilitating locomotion and operant response circuits. Dopamine might potentiate any behavior, but we know that homeostatic needs can alter sensory input. For example in the rat, salt deprivation can make salt solutions give a sweet-type response in the NST, and illness paired with a sweet solution can make it give a bitter-type response. Thus taste is coded, in part, for homeostatic benefit and safety (Scott and Mark, 1987). The deprivation conditions which produce the angiotensin also potentiate circuits for appropriate sensory input to rectify the deprivation. Thus acts leading to appropriate sensory input are what will stimulate the LH, release dopamine and be reinforced.

Changes in this model will come with the discovery of new neurotransmitters, new pathways, and finer subdivisions of the gross indications given. For a start at least, this represents an advance over the classic arrow that covered the whole brain to represent the reticular activation system (Moruzzi & Magoun, 1949). Stellar (1954) added functional labels to the medial and lateral hypothalamus with arrows signifying their role in the integration of internal and external stimuli. Lindsley (1951) in the original *Handbook of Experimental Psychology* drew a brain full of arrows that is surprisingly accurate based just on lesion and EEG data; almost nothing was known of neurochemistry thirty years ago. I can only hope that thirty years from now the present attempt will be viewed as hopelessly outdated but correct as far as it goes. Perhaps the major lesson of the past is that scientists and clinicians should take this as a snapshot of a rapidly-expanding field, not an enduring medical truth. L-DOPA, the precursor of dopamine, can restore motivation to a Parkinson patient, but the effect does not last. Other treatments and techniques for replacing neurons are being discovered. As for psychosis, the frontal lobotomy of yesteryear is the dopamine blocker of today

and the specific peptide blocker of tomorrow. The neuroscience of motivation is in its infancy. It will have much to offer through a combination of drug and nutritional therapy for circuits that need chemicals and through behavior therapy for circuits that need exercise. Growth of this science depends on discovering the functionally defined circuits for motivation.

REFERENCES

Acher, R. (1983). Principles of evolution: The neural hierarchy model. In D.T. Krieger, M.J. Brownstein, & J.B. Martin (Eds.), *Brain Peptides* (pp. 135–163). New York: Wiley.

Alder, N.T. & Allen, T.O. (1983). The origin of sexual behavior: A functional analysis. In E. Satinoff & P. Teitelbaum (Eds.), *Handbook of Behavioral Neurobiology: Volume 6. Motivation* (pp. 475–509). New York: Plenum Press.

Ahlskog, J.E. & Hoebel, B.G. (1973). Overeating and obesity from damage to a noradrenergic system in the brain. *Science, 69*, 166–182.

Ahlskog, J.E., Randall, P.K., Hernandez, L., & Hoebel, B.G. (1984). Diminished amphetamine anorexia and enhanced fenfluramine anorexia after midbrain 6-hydroxydopamine. *Psychopharmacology, 82*, 118–121.

Andrews, J.S. & Sahgal, A. (1983). Central administration of thyrotropin-releasing hormone and histidyl-proline-diketopiperazine disrupts the acquisition of a food rewarded task by a non-aversive action. *Regulatory Peptides, 7*, 373–383.

Angevine, J.B. & Cotman, C.W. (1981). *Principles of Neuroanatomy*. New York: Oxford University Press.

Antelman, S.M. & Chiodo, L.A. (1983). Amphetamine as a stressor. In I. Creese (Eds.), *Stimulants: Neurochemical, Behavioral and Clinical Perspectives* (pp. 269–299). New York: Raven Press.

Appel, J.A., White, F., & Kuhn, D.M. (1978). The use of drugs as discriminative stimuli in behavioral pharmacodynamics. In F.C. Colpaert & J.A. Rosecrans (Eds.), *Stimulus Properties of Drugs: Ten Years of Progress* (pp. 7–51). Amsterdam: Elsevier/North-Holland.

Aston-Jones, G. & Bloom, F.E. (1981). Norepinephrine-containing locus coeruleus neurons in behaving rats exhibit pronounced responses to non-noxious environmental stimuli. *Journal of Neuroscience, 1*, 887–900.

Axelrod, J. & Reisine, T.D. (1984). Stress hormones: Their interaction and regulation. *Science, 224*, 452–459.

Baile, C.A. & Della-Fera, M.A. (1984). Peptidergic control of food intake in food-producing animals. *Federation Proceedings*, *43*, 2898–2902.

Bannon, M.J. & Roth, R.H. (1983). Pharmacology of mesocortical dopamine neurons. *Pharmacological Reviews*, *35*, 53–68.

Bartness, T.J. & Waldbillig, R.J. (1984). Cholecystokinin-induced suppression of feeding: An evaluation of the generality of gustatory-cholecystokinin interactions. *Physiology & Behavior*, *32*, 409–415.

Beckwith, B.E., Petros, T., Kanaan-Beckwith, S., Couk, D.I., & Haug, R.J. (1982). Vasopression analog (DDAVP) facilitates concept learning in human males. *Peptides*, *3*, 627–630.

Belluzzi, J.D. & Stein, L. (1982). Endorphin mediation of feeding. In B.G. Hoebel & D. Novin (Eds.), *The Neural Basis of Feeding and Reward* (pp. 479–484). Brunswick, ME: Haer Institute.

Berridge, K.C., Flynn, F.W., Schulin, J., & Grill, H.J. (1984). Sodium depletion enhances salt palatability in rat. *Behavioral Neuroscience*, *98*, 652–660.

Berthoud, H.R. & Baettig, K. (1974). Effects of insulin and 2-deoxy-d-glucose on plasma glucose level and lateral hypothalamic eating threshold in the rat. *Physiology and Behavior*, *12*, 547–556.

Blundell, J.E. (1983). Problems and processes underlying the control of food selection and nutrient intake. In R.J. Wurtman & J.J. Wurtman (Eds.), *Nutrition and the Brain: Vol. 6* (pp. 163–221). New York: Raven Press.

Booth, D.A. (1980). Acquired behavior controlling energy intake and output. In A.J. Stunkard (Ed.), *Obesity* (pp. 101–143). Philadelphia: W.B. Saunders Co.

Boulant, J.A. (1980). Hypothalamic control of thermoregulation. In P.J. Morgane & J. Panksepp (Eds.), *Handbook of the Hypothalamus: Volume 3. Part A, Behavioral Studies of the Hypothalamus* (pp. 1–82). New York: Marcel Dekker, Inc.

Bozarth, M.A. (1983). Opiate reward mechanisms mapped by intracranial self-administration. In J.E. Smith & J.D. Lane (Eds.), *The Neurobiology of Opiate Reward Processes* (pp. 331–360). Amsterdam: Elsevier Biomedical Press.

Bozarth, M.A. (Ed.). (1987). *Methods of Assessing the Reinforcing Properties of Abused Drugs*. New York: Springer-Verlag.

Bray, G.A. & York, D.A. (1979). Hypothalamic and genetic obesity in experimental animals: An autonomic and endocrine hypothesis. *Physiological Review*, *59*, 719–809.

Brink, Jr., F. (1951). Excitation and conduction in the neuron. In S.S. Stevens (Ed.), *Handbook of Experimental Psychology* (pp. 50–93). New York: Wiley.

Britt, M.D. & Wise, R.A. (1983). Ventral tegmental site of opiate reward: Antagonism by a hydrophilic opiate receptor blocker. *Brain Research*, *258*, 105–108.

Brody, M.J. & Johnson, A.K. (1980). Role of the anteroventral third ventricle region in fluid and electrolyte balance, arterial pressure regulation, and hypertension. In L. Martini & W.F. Ganong (Eds.), *Frontiers in Neuroendocrinology: Vol. 6* (pp. 249–292). New York: Raven Press.

Bunney, B.S. (1984, June). Antipsychotic drug effects on the electrical activity of dopaminergic neurons. *Trends in Neuroscience*, 212–215.

Burbach, J.P.H., Kovacs, G.L., & De Wied, D. (1983). A major metabolite of arginine vasopressin the brain is a highly potent neuropeptide. *Science*, *221*, 1310–1312.

Cabanac, M. (1971). Physiological role of pleasure. *Science*, *173*, 1103–1107.

Caggiula, A.R. & Hoebel, B.G. (1966). A "copulation-reward" site in the posterior hypothalamus. *Science*, *153*, 1284–1285.

Caldwell, J. (Ed.). (1980). *Amphetamines and Related Stimulants: Chemical, Biological, Clinical, and Sociological Aspects*. Boca Raton, FL: CRC Press.

Campbell, B.A. & Randall, P.J. (1977). Paradoxical effects of amphetamine on preweaning and postweaning rats. *Science*, *195*, 888–891.

Carr, K.D. & Simon, E.J. (1983). The role of opioids in feeding and reward elicited by lateral hypothalamic electrical stimulation. *Life Sciences*, *33*, Suppl. I, 563–566.

Chang, F.-C.T. & Scott, T.R. (1984). Conditioned taste aversions modify neural response in the rat nucleus tractus solitarius. *Journal of Neuroscience*, *4*, 1850–1862.

Chronister, R.B. & DeFrance, J.F. (Eds.). (1981). *The Neurobiology of the Nucleus Accumbens*. Brunswick, ME: Haer Institute.

Clark, G.A. & Kandel, E.R. (1987). Serotonin produces long-term potentiation at peripheral synapses when applied selectively to synaptic regions of *Aplysia* siphon sensory cells. *Society for Neuroscience Abstracts*, *13*, 390.

Clavier, R.M. & Routtenberg, A. (1980). In search of reinforcement pathways: A neuroanatomical odyssey. In A. Routtenberg (Ed.), *Biology of Reinforcement: Facets of Brain-Stimulation Reward* (pp. 81–107). New York: Academic Press.

Collier, G.H. & Rovee-Collier, C.K. (1983). An ecological perspective of reinforcement and motivation. In E. Satinoff & P. Teitelbaum (Eds.), *Handbook of Behavioral Neurology: Vol. 6. Motivation* (pp. 427–441). New York: Plenum Press.

Cooper, S.J. (1981). Prefrontal cortex, benzodiazepines and opiates: Case studies in motivation and behaviour analysis. In S.J. Cooper (Eds.), *Theory of Psychopharmacology: Volume 1* (pp. 277–322). New York: Academic Press.

Cooper, S.J. & Sanger, D.J. (1984). Endorphinergic mechanisms in food, salt and water intake: an overview. *Appetite*, 5, 1–6.

Costa, E. & Trabucchi, M. (Eds.). (1980). *Neural Peptides and Neural Communication*. New York: Raven Press.

Coyle, J.T. & Enna, S.J. (Eds.). (1983). *Neuroleptics: Neurochemical, Behavioral, and Clinical Perspectives*. New York: Raven Press.

Cramer, C.P. & Blass, E.M. (1982). Rate versus volume in the milk intake of suckling rats. In B.G. Hoebel & D. Novin (Eds.), *The Neural Basis of Feeding and Reward* (pp. 67–74). Brunswick, ME: Haer Institute.

Crawley, J.N. & Schwaber, J.S. (1984). Abolition of the behavioral effects of cholecystokinin following bilateral radiofrequency lesions of the parvocellular subdivision of the nucleus tractus solitarius. *Brain Research*, 295, 289–299.

Creese, I. (1981). Dopamine Receptors. In H.I. Yamamura & S.J. Enna (Eds.), *Neurotransmitter Receptors: Part 2, Biogenic Amines* (pp. 129–183). London: Chapman & Hall, Ltd.

Creese, I. (Ed.). (1983). *Stimulants: Neurochemical, Behavioral, and Clinical Perspectives*. New York: Raven Press.

Davis, W.J. & Kovac, M.P. (1981, March). The command neuron and the organization of movement. *Trends in Neuroscience*, 73–76.

DeFrance, J.F., Sikes, R.W., & Chronister, R.B. (1984). Effects of CCK-8 in the nucleus accumbens. *Peptides*, 5, 1–6.

Delgado, J.M.R., Roberts, W.W., & Miller, N.E. (1954). Learning motivated by electrical stimulation of the brain. *American Journal of Physiology*, 179, 587–593.

Della-Fera, M., Baile, C.A., Schneider, B.S., & Grinker, J.A. (1981). Cholecystokinin antibody injected in cerebral ventricles stimulates feeding in sheep. *Science*, 212, 687–689.

DeLong, M.R., Georgopoulos, A.P., & Crutcher, M.D. (1983). Cortico-basal ganglia relations and coding of motor performance. In J. Massion, J. Paillard, W. Schultz, & M. Wiesendanger (Eds.), *Neural Coding of Motor Performance, Experimental Brain Research Supplementum 7* (pp. 30–40). Berlin: Springer-Verlag.

DeRyck, M. & Teitelbaum, P. (1983). Morphine versus haloperidol catalepsy in the rat: An electromyographic analysis of postural support mechanisms. *Experimental Neurology*, 79, 54–76.

Dethier, V.G. (1976). *The Hungry Fly*. Cambridge, MA.: Harvard University Press.

Dethier, V.G. (1982). The contribution of insects to the study of motivation. In A.R. Morrison & P.L. Strick (Eds.), *Changing Concepts of the Nervous System* (pp. 445–456). New York: Academic Press.

Deutsch, J.A. (1976). The drive-reward theory of brain reward. In A. Wauquier & E.T. Rolls (Eds.), *Brain-Stimulation Reward* (pp. 593–600). New York: Elsevier/North Holland, Inc.

Deutsch, J.A. (1979). Drive—another point of view. *Trends in Neuroscience*, 2, 242–244.

Deutsch, J.A. (1982). Controversies in food intake regulation. In B.G. Hoebel & D. Novin (Eds.), *The Neural Basis of Feeding and Reward* (pp. 137–145). Brunswick, ME: Haer Institute.

Devor, M.G., Wise, R.A., Milgram. N.W., & Hoebel, B.G. (1970). Physiological control of hypothalamically elicited feeding and drinking. *Journal of Comparative and Physiological Psychology*, 73, 226–232.

Domesick, V.B. (1981). Further observations on the anatomy of nucleus accumbens and caudatoputamen in the rat: similarities and contrasts. In R.B. Chronister & J.F. DeFrance (Eds.), *The Neurobiology of the Nucleus Accumbens* (pp. 7–39). Brunswick, ME: Haer Institute.

Ellison, G.D. (1968). Appetite behavior in rats after circumsection of the hypothalamus. *Physiology and Behavior*, 3, 221–226.

Engel, J. et al. (1987). *Brain Reward Systems and Abuse*. New York: Raven Press.

Epstein, A.N. (1981). Angiotensin-induced thirst and sodium appetite. In J.B. Martin, S. Reichlin, & K.L. Bick (Eds.), *Advances in Biochemical Psychopharmacology: Vol. 28. Neurosecretion and Brain Peptides* (pp. 373–387). New York: Raven Press.

Epstein, A.M. (1982a). Instinct and motivation as explanations for complex behavior. In D.W. Pfaff (Eds.), *The Physiological Mechanisms of Motivation* (pp. 25–58). New York: Springer-Verlag.

Epstein, A.M. (1982b). The physiology of thirst. In D.W. Pfaff (Ed.), *The Physiological Mechanisms of Motivation* (pp. 164–214). New York: Springer-Verlag.

Ettenberg, A. & Koob, G.F. (1984). Different effects of cholecystokinin and satiety on lateral hypothalamic self-stimulation. *Physiology & Behavior*, 32, 127–130.

Ettenberg, A., Koob, G.F., & Bloom, F.E. (1981). Response artifact in the measurements of neuroleptic induced anhedonia. *Science*, 213, 357–359.

Ettenberg, A. & White, N. (1978). Conditioned taste preferences in the rat induced by self-stimulation. *Physiology & Behavior*, 21, 363–368.

Evarts, E.V., Kimura, M., Wurtz, R.H. & Hikosaka, O. (1984). Behavioral correlates of activity on basal ganglia neurons. *Trends in Neuroscience, 7*, 447–453.

Fentress, J.C. (1983). Ethological methods of hierarchy and patterning of species-specific behavior. In E. Satinoff & P. Teitelbaum (Eds.), *Handbook of Behavioral Neurobiology: Volume 6. Motivation* (pp. 185–234). New York: Plenum Press.

Fibiger, H.C. & Phillips, A.G. (1986). Reward, motivation and cognition: Psychobiology of mesotelencephalic dopamine systems. In F.E. Bloom (Ed.), *Handbook of Physiology: Vol. IV Intrinsic Regulatory Systems of the Brain.* Bethesda: American Physiological Society.

Fluharty, S.J. & Epstein, A.M. (1983). Sodium appetite elicited by intracerebroventricular infusion of angiotensin II in the rat: II. Synergistic interaction with systemic mineralocorticoids. *Behavioral Neuroscience, 97*, 746–758.

Flynn, F.W. & Grill, H.J. (1985). The caudal brainstem and the integrated control of energy balance. In G. Bray & T. Castonguay (Eds.), *The Neural and Metabolic Bases of Feeding.*

Fonberg, E. (1969). The role of the hypothalamus and amygdala in food intake, alimentary motivation and emotional reactions. *Acta Biologica Exp., 29*, 335–358.

Franklin, K. & McCoy, S.N. (1979). Pimozide-induced extinction in rats: Stimulus control of responding rules out motor deficit. *Pharmacology, Biochemistry, and Behavior, 11*, 71–75.

Fray, P.J., Koob, G.F., & Iversen, S.D. (1982). Tail-pinch-elicited behavior in rats: Preference, plasticity and learning. *Behavioral and Neural Biology, 36*, 108–125.

Gallistel, C.R. (1980). From muscles to motivation. *American Scientist, 68*, 398–410.

Gallistel, C.R. (1981). Precis of Gallistel's *The Organization of Action: A New Synthesis. Behavioral and Brain Sciences, 4*, 609–650.

Gallistel, C.R. (1983). Self-stimulation. In J.A. Deutsch (Ed.), *The Physiological Basis of Memory* (pp. 269–349.) New York: Academic Press.

Gallistel, C.R. & Beagley, G. (1971). Specificity of brain stimulation reward in the rat. *Journal of Comparative and Physiological Psychology, 76*, 199–205.

Gallistel, C.R. & Karras, D. (1984). Pimozide and amphetamine have opposing effects on the reward summation function. *Pharmacology Biochemistry & Behavior, 20*, 73–77.

Gallistel, C.R., Shizgal, P., & Yeomans, J.S. (1981). A portrait of the substrate for self-stimulation. *Psychological Review, 88*, 228–273.

Ganten, D., Hermann, K., Bayer, C., Unger, T., & Lang, R.E. (1983). Angiotensin synthesis in the brain and increased turnover in hypertensive rats. *Science, 221*, 869–871.

Ganten, D., Speck, G., Schelling, P., & Unger, T. (1981). The brain renin-angiotensin system. In J.B. Martin, S. Reichlin, & K.L. Bick (Eds.), *Advances in Biochemical Psychopharmacology: Vol. 28. Neurosecretion and Brain Peptides* (pp. 359–372). New York: Raven Press.

Gelperin, A. (1983). Neuroethological studies of associative learning in feeding control systems. In F. Huber & H. Markl (Eds.), *Neuroethology and Behavioral Physiology* (pp. 189–205). Berlin: Springer-Verlag.

Gelperin, A. (1986). Complex associative learning in small neural networks. *Trends in Neurosciences, 9*, 323–328.

Glimcher, P., Giovino, A.A., Margolin, D.H., & Hoebel, B.G. (1984). Endogenous reward induced by an enkephalinase inhibitor, thiorphan, injected into the ventral midbrain. *Behavioural Neuroscience, 98*, 262–268.

Glimcher, P.V., Margolin, D.H., Giovino, A.A., & Hoebel, B.G. (1984). Neurotensin: A new "reward peptide." *Brain Research, 291*, 119–124.

Goeders, N.E., Lane, J.D., & Smith, J.E. (1984). Self-administration of methionine enkephalin into the nucleus accumbens. *Pharmacology Biochemistry & Behavior, 20*, 451–455.

Goeders, N.E. & Smith, J.E. (1983). Cortical dopaminergic involvement in cocaine reinforcement. *Science, 221*, 773–775.

Grace, A.A. & Bunney, B.S. (1984). The control of firing pattern in nigral dopamine neurons: burst firing. *Journal of Neuroscience, 4*, 2877–2890.

Grandison, L. & Guidotti, A. (1977). Stimulation of food intake by muscimol and beta-endorphin. *Neuropharmacology, 16*, 533–536.

Gratton, A. & Wise, R.A. (1985). Hypothalamic reward mechanism: Two first-stage fiber populations with a cholinergic component. *Science, 227*, 545–548.

Grevel, J. & Sadee, W. (1983). An opiate binding site in the rat brain is highly selective for 4, 5-epoxymorphinans. *Science, 221*, 1198–1200.

Groenewegen, H.J., Room, P., Witter, M.P., & Lohman, A.H.M. (1982). Cortical afferents of the nucleus accumbens in the cat, studied with anterograde and retrograde transport techniques. *Neuroscience, 7*, 977–995.

Gross, C.G., Desimone, R., Albright, T.D., & Schwartz, E.L. (1984). Inferior temporal cortex as a visual integration area. In E. Reinoso-Suarez & C. Ajmone-Marsan (Eds.), *Cortical Integration* (pp. 291–315). New York: Raven Press.

Grossman, S.P. (1962). Direct adrenergic and cholinergic stimulation of hypothalamic mechanism. *American Journal of Physiology*, *202*, 872–882.

Grossman, S.P. (1979). The biology of motivation. *Annual Review of Psychology*, *30*, 209–242.

Grossman, S.P. (1984). A reassessment of the brain mechanisms that control thirst. *Neuroscience and Biobehavioral Reviews*, *8*, 95–104.

Grossman, S.P., Dacey, D., Halaris, A.E., Collier, T., & Routtenberg, A. (1978). Aphagia and adipsia after preferential destruction of nerve cell bodies in hypothalamus. *Science*, *202*, 537–539.

Groves, P.M. (1983). A theory of the functional organization of the neostriatum and the neostriatal control of voluntary movement. *Brain Research Reviews*, *5*, 109–132.

Guerin, G.F., Goeders, N.E., Dworkin, S.I., & Smith, J.E. (1984). Intracranial self-administration of dopamine into the nucleus accumbens. *Society for Neuroscience Abstracts*, *10*, 1072.

Halberg, F. (1969). Chronobiology. *Annual Review of Physiology*, *31*, 675–725.

Halperin, R. & Pfaff, D.W. (1982). Brain-stimulated reward and control of autonomic function: Are they related? In D.W. Pfaff (Ed.), *The Physiological Mechanisms of Motivation* (pp. 337–376). New York: Springer-Verlag.

Hatton, G.I. & Armstrong, W.E. (1981). Hypothalamic function in the behavioral and physiological control of body fluids. In P.J. Morgane & J. Panksepp (Eds.), *Handbook of the Hypothalamus: Vol. 3. Part B, Behavioral Studies of the Hypothalamus* (pp. 1–105). New York: Marcel Dekker, Inc.

Hawkins, R.D. & Kandel, E.R. (1984). Is there a cell-biological alphabet for simple forms of learning? *Psychological Review*, *91*, 375–391.

Heck, G.L., Mierson, S., & DeSimone, J.A. (1984). Salt taste transduction occurs through an amiloride-sensitive sodium transport pathway. *Science*, *223*, 403–405.

Heimer, L., Switzer, R.D., & Van Hoesen (1982, March). Ventral striatum and ventral pallidum: Components of the motor system? *Trends in Neuroscience*, 83–87.

Hendricks, S.A., Roth, J., Rishi, S., & Becker, K.L. (1983). Insulin in the nervous system. In D.T. Krieger, M.J. Brownstein, & J.B. Martin (Eds.), *Brain Peptides* (pp. 903–939). New York: Wiley.

Herber, L., Stephens, D.N., & Franklin, K.B.J. (1980). Catecholamines and self-stimulation: Evidence suggesting a reinforcing role for noradrenaline and a motivating role for dopamine. *Pharmacology Biochemistry & Behavior*, *4*, 575–582.

Hernandez, L. (1976). Glucostatic influences on self-stimulation and hypothalamic neurons. In A.

Wauquier & E.T. Rolls (Eds.), *Brain-Stimulation Reward* (pp. 471–477). Amsterdam: Elsevier/North-Holland.

Hernandez, L. & Hoebel, B.G. (1978). Hypothalamic reward and aversion: A link between metabolism and behavior. In K. Lederis & W.L. Veale (Eds.), *Current Studies of Hypothalamic Function* (pp. 72–92). Basel: Karger.

Hernandez, L. & Hoebel, B.G. (1980). Basic mechanisms of feeding and weight regulation. In A.J. Stunkard (Eds.), *Obesity* (pp. 25–47). Philadelphia: W.B. Saunders Co.

Hernandez, L. & Hoebel, B.G. (1982). Overeating after midbrain 6-hydroxydopamine: Prevention by central injection of selective reuptake blockers. *Brain Research*, *245*, 333–343.

Hernandez, L., Auerbach, S., & Hoebel, B.G. (In press). Phencyclidine (PCP) injected in the nucleus accumbens increases extracellular dopamine and serotonin as measured by microdialysis. *Life Sciences*.

Hernandez, L., Lee, F., & Hoebel, B.G. (1987). Simultaneous microdialysis and amphetamine infusion in the nucleus accumbens and striatum of freely moving rats: Increase in extracellular dopamine and serotonin. *Brain Research Bulletin*, *19*, 623–628.

Hernandez, L., Paez, A., & Hamlin, C. (1983). Neurotransmitter extraction by local intracerebral dialysis in anesthetized rats. *Pharmacology Biochemistry and Behavior*, *18*, 159–162.

Hernandez, L., Stanley, B.G., & Hoebel, B.G. (1986). A small, removable microdialysis probe. *Life Sciences*, *39*, 2629–2637.

Hernandez, L. & Hoebel, B.G. (in press, a). Food reward and cocaine increase extracellular dopamine in the nucleus accumbens as measured by microdialysis. *Life Sciences*.

Hernandez, L. & Hoebel, B.G. (in press, b). Feeding increases dopamine turnover in the nucleus accumbens more than the ventral striatum as shown by microdialysis. *Brain Research Bulletin*.

Hess, W.R. (1954). *Diencephalon: Autonomic and extrapyramidal functions*. New York: Grune & Stratton.

Hoebel, B.G. (1969). Feeding and self-stimulation. *Annals of the New York Academy of Sciences*, 157-R2, 758–778.

Hoebel, B.G. (1971). Feeding: Neural control of intake. *Annual Review of Physiology*, *33*, 533–568.

Hoebel, B.G. (1974). Brain reward and aversion systems in the control of feeding and sexual behavior. In J.K. Cole and T.B. Sonderegger (Eds.) *Nebraska Symposium on Motivation*, *22*, 49–112.

Hoebel, B.G. (1976). Brain-stimulation reward and

aversion in relation to behavior. In A. Wauquier & E.T. Rolls (Eds.), *Brain-Stimulation Reward* (pp. 335–372). Amsterdam: Elsevier/North-Holland.

Hoebel, B.G. (1977a). Pharmacologic control of feeding. *Annual Review of Pharmacology and Toxicology, 17,* 605–621.

Hoebel, B.G. (1977b). The psychopharmacology of feeding. In L.L. Iversen, S.D. Iversen, & S.H. Snyder (Eds.), *Handbook of Psychopharmacology: Volume 8. Drugs, Neurotransmitters and Behavior* (pp. 55–129). New York: Plenum Press.

Hoebel, B.G. (1979). Hypothalamic self-stimulation and stimulation escape in relation to feeding and mating. *Federation Proceedings, 38,* 2454–2461.

Hoebel, B.G. (1980). Three anorectic drugs: Similar structures but different effects on brain and behavior. In G.A. Bray (Ed.), *Obesity: Comparative Methods of Weight Control* (pp. 59–68). London: John Libbey & Co.

Hoebel, B.G. (1982). The neural and chemical basis of reward: New discoveries and theories in brain control of feeding, mating, aggression, self-stimulation and self-injection. *Journal of Social and Biological Structures, 5,* 397–408.

Hoebel, B.G. (1984). Neurotransmitters in the control of feeding and its rewards: Monoamines, opiates and brain-gut peptides. In A.J. Stunkard & E. Stellar (Eds.), *Eating and Its Disorders* (pp. 15–38). Association for Research on Nervous and Mental Disease, Vol. 62. New York: Raven Press.

Hoebel, B.G. (1985a). Brain neurotransmitters in food and drug reward. *American Journal of Clinical Nutrition, 42,* 1133–1150.

Hoebel, B.G. (1985b). Integrative peptides. *Brain Research Bulletin, 14,* 525–528.

Hoebel, B.G., Hernandez, L., McClelland, R.C., & Schwartz, D. (In press). Dexfenfluramine and Feeding Reward. *Clinical Neuropharmacology.*

Hoebel, B.G., Hernandez, L., McLean, S., Stanley, B.G., Aulissi, E.F., Glimcher, P.G., & Margolin, D. (1982). Catecholamines, enkephalin and neurotensin in feeding and reward. In B.G. Hoebel & D. Novin (Eds.), *The Neural Basis of Feeding and Reward* (pp. 465–478). Brunswick, ME: Haer Institute.

Hoebel, B.G. & Leibowitz, S.F. (1981). Brain monoamines in the modulation of self-stimulation, feeding, and body weight. In H. Weiner, M.A. Hofer, & A.J. Stunkard (Eds.), *Brain, Behavior, and Bodily Disease* (pp. 103–142). Association for Research in Nervous and Mental Disease, Vol. 59. New York: Raven Press.

Hoebel, B.G., Monaco, A.P., Hernandez, L., Stanley, W.G., Aulisi, E.P., & Lenard, L. (1983). Self-injection of amphetamine directly into the brain. *Psychopharmacology, 81,* 156–163.

Hoebel, B.G. & Novin, D. (Eds.). (1982). *The Neural Basis of Feeding and Reward.* Brunswick, ME: Haer Institute.

Hoebel, B.G., Rosenquist, A.C., & Caggiula, A.R. (1969). *Hypothalamic Reward in Feeding, Running, and Mating Behavior.* Pennsylvania State University Psychological Cinema Register film #33018.

Hoebel, B.G. & Teitelbaum, P. (1966). Weight regulation in normal and hypothalamic hyperphagic rats. *Journal of Comparative and Physiological Psychology, 61,* 189–193.

Hokfelt, T., Lundberg, J.M., Skirbol, L., Johansson, O., Schultzberg, M., & Vincent, S.R. (1982). Coexistence of classical transmitters and peptides in neurons. In A.C. Cuello (Ed.), *Co-Transmission.* London: Macmillan.

Holaday, J.W. & Faden, A.I. (1983). Thyrotropin releasing hormone: Autonomic effects upon cardiorespiratory function in endotoxic shock. *Regulatory Peptides, 7,* 111–125.

Horovitz, Z.P. (Ed.), (1981). *Angiotensin Converting Enzyme Inhibitors: Mechanisms of Action and Clinical Implications.* Baltimore: Urban & Schwarzenberg.

Hughes, J. (Ed.) (1978). *Centrally Acting Peptides.* Baltimore: University Park Press.

Huston, J.P. (1982). Searching for the neural mechanism of reinforcement (of "stamping in"). In B.G. Hoebel & D. Novin (Eds.), *The Neural Basis of Feeding and Reward* (pp. 75–83). Brunswick, ME: Haer Institute.

Iversen, S.D. (1977). Brain dopamine systems and behavior. In L.L. Iversen, S.D. Iversen, & S.H. Snyder (Eds.), *Handbook of Psychopharmacology: Volume 8. Drugs, Neurotransmitters and Behavior* (pp. 333–384). New York: Plenum Press.

Iversen, S.D. (1983). Brain endorphins and reward function: Some thoughts and speculations. In J.E. Smith & J.D. Lane (Eds.), *The Neurobiology of Opiate Reward Processes* (pp. 439–468). Amsterdam: Elsevier Biomedical Press.

Jacobs, B.L. (1986). Single unit activity of brain monoamine-containing neurons in freely moving animals. *Annals of the New York Academy of Science, 473,* 70–77.

Jacobs, B.L., Heym, J., & Steinfels, G.F. (1984). Physiological and Behavioral Analysis of Raphe Unit Activity. In L.L. Iversen, S.D. Iversen, & S.H. Snyder (Eds.), *Handbook of Psychopharmacology: Volume 18. Drugs, Neurotransmitters, and Behavior* (pp. 343–396). New York: Plenum Press.

Jacquin, M.F. & Enfiejian, H. (1982). Trigeminal mediation of an oromotor fractional anticipatory goal response. In B.G. Hoebel & D. Novin (Eds.), *The Neural Basis of Feeding and Reward* (pp. 85–96). Brunswick ME: Haer Institute.

Johnson, A.K. (1979). Role of the periventricular tissue of the anteroventral third ventricle in body fluid homeostasis. In P. Meyer & H. Schmitt (Eds.), *Nervous System and Neurotensin* (pp. 106–114). New York: Wiley.

Johnson, A.K. (1982). Neurobiology of the periventricular tissue surrounding the anteroventral third ventricle (AV3V) and its role in behavior, fluid balance, and cardiovascular control. In O.A. Smith, R.A. Galosy, & S.M. Weiss (Eds.), *Circulation, Neurobiology, and Behavior* (pp. 277–295). New York: Elsevier.

Johnson, W.G. & Wildman, H.E. (1983). Influence of external and covert food stimuli on insulin secretion in obese and normal persons. *Behavioral Neuroscience, 97,* 1025–1028.

Kastin, A.J., Zadina, J.E., Banks, W.A., & Graf, M.V. (1984). Misleading concepts in the field of brain peptides. *Peptides,* Suppl. 1, *5,* 249–253.

Keesey, R.E. & Corbett, S.W. (1984). Metabolic defense of the body weight set-point. In A.J. Stunkard & E. Stellar (Eds.), *Eating and Its Disorders* (pp. 87–96). Association for Research on Nervous and Mental Disease, Vol. 61. New York: Raven Press.

Kelley, A.E. & Stinus, L. (1984). Neuroanatomical and neurochemical substrates of affective behavior. In N.A. Fox & R.J. Davidson (Eds.), *The Psychobiology of Affective Development* (pp. 1–75). Hillsdale, NJ: Erlbaum.

Kobashi, M. & Adachi, A. (1985). Convergence of hepatic osmoreceptic inputs on sodium-responsive units within the nucleus of the solitary tract of the rat. *Journal of Neurophysiology, 54,* 212–219.

Koob, G. & Bloom, F.E. (1983). Memory, learning, and adaptive behaviors. In D.T. Krieger, M.J. Brownstein, & J.B. Martin (Eds.), *Brain Peptides* (pp. 369–388). New York: Wiley.

Koob, G.F. & Bloom, F.E. (1985). Corticotropin-releasing factor and behavior. *Federation Proceedings, 44,* 259–263.

Koob, G.F., Dantzer, R., Rodriguez, F., Bloom, F.E., & Le Moal, M. (1985). Osmotic stress mimics effects of vasopressin on learned behavior. *Nature, 315,* 750–752.

Koob, G., Le Moal, M., & Bloom, F.E. (1984). The role of endorphins in neurobiology, behavior, and psychiatric disorders. In C.B. Nemeroff & A.J. Dunn (Eds.), *Peptides, Hormones, and Behavior* (pp. 349–383). New York: Spectrum Publications.

Koob, G., Pettit, H.O., Ettenberg, A., & Bloom, F.E. (1984). Effects of opiate antagonists and their quaternary derivatives on heroin self-administration in the rat. *Journal of Pharmacological and Experimental Therapeutics, 229,* 481–486.

Koob, G.F., Riley, S.J., Smith, S.C., & Robbins, T.W. (1978). Effects of 6-hydroxydopamine lesions of the nucleus accumbens septi and olfactory tubercle on feeding, locomotor activity, and amphetamine anorexia in the rat. *Journal of Comparative and Physiological Psychology, 92,* 917–927.

Kordower, J.H. & Bodnar, R.J. (1984). Vasopressin analgesia: Specificity of action and non-opioid effects. *Peptides, 5,* 747–756.

Kornblith, C.L., Ervin, G.N., & King, R.A. (1978). Hypothalamic and locus coeruleus self-stimulation are decreased by cholecystokinin. *Physiology & Behavior, 21,* 1037–1041.

Kornetsky, C. & Bain, G. (1983). Effects of opiates on rewarding brain stimulation. In J.E. Smith & J.D. Lane (Eds.), *The Neurobiology of Opiate Reward Processes* (pp. 237–256). Amsterdam: Elsevier Biomedical Press.

Krieger, D.T., Bronwstein, M.J., & Martin, J.B. (Eds.), (1983). *Brain Peptides.* New York: Wiley.

Kupferman, I. & Weiss, K.R. (1978). The command neuron concept. *Behavioral and Brain Sciences, 1,* 3–39.

Leibowitz, S.F. (1980). Neurochemical systems of the hypothalamus: Control of feeding and drinking behavior and water-electrolyte excretion. In P.J. Morgane & J. Panksepp (Eds.), *Handbook of the Hypothalamus: Vol. 3. Part A, Behavioral Studies of the Hypothalamus* (pp. 299–437). New York: Marcel Dekker, Inc.

Leibowitz, S.F. (1986a). Brain monoamines and peptides: Role in the control of eating behavior. *Federation Proceedings, 45,* 1396–1403.

Leibowitz, S.F. (1986b). Opiate, alpha-2-noradrenergic and adrenocorticotropin systems of hypothalamic paraventricular nucleus. In A. Baum (Ed.), *Perspectives on Behavioral Medicine: Volume V.* New York: Academic Press.

Leibowitz, S.F. & Hor, L. (1982). Endorphinergic and alpha-noradrenergic systems in the paraventricular nucleus: Effects on eating behavior. *Peptides, 3,* 421–428.

Leibowitz, S.F. & Stanley, B.G. (1986). Neurochemical controls of appetite, in R.C. Ritter, S. Ritter, & C.D. Barnes (Eds.), *Feeding Behavior: Neural and Humoral Controls* (pp. 191–234). New York: Academic Press.

Le Magnen, J. (1983). Body energy balance and food intake: A neuroendocrine regulatory mechanism. *Physiological Review, 63,* 314–386.

Le Magnen, J. (1985). *Hunger.* Cambridge: Cambridge University Press.

Levitt, P. (1984). A monoclonal antibody to limbic system neurons. *Science, 223,* 299–301.

Liebeskind, J.C., Dismukes, R.K., Barker, J.L., Berger, P.A., Creese, I., Dunn, A.J., Segal, D.S.,

Stein, L., and Vale, W.W. (1979). Peptides and behavior: A critical analysis of research strategies. *Neuroscience Research Program Bulletin, 16,* 489–635.

Liebeskind, J.C. & Paul, L.A. (1977). Psychological and physiological mechanisms of pain. *Annual Review of Psychology, 28,* 41–60.

Liebman, J.M. (1983). Discriminating between reward and performance: A critical review of intracranial self-stimulation methodology. *Neuroscience and Biobehavioral Reviews, 7,* 45–72.

Lind, R.W. & Johnson, A.K. (1982). Central and peripheral mechanisms mediating angiotensin-induced thirst. *Experimental Brain Research,* Suppl. 4, 343–364.

Lind, R.W., Swanson, L.W., & Ganten, D. (1984). Angiotensin II immunoreactivity in neural afferents and efferents of the subfornical organ of the rat. *Brain Research, 321,* 209–215.

Lindsley, D.B. (1951). Emotion. In S.S. Stevens (Ed.), *Handbook of Experimental Psychology* (pp. 473–516). New York: Wiley.

Livingston, K.E. & Hornykiewicz, O. (Eds.). (1976). *Limbic Mechanisms: The Continuing Evolution of the Limbic System Concept.* New York: Plenum Press.

Lombardini, J.B. & Kenny, A.D. (Eds.). (1980). *The Role of Peptides and Amino Acids as Neurotransmitters.* New York: Alan R. Liss, Inc.

Lytle, L.D. (1977). Control of eating behavior. In R.J. Wurtman & J.J. Wurtman (Eds.), *Nutrition and the Brain: Vol. 12* (pp. 1–145). New York: Raven Press.

MacLean, P.D. (1981). Role of transhypothalamic pathways in social communication. In P.J. Morgane & J. Panksepp (Eds.), *Handbook of the Hypothalamus: Volume 3. Part B, Behavioral Studies of the Hypothalamus* (pp. 259–287). New York: Marcel Dekker, Inc.

Margules, D.L. (1979). Beta-endorphin and endoloxone: Hormones of the autonomic nervous system for the conservation or expenditure of bodily resources and energy in anticipation of famine or feast. *Neuroscience and Biobehavioral Reviews, 3,* 155–162.

Margules, D.L., Moisset, B., Lewis, M.J., Shibuya, H., & Pert, C.B. (1978). Beta-endorphin is associated with overeating in genetically obese mice (ob/ob) and rats (fa/fa). *Science, 202,* 988–991.

Mark, G.P., Jacobs, K.M., & Scott, T.R. (1987). Taste responses in the NTS of sodium-deprived rats. *Society for Neuroscience Abstracts, 13,* 333.

Marshall, J.P. (1984). Brain function: Neural adaptations and recovery from injury. *Annual Review of Physiology, 35,* 277–308.

Martin, J.B., Reichlin, S., & Bick, K.L. (Eds.). (1981).

Neurosecretion and Brain Peptides: Implications for Brain Functions and Neurological Diseases. New York: Raven Press.

Martinez, J.L., Jensen, R.A., Messing, R.B., Rigter, H., & McGaugh, J.L. (Eds.). (1981). *Endogenous Peptides and Learning and Memory Processes.* New York: Academic Press.

McCaleb, M.L. & Myers, R.D. (1980). Cholecystokinin acts on the hypothalamic "noradrenergic system" involved in feeding. *Peptides, 1,* 47–49.

McGeer, P.L., Eccles, J.C., & McGeer, E.G. (1978). *Molecular Neurobiology of the Mammalian Brain.* New York: Plenum Press.

McKenzie, J.S., Kemm, R.E., & Wilcock, L.N. (Eds.). (1984). *The Basal Ganglia: Structure and Function.* New York: Plenum Press.

McLean, S. & Hoebel, B.G. (1983). Feeding induced by opiates injected into the paraventricular hypothalamus. *Peptides, 4,* 287–292.

Meisenberg, G. & Simmons, W.H. (1983). Peptides and the blood-brain barrier. *Life Sciences, 32,* 2611–2623.

Merzenich, M.M. & Kaas, J.H. (1980). Principles of organization of sensory-perceptual systems in mammals. *Progress in Psychobiology and Physiological Psychology, 9,* 1–42.

Miliaressis, E. & LeMoal, M. (1976). Stimulation of the medial forebrain bundle: Behavioral dissociation of its rewarding and activating effects. *Neuroscience Letters, 2,* 295–300.

Miselis, R.R. (1981). The efferent projections of the subfornical organ of the rat: A circumventricular organ within a neural circuitry subserving water balance. *Brain Research, 230,* 1–23.

Mittleman, G. & Valenstein, E.S. (1984). Ingestive behavior evoked by hypothalamic stimulation and schedule-induced polydipsia are related. *Science, 224,* 415–417.

Mogenson, G.J. (Eds.). (1977) *The Neurobiology of Behavior: An Introduction.* Hillsdale, NJ: Erlbaum.

Mogenson, G.J. (1982). Studies of the nucleus accumbens and its mesolimbic dopaminergic afferents in relation to ingestive behavior and reward. In B.G. Hoebel & D. Novin (Eds.), *The Neural Basis of Feeding and Reward* (pp. 275–288). Brunswick ME: Haer Institute.

Mogenson, G.J., Jones, D.L., & Yim, C.Y. (1980). From motivation to action: functional interface between the limbic system and the motor system. *Progress in Neurobiology, 14,* 69–97.

Mogenson, G.J. & Yim, C.Y. (1981). Electrophysiological and neuropharmacological-behavioral studies of the nucleus accumbens: Implications for its role as a limbic-motor interface. In R.B. Chronister & J.F. DeFrance (Eds.), *The Neurobiology of the*

Nucleus Accumbens (pp. 210–229), Brunswick, ME: Haer Institute.

Mondadori, C., Ornstein, K., Waser, P.G., & Huston, J.P. (1976). Post-trial reinforcing hypothalamic stimulation can facilitate avoidance learning. *Neuroscience Letters, 2,* 183–187.

Mook, D.G., Brane, J.A., Kushner, L.R., & Whitt, J.A. (1983). Glucose solution intake in the rat: The specificity of postingestive satiety. *Appetite, 4,* 1–9.

Moran, T.H. & Blass, E.M. (1982). Organized response patterns and self-stimulation induced by intrahypothalmic electrical stimulation in 3-day-old rats. In B.G. Hoebel & D. Novin (Eds.), *The Neural Basis of Feeding and Reward* (pp. 59–66). Brunswick, ME: Haer Institute.

Morgane, P.J. (1979). Historical and modern concepts of hypothalamic organization and function. In P.J. Morgane & J. Panksepp (Eds.), *Handbook of the Hypothalamus: Volume 1. Anatomy of the Hypothalamus* (pp. 1–64). New York: Marcel Dekker, Inc.

Morley, J.E. (1982). The ascent of cholecystokinin (CCK)–from gut to brain. *Life Sciences, 30,* 479–493.

Morley, J.E. & Levine, A.S. (1985). The pharmacology of eating behavior. *Annual Review of Pharmacology and Toxicology, 25,* 127–146.

Morley, J.E., Levine, A.S., Yim, G.K., & Lowy, M.T. (1983). Opioid modulation of appetite. *Neuroscience and Biobehavioral Reviews, 7,* 281–305.

Morruzi, G. & Magoun, H.W. (1949). Brainstem reticular formation and activation of the EEG. *Electroencephalography and Clinical Neurophysiology, 1,* 455–473.

Moss, C.F. & Dethier, V.G. (1983). Central nervous system regulation of finicky feeding by the blowfly. *Behavioral Neuroscience, 97,* 541–548.

Moss, R.L. & Dudley, C. (1984). The challenge of studying the behavioral effects of neuropeptides. In L.L. Iversen, S.D. Iversen, & S.H. Snyder (Eds.), *Handbook of Psychopharmacology: Volume 18. Drugs, Neurotransmitters, and Behavior* (pp. 397–454). New York: Plenum Press.

Mucha, R. & Iverson, S.D. (1986). Increased food intake after opioid microinjection into nucleus accumbens and ventral tegmental area of rat. *Brain Research, 397,* 214–224.

Murzi, E., Hernandez, L., & Baptista, T. (1986). Lateral hypothalamic sites eliciting eating affect medullary taste neurons in rats. *Physiology and Behavior, 36,* 829–834.

Myers, R.D. (1980). Hypothalamic control of thermoregulation. In P.J. Morgane & J. Panksepp (Eds.), *Handbook of the Hypothalamus: Volume 3, Part A, Behavioral Studies of the Hypothalamus* (pp. 83–210). New York: Marcel Dekker, Inc.

Myers, R.D. & McCaleb, M.L. (1980). Feeding: Satiety signal from intestine triggers brain's noradrenergic mechanism. *Science, 209,* 1035–1037.

Nauta, W.J.H. & Domesick, V.B. (1982). Neural associations of the limbic system. In A.L. Beckman (Eds.), *The Neural Basis of Behavior* (pp. 175–206). New York: Spectrum Publications.

Neill, D.B., Garr, L.A., Clark, A.S., & Britt, M.D. (1982). "Rate-free" measures of self-stimulation and microinjections: Evidence toward a new concept of dopamine and reward. In B.G. Hoebel & D. Novin (Eds.), *The Neural Basis of Feeding and Reward* (pp. 289–298). Brunswick ME: Haer Institute.

Nemeroff, C.B. & Dunn, A.J. (Eds.). (1984). *Peptides, Hormones, and Behavior.* New York: SP Medical & Scientific Books.

Nicolaidis, S. (1974). Rôle des récepteurs internes et externes dans la prise d'eau régulatrice et non régulatrice. *Rein et Foie, Maladies de la Nutrition, 16B,* 159–174.

Nielsen, E.B. & Scheel-Kruger, J. (1984). Amphetamine cue: Elicitation by intra-accumbens microinjection. *Society for Neuroscience Abstracts, 10,* 1072.

Niijima, A. (1977). Nervous regulatory mechanisms of blood glucose levels. In Y. Katsuki, M. Sato, S.F. Takagi, & Y. Oomura (Eds.), *Food Intake and Chemical Senses* (pp. 413–426).

Nishino, H., Ono, T., Fukuda, M., & Sasaki, K. (1982). Lateral hypothalamic neuron activity during monkey bar press feeding behavior: Modulation by glucose, morphine and naloxone. In B.G. Hoebel & D. Novin (Eds.), *The Neural Basis of Feeding and Reward* (pp. 355–372). Brunswick ME: Haer Institute.

Norgren, R. (1983). Afferent interactions of cranial nerves involved in ingestion. *Journal of the Autonomic Nervous System, 9,* 67–77.

Norgren, R. & Grill, H. (1982). Brain-stem control of ingestive behavior. In D.W. Pfaff (Ed.), *The Physiological Mechanisms of Motivation* (pp. 99–131). New York: Springer-Verlag.

Novin, D. & Oomura, Y. (Eds.). (1980). Integration of central and peripheral receptors in hunger and energy metabolism. *Brain Research Bulletin, 5,* Supplement 4.

Oberg, R.G.E. & Divac, I. (1981). The basal ganglia and the control of movement: Levels of motor planning. *Trends in Neuroscience, May,* 122–124.

Olds, J. (1977). *Drives and Reinforcements: Behavioral Studies of Hypothalamic Function.* New York: Raven Press.

Olds, J. & Milner, P. (1954). Positive reinforcement produced by electrical stimulation of septal area and other regions of rat brain. *Journal of Comparative and Physiological Psychology, 47,* 419.

Olds, M.E. & Williams, K.N. (1980). Self-administration of d-ala-2-met-enkephalinamide at hypothalamic self-stimulation sites. *Brain Research, 194,* 155–170.

Ono, T., Sasaki, K., Nakamura, K., & Norgren, R. (1985). Integrated lateral hypothalamic neural responses to natural and artificial rewards and cue signals in the rat. *Brain Research, 327,* 303–306.

Oomura, Y. (1980). Input-output organization in the hypothalamus relating to food intake behaviour. In P.J. Morgane & K. Panksepp (Eds.), *Handbook of the Hypothalamus: Vol. 2. Physiology of the Hypothalamus* (pp. 557–620). New York: Marcel Dekker, Inc.

Oomura, Y., Shimizu, N., Miyahara, S., & Hattori, K. (1982). Chemosensitive neurons in the hypothalamus: Do they relate to behavior? In B.G. Hoebel & D. Novin (Eds.), *The Neural Basis of Feeding and Reward* (pp. 551–566). Brunswick ME: Haer Institute.

Overton, D.A. (1984). State dependent learning and drug discriminations. In L.L. Iversen, S.D. Iversen, & S.H. Snyder (Eds.), *Handbook of Psychopharmacology: Volume 18, Drugs, Neurotransmitters, and Behavior* (pp. 59–128). New York: Plenum Press.

Panksepp, J. (1982). Toward a general psychobiological theory of emotions. *Behavioral and Brain Sciences, 5,* 407–467.

Panskepp, J. (1983). Hypothalamus integration of behavior: Rewards, punishments, and related psychological processes. In P.J. Morgane & J. Panksepp (Eds.), *Handbook of the Hypothalamus: Vol. 3b. Behavioral Studies of the Hypothalamus* (pp. 289–432). New York: Marcel Dekker, Inc.

Parada, M., Hernandez, L., Schwartz, D., & Hoebel, B.G. (In press). Lateral hypothalamic infusion of amphetamine increases extracellular serotonin, dopamine, and norepinephrine: a microdialysis study in freely moving rats. *Brain Research Bulletin.*

Pardridge, W.M. (1983). Neuropeptides and the blood brain barrier. *Annual Review of Physiology, 45,* 73–82.

Pearse, A.G.E. & Takor, T.T. (1979). Embryology of the diffuse neuroendocrine system and its relationship to the common peptides. *Federation Proceedings, 38,* 2288–2293.

Pettit, H.O., Ettenberg, A., Bloom, F.E., & Koob, G.F. (1984). Destruction of dopamine in the nucleus accumbens selectively attenuates cocaine but not heroin self-administration in rats. *Psychopharmacology, 84,* 167–173.

Pfaff, D.W. (1982). Motivational concepts: Definitions and distinctions. In D.W. Pfaff (Ed.), *The Physiological Mechanisms of Motivation* (pp. 1–24). New York: Springer-Verlag.

Phillips, A.G. (1984). Brain reward circuitry: A case for separate systems. *Brain Research Bulletin, 12,* 195–201.

Phillips, M.I. (1984). Angiotensin and drinking: A model for the study of peptide action in the brain. In C.B. Nemeroff & A.J. Dunn (Eds.), *Peptides, Hormones, and Behavior* (pp. 423–462). New York: SP Medical & Scientific Books.

Polak, J.M. & Bloom, S.R. (1984). Regulatory peptides–The distribution of two newly discovered peptides: PHI and NPY. *Peptides, 5,* Suppl. 1, 79–89.

Powley, T.L., Opsahl, C.A., Cox, J.E., & Weingarten, H.P. (1980). The role of the hypothalamus in energy homeostasis. In P.J. Morgane & J. Panksepp (Eds.), *Handbook of the Hypothalamus: Volume 3. Part A, Behavioral Studies of the Hypothalamus* (pp. 211–298). New York: Marcel Dekker, Inc.

Prange, A.J., Jr. & Nemeroff, C.B. (1982). The manifold actions of neurotensin: A first synthesis. In A.J. Prange, Jr. & C.B. Nemeroff (Eds.), *Annals of the New York Academy of Sciences: Vol. 400. Neurotensin, A Brain and Gastrointestinal Peptide* (pp. 368–375). New York: New York Academy of Sciences.

Prange, A.J., Jr., Nemeroff, C.B., & Lipton, M.A. (1978). Behavioral effects of peptides: Basic and clinical studies. In M.A. Lipton, A. DiMascio, & K.F. Killam (Eds.), *Psychopharmacology: A Generation of Progress* (pp. 441–458). New York: Raven Press.

Prange, A.J., Jr., Nemeroff, C.B., Loosen, P.T., Bissette, G., Osbahr, A.J., III, Wilson, I.C., & Lipton, M.A. (1982). Behavioral effects of thyrotropin-releasing hormone in animals and man: A review. In R. Collu, J.R. Ducharme, A. Barbeau, & G. Tolis, *Central Nervous System Effects of Hypothalamic Hormones and Other Peptides* (pp. 75–96). New York: Raven Press.

Quinn, W.G. & Greenspan, R.J. (1984). Learning and courtship in *Drosophila*: Two stories with mutants. *Annual Review of Neuroscience, 7,* 67–93.

Randrup, A., Divac, I., Fog, R., & Munkvad, I. (1984). Further development of "The Dopamine Hypothesis" suggested by recent findings from various areas of research. Poster, 14th Congress of Collegium Internationale Neuro-Psychopharmacologicum, Firenze.

Rebec, G.V. & Bashore, T.R. (1984). Critical issues in assessing the behavioral effects of amphetamine. *Neuroscience & Biobehavioral Reviews, 8,* 153–159.

Reid, I.A. (1984). Action of angiotensin II on the brain: Mechanisms and physiologic role. *American Journal of Physiology, 15,* F533–543.

Robbins, T.W. & Koob, G.F. (1980). Selective disruption of displacement behavior by lesions of the mesolimbic dopamine system. *Nature, 285,* 409–412.

Roberts, D.C.S., Koob, G.F., Klonoff, P., & Fibiger, H.C. (1980). Extinction and recovery of cocaine self-administration following 6-hydroxydopamine lesions of the nucleus accumbens. *Pharmacology Biochemistry & Behavior, 12,* 781–787.

Robinson, B.W. & Mishkin, M. (1968). Alimentary responses to forebrain stimulation in monkeys. *Experimental Brain Research, 4,* 330–366.

Rodriguez, E.M. (1984). Design and perspectives of peptide secreting neurons. In C.B. Nemeroff & A.J. Dunn (Eds.), *Peptides, Hormones, and Behavior* (pp. 1–36). New York: SP Medical & Scientific Books.

Rolls, B.J. (1979). How variety and palatability can stimulate appetite. *Nutrition Bulletin, 5,* 78–86.

Rolls, E.T. (1975). *The Brain and Reward.* Oxford: Pergamon Press.

Rolls, E.T. (1981). Processing beyond the inferior temporal visual cortex related to feeding, memory, and striatal function. In Y. Katsuki, R. Norgren, & M. Sato (Eds.), *Brain Mechanisms of Sensation* (pp. 241–269). New York: Wiley.

Rolls, E.T., Burton, M.J., & Mora, F. (1980). Neurophysiological analysis of brain-stimulation reward in the monkey. *Brain Research, 194,* 339–357.

Roper, S.D. & Atema, J. (1987). *Olfaction and Taste.* Annals of the New York Academy of Sciences. Vol. 510.

Rosell, S. (1982). The role of neurotensin in the uptake and distribution of fat. In C.B. Nemeroff & A.J. Prange, Jr. (Eds.), *Annals of the New York Academy of Sciences: Vol. 400. Neurotensin, A Brain and Gastrointestinal Peptide* (pp. 183–197). New York: New York Academy of Sciences.

Rossi, N.A. & Reid, L.D. (1967). Affective states associated with morphine injections. *Physiological Psychology, 4,* 269–274.

Routtenberg, A. (Eds.). (1980). *Biology of Reinforcement: Facets of Brain-Stimulation Reward.* New York: Academic Press.

Sadowski, B. (1976). Physiological correlates of self-stimulation. In A. Wauquier & E.T. Rolls (Eds.), *Brain-Stimulation Reward* (pp. 433–460). Amsterdam: Elsevier/North-Holland.

Sahgal, A. (1983). Vasopressin retards the acquisition of positively reinforced lever pressing in homozygous Brattleboro rats. *Regulatory Peptides, 5,* 317–326.

Samanin, R. & Garattini, S. (1982). Neuropharmacology of feeding. In T. Silverstone (Ed.), *Drugs and Appetite* (pp. 23–39). New York: Academic Press.

Sanger, D.J. (1983). Opiates and ingestive behaviour. In S.J. Cooper (Ed.), *Theory in Psychopharmacology: Volume 2* (pp. 75–113). New York: Academic Press.

Sasaki, K., Ono, T., Muramoto, K.-I., Nishino, H., & Fukuda, M. (1984). The effects of feeding and rewarding brain stimulation on lateral hypothalamic unit activity in freely moving rats. *Brain Research, 322,* 201–211.

Satinoff, E. (1983). A reevaluation of the concept of the homeostatic organization of temperature regulation. In E. Satinoff & P. Teitelbaum (Eds.), *Handbook of Behavioral Neurobiology: Volume 6. Motivation* (pp. 443–472). New York: Plenum Press.

Schallert, T., Pendergrass, M., & Farrar, S.B. (1982). Cholecystokinin-octapeptide effects on eating elicited by "external" versus "internal" cues in rats. *Appetite: Journal for Intake Research, 3,* 81–90.

Schallert, T., Whishaw, I.Q., De Ryck, M. & Teitelbaum, P. (1978). The postures of catecholamine-depletion catalepsy: Their possible adaptive value in thermoregulation. *Physiology & Behavior, 21,* 817–820.

Schneider, L.H., Alpert, J.E., & Iversen, S.D. (1983). CCK-8 modulation of mesolimbic dopamine: Antagonism of amphetamine-stimulated behaviors. *Peptides, 4,* 749–753.

Schultz, W., Ruffieux, A., & Aebischer, P. (1983). The activity of pars compacta neurons of the monkey substantia nigra in relation to motor activation. *Experimental Brain Research, 51,* 377–387.

Schwartz, D.H., Dorfman, D.B., Hernandez, L., & Hoebel, B.G. (In press). Cholecystokinin: 1, CCK antagonists in the PVN induce feeding, 2. effects of CCK in the nucleus accumbens on extracellular dopamine. In R.Y. Wang (Ed) *Cholecystokinin Antagonists.* New York: Alan R. Liss Inc.

Schwartz, D.H., Kloecker, J.B., Hernandez, L., & Hoebel, B.E. (1987). Fenfluramine increases extracellular serotonin measured by microdialysis. *Society for Neuroscience Abstracts, 13,* 336.

Sclafani, A. (1980). Dietary Obesity. In A.J. Stunkard (Ed.), *Obesity* (pp. 166–181). Philadelphia: W.B. Saunders Co.

Sclafani, A. & Kirchgessner, A. (1986). The role of the medial hypothalamus in the control of food intake: an update. In R.C. Ritter, S. Ritter & C.D. Barnes (Eds.), *Feeding Behavior: Neural and Humoral Controls* (pp. 27–66). Orlando, FL; Academic Press.

Scott, D.E., Paull, W.K., & Mitchell, J.K. (1984). Introduction. In W.K. Paull, D.E. Scott, & J.K. Mitchell (Eds.), *Brain-Endocrine Interaction V, The Schmitt Brain Symposium, Neuropeptides, Central and Peripheral Peptides, 5,* Suppl. 1, 1–2.

Scott, T.R. & Mark, G.P. (1987). The task system encodes stimulus toxicity. *Brain Research, 414*, 197–203.

Setler, P.E. (1977). The neuroanatomy and neuropharmacology of drinking. In L.L. Iversen, S.D. Iversen, & S.H. Snyder (Eds.), *Handbook of Psychopharmacology*: Vol. 8 (pp. 131–157). New York: Plenum Press.

Sgro, S., Ferguson, A.V., & Renaud, L.P. (1984). Subfornical organ-supraoptic nucleus connections: An electrophysiologic study in the rat. *Brain Research, 303*, 7–13.

Shephard, G.M. (1983). *Neurobiology*. New York: Oxford University Press.

Shivers, B.D., Harland, R.E., & Pfaff, D.W. (1983). Reproduction: The central nervous system role of leutinizing hormone releasing hormone. In D.T. Krieger, M.J. Brownstein, & J.B. Martin (Eds.), *Brain Peptides* (pp. 389–412). New York: Wiley.

Shizgal, P. & Matthews, G. (1977). Electrical stimulation of the rat diencephalon: Differential effects of interrupted stimulation on on- and off-responding. *Brain Research, 129*, 319–333.

Shizgal, P., Kiss, I., & Bielajew, C. (1982). Psychophysical and electrophysiological studies of the substrate for brain stimulation reward. In B.G. Hoebel & D. Novin (Eds.), *The Neural Basis of Feeding and Reward* (pp. 419–430). Brunswick ME: Haer Institute.

Siggins, G.R. (1981). Catecholamines and endorphins as neurotransmitters and neuromodulators. In G.R. Siggins (Ed.), *Regulatory Mechanisms of Synaptic Transmission* (pp. 1–27). New York: Plenum Press.

Simon, H., Stinus, L., Tassin, J.P., Lavielle, S., Blanc, G., Thierry, A.-M., Glowinski, J., & Le Moal, M. (1979). Is the dopaminergic mesocorticolimbic system necessary for intracranial self-stimulation? *Behavioral and Neural Biology, 27*, 125–145.

Simpson, J.B. (1981). The circumventricular organs and the central actions of angiotensin. *Neuroendocrinology, 32*, 248–256.

Simpson, J.B., & Routtenberg, A. (1973). Subfornical organ: Site of drinking elicitation by angiotensin II. *Science, 181*, 1172–1174.

Singer, G., Wallace, M., & Hall, R. (1982). Effects of dopaminergic nucleus accumbens lesions on the acquisition of schedule induced self injection of nicotine in the rat. *Pharmacology Biochemistry and Behavior, 17*, 579–581.

Skinner, B.F. (1953). *Science and Human Behavior*. New York: Macmillan.

Smith, H.W. (1953). *From Fish to Philosopher*. Boston: Little, Brown.

Smith, G.P. (1982a). Satiety and the problem of motivation. In D.W. Pfaff (Ed.), *The Physiological Mechanisms of Motivation* (pp. 133–143). New York: Springer-Verlag.

Smith, G.P. (1982b). Eliot Stellar and the physiological psychology of satiety. In A.R. Morrison & P.L. Strick (Eds.), *Changing Concepts of the Nervous System* (pp. 457–465). New York: Academic Press.

Smith, G.P. (1984). Gut hormones and feeding behavior: Intuitions and experiments. In C.B. Nemeroff & A.J. Dunn (Eds.), *Peptides, Hormones, and Behavior* (pp. 463–496). New York: SP Medical & Scientific Books.

Smith, G.P., Gibbs, J., & Kulkosky, P.J. (1982). Relationships between brain-gut peptides and neurons in the control of food intake. In B.G. Hoebel & D. Novin (Eds.), *The Neural Basis of Feeding and Reward* (pp. 149–165). Brunswick, ME; Haer Institute.

Smith, J.E. & Lane, J.D. (Eds.). (1983). *The Neurobiology of Opiate Reward Processes*. Amsterdam: Elsevier Biomedical Press.

Smith, O.A. & DeVito, J.L. (1984). Central neural integration for the control of autonomic responses associated with emotion. *Annual Review of Neuroscience, 7*, 43–65.

Smotherman, W.P. & Levine, S. (1980). $ACTH_{4-10}$ affects behavior but *not* plasma corticosterone levels in a conditioned taste aversion situation. *Peptides, 1*, 207–210.

Solomon, R.L. (1982). Affect and acquired motives. In A.R. Morrison & P.L. Strick (Eds.), *Changing Concepts of the Nervous System* (pp. 489–502). New York: Academic Press.

Stanley, B.G., Hoebel, B.G., & Leibowitz, S.F. (1983). Neurotensin: Effects of hypothalamic and intravenous injections on eating and drinking in rats. *Peptides, 4*, 493–500.

Stanley, B.G. & Leibowitz, S.F. (1984). Neuropeptide Y: Stimulation of feeding and drinking by injection into the paraventricular nucleus. *Life Sciences, 35*, 2635–2642.

Stanley, B.G., Leibowitz, S.F., Eppel, N., St.-Pierre, S., & Hoebel, B.G. (1985). Suppression of norepinephrine-elicited feeding by neurotensin: Evidence for behavioral, anatomical and pharmacological specificity. *Brain Research, 343*, 297–304.

Stein, L. (1980). The chemistry of reward. In A. Routtenberg (Ed.), *Biology of Reinforcement: Facets of Brain-Stimulation Reward* (pp. 109–132). New York: Academic Press.

Stein, L. & Belluzzi, J.D. (1987). Reward transmitters and drugs of abuse. In J. Engel & L. Oreland (Eds.), *Brain Reward Systems and Abuse*. New York: Raven Press.

Stein, L., Belluzzi, J.D., & Wise, C.D. (1976). Norepinephrine self-stimulation pathways: implications for long-term memory and schizophrenia. In A. Wauquier & E.T. Rolls (Eds.), *Brain-Stimulation Reward* (pp. 297–331). Amsterdam: Elsevier/North Holland.

Stellar, E. (1954). The physiology of motivation. *Psychological Review, 61*, 5–22.

Stellar, J.R. & Stellar, E. (1985). *The Neurobiology of Motivation and Reward*. New York: Springer-Verlag.

Stewart, J., de Wit, H., & Eikelboom, R. (1984). Role of unconditioned and conditioned drug effects in the self-administration of opiates and stimulants. *Psychological Review, 91*, 251–268.

Stivers, J.A. & Crawley, J.N. (1984). Cholecystokinin antagonists block the potentiation of dopamine-induced hyperlocomotion by cholecystokinin in the nucleus accumbens. *Society for Neuroscience Abstracts, 10*, 693.

Stricker, E.M. (1982). The central control of food intake: A role for insulin. In B.G. Hoebel & D. Novin (Eds.), *The Neural Basis of Feeding and Reward* (pp. 227–240). Brunswick, ME: Haer Institute.

Stricker, E.M. (1983a). Thirst and sodium appetite after colloid treatment in rats: Role of the renin-angiotensin-aldosterone system. *Behavioral Neuroscience, 97*, 725–737.

Stricker, E.M. (1983b). Brain neurochemistry and the control of food intake. In E. Satinoff & P. Teitelbaum (Eds.), *Handbook of Behavioral Neurobiology: Volume 6. Motivation* (pp. 329–366). New York: Plenum Press.

Stricker, E.M., Swerdloff, A.F., & Zigmond, M.J. (1978). Intrahypothalamic injections of kainic acid produce feeding and drinking deficits in rats. *Brain Research, 158*, 470–473.

Susswein, A.J., Weiss, K.R., & Kupfermann, I. (1984). Internal stimuli enhance feeding behavior in mollusc *Aplysia*. *Behavioral and Neural Biology, 41*, 90–95.

Swanson, L.W. & Mogenson, G.J. (1981). Neural mechanisms for the functional coupling of autonomic, endocrine and somatomotor responses in adaptive behavior. *Brain Research Review, 3*, 1–34.

Swanson, L.W. & Sawchenko, P.E. (1983). Hypothalamic integration: Organization of the paraventricular and supraoptic nucleus. *Annual Review of Neuroscience, 6*, 269–324.

Swerdlow, N.R. & Koob, G.F. (1984). Restrained rats learn amphetamine-conditioned locomotion, but not place preference. *Science, 84*, 163–166.

Swerdlow, N.R., Swanson, L.W., & Koob, G.F. (1984). Electrolytic lesions of the substantia innominata and lateral preoptic area attenuate the 'supersen-sitive' locomotor response to apomorphine resulting from denervation of the nucleus accumbens. *Brain Research, 306*, 141–148.

Swerdlow, N.R., van der Kooy, D., Koob, G.P., & Wenger, J.R. (1983). Cholecystokinin produces conditioned place-aversions, not place-preferences, in food-deprived rats: Evidence against involvement in satiety. *Life Sciences, 32*, 2087–2093.

Szego, C.M. (1984). Mechanisms of hormone action: Parallels in receptor-mediated signal propagation for steroid and peptide effectors. *Life Sciences, 35*, 2383–2396.

Teitelbaum, P. (1967). *Physiological Psychology: Fundamental Principles*. Englewood Cliffs, NJ: Prentice Hall.

Teitelbaum, P. (1977). Levels of integration of the operant. In W.K. Honig & J.E.R. Staddon (Eds.), *Handbook of Operant Behavior* (pp. 7–27). Englewood Cliffs, NJ: Prentice-Hall, Inc.

Teitelbaum, P. (1982a). Disconnection and antagonistic interaction of movement subsystems in motivated behavior. In A.R. Morrison & P.L. Strick (Eds.), *Changing Concepts of the Nervous System* (pp. 467–487). New York: Academic Press.

Teitelbaum, P. (1982b). What is the "zero condition" for motivated behavior? In B.G. Hoebel & D. Novin (Eds.), *The Neural Basis of Feeding and Reward* (pp. 7—23). Brunswick, ME: Haer institute.

Teitelbaum, P., Schallert, T., & Whishaw, I.Q. (1983). Sources of spontaneity in motivated behavior. In E. Satinoff & P. Teitelbaum (Eds.), *Handbook of Behavioral Neurobiology: Volume 6. Motivation* (pp. 23–65). New York: Plenum Press.

Tepperman, F.S., Hirst, M., & Gowdey, C.W. (1981). Hypothalamic injection of morphine: Feeding and temperature response. *Life Sciences, 28*, 2459–2467.

Toates, F.M. (1979). Homeostasis and drinking. *The Behavioral and Brain Sciences, 2*, 95–139.

Toates, F. (1986). *Motivational Systems*. Cambridge: Cambridge University Press.

Toates, F.M. & Halliday, T.R. (Eds.), (1980). *Analysis of Motivational Processes*. New York: Academic Press.

Ungerstedt, U. (1971). Adipsia and aphagia after 6-hydroxydopamine induced degeneration of the nigrostriatal dopamine system. *Acta Physiologica Scandinavica Supplementum, 367*, 95–122.

Ungerstedt, U. (1984). Measurement of noncotransmitter release by intracranial dialysis. In C.A. Marsden (Ed.) *Measurement of Neurotransmitter Release In Vivo* (pp. 81–105) New York, John Wiley & Sons.

Vaccarino, F.J., Bloom, P.E., Rivier, J., Vale, W., & Koob, G.F. (1985). Stimulation of food intake in rats by centrally administered hypothalamic growth hormone-releasing factor. *Nature, 314,* 167–168.

Vaccarino, F.J. & Koob, G.F. (1984). Microinjections of nanogram amounts of sulfated cholecystokinin octapeptide into the rat nucleus accumbens attenuates brain stimulation reward. *Neuroscience Letters, 52,* 61–66.

Valenstein, E.S. (Ed.). (1974). *Brain Control: A Critical Examination of Brain Stimulation and Psychosurgery.* New York: Wiley.

Valenstein, E.S. (1980). Stereotypy and sensory-motor changes evoked by hypothalamic stimulation: Possible relation to schizophrenic behavior patterns. In A. Routtenberg (Ed.), *Biology of Reinforcement: Facets of Brain-Stimulation Reward* (pp. 39–52). New York: Academic Press.

Van Der Kooy, D. & Phillips, A.G. (1977). Trigeminal substrates of intracranial self-stimulation in the brainstem. *Science, 196,* 447–449.

Vanderwolf, C.H. (1983). The role of cerebral cortex and ascending activating systems in the control of behavior. In E. Satinoff & P. Teitelbaum (Eds.), *Handbook of Behavioral Neurobiology: Volume 6. Motivation* (pp. 67–104). New York: Plenum Press.

Van Ree, I.M., Gaffori, O., & De Wied, D. (1983). In rats, the behavioral profile of CCK-8 related peptides resembles that of antipsychotic agents. *European Journal of Pharmacology, 93,* 63–78.

Van Wimersma Greidanus, T.B. & Versteeg, D.H.G. (1984). Neurohypophysial hormones—their role in endocrine function and behavioral homeostasis. In C.B. Nemeroff & A.J. Dunn (Eds.), *Peptides, Hormones, and Behavior* (pp. 385–421). New York: SP Medical & Scientific Books.

Waldbillig, R.J., Bartness, T.J., & Stanley, B.J. (1981). Increased food intake, body weight, and adiposity in rats after regional neurochemical depletion of serotonin. *Journal of Comparative and Physiological Psychology, 95,* 391–405.

Waldbillig, R.J. & O'Callahan, M. (1980). Hormones and hedonics cholecystokinin and taste: A possible behavioral mechanism of action. *Physiology and Behavior, 25,* 25–30.

Waldbillig, R.J., Steel, D.J., & Clemmons, R.M. (In preparation). Hyperphagia following intrahypothalamic microinfusion of 5,7-DHT: Potential modulation of the estrogenic control of feeding.

Wardener, H.E. & Clarkson, E.M. (1985). Concept of natriuretic hormone. *Physiological Reviews, 65,* 659–746.

Wauquier, A. & Rolls, E.T. (Eds.). (1976). *Brain-Stimulation Reward.* Amsterdam: Elsevier/North-Holland.

Wayner, M.J., Barone, F.C., & Loullis, C.C. (1981). The lateral hypothalamus and adjunctive behav-ior. In P.J. Morgane & J. Panksepp (Eds.), *Handbook of the Hypothalamus: Volume 3. Part B, Behavioral Studies of the Hypothalamus* (pp. 107–145). New York: Marcel Dekker, Inc.

Weiss, K.R., Koch, U.T., Koester, J., Rosen, S.C., & Kupfermann, I. (1982). The role of arousal in modulating feeding behavior of *Aplysia*: Neural and behavioral studies. In B.G. Hoebel & D. Novin (Eds.), *The Neural Basis of Feeding and Reward* (pp. 25–57). Brunswick, ME: Haer Institute.

West, D.B., Fey, D., & Woods, S.C. (1984). Cholecystokinin persistently suppresses meal size but not food intake in free-feedng rats. *American Journal of Physiology, 246,* R776–R787.

Westerink, B.H.C., Damsma, G., DeVries, J.B., & Horn, A.S. (1987). Scope and limitations of *in vivo* brain dialysis: A comparison of its application to various neurotransmitter systems. *Life Sciences, 41,* 1763–1776.

White, F.J. & Wang, R.Y. (1984). Interactions of cholecystokinin octapeptide and dopamine on nucleus accumbens neurons. *Brain Research, 300,* 161–166.

Whitnall, M.H., Gainer, H., Cox, B.M., & Molineaux, C.J. (1983). Dynorphin-A-(1-8) is contained within vasopressin neurosecretory vesicles in rat pituitary. *Science, 222,* 1137–1138.

Wise, R.A. (1978). Catecholamine theories of reward: A critical review. *Brain Research, 152,* 215–247.

Wise, R.A. (1982). Neuroleptics and operant behavior: The anhedonia hypothesis. *Behavioral Brain Science, 5,* 39–87.

Wise, R.A. (1983). Brain neuronal systems mediating reward processes. In J.E. Smith & J.D. Lane (Eds.), *The Neurobiology of Opiate Reward Processes* (pp. 405–437). Amsterdam: Elsevier Biomedical Press.

Wise, R.A. & Bozarth, M.A. (1984). Brain reward circuitry: Four circuit elements "wired" in apparent series. *Brain Research Bulletin, 12,* 203–298.

Wise, R.A. & Bozarth, M.A. (1987). A psychomotor stimulant theory of addiction. *Psychological Review, 94,* 469–492.

Wise, R.A. & Colle, L.M. (1984). Pimozide attenuates free feeding: Best scores analysis reveals a motivational deficit. *Psychopharmacology, 84,* 446–451.

Woods, S.C. (1977). Conditioned insulin secretion. In Y. Katsuki, M. Sato, S.F. Takagi, & Y. Oomura (Eds.), *Food Intake and Chemical Senses* (pp. 357–365). Baltimore: University Park Press.

Woods, S.C. & Porte, D., Jr. (1978). The central nervous system, pancreatic hormones, feeding, and obesity. *Advances in Metabolic Disorders, 9,* 293–311.

Wurtman, R.J. & Wurtman, J.J. (Eds.) (1983). *Nutri-*

tion and the Brain: Vol. 6. New York: Raven Press.

Yarbrough, G.G. (1983). Thyrotropin releasing hormone and CNS cholinergic neurons. *Life Sciences, 33,* 111–118.

Yim, C.Y. & Mogenson, G.J. (1983). Response of ventral pallidal neurons to amygdala stimulation and its modulation by dopamine projections to nucleus accumbens. *Journal of Neurophysiology, 50,* 148–161.

Young, A.M., Woods, J.H., Herling, S., & Hein, D.W. (1983). Comparison of the reinforcing and discriminative stimulus properties of opioids and opioid peptides. In J.E. Smith & J.D. Lane (Eds.), *The Neurobiology of Opiate Reward Processes* (pp. 147–174). Amsterdam: Elsevier Biomedical Press.

Zaborszky, L., Beinfeld, M.C., Palkovits, M., & Heimer, L. (1984). Brainstem projection to the hypothalamic ventromedial nucleus in the rat: A CCK-containing long ascending pathway. *Brain Research, 303,* 225–231.

Zarbin, M.S., Wamsley, J.K., Innis, R.B., & Kuhar, M.J. (1981). Cholecystokinin receptors: Presence and axonal flow in the rat vagus nerve. *Life Science, 29,* 697–705.

Zeigler, H.P. (1983). The trigeminal system and ingestive behavior. In E. Satinoff & P. Teitelbaum (Eds.), *Handbook of Behavioral Neurobiology: Volume 6. Motivation* (pp. 265–327). New York: Plenum Press.

Chapter 12

EMOTIONS

Carroll E. Izard and Patricia M. Saxton, *University of Delaware*

Scientific activity in the field of emotions has increased markedly in the past decade. The products of this activity reveal the interdisciplinary nature of the field and a multiplicity of theoretical orientations and levels of research. Any limited treatment of the subject requires some principles of selection and organization. The present chapter attempts to present material that is representative of major theoretical issues, substantive topics, and levels or domains of research. However, it is concerned primarily with human emotions, considered as complex phenomena with biological (neurophysiology and biochemical), social (neuromuscular-expressive), and personal (experimental or feeling) components. An exception is the section on the neurophysiology and biochemistry of emotions, where animal research plays a critical role. The contents of the chapter also reflect the premise that emotions have adaptive functions in phylogeny and ontogeny and specific organizing and motivational properties that influence individual and social behavior.

The recent literature includes detailed statements of the major theories of emotion by Arnold (1960a,b), Izard (1971, 1977), Lazarus (1968, 1974), Leventhal (1980), Mandler (1975),

Preparation of this chapter was supported by National Science Foundation Grant No. BNS 811832.

Plutchik (1962, 1980a), Schachter (1971), and Tomkins (1962, 1963). Summaries of these positions have appeared in several edited or multi-authored volumes by Candland, Fell, Keen, Leshner, Plutchik, and Tarpy (1977), Dienstbier (1979), and Plutchik (1980b); and these positions, along with other viable formulations, have been treated in one or the other of two volumes that qualify as textbooks on emotion, by Buck (1976) and Strongman (1978). Indeed, in the past 20 years authors concerned with emotions have generated far more pages of theoretical writings than of empirical research reports. This is not intended as a criticism, however, for the theories have begun to generate research.

In any case, the rich supply of theoretical treatises eliminates the need for a further one here. They set the stage, though, for an examination of similarities and differences among major theories regarding a number of critical issues, and may be expected to increase the already accelerating pace of empirical research on emotions.

ISSUES IN EMOTION THEORIES

Five major issues have shown an important influence on the investigator's efforts to conceptualize problems and formulate hypotheses for empirical test. The analysis of each of these issues raises a number of unanswered questions, but it also shows that different theoretical positions can lead to different problems, hypotheses, measurements, and inferences. The discussion may also suggest ways of framing studies that compare the predictive and explanatory power of the different theoretical positions.

The Activation of Emotion

A source of confusion in research on emotion has resulted from a failure to distinguish consistently between models of emotion activation and theories of emotion. The former focus on the problem of the generation of emotion. The production of emotion has been variously conceived in terms of linear causal relations (Arnold, 1960a; Mandler, 1975), additive functions (Schachter, 1971), sensory feedback (Tomkins, 1962, 1980), and complex feedback loops that are modulated by genetically influenced receptor thresholds and selectivity (Candland, 1977; Izard, 1977).

One model of emotion activation (Schachter & Singer, 1962) that derived from a study of the determinants of emotion had theory status thrust upon it by investigator's frequent reference to it as a theory of emotion. Subsequently a great deal of research on the determinants of emotion, much of which actually addressed the issue of subjects' causal attribution of emotion, led to a widespread misconception of emotion as an epiphenomenon of no real import in personality or behavior theory.

More recently, Dienstbier (1979) combined an emotion-activation model and some principles of attribution theory into a formulation of emotion-attribution theory. Unlike many of the investigators in attribution research, Dienstbier views emotions as central to human motivation, and he recognizes the complexity of the relation among emotion processes and the cognitive processes of attribution.

A central point here is that a model of emotion activation represents only one aspect of emotion theory, which is concerned not only with the generation of emotions but also with their functions in evolution, biology, motivation, human development, personality traits, and social behavior.

Early work on emotions reflected little interest in the problem of emotion activation. Darwin's

(1872) famous principles grew out of his observations of emotion expressions and his effort to explain their origins in phylogeny and their production in living species. Spencer (1855) and Wundt (1907) seem to have taken for granted the notion that emotions arise as a function of consciousness and concerned themselves chiefly with the characteristics of emotion experience and its relation to cognitive processes. As Zajonc (1980) recently pointed out, Wundt maintained, without the benefit of supporting data, that affective elements or feelings always precede acts of cognition or recognition.

Emotion as a Result of Sensory Feedback

James (1884, 1890) presented the first really influential model of emotion activation, and his notion of the differential qualitative effects of sensory feedback remain a part of some current formulations (Tomkins, 1962; Izard, 1971; Leventhal, 1980). He proposed, contrary to popular thought, that "bodily changes follow directly the perception of the exciting fact, and that our feeling of the same changes as they occur is the emotion." James's use of the term perception here is ambiguous; he fails to distinguish between cognitive processes involved in the "perceptions" that result when "we lose our fortune" and when "we meet a bear." In fact, these two examples of perception fall at nearly opposite ends of a continuum of complexity of perceptual-cognitive processes, and thus they may generate emotions via different neural pathways and structures. In the wild, the sense impression or percept of a bear can lead to escape behavior with little or no inferential process (cf. Zajonc, 1980), but the perception of a loss of fortune involves complex cognitive processes, including memory and anticipation.

In the original statement of his model, James described "bodily changes" resulting from both somatic and autonomic nervous system activities. The association of his work with that of Lange (1885), however, led to the James-Lange theory, in which bodily changes were synonymous with visceral activities. Later, on the basis of phsyiological experiments, Cannon (1927, 1929), argued that emotion, or rather its expression or emotional behavior, was independent of visceral feedback. This led to widespread rejection of the feedback hypothesis of emotion activation, but two disparate approaches revived it, though in different forms. F.H. Allport (1924), Jacobsen

(1929), Tomkins (1962), and Izard (1971) drew attention to somatic feedback, which was not considered by Cannon, and Schachter (Schachter & Singer, 1962) and Mandler (1975) held that undifferentiated arousal (autonomic nervous system activity) contributes to emotion experience, given certain mediating cognitive processes. The somatic factor was highlighted in the Tomkins (1962) claim, phrased essentially like James's, that awareness of facial feedback is the emotion. The evidence relating to the facial feedback hypothesis will be discussed in a later section.

Tomkins (1962), following Spencer, Darwin, and James, posits a number of innate emotions and explains their activation in terms of a single principle—"the density of neural firing or stimulation." For example, a sudden and rapid increase in the rate of neural firing activates startle, a less rapid increase produces fear, and a still less rapid increase activates interest. Thus, according to Tomkins, a particular gradient of neural firing over time produces a particular pattern of neuromuscular activity in the face, and the facial feedback is sensed as a specific emotion experience. The Tomkins model ignores the differential involvement of various brain structures in different emotions (see section 2 on Neuroanatomical and Neurochemical Substrates of Emotion). The same overall density of neural firing may activate very different emotions if the neural activity differentially involves limbic structures that are differentially involved in, say, anger and fear.

Emotion as a Function of Cognition

Arnold (1960a,b) presented a comprehensive theory of emotion, including a model of emotion activation that has become the cornerstone of contemporary cognitive theories of emotion. She maintains that emotions arise only as a consequence of perception and appraisal and that these two processes differ from each other. She defined perception as the "integration of sense impressions" and appraisal as an "integrative sensory function," but the distinction proved difficult to clarify, and most later cognitive models have ignored it. Lazarus, Kanner, and Folkman (1980) have described the cognitive antecedents of emotion as involving "learning memory, perception, and thought" (p. 192) and Plutchik's (1980a) model of "cognitive-emotional" functioning involves short- and long-term memory, evaluation, and prediction. Schachter (1971) and Mandler (1975) have taken similar positions.

The foregoing models lead to the conclusion that emotions do not emerge in infancy until the requisite cognitive capacities have developed. For one of these capacities—short-term memory —emergence does not occur until approximately 7 to 9 months of age (Kagan, Kearsley, & Zelazo, 1978). There is clear evidence, however, that infants have developed a substantial repertoire of adaptive responses, including the signaling functions inherent in the expressions of several basic emotions, prior to the emergence of the storage-retrieval processes of memory.

A variation of the appraisal model described by developmental psychologists ascribes emotion or motivation to information processing (Hunt, 1965). Positive affect arises from the assimilation of information; negative affect arises from difficulty or failure in assimilating information. In particular, negative emotion is activated by incongruity or discrepancy between the perceived object and a previously established schema or central representation of the object. The incongruity hypothesis was first described by Hebb (1946), though he later rejected it (1949). Explanation of emotion activation by the assimilation-discrepancy model requires either the assumption of innate schemata or the acquisition and storage of schemata in memory before emotion can be elicited. Thus this position, as presented by Kagan (1974), Schaffer (1974), and others, holds that emotion is dependent on the matching (assimilation) or mismatching (discrepancy) of the products of perceptual processes with learned schemata already existing in consciousness.

Leventhal (1980) holds that some form of cognitive process is always "active along with—if not prior to—emotion." However, he recognizes that the accompanying or preceding cognitive processes can vary from "minimally processed pre-attentive perception" to a "more deeply processed and specific schematic or conceptual code." Leventhal's position seems quite similar to that of Arnold.

Emotion as a Result of Arousal plus Cognitive Evaluation

Schachter and Singer (1962) proposed that undifferentiated and unexplained arousal leads to a cognitive evaluation or unbiased search for explanation. The search leads to a label that determines the quality of the emotion experience. In this formulation it is cognition involving symbolic processes that determines the quality of emotion. This model generated considerable research on cognitive manipulation of the labeling process under various experimental conditions, but the only direct tests of the model have been recent experiments intended to replicate the original Schachter-Singer study (Maslach, 1979; Marshall & Zimbardo, 1979). Both these experiments failed to replicate the original study, and the data suggested that undifferentiated, unbiased arousal leads to a negatively biased search and to predominantly negative labels and experiences. Schachter and Singer and Marshall and Zimbardo debated the merits of the original study and the failures at replication (Schachter and Singer, 1979; Marshall and Zimbardo, 1979).

Need for a Multifactor Model of Emotion Activation

Each of the foregoing models attempts to explain the activation of emotion on the basis of a single critical variable—density of neural firing (stimulation) or cognitive appraisal. Each of these principles offers a reasonable explanation of the activation of some emotions under certain circumstances. For example, a continued loud noise can elicit anger, as can a remark that is perceived as a personal insult.

Although there is no experimental evidence that bears directly on Tomkins's model, some developmental studies raise questions about its usefulness. Precisely the same painful stimulus e.g., DPT inoculation) activates different emotion expressions in different infants of the same age (Izard, Hembree, Dougherty, & Spizzirri, 1983). Tomkins could argue that there are individual differences in density of neural firing, but one could counter that the thresholds for pain and for the feeling or experience of emotion, could vary even when the density of neural firing remained constant. As already indicated, the same density of neural firing could involve different mechanisms that are differentially involved in different discrete emotions.

There is ample anecdotal and experimental evidence to indicate that cognitive processes trigger emotions. James (1890) called attention to the power of imagery to elicit emotions. Experimental evidence for the corrections of

James's observation has come from the work of Fridlund and Schwartz (1979), Izard (1972), Lang (1979), and Schwartz, Fair, Salt, Mandel, and Klerman (1976). The Schwartz et al. study provides a good example. They asked normal and depressed subjects to form images of happy, sad, and angry scenes, and of a typical day. They recorded electromyograms (EMG) from facial muscles involved in the expression of each of the target emotions and obtained post experimental self-reports of emotion experience on the Differential Emotions Scale (DES) (Izard, 1972). They obtained the predicted relation between EMG activity and DES scores. They also found that in the imagery of a typical day normal subjects showed EMG and DES profiles consistent with happiness or joy, while the depressives gave responses consistent with sadness and anger. The question, whether these findings were influenced by the demand characteristics of the study, has not been resolved, but the validity of the findings receives some support from Rusalova, Izard, and Simonov (1975), who found large changes in the heart rate and predicted EMG patterns in response to imagery.

Thus the crucial issue is not whether cognitive processes activate or trigger emotions, but whether there are other activating processes. Current evidence suggests that there are. The concept of emotion threshold, which is related to the concept of biological preparedness (Seligman & Hager, 1972), helps account for individual differences in responsiveness to emotion and for species- and age-related differences in emotion activation in response to particular stimuli. McDougall's (1923) notion that the "nervous system is peculiarly fitted to respond" affectively to certain sensory data and not to others helps explain why some stimuli, but not others, elicit a particular emotion. Strangeness (Emde, Gaensbauer, & Harmon, 1976) and heights (Campos & Stenberg, 1980) are differentially effective stimuli for fear in the second half-year of life.

Thus a satisfactory model of emotion activation must be multifactored or multidimensional in nature and must allow for developmental changes in emotion and in emotion-cognition processes. All the potentially relevant factors are not independent, and all may not be operative on all occasions or at all stages of development. The following factors or concepts must be taken into account: selectivity of receptors (McDougall, 1923; Izard, 1971), biological preparedness or genetically determined threshold (Bowlby, 1973; Gray, 1971; Izard, 1971), noninferential sensory-perceptual or preattentive processes, for example, uninterpreted sense impressions (McDougall, 1926; Izard, 1971), density of neural firing or stimulation gradients (Tomkins, 1962), feedback from physiological arousal or autonomic nervous system activity (Schachter, 1971; Mandler, 1975), feedback from facial patterning and activity of the somatic nervous system (Izard, 1977; Leventhal, 1980; Tomkins, 1962); immediate nonreflective cognitive appraisal or evaluation (Arnold, 1960a); thought, memory and higher-order cognitive processes (Lazarus, 1974; Lazarus, Kanner, & Folkman, 1980). Perhaps considerable empirical research on each of the foregoing concepts is in order before the multifactor model of emotion activation is formalized. In any case, a viable and comprehensive model will need to be a complex one.

The Components of Emotions

The failure to recognize that emotions involve processes in different systems has been a source of confusion and controversy. Some of the early views of emotion (e.g., Lange, 1885) held that emotion was essentially a vasomotor reaction, and visceral changes have continued to be emphasized by some investigators (Gasonov, 1974; Mandler, 1975). Other investigators have focused almost exclusively on neural structures and pathways (Flynn, 1967; Gellhorn, 1961, 1964, 1965; Lindsley, 1951, 1970; MacLean, 1972), hormones and neurotransmitters (Brady, 1970; Davis, 1970; Frankenhaeuser, 1979; Mason, 1975; Schildkraut, 1974), observable behavior, particularly facial expression (Ekman, Friesen, & Ellsworth, 1972), or subjective experience (Russell, 1979). While these specialists have made significant contributions to the field, they have typically presented information on only one system or component of emotion. Many of them leave open the question as to whether emotion has really been measured, since they present no evidence of concomitant emotion processes in other systems. Most emotion theorists now define emotions as having three components —neurophysiological-biochemical, behavioral-expressive, and feeling-experiential. The experiential component is usually thought to include action tendencies and cognitive cues. Each component can be viewed as a system that organizes

(noncognitive) information from other life systems.

The foregoing discussion makes it evident that the subject of emotions is interdisciplinary in nature and that the study of different component systems requires different conceptual tools and different methods to deal with very different variables. Research at the neurophysiological-biochemical level is facilitated by a sophisticated technology, whereas current techniques at the behavioral-expressive level depend on human observation. However, the measuring and studying of observable behavior are critical in emotion research since the best available criteria for the presence of a particular discrete emotion are the muscle movements or changes in appearance that characterize its innate, universal facial expression.

The remainder of the present section is devoted to an overview of the types of concepts and variables of emotion that are studied at each of the three levels or in each component system. Later sections will review representative experiments in each of the three domains of research.

The Neurophysiological-Biochemical Level

The neurophysiological domain includes anatomical and physiological studies of brain structures and neural pathways involved in emotions. This research has shown that the limbic system and certain limbic structures, such as the hypothalamus, hippocampus, amygdala, septum, and cingulate gyrus are differentially involved in different emotions (Gellhorn, 1968; MacLean, 1972). The evidence seems to support the notion that the neural substrate for a given emotion consists of complex interconnections among structures, and that different pathways may be involved in activation or amplification processes on the one hand and inhibition or attenuation processes on the other (Adams, 1979; Delgado, 1971; Isaacson, 1974).

The biochemistry of emotions includes psychoendocrinological and psychopharmacological studies of hormones and neurotransmitters involved in the limbic and limbic-neocritical processes in emotions. These studies have found that any of five neurotransmitters, or any of hundreds of different chains of these transmitters, may be involved in emotions. The existing evidence does not show strong relations between a specific hormone and a specific emotion. However, several studies, to be discussed in the next section, have suggested that the corticosteroids are implicated in stress (Frankenhaeuser, 1979; Selye, 1979), dopamine in anger (Kety, 1972), and the monomines in depression (Schildkraut, 1965; Schildkraut & Kety, 1967; Davis, 1970). The trend in psychopharmacology, psychoendocrinology, and psychophysiology is toward a search for profiles or patterns of neurophysiological functions underlying an emotion or a pattern of emotions (Mason, 1975; G.E. Schwartz, 1982).

In psychophysiological research on emotions the question of what functions to measure has been debated for years and still cannot be given an unqualified answer. Even the choice among neurophysiological systems has not proved simple. The pros and cons of measuring autonomic versus somatic functions have been discussed by several investigators (Izard, 1977; Mandler, 1975; Obrist, Light, & Hastrup, 1982). Evidence suggests that the best approach is to take multiple measures of two or more systems (G.E. Schwartz, 1982). At present, the best independent evidence of emotion-specific neurophysiological activity is provided by facial EMG, with electrodes on combinations of muscles that produce a particular expressive pattern, and observer-based measurement of the action of such muscles (Ekman & Friesen, 1978; Izard, 1979; Rusalova et al., 1975; G.E. Schwartz, Fair, Greenberg, Freedman, & Klerman, 1974; G.E. Schwartz et al., 1976). Hoffman (1982) has suggested that even the complex affective-cognitive phenomenon of empathy, at least in infants and children, is best indexed by facial behaviors. Even with measurement of facial muscle activity, however, it is necessary to show that the facial actions are involuntary or spontaneous if one wants to assume genuine emotion.

There is scant evidence of emotion-specific autonomic nervous system functions (Obrist et al., 1982), but that dearth may reflect the paucity of studies using a multilevel systems approach in a search for patterns or profiles of autonomic activities in relation to emotion experience and activities of the somatic nervous system (Schwartz, 1982). Another problem with the search for emotion-specific patterns of ANS activity has been the failure of many investigators to use empirically validated criteria for observable emotion expressions and objective measures to identify them. Objective, anatomically-based systems for coding facial expressions were used

successfully in two recent studies. Ekman, Levinson, and Friesen (1983) found that patterns of heart rate and skin temperature distinguished among subjects who were posing joy, surprise, sadness, anger, disgust, and fear according to established criteria for posing and coding these emotion expressions (Ekman & Friesen, 1978).

Cohen, Izard, and Simons (1986) found that patterns of heart rate and skin temperature distinguished among 4-1/2-month-old infants' spontaneous expressions of interest, joy, and anger. Emotion expressions were measured by the objective, anatomically based Maximally Discriminative Facial Movement Coding System (Izard, 1979) and ANS functions were recorded on line. The video system recording facial behavior and the polygraph recording ANS activity were time locked by signals on the computer. Preliminary analyses of follow-up data showed significant differences in patterns of ANS activity among the three foregoing emotions and the emotion of sadness. The initial studies of Ekman et al. and Cohen et al. suggest that rigorous methodology for measuring both behavioral and physiological activities may lead to a better understanding of the relations among specific emotion expressions and patterns of ANS functioning.

The Behavioral-Expressive Level

In the past decade research on facial expressions of emotion experienced a renaissance that has spread to the whole field. Robust evidence for Darwin's (1872) century-old hypothesis of the innateness and universality of the expressions of several discrete emotions sparked this upturn (Ekman et al., 1972; Izard, 1971; Eibl-Eibesfeldt, 1972). The emergence of ethology as a vigorous discipline and the presentation of a Nobel award to its leaders who claimed Darwin as their intellectual progenitor, fanned and fueled the spark. Two factors have given impetus to this resurgence: (1) the fact that facial expressions are observable behaviors and can be analyzed in terms of particular appearance changes, and (2) the rapid growth of interest in nonverbal communication. The confluence of these forces resulted in an increasingly wide acceptance of facial patterns as the best single index of the presence of emotion, particularly in infants and young children in whom cultural influences on expressive behavior are minimal and are more readily sorted out when present.

Facial behaviors occupy a unique place in emotion and hence in emotion research. They are at once integral to the neurophysiological processes of emotion and central to their social or communicative aspect. Facial feedback may be critical in generating the unique quality of consciousness that defines an emotion subjectively, but the evidence of this point is controversial (Buck, 1980a; Ekman, 1980; Izard, 1980; Laird, 1974; Laird, Wagener, Halal, & Szegda, 1982; Tomkins, 1981; Tourangeau & Ellsworth, 1979). Facial behaviors have been widely accepted as important social signals in development and in interpersonal interactions. Andrew (1963) has argued that the communicative value of facial behaviors accounts for their selection and transmission in evolution. (Ekman & Oster, 1979, give a somewhat different view of both the renaissance of emotion research and the status of research on facial expression.)

"Felt Emotion"—Feeling, Action Tendencies, Cognitive Cues

James (1890) argued that the ultimate verification of the existence of emotion depended on the self-report of the subject. He made a point of lasting value, and indeed the self-report scales to be discussed in a later section have proved valuable tools in the study of emotion. Self-report scales generally consist of ratings on (1) dimensions such as pleasantness, tension, and acceptance (Schlosberg, 1954) or (2) adjectives that define discrete categories of emotion experience such as happy, sad, angry, afraid (Izard, 1972). These two types have both high reliability and the support of some validity studies.

While it is generally accepted that emotion has an experiential or feeling component that can be measured only via self-report, it is not always clear whether self-reports relate more to words or thoughts about emotion that may be important in their own right or to genuine emotion experience. Another problem with self-reports is that of timing; since they are of necessity reflective in nature, they are influenced by learning and memory. Finally, unlike some of the measures of the other two components, self-report must be considered as a joint function of affective and cognitive processes. The strength of self-report data depends largely on evidence that the reports correlate in predictable ways with activity of the other components of emotion and help predict or account

for behavior subsequent to emotion-eliciting events.

Emotion and Cognition

Many of the early life scientists, like most other people, assumed that thinking and feeling were different but related processes. Spencer (1855/1890) maintained that "only in those rare cases in which both its terms and its remote associations are absolutely indifferent, can an act of cognition be absolutely free of emotion." Defining cognition to include perceptual processes, he went on to argue that "no emotion can be *absolutely* free of cognition" (1855/1890, pp. 474–475). In an even more dramatic statement on the issue, Wundt (1907) maintained that affect follows directly from sensory processes and precedes cognition.

James (1890/1950), like Spencer and Wundt, recognized that emotion and cognition involve different processes. He thought that without emotions one would have to "drag out an existence of merely cognitive or intellectual form" (1890/1950, p. 453). His discussion of the interaction of emotion and cognition could have been the framework for the recent research on imagery-induced emotion. He thought that memory for a felt emotion, for its particular quality of consciousness, was poor. "We can remember that we underwent grief or rapture, but not just how the grief or rapture felt" (p. 474). However, the mind can easily compensate for this deficiency of memory through imagery. "That is, we can produce, not remembrances of grief or rapture, but new griefs and raptures, by summoning up a lively thought of their exciting cause" (p. 474). James assumed that a good imagination was essential to "an abundant emotional life" and noted that "if the imagination be poor, the occasions for touching off the emotional trains will fail to be realized, and the life will be *pro tanto* cold and dry" (p. 475).

If we were to jump over the products of about a century of psychological research and writing and look at the issues now confronting cognitive science, as discussed by Zajonc (1980) and Norman (1980), we would be reminded of the statements of the earlier thinkers, but we would also see an effort on the part of some of our contemporaries to bridge a psychology divided between cognitive science, which has occupied a large part of experimental psychology during the past quarter century, and emotion science, which has just begun to emerge as a serious contender for a place among the subdisciplines of the behavioral and life sciences.

Zajonc, taking his inspiration from Wundt, argues that it is necessary to modify the typical information-processing model that begins with feature discrimination. New models must allow for important occasions in which affect precedes what is typically described as cognition. Norman does not argue for a principle of affective primacy, but he sees emotion as one of twelve "issues" or "topic matters" essential for cognitive science; and in the spirit of Spencer and Wundt, he maintains that the "pure cognitive sciences" of the past two decades have taught us little about how we learn to converse or read and write or remember what we said or how we forgot it. This is not to mention the enormous question of the why of these fundamental things. The need for the study of emotion-cognition relations is beginning to be recognized by experimental, social, and cognitive psychology.

Emotions, Behavior, and Personality

Biologists, who made the first scientific contributions to the study of emotions, conceptualized emotions as significant factors in behavior and adaptation. Darwin emphasized the signaling functions of emotion expressions, noting: "They serve as the first means of communication between mother and infant; she smiles approval, and thus encourages her child on the right path, or frowns disapproval. We readily perceive sympathy in others by their expression; our sufferings are thus mitigated and our pleasures increased; and mutual good feeling is thus strengthened" (Darwin, 1872/1965, p. 364). He also recognized functional relations between emotion, cognition, and action. He observed that in anger "the excited brain gives strength to the muscles, and at the same time energy to the will" (p. 239).

Cannon, like Darwin, assumed functional relations between emotions and behavior, and as an experimental physiologist he produced evidence for this assumption. In rage and fear "respiration deepens, the heart beats more rapidly, the arterial pressure rises, the blood is shifted away from the stomach and the intestines to the heart and central nervous system and the muscles, the processes in the alimentary canal cease, sugar is freed from the reserves

in the liver, the spleen contracts and discharges its contents of concentrated corpuscles, and adrenalin in secreted from the adrenal medulla. The key to these marvelous transformations in the body is found in relating them to the natural accompaniments of fear and rage—running away in order to escape from danger, and attacking in order to be dominant" (Cannon, 1929, pp. 227–228). Thus Cannon clearly saw the functional relations between emotion, preparation, and action, but his emphasis on the emergency functions of emotions in "life-or-death struggle" and on radical changes in activities of the autonomic nervous system misled later theorists and investigators into thinking of emotions as transitory phenomena that occurred only under extreme conditions and that were best indexed by autonomic functions. There is no experimental evidence contrary to the notion that the functional relations between emotion and behavior apply equally to mild and moderate intensities of positive as well as negative emotions. Nor is there evidence that precludes the role of the somatic nervous system in emotion.

Although the study of emotion has not been a central theme in biology, the topic continues to be pursued by a few present-day neuroscientists. They, like their predecessors, typically assume functional relations between emotion and adaptive behavior, and they focus their research on delineating the brain mechanisms, neural pathways, and neurotransmitters associated with different emotions or emotional behaviors (e.g., Delgado, 1971; Gellhorn, 1961; Mason, 1975; Hamburg, 1963; Schildkraut, Davis, & Klerman, 1968). For example, they have suggested that the amygdala, a limbic structure, and dopamine, a neurotransmitter, are implicated in anger and aggressive behavior (Hamburg, Hamburg, & Barchas, 1975; Moyer, 1971), and that the biogenic amines are involved in sadness and depressive behavior (Davis, 1970).

Most clinical psychologists and psychiatrists assume that emotions influence behavior and play some role in the etiology or symptomatology of psychopathology, and clinical investigators have provided some support for this assumption. However, they have typically reported on complex emotion-related phenomena such as anxiety and depression with little attention to discrete emotions.

Theorists who view emotions as motivational (Dienstbier, 1979; Izard, 1977; Plutchik, 1980a;

Tomkins, 1962) see them as direct and immediate determinants of cognitive and motor behavior. Most of the studies that support this premise have induced emotions experimentally, and in some cases the results are ambiguous because the investigators failed to test for the effects of the emotion induction on subjective experience. Nevertheless, these studies provide rather robust support for the direct effects of emotion on attention, learning, memory, and social behavior.

Some theories view emotion primarily as response, but they do not necessarily trivialize the role of emotions in influencing behavior. Although Lazarus (1968, p. 209) takes the "perspective of emotions as response" he argues that emotions are sometimes "integral aspects of the effort to cope with potential harm." He also argues that coping or adaptation results in "lowered levels of emotional response." Lazarus, Kanner, and Folkman (1980) take a position similar to that of emotion-as-motivation theorists in maintaining that positive emotions, like negative ones, can signal the need for coping. They go on to argue that "coping activity can be *aroused* and *sustained* . . . by positively toned emotions" (p. 207, emphasis added), which can also act as "breathers" (temporary relief from stress) and "restorers" (aids in recovery from stress).

A few theorists have attempted to apply their conceptual framework to the broad issues of personality development, defense mechanisms, and psychopathology. Izard has presented an empirical analysis of the affective component of anxiety and depression in terms of reliably identifiable patterns or combinations of discrete emotions (Izard, 1972; Izard & Schwartz, 1986). Plutchik, Kellerman, and Conte (1979) have argued that specific ego defense mechanisms are related to specific emotions and that diagnostic personality types are derived from particular defensive styles. Tomkins (1963) has presented a well-reasoned explanation of paranoid tendencies and paranoid schizophrenia in terms of the emotions of fear and shame.

A few developmental studies have shown continuity of emotion-expressive behavior over time (Hyson & Izard, 1985; Izard, Hembree, & Huebner, 1987; Washburn, 1929). Several other studies have demonstrated that measures of fear responses in infancy predicted shyness in the pre-school years (Bagley, 1956; Bronson, 1972; Kagan & Moss, 1962).

Two studies have shown that patterns of objectively measured emotion expressions in infancy predict aspects of personality in toddlerhood and the preschool years. Hyson, Izard, and Weston (1987) found correlations between emotion expressions in the mildly stressful strange-situation procedure (Ainsworth, Blehar, Waters, & Wall, 1978) and behaviors during a moderately frustrating problem-solving task. For example, anger expressions in the pre-verbal 14-month-old in the strange-situation procedure predicted anger expression and aggressive behavior at two years during problem solving at two years. They argued that the underlying experience or feeling of anger provided the motivation for functionally similar behaviors at the different ages and that the similarity of expression-feeling-behavior sequences over time reflects continuity or a trait-like phenomenon.

Huebner (1986) found continuity of expressive behavior from early infancy to preschool years. She found that infants' expressions of interest to the human face and face-like stimuli predicted their emotion-expression decoding ability and their mothers' ratings of their sociability at 5 years. Huebner argued that the invariant emotion feeling associated with interest expression is the common demoninator accounting for both greater attention to faces in infancy and sociability at 5 years of age.

Thus far this chapter has presented an overview of the field of emotions and considered a number of central issues and some evidence relating to them. The remaining three sections will review some of the research relating to each of the three components of emotions: the neurophysiological-biochemical component, the motor-expressive component, and the feeling-experimental component. Because investigators typically work within a special area relating to only one of the components of emotion, it is not possible to offer a neat integration of the following material. The research reviewed in the biological section especially stands in need of bridges to link it to research on the other two components of emotions.

THE NEUROANATOMICAL AND NEUROCHEMICAL SUBSTRATES OF EMOTION

Both peripheral and central nervous systems

are intrinsic to emotional activity. The peripheral nervous system—with somatic branches innervating the muscles and autonomic nervous system controlling heart rate, blood pressure, intestinal activity, and catecholamine secretion from the adrenal medulla—mediates the behavioral expression of emotion in the external and internal milieu. Not covered in this section is an extensive literature concerned with emotional correlates of the autonomic and neuroendocrine systems, especially as related to stress and coping behavior (e.g., see Frankenhaeuser, 1979; Mason, 1975). Rather, the present section emphasizes specific emotions and the central neural basis for emotions.

In studies of specific emotions, psychophysiological techniques have, except in a few important studies, been used only to index the loosely defined emotional constructs of anxiety, depression, and arousal. As Izard (1972), Marshall and Izard (1972), and Schwartz and Weinberger (1980) have shown, anxiety and depression are not discrete emotions but complex phenomena consisting of patterns of emotions, drives, and affective-cognitive structures. This may help to explain the low consistency among studies of psychophysiological correlates, especially those dealing with anxiety.

The construct of arousal, as related to emotional intensity, has never been satisfactorily defined. Schachter and Singer (1962) proposed that "unexplained, undifferentiated arousal" becomes a specific emotion when the individual evaluates the arousal-eliciting situation and labels the internal feelings accordingly. However, the meaningfulness of both the concept of undifferentiated arousal and the Schachter-Singer model of emotion activation has been seriously challenged in studies by Maslach (1979) and Marshall and Zimbardo (1979), who showed that undifferentiated arousal tended to elicit negative emotion labels. In animal studies, arousal is produced by stimulating the ascending reticular system of the midbrain. This system, based on activity in the mesencephalic reticular formation, is subject to input from all sensory modalities including the neocortex, and its stimulation results in a diffuse activation of all areas of the cortex and the subcortical integratory nuclei. Arousal is involved not only in emotional states, but in any behavioral activation such as waking, in the orienting responses to novel stimuli, or

in such motivated behavior as feeding or mating.

Autonomic activity may provide useful indexes of emotion-related constructs even though specific emotions are not identified. An example is Kagan's (1981) recent studies of heart-rate variability in Caucasian and Chinese children as a sign of a temperamental dimension in infants. Kagan found that a pattern of high heart rate and low range correlated significantly with the disposition to distress upon separation, when sex, type of care, and ethnicity were controlled.

G.E. Schwartz (1982) presented a systems approach to psychophysiology and concluded that, viewed in this frame of reference, the findings of the few investigators that have looked for patterns of psychophysiological activities in emotion-eliciting situations have been in fairly good agreement. Schwartz holds that by considering these systems as interrelated, consistent relation between event, emotion, and psychophysiological measures can be found when one uses multichannel recording techniques.

Schwartz and Weinberger (1980) replicated and extended Ax's (1953) early study of psychophysiological distinctions between anger and fear. Thirty-two college students, experienced in acting, were told to imagine and then express nonverbally one of four emotion states—joy, sadness, anger, or fear—while exercising (walking up and down a single step) or while relaxing. Heart rate and systolic and diastolic blood pressure were measured for each state. When exercise was combined with imagery, the authors found highly significant differences in diastolic blood pressure for anger and fear, replicating Ax's earlier finding. Moreover, the patterning of all three cardiovascular measures—heart rate and systolic and diastolic blood pressure—in anger and fear differed from the patterns in joy and sadness.

Although a systems approach may clarify the interrelations among the peripheral manifestations of an emotion, the peripheral and central nervous systems must also be considered as interacting with sensory and proprioceptive feedback, continuously modifying both subjective awareness and central nervous system (CNS) activation of emotion. The modulation of a sensory receptive field under the influence of emotion activation may be essential for emotional expression and may itself modulate that emotional state. For instance, Flynn (1967) and more recently Block, Siegel, and Edinger (1980), and Goldstein and Siegel (1980) have studied the gestation and inhibition of a trigeminal sensory receptive field on the lipline for the biting reflex in aggressive behavior. Stimulating the central brain structures that produce and inhibit aggressive behavior in cats also modified this receptive field.

At the neurophysiological and biochemical level, "emotion" is the CNS activity that underlies not only the awareness of feelings of joy and sadness, anger and fear, but also the expression of somatic and autonomic behavior associated with those feelings. Thus emotion at this level consists of patterns of neural activity mediated by specific chemical neurotransmitter systems in centran integratory structures of the brain.

The remainder of this section examines in more detail the neuroanatomical and neurochemical bases for emotion in the central nervous system. Much of this evidence comes from animal experimentation in which the mechanisms of behavior can be explored in single-unit recording of neural activity and pharmacological manipulation. However, the patterns of behavior that serve as indexes of emotional states are animal behaviors; thus the "rage" of rats with septal lesions or the "anxiety" of behaviorally inhibited rats (Gray, 1979), or the aggression anger of hypothalamically stimulated cats (Flynn, 1967)—these "emotional" behaviors in lower animal species may correspond to a very different type of subjective awareness and a less complex emotional differentiation than those experienced in our own species. Experimental results on animals are discussed in their inhibition or facilitation of certain behaviors, and the emotional experience of the animal must remain an inference.

Neuroanatomical Structures of the Emotion System

On the most simplistic level we can conceive of the brain as consisting of (1) incoming sensory pathways, both specific lemniscal systems and the diffuse arousal systems; (2) outgoing motor pathways; and (3) central integratory structures. These central subcortical integratory structures have until recently been thought to fall into two disparate groups: a limbic system concerned with the production, maintenance, or modulation of emotion, motivation, and autonomic activity, and a striatal or extrapyramidal system concerned with the integration and

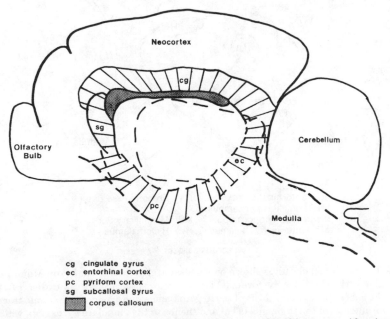

cg cingulate gyrus
ec entorhinal cortex
pc pyriform cortex
sg subcallosal gyrus
▨ corpus callosum

Figure 12.1. Limbic cortical areas of Broca are indicated by cross-hatching on a midsagittal section of cat brain. Note how these areas encircle the brainstem and include the palescortical areas of the entorhinal cortex (ec) overlying the hippocampus and the cingulate gyrus (cg) (compare with Figure 12.2).

control of motor patterns of behavior. In the past decade new anatomical techniques have made possible the identification of the pathways interconnecting striatal and limbic systems (Nauta & Domesick, 1978; Heimer, 1978; Heimer & Wilson, 1975; Beckstead, 1976).

Development of the Concept of the Limbic System

Just over 100 years ago, the French anatomist Broca referred to the cortical lobes forming a limbus or ring around the rostral end of the brainstem as "le grand lobe limbique" (see Figure 12.1). Broca observed that these older cortical areas, which have remained relatively stable throughout the phylogenetic development of mammals, were fundamental to the activation and maintenance of those feeling tones so essential for motivational engagement in behavior.

THE FIRST CONCEPTION OF AN EMOTION CIRCUIT

Papez (1937) proposed that the structurally prominent and phylogenetically old neural pathways interconnecting the hypothalamus with the older cortical areas referred to by Broca could serve as a substrate for a function as important as emotion. Papez suggested that the circulatory and reciprocal connections of his proposed limbic circuit would make possible the long-lasting neural activity required for motivating and sustaining goal-directed behavior. He considered this limbic circuit to be the physiological substrate of a "stream of feeling," which together with a "stream of movement" (through the striatal and motor nuclei) and a "stream of thought" (centered in the neocortex) made up neural activity in the most advanced mammalian brain. The limbic circuit of Papez is presented in Figure 12.2.

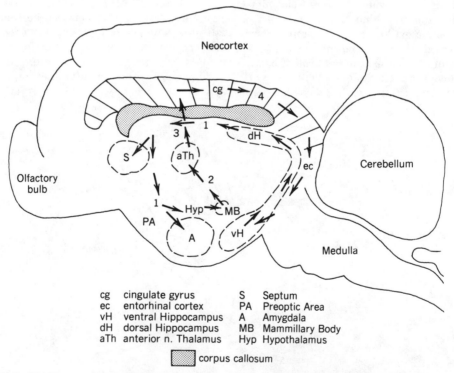

cg	cingulate gyrus	S	Septum
ec	entorhinal cortex	PA	Preoptic Area
vH	ventral Hippocampus	A	Amygdala
dH	dorsal Hippocampus	MB	Mammillary Body
aTh	anterior n. Thalamus	Hyp	Hypothalamus

▦ corpus callosum

Figure 12.2. The Papez emotion circuit is shown on a midsagittal section of cat brain. Major neural pathways from the hippocampus (dH and vH) via the fornix (1) terminate in septum (S), preoptic area (PA) and hypothalamus (Hyp). From the mammillary bodies (MB) of the hypothalamus, the mammillo-thalamic tract (2) projects to the ventral anterior nucleus of the thalamus (aTh) and thence to the cingulate gyrus (cg), which is connected through longitudinal striae (4) to the entorhinal cortex and back to the hippocampus. The more laterally situated amygdala (A) is shown projected onto the plane of this figure. Pathways to the amygdala are described in the text.

THE BRAIN AS A TRIPARTITTE ORGAN

MacLean (1952, 1975) proposed the term limbic system for those interconnected structures, including the limbic circuit of Papez, which had formerly been known as the rhinencephalon or "smell brain." He also included as a major limbic pathway the medial forebrain bundle, a neuronal tract containing both ascending and descending axons and connecting structures from the ventral forebrain to the hypothalamus, and from there to the mesencephalic brainstem. MacLean, like Papez, considered the brain as divisible into three levels of functioning arising phylogenetically as an ancient reptilian brain, an old mammalian brain, and a new mammalian brain, each level structurally overlying, expanding upon, and exerting controls over the earlier one.

MacLean (1954) conceived the old mammalian brain, centered in the limbic system, as adding a new dimension of emotionality to consciousness in order to act as a motivational force and to aid in the discrimination of desirable behavior, loosening the rigidity of the fixed behavior patterns of the more ancient reptilian brain. Emotion is a primitive response serving to help regulate behavior as it becomes more variable with phylogenetic development and with the enormous expansion of the neocortex. Emotion itself, as much as behavior, is subject to modification by interaction with memories, learning, and the complex evaluation of environmental stimuli that takes place in the neocortex. MacLean (1970) later emphasized the connections of the subcortical and paleocortical structures of the old mammalian brain with the newer prefrontal cortex, an association area receiving information from all areas of the neocortex. Recording from single neurons in the hippocampus and in Broca's cortical limbus, MacLean (1972) found units responding to visual, auditory, and somatic stimuli. He suggested that the convergence of exteroceptive and interoceptive information in the limbic system may give rise to the feeling of individuality, to a sense of familiarity and personal identification with what is visually experienced. In a similar vein, Izard (1978) has suggested that the experience and expression of emotion facilitate the development of the self-concept and personality in the prelingual child.

EXPANSION OF THE LIMBIC SYSTEM

The concept of the limbic system was further expanded by the anatomical work of Nauta (1960, 1963, 1972, 1979). Nauta emphasized the importance of the direct connections between limbic forebrain structures and what he describes as a limbic midbrain area in the ventral tegmental and midline raphe structures of the mesencephalon. This medial part of the mesencephalic brainstem, distinct from the reticular core and from the ascending sensory systems, has long ascending axons forming interconnections with forebrain limbic areas through the hypothalamus, thalamus, and habenula. The continuing evolution of the limbic system concept is more fully described in *Limbic Mechanisms* (Livingston & Hornykiewicz, 1978).

Major Structures and Pathways of the Limbic System

As indicated by the foregoing summary, the concept of the limbic system has gradually developed to include much more than Broca's original cortical limbus, but it retains a functional unity in its relation to emotional behavior. In addition to the major pathways connecting the limbic cortical areas of the hippocampus, and cingulate gyrus to the hypothalamus, as shown in the Papez circuit in Figure 12.2, four other pathways are important as part of the expanded limbic system.

THE AMYGDALOFUGAL PATHWAYS

The amygdala, composed of several cytoarchitectonically and functionally distinct subnuclei, has two major pathways connecting it to limbic forebrain areas. The older corticomedial nuclei send axons through the stria terminalis to the septum, thus influencing the septo-hippocampal axis. The phylogenetically more recently developed basolateral nuclei project to medial regions of the hypothalamus, some terminating in the key motivational area of the ventromedial nucleus while others join the medial forebrain bundle.

THE MEDIAL FOREBRAIN BUNDLE

The multineuronal pathway, prominent in all vertebrates, has ascending and descending axons with distinct monoamine components. It connects the whole ventral forebrain, including the septum and preoptic area, to the lateral hypothalamus and indirectly to the midbrain limbic areas.

THE DORSAL SEPTAL-MIDBRAIN PATHWAY

The midbrain limbic areas are also connected to the septum and forebrain areas by a medial dorsal pathway, the stria medullaris, arching over the top of the brainstem to the habenula and interpeduncular nucleus.

CONNECTIONS TO THE FRONTAL LOBES

Although not as frequently considered part of the limbic system, the prefrontal cortex has strong reciprocal interconnections with the thalamus, and through it with the hypothalamus, amygdala, and hence the whole limbic system. The prefrontal cortex is an association area, receiving information from much of the rest of the cortex. It is significant that this convergence area for an integrated response to sensory input and analysis, that is, an area responding to individual memories, is so strongly connected to subcortical limbic structures. This provides an anatomical basis for the interaction of emotion and memory, as discussed in theory (Tomkins, 1962; Izard, 1977) and as recently demonstrated in empirical research (Bower, 1981).

The limbic system as a whole receives its major afferent inflow from the reticular core and from the neocortex. Most of the major structures are polysensory; that is, they respond with evoked potentials, though often of long latency indicating multineuronal pathways, to sensory input of different modalities. McCleary and Moore (1965) and Leaton (1971) emphasize the dual importance of sensory convergence from the neocortex and dependence on the reticular arousal system through reciprocal connections with the mesencephalic reticular formation. The limbic structures are ideally situated anatomically to be subject to ascending arousal and descending neocortical influences, and, through their hypothalamic as well as recently discovered striatal interconnections (Nauta & Domesick, 1981), to influence motor patterns as well as autonomic behavior. Activity in the limbic system would thus appear to be capable of influencing all the peripheral manifestations of emotion: autonomic changes, behavior patterns, and subjective experience.

Experimental Evidence Relating Limbic Structures to Emotion

Experimental evidence for the involvement of limbic structures in emotional behavior comes from both human and animal studies. In clinical studies of accidental lesions in the human brain, as well as depth electrode stimulation in conscious patients (Heath & Mickle, 1960), patients report subjective feelings of emotions and changes in emotional behavior when the sites are in the limbic system. More accessible for direct experimentation are laboratory animals, and it is primarily lesion and stimulation in limbic system structures in the rat, cat, and monkey that show these structures to be involved in emotional behavior. However, in neither lesion nor stimulation studies are the results without ambiguity. Not only are lesions rarely confined to one cytoarchitectonically distinct subnucleus, but in addition, they necessarily interrupt the fiber tracts running through that area; and through deinnervation they change the activity of all secondary structures to which the damaged area projects. Similarly, in stimulation studies there may be confusion between stimulation of axon tracts running through the area and cell bodies as well as from the spread of current to adjacent areas. A more general argument against stimulation studies is that the parameters of stimulation are so overwhelming, compared with physiological neural activity, that it is only downstream from the site of stimulation that increased activity takes on normal physiological qualities and induces normal patterns of behavior. Thus the emotional changes induced by stimulation of a given structure may be due not so much to the activity of that specific structure as to activity in the whole system of which it is a part.

The Hypothalamus and Midbrain

The hypothalamus is a central structure in the expression and control of autonomic and visceral activity as well as in the expression of emotion (Sigg, 1975). The stimulation experiments of Hess (1954), conducted in 1951, showed a clear division of autonomic effects, with the anterior and medial hypothalamus showing parasympathetic domination, while stimulation of lateral or posterior portions of the hypothalamus is essential for integrated waking behavior; lesion in this area results in apathy, somnolence, and lack of emotional expression.

The hypothalamus also controls hormonal activity not only by the direct production and secretion of hormones from the posterior pituitary, but indirectly by regulatory hormones that affect the activity of the anterior pituitary, which in turn secretes hormones that regulate the thyroid, gonads, and adrenal cortex (see Wurtman, 1971, for a review of hypophysiotropic hormones and Mason, 1975, for emotion as reflected in patterns of endocrine integration).

The relation of the hypothalamus to emotional behavior has perhaps been most extensively explored in studies of feline predatory aggression by Flynn (1967). Stimulating the lateral areas of the hypothalamus of a previously unconcerned cat will so regularly elicit attack on a rat that this has become a standard experimental paradigm, used by many investigators to explore hormonal, biochemical, or electrophysiological mechanisms of behavioral control. Flynn was able to differentiate between lateral and more medial parts of the hypothalamus. Stimulation of lateral points evoked a predatory attack (a quiet crouching and stalking of the victim with a sudden deadly biting of the back of the neck), whereas more medial stimulation produced an autonomic display of rage with hissing, spitting, arched back, piloerection, and a dramatic attack on the rat (or the experimenter) with unsheathed claws. The aggressive behavior was shown to depend mainly on visual identification of the rat, but tactile stimuli also elicited attack. Intact facial sensation around the mouth was essential for biting to occur, and indeed lateral hypothalamic stimulation was found to produce the sensory field for this biting reflex. Conversely, Block, Siegel, and Edinger (1980) and Goldstein and Siegel (1980) have demonstrated that stimulating the subcortical structures that inhibit the aggressive behavior also reduces the sensory receptive field for biting. A behavior that is presumably motivated by emotion thus depends on peripheral sensory feedback for its expression. Proprioceptive feedback resulting from changes in facial expression might similarly be essential for full development of subjective awareness of that emotion.

Flynn (1967) found that stimulation of other parts of the brain, especially the midbrain limbic area and the thalamus, could also give rise to attack behavior. Stimulation of certain parts of the limbic system modulated aggressive behavior induced by stimulation of the lateral hypothalamus but did not initiate attack. In the amygdala, stimulation of a basomedial area delayed

attack, while a more posterior, lateral site facilitated it. Similarly inhibition of attack was obtained from sites in the dorsal hippocampus, whereas facilitation resulted from stimulation of the ventral hippocampus.

Lesion in the ventromedial nucleus produces directed rage both in rats (Thompson, 1978) and in humans (Reeves & Plum, 1969). This emotional behavior is successfully reversed by amygdaloid lesions (Narabayashi, Nagao, Saito, Yoshido, & Nagahata, 1963). (Note the anatomical connections between these two areas described previously.) Other studies on humans (Heath & Mickle, 1960) report subjective feelings of discomfort, anxiety, and autonomic sensations from stimulation of the rostral hypothalamus. Important as the hypothalamus is to the integration of specific motivated behaviors in the intact animal, its importance is not so much as a "center" with sole responsibility for an organized behavior but rather as part of a system. Damage to any part of such a system can be overcome to some degree by compensatory neural activity and biochemical changes.

The Amygdala

In contrast to the well-localized autonomic effects in the hypothalamus, stimulation of the amygdala produces a mixture of autonomic changes, frequently with quite opposite effects from sites very close together. Shortly after Papez proposed his emotional circuit in 1937, Kluver and Bucy (1939) reported on the marked effect they obtained by ablation of the tip of the temporal lobe in monkeys. The monkeys showed strong oral tendencies, that is, they examined everything in the mouth, and repetitively, as if they retained no memory of what they learned. They also showed hypersexuality and a definite decrease in emotionality. They became tamer and easier to handle, and showed less aggression toward other monkeys, and a complete loss of fear-induced reactions to normally arousing stimuli such as snakes. This syndrome was apparent also in human patients with temporal lobe lesions or lobectomies for the control of epilepsy. These ablations included not only the amygdala, but portions of the hippocampus and the entorhinal and periamygdaloid cortex surrounding these structures.

By making more discrete lesions it was determined that the amygdala itself was the critical structure for the emotional effects in the Kluver-

Bucy syndrome as well as in defense reactions of fear and flight, anger and attack. Schreiner and Kling (1956) showed that massive amygdaloid lesions produced doctility even in the fierce wild lynx and agouti, and similar results were found for the normally vicious wild Norway rat (Woods, 1956). Stereotaxic amygdalectomy has been found to relieve abnormal aggression uncontrollable by any other means in human patients with a variety of disorders (Narabayashi et al., 1963; Heimberger, Whitlock, & Kalsbeck, 1966). These effects on an active behavioral pattern such as aggression are not due to general interference with motor responses, since other motor patterns remain unaffected.

Although lesion of a major part of the amygdala has generally resulted in tamer behavior or decreased emotionality, some experimenters report facilitation of aggression and increases in rage behavior. Lesion of the central or basal nuclei of the amygdala can convert a friendly animal into one that attacks without provocation. Similarly, stimulation of specific areas of the amygdala blocks aggression in the normal mouser as well as in hypothalamically stimulated cats. Specific and contradictory effects of amygdaloid stimulation have been discussed by Block, Siegel, and Edinger (1980). Discrete stimulation and lesion experiments have revealed a functional organization of the subnuclei of the amygdala, with separate areas that facilitate or inhibit flight, defensive behavior, and predatory attack. Moyer (1971) has analyzed aggression in six different stimulus situations that produce slightly different forms of aggressive behavior (e.g., predation, territorial defense, intermale aggression), each of which has its own physiological substrate.

Gloor (1960, 1978) has suggested that input from neocortical areas concerned with perception and temporal patterns of auditory and visual stimuli might enable the amygdala to act as a decision center, controlling the response of the individual to meaningful environmental stimuli. The recent finding by Ahern and Schwartz (1979) that the right parietal cortex shows a more activated EEG in response to emotional questions may be related to these subcortical connections with the limbic system. In the frontal cortex, also anatomically connected to limbic structures, Davidson and his colleagues have found differential activation for negative emotions over the right and positive emotions over the left frontal cortex (Davidson, Schwartz, Saron, Bennett, & Coleman, 1979).

Adamec (1978) also considers the amygdala a source of emotive biasing. By testing with a variety of environmental threats, for example, the presence of humans, mice, rats, and a recording of fighting cats, Adamec distinguished four degrees of natural affective disposition in his cats—from fearless rat killers to fearful nonattackers who withdrew to a sheltered location in the face of even mild threat. Adamec found that the threshold for production of an afterdischarge when the amygdala was stimulated varied inversely with the continuum of sensitivity to threat found among his cats. In other words, the cats with the lowest after-discharge thresholds—indicative of a tendency to become neurally overactive—were also the most fearful. When he then used kindling techniques to lower the threshold for after-discharges in the amygdala of the fearless cats, Adamec found that with the same behavioral measures they now became more fearful. This experiment is one of the few that includes as parameters both the naturally occurring variations in affective disposition and responses to a variety of stimulus situations. Also unique is the use of a long-term alteration of neural activity as the experimental manipulation, with the result that the behavior measured both before and after the kindling situation occurs in the free unrestrained animal with no stimulation during the testing.

The construct of affective disposition, as measured behaviorally by Adamec, has a parallel in the concept of temperament, as studied in human personality and developmental psychology (Carey, 1970; Rothbart, 1977; Thomas & Chess, 1977). Adamec's study suggests that the basis of temperament may be conceived in terms of emotion thresholds and the related concept of emotional disposition, as discussed in differential emotions theory (Izard, 1977, 1978). These concepts provide part of the theoretical framework for studying important aspects of behavior that have been largely ignored by mainstream experimental psychologists.

The Septum

In contrast to the amygdala, where massive lesions produce an overall pacification, lesions of the septum in the rat have regularly been found to produce a hyperemotionality so extreme that it is known as the *septal rage syndrome*

(Brady & Nauta, 1955). Immediately after the operation the animal is extremely sensitive and irritable. The animal remains hyperirritable for several weeks, but then as in so many other brain dysfunctions, a process of recovery occurs and the rate regains its normal placidity. The stimulus situation or context is important, for if a septally lesioned rat is caged with a stronger male rat is shows less aggression than normal, that is, it shows a decrease in intermale aggression at the same time as an increase in irritable or fear-induced aggression (Blanchard, Blanchard, Takahashi, & Takahashi, 1977). Tumors affecting the septal region in human clinical patients were found to result consistently in physically aggressive behavior (Zeman & King, 1958). On the other hand, stimulation of the septum in humans (Heath & Mickle, 1960) produces alerting, rapid speech, reports of feeling good, and therapeutic relief from intractable pain.

The septal rage syndrome is reversed by amygdaloid lesions (McCleary & Moore, 1965; King & Meyer, 1958). Septum, amygdala, and hypothalamus appear to function together in the normal control of irritable aggression. McCleary (1966) regards septal lesions as producing primarily a response disinhibition, a decrease in the normal controls on behavior. McCleary's view is similar to that of Thomas, Hostetter, and Barker (1968), who suggest that the limbic system as a whole mediates a behavioral disposition, a tendency to act in a certain way in a given environment, whether it is to freeze, fight, or flee. For instance, it is the normal behavioral disposition of rats to explore and to remember and associate long sequences of stimuli, as in their feeding behavior. Humans may be considered to have a behavioral disposition toward visual exploration and oral communication. Since different species have very different behavioral dispositions, the behavioral alterations produced by ablation of individual limbic structures may be different, but in all instances they modulate motivated behavior, which especially in higher species involves emotion.

The Hippocampus

From the earliest studies of Broca and Papez the hippocampus has been seen as a central structure of the limbic system, but stimulation or lesion of this structure has yielded few observable responses, either autonomic or motor. Human stimulation studies and clinical experience show involvement of the hippocampus in placing new information into long-term memory, but this has been much more difficult to demonstrate in lower animals. The hippocampus, like the amygdala, appears to have modulatory effects on emotion that differ in different parts of the structure. Heath and Mickle (1960) have shown that stimulation of the hippocampus produces emergency reactions of rage or fear. Flynn (1967) found that stimulation of the dorsal hippocampus delayed hypothalamically induced predatory attack, while stimulation of the ventral hippocampus facilitated it. Lesions in the hippocampus result in behavioral deficits remarkably similar to those caused by lesions in the septum, namely, perseveration and a pronounced deficit in passive avoidance. This suggests that hippocampus and septum may form a system for certain types of behavior.

Gray (1979) has used a novel experimental approach to define the involvement of this septohippocampal axis in emotional behavior. Reasoning that drugs that have an antianxiety effect on humans will act on the same physiological substrate in laboratory animals, Gray has investigated the effect of these drugs on behaviors that involve septum and hippocampus and result from situations that would elicit anxiety in humans. The three experimental situations studied were: (1) response to anticipated punishing stimuli, (2) frustration or extinction of response to rewarded stimuli, and (3) response to novel stimuli. In each of these situations the animal tends to freeze or inhibit ongoing behavior, while at the same time showing increased arousal levels. Gray demonstrated that antianxiety drugs that have the effect of reducing this behavioral inhibition in both passive and two-way active avoidance as well as in extinction effects. He postulated that physiologically the effect of either antianxiety drugs or partial reinforcement was to block the pacemaker effect of the medial septal nuclei on the hippocampus as recorded by the theta rhythm, at and only at those frequencies that are selectively involved in this type of emotional behavior. However, the mechanism by which this blocking effect was carried out was not clear, since medial and lateral septal lesions resulted in the same kinds of behavior as did antianxiety drugs. The effect of these antianxiety drugs could be (1) inhibition of activity in the septum or (2) inhibition of activity effective in the hippocampus or (3) blocking of the input to the septum. Gray experimented with drugs blocking the monoaminergic and cholinergic systems and found that chemical lesion of the norepinephrine system produced the same behavioral effects as antianxiety drugs.

Neurotransmitter Systems: Chemical Substrates of Emotions

The activity of limbic system structures is clearly related to the kinds of behaviors that are termed emotional in humans. However, limbic system structures are complex integratory centers, modulating behavior not just as a result of immediate sensory input but also on the basis of their genetically determined biochemical activity. Emotional behavior is involved not only in preservation of self, but also in preservation of the species, and it must be examined, as Gray has begun to do for anxiety, on a cellular level, through study of those mechanisms that can differentiate within a nucleus between distinct patterns of activity.

Neurons communicate with each other in the vertebrate brain largely by means of chemical neurotransmitters. These chemical neurotransmitters, the drugs that affect them, and the neural activity controlled by them alter patterns of behavior and subjective feelings that we call emotion. Crow (1977) has reviewed the methods of histochemical analysis developed in the last few decades that have enabled experimenters to trace the synaptic pathways, the areas of cells of origin, and terminal fibers for certain chemicals accepted now as neurotransmitters. Histochemical fluorescent methods identify the catecholamines, norepinephrine (NE) and dopamine (DA), and the indole alkylamine, 5 hydroxytryptamine or serotonin (5HT). Similarly histochemical identification of the enzyme acetylcholine esterase, which must be present at synaptic sites were acetylcholine (ACh) is used as a neurotransmitter, has made possible the identification of a cholinergic system. Other categories of suspected neurotransmitters on the basis of their localization and release in specific brain areas include amino acids, such as gamma amino butyric acid (GABA), glutamic acid, aspartic acid, and glycine, and most recent:y-on explosion of neuroactive peptide molecules (Snyder, 1980; Iverson, Nicoll, & Vale, 1978). Some of these peptides were first isolated in the

brain, for example, the enkephalins, neurotensin and substance P, but others such as somatostatin, vasoactive intestinal peptide (VIP), and cholecystokinin have long been known as intestinal hormones and only recently, by new techniques of immunohistochemistry, have been identified in the brain.

These new peptide neurotransmitters have been found by double and even triple fluorescent labeling procedures to coexist in localized neurons with the monoamines, not indiscriminately but in regularly occurring groups or families of interacting compounds (Hökfelt, 1980; Snyder, 1980). For instance, substance P is frequently associated with serotinergic, cholecystokinin with dopaminergic, and VIP with cholinergic neurons. The possible effects of peptides in the brain on emotional behaviors offer exciting new possibilities for future research because of their localization within and influence on the monoaminergic neurons of the limbic system. The monoamine pathways are known to be phylogenetically ancient systems present in the most primitive animals. They represent chemical systems extending throughout forebrain structures but originating in and controlled largely by discrete brainstem sites. The monoamine and cholinergic pathways have been reviewed in detail by Hamilton (1976) and Crow (1977) and are only briefly summarized here before an examination of the experimental evidence linking these neurotransmitter systems with emotion.

Catecholamine Pathways

The biogenic monoamines are simple biologically active molecules with one amino subgroup. Those known to be active as neurotransmitters in CNS are classified as catecholamines or indolealkylamines. The catecholamines DA, NE, and E are sequentially synthesized from a common source, the amino acid tyrosine.

Substances that act as neurotransmitters between neurons are synthesized not only in the cell body, where the enzymes are formed, but also in the axon terminals to which the enzymes are transported and where the neurotransmitters are released. The activity of the neurotransmitter at the synaptic junction involves separate processes of synthesis, storage, release, interaction with receptor sites on the postsynaptic membrane, metabolism, and reuptake of all or part of the molecule. Each step in this process is subject to interference or facilitation by drugs. Cooper, Bloom, and Roth (1974) discuss the pharmacological effects on each of the catecholamine neurotransmitter systems in detail.

Dopamine (DA) Pathways

There are four known DA systems, whose cell bodies are restricted to very specific nuclei of the brainstem. The tuberoinfundibular system of the hypothalamus is a DA system concerned with neuroendocrine functioning. The other three DA systems have cell bodies in the ventral mesencephalon and in areas of the limbic midbrain, and they innervate specific parts of the forebrain. The best known of these, the nigrostriatal system, originates in the pars compacta of the substantia nigra and innervates the caudate-putamen complex (striatum) and the amygdala. The nigrostriatal system is important to motor behavior; Parkinson's disease is known to be due to a lesion in this system with a consequent loss of DA terminals. The nonstriatal DA systems originate in neurons in the medial ventral tegmental area and in an area caudal and lateral to the pars compacta. These neurons project to the nucleus accumbens of the ventral striatum (mesolimbic system) and the frontal cortex (mesocortical system). The DA systems have been subjected to intense scrutiny in the past few years (Costa & Gessa, 1977; Moore & Bloom, 1978) as pharmacological and clinical studies have increasingly suggested the importance of nonstriatal DA receptors in schizophrenia.

It is from a quite small number of brain cells that the extensive projections of the DA neurons derive. Furthermore, it has been shown that one inbred strain of rats may harbor as many as twice the number of DA neurons in the mesolimbic, mesocortical, and nigrostriatal systems as another strain (Ross, Judd, Pickel, Joh, & Ris, 1976). More recently Helmeste, Seeman, and Cascina (1980) demonstrated a particularly high density of a specific DA receptor in the F344 strain of rats and suggested that it was the cause of the behavioral differences observed. The genetic variability in these limbic DA systems may have significance in inherent susceptibility to psychopathological disorders and in individual variation in emotionality.

Norepinephrine (NE) Pathways

Like the DA system, the NE pathways in the brain originate from a discrete population of cells in the medullary brainstem. Isolated groups of nuclei in the ventral and caudal parts of the medulla give rise to descending axons to the spinal cord and ascending axons that terminate heavily in ventromedial parts of the brainstem in the hypothalamus, the medial preoptic nucleus, and the bed nucleus of the stria terminalis. Axons from this ventral pathway also follow the ventral amygdalofugal pathways to the amygdala and the internal capsule to the ventral basal ganglia and central nucleus of the amygdala.

The major source of NE in the brain, however, is the locus coeruleus, a small nucleus at the pontomedullary border, which in the rat contains only about 1600 neurons (Swanson, 1976). This nucleus innervates all the major structures of the limbic system as well as the cerebellum and neocortex. Moore & Bloom (1978) have estimated that an individual neuron of the locus coeruleus might have an axon 30 cm long with an average of 100,000 synapses. Locus coeruleus axons passing caudally through the cingulum give off collaterals that innervate not only the frontal cortex where there are many DA terminals, but also the more posterior neocortex (Moore & Bloom, 1978). Such widespread innervation of brain structures by a small discrete group of brainstem cells may provide a substrate for Tomkins' (1980) suggestion of an overall modulation of brain activity in the emotional motivation of behavior.

Serotonin (5 HT) Pathways

The neurons using 5 HT as a neurotransmitter are found in five discrete nuclei along the midline of the medullary and pontine brainstem (Taber, Brodal, & Walberg, 1960).

The ascending projections of the dorsal raphe and median raphe nuclei are of interest chiefly in connection with the limbic system and have been studied in the cat (Bobiller, Seguin, Petitjean, Salvert, Touret, & Jouvet, 1976) and rat (Geyer, Puereto, Menkes, Segal, & Mendell, 1976; Conrad, Leonard, & Pfaff, 1974). The pathways of the dorsal raphe parallel the dorsal NE pathway, innervating the central gray, the hypothalamus, septum, amygdala, nucleus accumbens, olfactory tubercle, the diagonal band of Broca, and the cingulate cortex and neocortex, but not the hippocampus (Azmitra & Segal, 1978; Kellar, Brown, Madrid, Bernstein, Vernikos-Danellis, & Mehler, 1977). In contrast, the median raphe innervates the mesencephalic reticular formation, the interpeduncular nucleus, the hypothalamus and the septal area, but not the amygdala. The projections of the median raphe continue into the hippocampus through both the fornix and the cingulum bundle (Moore & Halaris, 1975). Afferent projections to the raphe originate in the lateral habenula (a source of feedback connections from forebrain limbic structures), the nucleus of the diagonal band, and the locus coeruleus.

Acetylcholine (ACh) Pathways

Acetylcholine is a simple molecule made up of a choline moiety and an acetate ion. Its activity as a neurotransmitter requires its rapid break-down in the synaptic cleft by a specific acetylcholine esterase (AChE).

After breakdown the choline is taken up by the presynaptic terminals, and acetylcholine is resynthesized there with the aid of the enzyme choline acetyltransferase. AChE can be stained by histochemical techniques, and it is on the indirect evidence provided by the presence of AChE that the cell bodies, pathways, and terminals of the ACh system have been identified. In contrast to the monoamine systems, with their cell bodies restricted to the brainstem and with long branching axons, the ACh system is primarily a multisynaptic system of relatively short axons and widely scattered cell bodies (Krnjevic, 1969).

The brainstem origin of the ascending pathways to cholinergic neurons is primarily in the cuneiform nucleus of the mesencephalic tegmentum (Shute & Lewis, 1967b; Shute, 1973), from which a dorsal tegmental pathway passes through the tectum into the midline thalamic areas and on to the bed nucleus of the stria terminalis. A more ventral pathway originates in the ventral tegmental area and the substantia nigra, also known to be the major source of the forebrain dopaminergic projections. This ventral pathway innervates both limbic and striatal areas. Shute and Lewis (1967b) feel that this ascending cholinergic neurotransmitter system is the anatomical basis for the reticular activating system, whose activity is essential for behavioral and cortical arousal.

Secondary and tertiary cholinergic pathways lead to the limbic areas of amygdala, hippocampus, and septum, and to the cortex. These secondary pathways form the basis for a cholinergic limbic system with projections to and from the hippocampus and for cholinergic influences in the cortex. Shute and Lewis (1967a) suggest that the interpeduncular nucleus is a pivotal link between the cholinergic reticular activating pathways and the cholinergic limbic influences. Cholinergic-monoaminergic interactions were extensively reviewed in a recent symposium (Butcher, 1978).

Postsynaptic Effects

The excitatory and inhibitory effects of these monoamine and acetylcholine neurotransmitters have been studied in many parts of the brain. Acetylcholine generally acts as an excitatory neurotransmitter both peripherally at the neuromuscular junction and centrally. Norepinephrine produces a postsynaptic inhibition both in the spinal cord and centrally. In the cerebellum, cortex, and striatum, norepinephrine mediates a long-lasting inhibition of inhibitory gabaergic interneurons (Mogenson & Phillips, 1976), thus releasing programmed behavior. In contrast to these effects of NE on motivated behavior these authors believe that the dorsal-hippocampal NE pathways and nigrostriatal DA pathways are concerned more with motor behavior.

Serotonin is excitatory in the spinal cord but inhibitory in central structures. It mediates a much briefer inhibitory effect than NE in the same central structures. These neurophysiological effects of the chemical transmitters acting in discrete structures form the basis for the neural activity associated by Tomkins (1962) with emotional behavior.

Experimental Evidence Relating Neurotransmitter Systems to Emotion

We have seen that lesion and stimulation studies in controlled behavioral experiments in both humans and animals have led to the implication of limbic structures and pathways as the physiological substrate for emotion. Similarly experimental studies have led to the implication of the monoaminergic and cholinergic neurotransmitter systems in emotional behavior. These experimental studies have been of three types. In the first type, behavioral studies on animals have used electrophysiological or chemical lesion of the cell bodies of neurotransmitter systems or pharmacological manipulation of neurotransmitter effectiveness at the synaptic site of action in order to observe changes in behavior. A second type involves clinical observation of the effects of psychogenic drugs on human emotional behavior and illnesses and relates these observations to the effect of drugs on neurotransmitter systems. In the third type, the neurotransmitter systems have been implicated in emotional motivation in animals by self-stimulation studies that demonstrate their involvement in reward and punishment.

Animal Lesion and Drug Studies

The following studies demonstrate the modulatory effect that the cholinergic and monoamine neurotransmitters have on specific behaviors which, while not measuring emotion directly, are anthropomorphically associated with emotional states, for example, active or passive avoidance with fear, or aggression with anger.

ACETYLCHOLINE

Acetylcholine is known to be an important neurotransmitter in limbic structures, neocortex, and structures concerned with arousal. The cholinergic pathways are multisynaptic, however, and two or three neurons are interposed between brainstem and forebrain limbic structures. Thus, it is not possible for a lesion of the stimulation of any select area to influence this neurotransmitter system as a whole. On the other hand, either systematic or direct injection into the brain of acetylcholine itself, or any one of various drugs known to mimic or antagonize the effects of acetylcholine, can produce behavior that suggests that the limbic system is a central cholinergic system involved in the control of inhibitory processes (Leaton, 1971). For instance, Douglas and his associates implicated ACh activity in the production of normal activated behavior in response to frustration (Douglas, Mitchell, Slimp, Crist, Hammersla, & Peterson, 1972).

Gray (1979) obtained hippocampal theta activity during both voluntary movement and immobility (freezing), upon presentation of a novel stimulus that he considered to be anxiety provoking. Kolb and Whishaw (1977) found that atropine, an anticholinergic drug, would decrease hippocampal theta observed in the emotional situation, though it had no effect on hippocampal theta during ordinary voluntary movement. In other experiments atropine has been found to enhance active avoidance, whereas carbachol, which mimics the action of ACh, impairs active

avoidance when injected directly into the septum. These experiments implicate ACh in emotional behavior involving a septo-hippocampal circuit.

Small amounts of acetylcholine injected directly into the amygdala will cause a seizure focus there and produce a state of increased emotional reactivity for weeks or months after the seizure focus has disappeared. The animals are vicious and attack at the slightest provocation without regard for their own safety (Grossman, 1973). Indeed ACh has been suggested as an endogenous trigger for aggressive behavior (Sabelli, 1973). Cholinergic effects specifically within the amygdala also decrease active avoidance responses, indicating an interaction between amygdala and septum in this emotional behavior.

J.P. Flynn (see Reis, 1974) was able to show that monoamines and acetylcholine produced different effects on predatory and affective aggression resulting from lateral hypothalamic stimulation. Acetylcholine was the only substanced used that had a profound facilitatory effect on predatory attack.

NE AND DA

Systematically injected 6 hydroxydopamine does not pass the blood-brain barrier, but when injected directly into the ventricles or brain tissue it acts as a neurotoxin (Longo, 1975). It is taken up specifically by catecholaminergic neurons, thus causing a very specific chemical lesion. Discrete lesions can also be obtained by injection directly into specific monoamine pathways. Heyback, Coover, and Lints (1978) injected rats with 6 hydroxydopamine to produce chemical lesion of catecholamine pathways and 5,6 dihydroxytryptamine for lesions in the 5 HT pathways. They measured active and passive avoidance behavior, eating, and open-field activity. Lesion of the dorsal raphe serotonergic pathway had very little effect on behavior, but lesions in the median raphe serotonergic, the mesolimbic or nigrostriatal dopaminergic, or the ventral or dorsal noradrenergic bundles all produced deficits in one-way active avoidance and, in some animals, in passive avoidance behavior. In addition, lesion of the dorsal NE pathways from the locus coeruleus dramatically inhibited open-field activity.

Seiden, Brown, and Lewy (1973) studied conditioned avoidance and escape responses using reserpine, a drug that depletes all the catecholamines by interfering with the storage of these neurotransmitters. Reserpine completely suppresses avoidance activity and even interferes with escape behavior, thus affecting behavioral and presumably also emotional response to punishment. This response is reversed by injection of L-DOPA, a precursor of both DA and NE that can pass the blood-brain barrier. Disulfiram, which prevents the synthesis of NE from DA, decreased this reversal by half, indicating an equal involvement of both DA and NE pathways.

5 HT

A high concentration of serotonin is generally found in those areas of the brain that also have a high AChE—and presumably ACh—concentration (Costa, 1960). Serotonin, as is evident from the anatomical pathways, is also located in areas rich in NE and DA. Both 5 HT and NE terminals are found on both sympathetic and parasympathetic neurons (Fuxe, Hökfelt, & Ungerstedt, 1968).

Behavioral effects of the serotonergic system have been examined where lesions are made specifically in dorsal raphe (mesostriatal) or median raphe (mesolimbic) serotonergic pathways (Geyer et al., 1976). Dorsal raphe lesions showed few behavioral effects, but median raphe lesions produced a hyperactivity in novel environments, a hyperreactivity to air puffs (exaggerated startle response), and perseverative behavior after an unrewarded trial in alternation tasks. Notice the similarity of these behavioral effects of those obtained by septal-hippocampal lesions.

Self Stimulation

Most behavioral studies imply the arousal of negative emotions—fear in avoidance or escape reactions, fear or anger in aggressive studies. In contrast, self-stimulation studies involve positive feelings, presumed to mediate a sense of reward or pleasure. Since these studies have been conducted on lower animals, the relation of the constructs of reward or pleasure to the positive emotions of interest and joy found in humans is not addressed; however, the behavior associated with pleasure or reward is clearly distinct from that associated with pain or negative emotion.

Experimental evidence suggests that the pleasure-reward construct as studied in lower animals is related to physiological drive systems such as hunger and sex. Olds and Milner (1954) first discovered that a rat's behavior can be controlled positively by the direct administration of small electric currents to the brain through implanted electrodes. The rat not only goes where he finds stimulation in an open box or runway situation, but also works to obtain it by bar pressing or learning a maze. A hungry rat will suffer a stronger electric shock in order to obtain brain stimulation than it will to reach food. Those areas that mediate this rewarding result have been termed pleasure areas, and they extend throughout the limbic system in hypothalamus, cingulate, septum, amygdala, hippocampus, and midbrain. They are concentrated most heavily, however, in a medial strip through the ventral forebrain, that is, along the medial forebrain bundle. The highest rates of self stimulation in a bar-pressing situation are obtained around the interpeduncular nucleus (up to 7000 presses per hour).

There are many more rewarding sites of stimulation than aversive sites. Olds (1960) found that, while 60 percent of the electrode sites he stimulated were emotionally neutral, 35 percent were rewarding and only 5 percent aversive. Aversive sites are generally found very close to rewarding sites (McCleary & Moore, 1965). Olds (1960) found that many self-stimulation sites were specifically rewarding for certain behaviors, for example, self stimulation in the posterior hypothalamus or anterior preoptic regions was selectively increased by hunger, whereas other sites were self stimulating only when androgen levels were high, thus correlating with sexual motivation. Olds suggested that specific drive reward systems, that is to say, the pleasures associated with the consummation of behavior, are sensitive to different hormonal chemical effects.

Crow (1972b; Crow, Spear, & Arbuthnot, 1972) suggested that the DA pathways mediate appetitive or approach behaviors whereas the NE system is more involved in consummatory or reward behaviors. Crow (1977) subsequently proposed that this difference is due to the activation of nigrostriatal DA pathways by external incentive cues, whereas the dorsal NE pathway is activated by biologically significant events. An important role for DA in behaviors across species is suggested by a recent finding in human studies by Davidson et al. (1979) of hemispheric laterality for positive and negative emotion (mediating approach-avoidance behavior) over the frontal cortex, where the DA innervation of the neocortex is concentrated.

Serotonin has also been suggested as a mediator of self-stimulation effects. Electrodes implanted in the median raphe are self stimulating but after the injection of parachlorophenyl alanine (PCPA), a drug that interferes with the synthesis of serotonin, the raphe self stimulation is lowered dramatically. The neuroanatomical and neurochemical substrates for reinforcement have been extensively reviewed by Hall, Bloom, and Olds (1977) and Stellar and Corbit (1977).

General Effects of the Biogenic Amines on Behavior

Electrophysiological evidence has been found for sensory convergence not only on structures of the limbic system but also on specific monoamine systems. Under extracellular recording in the locus coeruleus, many presumably noradrenergic neurons responded to tactile stimulation of the skin as well as to optic-tract stimulation. Campbell (1973) suggests that, while the biogenic amine systems are activated by a certain level of sensory stimulation, it is the catecholamine terminals in limbic areas that are the mediators of reward. Campbell's studies with animals show that not only central brain stimulation but also peripheral sensory stimulation (access to means of turning on light or sound) is intrinsically rewarding for animals. He suggests that one of the major differences in brain functioning between primates and humans, on the one hand, and lower animal species, on the other, is that in the higher species cognitive or neocortical activity can also, by itself, activate reward centers and motivated behavior. The variety of neurotransmitter dysfunctions suggested as causes for any one behavioral abnormality indicates the complexity and difficulty of differentiating—in a behavioral activity that involves a variety of external and internal stimuli and cues—the function of any one transmitter system.

Peripherally, where the receptor structures are spatially and functionally dispersed, one neurotransmitter by itself can be shown to have a clearly defined function, for example, the excitatory effect of ACh at the neuromuscular synapse. In central integratory structures, however, where complex behavioral activities must somehow be mediated and kept separate within a relatively few structures, other means must be used for differentiation of specific functions. One means is the use of different neurotransmitters, which include not only the four monoamines and acetylcholine but many other substances such as gamma amino butyric acid (GABA), glutamate, aspartate, glycine, and possibly histamine, substance P, prostaglandins, VIP, cholecystokinin, and even cyclic AMP, which is likely to be a second messenger for both neurotransmitter and hormonal activity.

This section has examined the anatomical substrates for the concept of the limbic system and for the known neurotransmitter systems. Experimental evidence from many different perspectives has shown both directly and indirectly the involvement of specific structures as well as neurotransmitters in emotional behavior. We can say quite surely that it is central neural activity in the limbic system and in limbic-neocortical connections that is the physiological basis for emotion. We cannot say that it is the physiological basis for emotion only. These same structures and their neurotransmitters are involved in other behaviors, in fact in most of the behavior that animals engage in. However, some theorists (e.g., Izard, 1977) have postulated that emotions at widely varying levels of intensity affects consciousness and behavior continuously, and that the exploratory behavior of the relatively calm individual is motivated by the emotion of interest, just as more dramatic escape behavior is motivated by the emotion of fear. What is typically measured in animal experiments is relatively intense negative emotional behavior. Such intense emotion is indeed often transient and situational, and this has contributed to the widespread belief that emotions are transitory states. The hypothesis that emotion processes are continuous is consistent with the experimental evidence of the involovement of the neural and chemical substrates of emotion in virtually all of animal behavior.

THE BEHAVIORAL-EXPRESSIVE COMPONENT OF EMOTION

In humans the observable component of emotions consists primarily of actions of the musculature of the face and voice box—facial and vocal expressions and gaze behavior. The muscles that control posture are also involved, but their actions in emotions have been little studied. Some theorists view the facial, vocal, and postural activity of emotions as simply performing a "read-out" function (e.g., Buck, 1980a,b), whereas others view them not only as communicative acts but as an integral part of the emotion process that contributes to the specific quality of the conscious experience (Ekman, 1971; Izard, 1971; Leventhal, 1980; Plutchik, 1962; Tomkins, 1962).

Although there are differences of opinion as to causal and regulatory functions of the discrete patterns of facial muscle actions that we call expressions, no-one seriously challenges their status as correlates of genuine emotion experiences. Aside from common sense, three kinds of evidence link facial expressions with emotion experience and emotional behavior: (1) the existence of innate-universal facial patterns and their relation to particular classes of emotion-eliciting stimuli, (2) psychophysiological studies of imagery-induced emotions and facial electromyographic (EMG) responses, and (3) observations of prelingual infants in response to species-common emotion elicitors, such as pain and separation. Studies of each type—which will be reviewed in later sections of this chapter—support the following conclusions. (1) There are at least six innate universal expressions, and their conceptual definition in terms of feeling states or qualities of consciousness are essentially the same in widely different literate and preliterate cultures. (2) Cognitive instruction to visualize a situation that elicits a particular emotion produces a pattern of EMG activity from the muscles that results in the facial expression of that emotion, even when there are no observable appearance changes from muscle contractions. (3) Prelingual infants produce discrete emotion expressions that are predictable from stimulus situations that relate logically to particular emotion experiences.

Most of the research on the behavioral-expressive component of emotions reviewed here is concerned with observable facial behaviors and their communicative functions. Studies considered here also concern the role of facial behavior in activating and regulating emotion experience and in regulating or motivating the behavior of both the observer and the participants in social interaction.

Emotion-Related Facial, Vocal, and Postural Behaviors

Darwin's (1872) hypothesis of the innateness and universality of the expressions of emotions and his report of supporting data received relatively little attention for the first 50 years after their publication. For the next 40 or so years, efforts to test the hypothesis yielded some data that supported it and some that did not. Reviews of this literature by Ekman et al. (1972) and Izard (1971) showed that many of these studies were seriously flawed and that inferences from some of them were apparently unduly influenced by the stimulus-response behavioristic learning theories and cultural relativism that dominated psychology and the social sciences during that era.

Perhaps the most influential study that challenged the Darwinian hypothesis was that of Landis (1924). He raised the basic question of the correspondence of a particular facial expression and a particular emotion experience—does the face provide accurate information about the emotion being experienced? To produce emotion experiences in the laboratory, he exposed 25 subjects to a wide array of stimuli, including a bucket of live frogs (felt but not seen), the decapitation of a live rat, and electric shock. To complete the experiment subjects had to remain seated in a chair for approximately three hours, with their right arms restrained by a compression band (for measuring blood pressure) and a bracelet stethoscope. Methodological criticisms and reanalyses of Landis's data (Davis, 1934; Ekman et al., 1972; Izard, 1971) have shown that Landis was not justified in interpreting his data as weakening Darwin's position. Yet his study was cited frequently to refute the innateness or universality hypothesis, from the time of its publication until findings from cross-cultural research gained wide dissemination in the 1970s.

All the criticisms of Landis's study notwithstanding, it made an important contribution, though unfortunately it was little heeded by subsequent investigators. He showed (1) that there is a low probability that any stimulus will elicit the same emotion in all adult subjects and (2) that some stimulus situations elicit a limited and characteristic range of emotions, at least in terms of self-reported emotion experience.

The Search for Universals—Support for Darwin's Position

Cross-cultural evidence for the universality of what has been termed primary or fundamental emotions has come largely from three investigators and their colleagues. Ekman and Izard launched their research on this topic in the mid-sixties, and Eibl-Eibesfeldt began his a few years later.

Izard (1968, 1971) used emotion theory and earlier empirical work (Darwin, 1872; Tomkins, 1962, 1963; Tomkins & McCarter, 1964) to establish criteria for the expressions of the nine fundamental emotions of interest, joy, surprise, sadness, anger, disgust, contempt, fear, and shame or shyness. Photographs of these expressions were administered as a test of emotion labeling to American, English, French, and Greek subjects. Overall, the subjects' free-response verbal labels identified the expressions in terms of the a priori emotion categories approximately 60 percent of the time. The expression photographs were administered as a test of emotion recognition to subjects of American, English, German, Swedish, French, Swiss, Greek, Japanese, African, Indian, and Turkish cultures. Subjects were given a list of the fundamental emotion expressions and asked to place the photographs in the appropriate categories. For all the cultures the average accuracy in identifying the emotion expressions was 78 percent, strong evidence for the universality hypothesis.

However, the findings of these studies did not rule out the rather remote possibility that people in these diverse cultures are all socialized in terms of common stereotypes of the fundamental emotion expressions. Evidence against this alternative hypothesis came from the work of Ekman and his colleagues and Eibl-Eibesfeldt.

Ekman, working with photographs of Frois-Wittman (1930), Izard, Tomkins, and some of his own, did labeling and recognition studies for the six emotions of joy, surprise, sadness, anger, disgust, and fear with preliterate cultures in New Guinea and Borneo that had little or no contact with western civilization. This work, summarized by Ekman et al. (1972), effectively eliminated the alternative hypothesis of common cultural stereotypes for at least five of the six emotion expressions studied.

The cross-cultural studies of Izard and of Ekman and his colleagues have provided robust evidence for the universality of at least six fundamental emotion expressions. Their work has been complemented by studies of subjects born blind (summarized in Charlesworth & Kreutzer, 1973) and subjects congenitally deaf and blind, including thalidomide victims without arms and hence without the capacity for tactual learning of expressive patterns (Eibl-Eibesfeldt, 1979).

Allport (1924) suggested that the universality of emotion expressions did not necessarily mean that they were innate. He argued that they could be accounted for by species-common learning experiences, since all infants are exposed to certain stimulus situations such as pain, darkness, and separation or being left alone. Ekman (1971, 1980) and Oster and Ekman (1978), elaborating this position, outlined several ways in which they thought particular facial muscle actions could become associated with the same emotions in all cultures and then suggested a research strategy for resolving the issue.

The weight of recent evidence on the ontogeny of emotion expressions in relation to the development of cognitive capacities for learning and memory runs counter to the hypothesis of species-common learning. Oster and Ekman (1978) summarized the evidence that even premature newborns are capable of producing all the discrete facial muscle movements involved in the expressions of the fundamental emotions. For infants under nine months of age, meaningful relations between event and expression have been demonstrated for the expressions of interest, joy, surprise, sadness, anger, disgust, fear, and discomfort-pain, or physical distress (Emde et al., 1976; Izard, 1980; Langsdorf, Izard, Rayias, & Hembree, 1983; Campos & Stenberg, 1981). Since most experts agree that learning ability representational processes are severly limited in the early months of life (Kagan et al., 1978), it appears extremely unlikely that young infants could learn the complex motor patterns of the emotion expressions. Furthermore, the expressions of interest, disgust, endogenous smiling, physical distress, and at least some components of the sadness expression are present in the newborn (Emde et al., 1976; Hembree, Ansul, Huebner, & Izard, 1981; Peiper, 1963). In summary, the notion of species-common learning of facial expressions appears untenable. The evidence for the innateness and universality of the expressions of the fundamental emotions is sufficiently robust to consider Darwin's hypothesis as an established axiom of behavioral science.

The Ontogeny of Emotion Expressions

Current evidence suggests that some emotion expressions are present at birth, some become functional in the first four or five months, and others are not readily observable until the second half of the first year of life or the first half of the second year. The fact that some emotion expressions are determined in substantial degree by biological and maturational factors has been demonstrated in nonhuman primates. Sackett (1966) reared eight rhesus monkeys in complete social isolation. He projected color slides of adult monkeys in a threat pose, infant monkeys playing, and control slides of human beings and landscapes through translucent screen that formed one wall of the cage. The experimenter oberved the young monkeys' responses to the slides through a one-way screen. Slides of conspecifics consistently stimulated more activity than control slides, indicating what the author called an innate "species identity." The slides of adult monkeys in a threat pose evoked fear behaviors (fear grimace, rocking, shrinking back, especially when the subjects were 2.5 to 3.0 months old). The slides of infant monkeys elicited exploratory behavior and attempts to engage the image in play. From two to five months of age, the bar-pressing responses to operate the slide projector and view the slides decreased markedly for threat poses while it continued to rise in level for slides showing infants.

Harlow (1962, 1971) demonstrated that isolated rhesus monkeys showed a much higher than normal level of fearful and aggressive behaviors, suggesting that social animals require a social environment in order to develop the adaptive inhibitory mechanisms that are critical to the maintenance of social order. Observation of normal monkey infants revealed that exploratory and affectionate behaviors are present from birth, but that fear responses do not appear until a few weeks of age and are not well established until about six months. Infant monkeys become capable of fearful and aggressive behavior only after positive emotions have facilitated the development of affectional bonds with the mother and with peers. Deets and Harlow's (1971) suggestion that human infants also show positive emotions well before they display anger and fear has received support from studies of the ontogeny of human emotions.

Because much of the ontogenesis of human emotions is accomplished in the first year of life when infants are prelingual, the focus of research has to be on the ontogeny of the expression of emotion, and to be convincing such research has to use one of the objective systems for measuring facial behavior. Preferably, it should be longitudinal. Very little research has been done that meets these criteria. Most of the studies in the literature are cross-sectional and were completed before objective facial-movement coding systems were available. As already noted, acceptable data give some support for the presence of several expressions at birth.

Most of the data on the other expressions are not truly ontogenetic but rather they demonstrate event-expression relations at certain ages. For example, Campos and Stenberg (1981) found anger expression to arm restraint at 4 months; G.M. Schwartz, Ansul, and Izard (1982) observed fear expressions to discrepant facial stimuli at seven months, and Zahn-Waxler, Radke-Yarrow, and King (1979) showed that guilt, as judged by infants' verbal and instrumental responses to their mothers' distress, emerges in the second year.

Izard et al. (1983) showed that there is great regularity in the young infant's facial expression to acute pain (inoculation) and that there are developmental changes in pain-elicited facial patterns. The physical distress expression that characterizes the young infant in pain decreases markedly between 2 and 19 months of age, whereas the expression for anger in the pain situation increases markedly.

The question of the repertoire of emotion expressions is much simpler than that of their ontogeny. There is strong evidence for the presence of the emotion expressions of interest, joy, surprise, sadness, anger, disgust and for the affect expression of pain in the first half-year of life and of fear in the seventh month (Izard, Huebner, Risser, McGinnes, & Dougherty, 1980; Parisi, 1977; G.M. Schwartz et al., 1982).

There are only a few studies on the ontogeny of emotion expression discrimination or recognition, and findings are inconsistent among the few studies that have been reported. Most of these studies used a measure of time of observation as the index of discrimination. LaBarbera, Izard, Vietze, and Parisi (1976) showed that four-

and six-month-old infants looked longer at a joyful expression than at one that was angry or neutral. Using a procedure of habituation recovery, with an increase in looking time to the new stimulus as the dependent measure, Young-Browne, Rosenfeld, and Horowitz (1977) reported that three-month-old infants responded differently to expressions of surprise and happiness. Using a fixed-interval familiarization-comparison procedure, Nelson, Morse, and Leavitt (1979) found that seven-month-old infants looked longer at expressions of fear than at happy expressions. Schwartz and Izard (1982), using a similar procedure, found evidence for discrimination among sadness, anger, and fear expressions by five-month-olds. While the data did not permit an unequivocal interpretation of all the discriminative responses, there was substantial evidence that the infants avoided or showed less preference for the anger expression. (See Nelson, 1987, for a thorough review of the literature on the development of expression recognition.)

Emotion Expressions as Social Motivation

The earliest evidence of the motivational properties of emotion expression comes from studies of the crying sounds of newborns. Simner (1971) and Sagi and Hoffman (1976) showed that one- and three-day-old infants cried selectively in response to the vocal properties of another infant's cry. The investigators rejected the explanation of imitation or classic conditioning and interpreted the data as supporting Hoffman's (1975) notion that cry-induced crying is an innate precursor of emphatic distress.

Brazelton, Tronick, Adamson, Als, and Weise (1975) demonstrated that an infant responds to changes in the pattern of the mother's facial behavior. When mothers steadfastly maintained a poker face during a three-minute close-up interaction with their infants, the infants made jerky movements, averted their faces, and finally withdrew "into an attitude of helplessness . . . , body curled up and motionless" (p. 137). In a naturalistic study of the effects of infants' reduced expressiveness, Emde, Katz, and Thorpe (1978) showed that the damped emotional expressions of Down's Syndrome infants are disturbing to their parents, sometimes profoundly so. Main, Tomasini, and Tolan (1979) showed that infants of mothers who were more emotionally expressive were more likely to be classified as securely (rather than insecurely) attached, as measured with the Ains-worth strange-situation procedure. As infant's emotion expressions also affect the mother's phyiological responses, and such responsiveness varies with the mother's perception of her infant's temperament (Donovan & Leavitt, 1978; Frodi, Lamb, Leavitt, Donovan, Neff, & Sherry, 1978; Weisenfeld & Klorman, 1978).

Campos and Stenberg (1981) have delineated a conceptual framework for studying "social referencing," defined as the process whereby the infant obtains affective information from the mother's facial behavior. A number of experiments have demonstrated that social referencing mediates or regulates a variety of infant behaviors (Klinnert, Campos, Sorce, Emde, & Svejda, 1982). Sroufe and Wunsch (1972) and Rothbart (1973) studied the causes and effects of infants' laughter and concluded that laughter, by virtue of its motivational effect on the care-giver, tends to make interesting spectacles last, providing opportunities to develop knowledge and coping skills.

The motivational properties of emotion expression are clearly seen within the dyadic context of mothers and infants in face-to-face play. Malatesta (1980; Malatesta & Haviland, 1982) analyzed the facial behavior of mothers and their three- and six-month-old infants during five minutes of play and one minute of reunion following brief separation. Results of a sequential-lag contingency analysis demonstrated that maternal facial changes were not random but were contingent on changes in facial expression of their infants. The "pull" of the infant's emotion signals was clearly evident, in that mothers responded to the apparent change in their infants' emotional state with facial changes of their own, and those responses occurred within a fraction of a second. Reciprocal motivational effects were evident in the finding that mothers who scored high on emotionality (as judged by a temperament measure) had infants who showed more expressions of interest and joy during play than did less emotional mothers. The long-range consequences of maternal contingent responding to infant affective expressions became apparent in a six-month follow-up of the infants seen in the original study (Malatesta, 1982). Mothers who had the highest rate of contingent facial response when their infants were three and six months of age had the most positive infants six months later, as judged by changes in rating on a temperament scale, even when initial differences in infant positivity were statistically controlled.

Zahn-Waxler et al. (1979) studied the relation between mothers' emphatic care giving and responses of their 18- to 30-month-old infants to the mother's facial and vocal expressions of distress. The higher a mother's rating on emphatic care giving, the more likely was her expression of distress to elicit reparatory and altruistic behavior from her child.

Camras (1977) studied the role of children's facial expressions in a conflict situation. She coded the facial behaviors for signs of aggressiveness, using the system developed by the ethologist Blurton Jones (1972). She found that one aggressive and one unaggressive display were effective in warding off aggressive behavior and at least temporarily resolved the conflict in favor of the expresser. (For extensive reviews of socioemotional development, see Campos, Barrett, Lamb, Goldsmith, & Stendberg, 1983; Izard & Malatesta, 1987).

Orr and Lanzetta (1980) showed that conditioning of a skin-conductance response was more rapid and extinction slower when shock was paired with a fearful expression that with a joyful or happy expression. Compared with the incongruous CS-UCS pairing (happy face and shock), the congruous CS-UCS pairing (fearful face and shock), also produced a larger difference in CS+ than in CS− phasic skin-conductance responses. A second experiment by Vaughn and Lanzetta (1980) confirmed the finding of vicarious instigation and conditioning of autonomic responses and helped clarify the role of the observer's facial behavior. Their results indicated that the observer's facial responses, stimulated by the model's facial response to shock, are likely to be similar (i.e., expressions of pain or physical distress), whereas the observer's facial responses to the CS+ were considered indicative of fear.

Methods of Measuring Facial Behavior

Although Bell (1806), Darwin (1872), and Duchenne (1876) laid the foundation for the systematic study of facial behaviors, it was not until recently that investigators began to develop reliable and objective procedures. Two approaches have emerged: electromyographic (EMG) recording of changes in muscle potential and observational techniques based on appearance changes that result from actions of facial muscles.

G.E. Schwartz (1982) and his colleagues have described the EMG technique and demonstrated its usefulness in the assessment of emotions (G.E. Schwartz et al., 1982; Fridlund & Izard, 1982). An advantage of the EMG procedure is that it has the power to detect subtle changes in muscle potential that are difficult or impossible to measure reliably by naked eye observation. A disadvantage is that it is somewhat intrusive and restricts the movement of the subject. Certain basic research questions have been effectively studied with EMG, such as the relation between types of imagery, facial muscle movements, and self-reported emotion. The EMG can also be useful in determining the differential involvement of particular muscles in particular emotion expressions.

The observation procedures for measuring facial behaviors are essentially of two types— inductive approaches based on units of behavior defined by observation, and procedures based on anatomical structure and a knowledge of how the contraction of each facial muscle changes the appearance of the face. Work with these two types of procedures has been reviewed by Ekman (1982) and by Izard and Dougherty (1980).

Four observation systems based on facial anatomy have been developed by Ekman and Friesen (1978), Gergerian and Ermiane (1978), Izard (1979), and Izard and Dougherty (1980). In learning these systems, observers are trained to detect the presence or absence of appearance changes. The Ekman-Friesen system is concerned with all possible changes in facial appearance due to muscle actions, whereas Izard's is concerned only with appearance changes that contribute to the identification of emotion expressions. The Ekman-Friesen system uses mostly posed or spontaneous facial movements of the authors and other adults for illustrative and training material, and Izard's uses spontaneous expressions of infants and toddlers in a wide variety of stimulus situations.

Discrete-movement coding systems have the disadvantage that they are quite time consuming, since they require repeated slow-motion viewing of video records. Ekman (1982) has reviewed critically 14 techniques for measuring facial behavior.

Sensory Feedback and the Activation and Regulation of Emotion

In language more like casual observation than

scientific theory, Darwin (1872/1965) and James (1890/1950) observed that expressive behavior could be used to activate and regulate emotion experience. Darwin said "The free expression by outward signs of an emotion intensifies it" (1965, p. 365), and James said "Refuse to express a passion and it dies . . ." (1950, p. 463). Somewhat more formal statements of the role of sensory feedback from facial expression was incorporated in several emotion theories (Gellhorn, 1964; Izard, 1971; Leventhal, 1980; Tomkins, 1962). These emotion theories proposed that facial expression and its sensory feedback played a part in either the activation or the regulation of emotion experience or in both. Gellhorn (1970) and Izard (1971, ch. 15) went on to suggest that expressive behavior was a mechanism for emotion regulation that could be used systematically in socialization and psychotherapy.

An experimental social psychologist proposed the simple, yet radical, hypothesis that subject-blind, experimenter-manipulation of facial muscles into a configuration corresponding to an emotion expression would activate the corresponding specific emotion (Laird, 1974). In 10 of 12 relevant empirical reports, investigators claimed support for this version of the facial feedback hypothesis (for a summary, see Laird, 1984).

The two studies in which experimeter-manipulated facial movements had no effect on emotion experience limit the generalizability of the positive findings. More particularly, a careful study of all these experiments suggests that special care must be taken in implementing the experimental procedure. Typically the procedure requires the experimeter to manipulate (request) particular facial muscle movements that produce an emotion expression (or component of one) without the subjects' realizing the purpose of the experiment or that they are producing an emotion expression. It is also necessary to accomplish these apparently intrusive manipulations without irritating, embarrassing, or fatiguing the subjects.

Two recent reviews of the research on the facial feedback hypothesis (Winton, 1986; Matsumoto, 1987) have seriously questioned the evidence in favor of the categorical version of the FFH—the notion that an experimenter-manipulated specific expression leads to the corresponding specific emotion experience. Winton showed that the empirical evidence supported only a dimensional version of the FFH, which means that experimenter-manipulated expressions affect only the broad classes of emotion —positive and negative.

Matsumoto (1987) used meta-analytic techniques described by Rosenthal (1984) to determine the mean effect size for experimenter-manipulated facial expression. For 16 studies (reported in 11 articles) that used self-report measures of emotion experience as a dependent variable, the mean effect size (in Pearson r) was .343, indicating that only 11.8% of the total variance in emotion experience can be attributed to the experimenter-manipulated facial expression. This value is probably inflated, as Matsumoto noted, because most journals rarely publish negative results. Although Matsumoto did not distinguish between studies testing different versions of the FFH, all the studies used in his meta-analysis except the one with negative results (Tourangeau and Ellsworth, 1979) tested the dimensional version.

A close examination of the facial feedback studies reveal that the experiments fall into two general classes, those that employ subject-blind, experimenter-manipulated expressions to activate emotions and those that use self-regulated expressions to alter event- or imagery-induced emotion experience. Such self-regulated expression is behavior that the subject is apparently motivated to perform in pursuit of a desired goal, which may have been suggested by the experimenter. Six of the studies surveyed by Winton and Matsumoto employed self-regulated expressive behavior (Kopel & Arkowitz, 1974; Lanzetta et al., 1976, 2 studies; Zuckerman et al., 1981; Kleinke & Walton, 1982, Kraut, 1982). Two studies not included in these surveys also used manipulations that meet the criteria for self-regulated expression (McCanne & Anderson, 1987; Rusalova et al., 1975).

A re-analysis of Matsumoto's meta-analysis data reveal that the mean effect size (in Pearson r) for the six studies in his survey employing self-regulated expression was .457, more than 70 percent larger than that for the ten studies using subject-blind, experimenter-manipulated expression (.275). This is an impressive difference but none of these six studies of self-regulated expression tested the categorical version of the hypothesis. That is, none showed that emotion-specific expressive behavior altered the corresponding specific emotion feeling.

In summary, there is little or no support

for the notion that subject-blind, experimenter-manipulated facial expression is effective in activating or regulating emotion feelings or emotion experiences. If there is an effect for such expression manipulations, it is weak and non-specific. On the other hand, there is evidence for the hypothesis that self-regulated expressive behavior is an effective regulator of the broad classes of emotion experience. These data support Gellhorn's and Izard's idea that expressive-behavior techniques can be effective in psychotherapy and the socialization of emotions.

Nonverbal Behavior and Emotions

The past fifteen years have seen a large volume of research on nonverbal behavior. (For recent reviews see Buck, 1980b, DePaulo & Rosenthal, 1982; and volumes edited by Hinde, 1975; Von Cranach & Vine, 1973; Weitz, 1974; and Wolfgang, 1979. Although this work often has implications for the field of emotions, much of it makes no use of emotion or other motivational concepts. As implied by the term nonverbal, this work focuses on the communicative functions of motor activities, including gesture, body movement, and locomotion (Sogon & Izard, 1985; Ziven, 1985). The two types of nonverbal behavior that bear the closest relation to emotions or emotion communication are facial expressions and gaze patterns.

Facial Expression and Emotion Communication

Research on emotions and the study of nonverbal behavior converge in the domain of facial and vocal behavior, where the nonverbal behavior can be conceived as emotion communication. (For examples of such work on the face or facial expression of emotions see Buck, 1980b; Campos & Stenberg, 1981; Ekman et al., 1972; Izard, 1971; Izard et al., 1980; Klinnert et al., 1982; and for examples relating to the vocal characteristics of discrete emotions see Scherer, 1979, 1982). In summary, these studies have shown that, from early infancy, patterns of appearance changes brought about by contraction of the superficial musculature of the face signal emotion-specific messages that influence the behavior of parents and other observers. Similar findings hold for vocal expression, but to date relatively few studies have related patterns of acoustic characteristics

of voice to specific emotions. Available evidence summarized by Scherer shows, for example, that voice pitch is lower, narrower in range, and less variable in sadness than in anger or fear. And speech in sadness is lower in volume and slower in tempo than speech in joy.

Emotion investigators code facial behaviors as an index of emotion experience in the encoder (sender) and as an index of the social signal value of emotion expression for the decoder (receiver). A model for such studies was derived from Miller's cooperative conditioning procedure (see Miller, Banks, & Ogawa, 1962). The procedure as used by Buck (1978) and his colleagues requires senders (expression encoders who are televised unobtrusively) to view and describe their reactions to pleasant and unpleasant color slides. Receivers (or decoders) then view the video record of the senders' facial and gestural responses (without audio) and judge the pleasantness or unpleasantness of the senders' emotion responses to the slides. Studies using this paradigm found that (1) females showed greater sending accuracy than males; (2) sending accuracy was related to personality measures of extroversion and self-esteem; (3) one index of sending accuracy was negatively correlated with the senders' skin-conductance response to the slide presentation and to the senders' heart-rate acceleration while they discussed their feelings about the slides; and (4) sending accuracy of preschoolers was positively related to their teacher's rating of them as active, expressive, friendly, extroverted, and dominating, and negatively related to a rating of quiet, reserved, cooperative, shy, and introverted.

The Buck finding of a negative correlation between sending acuracy and physiological responding has revived interest in Jones's (1935) hypothesis that there are reliable individual differences in external (somatic: facial, postural, gestural) and internal (autonomic) modes of emotion expression, and that the two modes of expression are negatively correlated. A number of other studies have supported Jones's hypothesis of an inverse relation between somatic and autonomic expression (Prideaux, 1922; Landis, 1932; Block, 1957; Learmonth, Ackerly, & Kaplan, 1959; Lanzetta & Kleck, 1970). Lanzetta and Kleck also reported that "externalizers" were poorer judges of observable expression than "internalizers." Jones (1950) and Block (1957) reported that low autonomic (electrodermal) reactors (externalizers) tended to be sociable, extroverted, impulsive, and dominating, whereas high reactors (internalizers) tended to be cooperative, shy, inhibited, and introverted.

The Lanzetta et al. (1976) studies reviewed in the preceding section lead to a qualification of Jones's hypothesis. Deliberate efforts to regulate (e.g., attenuate) external (facial) expression resulted in regulation (e.g., attenuation) of internal arousal, suggesting that under certain circumstances the relation between internal and external expression is direct, not inverse.

Gaze Behavior and Emotion Communication

Even in the first hour of life, the gaze that an infant directs toward the mother's face has a measurable (positive, affective) impact on the mother (Klaus, Trause, & Kennell, 1975), and the suppression (or absence) of normal facial behavior on the part of the mother in infant-mother interactions has a strong (negative, affective) impact on the infant (Brazelton et al., 1975).

The visual motor system, which reaches maturity by about 3 months of age (White, Castle, & Held, 1964), is involved in the control of perceptual input and the self-regulation of affective arousal (Stechler & Carpenter, 1967; Walters & Parke, 1965). The infant can direct attention away from dull stimuli and toward interesting ones, thus increasing arousal (Fantz, 1964; Kagan & Lewis, 1965; McCall & Kagan, 1967). The work of the foregoing investigators suggests that the processes involved in the emotion of interest and those in gaze behavior operate in a kind of feedback loop whereby the emotion of interest directs and sustains gaze, and the resultant perceptual input in turn amplifies the interest.

Ethologists have documented for many species the effectiveness of the direct gaze as a threat display that increases arousal and the likelihood of aggression unless one member assumes a "cut-off" posture and averts its gaze from the other (Chance, 1962; Hinde & Rowell, 1962; Hall & DeVore, 1965). Exline and Yellin (1969) showed that monkeys (*Macaca mulatta*) responded to the steady stare of a human observer with threat displays and attack behaviors. Similar effects have been found in studies of human interactions where a bystander's steady expressionless stare at drivers stopped at a traffic light led to increased speed of starting up when the light changed (Ellsworth, Carlsmith, & Henson, 1972).

Exline, Paredes, Gottheil, and Winkelmayer (1979) have shown that there are some direct relations between gaze patterns and specific emotions or certain emotion-specific behaviors. They filmed adult women as they told of personal experiences of joy, sadness, and anger. With sound eliminated, trained coders viewed the films and determined gaze directions: direct (toward the eyes of the listener), direct side (gaze directly forward but to side of listener), and side-down (to the side of the listener and downward). Later, naive judges viewed the films (without sound) and guessed which of the three emotions was portrayed by the stimulus women as they told of their affective experiences. The fidelity of the stories to the prescribed emotions and the intensity of expressed emotions were rated by "blind" coders.

For stories that were judged to portray intense emotions, presenters showed consistent and different patterns of gazing behavior over the three stories. The presenters gazed most directly at the listener when recounting happy experiences, an intermediate amount for anger stories, and least for sad stories. The relatively low amount of direct gaze during the verbalization of a sad past experience is consistent with common conceptions of the effects of real sadness and with clinical descriptions of the posture and facial behavior of depressed patients. This suggests that the stimulus people either actually experience the emotion or act it out as they talk about it. Exline (1982) concluded that adults both emit and expect others to emit emotion-specific gaze patterns when describing intense emotion experiences.

EMOTION EXPERIENCE, MOTIVATION, AND BEHAVIOR

In common parlance and in much of the scientific writing on the topic, attributing a specific emotion to a person implies that the person has a certain "state of mind" (Darwin, 1872) or feeling, and this feeling component of emotion is generally assumed to be motivational in nature. Thus anger generates a tendency to defensive or aggressive behavior and fear to escape or avoidance. This logic fits well into an evolutionary biological approach and is easy to accept in any theoretical framework when the focus is on intense emotion and emergency behavior. However, emotion-as-motivation theories make much wider claims for the motivational properties of emotions than emergency functions. These theories hold that emotions not only motivate defense of life and limb but defense of self-esteem as well. They make a case for the role of emotions in behavior, ranging from simple approach and avoidance to exploratory behavior and creativity. This section explores the evidence relating emotion experience to motivation and behavior.

Emotions in Social Development and Social Behavior

Theorists who treat emotions as motivations assign an important role in social behavior to emotion experiences (emotional states or feelings). While major experimental efforts to delineate this role have begun only recently, the array of empirical findings is steadily mounting. Arguments have been made for a unique role for each emotion in personality and social development (Izard, 1978; Izard & Buechler, 1979), but most of the empirical data come from studies either of the affective-cognitive structure we call empathy or of the emotions of joy and sadness.

Empathy and Prosocial Behavior

Zahn-Waxler et al. (1979) trained mothers to achieve their 15- to 20-month-old child's reactions to real and simulated expressions of sorrow, discomfort, and pain on the part of both the mother and other people. Children whose mothers gave them clear and affectively intense reprimands for transgressions against other children were more likely to make amends. The inference that the act of conciliation was motivated by guilt induced by the mothers' verbalizations and expressive behaviors seems reasonable in the light of Bretherton and Beeghly-Smith's (1980) finding that the behavior of children as young as 18 months is guided by their emotion experiences, and that they have some understanding of their own and others' feelings.

Hoffman (1978) has developed a well-reasoned theory of empathy and has marshaled some empirical data to support it. He discusses five modes of empathic arousal that vary in degree of perceptual and cognitive involvement, type of

experience required, and type of eliciting stimulus (e.g., facial expression of another or symbolic representation). He argues that each mode of empathic response is based in part on emotion experience or feelings aroused in the one who empathizes.

The simplest mode of empathic response has been demonstrated in the newborn. Building on the earlier work of Simner (1971), Sagi and Hoffman (1976) showed that newborns cry more frequently in response to another infant's cry than to equally loud nonhuman sounds, including computer-simulated infant cries. Hoffman interpreted the infant's cry-induced cry as an early precursor of empathic arousal.

Hoffman reviewed a series of experiments that demonstrated that empathic responses could be mediated symbolically. In one of these studies, Stotland (1969) showed that subjects who imagined how they would feel if they were given the same painful treatment being applied to another person exhibited greater empathic distress (physiologically and verbally) than subjects instructed to attend to the pain recipient's physical movements.

Eibl-Eibesfeldt (1971) has discussed the advantages of sociability and of various forms of prosocial behavior for survival and adaptation. Averill (1968) has argued persuasively for the role of grief and communal empathy in maintaining group cohesiveness. One can infer from Jolly's (1966) work with lower primates that parental interest or empathic enjoyment of juveniles' play behavior contributed to the development of primate social life and primate intelligence. The ability to share feelings of negative as well as positive emotions by way of distal cues from another person and through symbolic processes is undoubtedly a part of the human evolutionary heritage, a significant contribution to our development as a social species and to our capacity for significant (and adaptive) prosocial behavior.

Emotions in Attachment and Separation

Emotions as motivating feelings or experiences also play a role in another important aspect of social development—the development of interpersonal attachment or social bonds (Bowlby, 1969; Hamburg, 1963). Bowlby has shown that the mother-infant attachment is always characterized by strong emotions. Breaking the bonds of this attachment even through brief separation elicits intense emotion expressions in infants (Bowlby, 1973; Shiller, Izard, & Hembree, 1986). Naturalistic studies (summarized in Bowlby, 1973) showed that moderately long-term separation of infants and young children from their mothers often produces severe depression with physiological complications.

The severe effects of long-term separation on the social and emotional development of non-human primates have been detailed by Harlow and his colleagues (Hansen, 1966; Harlow, Harlow, & Hansen, 1963) and by Kaufman (1977). The studies reviewed by Kaufman revealed species (pigtail versus bonnet macaque) differences in the effects of separation. The origin of this difference was traced to differences in the social structure (amount of social support available to the infant) in the two species (Kaufman & Rosenblum, 1969). Adolescent and adult members of both species spend about 80 percent of the time in positive, friendly interaction, but while pigtails direct almost all their attention to family members, bonnets spend as much time with nonkin as with kin. The pigtail mother forms a close, virtually exclusive relationship with her infant and threatens intruders. The bonnet mother welcomes or tolerates socializing with her infant by aunts, cousins, or virtually any member of the group. As a result of these biosocial differences, bonnet infants respond to separation with less protest and despair and show much quicker recovery than do pigtail infants. Soon after separation the bonnet infant is adopted by a relative or friend and receives the usual prosocial interactions from other members of the group. This kind of socio-emotional support system apparently protects the bonnet infant from the severe depression that debilitates the pigtail. Kaufman argues that within each species the behavior motivated by the separation-induced emotion is basically adaptive—that is, the protest normally serves to reunite infant and mother or to get someone else to take over the mothering functions, and the ultimate withdrawal serves to "conserve energy for better times."

Building on Bowlby's conceptualization of attachment, Ainsworth and her colleagues (Ainsworth, Blehar, Waters, & Wall, 1978; Ainsworth & Wittig, 1969) developed a procedure (strange situation) for classifying infants according to types of attachment—secure, insecure avoidant, insecure ambivalent. The assumption that emotions motivate attachment behaviors and influence the quality of attachment is supported by the finding that mothers who were more emotionally expressive were more likely to have securely attached infants (Main et al., 1979) and by studies showing that emotion indexes predict social-interactive behaviors in the strange-situation procedure (Gaensbauer et al., 1983). A few studies have found that type of attachment is predictive of later social and emotional adjustment, with secure attachment in infancy being associated with greater competence at 3 or 4 years of age (Arend, Gove, & Sroufe, 1979; Matas, Arend, & Sroufe, 1978; Waters, Wippman, & Sroufe, 1979).

Joy and Sadness in Altruistic and Self-Rewarding Behaviors

Several investigators have used a variety of techniques to induce specific emotions and have measured the effects on prosocial behavior. In some of these studies, the manipulation was conceived in terms of success and failure rather than in terms of specific emotion (e.g., Isen, 1970; Isen, Horn, & Rosenhan, 1973; Masters, 1971), but later studies showed that the induction of the "warm glow of success" and the "dejection of failure" yielded results very similar to induction of joy and sadness, respectively.

Isen (1970) found that subjects who achieved success on an experimental task contributed significantly more money to a stranger soliciting for a worthy cause than those who experienced failure. In follow-up studies she showed that the warm glow of success mediated other types of helpful behavior as well as a better memory for details about the experimental situation than did the experience of failure.

Rosenhan, Underwood, and Moore (1974) attempted to induce the specific emotions of joy and sadness by asking children in the second and third grades to reminisce on things that made them happy or sad. Children in both the "think-happy" and "think-sad" groups indulged in more self-gratification (took more candy that was made available) than children in a neutral state. However, altruistic behavior (sharing pennies with nonparticipants) showed a significant positive correlation with self-gratification in the happy condition and a significant negative correlation in the sad cognition. Follow-up studies by Rosenhan and his colleagues have shown that "egocentric" joy results in more altruistic behavior than "empathic" joy (Salovey & Rosenhan, 1982), and that the reverse is true for egocentric and empathic sadness (Thompson, Cowan, & Rosenhan, 1980). Fry (1975) also used the think-happy and think-sad emotion-induction technique and showed that induced joy resulted in greater resistance to temptation (playing with an attractive, forbidden toy) than did induced sadness.

Emotions and Cognitive Development

The theories of both Tomkins (1962) and Izard (1977) treat the emotion of interest as the principal motivation subserving exploratory behavior, adaptive learning, and cognitive development. They maintain that the feeling or motivational state of interest accounts for selective attention, attention focusing, and the sustained cognitive or behavioral effort necessary for information processing and problem solving. Other theorists have attributed to interest (sometimes termed curiosity or anticipation) an essential role in adaptation (Hass, 1970; Plutchik, 1980a) and copying (Berylne, 1960; Lazarus et al., 1980).

Despite these theoretical treatments, interest has enjoyed status as a variable in only two empirical studies. Langsdorf et al. (1983) studied interest, operationally defined in facial behavior (Izard, 1979), in relation to visual fixation and heart rate in infants 2, 4, 6, and 8 months of age while they viewed a live human face, a mannequin, and an inanimate object with scrambled facial features. The study showed that these stimuli elicited different amounts of visual fixation, heart-rate deceleration, and facial-movement indicators of interest. As with the other two dependent variables, infants showed most facial response to the person, next most to the mannequin, and least to the inanimate object. In a multiple regression analysis with age, heart-rate deceleration, and facial expression of interest as predictors of stimulus fixation time, interest was the only consistent predictor. Age was never a significant predictor and heart-rate deceleration was significant only for the mannequin. Interest accounted for a significant amount of unique variance in the fixation time of all three stimuli. These findings were considered consistent with the view that interest influences attention focusing and information processing.

Through naturalistic observations of play sessions in a nursery school Renninger and Wozniak (1985) determined the two toys in a large set that were of greatest interest to each child. Interest was measured in terms of the amount of attention given to the various toys in the play room. The selected toys were then embedded in tasks that measured attention-focusing, recognition memory, and recall. On the average, each child's performance relative to the selected toys was superior to that relative to the remaining toys.

Kagan (1976) and a number of other developmental psychologists hold that cognitive development precedes and sets the stage for emotional development. This is consistent with the position of emotion theorists such as Arnold (1960), Lazarus (1974), and Plutchik (1980a), who hold that some kind of cognitive appraisal or evaluative process is a necessary prerequisite to emotion. The research of Kagan (1976) and his colleagues (Kagan et al., 1978) on separation of infant from mother illustrates this approach. Kagan holds that there are two aspects to separation effects (variously termed anxiety, fear, protest, distress). The first is the growth function—the emergence, peaking, and decline of the effects over time—and the second consists of individual differences in their frequency and intensity. Kagan (1976) found that separation effects occur regularly and show a similar growth function in different cultures (Guatemalan Indian, Guatemalan Ladino, African Bushman, Israeli kibbutz) and in different social classes within cultures. His explanation of the growth function of this negative response to separation is based on his notion that the "primary incentive for the distress is the discrepant quality of the event" (Kagan et al., 1978, p. 106). He also assumes that a necessary though not sufficient condition is a certain level of memory capacity—the ability to store schemata and to retrieve and hold them in awareness long enough to compare them with the information currently being perceived and organized.

Despite this persuasive interpretation of the sequencing of cognitive and emotional attainments in relation to the separation effect, cognitive growth does not explain all event-emotion expression relation. For example, perceptual-cognitive development does not explain the emergence of negative emotion responses on the visual cliff (Campos, Hiatt, Ramsay, Henderson, & Svedja, 1978).

Apart from the question of the primacy of cognition or emotion in development, there is some evidence that event-emotion expression relations signal cognitive attainments. Ramsay and Campos (1978) have shown that the smiling response during search tasks is an excellent indicator of emergent representational memory at about 11 months of age. Haviland (1976) has argued cogently that emotion expressions generally provide essential information in any assessment of cognitive development in the preverbal infant.

Emotion Experience in Information Processing, Learning, and Memory

Although a few theorists have long maintained that affective experiences influence information processing in learning and memory, until recently there have been few empirical investigations relating directly to this issue.

Pleasant and Unpleasant Feelings in Personality and Cognitive Processes

Messick (1965) studied the effects of the assassinations of J.F. Kennedy on a number of personality and cognitive response measures, administering the test battery to the "experimental" group the day after the assassination and to a control group three months later. The experimental group performed significantly worse than the control group on two cognitive measures of flexibility of closure, and "were significantly more yielding and conventional than the comparison subjects . . ." (p. 122).

Another series of studies tested the effects of experimentally induced affect on perception, intellectual performance, and learning (Izard, Wehmer, Livsey, & Jennings, 1965). Their first study examined the effects of interpersonally induced positive and negative emotion on soldiers' stereoscopic perception of photographs of joyful and angry faces and of friendly and hostile interpersonal encounters (scenes). The emotion-induction procedure consisted of either warm, friendly responses from the experimenter, an officer with the rank of captain, or curt, critical responses. The stereoscopic picture stimuli were shown in 26 pairs, each pair made up of one friendly and one hostile scene. The subjects with negative-emotion induction reported seeing significantly more angry faces and hostile scenes than did the subjects in the positive-emotion induction group. Apparently the induced emotion determined the direction of the resolution of the binocular rivalry created by the stereoscopic presentation and led to emotion-congruent perceptions.

In their second study they used a role-playing technique to induce positive and negative emotion and measured the effects of induced emotion and self-esteem on measures of perception of experimenter and experiment, attitude change, and intellectual functioning. In the role-playing experiment the positive and negative emotion-induction conditions produced significantly different perceptions of the experimenter and the experiment in the predicted direction. Magnitude of self-esteem was also positively related to perception of experimeter and experiment. The induced positive affect produced significantly better performance on the measures of intellective functioning (multiple uses, digit span, problem solving) than did negative-affect induction. Finally, the positive-affect induction produced more favorable change in opinion (regarding a clinical report of a juvenile offender) than did negative affect induction.

In the third study the authors examined the effects of positive- and negative-emotion induction on subjects' learning efficiency on a paired-associate learning task. They found that subjects in the positive-emotion induction group performed significantly better on the learning task than did subjects in the negative-emotion induction condition. Recall scores obtained after the learning trials were completed gave the same result. The positive- and negative-emotion inductions produced no differences in subjects' self-reported anxiety, but the negative-emotion induction resulted in significantly higher hostility scores than did the positive-emotion induction. Izard et al. concluded that cognitively induced emotion altered subjects' emotion experiences, perceptions, learning efficiency, and performance on these intellectual tasks. In two additional studies Izard et al. tested the effects of background pictures with positive and negative affect on a paired-associate (trigrams) learning task. As predicted, the subjects learned the trigram pairs best when the background pictures were extremely positive, next best when either moderately positive or moderately negative (the only two groups that did not differ significantly), and most poorly when the background pictures were extremely negative.

Feelings, Preferences, and Cognitive Process

Zajonc and his colleagues completed a number of experiments that support the propositions that affect is primary and relatively independent of cognition. Building on the work of Matlin (1971), Moreland and Zajonc (1979) presented Japanese ideographs to subjects a varying number of times and required them to make a number of recognition and liking judgments. When only those stimuli that were not recognized in the first series of trials are considered, there is a correlation of 0.43 and 0.50 between frequency of exposure and rated attractiveness independent of cognitive recognition. Zajonc reviewed another series of studies on face recognition that showed "strong participation of affect in information processing." Bower and Karlin (1974) found that photographs judged on affective traits (honesty, likableness) were recognized more frequently on test trails than photographs judged for gender. Patterson and Baddeley (1977) found that recognition memory was substantially better for the photographs rated on personality traits than for those rated on specific facial features. Their results failed to confirm the depth-of-processing hypothesis and were consistent with Zajonc's thesis. The outcome of these studies is that even mildly affective components of a task influence cognitive performance.

Specific Emotions in Learning and Memory

Isen, Clark, Shalker, and Karp (1978) showed that a good mood, which can be considered as equivalent to the emotion of enjoyment or happiness, was "more likely to facilitate retrieval of positive than negative material from memory and that this improved access to positive material affects the decision-making process with regard to behavior . . . (especially behavior such as helping)" (p. 2). They conducted a study in a shopping mall where a confederate stopped passers by and gave them a small gift with explanation that it was part of a company's promotion scheme. Moments later another confederate, who did not know whether or not a gift had been presented, approached and asked the subject to participate in a consumer survey of evaluations of the performance and service records of products they owned. The results showed that subjects who had received a gift and presumably had experienced a "good mood" made significantly more positive judgments of products than did those without a gift. The authors interpreted their data as supporting their "accessibility hypothesis"—that the mood state functions as a cue in mediating the access of positive material in memory, material that in turn influences decision making and behavior. Other studies in this framework, reviewed in an earlier section, showed that induction of good mood resulted in more helping behavior in both field and laboratory settings (Isen & Levin, 1972).

Bower, Monteiro, and Gilligan (1978) conducted a series of experiments to test the effects of the specific emotions of joy and sadness on learning and memory. They took a lead from the research with animals that demonstrated state-dependent retention—that is, retention is better when training and testing occur in the same internal state than in a different state, with state typically being determined by drugs or sleep deprivation (Overton, 1973). The author also considered Blum's (1967) finding that matched arousal states (varied by depth of hypnotic trance) for learning and recall resulted in significantly greater retention than when states for input and output were mismatched. Bower et al. extended this line of research to emotion or mood states and showed that memory was better when hypnotically induced emotion state (joy or sadness) was matched for learning and recall than when input and output state was mismatched. They concluded that emotion functioned as an extra cue in the retrieval process since it had provided a different context for learning.

In another series of experiments Bower, Gilligan, and Monteiro (1981) investigated the relative effects of input and output emotion states on memory. They induced intensely sad or happy states by hypnosis and used posthypnotic suggestion to ensure that on a later occasion half the subjects would read a story while sad and half while happy. In Experiment 1 they found that the quality of the subjects' mood on input led to identification with the same-mood character (a character whose mood matched their own) and to the recall of a greater number of same-mood ideas. They concluded that mood-relevant material receives special attention and elaboration during encoding and hence is remembered better. Experiment 2 showed that emotion state during recall had no effect on material learned in a neutral mood. This null result suggested that the findings of Experiment 1 were not a function of the demand characteristics of hypnosis.

Experiment 3 showed that it was not the subjects' identification with the same-mood character in the story but rather the same-mood story's material that accounted for the selective learning of same-mood ideas. Experiment 4 reaffirmed the results of Experiment 2, leading to the conclusion that input or encoding mood is apparently more important for memory and retrieval than output mood. Experiment 5 was a more definitive test and confirmed the hypothesis that mood-relevant material is a more potent determinant of selective encoding and memory than character identification.

The investigators concluded that this series of experiments demonstrated that mood or emotion experience during input causes selective and improved learning of mood-congruent material over mood-incongruent material. They inferred that this effect is most likely produced by intensity of mood or emotion experience at the time of learning or encoding and by selective reminding —that is, the input event reminds the subject of an episode from the past and is more deeply and elaboratory processed.

Bower (1981) reported a number of other studies that extended the earlier findings on the influence of emotion on learning and memory. One of these experiments showed that the influence of emotion on memory generalized to real-life incidents. Subjects in a hypnotically induced happy mood at the time of testing recalled more of the happy than unhappy incidents they had recorded in a specially kept diary, and subjects in a sad mood at testing recalled more sad than happy incidents. A follow-up experiment showed the same result when the real-life incidents were remote childhood memories rather than events of the preceding week. Bower concluded that the mood-state retrieval effect (the effect of the emotion that is being experienced during output) is somewhat robust when subjects recall events in the same mood as the one in which they learned or experienced them. Emotion state during retrieval significantly influences recall only when it interacts with the emotion state at the time of learning. Another experiment showed varying effects on learning of moods that varied in the degree to which they matched the mood during recall.

Bower concluded that a person's current emotion state influences "associations, interpretative processes, imaginative reconstructions, perception, and selective learning" (1981, p. 147). These propositions and the supporting data are consistent with theories that treat emotions as basic motivational phenomena (Izard, 1971, 1977; Leventhal, 1980; Plutchik, 1962; 1980a; Tomkins, 1962, 1963).

At least in part, the empirical findings of Bower and his colleagues are consistent with the findings from the early experiments of Izard, Wehmer, Livsey, & Jennings (1965) and Messick (1965): these studies all show that emotion influences learning, memory, and personality processes. There is one difference. Both Messick and Izard found that learning was poorer with sadness or unpleasant emotion (or emotion-inducing stimuli) than with positive emotion, whereas Bower found no difference in speed of learning or retention for subjects in trance-induced emotion states. Izard obtained the effect in a laboratory experiment, and Messick in a naturalistic study of the impact of the assassination of President Kennedy. Further research is required to resolve this difference.

It is hoped that research will also help resolve the differences in the theoretical intepretations of the findings. Bower holds that the effects of emotion experience "are understandable in terms of ideas and mechanisms that are standard fare in cognitive psychology" (1981, p. 147). He considers an emotion as simply another node or concept in a semantic network and explains his findings in a "general theory of long-term semantic memory." Thus for Bower activation of an emotion node provides an additional cue in the retrieval process. Emotion-as-motivation theorists hold that emotion is not simply part of an associative network or just a concept or node from which "excitation spills over." Rather for those theorists emotion-as-motivation is generative, capable of producing cues and instigating, guiding, and regulating cognitive processes. Despite these differences in interpretation of the data, all the findings of Bower and his colleagues are generally consistent with theories that ascribe distinct motivational properties to each of the discrete emotions.

SUMMARY

For almost a century after Darwin's seminal work on the emotions, only sporadic attention was paid them by psychologists. In fact, it was not until a few investigators in the late 1960s produced robust evidence for Darwin's hypothesis of the innateness and universality of certain emotion expressions that the subject began to attract the attention of a number of investigators.

Along with the increasing volume of empirical research a number of comprehensive theories of emotion have emerged. These theories fall into the three broad classes: one that emphasizes emotions as motivational and adaptive, a second that views emotion as a product of cognition (appraisal, evaluation), and a third that emphasizes the response characteristics of emotion. These themes are neither mutually exclusive nor altogether contradictory, and each has generated a line of empirical research.

Theorists and investigators are generally agreed that emotions are complex phenomena, having neurophysiological-biochemical, behavioral-expressive, and feeling-experiential components. Of these the third is the most controversial as regards its definition and function.

Experimental evidence, based largely on lesion and stimulation studies in animals, suggested that specific parts of the hypothalamus are involved in aggression, and the septal-hippocampal axis in the control of emotional response. While emotional disposition and behavior are species specific in rats, cats, and humans, emotion appears in all species to involve modulation by the limbic structures discussed in this section. Behaviorally active monoamine neurotransmitters provide the neurochemical basis for the integration of complex emotional responses in relatively few anatomical structures.

Evidence for the modulatory effect of the monoamines and acetylcholine in emotional behaviors is provided by experimental studies of the behavioral effects of chemical lesion by neurotoxins, pharmacological studies of agonists and antagonists of these neurotransmitters, and studies of psychogenic drugs and their effects on neurochemicals. Self-stimulation studies, and the effect on self-stimulation of chemicals active in these monoamine neurotransmitter systems, indicate their involvement in feelings of reward and punishment. Experimental evidence from many different perspectives has implicated specific limbic structures and specific monoamine and cholinergic neurotransmitters as the physiological bases for emotional behavior.

Studies of the expressive component of emotion, particularly facial expression, have flourished recently, especially during the past dozen years. Research initiated on this topic by personality and clinical psychologists spread quickly to social and developmental psychology. Now there are studies on the role of emotion expression in various aspects of development, including attachment, prosocial behavior, and social competence. Another line of investigation has demonstrated the role of emotion expressions in social motivation. For example, whether an infant will cross the deep side of a visual cliff can be determined by the quality of the facial expression on the mother's face. Other studies have shown that infants' emotion expression affect mothers' physiological responses and overt behavior.

Perhaps, the most impressive of the developmental studies of emotion expression are those showing continuity of such behavior. Indexes of anger and sadness expression to a standard stimulus (DPT inoculation) aggregated over three occasions during early infancy predict anger and sadness expression to the same stimulus in the second half of the second year. And interest and attention to faces in early infancy predict sociability and shyness in the fifth year.

The evidence favoring the hypothesis that subject-blind, experimenter-manipulated facial expression activates expression-specific emotion experience has been rendered dubious by telling critiques. However, a number of studies favor the notion that self-regulated emotion expression plays a role in the regulation of emotion experience. The weight of empirical evidence is impressive but the nature of the mechanism that mediates the effects remains controversial. Any comprehensive model of emotion activation will probably have to be a multifactor one.

The research on emotion expression has also influenced the field of nonverbal communication. This is particularly evident in research on encoding and decoding facial patterns and in studies showing relations between gaze behavior and emotion experience.

Studies have ascribed a role to the third component of emotion—feeling or subjective experience—in cognition and behavior. Cognitively induced emotion has been shown to influence a wide variety of behaviors, including giving, helping, and the resisting of temptation. Increasing attention is being devoted to the relation between emotion and cognition, and there is some question as to whether these phenomena can indeed be studied as separate— though interrelated—processes. Some theorists argue that emotion and cognition are inseparable, but many impressive studies have already been generated in which emotion figures as an independent variable. With these studies contemporary cognitive psychology has made an impressive entry into the field of emotion or emotion-cognition relations. These studies have demonstrated significant effects of emotion experience on variables relating to such traditional topics as discrimination, learning, and recall. In one respect the psychologists conducting this research are following a long-standing historical trend. Many prominent experimentalists of the past have taken time out to do one or two studies on emotion—Titchener, Fernberger, Dunlap, Dashiell, Woodworth, Floyd Allport, and Boring. The present prospects for a more sustained effort in experimental psychology on the role of emotions in cognitive processes are improved by the gains that have already been made in other areas of the field of emotions.

REFERENCES

Adamec, R.E. (1978). Normal and abnormal limbic system mechanisms of emotive biasing. In K.E. Livingston & O. Hornykiewicz (Eds.), *Limbic mechanisms*. New York: Plenum Press.

Adams, D.B. (1979). Brain mechanisms for offense, defense, and submission. *Behavioral and Brain Science.*, 2, 201–241.

Ahern, G.L. & Schwartz, G.E. (1979). Differential lateralization for positive versus negative emotion. *Neuropsychologia*, 17, 693–697.

Ainsworth, M.D., Blehar, M.C., Waters, E., & Wall, S. (1978). A psychological study of the Strange Situation. In L. Erlbaum (Ed.), *Patterns of attachment*. New York: Wiley.

Ainsworth, M.D., Blehar, M.D., Water, E., & Wall, S. (1978). *Patterns of attachment: A psychological study of the strange situation*. Hillsdale, NJ: Erlbaum.

Ainsworth, M.D. & Wittig, B.A. (1969). Attachment and exploratory behavior of one-year-olds in a strange situation. In B.M. Foss (Ed.), *Determinants of infant behavior IV*. London: Methuen.

Allport, F.H. (1924). *Social psychology*. Cambridge, Mass.: Houghton Mifflin.

Afrend, R.A., Gove, F.L., & Sroufe, L.A. (1979). Continuity of early adaptation: From attachment in infancy to ego-resiliency and curiosity at age t. *Child Development*, 50, 950–959.

Arnold, M.B. (1960a). *Emotion and personality*. Vol. I. *Psychological aspects*. New York: Columbia University Press.

Averill, J.R. (1968). Grief: Its nature and significance. *Psychological Bulletin*, 70, 721–748.

Ax, A.F. (1953). The physiological differentiation between fear and anger in humans. *Psychosomatic Medicine*, 15, 433–442.

Azmitra, E.C. & Segal, M. (1978). An autoradiographic analysis of the differential ascending projections of the dorsal and median raphe nuclei in the rat. *Journal of Comparative Neurology*, 179, 641–668.

Bagley, N. (1956). Individual patterns of development. *Child Development*, 27, 45–74.

Beckstead, M. (1976). Convergent thalamic and mesencephalic projections to the anterior medial cortex in the rat. *Journal of Comparative Neurology*, 166, 403–416.

Bell, C. (1806). *Essays on the anatomy of expression in painting*. London: Longmans, Green.

Berlyne, D.E. (1960). *Conflict, arousal, and curiosity*. New York: McGraw-Hill.

Blanchard, D.C., Blanchard, R.J., Takahashi, L.K., & Takahashi, T. (1977). Septal lesions and aggressive behavior. *Behavioral Biology*, 21, 157–161.

Block, J. (1957). Studies in the phenomenology of emotions. *Journal of Abnormal and Social Psychology*, 54, 358–363.

Block, C.H., Siegel, A., & Edinger, H. (1980). Effects of amygdaloid stimulation upon trigeminal sensory fields of the lip that are established during hypothalamically-elicited quiet biting attack in the cat. *Brain Research*, 197, 39–55.

Blum, G.S. (1967). Hypnosis in psychodynamic research. In J.F. Gordon (Ed.), *Handbook of clinical and experimental hypnosis*. New York: Macmillan.

Blurton Jones, N.G. (1972). *Ethological studies of child behavior*. New York: Cambridge University Press.

Bobiller, P., Seguin, S., Petitjean, F., Salvert, D., Touret, M., & Jouvet, M. (1976). The raphe nuclei of the cat brain stem: A topographical atlas of their efferent projections as revealed by autoradiography. *Brain Research*, 113, 449–480.

Bower, G.H. (1981). Emotional mood and memory. *American Psychologist*, 36(2), 129–148.

Bower, G.H., Gilligan, S.G., & Monteiro, K.P. (1981). Selectivity of learning caused by affective states. *Journal of Experimental Psychology: General*, 110, 451–473.

Bower, G.H. & Karlin, M.B. (1974). Depth of processing pictures of faces and recognition memory. *Journal of Experimental Psychology*, 103, 751–757.

Bower, G.H., Monteiro, K.P., & Gilligan, S.G. (1978). Emotional mood as a context for learning and recall. *Journal of Verbal Learning and Verbal Behavior, 17,* 573–585.

Bowlby, J. (1969). *Attachment and loss:* Vol. I. New York: Basic Books.

Bowlby, J. (1973). *Attachment and loss:* Vol II. *Separation, anxiety, and anger.* New York: Basic Books.

Brady, J.V. (1970). Emotion: Some conceptual problems and psychophysiological experiments. In M.B. Arnold (Ed.), *Feelings and emotions: The Loyola Symposium* (pp. 69–100). New York: Academic Press.

Brady, J.V. & Nauta, W.J.H. (1955). Subcortical mechanisms in emotional behavior: The duration of affective changes following septal forebrain lesions in the albino rat. *Journal of Comparative and Physiological Psychology, 48,* 412–420.

Brazelton, T.B., Tronick, E., Adamson, L., Als, H., & Weise, S. (1975). *Early mother-infant reciprocity. Parent-infant interaction.* Amsterdam: CIBA Foundation, Associated Scientific Publishers.

Bretherton, I. & Beeghly-Smith, M. (1980). Talking about internal states: The acquisition of an explicit theory of mind. Unpublished paper.

Bronson, G.W. (1972). Infants' reactions to unfamiliar persons and novel objects. *Monographs of the Society for Research in Child Development, 37*(3), Ser. 148.

Buck, R. (1976). *Human motivation and emotion.* New York: Wiley.

Buck, R. (1978). The slide viewing technique for measuring nonverbal sending accuracy: A guide for replication. *Catalog of selected documents in psychology* (APA), Vol. 8, Ms 1723.

Buck, R. (1980a). Nonverbal behavior and the theory of emotion: The facial feedback hypothesis. *Journal of Personality and Social Psychology, 38,* 811–824.

Buck, R. (1980b). Emotion, emotion expression, and the nonverbal communication of emotion: Its evolution and development. In S. Brehm, S. Kassin, & F. Gibbons (Eds.), *Developmental social psychology.* New York: Oxford.

Butcher, L.L. (Ed.). (1978). *Cholinergic-monoaminergic interactions in the brain.* New York: Academic Press.

Campbell, H.J. (1973). *The pleasure areas.* New York: Delacorte Press.

Campos, J.J., Barrett, K.C., Lamb, M.E., Goldsmith, H.H., & Stenberg, C. (1983). Socioemotional development. In M.M. Haith & J.J. Campos (Eds.), *Handbook of child psychology: Vol. 2. Infancy and developmental psychology* (pp. 783–915). New York: Wiley.

Campos, J.J., Hiatt, S., Ramsay, D., Henderson, C., & Svedja, M. (1978). The emergence of fear on the visual cliff. In M. Lewis & L. Rosenblum (Eds.), *The development of affect* (pp. 149–182). New York: Plenum Press.

Campos, J. & Stenberg, C.R. (1981). Perception, appraisal and emotion: The onset of social referencing. In M. Lamb and L. Sherrod (Eds.), *Infant social cognition.* Hillsdale, NJ: Erlbaum.

Camras, L.A. (1977). Facial expressions used by children in a conflict situation. *Child Development, 48,* 1431–1435.

Candland, D.K. (1977). The persistent problems of emotion. In D.K. Candland, J.P. Fell, E. Keen, A.I. Leshner, R. Plutchik, & R.M. Tarpy (Eds.), *Emotion* (pp. 1–84). Belmont: Wadsworth.

Candland, D.K., Fell, J.P., Keen, E., Leshner, A.I., Plutchik, R., & Tarpy, R.M. (1977). *Emotion.* Belmont: Wadsworth.

Cannon, W.B. (1927). The James-Lange theory of emotions: A critical examination and an alternative theory. *American Journal of Psychology, 39,* 106–124.

Cannon, W.B. (1929). *Bodily changes in pain, hunger, fear and rage.* 2nd ed. New York: Appleton-Century-Crofts.

Carey, W.B. (1970). A simplified method for measuring infant temperament. *Journal of Pediatrics, 77,* 188–194.

Chance, M. (1962). An interpretation of some agnostic postures. *Symposium of the Zoological Society of London, 8,* 71–89.

Charlesworth, W.R. & Kreutzer, M.A. (1973). Facial expressions of infants and children. In P. Ekman (Ed.), *Darwin and facial expression, a century of research in review* (pp. 91–168). New York: Academic Press.

Cohen, B., Izard, C.E., & Simons, R.F. (1986, October). *Facial and physiological indices of emotions in mother-infant interactions.* Paper presented at the Twenty-Sixth Annual Meeting of the Society for Psychophysiological Research, Montreal, Canada.

Conrad, L.C., Leonard, C., & Pfaff, D.W. (1974). Connections of the median and dorsal raphe nuclei in the rat. An autoradiographic and degeneration study. *Journal of Comparative-Neurology, 156,* 179–206.

Cooper, J.R., Bloom, F.E., & Roth, R.H. (1974). *The biochemical basis of neuropharmacology.* New York: Oxford University Press.

Costa, E. (1960). The role of serotonin in neurobiology. *International Review of Neurobiology, 2,* 175–227.

Costa, E. & Gessa, G.L. (Eds.). (1977). *Nonstriatal dopaminergic neurons.* New York: Raven Press.

Crow, T.J. (1972a). Catecholamine-containing neurons and electrical self-stimulation. I. A review of some data. *Medicine, 2,* 414–421.

Crow, T.J. (1972b). A map of the rat mesocephalon

for electrical self stimulation. *Brain Research, 36,* 265–273.

Crow, T.J. (1977). Neurotransmitter-related pathways. The structure and function of central monoamine neurons. In A.N. Davison (Ed.), *Biochemical correlates of brain structure and function.* New York: Academic Press.

Crow, T.J., Spear, P.J., & Arbuthnot, G.W. (1972). Intracranial self-stimulation with electrodes in the region of the locus coeruleus. *Brain Research, 36,* 275–286.

Darwin, C.R. (1872). *The expression of emotions in man and animals.* London: John Murray. (Reprinted Chicago: University of Chicago Press, 1965). London: John Murray.

Davidson, R.J. (1978). Lateral specialization in the human brain: Speculations concerning its origins and development. *Behavioral and Brain Sciences, 1,* 291.

Davidson, R.J., Schwartz, G.E., Saron, C., Bennett, J., & Coleman, D. (1979). Frontal versus parietal EEG asymmetry during positive and negative affect. *Psychophysiology, 16,* 202–203.

Davis, J. (1970). Theories of biological etiology of affective disorders. *International Review of Neurobiology, 12,* 145–175.

Davis, R.C. (1934). The specificity of facial expressions. *Journal of General Psychology, 10,* 42–58.

Deets, A. & Harlow, H.F. (1971, December). Experience and the maturation of agnostic behavior. Paper presented at the convention of the American Association for the Advancement of Sciences, New York.

Delgado, J.M.R. (1971). *Physical control of the mind: Toward a psychocivilized society.* New York: Harper and Row.

Delgado, J.M. & DeFeudis, F.V. (Eds.). (1977). *Neural chemistry.* New York: Spectrum.

DePaulo, B.M. & Rosenthal, R. (1982). Measuring the development of sensitivity to nonverbal communication. In C.E. Izard (Ed.), *Measuring emotions in infants and children* (pp. 208–247). New York: Cambridge University Press.

Dienstbier, R.A. (1979). Emotion-attribution theory: Establishing roots and exploring future perspectives. In R.A. Dienstbier (Ed.), *Nebraska Symposium on Motivation.* Lincoln: University of Nebraska Press.

Donovan, W.L. & Leavitt, L.A. (1978). Early cognitive development and its relation to maternal physiologic and behavioral responsiveness. *Child Development, 49,* 1251–1254.

Douglas, R.J., Mitchell, D., Slimp, J., Crist, C., Hammersla, J., & Peterson, J. (1972) Drug enhancement of inhibition. *Proceedings of the 80th Conven-*

tion of the American Psychological Association, 7, 839–840.

Duchenne, G.B. (1876). *Mecanisme de la physionomie humaine.* Paris: Ballière.

Eibl-Eibesfeldt, I. (1971). *Love and hate: The natural history of behavior patterns.* New York: Holt, Rinehart & Winston.

Eibl-Eibesfeldt, I. (1972). Similarity and differences between cultures in expressive movements. In R.A. Hinde (Ed.), *Nonverbal communication* (pp. 20–33). Cambridge: Cambridge University Press.

Eibl-Eibesfeldt, I. (1979). Human ethology: Concepts and implications for the sciences of man. *Behavioral and Brain Sciences, 2,* 1–57.

Ekman, P. (1971). Universals and cultural differences in facial expressions of emotion. In J.K. Cole (Ed.), *Nebraska Symposium on Motivation* (pp. 207–283). Lincoln: University of Nebraska Press.

Ekman, P. (1980). Asymmetry in facial expression. *Science, 209,* 833–834.

Ekman, P. (1982). Methods for measuring facial action. In K. Spencer and P. Ekman (Eds.), *Handbook of nonverbal behavior.* New York: Cambridge University Press.

Ekman, P. & Friesen, W.V. (1978). *The facial action coding system (FACS).* Palo Alto, CA: Consulting Psychologists Press.

Ekman, P., Friesen, W.V., & Ellsworth, P. (1972). *Emotion in the human face: Guidelines for research and an integration of findings.* New York: Pergamon.

Ekman, P., Levenson, R.W., & Friesen, W.V. (1983). Autonomic nervous system activity distinguishes among emotions. *Science, 221*(4616), 1208–1210.

Ekman, P. & Oster, H. (1979). Facial expressions of emotions. In M.R. Rosenzweig & L.W. Porter (Eds.), *Annual review of psychology,* Vol. 30 (pp. 527–554). Palo Alto, CA: Annual Reviews.

Ellsworth, P., Carlsmith, J.M., & Henson, A. (1972). The stare as a stimulus to flight in human subjects: A series of field experiments. *Journal of Personality and Social Psychology, 21,* 302–311.

Emde, R.N., Gaensbauer, T.J., & Harmon, R.J. (1976). *Emotional expression in infancy.* New York: International Universities Press.

Emde, R., Katz, E.L., & Thorpe, J.K. (1978). Emotional expression in infancy. II. Early deviations in Down's syndrome. In M. Lewis & L. Rosenblum (Eds.), *The development of affect.* New York: Plenum Press.

Exline, R. (1982). Gaze behavior in infants and children: A tool for the study of emotions? In C.E. Izard (Ed.), *Measuring emotions in infants and children* (pp. 164–177). New York: Cambridge University Press.

Exline, R., Paredes, A., Gottheil, E., & Winkelmayer, R. (1979). Gaze patterns of normals and schizophrenics retelling happy, sad, and angry experiences. In C.E. Izard (Ed.), *Emotions in personality and psychopathology* (pp. 533–564). New York: Plenum Press.

Exline, R.V. & Yellin, A. (1969). Eye contact as a sign between man and monkey. *Proceedings, XIX International Congress of Psychology*. London: Methuen.

Fantz, R.L. (1964). Visual experience in infants: Decreased attention to familiar patterns relative to novel ones. *Science, 146,* 668–670.

Flynn, J.P. (1967). The neural basis of aggression in cats. In D.C. Glass (Ed.), *Neurophysiology and emotion*. New York: Rockefeller University Press.

Frankenhaeuser, M. (1979). Psychoneuroendocrine approaches to the study of emotion as related to stress and coping. In R.A. Dienstbier (Ed.), *Nebraska symposium on motivation*. Lincoln: University of Nebraska Press.

Fridlund, A.J. & Izard, C.E. (1982). Electromyographic studies of facial expressions of emotions and patterns of emotions. In J.T. Cacioppo & E.E. Petty (Eds.), *Social psychophysiology: A sourcebook*. New York: Guilford Press.

Fridlund, A.J. & Schwartz, G.E. (1979, October). Facial muscle patterning and emotion. I. Implementation of multivariate pattern-classification strategies. Paper presented at the 19th Annual Meeting of the Society for Psychophysiological Research, Cincinnati.

Frodi, A.M., Lamb, M.E., Leavitt, L.A., Donovan, W.L., Neff, C., & Sherry, D. (1978). Fathers' and mothers' responses to the faces and cries of normal and premature infants. *Developmental Psychology, 14,* 490–498.

Frois-Wittman, J. (1930). The judgment of facial expression. *Journal of Experimental Psychology, 13,* 113–151.

Fry, P.S. (1975). Affect and resistance to temptation. *Developmental Psychology, 11,* 466–472.

Fuxe, K., Hökfelt, T., & Ungerstedt, U. (1968). Localization of indolealkylamines in CNS. *Advances in Pharmacology, 6A,* 235–251.

Gaensbauer, T.J., Connell, J.P., & Schultz, L.A. (1983). Emotion and attachment: Interrelationships in a structured laboratory paradigm. *Developmental Psychology, 19*(6), 815–831.

Gasonov, G.G. (1974). Emotions, visceral functions, and limbic system. In G.G. Gasonov (Ed.), *Emotions and visceral functions*. Moscow: Elm Press.

Gellhorn, E. (1961). Prolegomena to a theory of the emotions. *Perspectives in Biology and Medicine, 4,* 403–436.

Gellhorn, E. (1964). Motion and emotion: The role of proprioception in the physiology and pathology of the emotions. *Psychological Review, 71,* 457–472.

Gellhorn, E. (1965). The neurophysiological basis of anxiety: A hypothesis. *Perspectives in Biology and Medicine, 8,* 488–515.

Gellhorn, E. (Ed.). (1968). *Biological foundations of emotion*. Glenview, IL: Scott, Foresman.

Gellhorn, E. (1970). The emotions and the ergotropic and trophotropic systems. *Psychologische Forschung, 34,* 48–94.

Gergerian, E. & Ermiane, R. (1978). *Album des expressions du visage*. Paris: La Pensée Universelle.

Geyer, M.A., Puereto, A., Menkes, D.B., Segal, D.S., & Mandell, A.J. (1976). Behavioral studies following lesions of the mesolimbic and mesostriatal serotonergic pathways. *Brain Research, 106,* 257–270.

Gloor, P. (1960). Amygdala. In J. Field, H.W. Magoun, & V.E. Hall (Eds.), *Handbook of physiology, Sec. I,* Vol. II, *Neurophysiology*. Washington DC: American Physiological Society.

Gloor, P. (1978). Inputs and outputs of the amygdala: What the amygdala is trying to tell the rest of the brain. In K.E. Livingston and O. Hornykiewicz (Eds.), *Limbic mechanisms*. New York: Plenum Press.

Goldstein, J. & Siegel, J. (1980). Stimulation of ventral tegmental area and nucleus accumbens reduce receptive fields for hypothalamic biting reflex in cats. *Experimental Neurology, 72,* 239–246.

Gray, J.A. (1971). *The psychology of fear and stress*. New York: McGraw-Hill.

Gray, J.A. (1979). A neuropsychological theory of anxiety. In C.E. Izard (Ed.), *Emotions in personality and psychopathology*. New York: Plenum Press.

Grossman, S.P. (1973). *Essentials of physiological psychology*. New York: Wiley.

Hall, K.R.L. & DeVore, I. (1965). Baboon social behavior. In I. DeVore (Ed.), *Primate behavior: Field studies of monkeys and apes*. New York: Holt, Rinehart & Winston.

Hall, R.D., Bloom, F.E., & Olds, J. (1977). Neuroanatomical and neuroanatomical substrates of reinforcement. *Neuroscience Research Program Bulletin, 15,* 134–312.

Hamburg, D.A. (1963). Emotions in the perspective of human evolution. In P.H. Knapp (Ed.), *Expression of the emotions in man* (pp. 300–317). New York: International Universities Press.

Hamburg, D.A., Hamburg, B.A., & Barchas, J.D. (1975). Anger and depression in perspective of behavioral biology. In L. Levi (Ed.), *Emotions, their parameters and measurement* (pp. 235–278). New York: Raven Press.

Hamilton, L. (1976). *Basic limbic system anatomy of the rat*. New York: Plenum Press.

Hansen, E.W. (1966). The development of material and

infant behavior in the rhesus monkey. *Behavior, 27*, 107–149.

Harlow, H.F. (1962). The heterosexual affectional system in monkeys. *American Psychologist, 17*, 1–9.

Harlow, H.F. (1971). *Learning to love.* San Francisco: Albion.

Harlow, H.F., Harlow, M.J., & Hansen, E.W. (1963). The material affectional system of rhesus monkeys. In H.L. Rheingold (Ed.), *Maternal behavior in mammals.* New York: Wiley.

Hass, H. (1970). *The human animal.* New York: Putman.

Haviland, J. (1976). Looking smart: The relationship between affect and intelligence in infancy. In M. Lewis (Ed.), *Origins of intelligence* (pp. 353–377). New York: Plenum Press.

Heath, R.G. & Mickle, W.A. (1960). Evaluation of seven years experience with depth electrode studies in human patients. In E.R. Ramey & D.S. O'Doherty (Eds.), *Electrical studies on the unanesthetized brain.* New York: Hoeber.

Hebb, D.O. (1946). On the nature of fear. *Psychological Review, 53*, 259–276.

Hebb, D.O. (1949). *The organization of behavior.* New York: Wiley.

Heimberger, R.F., Whitlock, C.C., & Kalsbeck, J.E. (1966). Stereotaxic amygdalectomy for epilepsy with aggressive behavior. *Journal of the American Medical Association, 198*, 741–745.

Heimer, L. (1978). The olfactory cortex and the ventral striatum. In K.E. Livingston & O. Hornykiewicz (Eds.), *Limbic mechanisms.* New York: Plenum Press.

Heimer, L. & Wilson, R.D. (1975). The subcortical projections of the allocortex: Similarities in the neural associations of the hippocampus, the piriform cortex and the neocortex. In M. Santini (Ed.), *Golgi centennial symposium: Perspectives in neurobiology.* New York: Raven Press.

Helmeste, D.M., Seeman, P., & Cascina, D.V. (1980). Genetic differences in catecholamine receptors and dopamine-mediated behavior in rats. *Society for Neuroscience Abstracts, 6*, 5–11.

Hembree, E.A., Ansul, S.E., Huebner, R.R., & Izard, C.E. (1981). Configurative facial movements in the newborn's response to pain. Unpublished manuscript, University of Delaware.

Hess, W.R. (1954). *Diencephalon: Autonomic and extrapyramidal functions.* London: Heinemann.

Heyback, J.P., Coover, G.D., & Lints, C.E. (1978). Behavioral effects of neurotoxic lesions of the ascending monoamine pathways in the rat brain. *Journal of Comparative and Physiological Psychology, 92*, 58–70.

Hinde, R.A. (1975). Mothers' and infants' roles: Distinguishing the questions to be asked. In M. O'Connor (Ed.), *Parent-infant interaction.* Amsterdam: Elsevier.

Hinde, R.A. & Rowell, T.E. (1962). Communication by postures and facial expressions in the rhesus monkey. *Proceedings of the Zoological Society of London, 138*, 1–21.

Hoffman, M.L. (1975). Developmental synthesis of affect and cognition and its implications for altruistic motivation. *Development Psychology, 11*, 607–622.

Hoffman, M.L. (1978). Empathy, its development and prosocial implications. *Nebraska symposium on motivation*, Vol. 25. Lincoln: University of Nebraska Press.

Hoffman, M.L. (1982). The measurement of empathy. In C.E. Izard (Ed.), *Measuring emotions in infants and children* (pp. 279–296). New York: Cambridge University Press.

Hökfelt, T. (1980). Peptide neurons. A new class of neurons or old neurons with a new content? Paper presented at Annual Meeting, Society for Neuroscience.

Huebner, R.R. (1986). *Emotions in early personality development: Two studies of children.* Unpublished doctoral dissertation. University of Delaware, Newark, DE.

Hunt, J. McV. (1965). Intrinsic motivation and its role in development. In D. Levine (Ed.), *Nebraska symposium on motivation* (pp. 189–282). Lincoln: University of Nebraska Press.

Hyson, M.C. & Izard, C.E. (1985). Continuities and changes in emotion expressions during brief separation at 13 and 18 months. *Developmental Psychology, 21*(6), 1165–1170.

Hyson, M.C., Izard, C.E., & Weston, K. (1987, April). *Emotion-related predictors of toddler's responses to a problem-solving task.* Paper presented at the meeting of the Society for Research on Child Development, Baltimore, MD.

Isaacson, R.L. (1974). *The limbic system.* New York: Plenum Press.

Isen, A. (1970). Success, failure, attention, and reaction to others: The warm glow of success. *Journal of Personality and Social Psychology, 15*, 294–301.

Isen, A., Horn, N., & Rosenhan, D.L. (1973). Effects of success and failure on children's generosity. *Journal of Personality and Social Psychology, 27*, 239–247.

Isen, A. & Levin, P. (1972). The effect of feeling good on helping: Cookies and kindness. *Journal of Personality and Social Psychology, 21*, 384–388.

Isen, A., Clark, M., Shalker, T., & Karp, L. (1978). Affect, accessibility of material in memory, and behavior: A cognitive loop? *Journal of Personality and Social Psychology, 36*, 1–12.

Iverson, L.L., Nicoll, R.A., & Vale, W.W. (1978). Neurobiology of peptides. *Neuroscience Research Program Bulletin, 16,* 211–370.

Izard, C.E. (1968). The emotions as a culture-common framework of motivational experiences and communicative cues. Technical Report No. 30, Vanderbilt University, Contract Nonr 2149(03)-NR 171-609, Office of Naval Research.

Izard, C.E. (1971). *The face of emotion.* New York: Appleton-Century-Crofts.

Izard, C.E. (1972). *Patterns of emotions: A new analysis of anxiety and depression.* New York: Academic Press.

Izard, C.E. (1977). *Human emotions.* New York: Plenum Press.

Izard, C.E. (1978). On the development of emotions and emotion-cognition relationships in infancy. In M. Lewis & L.A. Rosenblum (Eds.), *The development of affect.* New York: Plenum Press.

Izard, C.E. (1979). *The maximally discriminative facial movement coding system (Max).* Newark: University of Delaware, Instructional Resources Center.

Izard, C.E. (1980). The emergence of emotions and the development of consciousness in infancy. In J.M. Davidson & R.J. Davidson (Eds.), *The psychobiology of consciousness* (pp. 193–216). New York: Plenum Press.

Izard, C.E. & Buechler, S. (1979). Emotion expressions and personality integration in infancy. In C.E. Izard (Ed.), *Emotions in personality and psychopathology* (pp. 447–472). New York: Plenum Press.

Izard, C.E. & Dougherty, L.M. (1980). *System for identifying affect expressions by holistic judgments (Affex).* Newark: University of Delaware, Instructional Resources Center.

Izard, C.E., Hembree, E.A., Dougherty, L.M. & Spizzirri, C. (1983). Changes in facial expressions of 2- to 19-month-old infants following acute pain. *Developmental Psychology, 19,* 418–426.

Izard, C.E., Hembree, E.A., & Huebner, R.R. (1987). Infants' emotion expressions to acute pain: Developmental change and stability of individual differences. *Developmental Psychology, 23*(1), 105–113.

Izard, C.E., Huebner, R.R., Risser, D., McGinnes, G.C., & Dougherty, L.M. (1980). The young infant's ability to produce discrete emotion expressions. *Developmental Psychology, 16*(2), 132–140.

Izard, C.E. & Malatesta, C.Z. (1987). Perspectives on emotional development I: Differential emotions theory of emotional development. In J.D. Osofsky (Ed.), *Handbook of infant development* 2nd edition (pp. 494–554). New York: Wiley-Interscience.

Izard, C.E. & Schwartz, G.M. (1986). Patterns of emotion in depression. In M. Rutter, C.E. Izard, & P.B. Read (Eds.), *Depression in young people: Developmental and clinical perspectives* (pp. 33–70). New York: Guilford Press.

Izard, C.E., Wehmer, G.M., Livsey, W.J., & Jennings, J.R. (1965). Affect, awareness, and performance. In S. Tomkins & C. Izard (Eds.), *Affect, cognition, and personality* (pp. 2–41). New York: Springer.

Jacobsen, E. (1929). *Progressive relaxation.* Chicago: University of Chicago Press.

James, W. (1884). What is emotion? *Mind, 9,* 188–204.

James, W. (1950). *The principles of psychology.* New York: Holt. (Reprinted, New York: Dover, 1950.) (Original work published 1890.)

Jolly, A. (1966). Lemur social behavior and primate intelligence. *Science, 153,* 501–506.

Jones, H.E. (1935). The galvanic skin response as related to overt emotion expression. *American Journal of Psychology, 47,* 241–251.

Jones, H.E. (1950). The study of patterns of emotional expression. In M.L. Reymert (Ed.), *Feelings and emotions* (pp. 161–168). New York: McGraw-Hill.

Kagan, J. (1974). Discrepancy, temperament, and infant distress. In M. Lewis & L. Rosenblum (Eds.), *The origins of fear* (pp. 229–248). New York: Wiley.

Kagan, J. (1976). Emergent themes in human development. *American Scientist, 64,* 186–196.

Kagan, J. (1981). Heart rate and heart rate variability as signs of a temperamental dimension in infants. In C.E. Izard (Ed.), *Measuring emotions in infants and children* (pp. 38–66). New York: Cambridge University Press.

Kagan, J., Kearsley, R.B., & Zelazo, P.R. (1978). *Infancy: Its place in human development.* Cambridge, MA: Harvard University Press.

Kagan, J. & Lewis, M. (1965). Studies on attention in the human infant. *Merrill-Palmer Quarterly, 11,* 95–127.

Kagan, J. & Moss, H. (1962). *A birth to maturity.* New York: Wiley.

Kaufman, I.C. (1977). Developmental considerations of anxiety and depression: Psychobiological studies in monkeys. In T. Shapiro (Ed.), *Psychoanalysis and contemporary science,* Vol. 5 (pp. 317–363). International Universities Press.

Kaufman, I.C. & Rosenblum, L.A. (1969). The waning of the mother-infant bond in two species of macaque. In B.M. Foss (Ed.), *Determinants of infant behavior,* Vol. IV. London: Methuen.

Kellar, K.J., Brown, P.A., Madrid, J., Bernstein, M., Vernikos-Danellis, J., & Mehler, W.R. (1977). Origins of serotonin innervation of forebrain structures. *Experimental Neurology, 56,* 52–62.

Kety, S.S. (1972). Toward hypotheses for a biochemical component in the vulnerability to schizophrenia. *Seminars in Psychiatry, 4,* 233–237.

King, F.A. & Meyer, P.M. (1958). Effects of amygdaloid lesions upon septal hyperemotionality in the rat. *Science*, *128*, 655–656.

Klaus, M.H., Trause, M.A., & Kennell, J.H. (1975). Does human maternal behavior after delivery show a characteristic pattern? In *Parent-infant interaction*, Symposium 33. Amsterdam: CIBA, Associated Scientific Publishers.

Kleinke, C.L. & Walton, J.H. (1982). Influence of reinforced smiling on affective responses in an interview. *Journal of Personality and Social Psychology*, *4*(3) 557–565.

Klinnert, M., Campos, J., Sorce, J., Emde, R., & Svejda, M. (1982). Emotions as behavior regulators: The development of social referencing. In R. Plutchik & H. Kellerman (Eds.), *Emotion: Theory, research and experience*. Vol. 2. *Emotions in early development*. New York: Academic Press.

Kluver, H. & Bucy, P.C. (1939). Preliminary analysis of functions of the temporal lobes in monkeys. *Archives of Neurology and Psychiatry*, *42*, 979–1000.

Kolb, B. & Wishaw, I.Q. (1977). Effects of brain lesions and atropine on hippocampal and neocortical electroencephalograms in the rat. *Experimental Neurology*, *56*, 1–22.

Kopel, S. & Arkowitz, H.S. (1974). Role playing as a source of self-observation and behavior change. *Journal of Personality and Social Psychology*, *29*, 677–686.

Kraut, R.E. (1982). Social pleasure, facial feedback, and emotion. *Journal of Personality and Social Psychology*, *42*, 853–863.

Krnjevic, K. (1969). Central cholinergic pathways. *Federation Proceedings*, *28*, 113–120.

LaBarbera, J.D., Izard, C.E., Vietze, P., & Parisi, S.A. (1976). Four- and six-month-old infants' visual responses to joy, anger, and neutral expression. *Child Development*, *47*, 535–538.

Lacey, J.I. (1974). Somatic response patterning in stress. Some revisions of J.D. Laird, "Self-attribution of emotion: The effects of expressive behavior on the quality of emotional experience." *Journal of Personality and Social Psychology*, *29*, 475–486.

Laird, J.D. (1974). Self-attribution of emotion: The effects of expressive behavior on the quality of emotional experience. *Journal of Personality and Social Psychology*, *29*, 475–486.

Laird, J.D. (1984). The real role of facial response in the experience of emotion: A reply to Tourangeau and Ellsworth, and others. *Journal of Personality and Social Psychology*, *47*(4), 909–917.

Laird, J.D., Wagener, J.J., Halal, M., & Szegda, M. (1982). Remembering what you feel: Effects of emotion on memory. *Journal of Personality and Social Psychology*, *42*, 646–652.

Landis, C. (1924). Studies of emotion expression: General behavior and facial expression. *Journal of Comparative Psychology*, *4*, 447–498.

Landis, C. (1932). An attempt to measure emotional traits in juvenile delinquency. In K.S. Lashley (Ed.), *Studies in the dynamics of behavior*. Chicago: University of Chicago Press.

Lang, P.J. (1979). A bio-informational theory of emotional imagery. *Psychophysiology*, *16*, 495–512.

Lange, K. (1922). *The emotions*. Translated from the Danish 1985 ed. by Istar A. Haupt; K. Dunlap (Ed.). Baltimore: Williams & Wilkins.

Langsdorf, P., Izard, C.E. Rayias, M., & Hembree, E. (1983). Interest expression, visual fixation, and heart rate changes in 2- to 8-month-old infants. *Development Psychology*, *19*, 375–386.

Lanzetta, J.T., Cartwright-Smith, J.E., & Kleck, R.E. (1976). Effects of nonverbal dissimulation on emotional experience and autonomic arousal. *Journal of Personality and Social Psychology*, *33*, 354–370.

Lanzetta, J.T. & Kleck, R.E. (1970). Encoding and decoding of facial affect in humans. *Journal of Personality and Social Psychology*, *16*, 12–19.

Lazarus, R.S. (1968). Emotions and adaptation: Conceptual and empirical relations. In W.J. Arnold (Ed.), *Nebraska symposium on motivation* (pp. 175–270). Lincoln: University of Nebraska Press.

Lazarus, R.S. (1974). Cognitive and coping processes in emotion. In B. Weiner (Ed.), *Cognitive views of human motivation*. New York: Academic Press.

Lazarus, R.S., Kanner, A.D., & Folkman, S. (1980). Emotions: A cognitive-phenomenological analysis. In R. Plutchik & H. Kellerman (Eds.), *Emotion: Theory, research, and experience*, Vol. 1. New York: Academic Press.

Learmonth, G.J., Ackerly, W., & Kaplan, M. (1959). Relationships between palmar skin potential during stress and personality variables. *Psychosomatic Medicine*, *21*, 150–157.

Leaton, R.N. (1971). The limbic system and its pharmacological aspects. In R.H. Rech & K.E. Moore (Eds.), *An introduction to psychopharmacology*. New York: Raven Press.

Leventhal, H. (1980). Toward a comprehensive theory of emotion. In L. Berkowitz (Ed.), *Advances in experimental social psychology*, Vol. 13. New York: Academic Press.

Lindsley, D.B. (1951). Emotion. In S.S. Stevens (Ed.), *Handbook of experimental psychology*. New York: Wiley.

Lindsley, D.B. (1970). The role of nonspecific reticulo-thalamo-cortical systems in emotion. In P. Black (Ed.), *Physiological correlates of emotion*. New York: Academic Press.

Livingston, K.E. & Hornykiewicz, O. (Eds.). (1978).

Limbic mechanisms. New York: Plenum Press.

Longo, V.G. (1975). Behavioral consequences of the chemical destruction of central catecholaminergic terminals. In M. Santini (Ed.), *Perspectives in neurobiology*, Golgi centennial symposium. New York: Raven Press.

MacLean, P.D. (1952). Some psychiatric implications of physiological studies on frontotemporal portions of limbic system (visceral brain). *Electroencephalography and Clinical Neurophysiology, 4,* 407–418.

MacLean, P.D. (1954). The limbic system and its hippocampal formation: Studies in animals and their possible application to man. *Journal of Neurosurgery, 11,* 29–44.

MacLean, P.D. (1970). The limbic brain in relation to the psychosis. In P. Black (Ed.), *Physiological correlates of emotion*. New York: Academic Press.

MacLean, P.D. (1972). Implications of microelectrode findings on exteroceptive inputs to the limbic cortex. In C.H. Hockman (Ed.), *Limbic system mechanisms and autonomic function*. Springfield, IL: Thomas.

MacLean, P.D. (1975). Sensory and perceptive factors in emotional functions of the triune brain. In L. Levi (Ed.), *Emotions, their parameters and measurement* (pp. 71–92). New York: Raven Press.

Main, M., Tomasini, L., & Tolan, W. (1979). Differences among mothers of infants judged to differ in security. *Developmental Psychology, 15,* 472–473.

Malatesta, C.Z. (1980). Determinants of infant affect socialization: Age, sex of infant and maternal emotional traits. Unpublished doctoral dissertation, Rutgers University.

Malatesta, C.Z. (1982). The expression and regulation of emotion: A lifespan perspective. In T. Field & A. Fogel (Eds.), *Emotion and early interaction*. Hillsdale, NJ: Erlbaum.

Malatesta, C.Z. & Haviland, J.M. (1982). Learning display rules: The socialization of emotion expression in infancy. *Child Development, 53,* 991–1003.

Mandler, G. (1975). *Mind and emotions*. New York: Wiley.

Mandler, G. (1981). The construction of emotion in the child. In C.E. Izard (Ed.), *Measuring emotions in infants and children* (pp. 335–343). New York: Cambridge University Press.

Marshall, A.G. & Izard, C.E. (1972). Depression as a pattern of emotions and feelings: Factor-analytic investigations. In C.E. Izard, *Patterns of emotions: A new analysis of anxiety and depression* (pp. 237–254). New York: Academic Press.

Marshall, G.D. & Zimbardo, P.G. (1979). Affective consequences of inadequately explained physiological arousal. *Journal of Personality and Social Psychology, 37,* 970–988.

Maslach, C. (1979). Negative emotional biasing of unexplained arousal. *Journal of Personality and Social Psychology, 37,* 953–969.

Mason, J.W. (1975). Emotion as reflected in patterns of endocrine integration. In L. Levi (Ed.), *Emotions, their parameters and measurement*. New York: Raven Press.

Masters, J.C. (1971). Effects of social comparison upon children's self-reinforcement and altruism toward competitors and friends. *Developmental Psychology, 5,* 64–72.

Matas, L., Arend, R., & Sroufe, L.A. (1978). Continuity in adaptation: Quality of attachment and later competence. *Child Development, 49,* 547–556.

Matlin, M.W. (1971). Response competition, recognition, and affect. *Journal of Personality and Social Psychology, 19,* 295–300.

Matsumoto. D. (1987). The role of facial response in the experience of emotion: More methodological problems and a meta-analysis. *Journal of Personality and Social Psychology, 52*(4), 769–774.

McCall, R.B. & Kagan, J. (1967). Attention in the infant: Effects of complexity, contour, perimeter, and familarity. *Child Development, 38,* 939–952.

McCanne, T.R. & Anderson, J.A. (1987). Emotional responding following experimental manipulation of facial electromyographic activity. *Journal of Personality and Social Psychology, 52*(4), 759–768.

McCaul, K.D., Holmes, D.S., & Solomon, S. (1982). Voluntary expressive changes and emotion. *Journal of Personality and Social Psychology, 42,* 145–152.

McCleary, R.A. (1966). Response modulating functions of the limbic system: Initiation and suppression. In E. Stellar & J.M. Sprague (Eds.), *Progress in physiological psychology: Vol. 1.* New York: Academic Press.

McCleary, R.A. & Moore, R.Y. (1965). *Subcortical mechanisms of behavior*. New York: Basic Books.

McDougall, W. (1926). *An introduction to social psychology* (rev. ed.). Boston: Luce.

Messick, S. (1965). The impact of negative affect on cognition and personality. In S.S. Tomkins & C.E. Izard (Eds.), *Affect, cognition, and personality* (pp. 98–128). New York: Springer.

Miller, R.E., Banks, J.H., Jr., & Ogawa, N. (1962). Communication of affect in "cooperative conditioning" of rhesus monkeys. *Journal of Abnormal and Social Psychology, 64,* 343–348.

Mogenson, G.J. & Phillips, A.G. (1976). Motivation: A psychological construct in search of a physiological substrate. In J.M. Sprague & A.N. Epstein (Eds.), *Progress in psychobiology and physiological psychology*: Vol. 6. New York: Academic Press.

Moore, R.Y. & Bloom, F.E. (1978). Central catecholamine neuron systems: Anatomy and physiology of the dopamine systems. *Annual Review of Neuroscience, 1,* 129–169.

Moore, R.Y. & Halaris, A.E. (1975). Hippocampal innervation by serotonin neurons of the midbrain raphe in the rat. *Journal of Comparative Neurology, 164,* 171–184.

Moreland, R.L. & Zajonc, R.B. (1979). Exposure effects may not depend on stimulus recognition. *Journal of Personality and Social Psychology, 37,* 1085–1089.

Moyer, K.E. (1971). *The physiology of hostility.* Chicago: Markham.

Narabayashi, H., Nagao, T., Saito, Y., Yoshido, M., & Nagahata, M. (1963). Stereotaxic amygdalotomy for behavior disorders. *Archives of Neurology, 9,* 1–16.

Nauta, W.J.H. (1960). Some neural pathways related to the limbic system. In E.R. Ramey & D.S. O'Doherty (Eds.), *Electrical studies on the unanesthetized brain.* New York: Hoeber.

Nauta, W.J.H. (1963). Central nervous organization and the endocrine motor system. In A. Nalbandov (Ed.), *Advances in neuroendocrinology.* Urbana: University of Illinois Press.

Nauta, W.J.H. (1972). The central visceromotor system: A general survey. In C.H. Hockman (Ed.), *Limbic system mechanisms and autonomic function.* Springfield, IL: Thomas.

Nauta, W.J.H. (1979). Expanding borders of the limbic system concept. In T. Rasmussen & R. Marina (Eds.), *Functional neurosurgery.* New York: Raven Press.

Nauta, W.J.H. & Domesick, V.B. (1978). Crossroads of limbic and striatal circuitry: Hypothalamo-nigral connections. In K.E. Livingston & O. Hornykiewicz (Eds.), *Limbic mechanisms.* New York: Plenum Press.

Nauta, W.J.H. & Domesick, V.B. (1981). Neural associations of the limbic system. In A.L. Beckman (Ed.), *The neural basis of behavior.* New York: SP Medical & Scientific Books.

Nelson, C., Morse, P., & Leavitt, L. (1979). Recognition of facial expressions by seven-month-old infants. *Child Development, 50,* 1239–1242.

Nelson, C.A. (1987). The recognition of facial expression in the first two years of life: Mechanisms of development. *Developmental Psychology, 58*(4), 889–909.

Norman, D.A. (1980). Twelve issues for cognitive science. In D.A. Norman (Ed.), *Perspectives on cognitive science: Talks from the LaJolla conference.* Hillsdale, NJ: Erlbaum.

Obrist, P.A., Light, K.C., & Hastrup, J.L. (1982). Emotion and the cardiovascular system: A critical perspective. In C.E. Izard (Ed.), *Measuring emotions in infants and children.* New York: Cambridge University Press.

Olds, J. (1960). Differentiation of reward systems in the brain by self stimulation techniques. In E.R.

Ramey & D.S. O'Doherty (Eds.), *Electrical studies on the unanesthetized brain.* New York: Hoeber.

Olds, J. & Milner, P. (1954). Positive reinforcement produced by electrical stimulation of septal area and other regions of rat brain. *Journal of Comparative and Physiological Psychology, 47,* 419–427.

Orr, S.P. & Lanzetta, J.T. (1980). Facial expressions of emotion as conditioned stimuli for human autonomic responses. *Journal of Personality and Social Psychology, 38,* 278–282.

Oster, H. & Ekman, P. (1978). Facial behavior in child development. In W.A. Collins (Ed.), *Minnesota symposia on child pscyhology:* Hillsdale, NJ: Erlbaum.

Overton, D. (1973). State-dependent learning produced by addicting drugs. In S. Fischer & A. Freedman (Eds.), *Opiate addiction: Origins and treatment.* Washington, DC: Winston.

Papez, J.W. (1937). A proposed mechanism of emotion. *Archives of Neurology and Psychiatry, 38,* 725–743.

Parisi, S. (1977). Five-, seven-, and nine-month-old infants' facial responses to 20 stimulus situations. Unpublished master's thesis, Vanderbilt University.

Patterson, K.E. & Baddeley, A.D. (1977). When face recognition fails. *Journal of Experimental Psychology: Human Learning and Memory, 3,* 406–417.

Peiper, A. (1963). *Cerebral function in infancy and childhood.* New York: Consultants Bureau.

Plutchik, R. (1962). *The emotions: Facts, theories, and a new model.* New York: Random House.

Plutchik, R. (1980a). *Emotion: A psychoevolutionary synthesis.* New York: Harper & Row.

Plutchik, R.A. (1980b). A general psychoevolutionary theory of emotion. In R. Plutchik & H. Kellerman (Eds.), *Emotion: theory, research, and experience:* Vol. 1. New York: Academic Press.

Plutchik, R., Kellerman, H., & Conte, H. (1979). A structural theory of ego defenses and emotions. In C.E. Izard (Ed.), *Emotions in personality and psychopathology* (pp. 229–262). New York: Plenum Press.

Prideaux, E. (1922). Expression of the emotions in cases of mental disorders. *British Journal of Medical Psychology, 2,* 45.

Ramsay, D. & Campos, J. (1978). The onset of representation and entry into stage 6 of object permanence development. *Developmental Psychology, 14,* 79–86.

Reeves, A. & Plum, F. (1969). Hyperphagia, rage, and dementia accompanying a ventromedial hypothalmic neoplasm. *Archives of Neurology, 20,* 616–624.

Reis, D.J. (1974). Consideration of some problems encountered in relating specific neurotransmitters to specific behaviors or disease. *Journal of Psychiatric Research, 11,* 145–149.

Renninger, K.A. & Wozniak, R.H. (1985). Effect of

interest on attention shift, recognition, and recall in young children. *Developmental Psychology, 21*(4), 624–632.

Rosenhan, D.L., Underwood, B., & Moore, B. (1974). Affect moderates self-gratification and altruism. *Journal of Personality and Social Psychology, 30,* 546–552.

Rosenthal, R. (1984). *Meta-analytic procedures for social research.* Beverly Hills, CA Sage.

Ross, R.A., Judd, A.B., Pickel, V.M., Joh, T.H., & Reis, D.J. (1976). Strain dependent variations in number of midbrain DA neurons. *Nature, 264,* 654–656.

Rothbart, M.K. (1973). Laughter in young children. *Psychological Bulletin, 80,* 247–256.

Rothbart, M.K. (1977, March). Development of a caretaker report temperament scale for use with 3-, 6-, 9-, and 12-month old infants. Paper presented at SRCD meetings, New Orleans.

Rusalova, M.N., Izard, C.E., & Simonov, P.V. (1975). Comparative analysis of mimical and autonomic components of man's emotional state. *Aviation, Space, and Environmental Medicine, 46,* 1132–1134.

Russell, J.A. (1979). Affective space is bipolar. *Journal of Personality and Social Psychology, 37,* 345–356.

Sabelli, H.C. (Ed.). (1973). *Chemical modulation of brain function.* New York: Raven Press.

Sackett, G. (1966). Monkeys reared in isolation with pictures as visual input. Evidence for an innate releasing mechanism. *Science, 154,* 1468–1473.

Sagi, A. & Hoffman, M. (1976). Empathic distress in the newborn. *Developmental Psychology, 12,* 175–176.

Salovey, P. & Rosenhan, D.L. (1982). Effects of joy, attention, and recipient's status on helpfulness. Unpublished paper.

Schachter, S. (1971). *Emotion, obesity and crime.* New York: Academic Press.

Schachter, S. & Singer, J.E. (1962). Cognitive, social, and physiological determinants of emotional states. *Psychological Review, 69,* 379–399.

Schachter, S. & Singer, J.E. (1979). Comments on the Maslach and Marshall-Zimbardo experiments. *Journal of Personality and Social Psychology, 37,* 989–995.

Schaffer, H.R. (1974). Cognitive components of the infant's response to strangeness. In M. Lewis & L. Rosenblum (Eds.), *The origins of fear* (pp. 11–24). New York: Wiley.

Scherer, K.R. (1979). Non-linguistic vocal indicators of emotion and psychopathology. In C.E. Izard (Ed.), *Emotions in personality and psychopathology* (pp. 495–529). New York: Plenum Press.

Scherer, K.R. (1982). The assessment of vocal expression in infants and children. In C.E. Izard (Ed.), *Measuring emotions in infants and children*

(pp. 127–163). New York: Cambridge University Press.

Schildkraut, J.J. (1965). The catecholamine hypothesis of affective disorders: A review of supporting evidence. *American Journal of Psychiatry, 122,* 509–522.

Schildkraut, J.J. (1974). Biogenic amines and affective disorders. *Annual Review of Medicine, 25,* 333–348.

Schildkraut, J.J., Davis, J.M., & Klerman, G. (1968). Biochemistry of depression. In D.H. Efron, J.O. Cole, J. Levine, & J.R. Wittenborn (Eds.), *Psychopharmacology: A review of progress 1957–1967.* Washington, DC: Public Health Service Publication.

Schildkraut, J.J. & Kety, S.S. (1967). Biogenic amines and emotion. *Science, 156,* 21–30.

Schlosberg, H.S. (1954). Three dimensions of emotion. *Psychological Review, 61,* 81–88.

Schreiner, L. & Kling, A. (1956). Rhinencephalon and behavior. *American Journal of Physiology, 184,* 486–490.

Schwartz, G.E. (1982). Psychophysiological patterning and emotion revisited: A systems perspective. In C.E. Izard (Ed.), *Measuring emotions in infants and children* (pp. 67–93). New York: Cambridge University Press.

Schwartz, G.E., Fair, P.L., Greenberg, P.S., Freedman, M., & Klerman, J.L. (1974). Facial electromyography in the assessment of emotion. *Psychophysiology, 11,* 237.

Schwartz, G.E., Fair, P.L., Salt, P., Mandel, M.R., & Klerman, J.L. (1976). Facial muscle patterning to affective imagery in depressed and non-depressed subjects. *Science, 192,* 489–491.

Schwartz, G.E. & Weinberger, D.A. (1980). Patterns of emotional responses to affective situations: Relations among happiness, sadness, anger, fear, depression, and anxiety. *Motivation and Emotion, 4,* 175.

Schwartz, G.M. & Izard, C.E. (1982). The five-month-old's ability to discriminate adult facial expressions of emotions. Unpublished manuscript.

Schwartz, G.M., Ansul, S.E., & Izard, C.E. (1982, March). Facial and cardiac responses to novel stimuli. Paper presented at International Conference on Infancy, Austin, TX.

Seiden, L.S., Brown, R.M., & Lewy, A.J. (1973). Brain catecholamines and conditioned behavior: Mutual interactions. In H.C. Sabelli (Ed.), *Chemical modulation of brain function.* New York: Raven Press.

Seligman, M.E.P. & Hager, J.L. (1972). *Biological boundaries of learning.* New York: Appleton-Century-Crofts.

Selye, H. (1979). The stress concept and some of its implications. In V. Hamilton & D.M. Warburton (Eds.), *Human stress and cognition.* New York: Wiley.

Shiller, V.M., Izard, C.E., & Hembree, E.A. (1986). Patterns of emotion expression during separation in the strange-situation procedure. *Developmental Psychology, 22*(3), 378–382.

Shute, C.C.D. (1973). Cholinergic pathways of the brain. In L.V. Laitinen & K.E. Livingston (Eds.), *Surgical approaches in psychiatry.* Baltimore: University Park Press.

Shute, C.C.D. & Lewis, P.R. (1967a). The cholinergic limbic system: Projections to hippocampal formation, medial cortex, nuclei of the ascending cholinergic reticular system, and the subfornical organ and supraoptic crest. *Brain, 90,* 521–540.

Shute, C.C.D. & Lewis, P.R. (1967b). The ascending cholinergic reticular system: Neocortical, olfactory, and subcortical projections. *Brain, 90,* 497–520.

Sigg, E.B. (1975). The organization and functions of the central sympathetic nervous system. In L. Levi (Ed.), *Emotions: Their parameters and measurement* (pp. 93–122). New York: Raven Press.

Simner, M.L. (1971). Newborn's response to the cry of another infant. *Development Psychology, 5,* 136–150.

Snyder, S.H. (1980). Brain peptides as neurotransmitters. *Science, 209,* 976–983.

Sogon, S. & Izard, C.E. (1985). Ability to recognize emotion in normal and mentally retarded Japanese children. *Japanese Psychological Research, 27*(3), 125–132.

Spencer, H. (1890). *The principles of psychology,* Vol. I. New York: Appleton. (Original work published 1855.)

Sroufe, L.A. & Wunsch, J.P. (1972). The development of laughter in the first year of life. *Child Development, 42,* 1326–1344.

Stechler, G. & Carpenter, G. (1967). A viewpoint on early affective development. In J. Hellmuth (Ed.), *The exceptional infant:* Vol. 1. Seattle: Special Child Publications.

Stellar, E. & Corbit, J.D. (1977). Neural control of motivated behavior. In F.O. Schmitt, G. Adelman, & F.G. Worden (Eds.), *Neurosciences research symposium summaries.* Cambridge, MA: MIT Press, *8* 295–406.

Stotland, E. (1969). Exploratory investigations of empathy. In L. Berkowitz (Ed.), *Advances in experimental social psychology,* Vol. 4. New York: Academic Press.

Strongman, K.T. (1978). *The psychology of emotion.* New York: Wiley.

Swanson, L.W. (1976). The locus coeruleus: A cytoarchitectonic, golgi, and immunohistochemical study in the albino rat. *Brain Research, 110,* 39–56.

Switzer, D.K. (1968). A psychodynamic analysis of grief in the context of an interpersonal theory of self. *Dissertation Abstracts, 29*(13), 381.

Taber, E., Brodal, A., & Walberg, F. (1960). The raphe nuclei of the brain stem in the cat. *Journal of Comparative Neurology, 114,* 161–187, 239–281.

Thomas, A. & Chess, S. (1977). *Temperament and development.* New York: Bruner/Mazel.

Thomas, G.J., Hostetter, G., & Barker, D.J. (1968). Behavioral functions of the limbic system. In E. Stellar & J.M. Sprague (Eds.), *Progress in physiological psychology:* Vol. 2. New York: Academic Press.

Thompson, R. (1978). *A behavioral atlas of the rat brain.* New York: Oxford University Press.

Thompson, W.C., Cowan, C.L., & Rosenhan, D.L. (1980). Focus of attention mediates the impact of negative effect on altruism. *Journal of Personality and Social Psychology, 48,* 291–300.

Tinbergen, N. (1952). "Derived" activities: Their causation, biological significance, origin and emancipation during evolution. *Quarterly Review of Biology, 27,* 1–32.

Tinbergen, N. (1972). Functional ethology and the human sciences. *Proceedings of the Royal Society* (Lond.), *B1982,* 385–410.

Tomkins, S.S. (1962). *Affect, imagery, and consciousness:* Vol. 1. *The positive effects.* New York: Springer.

Tomkins, S.S. (1963). *Affect, imagery, consciousness:* Vol. 2. *The negative effects.* New York, Springer.

Tomkins, S.S. (1980). Affect as amplification: Some modifications in theory. In R. Plutchik & H. Kellerman (Eds.), *Emotion: Theory, research, and experience:* Vol. 1. New York: Academic Press.

Tomkins, S.S. (1981). The role of facial response in the experience of emotion: A reply to Tourangeau & Ellsworth. *Journal of Personality and Social Psychology, 40,* 355–357.

Tomkins, S.S. & McCarter, R. (1964). What and where are the primary affects? Some evidence for a theory. *Perceptual and Motor Skills, 18,* 119–158.

Tourangeau, R. & Ellsworth, P. (1979). The role of facial response in the experience of emotion. *Journal of Personality and Social Psychology, 37,* 1519–1531.

Vaughn, K.B. & Lanzetta, J.T. (1980). Vicarious instigation and conditioning of facial expressive and autonomic responses to a model's expressive display of pain. *Journal of Personality and Social Psychology, 38,* 909–923.

Von Cranach, M. & Vine, I. (Eds.). (1973). *Social communication and movement. Studies of interaction and expression in man and chimpanzee.* London: Academic Press.

Walters, R.H. & Parke, R.D. (1965). The role of distance receptors in the development of social responsiveness. *Advances in Child Development and Behavior, 2,* 59–96.

Washburn, R.W. (1929). A study of the smiling and laughing of infants in the first year of life. *Genetic Psychology Monographs, 6*(5), 397–535.

Waters, E., Wippman, J., & Sroufe, L.A. (1979). Attachment, positive affect, and competence in the peer group: Two studies in construct validation. *Child Development, 50,* 821–829.

Weisenfeld, A.R. & Klorman, R. (1978). The mother's psychophysiological reactions to contrasting affective expressions by her own and an unfamilar infant. *Development Psychology, 14,* 294–304.

Weitz, S. (Ed.). (1974). *Nonverbal communication.* New York: Oxford University Press.

White, B.L., Castle, P., & Held, R. (1964). Observations on the development of visually-directed reaching. *Child Development, 35,* 349–364.

Winton, W.M. (1986). The role of facial response in self-reports of emotion: A critique of Larid. *Journal of Personality and Social Psychology, 50,* 808–812.

Wolfgang, A. (1979). *Nonverbal behavior: Applications and cultural implications.* New York: Academic Press.

Woods, J.W. (1956). 'Taming' of the wild Norway rat by rhinencephalic lesions. *Nature, 178,* 869.

Wundt, W.W. (1907). *Outlines of psychology* (C.H. Judd, trans.). New York: Stechert.

Wurtman, E.B. (1971). Brain monamines and endocrine function. *Neuroscience Research Program Bulletin, 9,* 171–172.

Young-Browne, G., Rosenfeld, H.M., & Horowitz, F.D. (1977). Infant discrimination of facial expressions. *Child Development, 48,* 555–562.

Zahn-Waxler, C., Radke-Yarrow, M., & King, R.A. (1979). Child rearing and children's prosocial initiations toward victims of distress. *Child Development, 50,* 319–330.

Zajonc, R.B. (1980). Feeling and thinking: Preferences need no inferences. *American Psychologist, 35,* 151–175.

Zeman, W. & King, F.A. (1958). Tumors of the septum pellucidum and adjacent structures with abnormal affective behavior: An anterior midline structure syndrome. *Journal of Nervous and Mental Disorders, 127,* 490–502.

Zivin, G. (Ed.). (1985). Separating the issue in the study of expressive development. In G. Zivin (Ed.), *The development of expressive behavior.* Orlando, FL: Academic Press.

Zuckerman, M., Klorman, R., Larrance, D.T., & Spiegel, N.H. (1981). Facial, autonomic, and subjective components of emotion: The facial feedback hypothesis versus the externalizer-internalizer distinction. *Journal of Personality and Social Psychology, 41,* 929–944.

Chapter 13

BEHAVIORAL GENETICS

Gerald E. McClearn, *The Pennsylvania State University*

Terryl T. Foch, *Danville, California*

INTRODUCTION

The chapter by C.S. Hall on "The Genetics of Behavior" in the first edition of this *Handbook* was a significant development in the history of behavioral genetics. Not only did it provide a valuable review of a literature that was scattered hither and yon, but also, by its inclusion in a work describing the pillars of experimental psychology, it conferred a legitimacy and relevance on an area of study that had previously been unacceptable to the mainstream of social and behavioral sciences.

Hall's chapter cited 52 studies providing evidence that heredity had an influence on a variety of behavioral traits including spontaneous activity, sound-induced seizures, social dominance, and learning ability. A substantial part of the existing empirical work was included in this comprehensive review. It was thus indeed quite possible for a scholar to grasp the whole of the field. In the more than 30 years since the publication of the *Handbook*, research has increased exponentially, formal training programs have educated specialist scholars, textbooks have appeared, courses have been designed, a journal has been established, special programs have been organized at national and international meetings of behavioral and social scientists, and an international organization, the Behavior Genetics Association, has been founded and is flourishing.

Although behavioral genetics might, at first consideration, be regarded as a narrow specialty, the implications arising from the focusing of genetic theories and principles on behavioral issues and the empirical corpus of knowledge about the genetics of behavior that has been generated have significant implications for all branches of behavioral science.

The objective of this chapter is therefore emphatically not to provide a comprehensive review, which would be impossible in any case. It is rather to provide the conceptual framework that behavioral genetics offers to the behavioral sciences. Some basic genetics must be presented in this process, and the principles will be illustrated by behavioral examples. It is our hope

that this approach will present the reader with
the background to understand the future developments in behavioral genetics, as well as a
sampling of the current knowledge base, which
is rapidly changing. The reader seeking more
details of this current literature should consult
one or more of several textbooks (Ehrman &
Parsons, 1981; Fuller & Simmel, 1983; Fuller &
Thompson, 1960, 1978; Dixon & Johnson, 1980;
McClearn & DeFries, 1973; Plomin, DeFries, &
McClearn, 1980; Thiessen, 1972; Vale, 1980), or
review chapters (DeFries & Plomin, 1978; Henderson, 1982; Wimer & Wimer, 1985), in addition
to the journal *Behavior Genetics*.

A HISTORICAL PERSPECTIVE

The generation of knowledge is a cumulative
enterprise, and scientists have been characterized as standing on their predecessors'
shoulders, while providing their own shoulders
as platforms for their successors. For this reason
alone, it is justified to examine the history of a
subject matter—not just the recent history as
exemplified in contemporary periodicals, but
the earlier thought on the topic as well. In doing
so, we often find that earlier scholars had some
remarkable insights, though described in archaic terminology, based on methods we now
regard as flawed and analyzed by methods that
were, by our present standards, totally inadequate. Rather than proceeding in regular leaps
of progression, the organized thought about a
subject often undergoes gradual metamor-
phosis. Instead of a uniform advance along the
entire front, one finds salients that represent
sharp thrusts of knowledge acquisition. Some of
these salients may develop for a time, then halt
and become stale history. Some may be reac-
tivated when a discovery elsewhere removes a
block to progress. Thus a view of the history of
a field can often provide signposts to its future.

Some of the salients are real breakthroughs,
and we shall consider some of these vista-open-
ing discoveries here. The basic Mendelian laws
were such a contribution, as was the generalization of these laws to continuously variable
traits. These ideas, extended and expanded, are
the heart of behavioral genetics today. The discovery of the nature of the genetic material and
of the ways in which genes exert their influence
constitutes another ideational revolution whose

effects, not yet fully felt in behavioral genetics,
are certain to mold the field's future in a major
way.

Classical Philosophers

It is very likely the case that the origins of
individual differences were pondered in prehis-
toric times. For early recorded expression of
opinion on the matter, we may turn, naturally
enough, to the great Greek philosophers. Theog-
nis (Roper, 1913, p. 32), in the sixth century B.C.,
provided one of the earliest commentaries. He
clearly believed in the transmission of behavioral
propensities from generation to generation, and
he expressed a certain amount of outrage at
social mores that could lead to undesirable
consequences:

> We seek well-bred rams and sheep and horses
> and one wishes to breed from these. Yet a good
> man is willing to marry an evil wife, if she
> brings him wealth; nor does a woman refuse to
> marry an evil husband who is rich. For men
> reverence money, and the good marry the evil,
> and the evil the good. Wealth has confounded
> the race (1913, p. 32).

We find Plato somewhat later (Davis, 1849),
in designing his Republic, to believe similarly:

> It necessarily follows . . . from what has been
> acknowledged, that the best men should as
> often as possible form alliances with the best
> women, and the most depraved men, on the
> contrary, with the most depraved women, and
> the offspring of the former is to be educated, but
> not of the latter, if the flock is to be of the most
> perfect kind . . . ,p. 144.

Lucretius' comments (see Hutchins, 1952),
made about 50 B.C., are particularly pertinent,
because he made a distinction with which we are
still contending today; he identified as conceptually distinct entities the influence of teaching
and the basic nature of the person:

> And thus it is with mankind: however much
> teaching renders some equally refined, it yet
> leaves behind those earliest traces of the nature
> of each mind; and we are not to suppose that
> evil habits can be so thoroughly plucked up by
> the roots, that one man shall not be more prone
> than another to keen anger, a second shall not
> be somewhat more quickly assailed by fear, a

third shall not take some things more meekly than is right. In many other points there must be differences between the varied natures of men and the tempers which follow upon these . . . p. 34.

Lucretius had a definite bias in his estimate of the relative importance of teaching and nature, however, as can be perceived in his parting remark on this subject:

> What herein I think I may affirm is this: traces of the different natures left behind, which reason is unable to expel from us, are so exceedingly slight that there is nothing to hinder us from living a life worthy of gods. p. 34.

Another example of thought on the subject of heredity can be cited from the works of the renowned humanist, Montaigne, who confessed (see Hutchins, 1952) himself to be amazed at the process of inheritance:

> We need not trouble ourselves to seek out foreign miracles and difficulties; methinks, amongst the things we ordinarily see, there are such incomprehensible wonders as surpass all difficulties of miracles. What a wonderful thing it is that the drop of seed from which we are produced should carry in itself the impression not only of the bodily form, but even of the thoughts and inclinations of our fathers! Where can that drop of fluid matter contain that infinite number of forms? and how can they carry on these resemblances with so temerarious and irregular a progress that the son shall be like his great-grandfather, the nephew like his uncle? p. 367.

The Nineteenth Century Context

The second half of the nineteenth century was a time of revolution in the natural sciences. Of particular relevance to our present topic were the contributions of Francis Galton and Gregor Mendel—two scholars who could hardly have been more unlike in professional lifestyles and visibility but whose contributions provide the fundaments for our present conceptualizations of behavioral genetics.

Galton

Francis Galton was a cousin of Charles Darwin, sharing as grandfather the illustrious Erasmus

Darwin. While Darwin slowly and methodically consolidated his overwhelming case for evolution, Galton scintillated on the stage of Victorian science, conducting exploratory expeditions to Africa, inventing a printing telegraph, periscope, and other devices, playing a founder's role in the social sciences of sociology, anthropology and psychology, establishing fingerprinting as a mode of personal identification, making pioneering contributions to meteorology, and engaging in a wide variety of other activities (see Pearson, 1924).

Of particular importance to the present topic were Galton's contributions to the development of statistics, his insistence on the importance of quantification and measurement, and his development of methods for approaching issues of human genetics.

Basically, Galton was enchanted by human variability. He realized that the systematic study of this variability would require the sorts of quantification and measurement that had contributed to the success of the physical sciences. He therefore sought methods for measuring a wide variety of sensory, motor, and cognitive processes. The "Galton whistle" was devised to assess upper frequency limits of hearing; standardized presentation of printed text at different distances anticipated later tests of visual acuity; he also devised procedures and equipment for the measurement of color vision, touch, smell, weight, verticality, length, and memory span. Furthermore, he employed questionnaires to study mental imagery and the association of ideas.

The basic notions of descriptive statistics were in the early stages of development. Quetelet's law of deviation from an average, which we now know as the normal curve, had recently been introduced to the scientific world. Galton contributed the measures of medians and percentiles as ways of characterizing central tendency and distribution. His premier contribution, however, was with respect to the measurement of association between traits. The physical sciences had made spectacular progress, but it was not possible directly to apply physical science procedures to behavioral science. In particular, it was not always possible to devise a system in which cause and effect relationships could be laid bare with the clarity possible in Newtonian physics. In many behavioral science phenomena, there appeared to be a host of determinant or causal factors, many of which could not even be identified, much less measured. It was for dealing with this kind of situation, the situation of partial or incomplete determination, that Galton sought methods for expressing the degree to which two attributes or characteristics might vary together. The consequence of his deliberations on this topic was the development of the concepts of regression and correlation that have, of course, become major methodological approaches in behavioral and social sciences. It is also a fundamental concept in dealing with the inheritance of quantitatively graded characteristics.

A specific methodology for human genetics was also developed by Galton, who proposed the comparison of twins as a means of assessing the relative influences of "nature" and "nurture." He accepted the theory that there were two types of twins: Those of one-egg and of two-egg origin (Galton, 1883), but this distinction was not paramount in the logic of his analysis. In an empirical study based on questionnaires, biographical, and autobiographical information, Galton observed that those twins originally dissimilar did not seem to become more alike as they grew older (which could be taken as an indication of the effects of a common environment), nor did those originally highly similar become less so through diverse experiences. The evidence was largely anecdotal, and it is clear that there was much room for subjectivity in judging original twin similarity or the degree of diversity of environments. Nevertheless, Galton (1883, p. 241) concluded, in his typically vigorous style, that:

> There is no escape from the conclusion that nature prevails enormously over nurture when the differences of nurture do not exceed what is commonly to be found among persons of the same rank of society and in the same country. My fear is, that my evidence may seem to prove too much, and be discredited on that account, as it appears contrary to all experience that nurture should go for so little.

Whereas the relative strength of heredity might be claimed from observations such as Galton had made, the way in which heredity worked was only very dimly perceived. The predominant theory of the time was *pangenesis*, which decreed

that each part of the body gave off some factor or essence that in some fashion was distilled in the germ cells and transmitted to offspring. It was a theory or group of theories that explained some of the phenomena of transmission of attributes from generation to generation but left many phenomena unexplained. In fact, of course, it was quite wrong. The theory that illuminated the process of heredity with brilliant clarity had already been published but remained unheralded for many years until its rediscovery in 1900 launched the modern science of genetics. One wonders what Galton and his colleagues could have accomplished had their intellectual armament been enriched by the contents of a brief report by an obscure monk from Brunn, Moravia.

Mendel

In striking contrast to the effervescent career of Galton, Gregor Mendel lived the life of a quiet scholar and administrator of a monastery. He conducted research on the pea plant in the garden of the monastery and addressed his concern to the description of the results of breeding plants of different attributes. This approach, of course, was a standard one, and volumes had been written itemizing and detailing the particular results of various kinds of crosses within and between various species of plants. Mendel's unique contribution was to enumerate the results and to subject them to a form of mathematical analysis.

The basic Mendelian rules of inheritance, like many other major scientific discoveries, are elegantly simple. This is not to say, of course, that the field of genetics is without its complexities. The search for detailed understanding of the mode of transmission of hereditary factors and the basis of their effect has led investigators far into the realms of cytology, embryology, physiology, biochemistry, and mathematics. However, the fundamentals of Mendelism were established without knowledge of the physical or chemical nature of the hereditary material or its mechanism of action, and it is still convenient to introduce the topic of genetics by treating the hereditary determinants simply as hypothetical factors. The purpose of the next section is to provide such an introduction and to describe the evidence that has accumulated on the role of Mendelian factors in influencing behavior.

THE MENDELIAN RULES

Consider a hypothetical trait to be determined by a hereditary factor or *gene* that exists in two alternative forms (called *alleles*): *A* and *a*. A given individual will possess two alleles, one derived from its mother and one from its father. The genes exist in a linear array, like beads on a string, on the *chromosomes*. The specific address of a gene on a chromosome is its *locus*. There can be, therefore, three kinds of individual, as far as this particular allelic pair is concerned: *AA*, *Aa* and *aa*. Individuals possessing identical alleles (*AA* and *aa*) are known as *homozygotes*; individuals possessing unlike alleles (*Aa*) are called *heterozygotes*. The distinction made between the hereditary constitution, or *genotype*, and the observed trait, or *phenotype*, is of importance because the relationship between genotype and phenotype is not invariant. For some phenotypes the relationship to genotype is an *additive* one.

The meaning of additivity in this context may be seen in Figure 13.1. In this figure, genotypes are ordered from left to right in terms of the number of *A* alleles they possess, (0, 1, or 2), and phenotypic values are represented as increasing from bottom to top. The phenotypic difference attributable to having one *A* allele instead of none is shown by bracket Y, and the phenotypic difference consequent upon having two *A* alleles rather than one is shown by bracket X. In an additive system, as here, X = Y, and the total phenotypic difference between no *A* alleles and two *A* alleles is simply X + Y. Another way of expressing this, of course, is to note that the relationship is linear, the points representing phenotypic values being arrayed in a straight line.

For some phenotypes, as illustrated in Figure 13.2, the relationship to genotype is not a linear, additive one. In this example, the effect of one *A* allele is as great as the effect of two. Because the *a* allele has no apparent influence in the heterozygous condition (*Aa*), it is said to be *recessive* to the *A* allele. Alternatively, the *A* allele is said to be *dominant* over the *a* allele. The phenotypes studied by Mendel in his classical researches and much of the early work that extended Mendel's laws to a variety of phenotypes and a variety of species were concerned with dominant-recessive systems of this type.

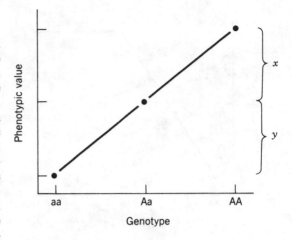

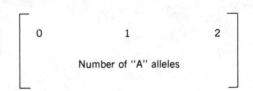

Figure 13.1 The relationship of genotype at a single hypothetical locus to phenotypic value under the condition of additive gene action.

The additive or dominant-recessive relationships are not the only ones possible. Any number of intermediate, *partially dominant* situations can be described in which the phenotypic value of the heterozygote is not exactly halfway between the phenotypic values of the homozygotes, but is not equal to either of them. Another conceivable circumstance is that of *overdominance* in which the heterozygote's phenotypic value lies outside the range of the homozygotes' values.

In the process of reproduction, the parents, although themselves possessing two alleles each of a given gene, can transmit but one each to their offspring. If the parent is a homozygote, it is of no consequence which of the identical alleles is transmitted; in effect, this parent can make only one kind of germ cell, or *gamete*, with respect to that particular gene. In the case of heterozygotes, two kinds of gamete can be produced. Consider the mating of a heterozygous *Aa* male with a heterozygous *Aa* female.

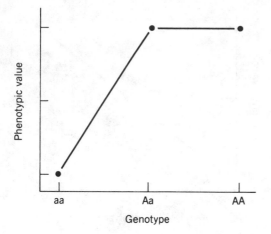

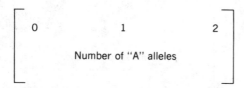

Figure 13.2. The relationship of genotype at a single hypothetical locus to phenotypic value under the condition of dominant gene action.

Half of the female's eggs will have an *A* allele and half will have an *a* allele. Similarly, half of the sperm of the male will contain an *A* and half will contain an *a* allele. An important Mendelian principle is that these alleles will unite randomly; there is, for example, no greater tendency for an *A* bearing sperm to fertilize an *A* bearing egg than an *a* bearing egg. Under these circumstances of random gamete union, the offspring genotypes that can be generated by mating of heterozygotes can be represented as in Table 13.1.

The four cells of the table contain the genotypes of the offspring that would result from the

Table 13.1. Genotypes produced by mating of two heterozygotes.

		Allele in egg	
		A	a
Allele in sperm	A	AA	Aa
	a	Aa	aa

union of the sperm of that row and the egg of that column. It is immaterial whether a heterozygote has received its *A* allele, say, from its mother or from its father, so the two heterozygous classes are indistinguishable. Thus, in matings of this type we may expect three genotypic classes of offspring, with equal numbers of the two kinds of homozygotes and twice as many heterozygotes, on the average. If the system involves dominance, however, it will not be possible to distinguish the heterozygotes from one of the homozygotes, so that the classic Mendelian phenotypic ratio of 3 : 1 will be observed.

Just as alleles of the same gene are independent of each other in *segregation* during gamete formation, so are different genes independent of each other (with some important exceptions to be described later). Consider two separate genes, each of which exists in two allelic forms: *A* and *a*; *B* and *b*. Let us examine the segregation process of an individual who is heterozygous for both genes. Such an individual is referred to as a double heterozygote, or *dihybrid*. In forming any particular gamete, the *A* or *a* allele is equally likely to be "selected." If the outcome of *A-a* segregation has no influence on *B-b* segregation, the *B* or *b* allele is equally likely to be selected for that half of the gametes containing *A* and also for that half of the gametes containing *a*. The consequence is indicated in Table 13.2. It may be seen that a dihybrid can generate four kinds of gamete, and that these four kinds will occur with equal frequency. Now, the gametes themselves, the eggs and the sperm, do not display the phenotypes with which we are concerned. The independent segregation (or independent assortment, as it is often termed) is revealed in the phenotypes of offspring. To illustrate this point, consider the possible outcome of a mating between dihybrids as shown in Table 13.3.

Table 13.2. Gametes produced by independent segregation at two loci.

A-a segregation	B-b segregation	gametes
A	B	AB
	b	Ab
a	B	aB
	b	ab

Table 13.3. Progeny arising from a dihybrid mating.

		Gametes producible by female parent			
		AB	Ab	aB	ab
Gametes	AB	AABB	AABb	AaBB	AaBb
producible	Ab	AABb	AAbb	AaBb	Aabb
by male	aB	AaBB	AaBb	aaBB	aaBb
parent	ab	AaBb	Aabb	aaBb	aabb

Although sixteen cells occur in this table, inspection will reveal that there are some duplicate entries, so that this type of mating can generate nine different genotypes in the indicated relative ratios:

1	AABB
2	AABb
1	AAbb
2	AaBB
4	AaBb
2	Aabb
1	aaBB
2	aaBb
1	aabb

If each genotype resulted in a distinct phenotype, these ratios would be directly observable. The actually observed phenotypic ratios from a dihybrid cross will depend upon dominance relationships, of course, since dominance can make some genotypes indistinguishable from others.

The above model was meant to illustrate independent assortment of two different genes. It is clear that, even with only two genes involved, a great amount of diversity can result. Given estimates that human beings may possess on the order of 100,000 genes (Stern, 1973; Watson, Tooze, & Kurtz, 1983), the power of Mendelian segregation in creating individuality may be appreciated.

The model to this point has assumed, in addition to independent segregation and transmission, that the two gene pairs were independent in effect. Further complications may arise when the effect of the allelic combination for one gene is dependent upon the allelic state of affairs of another gene. Just as dominance represents interaction between alleles of a given gene, these situations, described as *epistatic*, are interactions between different genes.

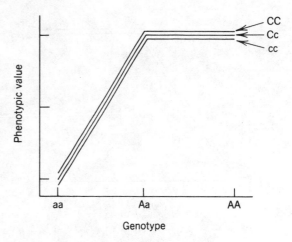

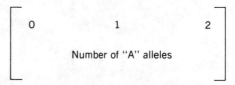

Figure 13.3. The absence of epistasis between two hypothetical loci, A/a and C/c.

In order to illustrate epistasis in graphic form, it is convenient first to illustrate its absence, as in Figure 13.3. The phenotypic values of genotypes *AA*, *Aa*, and *aa* are displayed separately for individuals who are *CC*, *Cc*, and *cc*. The functions overlap completely, being separated only for convenience of display, showing that the effect of the *A-a* gene is independent of the *C-c* gene. In Figure 13.4, however, it may be seen that, whereas possession of the *DD* or *Dd* genotype does not influence the effect of the *A-a* gene, the latter is completely overridden by the *dd* genotype. Various other types of epistasis can be imagined and have indeed been observed. Our present purpose does not require any more detailed examination of intergene interaction, however.

The foregoing has been a brief account of some of the principal features of transmission and manifest effects of single genes. In such a short space, of course, nothing approaching completeness can be claimed. This background will permit us to turn now to some behavioral examples, however. Further examinations of Mendelian concepts will be undertaken, as

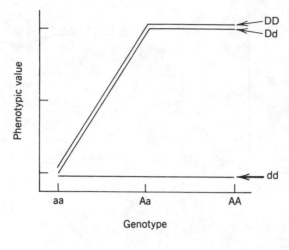

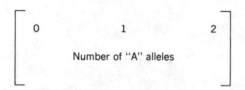

Figure 13.4. Epistasis between two hypothetical loci.

required for the understanding of particular problems.

THE EARLY POST-MENDELIAN PERIOD: FASHIONING THE TOOLS FOR ANIMAL RESEARCH

The rediscovery of the Mendelian principles in 1900 was followed by widespread attempts to determine their generality. In this quest, a variety of phenotypes was examined to determine if differences conformed to the Mendelian rules. Among the phenotypes investigated were behavioral ones. In animal research, the earliest example is the phenotype of "waltzing" in mice. This behavior, characterized by circling and head shaking, had been known to mouse fanciers for some time and in 1898, Von Guita, slightly before the rediscovery of the Mendelian laws, attempted to clarify its inheritance with inconclusive results. Just six years later, Darbishire (1904) was able to examine this phenotype from the Mendelian view. We now know that a single major locus does determine the waltzing phenotype, but, being misled by reduced viability of

the recessive homozygotes, Darbishire judged that the departure of the results from the expected 3:1 ratio indicated that Mendelian inheritance was not at work.

In the ensuing years there were numerous attempts to identify single loci that influence behavior, but these attempts were generally inconclusive, largely because the phenotypes of interest from the behavioral perspective tended to be continuously distributed rather than dichotomous. The methods for dealing with these continuously distributed characteristics were just in process of being worked out; indeed there existed for some considerable time uncertainty as to whether completely different sets of laws of inheritance applied to the continuous as compared with the dichotomous variables.

It was perceived that if two separate breeding groups, maintained under the same laboratory conditions, displayed differences in behavior it was likely that hereditary factors were involved. Such groups were at hand in the form of differing, more-or-less closed, breeding populations of animals in different laboratories, or in some cases, within the same laboratory. The temperament of rats (Utsurikawa, 1917; Yerkes, 1913) and mice (Coburn, 1922; Dawson, 1932) attracted the attention of early workers using this sort of approach. The conclusions were that these phenotypes were, indeed, heritable, and that multiple genetic factors were involved.

During the same period, there were several investigations on rodent learning behavior. The first reported was that of Basset (1914) who compared rats of the Wistar (a strain that was then in process of being inbred) with random-bred rats on performance in a circular maze task and in a problem box task. Slight inferiority of the Wistar animals relative to the random-bred rats was described. A similar conclusion was reached by Yerkes (1916) in a brightness discrimination task.

In the same year, Bagg (1916) described his results with a group of albino and a group of colored mice tested in two learning situations: two-choice position discrimination and multiple-choice. Very substantial differences were found, with the pigmented animals being poor learners.

Five years later, Vicari (1921) reported results from a study using an adaptation of the maze utilized by Bagg and compared the Bagg albino strain with a group of Japanese waltzer mice.

Each of these strains had been inbred for nine or more years; it was appreciated that this inbreeding would result in an increasing genetic uniformity within the strains, with the consequence that they would be superior for this type of research to the unsystematically maintained stocks. The Bagg albino animals ran the maze much more quickly than the Japanese waltzers, and the F_1 hybrid animals showed superior performance not only on the running time but also with respect to errors.

These comparisons of behavior of different groups of animals were pointing the way to a methodology that has played a major role in behavioral genetics. However, at the time, neither adequate animal strains nor adequate theory and methodology were available to make the most of the method. This pioneering research did have the effect, however, of making clear that hereditary factors were indeed influential on an array of continuously distributed behavioral characteristics.

At about the same time, in 1924, the eminent learning theorist Edward Tolman became the first to apply another powerful tool to the study of the genetics of behavior. Just as it was understood that reproductively distinct groups would differ genetically and that inbreeding within the groups would lead to increasing genetic homo-

geneity, it was understood also that mating together animals of like phenotype over successive generations would have the effect of concentrating an increasing percentage of alleles making for the desired expression of the phenotype in the stock being so selectively bred. Selective breeding, of course, had been practiced since prehistory in the domestication of animals. Furthermore, animal fanciers had employed selective breeding techniques to develop special varieties of animals, and, indeed, Darwin's arguments concerning natural selection were buttressed in part by evidence of the enormous variety of pigeons that had been so generated. That Tolman appreciated the potential of this method is clear from his introductory paragraph:

The problem of this investigation might appear to be a matter of concern primarily for the geneticist. Nonetheless, it is also one of very great interest to the psychologist. For could we, as geneticists, discover the complete genetic mechanism of a character such as maze-learning ability—i.e., how many genes it involves, how these segregate, what their linkages are, etc.—we would necessarily, at the same time, be discovering what psychologically, or behavioristically, maze-learning ability may be said to be made up of, what component abilities it contains, whether these vary independently of one

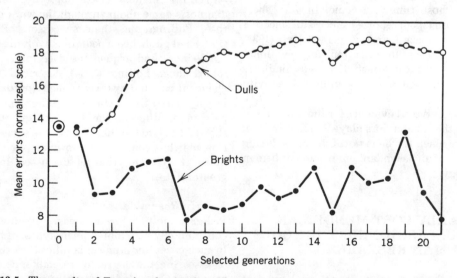

Figure 13.5. The results of Tryon's selective breeding for maze brightness and maze dullness. (From data provided through the courtesy of R.C. Tryon.) From "The Inheritance of Behavior" by G.E. McClearn, 1962, in *Psychology in the Making* (p. 213), L. Postman (ed.), New York: Random House. Copyright 1962 by Random House. Reprinted by permission.

another, what their relations are to other measurable abilities, as, say, sensory discrimination, nervousness, etc. The answers to the genetic problem require the answers to the psychological, while at the same time, the answers to the former point the way to those of the latter (1924, p. 1).

Although the results of selective breeding were well recognized, the process by which the effects were obtained was just coming to be understood in terms of quantitative genetics at the time of Tolman's research. He experienced some apparent difficulties in the third generation of selection. Perturbations of this type have been experienced in many subsequent selection studies and may simply represent sampling fluctuations or transient environmental effects. Had he persisted, Tolman's project may have succeeded; however, the blame was assigned to the questionable reliability of the maze that had been employed, and the project was turned over to Tryon who generated a highly reliable and automated maze, continued the work, and generated the maze bright and maze dull strains of rats whose descendants are still being studied today. The results from this classic study are shown in Figure 13.5.

The notion of manipulating genes by mating in this fashion and generating lines of animals differing in behavioral attributes was evidently an idea whose time had come. In very short order, Heron (1935) reported successful selective breeding for maze learning in rats, Hall (1938) reported success in selection for emotional defecation, and Rundquist (1933) was similarly successful in selective breeding for activity levels.

The unequivocal evidence for the influence of genes on these behaviors played a major role in holding a place for behavioral genetics during the period of an ascendant environmentalism in psychology.

THE EARLY POST-MENDELIAN PERIOD: FASHIONING THE TOOLS FOR HUMAN RESEARCH

As the methods of animal behavioral genetics were taking shape, other investigators were developing approaches to the study of the inheritance of behavior in human beings. Without the possibility of control of matings, of course, the human researcher must study individuals of varying degrees of genetic relatedness as they are found.

Pedigree Studies

One approach is the study of families in which a particular anomaly occurs. This sort of pedigree analysis was utilized in many early attempts to identify single locus conditions in human behavior. The array of behaviors addressed in this effort is quaint-sounding today—nomadism, harlotry, and so on—and most of the studies came to naught. In one domain, however, then called feeble-mindedness, the continuity of research begun in the 1920s has given rise to an extensive body of knowledge on Mendelian inheritance in what we now label mental retardation.

A classic effort in this field was that of Goddard (1914), who assessed the pattern of distribution of feeble-mindedness in families in terms of the Mendelian expectations. The outcome was rather confused, but Goddard concluded that Mendelian inheritance was, indeed, discernible. Unfortunately, the state of nosology in respect to feeble-mindedness was not well advanced, and Goddard was actually studying a melange of conditions of differing etiology.

The first major breakthrough in differential diagnosis came about through the work of Penrose, Fölling, and their successors. Penrose (1934) had published a pedigree involving feeble-mindedness and argued the case for recessive inheritance. Fölling (1934) described a biochemical peculiarity (excess phenylpyruric acid in the urine) in a retarded brother and sister pair in a different family. Subsequent work showed the two families to have the same condition that has come to be known as phenylketonuria (PKU) and that is discussed later in greater detail.

Family Resemblance

Pedigree methods are not easily applicable to continuously distributed phenotypes, of course. In such cases, the study of families took the form of assessing the degree of resemblance among relatives. Galton's invention of regression and correlation anayses was extended and applied vigorously by Pearson and others in a series of researches. There remained skepticism that

Mendelian principles could be applied to continuously distributed traits, and the interpretation of the obtained correlations among relatives was made on other grounds entirely.

Subsequent research was able to use more objective and standardized measures of intellectual performance. Starch (1917), for example, obtained sibling correlations for a variety of cognitive variables. The logic in this case was to compare resemblance for traits judged *a priori* to be susceptible to environmental (educational) influence (arithmetical and reading ability, spelling proficiency, and vocabulary) with those judged less susceptible to these influences (tapping rate, canceling of A's). The correlations were about the same, and Starch concluded that hereditary forces were equally important for these two classes of phenotype.

Later, Thorndike (1928) also compared sibling resemblance on several physical traits and intelligence, and also used Pearson's value (.52 $\pm$ .016) as an empirical benchmark of the degree of resemblance for traits free from environmental influence. It was found that resemblance for intelligence was somewhat higher than for physical traits, and it was concluded that the difference reflected the effects of environment.

One abiding problem with family resemblance studies is the difficulty of disentangling genetic from environmental sources of covariance. Just as parent and offspring or siblings share genes, so do they share environments. Thus, the study of correlations among members of conventional families really examines what might be called familiality. A degree of familiality is necessary for an interpretation either of genetic or of environmental transmission but, without other evidence, is insufficient to be conclusive about either.

Twin Studies

The occurrence of multiple births in the typically monotocous human species was perceived by Galton to provide an opportunity to distinguish between the influence of environment and the influence of heredity. In a catch phrase that is with us still, he spoke of the capability of twin studies to separate "nature from nurture."

The way in which Galton thought this would be accomplished was by examining twin pairs that were alike at birth and those that were unlike at birth.

The next major utilization of twins in behavioral research was undertaken by Thorndike (1905) who used the same basic logic as had Galton, though with cross-sectional rather than longitudinal comparisons. More objective data —efficiency in arithmetic computations, naming word opposites, finding misspelled words, or crossing out letters—were gathered, and a conclusion similar to that of Galton's was reached. Incidentally, the evidence concerning the biology of twinning was sufficiently vague at this time that Thorndike rejected the proposition that there were two basic types of twin.

A long pause then occurred, and it was not until the mid-1920s that the next twin studies appeared; four were then reported within a few years.

In 1924, Merriman described a study of twins in which standardized Stanford-Binet, Army Beta, and National Intelligence Test scores were used. Comparing older (10 to 16 years) with younger (5 to 9) twin pairs revealed no difference in degree of resemblance, as had been the case with Thorndike's data.

Merriman also reopened the issue of twin types, concluded that there were fraternal and duplicate types, and suggested the type of comparison that is the basis of modern twin studies: the greater the difference between the similarity of duplicate pairs and fraternal pairs, the greater the genetic influence.

Shortly thereafter Wingfield (1928) reported a conclusion very similar to Merriman's. A fundamental problem with this new comparison was that of establishing which type of twin was which. The unlike-sex pairs were easy, of course. They had to be fraternals, of two egg origin. However, like-sex pairs could be either fraternal or duplicate (= identical), of single egg origin. The best procedure that could be devised was to segregate the like-sex twins into two categories based upon physical resemblance, establishing a presumptive identical and presumptive fraternal group. Then the groups could be compared for other attributes. So long as the phenotypes used for diagnosis are not causally connected with the ones under study, this procedure escapes circularity of reasoning. A superior method, developed later, involves the comparison of members of the twin pairs on a number of blood protein phenotypes that are known to be due to single loci.

Another problem with the twin method

revolves around one of the assumptions in the
logic. Fraternal twins share half of their segregating alleles, on the average. Identical twins
share 100 percent of their alleles. Differences in
the average similarity of the two groups will
therefore reflect this difference in genetic similarity, if it can be assumed that environmental
factors do not act differentially on the two types.
It was conjectured that identical twins have
more similar environments as well as more similar genotypes than do fraternal twins. To the
extent that those aspects of the environment
that are more shared by identical twins influence the phenotype under investigation, the
method is weakened. Considerable controversy
has surrounded this issue, and there continues a
cautionary attitude in spite of several recent
studies that have suggested that the problem is
not as serious as once was thought to be the case
(Loehlin & Nichols, 1976; Matheny, Wilson, &
Dolan, 1976; Plomin, Willerman, & Locklin,
1976; Scarr & Carter-Saltzman, 1979).

Adoption Studies

Another natural experiment that was identified
as of value in human genetics research was the
existence of families in which offspring were
adopted and thus genetically unrelated to the
rest of the family members. The comparison of
the resemblance of genetically unrelated individuals to the adults who reared them or the
children with whom they were reared with the
resemblance of individuals to their genetically
related fathers, mothers, and siblings should
illuminate the effects of genes and of environments in inducing familial resemblance.

Two major studies utilizing this method were
reported in 1928. The "Chicago Study" (Freeman, Holzinger, & Mitchell, 1928) utilized standardized tests (including the Stanford-Binet and
the Otis Self-Administering Test) in a multifaceted study. In one part, genetic siblings who
were adopted separately were examined, and
their correlations were found to be lower than
the approximate 0.5 value that was by now
expected of siblings reared normally together.

In another aspect of the study, the correlation
between the adopted child and a genetic child in
the same family was found to be 0.34. Similarly, the correlation of genetically unrelated
adoptees reared in the same home was 0.37.
These results were interpreted generally as

displaying the strong influence of rearing
environment.

The "Stanford Study" (Burks, 1928) was
another large and complex project, involving
comparisons of adopted children with adoptive
parents and, in a control group, genetic children
with their genetic parents. Intelligence was
measured by the Stanford-Binet. The correlations of adopted children's IQ with the mental
age of fathers and mothers respectively were
0.07 and 0.19. The correlations of control children with the mental ages of their fathers and
mothers were 0.45 and 0.46. The difference in
magnitude of these coefficients was interpreted
by Burks as strong evidence for the influence of
genetics.

There followed considerable speculation on
the factors that could result in such a difference
in outcome between these two major studies.
The issue has never been completely resolved,
but the discussion identified numerous important issues in the use of the adoption method.

One of the major potential confounding features is that of selective placement. In some
cases, placement agencies may make strong
efforts to place a child in an adoptive home
similar to that of the genetic mother or father or
both. To the extent that these efforts are successful, the null expectation of a correlation of
zero between adoptive parent and child no
longer pertains.

This and other difficulties have been vigorously addressed and to some extent resolved in
more recent years (DeFries & Plomin, 1978), and
the adoption study has emerged as one of the
major tools of human behavioral genetics.

THE MODERN PERIOD

The previous discussion has focused on the first
three decades of this century. During this period
the basic approaches to the study of heredity
and environment in the determination of individual differences in behavior were being laid
down. Work continued apace during the subsequent years, and a substantial fund of knowledge
was gradually built up that demonstrated clearly
that genes could influence a wide variety of
behaviors. As mentioned in the introduction,
the publication of Hall's review (1951) seemed to
legitimize the field as a respectable interdisciplinary domain. The publication of Fuller

and Thompson's textbook in 1960 marked a sharp upturn in research and graduate training. The following review will be principally concerned with the developments that have occurred since that signal event.

Basic Quantitative Genetic Models

One of the most important developments in behavioral genetics has been the assimilation of the quantitative genetic models that had been elaborated in other fields, particularly agricultural genetics, and modifying and extending them for application to behavioral phenotypes.

These models not only are the underpinnings of analytical methods; they represent as well a *Weltanschauung* of behavioral genetics. To gain an understanding of behavioral genetics, it is necessary, therefore, that an appreciation of this basic view be attained. The following is a relatively nontechnical presentation of some of its principal features. It is convenient to begin with a discussion of inbreeding, its consequences, and the utilization of inbred strains and the generations that can be derived from them.

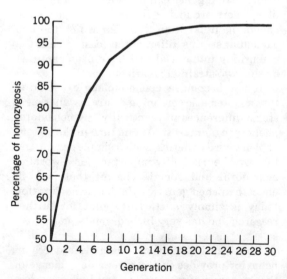

Figure 13.6. Homozygosis in successive generations of sibling mating. From "Experimental Methods in Behavior Genetics" by J.L. Fuller and W.R. Thompson, 1960, in *Behavior Genetics* (p. 82), New York: John Wiley & Sons, Inc. Copyright 1960 by John L. Fuller, Professor Emeritus, State University of New York at Binghamton, P.O. Box 543, York, ME 03909. Adapted by permission.

Table 13.4. Genotypes arising from mating of female and male heterozygotes with all unlike alleles.

		Sperm	
		A3	A4
Eggs	A1	A1A3	A1A4
	A2	A2A3	A2A4

Inbreeding

Because the use of inbred strains has provided such a large part of the data of behavioral genetics, it is important to understand how these strains are formed, exactly what their genetic condition is, and what they can and what they cannot reveal about the genetic basis of behavior.

As was indicated earlier, the effect of mating of relatives is to generate progeny who share more genes than would ordinary progeny of unrelated parents. The effect is cumulative, so that ultimately a condition is approached wherein the progeny are all homozygous in like allelic state for all loci. The rate at which this condition is approached varies with the intensity of inbreeding, being slower, for example, with cousin matings than with sibling matings. For the latter, the course of increasing homozygosity is shown in Figure 13.6.

The algebra of this relationship is beyond the scope of the present chapter, but a simple (though admittedly rather tedious) demonstration can make the principle apparent. Let us begin with one female and one male, each heterozygous and sharing no alleles in common. Thus, her genotype can be expressed as A_1A_2 and his as A_3A_4. With random uniting of gametes, as shown in Table 13.4, they will produce offspring having the genotypes A_1A_3, A_1A_4, A_2A_3, and A_2A_4 in equal numbers.

Now, if we assume that animals of all genotypes in Generation 0 are equally viable, equally fertile, and mate randomly, A_1A_3 can mate with A_1A_3, A_1A_4, A_2A_3, and A_2A_4, and so on. All of the mating types will occur with equal frequency under the random mating assumption. Table 13.5 presents the possibilities. The mating of A_1A_3 with A_1A_3 can produce A_1A_1, A_1A_3, A_3A_1, and A_3A_3 offspring (A_1A_3 and A_3A_1 are the same, of course; they are written differently here simply to record the difference of parental origin of

Table 13.5. Mating types and progeny from one generation of sib-mating.

Mating type (Gen 0)	Generation 1			
Random Matings from Generation 0				
A1A3 × A1A3	*A1A1*	A1A3	A3A1	*A3A3*
A1A3 × A1A4	*A1A1*	A1A4	A3A1	A3A4
A1A3 × A2A3	A1A2	A1A3	A3A2	*A3A3*
A1A3 × A2A4	A1A2	A1A4	A3A2	A3A4
A2A3 × A2A3	*A2A2*	A2A3	A3A2	*A3A3*
A2A3 × A1A3	A2A1	A2A3	A3A1	*A3A3*
A2A3 × A1A4	A2A1	A2A4	A3A1	A3A4
A2A3 × A2A4	*A2A2*	A2A4	A3A2	A3A4
A1A4 × A1A4	*A1A1*	A1A4	A4A1	*A4A4*
A1A4 × A1A3	*A1A1*	A1A3	A4A1	A4A3
A1A4 × A2A3	A1A2	A1A3	A4A2	A4A3
A1A4 × A2A4	A1A2	A1A4	A4A2	*A4A4*
A2A4 × A2A4	*A2A2*	A2A4	A4A2	*A4A4*
A2A4 × A1A3	A2A1	A2A3	A4A1	A4A3
A2A4 × A1A4	A2A1	A2A4	A4A1	*A4A4*
A2A4 × A2A3	*A2A2*	A2A3	A4A2	A4A3

the two alleles). Offspring of these genotypes will occur in equal numbers (the equal viability assumption). Two genotypes in this row are italicized, denoting that they are homozygous. The rest of the table may be similarly interpreted. It can be seen that one generation of sib-mating increases homozygosity from 0 (by definition) to 25 percent.

Similar tables can be constructed for each succeeding generation, in each of which the percentage of homozygosis is greater than in the preceding generation, as shown in Figure 13.6. The ultimate effect of continued sib-mating is to approach asymptotically the condition of homozygosity for all loci. Figure 13.6 shows that, after about 20 consecutive generations of transmitting a strain through a single sibling pair in each generation, F (the proportion of homozygous loci) = 0.99 (Falconer, 1981). It is for this reason that 20 generations is taken as the definitional requirement of an inbred strain.

In the prototypical case, only one sibling pair is chosen from each generation to propagate the strain, and only one strain is developed. Thus, the actual course of F for a single inbred strain in the process of being developed would be more erratic than the smooth function of Figure 13.6, which can be viewed as an average or expected

state of affairs, but it would ultimately arrive at the indicated levels.

We can now see that some of the pioneering work, such as that of Yerkes, Utsurikawa, Dawson, Basset, Bagg, and Vicari, was conducted while the strains they employed were at an intermediate stage of inbreeding. Results of their analyses, which assumed complete homozygosity at all loci in these early lines, could not be expected to provide results valid in detail concerning the genetic parameters; but they did serve well to demonstrate the fact of genetic influence on the behavioral traits they studied and to illustrate the relevance of quantitative genetic models.

The basic logic of inbred strain research is very simple. Clearly, strains inbred independently will become genetically unlike. For any two such strains, we can enumerate certain specific single loci, such as coat color loci, or blood proteins, for which they might differ, but we have no way at present of determining the exact total number and identity of differing loci. If animals of two inbred strains, raised in similar environments and tested by the same method, display a mean difference in a trait, this constitutes evidence that genes can influence the trait. Very likely there are loci that can also influence the phenotype other than those for which the two particular strains differ, but at least some of the potentially influential loci have been captured by this two-strain comparison.

It has become a commonplace expectation that a systematic screening of strains will reveal strain differences in practically any behavioral phenotype of interest. At one time in the history of behavioral genetics, such a simple demonstration was heuristically important for a world of behavioral and social sciences that had, in effect, banished genetics. Such a demonstration today is simply a starting point for further research and has very little dramatic impact *per se.*

The identification of strain differences in behavior provides incontrovertible evidence of the influence of genetic factors. It is of no less interest, however, to observe that substantial variability is usually found *within* the strains. Accepting that all animals within a strain are genetically alike, this variation must be of environmental origin. Given that the circumstances of a well-run colony and laboratory are highly controlled and uniform, this within strain variability is a striking testimony to the power of environmental nuances that have escaped the control of the experimenter. Thus, although inbred strains have not been used much for the purpose, they offer an approach of great potential for the detection of subtle environmental effects.

The fact that these inbred strains can reveal the power both of genetic and of environmental agencies should make it clear that the old simplistic conception that traits were genetic *or* environmental in origin is hopelessly inadequate.

The demonstration of strain differences is actually a fairly low order of genetic information —it shows only that genetic influence exists. Other research is then required to carry the issue forward. One method that has been utilized is a straightforward extension of the classical Mendelian procedure of mating animals from different inbred strains to generate F_1's, F_2's, and their backcrosses, which are derived by mating F_1 hybrids with individuals from the original, inbred lines. The relationship of the means of such groups to the percentage of alleles from each parent is instructive concerning the fact of genetic influence and the dominance relationship (Mather & Jinks, 1971).

But there is much more to be learned from these classical matings than can be determined from the relationship of means to allelic dosage. We have noted already that, because of the genetic uniformity of inbred strains, any variance within them must be due to environmental factors. From the earlier discussion of Mendelian principles, we saw also that the F_1 derived from a mating of parents who were homozygous for different alleles at a locus are uniformly heterozygous, but that segregation gives rise to heterogeneity of genotypes within the F_2. It is not surprising then that comparisons of groups whose variance is a reflection of environmental sources alone to groups with both genetic and environmental variance could be utilized to make inferences about the relative importance of these two sources of variability.

A nontechnical approach to the background for this approach not only will illuminate classical analyses but will serve as well as a foundation for understanding the quantitative genetic model in its other applications.

The Variance Model

In the description of the basic Mendelian phe-
nomena of independent assortment and segregation, consideration was given to two loci affecting different phenotypes. The present example will utilize similar notions but assumes that the two loci affect the *same* trait. Four of the groups identified in Column 1 of Table 13.6 have already been defined, but two, the backcrosses (B_1 and B_2), have not. Backcross progeny are generated from the matings of F_1 animals with one of the homozygous parents.

There are thus two backcrosses, and their genotypic possibilities can be derived by simple extension of the logic presented earlier. The genotypes of all of the groups involved in a classical mating scheme are shown in Column 2. In the case of the F_2, the relative frequencies are shown in parentheses.

In the first model, assume that both loci are acting in an additive fashion, and that each capital letter allele adds one point to the phenotype. We also assume, for the moment only, that environment has no effect whatever.

Individual scores are shown in Column 3, and the means of the various groups are shown in Column 4. Figure 13.7a displays graphically the relationship of these means to the increasing (capital letter) alleles of the different groups. The additivity assumptions built into the model have clearly generated a linear relationship between percentage of plus alleles and phenotypic mean. (See Bruell, 1962, for application of a similar representation.)

There are three groups within the classical analyses that are genetically uniform or, to put the matter in Mendelian terms, are nonsegregating. These groups, the P_1, P_2, and F_1, under our restricting assumption of lack of environmental influence, display zero phenotypic variance. Inspection of the table reveals that the maximum variance is that of the F_2, which has represented within it all of the genotypes that can possibly be generated by segregation and independent assortment of the two alleles at each of these two loci. The backcross groups are less variable than is the F_2, because each has only part of the total number of these possible genotypes. Under our assumption of additivity, the variance of the backcross group is one-half that of the F_2. The variance of the different groups under these restricting assumptions is shown in Column 5 of Table 13.6. We may display the relationship between the variance and the percentage of plus alleles graphically, as in

Table 13.6. Models of quantitative inheritance with two, two-allele loci, and various degrees of dominance and epistasis.

Generation	Genotype(s)	Model: Additive A/a Additive B/b			Model: Dominant A/a Additive B/b			Model: Dominant A/a Dominant B/b			Model: Epistatic		
		Individual Value	Group Mean	Group Variance	Individual Value	Group Mean	Group Variance	Individual Value	Group Mean	Group Variance	Individual Value	Group Mean	Group Variance
P1	aabb	0	0	0	0	0	0	0	0	0	0	0	0
B1	AaBb	2	1	0.5	3	1.5	1.25	4	2	2.0	2	.75	.69
	Aabb	1			2			2			0		
	aaBb	1			1			2			1		
	aabb	0			0			0			0		
F2	AABB (1)	4	2	1	4	2.5	1.25	4	3	1.5	4	1.625	0.41
	AABb (2)	3			3			4			3		
	AAbb (1)	2			2			2			0		
	AaBB (2)	3			4			4			3		
	AaBb (4)	2			3			4			2		
	Aabb (2)	1			2			2			0		
	aaBB (1)	2			2			2			2		
	aaBb (2)	1			1			2			1		
	aabb (1)	0			0			0			0		
F1	AaBb	2	2	0	3	3	0	4	4	0	2	2	0
B2	AABB	4	3	0.5	4	3.5	0.25	4	4	0	4	3	0.5
	AABb	3			3			4			3		
	AaBB	3			4			4			3		
	AaBb	2			3			4			2		
P2	AABB	4	4	0	4	4	0	4	4	0	4	4	0

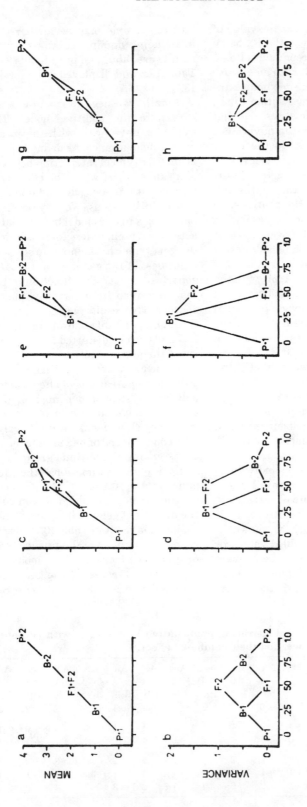

PERCENT P2 ALLELES

Figure 13.7. Relationships among means and variances of parental, F₁, F₂, and backcross generations in a hypothetical two locus situation with varying dominance and epistasis.

Figure 13.7b. Here, the function at the value of 50 percent is bifurcated, because the F_1, being genetically uniform with 50 percent plus alleles, has zero variance, while the F_2, with an *average* of 50 percent plus alleles, has the maximum variance of the groups. The resulting relationship is, however, a systematic and symmetrical one that displays the nonlinear relationship of variance to allelic frequency in contrast to the linear relationship of means to allelic frequency.

For the next step, we observe the consequences if there is some dominance in the system. Let us assume that locus B/b continues to act additively, but that the locus A/a acts in such a fashion that A is dominant over a, so that $AA = 2$, $Aa = 2$ and $aa = 0$. The result of this change in assumptions is to alter the values of the genotypes $AaBB$, $AaBb$, and $Aabb$, with the consequence of altering the means and variances of groups containing those genotypes. Individual phenotypic values under these new assumptions, and the new means and variances, are shown in Columns 6 through 8 of Table 13.6.

The new relationship between allelic frequencies and means under the assumption of dominance at one locus is shown in Figure 13.7c. The mean-allelic dose relationship is now bowed upward, reflecting the effects of dominance, and is bifurcated because of the fact that the F_2 individuals have the effect of dominance in only some of the cases, whereas the F_1 individuals have the influence of dominance in all cases. The symmetry of the relationship of variance to allelic frequency noted in the additive case is distorted under this new model, as shown in Figure 13.7d. From either the tabled values or the figure, it is clear that the variance of every group except the nonsegregating ones has been altered by this degree of dominance in the system.

The example may be further elaborated by introducing dominance now at both loci. The results are tabulated in Columns 9, 10, and 11 of Table 13.6 and displayed graphically in Figures 13.7e and 13.7f.

Finally, we need to examine another departure from the additive model. The previous examples have dealt with the intralocus deviations of dominance. As defined earlier, epistasis is another type of interaction between or among loci said to exist when the effects of allelic differences at one locus depend upon the genotype at some other locus. We may observe the effects of epistasis in our model by postulating an interaction in which, unless there is at least one B in the genotype, the phenotypic score will be zero, regardless of the genotype at the A/a locus. The departures from the functional relationships that pertained in our additive model are even sharper. The results may be seen in Columns 12 through 14 of Table 13.6 and in Figures 13.7g and 13.7h also to be distorted from the neat regularity of the additive situation.

These examples only touch upon some of the possible combinations of effects among loci in a polygenic system influencing a single phenotype, and they have concerned only two loci. However, they should make it intuitively acceptable that comparisons of phenotypic means and variances among the various groups in a classical analysis permit estimation of the effects of dominance and epistasis.

The foregoing model has been constrained to the display of genetic influences only. Our next example, laid out in Table 13.7, adds a postulated random environmental influence to the F_2 of our original two locus, additive model.

In the top two rows, the genotypes of the F_2 are displayed separately by locus. Beneath each

Table 13.7. A hypothetical scheme illustrating quantitative inheritance, with two-allele loci, two sources of environmental influence, and their combined effect.

Locus A-a	aa	aa	aa	Aa	Aa	aa	Aa	Aa	Aa	Aa	AA	Aa	Aa	AA	AA	AA
	0	0	0	1	1	0	1	1	1	1	2	1	1	2	2	2
Locus B-b	bb	Bb	Bb	bb	bb	BB	Bb	Bb	Bb	Bb	bb	BB	BB	Bb	Bb	BB
	0	1	1	0	0	2	1	1	1	1	0	2	2	1	1	2
Environment 1	0	−1	+1	+1	0	−1	−1	−1	+1	+1	0	0	0	0	0	0
Environment 2	0	+1	0	0	+1	−1	0	0	−1	0	+1	+1	−1	0	−1	0
G	0	1	1	1	1	2	2	2	2	2	2	3	3	3	3	4
E	0	0	+1	+1	+1	−2	−1	−1	0	+1	+1	+1	−1	0	−1	0
P	0	1	2	2	2	0	1	1	2	3	3	4	2	3	2	4

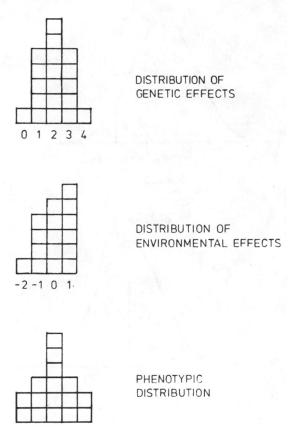

DISTRIBUTION OF
GENETIC EFFECTS

DISTRIBUTION OF
ENVIRONMENTAL EFFECTS

PHENOTYPIC
DISTRIBUTION

Figure 13.8. Distribution of genetic effects, environmental effects, and resulting phenotype in a hypothetical two locus, two environmental sources model.

genotype is given the genotypic value from the additive model of Table 13.6. The next two lines show the effects of two randomly assigned environmental agencies. The effects of these agencies are assumed to add one unit, subtract one unit, or leave unaltered the value generated by the genotype. It can be seen that the magnitude of genetic effects is the same for each locus. The joint distribution is the symmetrical binomial shown in the top of Figure 13.8.

The environmental effects were distributed at random over individuals, as shown in Table 13.7; the random outcome is revealed in the distribution of combined environmental effects in the center of Figure 13.8. The three rows at the bottom of Table 13.7 give respectively: the summed genetic influence, assuming additivity of genetic effects; the summed environmental influence, assuming additivity of environmental

effects; and the final phenotypic values, assuming additivity of genetic and environmental influences. Algebraically, we may describe this situation as one in which the total phenotypic variance (V_P) is the sum of a genetic variance (V_G) and an environmental variance (V_E):

$$V_P = V_G + V_E.$$

A figural representation of the phenotypic distribution is given at the bottom of Figure 13.8.

In this particular example, the contributions of the environmental and genetic sources are equal in generating this distribution. Thus, V_G/V_P, which describes the proportion of the phenotypic variance attributable to genetic sources and which is one measure of heritability, is 0.5; similarly, environmentality, $V_E/V_P = 0.5$.

This example has described the simplest case involving multiple genes and multiple environments (two each) in assuming random environmental effects, and with all effects being additive.

If we were to consider a situation in which environmental effects were not distributed randomly, but were biased so that, say, individuals with higher genotypic values were more likely to encounter favorable environments, then a covariance term must be added to the formulation:

$$V_P = V_G + V_E + 2\,CovGE.$$

In addition, we have seen in Table 13.6 and Figure 13.7 the sorts of complications that can arise if intralocus nonadditivity (dominance) and interlocus nonadditivity (epistasis) are permitted in the model. We may now contemplate that the environmental influences might interact with one another and that environmental influences might interact with genetic ones. In order to encompass these possibilities, the expression must include interaction terms:

$$V_P = V_G + V_E + 2\,CovGE + V_I + V_{G \times E}.$$

Here, V_I refers to variance associated with interlocus interactions, and $V_{G \times E}$ stands for variance caused by the interactive effects of particular combinations of genotypes and environments.

Referring to classical analyses of inbred strains and generations derived from them, we now can see that the variances of the nonsegregating generations have only the V_E component, whereas the F_2 variance may be constituted of the full complement of variance sources. With the environmental control possible in laboratories, the covariance and $G \times E$ terms can be substantially reduced. If V_I is ignored, then the estimates of V_E can be subtracted from the F_2 variance, leaving V_G. This last value, divided by the V_P, is a rough index of the heritability (h^2). It can be seen immediately that heritability is a descriptive statistic that characterizes a particular population only. In other populations, in another environmental milieu, or with other loci segregating, the result might be different.

We saw previously that the genetic variance can be regarded as consisting of an additive component (V_A) plus an intralocus nonadditive component due to dominance (V_D) plus an interlocus nonadditive component due to epistatic interactions (V_I). Thus,

$$V_G = V_A + V_D + V_I.$$

These distinctions permit another index of heritability in addition to the ratio of V_G to V_P, which we may now characterize as the broad sense heritability (Falconer, 1981). For certain purposes, such as prediction of response to selective breeding, to be discussed next, the narrow sense heritability, V_A/V_P, is a more useful index.

Selective Breeding

We saw earlier that inbreeding is a useful method of manipulation of the genotype. The process of mate assignment is under control of the experimenter, thus qualifying the procedure as manipulation of an independent variable in the conventional sense. However, there are uncertain aspects. The only rule for mate assignment is relatedness, and the two animals chosen as the progenitors for the next generation are chosen essentially at random within this constraint. Furthermore, the outcome of segregation, recombination, and random gamete union add a stochastic element to the procedure. Thus, in inbreeding, the genotype is being manipulated in general, in that homozygosity is increasing, but the specifics of the genotype—which alleles are becoming fixed at which loci—are not within experimental control.

In selective breeding, by contrast, there is a powerful increment in experimental control. As in inbreeding, the manipulation is the assignment of mates. However, in selective breeding, mate assignment is made upon the basis of phenotype. Animals of similar extreme phenotypes are mated, and, as we saw earlier, their offspring tend to have mean scores differing

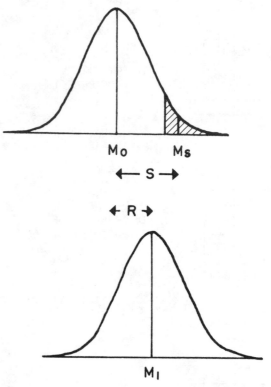

Figure 13.9. A representation of the principal parameters in a selective breeding program: group mean, mean of selected parents, mean of offspring, selection, and response.

from those of their parents' generation. The notion that such mating will result in an increasing number of favorable alleles is intuitively reasonable. The variance model provides more detailed insights into the workings of selective breeding.

The situation is represented in Figure 13.9. The distribution of the to-be-selected phenotype of the foundation population, or zero generation, is shown in the upper figure, with the shaded upper tail of the distribution identifying those individuals selected to be parents of Generation 1. M_0 identifies the mean of the entire foundation generation, and M_S identifies the mean of the selected animals from that generation. The difference between these two values is defined as S, the selection differential, or selection pressure.

The lower half of the figure shows the distribution of the offspring obtained by the mating of the selected animals. The mean of this first selected generation is described as M_1. The difference between M_0 and M_1 is the response to selection, defined as R.

This response to selection is a function of selection pressure and heritability, as follows:

$$R = h^2 S.$$

Thus, the greater the selectivity, the greater the mean shift from generation to generation. The relationship of heritability to selection response is apparent from consideration of two extreme cases. If heritability is zero, then the location of an individual in the phenotypic distribution is due entirely to environmental circumstances. Genetically speaking, selecting animals from the upper tail of the distribution is not different from random selection. Thus, the offspring of these parents should not differ from their parental generation. If heritability is 1.0, then the location of each individual is entirely due to additive genetic factors, and the offspring mean would be the same as the mean of their selected parents.

Most selection responses are intermediate to these extremes, reflecting some intermediate heritability of the phenotype. Indeed, the response to selection is used to estimate the heritability of the phenotype in the foundation population through the relationship

$$h^2 = R/S.$$

In many practical applications, such as agricultural ones, selection is undertaken only in the desirable direction. For research purposes, bidirectional selection is usually undertaken. Other refinements useful for research purposes include unselected control lines and replicated selected lines (McClearn, Deitrich, & Erwin, 1981).

Variability and the Hardy-Weinberg-Castle Equilibrium

The discussion above has presented a model for examining phenotypic variability under circumstances where relevant environmental factors are differentially distributed among individuals of a population, and where at least two alleles exist in that population at a minimum of one relevant locus. This model contrasts with the perception of variability as noise or error. The quantitative genetic-environmental model presents a systematic view of variance as a primary subject matter of study—not as an unwelcome error term in a statistical calculation.

Table 13.8. Relative frequencies of genotypes produced by random fertilization of A or a bearing eggs by A or a bearing sperm.

		Female gametes	
		(p)A	(q)A
Male	(p)A	(p^2)AA	(pq)Aa
gametes	(q)a	(pq)Aa	(q^2)aa

Further exploration of the fundamental genetic source of variance—the existence of differing alleles—has revealed a remarkable persistence that is not intuitively obvious. This persistence is due to an equilibrium state (named the Hardy-Weinberg-Castle equilibrium after its independent discoverers) that exists under certain circumstances. The H-W-C equilibrium is important to understand for several reasons. First, many analytical methods utilized in behavioral genetics begin with an assumption that the equilibrium exists; second, it makes vivid the quintessential nature of variability; and, third, it illuminates the conservative nature of a population's gene pool and the boundary conditions thereby imposed on eugenic views of the rate of deterioration or improvement of that gene pool.

Let us consider again a single locus with two alleles, A and a. We may characterize the relative frequency of these alleles in the population by assigning p to the frequency of A and q to the frequency of a. By definition, because in this example we postulate the existence of only two alleles, $p + q = 1$. Now, if we assume that these alleles meet at random during reproduction—an assumption involving random mating of individuals and random union of gametes—the frequency of the *genotypes* produced should be simply the product of the relative frequencies of the two alleles in the genotype. Table 13.8 describes the situation. As can be seen, the *genotypic* frequencies under these conditions for the homozygote AA, the heterozygote Aa and the homozygote aa, are, respectively, p^2, $2pq$, and q^2. As a simple numerical example, if eight of every ten alleles in the population are A, and two of every ten are a, then we expect $.8 \times .8 = .64$ or 64 percent of the population to be AA, $2 \times .8 \times .2 = .32$ or 32 percent to be Aa, and $.2 \times .2 = .04$ or 4 percent to be aa.

It may be noted that the frequency of a recessive allele for a rare condition is substantially higher than the frequency of the homozygous recessive genotype. Thus, the frequency of the homozygous recessive genotype for phenylketonuria in the population is approximately 1 in 10,000 (q^2 = .0001). The frequency of the recessive allele (q) is thus .01 or 1 in 100. The frequency of those carrying one recessive allele but with normal phenotype, the heterozygotes, is about 2 in 100 (2pq = 2 × .01).

It is possible to show that, in the absence of disturbing factors such as natural selection favoring one of the genotypes, these relative genotypic frequencies will persist indefinitely. [The interested reader should consult any of several works on population genetics, such as Wallace (1981) for discussions of the limiting conditions of the H-W-C equilibrium and of the circumstances under which allelic frequencies and, thus, genotypic frequencies, change.]

The conclusion is that the gene pool of a population is inherently a quite stable system with change occurring only slowly. For present purposes, the important point is that *variability* generated by the locus or loci under consideration is also a stable property of the system in the presence of random mating and the absence of selection.

The human genome has been estimated to consist of some 100,000 gene pairs or more, depending on whose estimate one reads. Approximately 30 percent or perhaps more of those gene pairs exist in multiple forms (i.e., have at least two alleles) in the population.

There are literally billions and billions of possible combinations of those genes, and each individual (with the exception of multiple births such as identical twins) is a unique combination of those genes—a combination that has never existed before and will never exist again. Add to this enormous genetic diversity the great range of environments to which individuals are exposed, and it becomes clear that individuality is quintessential—not just a regrettable error term.

Resemblance of Relatives

The preceding introduction to considerations of allelic frequency permits us to approach the topic of the genetic basis of resemblance of biological relatives.

We have seen that under H-W-C equilibrium conditions, the relative frequencies of *AA*, *Aa*, and *aa* genotypes are p^2, 2pq, and q^2, respect-

ively. If we assume additivity of allelic action and absence of environmental influence, the genetic correlation between parent and offspring can be shown (see, for example, Falconer, 1981) to be

$$pq/2pq = 1/2.$$

By similar calculations, it can be shown that this is also the expected value of the correlation between siblings. (For situations involving dominance, the expectations are dependent upon allelic frequency.) It may be noted that this value is very close to that obtained initially by Pearson (1904). That value was utilized as an empirical benchmark for the degree of resemblance of siblings for traits assumed to be highly heritable. The Mendelian expectation for this value was unknown to Pearson and his colleagues of the era. Indeed, many biometricians, of which group Pearson was a dominant figure, hotly contended the relevance of Mendelian inheritance to anything other than abnormal conditions. It was in 1918 that the Mendelian-biometrician dispute was resolved, with Fisher's fundamental demonstration that Mendelian elements, obeying Mendelian rules of segregation, each with a small influence on a common phenotype, would yield the statistical results that biometricians obtained.

A number of studies (including Jones, 1928; Cattell & Wilson, 1938; Roberts, 1941; Thorndike, 1944) from the late 1920s into the 1940s provided parent-offspring and sibling correlations for intellectual phenotypes that clustered around the value of 0.5. It is important to note, however, that empirical values that agree with theoretical ones derived with certain assumptions do not demonstrate that the assumptions are met in respect to the phenotypes under study. Thus, we cannot conclude from the results that all genes relevant to intelligence act additively, that the H-W-C equilibrium prevails, and that environment has no influence on intelligence. Departures from these assumptions would influence the predicted outcome in various ways. For example, assortative mating increases both parent-offspring and sibling correlations; dominant-recessive gene action, as already noted, reduces these correlations by an amount dependent upon allelic frequencies. Environmental influences could either augment or diminish correlations among relatives, depending upon whether these influences are common to families or randomly distributed. Thus, by themselves, the empirical values of relatives' correlations are capable of various interpretations. However, they play a valuable role in a total context of evidence from various sources.

The Corpus of Data: Animal Research

Over the past 20 years, the sophistication in application of the quantitative model to behavioral phenotypes has improved enormously. The species of greatest use have been mice, rats, and *Drosophila*, and the predominant methods have been comparison of inbred strains and derived generations, selective breeding, and the search for single major loci of interest.

Inbred Strains

Most of the research on inbred animals has involved mice, and, as noted earlier, the success in finding strain differences has been so great that it is now expected *a priori* that a screening of strains will reveal significant mean differences in almost any phenotype.

Sprott and Staats (1975, 1978, 1979) have provided a valuable compendium and categorization of behavioral genetic research using mice. Although animals other than inbred ones are included in their survey, inbred strains are the clear majority, and the trends overall can represent the trends of inbred strain research. Figure 13.10 shows the number of studies on genetically defined mice by year from 1926 through 1978. The growth of this literature has been very rapid, until over 100 papers a year are now being published. Of particular interest is the pattern of phenotypes examined. Figure 13.11 shows the relative emphasis on different behavioral domains by decades. Briefly summarized, inbred strain differences have been found in all of these domains, demonstrating that genetic influence on behavior is not peculiar or extraordinary, but quite common, if not, indeed, ubiquitous.

Only a few examples of this extensive literature can be cited here. Illustrative of the magnitude of strain differences that have been obtained are the results of Thompson (1953) who inspired a still continuing series of researches on activity level with his description of locomotor activity of 15 inbred mouse strains. The results are shown in Table 13.9. The range of mean activity,

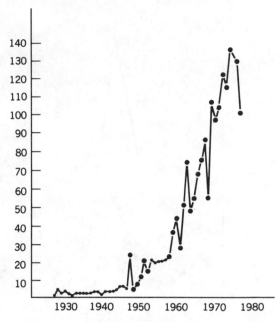

Figure 13.10. Number of behavioral studies on genetically defined mice published each year from 1926 through 1978. From "Selected Uses of the Mouse in Behavioral Research" by G.E. McClearn, 1982, in *The Mouse in Biomedical Research* (p. 39), H.L. Foster, J.D. Small, and J.G. Fox (eds.), New York: Academic Press. Copyright 1982 by Academic Press. Reprinted by permission.

from least active strain to most active, is almost twenty-three-fold!

Another example is provided by Silcock and Parsons (1973) who assessed temperature preference in a cage with a gradient of temperature along the floor. Table 13.10 shows results for three strains.

As a final example, strain differences in voluntary consumption of alcohol have been reported by McClearn and Rodgers (1961) and by Fuller (1964), using different assessment techniques. Although the different methods give different numerical outcomes, the rank ordering of the strains is the same. Animals of the C57BL strain drink over half of their total daily liquid from a 10 percent alcohol solution; most other strains avoid the alcohol. DBA mice in particular are extreme abstainers.

With this plethora of strain differences, it might appear that a useful research tactic to explore relatedness of different traits would be cross-tabulation using strains known to differ

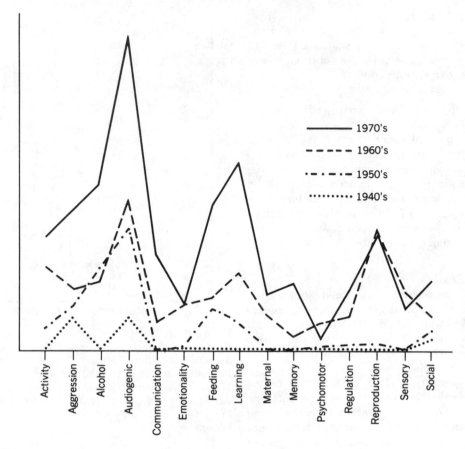

Figure 13.11 A decade-by-decade count of studies using genetically defined mice to investigate various types of behavior. From "Selected Uses of the Mouse in Behavioral Research" by G.E. McClearn, 1982, in *The Mouse in Biomedical Research* (p. 40), H.L. Foster, J.D. Small, and J.G. Fox (eds.), New York: Academic Press. Copyright 1982 by Academic Press. Reprinted by permission.

on one of the traits of interest. In the search for the mechanism of genetic influence, a general topic examined in more detail later, an obvious hypothesis was that the preference difference might be related to differences in metabolism of alcohol. Accordingly, Rodgers, McClearn, Bennett, and Hebert (1963) examined in these two strains the levels of activity of the enzyme, alcohol dehydrogenase (ADH), that mediates the first step in metabolism of alcohol. The results were that C57BL mice had significantly higher ADH activity. This outcome might appear to confirm the hypothesis, but careful examination of the situation reveals that only a negative outcome would be very informative. An apparently positive outcome is only permissive, in that it permits the investigator to retain the

hypothesis for a more rigorous test using some other method. Recall that inbreeding forces homozygosity at all loci, and that there are strong stochastic features in the determination of which alleles are fixed at which loci. Thus, any two strains will differ in numerous phenotypes that are not *necessarily* related to each other. C57BL and DBA mice will differ in hundreds of biochemical and other phenotypes that are unrelated to alcohol preference. Difference in ADH *may* be causally connected to the preference difference, but it cannot be demonstrated to be by two-strain cross-tabulations.

Multiple strain comparisons consistute a stronger approach, of course. Confidence in a causal relationship between two phenotypes would increase as rank orderings are preserved

Table 13.9. Exploratory activity in fifteen mouse strains (Thompson, 1953).

Rank	Strain	Mean Number Crossings	Probability of a Significant Difference*	
			.05	.01
1	C57BR/a	459	> 3	> 5
2	C57BL/6	361	> 7	> 10
3	C57BL/10	359	> 7	> 10
4	DBA/1	334	> 8	> 12
5	ND	308	> 8	> 12
6	BDP	286	> 10	> 13
7	DBA/2	253	> 11	> 14
8	LP	194	> 13	
9	AKR	188	> 13	
10	C3H	177	> 13	
11	Obese	149	> 15	
12	TC3H	117		
13	BALB/c	74		
14	AK/e	60		
15	A/Jax	20		

*This column is read as follows: the probability that the difference between rank 3 (C57BL/10) and rank 7 (DBA/2) and lower is due to chance is less than .05. The probability that the differences between C57BL/10 and strains of rank 10 and lower is due to chance is less than .01.

Note. From "Personality and Temperament" by J.L. Fuller and W.R. Thompson, 1960, in *Behavior Genetics*, New York: John Wiley & Sons, Inc. Copyright 1960 by J.L. Fuller. Reprinted by permission.

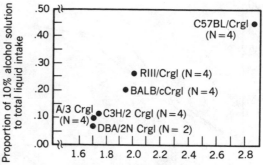

Figure 13.12. Relationship between strain differences in alcohol preference during deprivation and alcohol dehydrogenase activity. From "Alcohol Preference in Mice" by E.L. Bliss (ed.), 1962, in *Roots of Behavior* (p. 90), New York: Hoeber Medical Division, Harper & Brothers. Copyright © 1962 by Lippincott/Harper & Row. Reprinted by permission.

over an increasing number of strains. An example is given in Figure 13.12 that shows the relationship of ADH to preference in six strains.

An even stronger approach, however, is to investigate phenotypic correlations between the phenotypes in question in systematic, genetically heterogeneous stocks. For example, Anderson, McClearn, and Erwin (1979) examined the

Table 13.10. Temperature preference, three inbred strains of mice tested at age 55 to 58 days.

Strain	Temperature preference (°C)	
	Males	Females
BALB/c	25.67	26.30
C3H	36.78	35.92
C57BL	34.30	37.47

Note. Data from "The Genetics of Behavior: Rodents" by L. Ehrman and P.A. Parsons, 1976, in *The Genetics of Behavior* (p. 201), Sunderland, MA: Sinauer Associates, Inc. Copyright 1976 by Sinauer Associates, Inc. Adapted by permission.

relationship among several variables related to hepatic enzyme activity and ethanol consumption in the HS stock that was derived by intercrossing eight inbred strains. Among the results was a correlation of 0.25 between ADH activity per gram of liver and a measure of ethanol acceptance.

This result suggests that ADH activity is, indeed, a contributing factor, or related to a contributing factor, in determining alcohol ingestion, but that its contribution is modest, with only about 6 percent shared variance between preference and the enzyme activity.

Genetic Analyses Utilizing Inbred Strains

It has been noted previously that the existence of differences among inbred strains is *prima facie* evidence of genetic influence on the phenotype, but that these differences provide little information on the magnitude of that genetic influence relative to environmental influences. One way of approaching this question is by classical analysis utilizing inbred strains and F_1, F_2, and backcross generations derived from these. This method relates directly to the model presented earlier in explicating the quantitative genetic/environmental model.

An example of the use of the method is provided by DeFries and Hegmann (1970; see also DeFries, Gervais, & Thomas, 1978). Activity was assessed in an open field apparatus. The

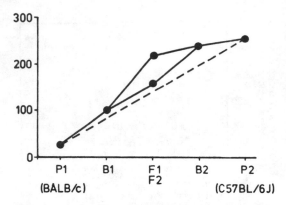

Figure 13.13. Means of activity of two inbred strains and derived generations. Data from "Development of Open-field Behavior in Mice: Effects of Age and Experience" by L.K. Dixon and J.C. DeFries, 1968, *Developmental Psychobiology, 1,* pp. 100–107. Copyright 1968 by L.K. Dixon and J.C. DeFries. Reprinted by permission.

parent strains were BALB/c and C57BL/6J. The means for the various groups plotted in Figure 13.13 can be compared to the didactic representation of Figures 13.7a and 13.7c. The empirical configuration clearly resembles that of Figure 13.7a. Some dominance is clearly present in the genetic system influencing open field activity.

This study also provided data from which broad sense heritability can be estimated. The pooled variance of the nonsegregating groups was 9.6; that of the F_2 was 16.1. From the earlier presentation, it will be recalled that the former value estimated V_E and the latter $V_G + V_E$. Subtracting V_E from $V_G + V_E$ (16.1 − 9.6) yields a value of 6.5, which estimates V_G. Then $V_G/V_E = 6.5/16.1$ for a broad sense heritability estimate of 0.40.

Another approach to the estimation of genetic and environmental sources of variance is the *diallel cross*. In this method, all possible F_1's among several strains are observed, but no segregating generations (F_2 or backcrosses) are required (Broadhurst, 1960; Mather & Jinks, 1971).

In very simplified terms, the average effect of a particular strain's genotype can be assessed by the consequences of mating with all of the other strains in the experiment. From these values, expectation can be specified for an additive model, and deviations of particular crosses from

expectation estimate nonadditive effects of dominance and epistasis.

The first usage of diallel analysis in behavior was by Broadhurst (1960) who evaluated activity and defecation in an open field by rats of six strains and their F_1's. Narrow sense heritability estimates of 0.59 and 0.62 were obtained for the two phenotypes, respectively. Another example is provided by Henderson's (1967) results on four strains of mice, also on the phenotype of open field activity. The broad sense heritability for activity was 0.40, but only 0.08 for defecation. Species, apparatus, and other differences exist between the two studies, so the reason for the discrepancy in heritability of open field defecation cannot be identified with confidence.

This diallel method is particularly useful for detecting and evaluating maternal effects and hybrid vigor. A good example is the work of Fulker (1966) on mating speed in males of six inbred strains of *Drosophila* and their F_1's. The broad and narrow sense heritability estimates were 0.72 and 0.37, respectively. Of particular interest was the fact that the hybrid F_1 animals evidenced much faster mating than their inbred parents. This outcome can be interpreted as indicating strong selection for rapid mating in natural populations of *Drosophila*.

Selective Breeding

As noted earlier, the classic selective breeding studies were performed with rats on the phenotypes of maze learning, activity, and emotional defecation. More recent selection studies also have utilized rats, and successful selection has been reported for alcohol consumption (Eriksson, 1969), avoidance learning (Bignami, 1965), water consumption (Roubicek & Ray, 1969), saccharin preference (Nachman, 1959), emotionality (Broadhurst, 1958), and maze learning (Thompson, 1954).

Mice also became subjects for selection studies, and successful response to selection has been obtained for activity (DeFries, Gervais, & Thomas, 1978), aggression (Lagerspetz & Lagerspetz, 1971) audiogenic seizure susceptibility (Deckard, Tepper, & Schlesinger, 1976; Frings & Frings, 1953), sensitivity to alcohol (McClearn & Kakihana, 1981), brain weight (Fuller & Herman, 1974; Roderick, Wimer, & Wimer, 1976), nesting (Lynch, 1981), and sensitivity to opiates (Belknap, Haltli, Goebel, & Lame, 1983). Several other selection programs are currently in

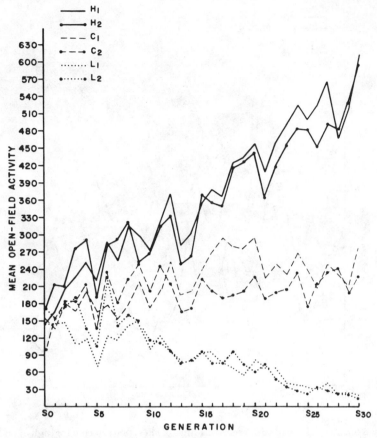

Figure 13.14. Mean open-field activity scores of six lines of mice: two selected for high open-field activity (H_1 and H_2), two selected for low open-field activity (L_1 and L_2), and two randomly mated within line to serve as controls (C_1 and C_2). From "Response to 30 Generations of Selection for Open-field Activity in Laboratory Mice" by J.C. DeFries, M.C. Gervais, and E.A. Thomas, 1978, *Behavior Genetics, 8,* p. 7. Copyright 1978 Plenum Publishing Corp. Reprinted by permission.

progress. More details of these studies may be found in the review by Hyde (1981).

The selective breeding study of DeFries and collaborators was particularly comprehensive. The genetically segregating foundation population was the F_3 of a cross between the C57BL/6 and BALB/c inbred strains, which, as noted above, differ substantially in open field activity level. Selection was bidirectional, and replicate high, low, and control lines were generated. The selection phenotype was the number of photocell beams interrupted in five minutes in an open field apparatus. The amount of defecation was also recorded. As Figure 13.14 shows, there is systematically increasing divergence between the high and low selected lines over 30 generations of selection. The realized heritability calculated from the first five selected generations was 0.26.

Figure 13.15 shows the correlated response of defecation tendency to selection for activity level. Clearly, the low activity lines have become high open field defecation lines, and *vice versa*. Such a correlated response to selection arises only when the two phenotypes share genes. In the present case, the genetic correlation was found to be −0.86. This remarkably high value reveals a large overlap of the genes influencing open field activity and those influencing open field defecation. In spite of the very great apparent differences between these phenotypes, they are very similar genetically.

Selective breeding has also proved to be a powerful tool in behavioral genetics research in

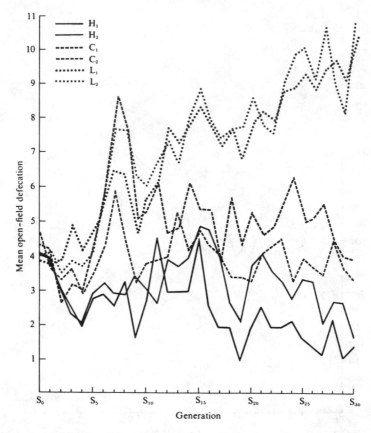

Figure 13.15. Mean open-field defecation scores of six lines of mice: two selected for high open-field activity (H_1 and H_2), two selected for low open-field activity (L_1 and L_2), and two randomly mated within line to serve as controls (C_1 and C_2). From "Response to 30 Generations of Selection for Open-field Activity in Laboratory Mice" by J.C. DeFries, M.C. Gervais, and E.A. Thomas, 1978, *Behavior Genetics, 8*, p. 9. Copyright 1978 Plenum Publishing Corp. Reprinted by permission.

the fruit fly, *Drosophila*. This genus is the invertebrate species of choice in such work because of the vast literature on its basic genetics, the great armamentarium of genetic techniques available, the obvious advantages of short generation time, and the possibility of maintaining and studying large populations.

A pioneering study in this area was that of Hirsch (1963), who selected for geotaxis in *D. melanogaster*. An ingenious maze presented the flies with successive choice points at which they could go either up or down. After 10 such choices, the animals emerged into collecting vials, having, in essence, classified themselves on an 11 point geotaxis scale. Dramatic selection progress was made, generating lines whose mean responses reflected strong negative geotaxis and strong positive geotaxis, respectively.

In addition, it was possible, by a series of chromosomal manipulations and test crosses, to determine the role of genes on three of the four chromosomes of this organism. The analysis revealed that geotaxis-relevant genes were on all three of the assayed chromosomes.

Other selection studies in *Drosophila* have generated lines differing in phototaxis (Hirsch & Boudreau, 1958; Hadler, 1964; Walton, 1970; Dobzhansky, 1968), and in optomotor response (Siegel, 1967).

Clearly, successful selection demonstrates the fact of genetic influence on the trait in question, permits the quantitative analysis of the magnitude of this influence relative to environmental sources, and addresses the genetic relatedness of different phenotypes through the study of correlated responses. Selection also generates lines of animals useful as model systems for all sorts of research on the phenotypes in question. For example, selectively bred rats and mice are of widespread current use in studies on senstivity to, tolerance to, metabolism of, and dependence liability to alcohol (see McClearn et al., 1981). The potential of the selection tool is just now coming to be appreciated in a variety of research areas and promises to be increasingly utilized in the future.

Single Loci and Animal Behavior

It is convenient to consider single loci separately from polygenic determinants, because the methods of analysis are different—not because there are fundamental differences in the nature of the gene action involved. In terms of the quantitative model presented earlier, the single locus is simply the limiting case where one gene pair has a sufficiently large effect to be detectable. In variance terms, it might be said that the percentage of phenotypic variance determined by genotypic differences at the single locus is so great that other sources of variance can be disregarded. To illustrate, one of the original single locus conditions described by Mendel was pea plant height. Homozygous recessive plants were dwarf, and heterozygotes and homozygous dominant plants were normal. Within each of these dichotomous categories, there was undoubtedly considerable variation, some due to environmental circumstances, some due to what might be called residual genotype—other loci that have an influence on plant height but that collectively do not obscure the major effect of the single locus.

To study single major locus effects on behavior, the original methods employed, for example by Darbishire, are still usable: animals with different phenotypes mated together to yield an F_1 generation; these mated together to yield F_2's, and so on. However, there are additional methods built upon inbred strains that now offer more powerful methods. With the large number of inbred mice in existence, it is, of course, inevitable that mutations will occur. When these are recognized and maintained, the result is an inbred strain, coisogenic to the original strain, genetically identical to it at all loci except for the locus at which the mutation occurred. Furthermore, if it is desired to place a particular allele on an inbred strain background, it is possible to do so by successive backcrossing to the strain. In each generation, the offspring possessing the desired allele are mated to the inbred strain. Gradually, the inbred strain is reconstituted except for the desired allele (plus genetic material adjacent to it on the chromosome, which would decline in amount with each generation). Strains generated in this way are called congenic. With either coisogenic or congenic strains, clear advantages obtain in the study of single loci because the residual genotype is controlled.

A number of coisogenic and congenic strains have been built upon the C57BL/6 background. Henry and Schlesinger (1967) compared animals of one of these, the coisogenic albino C57BL/6 strain, with animals of the standard C57BL/6 strain, with respect to alcohol preference, audiogenic seizure susceptibility, avoidance learning, and open field activity. Significant differences were observed for all behaviors except audiogenic seizure susceptibility; the albino animals were poorer in learning performance, drank less alcohol, and were less active than their pigmented peers. The nature of the coisogenic design allows clear attribution of these differences to the allelic differences at the albino locus.

This albino effect was confirmed with respect to activity by observations of DeFries in his selection study. It might be recalled that that study was begun with the F_3 generation between the C57BL/6 and the albino BALB/c strains. Thus, in this foundation population, allelic frequency (p) for the C allele was 0.5. and that for the c allele (q) was also 0.5. The frequency of the albino phenotype was thus $q^2 = 0.25$. If the albino allele indeed has an activity suppressing effect, it would be expected that selection for high activity would tend to eliminate the c allele, and that selection for low activity would tend to eliminate the C allele. The frequency of albinism became 100 percent by the eighth generation in one low line and by the twenty-second generation in the other, while it approached zero in both of the high lines. DeFries and Hegman (1970) have calculated that the single albino locus accounted for 12 percent of the variance in activity and 26 percent of the variance in defecation in the open field situation.

Yet another approach to the study of single loci in behavior has been provided by the recent development of recombinant inbred (RI) strains.

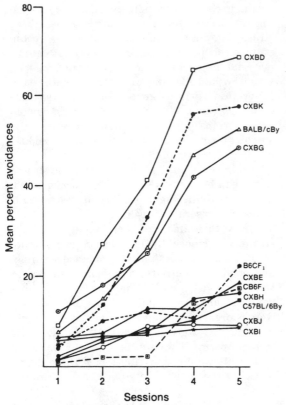

Figure 13.16. Mean percentage of avoidances per session for five days of seven RI lines, their two ancestral strains, and two reciprocal F₁ hybrids. Reprinted with permission from *Physiology and Behavior, 11,* A. Oliverio, B.E. Eleftheriou, and D.W. Bailey, "A Gene Influencing Active Avoidance Performance, Copyright 1973, Pergamon Press, Ltd.

These RI strains are generated by inbreeding from an F_2 between two different inbred strains. Recombination can occur in the F_2, and combinations of alleles differing from those in the parent strains will occur in the new recombinant inbred strains. If a large number of loci influence a phenotype, the RI strains should be distributed between the values of the original parent strains. However, if a single locus is involved, the RI strains should have only values like one or the other parent strain. A prime example of the use of this technique has been provided by Oliverio, Eleftheriou, and Bailey (1973), who compared C57BL/6, BALB/c, and seven RI strains with respect to avoidance learning. Figure 13.16 shows that the groups form two clusters: high performance BALB/c's

and three of the RI's, and low performance C57BL's and four of the RI's. It thus seems very likely that there is a major locus effect for this particular type of learning.

In another application of RI technique, Seyfried, Yu, and Glaser (1979) studied audiogenic seizures in C57BL, DBA, and 21 RI strains. Thirteen of the latter were intermediate to the parent strains, suggesting polygenic determination.

Other phenotypes for which single locus effects have been identified include a series of neuromuscular mutants in mice (including some affecting the cerebellum, to be discussed later), audible vocalization (Whitney, 1969), and mating success in *Drosophila* (Bastock, 1956).

These single locus examples provide dramatic and easily understood evidence of the potential of genes to influence behavior. That complex behaviors can be substantially influenced by a single gene is noteworthy. Furthermore, the clarity of the results makes easier the acceptance of the idea that these and other phenotypes may be influenced by large numbers of genes acting in concert.

The Corpus of Data: Human Research

The human behavioral phenotypes studied by behavioral geneticists have included traits from the domains of personality, temperament, attitudes, interests, mental illness, sensory and perceptual processing, cognitive and intellectual functioning, alcoholism, creativity, and criminality. Certainly, major aspects of human experience have been included in this effort, and some influence of genotype has been identified in all of the areas examined. Repeating our earlier apologia, it is clearly out of the question to review this literature comprehensively in this chapter. Two areas that have attracted particular interest will be presented to exemplify the approaches and results, but, even here, only a sampling of the major studies can be presented.

Intellectual Functioning

Because of the central position that concepts of intelligence and cognition have held in psychology, it was probably inevitable that behavioral geneticists would be concerned with studying the heritability of attributes from these key areas. Among the earliest concerns, as we have seen, were various forms of mental retardation. At first, the various types of retardation could not be clearly delineated, and the pattern of inheritance was sought for the collective category (as in the case of Goddard described above). With hindsight, we can see how this nosological limitation handicapped the earlier investigators, for we know that some of the (now) distinctive conditions of retardation are inherited as recessives, some as dominants, some polygenically, some are the result of chromosomal anomalies, and some arise from environmental insult. Small wonder that the early efforts were inconclusive.

As we have seen, a biochemical marker permitted the specification of a particular subtype of retardation—PKU. Intensive work following the discovery of that marker has revealed an autosomal recessive pattern of transmission. (As work has progressed, it has also become apparent that some variant forms exist that are likely due to other alleles at the same locus.)

Much has been learned of the biochemical pathways involved in PKU, of which more later. Here we note that this knowledge has led to rational therapeutic interventions that ameliorate the primary behavioral symptom of retardation. This success has spurred research on other single-locus-determined types of mental retardation involving inborn errors of metabolism of various types. Among the best understood of these monogenic conditions are Tay-Sachs disease, galactosemia, Hunter syndrome, Hurler syndrome, and Lesch-Nyhan syndrome, all involving severe mental retardation.

These conditions have important implications for public health in terms of clinical practice, genetic counseling, and population screening. Perhaps even more than the single locus demonstrations in animals, they also reveal the capability of genes to influence behavior and make plausible the genetic models that purport to account for variance in continuously distributed intellectual characteristics.

In the study of the genetics of the normal range of intelligence, all of the major sources of evidence have been exploited. Bouchard and McGue (1981) provide a current figural summary of 111 reports of correlations among relatives for performance on various intelligence tests. Figure 13.17 shows the median correlations and ranges of the reported values. In general, the genetic similarity of the compared individuals increases from top to bottom (with parent-child, sibling, and dizygotic twins the same, of course); there is also a trend to higher correlations from top to bottom. This outcome testifies to a genetic influence on intelligence, but we need to examine some selected studies for more detail to fill out this generalization.

FAMILY STUDIES

In discussing the early family studies on intelligence, it was mentioned that the family situation confounds genetic and environmental similarities, so that it is not possible to extract from parent-offspring or from sibling resemblance a clear estimate of heritability. However, recognizing the limitations of estimates derived from these correlations of relatives—that they provide upper limit estimates of heritability—family studies can be turned to informative purposes. For example, a recent large family study conducted in Hawaii (DeFries, Ashton, et al., 1976; DeFries, Johnson, et al., 1979) had an objective of characterizing the familiality of various specific cognitive abilities. Over 1800 families, each consisting of both parents and at least one child, were tested on 15 tests. The regressions of midchild on midparent for these tests and for four factors derived by multivariate analysis from families of European and families of Japanese ancestry are shown in Figure 13.18. Clearly, there are different levels of family resemblance: verbal abilities as a group show greatest similarity: visual memory shows the lowest. Among individual tests, Pedigrees shows the highest correlation and Immediate Visual Memory the lowest. Because of the confounding of genetic and environmental sources of influence, these results cannot be interpreted as demonstrating differential heritability, but they do suggest that variance in different components or factors of intellectual functioning may be differentially influenced by genetic and environmental factors. To explore this possibility further, other approaches must be utilized. It should be said that other studies have not shown evidence of differential heritable basis of specific cognitive factors (Loehlin & Nichols, 1976). The reasons for this disparity also require further investigation.

TWIN STUDIES

The twin design has continued to attract the attention of behavioral geneticists interested in

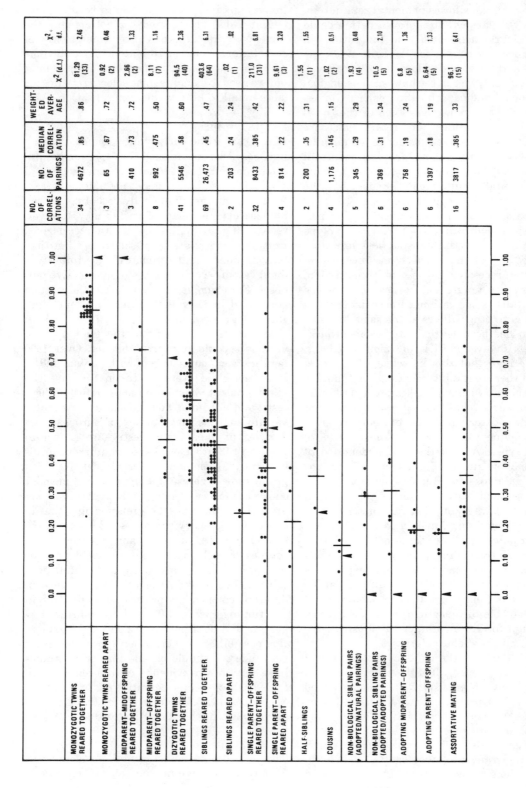

Figure 13.17. Familial correlations for IQ. The vertical bar in each distribution indicates the median correlation; the arrow indicates the correlation predicted by a single polygenic model. From "Studies of Intelligence: A Review" by T. Bouchard, Jr. and M. McGue, 1981, *Science, 212*, p. 1056. Copyright 1981 by the AAAS. Reprinted by permission.

	NO. OF CORREL- ATIONS	NO. OF PAIRINGS	MEDIAN CORREL- ATION	WEIGHT- ED AVER- AGE	χ^2 (d.f.)	$\frac{\chi^2}{d.f.}$
MONOZYGOTIC TWINS REARED TOGETHER	34	4672	.85	.86	81.29 (33)	2.46
MONOZYGOTIC TWINS REARED APART	3	65	.67	.72	0.92 (2)	0.46
MIDPARENT–MIDOFFSPRING REARED TOGETHER	3	410	.73	.72	2.66 (2)	1.33
MIDPARENT–OFFSPRING REARED TOGETHER	8	992	.475	.50	8.11 (7)	1.16
DIZYGOTIC TWINS REARED TOGETHER	41	5546	.58	.60	94.5 (40)	2.36
SIBLINGS REARED TOGETHER	69	26,473	.45	.47	403.6 (64)	6.31
SIBLINGS REARED APART	2	203	.24	.24	.02 (1)	.02
SINGLE PARENT–OFFSPRING REARED TOGETHER	32	8433	.385	.42	211.0 (31)	6.81
SINGLE PARENT–OFFSPRING REARED APART	4	814	.22	.22	9.61 (3)	3.20
HALF-SIBLINGS	2	200	.35	.31	1.55 (1)	1.55
COUSINS	4	1,176	.145	.15	1.02 (2)	0.51
NON-BIOLOGICAL SIBLING PAIRS (ADOPTED/NATURAL PAIRINGS)	5	345	.29	.29	1.93 (4)	0.48
NON-BIOLOGICAL SIBLING PAIRS (ADOPTED/ADOPTED PAIRINGS)	6	369	.31	.34	10.5 (5)	2.10
ADOPTING MIDPARENT–OFFSPRING	6	758	.19	.24	6.8 (5)	1.36
ADOPTING PARENT–OFFSPRING	6	1397	.18	.19	6.64 (5)	1.33
ASSORTATIVE MATING	16	3817	.365	.33	96.1 (15)	6.41

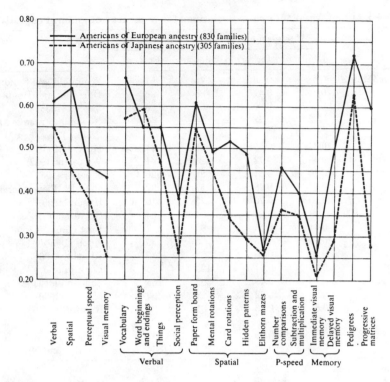

Figure 13.18. Family study of specific cognitive abilities. Regression of midchild on midparent for four group factors and 15 cognitive tests in two ethnic groups. Data from "Family Studies of Human Behavior" by R. Plomin, J. DeFries, and G. McClearn, 1980, in *Behavioral Genetics: A Primer* (p. 281), San Francisco: W.H. Freeman & Co. Copyright (c) 1980 by W.H. Freeman & Co. Reprinted by permission.

intellectual function. Table 13.11 summarizes 19 studies, spanning more than four decades, in which the focus of concern was general cognitive ability. Although the degree of correlation between monozygotic (MZ) twin pairs and between dizygotic (DZ) twin pairs differs from study to study, the MZ values are generally higher than the DZ values, suggesting a genetic influence. If we take as a rough summary the median MZ intraclass correlation of 0.85 and that of DZ's of 0.48, we may estimate broad sense heritability according to the method of Falconer (1981), doubling the difference between the correlation values, which yields a value of about 0.64. When fine tuning of this estimate is undertaken to correct for assortative mating and other factors that confound twin analysis, the result still suggests that between one-third and one-half of the variation in cognitive ability as measured by these various instruments is due to genetic factors. It is instructive to compare this value with the upper limit estimate of heritabil-

ity of the first principal component provided by the Hawaii family study. This multivariate index, which also can be regarded as a measure of general ability, provided a midchild-midparent regression that estimates upper-limit, narrow-sense heritability to be 0.60. This outcome suggests that both shared genes and shared environments contribute significantly to individual differences in cognitive abilities (see Plomin & DeFries, 1980, for comparison of older and more current research).

ADOPTION STUDIES

The most definitive evidence concerning the genetics of intelligence has been obtained from adoption studies. We have already reviewed the very substantial pioneering studies of Burks and of Freeman, et al. (1928). In the last decade, several major new studies have appeared (Scarr & Weinberg, 1976, 1983; Horn, 1983; Plomin & DeFries, 1983).

A major comparison of the adoption design is

Table 13.11. Identical and fraternal twin correlations for measures of general cognitive ability.

Test	Correlation		Number of pairs		Source
	Identical	Fraternal	Identical	Fraternal	
National and Multi-Mental	0.85	0.26	45	57	Wingfield and Sandiford (1928)
Otis	0.84	0.47	65	96	Herrman and Hogben (1933)
Binet	0.88	0.90	34	28	Stocks (1933)
Binet and Otis	0.92	0.63	50	50	Newman, Freeman, and Holzinger (1937)
I-Test	0.87	0.55	36	71	Husen (1947)
Simplex and C-Test	0.88	0.72	128	141	Wictorin (1952)
Intelligence factor	0.76	0.44	26	26	Blewett (1954)
JPQ-12	0.62	0.28	52	32	Cattell, Blewett, and Beloff (1955)
I-Test	0.90	0.70	215	416	Husen (1959)
Otis	0.83	0.59	34	34	Gottesman (1963)
Various group tests	0.94	0.55	95	127	Burt (1966)
PMA IQ	0.79	0.45	33	30	Koch (1966)
Vocabulary composite	0.83	0.66	85	135	Huntley (1966)
PMA total score	0.88	0.67	123	75	Loehlin and Vandenberg (1968)
General ability factor	0.80	0.48	337	156	Schoenfeldt (1968)
ITPA total	0.90	0.62	28	33	Mittler (1969)
Tanaka B	0.81	0.66	81	32	Kamitake (1971)
NMSQT total score:					
1962	0.87	0.63	687	482	Nichols (1965)
1965	0.86	0.62	1300	864	Loehlin and Nichols (1976)

Source: Adapted from Loehlin and Nichols, 1976.

Note. Adapted from Loehlin and Nichols, 1976. From "Twin Studies" by R. Plomin, J. DeFries, and G.E. McClearn, 1980, in *Behavioral Genetics: A Primer* (p. 308), San Francisco: W.H. Freeman & Co. Copyright 1980 by W.H. Freeman & Co. Reprinted with permission.

that between the resemblance of adopted child and adoptive parents on the one hand and the resemblance of appropriately selected control children and parents on the other hand. The work of Burks cited earlier showed that children in control families resembled their biological parents more than the children in adoptive families resembled their adoptive parents. Correlations of IQ from other studies, one published shortly after Burks, and another one recently making this comparison, are given in Table 13.12. The results are in very substantial agreement and argue for the importance of heredity in determining performance on intelligence tests.

Another comparison of interest is that of adoptive child-adoptive parent resemblance with adoptive child-biological parent resemblance. In approaching this analysis, earlier studies had to rely on indirect measures of intelligence of the biological parent—such as educational level.

In the Texas Adoption Project (Horn, Loehlin, & Willerman, 1979), IQ test scores of the mothers were available. Table 13.13 compares the correlations of adopted child with adoptive fathers, adoptive mothers, and biological mothers. Clearly, this comparison also implicates genetic factors in intelligence.

Many facets of the adoption design can be

Table 13.12. Correlations of IQ test scores of parents and children in adoptive and control families.

	Relationship	Adoptive family	Control family
Leahy (1935)	Father–child	.15	.51
	Mother–child	.20	.51
Scarr and Weinberg (1978)	Father–child	.16	.40
	Mother–child	.09	.41

Note. Data from "Adoption Studies" by R. Plomin, J. DeFries, and G.E. McClearn, 1980, in *Behavioral Genetics: A Primer* (p. 337), San Francisco: W.H. Freeman & Co. Copyright 1980 by W.H. Freeman & Co. Adapted by permission.

Table 13.13. Correlations of IQ test scores of children with adoptive parents and with biological mother.

Comparison	Correlation
Child–adoptive father	0.14
Child–adoptive mother	0.17
Child–biological mother	0.31

Note. Data from "Adoption Studies" by R. Plomin, J. DeFries, and G.E. McClearn, 1980, in *Behavioral Genetics: A Primer* (p. 339), San Francisco: W.H. Freeman & Co. Copyright 1980 by W.H. Freeman & Co. Adapted by permission.

examined other than those briefly described here. These include the degree of selective placement, the ages of placement of children and the ages at the time of measurement, the correlation of biological siblings adopted apart, and the correlations of unrelated children reared in the same adoptive family. For the additional perspectives (both clarifying and confusing) offered by these analyses, the original papers should be consulted. A particularly useful summary is provided by Scarr and Carter-Saltzman (1983).

Psychopathology

Just as it was understandable that behavioral geneticists should devote considerable effort to elucidating the role of genetics in variability in intellectual function, it was natural that they should do so as well for the broad area of mental illness. Among the specific illnesses or groups of illnesses that have been explored have been schizophrenia, affective psychosis, neuroses, criminality, homosexuality, and alcoholism. In all of these areas, some evidence has been produced implicating genetic factors in the liability to develop or display aberrant behavior. It is probably the case that schizophrenia has been the most intensively investigated, although alcohol-

ism has become in recent years an increasing focus of research efforts. The schizophrenia research can serve to illustrate the nature of the research designs and the nature of the data concerning genetics of psychopathology.

FAMILY STUDIES

Since the earliest description of schizophrenia as a diagnostic entity, there has been a suggestion that it has a heritable basis. This presumption was based on observations of a tendency for the affliction to run in families. Among the earliest formal evidence was morbidity risk estimates for relatives of differing degrees of genetic relatedness to proband cases. Rosenthal (1970) has summarized data from a number of studies. The results are contrasted in Table 13.14 with the general incidence in the population at large. It is clear that being a first-degree relative of a schizophrenic case increases the risk four- to tenfold over that of the population at large. Being a second-degree relative or third-degree relative also involves elevated risk but less than that of first-degree relatives. This picture is certainly consistent with the hypothesis of genetic transmission, but as we have seen in family studies in general, the family situation does not permit incisive attribution to either genetic or environmental sources—family members share genes, and they also share environments.

TWIN STUDIES

Once again, the twin study method has been employed to provide what was hoped to be superior data from the point of view of causal assignment. The classic work was that of Kallman (1938). The basic comparison was the *concordance*, or relative mutual incidence, in MZ and in DZ twin pairs in which at least one twin

Table 13.14. Median morbidity risk estimates for manic-depressive psychosis and schizophrenia for the general population and for relatives of manic-depressive index cases.

	Manic-depressive, %	Schizophrenic, %
General population	0.7	0.9
Parents of manic-depressives	7.6	0.6
Siblings of manic-depressives	8.8	0.8
Children of manic-depressives	11.2	2.5

Source: After Rosenthal, 1970.

Note. From "Family Studies of Human Behavior" by R. Plomin, J. DeFries, and G.E. McClearn, 1980, in *Behavioral Genetics: A Primer* (p. 286), San Francisco: W.H. Freeman & Co. Copyright 1980 by W.H. Freeman & Co. Reprinted by permission.

Table 13.15.　Schizophrenia: probandwise concordance in recent twin studies.

Investigator	Year	Country	Identical		Fraternal	
			Concordance %	Number of pairs	Concordance %	Number of pairs
Kringlen	1967	Norway	45	55	15	90
Fischer	1973	Denmark	56	21	26	41
Gottesman and Shields	1972	U.K.	58	22	12	33
Tienari	1971	Finland	35	17	13	20
Pollin et al.	1972	U.S.	43	95	9	125

Source: After Gottesman and Shields, 1976.

Note. From "Twin Studies" by R. Plomin, J. DeFries, and G. McClearn, 1980, in *Behavioral Genetics: A Primer* (p. 319), San Francisco: W.H. Freeman & Co. Copyright 1980 by W.H. Freeman & Co. Reprinted by permission.

was diagnosed as being schizophrenic. Of 174 monozygotic pairs, 59 percent were concordant; of 517 dizygotic pairs, 9 percent were concordant. These results immediately displayed two points that have subsequently been replicated in many observations: the lack of complete concordance in MZ twin pairs reveals that there is an important environmental source of variance, and the higher concordance in MZ pairs than in DZ pairs demonstrates a significant genetic component.

The late 1960s and early 1970s saw an outpouring of research in this area that Gottesman and Shields (1982) have summarized. Table 13.15 shows the principal results. Concordance in MZ pairs is higher than that in DZ pairs in all five of the studies summarized, based upon populations in Scandinavia, the United Kingdom, and the United States.

ADOPTION STUDIES

As we have seen, twin studies are not without their problems of interpretation. The contention that MZ twins' environments are more similar than those of DZ twins has been particularly appealing to critics who favor an exclusive, environmentalist interpretation of the etiology of schizophrenia. Again, the adoption study has emerged as the most definitive of the methods deployed in the investigation of this area. In 1966, Heston published the results of an analysis described as the adoptees study method. Children of 45 hospitalized chronic schizophrenic women were the adoptees at the focus of this study. They were compared to 50 adoptees whose biological parents did not have any known psychopathology. The adoptive parents of both groups were free of schizophrenia. The adoptees were assessed for psychopathology.

Results were that five (11 percent) of the 47 of the adoptees whose biological mothers were schizophrenic were themselves schizophrenic. Four other adoptees with biological schizophrenic mothers were regarded as borderline. None of the 50 control adoptees was schizophrenic. Overall, these results implicate genetic factors at work in determining liability to a schizophrenic condition.

As modern research in the genetics of schizophrenia has proceeded, it has become apparent that definitional and diagnostic criteria are of critical importance. Gottesman and Shields (1977) in their twin study, for example, examined concordance as a function of severity of the condition in the proband. The three levels of severity in increasing order were: (1) the proband spends less than two years in the hospital; (2) the proband spends more than two years in the hospital; and (3) the proband is unable to stay out of the hospital for at least six months. In this order, the concordance of MZ twins was 27 percent, 77 percent, and 75 percent. Heritability appears to be higher for the cases with the more severe manifestation. Another result showing the importance of differential analysis was obtained by Rosenthal et al. (1968) who classified the cases in terms of breadth of symptomatology included in the definition. First, they considered only chronic schizophrenic cases; second, they considered chronic, acute, borderline, and uncertain schizophrenia (called hard spectrum); and third, they considered these hard spectrum cases plus paranoid and schizoid personality (soft spectrum). An adoptees study method similar to that used by Heston was employed, with the results shown in Table 13.16. Naturally, as the definition is broadened, there is an increase in percent

Table 13.16. Schizophrenia and hard and soft schizophrenic spectrum in adopted offspring of schizophrenic and nonschizophrenic birth parents.

Birth parents	Adoptive parents	
	Normal	Affected
Normal	0% (0/67)*	–
	4% (3/67)†	–
	18% (12/67)‡	–
Affected	7% (3/44)*	–
	14% (6/44)†	–
	27% (12/44)‡	–

*Chronic schizophrenia.

†Chronic, acute, borderline, and uncertain schizophrenia (hard spectrum).

‡Hard spectrum plus paranoid and schizoid personality (soft spectrum).

Note. Source: Rosenthal et al., 1968. From "Adoption Studies" by R. Plomin, J. DeFries, and G.E. McClearn, 1980, in *Behavioral Genetics: A Primer* (p. 346), San Francisco: W.H. Freeman & Co. Copyright 1980 by W.H. Freeman. Reprinted by permission.

incidence of the condition. Moreover, under the more stringent definition, the disproportionality between the offspring of affected biological parents and those of unaffected biological parents (and thus, presumably, the magnitude of the genetic influence) decreases.

Another approach utilizing the natural experiment of adoption is the adoptees' family method. Kety, Rosenthal, Wender, and Schulsinger (1976) reported on a number of Danish adoptees in which the starting point was the identification of schizophrenic adoptees. The incidence of schizophrenia was then sought in their adoptive parents and in their biological parents, with whom the children never lived. A genetic hypothesis predicts that the incidence would be higher in the biological parents than in the rearing parents. Results from the schizophrenic adoptees were compared with a matched sample of nonschizophrenic adoptees. The results are shown in Table 13.17. In the biological and rearing parents of nonschizophrenic adoptees, there is an equal percentage of diagnosed schizophrenia. It may be seen that this incidence is relatively high compared to other reported general population values. This is an interesting phenomenon in its own right, requiring some explanation, but does not invalidate the use of this value as a baseline of expectation for adoptive parents under the prevailing cultural circumstances. In this particular study, adoptive parents of schizophrenic adoptive children have the same level of incidence as both the adoptive and biological parents of nonschizophrenic children. However, the incidence of schizophrenia in the biological parents of schizophrenic adoptees was three to four times as high. These results are generally confirmatory of the previous adoption studies, the twin material, and the family risk figures. The accumulated evidence leaves no doubt but that liability to schizophrenia has a genetic basis. Indeed, making certain assumptions of an underlying continuum of liability with a threshold, it is possible to calculate the heritability of this liability. Gottesman and Shields (1977), for example, calculated upper-bound estimates of this heritability to be between .45 and .73, depending upon the data base.

Chromosome Anomalies

Beginning about 25 years ago (LeJeune, Gauthier, & Turpin, 1959), another domain of behavioral genetics research was opened by methodological developments in cytogenetics that

Table 13.17. Hard schizophrenic spectrum (based on psychiatric interviews) in biological and adoptive relatives of schizophrenic and nonschizophrenic adoptees.

	Nonschizophrenic adoptees	Schizophrenic adoptees
First-degree biological relatives	4% (3/68)	12% (8/68)
Adoptive parents and adoptive siblings	4% (4/90)	3% (2/73)
Biological half-siblings (total sample)	3% (3/104)	16% (16/101)
Biological half-siblings (paternal only)	3% (2/64)*	18% (11/61)

*Both psychiatric interviews and hospital diagnoses.

Note. Source: Kety et al., 1976. From "Adoption Studies" by R. Plomin, J. DeFries, and G.E. McClearn, 1980, in *Behavioral Genetics: A Primer* (p. 347), San Francisco: W.H. Freeman & Co. Copyright 1980 by W.H. Freeman & Co. Reprinted by permission.

enhanced the identifiability of human chromosomes. As will be described later, chromosomes are composed of DNA and various proteins. The structure is folded in a complex, precise manner with the result that, at certain stages of the cell cycle, the compact chromosome is visible with a light microscope.

The chromosomes of an organism are paired, with one member of each pair having come from the mother and the other one from the father. In human beings, the normal number of chromosomes is 46. Twenty-two pairs are called autosomes; in these chromosomes, each member of the pair contains the same genetic material in the same linear order. The twenty-third pair comprises the sex chromosomes. One of these is a relatively large X chromosome; the other is a small Y chromosome. The genetic material on the X chromosome is generally not matched by loci on the Y chromosome. Females have two X's; males have one X and one Y.

Normally, when gametes are formed, one member of each chromosome pair is routed through the process of meiosis into each sperm and each egg. Upon fertilization, the normal chromosome number is then restored. Occasionally, an error occurs during meiosis, with the result that a gamete will have too many or too few chromosomes. Any zygote resulting from fertilization involving that gamete will then have an abnormal number of chromosomes. Many, perhaps most, of these individuals with anomalous chromosome complements succumb early in development. For example, about 50 percent of first trimester spontaneous abortuses have chromosomal defects. However, some of the anomalies, mostly of the smaller chromosomes, are compatible with continued, though abnormal, development until birth or beyond. Most of those with relevance to behavior are *trisomies*, with three instead of the normal pair of a particular chromosome.

The most frequent and best known of the autosomal trisomies is Down's syndrome, characterized by the possession of three chromosomes number 21 in addition to the normal pairs of other autosomes and sex chromosomes (LeJeune et al., 1959). The stigmata of Down's Syndrome are too well known to require elaboration here. Of special salience, of course, is the mental retardation that is typical of the syndrome. Other autosomal trisomies involve chromosomes 13 (Patau, Smith, Therman, Inhorn, &

Wagner, 1960) and 18 (Edwards, Harnden, Cameron, Crosse, & Wolff, 1960). Each of these trisomies involves multiple malformations and a life expectancy of less than a year. The prevalence of these disorders in live births is roughly as follows: trisomy 21—1/600; trisomy 13—1/15,000; trisomy 18—1/5000.

Anomalies of the sex chromosomes are relatively frequent. Individuals with an XXY constitution (see Jacobs, Brunton, Melville, Brittain, & McClemont, 1965) occur about 1 in 450 male births. These are phenotypic males, but display Klinefelter's syndrome involving testicular dysgenesis, gynecomastia, and, occasionally, mild retardation. XYY males (about 1 in 1000 male births) may be unusually tall and display a tendency toward criminality (see Jacobs, Price, Court Brown, Brittain, & Whatmore, 1968), but this latter issue remains controversial. XXX females (1 in 1000 female births) may be phenotypically normal, but there have been reports of retardation in some individuals with this chromosome constitution. The retardation seems to be more likely or more severe in persons with four or more X chromosomes.

Turner's syndrome (1 in 1500 female births), by contrast to the above examples, involves a shortage rather than a surplus of chromosomes. These phenotypic females have only a single X chromosome. They display failure of secondary sexual development and ovarian dysgenesis, short stature, and some other anomalies. Early reports described slight mental retardation, but subsequent work emphasized the normality of cognitive function except for spatial ability, which appears to be deficient (Shaffer, 1962; Money, 1968).

There are variants of all of these disorders, and the interested reader should consult recent texts of behavioral genetics for more details.

These chromosomal anomalies show the importance of a normal genetic complement to normal development. In no case are the mechanisms through which the genetic surplus or deficiency exerts its adverse effect on developmental processes clearly established, but this is an area of active research. Elucidation of these mechanisms, and the application of molecular techniques to pinpointing the loci whose triple representations are causally significant, will not only add to our comprehension of normal development and its genetic control, but might possibly also lead to early intervention to make development of persons with chromosomal anomalies more normal.

Recent Developments in Conceptual and Analytical Models

The last decade of research has been marked by an influx of sophisticated and powerful analytical tools. Most make use of maximum likelihood methods (Edwards, 1972) to fit specific models of transmission to family data and to estimate the values of the associated parameters (for general overview, see Elston, 1981; Elston & Rao, 1978; Schull & Weiss, 1980 or Reich, Suarez, Rice & Cloninger, 1981 and Rao & Morton, 1981). These techniques have been employed to study the transmission of schizophrenia, affective psychosis, and general intelligence. Our brief survey of these analytical methods will highlight some of this research; but the methods themselves are yet in their infancy, and there are still important questions about their adequacy as well as about the biases that might obscure or distort their results.

Segregation Analysis

For any trait under the control of alleles at a single locus in which there is a fairly strong determinant relation between genotype and phenotype, Mendelian theory predicts the expected proportions of offspring from the genotypes of the parents. Mendel's original experiments illustrate the essence of segregation analysis. In observing a cross of hybrids that were presumed to be heterozygous for alleles producing round and wrinkled seeds, he found the expected proportions of 75 percent round and 25 percent wrinkled among the offspring, thus confirming the suggested parental genotypes and demonstrating the law of segregation. For many traits, including metabolic disorders such as phenylketonuria or albinism, Mendelian transmission is obvious from the inspection of pedigree data. There are, however, many reasons why single-gene segregation may not be so obvious. The trait may vary in severity or in age-of-onset, or its expression may be influenced by sex or by other genetic and environmental factors. Consequently, the expression of the trait among individuals of the same genotype may vary considerably. The phenotypic ranges associated with different genotypes may

overlap to the extent that distinct, multiple modes are not apparent in sample distributions. For example, the enzyme red cell acid-phosphatase coded by a single locus with three alleles yields a continuous distribution of enzyme activity (Eze, Tweedie, Bullen, Wren, & Evans, 1974). In view of the potential for overlap, the absence of clear discontinuities in phenotypes cannot be taken as evidence against an hypothesis of a single gene accounting for a substantial part of phenotypic variation. On the other hand, the presence of distinctive phenotypic classes (i.e., the presence or absence of a disease) does not necessarily preclude polygenic transmission. A dichotomy at the phenotypic level may be determined by an underlying continuum of liability in which multiple genetic and environmental factors contribute to individual risk (Falconer, 1965). Pathology appears only if the sum of the risk factors exceeds a critical threshold. Current models of liability include the possibility of two or more such thresholds representing mild and severe forms of the same illness or different thresholds based on sex or on segregation at a single locus (Reich, James, & Morris, 1972; Reich, Rice, Cloninger, Wette, & James, 1979; Reich et al., 1981). In this last case, a complete genetic model would contain the effects of a single locus on a multifactorial background (Morton & MacLean, 1974; Reich et al., 1979). Other complexities are added by the fallibility of diagnostic instruments and by biases associated with the sampling methods used to ascertain families.

One of the first challenges in the development of segregation analysis was the problem of incomplete ascertainment. Cavalli-Sforza and Bodmer (1971) and Smith (1959) provide discussions of the early work on ascertainment bias. The potential bias introduced by ascertainment can be easily illustrated by considering the most common sort of sampling method, selecting families through an affected index case. If the trait were in fact transmitted as a simple, Mendelian recessive, we automatically exclude families in which the parents are heterozygotes but all of the offspring are normal, providing no probands to identify the family. Their exclusion would bias the estimates of gene frequency and, most important, the estimates of transmission probabilities would be inflated. Depending upon the exact method of sampling, families with two or more affected members might be more likely to be included, another source of bias. The early refinements of segregation analysis such as the Weinberg-Proband method have been greatly expanded by Morton (1959) and more recently by, among others, Stene (1977), Thompson and Cannings (1980), and Elston (1973, 1980).

Modern segregation analysis yields two major results: (1) a statistical test of the adequcy of particular models of transmission in the form of a likelihood and (2) estimates of the parameters used in the model (Elston & Stewart, 1971; Elston & Yelverton, 1975). Various factors enter into the likelihood expression, including the probabilities of the particular array of phenotypes and their presumed genotypes within families, as well as corrections for ascertainment. The overall likelihood is akin to a summary statement that reveals how well a particular model is suited to the data. Maximum likelihood procedures produce estimates of the parameters which are not fixed by the model being fitted (see Elston, 1981, for a discussion of likelihood equations in segregation analysis). The usual parameters in these analyses include the gene frequency, the phenotypic means and variances for each genotype, and the probability that individuals of particular genotypes will transmit specific genes (or polygenes) to their offspring (e.g., Elston & Yelverton, 1975). More complex analyses may also provide for multiple thresholds and effects of common environment within sibships (Morton, Yee, & Lew, 1971; Morton & MacLean, 1974; Reich et al., 1972; and Lalouel, 1984).

It is generally advisable, depending on the model, to demonstrate that a mixture of two (or more) distributions fit the data sufficiently well before testing models including a single locus effect (Go, Elston, & Kaplan, 1978; MacLean, Morton, Elston, & Yu, 1976). With positive results, segregation analysis is warranted. For each model tested, different parameters are restricted. In the case of a single major locus with dominance, for example, the transmission probabilities for parents of AA, Aa, and aa genotypes are set to 1.0, 0.5, and 0.0, respectively. Phenotypic distributions for each genotype must be estimated, in this case, with the restriction that the phenotypic mean of the homozygous AA individuals equals that of the heterozygotes, reflecting the hypothesis of dominance. Individuals are assigned conditional genotypes based upon the phenotypic distributions, and other

unrestricted parameters are estimated. After each iteration, the likelihood is calculated, and the iterations continue until a maximum is reached. The final likelihood is evaluated by comparing it with the likelihood obtained when none of the parameters is restricted or by comparing the likelihoods of alternative models. Twice the difference between the logarithms of the two likelihoods is distributed as a χ^2 with as many degrees of freedom as there are independent restrictions on parameters. If the difference between the two likelihoods is not significant, the tested model provides as good a fit to the data as the unrestricted one and cannot be rejected as a potential explanation.

Because of the sophistication required by these analyses and their intensive demands on sample size and structure, there have so far been only a few applications in behavioral genetics. Among these are analyses of schizophrenia (Matthyse & Kidd, 1976; McGue, Gottesman, & Rao, 1983; O'Rourke, Gottesman, Suarez, Rice, & Reich, 1982), specific reading disability (Lewitter, DeFries, & Elston, 1980), verbal and spatial ability (Borecki & Ashton, 1984), and affective psychosis (Baron, 1981; Baron, Mendlewicz, & Klotz, 1981; Crowe, et al., 1981; Leckman & Gershon, 1977; O'Rourke, McGuffin, & Reich, 1983).

Schizophrenia in particular, because of its prevalence and the substantial evidence in favor of genetic etiology, has been a favorite candidate for segregation analyses. Unfortunately, the results so far have not been conclusive. Depending on the precise nature of the model, both multifactorial-polygenic models and single-gene models have provided adequate fits to the data. In other cases, both have been rejected. Gottesman and Shields (1972) found that the single-locus model predicted an MZ twin concordance too far below the actual level, while the multifactorial model erred in the opposite direction. Analyzing the families of schizophrenic probands in a longitudinal study, Tsuang, Bucher, and Fleming (1982) were unable to fit models of simple Mendelian transmission, a result they attribute to possible genetic heterogeneity among the families or to limitations (such as the neglect of a common sibling environment factor) in the segregation model they employed (Elston & Yelverton, 1975). Using a mixed model analysis, Carter and Chung (1980) were unable to resolve a single-locus versus polygenic transmission.

In reviewing attempts to fit specific models of

transmission, O'Rourke et al. (1982) and Gottesman and Shields (1982) have argued that the positive correlations among the severity of the schizophrenia in the proband, the number of affected relatives, and the morbidity risks to relatives strongly suggest that the liability is multifactorial and polygenic. More recently, McGue et al. (1983) have argued that the failure to detect a single locus does not necessarily rule out a major gene effect; however, the equivocal results and the fact that identical twins are not fully concordant indicate that factors other than a single gene must be involved in the etiology of schizophrenia.

The interpretation of results from these complex segregation analyses is problematic, and the lack of clarity is especially apparent from the discordant results obtained when slightly different methods are applied to the same data. Elston and Campbell (1970), for example, found evidence in favor of a single-locus hypothesis using Kallman's (1938; 1946) data; but a subsequent reanalysis of the same pedigrees (Elston, Nambroodi, Spence, & Rainer, 1978) failed to fit a one-locus model. The failure to reject both polygenic and single-gene models in the same data (e.g., Matthyse & Kidd, 1976; Kidd & Cavalli-Sforza, 1982) or the inability to fit any model (Elston et al., 1978) may suggest that the models or methods are inadequate, or that there is considerable genetic heterogeneity (i.e., multiple forms with different etiologies). If there are multiple forms of schizophrenia, it may be necessary to distinguish them based on some biological marker, such as monoamine-oxidase activity (McGuffin, 1984; Buchsbaum & Haier, 1983; Deutsch & Davis, 1983), or on more specific diagnostic criteria before segregation analysis can produce more certain results.

Several other applications illustrate the use of these methods in behavioral studies. Lewitter et al. (1980) were unable to fit models of single-locus transmission (except for a small subsample of families with female probands) to family data on specific reading disability. Application of Morton and MacLean's (1974) complex segregation analysis to data from the Hawaii study of cognition has suggested the presence of a major-locus effect on vocabulary scores (Borecki and Ashton, 1984) and spatial ability (Ashton, Polovina, & Vandenberg, 1979). Such results must be interpreted with caution, however, because the analytical procedures are particularly sensitive to distributional aspects such as skew and kurtosis. In fitting simulated score data typical of psychometric tests, Eaves (1983) has shown that application of the mixed model often leads to false acceptance of the Mendelian model.

When Mendelian ratios are not obvious, segregation analysis may help to detect the effect of a single gene; but the results are often equivocal, and, for psychological phenotypes, the nature of the data may often fail to satisfy critical assumptions (e.g., normality). Where segregation or pedigree analysis suggests single-locus transmission, strong confirmation of the transmission model can be obtained from linkage analysis, the subject of our next section.

Linkage Analysis

Genes located near one another on the same chromosome do not assort independently during gametogenesis. Consider a person heterozygous at two loci ($AaBb$). If the loci were on separate chromosomes, the four gametic types (AB, Ab, aB, and ab) would be produced in equal proportions. If the genes were, instead, on the same chromosome (a condition described as linkage), two gametic types (e.g., AB and ab) would be more frequent than the others (e.g., aB and Ab). In this case, the A and B alleles would be together on one chromosome of the individual, while the a and b alleles would reside together on the homologue. (Another double heterozygote could have A and b linked and a and B linked, of course.) A gamete carrying the *recombinant* types (aB and Ab) would be produced only if there were a crossover involving the breakage and reunion between the arms of the homologous chromosomes. Such crossovers are frequent and generate much genetic variation by mixing the paternally and maternally derived chromosomal arrangements. For loci that are relatively far apart, the probability of multiple crossovers between them is so great that the genes assort independently. The closer the loci are, however, the less likely is such recombination.

Where matings can be controlled, it is relatively easy to detect linkage between genes by observing the transmission of two or more traits. In human studies, the investigators must select families that are *informative* in the sense that they are segregating for genetic markers in addition to the trait under analysis. Genetic markers are physical or chemical attributes, usually monogenic, for which the type of gene action and the chromosomal location are known. The rapid development of biochemical and molecular genetics has yielded an array of genetic markers including a variety of blood groups and enzyme variants, as well as unique chromosomal staining patterns and restriction sites—all of which are polymorphic, and many have been mapped to particular locations (see *American Journal of Human Genetics*, 1983, *35*, 134–156 for recent human gene map; Lalouel, 1977; Morton, 1984).

Linkage analysis requires that members of the pedigree be characterized for markers as well as for the phenotype under study. The extent to which the presence or absence of the trait coincides with the transmission of a particular marker is then evaluated to determine the degree of *discrepancy* from the association predicted by the null hypothesis of independent assortment (Fishman, Suarez, Hodge, & Reich, 1978; Ott, 1974; Lalouel, 1977). Maximum likelihood methods are used to select the recombination fraction.

This methodology has been applied to various behavioral pathologies. One example is reading disability, for which condition several family studies (Hallgren, 1950; Owen, Adams, Forrest, Stolz, & Fisher, 1971; DeFries, Singer, Foch, & Lewitter, 1978; Finucci, 1978) and twin studies (Bakwin, 1973) have indicated hereditary influence. The mode of transmission has remained unclear, however, (Lewitter et al., 1980) perhaps because of heterogeneity both in the phenotype and in the underlying genetic and environmental causes (Foch, 1979). Smith, Kimberling, Pennington, and Lubs (1983) applied quantitative linkage analysis, using the maximum likelihood procedure of Ott (1974), to nine families identified through a reading disabled proband. To maximize the chances of detecting a single-locus form, these investigators selected families in which reading disability appeared in two or more generations. Using 21 common genetic markers in addition to chromosamal banding patterns, they found evidence for significant linkage between specific reading disability and a marker on chromosome 15. Continued research is required to replicate this result and to determine whether a single-locus form of reading disability has in fact been identified.

From the time when Rosanoff, Handy, and Plessett (1935) first suggested that affective psychoses were influenced by an X-linked dominant gene, the hypothesis has been controversial. As described earlier, males are heteromorphic for the sex chromosomes, receiving an X chromosome from the mother and a Y chromosome from the father. Other than gender development, no traits have been clearly linked to the Y chromosome. Thus, early support for the hypothesis involved the greater incidence of depressive disorders in women and the relative infrequency of father-to-son transmission (Winokur, Clayton, & Reich, 1969; Taylor & Abrams, 1973). However, in 75 to 90 percent of the pedigrees published from other investigators, father-to-son transmission is present (Goetzl, Green, Whybrow, & Jackson, 1974; James & Chapman, 1975; Mendlewicz & Rainer, 1977; Perris, 1968; see recent review by Goldin & Gershon, 1983).

The appearance of X-linkage for a dominant allele in at least some families has prompted a continuing effort to test the purported linkage by applying maximum likelihood methods to estimate the recombination fraction between the incidence of affective psychosis in relatives of affected probands and traits known to be X-linked (protan and deutan forms of color blindness, Xg blood group, and glucose-6-phosphate dehydrogenase deficiency). The first reports of linkage between affective disorders and the X-chromosome markers, color blindness, and Xg in the families of *bipolar* probands (Mendlewicz, Fleiss, & Fieve, 1972; Mendlewicz & Fleiss, 1974; Reich, Clayton, & Winokur, 1969) were criticized heavily for methodological problems and especially for ascertainment bias (Gershon, Bunney, Leckman, Van Eerdewegh, & De Bauche, 1976). The critics also questioned the paradoxical result of linkage to both markers, since these had been found to be relatively distant from one another on the X-chromosome. In addition, Gershon, Targum, Matthysse, and Bunney (1979) and Leckman, Gershon, McGinniss, Targum, and Dibble (1979) were unable to detect linkage to either marker in their series of families. The differences between laboratories have prompted the reanalysis of the original data, supplemented by additional pedigrees and various improvements in methodology related to ascertainment biases and age-of-onset correction (Baron, 1977; Mendlewicz, Linkowski, Guroff, & Van Praag, 1979; Baron, Rainer, & Risch, 1981; Risch & Baron, 1982). These linkage analyses and reanalyses still confirm the close linkage between color blindness and affective disorders in the families of bipolar probands, but suggest only a weak association with the Xg locus. Recently, Mendlewicz, Linkowski, and Wilmotte (1980) reported linkage between bipolar psychosis and another X-chromosome marker, glucose-6-phosphate dehydrogenase; and Baron and Risch (1982) found linkage with affective disorders and color blindness in the families of schizoaffective probands. Whether the inconsistencies between the work of Mendlewicz, Baron, and their colleagues on the one hand, and Gershon and his colleagues on the other, indicate that there are multiple forms of bipolar illness, some X-linked and others not, remains uncertain. It is clear, however, that most pedigrees involve male-to-male transmission which rules out X-linkage as a sole mechanism in the transmission of all forms of bipolar illness.

Recent linkage analyses have suggested that liability to another form of bipolar illness may be transmitted autosomally. Turner and King (1981, 1983) and Weitkamp, Stancer, Persad, Flood, and Guttormsen (1981) reported linkage between bipolar disorder and the autosomal HLA locus (a complex of four or more polymorphic genes that produce the unique haptoglobin markers involved with immunologic identity). However, several investigators (Suarez & Reich, 1984; Goldin, Clerget-Darpoux, & Gershon, 1982; Johnson, Hunt, Robertson, & Doran, 1981) were unable to confirm these results.

Linkage analyses have also been attempted for schizophrenia. Turner (1979), adopting a model of autosomal dominance, showed linkage between the HLA locus and schizophrenia, but McGuffin, Festenstein, and Murray (1983) demonstrated that the positive result was dependent on the transmission model. They failed to replicate the positive linkage when a more flexible method (Green & Woodrow, 1977) was applied to data combined from Turner's study and their own cases.

Thus, the picture of psychiatric disorders yielded by linkage analysis has not yet come into clear focus. Some of the contradictory results may be due to ascertainment bias, to inappropriate applications of methods, or to violations of untested assumptions about the distribution or transmission of traits. Some results, however, may reflect true differences in the genetics of disorders that happen to be included in the same diagnostic category. The

resolution of genetic heterogeneity is, perhaps, the single most important goal of psychiatric genetics. If current nosological schemes lump together clinical types with diverse genetic and environmental etiologies, the search for biological markers is bound to produce equivocal results. The benefits to be yielded by the substantial effort required to identify etiologically unique subtypes will include more effective and earlier diagnosis and the capability of developing more specific preventive and therapeutic strategies.

Multiple-Threshold Models, Familial Incidence, and Genetic Heterogeneity

Examining the aggregation of psychiatric illness in family, twin, and adoption data has become an increasingly popular method for refining current nosological schemes (see McGuffin, Farmer, Gottesman, Murray, & Reveley, 1984). Principal among the diagnostic questions addressed has been the differentiation between the affective disorders and schizophrenia, as well as among clinical subtypes within these two major groupings. Recent investigators have shown that there is little overlap in the familial incidence of the major depressive disorders and the schizophrenia-related conditions (Kendler, Gruenberg, & Stauss, 1982; Baron, Gruen, Asnis, & Kane, 1983; Tsuang, Winokur, & Crowe, 1980; Loranger, 1981; Scharfetter, 1981). In general, relatives of schizophrenics exhibit increased rates of schizophrenia and of the schizophrenia spectrum disorders, namely, schizotypal and paranoid personality disorder (Kendler & Gruenberg, 1984; Kendler, Masterson, Ungaro, & Davis, 1984; Baron et al., 1983; Guze, Cloninger, Martin, & Clayton, 1983; Lowing, Mirsky, & Pereira, 1983). Affected relatives of probands with unipolar or bipolar illness typically receive a diagnosis within one of the major depressive categories (Kendler et al., 1982; Guze et al., 1983; Weissman et al., 1984; Gershon et al., 1982).

Nevertheless, the differentiation of schizophrenia from primary affective psychosis remains difficult. Guze et al. (1983) confirmed earlier reports of episodic depression in chronic schizophrenics whose relatives did not exhibit increased risk for affective disorders. Kendler and Hays (1983), however, found that major depression was far more likely to develop in

schizophrenics with depressed relatives compared to those without a family history of
unipolar disorder. Their follow-up study also
included a group of patients originally diagnosed as schizophrenic but who had a relative
with bipolar disorder. The symptoms and course
of the psychiatric illness in this third group
were characterized by more extreme variations
in affect, including episodes of both hypomania
and mania. Furthermore, these patients achieved
nearly full remission between psychotic episodes. This symptom pattern is more typical of
bipolar illness than of schizophrenia. Evidence
from several family and follow-up studies is
mounting in favor of the hypothesis that such
schizoaffective syndromes represent a severe
form of affective disorder (Abrams & Taylor,
1980; Baron et al., 1983; Guze et al., 1983) that, in
some pedigrees, may be X-linked (Baron &
Risch, 1982; Mendlewicz et al., 1980).

Familial studies have been marshalled to
study heterogeneity among affective and
schizoaffective disorders. Pooling data from
family studies conducted over two decades,
Schlesser and Altshuler (1983) found that the
morbidity risks for bipolar and unipolar forms
were each 11.5 percent among the 3213 first-
degree relatives of bipolar index cases and 1.0
percent and 13.9 percent, respectively, among
the 2219 first-degree relatives of unipolar index
cases. The prevalence of schizophrenia was not
elevated above that in the general population in
either proband group. Similar results have been
reported in the collaborative studies of Gershon
et al. (1982) and Weissman et al. (1982, 1984). In
these studies, unipolar disorder was the most
frequent diagnosis in the families of bipolar as
well as unipolar probands. Gershon et al. (1982)
included a group of schizoaffective probands
whose relatives exhibited the highest rates of
affective psychosis, confirming the suspicion
that schizoaffective disorder is a particularly
severe form of affective psychosis.

The familial aggregation of affective psychoses in these studies is consistent with the
hypothesis of a common liability, with unipolar,
bipolar, and schizoaffective variants representing increasing degrees of liability. Reich and his
colleagues (Reich et al., 1972; Reich et al., 1979)
have developed a series of analyses that test the
degree to which family prevalence data for such
related disorders fit a single liability distribution. The multiple-threshold model requires

several assumptions, including that genetic and
environmental determinants are additive, that
liability is normally distributed, and that individuals whose liability exceeds one or another
threshold manifest a particular form of the illness. Maximum likelihood estimates of the average liability in relatives of each type of proband
are derived from the prevalence data, and the
correlation between the liabilities of relatives
is calculated by assigning individuals the liability appropriate to their diagnosis. Finally, a
chi-square goodness-of-fit test is performed. If
independent estimates of prevalences in the
general population are included, the standard
errors of the estimated parameters are reduced,
and the goodness-of-fit test is more powerful.
Gershon et al. (1982) found that the three-
threshold model provided an adequate fit and
that the heritability of liability estimated from
the correlation of relatives was 78 percent (see
Figure 13.19). Since nongenetic, familial factors
may contribute to the correlation, the investigators point out that this value should be
interpreted as an index of familiality.

More complex models that combine multifactorial models with segregation analysis (Reich
et al., 1979; Morton & MacLean, 1974) may be
employed if the trait pattern in nuclear families
is analyzed rather than simple prevalence.
O'Rourke et al. (1983), for example, fit several
models of liability to families of bipolar index
cases. Models incorporating a major locus
effect, both with and without a multifactorial
background, provided reasonable likelihoods,
but these did not provide significantly better fit
than a complex multifactorial model that permitted heterogeneity among the six family
correlations (mother or father with son or
daughter and same sex and opposite sex sibling
sets).

Other applications of multiple-threshold
models have suggested that early-onset
(probands younger than 40 at onset) and late-
onset forms of affective disorder belong to a
single liability continuum, with higher genetic
loading for the early onset form (Baron et
al., 1981). Antisocial personality may share the
same etiological process as hysteria (Cloninger,
Reich, & Guze, 1975) but one that is apparently
independent of liability to alcoholism and
depression (Cloninger, Reich, & Wetzel, 1979).
Schizophrenia, too, has been the subject of
multiple-threshold analysis. Several failures to

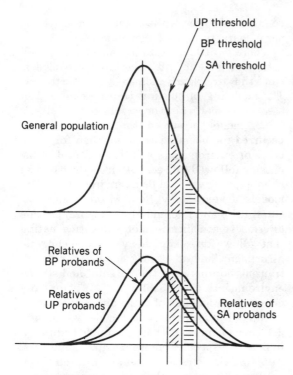

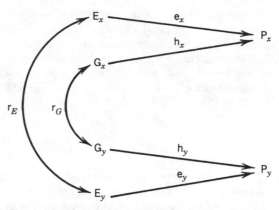

Figure 13.20. Path diagram of the phenotypic correlation between twin siblings (P_x and P_y) as a function of their genetic correlation (r_G) and their environmental correlation (r_E). From "Quantitative Genetic Theory" by R. Plomin, J. DeFries, G. McClearn, 1980, in *Behavioral Genetics: A Primer* (p. 229), San Francisco: W.H. Freeman & Co. Copyright (c) 1980 by W.H. Freeman & Co. Reprinted by permission.

Figure 13.19. Three-threshold, multifactorial model for genetic vulnerability to affective illness. UP indicates unipolar; BP, bipolar; and SA, schizoaffective. From "A Family Study of Schizoaffective, Bipolar I, Bipolar II, Unipolar, and Normal Control Probands" by E.S. Gershon, J. Hamovit, J.J. Guroff, E. Dibble, J.F. Leckman, W. Sceery, S.D. Targum, J.I. Nurnberger, L.R. Goldin and W.E. Bunney, 1982, *Archives of General Psychiatry*, *39*, p. 1162. Reprinted by permission.

fit multifactorial threshold models to schizophrenia and various spectrum disorders suggest that these diagnoses do not share a common liability distribution (Baron, 1982; Carter & Chung, 1980; Tsuang, Bucher, & Fleming, 1983). These negative findings pose a considerable problem in the development of biologically relevant diagnostic categories, since studies of identical twins (McGuffin et al., 1984; Gottesman & Shields, 1982), as well as the Danish adoption data (Kety, 1983; Kety, Rosenthal, & Wender, 1971; Kendler et al., 1984; Lowing et al., 1983), have repeatedly suggested that schizophrenia and various spectrum disorders are genetically related (see Torgersen, 1984, for an exception).

Path Analysis

Path analytic methods, first introduced by Sewall Wright (1921, 1978) comprise a subset of structural models that depict presumed relations among observed and hypothetical or latent variables. A simple path model portraying the causal connections that yield a correlation between the observed phenotypes of twins is shown in Figure 13.20. Single headed arrows represent causal linkages. Here, the phenotype, P_x, of twin X, is modeled as reflecting the additive combination of genotypic and environmental values, with $h_x = \sqrt{h_x^2}$ representing the correlation between genotype and phenotype and $e_x = \sqrt{1 - h_x^2}$ representing the correlation between environmental value and phenotype. In this case, h_y and e_y refer to the genetic and environmental correlations with the phenotype of twin Y and are equal to the respective correlations in twin X ($h_x = h_y = h$; $e_x = e_y = e$). The genetic correlation, r_G, as specified by quantitative genetic theory, is 1.0 for identical twins. According to the rules of path analysis (Li, 1975), the phenotypic correlation between the twins may be expressed as the sum of the paths that connect the phenotypes:

$$r_p = h_x h_y r_G + e_x e_y r_E = h^2 r_G + e^2 r_E.$$

In order to estimate the parameters, g, r_G, and r_E from the twin data alone, it is necessary to assume that the genotype and environment act additively (i.e., that dominance, epistasis, and gene-environment interaction and correlation are absent), that mating is random, and that r_E is similar in MZ and DZ twins. With these assumptions, $e^2 = 1 - h^2$ and $r_G = 0.5$ for DZ twins so that

$$r_{MZ} = h^2 + (1 - h^2)r_E$$
$$r_{DZ} = 1/2h^2 + (1 - h^2)r_E.$$

With two equations and two unknowns a perfect fit solution is possible—for example, $h^2 = 2(r_{MZ} - r_{DZ})$. This is, in fact, the traditional twin model. Laying the model out in path form makes explicit the untested assumptions and clarifies the limitations of the model. Additional path coefficients could be added, such as a connection between G and E to represent gene-environment correlation; but in the present model, additional paths could not be resolved with twin data alone. Correlations between other types of relatives are required to specify more elaborate models and to provide enough information to estimate parameters and test the overall fit.

Fulker (1982), for example, extended the path analytic model of twins to include the parents of twins. The extension allows for assortative mating between the parents, as well as for the gene-environment correlation induced by parental influences. Expectations for the correlations between spouses, between parents and offspring, and between MZ and DZ twins may be stated using just four parameters. Fulker's (1982) approach employs the covariances between relatives to derive maximum likelihood estimates of the parameters, which may then be used to solve equations for all of the path coefficients in the model. His illustrative application to data on shyness in twins and their parents yielded a heritability of 0.70, as well as a significant effect of familial environment, 0.09. The shared environmental effect was almost totally due to the *negative* correlation (-0.29 for mothers; -0.19 for fathers) between parental phenotype and child environment. Apparently, ". . . shy parents attempt to make their children less shy and vice versa. The effect is to counteract the children's own inherited tendencies and induce a negative gene-environmental correlation . . . (Fulker, 1982, p. 403)." Plomin, DeFries, and Loehlin (1977) had earlier predicted that positive gene-environment correlations might be common for

cognitive abilities, while negative ones might be more characteristic of temperament.

There is little uncertainty about the specification of genetic influences in these models since they are clearly defined by genetic theory. The modeling of cultural transmission and of assortative mating is more troublesome. Fulker's (1982) model presumed that mate selection occurred for phenotypes rather than for genotypes or environments and that cultural transmission followed a direct path from the parental phenotype to the child's environment. The models developed by Rao, Morton, and Yee (1974, 1976) and Rao and Morton (1978) provide alternative specifications of assortative mating that allow for social as well as phenotypic assortment and also include direct cultural transmission between the parental and sibling environments. (See Loehlin, 1978, 1979 for more critical comparisons of these different models.) With additional paths, their model was underdetermined, unless they incorporated additional indices of specific environmental influences. Adopting this strategy, Rao and Morton (1978) used an SES index in their analysis of published IQ data pooled from twin, family, and adoption studies. Rice, Cloninger, and Reich (1980) noted that the power of this analysis depends on the validity of the index and found that SES did not correspond with the transmissible cultural factor recovered in their path analysis of the same aggregation of IQ data.

Rice, Cloninger, and Reich (1978) and Cloninger, Rice, and Reich (1979) have implemented two path designs. Their models specify phenotypic assortment between spouses and direct cultural transmission between parent and child environment. They include an additional environmental effect that is shared by siblings but not directly correlated with transmissible environmental effects. Designed for use with data limited to nuclear families, the first model estimates the proportion of variance explained by transmissible factors but does not distinguish between genetic and environmental contributions. The second model can resolve cultural and genetic sources when the family data are supplemented by correlations from twin or adoption studies.

Their analyses of pooled IQ data reveal that the proportions of variance accounted for by genetic and cultural transmission were significant and approximately equal at 30 percent. An additional 8 percent is attributable to gene-environment correlation, yielding a total transmissibility of 68 percent. Furthermore, a model specifying equal environmental correlations between MZ and DZ or ordinary siblings could not be fit. The authors point out that this is not certain evidence of a stronger environmental correlation in MZ twins, but such an effect is suggested. The model does not specify genetic dominance. To the extent dominance exists, in this model it would be confounded with the environmental correlations of siblings. Thus, the unique MZ twin effect may also indicate that genetic dominance is present. The results of this analysis do clearly demonstrate that models of the transmission of IQ that incorporate cultural effects as well as assortative mating place lower bounds on estimates of heritability than do the simpler and less powerful designs.

Other phenotypes have also been analyzed with these flexible techniques. Vogler and Fulker (1983), for example, used the models proposed by Fulker (1982) and Rice et al. (1980) to study familial resemblance for educational attainment. In contrast to the IQ results, both models yielded a heritability near 60 percent with little evidence of either cultural transmission or effects of the sibling environment.

Rao et al. (1981) adapted their path analytic model to handle attribute data, namely the presence or absence of schizophrenia. In the absence of clear confirmation of Mendelian models through segregation analysis, the investigators suggest that path analysis is an appropriate method for understanding the nature of familial influences on liability. Assuming a population incidence of 0.85 percent, they found both heritability and cultural transmission to be significant, accounting for 71 percent and 20 percent, respectively, of the variance in liability. An environmental effect unique to twins and assortative mating were also found to be significant. The latter result is somewhat surprising since the prevalence in spouses of schizophrenics is not significantly different from the population figure. Rao et al. (1981) attribute this paradoxical result to the relatively high rate of psychiatric illness in children of schizophrenics.

While these rigorous methods provide a welcome alternative to the simpler, traditional approaches, they are not without some hazards. Collecting adequate data on multiple kinship types is essential if environmental and genetic influences are to be resolved. As implemented so far, the models specify only linear effects and do not yet allow for genotype-environment interactions. The models also assume that the variation underlying observed and latent variables is normally distributed. It is also important to remember that finding a model that meets the statistical criterion of a goodness-of-fit test means only that the hypothetical relations and derived parameters cannot be rejected as a possible explanation of the data. It does not prove that the model is, in fact, true. These issues, however, are hardly unique to path analysis, and the flexibility of the method is promising, as is well demonstrated by its extensions to multivariate and longitudinal data (DeFries, Kuse, & Vandenberg, 1979; Plomin & DeFries, 1979; Baker, DeFries, & Fulker, 1983).

The Birmingham Models

The Birmingham school, consisting of Jinks, Eaves, Martin, Fulker, and their colleagues, has developed various biometrical models that analyze the mean squares rather than correlations (Eaves, Last, Young, & Martin, 1978; Fulker, 1979; Jinks & Fulker, 1970; Mather & Jinks, 1971). These analytic models offer the advantage of including both within-family and between-family components of variance. The Birmingham formulations have a long history of application in animal behavioral genetics (see Fulker, 1979 for a concise overview). In addition to the classical analysis previously described (i.e., inbred parental, hybrid, and backcross generations), the biometrical analyses of the diallel design (Broadhurst, 1960; Mather & Jinks, 1971) and the triple-test cross (Hewitt & Fulker, 1981) provide the detailed assessment of genetic architecture required to make inferences about the adaptive significance of behavioral phenotypes (Broadhurst & Jinks, 1974; Broadhurst, 1979).

Since the 1970s, these methods have been extended to human behavioral genetics (Eaves et al., 1977b; Eaves et al., 1978). In brief, the expectations for the contributions of different genetic and environmental factors are set out in terms of the mean squares. For the simple case of the classical twin design, there are four mean squares between and within MZ and DZ pairs. Thus, four parameters can be fitted in this limited case: G1 and E1 are the genetic and

Table 13.18.   **Expectations of variance components and pairs of individuals for an additive biometrical model (G_1, G_2, E_1, E_2).**

	Component of variance	Mean square
(a) Twins raised together		
Between MZ	$G_1 + G_2 + E_2$	$2G_1 + 2G_2 + E_1 + 2E_2$
Within MZ	E_1	E_1
Between DZ	$G_2 + E_2$	$G_1 + 2G_2 + E_1 + 2E_2$
Within DZ	$G_1 + E_1$	$G_1 + E_1$
(b) Separated twins		
Between MZ	$G_1 + G_2$	$2G_1 + 2G_2 + E_1 + E_2$
Within MZ	$E_1 + E_2$	$E_1 + E_2$
Between DZ	G_2	$G_1 + 2G_2 + E_1 + E_2$
Within DZ	$G_1 + E_1 + E_2$	$G_1 + E_1 + E_2$
(c) Foster siblings raised together		
Between pairs	E_2	$G_1 + G_2 + E_1 + 2E_2$
Within pairs	$G_1 + G_2 + E_1$	$G_1 + G_2 + E_1$

Note. From "A Progressive Approach to Non-Additivity and Genotype-Environmental Covariance in the Analysis of Human Differences" by L.J. Eaves, K.A. Last, N.G. Martin, and J.L. Links, 1977, *The British Journal of Mathematical and Statistical Psychology, 30*, pp. 1–42. Copyright 1977 by The British Psychological Society. Adapted by permission.

environmental components of within-pair variance; G2 and E2 are the genetic and environmental components of the between-pair variance. With the usual assumptions of the twin method regarding additivity and assortative mating, the expectations for the mean squares are shown in the top section of Table 13.18.

The four parameters are estimated by the method of weighted least squares, and the fit of the model may be assessed by testing the deviation of the predicted from the observed mean squares. With twin data alone, it is possible, then, to test the fit of models that exclude one or more of the parameters. Rowe (1983a), for example, used this approach to study delinquency in twins. Models excluding G1 and G2 were clearly rejected, which suggests that there is, indeed, a significant genetic component.

The expectations for separated twins and foster siblings are also given in Table 13.18 to illustrate the extension of the biometrical model to other kinship relations. Eaves et al. (1978, 1977a) show how additional parameters, incorporating genotype-environment interactions and covariances, may be estimated when data from multiple kinship types are available. A variety of other designs including sex-specific effects and longitudinal analysis may be fitted (Eaves et al., 1978).

Multivariate Behavioral Genetic Analyses
The analyses we have discussed concern the apportionment of variance into genetic and environmental components. Since variance is simply a special case of covariance, it should be obvious that the covariances between two or among more variables is partitionable as well (Tukey, 1951; Plomin et al., 1980). The basic principle in multivariate genetic analysis can be illustrated by redefining the path model in Figure 13.20. The two phenotypes, P_X and P_Y, now stand for two measurements from the same individual, which could be different variables or different occasions or both. The observed correlation between the phenotypes may be expressed as:

$$r_p = h_x h_y r_G + e_x e_y r_E$$

where the subscripts denote the parameters of one or the other trait. Genetic correlations arise when the same gene or set of genes influences the development of both phenotypes, or when different genes affecting the two traits are linked, or when they have been forced into disequilibrium by nonrandom mating. Similarly, the same environmental factors may influence different traits. A general lesson from this formulation is that any correlation between variables may have both genetic and environmental sources.

Following the method used by Plomin and DeFries (1979), the matrix of correlations among different specific abilities is stated, in matrix notation, as:

$$R_P = HR_GH + ER_EE.$$

This is a simple, multivariate extension of the equation given previously for the univariate case. Here, R_P, R_G, and R_E are, respectively, the phenotypic, genotypic, and environmental correlation matrices in which off diagonal elements are the cross-correlations between different variables. H is a diagonal matrix of the square roots of the univariate heritabilities, and E is a diagonal matrix of the square roots of the environmentalities ($\sqrt{1 - h^2}$).

Multivariate analyses of kinship data do not escape the limitations of their univariate counterparts. The application to twin data requires the usual assumptions regarding additivity, gene-environment correlation and interaction, shared environment, and assortative mating. Then, the estimation of the genetic and environmental components proceeds in a manner directly analogous to the univariate case. Doubling the difference between the MZ and DZ phenotypic matrices estimates the matrix of phenotypically standardized genetic correlations:

$$2(R_{PMZ} - R_{PDZ}) = HR_GH.$$

The matrix of phenotypically standardized environmental correlations is then obtained by subtraction:

$$R_P - HR_GH = ER_EE.$$

The bivariate genetic and environmental correlations between measures may be calculated by standard matrix procedures. While the bivariate relations expressed in these derived matrices may reveal some theoretically or empirically useful information, the most important advantage offered by the multivariate method is the ability to examine the overall structure of genetic and environmental influences. That opportunity may be more fully exploited by factoring the derived matrices. If the principal goal is to understand the genetic and environmental structures that contribute to phenotypic correlations, then the phenotypically standardized genetic (HR_GH) and environmental (ER_EE) matrices can be factored. If, on the other hand, describing the congruences among genetic influences or among environmental influences is the goal, factor analysis can be applied to the matrices of genetic (R_G)

and environmental (R_E) correlations (Vogler, 1982).

Several multivariate procedures have been applied to twin and parent-offspring data on specific cognitive abilities and scholastic achievement (Bock & Vandenberg, 1968; Loehlin & Vandenberg, 1968; Loehlin & Nichols, 1976; Plomin & Vandenberg, 1980; DeFries, Kuse, & Vandenberg, 1979; Eaves & Gale, 1974; Page & Jarjoura, 1979). The typical result is that much of the genetic variance is found in a single factor, the residuals being specific to each test. A single major factor is typical of the environmental matrices as well. Individual differences in mental abilities appear to arise largely from single genetic and environmental dimensions. One exception to this general summary is Plomin and Vandenberg's (1980) analysis of primary mental abilities in five- to seven-year-old twins. Examination of the MZ and DZ cross-correlations between the verbal and spatial subsets indicates that these abilities were genetically independent.

Another common result of the multivariate analyses of mental abilities is that the patterns of the genetic and environmental factors are very similar. Loehlin and Vandenberg (1968) attribute the correspondence to a sort of positive feedback between human biological tendencies and cultural evolution. They speculate that, "the biological capacities of the human organism have historically had some bearing on what society has tended to recognize, name, and educate as a unit" (p. 275). Hegman and DeFries (1970), however, found that genetic and environmental dimensions underlying animal behavior were also correlated. They argue that the similar patterning of environmental and genetic sources of covariation is a consequence of commonality in physiological causal pathways through which both genes and environmental agents exert their influence. A model of this causal nexus is presented later in the discussion of the mechanisms of genetic effects.

The Birmingham group has provided an especially sophisticated approach to multivariate gene-environment analysis (Martin & Eaves, 1977). In adapting Jöreskog's confirmatory methods for analyzing covariance structures, they are able to formulate and test specific hypotheses about phenotypic covariation and the structure of gene-environment influences. As in the biometrical analysis of single variables, the expectations for a particular model of gene-environment effects are set out for the matrices of mean products both within and among kinship groups. The unconstrained parameters are then estimated by a maximum likelihood procedure. The adequacy of the model may be tested by comparing the log likelihood obtained from the restricted model and the one obtained from a perfect fit solution or from the solution of alternative models. Thus, a comparative test of the appropriateness of the assumptions in different models can be made. In contrast to methods employing additive decomposition of matrices, the expected cross-product matrices will be positive definite and therefore factorable. Another advantage of this method, shared by model-fitting procedures in general, is the flexibility to incorporate data from multiple kinship types into a single analysis.

Although we have heretofore used few examples involving research on genetics of personality and temperament, it must be recorded that these are lively research domains (see reviews by Scarr, Webber, Weinberg, & Wittig, 1981; Loehlin, 1982; Fuller & Thompson, 1978; Goldsmith, 1983; Plomin et al., 1980; Plomin, 1983). In general, familial and twin correlations are low compared to those obtained with cognitive abilities (Rowe & Plomin, 1981), and there is little evidence of E_2. Applying path analysis to personality data from twin, adoption, and family designs, Carey and Rice (1983) found that the three traits studied were each fit by a different model of gene-environment effects and sex differences.

The analysis of covariance structures is a particularly appropriate device in the domain of personality traits since both biometrical and psychological hypotheses about their organization can be analyzed simultaneously. Martin et al. (cited by Eaves et al., 1978) used twin data to test Eysenck's theory about the relations between major personality dimension (psychoticism, extraversion, and neuroticism) and other behavioral styles, which in this case were four measures each of sensation seeking and impulsivity. A model specified by the psychogenetic theory that restricted each of the major personality dimensions to separate genetic and environmental factors could not be fit. As usual, negative results are difficult to interpret. The failure may have resulted because twin data alone were inadequate for specifying an appropriate gene-

environment model. It may, however, indicate that Eysenck's personality dimensions do not exhaust the genetic covariation among measures of impulsiveness and sensation seeking.

In another application of the analysis of covariance structures, Eaves et al. (1977b) found that four aspects of impulsiveness were adequately explained by a simple G and E_1 model and that the structures of the underlying genetic and environmental components were similar. Extending the covariance analysis to model sex effects and interactions, Fulker (1978, 1979) fitted a model that suggested the possibility of sex differentiated genetic control in profiles of sensation seeking. Whether this model-fitting approach will become the wave of the future is yet a matter of speculation; but Eaves et al. (1977b) conclude that, with ingenious models and the right data, the causal analysis of trait covariation promises glimpses of the "subtleties of the mechanisms underlying the multivariate structure of individual differences" (p. 196).

THE IMPORTANCE OF WITHIN-FAMILY ENVIRONMENT

The methods of behavioral genetics clearly shed light on both environmental and genetic determinants of individual differences. No model or mode of analysis can specify heritable influences without explicitly including some treatment of environmental factors. Even the simple resolution of the within-families environmental influences (E_1) from the between-families component can (E_2) greatly inform theoretical development in psychology.

In their review of behavioral genetic research on personality, cognition, and psychopathology, Rowe and Plomin (1981) conclude that environmental factors that are *not* shared by siblings comprise the major part of environmental variance. E_1 effects predominate particularly in the domain of personality and psychopathology, where there is little evidence of E_2 effects. Even for intelligence, E_1 effects may be substantial (McCall, 1983). In the path analysis of kinship data on IQ, Rice et al. (1980) found that variance was apportioned equally among genetic, E_1, and E_2 compartments. Thus, E_1 accounts for roughly one-third of the variance in IQ. Recent adoption data suggest an even greater share for E_1 variance. The intraclass correlation of unrelated children reared in the same family is a direct estimate of E_2 variance. For IQ, these correlations are generally in the range of 0.20 to 0.30. In the only report of postadolescent adoptees (16 to 22 years of age) (Scarr & Weinberg, 1978), the correlation was essentially zero and suggests that shared family experiences become less important as children become more independent.

Outside of the domain of research concentrated on interactions within families, much empirical and theoretical research has emphasized E_2 variables or presumed that particular ones (i.e., SES, parental-style, divorce, etc.) have a unitary effect upon siblings (Maccoby & Martin, 1983). Indeed, it is possible that the effects of these influences are highly differentiated, depending upon the individual characteristics of each sibling, and should be considered as possible contributors to E_1 or gene-environment interaction components.

The E_1 component would, of course, include unreliability of measurement, as well as idiosyncratic and random factors. Some portion of E_1 variance, however, may include systematic effects such as those associated with family constellation. Gender and birth order, for example, do correlate with aspects of temperament and intellectual ability (Maccoby & Martin, 1983; Jacklin & Maccoby, 1974; Zajonc & Marcus, 1975), but these correlations generally account for less than five percent of the variance (Plomin & Foch, 1981; Scarr & Grajek, 1983). Rowe and Plomin (1981) proposed several other potential sources of systematic E_1 influences and formulated research designs that could elucidate their effects. See Rowe and Plomin (1979), Daniels, Dunn, Furstenberg, & Plomin (1985), Plomin & Daniels (1987) for specific applications.

Genotype-Environment Correlation and Interaction

Gene-environment interaction and correlation are often confused with ill-defined notions of interaction offered by some organismic theories of development. The basic organismic-development model states that the individual is a product of mutually reciprocal *interactions* among genetic and other constitutional factors and the environment. Accordingly, the differential influences of genes and environments are inseparable. Although it is certainly true that individual development is patterned by both genes and environments, the assertion that their effects are inseparable is wrong. Using the

simplest of single-subject designs, one can clearly demonstrate environmental effects. The new techniques promised by genetic engineering portend a time when the genes themselves may be subject to rather precise manipulation. Furthermore, for the study of differences among individuals, the biometrical and quantitative genetic analyses estimate the relative sizes of genetic and environmental components of variance. As discussed previously, some designs are better than others for distinguishing among particular components. Whether genetic and environmental influences interact or are correlated in their effects is an empirical question. The model-fitting approaches described previously have demonstrated that simple models involving only direct, linear effects of genes and environments often give an adequate account of the data. Even in laboratory research with animals, where it is possible to examine extremes of both genotype and environment, disordinal interaction effects that account for more than a small fraction of total variance are rare (Henderson, 1979; Fulker, Wilcock, & Broadhurst, 1972; Erlenmeyer-Kimling, 1972).

The possibility that gene-environment interaction may underlie some individual differences has been repeatedly emphasized in strong criticisms of behavioral genetic designs in general and of human behavior genetics more specifically (e.g., Feldman & Lewontin, 1975). The presence of gene-environment interaction, however, is not a difficulty for genetic interpretation alone; interaction effects limit the generalizability of environmental explanations as well. Henderson (1979) provides two illustrations of this principle. One involves Seligman's theory of conditioned helplessness. Broadhurst and Bignami (cited by Henderson, 1979) subjected rats from lines selectively bred for high versus low conditioned avoidance to inescapable shock. When tested later in a typical escape-avoidance procedure, the treated rats from the low line failed to escape. Treated rats from the high line were indistinguishable from controls of both lines that had not experienced the inescapable shock. "Since the two strains are both capable of learning to escape under normal control conditions, the study suggests an explanation of the pre-shock effect will require constructs in addition to those of learning theory, in which terms Seligman's explanation is exclusively couched (Henderson, 1979, p. 338)." Henderson's own elegant work (1968, 1970a, 1970b) has shown that the effects of early experience on later behavior depend in large part upon genotypic constitution. Thus, any social or psychological theory that fails to consider variation in genetic disposition may have little generality.

With laboratory animals, genotype-environment interaction is usually investigated via a standard, factorial design in which animals from two or more distinctive genetic groups are distributed into two or more treatment environments. For human studies, the identification of potential interactions is a little more difficult. Plomin et al. (1977) approximated a 2×2 factorial design with IQ data from adoption studies. Adoptees were classified into one of four cells defined on the genotypic dimension by having biological parents with higher than average SES versus lower SES and similarly on the environmental dimension by the SES of the adoptive parents. The application to two sets of adoption data yielded only one significant main effect, the genotypic dimension. Some other index of biological and adoptive parents might produce a significant interaction, but that is not the point at issue. The example is meant only to illustrate the analysis.

This approach was recently applied using regression analysis to test for the presence of gene-environment interaction. Cadoret, Cain, and Crowe (1983) found that adoptees whose biological parents were antisocial or alcoholic and who were exposed to adverse environments as children were far likelier to commit antisocial acts themselves than would be predicted from the simple additive combination of genotypic and environmental effects. The result suggests a gene-environment interaction. Other means of detecting gene-environment interactions are proposed by Martin and Eaves (1977).

Gene-environment correlation (CovGE) arises when genotypes are selectively exposed to environments. Plomin et al. (1977) proposed three kinds of CovGE that Scarr (1981; Scarr & McCartney, 1983) later elaborated in a theory of behavioral development. *Passive* CovGE arises if genetically related parents provide environments that correlate with the child's genotype. For example, intelligent parents may supply favorable genes and an intellectually stimulating environment. Alternatively, CovGE may be produced in an *evocative* way. That is, the reac-

tions of the physical and social environment may be influenced by the child's genotype. A very active, noisy child might continually meet with suppression (a negative CovGE). The third type of CovGE is *active*. Active CovGE is the consequence of individuals themselves seeking out environments concordant with their genetic dispositions.

Several methods to screen for CovGE have been suggested. Some of the model-fitting procedures discussed previously can incorporate CovGE if suitable kinship types are available. Plomin et al. (1977) noted that the extent of passive CovGE could be assessed in a full adoption study. Passive CovGE would contribute to the total variance in children reared by their biological parents. In the absence of selective placement, however, its value would be zero in adoptive families since genetic and cultural transmission are separated. If CovGE is an important source of individual differences, the phenotypic variance among control children should exceed that of adoptees.

Fischbein's (1978) approach relies on longitudinal data from twins. If a difference between MZ and DZ correlations is constant, genetic and environmental effects are probably linear and additive. If, however, the correlations diverge as DZ twins become progressively less similar, the more complex effects of GXE or CovGE may be involved. Examination of the longitudinal pattern of twin correlations suggested a simple additive model for growth and inductive reasoning, but the nonadditive components, GXE and CovGE, might explain the divergence of MZ and DZ correlations in verbal and mathematical abilities.

Scarr's (1981; Scarr & McCartney, 1983) recent consideration of developmental process puts CovGE in the limelight. She asserts that CovGE prescribes the nature of the environment that different individuals will experience. Accordingly, the uniqueness of experience and the directions it imposes on development are ultimately driven by the genotype. Early in childhood, correlations of the evocative and passive kind predominate. During later childhood and adolescence, active CovGE is progressively more important as individuals acquire more freedom in selecting their friends, their clothes, their physical settings, and their intellectual stimulation. Scarr does not mean to imply a rigid genetic determination but argues for a probabilistic connection in which certain combinations of genotypes and environments are more likely than others as a result of CovGE. In support of her theory, Scarr cites three general findings of twin and adoption studies that can be explained if CovGE does greatly influence development: (1) MZ and DZ intrapair differences diverge during childhood as MZ resemblance increases, while DZ resemblance declines to the level of ordinary, singleton siblings (Wilson, 1981, 1983); (2) the low correlations of young adoptees with their adoptive parents and siblings fall to zero by the end of adolescence (Scarr & Weinberg, 1978); and (3) MZ twins reared in separate environments are strikingly similar (Bouchard, 1983).

Scarr and McCartney (1983) developed several specific hypotheses from this CovGE theory and discussed research strategies to test them. For example, the theory predicts that parental treatment will be differential and correlated with the unique characteristics of each child. Another prediction is that naturalistic observations of children's behavior in problem solving situations ought to reveal correlations between their personalities or abilities and the particular solutions they employ. Adoption designs are particularly well suited to this endeavor. No doubt it will be relatively easy to demonstrate that individuals are active participants in their own development. The notion of an active and selective organism constructing its own development is increasingly popular (e.g., Lerner, 1982). Whether CovGE can be construed as a developmental *process* and genetic control accepted as the driving force are matters yet to be decided. The hypotheses, though, should stimulate research on the dynamic relation between genotype and environment during development.

Mechanisms of Gene Action

Following Mendel's elegant laws of heredity, and the gradual realization of the ubiquity of influence of the Mendelian elements, the nature of the genes—how they were constructed and how they functioned, both in their own replication and in their influence on phenotypes— became a central and fundamental problem of biology.

Garrod (1908) had provided a key observation in demonstrating an abnormal level of a meta-

bolite, homogentisic acid, in patients with alkaptonuria, a rare hereditary disorder that appeared to follow the then newly rediscovered laws of a Mendelian recessive condition. This observation showed that at least some genes might work by influencing biochemical pathways. Subsequent research, particularly on eye color in *Drosophila* (Beadle & Tatum, 1941; Ephrussi, 1942) and on nutritional requirements of a mold, *Neurospora crassa* (Beadle, 1959; Tatum, 1959), gave rise to the one gene-one enzyme hypothesis that, in brief, suggested that all biochemical processes are controlled by genes, and that each step in a biochemical reaction is under the control of a single specific gene that influences the enzyme mediating that step.

The field of biochemical genetics exploded in the early 1950s, drawing concepts from biology, chemistry, and physics into the towering intellectual achievement of molecular genetics.

The key discoveries occurred at about the same time as Hall's (1951) review chapter; behavioral genetics' renaissance was thus begun in the virtual absence of understanding of the mechanistic routes from genes to behavioral phenotypes, but the field has had the opportunity to incorporate the rapidly developing knowledge from molecular genetics into its conceptual framework as data have become available.

These dramatic advances have removed the mystical aura from gene action and have permitted its rationalization in terms of fundamental biochemical principles. A greatly condensed overview of these principles is necessary here in order to address the skeptical question, "How can genes, fixed chemical entities, possibly influence flexible, plastic behavior?"

The Structure and Replication of DNA

Following previous experiments that had identified deoxyribonucleic acid (DNA) as the molecule of heredity, Watson and Crick surmised its structure in 1953. As shown in Figure 13.21, DNA is a double stranded molecule. The two sides are composed of alternating sugar (deoxyribose) and phosphate groups. Ring structures called *bases* are bound to each sugar on both sides. The parallel sides are joined through the weak hydrogen bonds that form between parallel bases. There are only four kinds of bases: adenine (A), thymine (T), guanine (G), and cytosine (C). The physiochemical properties of the bases

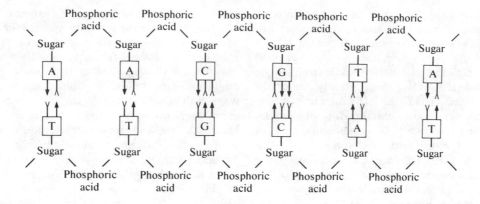

Flat representation of a DNA molecule. A = adenine; T = thymine; C = cytosine;
G = guanine. (From *Heredity, Evolution, and Society* by I. M. Lerner.
W. H. Freeman and Company. Copyright © 1968.)

Figure 13.21. Flat representation of a DNA molecule. A = adenine; T = thymine; C = cytosine, G = guanine.
From *Heredity, Evolution and Society* (p. 76) by I.M. Lerner, 1968, San Francisco: W.H. Freeman & Co. Copyright 1968 by W.H. Freeman & Co. Reprinted by permission.

permit the formation of stable, hydrogen bonds only between A and T or between G and C.

Each chromosome is composed of one very long strand of DNA and a variety of protein molecules that provide structural support for the DNA and that may also be involved in the regulation of gene activity. Whenever a cell divides, it is necessary to replicate the chromosomes precisely so that the genetic information they carry is transferred to the daughter cells. The critical information is the particular sequence of bases, and that sequence must be copied precisely when cells divide. Prior to cellular division, the duplication of DNA begins when the hydrogen bonds between bases are broken and the two strands separate from one another. The exposed bases are then free to attract free floating units of a base with a sugar and phosphate group. The specificity of the bonding ensures that each strand of the DNA will serve as a template for the synthesis of a replica of the original molecule. The result of replication as shown in Figure 13.22 is two identical molecules of DNA where there had been one. During somatic cell development and growth, all of the genes on all of the chromosomes are replicated prior to division and one copy of each chromosome migrates to each daughter cell. During the formation of gametes, sperm or ova, each chromosome is replicated,

but the replicas do not separate right away. Instead, the homologous pairs of chromosomes, each in its replicated state, separate one from the other into the daughter cells so that the total number of chromosomes is reduced by half. The replicas then separate and segregate into different daughter cells during a second division. Fertilization of an egg by a sperm restores the species-typical chromosome number since each gamete brings to the union exactly one member of each chromosome pair.

Transcription and Protein Synthesis

The information encoded in the DNA and sequestered in the nucleus of the cell must also be made available to the rest of the cell where the life functions are carried out. DNA is much too large to pass through the nuclear membrane. Hence, a messenger molecule that can carry information in the form of sequences of bases is required. Another type of nucleic acid, ribonucleic acid (RNA) fills this role. RNA is similar to DNA with three exceptions: (1) uracil (U) is substituted for thymine (T); (2) ribose sugar replaces deoxyribose; and (3) RNA is usually single-stranded.

During *transcription*, a small segment of the DNA is unwound, and the hydrogen bonds between base pairs in that segment are separated enough so that the sequence of bases

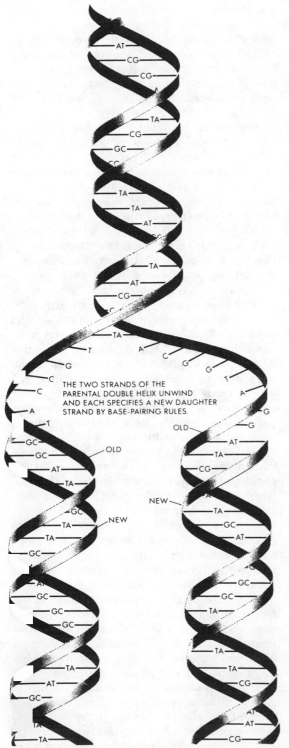

THE TWO STRANDS OF THE
PARENTAL DOUBLE HELIX UNWIND
AND EACH SPECIFIES A NEW DAUGHTER
STRAND BY BASE-PAIRING RULES.

on one side may serve as a template for the construction of a strand of RNA. That strand, called heterogeneous nuclear RNA (hnRNA), leaves the DNA and travels through the nuclear membrane into the cell's cytoplasm. After transcription the hnRNA is then processed by other enzymes. The resulting strand may be further operated on by various enzymes in the cell with pieces being removed and cut out, or the strand may be cleaved into several smaller segments. The modified RNA, called messenger RNA (mRNA), is then bound by ribosomes, where protein is synthesized. Ribosomes are made up of a number of associated proteins, enzymes, and yet another kind of RNA, ribosomal RNA (rRNA), which is also templated from the DNA. The ribosomal enzymes catalyze the biochemical reactions that *translate* the message carried in the sequence of bases in the mRNA into a sequence of amino acids. Amino acids are small molecules that are the building blocks of proteins. As illustrated in Table 13.19 each sequence of three bases in the mRNA specifies a single amino acid to be added to the protein chain. The decoding is accomplished by yet another form of RNA, transfer RNA (tRNA). These small RNA molecules have at one end a sequence of three bases called an *anti-codon*. At the other end of the tRNA is a specific amino acid. A tRNA carrying the anti-codon sequence, UUU, will bind only to the mRNA sequence, AAA. Consequently, a mRNA sequence of three adenine bases specifies that the amino acid phenylalanine, the only amino acid carried by the UUU tRNA, be added to the protein at that point. Each triplet of bases is decoded in this manner until all of the code is translated, and the protein molecule is finished. Thus, the linear sequence of amino acids in the protein is specified by a linear sequence of bases in DNA. These protein molecules may comprise structural components of the cell, or they may be enzymes or

Figure 13.22. Identical daughter double helices are generated through the semiconservative replication of DNA. From "DNA Is the Primary Genetic Material" by J.D. Watson, J. Tooze, D.T. Jurtz, 1983, in *Recombinant DNA: A Short Course* (p. 20), New York: Scientific American Books. Copyright (c) 1983 by W.H. Freeman & Co. Reprinted by permission.

Table 13.19. The genetic code.

First letter	Second letter				Third letter
	A	G	T	C	
A	Phe	Ser	Tyr	Cys	A
	Phe	Ser	Tyr	Cys	G
	Leu	Ser	chain end	chain end	T
	Leu	Ser	chain end	Try	C
G	Leu	Pro	His	Arg	A
	Leu	Pro	His	Arg	G
	Leu	Pro	Gln	Arg	T
	Leu	Pro	Gln	Arg	C
T	Ile	Thr	Asn	Ser	A
	Ile	Thr	Asn	Ser	G
	Ile	Thr	Lys	Arg	T
	Met	Thr	Lys	Arg	C
C	Val	Ala	Asp	Gly	A
	Val	Ala	Asp	Gly	G
	Val	Ala	Glu	Gly	T
	Val	Ala	Glu	Gly	C

Note: Each amino acid is coded by a triplet of three bases, as shown in the table, which is a compact way of setting out the 64 possible triplets.

The four bases are denoted by the letters A, G, T, and C. In DNA the four bases are: A = Adenine; G = Guanine; T = Thymine; C = Cytosine.

The 20 amino acids are identified as follows:

Ala = Alanine	Leu = Leucine
Arg = Arginine	Lys = Lysine
Asn = Asparagine	Met = Methionine
Asp = Aspartic acid	Phe = Phenylalanine
Cys = Cysteine	Pro = Proline
Glu = Glutamic acid	Ser = Serine
Gln = Glutamine	Thr = Threonine
Gly = Glycine	Try = Tryptophan
His = Histidine	Tyr = Thyrosine
Ile = Isoleucine	Val = Valine

Note. After Cavalli-Sforza and Bodmer, *The Genetics of Human Populations.* Data from Crick, 1966. From "Mechanisms of Heredity and Behavior" by R. Plomin, J. DeFries, and G.E. McClearn, 1980, in *Behavioral Genetics: A Primer* (p. 108), San Francisco: W.H. Freeman & Co. Copyright 1980 by W.H. Freeman & Co. Reprinted by permission.

parts of enzymes. Enzymes are essential to all activities of living cells. Respiration, digestion, movement, thought—all of these functions depend ultimately on enzymes.

Pathways of Genetic Influence on Behavior

One of the pieces of evidence in the early domain of biochemical genetics was, in fact, of direct relevance to behavioral genetics. This example was phenylketonuria, mentioned above. Affected individuals were distinguishable from other mentally retarded individuals through abnormal levels of certain metabolites in urine and blood. A series of studies (see Jervis, 1954) clarified the biochemical pathway that was involved and pinpointed the enzyme (phenylalanine hydroxylase) that was defective.

The search for biochemical, physiological, and anatomical routes through which genes influence behavior had begun by the time of Hall's *Handbook* review, and he identified this effort as the major objective of the field. The data to which he could refer for examples included a relationship between temperature preference and belly skin thickness (Herter, 1938), endocrine gland weights and emotionality (Yeakel & Rhoades, 1941), and metabolic rate and activity (Rundquist & Bellis, 1933).

Numerous other phenotypes have subsequently been studied. A particularly attractive area of research, for example, has been the phenomenon of audiogenic seizures and their neurochemical and neuroanatomical correlates (Ginsburg et al., 1969). As a proportion of the total behavioral genetics research effort, this area of study into mechanism has been rather small. However, it is gaining at an accelerating pace and will likely be a dominant focus of research in the near future.

One area that has achieved a vigorous momentum is that of behavioral pharmacogenetics (Plomin & Deitrich, 1982). The subject matter concerns the genetic basis of individuality in drug-related behaviors—avidity, sensitivity, tolerance, dependence—and their pharmacological mechanisms. The literature now includes strain differences and related analyses involving alcohol, amnesics, amphetamine, anxiolytics, barbiturates, convulsants, nicotine, and opiates. Broadhurst reviewed the field in 1978 and provided a reference list with over 450 entries. Obviously, only a suggestive representation can be provided here. Alcohol has been, perhaps, the drug most intensively investigated and will serve as exemplar.

It has already been noted that inbred mouse strains differ dramatically in voluntary consumption of alcohol. Similar differences have been reported for inbred rats (see Satinder, 1972) and for rats selectively bred for attributes other than alcohol preference (see Brewster, 1972). Selective breeding has also been successful in generating lines differing in alcohol consumption in rats (Eriksson, 1969; Li, Lumeng, McBride, & Waller, 1981) and mice (Anderson et al., 1979).

Sensitivity to the effects of alcohol has been explored by strain comparisons of mice using as behavioral measures open-field activity (Oliverio & Eleftheriou, 1976; Randall & Lester, 1975) and duration of loss of righting response after alcohol administration (Kakihana, Brown, McClearn, & Tabershaw, 1966; Tabakoff & Ritzmann, 1979; Randall & Lester, 1975; Rush & King, 1976). Mice have been selectively bred for differences in this measure (McClearn & Kakihana, 1981), and rats have been selectively bred for differences in motor impairment after alcohol administration (Riley, Worsham, Lester, & Freed, 1977). Mouse strains differ in functional tolerance to alcohol (Grieve, Griffiths, & Littleton, 1979; Tabakoff, Ritzmann, Raju, & Deitrich, 1980) and in severity of symptoms of alcohol withdrawal (Goldstein & Kakihana, 1975).

This wealth of evidence on genetic influence on alcohol-related behaviors, coupled with a rapidly enlarged body of knowledge concerning the physiology and metabolism of alcohol, has generated a rich field for exploring the causal pathways from gene to behavior.

As noted above, an early attractive hypothesis was that the enzymes alcohol dehydrogenase (ADH) and aldehyde dehydrogenase (ALDH) would be associated with strain differences in preference. That alcohol preferring C57BL/6 mice have higher activity levels of liver ADH than alcohol-avoiding DBA mice has been demonstrated by numerous authors (Rodgers et al., 1963; Sheppard, Albersheim, & McClearn, 1970; Damjanovich & MacInnes, 1973). Belknap, MacInnes, and McClearn (1972) and Sheppard et al. (1970) had similar findings for ALDH.

The vulnerability of two-strain, two-trait fortuitous associations has been discussed earlier. In the present topic, confirmation has been sought by use of heterogeneous groups. Anderson et al. (1979), for example, found a correlation of 0.25 between alcohol acceptance and liver ADH in a genetically heterogeneous stock of mice. The relevance of acetaldehyde metabolism to alcohol consumption is further intimated by results with rats selected for alcohol acceptance (Koivula, Koivualo, & Lindros, 1975).

The mouse lines selectively bred for sensitivity differences to first dose alcohol exposure have also been investigated for mechanisms underlying those differences. Collins (1981) summarized the then available literature, which suggests that the lines differ not in metabolic rate of alcohol but in central nervous system sensitivity to alcohol.

Another research focus within the general topic of mechanisms, and one that is growing particularly rapidly, is developmental neurogenetics. Progress in this field has been greatly facilitated by the availability of a wide array of behavioral mutants. A few such mutants were discovered by chance observations of aberrant behavior, but many were isolated from laboratory populations that had been purposefully exposed to chemical mutagens or irradiation. Initially, neuroscientists hoped that these genetic anomalies would provide such exquisitely precise lesions that the complex of structures and functions underlying behavior could be thoroughly analyzed by altering one component at a time. Before passing judgment on the degree to which this ambitious and optimistic goal has been reached, it is useful to review a few examples.

Although simple taxic responses of unicellular creatures to mechanical, electrical, and chemical stimuli are not the sorts of behavior that usually interest psychologists, they do provide simple behavioral systems which may serve as models of more complex ones. Kung, Chang, Saton, and Van Houten (1975), for example, described several single-gene mutations that disturb the normal chemotactic responses of *Paramecium aurelia*. Among these is *Pawn*, in which the animal fails altogether to reverse its forward swimming movement when it encounters aversive stimuli (e.g., excessive sodium concentrations). Like the chess piece for which it is named, it only moved forward and does not exhibit the normal avoidance reaction. Electrophysiological investigations of *Pawn* and related mutants suggest that the primary lesion involves a failure of the membrane-bound calcium ion gate. Its dysfunction prevents the generation of an all-or-none action potential. In another mutant, *Paranoiac*, the avoidance reaction is extraordinarily exaggerated, and encounters with aversive chemical stimuli lead to prolonged backward swimming. Electrophysiological recordings related this aberrant behavior to an overly long period of membrane depolarization and suggested a defect in the sodium channel. In other mutants, the electrophysiological responses appear to be entirely normal, and abnormal behavior is attributed to functional deficits in the cilia.

Parkinson (1977) employed the descriptions of similar behavioral mutants in bacteria to arrive at an integrated theory of chemotaxis. He identified among the various chemotactic mutants three major categories: (1) Some of the mutants are apparently unable to detect specific attractants or specific repellent stimuli. The defective chemoreception is the result of mutations in genes coding for various binding proteins that reside in the membrane. (2) Other mutations affect the structure and activity of the effectors, the flagella. (3) A third set of mutations was not associated with either sensory receptors or flagellar response *per se* but appeared instead to interrupt an intervening process. These were described as *signal deficient* and were associated with defects in both membrane-bound and cytoplasmic proteins. Parkinson proposed that these proteins accomplished the signal function through their interaction between the chemoreceptors and the effectors.

The genetic dissection of behavior in paramecia and bacteria provides a piecemeal approach to the analysis of gene-to-behavior pathways; but even with such simple systems, specification of all of the intermediary steps and their interactions remains to be done.

Recently, Scheller et al. (1984) applied molecular genetic techniques to the study of behavior in a more complex creature, the sea-slug *Aplysia*. The subject of this work was the coordinated sequence of behaviors that culminates in egg deposition. This behavioral sequence is highly stereotyped, species-typical, and does not seem to require any specific prior learning. It is, therefore, a behavior that fits the ethologist's notion of a fixed action pattern (FAP). Previously, researchers had discovered that injections of extract derived from a specific neuron cluster, the bag cells, elicited the FAP even though the animals had not mated and the eggs were unfertilized. An active factor, egg-laying hormone (ELH), consisting of just 36 amino acids, was isolated from the extract. Injection of the purified ELH elicits some but not all components of the FAP. With modern recombinant DNA techniques and cloning, Scheller et al. (1984) were able to construct a probe that pin-

pointed the ELH gene. The gene sequence encoded a long precursor or polyprotein that contained 10 other peptides in addition to ELH. Four of these had previously been isolated from bag-cell extract. Three of them, like ELH, were found to function as neurotransmitters at specific junctions.

ELH, like many other neuropeptides, functions as a hormone as well as a neurotransmitter. It diffuses through the circulatory system to the smooth-muscle of the reproductive tract where it triggers the contractions that expel the egg mass. The functions of the other peptides are yet unknown, but Scheller et al. (1984) suppose that they may direct other components of the FAP. Thus, they propose that this gene system encodes the neurohumoral agents responsible for the performance of a coordinated behavior. Additional analyses suggest that the ELH gene is regulated by yet another, related gene system.

A variety of peptides has been found in the mammalian brain as well (see Bolles & Fanselow, 1982, and Snyder, 1980, for reviews), and some are known to mediate stereotypical behavioral responses (Bloom, 1981). It is an obvious speculation to suggest that neuropeptides may constitute principal intermediaries of gene-to-behavior pathways.

The fruit fly, *Drosophila melanogaster*, is another laboratory animal that has been popular with geneticists but has not attracted much attention from psychologists. There is now substantial evidence for associative learning in *Drosophila* (McGuire, 1984; Tully, 1984), and genetic analyses have revealed some of the biochemistry involved. Conditioned olfactory avoidance has been the most widely used paradigm, and several single-gene mutants that disrupt it have been examined (Dudai, Jan, Byers, Quinn, & Benzer, 1976; Quinn, Sziber, & Booker, 1979; Duerr & Quinn, 1982; Aceves-Piña et al., 1983; Tully, 1984). *Dunce* and its five alleles (Dudai et al., 1976), along with *rutabaga* and *amnesiac*, have been mapped to specific locations on the X-chromosome. Two other learning deficient mutations, *turnip* and *cabbage*, are also X-linked but have not yet been mapped. A fifth mutation that interferes with learning, *dopamine decarboxylase deficiency* (Ddc), is located on autosomal chromosome II. Each recessive mutant has been associated with a fairly specific pattern of effects involving the nature of the conditioning paradigm, the stimuli, and varied aspects of acquisition, retention, and retrieval. (See Dudai, 1983; Tully, 1984; and McGuire, 1984 for detailed comparisons.) There is, nevertheless, substantial overlap in their effects which suggests that they disrupt a common causal pathway.

Byers, Davis, and Kiger (1981) noted that the loci for *dunce* and for the enzyme, phosphodiesterase (PdEII), were coincident. Biochemical analysis of homozygous *dunce* flies revealed very low levels of PdEII and high levels of the important cyclic nucleotide, cAMP, which has been widely accepted as an intracellular messenger. Thus, genetic and biochemical analysis of the *dunce* mutations implicated the involvement of cyclic nucleotides in *Drosophila* learning. Subsequently, three of the other mutations (*rutabaga*, *Ddc*, and *turnip*) were analyzed biochemically, and in each case the biochemical lesion interrupted one or another step in the monamine-activated cyclase system. As Tully (1984) concludes, this commonality in itself does not permit any grand synthesis regarding the molecular biology of learning. Nonetheless, the genetic dissection afforded by these learning-memory mutants has identified an important piece of the puzzle that should help to focus future research and theory.

Behavior-genetic analyses of learning in mice have been instrumental in correlating brain morphology with performance. Examining the brains of mice selectively bred for avoidance conditioning, Schwegler, Lipp, Vander Loos, and Buselmaier (1981) and Schwegler and Lipp (1983) noted a line difference in the distribution of mossy fiber fields in the hippocampus. Specifically, mice from the low-avoidance line had a relatively high proportion of mossy fiber connections with the basal dendritic fields of hippocampal neurons. High-avoidance mice had relatively more connections to the apical dendritic fields. Thus, the ratio of the areas of the mossy fiber synapses in the two areas was correlated with the line difference in avoidance. This difference in mossy fiber pattern between the lines may be merely coincidental, of course. Schwegler et al. (1983) tested the correlation in three ways. First, mice of seven different inbred strains known to differ in mossy fiber pattern or in avoidance conditioning were compared. Second, heterogeneous mice from a systematically outbred line were also

tested. Finally, mice from the selected lines were treated with the hormone, thyroxine, that modifies the development of the mossy fibers. In each test paradigm, the correlation between fiber pattern and avoidance performance was confirmed. Recently, Wimer, Wimer, and Wimer (1983) have also related other aspects of brain morphology to avoidance conditioning in mice by using genetic designs to assess the correlation. In sum, the results of these experiments demonstrate the unique power of behavior-genetic designs in analyzing complex and subtle brain behavior relations.

The Control of Gene Action

The genes whose messages are decoded into protein are called *structural* genes to distinguish them from genes with regulatory functions. For example, in certain bacterial cells (prokaryotes, without a cell nucleus) there are sequences of bases in the DNA that act as operators and promoters. Enzymes interacting with these segments of the DNA are responsible for turning on or turning off the transcription of structural genes. A set of structural genes and their regulators comprise an *operon*. One of the first operons to be thoroughly investigated was the *lac* operon of the intestinal bacterium, *E. coli*. In this organism, the presence of lactose induces the production of the enzymes necessary to metabolize it. As illustrated in Figure 13.23, transcription of the structural genes for these enzymes is usually inhibited by a repressor molecule that binds to the operator region of the lac operon. When lactose is present, it inactivates the repressor and transcription proceeds. Repressible systems have also been discovered in bacteria, where the structural genes are normally transcribed until an accumulation of their own products inhibits further transcription.

The issue of regulation of gene activity in eukaryotic (possessing cell nuclei), multicellular organisms has been much more difficult to resolve (see Lewin, 1985, for comprehensive review). In mammalian cells, for example, the enzymes involved in the process of transcription are more numerous, and the process is more complex. In some cases, the regulatory and structural components of a single genetic system appear to be distributed throughout the genome on different chromosomes. Changes in

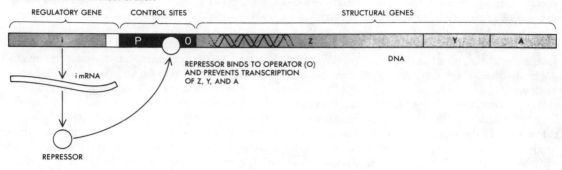

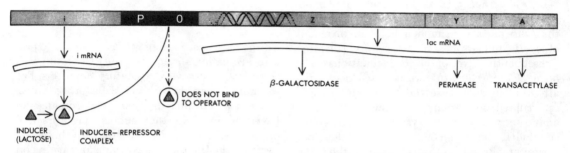

Figure 13.23. Repressors and inducers control the functioning of the genes belonging to the lactose (lac) operon. From *Recombinant DNA: A Short Course* (p. 46) by J.D. Watson, J. Tooze, and D.T. Jurtz, 1983, New York: Scientific American Books. Copyright (c) 1983 by W.H. Freeman & Co. Reprinted by permission.

the relative amounts of these different kinds of RNA-synthesizing enzymes and in their activities have been associated with changes in the developmental status of the organism as well as with the presence of particular hormones and nutrients (Lewin, 1985).

One of the striking differences between the DNA of eukaryotic organisms and that of prokaryotic cells is the existence in the former of segments of DNA that are extensively repeated throughout the chromosomes. There is speculation that these repeated sequences have both developmental and evolutionary significance (Davidson & Britten, 1979; Rose & Doolittle, 1983).

Still another difference between the protein synthesis in higher organisms and in bacteria is the post-transcriptional processing of RNA. One of the surprises encountered in the investigation of the genetics of higher organisms has been that transcripts of mRNA were much shorter when they reached the ribosome than were the hnRNA transcripts from which the mRNA was derived. Before that discovery, hnRNA had not been distinguished from mRNA.

It has been demonstrated that the initial transcript contains segments of bases that are never translated (see Crick, 1979, or Darnell, 1983, for reviews). These segments, called *introns*, are excised by enzymes, and the ends of the remaining pieces of RNA are spliced before the message reaches the ribosome. The significance of this additional complexity is that it may provide another mechanism for control and variation. Thus, gene activity may be regulated at several different levels. Furthermore, the RNA transcripts of structural genes are subject to processing. The same initial transcript could be differentially excised to provide a variety of structural products.

Gene regulation may also occur during the process of translation. It has been observed, for example, that, in some cells, some mRNA's are translated hundreds of times. Other mRNAs may be degraded by enzymes after they have been translated only a few times. Finally, the protein products themselves are subject to regulation by other proteins, hormones, and other substances.

Still another potential mechanism for gene

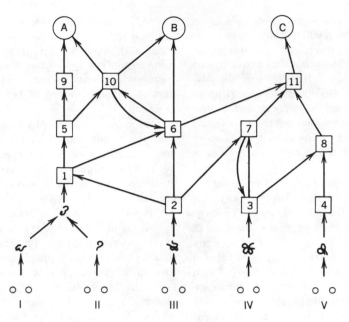

Figure 13.24. A summary schema representing the causal matrix between genes and phenotypes.

regulation and control involves the actual rearrangement of the physical location of genes on chromosomes. Half a century ago, McClintock interpreted the pattern of transmission of certain traits in corn to show that genes could move on chromosomes. Her work was largely ignored until very recently, when its great significance has come to be appreciated. Since her discovery, "jumping genes" have now been found in yeast cells, in invertebrates, and in mammalian cells (Shapiro, 1983).

Structural rearrangement of the immunoglobin genes occurs during the development and differentiation of immunocytes (Seidman & Leder, 1978) and may, in fact, be a decisive step in conferring specificity. Thus, mobile elements and chromosomal rearrangement may also be involved with developmental and evolutionary change.

All of these discoveries have dispelled the once accepted view of the genome as a static, rigidly fixed, and unvarying program. The old metaphor of a blueprint must now be rejected in favor of a model that conveys a much more dynamic picture.

A Summary Schema

A greatly oversimplified representation of the causal matrix through which genes influence the development of several characteristics is provided in Figure 13.24. At the bottom of the figure are six sets of genes shown as pairs of small circles. The irregular figures just above them represent the particular protein or protein portion that each gene specifies. As we have seen, these proteins constitute the array of structural and catalytic proteins that participate in the myriad of metabolic functions that constitute all living processes of the body including, of course, behavior. The complex of interacting metabolic pathways is represented by all the numbered boxes, each one an intermediate step in the pathway from the primary protein products of the genes to the phenotypes of interest at the end of the pathways. These phenotypic outcomes are represented by the circles labelled, A, B, and C, at the top of the figure.

Several points may be illustrated with this simple figure. First of all, we can discard the simple notion that there are any genes *for* a particular phenotype, whether it be eye color or personality trait. The only direct effect that any particular gene pair has is the conferring of specificity on its protein product. A second principle of gene action may be illustrated by following the paths of influence from a particular gene pair to the phenotypic outcomes. In the case of the first and second gene pair, for example, those paths lead to all three phenotypes. This is an example of *pleiotropy* in which a single gene pair influences two or more phenotypic outcomes. This phenomenon was exemplified above by the low activity and high defecation exhibited by albino mice when tested in the classical open-field apparatus. Various experimental and genetic analyses have supported the hypothesis that the albinism and the low activity are indeed pleiotropic effects of the same gene (DeFries et al., 1978).

Polygeny may be regarded, in a sense, as the complement of pleiotropy. In polygeny the effects of several different gene pairs converge to influence a single phenotype, as illustrated in the figure by the fact that all six gene pairs influence Phenotype C. Here, then, principles of the mechanism of gene action converge with principles of quantitative genetics. In the quantitative context presented earlier, we were essentially relating variability at the behavioral phenotype level to the level of the gene. But the gene was treated simply as a hypothetical Mendelian entity; now, we see that the phenotypic variability begins with the fact that base pair differences in the DNA of different individuals operate through the protein-producing machinery of the cell, through the anatomy, the biochemistry, and the physiology of the organism to eventuate in that variability that we approach quantitatively with concepts of variance and covariance partitioning.

Another important point to be made is that what constitutes a phenotype and what constitutes a mechanism in that phenotype's causal chain is an arbitrary matter. A researcher may enter this causal nexus at any point. The molecular biologist works at the level of the genes and their primary action. The physiologist works at what is represented here by the intermediate steps. The physiological psychologist bridges this level to the behavioral one. A psychologist typically works with complex phenotypes that are far removed from the primary actions of genes.

Behavioral geneticists may treat their subject matter quantitatively, relating the genetic level to the phenotypic level without consideration of the intermediate mechanisms, and the examples provided herein to this point have been mostly of this sort. However, the behavioral geneticist may also relate the behavioral phenotypes to some part or parts of the causal

nexus. Physiological, biochemical, anatomical, or basic gene action correlates may be included, along with genetic manipulation and behavioral measures. This type of study is increasingly frequent and can be expected to be a major part of the next wave of behavioral genetics research.

Our model so far is obviously incomplete in that the other major domain of influence on development, environment, remains to be incorporated. In Figure 13.25 environmental influences are represented by wavy lines drawn from particular environments on these phenotypes. An important point to be drawn from this figure is that, as in the case of the genes, there are no environments that have a direct effect on a particular distal phenotype. Environmental factors, like genes, operate through a complex series of biochemical and physiological processes. In this environmental realm there are analogs of pleiotropy where, for example, Environment 1 influences both Phenotype A and Phenotype B, and analogs of polygeny as in the case where Environments 2 through 3 all impinge upon Phenotype A. The definition of environment here is a very broad one, encompassing all factors that influence the phenotypes that are not encoded in the genes. Environmental influences range, therefore, from chemical gradients in the cytoplasm of the egg in which the individual began life to parental rearing styles to differences in diet and exercise, formal education, peer groups, and cultural trends.

Another salient point can be made by reference to this figure. Different phenotypes, for example Phenotypes A and B, may be correlated for two reasons. As illustrated in the diagram, the A and B phenotypes are influenced by common environments. Thus correlations observed at the phenotypic level between the two traits may be underlain by genetic correlations induced as pleiotropy or by environmental correlations, or both. Recognizing the importance of understanding the underlying correlational structure between different phenotypes, behavioral geneticists have increasingly employed multivariate designs that permit them to disentangle environmental and genetic contributions to the correlations among traits.

From this view we may see the vast potential for research programs that systematically integrate the molecular with the quantitative approaches to behavioral genetics.

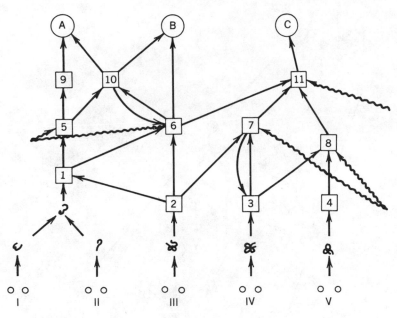

Figure 13.25. A summary schema representing genetic and environmental input to the causal matrix leading to phenotypes.

Developmental Behavioral Genetics

Figures 13.24 and 13.25 describe a static state of affairs at a particular frame of time. A model of relevance to development can be generated by extending notions of gene regulation. A series of frames is shown in Figure 13.26. A continuous developmental process would be ideally represented by an infinite succession of frames of vanishingly small intervals, of course, but for purposes of representation, only three are displayed.

In the earliest frame, loci III, IV, and V are shown to be operative, but I and II are not. In the intermediate frame, I and II are "on" and III is "off;" and in the last frame, IV is off, while I, II, III, and V are on. This representation makes the important point that the genotype of an individual is not a static conglomerate of alleles set at conception and thereafter functioning totally in all parts of the organism throughout the rest of its life. In any particular cell, only a small percentage of the genome will be expressed, and in all parts of the body, that fraction of the genome that is operative will change developmentally.

In brief summary, then, we can conceive of

both structural and regulatory genes, of movable genetic elements, of varying allelic frequencies, with additive and various types of intralocus (dominant) and interlocus (epistatic) nonadditive effects, and of environmental agencies of varying onset, duration and distribution, some contributing to family resemblance, some to dissimilarities within families, deployed over the entire range from the intimate chemical milieux of the DNA within the cell to the sociocultural influences of families, peers, and institutions.

It is, of course, the case that the demonstration of genetically influenced individual differences in any behavioral phenotype at any age is a genuine and legitimate demonstration of a genetic influence on a process of behavioral development. The phenotypes at the time of measurement had to be achieved by a development process. In this sense, the entire accumulation of the behavioral genetics literature could be presented as pertinent to developmental behavioral genetics. Here, we shall consider only those studies in which age was an explicit variable or in which elements in the process relating specific genes to specific behaviors are known.

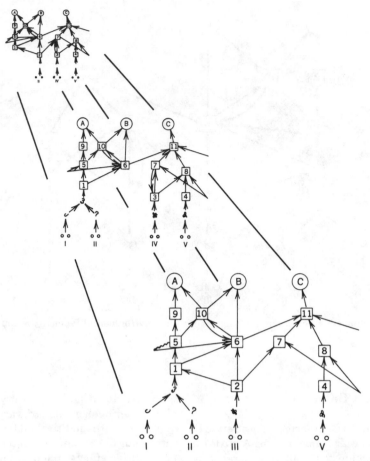

Figure 13.26. Successive frames of the causal matrix representing different gene action at different developmental stages.

Animal Model Studies

The animal research in the area can be categorized as either descriptive or intervention studies. In the former, animals of different genotypes are assessed for a specific phenotype at differing ages, either in a longitudinal or (more usually) a cross-sectional design. In the intervention studies, a typical design assesses the effects of an environmental treatment on animals of differing genotypes.

DESCRIPTIVE RESEARCH

An unambiguous demonstration of a genetic influence on a developmental process that includes motor behavior components is provided by the condition in mice known as *kreisler*. Kreisler is determined by a single autosomal locus, and animals that are homozygous for the recessive

allele begin, between 10 and 14 days of age, to show the anomalous behavior of crawling in circles, rigidity when placed on the back, head shaking and tossing, and running in small circles. Some insights into the causal elements in the route of gene influence have been provided by Deol (1964), who demonstrated that the affected individuals develop liquid-filled cysts under the pons that compress adjacent neural structures. A gross deformation of the telencephalon ensues. Although the behavioral anomaly appears 10 to 14 days after birth, the neurological defects are detectable as early as nine days of gestational age when the otic pit fails to make normal contact with the neural folds.

Another single-locus example has been described by Thiessen (1965), who examined various biological and behavioral attributes of young mice who were homozygous for another recessive allele called *Wabbler-lethal*. In this condition, hind limb motor incoordination and paralysis have an onset about two weeks after birth. The Wabbler-lethal condition provides an illustration of the degree of pleiotropy that can be attributable to the single locus. Prior to the onset of frank disability, a delayed developmental pattern was shown for measures of activity, of morphology, and of physiological functions. The pattern of deformities is not global, however. For example, liver and spleen weights are lower in Wabbler animals than in normal controls by 25 days of age, but adrenal weight is not. There is a reduced glucose level in Wabblers, but pituitary proteins and serum proteins appear to be normal. Among the earliest of the indications of the disorder is degeneration of myelin sheaths in the central funicular of the spinal cord and in the vestibulospinal and spinocerebellar tracts (Dickie, Schneider, & Harman, 1952). In reference to Figure 13.24, such an event could represent one of the elements of the causal nexus, relatively proximal to primary gene action, with the pleiotropic expression spreading through multiple branching pathways more distally.

The susceptibility of mice to convulsive seizures when exposed to high frequency sound is also under genetic control. A developmental function is clearly shown by a very sharp peak of susceptibility at 21 days of age in an inbred strain (DBA) of particularly high susceptibility (see Schlesinger & Griek, 1970). Fuller and Sjursen (1967) assessed mice of 11 inbred strains for seizure susceptibility from 21 to 42 days of age and found complex strain by age interactions both in susceptibility and in lethal outcomes.

Kakihana (1965) has provided an example of strain differences in development of a phenotype under polygenic influence in her work on sensitivity to the affects of administered alcohol. Using duration of loss of righting response subsequent to an intraperitoneally administered, hypnotic dose of ethanol, she found no differentiation among eight inbred strains studied at four weeks of age. By eight weeks of age, two of the strains (BALB/c and DBA) displayed markedly heightened sensitivity compared with the others, and by 16 weeks of age a pattern had emerged with the BALB/c and DBA strains extremely sensitive, the A and RIII

strains intermediate, and the C57BL and C3H/2 strains relatively insensitive as they had been at four weeks of age.

A similar demonstration of genotypically distinct developmental patterns for a polygenic trait was provided by Dixon and DeFries (1968). In this work, C57BL and BALB/c mice were assessed for open-field activity at various ages. The C57BL animals were more active than the BALB/c animals as early as 15 days of age. At older ages, the BALB/c activity increased only slightly, but the C57BL activity continued to rise so that, by three months of age, there was neary a fourfold activity difference. Further evidence of genetic influence was obtained in this study by the inclusion of hybrid F_1 animals whose developmental pattern resembled the C57BL parent most closely.

Some studies have given glimpses of intermediary steps in the causal-developmental system. Schlesinger and his colleagues, for example, discovered that in DBA mice the period of peak sensitivity to audiogenic seizures coincided with a developmental nadir in brain serotonin (Schlesinger & Uphouse, 1972). Susceptible animals could be made more seizure resistant by injecting serotonin precursors; genetically-resistant mice were made more susceptible by pharmacological depletion of brain serotonin.

Because learning is the vehicle through which many psychologically relevant environmental variables are presumed to operate, it is particularly important to note the work of Meier and Foshee (1963) and Meier (1964) who showed, in a cross-sectional study, that inbred strains not only differed substantially in learning performance in a water maze over a span from 21 to 147 days of age, but that there were dramatic strain differences in the developmental functions describing this learning performance. Animals of three strains (C57BL/6, DBA/2, CF/1) were uniformly good performers at all ages; another three strains (AKR, BALB/c and C3H) were inferior to the former, and in this group, age and sex differences were significant.

The foregoing has dealt principally with very early development, representing murine infancy, childhood, adolescence, or perhaps young adulthood in a few cases. That genetic programming continues throughout the lifespan is implied by a small but growing literature on gerontological genetics (see McClearn & Foch, 1983). Strain differences of the sort described above for early ages have been described for the aging mouse in activity level (Goodrick, 1967, 1974, 1975a; Elias, Elias, & Eleftheriou, 1975; Sprott & Eleftheriou, 1973; Wax, 1977), sensory processes (Sprott, 1975; Goodrick, 1975b; Wood, 1976; Henry, 1982), and learning (Sprott, 1972; Stavnes & Sprott, 1975; Sprott, 1978), among other phenotypes.

ENVIRONMENTAL INTERVENTION STUDIES
The intervention studies in development represent a special case of research on genotype-environment interactions. An extensive literature has developed on this topic (see Henderson, 1972; Plomin et al., 1977). Here, we shall be concerned only with those studies that have applied an environmental intervention at one stage of life with observations on outcome measures at some later stage of life. There are two types of research in this area, one in which the environmental intervention is a short, pulsed intervention, and the other in which long-term rearing circumstances are involved.

Of the pulsed environment studies, that of Lindzey and Winston (1962) constitutes a classic example. Animals of the C3H and C57BL strains were gentled by systematic handling and were subsequently compared to control animals on learning performance in a maze. The C57BL mice responded to the treatment by superior maze performance, but the treatment had almost no effect on C3H mice.

That prenatally administered environments can have a different effect depending upon genotype was demonstrated by Weir and DeFries (1964) who showed that daily exposure of pregnant females to three minutes of moderate stress throughout the last half of pregnancy had significant effects upon the adult open-field activity and defecation of the young who were *in utero* at the time the stress was administered. One major finding was that the treatment resulted in an increase in activity in the BALB/c animals, but a decrease in the C57BL animals. This situation has the interesting complexity of a two-organism interactive system: both the maternal genotype and the fetal genotype were of importance in determining the effectiveness of the environmental intervention (DeFries, Weir, & Hegmann, 1967).

A further example of a pulsed, short-term environmental intervention concerns susceptibility to audiogenic seizures. Henry (1967)

showed that animals of the normally nonsusceptible C57BL/6 strain could be made highly susceptible if they were acoustically primed in early life. The priming procedure involves exposure of anesthetized animals to the sound of an electric bell at 103 decibels for 30 seconds. A developmentally sensitive period was found to extend from 12 to 26 days, during which time the priming had an influence. For days 14 through 18 the priming treatment was so effective that it completely eliminated the strain differences in audiogenic seizure susceptibility as tested at 28 days of age.

A final example of brief, pulsed environment effects from mouse research is that of Mos et al. (1973) who examined the effects of shock, administered immediately after weaning on days 23 and 24, on a battery of tests, measuring seven factors of mouse emotionality, that was administered on day 50. The results are rather complex, but can be summarized for present purposes by noting that strain X treatment interactions were found on five of the seven factors.

Longer term interventions have been undertaken by Henderson (1970a). The treatment conditions involved rearing under normal laboratory conditions or rearing under enriched circumstances that offered the mice substantially more scope for exploration and varied stimulation. At six weeks of age, each mouse was motivated by 24-hour food deprivation and then placed in a large enclosure with a complex, circuitous route to a food basket. The dependent measure was time to obtain food. The analytic design permitted the estimation of various variance sources. Figure 13.27 presents an abstracted summary of these results. It is most noteworthy that the heritability of the phenotype in this case is four times as great when the animals have been reared under the enriched circumstances as it is for animals reared under the impoverished circumstances.

A similar study by Henderson (1972) examined the effects of enrichment on learning. Six inbred strains and their 30 possible F_1 crosses were tested in a diallel design. The difference in rearing circumstances was included in the overall variance analysis. An abstract of the results for a black-white and a vertical-horizontal discrimination task and for a T-maze is shown in Figure 13.28.

For all tasks, the variance due to the enriched environment and maternal environment is seen

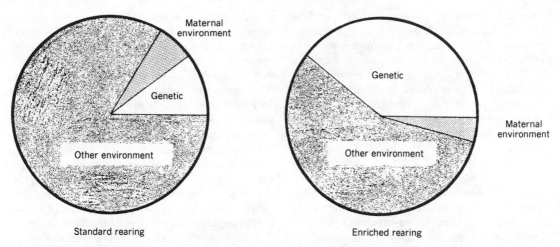

Figure 13.27. Components of variance estimated from groups reared under standard or enriched conditions in a "time to food" measure under hunger motivation (data from Henderson, 1970b).

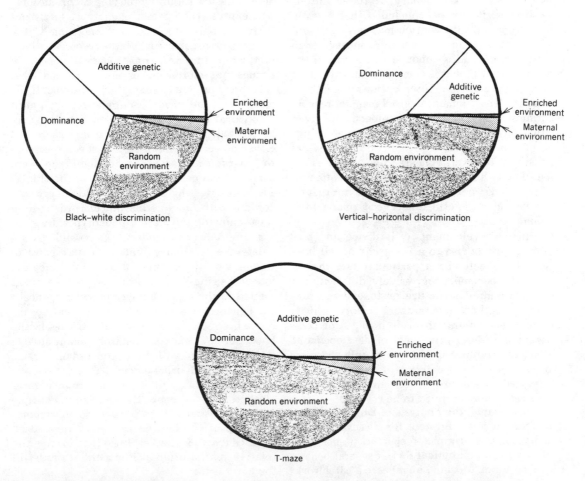

Figure 13.28. Components of variance in three learning situations estimated from groups reared under standard or enriched conditions (data from Henderson, 1974).

to be quite small relative to that arising from unidentified, random environmental factors. Broad sense heritability ranges from about 0.50 (for T-maze performance) to about 0.70 (for black-white discrimination). Narrow sense heritability ranges from 0.13 (for vertical-horizontal stripe discrimination) to 0.38 (for black-white discrimination). Clearly, the mix of determinant influences varies from measure to measure even within the general domain of learning.

Overall, the early enrichment and the maternal effects were found to be very small relative to the amount of genetic variation and to the amount of random environmental influence (E1) of unknown origin. In this particular case, the effects of genotype X environment interaction were relatively small.

As a succinct summary of these various researches, it can be concluded that a given environmental intervention may have very different consequences, either in magnitude or in direction, depending upon the genotype of the organism to which it is administered. The extent to which the various interventions of gentling, handling, environmental enrichment, or rearing permissiveness may be homologous to given situations with similar names in human beings is, of course, open to discussion. The general principle, however, appears to be solidly established and illustrates the inadequacy of attempting to build general theories of behavior that do not consider genetic differences among individuals.

During development, cells divide and proliferate, giving rise to a hierarchy of cell lineages. Each cell has a particular fate that is either to become progressively differentiated into a terminal structure or to undergo programmed cell death (Sternberg & Horvitz, 1984, p. 492). Identifying the cell lineages of body tissues is a descriptive goal of developmental biology. Establishing the causal influences on differentiation and cell death are the explanatory goals. In both of these missions, genetic approaches have proved to be essential.

For example, the analysis of *mosaic* animals has been a powerful tool for discovering the embryological origins of specific tissues and inferring the anatomical foci of several behavioral mutants. Mosaic animals are a patchwork quilt of tissues derived from distinctive cell lineages. *Gynandromorphs* constitute one type of mosaic, being composed of a mixture of male and female tissues. The discovery of the unstable, ring-X chromosome in *Drosophila* made the generation of the sex-mosaic gynanders possible. In the first stages of development, the ring-X chromosome behaves erratically and may be lost during early cell divisions. To produce a gynander, males from stock carrying multiple recessive markers on the morphologically normal X-chromosome are mated to females bearing the ring-X chromosome. Initially, then, the gynanders are heterozygous, having one normal X-chromosome and the ring-X. Cell lineages that retain both X-chromosomes are female (XX), but those derived from early cells that lost the ring-X will have only the one, marker-bearing X-chromosome. In *Drosophila*, these XO tissues become male. Wherever X-linked genes are active, tissues retaining the ring-X chromosome will express the normal phenotype. In tissues derived from cells that lost the ring-X, the phenotypes associated with the recessive alleles on the remaining X-chromosome will appear. In tissues that express one or more of the markers, it is then possible to score the phenotype. If the markers on the normal X-chromosome include a behavioral mutant, the aberrant behavior may be treated in the same fashion and scored as either present or absent. All tissues expressing the marker alleles are concordant and were derived from cell lineages that lost the ring-X. Tissues expressing the dominant alleles are concordant with one another but discordant from those showing the marker phenotypes. By scoring hundreds of gynanders, it is possible to calculate the frequency that particular pairs of tissues are concordant or discordant. Since the loss of the ring-X chromosome is a random event limited to the earliest stages of embryogenesis, the concordance rate reflects the relative distance between the origins of the tissues in the blastoderm. Tissues derived from remote sites in the blastoderm will have concordance rates close to chance or 50 percent. Those that have common origins will have concordance rates close to 100 percent. By analyzing multiple marker pairs, it is then possible to construct a fate map of the blastoderm (Sturtevant, 1929; Hall, Gelbart, & Kankel, 1976) that locates the relative spatial origins of primordial tissues in the early embryo.

Hotta and Benzer (1972, 1976) pioneered the fate-mapping approach in the analysis of behavioral mutants. The series of three body-surface markers they chose enabled them to trace the developmental history of the mutants to specific sites in the blastoderm. In some cases, the mutant behavior traced back to precursor tissues of the nervous system; in other cases, the precursors of muscles or sensory receptors were targeted. Since defects in one component are likely to have multiple effects upon the development of others, analysis of the adult phenotype may not reveal the primary effect of the mutation. By identifying the embryological origins of relevant tissues, the fate-mapping technique not only demonstrates the role of specific genetic influences in development but also directs neurobiological investigation to the primary lesion.

More recently, allelic variants of the X-linked enzymes, acid phosphatase (Kanel & Hall, 1976) and succinate dehydrogenase (Lawrence, 1981) were introduced into mosaic animals. Marking internal tissues, these enzyme variants allow the mosaic analysis to be carried out at the level of the cell. One of the behavioral systems studied in some detail in gynanders is courtship. Siegel, Hall, Gailey, and Kyriacou (1984), Tompkins (1984), and Wimer and Wimer (1985) provide excellent summaries of this work. The cell markers have allowed researchers to determine that the performance of stereotypical male display pattern, of female receptivity and of copulation depend upon the genetic sex of particular sites in brain.

The study of the development of mammalian nervous systems has been furthered by the use of several neurological mutants in mice. Mosaic mice are constructed by removing embryos at the morula stage when the embryo consists of a ball of undifferentiated cells. Morulae are dissociated, and the cells from genetically different embryos are mixed. During incubation of several hours, the mixed cells reaggregate and begin to form a blastocyst that may then be implanted into a female host. The resulting mosaic mouse is a patchwork of tissues originally derived from different donor morulae. Among the neurological mutations subjected to mosaic analysis are three different locomotor disorders that disrupt cerebellar development. For each mutation, morulae derived from mice doubly homozygous for the locomotor dysfunction and a unique cell marker were mixed with morulae taken from normal mice. Thus, the origins of individual cells can be determined as derived from either the mutant or the normal stock. In mice homozygous for the cerebellar mutant, pcd, the Purkinje cells grow and differentiate normally prior to birth but begin to degenerate postnally. In mosaic mice of mixed pcd and normal genotypes, the postnatal cerebella contained a mixture of healthy cells and degenerated ones. Histochemical analysis revealed that the healthy cells were all derived from the normal genotype. Hence, the defect, whatever it may be, has a primary focus specific to the Purkinje cell (Mullen, 1977). The effect of this gene is not limited to Purkinje cells. It is also responsible for the degeneration of photoreceptor, mitral, and sperm cells (see review by Stent, 1981).

Two other two cerebellar mutants, reeler (rl) and staggerer (sg), disrupt the developmental migration of cells. In staggerer mice, the granule cells arise normally on the surface of the developing cerebellum but begin to degenerate as they migrate inward through the Purkinje cell layer. The Purkinje cells are also abnormal, lacking the well branched dendritic processes that normally form synaptic junctions with the granule cells. In mosaic animals, the granule layer develops normally even though some cells are homozygous sg/sg. However, some of the Purkinje cells have branched dendritic trees; others do not. The sparsely branched ones are derived from the mutant stock. The sg mutation disrupts Purkinje cell development and only secondarily brings about the degeneration of the granule cells (Mullen & Herrup, 1979).

In reeler mice, the Purkinje cells fail to migrate. The cerebellar cortex of mosaic mice contains a mixture of Purkinje cells. Some migrate outward in the normal fashion; others fail to migrate and are embedded in deeper layers. The normal- and abnormal-migrants include cells of both genotypes. Apparently, the reeler mutation does not affect the Purkinje cells directly. It disrupts their migration by affecting some extrinsic source of guidance (Mullen & Herrup, 1979).

Some features of the interplay between gene activation and the spatiotemporal patterning of neurogenesis are revealed through these genetic analyses. For example, the fine grid of mixed Purkinje cells in the two locations of reeler mosaics suggests that guidance is rather specifically targeted to individual cells. The hypothesis of a chemical gradient field that exerts a homogeneous influence to draw the Purkinje cells up to the surface is not in agreement with these data. They do, however, affirm the elegant work of Goodman et al. (1984) who demonstrated the important role of precise and developmentally limited chemical affinities between individual cells during neurogenesis in grasshoppers. By following the origin and development of individual neurons, Goodman et al. (1984) suggest that these unique chemical identities seem to be established by the combined influences of cell lineage and intercellular interactions.

Goodman (1979) also described subtle variations in the neuronal patterns of different grasshoppers. Exploiting the grasshopper's parthenogenetic ability, Goodman developed several isogenic lines that are analogous to inbred mice. Grasshoppers within a single line are fully homozygous and genetic replicates of one another. Grasshoppers from different lines are genetically distinct. Variation within lines must be environmental in origin while average differences between lines reflect genetic factors. Goodman found that particular aspects of neuronal structure in some lines were invariant; but in others, some structures were more variable. Thus, differential susceptibility to nongenetic agents appears to be controlled by the genotype.

As cells in the developing embryo become progressively differentiated, it is clear from biochemical assays of their mRNA transcripts that different batteries of genes are active in different tissues at different times. One class of mutations, the *homeotic* mutants, may reveal a part of the mechanism that regulates gene activation. These bizarre mutants, first described in *Drosophila* (Morata & Lawrence, 1977; Ouweneel, 1976) and the nematode, *Caenorhabditis elegans* (Sternberg & Horvitz, 1984), have the intriguing effect of transforming cell fates. In *Drosophila*, for example, the *Antennapedia* mutation transforms the distal portion of the antenna into a leg, complete with sensory receptors. These receptors project sensory afferents to the brain in the same pattern as do the afferent fibers from the mechanoreceptors of normal antennae. Despite their ectopic location and antenna-like synaptic connections, the chemoreceptors of the homeotic leg are able to elicit the proboscis-extension reflex when stimulated by sugar (see review by Stent, 1981).

In *C. elegans*, a wide array of homeotic mutants has been studied. Some transform fates spatially. That is, tissues in one location take on the destiny of those in another. Of special interest are those that transform fates by altering the temporal ordering of development. Some retard a particular pathway; others speed it up. These heterochronic mutants can have as profound effect as the other homeotic types by disrupting the intercellular interactions that are important determinants of the sequential pattern of development.

Recently, homeotic genes have been isolated from *Drosophila* DNA (Marx, 1984). The DNA segments of the different mutations contain common sequences. Homologous sequences have just been located in several other species including the frog, *Xenopus laevis*, the mouse, and the human. The high degree of similarity suggests common evolutionary origins. There is, of course, speculation that these genes are developmental switches. They may represent the genetic part of inductive embryological processes by regulating the activities of other genes, turning some on and others off. Some of these, no doubt, regulate the activity of other switches. Thus, a hierarchy of determinative decisions about cell fates can be set into motion by a single gene. As tissues in the developing embryo become progressively differentiated from one another, it is easy to conceive that their biochemically unique cellular environments trigger specific genetic switches. The reciprocal feedback between gene activity and cytoplasmic constituents propels and guides development along specific channels. The obvious question in this scheme concerns the initiation of the dynamic feedback system: What turns on the first switch? The answer must involve the distribution of cytoplasmic factors in the fertilized ovum. Even minor biases in the apportionment of these factors to the first daughter cells may be sufficient to bring about differential gene activation.

However developmental processes are encoded and initiated, it is clear that the genome does not constitute a unilaterally acting program. If the program metaphor is to be useful, it must be elaborated into a hierarchical system of multiple programs and subprograms. Considering the pleiotropic effects of individual genes and of nongenetic factors as well, Stent (1981) suggested that development was better modeled as a historical process in which one thing leads to another. In sum, the techniques of both classical and molecular genetics will be essential to the study of causal antecedents and their rippling effects through multiple developmental pathways.

Human Studies

The principal evidence of human developmental behavioral genetics can be reviewed under the rubrics of single loci and quantitative behavioral genetics.

SINGLE-LOCUS CONDITIONS

Among the more dramatic and straightforward examples of genetic control of human cognitive development are the single-locus conditions of mental retardation. The prototype of these conditions is phenylketonuria (PKU), classical both in its priority of discovery and also in the degree of understanding of the causal mechanism through which the genetic effect is mediated. The evidence strongly suggests that some forms of PKU are caused by a single locus, although there are some complicating features (Murphey, 1983; Scriver & Clow, 1980). Affected individuals, homozygous for the recessive allele, have a defect in the enzyme phenylalanine hydroxylase. As a result, the ability of the affected individuals to metabolize phenylalanine, an amino acid nearly ubiquitous in food stuffs, is seriously impaired. The excess of unmetabolized phenylalanine or of its metabolites, generated in unusual quantities through alternate routes, evidently results in an internal chemical milieu that is incompatible with normal development of the central nervous system.

PKU is an effective counterexample to the naive view that, if a condition is genetic, it is unalterable. Indeed, because of the understanding of the genetic basis of the condition and the biochemical mechanism, it became possible to devise a *rational* environmental intervention (the provision of a diet with no or with very little phenylalanine).

In addition to phenylketonuria, a number of other amino acidurias are known, also apparently of single-gene origin, involving defects in protein metabolism and mental retardation (Rosenberg, 1981).

Single-gene influenced, metabolic defects of carbohydrates and of lipids can also result in mental retardation (Omenn, 1983). For some of these conditions there are rational dietary therapies that are, of course, environmental interventions tailored to the needs of these individuals.

Developmental implications of these conditions are obvious, but they are even more vivid in the case of Tay-Sachs disease, also known as infantile amaurotic idiocy (Omenn, 1983). This single-locus, recessive condition involves absence of an enzyme that metabolizes a particular lipid. Behavioral anomalies begin to appear at a few months of age, and the affected infants deteriorate to a state of blindness, paralysis, and profound idiocy, with death usually occurring before two years of age. Degenerative neuronal changes are related to this abnormality of lipid metabolism. At present, no effective therapy is available.

Still more evidence in countering the misconception that the genetic information of an individual is fully deployed at conception and operates unchanged thereafter for the whole life span is provided by the late onset of Huntington's disease, which is due to a dominant allele of a particular single gene. The first symptoms of this disease may appear as early as adolescence, but on the average, onset occurs at about 40 years of age. Early signs may include slight loss of motor control and irritability, proceeding to severe chorea, personality change, and dementia. Alzheimer's and Pick's diseases are other examples of late onset conditions, but their genetic basis is incompletely understood at the present time (see Heston & Mastri, 1977; Folstein & Breitner, 1982).

The foregoing examples have all involved serious anomalies with some distinctive pattern that has made possible the separate study of each entity. The enormous value of this potential can be appreciated by consideration of the confusion of results that would arise from studies of mechanism, if, for example, galactosemia, PKU, and Tay-Sachs disease were studied collectively. Yet it is very likely that many conditions of interest to developmental psychologists are, in fact, heterogeneous complexes with a variety of etiological mechanisms. Within these complexes may exist subentities with single-gene origins. For example, we have noted that there is general agreement on a familial component to reading disability (DeFries, Singer, Foch, & Lewitter, 1978; Finucci, 1978; Herschel, 1978) and have discussed the linkage analysis of Smith et al. (1983) that suggests there may exist a single, major gene influencing at least one subtype of this major problem of learning disability. Clearly, the identification of single-locus influenced subtypes could be of enormous value in the study of causal mechanisms in diagnosis and in the design of rational remedial and preventive interventions.

POLYGENIC CONDITIONS

The examples given to this point, dealing as they do with abnormalities of development, provide abundant demonstration of the capability of genes in influencing such processes adversely. But we are concerned as well with the origins of individual differences in developmental processes within the normal range. In these cases, we may again expect the applicability of the polygenic model involving both an environmental and a genetic source of variance, with the latter being attributed in the most part to many genes, each individually of small effect. How can we interpret the mechanisms of influence of these multifarious genes? Unlike the single major gene examples examined heretofore, where there is a clearly identifiable proximal genetic effect, we can expect a system in which the genes affect the fine tuning of a host of anatomical, biochemical, and physiological structures and processes that impinge upon the behavioral phenotype of interest. Little is actually known about the mechanism of action of specific polygenic systems. Reasonable speculations, can be made, however, by drawing from biopsychological disciplines as well as from the knowledge of the mechanisms of single genes. For example, with respect to individual differences in learning, one can imagine that the cognate polygenes influence minor alterations in neurotransmitter production, reuptake, receptor surfaces, neuron number, dendritic connection sites, the cellular electrolyte pump, interneural connections, refractory period of the neurons, fineness of the capillary beds, oxygen carrying capacity of the hemoglobin, pulmonary efficiency, and so on. Some of these variations will be positive with respect to, let us say, cognitive functioning, and others will be negative. For most of the individuals in a population, the net effect of these plus and minus influences places them in the phenotypic range that we define as normal or average. Those who have a preponderance of positive effects will constitute the upper tail of the distribution, and those with a preponderance of the negative attributes will be at the lower end of the distribution. A gross phenotypic measure, such as IQ, of these polygenic segregants may be similar to that of a single-locus case whose polygenic systems, though all within the normal range, are overridden by the effects of a gene of major effect. It can be seen, however, that the prospects for a rational intervention strategy are much different for the two classes of affected individuals. For the polygenic segregants, there is much less likelihood for the discovery of a "magic bullet." It is less easy to contemplate the fine retuning of a host of elements than the rectification of a single enzyme. In the former case, effective interventions will most likely be found to be more general in nature, and it will be necessary to apply them at a point in the causal nexus relatively distal from the genes. However, effective remediation or prevention, while made more challenging, is not made hopeless by these considerations. For example, it is entirely possible that physiological and embryological constraints lead to clustering, so that the polygenic segregants are not uniformly distributed through the n-space of the complex determinant systems. Differential diagnosis, aimed at the identification of such clusters, might lead to the identification of subgroups for which tailored remediations could be devised.

The study of genetic and environmental influences on these normal developmental processes has been the focus of intense recent activity, as documented by the recent special section on developmental behavioral genetics of *Child Development* (1983).

The stage for this recent research emphasis was set a couple of decades previously. For example, Sontag and Garn (1956–1957) reported briefly on a study of developmental patterns for IQ and an assortment of physical traits in sibling groups. They observed that certain developmental patterns were characteristic of families. In one family, for example, four siblings exhibited rapid growth, slow motor development, and poor coordination.

In a classic adoption study not previously mentioned, Skodak and Skeels (1949) examined the relationship between children's IQs and education level of mothers. The correlation of the IQ of the adopted child with the education level of either adoptive mother or adoptive father did not differ significantly from zero through the age range studied, which was from two to 14

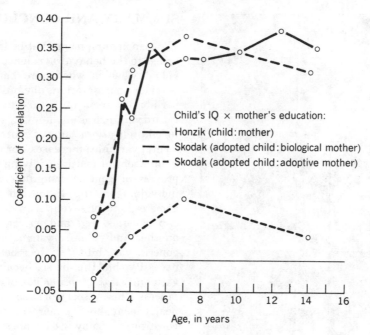

Figure 13.29. Coefficients of correlation at different ages between child's IQ and educational level of own or of foster mother. (After Honzik, M.P. (1957). Developmental studies of parent–child resemblance in intelligence. *Child Development*, 28, Figure 2. Used with permission of the Society for Research in Child Development.) From "The Inheritance of Behavior" by G.E. McClearn, 1962, in *Psychology in the Making* (p. 204, 213), L. Postman (ed.), New York: Random House, Inc. Copyright 1962 by Random House, Inc. Adapted by permission.

years of age. On the other hand, the correlation of the child's measured IQ with its biological mother's educational level rose from a baseline of zero at two years to 0.31 at four years, and remained fairly stable through the rest of the observation period. Honzik (1957) obtained similar data of children's IQ and parent's education level in normal families and found a striking similarity in the pattern of increasing relationship to biological parents in her study and in that of Skodak and Skeels. The developmental function, resulting in increasing resemblance to biological parents, and the level of resemblance attained would appear to be the same whether the children were reared by their biological parents or by adoptive parents. The frequently published representation of these results is given as Figure 13.29.

A major application of the twin study methodology to developmental behavioral genetics has been the Louisville Twin Study (Wilson, 1983). This longitudinal study has compared the phenotypic scores of MZ and DZ twin pairs over a 15-year span. One mode of analysis has been to examine the synchrony of developmental spurts and lags in mental development scores. Dramatic differences were observed in the degree of temporal concurrence of genetically identical twins and those who share only 50 percent of their genes. These classical results are reproduced in Figure 13.30.

Examination of the intraclass correlations for twin pairs at each age adds further evidence of genetic control of developmental process. During the first year, the value of the intraclass correlations was about the same for MZ and for DZ twin pairs. However, from 18 months onward the MZ twin pairs had significantly higher intraclass correlations than the DZs. The DZ correlations were highest at the value of 0.79 at 36 months of age, declining to a value of 0.54 at 15 years of age. Matheny (1983) has reported on changes in objective assessments of temperament during the first two years of life in this project and has shown a significant genetic contribution to longitudinal stability during this age.

As was true in the case of animal research, a growing literature on the genetics of human

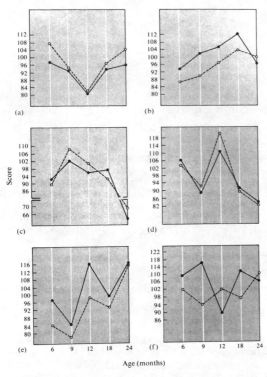

Figure 13.30 Profiles of mental development scores for MZ twins at ages 6 through 24 months. The pairs in (a) through (e) exhibit moderate to high profile congruence; the pair in (f) is obviously noncongruent. From "Twins: Early Mental Development" by R.S. Wilson, 1972, *Science*, *175*, p. 916. Copyright 1972 by the AAAS. Reprinted by permission.

behavioral aging fortifies the view that genes are involved in influencing developmental trajectories throughout the total lifespan (see McClearn & Foch, 1985, for review). A most dramatic example is provided by the Hutchinson-Gilford syndrome of progeria. Evidence suggests that this is due to a single locus. Growth retardation of homozygotes for the recessive allele is apparent by the end of the first year, and death usually occurs during the second decade of life after an apparently accelerated aging process. In spite of the multiple pathologies, intellectual and psychomotor development appears to be normal for these children.

With respect to quantitative cognitive attributes, the work of Jarvik, Kallmann, Falek, and Klaben (1957) comparing MZ and DZ twin similarities showed continuing evidence of genetic influence on cognitive measures after 60 years of age.

SUMMARY AND CONCLUSIONS

The principal message that behavioral genetics brings to the behavioral sciences concerns individuality, which, when more than one individual is under consideration, obviously translates to variability. It is quite a different matter to regard variance as an annoying error—reducible indefinitely as precision of control over environmental variables increases—or to regard it as a quintessential feature of living organisms. The process of genetic sampling from within the individual in the formation of his or her gametes, and of sexual reproduction, in which two gametes, egg and sperm, unite to begin another individual, systematically generates genetic variability. It has been a biological necessity that this be so, because intraspecific variability is the *sine qua non* of the evolutionary process. This system works so well that it is very nearly incapable of generating the same genetic constitution in any two members of a sexually reproducing species. (The exceptions, and they are trivial in terms of population dynamics, are the cases of identical twins and other multiple identical births.) Thus, if all of the sets of environmental influences that have been identified—nutrition, rearing mode, peer groups, education, and the rest—could be equally applied to all, there would still be differences among us. Furthermore, the genetic differences and the environmental differences that exist in the real world do not necessarily simply summate. Individuals of some genotypes may respond differently to a particular environment than individuals of other genotypes. The appropriate model, then, acknowledges that both genetics and environment are essential for the development of the organism and, thus, for any of its traits (McClearn, 1975).

Behavioral genetics has made enormous strides in the theoretical perspectives and the empirical data bases that provide at least a start in our comprehending of the origins and mechanisms of individuality. Certainly, there remains no excuse for continuing the archaic arguments of the nature-nurture controversy. We know that nature and nurture are both essential, and that they coact in the development of the organism and in the establishment of individual differences among organisms. (Indeed, it is perhaps ironic that the genetic methodologies have provided powerful designs for studying environment.)

As the new molecular genetic methodologies come to be applied increasingly to behavioral phenotypes, we can expect that our insights into mechanisms of genetic influence will grow exponentially. So will our capacity to intervene. That prospect can be auspicious or ominous, and we need to examine the issues before they are upon us. However, that is a matter for discussion in another forum.

REFERENCES

Abrams, R. & Taylor, M.A. (1980). Importance of schizophrenic symptoms in the diagnosis of mania. *American Journal of Psychiatry, 138*, 658–661.

Aceves-Piña, E.O., Booker, R., Duerr, J.S., Livingstone, M.S., Quinn, W.G., Smith, R.F., Sziber, P.P., Tempel, B.L., & Tully, T.P. (1983). Learning and memory in *Drosophila* studied with mutants. *Cold Spring Harbor Symposium on Quantitative Biology, 48*, 831–840.

American Journal of Human Genetics (1983). The human gene map, *35*, 134–156.

Anderson, S.M., McClearn, G.E., & Erwin, V.G. (1979). Ethanol consumption and hepatic enzyme activity. *Pharmacology, Biochemistry and Behavior, 11*, 83–88.

Ashton, G.C., Polovina, J.J., & Vandenberg, S.G. (1979). Segregation analysis of family data for 15 tests of cognitive ability. *Behavior Genetics, 9*, 329–347.

Bagg, H.J. (1916). Individual differences and family resemblances in animal behavior. *American Naturalist, 50*, 222–236.

Baker, L.A., DeFries, J.C., & Fulker, D.W. (1983). Longitudinal stability of cognitive ability in the Colorado adoption project. *Child Development, 54*, 290–297.

Bakwin, H. (1973). Reading disability in twins. *Developmental Medicine and Child Neurology, 15*, 184–187.

Baron, M. (1977). Linkage between an X-chromosome marker (deutan color blindness) and bipolar affective illness. *Archives of General Psychiatry, 24*, 721–727.

Baron, M. (1981). Genetic heterogeneity in affective disorders. Implications for psychobiological research. *Acta Psychiatrica Scandinavica, 64*, 431–441.

Baron, M. (1982). Genetic models of schizophrenia. *Acta Psychiatrica Scandinavica, 65*, 263–275.

Baron, M., Gruen, R., Asnis, L., & Kane, J. (1983). Familial relatedness of schizophrenia and schizotypal states. *American Journal of Psychiatry, 140*, 1437–1442.

Baron, M., Mendlewicz, J., & Klotz, J. (1981). Age-of-onset and genetic transmission in affective disorders. *Acta Psychiatrica Scandinavica, 64*, 373–380.

Baron, M., Rainer, J.D., & Risch, N. (1981). X-linkage in bipolar affective illness: Perspectives on genetic heterogeneity, pedigree analysis and the X-chromosome map. *Journal of Affective Disorders, 3*, 141–157.

Baron, M. & Risch, N. (1982). X-linkage in affective and schizoaffective disorders: Genetic and diagnostic implications. *Neuropsychobiology, 8*, 304–311.

Basset, G.C. (1914). Habit formation in a strain of albino rats of less than normal brain weight. *Behavioral Monograph, 2*, 1–46.

Bastock, M. (1956). A gene mutation which changes a behavior pattern. *Evolution, 10*, 421–439.

Beadle, G.W. (1959). Genes and chemical reactions in *Neurospora*. *Science, 129*, 1717–1719.

Beadle, G.W. & Tatum, E.L. (1941). Genetic control of biochemical reactions in *Neurospora*. *Proceedings of National Academy of Science, 27*, 499–506.

Belknap, J.K., Haltli, N.R., Goebel, D.M., & Lame, M. (1983). Selective breeding for high and low levels of opiate-induced analgesia in mice. *Behavior Genetics, 13*, 383–396.

Belknap, J.K., MacInnes, J.W., & McClearn, G.E. (1972). Ethanol sleep times and hepatic alcohol and aldehyde dehydrogenase activities in mice. *Physiology and Behavior, 9*, 453–457.

Bignami, G. (1965). Selection for high rates and low rates of conditioning in the rat. *Animal Behavior, 13*, 221–227.

Bloom, F.E. (1981). Neuropeptides. *Scientific American, 245*, 148–168.

Bock, R.D. & Vandenberg, S.G. (1968). Components of heritable variation in mental test scores. In S.G. Vandenberg (Ed.), *Progress in human behavior genetics* (pp. 233–260). Baltimore: Johns Hopkins University Press.

Bolles, R.C. & Fanselow, M.S. (1982). Endorphins and behavior. *Annual Review of Psychology, 33*, 87–101.

Borecki, I.B. & Ashton, G.C. (1984). Evidence for a major gene influencing performance on a vocabulary test. *Behavior Genetics, 14*, 63–80.

Bouchard, T.J. (1983). Do environmental similarities explain the similarity in intelligence of identical twins reared apart? *Intelligence, 7*, 175–184.

Bouchard, T.J. & McGue, M. (1981). Familial studies of intelligence: A review. *Science, 212*, 1055–1059.

Brewster, D.J. (1972). Ethanol preference in strains of rats selectively bred for behavioral characteristics. *Annals of the New York Academy of Sciences, 197*, 49–53.

Broadhurst, P.L. (1958). Studies in psychogenetics: The quantitative inheritance of behavior in rats investigated by selective and cross-breeding. *Bull British Psychological Society, 34*(2A). (Abstract).

Broadhurst, P.L. (1960). Experiments in psychogenetics: Applications of biometrical genetics to the inheritance of behavior. In H.J. Eysenck (Ed), *Experiments in personality: Vol. 1 Psychogenetics and psychopharmacology* (pp. 3–102). London: Routledge & Kegan Paul.

Broadhurst, P.L. (1978). *Drugs and the inheritance of behavior. A survey of comparative psychopharmacogenetics.* New York: Plenum.

Broadhurst, P.L. (1979). The experimental approach to behavioral evolution. In J.R. Royce & L.P. Mos (Eds.), *Theoretical advances in behavior genetics* (pp. 53–95). Alphen aan den Rijn, Netherlands: Sijthoff Noordhoff International.

Broadhurst, P.L. & Jinks, J.L. (1974). What genetical architecture can tell us about the natural selection of behavioral traits. In J.H.F. van Abeelen (Ed.), *The genetics of behavior.* Amsterdam: North Holland, 43–63.

Bruell, J.H. (1962). Dominance and segregation in the inheritance of quantitative behavior in mice. In E. Bliss (Ed.), *Roots of behavior.* New York: Harper & Row.

Buchsbaum, M.S. & Haier, R.J. (1983). Psychopathology: Biological approaches. *Annual Review of Psychology, 39*, 401–430.

Burks, B.S. (1928). The relative influence of nature and nurture upon mental development; a comparative study of foster parent–foster child resemblance and true parent–true child resemblance. *Yearbook of the National Society for the Study of Education, 27*(1), 219–316.

Byers, D., Davis, R.L., & Kiger, J.A. (1981). Deficit in cyclic AMP phosphodiesterase due to dunce mutation of learning in *Drosophila melanogaster, Nature, 289*, 79–81.

Cadoret, R.J., Cain, C.A., & Crowe, R.R. (1983). Evidence for gene-environment interaction in the development of adolescent antisocial behavior. *Behavior Genetics, 13*, 201–310.

Carey, G. & Rice, J. (1983). Genetics and personality temperament: Simplicity or complexity? *Behavior Genetics, 13*, 43–63.

Carter, C.L. & Chung, C.S. (1980). Segregation analysis of schizophrenia under a mixed genetic model. *Human Heredity, 30*, 350–356.

Cattell, R.B. & Wilson, J.L. (1938). Contributions concerning mental inheritance: I. Of intelligence. *British Journal of Educational Psychology, 8*, 129–149.

Cavalli-Sforza, L.L. & Bodmer, W.F. (1971). *The genetics of human populations.* San Francisco: Freeman.

Chaudhari, N. & Hahn, W.E. (1983). Genetic expression in the developing brain. *Science, 220*, 924–928.

Cloninger, C.R., Reich, T., & Guze, S.B. (1975). The multifactorial model of disease transmission: III. Familial relationship between sociopathy and hysteria (Briquet's Syndrome). *British Journal of Psychiatry, 127*, 23–32.

Cloninger, C.R., Reich, T., & Wetzel, R.D. (1979). Alcoholism and affective disorders: Familial associations and genetic models. In D. Goodwin & C. Erickson (Eds.), *Alcoholism and the affective disorders* (pp. 57–86). New York: Spectrum.

Cloninger, C.R., Rice, J., & Reich, T. (1979). Multifactorial inheritance with cultural transmission and assortative mating: II. A general model of combined polygenic and cultural inheritance. *American Journal of Human Genetics, 31*, 176–198.

Coburn, C.A. (1922). Heredity of wildness and savageness in mice. *Behavior Monographs, 4*, 1–71.

Collins, A.C. (1981). A review of research using short-sleep and long-sleep mice. In G.E. McClearn, R.G. Dietrich, & V.G. Erwin (Eds.), *Development of animal models as pharmacogenetic tools,* (DHEW Publication No [ADM] 81-1133). Washington, DC: U.S. Government Printing Office.

Crick, F. (1979). Split genes and RNA splicing. *Science, 204*, 264–271.

Crowe, R.R., Namboodiri, K.K., Ashby, H.B., & Alston, R.C. (1981). Segregation and linkage analysis of a large kindred of unipolar depression. *Neuropsychobiology, 7*, 20–25.

Damjanovich, R.P. & MacInnes, J.W. (1973). Factors involved in ethanol narcosis: Analysis in mice of three inbred strains. *Life Sciences, 13*, 55–65.

Daniels, D., Dunn, J., Furstenberg, F.F., Jr., & Plomin, R. (1985). Environmental differences within the family and adjustment differences between pairs of adolescent siblings. *Child Development, 56*, 764–774.

Daniels, D. & Plomin, R. (1985). Differential experience of siblings in the same family. *Developmental Psychology, 21*, 747–760.

Daniels, D., Plomin, R., & Greenhalgh, J. (1984). Correlates of difficult temperament in infancy. *Child Development, 55*, 1184–1194.

Darbishire, A.D. (1904). On the result of crossing Japanese waltzing with albino mice. *Biometrika, 3*, 1–51.

Darnell, J.E., Jr. (1983). The processing of RNA. *Scientific American, 249*, 90–100.

Davidson, E.H. & Britten, R.J. (1979). Regulation of gene expression: Possible role of repetitive sequences. *Science, 204*, 1052–1059.

Davis, N. (1849). *The works of Plato: Vol. II*. London: Bohn.

Dawson, W.M. (1932). Inheritance of wildness and tameness in mice. *Genetics, 17*, 296–326.

Deckard, B.S., Tepper, J.M., & Schlesinger, K. (1976). Selective breeding for acoustic priming. *Behavior Genetics, 6*, 375–383.

DeFries, J.C., Ashton, G.C., Johnson, R.C., Kuse, A.R., McClearn, G.E., Mi, M.P., Rashad, M.N., Vandenberg, S.G., & Wilson, J.R. (1976). Parent–offspring resemblance for specific cognitive abilities in two ethnic groups. *Nature, 261*, 131–133.

DeFries, J.C., Gervais, M.C., & Thomas, E.A. (1978). Response to 30 generations of selection for open-field activity in laboratory mice. *Behavior Genetics, 8*, 3–13.

DeFries, J.C. & Hegman, J.P. (1970). Genetic analysis of open-field behavior. In G. Lindzey & D.D. Thiessen (Eds.), *Contributions to behavior-genetic analysis: The mouse as a prototype* (pp. 23–56). New York: Appleton-Century-Crofts.

DeFries, J.C., Johnson, R.C., Kuse, A.R., McClearn, G.E., Polovina, J., Vandenberg, S.G., & Wilson, J.R. (1979). Family resemblance for specific cognitive abilities. *Behavior Genetics, 9*, 23–43.

DeFries, J.C., Kuse, A.R., & Vandenberg, S.G. (1979). Genetic correlations, environmental correlations, and behavior. In J.R. Royce & L.P. Mos (Eds.), *Theoretical advances in behavior genetics* (pp. 389–417). Germantown, MD: Sijthoff and Noordhoff.

DeFries, J.C. & Plomin, R. (1978). Behavioral genetics. *Annual Review of Psychology, 29*, 473–515.

DeFries, J.C., Singer, S.M., Foch, T.T., & Lewitter, F.I. (1978). Familial nature of reading disability. *British Journal of Psychiatry, 132*, 361–367.

DeFries, J.C., Weir, M.W., & Hegmann, J.P. (1967). Differential effects of prenatal maternal stress on offspring behavior in mice as a function of genotype and stress, *Journal of Comparative and Physiological Psychology, 63*, 332–334.

Deol, M.S. (1964). The abnormalities of the inner ear in *Kreisler* mice. *Journal of Embryology and Experimental Morphology, 12*, 475–490.

Deutsch, S.I. & Davis, K.L. (1983). Schizophrenia: A review of diagnostic and biological issues: II. Biological issues. *Hospital and Community Psychiatry, 34*, 423–437.

Dickie, M.M., Schneider, J., & Harman, P.J. (1952). A juvenile "Wabbler lethal" in the house mouse. *Journal of Heredity, 43*, 283–286.

Dixon, L.K. & DeFries, J.C. (1968). Development of open-field behavior in mice: Effects of age and experience. *Developmental Psychobiology, 1*, 100–107.

Dixon, L.K. & Johnson, R.C. (1980). *The roots of individuality*. Monterey, CA: Brooks/Cole.

Dobzhansky, T. (1968). On some fundamental concepts of Darwinian biology. *Evolutionary Biology, 2*, 1–4.

Dudai, Y. (1983). Mutations affect storage and use of memory differentially in *Drosophila*. *Proceedings of the National Academy of Sciences, USA, 80*, 5455–5448.

Dudai, Y., Jan, Y.N., Byers, D., Quinn, W.G., & Benzer, S. (1976). *Dunce*: A mutant of *Drosophila Deficient in Learning*. *Proceedings of the National Academy of Science, USA, 72*, 1684–1688.

Duerr, J.S. & Quinn, W.G. (1982). Three *Drosophila* mutations that block associative learning also affect habituation and sensitization. *Proceedings of the National Academy of Science, USA, 79*, 3646–3650.

Eaves, L.J. (1983). Errors of inference in the detection of major gene effects on psychological test scores. *American Journal of Human Genetics, 35*, 1179–1189.

Eaves, L.J. & Gale, J.S. (1974). A method for analyzing the genetic basis of covariation. *Behavior Genetics, 4*, 253–267.

Eaves, L.J., Last, K.A., Martin, N.G., & Jinks, J.L. (1977). A progressive approach to non-additivity and genotype-environmental covariance in the analysis of human differences. *British Journal of Mathematical and Statistical Psychology, 30*, 1–42.

Eaves, L.J., Last, K.A., Young, P.A., & Martin, N.G. (1978). Model fitting approaches to the analysis of human behavior. *Heredity, 41*, 429–430.

Edwards, A.W.F. (1972). *Likelihood: An account of the statistical concept of likelihood and its application to scientific inference*. London: Cambridge University Press.

Edwards, J.H., Harnden, D.G., Cameron, A.H., Crosse, V.M., & Wolff, O.H. (1960). A new trisomic syndrome. *Lancet*, i, 787–789.

Ehrman, L. & Parsons, P.A. (1981). *Behavor genetics and evolution*, New York: McGraw-Hill.

Elias, P.K., Elias, M.F., & Eleftheriou, B.E. (1975). Emotionality, exploratory behavior, and locomotion in aging inbred strains of mice. *Gerontologia, 21*, 46–55.

Elston, R.C. (1973). Ascertainment and age of onset in pedigree analysis, *Human Heredity, 23*, 105–112.

Elston, R.C. (1980). Likelihood models in human quantitative genetics. In C.F. Sing & M.H. Skolnick (Eds.), *The genetic analysis of common diseases* (pp. 391–406). New York: Alan R. Liss.

Elston, R.C. (1981). Segregation analysis. In J.H. Mielke & M.H. Crawford (Eds.), *Current developments in anthropological genetics: Vol. 1. Theory and methods* (pp. 327–354). New York: Plenum.

Elston, R.C. & Campbell, M.A. (1970). Schizophrenia: Evidence for the major gene hypothesis. *Behavior Genetics, 1*, 3–10.

Elston, R.C., Nambroodi, K.K., Spence, M.A., & Rainer, J.D. (1978). A genetic study of schizophrenia pedigrees. II. One-locus hypotheses. *Neuropsychobiology, 4*, 193–206.

Elston, R.C. & Rao, D.C. (1978). Statistical modeling and analysis in human genetics. *Annual Review of Biophysics and Bioengineering, 7*, 253–286.

Elston, R.C. & Stewart, J. (1971). A general model for the genetic analysis of pedigree data. *Human Heredity, 21*, 523–542.

Elston, R.C. & Yelverton, K.C. (1975). General models for segregation analysis. *American Journal of Human Genetics, 27*, 31–45.

Ephrussi, B. (1942). Chemistry of "eye-color hormones" of *Drosophila*. *Quarterly Review of Biology, 17*, 327–338.

Eriksson, K. (1969). Factors affecting voluntary alcohol consumption in the albino rat. *Annales Zoologici Fennici, 6*, 227–265.

Erlenmyer-Kimling, L. (1972). Gene-environment interactions and the variability of behavior. In L. Ehrman, G. Omenn, & E. Caspari (Eds.), *Genetics, environment and behavior: Implications for educational policy*, (pp. 181–208). New York: Academic Press.

Eze, L.C., Tweedie, M.C.K., Bullen, M.F., Wren, P.J.J., & Evans, D.A.P. (1974). Quantitative genetics of human red cell acid phosphatase. *Annals of Human Genetics, 37*, 333–340.

Falconer, D.S. (1965). The inheritance of liability of certain diseases, estimated from the incidence among relatives. *Annals of Human Genetics, 29*, 51–76.

Falconer, D.S. (1981). *Introduction to quantitative genetics* (2nd ed.), London: University of London Press.

Feldman, M.W. & Lewontin, R.C. (1975). The heritability hang-up. *Science, 190*, 1163–1168.

Finucci, J.M. (1978). Genetic considerations in dyslexia. In H.R. Myklebust (Ed.), *Progress in learning disabilities*: Vol. 4. New York: Grune & Stratton.

Fischbein, S. (1978). Heredity-environment interaction in the development of twins. *International Journal of Behavior Development, 1*, 313–322.

Fisher, R.A. (1918). The correlation between relatives on the supposition of Mendelian inheritance. *Transactions of the Royal Society of Edinburgh, 52*, 399–433.

Fishman, P., Suarez, B.K., Hodge, S.E., & Reich, T. (1978). A robust method for the detection of linkage in familial diseases. *American Journal of Human Genetics, 30*, 308–321.

Foch, T.T. (1979). *Differential diagnosis of specific reading disability: A typological study*. Unpublished doctoral dissertation, University of Colorado, Boulder.

Fölling, A. (1934). Uber Ausscheidung von Phenylbrenztraubensäure in den Harn als Stoffweckselanomalie in Verbindung mit Imbezillität. *Zeitschrift für Physiologischo Chemie, 227*, 160–176.

Folstein, M.F. & Breitner, J.C.S. (1982). Language disorder predicts familial Alzheimer's disease. In S. Corkin, K.L. Davis, J.H. Growden, E. Usdin, & R.J. Wurtman (Eds.), *Alzheimer's disease: A report of progress*: Vol. 19. (pp. 197–200). New York: Rowen Press.

Freeman, F.N., Holzinger, K.J., & Mitchell, B.C. (1928). The influence of environment on the intelligence, school achievement, and conduct of foster children. *Yearbook of National Social Studies Education, 27*(I), 103–217.

Frings, H. & Frings, M. (1953). The production of stocks of albino mice with predictable susceptibilities to audiogenetic seizures. *Behaviour, 5*, 305–19.

Fulker, D.W. (1966). Mating speed in male *Drosophila melanogaster*: A psychogenetic analysis. *Science, 153*, 203–205.

Fulker, D.W. (1978). Multivariate extensions of a biometrical model of twin data. In W.E. Nance, G. Allen, & P. Parisi (Eds.), *Twin research, Part A: Psychology and methodology* (pp. 217–236). New York: Alan R. Liss.

Fulker, D.W. (1979). Some implications of biometrical genetical analysis for psychological research. In J.R. Royce & L.P. Mos (Eds.), *Theoretical advances in behavior genetics* (pp. 337–380). Germantown, MD: Sitjhoff & Noordhoof.

Fulker, D.W. (1982). Extensions of the classical twin method. In B. Bonnê-Tamir, T. Cohen, & R.M. Goodman (Eds.), *Human genetics, Part A: The unfolding genome* (pp. 395–406). New York: Alan R. Liss.

Fulker, D.W., Wilcock, J., & Broadhurst, P.L. (1972). Studies in genotype-environment interaction. Methodology and preliminary multivariate analysis of a diallel cross of eight strains of rat. *Behavior Genetics, 2*, 261–287.

Fuller, J.L. (1964). Measurement of alcohol preference in genetic experiments. *Journal of Comparative and Physiological Psychology, 57*, 85–88.

Fuller, J.L. & Herman, B.H. (1974). Effect of genotype and practice upon behavioral development in mice. *Developmental Psychobiology, 7*, 21–30.

Fuller, J.L. & Simmel, E.C. (1983). *Behavior genetics:*

Principles and applications. Hillsdale, NJ: Lawrence Erlbaum Associates.

Fuller, J.L. & Sjursen, F.H. (1967). Audiogenic seizures in eleven mouse strains. *Journal of Heredity, 58*, 135–140.

Fuller, J.L. & Thompson, W.R. (1960). *Behavior Genetics,* New York: John Wiley & Sons.

Fuller, J.L. & Thompson, W.R. (1978). *Foundations of behavior genetics.* St. Louis: Mosby.

Galton, F. (1883). *Hereditary genius. Inquiries into human faculty and its development.* London: Mac-Millan.

Garrod, A.E. (1908). The Croonian lectures on inborn errors of metabolism I, II, III, IV. *Lancet, 2,* 73–79, 142–148, 214–220.

Gershon, E.S., Bunney, W.E., Leckman, J.F., Van Eerdewegh, M., & DeBauche, B.A. (1976). The inheritance of affective disorders: A review of data and of hypotheses. *Behavior Genetics, 6,* 227–261.

Gershon, E.S., Hamovit, J., Guroff, J.J., Dibble, E., Leckman, J.F., Sceery, W., Targum, S.D., Nurnberger, J.I., Goldin, L.R., & Bunney, W.E. (1982). A family study of schizoaffective, bipolar I, bipolar II, unipolar, and normal control probands. *Archives of General Psychiatry, 39,* 1157–1167.

Gershon, E.S., Targum, S.D., Matthysse, S., & Bunney, W.E., Jr. (1979). Color blindness not closely linked to bipolar illness. *Archives of General Psychiatry, 36,* 1423–1430.

Ginsburg, B.E., Cowan, S., Maxson, S.C., & Sze, P.Y. (1969). Neurochemical effects of gene mutations associated with audiogenic seizures. In A. Barbeau & J.R. Brunett (Eds.), *Progress in neurogenetics* (pp. 695–701). New York: Excerpta Medica Foundation.

Go, R.C.P., Elston, R.C., & Kaplan, E.B. (1978). Efficiency and robustness of pedigree segregation analysis. *American Journal of Human Genetics, 30,* 28–37.

Goddard, H.H. (1914). Feeble-mindedness, its causes and consequences. New York: Macmillan.

Goetzl, U., Green, R., Whybrow, P., & Jackson, R. (1974). X-linkage revisited: A further family study of manic-depressive illness. *Archives of General Psychiatry, 31,* 665–672.

Goldin, L.R., Clerget-Darpoux, F., & Gershon, E.S. (1982). Relationship of HLA to major affective disorder not supported. *Psychiatry Research, 7,* 29–45.

Goldin, L.R. & Gershon, E.S. (1983). Association and linkage studies of genetic marker loci in major psychiatric disorders, *Psychiatric Development, 1,* 387–418.

Goldsmith, H.H. (1983). Genetic influences on personality from infancy to adulthood. *Child Development, 54,* 331–355.

Goldstein, D.B. & Kakihana, R. (1974). Alcohol withdrawal reactions and reserpine effects in inbred strains of mice. *Life Sciences, 15,* 415–425.

Goldstein, D.B. & Kakihana, R. (1975). Alcohol withdrawal reactions in mice strains selectively bred for long or short sleep times. *Life Sciences, 17,* 981–986.

Goodman, C.S. (1979). Isogenic grasshoppers: Genetic variability and development of identified neurons. In X.O. Breakefield (Ed.), *Neurogenetics: Genetic approaches to the nervous system.* New York: Elsevier-North Holland.

Goodman, C.S., Bastiani, M.J., Doe, C.Q., duLac, S., Helfand, S.L., Kuwada, J.Y., & Thomas, J.B. (1984). Cell recognition during neuronal development. *Science, 225,* 1271–1279.

Goodrick, C. (1967). Behavioral characteristics of young and senescent inbred female mice of the C57BL/6J strain. *Journal of Gerontology, 22,* 459–464.

Goodrick, C.L. (1974). The effects of exercise on longevity and behavior of hybrid mice which differ in coat color. *Journal of Gerontology, 29,* 129–133.

Goodrick, C.L. (1975a). Life span and the inheritance of longevity for inbred mice. *Journal of Gerontology, 30,* 257–263.

Goodrick, C.L. (1975b). Behavioral differences in young and aged mice: Strain differences for activity measures, operant learning, sensory discrimination, and alcohol preference. *Experimental Aging Research, 1,* 191–207.

Gottesman, I.I. & Shields, J. (1972). *Schizophrenia and genetics: A twin study vantage point.* New York: Academic Press.

Gottesman, I.I. & Shields, J. (1977). Twin studies and schizophrenia a decade later. In B.A. Maher (Ed.), *Contributions to the psychopathology of schizophrenia.* New York: Academic Press.

Gottesman, I.I. & Shields, J. (1982). *Schizophrenia: The epigenetic puzzle.* London: Cambridge University Press.

Green, J.R. & Woodrow, J.C. (1977). Sibling method for detecting HLA-linked genes in disease. *Tissue Antigens, 9,* 31–35.

Grieve, S.J., Griffiths, P.J., & Littleton, J.M. (1979). Genetic influences on the rate of development of ethanol tolerance and the ethanol physical dependence syndrome in mice. *Drug and Alcohol Dependence, 4,* 77–86.

Guze, S.B., Cloninger, C.R., Martin, R.L., & Clayton, P.J. (1983). A follow-up and family study of schizophrenia. *Archives of General Psychiatry, 40,* 1273–1276.

Hadler, N.M. (1964). Genetic influence on phototaxis

in *Drosophila melanogaster*. *Biol. Bulletin*, *126*, 264–273.

Hall, C.S. (1938). The inheritance of emotionality. *Sigma Xi Quarterly*, *26*, 17–27.

Hall, C.S. (1951). The genetics of behavior. In S.S. Stevens (Ed.), *Handbook of experimental psychology*. New York: Wiley & Sons.

Hall, J.C., Gelbart, W.M., & Kankel, D.R. (1976). Mosaic systems. In M. Ashburner & E. Novitski, *The genetics and biology of Drosophila* (pp. 265–314). New York: Academic Press.

Hallgren, B. (1950). Specific dyslexia ("congenital word-blindness"): A clinical and genetic study. *Acta Psychiatrica et Neurologica Scandinavica*, Suppl. 65.

Hegman, J.P. & DeFries, J.C. (1970). Are genetic correlations and environmental correlations correlated? *Nature*, *226*, 284–286.

Henderson, N.D. (1967). Prior treatment effects on open field behavior of mice—A genetic analysis. *Animal Behaviour*, *15*, 365–376.

Henderson, N.D. (1968). The confounding effects of genetic variables in early experience research: Can we ignore them? *Developmental Psychobiology*, *1*, 146–152.

Henderson, N.D. (1970a). Brain weight increases resulting from environmental enrichment: A directional dominance in mice. *Science*, *169*, 776–778.

Henderson, N.D. (1970b). Genetic influences on the behavior of mice can be obscured by laboratory rearing. *Journal of Comparative and Physiological Psychology*, *72*, 505–511.

Henderson, N.D. (1972). Relative effects of early rearing environment on discrimination learning in housemice. *Journal of Comparative and Physiological Psychology*, *79*, 243–253.

Henderson, N.D. (1979). Adaptive significance of animal behavior: The role of gene-environment interaction. In J.R. Royce & L.P. Mos (Eds.) *Theoretical advances in behavior genetics* (pp. 243–287). Germantown, MD: Sijthoff & Noordhoff.

Henry, K.R. (1967). Audiogenic seizure susceptibility induced in C57BL/6J mice by prior auditory exposure. *Science*, *158*, 938–940.

Henry, K.R. (1982). Influence of genotype and age on noise-induced auditory losses. *Behavior Genetics*, *12*, 563–573.

Henry, K.R. & Schlesinger, K. (1967). Effects of the albino and dilute loci on mouse behavior. *Journal of Comparative and Physiological Psychology*, *63*, 320–323.

Heron, W.T. (1935). The inheritance of maze learning ability in rats. *Journal of Comparative Psychology*, *19*, 77–89.

Herschel, M. (1978). Dyslexia revisited: A review. *Human Genetics*, *40*, 115–134.

Herter, K. (1938). Die bezlehungen zwischen vorzugstemperatur und hautbeschattenheit bei mausen. *Zeitschrift für Wissenschaftliche Zoologie*, *11*, 48–55.

Heston, L.L. (1966). Psychiatric disorders in foster home reared children of schizophrenic mothers. *British Journal of Psychiatry*, *112*, 819–825.

Heston, L.L. & Mastri, A.R. (1977). The genetics of Alzheimer's disease: Associations with hematologic malignancy and Down's syndrome. *Archives of General Psychiatry*, *34*, 976–981.

Hewitt, J.K. & Fulker, D.W. (1981). Using the triple test cross to investigate the genetics of behavior in wild populations: I. Methodological considerations. *Behavior Genetics*, *11*, 23–36.

Hirsch, J. (1963). Behavior genetics and individuality understood. *Science*, *142*, 1436–1442.

Hirsch, J. & Boudreau, J.C. (1958). The heritability of phototaxis in a population of *Drosophila melanogaster*. *Journal of Comparative and Physiological Psychology*, *51*, 647–651.

Honzik, M.P. (1957). Developmental studies of parent–child resemblance in intelligence. *Child Development*, *28*, 215–228.

Horn, J.M. (1983). The Texas Adoption Project: Adopted children and their intellectual resemblance to biological and adoptive parents. *Child Development*, *54*, 268–275.

Horn, J.M., Loehlin, J.C. & Willerman, L. (1979). Intellectual resemblance among adoptive and biological relatives: The Texas Adoption Project. *Behavior Genetics*, *9*, 177–208.

Hotta, Y. & Benzer, S. (1972). Mapping of behavior in *Drosophila* mosaics. *Nature*, *240*, 527–535.

Hotta, Y. & Benzer, S. (1976). Courtship in *Drosophila* mosaics: Sex-specific foci for sequential action patterns. *Proceedings of the National Academy of Sciences, USA*, *73*, 4154–4158.

Hutchins, R.M. (1952). *Great book of the western world*. Lucretius, Epictetus, Marcus Aurelius. Chicago: Encyclopedia Britannica, *19*, 20.

Hyde, J. (1981). A review of selective breeding programs. In G.E. McClearn, R.A. Dietrich, & V.G. Erwin (Eds.), *Development of animal models as pharmacogenetic tools* (DHEW Publication No. [ADM] 81-1133). Washington, DC: U.S. Government Printing Office.

Jacklin, C.N. & Maccoby, E.E. (1974). The psychology of sex differences. Stanford, CA: Stanford University Press.

Jacobs, P.A., Brunton, M., Melville, M.M., Brittain, R.P. & McClemont, W.F. (1965). Aggressive behavior, mental sub-normality and the XYY male. *Nature, 208,* 1351–1352.

Jacobs, P.A., Price, W.H., Court Brown, W.M., Brittain, R.P., & Whatmore, P.B. (1968). Chromosome studies on men in a maximum security hospital. *Annals of Human Genetics, 31,* 339–358.

James, N.M. & Chapman, C.J. (1975). A genetic study of bipolar affective disorder. *British Journal of Psychiatry, 126,* 449–456.

Jarvik, L.F., Kallmann, F.J., Faleck, A., & Klaber, M.M. (1957). Changing intellectual functions in senescent twins. *Acta Genetica et Statistica Medica, 7,* 421–430.

Jervis, G.A. (1954). Phenylpyrvic oligophrenia (phenylketonuria). *Proceedings of the Association for Research in Nervous and Mental Disease, 33,* 259–282.

Jinks, J.L. & Fulker, D.W. (1970). Comparisons of biometrical genetical MAVA and classical approaches to the analysis of human behavior. *Psychological Bulletin, 73,* 311–349.

Johnson, G.F.S., Hunt, G.E., Robertson, S., & Doran, T.J. (1981). A linkage study of manic-depressive disorder with HLA antigens, blood groups, serum proteins and red cell enzymes. *Journal of Affective Disorders, 3,* 43–58.

Jones, H.E. (1928). A first study of parent–child resemblance in intelligence. *Yearbook of the National Society for the Study of Education, 27*(I), 61–72.

Kakihana, R. (1965). *Developmental study of preference for and tolerance to ethanol in inbred strains of mice.* Unpublished doctoral dissertation, University of California, Berkeley.

Kakihana, R., Brown, D.R., McClearn, G.E., & Tabershaw, I.R. (1966). Brain sensitivity to alcohol in inbred mouse strains. *Science, 154,* 1574–1576.

Kallman, F.J. (1938). *The genetics of schizophrenia.* Locus Valley, NY: J.J. Augustin.

Kallman, F.J. (1946). The genetic theory of schizophrenia: An analysis of 691 twin index families. *American Journal of Psychiatry, 103,* 309–322.

Kankel, D.R. & Hall, J.C. (1976). Fate mapping of nervous system and other internal tissues in genetic mosaics of *Drosophila melanogaster. Developmental Biology, 48,* 1–24.

Kendler, K.S. & Gruenberg, A.M. (1984). An independent analysis of the Danish Adoption Study of Schizophrenia: VI. The relationship between psychiatric disorders as defined by DSM-III in the relatives and adoptees. *Archives of General Psychiatry, 41,* 555–564.

Kendler, K.S., Gruenberg, A.M., & Strauss, J.S. (1982). An independent analysis of the Copenhagen sample of the Danish Adoption Study of Schizophrenia: IV. The relationship between major depressive disorder and schizophrenia. *Archives of General Psychiatry, 39,* 639–642.

Kendler, K.S. & Hays, P. (1983). Schizophrenia subdivided by the family history of affective disorder. *Archives of General Psychiatry, 40,* 951–955.

Kendler, K.S., Masterson, C.C., Ungaro, R., & Davis, K.L. (1984). A family history study of schizophrenia-related personality disorders, *American Journal of Psychiatry, 141,* 424–427.

Kety, S.S. (1983). Mental illness in the biological and adoptive relatives of schizophrenic adoptees: Findings relevant to genetic and environmental factors in etiology. *American Journal of Psychiatry, 140,* 720–727.

Kety, S.S., Rosenthal, D., Schulsinger, F., & Wender, P.H. (1971). Mental illness in the biological and adoptive families of adopted schizophrenics. *American Journal of Psychiatry, 138,* 302–306.

Kety, S.S., Rosenthal, D., Wender, P.H., & Schulsinger, F. (1976). Studies based on a total sample of adopted individuals and their relatives: Why they were necessary, what they demonstrated and failed to demonstrate. *Schizophrenia Bulletin, 2,* 413–428.

Kidd, K.K. & Cavalli-Sforza, L.L. (1982). An analysis of the genetics of schizophrenia. *Social Biology, 29,* 276–287.

Koivula, T., Koivualo, M., & Lindros, K.A. (1975). Liver aldehyde and alcohol dehydrogenase activities in rat strains genetically selected for their ethanol preference. *Biochemical Pharmacology, 24,* 1807–1811.

Kung, C., Chang, S.Y., Satow, Y., Van Houten, J., & Hansma, H. (1975). Genetic dissection of behavior in *Paramecium. Science, 188,* 898–904.

Lagerspetz, K.M.J. & Lagerspetz, K.Y.H. (1971). Changes in the aggressiveness of mice resulting from selective breeding, learning and social isolation. *Scandinavian Journal of Psychology, 12,* 241–248.

Lalouel, J.M. (1977). Linkage mapping from pair-wise recombination data. *Heredity, 38,* 61–77.

Lalouel, J.M. (1984). Segregation analysis: A gene or not a gene. *Progress in Clinical and Biological Research, 147,* 217–243.

Lawrence, P.A. (1981). A general cell marker for clonal analysis of *Drosophila* development. *Journal of Embryology and Experimental Morphology, 64,* 321–332.

Leckman, J.F. & Gershon, E.S. (1977). Autosomal models of sex effect in bipolar-related major affective illness. *Journal of Psychiatric Research, 13,* 237–261.

Leckman, J.F., Gershon, E.S., McGinniss, M., Targum, S.D., & Dibble, D.D. (1979). New data do not suggest linkage between Xg blood group and bipolar illness. *Archives of General Psychiatry, 36,* 1435–1441.

LeJeune, J., Gauthier, M., & Turpin, R. (1959). Etude des chromosomes somatiques de neuf enfants mongoliens. *Comptes Rendus de l'Academie des Sciences, Paris, 248,* 1721–1722.

Lerner, I.M. (1968). *Heredity, evolution, and society.* San Franciso: W.H. Freeman and Company.

Lerner, R. (1982). Children and adolescents as producers of their own development. *Environmental Review, 2,* 342–370.

Lewin, B. (1980). *Gene expression: Vol. 2. Eucaryotic chromosomes* (2nd ed). New York: Wiley.

Lewin, B. (1985). *Genes* (2nd ed.). New York: Wiley.

Lewitter, F.I., DeFries, J.C., & Elston, R.C. (1980). Genetic models of reading disability. *Behavior Genetics, 10,* 9–30.

Li, C.C. (1975). *Path analysis: A primer.* Pacific Grove, CA: Boxwood Press.

Li, T.K., Lumeng, L., McBride, W.J., & Waller, M.B. (1981). Indiana selection studies on alcohol-related behaviors. In G.E. McClearn, R.A. Dietrich, & V.G. Erwin (Eds.). *Development of animal models as pharmacogenetic tools,* (DHEW Publication No. [ADM] 81-1133). Washington, DC: U.S. Government Printing Office.

Lindzey, G. & Winston, H. (1962). Maze learning and effects of pre-training in inbred strains of mice. *Journal of Comparative and Physiological Psychology, 55,* 748–752.

Loehlin, J.C. (1978). Heredity-environment analysis of Jencks IQ correlations. *Behavior Genetics, 8,* 415–435.

Loehlin, J.C. (1979). Combining data from different groups in human behavior genetics. In J.R. Royce & L.P. Mos (Eds.), *Theoretical advances in behavior genetics* (pp. 303–334). Germantown, MD: Sijthoff & Noordhoff.

Loehlin, J.C. (1982). Are personality traits differentially heritable? *Behavior Genetics, 12,* 417–428.

Loehlin, J.C. & Nichols, R.C. (1976). *Heredity, environment, and personality.* Austin TX: University of Texas Press.

Loehlin, J.C. & Vandenberg, S.G. (1968). Genetic and environmental components in the covariance of cognitive abilities: An additive model. In S.G. Vandenberg (Ed.), *Progress in human behavior genetics* (pp. 261–285). Baltimore, MD: Johns Hopkins University Press.

Loranger, A.W. (1981). Genetic independence of manic-depression and schizophrenia. *Acta Psychiatrica Scandinavica, 63,* 444–452.

Lowing, P.A., Mirsky, A.F., & Pereira, R. (1983). The inheritance of schizophrenia spectrum disorders: A reanalysis of the Danish adoptee study data. *American Journal of Psychiatry, 140,* 1167–1171.

Lynch, C.B. (1981). Genetic correlation between two types of nesting in *Mus musculus*: Direct and indirect selection. *Behavior Genetics, 11,* 267–272.

MacLean, C.J., Morton, N.E., Elston, R.C., & Yee, S. (1976). Skewness in commingled distributions. *Biometrics, 32,* 695–699.

Maccoby, E.E. & Jacklin, C.N. (1974). *The psychology of sex differences.* Stanford, CA: Stanford University Press.

Maccoby, E.E. & Martin, J.A. (1983). Socialization in the context of the family. In P.H. Mussen (Ed.), *Handbook of child psychology: Vol. IV. Socialization, personality, and social development* (4th ed.). New York: Wiley.

Martin, N.B. & Eaves, L.J. (1977). The genetical analysis of covariance structure. *Heredity, 38*(1), 79–95.

Marx, J.L. (1984). Genes that guide fruit fly development. *Science, 224,* 1223–1225.

Matheny, A.P., Wilson, R.S., & Dolan, A.B. (1976). Relations between twins' similarity of appearance and behavioral similarity: Testing an assumption. *Behavior Genetics, 6,* 343–352.

Matheny, A.P., Jr. (1983). A longitudinal twin study of stability of component's from Bayley's Infant Behavior Record. *Child Development, 54,* 356–360.

Mather, K. & Jinks, J.L. (1971). *Biometrical Genetics* (2nd ed.). London: Chapman & Hall.

Matthyse, S.W. & Kidd, K.K. (1976). Estimating the genetic contribution to schizophrenia. *American Journal of Psychiatry, 133,* 185–191.

McCall, R.B. (1983). Environmental effects on intelligence: The forgotten realm of discontinuous non-shared within-family factors. *Child Development, 54,* 408–415.

McClearn, G.E. & DeFries, J.C. (1973). *Introduction to behavioral genetics.* San Franciso: Freeman.

McClearn, G.E., Deitrich, R.A., & Erwin, V.G. (Eds.). (1981). *Development of animal models as pharmacogenetic tools,* (DHEW Publication No. [ADM] 81-1133). Washington, DC: U.S. Government Printing Office.

McClearn, G.E. & Foch, T.T. (1985). Behavioral genetics. In J.E. Birren & K.W. Schaie (Eds.), *Handbook of the psychology of aging* (2nd ed.). (pp. 113–143). New York: Van Nostrand Reinhold.

McClearn, G.E. & Kakihana, R. (1981). Selective breeding for ethanol sensitivity: Short-sleep and long-sleep mice. In G.E. McClearn, R.A. Deitrich, & V.G. Erwin (Eds.), *Development of animal models as pharmacogenetic tools,* (DHEW Publication No. [ADM] 81-1133). Washington, DC: U.S. Government Printing Office.

McClearn, G.E. & Rodgers, D.A. (1961). Genetic factors in alcohol preference of laboratory mice. *Journal of Comparative and Physiological Psychology, 54*, 116–119.

McGue, M., Gottesman, I.I., & Rao, D.C. (1983). The transmission of schizophrenia under a multifactorial threshold model. *American Journal of Human Genetics, 35*, 1161–1178.

McGuffin, P. (1984). Biological markers and psychosis, *Psychological Medicine, 14*, 255–258.

McGuffin, P., Farmer, A.E., Gottesman, I.I., Murray, R.M., & Reveley, A.M. (1984). Twin concordance for operationally defined schizophrenia. Confirmation of familiality and heritability. *Archives of General Psychiatry, 41*, 541–545.

McGuffin, P., Festenstein, H., & Murray, R. (1983). A family study of HLA antigens and other genetic markers in schizophrenia. *Psychological Medicine, 13*, 31–43.

McGuire, T.R. (1984). Learning in three species of Diptera: The blow fly *Phormia regina*, the fruit fly *Drosophila melanogaster*, and the house fly *Musca domestica. Behavior Genetics, 14*, 479–526.

Meier, G.W. (1964). Differences in maze performances as a function of age and strain of house mice. *Journal of Comparative and Physiological Psychology, 58*, 418–422.

Meier, G.W. & Foshee, D.P. (1963). Genetics, age, and the variability of learning performances. *Journal of Genetic Psychology, 102*, 267–275.

Mendlewicz, J. & Fleiss, J.L. (1974). Linkage studies with X-chromosome markers in bipolar (manic-depressive) and unipolar (depressive) illness. *Biological Psychiatry, 9*, 261–294.

Mendlewicz, J., Fleiss, J.L., & Fieve, R.R. (1972). Evidence for X-linkage in the transmission of manic-depressive illness. *Journal of the American Medical Association, 222*, 1624–1627.

Mendlewicz, J., Linkowski, P., Guroff, J.J., & Van Praag, H.M. (1979). Color blindness linkage to bipolar manic-depressive illness. *Archives of General Psychiatry, 36*, 1442–1447.

Mendlewicz, J., Linkowski, P., & Wilmotte, J. (1980). Linkage between glucose-6-phosphate dehydrogenase deficiency and manic-depressive psychosis. *British Journal of Psychiatry, 137*, 337–342.

Mendlewicz, J. & Rainer, J.D. (1977). Adoption study supporting genetic transmission in manic-depressive illness. *Nature, 268*, 327–329.

Merriman, C. (1924). The intellectual resemblance of twins. *Psychological Monographs, 33*, 1–58.

Money, J. (1968). Cognitive deficits in Turner's syndrome. In S.G. Vandenberg (Ed.), *Progress in human behavior genetics* (pp. 27–30). Baltimore, MD: Johns Hopkins University Press.

Morata, G. & Lawrence, R. (1977). Homeotic genes, compartments and cell determination in *Drosophila. Nature, 265*, 211–216.

Morton, N.E. (1959). Genetic tests under incomplete ascertainment. *American Journal of Human Genetics, 11*, 1–16.

Morton, N.E. (1984). Linkage and association. *Progress in Clinical and Biological Research, 147*, 245–265.

Morton, N.E. & MacLean, C.J. (1974). Analysis of family resemblance: III. Complex segregation of quantitative traits. *American Journal of Human Genetics, 26*, 489–503.

Morton, N.E., Yee, S., & Lew, E. (1971). Complex segregation analysis. *American Journal of Human Genetics, 23*, 602–611.

Mullen, R.J. (1977). Site of *pcd* gene action and Purkinje cell mosaicism in cerebella of chimeric mice. *Nature, 270*, 245–247.

Mullen, R.J. & Herrup, K. (1979). Chimeric analysis of mouse cerebellar mutants. In D.R. Kankel & A. Ferrus (Eds.), *Neurogenetics: Genetic approaches to the nervous system* (pp. 173–196). New York: Elsevier North Holland.

Murphey, R.M. (1983). Phenylketonuria (PKU) and the single gene: An old story retold. *Behavior Genetics, 13*, 141–157.

Nachman, M. (1959). The inheritance of saccharin preference. *Journal of Comparative and Physiological Psychology, 52*, 451–457.

Oliverio, A. & Eleftheriou, B.E. (1976). Motor activity and alcohol: Genetic analysis in the mouse. *Physiology and Behavior, 16*, 577–581.

Oliverio, A., Eleftheriou, B.E., & Bailey, D.W. (1973). A gene influencing active avoidance performance in mice. *Physiology and Behavior, 11*, 497–501.

Omenn, G.S. (1983). Medical genetics, genetic counseling, and behavior genetics. In J.L. Fuller & E.C. Simmel (Eds.), *Behavior genetics, principles and applications* (pp. 155–187). Hillsdale, NJ: Lawrence Erlbaum.

O'Rourke, D., Gottesman, I.I., Suarez, B.K., Rice, J., & Reich, T. (1982). Refutation of the general single locus model for the etiology of schizophrenia. *American Journal of Human Genetics, 34*, 630–649.

O'Rourke, D.H., McGuffin, P., & Reich, T. (1983). Genetic analysis of manic-depressive illness. *American Journal of Physical Anthropology, 63*, 51–59.

Ott, J. (1974). Estimation of the recombination fraction in human pedigrees: Efficient computation of the likelihood for human linkage studies. *American Journal of Human Genetics, 26*, 558–597.

Ouweneel, W.S. (1976). Developmental genetics of homeosis. *Advances in Genetics, 18*, 179–248.

Owen, F.W., Adams, P.A., Forrest, T.S., Stolz, F.M., & Fisher, S. (1971). Learning disorders in children: Sibling studies. *Society for Research in Child Development, 36*(4), Serial No. 144.

Page, E.B. & Jarjoura, D. (1979). Seeking the course of correlations among mental abilities: Large twin analysis in a natural testing program. *Journal of Research and Development in Education, 12*, 108–117.

Parkinson, J.S. (1977). Behavioral genetics in bacteria. *Annual Review of Genetics, 11*, 397–414.

Patau, K., Smith, D.W., Therman, E., Inhorn, S.L., & Wagner, H.P. (1960). Multiple congenital anomaly caused by an extra autosome. *Lancet, i,* 790–793.

Pearson, K. (1904). On the laws of inheritance of man: II. On the inheritance of the mental and moral characters in man, and its comparison with the inheritance of the physical characters. *Biometrika, 3*, 131–190.

Pearson, K. (1924). *The life, letters and labours of Francis Galton.* London: Cambridge University.

Penrose, L.S. (1934). *The influence of heredity on disease.* London: H.K. Lewis.

Perris, C. (1968). Genetic transmission of depressive psychoses. *Acta Psychiatrica Scandinavica, 44*, Suppl. 203, 45–52.

Plomin, R. (1983). Childhood temperament. In B. Leahy & A. Kazdin (Eds.) *Advances in clinical child psychology* (Vol. 6). New York: Plenum.

Plomin, R. & Daniels, D. (1987). Why are children in the same family so different from each other? *The Behavioral and Brain Sciences, 10*, 1–16.

Plomin, R. & Dietrich, R.A. (1982). Neuropharmacogenetics and behavioral genetics. *Behavior Genetics, 12*, 111–121.

Plomin, R. & DeFries, J.C. (1979). Multivariate behavioral genetic analysis of twin data on scholastic abilities. *Behavior Genetics, 5*, 505–517.

Plomin, R. & DeFries, J.C. (1980). Genetics and intelligence: Recent data. *Intelligence, 4*, 15–24.

Plomin, R. & DeFries, J.C. (1983). The Colorado Adoption Project. *Child Development, 54*, 276–289.

Plomin, R., DeFries, J.C., & Loehlin, J. (1977). Genotype-environment interaction and correlation. *Psychological Bulletin, 84*, 309–322.

Plomin, R., DeFries, J.C., & McClearn, G.E. (1980). *Behavior genetics: A primer.* San Francisco: Freeman.

Plomin, R. & Foch, T.T. (1981). Sex differences and individual differences. *Child Development, 52*, 383–385.

Plomin, R. & Vandenberg, S.G. (1980). An analysis of Koch's (1966) primary mental abilities test data for 5- to 7-year-old twins. *Behavior Genetics, 10*, 409–412.

Plomin, R., Willerman, L., & Loehlin, J.C. (1976). Resemblance in appearance and the equal environments assumption in twin studies of personality traits. *Behavior Genetics, 6*, 43–52.

Quinn, W.G., Sziber, P.P., & Booker, R. (1979). The *Drosophila* memory mutant *amnesiac. Nature, 277*, 212–214.

Randall, C.L. & Lester, D. (1975). Social modification of alcohol consumption in inbred mice. *Science, 189*, 149–151.

Rao, D.C. & Morton, N.E. (1978). IQ as a paradigm in genetic epidemiology. In N.E. Morton & C.S. Chung (Eds.), *Genetic epidemiology* (pp. 145–181). New York: Academic Press.

Rao, D.C. & Morton, N.E. (1981). Path analysis of quantitative inheritance. In J.H. Mielke & M.H. Crawford (Eds.), *Current developments in anthropological genetics: Vol. 1. Theory and methods* (pp. 355–373). New York: Plenum Press.

Rao, D.C., Morton, N.E., & Yee, S. (1974). Analysis of family resemblance: II. A linear model for familial correlation. *American Journal of Human Genetics, 26*, 331–359.

Rao, D.C., Morton, N.E., & Yee, S. (1976). Resolution of cultural and biological inheritance by path analysis. *American Journal of Human Genetics, 28*, 228–242.

Reich, T., Clayton, P.J., & Winokur, G. (1969). Family history studies: V. The genetics of mania. *American Journal of Psychiatry, 125*, 1358–1369.

Reich, T., James, J.W., & Morris, C.H. (1972). The use of multiple thresholds in determining the mode of transmission of semi-continuous traits. *Annals of Human Genetics, 36*, 163–184.

Reich, T., Rice, J., Cloninger, C.R., Wette, R., & James, J. (1979). The use of multiple thresholds and segregation analysis in analyzing the phenotypic heterogeneity of multifactorial traits. *Annals of Human Genetics, 42*, 371–390.

Reich, T., Suarez, B., Rice, J., & Cloninger, C.R. (1981). Current directions in genetic epidemiology. In J.H. Mielke & M.H. Crawford (Eds.), *Current developments in anthropological genetics: Vol. 1. Theory and methods* (pp. 299–324). New York: Plenum Press.

Rice, J., Cloninger, C.R., & Reich, T. (1978). Multifactorial inheritance with cultural transmission and assortative mating: I. Description and basic properties of the unitary models. *American Journal of Human Genetics, 30*, 618–643.

Rice, J., Cloninger, C.R., & Reich, T. (1980). Analysis of behavioral traits in the presence of cultural transmission and assortative mating: Application to IQ and SES. *Behavior Genetics, 10*, 73–92.

Riley, E.P., Worsham, E.D., Lester, D., & Freed, E.X. (1977). Selective breeding of rats for differences in reactivity to alcohol: An approach to an animal model of alcoholism: II. Behavioral measures. *Journal of Studies on Alcohol, 38,* 1705–1717.

Risch, N. & Baron, M. (1982). X-linkage and genetic heterogeneity in bipolar-related major affective illness: Reanalysis of linkage data. *Annals of Human Genetics, 46,* 153–166.

Roberts, J.A.F. (1941). Resemblances in intelligence between sibs selected from a complete sample of an urban population. *Proceedings of the Seventh International Congress of Genetics,* 252.

Roderick, T.H., Wimer, R.E., & Wimer, C.C. (1976). Genetic manipulation of neuroanatomical traits. In L. Petrinovich & J.L. McGaugh (Eds.), *Knowing, thinking and believing.* New York: Plenum.

Rodgers, D.A., McClearn, G.E., Bennett, E.L., & Hebert, M. (1963). Alcohol preference as a function of its caloric utility in mice. *Journal of Comparative and Physiological Psychology, 56,* 666–672.

Roper, A.G. (1913). *Ancient eugenics.* Oxford: Blackwell.

Rosanoff, A., Jr., Handy, M., & Plessett, I.K. (1935). The etiology of manic-depressive syndromes with special reference to their occurrence in twins. *American Journal of Psychiatry, 91,* 725–762.

Rose, M.R. & Doolittle, W.F. (1983). Molecular mechanisms of speciation. *Science, 220,* 157–162.

Rosenberg, R.N. (1981). Biochemical genetics of neurological disease. *New England Journal of Medicine, 305,* 1181–1193.

Rosenthal, D. (1970). *Genetic theory and abnormal behavior.* New York: McGraw-Hill.

Rosenthal, D. (1972). Three adoption studies of heredity in the schizophrenic disorders. *International Journal of Mental Health, 1,* 63–75.

Rosenthal, D., Wender, P.H., Kety, S.S., Schulsinger, F., Welner, J., & Ostergaard, L. (1968). Schizophrenics' offspring reared in adoptive homes. *Journal of Psychiatric Research, 6,* 377–391.

Roubicek, C.G., & Ray, D.E. (1969). Genetic selection for adipsia and polydipsia in the rat. *Journal of Heredity, 60,* 332–335.

Rowe, D.C. (1983). A biometrical analysis of perceptions of family environment: A study of twin and singleton sibling kinships. *Child Development, 54,* 416–423.

Rowe, D.C. & Plomin, N. (1979). A multivariate twin analysis of within-family environmental influences in infants' social responsiveness. *Behavior Genetics, 9,* 519–525.

Rowe, D.C. & Plomin, R. (1981). The importance of nonshared (E_1) environmental influences in behav-ioral development. *Developmental Psychology, 17,* 517–531.

Rundquist, E.A. (1933). Inheritance of spontaneous activity in rats. *Journal of Comparative Psychology, 16,* 415–438.

Rundquist, E.A. & Bellis, C.J. (1933). Respiratory metabolism of active and inactive rats. *American Journal of Physiology, 106,* 670–675.

Rush, W.A. & King, R.A. (1976). Effect of the albino gene on sleep time in mice. *Behavior Genetics, 6,* 116 (Abstract).

Satinder, K.P. (1972). Behavior-genetic-dependent self-selection of alcohol in rats. *Journal of Comparative and Physiological Psychology, 80,* 422–434.

Scarr, S. (1981, April). *On the development of competence and the indeterminate boundaries between cognition and motivation: A genotype-environment correlation theory.* Invited address to the Eastern Psychological Association, New York.

Scarr, S. & Carter-Saltzman, L. (1979). Twin method: Defense of a critical assumption. *Behavior Genetics, 9*(6), 527–542.

Scarr, S. & Carter-Saltzman, L. (1983). In J.L. Fuller & E.C. Simmel (Eds.), Genetics and intelligence (pp. 217–335). *Behavior genetics: Principles and applications.* Hillsdale, NJ: Lawrence Erlbaum.

Scarr, S. & Grajek, S. (1983). Similarities and differences among siblings. In M.E. Lamb & B. Sutton-Smith (Eds.), *Sibling relationships: Their nature and significance across the life-sapn.* Hillsdale, NJ: Erlabum.

Scarr, S. & McCartney, K. (1983). How people make their own environments: A theory of genotype—environment effects. *Child Development, 54,* 424–435.

Scarr, S., Webber, P.L., Weinberg, R.A., & Wittig, M.A. (1981). Personality resemblance among adolescents and their parents in biologically related and adoptive families. *Progress in clinical and biological research: Vol. 69, Twin Research 3: Intelligence and Personality,* 99–120.

Scarr, S. & Weinberg, R.A. (1976). IQ test performance of black children adopted by white families. *American Psychologist, 31,* 726–739.

Scarr, S. & Weinberg, R.A. (1978). The influence of "family background" on intellectual attainment. *American Sociological Review, 43,* 674–692.

Scarr, S. & Weinberg, R.A. (1983). The Minnesota adoption studies: Genetic differences and malleability, *Child Development, 54,* 260–267.

Scharfetter, C. (1981). Subdividing the functional psychoses: A family hereditary approach. *Psychological Medicine, 11,* 637–640.

Scheller, R.H., Kaldany, R.R., Kreiner, T., Mahon,

A.C., Nambu, J.R., Schaefer, M., & Taussig, R. (1984). Neuropeptides: Mediators of behavior in aplysia. *Science, 225,* 1300–1308.

Schlesinger, K. & Griek, B.J. (1970). The genetics and biochemistry of audiogenic seizures. In G. Lindzey & D.D. Thiessen (Eds.), *Contributions to behavior-genetic analysis: The mouse as a prototype* (pp. 219–257). New York: Appleton-Century-Croft.

Schlesinger, K. & Uphouse, L.L. (1972). Pyridoxine dependencey and central nervous system excitability. *Advances in Biochemical Psychopharmacology, 4,* 105–140.

Schull, W.J. & Weiss, K.M. (1980). Genetic epidemiology: Four strategies. *Epidemiologic Reviews, 2,* 1–18.

Schwegler, H. & Lipp, H.P. (1983). Hereditary covariations of neuronal circuitry and behavior: Correlations between the proportions of hippocampal synaptic fields in the *regio inferior* and two-way avoidance in mice and rats. *Behavioral Brain Research, 7,* 1–38.

Schwegler, H., Lipp, H.P., vander Loos, H., & Buselmaier, W. (1981). Individual hippocampal mossy fiber distribution in mice correlates with two-way avoidance performance. *Science, 214,* 817–818.

Scriver, C.R. & Clow, C.L. (1980). Phenylketonuria: Epitome of human biochemical genetics. (First of two parts). *New England Journal of Medicine, 303,* 1136–1142.

Seidman, J.G. & Leder, P. (1978). The arrangement and rearrangement of antibody genes. *Nature, 276,* 790–795.

Seyfried, T.N., Yu, R.K., & Glaser, G.H. (1979). Genetic study of audiogenic seizure susceptibility in B6XD2 recombinant inbred strains of mice. *Genetics, 91,* 114.

Shaffer, J.W. (1962). A specific cognitive deficit observed in gonadal aplasia (Turner's syndrome). *Journal of Clinical Psychology, 18,* 403–406.

Shapiro, J.H. (1983). *Mobile genetic elements.* New York: Academic Press.

Sheppard, J.R., Albersheim, P., & McClearn, G.E. (1970). Aldehyde dehydrogenase and ethanol preference in mice. *Journal of Biological Chemistry, 245,* 2876–2882.

Siegel, I.M. (1967). Heritability and threshold determinations of the optomotor response in *Drosophila melanogaster. Animal Behavior, 15,* 299–306.

Siegel, R.W., Hall, J.C., Gailey, D.A., & Kyriacou, C.P. (1984). Genetic elements of courtship in *Drosophila*: Mosaics and learning mutants. *Behavior Genetics, 14,* 383–410.

Silcock, M. & Parsons, P.A. (1973). Temperature preference differences between strains of *Mus mus-*

culus, associated variables, and ecological implications. *Oecologia, 12,* 147–160.

Skodak, M. & Skeels, H.M. (1949). A final follow-up of one hundred adopted childern. *Journal of Genetic Psychology, 75,* 85–125.

Smith, C.A.B. (1959). A note on the effects of method of ascertainment on segregation ratios. *Annals of Human Genetics, 23,* 311–323.

Smith, S.D., Kimberling, W.J., Pennington, B.F., & Lubs, H.A. (1983). Specific reading disability: Identification of an inherited form through linkage analysis. *Science, 219,* 1345–1347.

Snyder, S.H. (1980). Brain peptides as neurotransmitters. *Science, 209,* 976–983.

Sontag, L.W. & Garn, S.M. (1956-1957). Human heredity studies of the Fels Research Institute. *Acta Genetica Statistica Medica, 6,* 494–502.

Sprott, R.L. (1972). Passive-avoidance conditioning in inbred mice: Effects of shock intensity, age, and genotype. *Journal of Comparative and Physiological Psychology, 80,* 327–334.

Sprott, R.L. (1975). Behavioral characteristics of C57BL/6J, DBA/2J, and B6D2F$_1$ mice which are potentially useful for gerontological research. *Experimental Aging Research, 1,* 313–323.

Sprott, R.L. (1978). The interaction of genotype and environment in the determination of avoidance behavior of aging inbred mice. In D. Bergsma & D.E. Harrison (Eds.), *Genetic effects on aging* (pp. 109–120). New York: Alan R. Liss.

Sprott, R.L. & Eleftheriou, B.E. (1974). Open-field behavior in aging inbred mice. *Gerontologia, 20,* 155–162.

Sprott, R.L. & Staats, J. (1975). Behavioral studies using genetically defined mice: A bibliography. *Behavior Genetics, 5,* 27–82.

Sprott, R.L. & Staats, J. (1978). Behavioral studies using genetically defined mice: A bibliography (July 1973–July 1976). *Behavior Genetics, 8,* 183–206.

Sprott, R.L. & Staats, J. (1979). Behavioral studies using genetically defined mice: A bibliography (July 1976–August 1978). *Behavior Genetics, 9,* 87–102.

Starch, D. (1917). The similarity of brothers and sisters in mental traits. *Psychology Review, 24,* 235–238.

Stavnes, K. & Sprott, R.L. (1975). Effects of age and genotype on acquisition of an active avoidance response in mice. *Developmental Psychobiology, 8,* 437–445.

Stene, J. (1977). Assumptions for different ascertainment models in human genetics. *Biometrics, 33,* 523–527.

Stent, G.S. (1981). Strengths and weaknesses of the genetic approach to the development of the nervous system. *Annual Review of the Neurosciences*, *4*, 163–194.

Stern, C. (1973). *Principles of human genetics* (3rd ed.). San Francisco: Freeman.

Sternberg, P.W. & Horvitz, H.R. (1984). The genetic control of cell lineage during nematode development. *Annual Review of the Genetics*, *18*, 489–524.

Sturtevant, A.H. (1929). The claret mutant type of *Drosophila simulans*: A study of chromosome elimination and cell lineage. *Zeitschrift für Wissenschaftliche Zoologie*, *135*, 325–356.

Suarez, B.K. & Reich, T. (1984). HLA and major affective disorder. *Archives of Genetic Psychiatry*, *41*, 103–106.

Tabakoff, B. & Ritzmann, R.F. (1979). Acute tolerance in inbred and selected lines of mice. *Drug and Alcohol Dependence*, *4*, 87–90.

Tabakoff, B., Ritzmann, R.F., Raju, R.S., & Deitrich, R.A. (1980). Characterization of acute and chronic tolerance in mice selected for inherent differences in sensitivity to ethanol. *Alcoholism: Clinical and Experimental Research*, *4*, 70–73.

Tatum, E.L. (1959). A case history in biological research. *Science*, *129*, 1711–1715.

Taylor, M. & Abrams, R. (1973). Manic states: A genetic study of early and late onset affective disorders. *Archives of Genetic Psychiatry*, *28*, 656–658.

Thiessen, D.D. (1972). *Gene organization and behavior*. New York: Random House.

Thompson, E.A. & Cannings, C. (1980). Sampling schemes and ascertainment. In C.F. Sing & M.H. Skolnick (Eds.), *The genetic analysis of common diseases*. New York: Alan R. Liss.

Thompson, W.R. (1953). The inheritance of behaviour: Behavioural differences in fifteen mouse strains. *Canadian Journal of Psychology*, *7*, 145–155.

Thompson, W.R. (1954). The inheritance and development of intelligence. *Proceedings of the Association for Research in Nervous and Mental Disorders*, *33*, 209–231.

Thompson, W.R. (1956). Traits, factors, and genes. *Eugenics Quarterly*, *4*, 8–16.

Thorndike, E.L. (1905). Measurements of twins. *Columbia University Contributions to Philosophy, Psychology and Education*, *13*, 1–64.

Thorndike, E.L. (1928). The resemblance of siblings in intelligence. *Yearbook of the National Society for the Study of Education*, *27*(I), 42–53.

Thorndike, E.L. (1944). The resemblance of siblings in intelligence-test scores. *Journal of Genetic Psychology*, *64*, 265–267.

Tolman, E.C. (1924). The inheritance of maze-learning ability in rats. *Journal of Comparative Psychology*, *4*, 1–18.

Tompkins, L. (1984). Genetic analysis of sex appeal in *Drosophila*. *Behavior Genetics*, *14*, 411–440.

Torgersen, S. (1984). Genetic and nosological aspects of schizotypal and borderline personality disorders: A twin study. *Archives of Genetic Psychiatry*, *41*, 546–554.

Tsung, M.T., Bucher, K.D., & Fleming, J.A. (1982). Testing the monogenic theory of schizophrenia: An application of segregation analysis to blind family study data. *British Journal of Psychiatry*, *140*, 595–599.

Tsuang, M.T., Bucher, K.D., & Fleming, J.A. (1983). A search for 'schizophrenia spectrum disorders.' An application of a multiple threshold model to blind family study data. *British Journal of Psychiatry*, *143*, 572–577.

Tsuang, M.T., Winokur, G., & Crowe, R.R. (1980). Morbidity risks of schizophrenia and affective disorders among first-degree relatives of patients with schizophrenia, mania, depression and surgical conditions. *British Journal of Psychiatry*, *137*, 497–504.

Tukey, J.W. (1951). Components in regression. *Biometrics*, *7*, 33–69.

Tully, T. (1984). *Drosophila* learning: Behavior and biochemistry. *Behavior Genetics*, *14*, 527–557.

Turner, W.D. (1979). Genetic markers for schizotaxia. *Biological Psychiatry*, *14*, 177–205.

Turner, W.J. & King, S. (1981). Two genetically distinct forms of bipolar affective disorder? *Biological Psychiatry*, *16*, 417–439.

Turner, W.J. & King, S. (1983). BPD2 an autosomal dominant form of bipolar affective disorder. *Biological Psychiatry*, *18*, 63–88.

Utsurikawa, N. (1917). Temperamental differences between outbred and inbred strains of the albino rat. *Journal of Animal Behavior*, *7*, 111–129.

Vale, J.R. (1980). *Genes, environment, and behavior*. New York: Harper & Row.

Vicari, E.M. (1921). Heredity of behavior in mice. *Yearbook of the Carnegie Institute of Washington*, 132–133.

Vogler, G.P. (1982). Multivariate behavioral genetic analysis of correlations vs. phenotypically standardized covariances. *Behavior Genetics*, *12*, 473–478.

Vogler, G.P. & Fulker, D.W. (1983). Familial resemblance for educational attainment. *Behavior Genetics*, *13*, 351–354.

Von Guaita, G. (1898). Versuche mit Kreuzungen von verschiedenen Rassen der Hausmaus. *Ber. Nat. Ges., Freiburg*, *10*, 317–332.

Wallace, B. (1981). *Basic population genetics*, New York: Columbia University Press.

Walton, P.D. (1970). The genetics of phototaxis in *Drosophila melanogaster*. *Canadian Journal of Genetic Cytology, 12*, 283–287.

Watson, J.D. & Crick, F.H.C. (1953). Genetic implications of the structure of deoxyribonucleic acid. *Nature, 171*, 964–967.

Watson, J.D., Tooze, J., & Kurtz, D.T. (1983). *Recombinant DNA: A short course*. New York: Freeman (Scientific American Books).

Wax, T.M. (1977). Effects of age, strain and illumination intensity on activity and self-selection of light-dark schedules in mice. *Journal of Comparative and Physiological Psychology, 91*, 51–62.

Weir, M.W. & DeFries, J.C. (1964). Prenatal maternal influence on behavior in mice: Evidence of a genetic basis. *Journal of Physiological Psychology, 58*, 412–417.

Weissman, M.M., Gershon, E.S., Kidd, K.K., Prusoff, B.A., Leckman, J.F., Dibble, E., Hamovit, J., Thompson, W.D., Pauls, D.L., & Guroff, J.J. (1984). Psychiatric disorders in the relatives of probands with affective disorders. The Yale University—National Institute of Mental Health collaborative study. *Archives of Genetic Psychiatry, 41*, 13–21.

Weissman, M.M., Kidd, K.K., & Pusoff, B.A. (1982). Variability in rates of affective disorders in relatives of depressed and normal probands. *Archives of Genetic Psychiatry, 39*, 1397–1403.

Weitkamp, L.R., Stancer, H.C., Persad, E., Flood, C., & Guttormsen, S. (1981). Depressive disorders and HLA. A gene on chromosome 6 that can affect behavior. *New England Journal of Medicine, 305*, 1301–1306.

Whitney, G.D. (1969). Vocalization of mice: A single genetic unit effect. *Journal of Heredity, 60*, 337–340.

Wilson, R. (1981). Synchronized developmental pathways for infant twins. In L. Gedda, P. Parisi, & W.E. Nance (Eds.), *Twin Research 3: Intelligence, personality, and development* (pp. 199–209). New York: Alan R. Liss.

Wilson, R.S. (1972). Twins: Early mental development. *Science, 175*, 914–917.

Wilson, R.S. (1983). The Louisville Twin Study: Developmental synchronies in behavior. *Child Development, 54*, 298–316.

Wimer, C., Wimer, R.E., & Wimer, J.S. (1983). An association between granule cell density in the dentate gyrus and two-way avoidance conditioning in the house mouse. *Behavior Neuroscience, 97*, 844–856.

Wimer, R.E. & Wimer, C.C. (1985). Animal behavior genetics: A search for the biological foundations of behavior. *Annual Review of Psychology, 36*, 171–218.

Wingfield, A.N. (1928). *Twins and orphans*. London: Dent.

Winokur, G., Clayton, P.J., & Reich, T. (1969). *Manic depressive illness*, St. Louis: Mosby.

Wood, W.G. (1976). Ethanol preference in C57BL/6 and BALB/c mice at three ages and eight ethanol concentrations. *Experimental Aging Research, 2*, 425–434.

Wright, S. (1921). Systems of mating. *Genetics, 6*, 111–178.

Wright, S. (1978). *Evolution and the genetics of populations: Vol. 4. Variability within and among natural populations*. Chicago: University of Chicago Press.

Yeakel, E.H. & Rhoades, R.P. (1941). A comparison of the body and endocrine gland (adrenal, thyroid and pituitary) weights of emotional and non-emotional rats. *Endocrinology, 28*, 337–340.

Yerkes, A.W. (1913). The heredity of savageness and wildness in rats. *Journal of Animal Behavior, 3*, 286–296.

Yerkes, A.W. (1916). Comparison of the behavior of stock and inbred albino rats. *Journal of Animal Behavior, 6*, 267–296.

Zajonc, R.B. & Markus, G.B. (1975). Birth order and intellectual development. *Psychological Review, 82*, 74–88.

Chapter 14

ETHOLOGY

Gerard P. Baerends, *University of Groningen*

INTRODUCTION

The Origin of the Discipline

Ethology is one way to approach the understanding of behavior. As a differentiated branch of the behavioral sciences it is little more than 50 years old. It first developed very much apart from the other branches. In the last decades, however, integration of the ethological approach has occurred increasingly in many fields of psychology, sociology, and cultural anthropology. Since this will be apparent in several other chapters of this handbook, my aim here is primarily to explain and clarify the ways ethologists pose problems—their angles of approach, methods of observing, experimenting, and thinking—rather than to strive for a comprehensive survey of what people identified as ethologists have found and concluded. For more extensive and detailed introductions to specific ethological studies, the reader is referred to compilations such as those by Alcock (1975), Brown (1975), Drickamer and Vessey (1982), Eibl-Eibesfeldt (1975), Huntingford (1984), Hinde (1970a), Manning (1979), Marler and Hamilton (1966), McFarland (1985) and Wilson (1975).

Because ethological research had its origins in zoology, its approach is characteristic of a branch of the biological sciences. By adopting the methods of science, ethologists wanted to distinguish their discipline methodologically from animal psychology, particularly as practised in Europe around the turn of the century, in which subjective feelings entered into the explanation for animal behavior, as is common in human psychology. Although the ethologists did not reject the possibility that subjective sensation might play a role in the causation of the behavior of animals (Griffin, 1976), they stressed the impossibility of knowing, identifying, or measuring such phenomena in animal subjects. Consequently they aimed at developing methods that would allow meaningful statements about causes of behavior in which speculations about feelings were not involved. In this respect the approaches of ethologists and behaviorists agree.

In another respect, however, they are very different. As biologists the ethologists are interested in the diversity of animal life and in its adaptiveness to environmental conditions. They are not only interested in the immediate causes of behavior and its development in the individual, but also in the functions of behavior patterns and the way they have developed in the course of evolution. Since it is generally accepted that evolution proceeds through natural selection of those alleles that are best adapted to the living conditions of a species, the studies of function and evolution are closely allied. The search for insight into how behavior may have evolved has led to an emphasis on comparing the behavior of related species, often with methods taken from comparative anatomy, which served as a model.

The early ethologists could be designated as naturalists. They loved to watch animals in the wild, or, under optimal conditions to hold and rear them in captivity. Their observations, mostly of birds or insects, inspired them to ask questions of the variety mentioned above, questions, which in turn stimulated a new generation of scientists.

In 1973 three ethologists from that generation collectively received the Nobel Prize for medicine and physiology. This recognition established the importance of the ethological approach which at that time had just begun to have an influence on human psychology and psychiatry. Each of these three scientists played a different role in founding ethology as a distinct discipline. Konrad Lorenz was interested in the phylogenetic approach and attempted to establish for ethology a theoretical framework of its own. This framework has proved to be of great stimulative and heuristic value. For this reason I shall use it as a guideline, even though several aspects of this complex of working hypotheses need to be revised and tested thoroughly. The second Nobel laureate, Niko Tinbergen, has led the way both in asking relevant questions that have arisen from theory and observation and in designing experiments to answer them by viewing animals under natural or seminatural conditions. Behind this experimental approach lies the work of the third member of this Nobel triumvirate, the physiologist Karl von Frisch who has taught us the art of how to make animals answer questions, and himself has led the way by his penetrating work into the behavior of the honeybee.

The Subjects Focused On

The naturalist background of most ethologists prompted them to focus their attention on the behavior that enables an animal to survive and reproduce in its natural environment. Usually a detailed systematic description of the observed behavior forms the basis for further research. Care is taken to describe behavior in an objective, noninterpretative way.

In a number of ethological studies, questions are asked concerning the mechanisms by which behavior is brought about. These questions deal with sensitivity to stimulation from the animal's surroundings, the rules by which this information is processed, and the principles underlying the control of motor patterns of different levels of complexity or integration. The questions also include the activities of chromatophores and of exocrine glands, which give off their products to the environment. The entire causal mechanism underlying the behavior of an animal must be in tune with its anatomy and physiology. Just as the anatomy of an individual can be said to be based on a blueprint that is typical of the species, so the corresponding behavioral mechanism must have a specific underlying organization that is based on genes. Mittelstaedt (1954) has coined the excellent German term *Wirkungsgefüge* for this concept, which I shall translate as *behavioral organization*. Thus, consistent differences in the structures of the organization of the behavior of different species are due to their genetic differences. The process by which the behavioral organization builds up in the individual animal in the course of its life —or the ways in which the information encoded in the genes comes to expression in interaction with the environment—is the subject of studies of the ontogeny of behavior.

The behavioral organization of an individual is a variant of the organization of the species to which that individual belongs. The species has developed in the course of evolution as a variant of the organization typical for a taxonomic group of a higher order (genus, family, etc.). The organizations of different genera of the same family are likely to have more in common than those of different families, and those of closely related families more than of families belonging to different orders, and so on. To answer questions on how behavioral organizations evolve requires on the one hand knowledge about the elements out of which the organization is composed and the procedures involved in building up its structure, and on the other hand knowledge about the various functions the behavioral organization and its parts must serve; and to assess the selective pressure that is exerted on the behavioral organization of a species through these functions, demands work of a combined ethological and ecological character.

Trend of the Chapter

In this chapter I shall attempt to construct on the basis of data from ethological studies a synthetic picture of how behavior is brought about. This presentation is also meant to show the ways of thinking in ethology. The choice of studies used here as examples is very much influenced by experience gained in my own work and in the work of close colleagues. Both the nature of this data base, and the influence of my own ideas in the attempt to build up a synthesis, will give this presentation a strongly personal touch. Since the purpose of the chapter is not so much to relate facts as to illustrate methods and to stimulate trains of thought, this approach seemed appropriate.

Although as a biologist I am well aware of species diversity, in this chapter I have often proceeded as though behavioral principles fundamental to one species also hold for others, even for species in very different taxonomic groups. Sometimes such an approach may be justified, as, for example, when the same principle has indeed been found in different groups; in other cases, however, evidence may be lacking. However, many principles in the organization of behavior appear to be phylogenetically old, like basic physiological mechanisms and such anatomical structures as the spinal cord.

In my survey of the ethological approach to understanding behavior I shall first consider work on the causal analysis of the structure of behavioral organizations; I shall then deal with studies of its ontogeny in the individual animal; and in the final section I shall discuss the problems of how functional demands might shape the behavioral organization through interactions of mutation and selection.

CAUSAL ETHOLOGICAL ANALYSIS

The Black-Box Approach

Most studies aimed at understanding the mechanisms through which behavior is brought about use physiological methods, and they generally employ operated animals or preparations rather than intact subjects. Hypotheses about the role of parts of the central nervous and endocrine systems are tested experimentally on a particular aspect of behavior. In this way a vast amount of knowledge has been gained on the potential capacities of elements of these physiological mechanisms. Nevertheless we are still far from having a satisfactory understanding of how these mechanisms manage to generate complex behavior as we observe it in an unrestrained animal in its natural surroundings.

To achieve that aim a second approach is needed, one that starts from complex behavior and this is complementary to the physiological one. Causal ethological analysis offers such an approach. It is based on detailed quantitative observations of normal behavior of the intact animal, preferably in a rich environment that can be experimentally manipulated. The animal is, in effect, considered as a black box; and by measuring under different circumstances the environmental input and comparing the result with the output, principles and rules can be derived about the procedures through which behavior is generated. As a result, the various tasks fulfilled by the underlying machinery can be described and defined. Then explicit questions on how the mechanisms proceed in accomplishing particular tasks can be formulated as a guide to the physiological research.

A detailed quantitative description of complex behavior requires the distinction of behavioral units. As such the modal action pattern is commonly used.

The Modal Action Pattern (MAP)

Distinct quantifiable units of behavior should preferably be chosen from integrated spatio-temporal patterns of muscle contractions and relaxations that are sequentially demarcated from other such units, as from a repetition of the same unit or from a behavioral pause. The units should be recurrent and sufficiently stereotyped so as to be easily recognizable on each occurrence. They should be distinguishable by descriptive features, thus without anticipation of what mechanism caused them.

In actually making a detailed description of the behavior of an animal, one tends intuitively to choose relatively small units corresponding to these demands. Such units usually subserve a limited discrete task, instrumental in fulfilling a need of the animal, mostly in interaction with the environment. Different elements of this type occur in almost the same form in all individuals of the same species, but they may also be detected, though somewhat modified, in related species. For this reason they are called *species specific*. In his early attempt to specify instinctive behavior, Lorenz (1935, 1937) chose this kind of activity as the core of his conception. He compared its stereotypy with that of anatomical features of an animal and argued that for taxonomic purposes such stereotyped behavior patterns could be used (Lorenz, 1941). He named them *instinctive activities*.

Since Lorenz felt that these elements were fundamental for the identity of a species, he looked for causal criteria that distinguished them from other categories, in particular from the apparently less species-specific reflexes. For this differentiation he advanced two arguments. First, he maintained that, although both instinctive activities and reflexes need a specific stimulus situation in order to be activated, only the instinctive activities would thereafter proceed without further input from peripheral stimulation. This would indicate that the motor pattern of an instinctive activity is mainly centrally controlled, in contast to the reflex, for which a continuous peripheral control is commonly assumed. This argument was based on a study by Lorenz and Tinbergen (1938) on the factors influencing the activity by which a goose moves an egg, placed outside the nest by the experimenter, back into its clutch. This is always done with the bill. The neck is stretched to bring the tip of the bill just behind the egg, and while bending the neck the bird shifts the egg toward and under its body. If, after the movement has started the experimenter takes the egg away, the bird nevertheless completes the full movement. The bird seems to notice the disappearance of the egg only when the next link in the chain, positioning the retrieved egg among the other eggs in the clutch, should be started. A single difference in performance distinguished the retrieval act with and without the egg when the egg was removed, the neck moved only in the medial plane of the bird; with the egg present, sideway movements were superimposed on the basic pattern to prevent the rolling egg from deviating too far from its path

on an uneven substrate. From this difference the authors concluded that two functionally different parts are present in the activity: a stereotyped core and a steering component. Lorenz generalized this finding to all instinctive activities, coining the term *Erbkoordination* for the normative stereotyped centrally generated part, and *Taxis* for the orientation component with its reflex character. *Erbkoordination* was first translated as *fixed action pattern* (FAP); but Barlow (1968) later glossed it as *modal action pattern* (MAP) to account for the variability between different performances by the same individual as well as between conspecifics.

Although it is questionable whether the distinction between the modal action pattern and the taxis can always be applied, it has been proved to hold in many cases. Consequently in triggering and in steering an activity, different external stimuli may be involved. For instance, Tinbergen and Kuenen (1939) found that in thrushes less than 10 days old a slight mechanical stimulation of the nest released the begging response, which was then gravitationally directed.

Although continuation of a fixed pattern after the releasing situation is removed has been found in other situations, it cannot be considered a general rule that modal action patterns do not need specific external stimulation in order to be maintained or continued. For instance, many fixed patterns will obviously need some control from feedback about their effect in order to fulfill their function. Prechtl and Schleidt (1950, 1951) found that the suckling act of mammalian babies is discontinued as soon as the milk flow stops. In an experimental study of incubation behavior in gulls, Baerends and Drent (1970) showed that, after incubation is set in motion or triggered by visual stimuli from the clutch, it is continued only as long as all three brood patches of the bird receive tactile stimuli from smooth rounded objects at 38° C.

Lorenz's second criterion was based on the fact that over longer periods the strength of the stimulus necessary to elicit an MAP was found to fluctuate. Sometimes the threshold for triggering an activity seemed to have been lowered so much that it existed in vacuo, that is, without any elements present of the adequate releasing situation so far as could be determined by the observer. In many cases, particularly cases involving sexual and feeding behavior, threshold lowering was observed more often after a long period in which the animal had been deprived of the appropriate external situation. This gave the impression that a specific internal factor controlling the triggering of an MAP accumulated with time. Lorenz drew the inference that each instinctive activity must be endogenously supplied by an internal impulse-generating factor, specific to that activity. He initially suggested that this factor was a substance that would be used up by performing the activity (*reizspezifische Erregungsstoff*). As will be shown in the next section, other and better interpretations can be offered for the phenomena advanced to support the existence of an impulse-generating factor specific to each MAP.

Lorenz's thinking about the differences between reflex and MAP was strongly influenced by von Holst's (1937) work on the physiological mechanisms underlying fish locomotion. Von Holst's evidence made the then-prevailing idea untenable that locomotion would only proceed by peripheral control, through chain reflexes. De-afferentiation experiments (in which the afferent nerves entering the spinal cord were severed) revealed both a central control of the patterning in locomotion, and a centrally induced rhythmicity for which the central nervous system (CNS) did not need a phasic input from the periphery. Nowadays it is generally agreed that locomotor activities are centrally patterned and generated but can, via reflexes, be peripherally adjusted and steered. This notion can be extended to the MAP.

The causal analysis of behavior requires a quantification of MAPs. Frequency per time unit is the most obvious parameter; other possibilities are duration, and latency between stimulus presentation and start. Since the performance of an MAP can reach different degrees of completeness, it may be important to take intensity into account. It is generally assumed (Barlow, 1968) that with increase of intensity the activity unfolds its components in a fixed order. An incipient MAP is in general easily identified.

The variation in details of the way in which conspecifics perform the same MAP may be genotypically as well as phenotypically caused. Lorenz (1935, 1965) has linked the MAP with the adjective *innate* because in many cases he had seen such activities correctly performed by animals reared in isolation who were thus deprived of the opportunity to learn the patterns by imitating conspecifics. With the adjective innate he wanted to express that the MAPs develop in all normal animals of the same species growing up under normal conditions, as the result of blueprint information carried by the genes. The term innate should not be taken to exclude all incorporation of experience and thus prejudice the design of research on the mechanisms of development (discussed below). However, the distinction between patterns specific for a species (or other taxon) and patterns characteristic for an individual only—such as acquired instrumental activities, operants, or habits—is fully justified. Nevertheless these learned activities may share with MAPs the characteristics of being stereotyped and elicited by a particular stimulus situation. Also their tendency to be performed may fluctuate and increase with time in the absence of the releasing stimulus. Usually, however, they will not be present in the same form in all members of the species, although through imitation they may be spread to members of the same population or group.

The following section analyzes the ways in which MAPs can be utilized by the animal within the framework of the behavioral organization. The question of how this organization deals with learned instrumental activities has had scant study, but may well be similar to what is here said of MAPs.

The Superimposed Control of Elementary Behavior Patterns

Modal action patterns can thus be considered as tools that enable an animal to interact in a functionally adaptive way with its environment. This section presents the methods used in ethological analysis to characterize the mechanisms and rules that control the use of these tools in an appropriate pattern of space and time.

At first Lorenz (1937) held the opinion that the occurrence of an instinctive activity would depend only on the presence of the appropriate external stimulus and on the strength of the particular endogenous factor for that MAP. He explicitly rejected theories, such as were advanced by McDougall (1923) who postulated that instrumental activities were controlled as a group by coordinating mechanisms of a higher level of integration corresponding to such major functions as feeding, sleeping, body care, or aggressive, sexual, parental, or escape behavior. Lorenz based his rejection on the absence of objective experimental evidence to support the concept of such superimposed mechanisms; he felt that those theories were no more than attempts to classify the behavioral elements by their functions. This argument is correct. In dealing with the causation of behavior we should build our picture of the behavioral mechanism on studies of causal relations only. The fact that these relations serve particular functions does not automatically imply that reliable deductions about their causal nature can be derived from the identification of those needs. Crucial for the acceptance of superimposed control mechanisms would be evidence that an internal factor, not immediately dependent on the presence of a specific external situation, was necessary for the occurrence of all members of a group of elementary activities. Experimental evidence of this type was first found and studied in two taxonomically widely separated animals: the digger wasp *Ammophila pubescens* (formerly called *A. campestris*) and the three-spined stickleback.

The females of the digger wasp care for their larvae alone and provide them with caterpillars (Baerends, 1941). In the course of the summer season a female successively digs a number of single nests in sand, each consisting of a 3-cm long shaft leading to a single chamber. The provisioning of each with caterpillars, which the wasp catches and paralyzes by stinging, takes place in three phases (Figure 14.1). In the first phase one caterpillar is stored and an egg is laid upon it; only if the egg hatches are more caterpillars provided. In the second phase when the larvae is still small one or two fresh caterpillars are added, and in the third phase another five to seven, after which the nest is closed. The wasp works at several nests (as far apart as 50 to 100 cm) during the same period. Between two phases in one nest, phases in one or two other nests may be executed. Each phase starts with a visit in which the wasp opens the shaft and enters the chamber without bringing food. It was proved experimentally that this initial visit serves for inspecting the nest's content. The size of the larva and the food reserve at that time determines the amount of prey to be supplied during the entire phase. Only the inspection visit had this effect; changes made in the chamber shortly before a provisioning visit did not

affect the amount of prey provided by the wasp until a new inspection visit occurred. Thus, during inspection a program is activated in the wasp that comprises activities related to brood care—hunting, catching, transporting, opening and closing the nest—to an amount that depends on the strength of the stimulus received during the inspection visit. Figure 14.1 shows how the wasp controlled the provisioning of different nests during the same period through a program that induced the wasp, after the termination of a phase in one nest, to pay an inspection visit to the oldest not-yet-completed (i.e., definitely closed) nest. Only when none of the existing nests can stimulate such a phase does the wasp start digging a new nest, the beginning of a new phase one. Although the provisioning program may be interrupted by feeding, and even by spending nights or periods of bad weather outside the

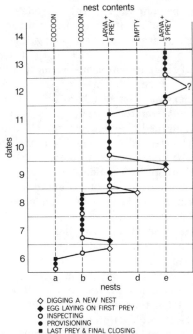

Figure 14.1. Record of the provisioning behavior of an individual digger wasp (*Ammophila pubescens*) in different nests (a to e) on consecutive days in August 1940. The heavy line connects the visits the wasp made in succession; on August 12 the wasp visited an unmarked nest (?) outside the area kept under constant observation. When the nests were dug out on August 14, nest d proved to be unfinished; it had probably been started too late on August 8 to be remembered on the next day.

nest, it is kept going as long as determined at the last inspection visit.

Within the motivational state controlling an entire phase, various lower levels of control can be demonstrated on the basis of differences in responsiveness to the same external stimulus. For instance, when the experimenter placed a caterpillar over the open nest entrance while the wasp was working on it, several different responses could follow: she either took the prey up and carried it away like a load of sand, or she used it as a plug to close the entrance, or she caught it, stung it, and drew it into the nest. Which activity occurred depended on how the wasp was occupied at the moment of the experiment; that is, whether she was still removing sand from the shaft, or had begun to fill it up again, or had started hunting for a new prey.

The other example not only suggests that the principle of specific behavioral states may have found a widespread application, but also provides possibilities for a more penetrating analysis of the phenomenon. It deals with work of Tinbergen's school on the behaviour of sticklebacks. Niko Tinbergen's choice of the three-spined stickleback as an experimental animal in ethology turned out to have been fortunate. This fish is highly suitable for behavioral experiments, and several fundamental ethological phenomena have been detected through it.

In order to show reproductive behavior of any kind, a stickleback, after reaching maturity, must be exposed to an increase in day length (Baggerman, 1972). It then starts its migration to shallow fresh water where a territory is established and defended against competing males, provided green plants are present. While maintaining its territorial status the male passes successively through three phases (Figure 14.2). The first consists mainly of nest-building behavior; the male digs a shallow pit and builds a tunnel of algae in it. Its responsiveness to ripe females is still relatively low. In the second phase, when the nest is ready, ripe females entering the territory are courted, guided to the nest, and induced to spawn. After spawning they are chased away. Usually up to five females spawn in the nest. In the third phase, the male cares for the offspring, spending most of the time ventilating the nest and protecting it against predation. In each phase the male has a different set of MAPs at his disposal. Some MAPs are restricted to one phase, others may occur in different phases. External and internal stimuli in combination were found to induce these phases.

Van Iersel (1953) studied the causation of the parental phase. Aerating the developing eggs is effected through fanning, an MAP quantified as the number of seconds of fanning per half-hour. When regularly measured during the first 10 days of the parental cycle (after which the young leave the nest), fanning was found to increase until day six or seven, and to drop steeply thereafter, about one day before the eggs were to hatch (Figure 14.3). It was shown experimentally that the amount of carbon dioxide produced by the developing embryos influences

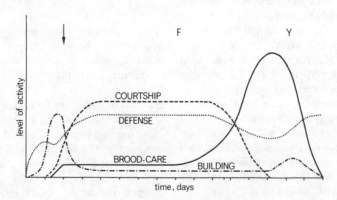

Figure 14.2. Schematic diagram of the level of activation of different behavior systems during a breeding cycle of the male three-spined stickleback. Agonistic activity (dots), nestbuilding (dot-dash), courting (dashes), parental care (solid). The arrow indicates the first occurrence of creeping through, which marks the end of the nest-building phase. F indicates fertilization (transition of sexual into parental phase), and Y indicates the hatching of young (after Sevenster, 1961).

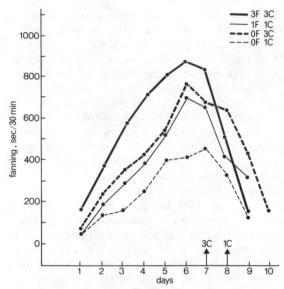

Figure 14.3. The average state of the parental system on successive days of the parental cycle of male sticklebacks (measured as the number of seconds spent fanning during 30-min daily test periods) is dependent on the number of times a male has fertilized (F) and the number of clutches (C) it has in its nest. Day 1 is the day after fertilization, and the arrows mark the average hatching day of the young (after Van Iersel, 1953).

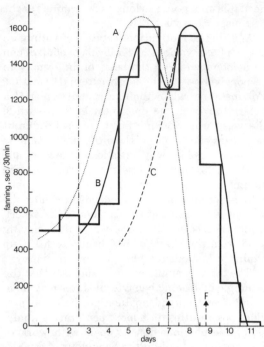

Figure 14.4. Frequency of fanning (real data indicated by histogram; smoothed in curve B) of a male three-spined stickleback whose original clutch was replaced by a fresh one on the second day of the parental cycle. To demonstrate the causes for bimodality, the expected frequency curves have been drawn for the original clutch, had it not been removed (curve A), and for the foster clutch, had the male not been influenced by the clutch originally present in the nest (curve C). Arrow P indicates the hatching day of the original clutch, and arrow F the hatching day of the foster clutch (after van Iersel, 1953).

the frequency at which fanning occurs. The drop in the fanning curve before the eggs hatched —when great quantities of carbon dioxide are still being produced in the nest—indicates an additional internal influence. Van Iersel demonstrated this factor experimentally by exchanging, in the beginning of the parental cycle, the original nest content for newly laid eggs. The effects of this manipulation, when carried out at the end of day two, are shown in Figure 14.4. Immediately after the exchange the fanning curve dropped, but not down to the level at which it had started. At day seven the level reached a peak, as would have been expected had the original clutch been left in the nest. The decline, however, was small and lasted only for one day, to be followed by a second rise, this time corresponding with the age of the exchange clutch. One day before this clutch hatched the steep ultimate drop of the curve set in.

The failure of the curve to fall back to zero level on day three and the incipient drop that appeared on day eight must be explained by the influence of an internal factor resulting from the contact with the original batch of eggs. In

the exchange experiment this factor was brought in competition with the effect of the external stimulation. Van Iersel found that more days of contact with the original clutch lent it a more powerful influence after exchange, the first drop becoming less, and the second one, more pronounced. From these experiments the conclusion was drawn that during contact with the eggs in the beginning of the fanning period an internal factor is generated that persists for at least eight days. Besides influencing the frequency of fanning, this factor also appeared to affect the occurrence of other activities directed to the nest and the young.

Figure 14.3 shows that the level reached by the fanning curve is influenced by the number of eggs (or number of clutches from different females) in the nest. This is to be expected in view of the effect of the carbon dioxide produced. In addition, when Van Iersel manipulated the number of times a male could fertilize, he found the steepness of the fanning curve and the maximum height attained to depend on the number of fertilizations. Thus fertilization has a positive aftereffect on the generation of the internal factor controlling the frequency of fanning, and probably also of other parental activities.

The experimental demonstration that internal factors as a group exert control on the occurrence of a number of activities led Tinbergen (1950) to postulate that the mechanisms underlying the causation of behavior are hierarchically organized. This meant a revival of the above-mentioned classification of instincts, but now based on the results of causal ethological analysis. Instead of continuing to use the terms *instinct* and *centre* in this sense, as Tinbergen did, I prefer to call a set of behavioral motor elements sharing the same causal factor a *behavioral control system* or *motivational system*. In addition to controlling the threshold for the activation of these elements by external factors, such a system is thought to be selectively responsive to particular external stimuli. A number of systems controlling MAPs (and possibly other elementary activities) may in turn be controlled in a superimposed system of a higher order of integration. The skeleton of the behavioral organization is usually formed of more than one such pyramid (Figure 14.5). Different systems or subsystems usually subserve different biological functions in the life of the animal.

This hierarchy hypothesis is further tested below. As a first step we shall look at the organization of a single system of low order.

Appetitive Behavior and Consummatory Act

When a herring gull settles on its nest to incubate its clutch of three eggs, it first performs several actions by which it manages to place each egg in a brood patch and surround it with feathers (Baerends and Drent, 1970). The performance of these MAPs is continued until the appropriate contact with the eggs is reached. The MAPs tend to ocur in a particular sequence because some of them prepare the eliciting external stimulus situation for others, but their

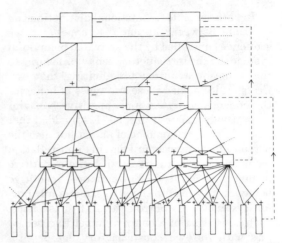

Figure 14.5. Hypothetical schematic representation of the hierarchical organization (functional network) of behavior. The rectangles on the bottom row represent modal action patterns (MAPs); the squares represent systems of different orders coordinating other systems or MAPs through activation (+) or inhibition (−). Systems of the same order have mutually inhibiting relations. The dashed lines represent two of the many feedback connections that are thought to be present in the network. The diagram can be extended to both sides (after Baerends, 1971).

order of occurrence is not strictly fixed internally. They can all be shown, however, to be subordinate to a common incubation system.

A male three-spined stickleback, when he observes a female entering his territory, approaches her with the zigzag dance. A ripe female responds by presenting her swollen abdomen; the zigzagging of the male then passes into motion toward the nest. When the female follows, the male takes up a position in front of the nest and, lying on his side with his nose just above the nest entrance, shows it to her. If she stays behind, assuming the courting posture without following, the male repeats his zigzagging and leading alternately. After she has been induced to approach the nest, she enters the tunnel and, provided the male performs trembling against her tail while she is inside, releases her batch of eggs. The male concludes the ceremony by creeping through the nest in turn and fertilizing. The spent female is chased away. Although each component of this courtship is elicited by another external situation, none of these activities is performed until the motivational state of the sexual system is sufficiently activated in the male.

In both examples a functional distinction can be made between the act that concludes the sequence controlled by the activated behavioral system and the introductory behavior leading to the situation required for eliciting that act. Craig (1918) named these two types of behavior the consummatory act and appetitive behavior respectively. Later Holzapfel (1940) added that not only the performance of an act but also the perception of a specific stimulus constellation (consummatory situation) can bring appetitive behavior to an end. Furthermore appetitive behavior may lead to the activation of a behavior system that controls several subsystems, each consisting of a chain of appetitive behaviors with its own consummatory act or situation.

Lorenz (1935, 1937, 1978) used the occurrence of appetitive behavior as an argument in support of his opinion that each *Erbkoordination* (MAP) would possess its own endogenous impulse-generating factor. In his view, this factor would continue to stimulate the appetitive behavior preceding that act until the act was elicited or the consummatory situation was perceived. Whereas Lorenz's consummatory act would always be an *Erbkoordination*, appetitive behavior could contain any kind of activity, varying from reflexes and MAPs to behavior controlled by learning and insight.

The recognition of group control of several acts by common internal factors within the framework of behavioral systems raised questions about the Lorenzian postulate that each separate act had its own specific endogenous factor. Instead it seemed more parsimonious to postulate that the consummatory act and the appetitive behavior preceding it are both controlled by the internal factors specific to the directly superimposed system, but that the effect of performance on the activation state of the system differs between appetitive and consummatory acts (Hinde, 1953). The observation, for example, that satiated carnivores no longer willing to eat can still be seen to perform activities of tracking, catching, or killing a prey—which led to Lorenz's concept of action-specific endogenous stimulus production—can also be interpreted by assuming that the different acts are controlled by quantitatively different levels of the same internal factor. The problem raised here can only be solved by clear experimental evidence on the effects of performance of the various activities of a system on its internal control.

The Effect of Feedback from Behavior on the Motivational State Underlying it

The foregoing considerations raise two questions: (1) What effect does the performance of a particular act have on the indicidence of the same act and other acts reckoned to belong to the same motivational system in a subsequent time span? (2) Does the probability that an activity will recur change as a function of the time passed since its last performance, and if so in which direction and to what extent?

For question (1) experiments on sexual behavior in the three-spined stickleback are again relevant. Van Iersel (1953) has compared the level of the sexual system in the male before and after fertilization, and before and after different lengths of time in which the male could only court. At daily intervals and under standard conditions he presented a female confined in a glass tube to a nest-owning male. The amount of time spent zigzagging was taken to be a representative measure of the level of the sexual system. A courtship of 15–50 minutes caused a slight rise in the level of zigzagging over a couple of days; one fertilization did not significantly affect the level. Three fertilizations, taking about 15 minutes, caused a drop of 40 percent in zigzagging, and 120 minutes of courtship, a drop of 50 percent. Fertilization and zigzagging recovered at the same rate (one to two days). It appears, therefore, that in this instance both the appetive behavior and the consummatory act reduced the internal stimulation underlying zigzagging, but to a different extent per time spent on these activities. When five fertilizations were allowed, the decrement in zigzagging was 10 to 20 percent higher than with three, but, more important, the rate of recovery was much slower, taking more than a week. This indicates that with the act of fertilization more than one decremental process is involved. After several fertilizations, each followed by experimental removal of the clutch, the male broke off the cycle but in the course of time began it all over again. This suggests that fertilization, besides influencing the sexual system, also influences a higher-order system superimposed on it.

The problem of how the performance of

fertilization and courtship exerts the reducing effect on the superimposed system was studied by Sevenster-Bol (1962). Using the same experimental setup, she prevented the courting male from finally creeping through by mounting a wire ring in front of the tunnel. So long as the male could smell eggs while lingering with his nose in the nest entrance and performing the quivering display, the level of zigzagging dropped to the same level as when sperm had been released. Thus the feedback stimulation resulting from the performance of courtship was shown to reduce the level of the motivational state that had generated it.

Similarly Hinde (1965) found that nest-building activity in canaries came gradually to a stop after repeated stimulation from a narrowing and better-lined nest cup. In the herring gull the consummatory situation conditional for the continuation of incubation consists in the bird's being seated on a completed nest with an egg at body temperature in each of the three brood patches. Deviation from this expected feedback leads to a resumption of appetitive behavior and, if the consummatory situation is not restored, to other behavioral phenomena to be discussed later (Baerends & Drent, 1970).

Studies of feeding behavior have also shown an incremental effect in the performance of certain acts. Wiepkema (1971) found an increase in the duration of successive feeding bouts when hungry mice were given palatable food, but a decrease with bitter food. He concluded that oral taste factors must act here as a positive feedback to keep the current behavior going. In contrast, alimentary loading factors (e.g., gastric distension, blood glucose) provide negative feedback, playing a role in establishing satiation

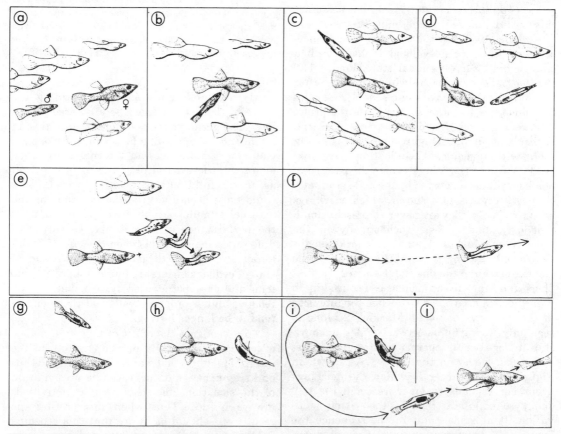

Figure 14.6. The courtship of the guppy, *Poecilia reticulata*. First phase: selecting (a, b) and following (c) a female; posturing (d); sigmoid display, increasing in intensity from left to right (e); display jump (f). Second phase: approach (g); halting (h); copulation attempt (i). The different marking patterns of the male are shown in succession (after Baerends et al., 1955).

(de Ruiter, 1963). A different effect of the performance of feeding behavior is the stimulation of other behavior, for example, drinking, which forestalls a consequence of eating, that is, thirst. This phenomenon has been called *feed-forward* by Fitzsimons and Le Magnen (1969).

Both decremental and incremental processes are likely to be important in determining the course of courtship sequences, which often comprise different displays performed in succession before mating takes place. Sometimes each link in such a chain must be elicited by a specific display of the mate; the exchange of displays may serve as a mechanism for partner selection. Sometimes merely the continued presence of a potential mate suffices for the performing animal to pass from one display to the next, suggesting that the motivational level suitable for mating is achieved by the effect of carrying out the successive displays. For the live bearing guppy (*Poecilia reticulata*), a fish that possesses this type of courtship, Baerends, Brouwer, and Waterbolk (1955) have shown that the advancement of sequence goes hand in hand with a change in the motivational state. Figure 14.6 surveys the behavior by which a male, after having selected a female in a school, first tries to induce her to follow him outside the group (Figure 14.6, a–f), and then stops her and attempts to copulate (Figure 6, g–i), transferring sperm with his penis, a modification of the anal fin. In the course of these events the pattern of black markings displayed by the male gradually changes. Figure 14.7 shows which markings occur in a male; they are never all present simultaneously, but appear stochastically in the order given. Marking 1, an overall darkening, is shown only during the initial selection of the female; marking 4 is characteristic for the first phase and 6 for the second phase of courtship. In both those phases 5 is added when the intensity of the activity increases. Marking 2 alone is seen only during fights between males; in courtship it may occur together with 4 in the first phase, but never in the second. As shown in Figure 14.7 the order in which the markings occur corresponds to an increase in the tendency to copulate, thus to the sexual motivation. If at some point in the sequence the female fails to respond in spite of repeated performance of the displays the markings of the male shift in the reverse order.

Summarizing this type of evidence, as currently available, question (1) concerning the effect of the act itself can be answered as follows. The performance of different activities, in a sequence of appetitive behavior and consummatory act, influences an internal state, common to all these activities. Decremental as well as incremental effects occur. Several cases could have been due to feedback from specific external stimulus situations brought about by the performance of an activity. Quantitative differences may exist between the effects of different situations on the level of the motivational state. Feedback effects are found not only on the immediately superimposed system, but on systems of higher order as well, and these effects tend to be longer lasting.

To investigate the effect of the performance of a particular activity on the strength of the internal factor(s) that may be involved (and thus on its tendency to occur) repeated presentation of the situation able to elicit that activity is always needed. Thus when interpreting the results one should be aware that this repeated presentation alone may cause a decrement in the frequency and intensity of the response. If so the decrement must be due to a change in the channel receiving information about the external

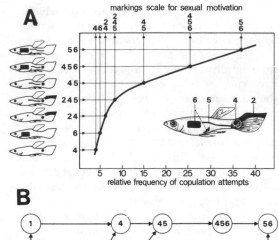

Figure 14.7 (A) Relation between patterns of black markings that can be displayed by the male guppy and the level of its sexual activity. Insert: Code numbers of markings; overall darkness is indicated by (1). (B) The order in which the various marking patterns tend to appear during courtship (after Baerends et al., 1955).

situation and transporting it to the mechanisms controlling the motor activity, a phenomenon usually classified as either *sensory adaptation* or *habituation* (Hinde, 1970b). For instance, the begging response (gaping) of songbird nestlings can be elicited by visual, acoustic, or tactile stimulation. Prechtl (1953) found that, if a dozen presentations of stimuli of one kind at intervals of about two seconds were not followed by presentation of food, the gaping response could no longer be elicited by the same stimulus. Another stimulus modality, however, immediately evoked the response at full strength. Consequently, this decrement was not due to reduction of the responsiveness of the motor mechanisms involved in gaping but should be sought in the affector mechanisms. Since after complete waning of the begging response to a particular stimulus the young birds still reacted to that stimulus with a fright response, Prechtl concluded that the reduced responsiveness should not be attributed to a decrease in the sensitivity of the receptor.

To give another example, in the waterbug *Notonecta glauca*, which locates its food by perceiving vibrations along the water surface, repeated stimulation from one direction led selectively to a decrement in the response rate to stimuli from that direction, in contrast to vibrations reaching it from other directions (Wolda, 1961). A study of mobbing in chaffinches (Hinde, 1960), a response which can be elicited by different kinds of potential predators of these birds, suggested the existence of two decremental processes, one more specific to the stimulus object and the other to the kind of response.

An attempt to answer question (2), on whether the passage of time would result in accumulation or depletion of the internal factor, was made by Rasa (1971) in a study of the appetite for territory defense in juveniles of the damsel fish *Microspatodon chrysurus*. These fish hold feeding territories on coral reefs, which they defend with attack and display. Rasa let single fish establish themselves in an aquarium divided by an opaque partition. On the side ocupied by the fish an opaque L-shaped tube, wide enough for a fish to enter, was mounted on the screen. This tube provided an entrance to a clear glass bottle, protruding into the other part of the aquarium. In that part a fish or a dummy could be introduced, which for the territory holder became visible only when it entered the bottle via the L-maze. Once the test fish had learned that potential opponents might be visible in the part of the aquarium at the other end of the maze and had threatened them with attacks (behind the glass wall) and displays, the frequency of his visits to the bottle increased. Rasa classified entering the tube as appetitive behavior. In this context the L-maze was learned, with the internal factor of the behavioral systems involved acting as a drive and the confrontation with the intruder as a reinforcement. Rasa speaks of appetence for aggression; one could, however, also see it as appetence for keeping the area clear of intruders, and could consider aggression as one of the implements for achieving this. The performance of threat display had an immediate incremental effect on this appetitive behavior: after the test fish was given an opportunity to threaten an opponent, it stayed in the bottle longer than if it had not displayed. On the other hand, a decremental effect was also found: after an aggressive encounter, more time elapsed between its leaving the bottle and returning to it than if no fight had occurred. Apparently the level of the motivational state dropped. In contrast, when the test fish was deprived for a longer time of the opportunity to interact with the intruder, the internal factor for territorial defense demonstrated accumulation. One day without an intruder doubled the time spent in the bottle after the intruder was put back; seven days of isolation increased it fourfold.

We may conclude that the evidence now available supports the early insights of Craig and Lorenz who considered the combination of a consummatory act and the appetitive behavior leading to it as a single compound unit on an intermediate level of integration in the behavioral organization. This unit is a control system in which the level of an internal (motivational) factor determines which activities belonging to the system can be elicited by specific external stimulus situations. Stimuli perceived as a result of the performance of particular activities may affect the level of the internal factor. Numerous variations are possible—between different systems in the same species and between similar systems in different species—in the way the different components are wired. Such variations are expressed in the characteristics of the different types of behavior sequences found (Hinde & Stevenson, 1969).

It follows from these considerations that the

specification of the complex of factors that determine the activation level of a system is a major problem in causal ethological analysis. A possible approach to finding answers is to build flow-diagram models of the type used in systems analysis and cybernetics, a technique now increasingly applied by ethologists (Hassenstein, 1971, 1980; McFarland, 1971, 1974a; McFarland and Houston, 1981). Such models should represent the various relations. Making such a model forces one to realize what arguments are available for mechanisms and relations that are assumed both to exist and to be excluded from the model. Examples of such models are given in Figures 14.11 and 14.16. After the models have resulted in the design of observations and experiments, and thus led to an accumulation of data, computer simulation is an attractive possibility for testing them.

The more highly the animal is differentiated, the greater the number of functions its behavioral organization has to fulfill, and the more behavioral control systems of the type discussed in this section can be expected to be present within this organization. The next section deals with attempts to detect and identify these systems.

The Identification of Behavioral Systems

The study of the organization of behavior requires identification of the various sytems involved, on the basis of causal arguments only. An obvious start for such a study is to seek temporal and sequential linkages of different elements into more-or-less separate groups. For this purpose the behavior of different individuals of a species is observed and recorded in detail on a time scale over relatively long periods, preferably under varied conditions approaching those in the natural environment. Since most behavioral sequences have a probabilistic rather than a deterministic character, various statistical techniques, mostly forms of multivariate analysis, have been used to interpret the resulting data and to permit the formulation of hypotheses on the causality involved (Colgan, 1978; Van Hooff, 1982). Such statistical methods aim at detecting positive and negative associations in the occurrence over time of different elementary activities. Although the exact value of these methods for our purpose is debatable in

each particular case, chiefly because the behavioral data can rarely be collected in accordance with the mathematical requirements inherent to the techniques, the methods have so far proved to be most effective in obtaining a quantitative description of the temporal relations between the many components of a species' behavior repertoire. One problem with these statistical methods is that the results—in particular those of reducing correlations between a large number of variables to a smaller number of common factors—may be interpreted prematurely in a causal sense. A common error is to consider such factors as internal causes, without checking whether they may be due simply to specific external stimulus situations. The statistical results should lead only to the formulation of hypotheses about causation, which then should be checked experimentally.

Wiepkema (1961) was the first ethologist to attempt the system analysis of complicated behavior. His subject was the fascinating reproductive behavior of the bitterling, *Rhodeus amarus*, a fish that deposits its eggs in freshwater mussels. In this species the male defends a territory around the mussel and courts ripe females, leading them to the mussel and inducing them to push their long (up to 2 cm) ovipositor tube into the exhalent siphon. In this way the eggs reach the gill cavity where they stay, well protected against predators, until the embryos have hatched and have used up most of the yolk. During each spawning act one to four eggs are laid, the female spawning at intervals of five to ten minutes. Males fertilize by spraying their sperm over the siphons of the mussel. In the interactions of the male with other males, the mussel, and females, Wiepkema distinguished 12 MAPs for incorporation into a factor analysis. Since about 90 per cent of the correlations were found to be explained by only three factors, it was possible to give a pictorial representation of the pattern of correlations among the 12 activities or vectors (Figure 14.8). This picture shows three clusters of vectors: the first consists of four fighting activities, the second of three acts involved in leading the female and ejaculation, and the third of fleeing and two cleaning activities. The feeding activity of snapping occupies a position at some distance from the third factor.

In order to check whether clustering in the factor analysis model of behavior of the male

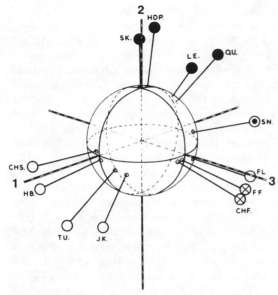

Figure 14.8. Vector model of the temporal relations between different behavioral elements of the male bitterling in encounters with other males and females near the mussel. The positive side of the factors are indicated by the numerals 1, 2, and 3. The vectors of the 12 variables are determined by their factor loadings (projections) on the three main axes. Axis 1 corresponds to aggressive factors, axis 2 to sexual factors, and axis 3 to nonreproductive factors. The vectors marked with filled circles, i.e., skimming (SK), head-down posture (HDP), leading (LE), and quivering (QU), represent courtship activities; those with open circles, i.e., chasing (CHS), head butting (HB), turn beating (TU), and jerking (JK), represent agonistic activities; the rest represent nonreproductive activities: the feeding activity of snapping (SN), the cleaning activities of fin flickering (FF) and chafing (CHF), and fleeing (FL) (after Wiepkema, 1961).

bitterling could be taken to reflect the effects of different motivational systems or should be attributed simply to direct influences of the external situation on each of the activities separately. Wiepkema carried out several experiments. He varied the size and distance of presentation of intruding males and females, as well as the accessibility to the mussel, measuring the frequency and orientation of the activities shown by the test fish. The results were consistent with the idea that the experimental manipulations influenced the various behavior patterns through the medium of three motivational control systems, one each for attack, escape, and sexual behavior, to which these patterns are subordinate.

With a combination of statistical and experimental methods, evidence for group control of different elementary activities by superimposed causal mechanisms has also been demonstrated in birds and mammals. Stokes (1962) and Blurton Jones (1968) have argued that mechanisms for attack, fleeing, and feeding underlie the form and sequencing of the social behavior of tits on a feeding table. In a study of the social behavior and display of the chimpanzee, Van Hooff (1973) distinguished five systems of elementary activities that control patterns involved in play and aggression and in affinitive, excitatory, and submissive behavior. The first two and last three appeared to be organized in turn into systems of a higher order.

Behavioral systems in this sense can be defined as integrating mechanisms, each controlling a particular set of behavior patterns, and sensitive to particular stimulus situations. Activation of a system implies that the elements belonging to the system can be elicited by their appropriate simulus situation for as long as this condition or motivational state lasts. Different systems should not be taken to be rigorously separated from each other. For one thing, the same element (or system of lower order) may belong to more than one superimposed system in the way schematically pictured in Figure 14.5. Thus the behavioral organization is made up of closely interwoven, hierarchically structured systems. Each system of higher order may stimulate or inhibit lower order ones, while systems of the same order are supposed to inhibit each other. At each level systems, subsystems, or patterns can be influenced by information from sensory organs, including feedback information about the effect of behavior performed at a particular moment (Baerends, 1976). It needs to be emphasized that the term system is meant in a software sense. No implications about the nature of the hardware involved are intended, and one should remain aware of the possibility that this hardware differs considerably between different systems in the same or different species. The concept of the hierarchical organization of behavior is a powerful explanatory concept in ethology (Dawkins, 1976a). As will be shown in the next section several conspicuous phenomena in normal and abnormal behavior can be interpreted as consequences of the hierarchical structure.

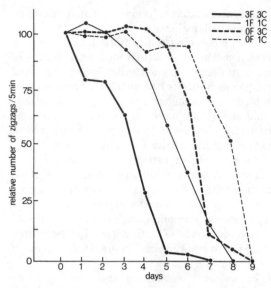

Figure 14.9. The average frequency of courting on successive days of the parental cycle of male stickle-backs, measured as number of zigzags per 5 min and expressed as a percentage of the value on the day of fertilization: F indicates the number of times the male has fertilized eggs, and C indicates the number of clutches in the nest. Day 1 is the day after fertilization (after van Iersel, 1953).

The Interaction of Behavioral Systems

Hierarchically organized behavior systems interact. Interaction between systems of the same order has been demonstrated by Van Iersel (1953) in the transition from the sexual into the parental phase in the three-spined stickleback. As Figure 14.4 demonstrated, the development of the parental phase is promoted by the number of clutches in the nest and the number of times the male has fertilized. Figure 14.9 shows a reciprocal effect of the same factors on zigzagging, a parameter for the state of the sexual system. Thus both the quantity of eggs in the nest and the number fertilizations achieved exert a long-term inhibiting effect on this system. The stronger these factors are, the earlier the decline of zigzagging sets in, and the steeper is it course.

The interaction between different systems is of great importance for the patterning of behavioral sequences. Ethologists first became aware of this when trying to find explanations for

the occasional ocurrence in sequences of goal-directed behavior of elements whose presence was difficult to understand from a functional point of view. For instance, it seems to serve no purpose when two birds in a boundary dispute interrupt their attacking, defending, and threatening behavior for an interval of feather trimming, or when, in a similar dispute between cocks, both pick up grains from the ground. Kortlandt (1940a) and Tinbergen (1940), each of whom reported this phenomenon independently, gave it the German name *Uebersprungbewegung*, which was first translated into English as *substitute* but later as *displacement* activity. Since in ethology both words have become tied to particular interpretations about causation, and because in psychiatry the terms are used in still a different sense, I prefer at this stage to use the more neutral term *interruptive* activity. With this term I want only to express that a functionally understandable chain of activities is interrupted briefly, and the achievement of the consummatory activity or situation is thus postponed.

A further example can be taken from Wiepkema's (1961) study on the bitterling. At intervals of five to ten minutes a female is willing to follow a male and lay one to four eggs in the mussel. About one minute after the egg laying, a drop occurs in the frequency of sexual activities in the male, such as quivering and ejecting sperm, although chasing and butting the female increases. As with the stickleback, the smell of the egg was found to be the direct cause of the motivational change. Figure 14.10 shows that, when the switch from the sexual to the aggressive system takes place, snapping begins to rise to a peak, followed slightly later by fin flickering and chafing. Functionally, snapping is a feeding activity, and chafing and fin flicking subserve body care. Thus all three activities belong to systems other than those for sex and aggression.

Originally Tinbergen and Kortlandt postulated that such apparently functionally irrelevant activities occurred because the primarily activated system had no opportunity to express itself. Tinbergen mentioned four possible causes: inhibition by another system, absence of the appropriate external situation, deficiency of the internal factor, or sudden attainment of the goal. Theoretically the first of these causes might also underlie the other three. Since Kortlandt

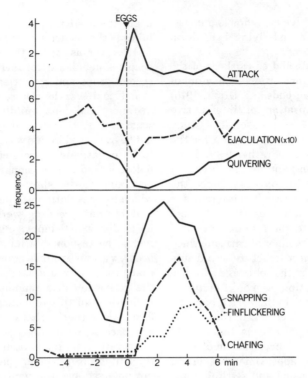

Figure 14.10. The frequencies of a male bitterling's behavior toward the female in the minutes before and after egg laying. Top: attack; middle: two sexual patterns (quivering and sperm ejection); bottom: interruptive activities (chafing, fin flickering, snapping).

assumed such indirectly produced activities to be supplied by the frustrated internal factor (surplus hypothesis), he suggested the term *allochthonous*, in contrast to *autochthonous* for activities supplied by their own system.

One of the most thorough studies of the causal factors underlying a displacement activity was also carried out on the three-spined stickleback. Sevenster (1961) investigated the causation of fanning (which is primarily functional in the parental phase for aerating the eggs) in the earlier nest building and sexual phases when the nest is still empty. Using methods similar to those of van Iersel, he measured the levels of the tendencies to attack intruders in the territory, to court females, and to perform parental behavior. These measurements revealed that the bouts of displacement fanning occurred at times when the tendencies to attack and to court were aroused simultaneously. Assuming that competition exists between different systems, Sevenster concluded that interaction between two systems suppresses their inhibiting force on other systems, thus providing the other systems with an

opportunity for manifestation. Under these circumstances of internal conflict the adequate external releasing situation of the disinhibited system (in this case the nest, with or without eggs) would facilitate its expression. This disinhibition hypothesis contrasts with the original surplus hypothesis. For displacement fanning Sevenster rejected the surplus hypothesis on the grounds that he could show that autochthonous internal and external factors were producing the fanning in the displacement situation also, whereas there was no indication that either the sexual or the aggressive system had a direct influence on the fanning. Other studies in which both the internal state and the external situation were manipulated—for example, Rowell (1961) for displacement grooming in chaffinches, and McFarland (1965) for displacement food pecking in the barbary dove —confirmed the role of disinhibition in facilitating the occurrence of such interruptive activities but also showed the importance of the external situation in determining composition and frequency. We must conclude therefore, that the occurrence of interruptive behavior is a consequence of the way the underlying behavioral organization is structured.

A study by Baerends and co-workers of the organization of the incubation behavior of the herring gull (in Baerends and Drent, 1970) revealed that the causation of interruptive behavior may differ between cases. The study was undertaken to find an explanation for the occurrence of short bouts of rather frantic and incomplete nest building and feather preening during a period of sitting on eggs. Since the temperature of the eggs drops when interruptive behaviors occur, these activities cannot be considered to contribute to the function of incubation. Neither did the manner of carrying them out contribute to the nest structure or aid substantially in trimming the plumage. In the course of the incubation season functional building occurred mainly in the period between the formation or reestablishment of the pair on the territory and the laying of eggs. Later, without experimental interference, the incubation act was interrupted only approximately every 20 minutes by the bird's rising and settling down again (resettling), often after changing its orientation and sometimes after shifting the eggs in the nest pit; some building occurred on such occasions but preening on the nest was rare.

In contrast, during the incubation period, resettling, building, and preening activities increased when the nest content was changed experimentally away from its optimal value of three natural gull eggs at 38°C in a well-shaped nest pit. Of these activities resettling is the appetitive behavior pattern leading to the situation that releases the consummatory act of incubating (eggs neatly placed in the brood patches); it can therefore be seen as functional in restoring the consummatory situation. The main question was why building sometimes and preening at other times accompanied the interruptive activity of resettling. Correlations of the occurrence of these activities revealed a close association between building, settling, and shifting or retrieving eggs. For this reason these activities were taken to belong to the same system, called the incubation system. Further evidence led to the conclusion that building corresponds to an activation level of this system that is lower than incubation. Feedback from the complete consummatory situation for incubation keeps the system at the highest level and also inhibits the occurrence of lower level activities.

However, as soon as the feedback stimulation becomes deficient, the level of the incubation system drops and activities appear that correspond to lower levels: resettling in the first instance, and nest building activities in the second. Only the occurrence of preening could not be explained in this way. Its incidence tended to be negatively associated with that of nest building, and this incompatibility became more pronounced, the shorter the time span over which the correlation was determined. Obviously building and preening were commonly caused by feedback deficiency, but additional factors had to be responsible for one or the other to occur. Various grounds permitted the conclusion that preening was associated in the bird with the activation of a tendency to escape. Since indications of this tendency also became more frequent as the feedback stimulation from the nest became increasingly deficient (lowering the temperature, taking two instead of one egg from the clutch), it was clear that deficient feedback not only reduced the tendency to incubate but also activated the tendency to escape. These two tendencies are obviously incompatible at high intensity; a conflict must therefore be expected, and during this conflict the bursts of preening appear. Since the preening activities can be considered to belong to a separate system, their occurrence in a bird sitting on a deficient clutch is likely to be caused by disinhibition, in conformity with Sevenster's explanation of displacement fanning in the stickleback. Figure 14.11 illustrates the proceedings described in the form of a pathway diagram.

The appearance of an activity that seems to fit into the context of the ongoing behavior is not the only means for a conflict between systems to express itself in overt behavior. Another is the combination of elements of several systems, and this can be effected in different ways. First, activities of the opposing systems can be carried out briefly in alternation. This alternation, called *successive ambivalence*, is evident when, for instance, animals in agonistic situations alternatively move toward and away from each other over small distances. Another possibility is the simultaneously ambivalent combination of incomplete elements of different systems in a *compromise activity* (Andrew, 1956). This compromise may concern only the

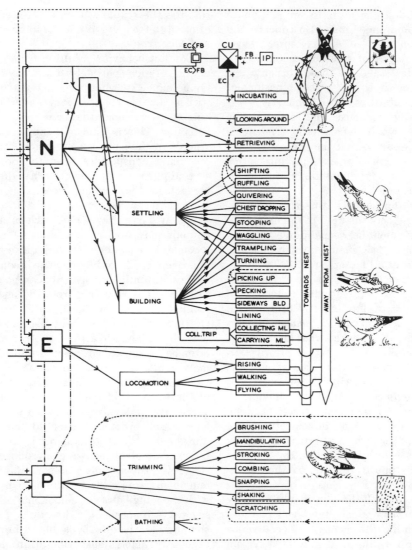

Figure 14.11. Model for the occurrence of interruptive behavior during incubation in herring gulls (after Baerends & Drent, 1970). The modal action patterns are in the right-hand column, and superimposed control systems of first and second order are represented to the left (N = incubation system, E = escape system, P = preening system). The large vertical arrows represent orientation components toward and away from the nest. Incubation is the consummatory act; feedback stimulation from the clutch, after being processed in IP, flows to a unit (CU) where it is compared with expectancy, an efference copy or corollary (EC) to the input for incubation. This input is fed through a unit (I) necessary to explain the inhibition of settling and building when feedback matches expectancy. The effect of feedback discrepancy on N (and I), E, and P can be read from the arrows. The main systems mutually suppress one another; P is thought to occur as interruptive behavior through disinhibition of N and E; P can be activated directly by external stimuli like dust, rain or parasites; E can also be stimulated by disturbances other than deficient feedback from the clutch.

orientation components of the MAPs involved. In that case an element belonging to the more strongly activated system is performed but is oriented inadequately relative to the opponent or the object releasing it. It is then given a direction that can be seen as a result of the orientations typical for the conflicting system. Such re-directed activities can often be seen in agonistic situations when the attack against the actual opponent is inhibited but redirected to another individual or even to an inanimate object. The compromise may also concern the normative components of MAPs of different systems. In such cases of simultaneous ambivalence, the initial stages of these elements are fused. As will be shown below, combinations of the various possibilities occur frequently.

It is usually assumed that ambivalence occurs mainly when both conflicting tendencies are relatively weak so that they do not inhibit one another completely. At high intensities displacement through disinhibition would be expected to prevail.

The interaction between differential behavioral systems reflects the need of the animal to decide at any moment between different courses of action stimulated simultaneously by the external and internal factors present. The number of muscular activities possible at the same time is limited; all motivational systems converge upon what McFarland and Sibly (1975) have called the *behavioral final common path*. So the question should be asked what mechanisms exist to determine which has priority in this path at a given moment and thus gains overt expression in the behavior sequence. The frequent occurrence of conflict behavior in sequences suggests that competition between systems is a major element. In competition the manifestation of a system at a particular moment depends on its level of activation (by internal and external stimuli) relative to the simultaneous levels of other systems. In contrast, if a system manifests itself through disinhibition by one or more other systems, the levels of those systems determine the moment of occurrence and its duration, while the disinhibited system expresses its level only in the intensity of the activity through which it becomes overt. McFarland (1974b) coined the name *time-sharing* for a form of disinhibition in which an alternating behavior sequence is caused by a dominating system that permits the temporary expression of a subdominant system. For instance, in male rats the sexual system takes precedence over feeding. Sexual behavior was found to be interrupted by feeding bouts only when the sexual tendency was low, mostly after ejaculation. Although food deprivation increased the number of feeding bouts, the time spent eating, and the food consumed, it did not alter the frequency of sexual behavior; it only increased the latency of the sexual activities. Thus in hungry rats too the sexual system controlled the time allotted to feeding but not the intensity (Brown and McFarland, 1979).

Conflict behavior resulting from mild interactions of incompatible systems may in particular be expected when an animal is confronted with an ambiguous situation, that is, a situation able to carry more than one system to overt behavior. This is likely to happen when individuals of the same species meet, since on the one hand conspecifics need to cooperate for several purposes, and on the other they have to compete for the same resources. An approaching conspecific may be a rival or a potential partner, or merely a passer-by. Under such circumstances animals may perform incomplete forms of the locomotor elements of moving off or fleeing, of approach, or of staying put. The incompleteness of these intention movements can be attributed to inhibitions resulting from the motivational conflict. Tinbergen (1940, 1952) and Daanje (1950) have pointed out that displays that serve both to repel and to attract another animal can often be recognized as combinations of incipient movements belonging to antagonistic motivational systems. For instance, the zigzag dance of the male stickleback can be interpreted as successive ambivalence between attacking the female and swimming back to the nest. The upright display of gulls can be seen as simultaneous ambivalence, a compromise between stretching the neck as a preparation for fleeing and downward pecking of the bill while beating with the wing bows as components of attack. In several gull species the direction of the bill is emphasized visually by a black hood. Simultaneously ambivalent orientation, leading to redirected attacks on grass tufts, has an important signal value in boundary disputes between herring gulls. Many displays shown in such agonistic disputes by fish, birds, and mammals can be recognized as—mostly incomplete—feeding, cleaning, nest building, and even sleeping acts. Since they are apparently out of context under such circumstances, their occurrence is likely to be due to the displacement phenomenon. The conflict hypothesis developed by Tinbergen and his associates (Tinbergen, 1952; Morris, 1956a; for a review see Baerends, 1975) postulates that in the evolutionary development of nonverbal communication, interruptive activities resulting from motivational conflicts have obviously been selected.

To test the conflict hypothesis, attempts have been made to measure the levels of the systems assumed to be involved in displays by quantifying overt behavior, in particular the occurrence of approach and withdrawal or attack and flight, in temporal association with displays. An example taken from a study by Kruijt (1964) concerns the causation of a threat activity in fowl. Fighting cocks often interrupt their movements of attack and retreat with the activities listed in Figure 14.12. The most conspicuous of these movements is a downward-directed zigzagging of the head, supported by erection of the conspicuous yellow-colored ruff. Film analysis revealed that the head zigzagging consists of a combination of pecking at the ground (as in attacking a prey) and head shaking (a comfort activity), movements that both occur as interruptive behavior during the conflict. The fact that ground pecking occurs mainly in the winners of the fight, and head shaking and other forms of preening in the losers, argues for their dependence on a particular range of attack and flight. This suggests the interpretation of ground pecking as redirected attack and of head shaking as a result of disinhibition of the preening system through the strong interference of a system that controls fleeing by one for attack.

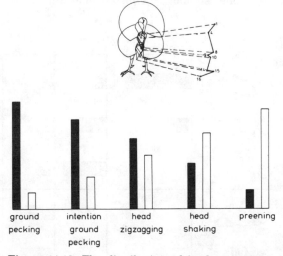

Figure 14.12. The distribution of irrelevant movements of different types among winners (black) and losers (white) in a cock fight. A reconstruction of the course of the bill tip from ciné film (24 frames per second, frame-numbers indicated) demonstrates the ambivalent character of head zigzagging: ground pecking and head shaking are being combined (after Kruijt, 1964).

Head zigzagging, as a combination of the two, appears to correspond to matching strengths of the opposing systems. Kruijt obtained evidence for his interpretation of ground pecking as redirected attack by inducing cocks to fight a colored stick after grains dyed in different colors had been spread on the ground. During their interruptions for ground pecking the cocks showed a preference for grains the color of the stick fought.

As with the head zigzagging of fowl, the evolution of an interruptive behavior pattern into a signal is in many cases combined with changes in anatomical structures supporting its effect. The behavioral form also tends to become more formalized and conspicuous. Morris (1957) has pointed out that this effect often appears to have been reached by a reduction in the variation originally shown by the response at different intensities. Furthermore, when there is ambivalence, certain compromise forms are often selected for communication, while transitory forms occur more rarely. In many other cases, however, a graded scale of compromise forms, covering a wide range of attack-flight ratios, seems to serve communication, for example, facial expression and body postures in mammals (Leyhausen, 1967). All changes in appearance by which an activity increases the adaptation to its signal value are called *ritualization*.

The conflict hypothesis was originally meant to provide an explanation for the development and shaping of communicative activities in phylogeny. Tinbergen has suggested that, with the ritualization of their form, the causation of communicative elements is emancipated from the incompatible tendencies originally underlying them and is assimilated into the systems in which they function as signals, such as the sexual or parental system. Different transitional phases toward complete emancipation can be hypothesized. If emancipation of a communicative activity were complete one would expect that correlations with the original underlying tendencies would no longer exist. The existence of relations between the incidence of a particular signal and the frequency of overt attack and flight following it could indicate that complete emanicipation of signals has not commonly occurred. In my opinion it has never been proved conclusively, though the occurrence of transitory stages is indicated. For instance, although the two components of the zigzag dance of the male stickleback have been shown by Tinbergen (1951) to be controlled by the antagonistic tendencies to attack an intruder (zig) and to withdraw toward the nest (zag), these tendencies are not free to vary the dance in every possible way; within a certain range of variability the zigzag form is stereotyped. Correspondingly, Van Iersel (1953) and Sevenster (1961) found the frequency of zigzagging, thus of the composite act, to be a suitable measure of the level of the sexual system. This agrees with the hypothesis of Kruijt (1964) who, on the basis of his study of the ontogeny of social behavior in jungle fowl, has suggested that the activated sexual state exerts a stabilizing influence on agonistic tendencies. Kruijt found that, when copulatory behavior started to occur in socially reared cockerels at the age of 120 days, overt attack and escape became moderated, whereas displays thought to be phylogenetically derived from conflicts between these tendencies became increasingly common.

The occurrence of the same display act in an almost identical form in agonistic as well as sexual or parental functional contexts was originally explained with the surplus hypothesis for displacement (sparking over, according to Tinbergen, 1940; Kortlandt, 1940a). The stabilizing hypothesis opens up the possibility of a more parsimonious interpretation of signal activities serving communication with a partner, as well as those used in interactions between parents and young. They can now be seen as directly produced by the attack and escape tendencies, but under a superimposed control of the systems regulating courtship or information exchange between parent and young. It is then assumed that, during the occurrence of a particular display in a sexual or parental context, this superimposed system would bring about the same quantitative balance between the tendencies to attack and escape, as would the systems controlling that display in a purely agonistic context. This conception implies that each display derived from a conflict would correspond to a motivational state to which at least two systems contribute to a quantitatively characteristic extent. It should be envisaged that the type of display produced could depend on the ratio or the absolute values of the levels of the conflicting motivational states, as well as on the two in combination.

Progress in verifying these hypotheses is

slow because of the methodological difficulties involved in measuring motivation (see Baerends, 1975). Against methods based on correlating particular displays with the type and frequency of the behavior preceding or following it objections can be raised that are not easy to overcome. The use of indicators that are simultaneous with the display to be assessed would be preferable. In this sense the variable color patterns of many fish species have proved useful. Different motivational systems may each control their own type of chromatophores, and simultaneous activation of two systems will then lead to a mixed pattern in which each element can be separately assessed. As an example, Figure 14.13 shows five patterns of black markings that can be exhibited by territorial males of *Cichlasoma meeki* and gives the relative frequencies at which the various patterns were observed during patrolling the territory and courting females, during fights with an intruder, and during flight after being beaten. In the escape state vertical bars and an overall darkening dominate, whereas in the sexual state it is the lateral row of patches. Mixtures of these patterns coincide with ambivalent agonistic behavior.

To test the conflict hypothesis experimentally, one should administer simultaneously

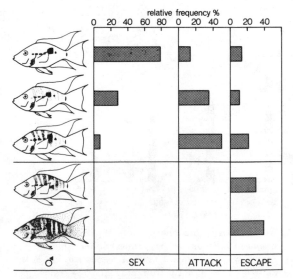

Figure 14.13. The relation between different marking patterns and three types of social behavior in *Cichlasoma meeki* (data from F.J. Engelsma, unpublished).

attack- and escape-evoking stimuli that can be varied independently. Blurton Jones (1960) achieved this by approaching captive Canada geese in either familiar or unfamilar clothing and with or without a stick. Unfamilar clothing induced attack, a stick induced fleeing; a combination of the two elicited threat postures, whose type seemed to be determined by the strength of the attack- and escape-evoking stimuli used.

Probably the most elaborate attempt made so far to test the conflict hypothesis experimentally is Vodegel's (1978) study of the motivation of the displays shown by the cichlid fish *Pseudotropheus zebra* in response to an intruder into its territory. By presenting intruder dummies of different sizes she manipulated the occurrence of behavior associated with the dummy, such as approaching and leaving and a number of displays, as well as of behavior carried out away from the dummy during presentation and control periods. Several parameters of these activities were measured. Attempts to interpret the data on the basis of a single motivational system failed. On the assumption of interaction between two systems, one for attack and one for escape, however, it was possible to develop a mathematical model to cover all qualitative and quantitative phenomena found, and to make simulation of the behavior of a hypothetical individual under the experimental conditions possible. The displays were each found to correspond to different ranges of the quotient of the level of attack divided by the level of escape (relative aggressiveness). Butting corresponded with the highest relative aggressiveness. As the quotient gradually decreased, butting was successively replaced by three different displays in a definite order, and finally by overt escape behavior. Each successive display was less oriented to the dummy and performed at greater distances from it than the preceding one. The latency before the test fish started its approach to the dummy increased with a decrease in the aggressiveness quotient.

These and similar studies lead to the conclusion that the two tendencies to attack and to flee may be continuously involved in causing behavior that is functionally labeled as sexual, parental, or filial. In addition to its importance for ethology itself, this notion may be essential for a correct interpretation of physiological studies of apparently nonagonistic behavior. It

may also be enlightening to our understanding of the processes of socialization, particularly of forming and maintaining bonds and the causes of disturbances in these processes in animals as well as in humans.

The concept of *motivational system* has led to important insight into how behavior is brought about. Nevertheless there is no general agreement on how a motivational system should be defined and to what extent different motivational systems can be distinguished from each other. Although motivational system is meant as a causal concept, the task of a system in serving a particular survival function is usually obvious. In this chapter the concept is intended to imply a complex of mechanisms in an animal controlling a group of causally and functionally related activities. Sensitivity to external stimuli effective in this control is considered part of the system, but I do not include in the definition the external stimuli themselves.

In the context of a system the various activities belonging to it serve different functions. This implies that each is controlled by a different set of external factors and that the internal factors determining their tendency to be performed may also be to some extent unequal. Consequently the correlations in the incidence of different activities of the same system need not be high. In this sense they are not simply and equally controlled by the same unitary drive (Hinde, 1956a).

The Processing of External Stimulation

As seen above, the triggering, steering, and maintenance of elementary activities, as well as the activation or priming of behavioral systems are often brought about by particular external stimulus situations. This section will deal with ethological research aimed at detecting what kind of information-processing procedures are involved in selecting the adequate stimuli in each case. In studies of this kind observing the animal under natural conditions may suggest insights about the nature of the adequate situation for obtaining a particular response. Experiments with natural objects are useful for further specification of this situation. However, analyzing which of the stimulus components in a situation may actually be effective and to what extent usually calls for experiments with dummies representing aspects of the situation so that the various features can be changed at will. Such experiments showed that different features of the same stimulus situation, though essential to the production of certain responses, may not be simultaneously selected and processed. This can be illustrated with Tinbergen's (1935) analysis of the control of the behavior of the digger wasp *Philanthus triangulum* when hunting for bees. This wasp preys on bees as food for its larvae. It catches the bees when they are visiting flowers, paralyzes them by stinging them near the ganglia of the ventral cord, and then transports them to a burrow in the ground that was dug earlier. Hunting starts as the wasp patrols the flowering heather. When it perceives a bee it halts, hovering in the air. Experiments with freshly killed bees, either tied to a twig or suspended from a thread so that they move in the wind, showed hovering to be triggered by a moving object. The wasp then takes a position downwind of the bee, from which it launches its attack, provided it perceives bee scent (from a bee or a bee-scented dummy, but not a deodorized bee or an untreated dummy). By placing a bee-scented dummy just upwind of an unscented one, Tinbergen could show that the pounce at the prey object was directed not by scent but by sight only; in this case the nearest scentless object was taken. After the object was grasped it was tactually and chemically tested. Thus different stimuli emanating from the prey are involved in the entire catching procedure, but they are effective at different stages for different elements of the chain. In another situation, when the wasp lost the bee during transport and tried to recover it, the procedure was different. The wasp did not—as in hunting—react first to visual stimuli; it immediately used scent.

The course of these experiments shows that the animal's appropriate response to an object may be brought about by running a program of preset perceptions and reactions. As a consequence the effectiveness of a particular stimulus may differ for different responses, or for different phases of one complex response in the same animal; it is not determined by receptor sensitivity alone.

Different features may also be effective simultaneously. For instance, the sexual pursuit flight of the greyling butterfly *Eumenis semele* can be triggered by any moving object, but this triggering grows more frequent as the number of effective features represented in that object—dark color, length/width < 3, fluttering movements—becomes greater (Tinbergen, Meeuse, Boerema and Varossieau, 1942). In a study of the characters releasing agonistic behavior in a cichlid fish, Seitz (1940) found indications that the power of a situation to induce a fight was determined by a process of summation of the values contributed by each of the effective stimuli present. The higher the total value present, the more complete was the agonistic display. Seitz called this principle of evaluation *Reizsummenphenomen*, translated as the rule of *heterogeneous summation*. He stressed as one of the consequences that when in an incomplete releasing situation one or more effective features were interchanged with different features of equal value, the situation for triggering the corresponding response remained equally effective.

To denote the response-specific stimulus-selecting mechanisms that enables a particular response to a specific set of incoming stimuli and thus underlies the phenomena just described, Lorenz (1935, 1950) coined the German name *auslösender Mechanismus*, translated as *releasing mechanism* (RM). He chose the verb "to release" because in his model for the mechanism that activates MAPs the accumulated reaction-specific energy that he thought supplied such activities would be set free after perception of the adequate stimulus situation. Most investigators, including Lorenz (1978), now believe that external and internal stimulation acts similarly on the control system of the response. Likewise it is parsimonious, so long as the facts permit, to assume similarity between the mechanisms through which the external stimuli that release and direct patterns are processed. It is well to remember that biases can be induced by the term releasing.

The releasing mechanism concept occurred to Lorenz when he realized that in the course of evolution many animals developed specialized structures and activities to release a specific response in another animal, usually a conspecific. For such developments he coined the term *Auslöser*, or social releaser (Tinbergen, 1948; Baerends, 1950). He reasoned that the social releasers in the sender would have developed simultaneously with the characteristics of the also evolving information-processing mechanisms in the receiver. Consequently such mechanisms would be maintained through genes, and this made Lorenz speak of innate releasing mechanisms (IRM). A critical discussion of the use of innate will be taken up later.

It should be clear that, although the concept of a social releaser inspired Lorenz to postulate releasing mechanisms, such affector mechanisms are also thought to be involved in responses to stimuli emanating from objects that do not benefit from evoking the response, such as potential prey animals or hosts of parasites. In such cases the adjective social is inappropriate.

The IRM concept has inspired a considerable number of ethological studies on how information from objects in the natural environment of animals is processed to evoke specific responses to such objects. Because of the predominance of visual perception in our own life, relatively more attention has been paid to analyzing the perception of visual signals than of signals concerning other sensory modalities. This research was stimulated by early findings —in particular on the stickleback (Tinbergen, 1948, 1951)—suggesting unexpectedly that not in invertebrates only was the responsiveness based on a few simple key stimuli instead of on the entire complexity of the adequate situation. Territorial male three-spined stickleback were found to respond differentially with aggressive or sexual behavior when dummies of modeling clay with features of male or female fish were moved about in the territory. A realistic fish shape was not essential for these responses. Attack responses were promoted by painting a dummy red underneath; light blue dorsal parts and a dark blue eye further increased the dummy's effectiveness for releasing aggressive responses. In contrast, a silvery coloration induced zigzagging, and a swollen ventral part on such a model promoted a response with courtship activities even more.

Various aspects of the studies initiated by the IRM concept will be discussed here in the context of an extensive study of the effectiveness of different stimuli emanating from eggs in inducing incubation behavior in the herring gull (Baerends & Drent, 1982). This analysis was concentrated on visual stimuli only after it had turned out that other sensory modalities hypothesized to play a role in the first response to eggs were not involved. In tests carried out in the field, wooden-egg dummies on which the shape, size, color, and speckling were varied, were presented on the nest rim in pairs to incubating birds. The egg-retrieval response was used as a criterion for stimulus selection; the dummy that was consistently retrieved first in a series of similar tests was taken to be the most effective one.

The results were surprising. When black-speckled dummies with different-colored ground tints (brown, blue, green, yellow, and red) were compared, green was greatly preferred to all other colors. Yellow came next, followed by brown and blue. The lowest scores were found for red and for shades of gray. Of the colors used, brown matched the real egg color best; blue and gray were also more like the real egg color than the much preferred but unrealistic green and yellow hues. Moreover, the effectiveness of the speckling pattern was found to increase with the number of speckles and the degree of contrast with the background. When these were applied, a dummy whose appearance was quite unlike that of a normal egg was more effective than a neatly imitated speckled pattern. Similar results were obtained for size: dummies larger than normal eggs were found to be more effective, even when they were as much as twice the linear dimensions of the normal egg. Thus, as for color, size, and speckling, the birds were found to be more strongly affected by stimulus constellations deviating considerably from those of the real egg than by stimuli matching the natural situation. Only for shape were the natural features preferred. Egg-shaped dummies were retrieved first more often than any of abnormal shapes; block-shaped dummies with rounded edges scored higher than those with sharp edges. However, the preferences for features of shape appeared to be weaker than those for features of color, speckling, or size.

A difference between the two types of features also appeared in an analysis of the time elapsed between the arrival of the bird on the nest (after the disturbance caused by setting up the test) and the retrieval of the first dummy. As the latency period became longer, there was decrease in the percentage of tests in which a green dummy was preferred to any other color, a large sized dummy to a smaller one, or highly rated speckling patterns to those scoring lower. The percentage of preferences for a natural shape however, increased as the bird took more time before showing its decision. Figure 14.14

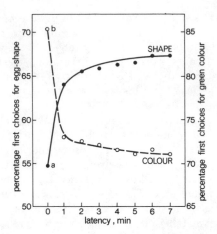

Figure 14.14. Change in the percent frequency of choices for the generally preferred dummy as latency increases stepwise between arrival on the nest and choice between two egg dummies laid on the nest rim for two groups of experiments: (a) egg-shaped dummies against abnormal shapes of equal volume and (b) green against other colors and shades of gray (after Baerends & Drent, 1982).

illustrates the contrasting latency characteristics for color and shape. The data suggest that two different types of stimuli can affect the selection of an object for the performance of incubation responses, namely, stimuli identical to features of the natural egg and stimuli that resemble only very roughly the natural features. In spite of their appearance, the unnatural stimuli are highly effective in inducing incubation behavior; consequently this type of stimulus is called supernormal. They deviate so much from the appearance of the real eggs that the responsiveness to them is unlikely to have been acquired from experience with handling eggs during incubation. In contrast, for the stimuli of the first type it is plausible that their linkages with the incubation responses are indeed due to learning. Thus when it takes longer for the bird to make its decision, the likelihood increases that the choice will favor a closer resemblance to the natural object, and such choices are probably based on acquired knowledge about the appearance of these objects. Longer latencies may be due to the activation of a tendency to escape. This interpretation is supported by both the relation of long latency periods to the incidence of postures and calls specific to more fearful situations, and the con-

siderable amount of preening in the interruptive behavior of birds that decide for a resemblance to natural eggs (an indication of interference by a tendency to escape). Thus the activation of a fear system appears to promote a preference for normal or natural features, whereas the preference for supernormally effective features occurs only when the bird is relatively free of fear.

This conclusion was confirmed by the observation that gulls that generally preferred the green, large, or better speckled dummy of a pair occasionally showed a temporary preference for a less conspicuous dummy that was closer in shape to the natural egg. In such cases the brown dummy would be retrieved before the generally more effective green or yellow dummy. Similarly a bird might consistently but temporarily prefer normal size to enlarged sizes, or a normal speckling pattern to an exaggerated one. Tests with this type of result indicted a greater than average tendency to escape. Such behavior was common in birds with little or no experience of the procedure of the test.

In many instances with different kinds of animals, but particularly with vertebrates, attempts to obtain specific responses to dummies failed. But even when the experiments were generally successful, some individual animals were impossible to work with, consistently or transiently, and were consequently disregarded. I think that these failures to respond to the dummies otherwise than by fleeing must have resulted from the animal's paying attention to a large number of features of the situation. It seems likely that this is the way in which experienced vertebrates initially react (Baerends, 1986). The animal's responsiveness to a small number of conspicuous key stimuli then become apparent only after the animal has become accustomed to the test procedure and reacts quickly without being frightened. Only under these circumstances is there revealed what Lorenz called innate releasing mechanisms, which he contrasted with a mechanism sensitive to a complex situation with many interacting stimuli. Lorenz asserted that in this latter mechanism, which he considered to be based on acquired knowledge, the lack of a single feature would make the situation quite ineffective. On the contrary, the dummy experiments demonstrate that the absence or poor representation of a feature merely reduces the effectiveness of the dummy.

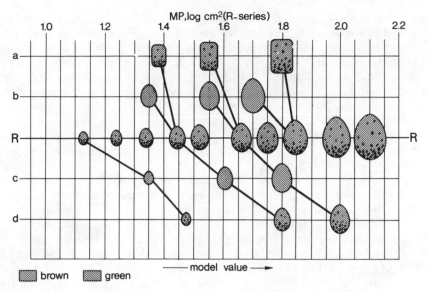

Figure 14.15. Heterogeneous summation. The stimulus values found for egg dummies, varied in different ways, compared with those of a reference series (R) of normally colored and shaped egg dummies of increasing size. The maximal projection surfaces (MP) of the eggs of the size series have been plotted along the logarithmic scale of the abscissa. Equal distances between points on this scale imply equal ratio values (Baerends & Drent, 1982). On the ordinate, (a) is block-shaped, (b) plain brown, (c) plain green, (d) speckled green.

The experiments on egg recognition presented an opportunity to test Seitz's rule. In order to quantify the stimulus values of different dummies, use was made of the finding that in the choice tests a bird often preferred one of the two sites on the nest rim where the dummies were presented. The resulting position preference in the choices could always be broken, however, by increasing the stimulus value of the dummy on the less preferred site. Consequently, the difference in the values attributed by a particular bird, during a sitting spell, to each of the two sites on the nest rim was measured by titration with a series of dummies of increasing size. In this procedure the smaller dummy of a pair was placed on the preferred site, and by trying different larger sized dummies on the other site it was determined which size ratio was needed to overcome the position preference during the experimental period. With a similar procedure the releasing value of every combination of features of a dummy could then be expressed with reference to that size series. Figure 14.15 shows the dummies measured and the relative values obtained. This figure permits a comparison, for dummies of different sizes, of the effect of changing from egg shape to block shape (a), of substituting the brown ground color for green

(c, d), and of omitting the speckles on brown (b) and on green (c) dummies. From the positions found for the various dummies when compared with the series of sizes and with each other, one can conclude that the different features distinguished must be evaluated independently by the bird. For instance, when the speckling is omitted on a brown egg-shaped dummy, the ratio at which its value is reduced is the same, regardless of the dummies' size; in Figure 14.15 the heavy lines connecting equal sized dummies tend to be parallel. The position a particular dummy occupies on the reference scale is the result of a combination of the stimulus values at which each of the features is represented in the dummy. Thus the response strength is determined by the total quantity of relevant information present, in accordance with Seitz's rule.

The rule of heterogeneous summation makes it possible to understand the increased responsiveness to an object in which particular features have been quantitatively exaggerated beyond the natural limits. In this way it is even possible to construct an object greatly deviating from the natural one, but considerably more effective and thus really supernormal. The incubation responses showed that a green-colored egg dummy 1.5 times the normal size, with a high density of small black spots, was significantly preferred to a real egg. Tinbergen (1951) found oystercatchers to prefer a nest with five eggs, or one with a naturally painted dummy the size of an ostrich egg, to a nest with a normal clutch of three or four eggs. Although the birds could not sit quietly on these abnormal clutches, they continued to make vigorous efforts.

Increased responsiveness to supernormality has also been reported in insects. Magnus (1958) found the sexual pursuit flight of males of the fritillary butterfly to be released by the fluttering movement of the yellow wings of the female. This movement could be imitated by a rotating drum with black and yellow stripes; rotation at a speed that suggested a higher flutter frequency than ever occurs in real butterflies induced a higher incidence of response than a speed corresponding to the natural flicker rate.

The findings on stimulus selection and responsiveness to supernormal stimulation raise questions about the underlying cause of these phenomena. Most likely they result from the potentialities and constraints that follow from the nature and characteristics of the afferent mechanisms. Insight into this matter can be obtained by penetrating further into the results of studies of releasing mechanisms in gulls.

The degree of effectiveness of a particular stimulus is often specific to a particular response, or rather to a group of responses controlled by the same superimposed system. For example, whereas green was highly effective and red much less so in evoking incubation responses in herring gulls, Tinbergen and Perdeck (1950), studying the stimuli that release the begging response in herring gull chicks, found red to be the most effective color. The gulls feed their chicks through regurgitation; their heads are white and the bill is yellow with a red patch near the tip. Interestingly, experiments on the begging response in other species of the family of gulls and terns all revealed selection for red in feeding situations, even in species without red on the outside of the bill and even though red was not a prominent color in their food. In most of these studies, however, the peak for red was accompanied by a peak about equally high for blue, a color absent in the food of most of these species. Thus the high effectiveness of red *and* blue for evoking begging does not appear as an obvious adaptation to the adequate natural situation.

Hailman (1967) was first to suggest that this bimodal color response curve for juvenile begging could be due primarily to characteristics of the information-processing system, and only secondarily to association with the adequate external stimulus. The character and the roughness of this adaptation can then be understood in connection with the marked preference for green displayed in the egg-retrieval response, a preference that also matches the real egg color only roughly. The facts that complementary colors are involved here, and that responsiveness to red seems to be tied to sensitivity to blue, urges one to look for an explanation in peculiarities of the mechanism for color discrimination. The system of color vision operative in birds is at least trichromatic and conceivably contains analyzers that might underlie the cases of stimulus selection found. One of them —an analyzer dipolarized by red and blue and hyperpolarized by green—seems a candidate for explaining the bimodality found in the color-response curve of the begging response (Emmerton & Delius, 1980; Gruber, 1979). If in order to characterize objects for feeding and incubation in an inexperienced animal a choice had to be made in evolution between a small number of color analyzers, then red would be more appropriate for evoking feeding reponses in a nonherbivorous bird, and green the better match for the egg color.

In addition to analyzers for wavelength, detectors for several other visual characteristics have been found in the afferent apparatus of vertebrates, such as for contrast, the direction of lines in space, curvatures, patches, and so forth. It must be possible to characterize particular stimulus situations roughly by combining the information from a selection of different detectors or analyzers. This could be the principle that underlies the innate releasing mechanism. A model, designed to represent various properties connected with this mechanism, and based on the work on egg recognition in the herring gull (Baerends & Drent, 1982), is given in Figure 14.16. The core of the model, corresponding to Lorenz's concept of IRM, is a selector unit connected with a specific set of detectors. To give an output, the selector must be activated by a motivational system to which it is subordinate, the system for incubation in the present case. In an animal still unfamiliar with the situation involved, the output of the selector

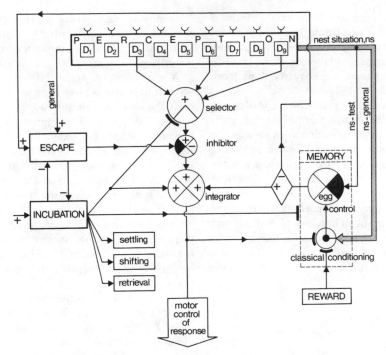

Figure 14.16. Flow diagram of the functioning of the mechanism underlying incubation responses of herring gulls toward eggs. Egg recognition is thought to be possible in two ways: (1) through identification of the object by way of linkages of particular detectors with a selector specifically representing the adequate object and activated by the motivational system concerned, and (2) through experience obtained while manipulating eggs (memory). The output of the selector, determined by heterogeneous summation of the inputs from the detectors, is integrated with the output from memory when determining the response and with the internal stimulation provided by the motivational system. Stimulation of the escape system, for instance, because the memory of the nest situation does not match the situation actually perceived, can reduce the input of the selector in favor of the influence of memorized information (after Baerends & Drent, 1982).

reaches a motor control unit of the motivational system unchanged. However, as the experiments on egg retrieval have shown, this input can become throttled when the escape system is activated simultaneously. For this purpose an inhibitor unit has been built in. The model further assumes that, from the moment the animal starts to perform in the adequate situation, knowledge concerning nest and eggs of a type more complicated than the information passed by the detectors begins to accumulate in memory. The experiment in which the relative stimulus value of different dummies was measured (Figure 14.15) has shown that this knowledge, which is derived from experience (e.g., egg shape), is combined with the output from the selector through the process of heterogeneous summation. This is thought to take place in an integrator that finally feeds the motor mechanism. The model further provides for the possi-

bility that discrepancies between the memorized template and the situation as observed increase the tendency to escape and thus reduce the input from the selector. This modification is needed to account for the occasional preference for a natural-looking dummy in the egg-retrieval experiments under the influence of a tendency to escape.

In a review of the historical development of the releasing-mechanism concept and its use, Schleidt (1962) has advocated distinguishing between innate releasing mechanisms, acquired releasing mechanisms, and innate releasing mechanisms modified by experience. He emphasized that in experienced vertebrates the modified type is the rule. The model in Figure 14.16 covers all these possibilities. The mechanism postulated provides the inexperienced animal with a primary potentiality to respond adequately to a number of vitally important situations in the animal's environment. Moreover, it forms a basis for acquiring additional knowledge about these situations through learning. This process as well as the dangers of labeling these types in accordance with the innate acquired dichotomy will be further discussed below.

The model also helps to clarify the occurrence of responses to supernormal stimuli, even in animals with highly developed capacities for detailed visual perception and for accumulating such details in memory. We must then assume that the input from the selector dominates over the input from memory in rapid reactions but loses primacy when the animal takes more time to decide on a response because of caution and possibly also for other reasons. In humans also responsiveness to supernormal situations plays an important role. It can account for the strong tendency to exaggerate particular anatomical features—often concerning sex differences—in pictorial arts, fashion, make-up, and the design of uniforms (Morris, 1977).

Two cases of sensitivity to supernormal stimuli in humans have been pursued; they concern the recognition of a laughing face and the release of parental responses by the facial characteristics of a baby. In order to analyze which characteristics of the human face contribute to the visual recognition of a laugh, Schmidt (1957) constructed a series of drawings in which different elements suspected of contributing to the laugh effect were represented or omitted in different combinations. Subjects were asked to arrange these dummies in order of increasing laughter effect. The scores obtained by each of them are given in Figure 14.17. First, these data show the validity of the rule of heterogeneous summation for this effect; absence of a feature, such as the eyes, can be compensated for by the presence of another, such as dimples near the corners of the mouth. Exaggeration beyond natural proportions, in particular of the mouth, considerably increases the laughter effect, a phenomenon commonly employed by cartoonists.

Lorenz (1943) was the first to point to the phenomenon illustrated in Figure 14.18, in which the combination of a steeply-rising forehead, relatively large eyes, rounded cheeks and a relatively smaller lower part of the face—all typical of human babies and many other mammalian young—evoked paternal care responses in humans. Humans also characterize these types of heads as cute, in contrast to the opposite

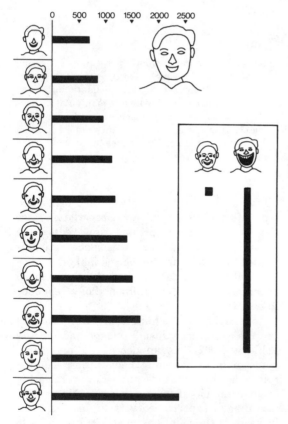

Figure 14.17. The relative effectiveness of different features of a human face in producing the effect of a laugh, and their heterogeneous summation (arbitrary laughing scale). Insert: supernormal model compared with natural laughing face (after Schmidt, 1957).

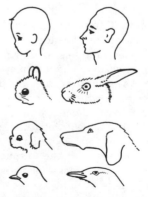

Figure 14.18. The contrast between the profiles of babies and adults (after Lorenz, 1943).

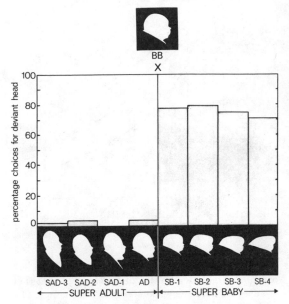

Figure 14.19. Percentage of choices for the natural baby profile (BB) when paired with super-baby profiles of four different degrees (SB), an adult profile (AD), and three super adults (SAD) (after Gardner & Wallach, 1965).

type displayed in the right-hand column of the figure. The toy industry tends to exaggerate these features in dolls and animal figures.

Gardner and Wallach (1965) carried out a series of tests in which subjects were asked to select the most attractive baby profile from a pair of drawings, one of a natural standardized baby profile and the other deformed to exaggerate either the baby traits or the adult features. The data, summarized in Figure 14.19 show a 70 percent preference for the supernormal baby profiles. Hückstedt (1965) went into more detail and found cephalic height to be more effective than the cephalic arch of the profile. The preference for supernormal profiles was distinctly present in females as young as 10 years of age and in males from 18 years on.

The combination of selector plus detectors is obviously essential for a naive animal to find its way in its particular environment. One may wonder, however, why evolution has not provided for the disappearance of its effect after the relevant information about the environment had been acquired. One reason may be that the possibility of a quick response continues to have survival value even though some misfirings may occur. The danger that such erroneous responses

will occur is already reduced through the inhibiting influence of the escape system on the output of the selector.

A preference for supernormal stimulation may also be based on a very different process, namely, a special conditioning procedure. When a positive reinforcement of responses at a particular value on a stimulus continuum is combined with negative reinforcement for values below or above that value, the generalization gradients will peak not at that value, but at some distance away on the side opposite the negative reinforcements. This peak shift has been found in experiments with pigeons tested on a wavelength scale (Hanson, 1957) and a scale of increasing density of spots (Hogan, Kruijt, and Frijlink, 1975).

Heterogeneous summation has been found in mechanisms for both triggering a response and directing it. Often, as in the analysis of egg retrieval and begging in gulls, it is operationally difficult or even impossible to disentangle these different effects of external stimulation. For both functions heterogeneous summation seems to provide an appropriate principle for information processing. It also holds for activating or priming motivational systems. In dealing with feedback information, however, when it is necessary to compare feedback stimulation with a template or an expectancy (such as tactile stimuli from three eggs of 38°C in an incubating herring gull), a principle based on pooling of information from different stimulus modes is unlikely to be applicable. Nor would sensitivity to supernormality play a role in that case.

The Interaction Between External and Internal Factors

The occurrence of an activity or the activation of a system results from the integration of external and internal stimulative factors. To reveal the rules for this integrative process it should be possible to measure both factors independently. Methodologically this is usually a difficult task, particularly for the internal factor.

Heiligenberg (1974) and his co-workers solved this problem elegantly in experiments on inducing attack behavior in territorial males of the cichlid fish *Haplochromis burtoni*. In these studies a single male was kept together with some small juvenile fish of another species. The level of the attack system of the male was measured continuously by the rate of attack at these constantly present targets. Since the small fish escaped quickly, the attacks were always brief. The attack rate was manipulated by offering, for 30 seconds, a dummy representing a conspecific intruder behind a glass plate. Each particular type of dummy was found to change the attack rate by a specific constant amount that was unrelated to the level of that rate just before presentation. A dummy with the markings and color of a territorial male, including a black bar through the eye, increased the attack rate, and did so most when the bar was roughly parallel and least when it was perpendicular to the forehead, regardless of the position of the body of the fish. An orange patch above the pectoral fins, normally present in a territorial male but not in an intruder, reduced the attack rate. A dummy in a vertical position with head down increased its effect, a posture with the head up decreased it. All these incremental and decremental effects were additive. After presentation of the dummy, the attack rate decreased exponentially over time to the previous level, the half-life of the increased attack rate being about two minutes. Thus the effect of the external stimulus was superimposed on that of the factors causing the base rate. However, in addition to this short-term increment in the attack tendency, Heiligenberg was also able to induce a long-term increment in the base rate by repeating the same presentation once every 15 minutes for eight hours, over a period of 10 days. At the end of this period the attack rate had gradually increased threefold. When stimulation was discontinued it slowly fell back to the prestimulatory base with a half-life of seven days. These results are not consistent with the Lorenzian concept that the external stimulus would only contribute through the release of "endogenous reaction-specific energy."

Baerends, Brouwer, and Waterbolk (1955) have exploited the motivationally controlled changes in the color patterns of the guppy to assess the internal state during the performance of courtship. The occurrence of changes in the black markings of the male while courting a female have already been mentioned above (see especially Figures 14.6 and 14.7). Figure 14.7 shows that the various patterns can be arranged along a scale of increasing sexual tendency. In a standardized experimental setup a male could be stimulated to any stage on this scale by allowing

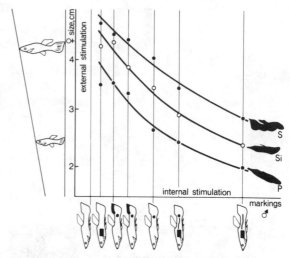

Figure 14.20. The combined influence of internal and external stimulation on the kind and completeness of the ensuing courting behavior of the male guppy. The different marking patterns that the male assumes during courtship are used as indicators of the tendency to perform sexual behavior (abscissa); the size of the female is a measure of the external stimulation. Displays of the male: posturing (P), sigmoid intention movement (Si), and fully developed sigmoid (S). The spacing of the marking patterns along the abscissa reflects the level of sexual activity as derived from Figure 14.7 (after Baerends et al., 1955).

it to court a female for some time. After a particular pattern had developed the female was removed and quickly replaced by another female confined in a glass tube. It was then observed to which stage courtship developed in the next two minutes. Since the effectiveness of a female had been found to increase with its size, the strength of the external factor could be manipulated by testing with females of different sizes.

The curves in Figure 14.20 show that a particular display could be released by quantitatively different combinations of the internal and external factors. The incipient sigmoid display corresponded to a lower value of the product than its high-intensity version (Figure 14.6e). The sigmoid as an advanced display needed a higher product value than the less advanced posturing (Figure 14.6c). Although the hyperbolic course of the curve for each display suggests a multiplicative relation, the reader should be aware of the influence the choice of scale has on the function's shape.

The curves confirm the rule, which Lorenz

had already enunciated, that with a high value of the internal factor a low value of the appropriate external stimulation suffices to have the response released. He called this phenomenon threshold lowering (see p. 768).

From a functional point of view, one would expect an animal to be more fastidious about the appropriate external situation when the corresponding internal factor was at a fairly high strength than at a low strength. This is indeed the case with feedback stimulation. Incubating gulls appeared to be most responsive to deviating tactile or temperature stimuli from the eggs when the tendency to incubate was high (Baerends and Drent, 1970). At the same time, however, they discriminated poorly between different dummies presented on the nest rim (Baerends and Drent, 1982).

THE ONTOGENY OF BEHAVIOR

Ontogenetical Processes

How does the behavioral organization of the individual animal develop in the course of its life? The fact that the specific structure of this organization is based on genes does not mean that all elements comprised in it can be called innate. In morphology and behavior, genes express themselves in interaction with the environment. For behavior this interaction may mean the incorporation of experience, that is, of sensory input. It is often insufficiently realized that in some way the selection and processing of this input has to be under the control of genes. Otherwise one could not expect behavior and structure to be mutually adapted, and recognizing any species from its behavior would be impossible. Watson's original idea that at birth only an animal's reflexes are present, and that genes play no role in the further development of behavior, cannot possibly be correct.

The genetics of behavior is treated separately in Chapter 13 of this book. The controlled or programmed acquisition of information in reaction to the environment will be the dominating topic in the present section.

Research on learning in animals was being carried out long before the rise of ethology. In those days animal psychologists were particularly interested in the abilities of animals to learn to solve problems, and they compared these capacities among the larger systematic groups. Experimental psychologists, using animals as a means to understand learning in man, were chiefly interested in factors facilitating learning, that is, in the underlying mechanism. Since they were not usually interested in the natural history of their animals as such, they did not realize that constraints on learning might exist, depending on the characteristics of a species and its way of life. The contribution of ethology lies mainly in this area, in the study of how learning contributes to the development of an animal into a normal representative of its species. In addition, following the example set by von Frisch, ethologists as well as physiologists have utilized conditioning techniques to investigate the sensory capacities of animals. In such studies attempts are made to train animals to respond to a more-or-less complex stimulus situation, often followed by an analysis of the relative effectiveness of the various stimuli that compare the situation under test. Examples are the work on the sensory capacities used by insects oriented toward food sources and nest locations (von Frisch, 1950, 1967; Tinbergen and Kruijt, 1938) and on the chemical and auditory senses in fish (von Frisch, 1926, 1936).

For the most part, between students of the development of anatomical structures and of the development of behavior, a remarkable difference in attitude exists. Developmental physiologists fully realize that genes can come to expression only through interaction with substances and forces outside the DNA molecule. They investigate which interactions take place and how. In contrast, behavioral studies pose the question again and again whether genes or experience have contributed to a trait, or, if both are involved, what was the share of each? The basis for this dichotomous thinking about the origin of behavioral elements in an individual lies in obsolete, but obstinate, philosophical concepts about how behavior is caused and in what aspects this causation is essentially different between humans and animals. About 350 years ago Descartes gave this question the pertinent answer that only humans possess reasoning whereas animals are merely automatons. That bold statement brought an unfortunate bias to the scientific approach to problems of the origin and development of behavior.

In the first place, the stress on reasoning in humans led to an emphasis on associations and thus of learning processes in human psychology. The failure to consider genetic factors, in particular by behaviorists, caused in zoologists studying behavior (i.e., the ethologists headed by Lorenz) an overemphasis on the genetic basis, commonly identified with the term instinct. The interest of the zoologists in the species-specificity of behavior led to attempts to distinguish such behavior sharply from behavior individually acquired through imitation of other animals. When an animal is reared in isolation from fellow members of its species—the so-called Kaspar Hauser experiment—and is found capable of performing motor patterns in the species-specific way and of responding to particular stimulus situations similarly to control animals reared under natural conditions, these capacities were said to be innate. As Lorenz (1965) pointed out, the use of innate in this sense is meant to imply that the information about the environment that is essential for eliciting the adequate response is not derived directly from that environment by the animal's own experience, but is collected indirectly through the mechanisms of evolution and is thus encoded in the genes. Whether particular environmentally adapted differences in behavior between related species are due to differences in their genetic codes can be checked experimentally with the appropriate genetic methods.

Although a genetic basis for behavior can be demonstrated in this way, the problems of what processes cause the development of behavior, or how expression of the genes is achieved, remain unsolved. Lehrman (1953) stressed this in his criticism of Lorenzian ethology. There is even a danger that the use of the term innate may discourage research on that topic; it is easy to forget that this term does not exclude the possibility that the genes act through stimulating the acquisition of information via experience. It will become clear in the following discussion that in ontogenetical studies dichotomous thinking is likely to inhibit deeply penetrating research.

The attempts made frequently in studies of behavioral development to discriminate sharply between *maturation* (i.e., growth and differentiation of the nervous and effector tissues through intrinsic forces within the animal) and *learning* (i.e., development through experience) as two alternative possibilities for causing changes in behavior elements with time result from dichotomous thinking. By stating that an element has up to a certain stage developed through maturation, one intends to express that it is thought to have developed without the influence of feedback from interactions with the environment that report about its functioning. However, feedback is not the only kind of input from the environment that can be conceived to influence development. The growth of differentiation of behavioral components sometimes depends on specific environmental input that may be independent of the activity of the animal.

Another result of dichotomous thinking is the persistent attempt to distinguish in the behavioral repertoire of a species between innate and learned elements, or within a single element between innate and acquired components. With his concept of instinct-learning intercalation Lorenz (1935) first postulated that mosaics between the two components could be formed, but he later stated that in those early days he had not yet realized that all learning is built on an instinctive or phylogenetically developed program (1978). Thinking in terms of intercalation may prevent us from understanding the merging of different types of information in the developmental process.

In spite of his contestable use of the term innate, it was Lorenz again who initiated what so far has been the most important contribution of ethologists to our insight into the process of the development of behavior. His experience in keeping and rearing animals of various kinds (Lorenz, 1935, 1952) had made him aware that different types of bonds, normally formed with specific classes of conspecifics, may in unnatural social situations be established with the wrong social or sexual partners. Lorenz distinguished five types of such bonds and accordingly five types of companions (German: *Kumpane*): parental, infant, sexual, social, and sibling companions. The formation of these bonds and their effect on the further development and success of the animals involved convinced Lorenz of the paramount importance of a learning phenomenon that he called *Prägung*, later translated as *imprinting*. Although this phenomenon had earlier been recognized in birds and mammals, including humans (e.g., by Spalding, Heinroth, Freud), the widespread experimental study of it was founded on Lorenz's stimulating observations, in particular, those on the gray lag goose. By exploiting goslings' tendency to form a practically undisruptable filial bond with a relatively large moving object present in their neighborhood just after they are hatched, Lorenz made himself the parental companion of a flock of goslings. While playing this role he followed the development of their behavior for several months on end (Lorenz, 1979). Exposure to conspecifics after the posthatching period did not change the interspecies bond. Lorenz concluded from his observations that imprinting differed essentially from the learning processes generally studied in the following ways: (1) the learning process was confined to a special phase or period in the ontogeny of the animal, (2) the learning situation appeared to be programmed, (3) rewards of the type commonly used in learning experiments were not required, (4) extinction would not take place, (5) the engram would be irreversible. The apparent divergences from the types of learning so far studied, and the potentialities imprinting seemed to have as an ontogenetic principle, gave rise to many studies aimed at testing Lorenz's claims and at penetrating further into the nature of this process and its impact. However, before looking at some of these studies and at some corrections and amendments of Lorenz's criteria that these studies have stimulated, I shall demonstrate the importance of the principle by means of the example most intensively studied so far, the development of bird song.

Like many other animals, birds possess vocalizations that are essentially species-specific; in the passerine birds these vocalizations have often become elaborated into complex songs. Among conspecifics of the same population, individual variations of the same song occur, but these are relatively small, and the songs fulfill all criteria given above for MAPs. Does that mean that in their development learning is not involved? The isolation experiment offers a first answer to this question. Rearing experiments with chaffinches (Thorpe, 1961) and with white-crowned sparrows (Marler and Tamura, 1964) have shown that to develop a species-specific song learning is necessary. However, this learning follows a specifically fixed program that guarantees that under natural environmental conditions the correct song develops. But individuals of these species, hatched and raised in isolation in soundproof rooms, produced a simple monotonous song as adults. Some characteristics of the normal song can nevertheless be

recognized in this vocalization, for example, in the chaffinch the specific rhythm. When a tape-recorded song of their own species was played to isolated sparrows or chaffinches, they later sang that song. In the chaffinch, tutoring was successful when applied during the first ten months of life, but in sparrows it succeeded only during the first three months. After those periods both species were found unreceptive to song learning. Thus these birds have critical sensitive periods, but different ones. When the song of their own species is played into the acoustical chamber in addition to the songs of alien species, only their own song is learned. Some species, such as the chaffinch, do learn alien songs, for instance, the songs of canaries or tree pipits (Thorpe, 1961) when their own specific song is withheld. By splicing tape recordings from songs in various ways, Marler and Peters (1977) showed that the swamp sparrow recognizes its own specific song by means of particular sound elements or syllables. This capacity was also present in birds reared in isolation.

Although the male white-crowned sparrow has, by the age of four months, learned the acoustic pattern of its song, it is not yet able to perform it; its vocal apparatus is ready only several months later, at the beginning of the new breeding season. The male then begins to practice and continues to change its production until the auditory feedback received from its vocal output matches the model or template acquired several months earlier. If the male is deafened before it starts to practice, a vocalization develops that is similar to that of a bird deafened shortly after hatching. Its vocalization is also very different from the song of a bird with unimpaired hearing but reared in isolation. This means that the ontogeny of this latter song must have been influenced by auditory feedback.

Thus in the ontogeny of the song of the white-crowned sparrow several developmental principles are involved. The species-specific pattern of notes is learned in a critical period from a template that the young has acquired on the basis of a predisposition, whose nature is as yet not understood. When the vocal organs are ready, the bird tries to match the template, and when it succeeds the motor pattern becomes definitely fixed in that form. From then on it tends to remain unchanged, even if the bird is deafened; nonauditory feedback may then have taken over control. The way in which the various principles interact and follow each other is laid down in a developmental program whose basis must lie in the genes. In different species of birds the stages and places in this program at which the different principles are applied vary; so does the irreversibility of the song and the possibility of acquiring new songs later in life. However, it is impossible to distinguish between learned and innate components, because each element is a product of the interaction of the influence of genes and environment.

The example for bird song illustrates how the idea of constrained learning as an important basic mechanism for the development of behavior—which grew out of the postulation of the imprinting concept—has led to the wider and more flexible conception that learning programs exist. In these programs the various characteristics given by Lorenz to define imprinting may occur independently in combinations varying from case to case. Some recent work done on this criteria will elucidate this thesis.

Critical Period

For many processes of programmed learning, a particular period in the life of an animal appears optimal for acquiring a particular kind of knowledge or skill. This is probably not so much because the animal would at other times be unable to make the association, as because in the sensitive period morphological or physiological circumstances or both have a maximum facilitating effect. In one of the first studies to test Lorenz's statements in a more sophisticated laboratory setup, Hess (1958) confronted single ducklings, at ages varying from one to 32 hours, with a slowly moving dummy. After an imprinting period of 10 minutes the duckling was given the choice between the familiar and a strange dummy; preference for the familiar predominated. The ducklings' choice for the stimulus object imprinted on peaked at 92 percent at the age of 16 hours. Hess has argued that the upward phase of this peak is due to the increase in locomotor skill with age, and the downward phase to an increasing tendency to flee from unfamiliar objects.

The possibility that particular hormonal levels may cause a sensitive period is suggested by Nottebohm's (1969) finding of a facilitative effect of exogeneously administered testosterone on the learning of recorded song themes

by a two-year old castrated chaffinch without previous singing experience.

Schutz (1965), who did extensive experiments on imprinting on the sexual partner in ducks, maintains that in the mallard the sensitive period for sexual imprinting is different from that of the filial imprinting (zero to 30 hours) mentioned above. About one-third of the male mallard ducklings whom he kept with their own mother from one to three weeks, and from then on for five to six weeks with a foster parent, later paired with the foster species after adulthood was reached. It is clear that in these ducklings the imprinting on the alien species must have taken place after the critical period for filial imprinting. Although Lorenz initially thought that imprinting was an instantaneous process, there are now several indications that the strength of the imprinted engram is dependent on the parameters (e.g., length) of the exposure to the imprinting object (Bateson, 1966). However, the length of exposure needed for imprinting is not constant throughout the sensitive period. Immelmann (1972) reports a decline toward the end of the period. In a critical review of the data on sensitive periods, Bateson (1979) has argued that imprinting is a self-terminating process because it narrows social perferences to familiar objects.

Reward

With his statement that a reward would not be necessary for establishing effective imprinting, Lorenz meant a reward corresponding to the biological function or goal of the activity concerned. The duck following a dummy mother needed not to be warmed or fed by the dummy to form a bond with it; sexual imprinting can take place long before a sexual act is successfully performed. However, the fact that a reward of this kind is not involved does not imply that, in the establishing of a learning code, a match between the feedback perceived during the response and a particular preprogrammed sensory input (expectation) would not play a part. This possibility certainly holds for the acquisition of the motor pattern of avian song, where the white-crowned sparrow's template for this expectation is programmed to be learned long before the vocal apparatus is ready. Stevenson (1969) has shown that playback of a conspecific song could also act as a reinforcer for other activities than singing, that is, to teach chaffinches to alight on a particular perch, provided the birds had been sensitized by testosterone injection.

Absence of Extinction

The criterion of absence of extinction is uncontested. White-crowned sparrows, deafened after they had developed the motor pattern of their song, kept that ability unimpaired for at least a year. Ducks and zebra finches, sexually imprinted to foster species, preferred foster parents even when kept in isolation during the long period between separation from the parent and reaching sexual maturity (Schutz, 1971; Immelman, 1972).

Irreversibility

Immelmann reported that zebra finch males who were imprinted on Bengalese finch females in the period between 15 and 43 days old always maintained a strong preference for mating with the foster species. Only when that species was not available might they mate with females of their own species. Schutz found that mallards keep their preference for foster parents such as other species of ducks, geese, and even fowl for up to nine years, in spite of having continuous access to potential mates of their own species. Altogether there is considerable evidence that in many species imprinting processes occur that lead to stimulus preferences that last for years.

More recent work on imprinting should warn us that the establishment of preferences through this kind of learning may be not only more complicated than hitherto thought, but also more variable from one species to another and in the types of bond concerned. For instance, Kruijt and his co-workers (Kruijt, Bossema, and Lammers, 1982; Bossema and Kruijt, 1982; ten Cate, 1982) have shown that the formation of a sexual bond in the mallard and the zebra finch may be due to a combination of different imprinting processes. The authors demonstrated that later sexual preference was influenced not only by the appearance of the birds that cared for them parentally but also by the appearance of siblings present during the rearing period. Bateson (1978, 1980) found that the mating preference of the Japanese quail is influenced by the external appearance of the siblings reared with them. Birds moderately different from the sibling appearance were preferred to closely similar or largely different birds; choices were greatest for a first cousin of the opposite sex. Bateson suggests that this preference enables the birds to strike an optimal balance between inbreeding and outbreeding. Kruijt et al. found that female mallards and zebra finches tended to direct their preferences to the most actively courting males; this preference largely superseded a preference based on the appearance of the plumage.

The findings on imprinting indicate that one learning process may differ from another by various features. The amount of variation possible suggests that it may be better to forego distinguishing a great many different classes of learning, and instead to recognize that each of the features possible may in any combinations with others, become attached to a given learning process, in accordance with further functional demands. In this way learning processes in many variations are tools, so to speak, that can be used in the building of some segments in the species-specific behavioral organization.

The example of the development of bird song involved both the sensory or afferent aspects of the response and the motor or efferent aspects, and the same holds for the discussion on the criteria used for imprinting. The following two sections deal more specifically with each of these aspects.

The Development of Responsiveness to Stimulus Situations

There are good reasons to assume that when an object is manipulated by an animal, learning about its features takes place. When begging for food naive gull chicks peck rather indiscriminately at a contrasting spot on long and thin objects, particularly when they are red or blue. In the course of several days' experience with the parent, however, the chicks gradually develop a preference for the correct shape and color patterns of the head and bill of these adult birds (Hailman, 1967). It is likely that the stimulus-response links (innate releasing mechanisms, see above) present in the naive animal facilitate the acquisition of more extensive information about the stimulus situation involved. Some evidence suggests that an animal learns about various features of an object handled more rapidly when the object contains features that the animal is sensitive to in the motivational state activated than when such guiding features are absent. Herring gulls learned more quickly to refrain from retrieving an egg dummy that was immovably pegged to the nest rim when the dummy was green or speckled brown than when it was red or plain brown (Kruijt and Baerends, 1982). The linkages connecting the detectors with a selector and a motor control unit were supposed to have developed as a result of morphogenetic processes similar to those underlying the coordination of muscular activity. However, specific external stimulation may influence such growth processes. For instance, in order for cats to develop detectors for particular angles of lines in their visual field, they must have experience with an environment containing such lines (Blakesmore, 1973).

Tinbergen (1951) has expressed the opinion that, even without prior experience with the adequate object, animals would be able to respond to relations between features of the object that could be classified as simple gestalts. One of his examples concerns the orientation of the gaping response in nestling thrushes. This response can be released by approaching the young with a cardboard disk (Tinbergen and Kuenen, 1939). When a dummy was used consisting of a large disk to whose edge were attached two smaller disks of different sizes, young birds reared without contact with parents directed their gaping response toward whichever projecting disk seemed in comparison to the main disk, to match best the head-body relation in the adult thrush. A well-known case is the response of goslings to the silhouette of a flying predator. When the silhouette was flown with a short neck in front, the young birds ran for cover. When the direction of the dummy's movement was reversed so that the long tail now led, suggesting a long goose neck, they were attracted to the dummy (Tinbergen, 1939). More recently, however, Schleidt (1961) has shown that the dual discrimination of hawk-goose dummy, depending on its direction of movement, was in fact learned. Working with turkey chicks reared under controlled environmental conditions, he showed that the differentiation between the two forms of dummy was due to a difference in habituation that corresponded to the frequency with which flying predators and conspecifics were seen under natural conditions. The escape response persisted toward silhouettes that occurred rarely, whereas the response to the familiar silhouette became habituated.

The Development of Motor Patterns

Several kinds of experiments have been carried out on the influence of experience on the development of motor patterns, especially loco-motor activities. Carmichael (1926, 1927) immobilized newt larvae through narcosis during the period of their early life in which the nerve connections needed for the undulating swimming movement were growing. Grohman (1939) reared pigeons in narrow tubes that prevented them from moving their wings. Neither of these treatments retarded or otherwise impaired the development of the locomotor ability involved. Weiss (1941) transplanted limb rudiments of newts to abnormal positions (dorsal, contralateral, reversed) and found that after the nerve connections had been established the grafted limb moved just as it would have done if left in its original position. Adjustment to the stimulation received in the new position did not take place. The nature of the intrinsic developmental processes involved, although studied intensively, is as yet only partly understood.

Motor patterns of the reflex type are also generally assumed to develop without feedback from their effect. Nevertheless Prechtl (1965) has found differences in the postures and reflex patterns of the legs between face and breech presentations in otherwise normal babies. The author attributes these phenomena to central effects of abnormal proprioceptive input during the intrauterine phase.

When animals reared in deprivation of normal living conditions are first confronted with these environmental aspects and enabled to interact with them, they usually appear to have the major part of their species-specific behavior repertoire at their disposal. The basic form of the patterns is usually recognized easily; if deviations occur from modality they tend to involve details. However, the patterns are often not oriented appropriately, or they may fail to be elicited by the normally adequate situation. The scanty evidence available indicates that such MAPs (with the exception of song in several birds investigated) also develop mainly through instrinsic growth processes. In this context the study of Fentress and his co-workers on the development of face grooming in mice should be mentioned. This behavior was filmed in a standardized experimental setup and analyzed on the basis of the Eskol-Wachmann notation developed for choreographic descriptions. Various components of grooming the face with the paws developed in early stages. The fact that the same movements also developed after amputation of the lower part of the forelimbs, so that the face could not be reached, speaks for little effect of feedback stimulation in this phase. Mice with these amputations kept protruding the tongue to wet the missing paw. This coordination linkage of limb and tongue movements was not yet present in an earlier phase when the limbs moved largely independently of each other. Since this coordination failed to take place after deafferentation of the limbs, it is likely to depend on the feedback. The authors noticed that variation in patterns between individuals, present in early stages, had later disappeared (Fentress, 1972).

Baerends-van Roon and Baerends (1979) have described how in kittens the various motor patterns seem to emerge gradually from undulating locomotor movements through increasing differentiation of discrete coordinated movement patterns involving more distal parts of the body. Plooy (1983) has described this phase of development through differentiation in chimpanzee babies and Humphrey (1969), studying it in humans, has attempted to relate this process to the neuroanatomical changes similtaneously taking place. Plooy (1983) has pointed out that the early movements of neonates on the body of the mother strive to find consummatory stimuli, such as a particular temperature or milk, and stop when these are reached. He suggests that, as in bird song, matching the perception of feedback stimulation that correspond to preset stimulus patterns may play an important role in the development of more complicated motor behavior.

In addition to development through differentiation, ascending development through the integration of differentiated patterns has been recognized as a principle of development. For instance, Kortlandt (1940b, 1955) has shown how in the cormorant simple action patterns present at the end of the second month later aggregate into more-or-less complicated sequences and become organized into behavioral systems. In chimpanzee babies Plooy found evidence that integrating development takes place after the differentiation of separate patterns have come to an end at the age of five months.

Differentiation is probably the dominating process so long as the developing animal is still inside the egg or the uterus. Postnatally ascending development is likely to increase in importance at a younger age in species with nidifugous young than in species with altricial young that are intensively cared for by the parents. Ascending development is the main subject of the next section.

The Development of Complex Behavior

As was shown above, modal action patterns and simple acquired operants or habits tend to occur in specific combinations, organized into systems or subsystems, each of which serves a particular function in the life of the animal. The performance of these elementary patterns occurs in close integration with selective responsiveness to sensory stimulation. Some insight into the processes involved in the ontogeny of such behavioral complexes can be derived from an as-yet small number of studies on animals of different taxonomic groups. The ontogeny of two levels of integration are considered here: (1) the integration of appetitive behavior and consummatory act within a behavior system and (2) the interaction between such motivational systems.

Appetitive Behavior

The release of a consummatory act as well as the attainment of a consummatory situation is, as a rule, reached after the performance of appetitive behavior, usually consisting of a chain of acts. In lower animals the composition of this chain is often fixed, each link producing the releasing situation for the next one. In higher animals more flexibility is often possible, and the exact composition of the sequences of activities may differ in detail between individuals. Several indications point to learning processes as important causes for such variations. In the higher vertebrates, and in particular in mammals, the opportunity for such learning is amply provided for in play. Most likely, classic and instrumental conditioning are the important processes involved.

A few examples may illustrate this role of learning. The red jungle fowl utilizes a display called cornering—derived from nesting behavior —to attract females. Whereas the form of cornering is probably determined intrinsically,

Kruijt (1964) could manipulate its relative occurrence considerably through instrumental conditioning, by releasing a hen from a cage every time the cock performed this display. Jungle fowl cocks also use courtship feeding (tidbitting) as a display to attract females. Stokes (1971) found that only adult cocks are usually able to apply this activity with success. Yearling males gain experience in tidbitting as well as in dealing with (yearling) rivals by consorting with hens rearing chicks. Eibl-Eibesfeldt (1956) has shown that young squirrels must learn to integrate a number of different MAPs to a functional whole in order to open hard-shelled nuts successfully with the least possible effort. In several series of experiments Baerends-van Roon and Baerends (1979) have tried to influence the prey-catching behavior of young cats by manipulating the kinds of prey with which they were confronted and the surroundings in which this took place, before the kittens were eight weeks old. They concluded that the motor patterns for seizing and killing a prey developed independently of experience in handling it, but that, in the organization of the appetitive behavior leading to seizing, individual differences occur that may be related to the experience obtained. Experience in the second month contributes to building up individually preferred sequences of appetitive behavior, with MAPs as the constitutents. The experience of killing and eating a prey was found to be of great importance in fixing the appetitive sequence. The acquisition of experience in prey catching is facilitated by the mother's bringing the prey to the nest—first dead, later stunned and still living—from the third week on.

Play

The behavior of kittens when presented with a more-or-less stunned prey is often designated as play. Many ideas exist about the causation and functions of play behavior, and consequently many definitions have been proposed (Bruner, Jolly and Sylva, 1976; Loizos, 1966). General agreement exists that play is important for the development of behavior, although the opinions may differ on detailed questions concerning when, where, and how. In general, one might say that play occurs in species in which an adult needs to develop a special kind of skill or has to cope regularly with solving relatively complicated problems in variable situations, for instance, in obtaining food (as in carnivores) and living in elaborately structured societies (as in monkeys and apes). Play occurs particularly in species with relatively long developmental periods and young that remain long with the parents.

Although it is usually easy to recognize play when it occurs by a number of vague criteria (direction toward inappropriate objects, inconsistency in aiming at goals, incompleteness, exaggeration), a sharp distinction between play and serious behavior is in my opinion impossible. This is not surprising when the chief function of play is to contribute to the development of behavior that is of direct and vital importance to the animal. During play an important part of the behavior repertoire of an animal is repeatedly tested against various conditions and adjusted accordingly. However, it seems characteristic that in play the behavior patterns appear to occur with little or no control from hierarchically superimposed systems, but are induced mainly by external stimulation (Eibl-Eibesfeldt, 1951; Barrett & Bateson, 1978). The motivational state of play seems to be characterized by a certain degree of uncoupling of the hierarchical organization. There are strong indications that particular external factors favor the occurrence of play. Special signals serve to invite play, such as characteristic tail movements in carnivores (Bekoff, 1974) and the play face in chimpanzees (Van Hooff, 1973). Play is facilitated by the mother's being quietly present. It often starts after contact with the mother and is interspersed with seeking contact with her again (Harlow, 1959). Alarm inhibits play.

Play has an important exploratory function, but not all exploratory behavior can be called play. Exploratory behavior can be subordinate to different motivational systems; it always comprises appetitive behavior and leads to a consummatory act or consummatory situation. Play does not lead directly to an ultimate goal.

In the human species with its extremely long developmental period, a strikingly large amount of time and effort is put into play. This difference from other animal species appears proportional to the relatively greater importance of learning processes for the development of human behavior and, in particular, to the role of a transference of habits through tradition (culture).

Social Behavior

Interactions between clutch or litter mates are an important aspect of play behavior. They always have an agonistic character; the young animals attack, chase, and flee from each other. In view of the notion that communication behavior has evolved as a result of the conflicting tendencies to attack conspecifics and to flee from them, and may still be controlled by these tendencies, it makes sense to ask whether social communication suffers when young animals are deprived of the possibility to interact with members of their species.

Such experiments have been done in red jungle fowl (Kruijt, 1964, 1971) and in rhesus monkeys (Harlow, 1959; Harlow and Harlow, 1962). From a few days after hatching, red jungle fowl chicks regularly interact with each other with mild attack and escape behavior. From about the third week on, interruptive activities occur, some of which serve as, or develop into, communicative displays. After seven weeks, side display and waltzing appear, displays that can both be considered as a compromise between incomplete attack and escape patterns and both of which are used in rank order disputes between cocks and as introductory displays in male courtship. Incomplete copulatory behavior starts between the second and third months, and full copulatory behavior when the fourth month is reached. Spatial and visual isolation of cocks for a year or more from the time of hatching was found to lead to a complete loss of the ability to copulate, even when the cocks were then kept continuously with conspecifics of both sexes. The same was true when isolation began at the age of six weeks. When isolation started at 10 weeks, however, the ability to copulate was not lost, even when this isolation lasted for more than 16 months. These data indicate that during the first two months a process takes place in the chicks that tunes them for later sexual behavior. This tuning does not concern the execution of the single behavior patterns of courtship and copulation, since isolates can occasionally be seen to perform them. However, they do not perform them in regular sequences, and they are usually badly oriented and sometimes not directed toward a female. A cock may execute the movements of copulation with only a feather in its bill. It is characteristic that, instead of passing through the courtship ceremony, the early deprived cock may frantically pursue a female, alternately pecking her viciously and showing extreme escape behavior. This suggests that during the tuning period a basis for a harmonious interaction between the system for sex, attack, and fleeing has to be established under the influence of experience obtained in interactions with other individuals.

Harlow and his co-workers did similar deprivation experiments with rhesus monkey babies. Several different rearing situations were used: complete spatial and visual isolation, raising young with a surrogate mother (i.e., a cylinder with built-in milk bottle, covered with terry cloth), raising with a normal mother (with and without access to peers) raising with a mother who had herself been raised motherless (with access to peers) or raised with peers with and without a surrogate mother. The monkeys were repeatedly tested over several months or even years after this isolation was discontinued. For the development of normal agonistic and sexual behavior, regular opportunities to play with peers were needed. In monkeys kept in complete isolation from birth, this behavior became almost normal provided separation was not continued for longer than 80 days. After isolation for six months or more the monkeys, when placed together with others, were not able to join the others in play, agonistic, or sexual behavior; presence of a surrogate mother during isolation did not make a difference. The isolates responded to other monkeys with extreme fear; they showed fits of strong and often paradoxical aggression; they engaged in little social exploration; and they often made queer ritualistic and idiosyncratic movements. When a motherless mother gave birth, she also behaved abnormally to the baby. She did not treat it with the gentleness that normally raised mothers show to their infants and frequently attacked or avoided it.

Baerends-van Roon and Baerends (1979) have followed the development of agonistic behavior in the social play of domestic kittens. During the first months this behavior is restricted to attempts between litter mates to push one another away, while crawling with sigmoid body movements and slow alternate beating of the legs. At the end of that month, when the kittens have become capable of moving about, they begin to launch direct attacks on each other. In the beginning these attacks are uninhibited. The kittens strike with all the force they possess, with stretched nails, and an attack may end with fierce biting. The attacked kitten reacts with screams and escape behavior. However, the attacks are launched mutually by the littermates, and consequently between the fourth and eighth weeks a versatile chasing-wrestling-fleeing interaction characterizes the social play. After some encounters the approach and attack of the nestmates becomes more inhibited; the nails are retracted, and beating and biting tend to be superficial. In the course of this behavior the kittens appear to learn to control the motivational systems for attack and escape.

Imitation; Culture

In addition to the transfer of information through genes and through acquisition in trial-and-error behavior, possibly stimulated by social facilitation, transference through tradition provides a third means of acquiring knowledge. The species specificity of a behavior pattern is not as a rule due to copying a model observed in a conspecific. Isolation from conspecifics—the Kasper Hauser experiment—has shown this to be true in animals of widely different groups. The only known exception is the species-specific song pattern of some birds, discussed above. I suggest that the rare occurrence of close imitations may result when an animal, observing an activity in another animal, builds a template that it can use later as a continuously present guide in order to achieve a match gradually by trial-and-error learning. This seems easier for a melody than for the temporal and spatial coordination of body and limb movements, possibly because the melody offers a frame of reference, a time matrix (rhythm) on which the notes can be built.

Crude imitation of the behavior of a conspecific through observational learning is, however, far more common. It can be important in socially feeding animals, primarily in detecting a special kind of food, and then in developing a technique for obtaining it. However, techniques acquired in this way vary considerably between individuals, since after having been socially stimulated to peck or scrape at certain places each individual develops by trial and error its own variations on the crudely imitated pattern. In natural situations the imitation of largely new motor patterns by monkeys and apes has been reported, in particular in the Japanese macaque in which innovations in feeding techniques made by one monkey gradually spread to others in the group. In 1953 a female was for the first time seen to wash sand from sweet potatoes before eating them; by 1962 this habit had been taken over by all members of the group except for infants less than one year old and adults older than twelve years (Kawai, 1965). The same monkey invented a technique for separating wheat from sand with which the food had become mixed, by throwing a handful of the mixture into water and scooping up the wheat after the sand had sunk (Tsumori, 1967). Habits spread first to playmates, and in general they are more likely to be taken up by monkeys of lower than of higher rank (Miyadi, 1967).

Transfer of acquired behavior patterns between individuals of a group means culture. Not only does it occur in monkeys, but it has also been observed in other animal groups, for example, in birds opening milk bottles (tits studied by Hinde & Fisher, 1951). Only in our own species, however, has it become of paramount importance, thanks to the development of articulated speech, later followed by writing. It is interesting to realize that tradition, as a means of information transference, contains a much greater risk of passing on erroneous or even harmful information to further generations than does genetic transference, where a rigorous testing through the mechanism of selection has taken place. Therefore one would expect that it would be important for information transfered through tradition to be accompanied by an evolutionary development of mechanisms for testing the reliability of tutors and leaders.

FUNCTION AND EVOLUTION

Principles Underlying the Evolution of Behavior

In the preceding sections we have tried to break down the species-specific behavioral organization into various causally defined units and their constituent elements. We have also discussed various principles underlying its ontogeny. In this section we shall consider the processes which in evolution could have promoted the adaptive differentiation of the behavioral organization to the species' functional needs.

Genes are the primary bases for the maintenance of the identity of the specific behavioral organization. They guarantee that members of a species or subspecies fit into their ecological niche. The individuals forming such a taxonomic unit are phenotypes, that is, the results of interaction between genes and environment. Two fundamental processes are involved in the assemblage of a collection of genes adapted to an ecological niche: (1) the formation of mutations or alleles of existing genes, and (2) the selection of those alleles that provide for the highest fitness in the given environment, that is, for the largest number of optimally viable progeny.

So far we have been dealing with factors directly influencing the occurrence of behavior by eliciting, orienting, priming, or controlling it. Such factors are denoted as *proximate* to distinguish them from so-called *ultimate* factors, which in the course of evolution have induced the development of the proximate processes. For instance, for many insect-feeding songbirds living in a temperate zone, it is of vital importance for their eggs to be hatched when food starts to become abundant. The right timing is brought about by sensitivity to a particular day length, activating the gonads to produce eggs. Day length, therefore, is the proximate controlling factor, selected under the pressure of food supply as the ultimate factor. Thus, whereas the preceding sections dealt with proximate factors, in this section we are interested in the nature of ultimate factors, and in the ways they have influenced the behavioral organization of a species.

A first problem is at what level of organization—population, individual, or single gene—ultimate factors exert a selective force. Darwin considered the individual as the target of selection. This means that phenotypes are mediating the selection of genes. In the selection of particular genes, their interactions with the environment as well as with other genes of the gene pool must be involved. This model is generally accepted for the evolution of structures, but difficulties arise with behavior when the evolution of activities carried out for the benefit of other individuals has to be understood. This problem was first raised for the evolution of warning coloration, that is, conspicuous color patterns combined with distastefulness as an antipredator mechanism. It works only when the predator, after tasting the prey, associates the unpleasant experience with the particular colors. Members of the same species with similar color patterns may benefit from this learning process in their common enemy, but only at the cost of the fitness of the individuals that fell victim when the predator was still naive. Fisher (1930) realized that genetic factors for warning coloration are likely to be carried also by siblings of the victims. Their fitness would be increased by the sacrifice, and along this line the incidence of those genes involved would be promoted. This implies that, although mediated through the individual, selection would in fact act on the genes. Recently this point of view has been taken by Dawkins (1976b) and ardently defended; he considers the individuals a vehicle for the replication of genes.

For a long time, however, phenomena such as the occurrence of warning coloration and behavior in assistance of conspecifics or group members was considered to be "for the good of the species or the group" without asking the question how such characteristics could have evolved. This casual attitude dramatically changed when Wynne-Edwards (1962) advanced the proposition that species, particularly those living in societies, would homeostatically adjust their population density to prevent overpopulation through behavioral mechanisms evolved as a result of competition between genetically differing populations of a species. Thus in this view the group is the target on which the selective forces act (group selection). However, it is difficult to conceive of how the principle of selection based on maximizing the progeny of the individual could be reconciled with the evolution of behavior that would be primarily of benefit to the group. While ecological research was increasingly producing evidence refuting Wynn-Edwards' group-selection concept (e.g., Lack, 1966), population geneticists embarked on an analysis of the fundamental processes taking place by designing mathematical models, in particular to explain the evolution of behavior in which individuals assist others at the cost of their own fitness. Such behavior is often called altruistic, in contrast to selfish behavior which would benefit primarily the performing individual and its offspring. The introduction of these anthropomorphic terms has proved to be unfortunate because of their value-ridden connotation in normal usage.

Several models have been produced that explain satisfactorily the occurrence of altruistic behavior. One is based on the idea that an individual can contribute to the representation of part of its genes in future generations by helping relatives, since it shares genes with them—to a degree decreasing with increasing distance of the relationship (called *kinship selection* or *inclusive fitness*; Hamilton, 1963). A second model is that of *reciprocal altruism* (Trivers, 1971). This principle can also work between unrelated individuals, provided there is a high probability that assistance given at some cost of the animal's own fitness is reciprocated by assistance received to an amount exceeding that cost and thus favorably influencing the fitness of the giver. Models of group selection have also been developed. They indicate that this type of selection is possible, provided the group is small and already formed, for instance, by genetic drift, and is well protected against immigration of a selfish trait (Maynard Smith, 1976a). However, we may conclude that selection is most likely to act on the individual, as the intermediary in the replication of genes.

Genes code for the synthesis of specific proteins that act as enzymes for catalyzing specific chemical reactions. Many of these reactions function for the maintenance and reproduction of the organism. Some play a role in regulating its ontogeny. Mutation of such a gene therefore causes some change in development. Consequently evolution is based on modification in the ontogenetical process (de Beer, 1940). Since ontogenetic development consists of a complicated branching series of processes superimposed on each other, the chance that a mutant that manifests itself in an early stage of development will disturb the harmony of further processes and cause the death of its bearer is considerably greater than if a mutant comes to expression in a later stage. As a result, different taxonomic groups have more features in common in early than in late development stages. This phenomenon led Haeckel to state that "ontogeny recapitulates phylogeny," an unfortunate formulation because it has masked the real direction of the underlying causal relation. Ontogeny can explain the course of phylogeny, but phylogeny does not explain ontogeny at all. A most important consequence of the rule that phylogeny is based on modified ontogeny is that the development of

new structures, as well as principles underlying behavior, is only possible on the basis of the existing situation. Therefore this situation also implies constraints for the possibilities of further adaptive developments.

The formation of a gene pool through mutation and selection, by which a species is adapted to a particular set of environmental conditions, takes a great many generations. It is a secure but time-consuming method. More adaptive flexibility is provided when genes allow for a certain amount of phenotypic adaptation, brought about within the life span of an individual through interaction with the environment. Morphological processes, such as those underlying the growth of structures, may in this way be modified within a range controlled by the genes. When behavior is involved, a possibility for incorporating experience may be laid down in the developmental program. According to whether a developmental program is controlled preponderantly by inherited determinants or by acquired ones, it may be called *open* or *closed* (Mayr, 1974). Programmed learning can be considered a compromise between maintaining the core of the species-specific behavioral organization and allowing flexibility for individual adaptation. Where, in the ontogeny of the behavioral organization, learning is applied and how the acquisition of the needed information is assured should then be determined by natural selection of the appropriate regulating genes. Programmed learning may concern the acquisition of knowledge in order to evaluate a stimulus situation, the establishment of stimulus-response links, and the acquisition of motor skills. The programs provide more commonly for learning of motor behavior through trial and error than through watching conspecifics (observational learning).

Evolution selects for morphological structures, physiological processes, and forms of behavioral organization, which in combination enable the individual to maximize its reproductive success. To reach that goal, the individual should possess mechanisms enabling it to strive to perform its behavior in such a way that the trade-off between benefits and costs to its reproductive success results in a maximum net benefit. Behavior should thus be optimized intrinsically. The optima must be the result of economy-based compromises in the ways different functions are fulfilled.

To check this notion of optimization, qualitative observations on how various functions are fulfilled should be supplied with quantification of these procedures. Mathematical optimality models should be constructed permitting testable predictions. This method, introduced by MacArthur in behavioral ecology (MacArthur and Pianka, 1966), has now been applied to single aspects of behavior in a considerable number of cases. The results, some of which will be treated below, strongly support the opinion that, in the evolution of the organization of species-specific behavior, the costs and benefits have been carefully weighed (Wilson, 1975; Barash, 1977; Krebs and Davies, 1978, 1981). In considering the cost-benefit relations it must be specified which aspect of the behavior is thought to be maximized, what constraints on its performance cause it to reach an optimum instead of the maximum, and what "currency" could appropriately be used in the calculations. Food or energy can prove a suitable currency, which is not surprising since as a result of competition food is usually in limited supply. A number of studies stimulated by the optimality theory have revealed how critical in the life of an animal the food supply tends to be. Often the circumstances under which a behavior has to be carried out are variable, for instance, in the character of the habitat or of the behavior of other individuals involved. In such cases there is not one optimal solution for maximizing the goal. The individual has alternative strategies available and means to choose the one most adequate for the prevailing situation.

Particular behavioral strategies may also develop in evolution as the result of competition between alternatives. For analyzing the principles at work in such competition, Maynard Smith (1979) has introduced the application of game theory to the study of evolution. He designed models that can predict which of the strategies under the conditions given is stable against invasion into the population of other strategies of a species (*evolutionary stable strategy*—ESS), or whether alternative strategies can coexist as a mixed ESS, and what then the relative frequency of each strategy should be in a stable situation. These models are all based on selection acting on the individual, not on the group.

Functional Demands on Behavior and Their Consequences

The number of descendants an individual brings forth depends on its capacity to maintain itself and to reproduce. To achieve this state, various functions have to be fulfilled by the organism. This section attempts to show how the selective forces corresponding to these functions have made demands on the species-specific behavioral organization and shaped it in the evolutionary process. A rough classification of functions has been used. The principles and considerations set forth in the preceding section will therefore be used as a key.

Maintenance of the Body

Various physiological functions, such as respiration, thermoregulation, digestion, and blood circulation, require behavioral processes. Some of these processes take place internally, but externally observable behavior is also needed for many physiological functions. Aquatic animals with tracheal or lung respiration possess adaptive behavior to refill their respiratory organs. Insects, reptiles, birds, and mammals may assume particular postures, or move to sites with a suitable microclimate on behalf of their thermoregulation. In birds and mammals, positioning of the features and hair play a role in body temperature control.

Behavior patterns for cleaning occur commonly and are often centrally controlled by relatively closed programs. The evolution of cleaning is interesting, particularly that of cleaning parts of the body the animal cannot reach. Bathing and the use of some substrate for chafing or scratching are common solutions, but assistance by other animals is a more sophisticated one. These other animals may be conspecifics, that is, a mate (as in mutual preening in birds), a parent, or another member of the group. In primates, grooming behavior has developed further into an important communicatory activity (Sparks, 1967). In shrimps, fish, and birds the need to be cleaned, especially from parasites, has further led to the development of symbiotic relationships in which specialized foraging behavior is practiced.

Foraging Behavior

The competition for resources that generally

exists between members of the same species, since they occupy the same ecological niche, is an important factor in intensifying selection for efficiency in feeding habits, involving searching, selecting, uptake, and digestion of food. In the evolution of a species a type of foraging behavior is selected that maximizes the inclusive fitness of the individual. The theory of optimal foraging (MacArthur and Pianka, 1966) postulates that this long-term goal is reached through maximizing one or more short-term goals. To study this proposition, hypotheses are designed about the way in which in a special case the animal manages to achieve a maximum net gain from the trade-off between the costs and benefits of the behavior performed. The hypotheses are described mathematically in optimality models that make possible quantitative and testable predictions when measured values for the costs and benefits of the behaviors concerned are entered. For foraging behavior the obvious currency for comparing benefit and cost is energy expended and gained per time unit. A few cases may illustrate how optimization of feeding behavior can be realized by the way in which this behavior is organized. For more examples, refer to Krebs and Davies (1981).

Drent (1980) studied the efficiency of brant geese, *Branta bernicla* in the utilization of an important component of saltmarsh vegetation, the plantain, *Plantago maritima*. On a given visit the geese were found to remove on average 35 percent of the blades of this plant. An experiment in which the daily growth rate of the plantain was measured after the blades were clipped by lengths varying from 0 to 100 percent, revealed an optimum growth rate after 30 to 50 percent of the blade length was removed. At that rate the loss to the plants was restored after five days, which was the length of the interval between successive grazings by the geese on the same plot. At each visit the geese were found to crop the increment added during their absence. Repeated cropping maintains the protein content of many plants. The behavior of the birds is thus adjusted in detail to obtaining the maximum yield from the sward.

When optimizing its feeding behavior an animal generally has to take into account several requirements. Moose for instance eat aquatic and terrestrial plants that contribute differentially to the energy and sodium demands of the animal; the water plants are rich in sodium and poor in energy, whereas the reverse holds for the land plants. Moreover, the size of the stomach sets an upper limit on the food intake, and aquatic plants are bulkier than terrestrial ones. The quantities of the two types of food actually taken were found to correspond to the prediction that follows when all three constraints are taken into account (Belovsky, 1978).

An animal needs to adjust its foraging behavior not only to the net energy yield of a food item, but also to the time needed to obtain it (Royama, 1970). The quotient between the two values is an index of the profitability of a type of foraging. Crabs feeding on mussels, for instance, were found to prefer mussels of intermediate size to larger ones. The energy gain per time unit from the former proved to exceed that of the latter.

Different foods vary in qualitative and quantitative composition, profitability, and distribution. As a consequence the animal may have to weigh the pros and cons before deciding when and where to forage and on what. J.M. Tinbergen (1981) studied this problem in starlings foraging to supply their brood. Individually marked breeding birds, in nest boxes, were kept under observation in their nest area and in the field. The prey delivered was automatically filmed in a way that made species identification and measurement of size possible. Search paths and prey captures could be measured synchronously. Two kinds of prey were found to be important, the leatherjacket (a fly larva) and the caterpillar of a moth. The starlings preferred caterpillars although they were much less abundant and were found farther away from the nest area. Leatherjackets were more numerous and easier to obtain, but according to several indications their quality was lower. Especially when the demand for food among the young in the nest was great (which could be experimentally manipulated by depriving them of food or by adding extra young), leatherjackets were brought in large numbers. Tinbergen concluded that for a foraging trip several decisions were taken in a hierarchical order. First, a bird decided which kind of prey it should go for; this decision depended on a compromise between the physiological demands (nutrient balance) of the brood and the foraging limits of the parents. Second, the bird decided on the area to search for this prey if different alternatives were available; this choice was made in accordance with experience recently gained on the intake rate in different areas. Thus the first and second decisions concerned the profitability of the prey. The third decision was made on the site in the area where the search was started (the prey had a patchy distribution); the higher the intake rate during the previous visits, the closer the birds landed to the point from which they took off after the preceding visit. Topographical memory was very likely to be used for the second and third decision. Finally a bird who collected a number of prey on a visit had to decide when to return to the nest; the birds tended to carry heavier loads when the flight distance was longer.

The examples reveal the organized character of foraging behavior and its guidance by a program that allows for but also controls an amount of flexibility. In such a program the acquisition of specified information through learning is often dictated, for instance, for updating estimates about the availability of food. One would expect the specific effectiveness of reinforcement schedules found in experimental psychology (variable and fixed ratios or intervals) to be applied in the programs in a functionally adaptive way. This point of view is only recently receiving attention (e.g., Herrnstein and Loveland, 1975; Staddon, 1980).

Sexuality

In most animal species sexuality, leading to recombination of genes through fusion of two types of gametes to a zygote, is needed for the prediction of progeny. The costs of this behavior are often considerable. What then may the selective advantages of recombination and sexuality have been that they could have promoted this spectacular development in evolution?

It is possible to see recombination as an imperfect replication of DNA that has been selected for, since such imperfections may increase the stability of the double helix. Maynard Smith (1971) has shown with mathematical models that recombination of genes from individuals adapted to different environments must influence the offspring of the individuals possessing those traits favorably, because it considerably increases the potentiality of its descendants to survive in a wide range of environmental conditions. However, this holds only when fecundity is very high, as it is in many invertebrates and fish. Consequently

the common occurrence of recombination in vertebrates with lower fecundity and brood care can be seen as a relict, possibly preserved through competition between groups that kept and groups that lost this trait.

More than one advantage is likely to have promoted the recombination of DNA molecules between different conspecific individuals and morphologically different cells. First, differentiation of individuals into either egg-cell or sperm-cell producers reduces the chance of self-fertilization and thus protects against inbreeding. Furthermore cross-breeding is promoted by the combination of the strategy of females to maximize on the survival of their genes by storing a quantity of food in the eggs (which necessarily restricts the number of eggs), and the strategy of the males to maximize on the chances of fertilization by producing great numbers of small, highly mobile cells, each at low cost. Mathematical modeling again has shown that in a population fusion between gametes varying in size, and with the fitness of the zygote increasing with its size, individuals with either very small or large gametes will have the greatest survival value, provided the large ones are sufficiently numerous (Parker, Barker, and Smith, 1972). Thus sexuality may be considered a mixed ESS.

Sexual differentiation creates a selection pressure for the development of behavior to bring the two sexes together so that fertilization can take place. This behavior should make it possible to select an individual of the same species, of the opposite sex, and of the proper stage of maturity. Considering the investment made by each partner, it would also be important to be able to assess the quality of a potential mate.

Investment in the zygote tends to lead to further investments to protect and raise the brood. Since the investment of the female in a zygote is larger than that of the male, selection leading to the development of parental care will more readily take place in the female than in the male.

The argument that selection acts chiefly on the individual rather than on the group is strongly supported by the fact that the sex ratio of a species rarely deviates appreciably from 1:1. Since there are so many more sperm than egg cells, one would expect the group to benefit if females greatly outnumbered males, so that more eggs would be fertilized. However, such a sex ratio is unstable. Mutations promoting the number of daughters of an individual would readily take over and reduce the number of males in the population far below the optimum. If, on the other hand, mutations were to cause the number of sons to increase above 50 percent of the population, the chance that the sperm of such males would fertilize an egg would be correspondingly reduced; at the same time mutation favoring the production of daughters would be promoted by the increased chance of being fertilized (Fisher, 1930). If the investment in sons and daughters were to be different, the ESS would favour equal investment in the two sexes rather than equal numbers.

Partner Selection, Pair Bond, and Parental Care

In many animal species living in the sea, the sperm, and often the eggs as well, are merely discharged into the water. Synchronization of this discharge (as induced by lunar periodicity) and chemical orientation of the spermatozoa may enhance the probability that the gametes actually meet. Obviously any behavior that brings the two sexes near to each other will increase the number of fertilized eggs and thus tends to be preserved and further developed in evolution. Spawning concentrations of aquatic animals reflect a simple form of sexual behavior. During spawning, contact between male and female may be promoted by behavior patterns through which the genital pores are brought close together.

The opportunity for active partner selection seems favorable in species in which sexually mature individuals do not stay in a group but isolate themselves in a location that they defend against conspecifics of their own sex, advertising their presence by visual or acoustic displays or both, and thus trying to attract mates. This is in most species a role for the males. Ripe females move from one displaying male to another before they finally stay with one.

The duration and complexity of the contacts between sexes in a species is closely related to the degree of parental care. When fertilization is internal it is nearly always the female who cares for eggs or young—a consequence of being left with the zygote. In most fish species that require parental care, however, the female abandons the eggs in the male's territory immediately after

laying. This gives her ample opportunity to feed and recuperate, and possibly to produce a new batch of eggs. In contrast, the males continue to stay on at the location, trying to induce other females to let them fertilize their eggs. It is not surprising, therefore, that in fish (and in similarly behaving amphibia such as frogs and toads) parental care has evolved mostly as a role of males. This care varies from merely defending the spawning site on a lek, to the aerating, cleaning, and defending of the clutch, to the building of a nest (Loiselle and Barlow, 1978). In several species of Cichlidae, a family of tropical perchlike fish with a spectacularly diversified evolution, parental care shared by both partners has developed and led to monogamy. Probably as a derivation from joint care, parental care by the female exclusively has also evolved in cichlids. The female, after the eggs and sperm have been discharged in the nest pit, collects the spawn in her mouth and leaves the arena. From then on she invests one or two weeks in caring for the young before starting to produce a new batch of eggs, whereas the male immediately resumes soliciting and fertilizing other females.

This reproductive behavior is similar to that of birds in which the females visit the—usually small—territories of the males to be fertilized. This occurs, for instance, in many grouse species (de Vos, 1979) and in some wader birds (e.g., the ruff, *Philomachus pugnax*; Van Rhijn, 1973), where displaying males concentrate in a restricted area, called an arena or lek. After fertilization the females leave the lek, and care for eggs and young without any male assistance. With the entry of internal fertilization in birds and mammals, females have nearly always become involved in parental care; the strategy of protecting and raising the relatively costly eggs and developing young has won out over the strategy of maximizing the number of eggs produced. However, in a few exceptional cases in which birds live under extraordinary climatic conditions, the latter strategy is still found. In the spotted sandpiper, for instance (Oring, 1981), which breeds in the Arctic on grounds with intense but brief food productivity, most females produce up to five clutches in six weeks, leaving each clutch for a male to incubate. In this example of polyandry, females compete with one another to attract males.

Although this arena system leaves males with nothing to offer to females but fertilization, in many other species an evolutionary tendency can be recognised in males to provide other commodities as well in their territory, thus increasing their attractiveness and means of competing with rivals. By enlarging the defended area, a male can become the holder of resources, which may allow him not only to increase his attractiveness to females, but also to monopolize one or more females and protect the offspring he has sired. Such a harem system has been found in some species of cichlid and labroid fish (Robertson & Hoffmann, 1977). It occurs also in pheasants and wild fowl, but it is most common in mammals. The largest harems occur in various species of seals, where a few males may herd a considerable number of females who are assembled on a beach to deliver their pups and nurse them, in order to have the opportunity to mate with them before they leave at the end of the nursing period (Le Boeuf, 1972). In some species of ungulates (antelope, deer) the resource-holding male offers a grazing area and protection against predators. The reproductive success of a harem holder equals the number of females multiplied by their success. When competition for the resource exists between the females of a harem, the male should not maximize but optimize the number of females under his control. In contrast, a female is likely to gain maximum profit from monogamy. Thus conflict of interests may exist between the sexes.

To hold a resource that permits one or more females to stay for some time in his domain implies that a male has included parental care in his strategy for maximizing offspring, most likely at the cost of the number of fertilizations he can achieve. If the ecological circumstances so dictate, it may then become even more profitable for the male to turn to monogamy and concentrate his efforts on the care of the brood of one female only. In cichlid fish this has commonly happened in those species that deposit their eggs on a substrate and continue caring for the brood for several weeks; partners usually stay together for several broods and are able to recognize one another individually. Monogamy is the most common mating system in birds, where it occurs in 92 percent of all species. In mammals monogamy is much less common; however in some species of primates (gibbon, siamang, titi monkeys) it is the rule, and in wolves its occurrence depends on the ecological circumstances. This difference in the incidence of monogamy between mammals and birds can be attributed to the fact that in birds male care can start shortly after fertilization, whereas in mammals there is no task for the male during the period of pregnancy. Under these circumstances the male can more profitably spend this time maximizing his progeny by mating with other females (Daly and Wilson, 1978).

In view of the rearing of young, monogamy may be more profitable for a female than polygyny when polygyny entails serious competition for commodities with other females in the same territory. Sharing a rich territory with another female, however, may be more advantageous than joining an unimpaired male defending a poor area (Orians, 1969).

Thus ecological conditions have a great influence on the type of mating system evolved in a species. In many species different mating systems are possible, enabling the animals to choose the most suitable system for the prevailing conditions.

Parental Behavior

To counteract the effect of mortality on the number of progeny, two life-history strategies exist that are opposite in their extremes (Pianka and Parker, 1975). One, the r strategy, is directed toward maximizing the production of offspring through early maturity, high fecundity, rapid development and growth, and strong dispersal. The other, the k strategy, is directed toward reduction of mortality where parental care is the most effective way of achieving this. It has been argued above why, when fertilization is internal, selection will favor the involvement of the female in parental care.

Important objectives of parental care are protection against predation and diseases (cleaning), thermoregulation, and feeding. The latter two functions, in particular, feeding through lactation, imply a considerable protection against the dangers of fluctuations in environmental conditions.

Control of the rate of development of the brood through parental behavior first developed on a wide scale in the incubation behavior of birds. The organization of the most common form of incubation has been discussed above. In primates, particularly apes, behavior patterns securing thermoregulation and feeding of the baby via close contact with the body of the mother play an important role in the establishment of the relations between mother and infant (Plooy, 1983) and facilitate learning processes essential for the socialization of the young animal among members of its species. In recent years the importance of these attachment processes for the behavioral development of human babies has been increasingly recognized (Hinde, 1974; Bowlby, 1980).

For the interaction between parents and young, specially adapted communicatory activities often exist in which different sensory modalities can be involved. These signals may characterize the individual (e.g., olfactory cues in mammals, vocalizations in birds). By means of an individually varying call that cliff-bred chicks learn during their first 10 days after hatching the parents can recognize their own chick when, in its third week it jumps off the ledges into the sea (Ingold, 1973).

Prolonged contact of the developing young with a parent provides a very important opportunity for programmed learning. Since parental care often goes hand in hand with living in family groups, learning may come not only from parents but from other adults and juveniles of various ages. The transfer of information through tradition is based on these contacts.

The opportunities to learn through parental and peer influence increase with protraction of the phase of juvenile and adolescent behavior. A tendency toward longer developmental periods occurs in primates and culminates in our own species.

Other Conspecific Relations

Individuals of the same species make corresponding demands on the environment and thus tend to concentrate in the same areas. It may be advantageous for individuals to assemble closely with conspecifics. Several species of invertebrates aggregate as a protection against low temperatures or drying out. The chicks of the emperor penguin and breeding herds of musk oxen also reduce their heat losses in the Antarctic winter by packing together. Probably the most widespread function of aggregate behavior is defense against predators; this occurs even though groups are usually more conspicuous than dispersed individuals (Bertram, 1978; Hobson, 1978). The increased capacity to detect predators even when each individual spends less time on vigilance, the fact that the predator is more easily confused and deterred, and the

dilution of the chance of capture all act favorably on the development of aggregate behavior in animals vulnerable to predation. Unpalatable animals with warning coloration often crowd together, thus maximizing the effect of aversive conditioning in predators. Groups of conspecifics may also forage more efficiently than single individuals, in particular, when the distribution of food is irregular and unpredictable. Aggregate behavior is probably also advantageous to colonial breeding in sea birds, since the colonies can act as information centers (Ward and Zahavi, 1973).

Whenever an assemblage of conspecifics involves mutual attraction between individuals, one can speak of a social system. The simplest form of such a system is a school of fish, a flock of birds, or a herd of ungulates, in which all members are equal, and they keep together actively by means of visual, chemical, auditory, or tactile cues. More complicated social systems have arisen in animals that have balanced the profits of aggregating against the costs of competing with conspecifics, all of whom have the same demands for food, shelter, breeding areas, and so on. This need implies a selective force for the evolution of behavior for attack and defense against competitors. Thus social systems can be considered to have resulted from different selection pressures: those favoring approach and those favoring avoidance of conspecifics. Two main types of compromise between these opposing selection pressures are reached in the various social systems found among animals: (1) the defense of territories with distinct boundaries, harboring one or more of the necessary commodities and (2) the dependence for access to such commodities on the position of an individual in relation to other members of a group (rank or role). Sometimes these two compromises occur in combination.

Territorial Societies

The interests protected through the defense of territories may differ greatly between species; correspondingly substantial species differences in territorial size occur (Etkin, 1967). Roughly one can distinguish between territories subserving the following functions:

1. Sexual contact only. Territories that serve spawning or copulation exclusively are typical for species with polygamous

mating systems. As mentioned above, such territories are usually small and situated close together (lek). In nearly all cases only males occupy and defend such mating territories. They have been found with insects (dragon flies, solitary bees) and all classes of vertebrates.

2. Isolation and protection of brood. Territories that mainly serve to isolate eggs and young from interference by conspecifics are typical of monogamous colonial birds who collect their food outside the breeding colony (gulls, terns, gannets, penguins). Many of the advantages of aggregation hold for this type of society, even though it is at the cost of devoting much energy to territorial defense.

3. The reservation of a food supply or other commodities, often but not always combined with mating and raising a brood. Territories of this type are larger than those of types (1) and (2), at least in relation to the size of the occupants. They occur among fish, many birds, and various groups of mammals. Such territories may be occupied by a monogamous pair—a situation common among birds—but are also found for small antelopes such as duikers. In mammals they are often defended by a harem-holding male, as, for instance, among many medium-sized antelope species. Territories of type (3) may not provide all the food the occupants need, but they provide at least a quantity for periods of bad weather or high food uptake, due to young, when it would be difficult or time consuming to collect food at great distances (especially for songbirds). In general, since this type of territory is more resistant that the other types to pressure from newly arriving conspecifics trying to settle, it is often considered a means of regulating population density. An area that is regularly frequented for foraging by a particular individual, pair, or small group—but is not defended as a whole by means of consolidated boundaries—is called a home range of the individual or group. Home ranges of different groups, such as monkeys and apes, may partly overlap; agonistic behavior may occur at encounters, but different units mostly avoid each other.

Structured Groups

The members of a swarm, school, flock, or herd usually have equal social positions so long as the group is traveling around or resting. This equality generally disappears when the group members embark on an activity involving competition for some commodity. In that case agonistic encounters between members tend to occur, and larger groups often disintegrate into smaller ones that are likely to become structured through the appearance of differences in social status or role between the members. Status differences may be emphasized by morphological distinctions as well as by the type of behavior shown. Members of the same group are found to behave agonistically toward others and are themselves the recipients of such behavior; long-term observations of marked individuals reveal the existence of rules on who is aggressive toward whom.

A simple type of social system is the straight-line hierarchy in which an α individual dominates all other members of the group, whereas an ω individual is submissive to all others. Individuals in between are consistently submissive to some and dominant to other group members. The dominance-subordinance relations may have a deterministic or only a probabilistic character. Often the relationships are more pronounced at the top than further down the hierarchy. Furthermore, triangular or more complicated relationship chains may develop between individuals. Complications in the system may also occur when mature and immature individuals of both sexes belong to the group.

The rank of an individual is important in determining priorities of access to such objects as food, places to roost or shelter, and social or sexual partners. Fights of longer or shorter duration often occur in a first encounter between two individuals, but when the dominance-subordinate relation has been established fighting is greatly reduced, provided the relation is from time to time reinforced or confirmed by displays. Fighting is not the only way to establish a difference in rank between individuals; success or failure for other reasons (greater skill or sheer luck) in obtaining the desired object when competing with another group member can also be effective (Rowell, 1974). Moreover, factors such as age, size, sex, sexual maturity, and rank of close relatives play a role. Individual recognition is obviously of great importance in the respecting of ranks; low-ranking members avoid higher-ranking ones and the aggressiveness in the high ranks is directed mainly at potential challengers. Evidence has been obtained that not only do monkeys know to which members they are submissive and over whom they are dominant, but they also recognize the relative position of each member in the hierarchy. For instance, in baboons the amount of grooming that females direct to one another decreases with their distance apart in rank (Seyfarth, 1977), and in stump-tailed macaques the treatment of infants by various group members differs with the relative rank of their mother in the group (Gouzoules, 1975).

Rank orders can be measured in various ways and with respect to different factors. The results of different methods frequently disagree, and caution therefore must be exercised when treating dominance or subordinance as absolute characteristics typifying a specific individual. A balanced discussion of the rank-order concept applied to primates can be found in Chalmers (1979).

The second factor that causes complications in the structure of a group—not only because it may influence rank order—is heterogeneity in composition. Differences in composition are loosely related to the types of mating system and parental care. In many mammals (macaques, yellow baboons, the African buffalo, and various rodents) the group comprises several adult and juvenile animals of both sexes. In the baboons mentioned, only the most dominant males of the group win any females with which they form only brief liasons when the female is in oestrus. Lower-ranking adult and adolescent males stay more on the periphery of the group, while the high-ranking females with infants are kept in the center (Hall and DeVore, 1965).

In many other species adolescent males leave the group, which then remains as a harem headed by an adult male. The adolescent males often assemble in large hierarchically structured bachelor groups (deer: Clutton Brock, Albon, Gibson, and Guinness, 1979; antelopes: Jarman, 1974). Not before a male has reached the top of his group is he likely to make an attempt to reproduce, often by claiming a territory and trying to build up his own harem. The harem of the hamadryas baboons—consisting of a male with one or more females, often with young—originate from an adolescent male who

adopts and mother a young female, and in this way forms a lasting bond with her. In a later stage other females can be incorporated into the harem. In this species, moreover, a number of harems of different size, together with groups comprizing adult and adolescent bachelor males, are organized into larger troops (Kummer, 1971).

In contrast to the harem system, there are several species—for instance, the African elephant (Douglas-Hamilton and Douglas-Hamilton, 1975)—in which a female heads a group consisting of females, adolescents, and juveniles of both sexes. Only temporarily may an adult male be in control of such a breeding herd so that it becomes his harem. In all subhuman primates, bonds between individuals are of a matrilineal nature. The social relations between mother and child and between siblings are strong. There is no social bond with the father.

Since females tend to stay in the group in which they were born, breeding herds are usually families or groups of families comprising several generations. In contrast, any adult male that is involved with these herds has as a rule no family relations with the members of the group. Family groups may also be formed around a nucleus of a monogamous pair, or a male that has formed a seasonally permanent bond with two or more females (wolves: Mech, 1970). In the zebra several such family groups aggregate into large herds, whereas the bachelor males group separately (Klingel, 1974).

With such a variety in the structure of groups it is not surprising that the rank-order principle is often not realized in the simple straight-line hierarchy form mentioned above. When both sexes are present in a group, males and females may form separate hierarchies in some species and mixed rank orders in others. Changes in the oestrus cycle or the presence of young often cause changes in rank. Although in a great many species males rather than females and older rather than young animals hold the top ranks, these are not general rules, and variations between species can always be expected.

In a number of primate species group members have been observed to form alliances that were effective in maintaining or improving their position in the rank order. De Waal (1978) has conducted a longitudinal study on rank-order conflicts and rank reversals among individuals in a mixed colony of chimpanzees living in captivity in a forest area of about one hectare. The two contesting males at the top of the group often received support from other members. A distinct difference divided the two sexes concerning which animal was supported. The adult females, whose rank order was stable, supported the α male against its challenger until a reversal took place. Consequently, they had a stabilizing influence. The strategy of the males was more opportunistic and was directed to improving their own position; attempts to disturb friendly interactions between other group members were part of their tactics.

Cooperation between group members need not have evolved through group selection. Often cooperation or coalition formation involves relatives (e.g., lion brothers working together in taking over a pride by chasing off the attending males). Then the principle of inclusive fitness applies—thus kin selection—acting through the individual. Sometimes the principle of reciprocal altruism holds (e.g., as in chimpanzees when females support a leading male).

In some fish, birds (Emlen, 1978), and mammals (dwarf mongoose: Rood, 1978) groups may be composed of a pair, its offspring, and a number of helpers who aid in raising and defending the brood. Helpers are usually younger individuals that have not been able to reserve their own breeding location. For such animals the alternative route to having a proportion of their genes represented in future generations is the promotion of the survival of siblings. As a matter of fact, helpers are often earlier offspring of the animals they assist. Yet this is not always the case, and the question thus arises, how such assistance to young that are not kin could have evolved on the basis of individual selection. Most likely the selective value for helping individuals lies in the investment in opportunities for future breeding, for instance, through extending the infiltrated territory and ultimately claiming part of it, or through pairing with one of the parents if the other dies. The activity of helpers has proved beneficial to the brood, and some helpers were found to achieve breeding themselves via this dependent start. In the pied kingfisher, unrelated helpers were accepted only when they assisted the breeding pair effectively (Reyer, 1980).

Social organization in groups and the defense of territories need not exclude one another. Individuals may defend territories within the groups, and the group may live within a defended territory.

The diversity in the structure of the societies of different species can be understood as the result of adaptation to the ecological conditions of the niches they occupy. Evidence in support of this statement has been presented by Crook (1964) who compared mating system, social organization, territory size, types of nest built, feeding habits, antipredator defense, and so on, in the 100 different species of weaver birds (*Ploceinae*), a subfamily of finches widely distributed in Africa and Asia. He found food and predation to be the main selective factor by which the diversity could be explained. In a similar study on African antelopes, Jarman (1974) has argued that the species-specific selection of food and the utilization of vegetation have led to diversity in feeding styles between species that are related by body size, group size, habitat choice, and annual movement patterns over the home range. These characteristics also interact with antipredator behavior.

Several species are able to live in different kinds of habitats and may correspondingly adapt their social organization. For instance, the topi antelope inhabits woodlands and open plains. In the woodlands female groups averaged four members, their home range was $1.5\,km^2$, and the male territory was $1.2\,km^2$. On the plains the group size averaged 1098 animals with female territories of $184\,km^2$, whereas the male territories were extremely small (mean $0.17\,km^2$). In some places leks were found with clusters of territories that averaged $0.006\,km^2$ (Jarman and Jarman, 1979). In the Serengeti lion, a distinction can be made between residents, who are territorial during their whole lives and wait for prey animals to pass their home range, and nomads that follow the migrating herds. Most individuals keep to one type of life, but changes from one type to the other have also been observed (Schaller, 1972).

The Timing of Behavior

Optimization of behavior demands that, under the pressure of ultimate factors, proximate time markers are built into the behavioral organization to ensure that various functional types of activity—such as foraging, sleeping, migrating, mating, egg laying—are carried out at the most profitable time. Periodic environmental changes, such as a rise or drop in the ambient temperature or the onset or termination of a rainy season, may be selected as proximate factors for attaining this end.

Another possibility is the use of biological rhythms. It has been demonstrated in birds (Farner, 1967) and fish (Baggerman, 1972) that the changes in the length of the daily photoperiod, which have been selected as proximate time markers for controlling the annual reproductive cycle, are perceived by means of a circadian rhythm in the animals' sensitivity to light. Baggerman (1980) has presented evidence that in the stickleback an approximately annual rhythm determines that this circadian rhythm in light sensitivity exerts its effect only at the functionally correct time of the year.

Daan (1981) has surveyed our knowledge about the daily timing of functional types of activities by means of circadian rhythms. One example should suffice here. When chicks of the Brunnich's guillemot are about to leave the breeding ledges for the sea below at the age of three weeks, they concentrate their jumping activity in the period betwen 8 p.m. and midnight. During these hours predation from gulls is relatively low. Synchronization also reduces the risk of predation for each individual.

The Function and Content of Communicative Behavior

Social, sexual, and parent-young relations between animals are established and maintained through communication, that is, behavior that serves to adjust the behavior of group members to the benefit of the actor, and enables the actor to respond advantageously to the behavior of the others. Communication may, for instance, serve synchronous movements of a group, selection of a sexual partner, maintenance and adjustment of contacts between social and sexual partners or between partners and offspring, and may exhibit resource-holding potential or social status, and so on. In comparison with fighting, communicating is a cheap way to settle a dispute.

Although communication is often to mutual benefit to actor and reactor and to the functioning of the group, attempts to explain its evolution are best based, for the reasons of parsimony mentioned above, on selection acting on the sender of the signal. It is important to

observe this rule in considering what might be the exact content of messages transmitted by one animal to another. The following possibilities present themselves: (1) information on the identity (species, sex, individual) of the sender and on its general condition (age, reproductive state, health); (2) information about its individual capacities (strength, stamina, skill) to perform particular kinds of behavior and about its control of particular resources; (3) information about its transitory motivational state; and (4) transfer of acquired knowledge.

Function (1), which may serve the selection of the correct social or sexual partner or the mutual recognition of parents and young, was the first to be recognized. As a result, the concept social releaser was postulated (see above). Function (2) allows an assessment of qualities of the communicating animal. This could guide females when selecting a partner from among several competing males. It may also enable such males to compare each other's strength. For instance, instead of fighting, red deer stags may embark on a roaring contest in which each tries to increase its rate of roaring until one of them gives up. Roaring is exhausting, and the rate of performing this vocalization is likely to be a measure of strength (Clutton-Brock and Albon, 1979). However, greater strength may not be the only factor to underlie the power of an assessment display for overcoming an opponent. Resource holdings may also affect some of the parameters of such a display, for instance, by determining the persistence of singing in territorial birds.

The survival value for the individual of sending and receiving type (3) information is obvious in several situations, such as the signaling by a female of her receptive state, by a young animal of a hunger state, or by members of a foraging group of an alarm state. A well-known case of transfer of knowledge (4) is the dancing of honey bees by which information on nature and location of food sources or potential nest sites is passed from one individual to another (von Frisch, 1967). Transfer of type (4) is also basic to the development of culture.

The Strategy of Communication

In considering the function and evolution of communicative behavior, ethologists have long assumed rather gratuitously that honesty in the transfer of information about an animal's own motivational state and intentions would have great selective value. The use of display for comparing strength would be beneficial to the numerical strength of a species, because it would reduce the number of damaging fights. The introduction of game theory into the search for the most likely paths of evolution and the recognition that individuals are the most likely targets for selection to act upon have led to a reappraisal and refinement of ethological thinking about how communication is applied. In particular, a weighing of the values of different possible strategies for action might take place —in the ultimate sense during the evolution of behavior, as well as proximately in each decision of a communicating individual.

In game-theory models the pay-offs (cost or benefit) of different strategies, played against each other in every possible combination, are compared. Maynard Smith's 1979 models predict that if the opponents are equal in all aspects (symmetric contest) neither of the two opposite strategies—fight and display but retreat before hurt—is an evolutionarily stable strategy (ESS) that cannot be invaded by the other. Only a mixture of the two strategies, in a proportion depending on their respective pay-offs, is stable. The mixture can be achieved in a population of two types of individuals, each playing only one strategy, if the ratio between the two types corresponds to the ratio required for the mixed ESS. However, it can also be reached when all individuals are able to play both strategies, and do so in random order but in the proportion required.

If, by contrast, the opponents are unequal (asymmetric contest)—for instance, because one of them is stronger or is the holder of a resource so that they differ in the gain or loss to be expected—there is only one stable strategy, namely, using the asymmetry as a cue for deciding between persisting or retreating. In this model the provision must be made that the asymmetry is unambiguously perceptible to the contestants and not easy to gain. This raises the problem of how much and in what way ESSs are protected against cheating. Thus the possible advantage to an individual to lie about its motivational state or potentialities has to be taken into account.

According to Wallace (1973), when a mutant in a gene population would benefit from cheating, its frequency must increase and its relative advantage be reduced correspondingly. Elements of cheating that have indeed become general practice between conspecifics can be found in many communicative displays in which the body is apparently enlarged, for example, by the raising of fins, feathers, or hair, or by inflation. These are all cases of bluffing about size. In contrast, cheating in interspecific relations— such as the demonstration of warning coloration by harmless animals or luring devices in predatory fish—can only be ESSs so long as the model individuals largely outnumber the mimics. Under these circumstances protective mechanisms against being cheated have little chance to develop.

Cheating is counteracted by selection for responsiveness to communicative activities including phenomena that are tied physiologically to a motivational state, such as changes in blood circulation, respiration, or secretion. In the evolution of some displays selection does indeed seem to have taken place for movements or vocalizations that quantitatively reflect a relevant quality of an animal, for example, strength or endurance (the roaring of red deer: Clutton-Brock and Albon, 1979). Zahavi (1975, 1977) went still further in suggesting that such assessment displays would usually involve a handicap to the actor (e.g., antlers on a stag or the long tail of a peacock), and thus inform the reactor about the viability of a bearer that could survive despite such extra costs. Although many display movements and structures could be seen as handicaps, it is difficult to see how they could have evolved on the basis of this principle, or how this hypothesis could be tested (Maynard Smith, 1976b).

Maynard Smith and Parker (1976) have pointed out that it would be a bad strategy for an animal during a contest to convey information about the strength of its intention to attack, or to signal a high tendency to retreat before being seriously threatened. Such behavior would encourage cheating and thus reinforce the value of such messages. These and other authors (e.g., Caryl, 1979) suggest that the displays observed during contests in several studies and until now assumed to transfer information on the strength of their underlying agonistic tendencies—are in fact displays by which particular qualities of the sender and its resources are advertised. Only when an animal is about to surrender would it be good strategy to signal this intention, since that might keep its opponent from launching a damaging attack.

However, although the game-theory models are illuminating for improving the versatility and clearness of our thinking about the selective factors that may have been at work in an evolutionary process, the models are as yet too simple to match reality. For instance, it has been assumed in these models that the opponents do not know each other individually and thus are not taking into account experiences with an individual in earlier contests. This does not hold in many cases. Using Maynard Smith's methods, Van Rhijn and Vodegel (1980) have shown that giving away information about one's intention can be a good strategy when the opponents know each other individually.

Moreover, these models insufficiently take into account that the interchange of displays often does not lead to an immediate decision but serves a decision-making process. This process takes time during which the contestants assess each other's motivational state, which need not remain stable during that period. Displays expressing an intention at a particular moment in this period tend to induce in response displays that transfer information about the instantaneous motivation of the opponent. This information, together with the results of probes made at other times, could be used by the receiver to predict his chances against the sender. In this sense communication serves not only to manipulate an opponent to reveal information about its motivation state, but also to adjust that state, possibly to the advantage of the sender (Dawkins and Krebs, 1978; Hinde, 1981).

The Evolutionary Origin of Elementary Activities

Along which routes and by means of which processes may the behavior repertoire of newly evolving species have become extended? For anatomical structures, the method of comparing similar constructions within an individual and between different species has become classic. With the MAP as a unit suitable for comparison, Lorenz has introduced this comparative method into ethology and with it the use of the terms homology and analogy. Behavior patterns in the same or different kinds of animals are called *homologous* to express the opinion that they

have originated from the same ancestral form. For similarity in form or function as a result of similarity in selection pressure only (convergence), *analogous* is used. The term homology is useful to indicate the kind of relation that is thought to underlie resemblance between two morphological structures or behavior patterns.

Comparative studies aimed at disclosing the phylogeny of behavior patterns have concentrated mainly on communicative behavior, probably because the often bizarre appearance of visual signals need explanation more urgently than do activities that directly serve as implements for achieving some goal (e.g., picking up food, digging, nest building, cleaning).

For illustration I have chosen work on the visual displays of the duck family (Anatidae). A comparison of different activities in a single species has shown a close resemblance—suggesting homology—between ritualized communicative activities and particular implemental MAPs. For instance, in the blue-winged ducks (shovelers and teals) three displays—lateral dabbling, head digs, and up-ending—closely resemble the feeding patterns of these ducks (McKinney, 1970). Moreover, several duck displays show great similarity to comfort movements (e.g., body shake and belly preen and preening behind wing), as well as to two initial phases of locomotion (e.g., the bow and the stretch in preparation for jumping, Daanje, 1950). Turning the back of the head, a very common display in ducks, could be interpreted as a movement showing an intention of leaving (facing away).

I have earlier mentioned that the interactions between incompatible motivational systems occurring when conspecifics meet are thought to cause the phenomena of partial inhibition and ambivalence of modal action patterns and their orientation components (redirection) and displacement. These phenomena may account for the production of the precursors from which the above-mentioned signal activities could have been selected in evolution. Thus it is plausible that signal activities were phylogenetically derived from activities with direct implemental function. Since little research has been done on the equally important problem of the derivation of this group of activities, this issue remains speculative; nevertheless it deserves to be touched upon.

This discussion is restricted to vertebrates.

The most elementary behavioral interactions with the environment necessary to all representatives of this subphylum of the chordates are respiration, feeding, discharge of metabolic waste and gametes, and locomotion. The original chordates and their ancestors were filter feeders. In the subphyla of the tunicates and the lancelets, and in the jawless Agnata, the most primitive group of fish, suspended food and oxygen are taken up in the pharynx into which water is pumped through the mouth to be expelled through the gill slits. Locomotion occurs in these groups through undulating movements of the body. Contractions of the musculature of the abdominal body wall facilitate discharge.

Undulating body movements remained the basis for locomotion, even after extremities were developed. Extremities appeared in fish (the Agnata excepted) first as paired appendages, along with movable jaws. Through these developments the more passive filter feeding could be replaced by actively catching food. Thus a much wider range of organisms became potentially available as food, and foraging was no longer exclusively dependent on suspended matter. Food could also be collected in a greater diversity of locations, the more so since, with the appearance of the appendages, the possibilities to maneuver were improved. Although the jaws also became involved in the movement of respiration, separate action patterns evolved for respiratory and foraging functions. The difference in demands for the two functions went together with emancipation of the superimposed control mechanisms and the formation of a relatively independent feeding system. Incorporation in foraging behavior of movements of extremities has already occurred in some fishes (e.g., foward-beating movements of the pectoral fins for stirring up food). Some reptiles use their forelegs for digging up food, several carnivores for grasping prey.

Nonpredatory attack too is usually based on forward locomotion, ending in pushing the adversary and often damaging it with movements that are also used to take up food. For an attack mechanism not to endanger the attacker itself it requires that the attacker be able to keep it in check. Accordingly, attack is found to be increasingly inhibited by escape, the closer the opponent is approached. As a result, pure attack behavior is rarely realized. Considering

the weight of their survival value and their widespread distribution in the animal kingdom, mechanisms for escape must by phylogenetically old. At least two different types of escape behavior have been distinguished throughout the vertebrates: rapid moving away and freezing. The first type is based on locomotion away from the opponent; the other uses a static pattern such as posturing or crouching. In encounters both are found to interact with attack.

The manipulation of material in constructing some kind of nest is a type of implemental behavior that may have evolved from a conflict between agonistic tendencies. Nest digging in fish, and the collection and arrangement of nest material in gulls and terns have been observed to be stimulated by the near presence of a conspecific in a way suggestive of redirected aggression.

Another example of an implemental behavior pattern derived from the interaction of attack and withdrawal may be derived from fertilization in the three-spined stickleback. The fertilizating act consists of two components: a nest-building activity (creeping through the tunnel) and the actual ejaculation. A measurement of the level of the tendencies either to attack or to swim away from the female toward the nest (when a confined male or female is presented, respectively), makes it seem plausible that creeping through is caused by disinhibition of nest-building behavior when the two opposite tendencies are present and in equal strength. Thus in this case an activity caused by displacement serves as a vehicle for fertilization (Sevenster-Bol, 1962).

Besides the tendency to attack (or move toward) and the tendency to escape (or move away), a third tendency that urges an animal to remain is likely to play an important role in the formation of signal activities (Blurton Jones, 1968; Baerends, 1975). For activities with a direct implemental function this possibility has not yet been considered.

There are often few differences between signal activities used to threaten an opponent, court a female, or entice young. Tinbergen (1940) originally suggested that a display developed for one of these functions had invaded another functional context through 'sparking over'. However, it is more parsimonious to assume, in the light of the conflict hypothesis that an equal balance between aggression, escape, and staying put may occur in different contexts and thus lead to the same activity. The internal factor for sexual or parental behavior could then be taken to have a stabilizing influence on this balance, as suggested by Kruijt (1964). Diversity of homologous displays among related species (radiation) can be brought about by specific differences in the average motivational balance between the incompatible tendencies (birds: Hinde, 1956b, 1959; fish: Baerends, 1975). Ecological factors are likely to have selected for such motivational threshold differences. McKinney (1970, 1975) found the various displays that occur in different duck species to be related to their differences in the social system, which are themselvs adapted to variations in ecology. He is of the opinion that the blue-winged ducks have specialized in feeding while swimming, using the dabbling and dipping techniques that are reflected in their courtship. These species use localized rich food sources which a pair monopolizes by claiming a discrete territory. The territory is continuously defended by the male who forms a strong and lasting bond with a female. The displays they select are functional in establishing and maintaining the monogamous bond. In contrast, the social system of the pintail and the mallard is based on ranging over a much wider area and using it more opportunistically. Although these

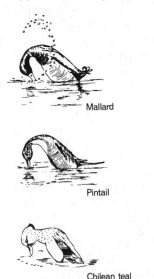

Figure 14.21. The grunt-whistle display in the mallard (*Anas platyrhynchos*), the pintail (*Anas acuta*), and the Chilean teal (*Nettion flavirostra*) (after Lorenz, 1941).

ducks also form pairs, the males in addition spend part of their time trying to copulate with other females. Movements have been selected in their courtship that are suitable for attracting the attention of females, such as the grunt whistle, pictured in Figure 14.21 for three different species.

Some authors have suggested that reflexes provide a source from which signal activities could have developed. Andrew (1963) maintains that facial expressions, such as greeting displays and grinning in primates, are more likely to have derived from protective reflexes than from conflicts between motivational systems. The position of hairs and feathers is important in many displays (Morris, 1956b). Autonomic responses are also involved in scent signals, color changes, vocalizations, inflation displays, and territorial marking through urination and defecation.

CONCLUDING REMARKS

The impulse of evolution is the increase in fitness (i.e., number of viable offspring) gained by successfully invading hitherto unexploited niches. Since every niche demands another set of adaptations, plural forms are promoted in anatomical features, in physiological mechanisms, and in the structure of behavioral organizations. Pluralism is found not only in the ways in which a particular function is fulfilled in different species, but also in the number of functions that can be distinguished. Increased complication in the way of life—for instance in the formation of social systems—leads to differentiation of new ecological niches. I have tried to give insights into the nature and variety of functions that evolution has managed to implement, and into the extension of the assortment of functions when higher taxonomic groups are compared with lower ones, that is to say phylogenetically older with younger forms.

To understand how the behavioral organization has managed to cope with this increasing demand for complexity, we need to know about the elements of the behavioral organization and its construction and about the nature of the selective forces acting on this causal substrate through the phenotype. I have dealt with the properties of this substrate and have tried to indicate how functions distinguished in the life history of an animal can be translated into selective forces. In the course of evolution these forces will modify the existing substrate of afferent and efferent components and their possible interaction. I have then discussed some ways in which this could be achieved. Thus, the selective forces compose the behavioral organization of a species by selecting and assembling the various elements available in an optimally adapted way. In addition, they may stimulate the development of new types of elements or construction principles.

A separate section dealt with the principles through which the behavioral organization develops in the individual. The genes selected in the course of evolution maintain the species specificity of behavior by controlling ontogeny. This guarantees harmony between anatomy, physiology, and behavior, and their adaptation to the ecological niche. The ontogenetic proceedings comprise processes usually described as maturation, but learning processes of various kinds are also amply utilized in building up the behavioral organization of the individual. To ensure that the appropriate information is acquired in these learning processes, learning is often confined to genetically controlled programs that determine when and what is learned and how stable the engram is going to be.

Learning may be of great value for an individual to adapt quickly to short-term changes in its environment. However, since developmental processes are often superimposed on each other during ontogeny, flexiblity through learning must be kept in check. Great flexibility in the development of individual behavior through learning processes that are not rigidly controlled can be expected only after much of the behavioral organization has been realized, with its species specificity thus secured.

The higher a species stands on the phylogenetic scale, the more we expect it to use learning processes in the ontogeny of its behavioral organization. Learning through tradition, in particular, shows a steep increase in the highest mammals and culminates in man. The possibility of accumulating knowledge this way, greatly augmented by the capacity for articulate speech and the invention of writing, can account for much of the unique achievements of our species. Nevertheless, there must be a danger in the passing on from one generation to the next of information whose value has not been as sharply checked as occurs in genetic selection. Since culture too is made possible by characteristics of the specific behavioral organization, one wonders whether and how in species possessing this faculty the behavioral organization provides for ways to prevent the development of traits of cultural behavior that would be incompatible with important aspects of the species-specific nature. This question appears particularly relevant for the survival of our own species.

ACKNOWLEDGMENTS

I gratefully acknowledge the assistance of Dr. Kathy Carlstead in writing this chapter. I am also indebted to Dr. Gethin Thomas for his comments after critically reading the manuscript.

REFERENCES

Alcock, J. (1975). *Animal behavior*. Sunderland, MA: Sinauer.

Andrew, R.J. (1956). Some remarks on behaviour in conflict situations, with special reference to *Emberiza sp. British Journal of Animal Behaviour, 4*, 41–45.

Andrew, R.J. (1963). The origin and evolution of the calls and facial expressions of the primates. *Behaviour, 20*, 1–109.

Baerends, G.P. (1941). Fortpflanzungsverhalten und Orientierung der Grabwespe *Ammophila campestris* Jur. *Tijdschrift voor Entomologie, 84*, 68–275.

Baerends, G.P. (1950). Specializations in organs and movements with a releasing function. In *Symposia Society of Experimental Biology, 4*, 337–360.

Baerends, G.P. (1975). An evaluation of the conflict hypothesis as an explanatory principle for the evolution of displays. In G.P. Baerends, C. Beer, & A. Manning (Eds.), *Function and evolution of behaviour*. Oxford: Clarendon Press.

Baerends, G.P. (1976). The functional organization of behaviour. *Animal Behaviour, 24*, 726–738.

Baerends, G.P. (1985). Do the dummy experiments with sticklebacks support the IRM-concept? *Behaviour, 93*, 258–277.

Baerends, G.P., Brouwer, R., & Waterbolk, H.T. (1955). Ethological studies on *Lebistes reticulatus* (Peters). I. An analysis of the male courtship pattern. *Behaviour, 8*, 249–334.

Baerends, G.P., & Drent, R.H. (Eds.) (1970). The

herring gull and its egg. Part I. *Behaviour, Suppl. 17*, 312 pp.

Baerends, G.P., & Drent, R.H. (Eds.) (1982). The herring gull and its egg. Part II. *Behaviour, 82*, 417 pp.

Baerends-van Roon, J.M., & Baerends, G.P. (1979). The morphogenesis of the behaviour of the domestic cat. *Verhandelingen Koninklijke Nederlandse Akademie van Wetenschappen*, Afd. Natuurkunde, *72*, 116 pp.

Baggerman, B. (1972). Photoperiodic responses in the stickleback and their control by a daily rhythm of photosensitivity. *General and Comparative Endocrinology, Suppl. 3*, 466–476.

Baggerman, B. (1980). Photoperiodic and endogenous control of the annual reproductive cycle in teleost fishes. In M.A. Ali (Ed.), *Environmental physiology of fishes*. New York: Plenum Press.

Barash, D.P. (1977). Sociobiology and behavior. New York: Elsevier.

Barlow, G.W. (1968). Ethological units of behavior. In David Ingle (Ed.), *The central nervous system and fish behavior*. pp. 217–232. Chicago: University of Chicago Press.

Barrett, P., & Bateson, P.P.G. (1978). The development of play in cats. *Behaviour, 66*, 106–120.

Bateson, P.P.G. (1966). The characteristics and context of imprinting. *Biological Reviews, 41*, 177–220.

Bateson, P.P.G. (1978). Early experience and sexual preferences. In J.B. Hutchison (Ed.), *Biological determinants of sexual behaviour*. pp. 29–53. New York: Wiley.

Bateson, P.P.G. (1979). How do densitive periods arise and what are they for? *Animal Behaviour, 27*, 470–486.

Bateson, P.P.G. (1980). Optimal outbreeding and the development of sexual preferences in Japanese quail. *Zeitschrift für Tierpsychologie, 53*, 231–244.

Beer, G.R. de (1940). *Embryos and ancestors*. Oxford: Clarendon Press.

Bekoff, M. (1974). Social play and play-soliciting by infant canids. *American Zoologist, 14*, 323–340.

Belovsky, G.E. (1978). Diet optimization in a generalist herbivore: The moose. *Theoretical Population Biology, 14*, 105–134.

Bertram, B.C.R. (1978). Living in groups: Predators and prey. In J.R. Krebs & N.B. Davies (Eds.), *Behavioral ecology, an evolutionary approach*, pp. 64–96. Oxford: Blackwell.

Blakemore, C. (1973). Environmental constraints on development in the visual system. In R.A. Hinde & J. Stevenson-Hinde (Eds.), *Constraints on learning* (pp. 51–73). London: Academic Press.

Blurton Jones, N.G. (1960). Experiments on the causation of the threat postures of Canada geese. Wildfowl Trust, 11th Annual Report, 1958–59. (pp. 46–52). Slimbridge, UK.

Blurton Jones, N.G. (1968). Observations and experiments on causation of threat displays of the great tit. *Animal Behaviour Monographs, 1*, 75–158.

Bossema, I., & Kruijt, J.P. (1982). Male activity and female mate acceptance in the mallard (*Anas platyrhynchos*). *Behaviour, 79*, 313–324.

Bowlby, J. (1980). By ethology out of psycho-analysis: An experiment in interbreeding. *Animal Behaviour, 28*, 649–656.

Brown, J.L. (1975). *The evolution of behavior*. New York: Norton.

Brown, R.E., & McFarland, D.J. (1979). Interaction of hunger and sexual motivation in the male rat: A time-sharing approach. *Animal Behaviour 27*, 887–889.

Bruner, J.S., Jolly, A., & Sylva, K. (Eds.), *Play—Its role in development and evolution*. New York: Basic Books.

Carmichael, L. (1926). The development of behavior in vertebrates experimentally removed from the influence of external stimulation. *Psychological Reviews, 33*, 51–58.

Carmichael, L. (1927). A further study of the development of behavior in vertebrates experimentally removed from the influence of external stimulation. *Psychological Reviews, 34*, 34–47.

Caryl, P. (1979). Communication by agonistic displays: What can games theory contribute to ethology? *Behaviour, 68*, 136–169.

Cate, C. ten (1982). Behavioural differences between zebrafinch and Bengalese finch (foster) parents raising zebrafinch offspring. *Behaviour, 81*, 152–172.

Chalmers, N. (1979). *Social behaviour in primates*. London: Arnold.

Clutton-Brock, T.H., & Albon, S.D. (1979). The roaring of red deer and the evolution of honest advertisement. *Behaviour, 69*, 145–170.

Clutton-Brock, T.H., Albon, S.D., Gibson, R.M., & Guinness, F.E. (1979). The logical stag: Adaptive aspects of fighting in red deer (*Cervus elaphus* L.). *Animal Behaviour, 27*, 211–225.

Colgan, P.W. (1978). Quantitative ethology. New York: Wiley.

Craig, W. (1918). Appetites and aversions as constituents of instincts. *Biological Bulletin* (Woods Hole), *34*, 91–107.

Crook, J.H. (1964). The evolution of social organization and visual communication in the weaver birds (*Ploceinae*). *Behaviour, Suppl. 10*, 178 pp.

Daan, S. (1981). Adaptive daily strategies in behavior. In J. Aschoff (Ed.), *Handbook of behavioral neurobiology*. (pp. 275–298). New York: Plenum Press.

Daanje, A. (1950). On locomotory movements in birds

and the intention movements derived from them. *Behaviour, 3,* 48–98.

Daly, M., & Wilson, M. (1978). *Sex, evolution and behavior.* North Scituate, MA: Duxbury Press.

Dawkins, R. (1976a). Hierarchical organization: A candidate principle for ethology. In P.P.G. Bateson & R.A. Hinde (Eds.), *Growing points in ethology.* (pp. 7–54). Cambridge: Cambridge University Press.

Dawkins, R. (1976b). *The selfish gene.* New York: Oxford University Press.

Dawkins, R., & Krebs, J.R. (1978). Animal signals: Information or manipulation? In J.R. Krebs & N.B. Davies (Eds.), *Behavioral ecology.* (pp. 282–309). Oxford: Blackwell.

Douglas-Hamilton, I., & Douglas-Hamilton, O. (1975). *Among the elephants.* London: Collins & Harvill.

Drent, R.H. (1980). Goose flocks and food exploitation: How to have your cake and eat it. *Proceedings, 18th International Ornithological Congress,* (pp. 800–806). Berlin.

Drickamer, L.C., & Vessey, S.H. (1982). *Animal behavior: Concepts, processes and methods.* Boston: Grant.

Eibl-Eibesfeldt, I. (1951). Beobachtungen zur Fortpflanzungsbiologie und Jugendentwicklung des Eichhörnchens (*Scirurus vulgaris* L.). *Zeitschrift für Tierpsychologie, 8,* 370–400.

Eibl-Eibesfeldt, I. (1956). Ueber die ontogenetische Entwicklung der Technik des Nüsseöffnens vom Eichhörnchen (*Sciurus vulgaris* L.). *Zeitschrift für Säugetierkunde, 21,* 132–134.

Eibl-Eibesfeldt, I. (1975). *Ethology, the biology of behavior.* New York: Holt, Rinehart & Winston.

Emlen, S.T. (1978). The evolution of co-operative breeding in birds. In J.R. Krebs & N.B. Davies (Eds.), *Behavioral ecology.* (pp. 245–281). Oxford: Blackwell.

Emmerton, J., & Delius, J.D. (1980). Wavelength discrimination in the 'visible' and ultraviolet spectrum by pigeons. *Journal of Comparative Physiology, 141,* 47–52.

Etkin, W. (1967). *Social behavior from fish to man.* Chicago: University of Chicago Press.

Farner, D.S. (1967). The control of avian reproductive cycles. *Proceedings, 14th International Ornithological Congress.* (pp. 107–113). Oxford.

Fentress, J.C. (1972). Development and patterning of movement sequences in inbred mice. In J.A. Kiger, Jr. (Ed.), *The biology of behavior.* (pp. 83–131). Corvallis: Oregon State University Press.

Fisher, R.A. (1930). *The genetical theory of natural selection.* Oxford: Clarendon Press.

Fitzsimons, J.T.. & Le Magnen, J. (1969). Eating as a regulatory control of drinking in the rat. *Journal of Comparative and Physiological Psychology, 68,* 308–314.

Frisch, K. von. (1926). Vergleichende Physiologie des Geruchs- und Geschmacksinnes. In *Handbuch der Normalen und Pathologischen Physiologie, 11,* (pp. 203–240). Berlin: Springer.

Frisch, K. von. (1936). Ueber den Gehörsinn der Fische. *Biological Reviews, 11,* 210–246.

Frisch, K. von. (1950). *Bees, their vision, chemical senses and language.* Ithaca: Cornell University Press.

Frisch, K. von. (1967). *The dance language and orientation of bees.* Cambridge, MA: Harvard University Press.

Gardner, B.T., & Wallach, L. (1965). Shapes of figures identified as a baby's head. *Perceptual and Motor Skills, 20,* 135–142.

Gouzoules, H. (1975). Maternal rank and early social interactions of infant stumptail macaques, *Macaca arctoides. Primates, 16,* 405–418.

Griffin, D.R. (1976). *The question of awareness.* New York: Rockefeller University Press.

Grohman, J. (1939). Modifikation oder Funktionsreifung. *Zeitschrift für Tierpsychologie, 2,* 132–144.

Gruber, S.H. (1979). Mechanisms of color vision: An ethologist's primer. In E.H. Burt, Jr. (Ed.), *The behavioral significance of color.* (pp. 183–236). New York: Garland.

Hailman, J.P. (1967). The ontogeny of an instinct. *Behaviour, Suppl. 15,* 159 pp.

Hall, K.R.L., & DeVore, I. (1965). Baboon social behavior. In I. DeVore (Ed.), *Primate behavior.* (pp. 53–110). New York: Holt.

Hamilton, W.D. (1963). The evolution of altruistic behaviour. *American Naturalist, 97,* 354–356.

Hanson, H.M. (1957). Discrimination training effect on stimulus generalization gradient for spectrum stimuli. *Science, 125,* 888–889.

Harlow, H.F. (1959). Love in infant monkeys. *Scientific American, 200, 6,* 68–74.

Harlow, H.F., & Harlow, M.K. (1962). Social deprivation in monkeys. *Scientific American, 207, 5,* 136–146.

Hassenstein, B. (1971). *Information and control in the living organism.* London: Chapman & Hall.

Hassenstein, B. (1980). *Instinkt, Lernen, Spielen, Einsicht.* München: Piper.

Heiligenberg, W. (1974). Processes governing behavioral states of readiness. *Advances in the Study of Behavior, 5,* 173–200.

Herrnstein, R.J., & Loveland, D.H. (1975). Maximizing and matching on concurrent ratio schedules. *Journal for the Experimental Analysis of Behavior, 24,* 107–116.

Hess, E.H. (1958). Imprinting in animals. *Scientific*

American, 198, 3, 81–88.

Hinde, R.A. (1953). Appetitive behaviour, consummatory act, and the hierarchical organisation of behaviour—with special reference to the great tit (*Parus major*). *Behaviour, 5,* 189–224.

Hinde, R.A. (1956a). Ethological models and the concept of 'drive'. *British Journal for the Philosophy of Science, 6,* 321–331.

Hinde, R.A. (1956b). A comparative study of the courtship of certain finches (*Fringillidae*). *Ibis, 98,* 1–23.

Hinde, R.A. (1959). Behaviour and speciation in birds and lower vertebrates. *Biological Reviews, 34,* 85–128.

Hinde, R.A. (1960). The interaction of short-term and long-term incremental and decremental effects. *Proceedings of the Royal Society (Lond.), B153,* 398–420.

Hinde, R.A. (1965). Interaction of internal and external factors in integration of canary reproduction. In F.A. Beach (Ed.), *Sex and behavior.* (pp. 381–415). London: Wiley.

Hinde, R.A. (1970a). *Animal behaviour, A synthesis of ethology and comparative psychology.* (2nd ed.). New York: McGraw-Hill.

Hinde, R.A. (1970b). Behavioural habituation. In G. Horn and R.A. Hinde (Eds.), *Short-term changes in neural activity and behaviour.* (pp. 1–40). Cambridge: Cambridge University Press.

Hinde, R.A. (1974). Biological bases of human social behaviour. London: McGraw-Hill.

Hinde, R.A. (1981). Animal signals: Ethological and games-theory approaches are not incompatible. *Animal Behaviour, 29,* 535–542.

Hinde, R.A., & Fisher, J. (1952). Further observations on the opening of milk bottles by birds. *British Birds, 44,* 393–396.

Hinde, R.A., & Stevenson, J.G. (1969). Sequences of behavior. *Advances in the Study of Behavior, 2,* 267–296.

Hobson, E.S. (1978). Aggregating as a defense against predators in aquatic and terrestrial environments. In E.S. Reese & F.J. Lighter (Eds.), *Contrasts in behavior.* (pp. 219–234). New York: Wiley.

Hogan, J.A., Kruijt, J.P., & Frijlink, J.H. (1975). 'Supernormality' in a learned situation. *Zeitschrift für Tierpsychologie, 38,* 212–218.

Holst, E. von. (1937). Vom Wesen der Ordnung im Zentralnervensystem. *Naturwissenschaften, 25,* 625–631; 641–647.

Holzapfel, M. (1940). Triebbedingte Ruhezustände als Ziel von Appetenzhandlungen. *Naturwissenschaften, 28,* 273–280.

Hooff, J.A.R.A.M. van. (1973). A structural analysis of the social behaviour of a semi-captive group of chimpanzees. In M. von Cranach & I. Vine (Eds.), *Expressive movement and non-verbal communication.* (pp. 75–162). London: Academic Press.

Hooff, J.A.R.A.M. van. (1982). Categories and sequences of behavior: Methods of description and analysis. In *Handbook of methods in nonverbal behavior research.* (pp. 362–439). Cambridge: Cambridge University Press.

Hückstedt, B. (1965). Experimentelle Untersuchungen zum 'Kindchenschema'. *Zeitschrift für experimentelle und angewandte Psychologie, 12,* 421–450.

Humphrey, T. (1969). Postnatal repetition of human prenatal activity sequences with some suggestions of their neuro-anatomical basis. In R.J. Robinson (Ed.), *Brain and early behavior.* (pp. ˅43–84). London: Academic Press.

Huntingford, F. (1984). *The study of animal behaviour.* London, New York: Chapman and Hall.

Iersel, J.J.A. van. (1953). An analysis of the parental behaviour of the male three-spined stickleback (*Gasterosteus aculeatus* L.). *Behaviour, Suppl. 3,* 159 pp.

Immelmann, K. (1972). The influence of early experience upon the development of social behaviour in estrildine finches. *Proceedings, 15th International Ornithological Congress.* (pp. 316–338). The Hague.

Ingold, P. (1973). Zur lautlichen Beziehung des Elters zu seinem Küken bei Tordalken (*Alca torda*). *Behaviour, 45,* 154–190.

Jarman, P.J. (1974). The social organisation of antelope in relation to their ecology. *Behaviour, 48,* 215–267.

Jarman, P.J., & Jarman, M.V. (1979). The dynamics of ungulate social organization. In A.R.E. Sinclair & M.N. Griffith (Eds.), *Serengeti, dynamics of an ecosystem.* (pp. 130–163). Chicago: University of Chicago Press.

Kawai, M. (1965). Newly acquired pre-cultural behavior of the natural troop of Japanese monkeys of Kishima islet. *Primates, 6,* 1–30.

Klingel, H. (1974). A comparison of the social behaviour of *Equidae*. In V. Geist and F. Walther (Eds.), *The behaviour of ungulates and its relation to management.* (pp. 124–132). Switzerland: Morges, IUCN.

Kortlandt, A. (1940b). Eine Uebersicht der angeborenen Verhaltensweisen des mittel-europäischen Kormorans (*Phalacrocorax carbosinensis* Shaw & Nodd), ihre Funktion, ontogenetische Entwicklung und phylogenetische Herkunft. *Archives néerlandaises de Zoologie, 4,* 401–442.

Kortlandt, A. (1940a). Wechselwirkungen zwischen Instinkten. *Archives néerlandaises de Zoologie, 4,* 442–520.

Kortlandt, A. (1955). Aspects and prospects of the content of instinct (Vicissitudes of the hierarchy theory). *Archives néerlandaises de Zoologie, 13,* 196–229.

Krebs, J.R., & Davies, N.B. (1978). *Behavioural ecology, an evolutionary approach.* Oxford: Blackwell.

Krebs, J.R., & Davies, N.B. (1981). *An introduction to behavoural ecology.* Oxford: Blackwell.

Kruijt, J.P. (1964). Ontogeny of social behaviour in Burmese red jungle-fowl. *Behaviour, Suppl. 12,* 201 pp.

Kruijt, J.P. (1971). Early experience and development of social behaviour in junglefowl. *Psychiatria, Neurologia Neurochirurgia, 74,* 7–20.

Kruijt, J.P. & Baerends, G.P. (1982). The influence of experience with respect to incubation responses. In G.P. Baerends & R.H. Drent (Eds.), *Behaviour, 82,* 247–275.

Kruijt, J.P., Bossema, I., & Lammers, G.J. (1982). Effects of early experience and male activity on mate choice in mallard females (*Anas platyrhynchos*). *Behaviour, 80,* 32–43.

Kummer, H. (1971). *Primate societies; group techniques of ecological adaptations.* Chicago: Aldine-Atherton.

Lack, D. (1966). *Population studies in birds.* Oxford: Clarendon Press.

Le Boeuf, B.J. (1972). Sexual behaviour in the northern elephant seal, *Mirounga angustirostus. Behaviour, 41,* 1–26.

Lehrman, D.S. (1953). A critique of Konrad Lorenz's theory of instinctive behavior. *Quarterly Review of Biology, 28,* 337–363.

Leyhausen, P. (1967). The biology of expression and impression. In K. Lorenz & P. Leyhausen (Eds.), *Motivation of human and animal behavior* (Behavioral Science Series). (pp. 272–380). New York: Van Nostrand Reinhold.

Loiselle, P.V., & Barlow, G.W. (1978). Do fishes lek like birds? In E.S. Reese & F.J. Lighter (Eds.), *Contrasts in behavior.* (pp. 31–75). New York: Wiley.

Loizos, C. (1966). Play in mammals. *Symposia of the Zoological Society of London, 18,* 1–10.

Lorenz, K. (1935). Der Kumpan in der Umwelt des Vogels. Translation in K. Lorenz, 1970, Vol. I (q.v.).

Lorenz, K. (1937). Ueber den Begriff der Instinkthandlung. Translation in K. Lorenz, 1970, Vol. I (q.v.).

Lorenz, K. (1941). Vergleichende Bewegungsstudien an Anatinen. Translation in K. Lorenz, 1971, Vol. II (q.v.).

Lorenz, K. (1943). Die angeborenen Formen möglicher Erfahrung. *Zeitschrift für Tierpsychologie, 5,* 235–409.

Lorenz, K. (1950). The comparative method in studying innate behaviour patterns. *Symposia, Society for Experimental Biology, 4,* 221–268.

Lorenz, K. (1952). *King Solomon's ring; new light on animal ways.* London: Methuen.

Lorenz, K. (1965). *Evolution and modification of behavior.* Chicago: University of Chicago Press.

Lorenz, K. (1970–1971). *Studies in animal and human behaviour.* (R. Martin, Trans.). Vol. I, 1970; Vol. II, 1971. Cambridge, MA: Harvard University Press.

Lorenz, K. (1978). *Vergleichende Verhaltensforschung.* Vienna: Springer.

Lorenz, K. (1979). *The year of the greylag goose.* London: Eyre Methuen.

Lorenz, K., & Tinbergen, N. (1938). Taxis und Instinkthandlung in der Eirollbewegung der Graugans I. Translation in K. Lorenz, 1979, Vol. I. (q.v.).

MacArthur, R.H., & Pianka, E.R. (1966). On the optimal use of a patchy environment. *American Naturalist, 100,* 603–609.

Magnus, D.B.E. (1958). Experimental analysis of some 'overoptimal' sign-stimuli in the mating behaviour of the fritillary butterfly *Argynnis paphia* L. *Proceedings, 10th International Congress of Entomology, 1956, 2,* 405–418.

Manning, A. (1979). *An introduction to animal behaviour* 3rd ed. London: Arnold.

Marler, P.R., & Hamilton, W.J., III. (1966). *Mechanisms of animal behavior.* New York: Wiley.

Marler, P.R., & Peters, S. (1977). Selective vocal learning in a sparrow. *Science, 198,* 519–521.

Marler, P., & Tamura, M. (1964). Cultural transmitted patterns of vocal behavior in sparrows. *Science, 146,* 1483–1486.

Maynard Smith, J. (1971). What use is sex? *Journal of Theoretical Biology, 30,* 319–335.

Maynard Smith, J. (1976a). Group selection. *Quarterly Review of Biology, 51,* 277–283.

Maynard Smith, J. (1976b). Evolution and the theory of games. *American Scientist, 64,* 41–45.

Maynard Smith, J. (1979). Game theory and the evolution of behaviour. *Proceedings, Royal Society* (Lond.), *B205,* 475–488.

Maynard Smith, J., & Parker, G.A. (1976). The logic of asymmetric contests. *Animal Behaviour, 24,* 159–175.

Mayr, E. (1974). Behavior programs and evolutionary strategies. *American Scientist, 62,* 650–659.

McDougall, W. (1923). *An outline of psychology,* London: Methuen.

McFarland, D.J. (1965). Hunger, thirst and displacement pecking in the Barbary dove. *Animal Behaviour, 13,* 293–300.

McFarland, D.J. (1971). *Feedback mechanisms in animal behaviour.* London: Academic Press.

McFarland, D.J. (1974a). Motivational control systems analysis. In D.J. McFarland (Ed.), *Experi-*

mental investigation of motivation state. (pp. 251–282). London: Academic Press.

McFarland, D.J. (1974b). Time sharing as a behavioral phenomenon. *Advances in the Study of Behavior, 5,* 201–225.

McFarland, D.J. (1985). *Animal behaviour.* London: Pitman.

McFarland, D.J., & Houston, A.I. (1981). *Quantitative ethology. The state space approach.* Boston: Pitman.

McFarland, D.J., & Sibly, R.M. (1975). The behavioural final common path. *Philosophical Transactions, Royal Society* (Lond.), *B270,* 265–293.

McKinney, F. (1970). Displays of four species of blue-winged ducks. *Living Bird, 9,* 29–64.

McKinney, F. (1975). The evolution of duck displays. In G.P. Baerends, C. Beer, & A. Manning (Eds.), *Function and evolution of behaviour.* (pp. 331–357). Oxford: Clarendon Press.

Mech, L.D. (1970). *The wolf: The ecology and behavior of an endangered species.* New York: Natural History Press.

Mittelstaedt, H. (1954). Regelung und Steuerung bei der Orientierung der Lebewesen. *Regelungstechnik, 2,* 226–235.

Moyadi, D. (1967). Differences in social behavior among Japanese macaque troops. In D. Starck, R. Schneider & H.J. Kühm (Eds.), *Neue Ergebnisse der Primatologie.* Stuttgart: Fisher.

Morris, D. (1956a). The function and causation of courtship ceremonies. In *L'instinct dans le comportement des animaux et de l'homme.* (pp. 261–286). Paris: Masson.

Morris, D. (1956b). The feature postures of birds and the problem of the origin of social signals. *Behaviour, 9,* 75–113.

Morris, D. (1957). 'Typical intensity' and its relation to the problem of ritualisation. *Behaviour, 11,* 1–12.

Morris, D. (1977). *Manwatching.* London: Cape.

Nottebohm, F. (1969). The critical period for song learning. *Ibis, 111,* 386–387.

Oriens, G.H. (1969). On the evolution of mating systems in birds and mammals. *American Naturalist, 103,* 589–603.

Oring, L.W. (1981). Avian mating systems. In D.S. Farner & J.R. King (Eds.), *Avian biology,* Vol. 6. London: Academic Press.

Parker, G.A., Baker, R.R., & Smith, V.G.F. (1972). The origin and evolution of gamete dimorphism and the male-female phenomenon. *Journal of Theoretical Biology, 36,* 529–553.

Pianka, E.R., & Parker, W.S. (1975). Age-specific reproductive tactics. *American Naturalist, 109,* 453–464.

Plooy, F.X. (1983). The behavioural development of free-living chimpanzee babies and infants. Norwood, NJ: Ablex.

Prechtl, H.F.R. (1953). Zur Physiologie der angeborenen auslösenden Mechanismen. I. Quantitative Untersuchungen über die Sperrbewegung junger Singvögel. *Behaviour, 1,* 32–50.

Prechtl, H.F.R. (1965). Problems of behavioral studies in the newborn infant. *Advances in the Study of Behavior, 1,* 75–98.

Prechtl, H.F.R., & Schleidt, W.M. (1950). Auslösende und steuernde Mechanismen des Saugaktes I. *Zeitschrift für vergleichende Physiologie, 32,* 257–262.

Prechtl, H.F.R., & Schleidt, W.M. (1951). Auslösende und Steuernde Mechanismen des Saugaktes II. *Zeitschrift für vergleichende Physiologie, 33,* 53–62.

Rasa, O.A.E. (1971). Appetence for aggression in juvenile damsel fish. *Zeitschrift für Tierpsychologie, Suppl. 7,* 7–67.

Reyer, H.-U. (1980). Flexible helper structure as an ecological adaptation in the pied kingfisher, *Ceryle rudis rudis* L. *Behavioural and Ecological Sociobiology, 6,* 219–227.

Rhijn, J.G. van. (1973). Behavioural dimorphism in male Ruff (*Philomachus pugnax*), *Behaviour, 47,* 153–229.

Rhijn, J.G. van, & Vodegel, R. (1980). Being honest about one's intentions: An evolutionary stable strategy for animal conflicts. *Journal of Theoretical Biology, 85,* 623–641.

Robertson, D.R., & Hoffmann, S.G. (1977). The roles of female mate choice and predation in the mating systems of some tropical labroid fishes. *Zeitschrift für Tierpsychologie, 45,* 298–320.

Rood, J.P. (1978). Dwarf mongoose helpers at the den. *Zeitschrift für Tierpsychologie, 48,* 277–287.

Rowell, C.H.F. (1961). Displacement grooming in the chaffinch. *Animal Behaviour, 9,* 38–63.

Rowell, T.E. (1974). The concept of social dominance. *Behavioural Biology, 11,* 131–154.

Royama, T. (1970). Factors governing the hunting behaviour and the selection of food by the great tit (*Parus major* L.,). *Journal of Animal Ecology, 30,* 619–668.

Ruiter, L. de (1963). The physiology of vertebrate feeding behaviour: Towards a synthesis of the ethological and physiological approaches to problems of behaviour. *Zeitschrift für Tierpsychologie, 20,* 498–516.

Schaller, G.B. (1972). *The Serengeti lion.* Chicago: University of Chicago Press.

Schleidt, W.M. (1961). Reaktionen von Truthühnern auf fliegende Raubvögel und Versuche zur Analyse ihrer AAM's. *Zeitschrift für Tierpsychologie, 18,* 435–560.

Schleidt, W.M. (1962). Die historische Entwicklung

der Begriffe 'Angeborenes auslösendes Schema' und 'Angeborener Auslösemechanismus' in der Ethologie. *Zeitschrift für Tierpsychologie, 19,* 697–722.

Schmidt, W. (1957). Attrappenversuche zur Analyse des Lachens. *Psychologische Beiträge, 3,* 223–264.

Schutz, F. (1965). Sexuelle Prägung bei Anatiden. *Zeitschrift für Tierpsychologie, 22,* 50–103.

Schutz, F. (1971). Prägung des Sexualverhaltens von Enten und Gänsen durch Sozialeindrücke während der Jugendphase. *Journal of Neuro-Visceral Relations, Suppl. 10,* 339–357.

Seitz, A. (1940). Die Paarbildung bei einigen Cichliden I. *Astatotilapia strigigena* Pfeffer. *Zeitschrift für Tierpsychologie, 4,* 40–84.

Sevenster, P. (1961). A causal analysis of displacement activity (fanning in *Gasterosteus aculeatus* L.). *Behaviour, Suppl. 9.* 170 pp.

Sevenster-Bol, A.C.A. (1962). On the causation of drive reduction after a consummatory act (*Gasterosteus aculeatus* L.). *Archives néerlandaises de Zoologie, 15,* 175–236.

Seyfarth, R.M. (1977). A model of social grooming among adult female monkeys. *Journal of Theoretical Biology, 65,* 671–698.

Sparks, J. (1967). Allogrooming in primates: A review. In D. Morris (Ed.), *Primate ethology.* (pp. 148–175). London: Weidenfeld and Nicholson.

Staddon, J.E.R. (1980). Optimality analyses of operant behaviour and their relation to optimal foraging. In J.E.R. Staddon (Ed.), *Limits to action. The allocation of individual behavior.* (pp. 101–141). London: Academic Press.

Stevenson, J.G. (1969). Song as reinforcer. In R.A. Hinde (Ed.), *Bird vocalizations in relation to current problems in biology and psychology,* (pp. 49–60). Cambridge: Cambridge University Press.

Stokes, A.W. (1962). Agonistic behaviour among blue tits at a winter feeding station. *Behaviour, 19,* 118–138.

Stokes, A.W. (1971). Parental and courtship feeding in red jungle fowl. *Auk, 88,* 21–29.

Thorpe, W.H. (1961). *Bird song.* Cambridge: Cambridge University Press.

Tinbergen, J.M. (1981). Foraging decision in starlings (*Sturnus vulgaris* L.). *Ardea, 69,* 1–67.

Tinbergen, N. (1935). Ueber die orientierung des Bienenwolfes. II Die Bienenjagd. Translation in N. Tinbergen, 1972, Vol. I. (q.v.).

Tinbergen, N. (1939). On the analysis of social organization in vertebrates, with special reference to birds. *American Midland Naturalist, 21,* 210–235.

Tinbergen, N. (1940). Die Uebersprungbewegung. *Zeitschrift für Tierpsychologie, 4,* 1–40.

Tinbergen, N. (1948). Social releasers and the experimental method required for their study. *Wilson Bulletin, 60,* 6–51.

Tinbergen, N. (1950). The hierarchical organisation of nervous mechanisms underlying instinctive behaviour. *Symposia of the Society of Experimental Biology, 4,* 305–312.

Tinbergen, N. (1951). *The study of instinct.* Oxford: Clarendon Press.

Tinbergen, N. (1952). Derived activities: Their causation, biological significance, origin and emancipation during evolution. *Quarterly Review of Biology, 27,* 1–32.

Tinbergen, N. (1972–1973). *The animal in its world.* London: Allen and Unwin, Vol. I, 1972; Vol. II, 1973.

Tinbergen, N., & Kruijt, W. (1938). On the orientation of the digger wasp *Philanthus triangulum* Fabr. III. Selective learning of landmarks. In N. Tinbergen, 1972, Vol. I, pp. 146–197 (q.v.).

Tinbergen, N., & Kuenen, D.J. (1939). Ueber die auslösenden und die richtunggebenden Reizsituationen der Sperrbewegung von jungen Drosseln (*Turdus m.merula* L. and *T.e.ericetorum* Turton). In N. Tinbergen, 1973, Vol. II, pp. 17–51 (q.v.).

Tinbergen, N., Meeuse, B.J.D., Boerema, L.K., & Varossieau, W. (1942). Die Balz des Samtfalters, *Eumenis* (= *Satyrus*) *semele* (L.). In N. Tinbergen, 1972, Vol. I, pp. 197–249 (q.v.).

Tinbergen, N., & Perdeck, A.C. (1950). On the stimulus situation releasing the begging response in the newly hatched herring gull chick (*Larus argentatus argentatus* Pont). *Behaviour, 3,* 1–39.

Trivers, R.L. (1971). The evolution of reciprocal altruism. *Quarterly Review of Biology, 46,* 35–57.

Tsumori, A. (1967). Newly acquired behavior and social interaction. In S.A. Altman (Ed.), *Social communication among Primates,* (pp. 207–219). Chicago: Chicago University Press.

Vodegel, N. (1978). A study of the underlying motivation of some communicative behaviours of *Pseudotropheus zebra* (*Pisces: Cichlidae*): a mathematical model. *Proceedings Koninklijke Nederlandse Akademie van Wetenschappen,* Ser. C, *81,* 211–240.

Vos, G.J. de. (1979). Adaptedness of arena behaviour in black grouse *Tetrao tetrix* and other grouse species (*Tetraonidae*). *Behaviour, 68,* 277–314.

Waal, F.B.M. de. (1978). Exploitative and familiarity-dependent support strategies in a colony of semi-free living chimpanzees. *Behaviour, 66,* 268–282.

Wallace, B. (1973). Misinformation, fitness and selection. *American Naturalist, 107,* 1–7.

Ward, P., & Zahavi, A. (1973). The importance of certain assemblages of birds as 'information-centres' for food finding. *Ibis*, 115, 517–534.

Weiss, P. (1941). Self-differentiation of the basic patterns of coordination. *Comparative Psychological Monographs*, *17*, 1–96.

Wiepkema, P.R. (1961). An ethological analysis of the reproductive behaviour of the bitterling (*Rhodeus amarus* Bloch). *Archives néerlandaises de Zoologie*, *14*, 103–199.

Wiepkema, P.R. (1971). Positive feedbacks at work during feeding. *Behaviour*, *39*, 266–273.

Wilson, E.O. (1975). *Sociobiology, the new synthesis*. Cambridge MA: Harvard University Press.

Wolda, H. (1961). Response decrement in the prey catching activity of *Notonecta glauca* L. (*Hemiptera*). *Archives néerlandaises de Zoologie*, *14*, 45–60.

Wynne-Edwards, V.C. (1962). *Animal dispersion in relation to social behaviour*. Edinburgh: Oliver and Boyd.

Zahavi, A. (1975). Mate-selection—a selection for a handicap. *Journal of Theoretical Biology*, *53*, 205–214.

Zahavi, A. (1977). The cost of honesty (further remarks on the handicap principle). *Journal of Theoretical Biology*, *67*, 603–605.

AUTHOR INDEX

Entries for Volume 1 are in regular text type; entries for Volume 2 are in **bold type**.

SUBJECT INDEX

Entries for Volume 1 are in regular text type; entries for Volume 2 are in **bold type**.

Figural flexibility, **845**, **852**
Figurative language, **424-428**
Figure-ground phenomenon, 219, 220
Figure illusions, **850**
Figure(s)
    impossible, 238, 239, 256
    inspection, 235
    Penrose, 238
    test, 235
Filial imprinting, **294-295**
Filiform papillae, 461
Filter bandwidth, and dissonance, 385
Filtering, **793**
Filter theory, **788**, **789**
Fine grain, of visual space, 169-173
Fine sound discrimination, **892**
Finger dexterity, **845**, **853**
Fitts' law, **480**, **497-498**
Fixation, visual field of, 166
Fixed action pattern (FAP), 598-599, 734, 768
Fixed-delay schedules, **230**
Fixed interval (FI) reinforcement, **169-170**
Fixed interval method, **678**
Fixed-interval schedules, **77**
Fixed ratio (FR) reinforcement, **169-170**
Fixed-ratio schedules, **77**
Fixed schedules, **187-188**
Flat bipolars, 135
Flavor-aversion learning, **28**
Flexibility, **845**, **849**, **850**, **852**
Flexible mapping, **372**
Flow diagrams, **719**
Fluency, **845**, **851-852**, **859**
Fluid control peptides, and learning, 573-574
Fluid general ability, **849**
Fluid intelligence factors (Gf), **844**, **848**, **854**
Fluid pressure, and angiotensin, 569-571
Flurothyl, **274**
Focus, region of, **781**
Focused attention
    attentional spotlights, **783-784**
    defined, **775**
    inhibition of objects in nonfo-
        cused regions, **785**
    upon location, **782-783**, **794**
    upon size and/or globality, **784-785**
    switching attention, **788**
Focusing, **393-394**, **781-785**
Focusing strategies, **642**
Focus sample, **394**
Foliate papillae, 461, 463, 464, 479
Food
    capture and handling of, 534
    identification of, 534
    recognition of, and autoshaping, 530
    search for, 533-534
    selection of, 527-533
Food-aversion learning, **27**, **28**
Foraging, and optimality theory, 531-533
Foraging behavior, 809-811
Forgetting, **378**, **379**, **382-383**
    (*see also* Retention)

Formal logic, **521**, **660**
Formants
    and timbre, 383-384
    in vowel theory, 382, 396, 397, 398, 402
Formant transition, **893**
Form perception, and lie group algebra, 182
Forms, wholes and parts of, 238
Forward masking technique, 338, 339, 340
Fourier analysis, and pitch perception, , 347-349, 351
Fourier optics, 89, 91-94
Fourier series, 284, 286, 299
Fourier theory of vision, 182
Fourier transform, 284
Fovea, 97, 99, 100, 166, 171, 207, 208
Fractile method, **678**
Fractional method, 49
Fragmentation hypothesis, **366-367**
Frames, **523**, **536-545**
Frame size, **746**
Frame time, **756**
Framing, **702-703**, **727**
Frank's classification of taste fiber types, 477-482
F-ratio tests, **813**
Fraunhofer far-field diffraction pattern, circular aperture, 90, 91
Free-operant procedures, **63**, **66**, **169**, **170**
Free recall, **355**, **359-360**, **362**, **379**, **380**, **381**, **384**, **385**, **390**
Free recall tasks, **820**, **840**
Frequency, **368-373**, **374**, **378**, **392**, **394**
Frequency-based probabilities, **678**
Frequency characteristics, of mask-
    ing data, 337
Frequency distortion and speech perception, 398
Frequency glides, 387, 390, 397
Frequency judgment, **368**, **369**
Frequency learning, **372**
Frequency matching, **369**, **372**
Frequency-of-seeing curve, 43
Frequentists, **676**
Frontal cortex, self-injection in, 595
Frontal lobes, **288-289**
Frontal lobotomy, **288**
Fructose, 466, 467, 468, 481
Full report procedure, **354-355**
Function, **290-292**, **520-521**
    and evolution, 806-822
Function, principles, and mecha-
    nisms of behavior, 520-525
Functional fixity, **635-636**
Functional measurement, 22, 53, **717**
Functional relations, **824-826**
Fundal reflectometry, 111-112
Fundamental sensations, 212
Fungiform papillae, 461, 462, 464, 479
Fuzzy categories, **392-393**, **397**
Fuzzy logic, **578**
Fuzzy set theory, **578**

Galactosemia, 707
Galton whistle, 679
Gambles, **693-694**, **696**, **698**, **724**
Game strategy, **632**
Gametes, 681, 682
Game theory, and evolution, 809, 819, 820
Ganglion cells, 134, 135, 137-141, 146-148
Gaping response, 802
Gaussian distribution, 20, 26, 43, 65
Gaussian noise, 331
Gaussian region, 86, 89
Gaze behavior, and emotion communication, 657-658
Gene action
    control of, 735-737
    mechanisms of, 729-732
General auditory perception factors, **844**, **850-851**
Generality
    degrees of, 518
    forces of, 516-517
Generalization
    and categorization, **400-402**
    and generalized schema, **579**
    gradients, **52**, **112**
    information-processing models of, **145**
    mediated, **147-148**
    in Pavlovian conditioning, **51-52**
    in representation, **578-580**
    stimulus, **15**, **21**, **143-144**, **145**
    superpositional models of, **580**
    without specific generalized concepts, **579-580**
Generalized invariance theory, 224
Generalized matching law, **180-183**, **185**
General memory capacity, **851**
General memory factors, **845**, **851**
General Problem Solver (GPS), **596-598**, **600**, **602**, **608**, **622**
General processes, and natural selection, 516-517
General process learning abilities, 507
General process theory, 504, 505, 506, 507-508, 509-510
General reasoning, **844**, **848**
General retrieval capacity, **852**
General visual perception factors (Gv), **844**, **849-850**
Genes, 681, 682
    causal matrix between pheno-
        types and, 737-738
    and specific behavioral organiza-
        tion, 807, 808
Genetic code, 732
Genetic influence on behavior, pathways of, 732-735
Genetic models, quantitative, 689-699
Genetics, behavioral (*see* Behavioral genetics)
Genetic structure, **639**
Genotype-environment correlation and interaction, 727-729, 742-747

SUBJECT INDEX

OEMCO